Patent Prosecution

Practice & Procedure
Before the U.S. Patent Office

Second Edition

2001 Cumulative Supplement

Patent Prosecution

Practice & Procedure Before the U.S. Patent Office

Second Edition

2001 Cumulative Supplement

Irah H. Donner

Hale and Dorr LLP
Washington, D.C.

The Bureau of National Affairs, Inc., Washington, D.C.

Library of Congress Cataloging-in-Publication Data

Donner, Irah H.
Patent prosecution: practice & procedure before the U.S. Patent Office / Irah H. Donner.--2nd ed.
p. cm.
Includes index.
ISBN 1-57018-188-8
1. Patent laws and legislation--United States. 2. United States. Patent Office--Rules and practice. I. Title.
KF3120.D66 2000
346.7304'86--dc21

99-048597

Published by BNA Books
1231 25th St. NW, Washington, DC 20037
http://www.bnabooks.com

International Standard Book Number: 1-57018-276-0
Printed in the United States of America

To Batsheva

Foreword to the First Edition

The patent practitioner will find this book to be a well developed approach to solving the mystery of successful patent prosecution. It provides detailed and comprehensive explanations of virtually every step in the prosecution process and allows the reader to benefit from the author's extensive experience and innovative methods.

Patent Prosecution: Practice and Procedures Before the U.S. Patent Office includes a good mixture of law, procedure, practice, and strategy that the experienced practitioner will find helpful and the new practitioner will find invaluable. Patent litigators, too, will find the book to be a useful reference for explaining patent prosecution as it affects the issues in patent infringement cases.

A particular strength of the book is the innovative approach that the author advocates when responding to rejections from the PTO. He provides insights that will be thought provoking for the seasoned practitioner. And while every new practitioner must spend painstaking years mastering the intricacies of effective prosecution, I am sure he or she will consult this treatise regularly in accomplishing that task.

The author, Irah H. Donner, is to be congratulated for a substantial contribution to the profession.

Don Martens
Knobbe, Martens, Olson & Bear
Newport Beach, California

Foreword

The Federal Circuit Court of Appeals, and predecessor court, the Court of Customs and Patent Appeals, have designed an excellent framework for use by the U.S. Patent Office in examining patent applications called the prima facie case of unpatentability. As stated by Federal Circuit Judge Plager:

> [t]he examiner cannot sit mum, leaving the applicant to shoot arrows in the dark hoping to somehow hit a secret objection harbored by the examiner. The 'prima facie' case notion, the exact origin of which appears obscure . . . , seemingly was intended to leave no doubt among examiners that they must state clearly and specifically any objections (the prima facie case) to patentability, and give the applicant fair opportunity to meet those objections with evidence and argument. To that extent the concept serves to level the playing field and reduces the likelihood of administrative arbitrariness.[1]

It is this concept of the prima facie case that has been employed by the author in this book, *Patent Prosecution.*

The author has gone to great lengths to institutionalize the prima facie case for the basic substantive rejections encountered at the U.S. Patent Office. The author has provided an element-by-element prima facie case for major areas in U.S. patent law. *Patent Prosecution* should be a valuable tool for patent attorneys preparing and prosecuting patent applications. *Patent Prosecution* will also be a welcome addition to patent litigators, when either attempting to invalidate or maintain a granted U.S. patent in a patent infringement/declaratory judgment lawsuit. Irah Donner should be congratulated for his efforts.

October 1999

Harry F. Manbeck, Jr.
Former U.S. Commissioner of U.S. Patent and Trademark Office
Former Assistant Secretary of Commerce

[1]In re Oetiker, 977 F.2d 1443, 24 USPQ 2d 1443, 1447 (Fed. Cir. 1992) (Plager, J., concurring).

Preface to the 2001 Cumulative Supplement

New material in this 2001 Supplement addresses various significant changes in U.S. patent law resulting from laws passed by Congress and recent decisions by the U.S. Supreme Court and the Federal Circuit. Please refer to the Preface for the 2000 Supplement for additional changes in this cumulative supplement.

Examples of these changes include the following:

Chapter 1 describes new procedures under the American Inventors Protection Act (AIPA) for 18-month publication of patent applications, including Request for Non-Publication, Request to Rescind Non-Publication Request, and Request for Deferral of Examination. Chapter 1 also discusses Request for Continued Examination (RCE) practice and differences from Continued Prosecution Application (CPA) practice.

Chapter 2 describes in detail the Federal Circuit decision in *Festo Corp. v. Shoketsu Kinzoku Kogyo Kabushiki Co.* In *Festo*, the Federal Circuit held that any narrowing amendment for any reason relating to patentability will be a complete bar to the doctrine of equivalents for the amended claim element, thereby overruling the previous flexible bar approach to the doctrine of equivalents. Chapter 2 also discusses *In re Gartside*, in which the Federal Circuit held that the standard of review under the Administrative Procedure Act (APA) requires substantial evidence to support the Patent Office's decision, as opposed to the arbitrary and capricious standard. Chapter 2 also discusses a change in procedure with respect to an Examiner's Reasons for Allowance.

Chapter 3 has been supplemented with discussion of the Federal Circuit decision of *Banks v. Unisys Corp.*, holding that an employee's refusal to sign a work-for-hire agreement is a factor to be considered in determining whether an employer may assert the employed-to-invent exception.

Chapter 6 includes additional discussion of the AIPA with respect to the prior art effect of published patent applications under Section 102(e).

Chapter 7 discusses various Federal Circuit decisions further clarifying criteria for an obviousness rejection. In *Winner International Royalty Corp. v. Wang*, for example, the Federal Circuit held that motivation to combine requires a desirable result, and is not directly related to trade-offs that may only be for convenience. Chapter 7 also discusses additional Federal Circuit decisions delineating when a claim element is or is not considered to be an equivalent.

Chapter 9 discusses the Federal Circuit decision in *Amtel Corporation v. Information Storage Devices, Inc.*, which held that the corresponding structure under Section 112, sixth paragraph, must be described in the specification, and that incorporating structure by reference to another patent or publication is not itself sufficient. Chapter 9 also discusses the Federal Circuit decision in *Solomon v. Kimberly-Clark Corporation*, holding that an inventor's statements during prosecution of the patent application may be used to support a rejection based on Section 112, second paragraph, that a claim does not correspond in scope to what the inventor *regards* as the invention. Chapter 9 also provides additional words and phrases commonly used in patent claims that have been the subject of Federal Circuit decisions.

Chapter 12 describes the new third party or inter partes reexamination procedure and its benefits and costs. Chapter 12 also discusses *Southwest Software Inc. v. Harlequin Inc.*, in which the Federal Circuit held that even though the Patent Office made a printing mistake in the patent, a subsequently filed certificate of correction is effective as of the date the Patent Office issues such a certificate. Accordingly, a patent might be invalid until the certificate of correction issues.

This book can greatly benefit from the comments of those who use it. I therefore ask for your help as a reader. If any text is incorrect, incomplete, or misleading, I would very much like to hear about it. If relevant subject matter has been omitted or needs to be treated in greater depth, I would also like to hear about it. All suggestions for improvements in this book are welcome.

You may contact me in care of BNA Books, The Bureau of National Affairs, Inc., 1231 25th St., NW, Washington, DC 20037-1197; or by e-mail at books@bna.com.

My sincere appreciation is extended to James F. Fattibene, Joseph Dundin, and Richard Cornfield of BNA Books Division. I would like to express special thanks to Karen Hinson, librarian at the Washington, DC, offices of Hale and Dorr, for checking the citations in the supplement and re-checking those in the main volume. Finally, I would like to acknowledge the patience and love of my wife Batsheva and my children, Zachary, Avital, J.J., and Loni.

Irah H. Donner
Washington, DC
September 2001

Preface to the 2000 Supplement

The 2000 Supplement to *Patent Prosecution* addresses various significant changes in U.S. patent law resulting from new laws passed by Congress and recent decisions by the U.S. Supreme Court and the Federal Circuit. Examples of these changes include the following:

Chapter 1—In *Dickinson v. Zurko,* the U.S. Supreme Court held that the standard the Federal Circuit must apply when reviewing decisions by the Board of Patent Appeals and Interferences is the standard set forth in the Administrative Procedures Act (APA). Thus reversal is only appropriate if there is no substantial evidence to support the Board's holding or if the Board acted arbitrarily or capriciously.

Chapter 2—Recent decisions include a significant number of examples of prosecution history estoppel, illustrating the potentially devastating effects arguments and amendments to patent claims may have on the scope of the patent protection as ultimately determined by the courts. In *Sextant Avionique, S.A., v. Analog Devices, Inc.,* for example, the Federal Circuit, applying the U.S. Supreme Court's *Warner-Jenkinson presumption,* held that where the reason for an amendment is unclear, prosecution history estoppel is a total and complete "bar" to the doctrine of equivalents as to the amended limitation.

Chapter 3—Additional decisions have been added dealing with ownership of inventions made by U.S. Government employees.

Chapter 5—This chapter includes a discussion of the Federal Circuit decision in *Juicy Whip, Inc. v. Orange Bang, Inc.,* holding that the fact that one product can be altered to make it look like another product is a specific benefit sufficient to satisfy the statutory requirement of utility. Chapter 5 also discusses the Federal Circuit decision in *AT&T Corp. v. Excel Communications, Inc.,* holding that a method using a data field to indicate a primary exchange carrier was statutory (i.e., patentable) subject matter since the algorithm produced a tangible and useful result. *AT&T Corp. v. Excel* also re-affirmed the Federal Circuit holding in *Signature Financial Group v. State Street Bank.*

Chapter 6—This chapter includes discussion of the Intellectual Property and Communications Omnibus Reform Act of 1999, which authorizes the publication of U.S. patent applications eighteen months after filing, subject to various conditions. The Act also provides that a published patent application in the United States is entitled to the prior art effect of its filing date under Section 102(e). Chapter 6 also discusses the Federal Circuit decision in *Atlas Powder Company v. IRECO Incorporated,* which explained that an insufficient scientific understanding of the invention in the prior art does not defeat a showing of inherency and anticipation.

Chapter 7—The Intellectual Property and Communications Omnibus Reform Act 1999 is discussed in connection with limitations on when prior art owned by a common assignee can be used in an obviousness rejection, as well as its effective overruling of the Court of Customs and Patent Appeals (CCPA) decision of *In re Land.*Chapter 7 also discusses recent Federal Circuit decisions further clarifying criteria for an obviousness rejection. In *Tec Air, Inc. v. Denso Manufacturing Michigan Inc.,* for example, the invention was held to be nonobvious over the prior art because the proposed combination resulted in one of the patent references being inoperable for its intended purpose. In addition, *Interactive Technologies, Inc. v. Pittway Corporation* held that a "general relationship" between the fields of the prior art references to be combined is insufficient to suggest the motivation.

Chapter 7 also includes significant discussion of criteria governing when a claimed process will be considered a step-plus-function element under section 112, sixth paragraph, as outlined in Judge Rader's concurring opinion in *Seal-Flex, Inc. v. Athletic Track and Court Construction.*

Chapter 7 further discusses recent Federal Circuit decisions delineating when a claim element is or is not considered to be an equivalent. These decisions provide insight for applicants arguing before the U.S. Patent Office that their invention is not an equivalent over the prior art and therefore deserves the grant of a patent. Among other cases discussed in this connection, *General Electric Company v. Nintendo Company, Ltd.,* held that a disrupting signal path was not equivalent to a bypassing signal path, and *Nagle Industries, Inc. v. Ford Motor Company,* held that a spring adjustment device was not equivalent to manual adjustment device.

Chapter 8—This chapter addresses the Federal Circuit's use of the written description requirement in defining the scope of patent claim interpretation. In *Total Containment, Inc. v. Intelpro Corporation,* for example, the Federal Circuit held that a liberal written description will not narrow the scope of patent claims, particularly where the written description of the invention described multiple embodiments. Revised PTO guidelines addressing the written description requirement are included in Appendix C.

Chapter 9—Additional words and phrases commonly used in patent claims have been added which have been the subject of Federal Circuit decisions providing guidance on their interpretation. For example, *Pitney Bowes Inc. v. Hewlett-Packard Co.* held that more than one definition of the same claim term may be used and the claims may nevertheless be considered definite. Additional new commonly used terms that are discussed include "permanently affixed," "enlarged," "predetermined," "at least one," and "uniformly." The decision in *WMS Gaming Inc. v. International Game Technology,* describing how to interpret means-plus-function claims when the disclosed structure is a general purpose computer, is also discussed.

Chapter 10—The Federal Circuit decision in *Ricoh Company, Ltd. v. Nashua Corporation* is discussed, which reaffirmed that there is no time limit for submitting broadened claims in continuation applications. Discussion also includes the Federal Circuit decision in *Merck & Co., Inc. v. Mylan Pharmaceuticals, Inc.,* which held that an estoppel may arise through failure to prosecute claims in a divisional application in the face of a prior art rejection.

Chapter 12—This chapter is entirely new, and deals with reissue, reexamination, certificates of correction, and maintenance fees.

This book can greatly benefit from the comments of those who use it. I therefore ask for your help as a reader. If any text is incorrect, incomplete, or misleading, I would very much like to hear about it. If relevant subject matter has been omitted or needs to be treated in greater depth, I would also like to hear about it. All suggestions for improvements in this book are welcome.

You may contact me in care of the BNA Books Editorial Offices, 1231 25th St., N.W., Washington, DC 20037-1197; or by e-mail at books@bna.com.

My sincere appreciation is extended to James F. Fattibene, Joseph Dundin, Susan Sproul, and Richard Cornfield of the BNA Books Division. Finally, I would like to acknowledge the patience and love of my wife Batsheva and my children, Zachary, Avital, J.J., and Loni.

Irah H. Donner
Washington, DC
October 2000

Summary Table of Contents

Detailed Table of Contents

1

Patent Protection

I. Introduction to U.S. Patent Laws

[Insert after footnote 12.]

Pursuant to 28 U.S.C. Section 1338, exclusive jurisdiction lies in the federal courts for actions arising under the patent laws:

> The district courts shall have original jurisdiction of any civil action arising under any Act of Congress relating to patents, plant variety protection, copyrights and trademarks. Such jurisdiction shall be exclusive of the courts of the states in patent, plant variety protection and copyright cases.[1]

[Insert after footnote 13.]

Congress "may leave it to administrative officials to establish rules within the prescribed limits of the statute."[2] In the patent field, Congress has done precisely that by providing that the Director "may, subject to the approval of the Secretary of Commerce, establish regulations, not inconsistent with law, for the conduct of proceedings in the Patent and Trademark Office."[3] In this type of situation, "the validity of a regulation promulgated thereunder will be sustained so long as it is 'reasonably related to the enabling legislation.'"[4]

---

[1] 28 U.S.C. § 1338(a) (1988).

[2] Ethicon v. Quigg, 849 F.2d 1422, 1425, 7 USPQ 2d 1152, 1154 (Fed. Cir. 1988) (quoting Patlex Corp. v. Mossinghoff, 758 F.2d 594, 605, 225 USPQ 243, 251 (Fed. Cir. 1985), and citing United States v. Grimaud, 220 U.S. 506, 517 (1911)).

[3] 35 U.S.C. § 6(a) (1994).

[4] Mourning v. Family Publications Serv., Inc., 411 U.S. 356, 369 (1973) (quoting Thorpe v. Housing Auth. of Durham, 393 U.S. 268, 280 (1969)). *See* Chevron U.S.A. Inc. v. Natural Resources Defense Council, Inc., 467 U.S. 837, 844 (1984).

Main volume footnote updates begin on page 21.

II. Utility Patents

[Insert after footnote 24.]

Inventions may embody a combination of old elements, a combination of old and new elements or one or more new elements. Accordingly, claims that may be drafted to secure legal protection for inventions may consist of a combination of elements (combination claims) or single element claims. Combination claims can therefore be drafted as a new combination of old elements or combinations of new and old elements.[5] Because old elements are part of these combination claims, claim limitations may, and often do, read on the prior art. It is well established in patent law that a claim may consist of all old elements, such as the rigid-conduit system, for it may be that the combination of the old elements is novel and patentable. Similarly, it is well established that a claim may consist of all old elements and one new element, thereby being patentable.[6]

It is no secret that patent applications are extremely difficult to draft. In this context, the Supreme Court observed:

> The specification and claims of a patent, particularly if the invention be at all complicated, constitute one of the most difficult legal instruments to draw with accuracy, and in view of the fact that valuable inventions are often placed in the hands of inexperienced persons to prepare such specifications and claims, it is no matter of surprise that the latter frequently fail to describe with requisite certainty the exact invention of the patentee, and err either in claiming that which the patentee had not in fact invented, or in omitting some element which was a valuable or essential part of his actual invention. . . . The object of the patent law is to secure to inventors a monopoly of what they have actually invented or discovered, and it ought not to be defeated by a too strict and technical adherence to the letter of the statute, or by the application of artificial rules of interpretation.[7]

[Delete the paragraph following footnote 26 and replace with the following.]

Prior to the American Inventor's Protection Act (AIPA) of 1999, the entire negotiation process conducted before the Patent Office, typically called ex parte prosecution, was confidential.[8] Accordingly, the public had no participation in or knowledge about the details of the invention or the prosecution process. However, with the passage of the AIPA,

[5] Clearstream Wastewater Sys., Inc. v. Hydro-Action, Inc., 206 F.3d 1440, 54 USPQ 2d 1185, 1189 (Fed. Cir. 2000); Intel Corp. v. U.S. Int'l Trade Comm'n, 946 F.2d 821, 842, 20 USPQ 2d 1161, 1179 (Fed. Cir. 1991); Panduit Corp. v. Dennison Mfg., 810 F.2d 1561, 1575, 1 USPQ 2d 1593, 1603 (Fed. Cir. 1987).

[6] *Clearstream*, 54 USPQ 2d at 1189.

[7] Topliff v. Topliff, 145 U.S. 156, 171 (1892).

[8] 35 U.S.C. § 31 (1988); 37 C.F.R. § 1.31.

Main volume footnote updates begin on page 21.

patent applications are published after 18 months from the earliest priority date.[9] The public is permitted only limited participation in the prosecution process prior to the application being published in the form of a prior art submission.[10] Once the application is published, any prior art received by the Patent Office will not be considered without the permission of the patent applicant/owner if filed after the patent application has been published for more than two months or after a Notice of Allowance has been mailed, whichever is earlier.[11] Importantly, the publication of a patent application will open the file wrapper to public inspection during its pendency in the Patent Office.

Prior to publication of the patent application, the applicant who decides that the patent acquisition process is too cumbersome may discontinue the process and allow the application to be abandoned. In this situation, although the invention remains confidential prior to publication, the applicant will lose filing and priority dates.[12] The loss of priority is significant only if the applicant chooses to apply for a patent on the same invention at a later time, assuming that the earlier published patent application does not completely bar the later patent application. Once the patent application is published, it will be considered prior art as of its earlier filing date, as opposed to its publication date.[13] A comparison document showing the substantive statutory changes as a result of the AIPA is included in Appendix C. A copy of the internal Patent Office procedures implementing the publication of patent applications is included in Appendix D.

[On page 8, in the paragraph following footnote 35, beginning "The specific date on which . . .," delete the first sentence and substitute the following.]

The specific date on which the patent grant expires for patent applications filed before May 29, 2000 is governed by the Uruguay Round Agreements Act (URAA), enacted in 1994.

[On page 9, prior to the paragraph beginning "In addition to the patent term extension . . .," insert the following.]

The AIPA further amended the patent laws to provide additional patent term extensions based on prosecution delays at the Patent Office. These amendments to the patent term took effect on May 29, 2000 and apply to any patent, except a design patent, issuing on any

[9] American Inventors Protection Act (AIPA) § 4503 (Nov. 29, 1999); 37 C.F.R. § 1.211(a) (Supp. 2000).

[10] 37 C.F.R. § 1.99 (2000).

[11] *Id.*

[12] *See infra* Chapter 4 for a detailed discussion of priority of invention.

[13] 35 U.S.C. § 102(e) (Supp. 2000).

Main volume footnote updates begin on page 21.

application filed on or after May 29, 2000. These new provisions provide extensions of the 20-year patent term for certain periods of delay in issuance that are beyond the applicant's control.

Term extensions are assessed by determining the actual days qualifying for a delay in issuance due to (1) untimely action on the part of the Patent Office, (2) delays in issuance due to interferences or secrecy orders imposed on the application, and (3) delays in issuance due to improper rejections of claims subsequently reversed by the Board or a court. Term extensions are then reduced by the number of days of delay in issuance due to the applicant's lack of diligence in prosecuting the application.[14] A copy of the initial proposed rules for patent term extension is included in Appendix D and a copy of the final rules for patent term extension is included in Appendix C.

[On page 9, in the paragraph beginning "In addition to the patent term extension, . . ." delete the first sentence and insert the following.]

In addition to patent term extension under the URAA and AIPA for prosecution delays, the Hatch-Waxman Act provides owners of approved patented products with an extended patent term to compensate for the delay in obtaining Food and Drug Administration (FDA) regulatory approval.[15]

[Insert after footnote 43.]

A listing of the different patent applications subject to a patent term of 20 years from filing or greater than 20 years from filing/17 years from issue is provided in Appendix C.

[Insert after footnote 45.]

As stated by the Federal Circuit:

> A patent represents the legal right to exclude others from making, using, selling, or offering to sell a patented invention in the United States, and from importing the invention into the United States. . . . Implicit in the right to exclude is the ability to waive that right, i.e., to license activities that would otherwise be excluded, such as making, using and selling the patented invention in the United States. Those activities, of course, may be subject to further limitations such as governmental restrictions or "blocking" patents. . . . A "blocking patent" is an earlier patent that must be licensed in order to practice a later patent. This often occurs, for instance, between a pioneer patent and an improvement patent.[16]

[Insert after footnote 47.]

---

[14] 35 U.S.C. § 154(b) (Supp. 2000).

[15] *Id.*

[16] Prima Tek II, L.L.C. v. A-Roo Co., 222 F.3d 1372, 55 USPQ 2d 1742, 1747 & n 2 (Fed. Cir. 2000).

Main volume footnote updates begin on page 21.

That is, actions predicated on direct patent infringement do not require any showing of intent to infringe; instead, knowledge and intent are considered only with respect to damages.[17]

[Insert after footnote 48.]

Patents have long been considered a species of property.[18] As such, they are surely included within the "property" of which no person may be deprived by a state without due process of law.[19]

A. Publication of U.S. Patent Applications [New]

Under the American Inventors Protection Act (AIPA), almost all U.S. patent applications filed on or after November 29, 2000 which have been, or will be, filed in a foreign country, or under a multilateral agreement, that requires publication at 18 months, will now be published by the U.S. Patent Office. The new publication provisions do not require any additional information to be disclosed to the public since they only require publication of U.S. patent applications that are already being published abroad. However, the 18-month publication under the AIPA also applies to divisionals, continuations, continuations-in-part, and international applications entering the national phase in the United States under 35 U.S.C. Section 371. Applications will be published 18 months after their earliest claimed priority date.

The new law provides for provisional protection in the United States based on the claims published in the U.S. patent application or in an international application designating the United States as a possible country to enter the national stage of the patent application. Provisional rights include a reasonable royalty for infringement of claims substantially similar to claims in the issued patent.[20] Since the priority date must be known in advance for the date of publication to be set, the statute was amended to give the U.S. Patent Office the authority to require applicants to timely claim priority.

Nonpublished patent applications will remain secret until published. Patent applications will be published 18 months after their earliest claimed priority date, unless the applicant specifically requests no publication and certifies that no foreign application for the invention

---

[17] Florida Prepaid Postsecondary Educ. Expense Bd. v. College Savs. Bank, 527 U.S. 627, 51 USPQ 2d 1081, 1087 (1999).

[18] *See* Brown v. Duchesne, 60 U.S. (19 How.) 183, 197, (1857) ("For, by the laws of the United States, the rights of a party under a patent are his private property."); Consolidated Fruit-Jar Co. v. Wright, 94 U.S. 92, 96 (1877) ("A patent for an invention is as much property as a patent for land.").

[19] Florida Prepaid Postsecondary Educ. Expense Bd. v. College Savs. Bank, 527 U.S. 627, 51 USPQ 2d 1081, 1087 (1999).

[20] 35 U.S.C. § 154(d) (Supp. 2000).

has been filed. In addition, pre-issuance oppositions to published applications are not permitted once the application has been published for longer than two months or after a Notice of Allowance has been mailed, whichever is earlier.[21] If a nonpublication request is filed with an application, the filing receipt for the application will indicate "No Publication" to confirm receipt of the nonpublication request to the applicant. If a foreign filing is subsequently made in another country, or under a multilateral agreement, that requires publication at 18 months, the applicant must withdraw the request within 45 days of the foreign filing or the U.S. application will be considered abandoned.[22] Such an abandoned application may be subject to revival if it is shown that the delay in submitting the notice of withdrawal was unintentional.[23] Appendix B includes samples of a nonpublication request and a request to rescind a previous nonpublication request. Examination of published applications may also be deferred for up to three years from the priority date. A sample request for deferred examination is included in Appendix B.

Provisional rights for published applications include the ability to receive a reasonable royalty from the time a U.S. national application or an English language Patent Cooperation Treaty (PCT) application is published until the time the patent issues for infringement of any claim in the published application that is substantially identical to a claim in the issued patent. The statute of limitations for actions for a reasonable royalty for infringement of the published application runs six years from the issue date of the patent.[24]

A copy of the initial proposed rules for 18-month publication is included in Appendix D, and a copy of the final rules for 18-month publication is included in Appendix C. A comparison document showing the substantive statutory changes as a result of the AIPA is included in Appendix C.

III. Comparative Intellectual Property Protections

A. Trade Secret Protection

[On page 12, in the paragraph beginning "A patent and a trade secret in the same subject matter . . ., delete the second sentence and insert the following.]

When an inventor decides to patent the subject matter, disclosure of the subject matter in a patent when published or granted immediately voids any trade secrets in it.

---

[21] 35 U.S.C. § 122(b) (Supp. 2000).

[22] 37 C.F.R. § 1.213(c) (2000).

[23] 37 C.F.R. § 1.137(f) (2000).

[24] 35 U.S.C. § 154(d) (Supp. 2000).

Main volume footnote updates begin on page 21.

B. Copyright Protection

[Insert after footnote 60.]

Not all copying from a copyrighted work is necessarily an infringement of the copyright. Certain elements of a copyrighted work are not protected—even against intentional copying. For example, it is a basic principle of copyright law that ideas, concepts, and processes are not protected from copying.[25] A copyright thus protects not the author's ideas, but only his or her expression of them[26] For example, architectural plans or engineering designs include generalized notions of where to place functional elements, how to route the flow of traffic, and what methods of construction and principles of engineering to rely on—all ideas that may be copied and utilized without violating the copyright of the original author or designer. However, to the extent that the copier takes not only the architectural plans or engineering drawings, but also the author's expression of them, copyright infringement may be found.[27]

E. Trade Dress Protection

[Insert after footnote 101.]

The Federal Circuit and its predecessor, the Court of Customs and Patent Appeals (CCPA), have addressed the interaction between patent law principles and trade dress protection on several occasions. While recognizing that trade dress protection can serve important ends by facilitating customers' recognition of products and protecting producers' good will, the CCPA cautioned that exclusive rights in trade dress, if granted too freely, would conflict with the policy in favor of encouraging "competition by all fair means," which "encompasses the right to copy, very broadly interpreted, except where copying is lawfully prevented by a copyright or patent."[28]

To guard against such anticompetitive effects, the CCPA invoked the doctrine of "functionality" to limit the scope of trade dress protection. The CCPA held that a seller of goods could not obtain trademark protection for a trade dress or product configuration that was primarily utilitarian, or "functional." The CCPA defined as "functional" any

---

[25] Attia v. Society of N.Y. Hosp., 201 F.3d 50, 53 USPQ 2d 1253, 1256 (2d Cir. 1999), *cert. denied*, 121 S. Ct. 109 (2000).

[26] Feist Publications, Inc. v. Rural Tel. Serv. Co., 499 U.S. 340, 349–50, 18 USPQ 2d 1275, 1277 (1991).

[27] Attia v. Society of N.Y. Hosp., 201 F.3d 50, 53 USPQ 2d 1253, 1257 (2d Cir. 1999), *cert. denied*, 121 S. Ct. 109 (2000).

[28] *In re* Deister Concentrator Co., 289 F.2d 496, 501, 129 USPQ 314, 319 (C.C.P.A. 1961).

Main volume footnote updates begin on page 21.

feature that possessed such utility that its protection would hinder competition.[29]

The Supreme Court has adopted the same approach, explaining the role of the "functionality" doctrine as follows:

The functionality doctrine prevents trademark law, which seeks to promote competition by protecting a firm's reputation, from instead inhibiting legitimate competition by allowing a producer to control a useful product feature. It is the province of patent law, not trademark law, to encourage invention by granting inventors a monopoly over new product designs or functions for a limited time . . . after which competitors are free to use the innovation. If a product's functional features could be used as trademarks, however, a monopoly over such features could be obtained without regard to whether they qualify as patents and could be extended forever (because trademarks may be renewed in perpetuity).[30]

The Supreme Court defined a product feature as "functional" if it is "essential to the use or purpose of the article or if it affects the cost or quality of the article."[31] That is, a feature is functional "if exclusive use of the feature would put competitors at a significant non-reputation-related disadvantage."[32]

For example, where the whole product configuration is

> nothing other than the assemblage of functional parts, and where even the arrangement and combination of the parts is designed to result in superior performance, it is semantic trickery to say that there is still some sort of separate "overall appearance" which is non-functional. If it is permissible to draw a distinction between such an object and its "general appearance," then virtually the only product designs which could be copied faithfully are those which are widely used and therefore in the public domain.[33]

There are two general opinions as to whether a patented product or feature may also receive trade dress protection. Main circuit courts, including the Fifth, Sixth, Seventh, and Federal Circuit's, hold that

---

[29] *See In re* Penthouse Int'l Ltd., 565 F.2d 679, 682, 195 USPQ 698, 700–01 (C.C.P.A. 1977) (functionality is addressed to whether protection of a design would "hinder competition"); *In re* Mogen David Wine Corp., 328 F.2d 925, 933, 140 USPQ 575, 581 (C.C.P.A. 1964) (Rich, J., concurring) ("Whether competition would in fact be hindered is really the crux of the matter."); Brunswick Corp. v. British Seagull Ltd., 35 F.3d 1527, 1530–31, 32 USPQ 2d 1120, 1122 (Fed. Cir. 1994) ("the policies underlying the functional limitation on trademark protection explicitly invoke an inquiry into competitive fairness"); New England Butt Co. v. U.S. Int'l Trade Comm'n, 756 F.2d 874, 879, 225 USPQ 260, 263 (Fed. Cir. 1985) ("functionality is to be determined in light of the competitive necessity to copy").

[30] Qualitex Co. v. Jacobson Prods. Co., 514 U.S. 159, 164–65, 34 USPQ 2d 1161, 1163 (1995).

[31] *Id.* at 165, 34 USPQ 2d at 1163–64 (quoting Inwood Lab., Inc. v. Ives Lab., Inc., 456 U.S. 844, 850 n.10, 214 USPQ 1, 4 n.10 (1982)).

[32] *Id.* at 165, 34 USPQ 2d at 1164.

[33] Leatherman Tool Group Inc. v. Cooper Indus. Inc., 199 F.3d 1009, 53 USPQ 2d 1196, 1200 (9th Cir. 1999), *cert. granted in part*, 121 S. Ct. 297 (2000).

Main volume footnote updates begin on page 21.

trade dress protection is not precluded by a patent on a product or feature.[34]

For example, the CCPA and Federal Circuit are of the opinion that the availability of trade dress protection does not depend on whether a patent has been obtained for the product or feature in question.[35] For example, in *In re Mogen David Wine Corp.*,[36] the CCPA explained that trademark rights, or rights under the law of unfair competition, do not prolong the patent monopoly. Rather,

> they exist independently of it, under different law and for different reasons. The termination of either has no legal effect on the continuance of the other. When the patent monopoly ends, it ends. The trademark rights do not extend it. We know of no provision of patent law, statutory or otherwise, that guarantees to anyone an absolute right to copy the subject matter of any expired patent. Patent expiration is nothing more than the cessation of the patentee's right to exclude held under the patent law.[37]

Further, the Federal Circuit has explained that in resolving the question of product design functionality for purposes of the Lanham Act, "reference to utility patent claims that are, or have been, asserted to read on either product, or to the appearance of the device depicted in figures included in the patent specification supporting such claims, must be done with caution."[38] Statements in a patent may provide evidence that the asserted trade dress is functional, and thus not entitled to legal protection.[39] However, according to most circuit courts, the fact that a patent has been acquired does not convert what otherwise would have been protected trade dress into nonprotected matter. "[W]e are not seriously concerned with whether he who claims trademark rights of unlimited duration now has or did have patent protection, or what that protection was."[40]

As indicated above, other courts of appeals have followed the lead of the CCPA in holding that a product may be entitled to trade dress protection for distinctive, nonfunctional features, even if the product is, or has been, the subject of a patent.[41]

---

[34] Marketing Displays Inc. v. TafFix Devices Inc., 200 F.3d 929, 53 USPQ 2d 1335, 1343 (6th Cir. 1999), *reversed on other grounds*, 121 S. Ct. 1255, 58 USPQ 2d 1001 (2001).

[35] Midwest Indus., Inc. v. Karavan Trailers, Inc., 175 F.3d 1356, 50 USPQ 2d 1672, 1677 (Fed. Cir. 1999).

[36] *In re* Mogen David Wine Corp., 328 F.2d 925, 140 USPQ 575 (C.C.P.A. 1964).

[37] *Id.* at 930, 140 USPQ at 579.

[38] Cable Elec. Prods., Inc. v. Genmark, Inc., 770 F.2d 1015, 1031, 226 USPQ 881, 891 (Fed. Cir. 1985).

[39] *In re* Bose Corp., 772 F.2d 866, 872, 227 USPQ 1, 6 (Fed. Cir. 1985); *In re* Morton-Norwich Prods., Inc., 671 F.2d 1332, 1340–41, 213 USPQ 9, 15–16 (C.C.P.A. 1982); *In re* Honeywell, Inc., 497 F.2d 1344, 1348, 181 USPQ 821, 824 (C.C.P.A. 1974).

[40] *In re* Deister Concentrator Co., 289 F.2d 496, 501, 129 USPQ 314, 319 (C.C.P.A. 1961).

[41] Pebble Beach Co. v. Tour 18 I Ltd., 155 F.3d 526, 548, 549 n.16, 48 USPQ 2d 1065, 1080–81, 1081 n.16 (5th Cir. 1998); Thomas & Betts Corp. v. Panduit Corp., 138 F.3d 277,

Main volume footnote updates begin on page 21.

The Tenth Circuit stands alone in holding to the contrary, ruling that trade dress protection is unavailable for a product configuration that is claimed in a patent and is a described, significant inventive aspect of the patented invention, even if the configuration is nonfunctional.

[Insert after footnote 102.]

under the Tenth Circuit viewpoint

IV. Different Types of U.S. Patent Applications

B. Continuation Applications

[Insert after footnote 112.]

There is no time limit with respect to the filing of a continuation application so long as the continuation application maintains co-pendency with the earlier-filed application. In addition, there is no limit to the number of continuation applications filed in a chain of continuation applications. Thus, an applicant is free to submit broader claims in a continuation application, subject to the enablement, written description, and double patenting requirements, more than two years after the earliest application was filed, even though broadened claims under reissue practice are not possible.

According to the Federal Circuit, "Section 120, governing continuation applications, does not contain any time limit on an applicant seeking broadened claims. In contrast, section 251, governing reissue proceedings, does contain a specific time limit of two years."[42] "[A] limit upon continuing applications [i.e., similar to the two-year limit in reissue proceedings] is a matter of policy for Congress, not for us."[43] Similarly, the Federal Circuit has recognized the practice of filing continuation applications containing claims broader than those in a parent application, subject to double patenting objections, in order to encompass a competitor's product.[44]

287–89, 46 USPQ 2d 1026, 1032–33 (7th Cir.), *cert. denied*, 525 U.S. 929 (1998); Ferrari S.P.A. Esercizio Fabriche Automobile Corse v. Roberts, 944 F.2d 1235, 1241, 20 USPQ 2d 1001, 1006–07 (6th Cir. 1991); Ideal Toy Corp. v. Plawner Toy Mfg. Corp., 685 F.2d 78, 81, 216 USPQ 102, 105 (3d Cir. 1982); Dallas Cowboys Cheerleaders, Inc. v. Pussycat Cinema, Ltd., 604 F.2d 200, 203, 203 USPQ 161, 163–64 (2d Cir. 1979); Truck Equip. Servs. Co. v. Fruehauf Corp., 536 F.2d 1210, 1214–15, 191 USPQ 79, 82–83 (8th Cir. 1976); Pachmayr Gun Works, Inc. v. Olin Mathieson Chem. Corp., 502 F.2d 802, 806–07, 183 USPQ 5, 8–9 (9th Cir. 1974).

[42] Ricoh Co. v. Nashua Corp., Civ. App. No. 97-1344, slip op. at 5 (Fed. Cir. Feb. 18, 1999) (unpublished), *cert. denied*, 528 U.S. 815 (1999).

[43] *In re* Hogan, 559 F.2d 595, 604 n.13, 194 USPQ 527, 536 n. 13 (C.C.P.A. 1977).

[44] *See, e.g.*, Texas Instruments, Inc. v. U.S. Int'l Trade Comm'n, 871 F.2d 1054, 1065, 10 USPQ 2d 1257, 1265 (Fed. Cir. 1989).

Main volume footnote updates begin on page 21.

In fact, Congress addressed this issue of continuation applications using a different solution when Congress passed the Uruguay Round Agreements Act in 1994.[45] This act conformed U.S. law to the April 1994 Uruguay Round trade negotiations agreement under the General Agreement on Tariffs and Trade on "Trade-Related Aspects of Intellectual Property." In particular, Congress amended 35 U.S.C. Section 154 to provide for a patent term of 20 years from the date of the earliest-filed priority application, rather than 17 years from the date of issue of the patent.[46] This amendment in effect addressed the perceived problem of so-called submarine patents, i.e., the use of continuation applications to claim previously disclosed but unclaimed features of an invention many years after the filing of the original patent application.[47]

[Insert at the end of the section.]

Effective May 29, 2000, a new procedure for requesting continued examination in an application was created under 37 C.F.R. Section 1.114. Under this new procedure, an applicant may obtain continued examination of an application by filing a submission and paying a specified fee, even if the application is under a final rejection, appeal, or a notice of allowance. This new procedure is not available for: (1) an application for a utility or plant patent filed before June 8, 1995; (2) an international application filed under 35 U.S.C. Section 363 before June 8, 1995; (3) an application for a design patent; or (4) a patent under reexamination.[48]

This procedure for request for continued examination (RCE) is not generally available in any application unless prosecution is closed. Prosecution is closed where, for example, the application is under appeal, the last Office Action was a final action, or a notice of allowance was issued. This means, for example, that an RCE could not be filed in response to a notice of missing parts indicating that an oath or declaration or a filing fee should be filed within a specified period of time. Also an RCE could not be filed after a reply to a non-final Office Action. An RCE is not available in an application after the filing of a notice of appeal to the Federal Circuit or the commencement of a civil action, unless the appeal or civil action is terminated and the application is still pending.

In addition to the request and the payment of a fee, the RCE requires the filing of a submission or a response to the previous communication. This submission includes, but is not limited to, an information

---

[45] Uruguay Round Agreements Act, Pub. L. No. 103-465, 108 Stat. 4809 (Dec. 8, 1994).

[46] 35 U.S.C. § 154 (1994).

[47] Ricoh Co. v. Nashua Corp., Civ. App. No. 97-1344, slip op. at 6 n.3 (Fed. Cir. Feb. 18, 1999) (unpublished), *cert. denied*, 120 S. Ct. 580 (1999).

[48] 37 C.F.R. § 1.114(e) (2000).

Main volume footnote updates begin on page 21.

disclosure statement; an amendment to the written description, claims, or drawings; new arguments; or new evidence in support of patentability. If a reply to an Office Action is outstanding, the submission must include a complete reply to all the outstanding requirements, objections, and rejections contained in the outstanding Office Action.

Upon receiving the RCE, the Patent Office will withdraw the finality of any previous Office Action and will enter and consider the submission which must accompany the request. The Examiner is authorized to make the next Office Action final if the criteria for making the first Office Action final in a continuing application are satisfied. For example, if an amendment submitted after a final Office Action is denied entry, an RCE requesting entry of that amendment would preclude the next Office Action being final.

Since the filing of a new application requires the payment of filing and additional claim fees, the filing of a continuing application may be more costly than the filing of a Request for Continued Examination which requires only the payment of the request fee. An applicant may defer the payment of the filing and claim fees when filing a continuing application, while the Request for Continued Examination requires that the fee be paid on filing.

The filing of any new application starts a new period for determining the length of any term adjustments that can be accumulated because of Patent Office delays in granting the patent. The filing of an RCE, on the other hand, would lock in any term adjustments accumulated up to the time of filing the request, but would preclude any adjustment based on the three-year pendency rule for delays occurring after the RCE is filed. The filing of an RCE, however, would not preclude the accumulation of term adjustments based on delays other than the three-year pendency rule.

An applicant is limited to the examination of the same invention that was being prosecuted in the application in which the RCE is filed. Accordingly, a continuing application must be filed to obtain examination of inventions other than the inventions being currently examined. Finally, the filing of a new application will trigger the 18-month publication rules if filed on or after November 29, 2000, whereas the RCE would not trigger patent application publication.

Thus, there are a number of considerations that may affect the choice of procedure for continuing prosecution in an application. These considerations include: (1) the invention to be examined; (2) the stage of prosecution of the application; (3) whether a reply to any outstanding Office Action is available; (4) whether patent term adjustments have been accumulated or are likely during future prosecution; (5) the fee to be paid for continuing examination; (6) whether the application will be subject to publication or republication; and (7) whether the new provisions of 35 U.S.C. Section 103(a) are available as applied to Section 102(e) prior art.

Main volume footnote updates begin on page 21.

A sample RCE form is included in Appendix B, and a copy of the Patent Office rules implementing RCEs is included in Appendix C. A copy of questions and answers regarding RCEs and a comparison between RCEs and Continued Prosecution Applications (CPAs) are included in Appendix D.

E. Provisional Applications

[Insert after footnote 116.]

The pendency period of a provisional application, however, will extend beyond the 12 months to the next succeeding secular business day if the 12-month period expires on a holiday observed in the District of Columbia.[49] Accordingly, there is no co-pendency requirement for a provisional application and either a national or Patent Cooperation Treaty (PCT) application, for the provisional application to be relied upon in any proceeding in the Patent Office.[50] A copy of the Patent Office rules implementing these changes is included in Appendix C.

[Insert at the end of the section.]

A description of provisional applications is provided in Appendix C.

F. Statutory Invention Registration

[Insert after footnote 120.]

See Appendix B for a U.S. Patent Office form that can be used to convert a patent application into a statutory invention registration.

V. General Parts of a Patent Application

[Insert after footnote 122.]

The Patent Office has also created an optional Application Data Sheet that can be filed with the application which is supposed to improve the accuracy of filing receipts. A copy of the requirements for the Application Data Sheet is provided in Appendix C. A guide for filing utility patent applications is provided in Appendix C. In addition, the procedure relating to according a filing date to a patent application is provided in Appendix C.

---

[49] 35 U.S.C. § 119(e) (Supp. 2000).

[50] *Id.*

Main volume footnote updates begin on page 21.

A. Specification

1. Title of Invention

[Insert at the end of the subsection.]

The Federal Circuit has subsequently clarified that the *Exxon* decision was not used to directly interpret a patent claim, but merely to make an illustrative point. Specifically, in *Pitney Bowes Inc. v. Hewlett-Packard Co.*,[51] the Federal Circuit reversed a district court's claim interpretation based on an amendment made to the patent application title. The Federal Circuit acknowledged that according to Patent Office procedure, "where the title is not descriptive of the invention claimed, the examiner should require the substitution of a new title that is clearly indicative of the invention."[52]

The Federal Circuit emphasized that, as indicated by the Manual of Patent Examining Procedure (MPEP), the purpose of the title is not to demarcate the precise boundaries of the claimed invention, but rather to provide a useful reference tool for future classification purposes. The Federal Circuit also reasoned that if limitations are not read into the claims from the specification, then limitations from the patent title will most surely not be read into the claims.[53] Consequently, the Federal Circuit held that an amendment of the patent title during prosecution should not be regarded as having the same or similar effect as an amendment of the claims themselves by the applicant.[54]

The near irrelevancy of the patent title to claim construction, the Federal Circuit reasoned, was demonstrated by the dearth of case law in which the patent title had been used as an aid to claim construction. According to the Federal Circuit, "[w]e are only aware of one case [*Exxon Chemical Patents*] from this court in which the patent title was accorded any significance whatsoever in a claim construction."[55] According to the Federal Circuit:

> While the court in *Exxon Chemical Patents* mentioned the patent title in its claim construction, this one-sentence statement was made simply to illustrate the point that the patent-in-suit claimed a product containing certain ingredients. Indeed, the claim construction relied, not upon the patent title, but upon the standard sources of the claims, the specification, and the prosecution history. . . . Consequently, that the patent title has only been mentioned once by this court in the context of claim con-

[51] Pitney Bowes Inc. v. Hewlett-Packard Co., 182 F.3d 1298, 51 USPQ 2d 1161 (Fed. Cir. 1999).

[52] Manual of Patent Examining Procedure § 606.01 (6th ed., 1995) [hereinafter MPEP].

[53] Pitney Bowes, 51 USPQ 2d at 1171 (citing E.I. du Pont de Nemours & Co. v. Phillips Petroleum Co., 849 F.2d 1430, 1433, 7 USPQ 2d 1129, 1132 (Fed. Cir. 1988)).

[54] *Id.*

[55] *Id.*

Main volume footnote updates begin on page 21.

struction and, even then, merely to make an illustrative point in one sentence, makes a powerful statement as to the unimportance of a patent's title to claim construction.[56]

7. *Description of the Preferred Embodiments*

[Insert after footnote 140.]

Incorporation by reference is a common drafting tool used throughout the law.[57] "As the expression itself implies, the purpose of 'incorporation by reference' is to make one document become a part of another document by referring to the former in the latter in such a manner that it is apparent that the cited document is part of the referencing document as if it were fully set out therein."[58] Therefore, unless Congress deviated from this accepted norm, material is "in" the specification if it is incorporated by reference.[59]

8. *Claims*

a. Basic Parts of a Claim

[Insert after footnote 156.]

If the claim preamble, when read in the context of the entire claim, recites limitations of the claim, or, if the claim preamble is "necessary to give life, meaning, and vitality" to the claim, then the claim preamble should be construed as if in the balance of the claim.[60] According to the Federal Circuit:

> Indeed, when discussing the "claim" in such a circumstance, there is no meaningful distinction to be drawn between the claim preamble and the rest of the claim, for only together do they comprise the "claim." If, how-

---

[56] *Id.*

[57] *See In re* Hawkins, 486 F.2d 569, 573, 179 USPQ 157, 161 (C.C.P.A. 1973) (incorporation by reference has "longstanding basis in the law"); General Elec. Co. v. Brenner, 407 F.2d 1258, 1261–62, 159 USPQ 335, 337–38 (D.C. Cir. 1968).

[58] *In re* Lund, 376 F.2d 982, 989, 153 USPQ 625, 631 (C.C.P.A. 1967) (emphasis added); Interstate Consol. St. Ry. v. Massachusetts, 207 U.S. 79, 84 (1907) ("If the charter, instead of writing out the requirements of Rev. Laws, 112, Section 72, referred specifically to another document expressing them, and purported to incorporate it, of course the charter would have the same effect as if it itself contained the words."); Black's Law Dictionary 907 (4th ed. 1968) (defining "incorporate" as "[t]o declare that another document shall be taken as part of the document in which the declaration is made as much as if it were set out at length therein").

[59] Atmel Corp. v. Information Storage Devices, Inc., 198 F.3d 1374, 1378, 53 USPQ 2d 1225, 1227 (Fed. Cir. 1999) (Mayer, J., dissenting).

[60] Kropa v. Robie, 187 F.2d 150, 152, 88 USPQ 478, 480–81 (C.C.P.A. 1951); Rowe v. Dror, 112 F.3d 473, 478, 42 USPQ 2d 1550, 1553 (Fed. Cir. 1997); Corning Glass Works v. Sumitomo Elec. U.S.A., Inc., 868 F.2d 1251, 1257, 9 USPQ 2d 1962, 1966 (Fed. Cir. 1989).

Main volume footnote updates begin on page 21.

ever, the body of the claim fully and intrinsically sets forth the complete invention, including all of its limitations, and the preamble offers no distinct definition of any of the claimed invention's limitations, but rather merely states, for example, the purpose or intended use of the invention, then the preamble is of no significance to claim construction because it cannot be said to constitute or explain a claim limitation.[61]

[Insert on page 44 before the paragraph beginning "The body of a claim . . ."]

As summarized by the Federal Circuit:

> The phrase "consisting of" is a term of art in patent law signifying restriction and exclusion, while, in contrast, the term "comprising" indicates an open-ended construction. . . . In simple terms, a drafter uses the phrase "consisting of" to mean "I claim what follows and nothing else." A drafter uses the term "comprising" to mean "I claim at least what follows and potentially more."[62]

9. *Abstract*

[On page 51 change the second sentence to the following.]

The abstract must be short and easy to read, containing no more than 150 words.

[Change the last sentence to the following.]

Even though the Patent Office regulations specify that the abstract has no legal significance with respect to interpreting the scope of the claims defining the metes and bounds of the invention,[63] the Federal Circuit has not exactly adopted this view of the regulations. In fact, the Federal Circuit has held that in determining the scope of a claim, the abstract of a patent is a potentially useful source of intrinsic evidence as to the meaning of a disputed claim term.[64]

B. Drawings

[Add the following at the end of the section.]

Patent drawings do not generally define the precise proportions of the elements depicted therein, and therefore, may not generally be

---

[61] Pitney Bowes Inc. v. Hewlett-Packard Co., 182 F.3d 1298, 51 USPQ 2d 1161, 1166 (Fed. Cir. 1999).

[62] Vehicular Techs. Corp. v. Titan Wheel Int'l, Inc., 212 F.3d 1377, 54 USPQ 2d 1841, 1845 (Fed. Cir. 2000).

[63] 37 C.F.R. § 1.72(b).

[64] Hill-Rom Co. v. Kinetic Concepts, Inc., 209 F.3d 1337, 1341 n.1, 54 USPQ 2d 1437, 1440 n.1 (Fed. Cir. 2000).

Main volume footnote updates begin on page 21.

relied on to show particular sizes if the specification is completely silent on the issue.[65] Thus, the Federal Circuit has held that a reasonable competitor, being aware that figures in a patent are not drawn to scale unless otherwise indicated, may interpret the scope of the patent claims and interpret the prosecution history and possible estoppels, accordingly.[66] Thus, whenever possible, specific dimensions or dimensional relationships depicted in the drawings should be described in the specification. In addition, any potential dimensional equivalents should also be described in association with the drawings.

C. Inventor Declaration

[Insert at the end of the section.]

In view of the sensitive nature of the declaration document, the specific rules associated with the declaration should be carefully followed. For example, 37 C.F.R. Section 1.69 requires that

> [w]henever an individual making an oath or declaration cannot understand English, the oath or declaration must be in a language that such individual can understand and shall state that such individual understands the content of any documents to which the oath or declaration relates.[67]

Failure to adhere to the rules may raise issues that easily could have been disposed of had compliance occurred. For example, in *Seiko Epson Corp. v. Nu-Kote International, Inc.*,[68] the U.S. patent attorney prosecuting Seiko's patents (the Suzuki patents), which originated in Japan, had filed declarations in order to correct a description of certain patent drawings as prior art. These declarations were in the English language and had not been translated into Japanese when signed by the Japanese inventors. The district court held that this was a per se violation of 37 C.F.R. Section 1.69 and rendered the patents permanently unenforceable for inequitable conduct.

The district court relied solely on the undisputed fact that the declarations were in the English language when they were signed. The district court ruled that although none of the declarations were false, it sufficed, per se, that the documents had not been presented in the Japanese language. The court held that this of itself served to invalidate the patents and that it was irrelevant that two of the three Japanese inventors testified that they could read and understand

---

[65] Hockerson-Halberstadt, Inc. v. Avia Group Int'l, Inc., 222 F.3d 951, 55 USPQ 2d 1487, 1491 (Fed. Cir. 2000) (citing *In re* Wright, 569 F.2d 1124, 1127, 193 USPQ 332, 335 (C.C.P.A. 1977) ("Absent any written description in the specification of quantitative values, arguments based on measurement of a drawing are of little value."); *In re* Olson, 212 F.2d 590, 592, 101 USPQ 401, 402 (C.C.P.A. 1954)).

[66] *Id.*

[67] 37 C.F.R. § 1.69.

[68] Seiko Epson Corp. v. Nu-Kote Int'l, Inc., 190 F.3d 1360, 52 USPQ 2d 1011 (Fed. Cir. 1999).

Main volume footnote updates begin on page 21.

English, and the third testified that the document was fully explained to him by a co-inventor, who also so testified.

On appeal, the Federal Circuit reversed. Epson argued that the requirement for foreign language oaths related to ensuring that foreign inventors fully understood the obligations and representations in the inventors' original or supplemental oaths. Epson also argued that even if 37 C.F.R. Section 1.69 did apply, any technical violation was cured by subsequently filed documents. That is, the challenged English language declarations were followed by Supplemental Declarations of Inventorship, which were executed in parallel English and Japanese format, in full accordance with the regulations. Thus, the challenged English language declarations were followed by Japanese language declarations that referred to the subject matter of the challenged declarations. Nu-Kote argued that the inventors did not know what they were signing, whether or not they understood English.

The Federal Circuit specifically declined to reach the general question of whether the correct scope of Section 1.69 is that every declaration of a nonEnglish-speaking declarant, at every stage of patent prosecution, must be executed in the declarant's language.[69] The Federal Circuit agreed with Epson that the Japanese declarations remedied any technical flaw in the declarations accompanying the amendment correcting the drawing figures.

The Federal Circuit also held that a ruling of inequitable conduct in the Patent Office must be supported by clear and convincing evidence of material misrepresentation, made with the intent to deceive or mislead the patent examiner. "Technical violations of PTO procedures, absent fraud or intentional deception, are not inequitable conduct as would invalidate the patent."[70] The Federal Circuit pointed out that the notion of per se forfeiture based on nonfraudulent failure to comply with a rule of practice before the Patent Office has been consistently rejected.[71]

Thus, the practitioner should not underestimate the complication that may result when preparing the declaration document, and should follow the Patent Office regulations closely, as appropriate.[72]

Additional Declarations are provided in Appendix B in the Korean, Russian, and Chinese languages.

---

[69] *Id.*, 52 USPQ 2d at 1017 n.4.

[70] *Id.* at 1017.

[71] *Id.* (citing Hebert v. Lisle Corp., 99 F.3d 1109, 1116, 40 USPQ 2d 1611, 1615–16 (Fed. Cir. 1996) ("A holding of unenforceability based on the filing of a false oath requires that the oath was false, and made with knowledge of the falsity .... Knowledge of falsity is predicate to intent to deceive."); Molins PLC v. Textron, Inc., 48 F.3d 1172, 1184, 33 USPQ 2d 1823, 1832 (Fed. Cir. 1995) ("intent to deceive should be determined in light of the realities of patent practice, and not as a matter of strict liability whatever the nature of the action before the PTO").

[72] *See also* Ajinomoto Co. v. Archer-Daniels-Midland Co., 228 F.3d 1338, 56 USPQ 2d 1332, 1336 (Fed. Cir. 2000) *cert. denied*, 121 S.Ct. 1957 (2001) (noting that inventor cannot authorize another to sign declaration on his or her behalf).

Main volume footnote updates begin on page 21.

D. Filing Fee

[Insert after footnote 185.]

The Patent Office has eliminated the requirement of a verified statement from a small entity, and has adopted simplified procedures for claiming small entity status. These procedures include a simple written assertion of entitlement to small entity status that can be signed by an attorney or agent registered to practice before the Patent Office.[73] However, a written assertion is not required where the basic filing fee is submitted in a small entity amount. The Patent Office will consider the payment of the basic filing fee in the small entity amount to constitute a written assertion of entitlement to small entity status.[74] However, if a change in status from a large entity to a small entity occurs during the prosecution of a patent application, after the filing fees have been paid in large entity amount, it is no longer sufficient to submit small entity fees in the absence of a written assertion of entitlement to small entity status.[75] A copy of the Patent Office rules implementing the Patent Office business goals is included in Appendix C, and copies of an overview and questions and answers regarding the Patent Office business goals are included in Appendix D.

[Change the text following footnote 188.]

The regulation additionally provides:

(1) Any attempt to fraudulently establish status as a small entity, or pay fees as a small entity shall be considered as a fraud practiced or attempted on the Office.

(2) Improperly, and with intent to deceive, establishing status as a small entity, or paying fees as a small entity, shall be considered as a fraud practiced or attempted on the Office.[76]

---

[73] 37 C.F.R. § 1.27(c)(1) and (2)(i) (2000).

[74] 37 C.F.R. § 1.27(c)(3).

[75] 37 C.F.R. § 1.27(c)(3)(ii).

[76] 37 C.F.R. § 1.27(h) (2000).

Main volume footnote updates begin on page 21.

MAIN VOLUME FOOTNOTE UPDATES

[7]**[Replace the S. Ct. cite with the following.]** 525 U.S. 929.

[19]**[Replace the S. Ct. cite with the following.]** 518 U.S. 1018.

[34]**[Replace the S. Ct. cite with the following.]** 524 U.S. 940.

[36]**[Replace the S. Ct. cite with the following.]** 519 U.S. 1101.

[42]**[Replace the S. Ct. cite with the following.]** 519 U.S. 1101.

[45]**[In Hunter Douglas Inc. v. Harmonic Design Inc., replace the LEXIS cite with the following.]** 525 U.S. 1143.

[51]**[Replace the LEXIS cite with the following.]** 57 F.3d 1067.

[61]**[Replace the S. Ct. cite with the following.]** 516 U.S. 1040.

[71]**[Replace the S. Ct. cite with the following.]** 525 U.S. 929.

[87]**[Replace "(95–524 Jan. 9, 1996)" with the following.]** 516 U.S. 1067 (1996).

[102]**[Replace existing footnote 102 with the following.]** Vornado Air Circulation Sys., Inc. v. Duracraft Corp., 58 F.3d 1498, 35 USPQ 2d 1332 (10th Cir. 1995), *cert. denied*, 516 U.S. 1067 (1996).

[103]**[Replace the S. Ct. cite for Thomas & Betts Corp. v. Panduit Corp. with the following.]** 516 U.S. 1159.

[117]**[In Hyatt v. Boone, replace the LEXIS cite with the following.]** 525 U.S. 1141.

[125]**[Replace the S. Ct. cite in footnote 125 with the following.]** 518 U.S. 1020

[145]**[Replace the S. Ct. cite in footnote 145 with the following.]** 518 U.S. 1020

2

Prosecution and Appeals

VI. Response/Amendment by the Applicant

[Insert after footnote 43.]

The Patent Office requires all business before it to be conducted, or at least documented, in writing.[1] It is the responsibility of the applicant to ensure that the substance of any interview with an Examiner is included in the written record of the application, unless the Examiner provides the written record, for example, in an interview summary record.[2]

XII. Notice of Allowance

[Delete the second, third, fourth, and fifth sentences in the section and replace them with the following.]

The Notice of Allowance (also known as the Notice of Allowability), may optionally be accompanied by an Examiner's Statement of Reasons for Allowance.[3] These reasons for allowance may be considered in in-

[1] Li Second Family v. Toshiba Corp., 231 F.3d 1373, 56 USPQ 2d 1681, 1685 (Fed. Cir. 2000), *cert. denied*, 69 USLW 3673 (U.S. 2001); Litton Sys., Inc. v. Whirlpool Corp., 728 F.2d 1423, 1439, 221 USPQ 97, 106 (Fed. Cir. 1984).

[2] Li Second Family v. Toshiba Corp., 231 F.3d 1373, 56 USPQ 2d 1681, 1685 (Fed. Cir. 2000), *cert. denied*, 69 USLW 3673 (U.S. 2001).

[3] 37 C.F.R. § 1.104(e) (1998).

Main volume footnote updates begin on page 72.

terpreting the patent claims, particularly if the applicant fails to respond. For example, the Patent Office is of the view that the applicant is required "to set forth his or her position in the file if he or she disagrees with the examiner's reasons for allowance, or be subject to inferences or presumptions to be determined on a case-by-case basis."[4] It follows, therefore, that the reasons for allowance may also produce prosecution history estoppel. Applicants are cautioned, therefore, that confirming that the reasons should not be used to interpret the patent claims may be advisable.

XIII. Appeal to Patent Office

[Insert after footnote 109.]

Applicants should be cautious when appealing a plurality of rejected claims, preferably arguing each claim separately. That is, an applicant should not generally stipulate that one claim or a subset of claims are representative of all claims being appealed. If certain claims are designated as representative claims, then patentability of the remaining claims will be based on the representative claims.

The Federal Circuit has indicated, however, that an applicant may still request reconsideration of all claims even though initially all claims were not separately argued. As stated by the Federal Circuit, "[w]e do not believe that such legalistic rigidity is appropriate in the proceeding before the Board, particularly when appeal to the Board was taken to all the rejected claims."[5]

Applicants should be cautious that the record is clear on appeal, and that the issues are ripe or clearly set forth for decision by the Board. For example, the Board has commented in this regard as follows:

> The appeal is is manifestly not ready for a decision on the merits. We start out with the proposition that an appeal is just that—an appeal. The review authorized by 35 U.S.C. § 134 is not a process whereby the examiner and the applicant invite the board to examine the application and resolve patentability in the first instance. But, that is what both examiner and applicant have asked us to do. The examiner has not clearly set out the basis for his rejection because he has failed to precisely identify the differences between the claimed subject matter and [the prior art]. Applicant likewise has not been much help because he wants us to locate and then consider material not introduced into evidence.[6]

---

[4] Fed. Reg., Vol. 65, No. 175, 54633 (Sept. 8, 2000).

[5] *In re* Duve, Civ. App. 97–1095, slip op. at 5, n. 1 (Fed. Cir. Feb. 26, 1999) (unpublished).

[6] *Ex parte* Braeken, 54 USPQ 2d 1110 (B.P.A.I. 1999) (unpublished).

Main volume footnote updates begin on page 72.

XIV. Appeal to Federal Court

[On page 80, insert after the paragraph containing footnote 110.]

In the context of an appeal to the District Court under 35 U.S.C. Section 145, in which the Board has conducted an ex parte proceeding, the admission of live testimony at trial requires the factfinder to make its own findings, i.e., a de novo review.[7] The rationale is that the applicant was at least partly unable to present the live testimony in the ex parte proceeding before the Board. The district court, therefore, can reach a different conclusion on the same evidence that was before the Patent Office since the form in which the evidence is presented is fundamentally different.[8] As noted by the Federal Circuit:

> In its evaluation of the evidence on which this conclusion was based, the district court had a powerful advantage over the patent examiner and the Board, an advantage characteristic of section 145 appeals, in that the court heard and saw witnesses, testifying under examination and cross-examination, and had the benefit of extensive discussion and argument.[9]

The district court may therefore hear live testimony, give more weight to some witnesses than to others, and come to a different conclusion than that reached by the Board. According to the Federal Circuit:

> This trial before the district court partook of the quality that is available only with the examination and cross-examination of live witnesses. . . . If the evidence adduced before the district court led to a decision different from that reached by the PTO, that is not contrary to the legislative purpose of section 145 de novo review. Indeed, it is in fulfillment of that purpose.[10]

[Insert after footnote 112.]

When appealing from the Patent Office, all appeals within the Patent Office must be exhausted. For example, in *Teacherson v. Patent and Trademark Office,*[11] the applicant claimed that the Patent Office violated its own regulations. Rather than appealing to the Board, the applicant attempted to appeal the Examiner's rejections directly to the

[7]Burlington Indus., Inc. v. Quigg, 822 F.2d 1581, 1584, 3 USPQ 2d 1436, 1439 (Fed. Cir. 1987).

[8]Winner Int'l Royalty Corp. v. Wang, 202 F.3d 1340, 53 USPQ 2d 1580, 1585 (Fed. Cir.), *cert. denied*, 530 U.S. 1238 (2000).

[9]Burlington Indus., Inc. v. Quigg, 822 F.2d 1581, 1584, 3 USPQ 2d 1436, 1437–38 (Fed. Cir. 1987).

[10]*Id.* at 1584, 3 USPQ 2d at 1439.

[11]Teacherson v. Patent and Trademark Office, Civ. App. No. 99-1465 (Fed. Cir. Mar. 10, 2000) (unpublished), *cert. denied*, 121 S. Ct. 493 (2000).

U.S. District Court for the District of Columbia. The district court held that it had no jurisdiction since the applicant failed to appeal the rejection to the Board. The Federal Circuit subsequently affirmed the holding of the district court and sent the applicant back to the Patent Office to appeal the rejection to the Board. The Federal Circuit stated:

> The Patent Act created the PTO review process, imposing the duty to follow a specified appeal process on both applicant and PTO. The Act does not create jurisdiction to circumvent these statutory appeal routes. Mr. Teacherson claims that the PTO violated own regulations, but by avoiding the statutory appeal routes he has not allowed PTO to correct those errors, if any.[12]

[Insert after footnote 138.]

The Supreme Court granted certiori and reversed, holding that the standard the Federal Circuit must apply is the standard set forth in the Administrative Procedures Act (APA).[13]

The APA establishes standards governing judicial review of findings of fact made by federal administrative agencies.[14] The issue in *Zurko* was whether the APA applies when the Federal Circuit reviews findings of fact made by the Patent and Trademark Office (PTO).

Section 706 of the APA, originally enacted in 1946, sets forth standards that govern the scope of review of agency factfinding (court/agency review). Section 706 states that a reviewing court shall:

> (2) hold unlawful and set aside agency . . . findings . . . found to be—
>
> (A) arbitrary, capricious, [or] an abuse of discretion, or . . .
>
> (E) unsupported by substantial evidence in a case subject to sections 556 and 557 of this title or otherwise reviewed on the record of an agency hearing provided by statute; . . .
>
> In making the foregoing determinations, the court shall review the whole record or those parts of it cited by a party . . . .[15]

Federal Rule of Civil Procedure 52(a) sets forth standards that govern appellate court review of findings of fact made by a district court judge (court/court review). Rule 52(a) states that the appellate court shall set aside those findings only if they are "clearly erroneous."[16] Traditionally, this court/court standard of review has been considered somewhat stricter (i.e., allowing a more detailed judicial review) than the APA's court/agency standards.

The patent statutes, however, did not and do not use the term "substantial evidence" or any other term to describe the standard of

---

[12]*Id.*, slip op. at 4–5.

[13]Dickinson v. Zurko, 527 U.S. 150, 50 USPQ 2d 1930 (1999).

[14]Administrative Procedure Act § 706, 5 U.S.C. § 706 (1988).

[15]Administrative Procedure Act § 706, 5 U.S.C. § 706 (1994)

[16]Fed. R. Civ. P. 52(a).

court review.[17] The Supreme Court noted that the appropriate standard of review remains in dispute to this day, a dispute that the Supreme Court did not settle, that is, precisely which APA standard—"substantial evidence" or "arbitrary, capricious, abuse of discretion"—would apply to court review of PTO factfinding, if the APA standard were to be applied.[18]

While the court/agency standard is somewhat less strict than the court/court standard, the Supreme Court noted that:

> the difference is a subtle one—so fine that (apart from the present case) we have failed to uncover a single instance in which a reviewing court conceded that use of one standard rather than the other would in fact have produced a different outcome.[19]

Thus, the Supreme Court outlined the following possibilities available to an applicant for appealing an adverse decision from the Board of Patent Appeals and Interferences. An applicant denied a patent can seek review either directly in the Federal Circuit or indirectly by first obtaining direct review in federal district court. The first path will now bring about Federal Circuit court/agency review; the second path might well lead to Federal Circuit court/court review, for the Federal Circuit now reviews federal district court factfinding using a "clearly erroneous" standard. The second path permits the disappointed applicant to present to the court evidence that the applicant did not present to the PTO. The presence of such new or different evidence makes a factfinder of the district judge. And nonexpert judicial factfinding calls for the court/court standard of review.[20]

Of course, the above standard under the APA applies to factual determinations by the Board of Patent Appeals and Interferences. Questions of law are reviewed de novo by the Federal Circuit.[21]

However, the Supreme Court decision in *Zurko*, did not explicitly determine whether the correct standard of review for Patent Office findings of fact is the "arbitrary, capricious" or the "substantial evidence" standards under the APA. In *In re Gartside*,[22] the Federal Circuit decided the issue and held that Supreme Court precedent and the law of the federal circuit courts indicated that "substantial evidence" review is appropriate for appeals from the Board of Patent Appeals

---

[17] 35 U.S.C. §§ 61, 62 (1994).

[18] Dickinson v. Zurko, 527 U.S. 150, 50 USPQ 2d 1930, 1934 (1999) (citing Association of Data Processing Serv. Orgs., Inc. v. Board of Governors of Fed. Reserve Sys., 745 F.2d 677, 683–84 (D.C. Cir. 1984) (finding no difference between the APA's "arbitrary, capricious" standard and its "substantial evidence" standard as applied to court review of agency factfinding)).

[19] *Id.*, 50 USPQ 2d at 1936.

[20] *Id.*

[21] *See In re* Donaldson, 16 F.3d 1189, 1192, 29 USPQ 2d 1845, 1848 (Fed. Cir. 1994); *In re* Beasley, Civ. App. 99-1055, slip op. at 4–5 (Fed. Cir. July 20, 1999) (unpublished); *In re* Case, Civ. App. 98-1531, slip op. at 6 (Fed. Cir. Aug. 31, 1999) (unpublished).

[22] *In re* Gartside, 203 F.3d 1305, 53 USPQ 2d 1769 (Fed. Cir. 2000).

Main volume footnote updates begin on page 72.

and Interferences. The Federal Circuit noted that the Supreme Court has stated generally that the "basic requirement" for "substantial evidence" review is that the agency hearing produce a record that serves as the foundation for the agency's action.[23]

The Federal Circuit also noted that in appeals from the Board, a comprehensive record is developed that contains the arguments and evidence presented by the parties, including all of the relevant information upon which the Board relied in rendering its decision.[24] This record is closed, in that the Board's decision must be justified within the four corners of that record. The record on appeal thus dictates the parameters of Federal Circuit review. The Federal Circuit commented that it cannot look elsewhere to find justification for the Board's decision. Furthermore, the record reflects the results of a proceeding in the Patent Office during which the applicant has been afforded an opportunity to bring forth the facts thought necessary to support his or her position. Accompanying the record is a detailed opinion from the Board. The Federal Circuit further emphasized that the Board's opinion must explicate its factual conclusions, enabling the Federal Circuit to verify readily whether those conclusions are indeed supported by "substantial evidence" contained within the record.[25]

The "substantial evidence" standard asks whether a reasonable fact finder could have arrived at the agency's decision,[26] and is considered to be a less deferential review standard than "arbitrary, capricious."[27] The Supreme Court has described "substantial evidence" in the following manner:

> Substantial evidence is more than a mere scintilla. It means such relevant evidence as a reasonable mind might accept as adequate to support a conclusion. . . . Mere uncorroborated hearsay or rumor does not constitute substantial evidence.[28]

The Supreme Court has emphasized that "substantial evidence" review involves examination of the record as a whole, taking into ac-

---

[23] *Id.*, 53 USPQ 2d at 1774 (citing Citizens to Preserve Overton Park, Inc. v. Volpe, 401 U.S. 402, 415 (1971); Camp v. Pitts, 411 U.S. 138, 141 (1973) (noting that "substantial evidence" review "is appropriate when reviewing findings made on a hearing record")).

[24] *Id.* (citing 35 U.S.C. § 143 (1994) ("[T]he Commissioner shall transmit to the United States Court of Appeals for the Federal Circuit a certified list of the documents comprising the record in the Patent and Trademark Office.")).

[25] *Id.* (citing Gechter v. Davidson, 116 F.3d 1454, 1460, 43 USPQ 2d 1030, 1035 (Fed. Cir. 1997) ("[W]e hold that the Board is required to set forth in its opinions specific findings of fact and conclusions of law adequate to form a basis for our review.")).

[26] Consolidated Edison Co. v. NLRB, 305 U.S. 197, 229 (1938).

[27] American Paper Inst., Inc. v. American Elec. Power Serv. Corp., 461 U.S. 402, 412–13 n.7 (1983) (characterizing the "arbitrary, capricious" standard as "more lenient" than the "substantial evidence" standard); Abbott Lab. v. Gardner, 387 U.S. 136, 143 (1967) (characterizing "substantial evidence" review as "more generous judicial review" than "arbitrary, capricious" review).

[28] Consolidated Edison Co. v. NLRB, 305 U.S. 197, 229–30 (1938).

Main volume footnote updates begin on page 72.

count evidence that both justifies and detracts from an agency's decision.[29] The Supreme Court has also clarified that the possibility of drawing two inconsistent conclusions from the evidence does not prevent an administrative agency's finding from being supported by substantial evidence.[30] "Indeed, if a reasonable mind might accept the evidence as adequate to support the factual conclusions drawn by the Board, then we must uphold the Board's determination."[31]

When a regulation promulgated by the Patent Office is challenged, the Patent Office's interpretation is provided great deference.[32] In connection with the review of a regulation, the Patent Office's interpretation of the statute which the regulation at issue implements must be reasonable and not arbitrary or capricious.[33]

[Insert after footnote 147.]

The soundness of the Federal Circuit rule regarding non-precedential opinions has been called into question by the U.S. Court of Appeals for the Eighth Circuit in *Anastasoff v. United States*,[34] holding the inability to cite unpublished opinions unconstitutional. In *Anastasoff*, Faye Anastasoff sought a refund of overpaid federal income tax. On April 13, 1996, Ms. Anastasoff mailed her refund claim to the Internal Revenue Service (IRS) for taxes paid on April 15, 1993. Although her claim was mailed within the appropriate period, it was received and filed by the IRS on April 16, 1996, three years and one day after she overpaid her taxes, i.e., one day late. The IRS denied her claim under 26 U.S.C. Section 6511(b), which limits refunds to taxes paid in the three years prior to the filing of a claim. Another section of the IRS statutes, 26 U.S.C. Section 7502, called "the Mailbox Rule," allows some IRS filings to be deemed received when postmarked.

The district court held that Section 7502 could not apply to Ms. Anastasoff's claim, and granted judgment for the IRS. On appeal, Ms. Anastasoff argued that Section 7502 should apply whenever necessary to fulfill its remedial purpose, i.e., to save taxpayers from the vagaries of the postal system, even when only part of the claim is untimely. The Eighth Circuit held that a prior non-precedential opinion, *Christie v. United States*,[35] prevented the Mailbox Rule from being

---

[29] Universal Camera Corp. v. NLRB, 340 U.S. 474, 487–88 (1951)

[30] Consolo v. Federal Maritime Comm'n, 383 U.S. 607, 620 (1966).

[31] *In re* Kotzab, 217 F.3d 1365, 55 USPQ 2d 1313, 1316 (Fed. Cir. 2000).

[32] Blacklight Power, Inc. v. Dickinson, 109 F. Supp. 2d 44, 55 USPQ 2d 1812 (D.D.C. 2000) (citing Chevron U.S.A., Inc. v. Natural Resources Defense Council, Inc. 467 U.S. 837, 842–44 (1984)).

[33] *Id.*, 55 USPQ 2d at 1819, 1820.

[34] Anastasoff v. United States, 223 F.3d 898, 56 USPQ 2d 1621 (8th Cir.), *vacated on rehearing en banc*, 235 F.3d 1054 (8th Cir. 2000).

[35] Christie v. United States, Civ. App. No. 91-2375MN (8th Cir. Mar. 20, 1992) (unpublished).

Main volume footnote updates begin on page 72.

applied to Ms. Anastasoff's claim. Ms. Anastasoff argued that *Christie* should not be used as precedent because it was an unpublished decision, and an Eighth Circuit rule prevented use of the opinion. In particular, the rule provides:

> Unpublished opinions are not precedent and parties generally should not cite them. When relevant to establishing the doctrines of res judicata, collateral estoppel, or the law of the case, however, the parties may cite any unpublished opinion. Parties may also cite an unpublished opinion of this court if the opinion has persuasive value on a material issue and no published opinion of this or another court would serve as well.[36]

The Eighth Circuit, however, disagreed, relying on the longstanding use of precedent in the U.S. legal system. The Eighth Circuit noted that the doctrine of precedent was well established by the time the Framers gathered in Philadelphia.[37] The doctrine of precedent was not merely well established; it was the historic method of judicial decision-making, and well regarded as a bulwark of judicial independence in past struggles for liberty.[38] According to the Eighth Circuit, the Framers of the Constitution considered these principles to derive from the nature of judicial power, and intended that they would limit the judicial power delegated to the courts by Article III of the Constitution. The doctrine of precedent was therefore well established in legal practice, despite the absence of a reporting system, regarded as an immemorial custom, and valued for its role in past struggles for liberty. The duty of courts to follow their prior decisions was understood to derive from the nature of the judicial power itself and to separate it from a dangerous union with the legislative power.

For these reasons, the Eighth Circuit rejected Ms. Anastasoff's argument that, under Eighth Cir. R. 28A(i), it could ignore the prior non-precedential decision in *Christie*. Federal courts, in adopting rules, are not free to extend the judicial power of the United States described in Article III of the Constitution; Rule 28A(i) allows courts to ignore this limit by designating an opinion as unpublished. According to the Eighth Circuit, this discretion is completely inconsistent with the doctrine of precedent; Rule 28A(i) expanded the judicial power beyond the limits set by Article III by allowing courts complete discretion to determine which judicial decisions would be binding, and which would not. Insofar as it limits the precedential effect of prior decisions, the Eighth Circuit held that Rule 28A(i) was unconstitutional.

The Eighth Circuit therefore held that Ms. Anastasoff's interpretation of Section 7502 was directly addressed and rejected in *Christie*,

---

[36] *Anastasoff*, 56 USPQ 2d at 1622 (quoting Eighth Circuit Rule 28A(i)).

[37] Morton J. Horwitz, *The Transformation of American Law: 1780–1860,* 8–9 (1977); J.H. Baker, *An Introduction to English Legal History,* 227 (1990); Sir William Holdsworth, *Case Law*, 50 L.Q.R. 180 (1934); 1 Sir William W. Blackstone, *Commentaries on the Laws of England,* 69 (1765) ("it is an established rule to abide by former precedents").

[38] *Anastasoff*, 56 USPQ 2d at 1623.

Main volume footnote updates begin on page 72.

and that Eighth Cir. R. 28A(i) required that decision to be followed. Accordingly, the judgment of the district court was affirmed. The Eighth Circuit has agreed to hear this case en banc, and the decision has been vacated pending the rehearing en banc.

XV. Prosecution Tips

A. Interpreting Scope of Patent Claims

[Insert after footnote 150.]

It is the claims of a patent, not the written description, that define the scope of the patentee's right to exclude.[39]

[Insert after footnote 151.]

If upon examination of this intrinsic evidence the meaning of the claim language is sufficiently clear, resort to the above-described extrinsic evidence, such as treatises and technical references, as well as expert testimony when appropriate, should not be necessary.[40] Unambiguous intrinsic evidence in turn provides sufficient input to the rules of claim construction, in particular the rule that explicit statements made by a patent applicant during prosecution to distinguish a claimed invention over prior art may serve to narrow the scope of a claim.[41]

---

[39] E.I. du Pont de Nemours & Co. v. Phillips Petroleum Co., 849 F.2d 1430, 1433, 7 USPQ 2d 1129, 1131 (Fed. Cir. 1988).

[40] Digital Biometrics, Inc. v. Identix, Inc., 149 F.3d 1335, 1347, 47 USPQ 2d 1418, 1424 (Fed. Cir. 1998).

[41] Spectrum Int'l, Inc. v. Sterilite Corp., 164 F.3d 1372, 49 USPQ 2d 1065, 1069 (Fed. Cir. 1998). *See also* K-2 Corp. v. Salomon S.A., 191 F.3d 1356, 52 USPQ 2d 1001, 1008–09 (Fed. Cir. 1999):

> The Johnson reference describes and depicts an in-line skate with an easily removable upper shoe portion that can be attached to the base of the skate. A second prior art reference, French Patent No. 2,688,072 (the "French reference"), teaches a soft upper bootie attached to the skate base with screws at the toe and the heel. Given these two pieces of prior art, and the undisputed fact that the accused skate utilizes a removable screw to attach the heel of the soft upper bootie to the base of the skate, we have no trouble concluding that the doctrine of equivalents cannot allow the '466 patent's "permanently affixed" limitation to expand to cover the accused device's removable screw.
>
> First, because the Salomon skate's removable heel screw is, at most, an obvious variation of the French reference's screw attachment and the Johnson reference's removable upper shoe (either alone or taken in combination), the doctrine of equivalents cannot, as a matter of law, expand the '466 patent to encompass the Salomon skate. To hold otherwise would allow the '466 patent, through the doctrine of equivalents, to cover subject matter that could not have been legally patented in the first instance;

Bayer AG v. Elan Pharm. Research Corp., 212 F.3d 1241, 54 USPQ 2d 1711, 1719 (Fed. Cir.), *cert. denied*, 121 S. Ct. 484 (2000):

Main volume footnote updates begin on page 72.

Claim interpretation begins with the language of the claims.[42] The general rule is that terms in the claim are to be given their ordinary and accustomed meaning.[43] General descriptive terms will ordinarily be given their full meaning; modifiers will not be added to broad terms standing alone.[44] In short, a court must presume that the terms in the claim mean what they say, and, unless otherwise compelled, give full effect to the ordinary and accustomed meaning of claim terms.[45]

In order to overcome this heavy presumption in favor of the ordinary meaning of claim language, it is clear that "a party wishing to use statements in the written description to confine or otherwise affect a patent's scope must, at the very least, point to a term or terms in the claim with which to draw in those statements."[46] That is, claim terms cannot be narrowed by reference to the written description or prosecution history unless the language of the claims invites reference to those sources.[47] In other words, there must be a textual reference in the actual language of the claim with which to associate a proffered claim construction.[48]

Federal Circuit case law demonstrates two situations where a sufficient reason exists to require the entry of a definition of a claim term other than its ordinary and accustomed meaning. The first arises if the patentee has chosen to be his or her own lexicographer by clearly

---

In short, through its statements to the PTO and the declarations it filed, Bayer made statements of clear and unmistakable surrender of subject matter outside the the claimed SSA range of 1.0 to 4 m^2/g. Bayer reportedly argued that its claimed range 1.0 to 4 m^2/g produced unique results and was a superior inventive range. . . . In this case, during prosecution, Bayer emphasized the inventive nature of its claimed SSA range and the disadvantages of SSAs outside its claimed range. Thus, Bayer's statements, in total, amount to a "clear and unmistakable surrender," so that a competitor would reasonably believe that Bayer had surrendered SSAs outside the claimed range.

[42]Renishaw PLC v. Marposs Societa' Per Azioni, 158 F.3d 1243, 1248, 48 USPQ 2d 1117, 1120 (Fed. Cir. 1998); AbTox, Inc. v. Exitron Corp., 122 F.3d 1019, 1023, 43 USPQ 2d 1545, 1548 (Fed. Cir. 1997); Bell Communications Research, Inc. v. Vitalink Communications Corp., 55 F.3d 615, 619–20, 34 USPQ 2d 1816, 1819 (Fed. Cir. 1995).

[43]*See Renishaw*, 158 F.3d at 1249, 48 USPQ 2d at 1121; York Prods., Inc. v. Central Tractor Farm & Family Ctr., 99 F.3d 1568, 1572, 40 USPQ 2d 1619, 1622 (Fed. Cir. 1996).

[44]*See, e.g.*, Virginia Panel Corp. v. MAC Panel Co., 133 F.3d 860, 865–66, 45 USPQ 2d 1225, 1229 (Fed. Cir. 1997) (unmodified term "reciprocating" not limited to linear reciprocation); *Bell Communications*, 55 F.3d at 621–22, 34 USPQ 2d at 1821 (unmodified term "associating" not limited to explicit association); Specialty Composites v. Cabot Corp., 845 F.2d 981, 987, 6 USPQ 2d 1601, 1606 (Fed. Cir. 1988) (unmodified term "plasticizer" given full range of ordinary and accustomed meaning).

[45]*See, e.g.*, Nike Inc. v. Wolverine World Wide, Inc., 43 F.3d 644, 646, 33 USPQ 2d 1038, 1039 (Fed. Cir. 1994); E.I. Du Pont de Nemours & Co. v. Phillips Petroleum, 849 F.2d 1430, 1433, 7 USPQ 2d 1129, 1131 (Fed. Cir. 1988); Envirotech Corp. v. Al George, Inc., 730 F.2d 753, 759, 221 USPQ 473, 477 (Fed. Cir. 1984).

[46]*Renishaw*, 158 F.3d at 1248, 48 USPQ 2d at 1121.

[47]*See, e.g.*, McCarty v. Lehigh Valley R.R., 160 U.S. 110, 116 (1895) ("If we once begin to include elements not mentioned in the claim in order to limit such claim . . . , we should never know where to stop."); *Renishaw*, 158 F.3d at 1249, 48 USPQ 2d at 1121.

[48]Johnson Worldwide Assocs., Inc. v. Zebco Corp., 175 F.3d 985, 50 USPQ 2d 1607, 1610 (Fed. Cir. 1999).

Main volume footnote updates begin on page 72.

setting forth an explicit definition for a claim term.[49] The second is where the term or terms chosen by the patentee so deprive the claim of clarity that there is no means by which the scope of the claim may be ascertained from the language used.[50] In these two circumstances, a term (or terms) used in the claim invites—or indeed, requires—reference to intrinsic or, in some cases, extrinsic, evidence to determine the scope of the claim language.[51]

However, "claims are not to be interpreted by adding limitations appearing only in the specification. . . . Although the specification may well indicate that certain embodiments are preferred, particular embodiments appearing in [the] specification will not be read into the claims when the claim language is broader than such embodiments."[52] On the other hand, claims must be interpreted to at least cover one embodiment disclosed in the specification. Failure of a claim to cover at least one embodiment of the invention would produce an anomaly of a specification that nowhere describes or depicts a single embodiment illustrating such breadth of interpretation.[53] In rare circumstances, however, it is possible for a patent claim to be interpreted to exclude the preferred embodiment. For example, the Federal Circuit has stated in one instance:

> Elekta argues that OSI's proposed claim construction should not be adopted because it would exclude the preferred and only embodiment disclosed in the specification. We have previously stated that "[s]uch an interpretation is rarely, if ever, correct and would require highly persuasive evidentiary support." . . . That proposition is correct. However,

---

[49]*In re* Paulsen, 30 F.3d 1475, 1480, 31 USPQ 2d 1671, 1674 (Fed. Cir. 1994); Intellicall, Inc. v. Phonometrics, Inc., 952 F.2d 1384, 1387–88, 21 USPQ 2d 1383, 1386 (Fed. Cir. 1992); Lear Siegler, Inc. v. Aeroquip Corp., 733 F.2d 881, 888–89, 221 USPQ 1025, 1031 (Fed. Cir. 1984).

[50]Eastman Kodak Co. v. Goodyear Tire & Rubber Co., 114 F.3d 1547, 1554, 42 USPQ 2d 1737, 1741 (Fed. Cir. 1997), *overruled on other grounds*, Cybor Corp. v. FAS Techs., Inc., 138 F.3d 1448, 46 USPQ 2d 1169 (Fed. Cir. 1998) (en banc); J.T. Eaton & Co. v. Atlantic Paste & Glue Co., 106 F.3d 1563, 1568, 41 USPQ 2d 1641, 1646 (Fed. Cir. 1997) (because "[the disputed claim term] is a term with no previous meaning to those of ordinary skill in the prior art[,] its meaning, then, must be found [elsewhere] in the patent."); North Am. Vaccine, Inc. v. American Cyanamid Co. 7 F.3d 1571, 1576, 28 USPQ 2d 1333, 1336 (Fed. Cir. 1993) (using the specification for guidance "when the meaning of a claim term is in doubt"); Comark Communications, Inc. v. Harris Corp., 156 F.3d 1182, 1187, 48 USPQ 2d 1001, 1005 (Fed. Cir. 1998) ("In this case, the [disputed term] has a clear and well-defined meaning. This term is not so amorphous that one of skill in the art can only reconcile the claim language with the inventor's disclosure by recourse to the specification.").

[51]Johnson Worldwide Assocs., Inc. v. Zebco Corp., 175 F.3d 985, 50 USPQ 2d 1607, 1611 (Fed. Cir. 1999) (citing Vitronics Corp. v. Conceptronic, Inc., 90 F.3d 1576, 1583, 39 USPQ 2d 1573, 1577 (Fed. Cir. 1996) (reference to extrinsic evidence is proper when intrinsic evidence cannot resolve ambiguity in claim language)).

[52]Electro Med. Sys. S.A. v. Cooper Life Sciences, 34 F.3d 1048, 1054, 32 USPQ 2d 1017, 1021 (Fed. Cir. 1994).

[53]Manchak v. Chemical Waste Mgmt. Inc., Civ. App. 98-1530, slip op. at 10–11 (Fed. Cir. Dec. 6, 1999) (unpublished), *cert. denied*, 530 U.S. 1231 (2000) (citing Laitram Corp. v. Morehouse Indus., 143 F.3d 1456, 1463, 46 USPQ 2d 1609, 1614 (Fed. Cir. 1993) (viewing it as relevant that nothing in the written description suggests the rejected construction)).

Main volume footnote updates begin on page 72.

in light of the prosecution history and the unambiguous language of the amended claim, we conclude that this is the rare case in which such an interpretation is compelled.[54]

[Insert after footnote 159.]

The Federal Circuit has delineated several rules for claim drafters to invoke the strictures of 35 U.S.C. Section 112, sixth paragraph. Specifically, if the word "means" appears in a claim element in combination with a function, it is presumed to be a means-plus-function element to which Section 112, sixth paragraph applies.[55] Nevertheless, according to its express terms, Section 112, sixth paragraph governs only claim elements that do not recite sufficient structural limitations. Therefore, the presumption that Section 112, sixth paragraph applies is overcome if the claim itself recites sufficient structure or material for performing the claimed function.[56]

Although use of the phrase "means for" (or "step for") is not the only way to invoke Section 112, sixth paragraph, that terminology typically invokes Section 112, sixth paragraph while other formulations generally do not.[57] Therefore, when an element of a claim does not use the term "means," treatment as a means-plus-function claim element is generally not appropriate.[58] However, when it is apparent that the element invokes purely functional terms, without the additional recital of specific structure or material for performing that function, the claim element may be a means-plus-function element despite the lack of express means-plus-function language.[59]

The Federal Circuit has attempted to further define the criteria of when a claimed process will be considered a step-plus-function element under Section 112, sixth paragraph. In a concurring opinion, Judge Rader provided the following procedure for determining whether a process claim is to be interpreted as a step-plus-function claim under Section 112, sixth paragraph:

> The correlation between means-plus-function and step-plus-function claim elements assists the difficult process of identifying step-plus-function claim elements. This court has set forth a structured analysis

---

[54] Elekta Instrument S.A. v. O.U.R. Scientific Int'l, Inc., 214 F.3d 1302, 54 USPQ 2d 1910, 1914 (Fed. Cir., 2000) (quoting Vitronics Corp. v. Conceptronic, Inc., 90 F.3d 1576, 1583, 39 USPQ 2d 1573, 1578 (Fed. Cir. 1996)).

[55] Sage Prods., Inc. v. Devon Indus., Inc., 126 F.3d 1420, 1427, 44 USPQ 2d 1103, 1109 (Fed. Cir. 1997); Greenberg v. Ethicon Endo-Surgery, Inc., 91 F.3d 1580, 1583, 39 USPQ 2d 1783, 1785 (Fed. Cir. 1996).

[56] York Prods., Inc. v. Central Tractor Farm & Family Ctr., 99 F.3d 1568, 1574, 40 USPQ 2d 1619, 1623 (Fed. Cir. 1996); Cole v. Kimberly-Clark Corp., 102 F.3d 524, 531, 41 USPQ 2d 1001, 1006 (Fed. Cir. 1996).

[57] Al-Site Corp. v. VSI Int'l, Inc., 174 F.3d 1308, 50 USPQ 2d 1161, 1166 (Fed. Cir. 1999).

[58] Mas-Hamilton Group v. LaGard, Inc., 156 F.3d 1206, 1213-15, 48 USPQ 2d 1010, 1016-18 (Fed. Cir. 1998).

[59] *Al-Site Corp.*, 50 USPQ 2d at 1166.

Main volume footnote updates begin on page 72.

for determining whether the elements of a claim are in means-plus-function form. Specifically, if the word "means" appears in the claim element, there is a presumption that it is a means-plus-function element to which § 112, ¶ 6 applies. . . . This presumption is overcome if the claim itself recites sufficient structure or material for performing the claimed function or when it fails to recite a function associated with the means. . . .

When an element of a claim does not use the term "means," treatment as a means-plus-function claim element is generally not appropriate. . . . However, when it is apparent that the element invokes purely functional terms, without the additional recital of specific structure or material for performing that function, the claim element may be a means-plus-function element, despite the lack of express "means" language. . . .

Given the parallel format of the statute, a similar analysis applies to step-plus-function claim elements. Certain phrases trigger a presumption that § 112, ¶ 6 applies, but other aspects of the elements, such as the recitation of a specific act, may overcome that presumption. The difficulty of distinguishing acts from functions in step-plus-function claim elements, however, makes identifying step-plus-function claims inherently more problematic. This difficulty places a significant burden on the claim drafter to choose language with a definite and clear meaning. To invoke a presumption of § 112, ¶ 6 application, a claim drafter must use language that expressly signals the recitation of a function as distinguished from an act.

As used in § 112, ¶ 6, "step" is the generic term for "acts" in the same sense that "means" is the generic term for "structure" and "material." . . . The word "step," however, may introduce either an act or a function depending on context within the claim. Therefore, use of the word "step," by itself, does not invoke a presumption that § 112, ¶ 6 applies. For example, method claim elements may begin with the phrase "steps of" without invoking application of § 112, ¶ 6. . . . The phrase "steps of" colloquially signals the introduction of specific acts, rather than functions, and should therefore not presumptively invoke application of § 112, ¶ 6.

Unlike "of," the preposition "for" colloquially signals the recitation of a function. Accordingly, the phrase "step for" generally introduces functional claim language falling under § 112, ¶ 6. . . . Thus, the phrase "step for" in a method claim raises a presumption that § 112, ¶ 6 applies. This presumption gives legal effect to the commonly understood meanings of "of"—introducing specific materials, structure or acts—and "for"—introducing a function.

Even when a claim element uses language that generally falls under the step-plus-function format, however, § 112, ¶ 6 still does not apply when the claim limitation itself recites sufficient acts for performing the specified function.

As this court explained in *O.I. Corp.*:

> Of course, [Section 112, sixth paragraph] is implicated only when means plus function without definite structure are present, and that is similarly true with respect to steps, that the paragraph is implicated only when steps plus function without acts are present. The statute thus in effect provides that an element in a combination method or process claim may be recited as a step for performing a specified function without the recital of acts in support of the function.

. . . Therefore, when the claim language includes sufficient acts for performing the recited function, § 112, ¶ 6 does not apply. Again similar

> to a means-plus-function analysis, the absence of the phrase "step for" from the language of a claim tends to show that the claim element is not in step-plus-function form. However, claim elements without express step-plus-function language may nevertheless fall within § 112, ¶ 6 if they merely claim the underlying function without recitation of acts for performing that function. Unfortunately, method claim elements often recite phrases susceptible to interpretation as either a function or as an act for performing a function. Both acts and functions are often stated using verbs ending in "ing." For instance, if the method claim element at issue in this case had merely recited the "step of" "spreading an adhesive tack coating," it would not have been clear solely from this hypothetical claim language whether "spreading" was a function or an act. In such circumstances, claim interpretation requires careful analysis of the limitation in the context of the overall claim and the specification.
>
> In general terms, the "underlying function" of a method claim element corresponds to what that element ultimately accomplishes in relationship to what the other elements of the claim and the claim as a whole accomplish. "Acts," on the other hand, correspond to how the function is accomplished. Therefore, claim interpretation focuses on what the claim limitation accomplishes, i.e., its underlying function, in relation to what is accomplished by the other limitations and the claim as a whole. If a claim element recites only an underlying function without acts for performing it, then § 112, ¶ 6 applies even without express step-plus-function language.
>
> In sum, similar to means-plus-function claims, this court employs a straightforward analysis for identifying a step-plus-function claim. If the claim element uses the phrase "step for," then § 112, ¶ 6 is presumed to apply. Because the phrasing "step for" would appear to claim every possible act for performing the recited function, in keeping with § 112, ¶ 6, such a claim covers only the specific acts recited in the specification for performing that function, and equivalent acts. On the other hand, the term "step" alone and the phrase "steps of" tend to show that § 112, ¶ 6 does not govern that limitation. Accordingly, this court has similarly denied step-plus-function treatment to method claims which use the conventional "steps of" language.[60]

Although patentees are not necessarily limited to their preferred embodiment,[61] interpretation of a means-plus-function element requires the court to consult the structure disclosed in the specification, which often describes little more than the preferred embodiment.[62] Although the prosecution history serves as a tool for claim interpretation, the statutory requirements of 35 U.S.C. Section 112, sixth paragraph nonetheless apply to means-plus-function claims. Under Section 112, sixth paragraph, the specification limits the meaning of means-plus-function claim elements.[63] For example, the Federal Circuit has stated in this connection:

---

[60] Seal-Flex, Inc. v. Athletic Track & Court Constr., 172 F.3d 836, 50 USPQ 2d 1225, 1233–34 (Fed. Cir. 1999) (Rader, J., concurring) (quoting O.I. Corp. v. Tekmar Co., 115 F.3d 1576, 1583, 42 USPQ 2d 1777, 1782 (Fed. Cir. 1997)).

[61] Serrano v. Telular Corp., 111 F.3d 1578, 1583, 42 USPQ 2d 1538, 1542 (Fed. Cir. 1997).

[62] Signtech USA, Ltd. v. Vutek, Inc., 174 F.3d 1352, 50 USPQ 2d 1372, 1375 (Fed. Cir. 1999).

[63] *Id.*, 50 USPQ 2d at 1376.

Main volume footnote updates begin on page 72.

> Thus, this decision, like many others emanating from this court, . . . emphasizes the importance of careful language choices in the specification and, particularly, in the claims. To avoid having its claims limited to exclude the embodiments disclaimed in the specification, the claim drafter for this patent might have chosen language to avoid application of 35 U.S.C. § 112, ¶ 6. Otherwise, assuming that no intervening statutory bars had arisen, Signtech could have filed a new applications . . . without limitation in the specification or claims to the dual air sources. It did neither. Therefore, because of the statutory limitations governing the meaning of means-plus-function elements, courts must limit the scope of these claim elements to the corresponding structure disclosed in the specification and its equivalents. Signtech's arguments are therefore unavailing . . . .[64]

However, a carefully drafted patent specification may, in some circumstances, provide a broader scope of interpretation for means-plus-function claims than non-means-plus-function claims.[65] For example, when multiple embodiments in the specification correspond to the claimed function, proper application of Section 112, sixth paragraph generally reads the claim element to embrace each of those embodiments.[66] However, there is no requirement that a means-plus-function claim have a single claim construction that encompasses all the embodiments disclosed in the specification. Rather, all that is required is identification of the corresponding structure or structures in the specification that perform the recited function.[67]

---

[64] *Id.*

[65] *See* Overhead Door Corp. v. Chamberlain Group, Inc., 194 F.3d 1261, 52 USPQ 2d 1321, 1327–28 (Fed. Cir. 1999):

> The claim language and the specification explain that the "memory selection switch" functions to select memory locations. This claim element accomplishes its function by way of a mechanical switch. . . . As properly construed, the "memory selection switch" means a mechanical switch for selecting memory locations. . . .
>
> Although software operations do not fall within the literal scope of the "memory selection switch" in claim 1, the reissue prosecution history also discloses a broader reading for the "switch means" of claim 5. First, the patentees' representation to the Patent and Trademark Office in its November 29, 1989 sworn declaration indicated their intent to include the algorithm of Figure 3 as a "corresponding structure" for the switch means. . . . While this statement weighs against construing claim 1 to include software operations, it gives a broader reading to claim 5. This statement evinces the patentees' use of the term "switch means" to include microprocessor operations driven by software, i.e., "electronic" switches, as opposed to a mechanical switch of Figure 2. The patentees' use in claim 5 of the term "switch means" rather than "switch" and "being adapted to select" rather than "setable" and "set," to describe software operations, further support a broader construction.

[66] *Id.*, 52 USPQ 2d at 1264 (citing Serrano v. Telular Corp., 111 F.3d 1578, 1583, 42 USPQ 2d 1538, 1542 (Fed. Cir. 1997)). *See also* Eisenberg v. Alimed, Inc., Civ. App. No. 98-1317, slip op. at 5 (Fed. Cir. Aug. 8, 2000) (unpublished); TA Instruments, Inc. v. Perkin-Elmer Corp., Civ. App. No. 99-1358, slip op. at 30 (Fed. Cir. June 1, 2000) (unpublished), *cert. denied*, 121 S. Ct. 571 (2000):

> The function recited in the claim is "correcting automatically," and there is no limit on how this function is performed. The specification describes two structures that perform this function, the structure of Figure 1, which corrects automatically without interpolation, and the structure of Figure 3, which corrects automatically using interpolation. Both these structures are corresponding structures for the recited "computer means . . ." under 35 U.S.C. § 112, ¶ 6.

[67] Ishida Co. v. Taylor, 221 F.3d 1310, 55 USPQ 2d 1449, 1453 (Fed. Cir. 2000).

Main volume footnote updates begin on page 72.

Application of Section 112, sixth paragraph requires identification of the structure or acts in the specification that performs the recited function.[68] Therefore, Section 112, sixth paragraph requires both identification of the claimed function and identification of the structure or acts in the written description necessary to perform that function. The statute does not permit limitation of a means-plus-function claim by adopting a function different from that explicitly recited in the claim. Nor does the statute permit incorporation of structure from the written description beyond that necessary to perform the claimed function.[69] Correct identification of the function is imperative to identify the corresponding structure disclosed in the application.[70] "[I]ndividual components, if any, of an overall structure that corresponds to the claimed function are not claim limitations. Rather the claim limitation is the overall structure corresponding to the claimed function."[71]

After identifying the function of the means-plus-function element, the court looks to the written description to identify the structure corresponding to that function. Identification of corresponding structure may embrace more than the preferred embodiment. A means-plus-function claim encompasses all structure in the specification corresponding to that element and equivalent structures.[72] When multiple embodiments in the specification correspond to the claimed function, proper application of Section 112, sixth paragraph generally reads the claim element to embrace each of those embodiments.[73]

In a means-plus-function claim in which the disclosed structure is a computer, or microprocessor, programmed to carry out an algorithm, the disclosed structure is not the general purpose computer, but rather the special purpose computer programmed to perform the disclosed algorithm.[74] The structure of a microprocessor programmed

---

[68] Rodime PLC v. Seagate Tech., Inc., 174 F.3d 1294, 1302, 50 USPQ 2d 1429, 1435 (Fed. Cir. 1999), *cert. denied*, 528 U.S. 1115 (2000).

[69] Micro Chem., Inc. v. Great Plains Chem. Co., 194 F.3d 1250, 52 USPQ 2d 1258, 1263 (Fed. Cir. 1999).

[70] *See, e.g.*, Smiths Indus. Med. Sys., Inc. v. Vital Signs, Inc., 183 F.3d 1347, 51 USPQ 2d 1415, 1421 (Fed. Cir. 1999):

> The court erred in the next step of the claim construction process by interpreting the claim language "means for supplying gas" to require a means for supplying gas under pressure. It is improper to import the limitation "under pressure" from the written description into the claim because the claim language is clear on its face. . . . Instead, the function recited by the means-plus-function claim limitation is simply the function of "supplying gas," and it is this function alone that serves as the touchstone identifying the disclosed, corresponding structure that is recited by the means-plus-function claim limitation.

[71] Odetics, Inc. v. Storage Tech. Corp., 185 F.3d 1259, 51 USPQ 2d 1225, 1230 (Fed. Cir. 1999).

[72] Serrano v. Telular Corp., 111 F.3d 1578, 1583, 42 USPQ 2d 1538, 1542 (Fed. Cir. 1997).

[73] *Micro Chem. Inc.*, 52 USPQ 2d at 1264.

[74] WMS Gaming Inc. v. International Game Tech., 184 F.3d 1339, 51 USPQ 2d 1385, 1391 (Fed. Cir. 1999); *In re* Alappat, 33 F.3d 1526, 1545, 31 USPQ 2d 1545, 1558 (Fed. Cir. 1994) (en banc).

Main volume footnote updates begin on page 72.

to carry out an algorithm is limited by the disclosed algorithm.[75] A general purpose computer, or microprocessor, programmed to carry out an algorithm creates "a new machine, because a general purpose computer in effect becomes a special purpose computer once it is programmed to perform particular functions pursuant to instructions from program software."[76] The instructions of the software program that carry out the algorithm electrically change the general purpose computer by creating electrical paths within the device. These electrical paths create a special purpose machine for carrying out the particular algorithm.

[Insert after footnote 161.]

When a claim, whether drafted in means-plus-function or non-means-plus-function format, is not met literally, the claim may nevertheless be infringed under the doctrine of equivalents. Any analysis of infringement under the doctrine of equivalents "necessarily deals with subject matter that is 'beyond,' 'ignored' by, and not included in the literal scope of a claim. Such subject matter is not necessarily 'specifically excluded' from coverage under the doctrine unless its inclusion is somehow inconsistent with the language of the claim. Literal failure to meet a claim limitation does not necessarily amount to 'specific exclusion.' "[77] "An equivalent must be found for every limitation of the claim somewhere in an accused device, but not necessarily in a corresponding component, although that is generally the case."[78] The doctrine of equivalents does not "expand" or "broaden" claims, but instead expands the right to exclude.[79]

One-to-one correspondence of components is not required, and elements or steps may be combined without ipso facto loss of equivalency.[80] In other words, two physical components of an accused device may be viewed in combination to serve as an equivalent of one element of a claimed invention, as long as no claim limitation is thereby wholly vitiated.[81] Thus, "[e]quivalency is not defeated by using an additional

[75] *WMS Gaming Inc.*, 51 USPQ 2d at 1391.

[76] *Alappat*, 33 F.3d at 1545, 31 USPQ 2d at 1558; *In re* Bernhart, 417 F.2d 1395, 1399–1400, 163 USPQ 611, 615–16 (C.C.P.A. 1969) ("If a machine is programmed in a certain new and unobvious way, it is physically different from the machine without that program; its memory elements are differently arranged.").

[77] Ethicon, Inc. v. United States Surgical Corp., 149 F.3d 1309, 47 USPQ 2d 1272, 1277 (Fed. Cir. 1998).

[78] Corning Glass Works v. Sumitomo Elec. U.S.A., Inc., 868 F.2d 1251, 1259, 9 USPQ 2d 1962, 1968 (Fed. Cir. 1989).

[79] Wilson Sporting Goods Co. v. David Geoffrey & Assocs., 904 F.2d 677, 684, 14 USPQ 2d 1942, 1948 (Fed. Cir. 1990).

[80] A.C. Aukerman Co. v. R.L. Chaides Constr. Co., 960 F.2d 1020, 1038–39, 22 USPQ 2d 1321, 1333 (Fed. Cir. 1992).

[81] Ethicon, Inc. v. United States Surgical Corp., 149 F.3d 1309, 47 USPQ 2d 1272, 1280 (Fed. Cir. 1998).

Main volume footnote updates begin on page 72.

step to achieve what the patentee does in one step."[82] Rather, "the accused product is equivalent to a claimed element if the differences between the two are 'insubstantial' to one of ordinary skill in the art."[83]

More succinctly, the Federal Circuit has summarized the overall test for equivalency as follows:

> [u]nder the doctrine of equivalents, a patentee must show that the accused device performs substantially the same function, in substantially the same way, to achieve substantially the same result. . . . "The 'substantially the same way' prong of the test may be met if an equivalent of a recited limitation has been substituted in the accused device." . . . . Thus, infringement requires that each limitation of a claim be met exactly or by a substantial equivalent.[84]

In *Warner-Jenkinson Co. v. Hilton Davis Chemical Co.*,[85] the Supreme Court elaborated as follows on the substance of infringement under the doctrine of equivalents:

> Each element contained in a patent claim is deemed material to defining the scope of the patented invention, and thus the doctrine of equivalents must be applied to individual elements of the claim, not to the invention as a whole. It is important to ensure that the application of the doctrine, even as to an individual element, is not allowed such broad play as to effectively eliminate that element in its entirety.[86]

The Supreme Court further elaborated:

> The known interchangeability of substitutes for an element of a patent is one of the express objective factors noted by *Graver Tank* as bearing upon whether the accused device is substantially the same as the patented invention. Independent experimentation by the alleged infringer would not always reflect upon the objective question whether a person skilled in the art would have known of the interchangeability between two elements, but in many cases it would likely be probative of such knowledge.[87]

The Supreme Court summed up the overall inquiry under the doctrine of equivalents as follows:

> In our view, the particular linguistic framework used is less important than whether the test is probative of the essential inquiry: Does the accused product or process contain elements identical or equivalent to each claimed element of the patented invention? Different linguistic frameworks may be more suitable to different cases, depending on their par-

---

[82] EMI Group N. Am., Inc. v. Intel Corp., 157 F.3d 887, 48 USPQ 2d 1181, 1188 (Fed. Cir. 1998), *cert. denied*, 526 U.S. 1112 (1999).

[83] Marquip, Inc. v. Fosber Am., Inc., 198 F.3d 1363, 53 USPQ 2d 1015, 1018 (Fed.Cir. 1999).

[84] Read Corp. v. Portec, Inc., 970 F.2d 816, 23 USPQ 2d 1426, 1431 (Fed. Cir. 1992) (quoting Malta v. Schulmerich Carillons, Inc., 952 F.2d 1320, 1325–26, 21 USPQ 2d 1161, 1164–65 (Fed. Cir. 1991), *cert. denied*, 112 S. Ct. 2942 (1992), and citing Graver Tank & Mfg. Co. v. Linde Air Prods. Co., 339 U.S. 605, 607 (1950)).

[85] Warner-Jenkinson Co. v. Hilton Davis Chem. Co., 520 U.S. 17, 41 USPQ 2d 1865 (1997).

[86] *Id.*, 41 USPQ 2d at 1871.

[87] *Id.* at 1874.

Main volume footnote updates begin on page 72.

> ticular facts. A focus on individual elements and a special vigilance against allowing the concept of equivalence to eliminate completely any such elements should reduce considerably the imprecision of whatever language is used. An analysis of the role played by each element in the context of the specific patent claim will thus inform the inquiry as to whether a substitute element matches the function, way, and result of the claimed element, or whether the substitute element plays a role substantially different from the claimed element.[88]

As an aid in determining infringement under the doctrine of equivalents, the Federal Circuit has developed a hypothetical claim methodology. Under the hypothetical claim methodology, the patentee may propose a hypothetical claim that is broad enough in scope to literally read on the accused device.[89] If the hypothetical claim could have been allowed by the Patent and Trademark Office (PTO) in view of the prior art, then the prior art does not preclude the application of the doctrine of equivalents and infringement may be found. On the other hand, as in the PTO's examination process, references may be combined to prove that the hypothetical claim would have been obvious to one of ordinary skill in the art and thus would not have been allowed.[90]

A hypothetical claim analysis is not an opportunity to freely redraft granted claims. That opportunity existed in the PTO, where the submitted claims were examined for patentability.[91] While use of a hypothetical claim may permit a minor extension of a claim to cover subject matter that is substantially equivalent to that literally claimed, a claim cannot, in the course of litigation and outside of the PTO, cut and trim, expanding here and narrowing there, to arrive at a claim that encompasses an accused device, but avoids the prior art. Slight broadening is permitted at that point, but not narrowing.[92]

Wholesale redrafting of granted claims during litigation by narrowing and expanding the claims at the same time in creating a hypothetical claim is not supported by Federal Circuit case law, and it avoids the examination process. It is contrary to the statutory requirement that an applicant "particularly point[] out and distinctly claim[] the subject matter which the applicant regards as his [or her] invention,"[93] a requirement that presupposes a Patent Office examination,

---

[88] *Id.* at 1875.

[89] Wilson Sporting Goods Co. v. David Geoffrey & Assocs., 904 F.2d 677, 684, 14 USPQ 2d 1942, 1948 (Fed. Cir. 1990).

[90] *Id.*

[91] Streamfeeder, LLC v. Sure-Feed Sys., Inc., 175 F.3d 974, 50 USPQ 2d 1515, 1521 (Fed. Cir. 1999).

[92] Jurgens v. McKasy, 927 F.2d 1552, 1561, 18 USPQ 2d 1031, 1038 (Fed. Cir. 1991) ("It may be helpful to 'conceptualize' the prior art limitation on the doctrine of equivalents by envisioning a hypothetical patent claim—similar to the asserted claim but broad enough to literally cover the accused products—and testing whether that claim would have been patentable in view of the prior art.").

[93] 35 U.S.C. § 112 (1994).

Main volume footnote updates begin on page 72.

which does not occur with a hypothetical claim. Hypothetical claim analysis thus cannot be used to redraft granted claims in litigation by narrowing and broadening a claim at the same time.[94]

The Federal Circuit found a narrow, counterintuitive exception to the general principle that when one does not infringe a broader claim, one cannot infringe a dependent claim containing all of that broader claim's limitations plus more:

> While this proposition is no doubt generally correct, it does not apply in the circumstances of this case. Here, we have reversed the judgment of infringement of independent claim 1 solely because the asserted range of equivalents of the claim limitations would encompass the prior art Uniroyal ball. The dependent claims, of course, are narrower than claim 1; therefore, it does not automatically follow that the ranges of equivalents of these narrower claims would encompass the prior art, because of their added limitations.[95]

[Insert after footnote 162.]

A key feature that distinguishes "equivalents" under Section 112, paragraph 6 from "equivalents" under the doctrine of equivalents is that Section 112, paragraph 6 equivalents must perform the identical function of the disclosed structure, while equivalents under the doctrine of equivalents need only perform a substantially similar function.[96]

> These principles . . . suggest that title 35 will not produce an "equivalent of an equivalent" by applying both §112, ¶6 and the doctrine of equivalents to the structure of a given claim element. A proposed equivalent must have arisen at a definite period in time, i.e., either before or after patent issuance. If before, a §112, ¶6 structural equivalents analysis applies and any analysis for equivalent structure under the doctrine of equivalents collapses into the §112, ¶6 analysis. If after, a non-textual infringement analysis proceeds under the doctrine of equivalents. Patent policy supports application of the doctrine of equivalents to a claim element expressed in means-plus-function form in the case of "after-arising" technology because a patent draftsman has no way to anticipate and account for later developed substitutes for a claim element. Therefore, the doctrine of equivalents appropriately allows marginally broader coverage than §112, ¶6.[97]

As stated by the Federal Circuit:

> [P]reclusion of a finding of infringement under the doctrine of equivalents for pre-existing technology after an adverse holding of no literal infringe-

---

[94] Streamfeeder, LLC v. Sure-Feed Sys., Inc., 175 F.3d 974, 50 USPQ 2d 1515, 1521 (Fed. Cir. 1999).

[95] Wilson Sporting Goods Co. v. David Geoffrey & Assocs., 904 F.2d 677, 686, 14 USPQ 2d 1942, 1949 (Fed. Cir. 1990).

[96] Kemco Sales, Inc. v. Control Papers Co., Inc., 208 F.3d 1352, 54 USPQ 2d 1308 (Fed. Cir. 2000); Al-Site Corp. v. VSI Int'l, Inc., 174 F.3d 1308, 1320–21, 50 USPQ 2d 1161, 1168 (Fed. Cir. 1999).

[97] Al-Site Corp. v. VSI Int'l, Inc., 174 F.3d 1308, 50 USPQ 2d 1161, 1168 n.2 (Fed. Cir. 1999).

Main volume footnote updates begin on page 72.

> ment for the same technology applies only to means-plus-function claim limitations. Where the patentee does not use the means-plus-function format, the resolution of infringement under the doctrine of equivalents would not allow the patentee "two bites at the apple," since the resolution of the literal infringement question would not address the issue of equivalence in a claim drawn to structure rather than to a means-plus-function. Thus, for a claim limitation not drafted in means-plus-function language, the mere fact that the asserted equivalent structure was pre-existing technology does not foreclose a finding of infringement under the doctrine of equivalents.[98]

While acknowledging that there are differences between Section 112, sixth paragraph and the doctrine of equivalents, the court on several occasions has indicated that the tests for equivalence under Section 112, sixth paragraph and the doctrine of equivalents are "closely related," involving "similar analyses of insubstantiality of the differences."[99] Thus, a reduced version of the well-known tripartite test for the doctrine of equivalents has alternatively been applied in the Section 112, sixth paragraph context to determine if the differences are insubstantial, i.e., after determining that the accused device performs the identical function, as required by statute, whether it performs the function in substantially the same way to achieve substantially the same result.[100] Evidence of known interchangeability between structure in the accused device and the disclosed structure has also been considered an important factor.[101]

The Federal Circuit has clarified the relationship between the doctrine of equivalents and equivalents under Section 112, sixth paragraph as follows:

> In light of the similarity of the tests for equivalence under Section 112, Para. 6 and the doctrine of equivalents, the context of the invention should be considered when performing a Section 112, Para. 6 equivalence analysis just as it is in a doctrine of equivalents determination. . . . As a result, two structures that are equivalent in one environment may not be equivalent in another. More particularly, when in a claimed "means" limitation the disclosed physical structure is of little or no importance to the claimed invention, there may be a broader range of equivalent structures than if the physical characteristics of the structure are critical in per-

---

[98] Kraft Foods, Inc. v. International Trading Co., 203 F.3d 1362, 53 USPQ 2d 1814, 1822 (Fed. Cir. 2000).

[99] Chiuminatta Concrete Concepts, Inc. v. Cardinal Indus., Inc., 145 F.3d 1303, 1310, 46 USPQ 2d 1752, 1757–58 (Fed. Cir. 1998). *See also* Warner-Jenkinson Co. v. Hilton Davis Chem. Co., 520 U.S. 17, 28, 41 USPQ 2d 1865, 1870 (1997) (stating that application of Section 112, para. 6 "is an application of the doctrine of equivalents in a restrictive role. . . .");Valmont Indus., Inc. v. Reinke Mfg. Co., 983 F.2d 1039, 1043, 25 USPQ 2d 1451, 1455 (Fed. Cir. 1993) ("The word 'equivalent' in section 112 invokes the familiar concept of an insubstantial change which adds nothing of significance.").

[100] Odetics, Inc. v. Storage Tech. Corp., 185 F.3d 1259, 1267, 51 USPQ 2d 1225, 1229–30 (Fed. Cir. 1999).

[101] Al-Site Corp. v. VSI Int'l, Inc., 174 F.3d 1308, 1316, 50 USPQ 2d 1161, 1165 (Fed. Cir. 1999); *Chiuminatta*, 145 F.3d at 1309, 46 USPQ 2d at 1757 (citing Graver Tank & Mfg. Co. v. Linde Air Prods. Co., 339 U.S. 605, 609, 85 USPQ 328, 331 (1950)).

Main volume footnote updates begin on page 72.

forming the claimed function in the context of the claimed invention. Thus, a rigid comparison of physical structures in a vacuum may be inappropriate in a particular case. Indeed, the statute requires two structures to be equivalent, but it does not require them to be "structurally equivalent," i.e., it does not mandate an equivalency comparison that necessarily focuses heavily or exclusively on physical structure.

In some cases, an analysis of insubstantial differences in the context of the invention results in a finding of equivalence under Section 112, Para. 6 even though two structures arguably would not be considered equivalent structures in other contexts, e.g., if performing functions other than the claimed function. . . . In other cases, in which the specific physical features of the structure corresponding to the "means" limitation may have more relevance to the claimed invention, a finding of noninfringement results.[102]

[Insert after footnote 164.]

While examples disclosed in the preferred embodiments may aid in the proper interpretation of a claim term, the specific embodiments appearing in the written description of the patent will not be read into the claims when the claim language is broader than such embodiments.[103]

D. Prosecution History Estoppel Considerations

[Insert after footnote 177.]

The prior art may aid in determining the scope of an estoppel.[104] "[A] patentee is estopped from recovering through equivalency that which was deemed unpatentable in view of the prior art."[105] After adding a claim limitation during prosecution to overcome prior art, the applicant cannot later assert that the distinguished feature of the prior art is equivalent to the added limitation. Similarly, the patentee may not assert coverage of a "trivial" variation of the distinguished prior art feature as an equivalent.[106]

[Insert after footnote 191.]

For a patentee to be bound by a statement made to the Patent Office in connection with a later prosecution of a different patent, the statement would have to be one that the Examiner relied upon in al-

---

[102] IMS Tech., Inc. v. Haas Automation, Inc., 206 F.3d 1422, 54 USPQ 2d 1129, 1138 (Fed. Cir. 2000).

[103] Electro Med. Sys. S.A. v. Cooper Life Sciences, Inc., 34 F.3d 1048, 1054, 32 USPQ 2d 1017, 1021 (Fed. Cir. 1994).

[104] Augustine Med., Inc. v. Gaymar Indus., Inc., 181 F.3d 1291, 50 USPQ 2d 1900, 1905 (Fed. Cir. 1999).

[105] Pall Corp. v. Micron Separations, Inc., 66 F.3d 1211, 1219, 36 USPQ 2d 1225, 1230 (Fed. Cir. 1995).

[106] Augustine Med., Inc. v. Gaymar Indus., Inc., 181 F.3d 1291, 50 USPQ 2d 1900, 1905 (Fed. Cir. 1999).

Main volume footnote updates begin on page 72.

lowing the claims in the patent at issue.[107] For example, the Federal Circuit has stated that "[i]n cases where a patentee's amendments were not required in response to an examiner's rejection or critical to the allowance of the claims, no estoppel has been found."[108]

On the other hand, the fact that claim amendments and arguments were not necessary to overcome the prior art does not prevent prosecution history estoppel or a narrow claim interpretation from taking effect.

For example, in *Antonious v. Spalding & Evenflo Cos.*,[109] the invention related to iron-type golf club heads. The invention was directed to a club head design incorporating a cavity back bar weight mass configuration that was described as increasing golf club performance during a golf swing. Antonious sued Spalding, claiming that Spalding's Top-Flite Tour and Tour Edition irons infringed the patent.

The district court interpreted the phrase "formed on and attached solely to said rear wall within said cavity" to mean that the weight member must be attached solely (i.e., only) to the rear wall (back side of the striking surface) and not attached also to the peripheral mass within the cavity.[110]

On appeal, the Federal Circuit affirmed the district court. The Federal Circuit noted that during prosecution, the Examiner rejected the claims in a parent application based on prior art. As part of his office action response, Antonious added the "attached solely to said rear wall" language. Antonious argued that the addition of the claim language was not necessary to overcome the prior art rejection and, therefore, the claim should not be limited to such a narrow interpretation. The Federal Circuit was not persuaded. According to the Federal Circuit:

> We do not disagree with Antonious's suggestion that the addition of this claim language may not have been needed in order to distinguish Sugioka. However, an applicant is free to give up more claim scope than is necessary to overcome a reference. . . . We are satisfied that, whether he needed to or not, Antonious gave up a claim scope that could include a weight bar attached to the peripheral mass and the rear wall when he added the "attached solely to said rear wall" limitation.[111]

---

[107] Georgia-Pacific Corp. v. United States Gypsum Co., 195 F.3d 1322, 52 USPQ 2d 1590, 1599 (Fed. Cir. 1999), *cert. denied*, 121 S. Ct. 54 (2000).

[108] Mannesmann Demag Corp. v. Engineered Metal Prods. Co., 793 F.2d 1279, 1284–85, 230 USPQ 45, 48 (Fed. Cir. 1986).

[109] Antonious v. Spalding & Evenflo Cos., Civ. App. No. 98-1478 (Fed. Cir. Aug. 31, 1999) (unpublished).

[110] *Id.*, slip op. at 3.

[111] *Id.* at 9 (citing Bai v. L & L Wings, Inc., 160 F.3d 1350, 1356, 48 USPQ 2d 1674, 1678–79 (Fed. Cir. 1998); Lemelson v. General Mills, Inc., 968 F.2d 1202, 1206, 23 USPQ 2d 1284, 1288 (Fed. Cir. 1992) ("The prosecution history gives insight into what the applicant originally claimed as the invention, and often what the applicant gave up in order to meet the Examiner's objections."); Standard Oil Co. v. American Cyanamid Co., 774 F.2d 448, 452, 227 USPQ 293, 296 (Fed. Cir. 1985) (prosecution history "limits the interpretation of claims so as to exclude any interpretation that may have been disclaimed or disavowed during prosecution in order to obtain claim allowance")).

Main volume footnote updates begin on page 72.

Thus, claim amendments and arguments that are not necessary to overcome a prior art rejection may still be used in interpreting the scope of the patent claim.

1. *Prosecution History Estoppel Applied Even When Claims Not Amended*

[Insert at the beginning of the section.]

Arguments made during the prosecution of a patent application may be given the same weight as claim amendments.[112] Because it is the totality of the prosecution history that must be assessed, not the individual segments of the presentation made to the Patent Office by the applicant, it is irrelevant whether the applicant relinquished this potential claim construction in an amendment to the claim or in an argument to overcome or distinguish a reference.[113]

2. *Prosecution History Estoppel Does Not Automatically Apply When a Claim Is Amended*

Amend the section heading as follows:

2. *Prosecution History Estoppel Does Not Automatically Apply When a Claim Is Amended — Or Does It?*

[Insert after footnote 202.]

However, for amendments made for reasons related to patentability, "[a] careful reading of the Supreme Court's opinion in context shows that *Warner-Jenkinson* did not effect a change in the scope of subject matter precluded by an estoppel, but only in the circumstances that may trigger an estoppel."[114]

As a practical matter, anyone desiring to assess the possible scope of an estoppel arising from the operation of the *Warner-Jenkinson* presumption faces a difficult task. In the circumstance in which a pre-

[112] Standard Oil Co. v. American Cyanamid Co., 774 F.2d 448, 452, 227 USPQ 293, 296 (Fed. Cir. 1985) ("[The prosecution history includes] all express representations made by or on behalf of the applicant to the examiner to induce a patent grant. . . . Such representations include amendments to the claims and arguments made to convince the examiner.").

[113] Elkay Mfg. Co. v. Ebco Mfg. Co., 192 F.3d 973, 52 USPQ 2d 1109, 1113 (Fed. Cir. 1999), *cert. denied*, 529 U.S. 1066 (2000); Bai v. L & L Wings, Inc., 160 F.3d 1350, 1356, 48 USPQ 2d 1674, 1678–79 (Fed. Cir. 1998).

[114] Litton Sys., Inc. v. Honeywell, Inc., 140 F.3d 1449, 1457, 46 USPQ 2d 1321, 1327 (Fed. Cir. 1998).

sumption is operative, because the record is unclear concerning the reason for an amendment, it is unlikely that the prior art or the patentee's arguments, if any, will be of assistance in an estoppel analysis. The lack of relevant information concerning the scope of surrendered subject matter is further exacerbated if the patentee does not provide clarification during rebuttal. Unguided by the prosecution history the prior art, the applicant's argument during prosecution, and sufficient evidence in rebuttal to the presumption, there may be no effective way to set reasonable limits on how far the estoppel will allow the doctrine of equivalents to reach. Reasonable competitors assessing the file history will be equally puzzled as to the scope of any potential estoppel. Thus, the Federal Circuit has held that:

> it is logical and fair that prosecution history estoppel arising from the operation of the *Warner-Jenkinson* presumption allows the doctrine of equivalents no room to operate. Finding the Supreme Court's language clear, we hold that in circumstances in which the *Warner-Jenkinson* presumption is applicable, i.e., where the reason for an amendment is unclear from an analysis of the prosecution history record, and unrebutted by the patentee, the prosecution history estoppel arising therefrom is total and completely "bars" the application of the doctrine of equivalents as to the amended limitation.[115]

According to the Federal Circuit, the Supreme Court's language is unequivocal: "In those circumstances [i.e., when the *Warner-Jenkinson* presumption applies], prosecution history estoppel would bar the application of the doctrine of equivalents as to that element."[116]

In the aftermath of *Warner-Jenkinson*, the Federal Circuit issued its long awaited decision in *Festo Corp. v. Shoketsu Kinzoku Kogyo Kabushiki Co.*[117] In the decision, the Federal Circuit, sitting *en banc*, held that a patent claim limitation is entitled to no range of equivalents if it is narrowed by amendment during patent prosecution for any reason related to patentability, including any of the statutory requirements for a patent. Several dissenting judges argued that this decision will increase the costs of patent protection to prohibitively high levels for individual inventors and startup companies and permit easy circumvention of patents.

The case involved the potential infringement of two patents owned by Festo Corp. for magnetically coupled rodless cylinders. The accused device was found not to literally meet every patent claim limitation, so Festo asserted infringement under the doctrine of equivalents. That is, Festo argued that the differences between the claimed invention and

---

[115] Sextant Avionique, S.A. v. Analog Devices, Inc., 172 F.3d 817, 49 USPQ 2d 1865, 1875 (Fed. Cir. 1999).

[116] Warner-Jenkinson Co. v. Hilton Davis Chem. Co., 520 U.S. 17, 41 USPQ 2d 1865, 1873 (1997).

[117] Festo Corp. v. Shoketsu Kinzoku Kogyo Kabushiki Co., 234 F.3d 558, 56 USPQ 2d 1865 (Fed. Cir. 2000) (en banc), *cert. granted*, 121 S. Ct. 2519 (2000).

Main volume footnote updates begin on page 72.

Shoketsu's modified device were insubstantial. Shoketsu argued, however, that amendments made to narrow the patent claims during prosecution created prosecution history estoppel, which barred a finding of infringement under the doctrine of equivalents.

The district court granted summary judgment of infringement in favor of Festo on one patent, and the jury found infringement of the other. Both infringement determinations were under the doctrine of equivalents. On appeal, the Federal Circuit affirmed. The case was then appealed to the Supreme Court, which granted certiorari, vacated the Federal Circuit decision, and remanded the case to the Federal Circuit for reconsideration in light of the Supreme Court's decision in *Warner-Jenkinson Co. v. Hilton Davis Chemical Co.* On remand from the Supreme Court, the Federal Circuit, sitting *en banc*, reversed the district court judgment, finding that neither patent was infringed under the doctrine of equivalents based on prosecution history estoppel.

For the appeal, the Federal Circuit requested briefing directed to five specific questions concerning the doctrine of equivalents and prosecution history estoppel. These five questions, and the Federal Circuit's holding regarding each, are discussed below.

QUESTION 1

> For the purposes of determining whether an amendment to a claim creates prosecution history estoppel, is it a "substantial reason it related to patentability," Warner-Jenkinson Co. v. Hilton Davis Chem. Co., . . . limited to those amendments made to overcome prior art under ¶ 102 and ¶ 103, or does "patentability" mean any reason affecting the issuance of a patent?

The Federal Circuit answered Question 1 as follows: "For the purposes of determining whether an amendment gives rise to prosecution history estoppel, a 'substantial reason related to patentability' is not limited to overcoming or avoiding prior art but instead includes any reason which relates to the statutory requirements for a patent."[118] Accordingly, "a narrowing amendment made for any reason related to the statutory requirements for a patent will give rise to prosecution history estoppel with respect to the amended claim element."[119]

The Federal Circuit noted that there were various statutory requirements for patentability, including: novelty, nonobviousness, patentable subject matter and usefulness, written description, enablement, best mode, and definiteness requirements. Because "any one of these requirements may be a ground for invalidating an issued patent . . . , [a]n amendment related to any of these statutory requirements is an amendment made for 'a substantial reason related to patentability.' "[120] Such an amendment will thus trigger prosecution

---

[118] *Id.*, 56 USPQ 2d at 1870.

[119] *Id.*

[120] *Id.* at 1871.

Main volume footnote updates begin on page 72.

history estoppel. However, the Federal Circuit noted that "if a patent holder can show from the prosecution history that a claim amendment was not motivated by patentability concerns, the amendment will not give rise to prosecution history estoppel."[121] The Federal Circuit, however, did not provide any description as to which types of amendments qualify as those "not motivated by patentability concerns."[122]

QUESTION 2

Under Warner-Jenkinson, should a "voluntary" claim amendment—one not required by the examiner or made in response to a rejection by an examiner for a stated reason—create prosecution history estoppel?

The Federal Circuit answered Question 2 as follows: "Voluntary claim amendments are treated the same as other amendments. Therefore, a voluntary claim amendment that narrows the scope of a claim for a reason related to the statutory requirements for a patent will give rise to prosecution history estoppel as to the amended claim element."[123]

In answering Question 2, the Federal Circuit explained that both "voluntary amendments and amendments required by the Patent Office signal to the public that subject matter has been surrendered."[124] The Court believed this holding was consistent with the doctrine of argument-based estoppel, i.e., those situations where an applicant, in making arguments for patentability, voluntarily surrenders subject matter and thus subjects himself or herself to prosecution history estoppel based on those arguments. The Court therefore reasoned that there is "no reason why an amendment-based surrender of subject matter should be given less force than an argument-based surrender of subject matter."[125]

QUESTION 3

If a claim amendment creates prosecution history estoppel, under Warner-Jenkinson what range of equivalents, if any, is available under the doctrine of equivalents for the claim element so amended?

In answering Question 3, the Federal Circuit majority opinion (8 of the 12 judges) ended the conflict in its prior decisions and held that "when a claim amendment creates prosecution history estoppel with regard to a claim element, there is no range of equivalents available for the amended claim element. Application of the doctrine of equivalents to the claim element is completely barred (a 'complete bar')."[126]

[121] *Id.*

[122] *Id.*

[123] *Id.*

[124] *Id.* at 1871–72.

[125] *Id.* at 1872.

[126] *Id.*

Main volume footnote updates begin on page 72.

The Federal Circuit majority opinion expressly repudiated its prior "flexible bar" approach in determining the scope of the estoppel.

The Federal Circuit majority reasoned that "the notice function of patent claims has become paramount, and the need for certainty as to the scope of patent protection has been emphasized."[127] The Federal Circuit explained:

> We believe that the current state of the law regarding the scope of equivalents that is available when prosecution history estoppel applies is "unworkable." In patent law, we think that rules qualify as "workable" when they can be relied upon to produce consistent results and give rise to a body of law that provides guidance to the marketplace on how to conduct its affairs. . . .
>
> We also believe that the flexible bar approach "poses a direct obstacle to the realization of important objectives." . . . These objectives include giving effect, when prosecution history estoppel arises, to a narrowing amendment's operation as a disclaimer of subject matter, . . . preserving the notice function of patent claims, . . . and promoting certainty in patent law, ... The realization of these objectives cannot help but be frustrated by the uncertainty inherent in the flexible bar approach.
>
> By making prosecution history estoppel act as a complete bar, we enforce the disclaimer effect of a narrowing claim amendment. By narrowing his claims, a patentee disclaims subject matter encompassed by the original claims.[128]

The Federal Circuit further commented regarding this new rule as follows:

> A complete bar, unlike a flexible bar, thus lends certainty to the process of determining the scope of protection afforded by a patent. With a complete bar, both the public and the patentee know that once an element of a claim is narrowed by amendment for a reason related to patentability, that element's scope of coverage will not extend beyond its literal terms. There is no speculation or uncertainty as to the exact range of equivalents that might be available. This certainty aids both the public and the patentee in ascertaining the true scope and value of the patent without having to resort to litigation to obtain a case by case analysis of what subject matter the claims can cover. With a complete bar, neither the public nor the patentee is required to pay the transaction costs of litigation in order to determine the exact scope of subject matter the patentee abandoned when the patentee amended the claim.
>
> Thus, under the complete bar approach, technological advances that would have lain in the unknown, undefined zone around the literal terms of a narrowed claim under the flexible bar approach will not go wasted and undeveloped due to fear of litigation. The public will be free to improve on the patented technology and design around it without being inhibited by the threat of a lawsuit because the changes could possibly fall within the scope of equivalents left after a claim element has been narrowed by amendment for a reason related to patentability. This certainty will stimulate investment in improvements and design-arounds because the risk

---

[127] *Id.* at 1877.

[128] *Id.* at 1877–88 (quoting Patterson v. McClean Credit Union, 491 U.S. 164, 173 (1989) (setting forth the "traditional justification[s] for overruling a prior case")).

Main volume footnote updates begin on page 72.

of infringement will be easier to determine. In general, the difficulty in counseling the public and the patentee on the scope of protection provided by an amended element is greatly reduced under the complete bar approach due to the certainty and predictability such a bar produces.[129]

QUESTION 4

When "no explanation [for a claim amendment] is established," Warner-Jenkinson, . . . thus invoking the presumption of prosecution history estoppel under Warner-Jenkinson, what range of equivalents, if any, is available under the doctrine of equivalents for the claim element so amended?

The Federal Circuit disposed of this question in accordance with the Supreme Court holding of *Warner-Jenkinson* as follows: "When no explanation for a claim amendment is established, no range of equivalents is available for the claim element so amended."[130]

QUESTION 5

Would a judgment of infringement in this case violate *Warner-Jenkinson*'s requirement that the application of the doctrine of equivalents "is not allowed such broad play as to eliminate [an] element in its entirety," 520 U.S. at 29. In other words, would such a judgment of infringement, post *Warner-Jenkinson*, violate the "all elements" rule?

The Federal Circuit declined to answer Question 5. The Federal Circuit indicated that the specific facts of the *Festo* case did not require it to decide this question. Specifically, the Federal Circuit explained that the claim elements that the patentee Festo was trying to show were present in the defendant's devices under the doctrine of equivalents were added by amendment during prosecution. The Federal Circuit held that the record showed the amendments narrowed the scope of the original claim, and that Festo could not establish that the amendments were made for reasons unrelated to patentability. Thus, the Federal Circuit found that prosecution history estoppel applied, and as such Festo was entitled to no range of equivalents for the elements added by amendment. The Federal Circuit, therefore, reversed the finding of infringement under the doctrine of equivalents.

In reviewing the specific facts in the *Festo* case, the Federal Circuit majority opinion set forth the new analysis a court should apply in determining whether infringement under the doctrine of equivalents is available to a patentee:

> When infringement is alleged to occur under the doctrine of equivalents, two primary legal limitations on the doctrine "are to be determined by the court, either on a dispositive pretrial motion or on a motion for judgment as a matter of law at the close of evidence and after the jury ver-

[129] *Id.* at 1879.

[130] *Id.* at 1880.

> dict." *Warner-Jenkinson*, 520 U.S. at 39 n.8. Those legal limitations are prosecution history estoppel and the "all elements" rule. . . .
>
> The first legal limitation a court should consider is prosecution history estoppel, because prosecution history estoppel may completely bar the application of the doctrine of equivalents to a given claim element. The first step in a prosecution history estoppel analysis is to determine which claim elements are alleged to be met by equivalents. Then, the court must determine whether the elements at issue were amended during prosecution of the patent. If they were not, amendment-based estoppel will not bar the application of the doctrine of equivalents. However, the court still may need to consider whether statements made during prosecution give rise to argument-based estoppel. . . .
>
> If the claim elements at issue were amended, the court first must determine whether the amendment narrowed the literal scope of the claim. If so, prosecution history estoppel will apply unless the patent holder establishes that the amendment was made for a purpose unrelated to patentability. . . . If the patent holder fails to do so, prosecution history estoppel will bar the application of the doctrine of equivalents to that claim element.
>
> In *Warner-Jenkinson*, the Supreme Court explained the purpose of placing on the patent holder the burden of establishing the reason for an amendment: allocating the burden in this manner "gives proper deference to the role of claims in defining an invention and providing public notice." *Id.* at 33. Public notice consideration also have been fundamental to our decisions regarding the scope of prosecution history estoppel. . . . In order to give due deference to public notice considerations under the *Warner-Jenkinson* framework, a patent holder seeking to establish the reason for an amendment must base his arguments solely upon the public record of the patent's prosecution, i.e., the patent's prosecution history. To hold otherwise—that is, to allow a patent holder to rely on evidence not in the public record to establish a reason for an amendment—would undermine the public notice function of the patent record. If the reasons for the amendment do not appear in the public record of the patent's prosecution, the reasons in most cases will be known only to the patent holder. . . . We therefore hold that a narrowing amendment will give rise to prosecution history estoppel unless the prosecution history of the patent reveals that the amendment was made for a purpose unrelated to patentability concerns.
>
> If prosecution history estoppel does not bar the application of the doctrine of equivalents, the court should consider the second legal limitation on the doctrine, the "all elements" rule . . . . If the court determines that a finding of infringement under the doctrine of equivalents "would entirely vitiate a particular claim element," then the court should rule that there is no infringement under the doctrine of equivalents.[131]

Thus, the Federal Circuit majority opinion further refined or limited when an amendment that narrows a claim element is to be considered an amendment with respect to patentability, i.e., when the prosecution history of the patent reveals that the amendment was made for a purpose unrelated to patentability concerns.

---

[131] *Id.* at 1886–87.

Main volume footnote updates begin on page 72.

The Federal Circuit majority opinion also further defined what constitutes an amendment to a claim that triggers the possibility of prosecution history estoppel. According to the Federal Circuit, a narrowing amendment to a claim may result when a broader claim is replaced with a new claim that is narrower that the original claim.[132] In addition, the Federal Circuit also indicated that amending a claim element written in means-plus-function format with a recitation of the corresponding structure also is considered a narrowing amendment. According to the Federal Circuit, a claim element recited in means-plus-function language literally encompasses the corresponding structure and its equivalents, whereas a claim element that recites the corresponding structure does not literally encompass equivalents of that structure. Thus, the Federal Circuit concluded that "a claim amendment that replaces means-plus-function language with language reciting the corresponding structure narrows the literal scope of the claim."[133]

The Federal Circuit majority opinion also defined when an amendment relates to patentability. According to the Federal Circuit, any amendment made to satisfy the patent statutes is an amendment made for a reason related to patentability.[134] The Federal Circuit further indicated that an Examiner's reasoning for allowing an application can also be used to indicate that the amendment to the claim was for a reason related to patentability.[135]

The dissenters with respect to Question 3 comprised four judges, each of whom wrote their own opinion. All dissenting judges essentially argued that the majority ignored established Supreme Court precedent, significantly reduced the value of existing patents, enhanced the ability of copyists to escape infringement, and increased the cost of the patent prosecution process to prevent many inventors from being able to protect their inventions, thereby increasing the use of trade secret protection and depriving the public of technological advances, perhaps forever.[136]

[On page 98, delete the first three sentences in the second paragraph and delete the sentence following footnote 206.]

[On page 99, insert after the first sentence in the last paragraph.]

The Federal Circuit has stated that "[i]n cases where a patentee's amendments were not required in response to an examiner's re-

[132] *Id.* at 1887.

[133] *Id.* at 1888.

[134] *Id.*

[135] *Id.* at 1890.

[136] *See e.g., Id.* at 1912 (Michel, J., concurring-in-part, dissenting-in-part).

Main volume footnote updates begin on page 72.

jection or critical to the allowance of the claims, no estoppel has been found."[137]

[Page 100, change the following in the last full paragraph.]

On appeal, the Federal Circuit affirmed.

[Page 102, insert the following after the first full paragraph.]

Of course, the specific statements in *Southwall* regarding amendments to claims and prosecution history estoppel resulting therefrom are subject to *Festo Corp. v. Shoketsu Kinzoku Kogyo Kabushiki Co.*,[138] described above.

[Insert the following at the end of the section.]

Of course, the specific statements in *Read Corp.* regarding amendments to claims and prosecution history estoppel resulting therefrom are subject to *Festo Corp. v. Shoketsu Kinzoku Kogyo Kabushiki Co.*,[139] described above.

6. *Prosecution History Estoppel May Prevent Infringement Under the Doctrine of Equivalents*

[Move this heading from after footnote 235 to after footnote 236.]

8. *New Claims Added During Prosecution That Include Narrow Limitations May Create Estoppel [New Topic]*

That a claim was added, and therefore not amended during prosecution, does not preclude the application of prosecution history estoppel.[140] Thus, when a claim limitation is added in order to overcome a specific cited reference, estoppel as to that limitation is generated whether the limitation is added by amendment to pending claims or by the submission of new claims containing the limitation.[141]

---

[137] Mannesmann Demag Corp. v. Engineered Metal Prods. Co., 793 F.2d 1279, 1284–85, 230 USPQ 45, 48 (Fed. Cir. 1986).

[138] Festo Corp. v. Shoketsu Kinzoku Kogyo Kabushiki Co., 234 F.3d 558, 56 USPQ 2d 1865 (Fed. Cir. 2000) (en banc), *cert. granted*, 121 S. Ct. 2519 (2001).

[139] Festo Corp. v. Shoketsu Kinzoku Kogyo Kabushiki Co., 234 F.3d 558, 56 USPQ 2d 1865 (Fed. Cir. 2000) (en banc), *cert. granted*, 121 S. Ct. 2519 (2001).

[140] Pall Corp. v. Hemasure Inc., 181 F.3d 1305, 50 USPQ 2d 1947, 1951 (Fed. Cir. 1999).

[141] Builders Concrete, Inc. v. Bremerton Concrete Prods. Co., 757 F.2d 255, 225 USPQ 240 (Fed. Cir. 1985) ("The fact that the 'passage' clause of patent claim 10 was not itself amended during prosecution does not mean that it can be extended by the doctrine of equivalents to cover the precise subject matter that was relinquished in order to obtain allowance of claim 1.").

Main volume footnote updates begin on page 72.

9. Amendments/Arguments With Respect to Certain Claims May Not Necessarily Be Used to Interpret Other Claims [New Topic]

In *Johnson Worldwide Associates, Inc. v. Zebco Corp.*,[142] the Federal Circuit held that an applicant's interpretation of certain claims during prosecution was not to be used to interpret other claims, where these other claims did not include certain limitations. Zebco argued that the applicant's statement, in a June 17, 1992, amendment that the claim language "the heading signal . . . is dependent solely on the heading of the motor, and totally independent of the orientation of the vessel," was a clear definition of "heading signal" as being limited to the direction of the thrust motor.[143] However, the Federal Circuit disagreed and noted that Zebco overlooked the fact that the claims referred to in that passage, claims 4 and 14, expressly included an additional limitation: that the compass be "in a substantially fixed relationship to said propulsion device" (claim 4) or likewise "in a predetermined relationship with said propulsion device" (claim 14).[144]

According to the Federal Circuit, the argument referenced by Zebco was unquestionably focused on the requirement, in claims 4 and 14, that the compass be attached to the trolling motor. The applicant's suggestion that, where the "substantially fixed relationship" or "in a predetermined relationship" claim limitation was present, the feedback signal (i.e., the heading signal) was dependent on the heading of the motor "sheds no light on the meaning of 'heading signal' in claims where that very limitation is not present."[145] The Federal Circuit emphasized:

> Rather, this exchange is an example of how carefully-crafted arguments in support of patentability can avoid creating ambiguous or adverse prosecution history. By stating clearly and particularly that the context of his remarks was in regards to claims 4 and 14, the applicant ensured that those of ordinary skill in the art—as well as courts, if need be—could evaluate the import and scope of his statements. Thus, because this argument was plainly limited to claims including a "fixed" or "predetermined" relationship between the compass and the trolling motor, it cannot be said to be a clear statement limiting the scope of "heading signal" in general. Zebco thus has not shown that sufficient reasons exist to import a limited definition of this term into the clear language of the claim.[146]

---

[142]Johnson Worldwide Assoc., Inc. v. Zebco Corp., 175 F.3d 985, 50 USPQ 2d 1607, 1611 (Fed. Cir. 1999).

[143]*Id.*, 50 USPQ 2d at 1612.

[144]*Id.*

[145]*Id.*

[146]*Id.*

Main volume footnote updates begin on page 72.

Thus, *Johnson* teaches that arguments with respect to certain claims may not necessarily be used to interpret other claims, particularly where the claims also contain different limitations.[147]

10. Amendments/Arguments With Respect to Claims in One Patent May Create an Estoppel for Claims in Another Patent Having Similar Language [New Topic]

The prosecution history of a parent application may limit the scope of a later application using the same claim term.[148] For example, in *Augustine Medical, Inc. v. Gaymar Industries, Inc.*,[149] the invention related to convective thermal blankets. During prosecution, Augustine Medical amended the claims to recite the limitation that the blankets were "self-erecting" and also argued this feature.[150] Augustine Medical sued Gaymar, and Gaymar argued that the claims were not infringed, literally or by equivalents, because its blankets did not satisfy the "self-erecting" limitation.

On appeal, the Federal Circuit agreed with Augustine Medical, noting that:

> The prosecution histories of the Augustine patents show that the applicant expressly surrendered coverage of any forced-air blanket other than a "self-erecting" convective thermal blanket which stands off of a patient when in operation. During prosecution of application No. 07/227, 189 (the '189 application), a parent application to later applications result-

[147] *See also* Fiskars Inc. v. Hunt Mfg. Co. 221 F.3d 1318, 55 USPQ 2d 1569, 1573 (Fed. Cir. 2000), *cert. denied*, 121 S. Ct. 1603 (2001):

> Fiskars points out that the only asserted claim that was amended to include a supporting as well as a biasing function was claim 6, and that claim 6 is the only asserted claim in which the support function was mentioned in prosecution argument. Although claim 6 may be subject to prosecution history estoppel as to this element, the other claims in suit are not. Claims whose allowance was not due to a particular argument are not subject to estoppel deriving from that argument. We agree with the district court that there was no estoppel barring the jury question of equivalency of the biasing springs;

Princeton Biochemicals, Inc. v. Beckman Instruments, Inc., Civ. App. 98-1525, slip op. at 10–11 (Fed. Cir. Aug. 19, 1999) (unpublished):

> We also hold that the applicant did not limit claim 32 to a vertically moving holder during prosecution as the amendments and arguments cited by the district court were directed to claims other than those that were combined as issued claim 32. . . . See *Johnson Worldwide Assocs., Inc. v. Zebco Corp.,* 175 F.3d 985, 992, 50 USPQ 2d 1607, 1612 (Fed. Cir. 1999) ("carefully-crafted arguments" clearly directed to certain claims and not others will "avoid creating ambiguous or adverse prosecution history"). Beckman's reliance on certain amendments and remarks made by the applicant during prosecution concerning holder limitations specifically limited to a vertically movable holder is misplaced. Those amendments and remarks were directed primarily at application claim 8, a picture claim containing numerous other limitations and directed to the specific embodiment of a vertically moving holder, and not to the broader holder limitation in claim 1 that eventually resulted in issued claim 32).

[148] Jonsson v. Stanley Works, 903 F.2d 812, 818, 14 USPQ 2d 1863, 1870 (Fed. Cir. 1990).

[149] Augustine Med., Inc. v. Gaymar Indus., Inc., 181 F.3d 1291, 50 USPQ 2d 1900 (Fed. Cir. 1999).

[150] *Id.*, 50 USPQ 2d at 1906.

Main volume footnote updates begin on page 72.

> ing in the '102, '320 and '371 patents, Augustine Medical canceled or amended all of the original claims in favor of new claims containing the "self-erecting" limitation. Augustine Medical made these amendments in response to the examiner's rejections over the prior art.[151]

Because the prosecution history of a parent application may limit the scope of a later application using the same claim term, the Federal Circuit held that the "self-erecting" claim amendments and arguments restricted the scope of the claims in each of the later-issued patents containing the "self-erecting" limitation.[152]

11. Estoppels in Earlier Application Will Not Extend to Broader Claims in Later Application [New Topic]

Estoppels relating to an applicant's amendments/arguments in earlier applications will not generally extend to broader claims allowed in later applications.[153] This is contrary to the usual rule that the entire prosecution history, including parent and grandparent applications, be analyzed in interpreting a claim.[154]

For example, in *Princeton Biochemicals, Inc. v. Beckman Instruments, Inc.*,[155] the invention related to an apparatus for use in the process of capillary electrophoresis whereby molecules and proteins are separated from fluid samples as a result of application of an electrical charge. Princeton sued Beckman for patent infringement, asserting that Beckman's patent infringed claim 32 of U.S. Patent No. 5,045,172 ("the '172 patent"). The parties disputed whether the claim covered only the embodiment where the holder and the capillary tube moved vertically toward a stationary sample cup and table, or also the alternative embodiment in which the sample cup and table moved vertically toward a stationary holder and capillary tube as in the accused devices.

Princeton argued that the district court erred in construing the "holder limitation" of claim 32. In particular, Princeton asserted that the district court erred by requiring a "vertically moving" holder, as no such limitation was present in the asserted claim. Nor, argued Princeton, were any arguments made during the prosecution of the application that resulted in the '172 patent and directed at claim 32 that would support reading a vertical movement limitation into that claim.

---

[151] *Id.*

[152] *Id.* at 1907.

[153] Princeton Biochemicals, Inc. v. Beckman Instruments, Inc., Civ. App. 98-1525, slip op. at 10 (Fed. Cir. Aug. 19, 1999) (unpublished).

[154] Mark I Mktg. Corp. v. Donnelley & Sons Co., 66 F.3d 285, 291, 36 USPQ 2d 1095, 1100 (Fed. Cir. 1995).

[155] Princeton Biochemicals, Inc. v. Beckman Instruments, Inc., Civ. App. 98-1525 (Fed. Cir. Aug. 19, 1999) (unpublished).

Main volume footnote updates begin on page 72.

On appeal, the Federal Circuit agreed, stating that "[a] careful review of the prosecution history reveals that Princeton is correct."[156] The Federal Circuit noted that a continuation-in-part (CIP) application was filed in which claim 32 (claim 1 as originally filed) was returned to its original, unamended form. Thereafter, claim 32 was rejected as obvious over prior art, but was not subsequently amended to include any requirement of vertical movement and in fact was not amended to distinguish over the cited prior art. The Examiner thus allowed the combined claim to issue as claim 32 without any amendment being made or any argument being espoused that would limit the holder limitation to the embodiment where the holder/capillary was vertically moving in relation to a stationary sample cup/table.

On this basis the Federal Circuit held the following:

> We hold that the prosecution history does not limit the holder limitation of claim 32 to only vertically movable holders. Although the applicant amended claim 1 to include a vertical movement requirement of the holder in the original application, the subsequent filing of the CIP application and the return of claim 1 to its original, unamended form, counsels against applying the usual rule that the entire prosecution history, including parent and grandparent applications, be analyzed in interpreting a claim.[157]

Thus, *Princeton Biochemicals* teaches that estoppels relating to an applicant's amendments/arguments in earlier applications will not generally extend to broader claims allowed in later applications that do not include those specific limitations. A similar situation occurred in *Al-Site Corp. v. VSI International, Inc.*,[158] wherein the Federal Circuit stated the following:

> In a further attempt to overturn the jury verdict of infringement under the doctrine of equivalents with respect to the '345, '726, and '911 patents, VSI relies on prosecution history estoppel. This court has reviewed VSI's prosecution history estoppel argument and finds it unpersuasive. To overcome prior art objections by the Examiner, Magnivision amended what became claim 8 of the '532 patent to require that the extension project from the bottom edge portion of the hanger tag. . . . VSI argues that because all of Magnivision's patents arose from related applications, the same prosecution history estoppel applies to them as well. VSI therefore contends that because the arms of its Version 2 hanger tag extend from the sides of the body of the tag, it cannot infringe the claims of these patents under the doctrine of equivalents as restricted by prosecution history estoppel. While in some cases, the prosecution history of a related application may limit application of the doctrine of equivalents in a later filed patent, in this case the specific limitation added in the claims of an earlier issued patent is not present in the claims of the later issued patents. The '345, '726, and '911 patents all have limitations not found in the '532 patent and did not necessarily require the specific limitation added to the claims of the '532 patent to be patentable. The specific limitations added to gain allowance of the '532 patent are not

---

[156] *Id.*, slip op. at 9.

[157] *Id.* at 10.

[158] Al-Site Corp. v. VSI Int'l, Inc., 174 F.3d 1308, 50 USPQ 2d 1161 (Fed. Cir. 1999).

Main volume footnote updates begin on page 72.

included in and are therefore not relevant to determining the scope of the claims of the later issued patents.[159]

On the other hand, when the earlier and later applications share the same claim terminology and/or arguments, an estoppel with respect to an earlier application will generally apply to one or more later applications, particularly when an applicant links the two or more applications during prosecution. For example, the Federal Circuit stated the following in *Elkay Manufacturing Co. v. Ebco Manufacturing Co.*:[160]

> When multiple patents derive from the same initial application, the prosecution history regarding a claim limitation in any patent that has issued applies with equal force to subsequently issued patents that contain the same claim limitation. . . . The facts in the present case are even more compelling than in Jonsson for applying the prosecution history of the first issued patent to the second issued patent. Here, Elkay added new claims 26-28 during the prosecution of the '639 application, which issued as claims 1-3, respectively, in the '855 patent. In describing the claims, *Elkay stated that "new claim 26 is patterned after a combination of claims 1, 3 and 5 of [the '531 patent] with the 'feed tube' changed to—feed probe—. . . ."* By making this statement, Elkay affirmatively linked the meaning of claim 26 of the '639 application to claims 1, 3, and 5 of the '531 patent. Because Elkay's statement put competitors on clear notice of that *linkage* and because the '531 and '855 patents stem from the same genus, it is proper to consider the prosecution history of claim 1 of the '855 patent to be an amalgam of the prosecution histories of both patents.[161]

12. Examiner Amendments/Reasons for Allowance May Be Used to Interpret Claim or Create an Estoppel [New Topic]

Examiner amendments or Examiner statements on reasons for allowance may be used to interpret a patent claim or create an estoppel.[162] For example, in *Elkay Manufacturing Co. v. Ebco Manufacturing Co.*,[163] the technology concerned "no-spill" adapters for bottled water coolers that permit jugs of water to be inserted into coolers with the cap still on the bottle, thereby eliminating the potential problems of spilling or contaminating water when, for example, a bottle is inserted into a cooler.

Elkay sued Ebco, claiming that Ebco's WaterGuard devices infringed various claims of its patents. Ebco argued that the patents were not infringed, literally or under the doctrine of equivalents, because its feed tube structure was not limited to a single passageway

---

[159] *Id.*, 50 USPQ 2d at 1170.

[160] Elkay Mfg. Co. v. Ebco Mfg. Co., 192 F.3d 973, 52 USPQ 2d 1109 (Fed. Cir. 1999), *cert. denied*, 529 U.S. 1066 (2000).

[161] *Id.*, 52 USPQ 2d at 1114 (emphasis added).

[162] Alpex Computer Corp. v. Nintendo Co., 102 F.3d 1214, 40 USPQ 2d 1667 (Fed. Cir. 1996), *cert. denied*, 521 U.S. 1104 (1997).

[163] Elkay Mfg. Co. v. Ebco Mfg. Co., 192 F.3d 973, 52 USPQ 2d 1109 (Fed. Cir. 1999), *cert. denied*, 529 U.S. 1066 (2000).

Main volume footnote updates begin on page 72.

for both water and air. Ebco cited the Examiner's Statement of Reasons for Allowance in support of its argument.

On appeal, the Federal Circuit agreed with Ebco:

> Elkay's argument that its statement distinguishing [prior art] Krug on the basis of Krug's use of separate feed tubes was insignificant is particularly unpersuasive in view of the Examiner's response to that statement. In the Examiner's Statement of Reasons for Allowance, dated March 30, 1993, the Examiner wrote that he allowed claim 22 (i.e., claim 7 in the '531 patent) because he understood the claim to describe a single feed tube with a single flow path for both liquid and air. . . . Elkay did not respond to this statement.[164]

The Federal Circuit concluded that during prosecution Elkay disavowed a potential interpretation of the feed tube limitations that would include separate feed tubes or flow paths for liquid and air and, therefore, was limited to a single feed tube with a single flow path for both liquid and air.

Whether the amendments were made by an applicant or entered by an Examiner to advance the application to the stage of allowance is irrelevant if the amendments were made for a substantial reason related to patentability.[165] For example, in one case, the Federal Circuit has stated the following:

> In this case, our review of the prosecution history makes it plain that the amendments relevant here were made for a "substantial reason related to patentability." . . . The "heel-and-toe" amendments, which were entered by the examiner during reexamination after a telephone conference with the patentee, were made for such a reason. . . . These amendments were entered after the citation of additional prior art to the examiner . . . , and unquestionably in light of the earlier art cited against the claims . . . . The fact that the words were formally entered by the examiner (after conversation with the applicant) rather than the applicant does not affect the question of whether a substantial reason related to patentability precipitated their addition.[166]

13. *Estoppel May Arise by Failure to Prosecute Claims in Divisional Application in Face of Prior Art Rejection [New Topic]*

Limiting a claim because of a restriction requirement does not necessarily invoke prosecution history estoppel.[167] An estoppel may arise, however, by failure to prosecute claims in divisional application in face of prior art rejection. The determination of whether an amendment was made for purposes of patentability on grounds of obvious-

[164] *Id.*, 52 USPQ 2d at 1113.

[165] Warner-Jenkinson Co. v. Hilton Davis Chem. Co., 520 U.S. 17, 33, 41 USPQ 2d 1865, 1875 (1997).

[166] K-2 Corp. v. Salomon S.A., 191 F.3d 1356, 52 USPQ 2d 1001, 1009–10 (Fed. Cir. 1999).

[167] Bayer Aktiengesellschaft v. Duphar Int'l Research B.V., 738 F.2d 1237, 1243, 222 USPQ 649, 653 (Fed. Cir. 1984).

Main volume footnote updates begin on page 72.

ness is adjudged from the viewpoint of a person of skill in the field of the invention and, when the issue includes consideration of formalities of patent practice, experience in patent law and procedures is presumed.[168] The court must determine what such a person would conclude from the prosecution record.[169]

Merck & Co. v. Mylan Pharmaceuticals, Inc.[170] is an example of an estoppel found when the applicant Merck failed to prosecute claims in divisional application in face of prior art rejection. The invention was directed to a controlled release formulation of a combination of the drugs levodopa and carbidopa, used to treat Parkinson's disease. The desired controlled release was achieved by delivering these drugs in a polymer vehicle, the specific composition of which was the issue in this dispute.

The district court ruled that Merck had surrendered coverage of a HPC/HPMC polymer vehicle during prosecution, by amending and narrowing the claims in response to the Examiner's rejection of Merck's broad claims on the ground of obviousness in view of certain prior art. Merck argued to the district court that it was compelled by the Examiner to elect a species from the proposed Markush genus, and that it amended its claims for this reason and not because the claims were unpatentable under Section 103. Merck further argued that it simply complied with the Examiner's formal requirement of an examination expedient and did not yield anything in response to the rejection on obviousness. According to Merck, once it had elected a species, the Examiner's rejection based on the prior art simply became irrelevant to the prosecution. Thus, Merck argued that its election to prosecute a claim covering its commercial formulation when the Examiner required an election of species did not effect an estoppel against equivalent polymer combinations.

The district court found that Merck limited its claims to the particular polymer species in response to the Examiner's obviousness rejection, notwithstanding that the Examiner had also imposed a restriction requirement, and, therefore, an estoppel occurred.

On appeal, the Federal Circuit affirmed the district court decision. According to the Federal Circuit:

> Although Merck carried the Markush-group polymers into the divisional application, upon rejection under §103 and the formal requirement for an election of species Merck again elected the HPC/PVACA combination. Although this action also resolved the requirement of an election of species, we conclude that the controlling fact is that Merck no longer sought to claim any of the several other polymer vehicles. . . . We therefore conclude that the most reasonable reading of the prosecution history is that Merck's

[168] Merck & Co. v. Mylan Pharms., Inc., 190 F.3d 1335, 51 USPQ 2d 1954, 1958 (Fed. Cir. 1999).

[169] EMI Group N. Am., Inc. v. Intel Corp., 157 F.3d 887, 898, 48 USPQ 2d 1181, 1189 (Fed. Cir. 1998), *cert. denied*, 526 U.S. 1112 (1999); Modine Mfg. Co. v. United States Int'l Trade Comm'n, 75 F.3d 1545, 1555–56, 37 USPQ 2d 1609, 1616 (Fed. Cir. 1996).

[170] Merck & Co. v. Mylan Pharms., Inc., 190 F.3d 1335, 51 USPQ 2d 1954 (Fed. Cir. 1999).

> actions in limiting all of the claims of both patents to a single species of combined polymer vehicle, without further pursuit of the broader polymer claims, were primarily in consideration of the patentability rejection . . . . Thus we conclude that prosecution history estoppel arises.[171]

14. No Prosecution History Estoppel When Claim Rewritten in Independent Form or to Correct Antecedent Basis Problem [New Topic]

In general, when a patent application is drafted, a variety of patent claims are submitted of varying scope by generally submitting a variety of independent and dependent claims. Dependent claims depend from, or provide additional features, upon the claim from which they depend. Accordingly, during the examination stage of prosecution, the Patent Office Examiner may indicate that a dependent claim is allowable over the prior art of record. If the patent applicant agrees with the Examiner, the patent applicant may cancel all claims that are not allowable, and rewrite the allowable dependent claim in independent form. The Federal Circuit has indicated that this type of amendment is not the kind of amendment that will trigger the prosecution history estoppel doctrine to limit the scope of equivalents.[172]

Similarly, with regard to correcting claim language relating to an antecedent basis informality, the Federal Circuit has also indicated that this type of claim amendment will not trigger the prosecution history estoppel doctrine.[173]

15. Prosecution History Estoppel Applies When Claim Amended After Notice of Allowance [New Topic]

Prosecution history estoppel may apply even though a patent claim is amended after the Examiner issues a Notice of Allowance if the reason for the amendment related to patentability. Narrowing amendments after a Notice of Allowance are rare because there is no incentive for the applicant to further limit the invention; substantive

---

[171] *Id.*, 51 USPQ 2d at 1958.

[172] Vermeer Mfg. Co. v. Charles Mach. Works, Inc., Civ. App. No. 00-1119, slip op. at 4 (Fed. Cir. Nov. 27, 2000) (unpublished). *But see* Festo Corp. v. Shoketsu Kinzoku Kogyo Kabushiki Co., 234 F.3d 558, 56 USPQ 2d 1865, 1870–71 (Fed. Cir. 2000) (en banc):

> [A narrowing amendment made for any reason related to the statutory requirements for a patent will give rise to prosecution history estoppel with respect to the amended claim element. . . . [T]here are a number of statutory requirements that must be satisfied before a valid patent can issue and that thus relate to patentability. . . . [T]he second paragraph of section 112 requires that the claims set forth the subject matter that the applicant regards as his invention and that the claims particularly point out and distinctly define the invention. . . . An amendment related to any of these statutory requirements is an amendment made for a substantial reason related to patentability.

[173] *Id.*

Main volume footnote updates begin on page 72.

examination has been completed. Thus, one would normally infer that the claim was amended for reasons other than patentability, and therefore, no prosecution history estoppel should normally take place.

Ramp R&D Co. v. Structural Panels, Inc.,[174] is an example of when the applicant amended the patent claim after Notice of Allowance, and the amendment created prosecution history estoppel. In *Ramp R&D Co.*, the invention related to interlocking insulated building panels. The district court found that the Ramp panels did not literally infringe claim 1 of U.S. Patent No. 5,086,599 ('599 patent), but did infringe the claim under the doctrine of equivalents. Ramp appealed and the Federal Circuit reversed and held no infringement by equivalents based on prosecution history estoppel.

Claim 1 of the '599 patent reads in pertinent part as follows:

> 1. A building panel comprising, in combination, a core portion having insulating and structural properties, a skin secured to the core portion having formed lateral edges which extend beyond the core on one lateral edge of the panel.[175]

Ramp argued that the district court failed to consider the prosecution history, and that statements were made during the prosecution of the '599 patent that estopped Structural from asserting that the accused panel infringed under the doctrine of equivalents. Specifically, Ramp contended that Structural was estopped from asserting that the Ramp panel, which had an aluminum "skin" that extended beyond the core material on both ends of the panel, met the "skin secured to the core portion having formed lateral edges which extend beyond the core on one lateral edge of the panel" limitation.

Ramp noted that after claim 1 was allowed, the applicant amended the claim to correct an error. The applicant added the limitation "on one lateral edge of the panel" to the claim, and stated that "[t]he skin extends from one lateral edge of the panel, and the nose extends from the other. As originally allowed, line 6 of claim 1 would imply that the skin extends beyond the core on all of the edges."[176] Ramp argued that having amended the claim to make it clear that the skin extended beyond the core only on one lateral edge, not on two, Structural could not assert that having the skin extend beyond the core on both edges of the panel was equivalent to having the skin extend beyond the core on one edge, as the claim required.

The Federal Circuit agreed with Ramp that these statements evinced a clear surrender of the subject matter accused of infringing under the doctrine of equivalents. According to the Federal Circuit, the claims and prosecution history perform an important function of

---

[174] Ramp R&D Co. v. Structural Panels, Inc., Civ. App. No. 97-1357 (Fed. Cir. Feb. 8, 2000) (unpublished).

[175] *Id.*, slip op. at 11.

[176] *Id.*

Main volume footnote updates begin on page 72.

providing the public with written notice as to the scope of what the applicant claims as his or her invention.[177] The applicant clearly stated that his invention was not a panel that had "skin" protruding on both edges of the core portion, reasoned the Federal Circuit. Ramp, as a member of the public, had a right to rely on that statement.[178] On this basis the Federal Circuit held that Structural was estopped from asserting that Ramp's panel, which did have skin protruding on both sides of the inner core, fell within the scope of the claimed invention under the doctrine of equivalents. The district court's decision on infringement of the '599 patent was thus reversed.

Thus, *Ramp R&D Co.* underscores the importance of clarifying the prosecution record with regard to claim amendments. In this case, if the claim amendment was not for reasons of patentability, but rather to correct an informality, the applicant should have clearly made such a statement, supported by sufficient reasoning. The reasoning provided by the applicant in *Ramp R&D Co.* was used by the Federal Circuit to interpret and limit the scope of the claim at issue.

16. Drawings May be Used to Determine Whether Prosecution History Estoppel Applies [New Topic]

Drawings may be used to determine whether prosecution history estoppel applies. For example, in *Hockerson-Halberstadt, Inc. v. Avia Group International, Inc.*,[179] that fact that drawings are typically not drawn to scale was used in interpreting the prosecution history to exclude or disclaim a particular claim interpretation. Hockerson-Halberstadt, Inc. ("HHI") sued Avia Group International, Inc. ("Avia") for infringement of U.S. Patent No. 4,259,792 ("the '792 patent"), covering an article of outer footwear. The '792 patent more specifically related to athletic shoes having a heel that was bisected by a central groove creating two peripheral fins. The central groove and double fin structure provided the user with a cushioning effect by distributing the downward force of footfall over a wide area of the heel.

During prosecution of the '792 patent, the inventor made various arguments to distinguish the new claims from the prior art. In one of his arguments, the inventor submitted drawings, and pursuant to the drawings, the inventor argued that the invention "is providing a much narrower groove for a totally different purpose, namely to provide fins

---

[177] *Id.* at 12 (citing Warner-Jenkinson Co. v. Hilton Davis Chem. Co., 520 U.S. 17, 29, 41 USPQ 2d 1865, 1871 (1997); Spectrum Int'l, Inc. v. Sterilite Corp., 164 F.3d 1372, 1378, 49 USPQ 2d 1065, 1069 (Fed. Cir. 1998)).

[178] *Id.* (citing Digital Biometrics, Inc. v. Identix, Inc., 149 F.3d 1335, 1347, 47 USPQ 2d 1418, 1427 (Fed.Cir.1998) ("The public has a right to rely on [ ] definitive statements made during prosecution.")).

[179] Hockerson-Halberstadt, Inc. v. Avia Group Int'l., Inc., 222 F.3d 951, 55 USPQ 2d 1487 (Fed. Cir. 2000).

Main volume footnote updates begin on page 72.

which can be compressed outwardly and upwardly. Such fins are not provided on the shoe of the prior art."[180] Following these arguments, the Examiner allowed the new claims, which issued as independent claims 1, 2, and 3 of the '792 patent. The inventor then assigned the '792 patent to HHI.

The district court analyzed the '792 patent and its prosecution history, and construed the term "central longitudinal groove" as being a relatively long and narrow structure that extended longitudinally or lengthwise completely through the center so as to divide the heel part into a pair of fins. On appeal, HHI asserted that the district court incorrectly analyzed the prosecution history. HHI contended that a reasonable competitor would understand that the inventor's "much narrower groove" statement was an erroneous statement rather than a disavowal of a particular width relationship because the statement was made in reference to drawings submitted during prosecution, and the specification contains figures depicting a groove that was wider than the fins.

The Federal Circuit disagreed with HHI and affirmed the district court's claim interpretation. The Federal Circuit noted that review of the prosecution history revealed that the inventor disclaimed a particular interpretation of groove, thereby modifying the term's ordinary meaning.

Specifically, during prosecution of the '792 patent, the inventor submitted drawings comparing the features of the claimed invention to a hypothetical combination of the prior art Lombard and Bowerman patents. The inventor then distinguished the prior art by arguing that the claimed invention "provid[es] a much narrower groove for a totally different purpose, namely . . . to involve as much of the underneath surface of the footwear as possible in a cushioning and supporting function."[181] According to the Federal Circuit, flowing from this statement was the inventor's clear disavowal of footwear having a groove width greater than that disclosed in the prior art. Thus, it ruled that the district court correctly held that the inventor necessarily defined the central longitudinal groove as requiring a width that must be less than the combined width of the two fins.

The Federal Circuit also noted that the '792 patent lacked any indication that the proportions of the groove and fins were drawn to scale. The Federal Circuit reasoned that HHI's argument hinged on an inference drawn from certain figures about the quantitative relationship between the respective widths of the groove and fins. However, the Federal Circuit pointed out that "it is well established that patent drawings do not define the precise proportions of the elements and may not be relied on to show particular sizes if the specification

[180] *Id.*, 55 USPQ 2d at 1489.

[181] *Id.*

Main volume footnote updates begin on page 72.

is completely silent on the issue."[182] Thus, the Federal Circuit held that a reasonable competitor, being aware that figures in a patent are not drawn to scale unless otherwise indicated, would understand the arguments in the prosecution history as clearly disclaiming a groove having a width greater than the combined width of the fins.[183]

F. Drafting the Patent Specification and Claims for Proper Scope

[Insert after footnote 252.]

The Federal Circuit has become increasingly reluctant to provide a claim interpretation of broader scope covering an alternative embodiment of the invention when the patent specification provides no appreciation of a potential alternative embodiment as understood by one of ordinary skill.[184] The prior art may assist in interpreting the scope of the patent claim. In general, the prior art will restrict or limit the scope of patent claims, particularly those claims drafted in means-plus-function format.[185] However, when the invention is a combination of old elements, and the specification specifically references or describes alternative prior art components, the patent claims will be in-

[182] *Id.* At 1491 (citing *In re* Wright, 569 F.2d 1124, 1127, 193 USPQ 332, 335 (C.C.P.A. 1977) ("Absent any written description in the specification of quantitative values, arguments based on measurement of a drawing are of little value."); *In re* Olson, 212 F.2d 590, 592, 101 USPQ 401, 402 (C.C.P.A. 1954)).

[183] *Id.*

[184] Wang Labs., Inc. v. America Online, Inc., 197 F.3d 1377, 53 USPQ 2d 1161, 1165 (Fed. Cir. 1999):

> The usage "preferred" does not of itself broaden the claims beyond their support in the specification. . . . General American Transportation Corp. v. Cryo-Trans, Inc., 93 F.3d 766, 770, 772, 39 USPQ 2d 1801, 1803, 1805–06 (Fed. Cir. 1996) (the teaching in the specification was "not just the preferred embodiment of the invention; it is the only one described"). The only embodiment described in the '669 patent specification is the character-based protocol, and the claims were correctly interpreted as limited thereto;

Mitek Surgical Prods., Inc. v. Arthrex, Inc., Civ. App. No. 99-1004, slip op. at 4–5 (Fed. Cir. Feb. 22, 2000) (unpublished):

> Mitek admits that the specification only discloses the structure of a means for securing that contains a retention disk attached to the means. . . . Mitek misses the focus of means-plus-function claim construction. There was no error in the district court's construction of "means for securing" because section 112 ¶ 6 expressly restricts coverage of a means-plus-function claim to the structure disclosed in the specification and the equivalents of that structure. The internal retention disk is the only means for securing structure disclosed in the specification.

[185] Mitek Surgical Prods., Inc. v. Arthrex, Inc., Civ. App. No. 99-1004, slip op. at 5 (Fed. Cir. Feb. 22, 2000) (unpublished):

> The internal retention disk is the only means for securing structure disclosed in the specification. Mitek argues that alternative embodiments of means for securing are disclosed in the prior art. These embodiments are irrelevant when attempting to outwardly expand claim scope as here. Structure in the prior art may be used to limit, but not broaden the scope of means-plus-function structures. See Biodex Corp. v. Loredan Biomedical, Inc., 946 F.2d 850, 863, 20 USPQ 2d 1252, 1262 (Fed. Cir.1991) (stating that prosecution history may be used to limit scope of means-plus-function claims).

Main volume footnote updates begin on page 72.

terpreted broadly to encompass those alternatives, as well as other alternatives that one of ordinary skill would understand from the specification. For example, combination claims can be drafted as a new combination of old elements or combinations of new and old elements.[186]

[Insert after footnote 263.]

However, a carefully drafted patent specification may, in some circumstances, provide a broader scope of interpretation for means-plus-function claims than non-means-plus-function claims.[187] For example, when multiple embodiments in the specification correspond to the claimed function, proper application of Section 112, sixth paragraph generally reads the claim element to embrace each of those embodiments.[188]

[Insert at the end of the section.]

See Chapter 9, Section VII for a more detailed discussion on interpreting claims under Section 112, sixth paragraph.

H. Patent Written Description May Set Forth More Than One Definition for the Same Claim Term Used in Different Contexts [New Topic]

As a general principle, "the same word appearing in the same claim should be interpreted consistently."[189] However, in circum-

---

[186]Clearstream Wastewater Sys., Inc. v. Hydro-Action, Inc., 206 F 3d 1440, 54 USPQ 2d 1185, 1189 (Fed. Cir. 2000); Intel Corp. v. U.S. Int'l Trade Comm'n., 946 F.2d 821, 842, 20 USPQ 2d 1161, 1179 (Fed. Cir. 1991); Panduit Corp. v. Dennison Mfg., 810 F.2d 1561, 1575, 1 USPQ 2d 1593, 1603 (Fed. Cir. 1987).

[187]*See* Overhead Door Corp. v. Chamberlain Group, Inc., 194 F.3d 1261, 52 USPQ 2d 1321, 1327–28 (Fed. Cir. 1999):

> The claim language and the specification explain that the "memory selection switch" functions to select memory locations. This claim element accomplishes its function by way of a mechanical switch. . . . As properly construed, the "memory selection switch" means a mechanical switch for selecting memory locations. . . .
>
> Although software operations do not fall within the literal scope of the "memory selection switch" in claim 1, the reissue prosecution history also discloses a broader reading for the "switch means" of claim 5. First, the patentees' representation to the Patent and Trademark Office in its November 29, 1989 sworn declaration indicated their intent to include the algorithm of Figure 3 as a "corresponding structure" for the switch means. . . . While this statement weighs against construing claim 1 to include software operations, it gives a broader reading to claim 5. This statement evinces the patentees' use of the term "switch means" to include microprocessor operations driven by software, i.e., "electronic" switches, as opposed to a mechanical switch of Figure 2. The patentees' use in claim 5 of the term "switch means" rather than "switch" and "being adapted to select" rather than "setable" and "set," to describe software operations, further support a broader construction.

[188]*Id.*, 52 USPQ 2d at 1264 (citing Serrano v. Telular Corp., 111 F.3d 1578, 1583, 42 USPQ 2d 1538, 1542 (Fed. Cir. 1997)).

[189]Digital Biometrics, Inc. v. Identix, Inc., 149 F.3d 1335, 1345, 47 USPQ 2d 1418, 1425 (Fed. Cir. 1998); Fonar Corp. v. Johnson & Johnson, 821 F.2d 627, 632, 3 USPQ 2d 1109, 1113 (Fed. Cir. 1987).

Main volume footnote updates begin on page 72.

stances where the patent specification is sufficient to put a reader on notice of the different uses of a term, and where those uses are further apparent from publicly available documents referenced in the patent file, the same claim term may be interpreted differently.[190]

Pitney Bowes Inc. v. Hewlett-Packard Co.[191] is an example of a case in which the same claim term received different interpretations in different claims of the same patent. In *Pitney Bowes*, the district court placed significant weight on Pitney Bowes's concession that in 42 out of 44 uses of the term "spot" in the written description, that usage referred to the spots of light generated by the beam of light and not the spots of discharged area on the photoreceptor. Pitney Bowes, however, argued that the term "spot" should be interpreted to mean a spot of discharged area on the photoreceptor.

On appeal, the Federal Circuit agreed with Pitney Bowes. The Federal Circuit noted that the usage of the term "spot" was noticeably different in the earlier portions of the written description. These earlier uses of the term referred to a "spot" in the sense of a moving spot, such as a spot of light produced by the beam. The Federal Circuit also noted that the two uses of the term "spot" in the later part of the written description did not refer to "spot" in the context of a moving spot, but rather in the context of the "spot size" to be employed to avoid roughed edges and improve character formation.[192] This usage of the term was quite distinct from the dynamic spot referred to earlier in the written description, according to the Federal Circuit.

The Federal Circuit then held the following:

> In circumstances such as this, where the language of the written description is sufficient to put a reader on notice of the different uses of a term, and where those uses are further apparent from publicly-available documents referenced in the patent file, it is appropriate to depart from the normal rule of construing seemingly identical terms in the same manner. . . . Parsing the written description, in the context of the prosecution history, puts the reader on notice that the term "spot" has different meanings in the written description depending on its context. . . . [T]he term must be read to correspond to the only plausible meaning in each context. In light of the prosecution history, the only plausible meaning of the term "spot size," as used in the disputed part of the written description, is the area of discharge on the photoreceptor.[193]

---

[190] Genentech, Inc. v. Wellcome Found., Ltd., 29 F.3d 1555, 1564, 31 USPQ 2d 1161, 1167 (Fed. Cir. 1994) ("there are at least four possible definitions of the phrase set forth in the specification . . . [and] avoid those definitions upon which the PTO could not reasonably have relied when it issued the patent").

[191] Pitney Bowes Inc. v. Hewlett-Packard Co., 182 F.3d 1298, 51 USPQ 2d 1161 (Fed. Cir. 1999).

[192] *Id.*, 51 USPQ 2d at 1170.

[193] *Id.*

Main volume footnote updates begin on page 72.

The Federal Circuit therefore held that the district court erred when it relied upon the frequency of occurrences of the term "spot" to draw the conclusion that the two disputed occurrences of the term in the written description and all the occurrences of the term in the claims must also have that meaning.[194]

---

[194] *Id.*

Main volume footnote updates begin on page 72.

MAIN VOLUME FOOTNOTE UPDATES

[58]**[Add at the end of footnote 58.]** (unpublished).

[62]**[Replace the S. Ct. cite with the following.]** 522 U.S. 1090.

[79]**[Replace existing footnote 79 with the following.]** Kamyr, Inc. v. Clement, Civ. App. 97-1262 (Fed. Cir. Jan. 12, 1998) (unpublished).

[80]**[Add the following to the end of footnote 80.]** *See also* Stanis v. Allied Signal Inc., Civ. App. 98-1515, slip op. at 3 (Fed. Cir. Jan. 29, 1999) (unpublished) ("In fact, as the district court noted, these two limitations distinguished Stanis' claimed invention from the prior art as evidenced by the examiner's statement in his reasons for allowance.").

[109]**[Add the following at the end of in footnote 109.]**; *In re* Baker Hughes Inc., 215 F.3d 1297, 55 USPQ 2d 1149, 1153 (Fed. Cir. 2000) ("In its reexamination decision, the examiner allowed another claim, claim 37 (added during reexamination), that is identical to claim 1 except that it explicitly recites a "liquid hydrocarbon." . . . Since the examiner concluded that claim 37 would not have been obvious over the Doerges reference, we can safely assume that he would have concluded that claim 1 would not have been obvious over the Doerges reference had he construed the claim as we have.").

[113]**[Replace "*cert. granted sub nom.* Lehman v. Zurko, 119 S. Ct. 401 (1998)" with the following.]** *rev'd and remanded,* 527 U.S. 150, 50 USPQ 2d 1930 (1999).

[137]**[Replace "*cert. granted sub nom.* Lehman v. Zurko, 119 S. Ct. 401 (1998)" with the following.]** *rev'd and remanded,* 527 U.S. 150, 50 USPQ 2d 1930 (1999).

[162]**[Add the following to the end of footnote 162.]** *See also* Al-Site Corp. v. VSI Int'l, Inc., 174 F.3d 1308, 50 USPQ 2d 1161, 1168 (Fed. Cir. 1999):

> One important difference between §112, ¶6 and the doctrine of equivalents involves the timing of the separate analyses for an "insubstantial change." As this court has recently clarified, a structural equivalent under §112 must have been available at the time of the issuance of the claim. . . . An equivalent structure or act under §112 cannot embrace technology developed after the issuance of the patent because the literal meaning of a claim is fixed upon its issuance. An "after arising equivalent" infringes, if at all, under the doctrine of equivalents. . . . Thus, the temporal difference between patent issuance and infringement distinguish an equivalent under §112 from an equivalent under the doctrine of equivalents. . . . In other words, an equivalent structure or act under §112 for literal infringement must have been available at the time of patent issuance while an equivalent under the doctrine of equivalents may arise after patent issuance and before the time of infringement. . . . An "after-arising" technology could thus infringe under the doctrine of equivalents without infringing literally as a §112, ¶6 equivalent. Furthermore, under §112, ¶6, the accused device must perform the identical function as recited in the claim element while the doctrine of equivalents may be satisfied when the function performed by the accused device is only substantially the same.

See also Nagle Indus., Inc. v. Ford Motor Co., Civ. App. 97-1449, slip op. at 15 (Fed. Cir. June 22, 1999) (unpublished) (quoting *Chiuminatta Concrete Concepts, Inc.*, 46 USPQ 2d at 1758):

> As this court has stated, the doctrine of equivalents was developed in part because a patentee cannot predict the future and disclose equivalent embodiments not yet developed. Therefore, we have concluded that if an equivalent is from later developed technology, "even if such an element is found not to be a §112, ¶6, equivalent because it is not equivalent to the structure disclosed in the patent, this analysis should not foreclose it from being an equivalent under the doctrine of equivalents." . . . As in *Chiuminatta*, however, the spring technology used by Ford to adjust the slack means predates the invention itself. Because such structure could have been disclosed in the written description, the finding of non-equivalence for §112, ¶6 purposes precludes a contrary finding under the doctrine of equivalents.

[163]**[Add to the end of the cite.]** *cert. denied,* 516 U.S. 987 (1995).

[168]**[Add the following to the end of footnote 168.]** *See also In re* Beasley, Civ. App. 99-1055, slip op. at 6 (Fed. Cir. July 20, 1999) (unpublished):

> The issue before us is one of claim construction—viz., whether the claims require a one-to-one correspondence between particular memory locations and particular points on the display. We conclude that they do not. In drawing this conclusion we rely on the premise that the PTO is required to give claims their broadest reasonable interpretation during prosecution. . . . As asserted by Beasley, the claims do require a "correspondence" between sequentially-addressed memory locations and different points on the screen, but this claim language *is not sufficiently narrow to require a one-to-one correspondence* in which a particular memory location corresponds to a pre-determined point on the screen display. . . . While we recognize that the system disclosed in Beasley's specification does disclose one-to-one correspondence, we cannot read this attribute of the disclosed system into the claims as a limitation.

(Emphasis added, citations omitted.)

[176]**[Replace the S. Ct. cite with the following.]** 525 U.S. 923.

[179]**[Replace the S. Ct. cite with the following.]** 525 U.S. 923.

[182]**[Add the following to the end of footnote 182.]**; Bai v. Toy Island Mfg. Co., Civ. App. 00-1178, slip op. at 4 (Fed. Cir. Oct. 10, 2000) (unpublished) ("A patentee is estopped from recovering through equivalency that which was deemed unpatentable in view of the prior art. See Litton Sys., Inc. v. Honeywell, Inc., 140 F.3d 1449, 1462, 46 USPQ 2d 1321, 1330 (Fed. Cir. 1998). An applicant who responds to an examiner's prior art rejection by narrowing his claim cannot later assert that the surrendered subject matter is an equivalent of the amended limitation. See id. The dish-shaped subject matter surrendered by insertion of the term "hemispherical" is precisely what Bai needs to recover in order to encompass the CATCH & STICK within the instant claim. He is therefore estopped from asserting that the CATCH & STICK infringes Claim 1 of the '076 patent under the doctrine of equivalents.")

[189]**[Replace existing footnote 189 with the following.]** Alpex Computer Corp. v. Nintendo Co., 102 F.3d 1214, 40 USPQ 2d 1667 (Fed. Cir. 1996), *cert. denied,* 521 U.S. 1104 (1997).

[192]**[Replace the S. Ct. cite with the following.]** 522 U.S. 1027.

[196]**[Replace the L. Ed. cite with the following.]** 516 U.S. 987.

[199]**[Replace the S. Ct. cite with the following.]** 520 U.S. 17.

[207]**[Replace the LEXIS cite with the following.]** 525 U.S. 1177.

[214]**[Replace the S. Ct. cite with the following.]** 520 U.S. 1115.

[219]**[Replace the L. Ed. cite with the following.]** 516 U.S. 987.

[239]**[Replace the S. Ct. cite with the following.]** 520 U.S. 1115.

[257]**[Replace existing footnote 257 with the following.]** G&S Metal Prods. Co. v. Ekco Housewares, Inc., Civ. App. 97-1188, 97-1210 (Fed. Cir. Mar. 17, 1998) (unpublished).

[269]**[Add at the end of footnote 269.]** (unpublished).

3

Inventorship

I. INVENTORSHIP

[Insert after footnote 8.]

As stated by the Federal Circuit:

> A primary purpose of patent law is to reward invention. . . . The law of inventorship, which has heretofore developed solely under federal law, supports this purpose by identifying the actual inventors of an invention eligible for patent protection. With its advent in Article 1 of the Consti-

> tution, patent law has developed under federal law to achieve the objective of national uniformity.[1]

The actual inventors must apply for the patent in their names. This is generally accomplished through the requirement that an oath or declaration be filed in the names of the inventors stating "[a]n application for patent shall be made, or authorized to be made, by the inventor. . . . Such application shall include . . . an oath by the applicant as prescribed by section 115 of this title."[2] Under the patent laws, "[t]he applicant shall make oath that he believes himself to be the original and first inventor of the process, machine, manufacture, or composition of matter, or improvement thereof, for which he solicits a patent. . . ."[3] "A patent which is not supported by the oath of the inventor, but applied for by one who is not the inventor, is unauthorized by law and void. . . ."[4]

The federal Patent Act leaves no room for states to supplement the national standard for inventorship.[5] Moreover, federal law has provided the Federal Circuit with jurisdiction to enforce these comprehensive provisions to provide a uniform national standard for inventorship.[6] Therefore, the field of federal patent law preempts any state law that purports to define rights based on inventorship.[7]

V. Ownership of Invention

B. Employed-to-Invent Exception

[Insert after footnote 152.]

> Generally, an invention is the property of the inventor who conceived, developed, and perfected it. Hence, the mere fact that the inventor was employed by another at the time of the invention does not mean that the inventor is required to assign the patent rights to the employer. The right, if any, of an employer to inventions of its employee is determined primarily by the contract of employment. If, as here, the contract of employment does not contain an express provision respecting the subject,

---

[1] University of Colo. Found., Inc. v. American Cyanamid Co., 196 F.3d 1366, 52 USPQ 2d 1801, 1805 (Fed. Cir. 1999), *cert. denied*, 529 U.S. 1130 (2000) (citing Kewanee Oil. Co. v. Bicron Corp., 416 U.S. 470, 480, 181 USPQ 673, 678 (1974), and quoting Florida Prepaid Postsecondary Educ. Expense Bd. v. College Savs. Bank, 527 U.S. 627, 51 USPQ 2d 1081, 1088 (1999) ("The need for uniformity in the construction of patent law is undoubtedly important.")).

[2] 35 U.S.C. § 111 (Supp. 2000).

[3] 35 U.S.C. § 115 (1994).

[4] Kennedy v. Hazelton, 128 U.S. 667, 672 (1888). *See also* Ajinomoto Co. v. Archer-Daniels-Midland Co., 228 F.3d 1338, 56 USPQ 2d 1332, 1336 (Fed. Cir. 2000), *cert. denied*, 121 S. Ct. 1957 (2001).

[5] *Id.*

[6] *In re* Snap-On Tools Corp., 720 F.2d 654, 655, 220 USPQ 8, 9 (Fed. Cir. 1983).

[7] University of Colo. Found., Inc., 52 USPQ 2d at 1805.

Main volume footnote updates begin on page 90.

an employer, is nonetheless, not necessarily precluded from claiming a right to the invention.

If an employee's job duties include the responsibility for inventing or for solving a particular problem that requires invention, any invention created by that employee during the performance of those responsibilities belongs to the employer. Hence, such an employee is bound to assign to the employer all rights to the invention. This is so because, under these circumstances, the employee has produced only that which he was employed to produce, and the courts will find an implied contract obligation to assign any rights to the employer. . . .

On the other hand, if an employee is not employed to invent or to solve a particular problem, that employee owns the right to any invention made by the employee during the term of employment. However, under such circumstances, if the employer has contributed to the development of the invention, such as by paying for the employee's efforts, the employer has a "shop right" to use it free of charge and without liability for infringement.[8]

[Insert after footnote 154.]

When applying the "employed-to-invent" exception, "a court must examine the employment relationship at the time of the inventive work to determine if the parties entered an implied-in-fact contract to assign patent rights."[9] State contract principles provide the rules for identifying and enforcing implied-in-fact contracts.[10]

[Insert at the end of the section.]

Depending on state law, a corporate officer may have a fiduciary duty to assign any invention created during employment to the employer. For example, it should be clear that all officers and directors of a corporation owe a fiduciary duty to the corporation and to its stockholders. They are required to act in good faith and in a reasonable manner in the best interests of those parties.[11] Such a fiduciary duty obligates an officer or director to assign a patent to the corporation if the invention was developed while he or she was employed by the corporation and it is related to the corporation's business.[12]

The failure of an employee to sign an assignment agreement, and the failure of the employer to pursue the signing of the agreement creates a reasonable inference that the employer acquiesced to the employee's refusal to convey ownership, thereby preventing formation of an implied-in-fact contract.[13]

---

[8]Scott Sys., Inc. v. Scott, 996 P.2d 775, 53 USPQ 2d 1692, 1693–94 (Colo. App. 2000).

[9]Teets v. Chromalloy Gas Turbine Corp., 83 F.3d 403, 407, 38 USPQ 2d 1695, 1698 (Fed. Cir. 1996).

[10]Banks v. Unisys Corp., 228 F.3d 1357, 56 USPQ 2d 1222, 1224 (Fed. Cir. 2000).

[11]Scott Sys., Inc. v. Scott, 996 P.2d 775, 53 USPQ 2d 1692, 1695 (Colo. App. 2000).

[12]*Id.*

[13]Banks v. Unisys Corp., 228 F.3d 1357, 56 USPQ 2d 1222, 1224 (Fed. Cir. 2000).

Main volume footnote updates begin on page 90.

C. Contractual Right to Assign

[On page 52, insert before the paragraph beginning "Parties may transfer patent rights . . .".]

While intellectual property is

> the most intangible form of property, it still, in many characteristics, is closer in analogy to real than to personal estate. Unlike personal property, it cannot be lost or found; it is not liable to casualty or destruction; it cannot pass by manual delivery. Like real property, it may be disposed of, territorially, by metes or bounds; it has its system of conveyancing by deed and registration; estates may be created in it, such as for years and in remainder; and the statutory action for infringement bears a much closer relation to an action of trespass than to an action in trover and replevin. It has, too, what the law of real property has, a system of user by license.[14]

It is settled law that between the time of an invention and the issuance of a patent, rights in an invention may be assigned and legal title to the resulting patent will pass to the assignee upon grant of the patent.[15]

If an assignment of rights in an invention is made prior to the existence of the invention, this may be viewed as an assignment of an expectant interest. An assignment of an expectant interest can be a valid assignment.[16] In such a situation, the assignee holds at most an equitable title.[17] No further act is required to perfect the assignment of the invention once the invention comes into being or is created; the transfer of title occurs by operation of law.[18]

It is well established that when a legal title holder of a patent transfers his or her title to a third-party purchaser for value without notice of an outstanding equitable claim or title, the purchaser takes the entire ownership of the patent, free of any prior equitable encumbrance.[19] This is an application of the common law bona fide purchaser for value rule.

Section 261 of Title 35 goes a step further. It adopts the principle of the real property recording acts and provides that the bona fide purchaser for value cuts off the rights of a prior assignee who has failed to record the prior assignment in the Patent and Trademark Office by the dates specified in the statute. Although the statute does not expressly

---

[14] A.S. Solomons v. United States, 21 Ct. Cl. 479, 483 (1886), *aff'd* 137 U.S. 342 (1890).

[15] Gayler v. Wilder, 51 U.S. (10 How.) 477, 493 (1850).

[16] Mitchell v. Winslow, 17 F. Cas. 527, 531–32 (C.C.D. Me. 1843) (nonexisting [personal] property may be the subject of valid assignment).

[17] *Id.* at 532.

[18] Speedplay, Inc. v. Bebop, Inc., 211 F.3d 1245, 53 USPQ 2d 1984, 1989 (Fed. Cir. 2000).

[19] Hendrie v. Sayles, 98 U.S. 546, 549 (1879).

Main volume footnote updates begin on page 90.

so say, it is clear that the statute is intended to cut off prior legal interests, which the common law rule did not.[20] "Both the common law rule and the statute contemplate that the subsequent purchaser be exactly that—a transferee who pays valuable consideration, and is without notice of the prior transfer."[21]

The subsequent purchaser must be in fact a purchaser for valuable consideration. According to the Federal Circuit:

> This requirement is different from the classic notion of a purchaser under a deed of grant, where the requirement of consideration was a formality, and the proverbial peppercorn would suffice to have the deed operate under the statute of uses. Here the requirement is that the subsequent purchaser, in order to cut off the rights of the prior purchaser, must be more than a donee or other gratuitous transferee.[22]

There must be in fact valuable consideration paid so that the subsequent purchaser can, as a matter of law, claim record reliance as a premise upon which the purchase was made.[23] In addition, the subsequent transferee/assignee must be without notice of any such prior assignment.[24]

[Insert after footnote 169.]

Standing to sue for patent infringement derives from the Patent Act, which provides that "[a] patentee shall have remedy by civil action for infringement of his patent."[25] The term "patentee" includes "not only the patentee to whom the patent was issued but also the successors in title to the patentee."[26]

[Insert after footnote 171.]

The patent laws recognize, and courts have long held, that an exclusive, territorial license is equivalent to an assignment and may therefore confer standing upon the licensee to sue for patent infringement.[27] Conversely, a "bare licensee"—one who enjoys only a non-

---

[20] Filmtec Corp. v. Allied-Signal Inc., 939 F.2d 1568, 19 USPQ 2d 1508, 1512 (Fed. Cir. 1991).

[21] *Id.*

[22] *Id.*, 19 USPQ 2d at 1513.

[23] *Id.*

[24] 35 U.S.C. § 261 (1994).

[25] 35 U.S.C. § 281 (1994).

[26] 35 U.S.C. § 100(d) (1994).

[27] 35 U.S.C. § 261 (1994); Waterman v. Mackenzie, 138 U.S. 252, 255 (1891); Enzo APA & Son, Inc. v. Geapag A.G., 134 F.3d 1090, 1093, 45 USPQ 2d 1368, 1370 (Fed. Cir. 1998); Rite-Hite Corp. v. Kelley Co., 56 F.3d 1538, 1551, 35 USPQ 2d 1065, 1074 (Fed. Cir. 1995) (en banc); Vaupel Textilmaschinen KG v. Meccanica Euro Italia S.p.A., 944 F.2d 870, 875, 20 USPQ 2d 1045, 1049 (Fed. Cir. 1991).

Main volume footnote updates begin on page 90.

exclusive license—has no standing to sue for infringement under the Patent Act.[28]

A party that has been granted all substantial rights under the patent is considered the owner regardless of how the parties characterize the transaction that conveyed those rights.[29] A written instrument documenting the transfer of proprietary rights in the patent must be produced to prove ownership of a sufficient proprietary interest to bring a lawsuit in their name.[30]

[Insert after footnote 174.]

For example, the Supreme Court has held that, where a patent owner mortgaged her patent to secure a loan, the mortgagee—as equitable owner of the patent during the loan period—had standing to sue for infringement without being joined by the patent owner. Thus, while acknowledging the possibility that title to the patent could revert back to the mortgagor prior to the expiration of the patent term, the Supreme Court concluded that this, alone, did not make the mortgagor an indispensable party to the infringement suit.[31] The Federal Circuit has applied the Supreme Court's reasoning to a license agreement in which the patent owner retained a reversionary right in the patent. The agreement in question contained a termination clause whereby the license would terminate automatically if the licensee filed for bankruptcy or stopped production of the patented product. The Federal Circuit held that the termination clause was "entirely consistent with an assignment," and therefore, did not preclude the licensee from having standing to sue in its own name.[32]

[Insert on page 153, in the paragraph beginning "Infringement harms . . ." after the sentence ending ". . . unless the assignment agreement manifests and intent to transfer this right."]

As stated by the Federal Circuit:

> As a general rule, only a party that possessed legal title to a patent at the time the infringement occurred can bring suit to recover damages for such infringement. . . . A narrow exception to the foregoing rule is that a

---

[28] Prima Tek II, L.L.C. v. A-Roo Co., 222 F.3d 1372, 55 USPQ 2d 1742, 1745 (Fed. Cir. 2000); Rite-Hite, 56 F.3d at 1553, 35 USPQ 2d at 1076.

[29] Speedplay, Inc. v. Bebop, Inc., 211 F.3d 1245, 53 USPQ 2d 1984, 1986 (Fed. Cir. 2000).

[30] 35 U.S.C. § 261 (1994); Speedplay, Inc. v. Bebop, Inc., 211 F.3d 1245, 53 USPQ 2d 1984, 1986–87 (Fed. Cir. 2000); Enzo APA & Son, Inc. v. Geapag A.G., 134 F.3d 1090, 1093, 45 USPQ 2d 1368, 1370–71 (Fed. Cir. 1998).

[31] Waterman v. Mackenzie, 138 U.S. 252, 260–61 (1891).

[32] Vaupel Textilmaschinen KG v. Meccanica Euro Italia S.p.A., 944 F.2d 870, 874, 20 USPQ 2d 1045, 1048 (Fed. Cir. 1991).

Main volume footnote updates begin on page 90.

party may sue for infringement transpiring before it acquired legal title if a written assignment expressly grants the party a right to do so; that right, however, must be articulated explicitly in the assignment and will not be inferred by the court.[33]

[Insert at the end of the subsection.]

To perfect the assignment of the invention, the assignee is generally required to record the assignment in the U.S. Patent Office. If the assignee fails to record, the assignee may lose ownership to a bone fide purchaser for value. The Patent Office permits the assignee to record the assignment through various methods, including facsimile transmissions. A copy of the recording requirements for facsimile transmissions is included in Appendix C.

E. Rights of Co-Owners of Invention

[Insert after footnote 189.]

Accordingly, it is a well established principle of patent law that a patent cannot be found to be infringed by one of its co-owners.[34]

F. U.S. Government Rights in Inventions Made by Government Employees

[Insert after first paragraph in the section.]

Paragraph 1(a) of Executive Order 10096 provides that the Government shall obtain the entire right, title, and interest in and to all inventions made by any Government employee (1) during working hours,

---

[33] Messagephone, Inc. v. SVI Sys., Inc., Civ. App. No. 99-1471, slip op. at 8–9 (Fed. Cir. Aug. 11, 2000) (unpublished) ("In the present case, the November 7, 1996 assignment grants Messagephone the "entire right, title, and interest" in the '448 and '740 patents. The assignment, however, is silent as to Messagephone's right to sue for infringement that occurred prior to that date. Accordingly, in the absence of any explicit language conveying such a right, we hold that Messagephone lacked standing to sue for infringement of the '448 and '740 patents that occurred before November 7, 1996.") (citing Moore v. Marsh, 74 U.S. (7 Wall.) 515, 522 (1868) ("[I]t is a great mistake to suppose that the assignment of a patent carries with it the right to damages for an infringement committed before such assignment."); Mas-Hamilton Group v. LaGard, Inc., 156 F.3d 1206, 1210, 48 USPQ 2d 1010, 1013 (Fed. Cir. 1998); Arachnid, Inc. v. Merit Indus., Inc., 939 F.2d 1574, 1579 & n.7, 19 USPQ 2d 1513, 1517 & n.7 (Fed. Cir. 1991); Crown Die & Tool Co. v. Nye Tool & Mach. Works, 261 U.S. 24, 40–41 (1923) (explaining that "plaintiff in an action at law must be the person . . . in whom the legal title of the patent resided at the time of the infringement")

[34] Corry v. CFM Majestic Inc., Civ. App. 00-1019, slip op. at 9 (Fed. Cir. Nov. 16, 2000) (unpublished) (citing 35 U.S.C. § 262 (1994) ("[E]ach of the joint owners of a patent may make, use, offer to sell, or sell the patented invention . . . without the consent of and without accounting to the other owners."); Schering Corp. v. Roussel-UCLAF SA, 104 F.3d 341, 344, 41 USPQ 2d 1359, 1361 (Fed. Cir. 1997) (interpreting Section 262 to preclude infringement by a co-owner)).

Main volume footnote updates begin on page 90.

or (2) with a contribution by the Government of facilities, equipment, materials, funds or information or of time or services of other Government employees on official duty, or (3) which bear a direct relation to or are made in consequence of the official duties of the inventor.[35]

Paragraph 1(c) of the Executive Order provides that an invention made by an employee hired to (1) invent, (2) conduct research, (3) supervise government-financed or -conducted research, or (4) act as a liaison among government or nongovernment agencies conducting such research, is presumed to be made under paragraph 1(a).[36] The presumption may be overcome by the facts and circumstances of a given case. There is no requirement that an invention be patentable for the U.S. government to obtain title.[37]

[On page 164 insert new heading before the paragraph beginning "The U.S. government will . . .".]

1. U.S. Government Will Receive At Least a Nonexclusive License When Government Resources Used to Test Invention [New Topic]

[Insert at the end of the section.]

2. U.S. Government Owns Invention When Invention Reduced to Practice While Inventor Government Employee on Official Duty [New Topic]

The U.S. government will generally own all rights and title to an invention reduced to practice while the inventor was a government employee or created by the inventor while on official duty. Paragraph 1(a) of Executive Order 10096 provides that the government shall obtain the entire right, title, and interest in and to all inventions made by any government employee with a contribution by the government of facilities, equipment, materials, funds, or information or of time or services of other government employees on official duty.[38] However, the contribution may be insufficient equitably to justify an assignment.[39]

Fretheim v. Department of the Air Force[40] is an example of a case in which the U.S. government obtained the entire title and interest in

---

[35] Freund v. Department of the Navy, 49 USPQ 2d 1700, 1702 (U.S. Dep't Comm. 1998). *See also* 37 C.F.R. § 501.6(a)(1).

[36] *Freund*, 49 USPQ 2d at 1702. *See also* 37 C.F.R. § 501.6(a)(3).

[37] *Freund*, 49 USPQ 2d at 1701 n.3.

[38] *See* 37 C.F.R. § 501.6(a)(1).

[39] 37 C.F.R. § 501.6(a)(2).

[40] Fretheim v. Department of the Air Force, 49 USPQ 2d 1316 (U.S. Dep't Comm. 1998).

Main volume footnote updates begin on page 90.

an invention created by a government employee while on official duty. Erik J. Fretheim appealed a determination by the Department of the Air Force (AF) that the government obtained his entire domestic right, title, and interest in a joint invention he made with Joanne E. DeGroat (DeGroat) and Michael W. Scriber (Scriber). DeGroat did not appeal her rights determination, and Scriber signed an assignment of his undivided interest to the Air Force.

The invention related to a new signal selection adder architecture in a computer that allowed for the addition of large numbers in logarithmically increasing time with only limited increases in circuitry complexity by combining certain redundant logic functions in parallel processed adder cells of a binary tree adder. Fretheim acknowledged using some computer work stations and laboratory facilities and making a test circuit with $250 from government funds after he reported the invention to the Air Force. Fretheim argued, however, that these activities were insufficient to confer his entire right, title, and interest in the invention to the government.

The Air Force Legal Services Agency (AFLSA) relied on the government's contribution to the invention in the form of the many official hours spent by the other co-inventors of the invention, all at the Air Force Institute of Technology (AFIT) in Ohio. Fretheim and Scriber were both graduate students as well as military officers and DeGroat was an instructor in Electrical Engineering.

On appeal to the U.S. Department of Commerce, the decision of the AFLSA was affirmed. Commerce noted that the first reduction of practice may have occurred at AFIT when the adder was implemented in a test chip for a proof of concept. According to Commerce, "[s]uch a reduction of practice would entitle the Air Force to ownership."[41] Commerce also found significant the participation of the other government employees in making the invention, as recognized by their inclusion as inventors in the patent applications and resulting patent. On this basis, Commerce held that the contributions to the invention by the co-inventors and Fretheim's use of government equipment, funds, and materials could not be said to be insufficiently equitable to justify an assignment. Commerce did note that Fretheim was entitled to share royalties with the other inventors from any license of the invention by the Air Force.

3. *U.S. Government Owns Invention by Employee Hired for Research Even Though Not Hired to Invent [New Topic]*

The U.S. government is entitled to obtain the entire right, title, and interest in and to all inventions made by any government employee hired to (a) invent, (b) conduct research, (c) supervise government-

[41] *Id.* at 1318.

Main volume footnote updates begin on page 90.

financed or -conducted research, or (d) act as a liaison among government or nongovernment agencies conducting such research. Any one of the above categories is sufficient to confer title to the U.S. government.[42]

Freund v. Department of the Navy[43] is an example of a case in which the government employee was only hired for research and the government obtained the entire title in the invention even though the employee was not hired to invent. Richard F. Freund appealed a determination by the Department of Navy (Navy) that the government owned the entire right, title, and interest in his invention on "A Scheduling Framework for a Heterogeneous Computer Network."

The invention related to a scheduling framework for assigning a set of problems to computers in a heterogeneous computer network to achieve an optimal matching of the problems to the computers so as to minimize the amount of time required to solve the problems. The framework was part of the system called "Smartnet."

The Navy's position in the rights determination dated February 19, 1998 was that the government was entitled to the entire right, title, and interest to the invention because it was made during working hours with a contribution by the government of facilities, equipment, materials, funds, or information or of time or services of other government employees on official duty or because it bore a direct relation to, or was made in consequence of, the official duties of the inventor.

Freund questioned the application of the presumption of title to the government in paragraph 1(a) of Executive Order 10096 because he was not hired to invent or improve devices. The Department of Commerce, however, noted that there are three other categories in paragraph 1(a), including one that relates to research and development duties, which Freund acknowledged having. According to Commerce, since the different categories are connected by the disjunctive ("or"), any one of them would give rise to the presumption of title. Accordingly, Commerce found that the presumption was properly applied by the Navy.

Commerce noted that in a previous case, the agency's determination of title to the government was upheld, notwithstanding that the inventor spent 500 hours of his personal time and only 40 hours of government time in making the invention.[44] The determination by the Navy that the government was entitled to the entire right, title, and interest in the invention was therefore affirmed. Commerce further noted that Freund could still receive a share of royalties from the licensing of the invention by the Navy.[45]

---

[42]Schlie v. Department of the Air Force, 37 USPQ 2d 1215, 1217 (U.S. Dep't Comm. 1993).

[43]Freund v. Department of the Navy, 49 USPQ 2d 1700 (U.S. Dep't Comm. 1998).

[44]*See In re* Phillips, 230 USPQ 350, 352 (Comm'r Pat. 1986).

[45]15 U.S.C. § 3710c (1994).

Main volume footnote updates begin on page 90.

4. Government Desire to Publish Invention Does Not Forfeit Government's Rights [New Topic]

An agency's desire to publish an invention does not necessarily mean that it is not interested in the invention. Therefore, the fact that the government wants to publish an invention does not constitute an "insufficient interest in the invention" that would preclude the government from claiming ownership in an invention.[46]

Wright v. United States[47] is an example of a case in which an agency's desire to publish an invention did not preclude the government from obtaining the entire right, title, and interest to the invention. Dr. James Wright, while working for the U.S. Department of Agriculture (USDA), isolated a specific strain of BB fungus effective against boll weevils and other crop-damaging insects. Combined with an attractant and a food source, the strain would infect the insect either by ingestion or by physical contact and provide an effective means for controlling these pests.

Wright petitioned the government to grant him the ownership rights to the invention. The Office of the General Counsel of the USDA issued a formal determination stating that the domestic patent rights in the invention belonged to the government. Wright appealed this decision to the Department of Commerce. Following an administrative hearing, the Department of Commerce affirmed the USDA's ownership rights to the invention.

Wright appealed to the U.S. Court of Appeals for the Fifth Circuit. The issue presented was whether, pursuant to Commerce Department regulations, the invention belonged to the government under Section 501.6(a)(1) of the regulations, or whether Wright had a valid ownership claim under Section 501.6(a)(2). The relevant parts of Section 501.6 read as follows:

> (a) The following rules shall be applied in determining the respective rights of the Government and of the inventor in and to any invention that is subject to the provisions of this part:
>
> (1) The Government shall obtain, except as herein otherwise provided, the entire right, title and interest in and to any invention made by any Government employee. . . .
>
> (2) In any case where the contribution of the Government, as measured by any one or more of the criteria set forth in paragraph (a)(1) of this section, to the invention is insufficient equitably to justify a requirement of assignment to the Government of the entire right, title and interest in and to such invention, or in any case where the Government has insufficient interest in an invention to obtain the entire right, title and interest therein (although the Government could obtain same under paragraph (a)(1) of this section), the Gov-

[46] *See* 37 C.F.R. § 501.6(a)(2).

[47] Wright v. United States, 164 F.3d 267, 49 USPQ 2d 1542 (5th Cir. 1999).

Main volume footnote updates begin on page 90.

> ernment agency concerned shall leave title to such invention in the employee, subject however to the reservation to the Government of a nonexclusive, irrevocable, royalty-free license in the invention with power to grant licenses for all governmental purposes.[48]

It was undisputed that Wright made the invention during working hours as a government employee, that government funds were used for the discovery and that the discovery was directly related to the duties of Wright's employment. Wright claimed that the government was only interested in publishing his invention and did not initially file an application for a patent. This, Wright asserted, impliedly granted him the right to patent the invention under Section 501.6(a)(2).

The USDA argued that an agency's desire to publish an invention does not necessarily mean that it is not interested in the invention. Therefore, the fact that the government wanted to publish the invention did not constitute an "insufficient interest in the invention" under Section 501.6(a)(2). The Department of Commerce held that Wright did not have a valid claim to the invention under Section 501.6(a)(2) because the government's rights remained solely within the purview of the regulation.

The Fifth Circuit concluded that there was no abuse of discretion in the Commerce Department determining that the USDA had the right of ownership over this invention.[49] As stated by the Fifth Circuit:

> This Court grants great deference to the USDA's interpretation of the words "insufficient interest" in 501.6(a)(2). We do not find any language in this section which would lead us to believe that the district court's holding is blatantly inconsistent with 501 and its relevant sub-parts.[50]

5. *U.S. Government Owns Invention When Invention Conceived While Not on Official Duty But Tested Using Government Time and Facilities [New Topic]*

The fact that the inventors may have conceived the invention while off the job does not rebut the presumption of the government's right to the title of the invention if the inventors tested the invention at work using government time, equipment, and money. For example, the Director (former title Commissioner) of Patents has held that "[i]t would be curious indeed if a Government employee could decide on his own to use Government time and facilities to test an invention while at the same time contend that he is entitled to title subject to a license to the Government."[51]

---

[48] 37 C.F.R. § 501.6.

[49] *Id.*, 49 USPQ 2d at 1544.

[50] *Id.*

[51] *In re* Schroeder, 3 USPQ 2d 1057, 1059 (Comm'r Pat. 1986).

Main volume footnote updates begin on page 90.

Goldberg v. Department of the Army[52] involved a situation where the inventor conceived the invention not using government time or facilities, but tested the invention using government facilities and six hours of government time. The invention related to a device that automatically hoists people or loads on ropes. The Army argued that the government was entitled to the entire right, title, and interest to the invention because it was made with a contribution of government resources of facilities, equipment, materials, funds, and information.

Goldberg argued that the presumption of title to the government should not apply because he and the other inventors were not hired to invent or improve devices. The Department of Commerce noted, however, that there are three other categories in paragraph 1(a) of Executive Order 10096, including one that relates to research and development duties, which the inventors each acknowledged having. Since the three categories are connected by the disjunctive ("or"), any one of them can give rise to the presumption of title.[53] Accordingly, the Department of Commerce found that the presumption was properly applied by the Army.

The Department of Commerce noted that the fact that the inventors may have conceived the invention off their job did not rebut the presumption because they tested their invention at work with government time, equipment, and money. Commerce rejected the argument that the government contribution to the invention of facilities for testing be considered as being "insufficient equitably" to justify an assignment.[54] Accordingly, the determination by the Army that the government was entitled to the entire right, title, and interest was affirmed.

VI. Correction of Inventorship

B. Correction After Patent Granted

[Insert after footnote 247.]

Section 256, and its implementing regulation 37 C.F.R. Section 1.324, allows not only the addition of an inventor, but the complete substitution of one inventor for another, provided that the true inventor acted without deceptive intent.[55] The Patent Office has recently

---

[52] Goldberg v. Department of the Army, 49 USPQ 2d 1382 (U.S. Dep't Comm. 1998).

[53] *Id.* at 1383 (citing Schlie v. Department of the Air Force, 37 USPQ 2d 1280, 1281–82 (U.S. Dep't Comm. 1993)).

[54] *Id.* at 1383-84 (citing *In re* Phillips, 230 USPQ 350, 352 (Comm'r Pat. 1986) (affirming agency determination of title to the government notwithstanding that inventor spent 500 hours of his personal time and only 40 hours of government time in making invention)).

[55] Stark v. Advanced Magnetic, Inc., 119 F.3d 1551, 1556, 43 USPQ 2d 1321, 1325 (Fed. Cir. 1997); Virginia Elec. & Lighting Corp. v. National Serv. Indus., Inc., Civ. App. No. 99-1226, slip op. at 9 (Fed. Cir. Jan. 6, 2000) (unpublished), *cert. denied*, 120 S. Ct. 2743 (2000).

Main volume footnote updates begin on page 90.

amended the regulations to eliminate the requirement for a statement from an inventor being deleted stating that the inventorship error occurred without deceptive intent.[56] A copy of the Patent Office rules implementing these changes is included in Appendix C relating to the Patent Office business goals. A pamphlet from the Patent Office describing this change relating to correction of inventorship is included in Appendix D.

D. General Factors Involved in Correcting Inventorship

2. *Deceptive Intent*

[Replace the sentence containing footnote 270 with the following sentence.]

Stark v. Advanced Magnetic, Inc.[57] is a case in which the deceptive intent requirement was applied only to nonjoinder of inventors, and not to misjoinder of inventors.

[Insert after footnote 271.]

Thus, correction of inventorship will be permitted even if all inventors were deceptively listed and the true inventor was omitted, so long as the true inventor did not have any deceptive intent. That is, "correction of nonjoinder of entitled inventors does not invalidate a patent."[58]

---

[56] 37 C.F.R. § 1.324 (Supp. 2000).

[57] Stark v. Advanced Magnetic, Inc., 119 F.3d 1551, 43 USPQ 2d 1321 (Fed. Cir. 1997).

[58] University of Colo. Found., Inc. v. American Cyanamid Co., 196 F.3d 1366, 52 USPQ 2d 1801, 1805 (Fed. Cir. 1999), *cert. denied*, 529 U.S. 1130 (2000).

Main volume footnote updates begin on page 90.

MAIN VOLUME FOOTNOTE UPDATES

[36]**[Replace the S. Ct. cite with the following.]** 520 U.S. 1277.

[84]**[Replace the S. Ct. cite with the following.]** 525 U.S. 923

[88]**[Replace the S. Ct. cite with the following.]** 525 U.S. 923

[93]**[Replace the S. Ct. cite with the following.]** 525 U.S. 923

[152]**[Replace the S. Ct. cite for Teets v. Chromalloy Gas Turbine Corp. with the following.]** 519 U.S. 1009.

[152]**[Replace the S. Ct. cite for McCoy v. Mitsuboshi Cutlery, Inc. with the following.]** 516 U.S. 1174 (1996).

[156]**[Replace the S. Ct. cite with the following.]** 519 U.S. 1009.

[161]**[Replace the S. Ct. cite with the following.]** 519 U.S. 1009.

[184]**[Replace the LEXIS cite with the following.]** 57 F.3d 1067.

[186]**[Replace the S. Ct. cite with the following.]** 519 U.S. 1009.

[197]**[Replace the S. Ct. cite with the following.]** 525 U.S. 923

4

Antedating Prior Art References Under Rule 131

I. Introduction to Rule 131

[Replace the block quote preceding footnote 3 and footnote 3 itself with the following.]

(a) When any claim of an application or a patent under reexamination is rejected, the inventor of the subject matter of the rejected claim, the owner of the patent under reexamination, or the party qualified under §§ 1.42, 1.43, or 1.47 may submit an appropriate oath or declaration to establish invention of the subject matter of the rejected claim prior to the effective date of the reference or activity on which the rejection is based. The effective date of a U.S. patent, U.S. patent application publication, or international application publication under PCT Article 21(2) is the earlier of its publication date or the date that it is effective as a reference under 35 U.S.C. 102(e). Prior invention may

Main volume footnote updates begin on page 96.

not be established under this section in any country other than the United States, a NAFTA country, or a WTO member country. Prior invention may not be established under this section prior to December 8, 1993, in a NAFTA country other than the United States, or before January 1, 1996, in a WTO member country other than a NAFTA country. Prior invention may not be established under this section if either:

(1) The rejection is based upon either a U.S. patent or a U.S. patent application publication of a pending or patented application to another or others which claims the same patentable invention as defined in § 1.601(n); or
(2) The rejection is based upon a statutory bar.[1]

II. Prior Art That May Be Overcome Under Rule 131

[On page 188, delete the first sentence and replace it with the following.]

Part (a) of Rule 131 does not specify the specific references or prior art that may be overcome; rather, Rule 131 only specifies that the references or prior art that may not be overcome include prior art that is a statutory bar or prior art U.S. patents or U.S. patent application publications that claim the same patentable inventions. Accordingly, the following is a list of exemplary prior art that may be overcome by a Rule 131 affidavit or declaration:

1. Foreign patents
2. Publications
3. U.S. patents or U.S. published patent applications that do not contain the same invention
4. Prior use or knowledge under 35 U.S.C. Section 102(a)[2].

[Delete the sentence following footnote 21 and replace with the following.]

With the passage of the American Inventors Protection Act of 1999, which includes 18-month publication of U.S. patent applica-

[1] Fed. Reg., Vol. 65, No. 183, 57057 (Sept. 20, 2000).

[2] Fed. Reg., Vol. 65, No. 175, 54640 (Sept. 8, 2000) ("Section 1.131(a) is amended to eliminate the provisions that specify which bases for rejection must be applicable for § 1.131 to apply. . . . This avoids the situation in which the basis for rejection is not a statutory bar (under 35 U.S.C. 102(a) based upon prior use by others in the United States) and should be capable of being antedated, but the rejection is not specified as a basis for rejection that must be applicable for § 1.131 to apply."). The effective date of this change is for all pending applications as of September 8, 2000. See *Id.* ("Affidavits under § 1.131 to overcome rejections based on prior knowledge or use under 35 U.S.C. 102(a) are effective on the date of publication in the Federal Register for all pending applications where such issue needs to be addressed (to include appropriately filed requests for reconsideration.").

Main volume footnote updates begin on page 96.

tions,[3] the effective date of a U.S. patent application publication, or international application publication under PCT Article 21(2), is the earlier of its publication date or the date that it is effective as a reference under 35 U.S.C. § 102(e); therefore, the date to be overcome under Rule 131 is the filing date of the U.S. application or international application publication under PCT Article 21(2), and not the foreign country priority date.

III. Prior Art That May Not Be Overcome Under Rule 131

C. U.S. Patent that Claims Same Invention

[Replace the sentence containing footnote 44, and replace footnote 44 as follows.]

Rule 131 expressly states that it may not be used to antedate a U.S. patent or U.S. patent application publication and establish prior invention with respect to an application that "claims the same patentable invention, as defined in § 1.601(n) [of the interference rules]."[4]

V. General Requirements Under Rule 131

C. Reduction to Practice

1. Actual Reduction to Practice

[Insert after footnote 222.]

The requirement that an inventor know that the invention is useful may be satisfied when an agent of the inventor obtains such knowledge.[5] As summarized by the Federal Circuit, there are

> at least three requirements that must be met before a non-inventor's recognition of the utility of an invention can inure to the benefit of the inventor. First, the inventor must have conceived of the invention. Second, the inventor must have had an expectation that the embodiment tested would work for the intended purpose of the invention. Third, the inventor must have submitted the embodiment for testing for the intended purpose of the invention.[6]

---

[3] 35 U.S.C. § 122(b)(1)(A) (Supp. 2000); Fed. Reg., Vol. 65, No. 183, 57024–57061 (Sept. 20, 2000).

[4] Fed. Reg., Vol. 65, No. 183, 57057 (Sept. 20, 2000).

[5] Estee Lauder, Inc. v. L'Oreal, S.A., 129 F.3d 588, 593, 44 USPQ 2d 1610, 1614 (Fed. Cir. 1997).

[6] Genentech, Inc. v. Chiron Corp., 220 F.3d 1345, 55 USPQ 2d 1636, 1643 (Fed. Cir. 2000).

Main volume footnote updates begin on page 96.

2. *Constructive Reduction to Practice*

[Change footnote 239 to the following.]

Hyatt v. Boone, 146 F.3d 1348, 47 USPQ 2d 1128, 1130 (Fed. Cir. 1998), *cert. denied*, 525 U.S. 1141 (1999) (interference context).

E. Antedating Acts in the United States or in a WTO/NAFTA Country

[Insert after footnote 248.]

35 USC Section 119 has also been amended to extend the Paris Convention right of priority to any member of the WTO. This section states:

> An application for patent for an invention filed in this country by any person who has, or whose legal representatives or assigns have, previously regularly filed an application for patent for the same invention in a foreign country which affords similar privileges in the case of applications filed in the United States or to citizens of the United States or in a WTO member country, shall have the same effect as the same application would have if filed in this country on the date on which the application for patent for the same invention was first filed in such foreign country.[7]

The effective date of this change to Section 119 was November 29, 1999.

[Replace the paragraph ending with footnote 249, and also replace footnote 249 as follows.]

Prior invention may not be established under this section in any country other than the United States, a NAFTA country, or a WTO member country. Prior invention may not be established under this section prior to December 8, 1993, in a NAFTA country other than the United States, or before January 1, 1996, in a WTO member country other than a NAFTA country.[8]

---

[7] 35 U.S.C. § 119(a) (Supp. 2000).

[8] Fed. Reg., Vol. 65, No. 183, 57057 (Sept. 20, 2000).

Main volume footnote updates begin on page 96.

MAIN VOLUME FOOTNOTE UPDATES

[232]**[Replace the LEXIS cite with the following.]** 525 U.S. 1141.

[239]**[Replace the LEXIS cite with the following.]** 525 U.S. 1141.

[250]**[Replace footnote 250 with the following.]** *Id.*

5

Exceptions to Patentable Subject Matter

I. General Purposes of Section 101

[Insert at the end of the section.]

A. Seeds and Seed Grown Plants Are Statutory Subject Matter [New Topic]

The Supreme Court noted some time ago the importance of the "increasing adaptation [of the patent laws] to the uses of society."[1] The Supreme Court in *Diamond v. Chakrabarty*,[2] stated that "Con-

---

[1] Kendall v. Winsor, 62 U.S. (21 How.) 322, 328 (1859).

[2] Diamond v. Chakrabarty, 447 U.S. 303, 309, 206 USPQ 193, 197 (1980).

Main volume footnote updates begin on page 111.

gress intended statutory subject matter to 'include anything under the sun that is made by man.' "[3] The Supreme Court confirmed that there is no basis in law for excluding living things from the subject matter included in Section 101:

> Whoever invents or discovers any new and useful process, machine, manufacture, or composition of matter, or any new and useful improvement thereof, may obtain a patent therefor, subject to the conditions and requirements of this title.[4]

In *Chakrabarty*, the Supreme Court dealt directly with the issue of whether a new bacterium that was engineered to consume oil spills was statutory subject matter and eligible for utility patent protection. In holding that engineered microorganisms were eligible for patent protection, the Supreme Court explained that the patent system is directed to the inventive works of mankind, and is not otherwise limited. According to the Supreme Court: "In choosing such expansive terms as 'manufacture' and 'composition of matter,' modified by the comprehensive 'any,' Congress plainly contemplated that the patent laws would be given wide scope."[5]

The Board of Patent Appeals and Interferences has included seeds and seed-grown plants in the category of living things eligible for patent protection, even though alternative protection is also available under the Plant Protection Act and the Plant Variety Protection Act.[6]

In *Pioneer Hi-Bred International, Inc. v. J.E.M. Ag Supply, Inc.*,[7] the Federal Circuit confirmed this interpretation by the Board. The patents-in-suit, owned by Pioneer Hi-Bred International, Inc., were directed to plants and seed for new varieties of hybrid and inbred corn. The district court ruled that seeds and plants grown from seed, that is, sexually reproduced plants, are patentable subject matter within the scope of 35 U.S.C. Section 101. The district court observed that the Patent and Trademark Office has been granting patents on new and nonobvious varieties of seed-grown plants for at least 15 years. The district court found no historical basis for excluding seed-grown plants from the scope of Section 101. Although there remain traditional categories that have never been viewed as patentable subject matter, such as laws of nature, natural phenomena, and abstract ideas, the district court reasoned that the policy underlying the patent system fosters its application to all areas of technology-based commerce, including sexually reproduced plants and seeds.[8]

---

[3] *Id.* at 309, 206 USPQ at 197 (quoting S. Rep. No. 1979 at 5 (1952)).

[4] 35 U.S.C. § 101 (1994).

[5] *Chakrabarty*, 447 U.S. at 308, 206 USPQ at 197.

[6] *In re* Hibberd, 227 USPQ 443, 444 (B.P.A.I. 1985).

[7] Pioneer Hi-Bred Int'l., Inc. v. J.E.M. Ag Supply, Inc., 200 F.3d 1374, 53 USPQ 2d 1440 (Fed. Cir. 2000), *cert. granted*, 121 S. Ct. 1077, (2001) (No. 99-1996).

[8] *Id.*, 53 USPQ 2d at 1441.

Main volume footnote updates begin on page 111.

The defendants argued that sexually reproduced plants and seeds are not eligible for utility patent protection because such plants were intended to be excluded from the patent system, as evidenced by the enactment of other statutes to provide protection to plants. Thus, the defendants argued that seeds and seed-grown plants were excluded from Title 35 and may be protected only under the Plant Variety Protection Act.[9] The district court was unpersuaded, and concluded that a person who develops a new plant variety may have recourse either to patenting under Title 35 or to registration under the PVPA. The defendants appealed.

On appeal, the Federal Circuit affirmed the district court. The Federal Circuit first noted that the first statute that related specifically to plant protection was the Townsend-Purnell Plant Patent Act of 1930 (PPA), codified at 35 U.S.C. Section 161–164. This statute provided patent protection for asexually reproduced plants, and relaxed the written description requirement to accommodate the then-available modes of describing plant varieties:

> Whoever invents or discovers and asexually reproduces any distinct and new variety of plant, including cultivated sports, mutants, hybrids, and newly found seedlings, other than a tuber propagated plant or a plant found in an uncultivated state, may obtain a patent therefor, subject to the conditions and requirements of this title. The provisions of this title relating to patents for inventions shall apply to patents for plants, except as otherwise provided.[10]

The 1930 Act did not include seed-grown plants. In 1970, the Plant Variety Protection Act (PVPA) established a form of protection for new varieties of seed-grown and tuber propagated plants. The Act does not include the extensive examination system that is applied to applications for patents, contains several provisions specific to agricultural crops, and is administered by the Department of Agriculture. The basic requirements are as follows:

> The breeder of any sexually reproduced or tuber propagated plant variety (other than fungi or bacteria) . . . shall be entitled to plant variety protection for the variety, subject to the conditions and requirements of this chapter, if the variety is (1) new . . . (2) distinct . . . (3) uniform . . . and (4) stable . . . .[11]

The defendants argued that Congress excluded sexually reproduced plants and seeds from utility patent protection via the enactment of the PVPA. However, the Federal Circuit responded that the PVPA did not purport to remove plants from the patent statute. Neither Con-

---

[9] *See* 7 U.S.C. § 2321 (1994).

[10] 35 U.S.C. § 161 (1994).

[11] 7 U.S.C. § 2402(a) (1994).

Main volume footnote updates begin on page 111.

gress nor the courts excluded new plant varieties from the patent statute; the enactment of the PVPA did not effect such an exclusion.[12]

The defendants also argued that Pioneer obtained utility patents as well as certificates under the PVPA, and stated that the corresponding statutes are in conflict. The Federal Circuit, however, noted that it is not unusual for more than one statute to apply to a legal or property interest. For example, an ornamental design may qualify for protection under both copyright and design patent laws. The fact that laws are of different scope does not invalidate the laws.[13] Accordingly, the Federal Circuit held that patentable subject matter under 35 U.S.C. Section 101 includes seeds and seed-grown plants.

II. Utility Rejections

[Insert at the end of the section.]

The revised utility examination guidelines are also provided in Appendix C.

A. Introduction to Prima Facie Case of Nonutility

[Insert after footnote 23.]

The threshold of utility is not high: "An invention is 'useful' under section 101 if it is capable of providing some identifiable benefit."[14]

[Insert the following footnote [37a] at the end of the last sentence of the section.]

[37a]*See also* Juicy Whip, Inc. v. Orange Bang, Inc., 185 F.3d 1364, 51 USPQ 2d 1700, 1702 (Fed. Cir. 1999) ("[Y]ears ago courts invalidated patents on gambling devices on the ground that they were immoral . . . but that is no longer the law. . . . ").

B. Attacking a Prima Facie Case of Nonutility

[Add the following text at the end of the subsection.]

[12]Pioneer Hi-Bred Int'l., Inc. v. J.E.M. Ag Supply, Inc., 200 F.3d 1374, 53 USPQ 2d 1440, 1442 (Fed. Cir. 2000), *cert. granted*, 121 S. Ct. 1077 (2001).

[13]*Id.*, 53 USPQ 2d at 1442.

[14]Juicy Whip, Inc. v. Orange Bang, Inc., 185 F.3d 1364, 51 USPQ 2d 1700, 1702 (Fed. Cir. 1999). *See also* Brenner v. Manson, 383 U.S. 519, 534, 148 USPQ 689, 696 (1966); Brooktree Corp. v. Advanced Micro Devices, Inc., 977 F.2d 1555, 1571, 24 USPQ 2d 1401, 1412 (Fed. Cir. 1992) ("To violate 101 the claimed device must be totally incapable of achieving a useful result.").

Main volume footnote updates begin on page 111.

1. Invention Useful Even Though It Has Capacity to Fool Some Members of Public [New Topic]

The fact that one product can be altered to make it look like another is in itself a specific benefit sufficient to satisfy the statutory requirement of utility.

Juicy Whip, Inc. v. Orange Bang, Inc.[15] is a case in which the invention claimed was a postmix beverage dispenser that was designed to look like a premix beverage dispenser. A postmix beverage dispenser stores beverage syrup concentrate and water in separate locations until the beverage is ready to be dispensed. The syrup and water are mixed together immediately before the beverage is dispensed, which is usually after the consumer requests the beverage. In contrast, in a premix beverage dispenser, the syrup concentrate and water are premixed and the beverage is stored in a display reservoir bowl until it is ready to be dispensed. The display bowl is said to stimulate impulse buying by providing the consumer with a visual beverage display. A premix display bowl, however, has a limited capacity and is subject to contamination by bacteria. It therefore must be refilled and cleaned frequently.

Juicy Whip sued defendant Orange Bang, Inc. for infringement of its patent on the postmix beverage dispenser. Orange Bang moved for summary judgment of invalidity. The district court granted Orange Bang's motion on the ground that the invention lacked utility and thus was unpatentable under 35 U.S.C. Section 101. The district court concluded that the invention lacked utility because its purpose was to increase sales by deception, i.e., through imitation of another product. The district court explained that the purpose of the invention was to create an illusion, whereby customers believed that the fluid contained in the bowl was the actual beverage that they were receiving, when it was not.[16]

On appeal, the Federal Circuit reversed. The Federal Circuit noted that it is not at all unusual for a product to be designed to appear to viewers to be something it is not. For example, cubic zirconium is designed to simulate a diamond, imitation gold leaf is designed to imitate real gold leaf, synthetic fabrics are designed to simulate expensive natural fabrics, and imitation leather is designed to look like real leather. "In each case, the invention of the product or process that makes such imitation possible has 'utility' within the meaning of the patent statute, and indeed there are numerous patents directed toward making one product imitate another."[17] According to the Federal Circuit, the claimed

[15]Juicy Whip, Inc. v. Orange Bang, Inc., 185 F.3d 1364, 51 USPQ 2d 1700, 1702 (Fed. Cir. 1999).

[16]*Id.,* 51 USPQ 2d at 1702.

[17]*Id.* at 1703.

Main volume footnote updates begin on page 111.

postmix dispenser meets the statutory requirement of utility by embodying the features of a postmix dispenser while imitating the visual appearance of a premix dispenser. The fact that customers may believe they are receiving fluid directly from the display tank does not deprive the invention of utility, commented the Federal Circuit.[18]

The Federal Circuit further noted:

> The requirement of "utility" in patent law is not a directive to the Patent and Trademark Office or the courts to serve as arbiters of deceptive trade practices. Other agencies, such as the Federal Trade Commission and the Food and Drug Administration, are assigned the task of protecting consumers from fraud and deception in the sale of food products. . . . As the Supreme Court put the point more generally, "Congress never intended that the patent laws should displace the police powers of the States, meaning by that term those powers by which the health, good order, peace and general welfare of the community are promoted." Of course, Congress is free to declare particular types of inventions unpatentable for a variety of reasons, including deceptiveness. . . . Until such time as Congress does so, however, we find no basis in section 101 to hold that inventions can be ruled unpatentable for lack of utility simply because they have the capacity to fool some members of the public.[19]

Thus, *Juicy Whip* illustrates that an invention will be considered useful even though it fools the public in some manner.

F. Relationship Between Utility and Operability

[Insert after the second sentence of the first paragraph in this section.]

Lack of enablement and absence of utility are closely related grounds of unpatentability.[20] The enablement requirement of 35 U.S.C. Section 112, first paragraph requires that the specification adequately disclose to one skilled in the relevant art how to make, or in the case of a process, how to carry out, the claimed invention without undue experimentation.[21] The utility requirement of 35 U.S.C. Section 101 mandates that any patentable invention be useful and, accordingly, the subject matter of the claim must be operable.[22] If a patent claim fails to meet the utility requirement because it is not useful or operative, then it also fails to meet the how-to-use aspect of the enablement requirement.[23]

---

[18] *Id.*

[19] *Id.* (quoting Webber v. Virginia, 103 U.S. 344, 347–48 (1880)).

[20] Raytheon Co. v. Roper Corp., 724 F.2d 951, 956, 220 USPQ 592, 596 (Fed. Cir. 1983).

[21] Genentech, Inc. v. Novo Nordisk, A/S, 108 F.3d 1361, 1365, 42 USPQ 2d 1001, 1004 (Fed. Cir. 1997).

[22] Brooktree Corp. v. Advanced Micro Devices, Inc., 977 F.2d 1555, 1571, 24 USPQ 2d 1401, 1412 (Fed. Cir. 1992).

[23] Process Control Corp. v. HydReclaim Corp., 190 F.3d 1350, 52 USPQ 2d 1029, 1034–35 (Fed. Cir. 1999).

Main volume footnote updates begin on page 111.

The Federal Circuit has held certain process claims invalid, stating:

> [B]ecause it is for the invention as claimed that enablement must clearly exist, and because the impossible cannot be enabled, a claim containing a limitation impossible to meet may be held invalid under 112. Moreover, when a claim requires a means for accomplishing an unattainable result, the claimed invention must be considered inoperative as claimed and the claim must be held invalid under either 101 or 112 of 35 U.S.C.[24]

When an impossible limitation, such as a nonsensical method of operation, is clearly embodied within the claim, the patent must be held invalid.[25] While an otherwise valid patent covering a meritorious invention should not be struck down simply because of the patentee's misconceptions about scientific principles concerning the invention,[26] when "the claimed subject matter is inoperable, the patent may indeed be invalid for failure to meet the utility requirement of 101 and the enablement requirement of 112."[27]

Process Control Corp. v. HydReclaim Corp.[28] is an example in which the invention being claimed recited a mathematical impossibility resulting in the claim being held inoperative and invalid. HydReclaim is the owner of U.S. Patent No. 5,148,943 (the '943 patent) directed to continuous gravimetric blenders used in the plastics industry. These blenders mix multiple solid ingredients in appropriate proportions based on weight and feed the mixture to a weighed common hopper. The invention described in the '943 patent measures the weight, rather than the volume, of the material in the common hopper, and maintains that weight in the common hopper at a constant value.

Process Control filed a declaratory judgment action asserting the invalidity of the '943 patent. The district court construed the claims as urged by HydReclaim, sustained the validity of the '943 patent, and found that Process Control had willfully infringed claims.

On appeal, the Federal Circuit reversed. The Federal Circuit noted that it was undisputed by both HydReclaim and Process Control that a consistent definition of "discharge rate" in clauses [b] and [d] of claim 1 led to a nonsensical conclusion. Due to the principle of conservation of mass, the material processing rate of the processing machine must necessarily be equal to the discharge rate of the material from the common hopper to the processing machine in a steady-state process. Clause [d] of claim 1 read:

---

[24] *Raytheon*, 724 F.2d at 956, 220 USPQ at 596.

[25] *Process Control Corp. v. HydReclaim Corp.*, 190 F.3d 1350, 52 USPQ 2d 1029, 1035 (Fed. Cir. 1999).

[26] Fromson v. Advance Offset Plate, Inc., 720 F.2d 1565, 1570, 219 USPQ 1137, 1140 (Fed. Cir. 1983).

[27] *Brooktree Corp.*, 977 F.2d at 1571, 24 USPQ 2d at 1412 (citing *Raytheon Co.,* 724 F.2d at 956, 220 USPQ at 596).

[28] Process Control Corp. v. HydReclaim Corp., 190 F.3d 1350, 52 USPQ 2d 1029 (Fed. Cir. 1999).

Main volume footnote updates begin on page 111.

[d] determining the material processing rate of the processing machine from the sum of the material discharge rates of the ingredients to the common hopper and the discharge rate of the material from the common hopper to the processing machine.

Clause [d] embodied an inoperable method that violated the principle of conservation of mass. According to the Federal Circuit:

> In other words, clause [d] requires determining a quantity from the sum of that exact same quantity and something else, or symbolically, A = A + B, which is impossible, where, as here, B is not equal to zero. Accordingly, we hold that the correctly construed claims are invalid because they are inoperative, and thus the claims fail to comply with the utility and enablement requirements of 35 U.S.C. 101 and 112, 1, respectively.[29]

On this basis, the Federal Circuit held that claim 1 was invalid as lacking utility.

IV. Business Method Rejections

B. Cases Involving Business Method Rejections

10. Computer Implemented Investment Structure— Not a Business Method

[Insert at the end of the section.]

The holding in *State Street Bank* was subsequently reaffirmed by the Federal Circuit in *AT&T Corp. v. Excel Communications, Inc.*[30] In *AT&T Corp.* the Federal Circuit summarized the holding in *State Street Bank* as follows:

> In our recent decision in *State Street*, this court discarded the so-called "business method" exception and reassessed the "mathematical algorithm" exception, . . . both judicially-created "exceptions" to the statutory categories of 101. . . . In *State Street*, we held that the processing system there was patentable subject matter because the system takes data representing discrete dollar amounts through a series of mathematical calculations to determine a final share price—a useful, concrete, and tangible result.[31]

---

[29] *Id.*, 52 USPQ 2d at 1035.

[30] AT&T Corp. v. Excel Communications, Inc., 172 F.3d 1352, 50 USPQ 2d 1447 (Fed. Cir. 1999).

[31] *Id.*, 50 USPQ 2d at 1450, 1452. *See also id.* at 1451 (quoting *State Street Bank*, 149 F.3d at 1373, 47 USPQ 2d at 1601:

> As previously noted, we most recently addressed the "mathematical algorithm" exception in *State Street*. . . . In *State Street*, this court, following the Supreme Court's guidance in *Diehr*, concluded that "unpatentable mathematical algorithms are identifiable by showing they are merely abstract ideas constituting disembodied concepts or truths that are not 'useful.' . . . To be patentable an algorithm must be applied in a 'useful' way." . . . In that case, the claimed data processing system for implementing a financial management structure satisfied the 101 inquiry because it constituted a "practical application of a mathematical algorithm, . . . [by] producing 'a useful, concrete and tangible result.'".

Main volume footnote updates begin on page 111.

The Patent Office's "unofficial" opinion on the *State Street Bank* case is presented in an article entitled "Patent Eligibility in View of *State Street* and *AT&T v. Excel Communications*," by Stephen G. Kunin, Deputy Assistant Commissioner for Patent Policy and Projects of the U.S. Patent Office.[32] The Patent Office Business Method Patent Initiative and White Paper on Automated Financial or Management Data Processing Methods (Business Methods) are included in Appendix D.

V. Mathematical Algorithm Rejections

G. Federal Circuit Reevaluation of Algorithm Rejections

6. *Method Using Data Field to Indicate Primary Exchange Carrier—Statutory Subject Matter [New Topic]*

The mathematical algorithm rejection was further narrowed by the Federal Circuit in *AT&T Corp. v. Excel Communications, Inc.*[33] The invention related to a message record for long-distance telephone calls that was enhanced by adding a primary interexchange carrier (PIC) indicator. The addition of the indicator aided long-distance carriers in providing differential billing treatment for subscribers, depending upon whether a subscriber called someone with the same or a different long-distance carrier.

The Federal Circuit focused on whether a mathematical algorithm is statutory subject matter, writing: "A mathematical formula alone, sometimes referred to as a mathematical algorithm, viewed in the abstract, is considered unpatentable subject matter."[34] The Federal Circuit noted that courts have used the terms "mathematical algorithm," "mathematical formula," and "mathematical equation" to describe types of nonstatutory mathematical subject matter without explaining whether the terms are interchangeable or different. Even assuming the words connote the same concept, the Federal Circuit reasoned, there is considerable question as to exactly what the concept encompasses.[35]

The Federal Circuit commented that since the process of manipulation of numbers is a fundamental part of computer technology, the rules that govern the patentability of such technology should be reexamined. The Federal Circuit also noted that "the sea-changes in

[32] Stephen G. Kunin, *Patent Eligibility in View of* State Street *and* AT&T v. Excel Communications, 81 J. Pat. & Trademark Off. Soc'y 671 (1999).

[33] AT&T Corp. v. Excel Communications, Inc., 172 F.3d 1352, 50 USPQ 2d 1447 (Fed. Cir. 1999).

[34] *Id.*, 50 USPQ 2d at 1450.

[35] *Id.*

Main volume footnote updates begin on page 111.

both law and technology stand as a testament to the ability of law to adapt to new and innovative concepts, while remaining true to basic principles."[36]

The Federal Circuit specifically emphasized the narrow application of the mathematical algorithm rejections to "abstract" mathematical algorithms having no practical value:

> Because Section 101 includes processes as a category of patentable subject matter, the judicially-defined proscription against patenting of a "mathematical algorithm," to the extent such a proscription still exists, is *narrowly limited* to mathematical algorithms in the *abstract*.[37]

The Federal Circuit rejected the notion that the method claims should be treated differently than the apparatus claims in *State Street Bank*. Whether stated implicitly or explicitly, the Federal Circuit considered the scope of Section 101 to be the same regardless of the form, machine, or process in which a particular claim was drafted.[38] Thus, the Federal Circuit stated, "we are comfortable in applying our reasoning in *Alappat* and *State Street* to the method claims at issue in this case."[39]

The Federal Circuit then noted that AT&T's claimed process employed subscribers' and call recipients' PICs as data, applied Boolean algebra to those data to determine the value of the PIC indicator, and applied that value through switching and recording mechanisms to create a signal useful for billing purposes. Referring to *State Street*, the Federal Circuit commented, "we held that the processing system there was patentable subject matter because the system takes data representing discrete dollar amounts through a series of mathematical calculations to determine a final share price—a useful, concrete, and tangible result."[40]

The Federal Circuit emphasized that the written description was clear that AT&T was only claiming a process that used the Boolean principle in order to determine the value of the PIC indicator. The PIC indicator represented information about the call recipient's PIC, a useful, nonabstract result that facilitates differential billing of long-distance calls made by an interexchange carrier's subscriber. According to the Federal Circuit, "[b]ecause the claimed process applies the Boolean principle to produce a useful, concrete, tangible result without pre-empting other uses of the mathematical principle, on its face the claimed process comfortably falls within the scope of 101."[41]

---

[36] *Id.*

[37] *Id.*

[38] *Id.* at 1451 (citing *In re* Alappat, 33 F.3d 1526, 1581, 31 USPQ 2d 1545, 1589 (Rader, J., concurring)).

[39] *Id.*

[40] *Id.* at 1452.

[41] *Id.* (citing Arrhythmia Research Tech. Inc. v. Corazonix Corp., 958 F.2d 1053, 1060, 22 USPQ 2d 1033, 1039 (Fed. Cir. 1992) ("That the product is numerical is not a criterion of whether the claim is directed to statutory subject matter.")).

Main volume footnote updates begin on page 111.

The Federal Circuit noted that the inquiry as to whether an invention including a mathematical algorithm is statutory subject matter focuses on whether the mathematical algorithm is applied in a practical manner to produce a useful result. According to the Federal Circuit, *mere* laws of nature, natural phenomena, and abstract ideas are not within the categories of inventions or discoveries that may be patented under Section 101.[42]

The Federal Circuit concluded:

> [I]t is now clear that computer-based programming constitutes patentable subject matter so long as the basic requirements of 101 are met. . . . [T]he focus is understood to be not on whether there is a mathematical algorithm at work, but on whether the algorithm-containing invention, as a whole, produces a tangible, useful, result.[43]

Thus, the *AT&T* decision illustrates that the only inquiry the reviewing court need make is whether the algorithm produces a tangible and useful result. The Patent Office's "unofficial" opinion on the *AT&T* case is presented in an article entitled "Patent Eligibility in View of *State Street* and *AT&T v. Excel Communications*," by Stephen G. Kunin, Deputy Assistant Commissioner for Patent Policy and Projects of the U.S. Patent Office.[44]

H. Combating Algorithm Rejections

[Insert before the last sentence of the section.]

The techniques for combating algorithm rejections, described below, were developed in response to the decisions that developed over the years. The most current practice, however, is to apply the decisions of *State Street Bank* and *AT&T Corp.* where the overall inquiry is whether the mathematical algorithm provides a useful, practical result.[45]

---

[42] *Id.* at 1453 (emphasis added).

[43] *Id.* at 1454.

[44] Stephen G. Kunin, *Patent Eligibility in View of* State Street *and* AT&T Excel Communications, 81 J. Pat. & Trademark Off. Soc'y 671 (1999).

[45] *See infra* Section V.G.5–6.

Main volume footnote updates begin on page 111.

MAIN VOLUME FOOTNOTE UPDATES

[256]**[Add at the end of footnote 256.]** (unpublished).

[308]**[Replace the existing footnote with the following.]** State St. Bank & Trust Co. v. Signature Fin. Group, Inc., 149 F.3d 1368, 47 USPQ 2d 1596 (Fed. Cir. 1998), *cert. denied,* 525 U.S. 1093 (1999).

[597]**[Replace the existing footnote with the following.]** State St. Bank & Trust Co. v. Signature Fin. Group, Inc., 927 F. Supp. 502, 38 USPQ 2d 1530, (D. Mass. 1996), *rev'd,* 149 F.3d 1368, 47 USPQ 2d 1596 (Fed. Cir. 1998), *cert. denied,* 525 U.S. 1093 (1999).

[600]**[Replace the existing footnote with the following.]** State St. Bank & Trust Co. v. Signature Fin. Group, Inc., 149 F.3d 1368, 47 USPQ 2d 1596 (Fed. Cir. 1998), *cert. denied,* 525 U.S. 1093 (1999).

6

Anticipation Standard Under 35 U.S.C. Section 102

III. Some Basics Regarding Terminology Used in Section 102 Rejections

C. Patent Versus Printed Publication

1. Printed Publication

[Insert after footnote 47.]

A published U.S. application for a patent by another filed in the United States or a Patent Cooperation Treaty (PCT) international application are additional forms of printed publications that may be used as prior art references.[1] Since these types of publications are specifically identified by statute, i.e., 35 U.S.C. Section 102(e), by definition, these forms of published patent applications are sufficiently accessible on their publication date, assuming that the application is in fact published.

a. Effective Date of Publication

[Insert after footnote 53.]

[1] 35 U.S.C. § 102(e)(1) (Supp. 2000).

Main volume footnote updates begin on page 142.

The effective date of a published U.S. application, or published PCT international application under 35 U.S.C. Section 122(b) designating the United States that was published in the English language, is the filing date.[2] A published application's prior art effect will be as of its filing date if the application (1) was a U.S. national application pending on or after November 29, 2000 or (2) was a PCT application filed on or after November 29, 2000 and which was published in English.[3]

IV. Prima Facie Anticipation Based on Prior Art

[On page 411, replace 35 U.S.C. Section 102(e) with the following.]

(e) The invention was described in—

(1) an application for patent, published under section 122(b), by another filed in the United States before the invention by the applicant for patent, except that an international application filed under the treaty defined in section 351(a) shall have the effect under this subsection of a national application published under section 122(b) only if the international application designating the United States was published under Article 21(2)(a) of such treaty in the English language; or

(2) a patent granted on an application for patent by another filed in the United States before the invention by the applicant for patent, except that a patent shall not be deemed filed in the United States for the purposes of this subsection based on the filing of an international application filed under the treaty defined in section 351(a); or[4]

[On page 411, replace 35 U.S.C. Section 102(g) with the following.]

(g)(1) during the course of an interference conducted under section 135 or section 291, another inventor involved therein establishes, to the extent permitted in section 104, that before such person's invention thereof the invention was made by such other inventor and not abandoned, suppressed, or concealed, or (2) before such person's invention thereof, the invention was made in this country by another inventor who had not abandoned, suppressed, or concealed it. In determining priority of invention under this subsection, there shall be considered not only the respective dates of conception and reduction to practice of the invention, but also the reasonable diligence of one who was first to conceive and last to reduce to practice, from a time prior to conception by the other.[5]

---

[2] 35 U.S.C. § 102(e)(1) (Supp. 2000).

[3] It is unclear from 35 U.S.C. § 102(e) if the PCT application must also comply with 35 U.S.C. § 371 (entry into the national stage) requirements in order to be 35 U.S.C. § 102(e) prior art. A technical revision to Section 102(e) is currently pending in Congress that would clarify this issue.

[4] Intellectual Property and Communications Omnibus Reform Act of 1999, Pub. L. No. 106–113, § 4505, Nov. 29, 1999.

[5] 35 U.S.C. § 102(g) (Supp. 2000).

Main volume footnote updates begin on page 142.

V. Alternative 1: Attacking the Prima Facie Case

A. Element 1: Single Reference

[Insert after footnote 137.]

Admissions may also take the form of a statement made by a patent owner accusing another party of manufacturing a device that infringes the patent. If the accused device also turns out to have been sold more than one year prior to the filing date of the patent, the patent may be held to be invalid.[6] However, a mere allegation of infringement, prior to full discovery and analysis, should be unlikely to trigger such an admission.

1. References for Novelty Provisions Under Subsections 102(a), (e), (g)

a. Section 102(a) Reference

[Insert after footnote 148.]

A presentation indicative of the state of knowledge and use in this country qualifies as prior art for anticipation purposes under Section 102(a).[7]

b. Section 102(e) Reference

[Delete the paragraph containing footnote 206.]

[Insert at the end of the section.]

The Intellectual Property and Communications Omnibus Reform Act of 1999, which became law in 1999, authorized the publication of U.S. patent applications after 18 months from filing, subject to various conditions.[8] The Act provided that a published patent application in the United States is also entitled to prior art effect of its filing date under Section 102(e). Section 4505 of the Act, entitled "Prior Art Effect of Published Applications," states:

---

[6] Vanmoor v. Wal-Mart Stores, Inc., 201 F.3d 1363, 53 USPQ 2d 1377, 1379 (Fed. Cir.), *cert. denied*, 121 S. Ct. 63 (2000).

[7] Ecolochem, Inc. v. Southern Cal. Edison Co., 227 F.3d 1361, 56 USPQ 2d 1065, 1071 (Fed. Cir. 2000), *cert. denied*, 121 S. Ct. 1607 (2001).

[8] Intellectual Property and Communications Omnibus Reform Act of 1999, Pub. L. No. 106–113, 4505, Nov. 29, 1999.

Main volume footnote updates begin on page 142.

> Section 102(e) of title 35, United States Code, is amended to read as follows: (e) The invention was described in—
>
> (1) an application for patent, published under section 122(b), by another filed in the United States before the invention by the applicant for patent, except that an international application filed under the treaty defined in section 351(a) shall have the effect under this subsection of a national application published under section 122(b) only if the international application designating the United States was published under Article 21(2)(a) of such treaty in the English language; or
>
> (2) a patent granted on an application for patent by another filed in the United States before the invention by the applicant for patent, except that a patent shall not be deemed filed in the United States for the purposes of this subsection based on the filing of an international application filed under the treaty defined in section 351(a);. . . .[9]

The effective date of this amendment is described in Section 4508 as follows:

> Sections 4502 through 4507, and the amendments made by such sections, shall take effect on the date that is 1 year after the date of the enactment of this Act and shall apply to all applications filed under section 111 of title 35, United States Code, on or after that date, and all applications complying with section 371 of title 35, United States Code, that resulted from international applications filed on or after that date.[10]

Thus, patent applications filed on or after November 29, 2000, which will be published on or after May 29, 2002, unless an earlier priority date is claimed, will fall under this amendment of Section 102(e).

The effective date of a published U.S. application, or a published PCT international application under 35 U.S.C. Section 122(b) designating the United States that was published in the English language, is the filing date.[11] A published application's prior art effect will be as of its filing date if the application (1) was a U.S. national application pending on or after November 29, 2000 or (2) was a PCT application filed on or after November 29, 2000 and which was published in English.[12]

c. *Section 102(g) Reference*

[Change the Section 102(g) text after footnote 221 as follows:]

Specifically, Section 102(g) excludes a patent when

> (g)(1) during the course of an interference conducted under section 135 or section 291, another inventor involved therein establishes, to the ex-

---

[9] *Id.*

[10] *Id.* at 4508.

[11] 35 U.S.C. § 102(e) (1) (Supp. 2000).

[12] It is unclear from 35 U.S.C. § 102(e) if the PCT application must also comply with 35 U.S.C. § 371 (entry into the national stage) requirements in order to be 35 USC 102(e) prior art. A technical revision to Section 102(e) is currently pending in Congress that would clarify this issue. See Appendix C.

Main volume footnote updates begin on page 142.

tent permitted in section 104, that before such person's invention thereof the invention was made by such other inventor and not abandoned, suppressed, or concealed, or (2) before such person's invention thereof, the invention was made in this country by another inventor who had not abandoned, suppressed, or concealed it. In determining priority of invention under this subsection, there shall be considered not only the respective dates of conception and reduction to practice of the invention, but also the reasonable diligence of one who was first to conceive and last to reduce to practice, from a time prior to conception by the other.[13]

[Insert after footnote 223.]

The Federal Circuit has stated in this connection:

> As the second sentence in the subsection indicates, 102(g) was written merely to provide a statutory basis for determining priority of invention in the context of interference proceedings before what was then the United States Patent Office. . . . Nevertheless, the first sentence is clear and, as the cases show, has been taken to have independent significance as a basis for prior art outside of the interference context.[14]

The Federal Circuit has remarked on the policy concerns surrounding Section 102(g):

> This result makes sense. The first to invent who has invested time and labor in making and using the invention—but who might have opted not to apply for a patent—will not be liable for infringing another's patent on that same invention, while the public will have benefited because the invention was not abandoned, suppressed, or concealed. However, in view of these and other related policy concerns, and amendment of the statute, we have made clear that art qualifying only under subsection 102(g) may not be used under 103 to invalidate other patents of fellow employees engaged in team research.[15]

The Federal Circuit has interpreted the first sentence of Section 102(g) to permit qualifying art to invalidate a patent claim even if the same art may not qualify as prior art under other subsections of Section 102.[16]

[On page 435, replace the quotation preceding footnote 272 with the following.]

---

[13] 35 U.S.C. § 102(g) (Supp. 2000).

[14] Thomson S. A. v. Quixote Corp., 166 F.3d 1172, 49 USPQ 2d 1530, 1532 (Fed. Cir.), *cert. denied*, 527 U.S. 1036 (1999) (citing P.J. Federico, Commentary on the New Patent Act 19, in 35 U.S.C.A. (1954 ed., discontinued in subsequent volumes) (reprinted in 75 J. Pat. & Trademark Off. Soc'y 161, 180 (1993))).

[15] *Id.*, 49 USPQ 2d at 1532 n.3 (citing Oddzon Prods., Inc. v. Just Toys, Inc., 122 F.3d 1396, 1402–03, 43 USPQ 2d 1641, 1644–45 (Fed. Cir. 1997) (discussing *In re* Bass, 474 F.2d 1276, 1290, 177 USPQ 178, 189 (C.C.P.A. 1973), and the 1984 amendments to 103)).

[16] *See, e.g.*, Checkpoint Sys., Inc. v. United States Int'l Trade Comm'n, 54 F.3d 756, 761, 35 USPQ 2d 1042, 1046 (Fed. Cir. 1995); Amgen, Inc. v. Chugai Pharm. Co., 927 F.2d 1200, 1205, 18 USPQ 2d 1016, 1020 (Fed. Cir. 1991).

Main volume footnote updates begin on page 142.

"[S]ubject matter developed by another person, which qualifies as prior art only under subsection (e), (f) and (g) of section 102 of this title, shall not preclude patentability under this section where the subject matter and the claimed invention were, at the time the invention was made, owned by the same person or subject to an obligation of assignment to the same person."[17]

2. *References for Statutory Bar Provisions Under Subsections 102(b), (d)*

a. Section 102(b) Reference

ii. Use or Sale Under Section 102(b).

[Insert after footnote 279.]

The "invention" that has been offered for sale or in public use must, of course, be something circumscribed by metes and bounds of the claim.[18] Therefore, the first determination in the Section 102(b) analysis must be whether the subject of the barring activity met each of the limitations of the claim.[19]

Public use relates to the invention being claimed, and not to unclaimed features of the invention. Unclaimed features of the invention that may not have been publicly available do not negate novelty.[20] An evaluation of a question of public use depends on "how the totality of the circumstances of the case comports with the policies underlying the public use bar."[21] These policies include:

> (1) discouraging the removal, from the public domain, of inventions that the public reasonably has come to believe are freely available; (2) favoring the prompt and widespread disclosure of inventions; (3) allowing the inventor a reasonable amount of time following sales activity to determine the potential economic value of a patent; and (4) prohibiting the inventor from commercially exploiting the invention for a period greater than the statutorily prescribed time.[22]

The public use bar of Section 102(b) requires that the invention (1) was used in public and (2) was not primarily experimental in purpose.[23] "The use of an invention by the inventor himself, or of any other

---

[17] 35 U.S.C. § 103(c) (Supp. 2000).

[18] Graver Tank & Mfg. Co. v. Linde Air Prods. Co., 339 U.S. 605, 607 (1950).

[19] Scaltech Inc. v. Retec/Tetra, L.L.C., 178 F.3d 1378, 51 USPQ 2d 1055, 1058 (Fed. Cir. 1999); Tec Air, Inc. v. Denso Mfg. Mich. Inc., 192 F.3d 1353, 52 USPQ 2d 1294, 1296–97 (Fed. Cir. 1999).

[20] Lockwood v. American Airlines, Inc., 107 F.3d 1565, 41 USPQ 2d 1961 (Fed. Cir. 1997).

[21] Tone Bros. v. Sysco Corp., 28 F.3d 1192, 1198, 31 USPQ 2d 1321, 1324 (Fed. Cir. 1994), *cert. denied*, 514 U.S. 1015 (1995).

[22] *Id.* at 1198, 31 USPQ 2d at 1324–25.

[23] Allied Colloids Inc. v. American Cyanamid Co., 64 F.3d 1570, 35 USPQ 2d 1840, 1843 (Fed. Cir. 1995).

Main volume footnote updates begin on page 142.

person under his direction, by way of experiment, and in order to bring the invention to perfection, has never been regarded as [a public] use."[24] This doctrine is based on the underlying policy of giving an inventor time to determine if the invention is suitable for its intended purpose—in effect, to reduce the invention to practice.[25]

The determination of these aspects requires weighing such factors as the nature of the activity that occurred in public, public access to and knowledge of the public use, whether any confidentiality obligation was imposed on people who observed the use, whether progress records or other indicia of experimental activity were kept, whether people other than the inventor or those acting for the inventor conducted the experiments, how many tests were conducted, the scale of the tests compared with commercial conditions, the length of the test period in comparison with tests of similar products, and whether payment was made for the product of the tests.[26] The factor of whether the inventor controlled the experiment is critically important, because an inventor who has no control over the alleged experiments is not experimenting.[27] Similarly, if the inventor does not inquire about the testing or receive reports concerning the results, the inventor is not experimenting.[28] The Federal Circuit has clarified that the level of control the inventor must exert is flexible and is dependent on the facts in each case. As stated by the Federal Circuit:

> In order to justify a determination that legally sufficient experimentation has occurred, there must be present certain minimal indicia. The framework might be quite formal, as may be expected when large corporations conduct experiments, governed by contracts and explicit written obligations. When individual inventors or small business units are involved, however, less formal and seemingly casual experiments can be expected. Such less formal experiments may be deemed legally sufficient to avoid the public use bar, but only if they demonstrate the presence of the same basic elements that are required to validate any experimental program.[29]

Public acts may range from experimentation in which there are many unknowns to simply using an already proven product in an unrestricted public location. The experimental use exception does not

---

[24] City of Elizabeth v. American Nicholson Pavement Co., 97 U.S. (7 Otto.) 126, 134 (1878).

[25] Lough v. Brunswick Corp., 86 F.3d 1113, 39 USPQ 2d 1100, 1104–05 (Fed. Cir. 1996), *cert. denied*, 526 U.S. 806 (1997).

[26] *See* Baker Oil Tools, Inc. v. Geo Vann, Inc., 828 F.2d 1558, 1564, 4 USPQ 2d 1210, 1214 (Fed. Cir. 1987); *In re* Brigance, 792 F.2d 1103, 1107–08, 229 USPQ 988, 991 (Fed. Cir. 1986); Hycor Corp. v. Schlueter Co., 740 F.2d 1529, 1535, 222 USPQ 553, 557 (Fed. Cir. 1984); TP Lab., Inc. v. Professional Positioners, Inc., 724 F.2d 965, 971–72, 220 USPQ 577, 582 (Fed. Cir.), *cert. denied*, 469 U.S. 826 (1984).

[27] Lough v. Brunswick Corp., 86 F.3d 1113, 39 USPQ 2d 1100, 1105 (Fed. Cir. 1996), *cert denied*, 522 U.S. 806 (1997).

[28] *Id.*

[29] *Id.*

Main volume footnote updates begin on page 142.

extend to an offer for sale of the invention while the invention is being tested.[30]

"A sale is a contract between parties to give and to pass rights of property for consideration which the buyer pays or promises to pay the seller for the thing bought or sold."[31]

[Insert after footnote 282.]

One of the primary purposes of the on-sale bar is to prohibit the withdrawal of inventions that have been placed into the public domain through commercialization. For example, this policy prohibits a person from buying or selling a compound whose exact nature had not been determined and then, years after those sales or purchases, filing a patent application claiming the compound by characteristics newly discovered. The on-sale bar does not permit such a withdrawal of subject matter already available to the public.[32]

[Insert before paragraph containing footnote 289.]

The Federal Circuit subsequently summarized the Supreme Court's holding as follows:

> The Supreme Court has recently addressed the standards for application of the on-sale bar. . . . In *Pfaff*, the inventor showed detailed engineering drawings of his computer chip socket invention to Texas Instruments. Before the critical date, Texas Instruments provided the inventor with a written order for over 30,000 of his new sockets. In accord with the inventor's normal practice, he had not made any prototypes before offering his invention for commercial sale. After receiving Texas Instruments' purchase order, the inventor set out to make the device in commercial quantities. The inventor did not reduce his invention to practice or fill Texas Instruments' order until after the critical date. The Supreme Court determined that "the invention had been on sale for more than one year in this country before [the inventor] . . . filed his patent application."[33]

[Insert after footnote 289.]

It is well settled in the law that there is no requirement that a sales offer specifically identify all the characteristics of an invention offered for sale or that the parties recognize the significance of all these characteristics at the time of the offer. If a product that is offered for sale inherently possesses each of the limitations of the claims, then the

---

[30] Scaltech Inc. v. Retec/Tetra, L.L.C., 178 F.3d 1378, 51 USPQ 2d 1055, 1059 n.1 (Fed. Cir. 1999).

[31] *In re* Caveney, 761 F.2d 671, 676, 226 USPQ 1, 4 (Fed. Cir. 1985).

[32] Abbott Labs. v. Geneva Pharms., Inc., 182 F.3d 1315, 51 USPQ 2d 1307, 1309–10 (Fed. Cir. 1999).

[33] Weatherchem Corp. v. J. L. Clark, Inc., 163 F.3d 1326, 49 USPQ 2d 1001, 1006 (Fed. Cir. 1998) (citing Pfaff v. Wells Elecs., Inc., 525 U.S. 55, 48 USPQ 2d 1641 (1998)).

Main volume footnote updates begin on page 142.

invention is on sale, whether or not the parties to the transaction recognize that the product possesses the claimed characteristics.[34]

[Delete the text beginning with the first full paragraph on page 440 and ending with the first sentence in the first full paragraph on page 441.]

[Insert after footnote 311.]

An invention is "ready for patenting" when a foreign manufacturer had already reduced it to practice.[35]

[Insert before paragraph containing footnote 319.]

Commercial exploitation, if not incidental to the primary purpose of experimentation, will result in an on-sale bar, even if the invention was still in its experimental stage, if the invention was ready for patenting or reduction to practice.[36] The fact that a sale is made in the context of a research and development contract and that there is no fixed price set does not suffice to avoid the on-sale bar.[37] For example, a cost-plus contract to supply experimental systems incorporating an invention that was reduced to practice was held by the Federal Circuit to constitute an invalidating offer for sale.[38] Likewise, the fact that the products sold are to be used for testing rather than as routine production units, is not sufficient to avoid the effect of the on-sale bar.[39] A contract to supply goods is a sales contract, regardless of the means used to calculate payment and regardless of whether the goods are to be used for testing in a laboratory or for deployment in the field.[40]

[Delete the paragraph and quote ending in footnote 327.]

[Insert after footnote 337.]

---

[34] Abbott Labs. v. Geneva Pharms., Inc., 182 F.3d 1315, 51 USPQ 2d 1307, 1309–10 (Fed. Cir. 1999); J.A. LaPorte, Inc. v. Norfolk Dredging Co., 787 F.2d 1577, 1582–83, 229 USPQ 435, 439 (Fed. Cir. 1986) ("The question is not whether the sale, even a third party sale, 'discloses' the invention at the time of the sale, but whether the sale relates to a device that embodies the invention.").

[35] Pfaff v. Wells Elecs., Inc., 525 U.S. 55, 48 USPQ 2d 1641, 1642 n.2 (1998) ("A composition of matter is reduced to practice when it is completely composed.").

[36] Scaltech Inc. v. Retec/Tetra, L.L.C., 178 F.3d 1378, 51 USPQ 2d 1055, 1059 n.1 (Fed. Cir. 1999) (citing Paragon Podiatry Lab., Inc. v. KLM Labs., Inc., 984 F.2d 1182, 1185, 25 USPQ 2d 1561, 1563 (Fed. Cir. 1985)).

[37] Zacharin v. United States, 213 F.3d 1366, 55 USPQ 2d 1047, 1050 (Fed. Cir. 2000).

[38] RCA Corp. v. Data Gen. Corp., 887 F.2d 1056, 1062–63, 12 USPQ 2d 1449, 1454–55 (Fed. Cir. 1989).

[39] Zacharin v. United States, 213 F.3d 1366, 55 USPQ 2d 1047, 1050 (Fed. Cir. 2000) (citing General Elec. Co. v. United States, 654 F.2d 55, 59 & n.6, 211 USPQ 867, 871 & n.6 (Ct. Cl. 1981)).

[40] Zacharin v. United States, 213 F.3d 1366, 55 USPQ 2d 1047, 1050 (Fed. Cir. 2000).

Main volume footnote updates begin on page 142.

As stated by the Federal Circuit, "the statutory on-sale bar is not subject to exceptions for sales made by third parties either innocently or fraudulently."[41] It is also of no consequence that the product was constructed and the sale made pursuant to the buyer's directions.[42]

[Replace the text beginning on the top of page 448 and ending at footnote 344 with the following.]

Thus, the *Evans* holding indicates that even though the invention may have been stolen, the sale of the invention was still effective to implicate the Section 102(b) bar.

A sale or offer for sale of the invention still falls under Section 102(b) even if the invention is hidden from view as part of a larger machine or device.[43] For example, the Board has stated in this connection:

> With respect to appellant's argument that the public did not see the inner workings of the [invention], we are not aware of any requirement that the person to which an invention is publicly disclosed has to understand the significance and the technical complexities of the invention.[44]

As stated by the Federal Circuit in a similar context, "an insufficient understanding does not defeat a showing of [anticipation]."[45]

Any nonsecret use of an invention in the ordinary course of business by a third party not authorized by the inventor may be considered a public use under Section 102(b). On the other hand, if the details of an inventive process are not ascertainable from the product sold or displayed by a third party not authorized by the inventor, and the third party has kept the invention secret, the secret use of the invention by the third party will not be considered a public use against an inventor unconnected to the third party.[46] As stated by the Federal Circuit:

---

[41] Abbott Labs. v. Geneva Pharms., Inc., 182 F.3d 1315, 51 USPQ 2d 1307, 1309 (Fed. Cir. 1999).

[42] Brasseler, U.S.A. I, L.P. v. Stryker Sales Corp., 182 F.3d 888, 891, 51 USPQ 2d 1470, 1473 (Fed. Cir. 1999).

[43] *In re* Blaisdell, 242 F.2d 779, 113 USPQ 289, 292 (C.C.P.A. 1957).

[44] *Ex parte* Kuklo, 25 USPQ 2d 1387, 1390 (Bd. Pat. App. & Inter. 1992). *See also* Comfort Silkie Co. v. Seifert, Civ. App. No. 98-1476, slip op. at 4 (Fed. Cir. July 16, 1999) (unpublished), *cert. denied*, 529 U.S. 1019 (2000) (citing Egbert v. Lippmann, 104 U.S. 333 (1881)):

> Upon looking at the whole record, we agree that there is clear and convincing evidence that, as a matter of law, the patented blanket was used publicly more than a year before the patent application was filed. Furthermore, the use was sufficiently public to render invalid Comfort Silkie's patent under 35 U.S.C. 102(b). Although Comfort Silkie argues that a baby blanket cannot be considered to have been in public use because it was within the baby's realm of privacy and could not be touched by strangers, we note that if the Supreme Court has held that a woman wearing a corset stay, under her clothes, is a public use, then a fortiori, a baby playing with a blanket in public locations observable by others is a public use.

[45] Atlas Powder Co. v. IRECO Inc., 190 F.3d 1342, 51 USPQ 2d 1943, 1947 (Fed. Cir. 1999). *See also In re* Caveney, 761 F.2d 671, 675–76, 226 USPQ 1, 3–4 (Fed. Cir. 1985).

[46] W.L. Gore Assocs. v. Garlock, Inc., 721 F.2d 1540, 220 USPQ 303, 310 (Fed. Cir. 1983), *cert. denied*, 469 U.S. 851 (1984).

Main volume footnote updates begin on page 142.

An exception to this rule exists where a patented method is kept secret and remains secret after a sale of the unpatented product of the method. Such a sale prior to the critical date is a bar if engaged in by the patentee or patent applicant, but not if engaged in by another.[47]

It is immaterial that the record shows no delivery of the later patented invention and no exchange of money until after the critical date. Record evidence of a signed purchase agreement before the critical date establishes an offer for sale sufficient to invoke the on-sale bar.[48] The fact that delivery was set for dates after the critical date is irrelevant to the finding of a commercial offer for sale.[49]

[Insert after footnote 348.]

On the other hand, the fact that a sales agreement was forged as part of a settlement of a dispute will not preclude a finding that the invention was on sale as of the time of the sales agreement. "It is enough that the parties were separate entities and that the agreement was an arm's-length transaction that bore all the earmarks of a commercial sale."[50] For example, the buyer and seller may be considered separate entities for purposes of Section 102(b) despite the fact that the corporate entity that wholly owned the seller also owned 49 percent of buyer, which was formed to be the seller's exclusive seller in the United States.[51] The fact that the buyer may have retained control over the manufacturing of the patented invention as a result of the alleged exclusive relationship between it and the seller says nothing about the basic corporate relationships between the entities and whether the entities are separate.[52]

A sale between joint developers in of itself is not sufficient to remove or except the sale from the on-sale bar.[53] In addition, the fact that the buyer had ownership rights in the invention when an embodiment thereof was produced and sold to it does not per se prevent the sale from being considered within the on-sale bar.[54] The sale may

---

[47] *In re* Caveney, 761 F.2d 671, 226 USPQ 1, 3–4 (Fed. Cir. 1985); W.L. Gore Assocs. v. Garlock, Inc., 721 F.2d 1540, 220 USPQ 303, 310 (Fed. Cir. 1983), *cert. denied*, 469 U.S. 851 (1984); D.L. Auld Co. v. Chroma Graphics Corp., 714 F.2d 1144, 219 USPQ 13, 16 (Fed. Cir. 1983).

[48] Weatherchem Corp. v. J.L. Clark, Inc., 163 F.3d 1326, 49 USPQ 2d 1001, 1007 (Fed. Cir. 1998).

[49] STX LLC v. Brine Inc., 211 F.3d 588, 54 USPQ 2d 1347, 1349 (Fed. Cir. 2000).

[50] IGT v. Global Gaming Tech., Inc., Civ. App. 98–1246, slip op. at 7–8 (Fed. Cir. June 17, 1999) (unpublished); *In re* Caveney, 761 F.2d 671, 676, 226 USPQ 1, 4 (Fed. Cir. 1985) ("a sale or offer to sell under 35 U.S.C. 102(b) must be between two separate entities").

[51] *In re* Caveney, 761 F.2d 671, 673–74, 676, 226 USPQ 1, 2, 4 (Fed. Cir. 1985).

[52] Brasseler, U.S.A. I, L.P. v. Stryker Sales Corp., 182 F.3d 888, 51 USPQ 2d 1470, 1472 (Fed. Cir. 1999).

[53] Buildex Inc. v. Kason Indus., Inc., 849 F.2d 1461, 1465, 7 USPQ 2d 1325, 1328 (Fed. Cir. 1988).

[54] Brasseler, U.S.A. I, L.P. v. Stryker Sales Corp., 182 F.3d 888, 51 USPQ 2d 1470, 1472 (Fed. Cir. 1999).

Main volume footnote updates begin on page 142.

still be considered within the on-sale bar even though the buyer initiated development of the invention.[55] "[A]dditional steps undertaken for marketing of the product do not change the basic transaction—a sale of completed product in quantity, constituting a commercial sale of a product ready for patenting."[56]

[Insert at the end of the last paragraph on p. 450.]

The *Feraq* decision also explains that a sale or offer for sale may still occur between related or affiliated companies when the companies are separately controlled.

B. Element 2: Reference That Teaches or Discloses

[Insert after footnote 380.]

The disclosure of a reference is not limited to specific working examples disclosed therein.[57]

1. *Reference That Incorporates Another Reference*

[Add the following at the end of the subsection.]

To support an anticipation rejection, the Federal Circuit appears to have adopted a more rigorous test than in other areas of incorporation by reference, and rightfully so since an anticipation rejection requires all elements to be found in the prior art as arranged in the claim. For example, the Federal Circuit has stated "[i]ncorporation by reference provides a method for integrating material from various documents into a host document—a patent or printed publication in an anticipation determination—by citing such material in a manner that makes clear that the material is effectively part of the host document as if it were explicitly contained therein."[58] To incorporate material by reference for anticipation, the host document must identify with de-

---

[55] *See* Buildex Inc. v. Kason Indus., Inc., 849 F.2d 1461, 1465, 7 USPQ 2d 1325, 1328 (Fed. Cir. 1988) ("[The buyer] may have provided the impetus for making the invention, but that does not make the transaction any less an offer for sale.").

[56] Brasseler, U.S.A. I, L.P. v. Stryker Sales Corp., 182 F.3d 888, 51 USPQ 2d 1470, 1473 (Fed. Cir. 1999).

[57] *In re* Fracalossi, 681 F.2d 792, 794 n.1, 215 USPQ 569, 570 n.1 (C.C.P.A. 1982).

[58] Advanced Display Sys., Inc. v. Kent State Univ., 212 F.3d 1272, 54 USPQ 2d 1673, 1679 (Fed. Cir. 2000), *cert. denied*, 121 S. Ct. 1226 (2001) (citing General Elec. Co. v. Brenner, 407 F.2d 1258, 1261–62, 159 USPQ 335, 337 (D.C. Cir. 1968); *In re* Lund, 376 F.2d 982, 989, 153 USPQ 625, 631 (C.C.P.A. 1967)).

Main volume footnote updates begin on page 142.

tailed particularity what specific material it incorporates and clearly indicate where that material is found in the various documents.[59]

2. *Restriction Requirement in Application Does Not Have Any Bearing on Enablement of Prior Art Reference [New Topic]*

The Patent Office's determination or opinion regarding an application under examination has no general relevance or bearing with respect to the suitableness or enablement of a prior art reference. For example, the fact that a restriction requirement is issued in an application between the method claims and the system claims, thereby indicating that the claimed method may be performed by other systems than the claimed system, does not have any bearing on enablement of a prior art reference that describes a different system used to implement the claimed method.

For example, in *Helifix Ltd. v. Blok-Lok, Ltd.*,[60] the invention was directed to a method of securing layers of masonry ("wythes"), such as an exterior brick wall and an interior concrete wall, by means of ties. The typical tie was described as spiral-shaped, 7–8 inches long, and made of solid stainless steel. In January 1993, representatives of Helifix attended the World of Concrete trade show in Las Vegas, Nevada, where they displayed and distributed a brochure ("the '93 brochure"). The '93 brochure described Helifix stainless steel ties and their use in masonry refacing and new construction, including methods of construction.

During initial prosecution, the grandparent application of the Helifix patent was filed with claim 1 to a method of securing wythes with a helical tie, claim 2 to a tool for driving a helical tie into a wall, and claims 3 and 4 to helical ties. The Patent Office issued a restriction requirement between the method, tool, and tie claims. With respect to the method and tool claims, the Patent Office asserted that the tool is not required to insert the tie. Helifix elected to pursue the method claim. In due course, the grandparent application was abandoned in favor of the parent application of the Helifix patent.

The parent application was filed with claim 1 to the method, claims 2 and 5–7 to the tool, and claims 3 and 4 to the helical tie. The Patent Office again issued a restriction requirement along the same lines as the restriction requirement issued in the grandparent application,

---

[59] *Id.*, 54 USPQ 2d at 1679 (citing *In re* Seversky, 474 F.2d 671, 674, 177 USPQ 144, 146 (C.C.P.A. 1973) (providing that incorporation by reference requires a statement "clearly identifying the subject matter which is incorporated and where it is to be found"); *In re* Saunders, 444 F.2d 599, 602–03, 170 USPQ 213, 216–17 (C.C.P.A. 1971) (reasoning that a rejection for anticipation is appropriate only if one reference "expressly incorporates a particular part" of another reference)).

[60] Helifix Ltd. v. Blok-Lok, Ltd., 208 F.3d 1339, 54 USPQ 2d 1299 (Fed. Cir. 2000).

Main volume footnote updates begin on page 142.

asserting that the tool is not required to insert the tie. Helifix did not present any substantive arguments in response to this restriction requirement, and elected to pursue the tool claims.

The Helifix patent application was filed with the same claims as the parent application; however, the tool and tie claims were subsequently canceled, leaving only method claim 1. This claim of the Helifix patent recited:

> 1. A method of securing two or more wythes in a building structure utilizing a helical tie member having longitudinal helical flutes terminating at a cutting end at one end and terminating at a remote end opposite the cutting end comprising the steps of:
>
> drilling a first wythe to a diameter less than a diameter of the flutes on the tie to be inserted,
>
> drilling a pilot hole in a second wythe to a predetermined depth,
>
> inserting the remote end of the tie into a tool which impactingly drives the tie and rotatably permits the same to rotate as a helical bed is developed in the first wythe due to penetration by the tie,
>
> passing the flutes into the second wythe and continuing to impactingly drive the tie to a base of the pilot hole,
>
> removing the driving tool from the remote end of the tie,
>
> and thereafter finishing the remote end of the tie in accordance with mandates of the site.[61]

Helifix filed suit against Blok-Lok, alleging that Blok-Lok was infringing its patent. Blok-Lok filed a counterclaim which included a request for a declaratory judgment of patent invalidity. Blok-Lok asserted that the '93 brochure described the method claimed in the Helifix patent and that the claimed method was on sale at the January 1993 World of Concrete trade show. Because the earliest United States priority date of the Helifix patent was more than one year after the brochure was publicly distributed and more than one year after the trade show, Blok-Lok asserted that the method was unpatentable under 35 U.S.C. Section 102(b).

The district court construed claim 1 of the patent, focusing on the tool recited in the claim. The district court concluded that the claim was not limited to the specific tool described in the patent specification. The district court then determined that the patent was anticipated by the '93 brochure under 35 U.S.C. Section 102(b), and that activities at the World of Concrete trade show in January 1993 amounted to an on-sale bar under 35 U.S.C. Section 102(b). Although the '93 brochure did not describe the tool used to perform the claimed method, the district court determined that such a tool was enabled because the Patent Office had issued a restriction requirement between the claimed method and the specific tool described in the specification. Accordingly, the district court assumed that the restriction require-

[61] *Id.*, 54 USPQ 2d at 1300–01.

Main volume footnote updates begin on page 142.

ment indicated that any tool could perform the claimed method, and therefore, the fact the '93 brochure did not specifically describe a tool that could implement the claimed method was irrelevant to the enablement of the '93 brochure. The district court therefore granted Blok-Lok's motion for summary judgment of patent invalidity.

On appeal, the Federal Circuit reversed, holding that the '93 brochure was not enabling, and therefore, was not an anticipatory reference under Section 102. Helifix argued that the '93 brochure did not enable a tool capable of practicing the method recited in the patent and that such a tool was not available at the time of the World of Concrete trade show. The Federal Circuit concluded that Blok-Lok failed to provide clear and convincing evidence that the '93 brochure enabled a person of ordinary skill in the art to practice the claimed method. In particular, Blok-Lok did not present any evidence indicating that a person of ordinary skill in the art could have made or obtained a tool capable of being used in the claimed method without an undue amount of experimentation.[62]

The Federal Circuit explained that the Patent Office can issue a restriction requirement if it finds that two or more inventions claimed in a patent application are "independent and distinct."[63] A process and apparatus (tool) for its practice can be restricted if either "the process as claimed can be practiced by another materially different apparatus or by hand" or "the apparatus as claimed can be used to practice another and materially different process."[64] In response to a restriction requirement, an applicant must elect one invention for examination.[65] Claims to the non-elected invention(s) are withdrawn from consideration and must be canceled before the application is allowed to issue as a patent.[66]

The Federal Circuit rejected Block-Lok's argument that the Patent Office's repeated assertions that the tool claimed in the patent applications was not required to be inserted in the tie demonstrated that the '93 brochure need not describe the tool to enable the claimed method. According to the Federal Circuit:

> Both Block-Lok and the district court, however, have read too much into the restriction requirements in this case. The restriction requirements at issue merely reflect the Patent Office's conclusions that claim 1, by its terms, is not limited to a method using the tool recited in claim 2. Accordingly, the restriction requirements between the method claimed in

[62] *Id.* at 1304 (citing *In re* Sheppard, 339 F.2d 238, 242, 144 USPQ 42, 45 (C.C.P.A. 1981) (reversing a rejection under 35 U.S.C. Section 102(b) where the asserted prior art reference did not permit someone skilled in the art to possess the claimed invention without an undue amount of experimentation)).

[63] *Id.* (citing 35 U.S.C. § 121 (1994)).

[64] *Id.* (citing M.P.E.P. § 806.05(e) (7th ed. 1998)).

[65] *Id.* (citing 37 C.F.R. § 1.142(a) (1999)).

[66] *Id.* (citing 37 C.F.R. § 1.142(b) (1999)).

Main volume footnote updates begin on page 142.

> the [Helifix] patent and the specific tool described in the specification in no way bear on the enablement of a different tool.[67]

Accordingly, the Federal Circuit held that the action of U.S. Patent Office in issuing restriction requirements between the claimed method and a tool described in the specification of the patent to implement the method does not reflect the Patent Office's determination that other tools could be devised to practice the claimed method, and thus does not bear in any way on enablement of a prior art reference.

C. Element 3: Each of the Claimed Elements

[Insert after footnote 389.]

On the other hand, when the claimed invention recites a method and the specification of the patent describes a specific structure to perform the method, any prior art structure that describes or discloses the method will anticipate the claim.[68] This assumes that the claims at issue do not recite the specific structure used to implement the method.

3. Public Use of Manual Method Does Not Anticipate Automatic Method [New Topic]

A public use of a manual method does not anticipate an automatic method when, of course, the methods do not involve the identical steps. For example, in *Systemation, Inc. v. Engel Industries, Inc.*,[69] the invention was directed to machines and methods of connecting sections of duct at their adjacent ends. The connections were typically accomplished by fastening together flanges that were formed on the ends of the panels that formed the sides of the duct sections. To fasten the flanges together, L-shaped angle plates (also referred to as corner members) were inserted into the corners of the flanges, one on either side of the meeting flanges of two adjacent duct sections, and a fastener (e.g., a bolt) was inserted through the angle plates to connect them. The insertion of the angle plates in the flanges was carried out manually.

The patent disclosed an apparatus and method for automatically inserting angle plates in the duct flanges. The machine that carried out this process was not directly at issue. Systemation contended that Engel was practicing a method of inserting the angle plates that infringed method claim 1 of Systemation's patent. Engel attacked the validity of the patent on the ground that the prior art manual method

---

[67] *Id.*

[68] Helifix Ltd. v. Blok-Lok, Ltd., 208 F.3d 1339, 54 USPQ 2d 1299, 1306 (Fed. Cir. 2000).

[69] Systemation, Inc v. Engel Indus., Inc., Civ. App. No. 98-1489 (Fed. Cir. Mar. 10, 1999) (unpublished).

Main volume footnote updates begin on page 142.

of inserting such plates anticipated the claim. Systemation responded that the prior art method did not have positioned plates within a hopper that were part of an automated system and, therefore, the prior art manual method could not anticipate. The district court found that Systemation would likely withstand Engel's challenges to the validity of the claim because the prior art manual method of inserting plates could not anticipate the claimed automated method, which had additional steps.

On appeal, the Federal Circuit affirmed the district court, holding that the patent was not anticipated. The Federal Circuit noted that Systemation was likely to withstand Engel's validity challenges to the patent. The only prior art relevant to the patent was long public use of the manual method of inserting angle plates. Engel argued that the manual method anticipated the patent. Systemation, however, argued that the manual method could not anticipate the patent, which was clearly directed toward an automatic method. As stated by the Federal Circuit:

> It is clear, at least when claim 1 is read in light of the written description and the other claims, that the claim is directed to an automated method of inserting plates. . . . Such a method cannot be anticipated by a manual method for doing the same. The steps of the former are necessarily more in number. . . . We hold the district court did not clearly err in finding that claim 1 was unlikely to be proven invalid by Engel by clear and convincing evidence.[70]

Accordingly, the *Systemation* decision indicates that a public use of manual method does not anticipate an automatic method when the methods are different.

4. *Prior Art Racing Fuel Does Not Anticipate Automotive Fuel [New Topic]*

A holding of no anticipation may be found in instances where the general subject matter is the same, but the specific application or use is different. For example, in *Union Oil Co. of California v. Atlantic Richfield Co.*,[71] the invention related to automotive gasoline compositions that reduced automobile tailpipe emissions. The inventors sought to reduce the levels of carbon monoxide (CO), nitrous oxide (NOx), and hydrocarbons (HC) emitted from automobile tailpipes. After considerable experimentation, the inventors discovered relationships between the various petroleum characteristics described above and tailpipe emissions.

---

[70] *Id.*, slip op. at 10.

[71] Union Oil Co. of Cal. v. Atlantic Richfield Co., 208 F.3d 989, 54 USPQ 2d 1227 (Fed. Cir. 2000), *cert. denied*, 121 S. Ct. 1167 (2001).

Main volume footnote updates begin on page 142.

Atlantic Richfield originally sued Unocal in district court, seeking a declaratory judgment to invalidate the patent. Unocal counterclaimed, alleging willful infringement of the patent. The district court then construed the claims of the patent, and limited the claims to automotive fuels. As an example, dependent claim 117 recited, when placed in independent form:

> 117. [An unleaded gasoline fuel suitable for combustion in an automotive engine, said fuel having a Reid Vapor pressure no greater than 7.0 psi, and a 50% D-86 distillation point no greater than 200 degrees F., and a 90% D-86 distillation point no greater than 300 degrees F., and a paraffin content greater than 85 volume percent, and an olefin content less than 4 volume percent] wherein the maximum 10% distillation point is 158 degrees F (70 degrees C.).[72]

The district court emphasized that the claims of the patent recited either "[a]n unleaded gasoline suitable for combustion in an automotive engine" or "[a]n unleaded gasoline fuel suitable for combustion in a spark ignition automotive engine."[73] In addition, the district court noted that the specification also focused on automobile engines. On this basis, the district court held that the claims were not anticipated by prior art aviation and racing fuel compositions that were alleged to be the same by Atlantic Richfield.

On appeal, the Federal Circuit affirmed. The court reasoned:

> Because the '393 patent [U.S. Patent 5,288,393] covered only standard automotive fuel, the district court correctly determined that specialty fuels within other limitations of the claims do not anticipate under 35 U.S.C. Section 102. In other words, the aviation and racing fuels that allegedly invalidate the '393 claims do not anticipate because they do not contain each and every limitation of the claims. . . . Specifically, this alleged prior art does not include the limitation of being a standard automotive fuel composition. Moreover, the record does not show that the aviation and racing fuels otherwise have the claimed characteristics of the particular standard automotive fuels recited in the '393 patent. While the record shows that some properties of the aviation and racing fuels coincide with the properties of the '393 patent's claims, the record does not show the presence of each and every limitation.[74]

Accordingly, the Federal Circuit held that composition claims that cover only standard unleaded automotive gasoline were not anticipated by aviation and racing fuels, since the prior art compositions did not include the limitation of being, or applicable with, a standard automotive fuel. Therefore, the Federal Circuit held that the prior art racing and aviation fuels did not contain each and every limitation of the claims at issue, and were therefore not anticipated.

---

[72] *Id.*, 54 USPQ 2d at 1228.

[73] *Id.* at 1231.

[74] *Id.* at 1232.

Main volume footnote updates begin on page 142.

D. Element 4: Expressly or Inherently

[Insert after footnote 406.]

The operation of inherency in anticipation was also explained by the Federal Circuit in *Continental Can Co., U.S.A. v. Monsanto Co.*:[75]

> To serve as an anticipation when the reference is silent about the asserted inherent characteristic, such gap in the reference may be filled with recourse to extrinsic evidence. Such evidence must make clear that the missing descriptive matter is necessarily present in the thing described in the reference, and that it would be so recognized by persons of ordinary skill. . . . This modest flexibility in the rule that "anticipation" requires that every element of the claims appear in a single reference accommodates situations where the common knowledge of technologists is not recorded in the reference; that is, where technological facts are known to those in the field of the invention, albeit not known to judges.[76]

"Occasional results are not inherent."[77] On the other hand, subjective qualities inherent in a product cannot be used as an escape hatch to circumvent an anticipation holding.[78]

Inherency equally applies to nonpublished prior art, such as an offer for sale and/or public use. "If the process that was offered for sale inherently possessed each of the claim limitations, then the process was on sale, whether or not the seller recognized that his process possessed the claimed characteristics."[79] For example, the Federal Circuit has stated:

> It is well settled in the law that there is no requirement that a sales offer specifically identify all the characteristics of an invention offered for sale or that the parties recognize the significance of all of these characteristics at the time of the offer. . . . If a product that is offered for sale inherently possesses each of the limitations of the claims, then the invention is on sale, whether or not the parties to the transaction recognize that the product possesses the claimed characteristics.[80]

---

[75] Continental Can Co., U.S.A. v. Monsanto Co., 948 F.2d 1264, 20 USPQ 2d 1746 (Fed. Cir. 1991).

[76] *Id.* at 1268–69, 20 USPQ 2d at 1749–50. Also quoted in Finnigan Corp. v. United States International Trade Comm'n, 180 F.3d 1354, 51 USPQ 2d 1001, 1009 (Fed. Cir. 1999).

[77] Mehl/Biophile Int'l Corp. v. Milgraum, 192 F.3d 1362, 52 USPQ 2d 1303, 1306 (Fed. Cir. 1999)

[78] STX LLC v. Brine Inc., 211 F.3d 588, 54 USPQ 2d 1347, 1350 (Fed. Cir. 2000).

[79] Scaltech Inc. v. Retec/Tetra, L.L.C., 178 F.3d 1378, 51 USPQ 2d 1055, 1059 (Fed. Cir. 1999) (citing *In re* King, 801 F.2d 1324, 1326, 231 USPQ 136, 138 (Fed. Cir. 1986)).

[80] Abbott Labs. v. Geneva Pharms., Inc., 182 F.3d 1315, 51 USPQ 2d 1307, 1309–10 (Fed. Cir. 1999); J.A. LaPorte, Inc. v. Norfolk Dredging Co., 787 F.2d 1577, 1582–83, 229 USPQ 435, 439 (Fed. Cir. 1986) ("The question is not whether the sale, even a third party sale, 'discloses' the invention at the time of the sale, but whether the sale relates to a device that embodies the invention.").

Main volume footnote updates begin on page 142.

1. One of Ordinary Skill Need Not Recognize the Inherent Characteristics of Functions to Find Inherency [New Topic]

Inherency is not necessarily coterminous with the knowledge of those of ordinary skill in the art. Artisans of ordinary skill may not recognize the inherent characteristics or functioning of the prior art.[81]

In *Mehl / Biophile International Corp. v. Milgraum*,[82] a patent was held anticipated by a prior art publication, even though there was no description in the prior art application with respect to certain results that were specifically recognized by the patent owner, Mehl/Biophile International Corp. (Mehl).

Mehl asserted that Dr. Sandy Milgraum (Milgraum) infringed U.S. Patent No. 5,059,192 (the '192 patent). The '192 patent, entitled "Method of Hair Depilation," claimed a method for removing hair using a laser. The invention destroyed the papilla using the laser, thereby preventing hair regrowth.

Milgraum moved for summary judgment that all of the '192 patent claims were anticipated by a 1987 *Journal of Investigative Dermatology* article authored by Dr. Luigi Polla and others (the Polla article). The district court disagreed that the claims were anticipated by the Polla article, but nevertheless granted summary judgment of invalidity based on different prior art, and dismissed the action.

On appeal, the Federal Circuit affirmed the holding on invalidity, but used the Polla article for the anticipation analysis. The Polla article involved epilating guinea pigs with soft wax, holding the aperture of the laser in contact with the skin, and pulsing the laser. Using an electron microscope, the researchers observed disruption of melanosomes deep in the hair papillae of the guinea pigs.

The Federal Circuit noted that it was not a question of probabilities as to whether a person of ordinary skill following the teachings of the article would align the laser light applicator over a hair follicle. While the researchers focused their study on the epilated backs of guinea pigs, no one disputed that guinea pigs have hairy backs. Mehl's arguments that the Polla article concerned itself only with guinea pig, rather than human, skin, were irrelevant to the anticipation analysis. According to the Federal Circuit, nothing in the claim limited the method's reach to human skin.[83]

The Federal Circuit also noted that the Polla article's failure to mention hair depilation as a goal was similarly irrelevant. Mehl did not dispute that the laser operating parameters disclosed in the arti-

---

[81]*In re* King, 801 F.2d 1324, 1326, 231 USPQ 136, 138 (Fed. Cir. 1986).

[82]Mehl/Biophile Int'l Corp. v. Milgraum, 192 F.3d 1362, 52 USPQ 2d 1303 (Fed. Cir. 1999).

[83]*Id.*, 52 USPQ 2d at 1307.

Main volume footnote updates begin on page 142.

cle substantially coincided with those disclosed in the patent. Accordingly, the Federal Circuit reasoned that to the extent the embodiment in the patent achieves hair depilation, so does the Polla method. The Federal Circuit further stated, "[w]here, as here, the result is a necessary consequence of what was deliberately intended, it is of no import that the article's authors did not appreciate the results."[84]

On this basis, the Federal Circuit held that the Polla article anticipated the ′192 patent.

2. *Inherency Not Present When Prior Art Only Capable of Being Modified [New Topic]*

To establish inherency, the extrinsic evidence "must make clear that the missing descriptive matter is necessarily present in the thing described in the reference, and that it would be so recognized by persons of ordinary skill."[85] "Inherency, however, may not be established by probabilities or possibilities. The mere fact that a certain thing may result from a given set of circumstances is not sufficient."[86] The fact that a prior art reference is capable of being modified to arrive at the invention is not sufficient to support anticipation based on inherency.

In *In re Robertson*,[87] the Federal Circuit reversed an anticipation holding because the prior art was only capable of being modified and one of ordinary skill would not have recognized such modification. The invention was for an improved mechanical fastening system for disposable absorbent articles such as diapers that provided convenient disposal of the absorbent article. The claim at issue, claim 76, provided for two mechanical fastening means to attach the diaper to the wearer and a third such means for securing the diaper for disposal.

The prior art, the Wilson patent, disclosed two snap elements on fastening strips attached to the outer edges of the front and rear hip sections of the garment. The fastening strips additionally included secondary load-bearing closure means that functioned as additional fasteners to secure the garment. Wilson also stated:

> Disposal of the soiled garment upon removal from the body is easily accomplished by folding the front panel . . . inwardly and then fastening the rear pair of mating fastener members . . . to one another, thus neatly bundling the garment into a closed compact package for disposal.[88]

---

[84] *Id.* (citing W.L. Gore & Assocs. v. Garlock, Inc., 721 F.2d 1540, 1548, 220 USPQ 303, 309 (Fed. Cir. 1983)).

[85] Continental Can Co. v. Monsanto Co., 948 F.2d 1264, 1268, 20 USPQ 2d 1746, 1749 (Fed. Cir. 1991).

[86] *Id.* at 1269, 20 USPQ 2d at 1749 (quoting *In re* Oelrich, 666 F.2d 578, 581, 212 USPQ 323, 326 (C.C.P.A. 1981)).

[87] *In re* Robertson, 169 F.3d 743, 49 USPQ 2d 1949 (Fed. Cir. 1999).

[88] *Id.*, 49 USPQ 2d at 1950.

Main volume footnote updates begin on page 142.

Wilson, however, did not provide a separate fastening means to be used in disposing of the diaper. Instead, Wilson suggested that disposal of the used diaper may be "easily accomplished" by rolling it up and employing the same fasteners used to attach the diaper to the wearer to form "a closed compact package for disposal."[89]

According to the Federal Circuit, the Wilson patent did not expressly include a third fastening means for disposal of the diaper, as claim 76 required in Robertson's invention. The third fastening means was separate from and in addition to the other mechanical fastening means and performed a different function. The Federal Circuit commented that Wilson merely suggested that the diaper may be closed for disposal by using the same fastening means that are used for initially attaching the diaper to the body.

In holding that the invention claim 76 covered was anticipated by Wilson, the Federal Circuit indicated that the Board of Patent Appeals and Interferences did not hold that Wilson set forth a third fastening means. Instead, the Board found that Wilson anticipated claim 76 under principles of inherency. Applying the language of claim 76 to the operation of Wilson, the Board concluded that an artisan would readily understand the disposable absorbent garment of Wilson as being inherently capable of making the secondary load-bearing closure means mechanically engageable with the other snap fasteners on the fastening strip.[90]

In reversing the Board, the Federal Circuit noted that the Board ignored the "critical principles" of inherency.[91] The Board made no attempt to show that the fastening mechanisms of Wilson that were used to attach the diaper to the wearer also necessarily disclosed the third separate fastening mechanism of claim 76 used to close the diaper for disposal, or that an artisan of ordinary skill would so recognize. As stated by the Federal Circuit:

> [T]he Board ruled that one of the fastening means for attaching the diaper to the wearer also *could* operate as a third fastening means to close the diaper for disposal and that Wilson therefore inherently contained all the elements of claim 76. . . . The Board's theory that these two fastening devices in Wilson were *capable of* being intermingled to perform the same function as the third and first fastening elements in claim 76 is insufficient to show that the latter device was inherent in Wilson. Indeed, the Board's analysis rests upon the very kind of probability or possibility—the odd use of fasteners with other than their mates—that this court has pointed out is insufficient to establish inherency.[92]

On this basis, the decision of the Board of Patent Appeals and Interferences affirming the Examiner's rejection of claim 76 as anticipated by the Wilson patent was reversed.

---

[89] *Id.*

[90] *Id.*

[91] *Id.* at 1951.

[92] *Id.* (emphasis added).

Main volume footnote updates begin on page 142.

3. Insufficient Scientific Understanding Does Not Defeat a Finding of Inherency [New Topic]

Inherency is not necessarily coterminous with the knowledge of those of ordinary skill in the art. Artisans of ordinary skill may not recognize the inherent characteristics or functioning of the prior art.[93] However, the discovery of a previously unappreciated property of a prior art composition, or of a scientific explanation for the prior art's functioning, does not render the old composition patentably new to the discoverer.[94]

Atlas Powder Co. v. IRECO Inc.[95] is an example of a case in which the prior art inherently anticipated the invention even though it did not recognize the key aspect of the invention, which related to explosive compositions. To detonate, explosives generally require both fuel and oxidizers. The oxidizer rapidly reacts with the fuel to produce expanding gases and heat—an explosion. Composite explosives mix various sources of fuel and oxygen. The most widely used and economical composite explosive is ammonium nitrate and fuel oil (ANFO). ANFO explosives have two primary disadvantages. First, wet conditions dissolve the ammonium nitrate and make the explosive unusable in damp settings. Second, ANFO is a relatively weak explosive because interstitial air occupies considerable space in the mixture, thereby decreasing the amount of explosive material per unit of volume.

To address these shortcomings, explosive experts developed water-in-oil emulsions. These emulsions dissolved the oxidizer into water and then dispersed the solution in oil. Because oil surrounds the oxidizer, it is resistant to moisture, thus solving one of the problems with ANFO. Emulsions also increased the explosive's bulk strength by increasing the density of explosive material in the mixture. Emulsions, however, also have a disadvantage. Emulsions will not detonate unless sensitized, generally using gassing agents or adding microballoons throughout the mixture. The gassing agents or microballoons provide tiny gas or air bubbles throughout the mixture. Upon detonation, the gas pockets compress and heat up, thereby igniting the fuel around them. In other words, the tiny gas or air bubbles act as "hot spots" to propagate the explosion.

The invention was a composite explosive made from the combination of an ANFO blasting composition and an unsensitized water-in-oil emulsion. Atlas commenced this lawsuit against IRECO for

[93]*In re* Spormann, 363 F.2d 444, 150 USPQ 449, 452 (C.C.P.A. 1966) ("[The] inherency of an advantage and its obviousness are entirely different questions. That which may be inherent is not necessarily known. Obviousness cannot be predicated on what is unknown.").

[94]Titanium Metals Corp. v. Banner, 778 F.2d 775, 782, 227 USPQ 773, 778 (Fed. Cir. 1985) ("Congress has not seen fit to permit the patenting of an old [composition], known to others . . ., by one who has discovered its . . . useful properties.").

[95]Atlas Powder Co. v. IRECO Inc., 190 F.3d 1342, 51 USPQ 2d 1943 (Fed. Cir. 1999).

Main volume footnote updates begin on page 142.

infringing the patent. The district court found certain claims of the patent (the Clay patent) invalid as anticipated by either one of two prior art references, Egly or Butterworth. Egly and Butterworth each disclosed blasting compositions containing a water-in-oil emulsion and ANFO with ingredients identical to those of the Clay patent in overlapping amounts. The only element of the Clay patent that was arguably not present in the prior art compositions was the limitation that there be "sufficient aeration . . . entrapped to enhance sensitivity to a substantial degree."[96] The district court concluded that the claim term "sufficient aeration" included both interstitial air (between oxidizer particles) and porous air (within the pores of oxidizer particles).[97]

Based on this interpretation, the district court held that this sufficient aeration limitation was an inherent element in the prior art blasting compositions within the overlapping ranges.

On appeal, the Federal Circuit affirmed the holding of invalidity based upon anticipation and inherency. Atlas Powder argued that the sufficient aeration limitation was not present or inherent in the prior art since it was not recognized, but the Federal Circuit rejected this argument. According to the Federal Circuit:

> Because "sufficient aeration" was inherent in the prior art, it is irrelevant that the prior art did not recognize the key aspect of Dr. Clay's alleged invention—that air may act as the sole sensitizer of the explosive composition. An inherent structure, composition, or function is not necessarily known. . . . Once it is recognized that interstitial and porous air were inherent elements of the prior art compositions, the assertion that air may act as a sole sensitizer amounts to no more than a claim to the discovery of an inherent property of the prior art, not the addition of a novel element. Insufficient prior understanding of the inherent properties of a known composition does not defeat a finding of anticipation.[98]

Thus, the *Atlas Powder* decision explains that insufficient scientific understanding does not defeat a showing of inherency.

4. *Examiner Must Point to "Page and Line" of Prior Art to Support Inherency [New Topic]*

When an Examiner relies on inherency, it is incumbent on the Examiner to point to the page and line of the prior art which justifies a rejection that relies on inherency. For example, in *Ex parte Schricker*,[99] the invention related treating fish with a substance, porcine somatotropin, to increase protein content and protein accretion or decrease fat content and fat accretion. The Examiner rejected the claims based

---

[96] *Id.*, 51 USPQ 2d at 1946.

[97] *Id.*

[98] *Id.* at 1947.

[99] *Ex parte* Schricker, 56 USPQ 2d 1723 (B.P.A.I. 2000) (unpublished).

Main volume footnote updates begin on page 142.

on inherency. According to the Examiner, the [prior art] "system has not been demonstrated to be different than that claimed. That is, the claimed 'increasing the protein content and fat accretion of fish' would be inherent in the use of the porcine somatotropin of [the prior art]."[100]

On appeal, the Board reversed, stating:

> when an examiner relies on inherency, it is incumbent on the examiner to point to the "page and line" of the prior art which justifies an inherency theory. . . . The examiner has left applicant and the board to guess at the basis of the rejection and after having us guess would have us figure out (i.e., further guess) what part of which [prior art] document supports the rejection. We are not good at guessing; hence, we decline to guess[101].

E. Element 5: Interpreted By One of Ordinary Skill

[Insert after footnote 417.]

The hypothetical person of ordinary skill is not defined as one who is deemed to be aware of all relevant prior art or literature.[102] Rather, the hypothetical person of ordinary skill is defined by considering the educational level of the inventor; the types of problems encountered in the art; the prior art solutions to those problems; the rapidity with which innovations are made; the sophistication of the technology; and the educational level of workers in the field.[103] Once the person of ordinary skill has been defined, then a determination may be made as to whether that person of ordinary skill would have been familiar with the relevant literature, if such a consideration is appropriate when attempting to define the patent claims or the prior art.

IX. Special Topic: Anticipation and Preamble Limitations

[Insert after footnote 483.]

Preamble limitations may become important, in retrospect, if a prior art reference or activity is discovered after the patent application has been prosecuted. In such an instance, the patentee might want to rely on the additional preamble limitations to defend against a prior art rejection. For example, in *STX LLC v. Brine Inc.*,[104] the invention

---

[100] *Id.* at 1725.

[101] *Id.*

[102] Helifix Ltd. v. Blok-Lok, Ltd., 208 F.3d 1339, 54 USPQ 2d 1299, 1304 (Fed. Cir. 2000).

[103] Custom Accessories, Inc. v. Jeffrey-Allan Indus., Inc., 807 F.2d 955, 962, 1 USPQ 2d 1196, 1201 (Fed. Cir. 1986).

[104] STX LLC v. Brine Inc., 211 F.3d 1351, 54 USPQ 2d 1347 (Fed. Cir. 2000).

Main volume footnote updates begin on page 142.

related to a head frame for a lacrosse stick, with netting attached for catching and throwing the ball during play. STX filed a complaint against Brine, Inc. alleging that lacrosse sticks Brine made infringed the patent. Brine asserted that the patent was invalid on the ground that STX violated the on-sale bar of 35 U.S.C. Section 102(b).

STX argued that there could not have been a sale of the invention because it did not know at the time of the sale whether the head frame would have "improved playing and handling" characteristics while retaining the strength and durability exhibited by the prior solid sidewall design, as recited in the preamble of claim 1.

Claim 1, the only independent claim of the patent, recited the following:

> 1. A head for a lacrosse stick which provides improved handling and playing characteristics comprising a generally V-shaped frame constructed of a synthetic polymeric material defined by two sidewalls joined at a juncture and diverging therefrom, a traverse wall joining tile ends of said sidewalls opposite of said juncture, said frame being adapted to receive a web, and said sidewalls having openings therein, the area of said openings including string holes comprising in the range of from about 7% to 65% of the entire area of said sidewalls.[105]

The district court granted Brine's motion for summary judgment of invalidity, concluding that not only had STX failed to show a genuine issue of material fact suggesting the patented invention was not on-sale prior to the critical date, but that Brine had shown by clear and convincing evidence that STX's product was on-sale and in the public domain prior to that date. In addition, the district court held that the words relied on by Brine recited in the preamble of the claim were not limitations that could be used to avoid the on-sale bar.

On appeal, the Federal Circuit affirmed the holding of invalidity. The Federal Circuit reasoned that the statement in the claim preamble that the lacrosse stick invention of patent has "improved playing and handling characteristics" was not a structural limitation, since the preamble did not limit the claim. The Federal Circuit explained that the invention was defined structurally in the claim's body and used the preamble only to state the purpose or intended use for the invention, and the body of the claim was a self-contained description that could stand alone without the preamble. In addition, the Federal Circuit commented that the preamble language was not essential in distinguishing the invention over the prior art, and was not decisive in eventually securing allowance of the claim. Accordingly, the Federal Circuit affirmed the holding of invalidity based on the on-sale bar of Section 102(b).[106]

---

[105] *Id.*, 54 USPQ 2d at 1348.

[106] *See also* Heidelberg Harris, Inc. v. Mitsubishi Heavy Indus., Ltd., Civ. App. No. 99-1100, slip op. at 12–13 (Fed. Cir. Sept. 18, 2000) (unpublished):

Main volume footnote updates begin on page 142.

XIII. Special Topic: Anticipation and Genus/Species Claims

[Insert after footnote 530.]

Specifically, when a patent claims a chemical composition in terms of ranges of elements, any single prior art reference that falls within each of the ranges anticipates the claim.[107] In chemical compounds, a single prior art species within the patent's claimed genus reads on the generic claim and anticipates.[108]

While the phrase "for reducing vibrations and slippage" was originally added to the body of the '048 claims in the context of means-plus-function language, which indisputably would have acted to limit the claimed inventions, its movement to the preamble of the newly-added claims did not create a similar effect. The only relevance of the phrase "reducing vibrations and slippage" is to illustrate the intended purpose of the invention. See Pitney Bowes, Inc. v. Hewlett-Packard Co., 182 F.3d 1298, 1305, 51 USPQ 2d 1161, 1165–66 (Fed. Cir. 1999). The phrase is plainly not "necessary to give life, meaning, and vitality to the claim." Kropa v. Robie, 187 F.2d 150, 152, 88 USPQ 478, 480–81 (C.C.P.A. 1951). It does not, for example, provide an antecedent basis for terms later used in the body of the claim. See Gerber Garment Tech., Inc. v. Lectra Sys., Inc., 916 F.2d 683, 688–89, 16 USPQ 2d 1436, 1441 (Fed. Cir. 1990). Nor could such an expression of the intended use and function of the offset press have distinguished over the prior art. See In re Lechene, 277 F.2d 173, 176, 125 USPQ 2d 396, 399 (C.C.P.A. 1960). Consequently, we hold that the phrase "reducing vibrations and slippage" is not a claim limitation.

[107] Atlas Powder Co. v. IRECO Inc., 190 F.3d 1342, 51 USPQ 2d 1943, 1945–56 (Fed. Cir. 1999).

[108] *In re* Gosteli, 872 F.2d 1008, 1010, 10 USPQ 2d 1614, 1616 (Fed. Cir. 1989).

Main volume footnote updates begin on page 142.

MAIN VOLUME FOOTNOTE UPDATES

[136]**[Add the following at the end of footnote 136.]**; *see also* Cabinet Vision v. Cabnetware, Civ. App. No. 99-1050, slip op. at 13–14 (Fed. Cir. Feb. 14, 2000) (unpublished) ("More specifically, Cornwell declared during prosecution of the '207 patent that '[b]eginning in 1986, I sold a computer-based program that permitted the user to design one cabinet at a time, and then to display a series of cabinets in an elevational view on a wall. The user assembled the series of cabinets with computer assistance in the display.' Thus, the inventor admits selling a computer design program with many or all of the features of the claimed invention before the critical date of June 16, 1987.").

[178]**[Replace the existing cite with the following.]** Lough v. Brunswick Corp., 86 F.3d 1113, 39 USPQ 2d 1100 (Fed. Cir. 1996), *cert. denied,* 522 U.S. 806 (1997).

[179]**[Replace the S. Ct. cite with the following.]** 514 U.S. 1015.

[294]**[Replace the S. Ct. cite with the following.]** 514 U.S. 1015.

[298]**[Replace existing footnote 298 with the following.]** Lough v. Brunswick Corp., 86 F.3d 1113, 39 USPQ 2d 1100, 1104–05 (Fed. Cir. 1996), *cert. denied*, 522 U.S. 806 (1997).

[320]**[Replace the S. Ct. cite for Micro Chem., Inc. v. Great Plains Chem. Co. with the following.]** 521 U.S. 1122.

[328]**[Replace existing footnote 328 with the following.]** *Id.*, 48 USPQ 2d at 1041 (citing Tilghman v. Proctor, 102 U.S. (12 Otto.) 707, 711–12 (1880); Eibel Process Co. v. Minnesota & Ontario Paper Co., 261 U.S. 45, 66 (1923)).

[336]**[Replace the existing cite for Lough v. Brunswick Corp. with the following.]** Lough v. Brunswick Corp., 86 F.3d 1113, 39 USPQ 2d 1100 (Fed. Cir. 1996), *cert. denied,* 522 U.S. 806 (1997).

[338]**[Replace the S. Ct. cite with the following.]** 522 U.S. 1115.

[346]**[Replace the S. Ct. cite with the following.]** 516 U.S. 816.

[351]**[Replace the S. Ct. cite with the following.]** 516 U.S. 816.

[382]**[Replace the L. Ed. cite with the following.]** 525 U.S. 1106.

[407]**[Replace the existing cite with the following.]** Glaxo Inc. v. Novopharm Ltd., 29 USPQ 2d 1126, 1128 (E.D.N.C. 1993) (citing Stoller v. Ford Motor Co., 18 USPQ 2d 1545, 1547 (Fed. Cir. 1991) and *In re* Sovish, 769 F.2d 738, 226 USPQ 771 (Fed. Cir. 1985)), *aff'd,* 52 F.3d 1043, 34 USPQ 2d 1565 (Fed. Cir.), *cert. denied,* 516 U.S. 988 (1995).

[489]**[Replace existing footnote 489 with the following.]** R.A.C.C. Indus., Inc. v. Stun-Tech, Inc., 49 USPQ 2d 1793, 1796 (Fed. Cir. 1998) (unpublished).

7

Combating Obviousness Rejections Under 35 U.S.C. Section 103

II. Attacking Establishment of the Prima Facie Case of Obviousness

A. Element 1: References

[Insert after footnote 43.]

Admissions may also take the form of a settlement made by a patent owner accusing another party of manufacturing a device that infringes the patent. If the accused device for which the patent owner claims infringement also turns out to have been sold more than one year prior to the filing date of the patent, the patent may be held to be invalid.[1] However, a mere allegation of infringement, prior to full discovery and analysis, should be unlikely to trigger such an admission.

[Insert after footnote 45.]

The general skill in the art will rarely operate to supply missing knowledge or prior art to reach an obviousness judgment. As stated by the Federal Circuit:

> To imbue one of ordinary skill in the art with knowledge of the invention in suit, when no prior art reference or references of record convey or suggest that knowledge, is to fall victim to the insidious effect of a hindsight syndrome wherein that which only the inventor taught is used against its teacher.[2]

Skill in the art does not act as a bridge over gaps in substantive presentation of an obviousness case, but instead supplies the primary guarantee of objectivity in determining obviousness.[3] As also stated by the Federal Circuit in this connection:

[1] Vanmoor v. Wal-Mart Stores, Inc., 201 F.3d 1363, 53 USPQ 2d 1377, 1379 (Fed. Cir. 2000).

[2] W.L. Gore & Assocs. v. Garlock, Inc., 721 F.2d 1540, 1553, 220 USPQ 303, 312–13 (Fed. Cir. 1983).

[3] Ryko Mfg. Co. v. Nu-Star, Inc., 950 F.2d 714, 718, 21 USPQ 2d 1053, 1057 (Fed. Cir. 1991).

Main volume footnote updates begin on page 223.

The level of skill in the art is a prism or lens through which a judge or jury views the prior art and the claimed invention. This reference point prevents these deciders from using their own insight or, worse yet, hindsight, to gauge obviousness.[4]

B. Element 2: References Available to the Inventor

2. *Titanium Aircraft Screw Considered Analogous Prior Art to Bioabsorbable Screw [New Topic]*

In *In re Huene*,[5] the invention related to an absorbable screw bone and a tool for its insertion. The screw is used in surgery to attach bone fragments. Claim 1 of the application recited:

> A bone screw, comprising:
>
> a) a threaded shank having an axis of rotation;
>
> b) a head integral with said shank, said head including a surface disposed generally normal to said axis and said head and said shank formed from a bioabsorbable material;
>
> c) a plurality of driver means disposed about said surface wholly remote from said axis, each of said driver means adapted for engagement with a cooperating driver element of a rotary driver so that said head and thereby said shank may be rotated about said axis; and
>
> d) a threaded bore coaxial with said axis extending inwardly from said surface for threadedly engaging a cooperating threaded element of the rotary driver.[6]

The Examiner rejected the claim based on a combination of four references: U.S. Patent No. 5,275,601 to Gogolewski, which disclosed a self-locking absorbable bone screw and plate system with a threaded shaft; U.S. Patent No. 4,973,333 to Treharne, which disclosed a reabsorbable compressing screw for repairing bone fractures; U.S. Patent No. 4,466,314 to Rich, which disclosed a nonslip fastener torquing system that used threaded engagement to provide a solid base for torque applications primarily for the aerospace industry; and U.S. patent No. 4,466,315 to Boschetto, which disclosed a driving simultaneously a screw requiring a screw driver and a screw requiring a spanner wrench.

Huene argued that Rich was nonanalogous art and therefore, not combinable with the remaining prior art references. The Board rejected his argument. On appeal, the Federal Circuit affirmed the rejection.

Huene argued on appeal that Rich was nonanlogous art because it was directed to a titanium aircraft screw, whereas Gogolewski and

[4] Al-Site Corp. v. VSI Int'l, Inc., 174 F.3d 1308, 50 USPQ 2d 1161, 1171 (Fed. Cir. 1999).

[5] *In re* Huene, Civ. App. No. 99-1514 (Fed. Cir. Aug. 11, 2000) (unpublished).

[6] *Id.*, slip op. at 6.

Treharne were directed to bioabsorbable screws. According to Huene, the problem Rich sought to solve arose due to the hardness of titanium. By contrast, the problem Huene set out to solve—the failure of the bone screw to maintain proper alignment during insertion—arose as a result of the softness of the absorbable fastener material. According to Huene, nothing in Rich suggested its application to soft materials, such as an absorbable bone screw.

The Federal Circuit conceded that Rich was not in the same field of endeavor as Huene's invention. However, the Federal Circuit held that there was substantial evidence to support the Board's holding that Rich was reasonably pertinent to Huene's invention because both Rich and Huene sought to solve the same problem, i.e., the misalignment of a tool and a fastener and the camming out that can occur due to misalignment. The Federal Circuit rejected Huene's argument that the references were nonanalogous because Rich was directed to solving a problem relating to the hardness of titanium and Huene was directed to solving a problem due to the softness of the absorbable fastener. The Federal Circuit considered it significant that "neither Rich nor Huene points to the hardness or softness of the screw material as the cause of the problem he set out to solve."[7]

On this basis, the Federal Circuit affirmed the rejection of Huene's application as obvious in view of the prior art, and held that there was substantial evidence to support the Board's holding.

C. Element 3: References That Teach

[Insert after footnote 81.]

The disclosure of a reference is not limited to specific working examples disclosed therein.[8]

[Insert after footnote 84.]

However, the situations where an inherent teaching can be used in an obviousness rejection are relatively few. For example, the Federal Circuit has stated that the "inherency of an advantage and its obviousness are entirely different questions. That which may be inherent is not necessarily known. Obviousness cannot be predicated on what is unknown."[9] Similarly, the general skill in the art will rarely operate to supply missing knowledge or prior art to reach an obviousness judgment. As stated by the Federal Circuit:

---

[7] *Id.* at 17.

[8] *In re* Fracalossi, 681 F.2d 792, 794 n.1, 215 USPQ 569, 570 n.1 (C.C.P.A. 1982).

[9] *In re* Spormann, 363 F.2d 444, 150 USPQ 449, 452 (C.C.P.A. 1966). *See infra* Ch. 7, § II.E.6.a in the main volume.

Main volume footnote updates begin on page 223.

> To imbue one of ordinary skill in the art with knowledge of the invention in suit, when no prior art reference or references of record convey or suggest that knowledge, is to fall victim to the insidious effect of a hindsight syndrome wherein that which only the inventor taught is used against its teacher.[10]

Skill in the art does not act as a bridge over gaps in substantive presentation of an obviousness case, but instead supplies the primary guarantee of objectivity in determining obviousness.[11]

[Insert at the end of the section.]

1. Prior Art Interpreted Not to Teach Invention Particularly When Stated Objectives of the Prior Art Reinforced Interpretation [New Topic]

Prior art may be considered not to teach an invention and thereby fail to support an obviousness rejection, particularly when the stated objectives of the prior art reinforce such an interpretation.

For example, in *WMS Gaming Inc. v. International Game Technology*,[12] the invention, which was directed to an electronic gaming device utilizing a random number generator for selecting reel stop positions, was assigned to International Game Technology (IGT). The patent claimed a slot machine that decreased the probability of winning while maintaining the external appearance of a standard mechanical slot machine. The decreased probability of winning permitted higher payoffs, which attracted players.

At trial, WMS presented three prior art patents to support its contention of obviousness: U.S. Patent No. 4,095,795, entitled "Amusement Apparatus and Method," issued to James Saxton et al. on June 20, 1978 (the Saxton patent); U.S. Patent No. 3,918,716, entitled "Game Apparatus for Trying Coincidence between Randomly Selected Characters," issued to Hiroshi Nonaka et al. on November 11, 1975 (the Nonaka patent); and Australian Patent No. 280649, entitled "An Improved Electrically Operated Gaming Machine," issued to Albert Cohen et al. on April 6, 1967 (the Cohen patent).

WMS contended that the Saxton patent taught a reel-type slot machine under microprocessor control that uniformly mapped numbers to stop positions. WMS further contended that the Cohen and Nonaka patents taught the nonuniform mapping of numbers to stop positions (i.e., assigning a plurality of numbers to stop positions where

---

[10] W.L. Gore & Assocs. v. Garlock, Inc., 721 F.2d 1540, 1553, 220 USPQ 303, 312–13 (Fed. Cir. 1983).

[11] Ryko Mfg. Co. v. Nu-Star, Inc., 950 F.2d 714, 718, 21 USPQ 2d 1053, 1057 (Fed. Cir. 1991).

[12] WMS Gaming Inc. v. International Game Tech., 184 F.3d 1339, 51 USPQ 2d 1385 (Fed. Cir. 1999).

the plurality of numbers exceed the number of stop positions) to decrease the odds of winning. Based on these references, WMS argued that it would have been obvious to one of ordinary skill in the art to combine the nonuniform mapping of the Cohen or Nonaka patents with the reel-type slot machine of the Saxton patent to arrive at the claimed invention.

IGT contended that the Cohen and Nonaka patents taught the mapping of numbers to symbols, which merely simulated the occurrence of multiple symbols on a physical reel.

The district court agreed with IGT, and on appeal, the Federal Circuit affirmed the district court's holding. The Federal Circuit first noted with respect to interpreting the Cohen patent that, consistent with its stated objectives, the Cohen patent taught an electro-mechanical slot machine that does not use physical reels. Rather, according to the Federal Circuit, the Cohen patent employed symbol display devices to show the outcome of each actuation of the machine.[13]

In interpreting the Nonaka patent, the Federal Circuit noted that it disclosed a digital electronic slot machine, in which the results are displayed using three symbol display devices rather than reels. The Federal Circuit emphasized that the first of the listed objects of the invention in the Nonaka patent was to provide a game apparatus that eliminates the intrinsic deficiencies of the prior art mechanical machines, such as noise and wear of moving parts.

The Federal Circuit accepted the district court's finding that the Cohen and Nonaka patents merely simulate the physical reels of a standard mechanical slot machine. Thus, the Cohen and Nonaka patents were interpreted as teaching decreasing the odds of winning by increasing the range of numbers beyond the number of reel stop positions. The Federal Circuit emphasized that "[t]his conclusion is reinforced by the fact that the stated objectives of Cohen and Nonaka are to overcome the deficiencies of mechanical reels, such as noise and being susceptible to wear and tampering."[14]

Thus, in *WMS Gaming*, the prior art was interpreted not to teach the claimed invention while using the stated objectives described in the prior art to reinforce the interpretation.

2. *Proposed Combination That Creates an Inoperable Reference Teaches Away From Combination [New Topic]*

When the Examiner proposes a combination that makes a prior art reference inoperable for its intended purpose, the resulting inoperable prior art reference may be considered to teach away from the

[13] *Id.*, 51 USPQ 2d at 1397–98.

[14] *Id.* at 1400.

Main volume footnote updates begin on page 223.

proposed combination, i.e., not teach the combination, thereby supporting a showing of nonobviousness.[15]

Tec Air, Inc. v. Denso Manufacturing Michigan Inc.[16] is a case in which the invention was held to be nonobvious over the prior art because the proposed combination resulted in one of the patent references being inoperable for its intended purpose. The invention related to a method of and a device for making properly balanced, injected-molded fans. The invention inserted adjustable screws into hollowed-out sections of the mold insert that was used to form the fan hub. These screws were accessible from the front or cavity side of the mold.

Tec Air sued Denso for infringement because it manufactured radiator and condenser assemblies that included fans balanced according to the claimed method. Denso argued that the invention would have been obvious based on a combination of prior art references. The district court determined that Denso failed to establish a prima facie case of obviousness for lack of a suggestion to combine the cited references.

On appeal, the Federal Circuit affirmed the holding of nonobviousness. Denso argued that the court should have granted its motion for judgment as a matter of law because the invention of the claims would have been obvious over U.S. Patent No. 3,136,001 (the Gelbard patent) in combination with a prior art brass plug method. The Gelbard patent taught using adjustable screws to create balance lugs on the blade tips of a molded fan. Unlike the screws of Tec Air's patent, these screws were accessible from the rear of the mold. Because in the brass plug method the operator drilled the brass plugs from the cavity side of the mold, Denso argued that combining this method with the teachings of the Gelbard patent resulted in cavity-side accessible screws.

The Federal Circuit rejected this argument because the proposed modification to the Gelbard patent would make it inoperable for its intended purpose. According to the Federal Circuit:

> The Gelbard patent teaches, however, that each of its adjustable threaded members has "a non-threaded or smooth tip extending into a recess," which comes into contact with the molten plastic. Because the brass plugs-Gelbard patent combination would be inoperable for its intended purpose—no screw driver would be able to turn the smooth-headed screws from the cavity-side of the mold—the jury reasonably could have found that the Gelbard patent taught away from its combination with the brass plug method.[17]

---

[15] *In re* Gordon, 733 F.2d 900, 902, 221 USPQ 1125, 1127 (Fed. Cir. 1984) (finding no suggestion to modify a prior art device where the modification would render the device inoperable for its intended purpose).

[16] Tec Air, Inc. v. Denso Mfg. Mich. Inc., 192 F.3d 1353, 52 USPQ 2d 1294 (Fed. Cir. 1999).

[17] *Id.*, 52 USPQ 2d at 1298.

Main volume footnote updates begin on page 223.

D. Element 4: Suggestion to Combine or Modify the References

[Insert after footnote 91.]

In this connection, the Federal Circuit has indicated that the analysis begins with the phrase "at the time the invention was made."[18] It is this phrase that guards against entry into the "tempting but forbidden zone of hindsight"[19] when analyzing the patentability of claims pursuant to that section. "Measuring a claimed invention against the standard established by section 103 requires the oft-difficult but critical step of casting the mind back to the time of invention, to consider the thinking of one of ordinary skill in the art, guided only by the prior art references and the then-accepted wisdom in the field."[20] Close adherence to this methodology is especially important in the case of less technologically complex inventions, where the very ease with which the invention can be understood may prompt one "to fall victim to the insidious effect of a hindsight syndrome wherein that which only the inventor taught is used against its teacher."[21]

Federal Circuit case law makes clear that the best defense against the subtle but powerful attraction of a hindsight-based obviousness analysis is rigorous application of the requirement for a showing of the teaching or motivation to combine prior art references.[22] A general relationship between fields of the prior art patents to be combined is insufficient to establish the suggestion or motivation.[23]

[Insert after footnote 105]

Evidence of a suggestion, teaching, or motivation to combine may flow from the prior art references themselves, the knowledge of one of ordinary skill in the art, or, in some cases, the nature of the problem to be solved.[24] However, "the suggestion more often comes from the

---

[18] *In re* Dembiczak, 175 F.3d 994, 50 USPQ 2d 1614, 1616 (Fed. Cir. 1999).

[19] Loctite Corp. v. Ultraseal Ltd., 781 F.2d 861, 873, 228 USPQ 90, 98 (Fed. Cir. 1985), *overruled on other grounds by* Nobelpharma AB v. Implant Innovations, Inc., 141 F.3d 1059, 46 USPQ 2d 1097 (Fed. Cir.), *cert. denied*, 525 U.S. 876 (1998).

[20] *In re* Dembiczak, 175 F.3d 994, 50 USPQ 2d 1614, 1617 (Fed. Cir. 1999) (citing W.L. Gore & Assocs. v. Garlock, Inc., 721 F.2d 1540, 1553, 220 USPQ 303, 313 (Fed. Cir. 1983)).

[21] *Id.*

[22] *See, e.g.*, C.R. Bard, Inc. v. M3 Sys., Inc., 157 F.3d 1340, 1352, 48 USPQ 2d 1225, 1232 (Fed. Cir. 1998) (describing "teaching or suggestion or motivation [to combine]" as an "essential evidentiary component of an obviousness holding"); *In re* Rouffet, 149 F.3d 1350, 1359, 47 USPQ 2d 1453, 1459 (Fed. Cir. 1998) ("the Board must identify specifically . . . the reasons one of ordinary skill in the art would have been motivated to select the references and combine them").

[23] Interactive Techs., Inc. v. Pittway Corp., Civ. App. No. 98-1464, slip op. at 13 (Fed. Cir. June 1, 1999) (unpublished), *cert. denied*, 528 U.S. 1046 (1999).

[24] Pro-Mold & Tool Co. v. Great Lakes Plastics, Inc., 75 F.3d 1568, 1573, 37 USPQ 2d 1626, 1630 (Fed. Cir. 1996); Para-Ordnance Mfg. v. SGS Imports Int'l, Inc., 73 F.3d 1085, 1088, 37 USPQ 2d 1237, 1240 (Fed. Cir. 1995).

Main volume footnote updates begin on page 223.

teachings of the pertinent references."[25] The range of sources available, however, does not diminish the requirement for actual evidence. That is, the showing must be clear and particular.[26] Broad conclusory statements regarding the teaching of multiple references, standing alone, are not "evidence."[27] In addition to demonstrating the propriety of an obviousness analysis, particular factual findings regarding the suggestion, teaching, or motivation to combine serve a number of important purposes, including: (1) clear explication of the position adopted by the Examiner and the Board; (2) identification of the factual disputes, if any, between the applicant and the Board; and (3) facilitation of review on appeal.[28]

[Insert prior to the sentence containing footnote 108.]

A general relationship between the fields of the prior art references to be combined is insufficient to suggest the motivation.[29]

1. *"Trend" May Provide Suggestion or Motivation for Minor Changes*

[Insert after footnote 113.]

In re Gartside[30] is an example of a case in which the trend in the art provides the necessary motivation to combine two prior art references. The invention related to cracking processes, i.e., processes that generate low molecular weight, purified hydrocarbons of desired molecular composition by breaking down impure, high molecular weight hydrocarbon feed oil. Cracking is accomplished by reacting impure feed oil with solids or particulate matter that induces the breakdown of feed oil by either a thermal or catalytic reaction mechanism. The claims at issue were directed to catalytic cracking processes.

---

[25] *In re* Rouffet, 149 F.3d 1350, 1355, 47 USPQ 2d 1453, 1456 (Fed. Cir. 1998).

[26] *See, e.g.*, C.R. Bard, Inc. v. M3 Sys., Inc., 157 F.3d 1340, 1352, 48 USPQ 2d 1225, 1232 (Fed. Cir. 1998).

[27] McElmurry v. Arkansas Power & Light Co., 995 F.2d 1576, 1578, 27 USPQ 2d 1129, 1131 (Fed. Cir. 1993) ("Mere denials and conclusory statements, however, are not sufficient to establish a genuine issue of material fact."); *In re* Sichert, 566 F.2d 1154, 1164, 196 USPQ 209, 217 (C.C.P.A. 1977) ("The examiner's conclusory statement that the specification does not teach the best mode of using the invention is unaccompanied by evidence or reasoning and is entirely inadequate to support the rejection.").

[28] *In re* Dembiczak, 175 F.3d 994, 50 USPQ 2d 1614, 1617 (Fed. Cir. 1999).

[29] Interactive Techs. Inc. v. Pittway Corp., Civ. App. No. 98-1464, slip op. at 13 (Fed. Cir. June 1, 1999) (unpublished), *cert. denied*, 528 U.S. 1046 ("The sole evidence proffered of a motivation to combine was that several prior art patents mentioned there being a similarity between garage door openers and home security systems. However, such limited evidence of there being a general relationship between the fields does not suggest a motivation to combine the particular references here relied upon.").

[30] *In re* Gartside, 203 F.3d 1305, 53 USPQ 2d 1769 (Fed. Cir. 2000).

Main volume footnote updates begin on page 223.

Independent claim 41 was representative and recited:

> 41. A catalytic process, comprising the steps of:
>
> (a) delivering hot particulate catalytic cracking solids to a catalytic cracking reactor;
>
> (b) delivering a hydrocarbon feed to said reactors;
>
> (c) cracking said hydrocarbon feed in said reactor at a temperature of from 1100 to 1500 degrees F to produce a cracked product;
>
> (d) separating said catalytic solids from the cracked product;
>
> (e) Equenching said cracked product;
>
> wherein the total residence time from step (a) through step (e) ranges from 0.1 to 0.6 seconds.[31]

The Board held the claims unpatentable as obvious over a combination of references including Gartside's U.S. Patent 4,552,645, Gartside's U.S. Patent 4,288,235, and U.S. Patent 4,419,221 to Castagnos under Section 103. Gartside's U.S. Patent 4,552,645 disclosed a process of thermally cracking feed oil. Gartside's U.S. Patent 4,288,235 disclosed an apparatus used for both thermal and catalytic processes employing low residence times and quenching to prevent undesired cracking. Castagnos disclosed the precise kinetic residence time recited in the claim. The Board found that the motivation to combine the thermal cracking teachings with a catalytic cracking process with the precise kinetic residence time arose from the nature of the problem to be solved, i.e., undesired cracking due to the presence of thermal or catalytic solids and optimizing yields by avoiding undesired cracking.

On appeal, the Federal Circuit affirmed. Gartside argued that the Board erred in its holding that the claims were unpatentable under 35 U.S.C. Section 103 because there was no teaching or suggestion to use a 0.1 to 0.6 second kinetic residence time in a catalytic cracking process. The Commissioner (new title is Director) responded that the Board correctly held that the claims were unpatentable, arguing that the motivation to combine the references arose from the references themselves, as well as the nature of the problem to be solved, i.e., maximizing reaction conditions in cracking processes by minimizing residence time.

The Federal Circuit agreed with the Commissioner that substantial evidence supported the Board's finding that a motivation to combine the prior art patents arose from the teachings of the references themselves and the nature of the problem to be solved. As the Board found, use of low residence times to arrest undesired cracking was part of a "trend in the art towards short residence times." The Federal Circuit reasoned that in view of this trend, one of ordinary skill who was attempting to minimize undesired cracking reactions would have been directed by the two Gartside patents to utilize the Castagnos patent, which described low residence time catalytic reactions and

[31] *Id.*, 53 USPQ 2d at 1770.

which disclosed the precise residence time in the disputed claims. Accordingly, the Federal Circuit concluded that substantial evidence supported the Board's finding that a motivation existed to combine the patents, and therefore, held the invention to be unpatentable.

3. Selected Decisions

c. Simple Invention Not Obvious Where Prior Art Elements Are From Unrelated / Nonanalogous Fields

[Insert after footnote 125.]

Similarly, in *Carlisle Plastics, Inc. v. Spotless Enterprises, Inc.*,[32] the Federal Circuit stated the following:

> We agree with the district court that the commercial success of the embodiment of the invention and the failure of anyone (including Carlisle's predecessor) to combine the prior art elements before the inventor did so provide significant support for the conclusion that the invention was not obvious, notwithstanding that combining the elements in the prior art would seem, with the considerable benefit of hindsight, to be fairly elementary.[33]

[Insert the following new subsections.]

g. Invention Obvious Where Problem Being Addressed Provided Motivation [New Topic]

In what should be rare circumstances, the motivation to combine or modify the prior art to arrive at the invention may be based on the actual problem the inventor was seeking to solve. The reason why this situation should be relatively rare is that, in general, identification of the problem in the prior art is a factor that may show nonobviousness. For example, the CCPA has emphasized:

> It should not be necessary for this court to point out that a patentable invention may lie in the discovery of the source of a problem even though the remedy may be obvious once the source of the problem is identified. This is part of the "subject matter as a whole" which should always be considered in determining the obviousness of an invention under 35 U.S.C. 103.[34]

Thus, for the motivation to emanate from the problem in the prior art, the problem itself must also be known to one of ordinary skill in

---

[32] Carlisle Plastics, Inc. v. Spotless Enters., Inc., Civ. App. 98-1170 (Fed. Cir. Jan. 26, 1999) (unpublished).

[33] *Id.*, slip op. at 4.

[34] *In re* Nomiya, 509 F.2d 566, 184 USPQ 607, 612 (C.C.P.A. 1975) (quoting *In re* Sponnoble, 405 F.2d 578, 585, 160 USPQ 237, 243 (C.C.P.A. 1969)). *See supra* Ch. 7, § II.E.3 in the main volume.

Main volume footnote updates begin on page 223.

a manner that suggests or motivates the modification needed to arrive at the invention.

In *In re Greene*,[35] the Federal Circuit found an invention obvious where the motivation to modify the prior art came from the problem requiring solution. The patent related to an improved telephone directory wherein the telephone number identified the actual geographic location of the telephone and at the same time served as an individual's or organization's postal address. The Examiner rejected all of Greene's pending claims as obvious over a prior patent, U.S. Patent No. 4,757,267 to Riskin (Riskin), and the Board affirmed the rejection. The Riskin patent described a system for re-routing calls placed to a central number to a dealership or supplier located near the caller. For example, a call to 1-800-FLOWERS would be routed to a participating florist close to the caller. Riskin identified a caller's location using the National Plan Area (NPA), also known as the "area code" and the Central Office Code, or "exchange" (NNX).

The NPA-NNX corresponds to a telephone subscriber's location by way of a "V-H" file provided by a telephone company. The V-H system is a complex transformation of latitude and longitude used by telephone companies to calculate the distance between a caller and the location called, for billing purposes. A particular NPA-NNX combination corresponds to a particular V-H geographic coordinate, which is the location of the telephone company central office.

Greene argued that the Board committed a legal error in concluding that the claims at issue would have been obvious to a person of ordinary skill in the art at the time of the application filing date. According to Greene, Riskin was directed to a different problem. The Federal Circuit rejected this argument and held the following:

> The need for adaptation of the reference, however, does not defeat obviousness, unless the adaptation is outside the skill or knowledge of one skilled in the art. Here, decreasing the granularity to produce a more exact location is an adaptation that is clearly within the skill or knowledge of one skilled in the art. The missing element, prior to the Greene application, was the desire to identify the postal address via phone number. . . . Here Greene's proposed system was aimed at reducing the size of telephone directories, by removing the address line from the book. Greene's desire to reduce the directory size provided the motivation to decrease the granularity of the Riskin system. Thus, the very problem he was addressing provided the motivation to adapt Riskin.[36]

For these reasons, the Federal Circuit held that the Board's conclusion that Riskin did teach using a phone number to identify the location of a caller was based on substantial evidence, and therefore,

[35] *In re* Greene, Civ. App. No. 99-1317 (Fed. Cir. Dec. 6, 1999) (unpublished).

[36] *Id.*, slip op. at 10–11.

Main volume footnote updates begin on page 223.

the Patent Office met its burden of establishing a prima facie case of obviousness for the claims.[37]

h. Invention Obvious Where Motivation Arises From Gains in Convenience [New Topic]

In *In re Oggero*[38] the motivation to combine the prior art was based on the need or gains in convenience resulting from the combination in a crowded field of development. The invention related to an integral transparent disposable toothbrush and gel dispenser. The Board rejected the claims as obvious in view of the teachings of one or more of six patents in the prior art.

Oggero contended that the unitary integral container with an integrally formed brush head limitation imparted nonobviousness because, in addition to its unique shape, the invention mechanically pushed toothpaste up into the bristles when a dial was turned and a long screw rotated, moving a piston the length of the body. The Board, however, found that the disclosures in an O'Neal patent and an Italian patent teach an integral brush head and handle. In response to the mechanical means of urging gel from the container also stated in the claim, the Board noted that a person of ordinary skill in the art would have been taught from the disclosures of the cited prior art that the toothpaste could be discharged by a squeezable container or by the piston/screw arrangement disclosed in a British patent.

Oggero also argued that the transparency aspect further imparted nonobviousness. The Board however, disagreed and noted that the Italian patent disclosed the claimed subject matter but did not disclose a transparent housing or an integral brush head. According to the Board, the British patent taught a transparent housing for a toothbrush, and the O'Neal patent taught an integral brush head.

On appeal, the Federal Circuit affirmed the rejection of nonobviousness. The Federal Circuit reasoned as follows:

> We hold that in the crowded art of toothbrushes, no explicit suggestion in the references themselves is needed to combine their teachings, particularly as nothing in the prior art teaches away from this combination. The motivation to combine the named teachings of each of these three patents arises from the apparent gains in convenience, such as an integral brush head, which allows the user to urge toothpaste or gel

---

[37]*But see id.*, citing Motorola, Inc. v. Interdigital Tech. Corp., 121 F.3d 1461, 1472, 43 USPQ 2d 1481, 1489 (Fed. Cir. 1997):

> The information provided in Riskin about the V-H system, however, certainly does suggest that steps could be saved by using the latitude and longitude information directly rather than taking the extra steps of translating the information first to V-H and then to NPA-NNX. Cost and simplicity improvements are both factors that inherently motivate modification or combination of prior art references.

[38]*In re* Oggero, Civ. App. No. 99-1116 (Fed. Cir. Aug. 10, 1999) (unpublished).

Main volume footnote updates begin on page 223.

through the brush head, and transparency, which allows the user to see the amount of gel left in the container. . . . Therefore, an invention including an integral brush head and a transparency limitation would have been obvious in view of the combined teachings of the British, Italian, and O'Neal Patents.[39]

The Federal Circuit summarized the holding as follows:

> In short, despite individual and collective consideration of five limitations that the applicant asserts impart patentability, the toothbrush as claimed in all six claims was correctly held obvious in view of the various teachings of the six cited prior art patents, for which motivation to combine was found established by the nature of the problem the inventor addressed, the need for a "unitary integral transparent disposable toothbrush and gel container" and which finding, we hold, was not clearly erroneous.[40]

i. Invention Not Obvious Where One Prior Art Reference Taught Away From Combination With Second Prior Art Reference [New Topic]

An invention was held not obvious where one prior art reference taught away from the combination with a second prior art reference. In *In re Rudko*,[41] the invention related to a handpiece for a laser surgical scalpel adapted for use in a surgical procedure known as transmyocardial revascularization (TMR), in which a patient's heart was lased to form a number of small holes. These holes heal on the outside surface of the heart but remain open inside the heart, thus increasing the blood flow to the patient's heart tissue.

Prior art laser surgical scalpels terminated in a sharp tip and were therefore not well suited for TMR because they created increased pressure on the heart surface, possibly leading to arrhythmia or even puncture of the heart wall. Moreover, it is difficult to maintain the sharp-tipped prior art devices perpendicular to a patient's beating heart during the TMR procedure. Accordingly, two objects of Rudko's invention were to provide a handpiece with an increased contact surface area that reduced pressure at the area of contact and that more readily maintained perpendicularity with the heart tissue.

The Examiner rejected certain claims as obvious under Section 103(a) over a primary reference, U.S. Patent No. 3,865,113 to Sharon et al., entitled "Laser Device Particularly Useful as Surgical Scalpel" (Sharon patent), in view of a secondary reference, U.S. Patent No. 1,562,460 to McFee entitled "Fulgurator" (McFee). Sharon gener-

---

[39] *Id.*, slip op. at 3–4 (citing *In re* Edwards, 440 F.2d 1380, 1383, 169 USPQ 480, 483 (C.C.P.A. 1971)).

[40] *Id.* at 5.

[41] *In re* Rudko, Civ. App. No. 98-1505 (Fed. Cir. May 14, 1999) (unpublished).

Main volume footnote updates begin on page 223.

ally described a laser scalpel that allowed a surgeon to see a working area more easily and to focus the laser thereon. McFee disclosed a device for treating certain body tissues that were difficult to access with a high-frequency electrical discharge. McFee further showed a tubular glass protector that surrounded the electrode and isolated the tissue to be treated from tissue that was not to be treated.

McFee's first embodiment disclosed a tapered protector that was relatively narrow at its tip, used for treating a small localized area. A second embodiment of McFee, in contrast, disclosed a flared protector that allowed a larger surface area to be treated. The Board sustained the rejections based on the combination of Sharon and McFee.

On appeal, the Federal Circuit reversed. Rudko contended that the Board clearly erred in combining the Sharon and McFee references. Rudko argued that it was improper to combine Sharon with McFee because Sharon taught away from the flared end shown in McFee's second embodiment. The Board justified combining Sharon and McFee based on McFee's teaching that the flared end facilitated proper positioning between the electrode and the tissue to be treated, and acted as a barrier to exclude other tissue that was not to be treated. The Board found that one of ordinary skill in the art would have recognized that these teachings were applicable to Sharon's laser scalpel.

The Federal Circuit agreed with Rudko, noting that using the cited references alone, one of ordinary skill in the art would not have been motivated to combine the flared, enlarged end disclosed in McFee with Sharon's tapered laser scalpel. The Federal Circuit emphasized that Sharon taught away from the proposed combination with McFee. According to the Federal Circuit, Sharon disclosed that previous laser surgical scalpels were difficult to manipulate and aim precisely, and Sharon's invention addressed this problem by providing the surgeon with a clear unobstructed view of the working spot where the laser beam was focused by tapering the laser scalpel tip into a relatively small point. Sharon also disclosed that this feature could be achieved by removing a portion of the laser device tip. McFee's second embodiment, on the other hand, showed a flaring end that was significantly larger in diameter at the terminating end, rather than smaller as in Sharon.

In reversing the holding of obviousness, the Federal Circuit reasoned that "[s]uch an enlarged end [of McFee] runs counter to Sharon's explicit recital of an unobstructed field of view and an easily manipulable and precisely aimed device. Accordingly, the Board's combination of Sharon with McFee to reject the disputed claims was clear error."[42]

---

[42] *Id.*, slip op. at 6 (implementing standard of review prior to *In re* Zurko, 527 U.S. 150, 50 USPQ 2d 1930 (1999) (substantial evidence standard)). *See* Ch. 2, § XIV for additional discussion.

Main volume footnote updates begin on page 223.

j. Motivation to Combine Requires Desirability Not Merely Trade Off [New Topic]

Trade-offs often concern what is feasible, not what is necessarily desirable. Motivation to combine requires the latter. *Winner International Royalty Corp. v. Wang*,[43] is an example of a case in which a trade-off alone was insufficient to provide the motivation to combine. The invention related to the original steering wheel anti-theft device known as "The Club." The invention provided an automobile anti-theft device that was mounted across the steering wheel and was locked in place by use of a self-locking ratcheting mechanism. When locked in place, theft was prevented by blocking the steering wheel from turning. Wang also manufactured similar anti-theft devices in Taiwan and exported them to the United States where they were sold through a United States distributor. Wang's device was known commercially as "The Gorilla Grip."

Wang alleged that four prior art references rendered the invention of the patent obvious. These references were: U.S. Patent No. 4,738,127 (Johnson); U.S. Patent No. 3,462,982 (Moore); Taiwan-Patent App. No. 74,210,699 (WuROC); and French Patent App. No. 2,566,398 (Grimaldi). Winner also introduced evidence of the commercial success of its Super Club line of products. Like the device disclosed in Winner's patent, the mechanism of Johnson immobilized the steering wheel when the user inserted it within the steering wheel, telescoping its arms outward so that hooks on the end of the arms engaged the steering wheel, and then locked the arms in place. Unlike the Winner patent, which disclosed a self-locking ratcheting mechanism, Johnson used a dead-bolt to lock the device in place, which required the user to turn a key after putting the device on the wheel. Moore disclosed a steering wheel lock that unfolded into a "Y" shape and utilized a self-locking ratcheting mechanism that did not require a key. WuROC disclosed a wheel and brake pedal locking device with a versatile locking core that could accommodate either a dead-bolt or a self-locking ratcheting mechanism, but it did not disclose either of these locking mechanisms. Grimaldi disclosed a two-piece mechanism for locking a clutch or brake pedal to the floorboard or firewall of a car and its figures appeared to show a rod and pawl mechanism that locked it into place.

The Board held that there was sufficient proof of motivation to combine the four prior art references. The Board found that one skilled in the art: (1) would have considered Johnson's dead-bolt-type locking device to be disadvantageous compared to the Moore and WuROC devices to the extent that Johnson required a key for setting in position

[43] Winner Int'l Royalty Corp. v. Wang, 202 F.3d 1340, 53 USPQ 2d 1580 (Fed. Cir.), *cert. denied*, 530 U.S. 1238 (2000).

Main volume footnote updates begin on page 223.

and adjusting the device; and (2) would have been motivated to make Johnson easier to use, albeit less secure, by replacing the dead-bolt mechanism of Johnson with a suitable self-locking ratcheting mechanism. The district court found that these factual findings were clearly erroneous and held that adequate motivation to combine the references was not shown.

On appeal, the Federal Circuit affirmed. The Federal Circuit noted that the arguments of both parties on appeal focused on whether one of ordinary skill would have been motivated to combine the four references. The key references at issue were Johnson, which disclosed virtually all aspects of the invention claimed in the Winner patent except ratcheting, and Moore, which disclosed a self-locking ratcheting mechanism. The Federal Circuit explained that if there was no motivation or suggestion to combine Johnson with the ratcheting mechanism of Moore, one of ordinary skill in the art would not have viewed the invention of the Winner patent as obvious.

The Federal Circuit noted that the district court found that there was no motivation to combine Johnson with the ratcheting mechanism of Moore because: (1) there was no apparent disadvantage to the dead-bolt mechanism of Johnson, and therefore the motivation to combine would not stem from the "nature of the problem" facing one of ordinary skill in the art, because no "problem" was perceived; and (2) Johnson's written description taught away from the use of Moore. The Federal Circuit concluded that the district court did not clearly err in finding that one of ordinary skill in the art would not have reasonably elected trading the benefit of security for that of convenience. According to the Federal Circuit, "[t]rade-offs often concern what is feasible, not what is, on balance, desirable. Motivation to combine requires the latter."[44] In addition, the "fact that the motivating benefit comes at the expense of another benefit, however, should not nullify its use as a basis to modify the disclosure of one reference with the teachings of another. Instead, the benefits, both lost and gained, should be weighed against one another."[45]

Thus, the district court correctly concluded that there was no motivation to combine prior art automotive anti-theft device that used a dead-bolt lock with the prior art ratcheting mechanism to create an anti-theft device that employed a ratcheting mechanism to lock the device to the car's steering wheel. This was based on the fact that one of ordinary skill in the art would not have reasonably elected to trade the security of a dead-bolt lock for the convenience of a ratcheting mechanism, and thus was not shown to be combinable with such a mechanism.

---

[44] *Id.*, 53 USPQ 2d at 1587.

[45] *Id.* at 1587 n.8.

Main volume footnote updates begin on page 223.

k. No Suggestion to Modify Prior Art That One Sensor May Be Used to Control a Plurality of Valves [New Topic]

In *In re Kotzab*,[46] the invention involved an injection molding method for forming plastic articles. The temperature of the mold must be controlled so that the plastic can harden uniformly throughout the mold. Kotzab was confronted with the problem of providing optimal temperature control for an injection molding method to ensure the quality of the final product on the one hand, and achieving optimally short molding cycle times on the other hand. The Board held that the invention was not patentable because it would have been obvious for one of ordinary skill in the art to utilize only one temperature measurement to control the coolant pulses in light of the prior art Evans disclosure. Kotzab appealed.

On appeal, the Federal Circuit reversed. The Court noted that:

> A critical step in analyzing the patentability of claims pursuant to section 103(a) is casting the mind back to the time of invention, to consider the thinking of one of ordinary skill in the art, guided only by the prior art references and the then-accepted wisdom in the field. . . . Close adherence to this methodology is especially important in cases where the very ease with which the invention can be understood may prompt one "to fall victim to the insidious effect of a hindsight syndrome wherein that which only the invention taught is used against its teacher."[47]

Kotzab argued that the Board erred in holding the claims unpatentable under 35 U.S.C. Section 103(a) over Evans, or Evans in view of secondary references, because Evans did not teach or suggest the use of a single temperature sensor to control a plurality of flow control valves. The Federal Circuit agreed.

The Federal Circuit did not take issue with the argument that Evans suggested the concept of using the historic temperature obtained by one temperature measurement to control coolant pulses. However, the Federal Circuit reasoned, there was no substantial evidence of record to extrapolate this teaching to the multiple zone system described later in Evans. At most, the combined teachings suggested that the historic temperature of a mold zone may be measured by one sensor, and as part of a multiple zone system where multiple valves are controlled, that one sensor measurement could be used to control the valve for that zone. Thus, the Federal Circuit could not say that there was relevant evidence a reasonable mind might accept as adequate to support the conclusion that where there are a plurality of con-

[46] *In re* Kotzab, 217 F.3d 1365, 55 USPQ 2d 1313 (Fed. Cir. 2000).

[47] *Id.*, 55 USPQ 2d at 1316 (quoting *In re* Dembiczak, 175 F.3d 994, 999, 50 USPQ 2d 1614, 1617 (Fed. Cir. 1999)).

Main volume footnote updates begin on page 223.

trol valves in a multiple zone setting, only one temperature sensor provides the control for a plurality of valves.

On this basis, the Federal Circuit concluded that there was no substantial evidence to support the Board's finding of fact that Evans expressly taught that "one sensor" may be used to control a plurality of valves, and there was no substantial evidence of record, either expressly or implicitly, to modify the teachings of Evans to obtain a system in which one sensor controlled a plurality of valves.[48] The Federal Circuit then concluded:

> In this case, the Examiner and the Board fell into the hindsight trap. The idea of a single sensor controlling multiple valves, as opposed to multiple sensors controlling multiple valves, is a technologically simple concept. With this simple concept in mind, the Patent and Trademark Office found prior art statements that in the abstract appeared to suggest the claimed limitation. But, there was no finding as to the specific understanding or principle within the knowledge of a skilled artisan that would have motivated one with no knowledge of Kotzab's invention to make the combination in the manner claimed.[49]

E. Element 5: Combination or Modification Obvious to One of Ordinary Skill

[Insert after footnote 147.]

It is important to note that there must a reasonable expectation of success regarding the proposed combination.[50] However, there is no requirement that the proposed combination in the prior art have absolute predictability of success.[51]

2. *Determining Level of Ordinary Skill*

[Insert after footnote 175.]

The hypothetical person of ordinary skill is not defined as one who is deemed to be aware of all relevant prior art or literature.[52] Rather, the hypothetical person of ordinary skill is defined by con-

---

[48] *Id.* at 1318.

[49] *Id.*

[50] Brown & Williamson Tobacco Corp. v. Philip Morris Inc., 229 F.3d 1120, 56 USPQ 2d 1456, 1459 (Fed. Cir. 2000).

[51] *In re* O'Farrell, 853 F.2d 894, 903–904, 7 USPQ 2d 1673, 1681 (Fed. Cir. 1988); *In re* Longi, 759 F.2d 887, 897, 225 USPQ 645, 651–52 (Fed. Cir. 1985).

[52] Helifix Ltd. v. Blok-Lok, Ltd., 208 F.3d 1339, 54 USPQ 2d 1299, 1304 (Fed. Cir. 2000).

sidering the educational level of the inventor; the types of problems encountered in the art; the prior art solutions to those problems; the rapidity with which innovations are made; the sophistication of the technology; and the educational level of workers in the field.[53] Once the person of ordinary skill has been defined, then a determination may be made as to whether that person of ordinary skill would have been familiar with the relevant literature, if such a consideration is appropriate when attempting to define the patent claims or the prior art.

[Insert new heading at the beginning of the paragraph containing footnote 188.]

iv. Examples of Level of Ordinary Skill [New Topic]

[Insert after footnote 197.]

In *WMS Gaming Inc. v. International Game Technology*,[54] the invention was directed to an electronic gaming device utilizing a random number generator for selecting the reel stop positions, and assigned to International Game Technology (IGT). The patent claimed a slot machine that decreased the probability of winning while maintaining the external appearance of a standard mechanical slot machine. The decreased probability of winning permitted higher payoffs, which attracted players.

In *WMS Gaming*, the parties stipulated to the level of ordinary skill in the art at the time the invention was conceived. According to the stipulation, the person of ordinary skill completed at least several college-level courses in computer science or electrical engineering, would have been employed for several years in the field of engineering, developing and designing gaming devices, and would have had some knowledge of probability theory, random numbers, and computer programming.[55]

v. Independent Development Occurring After Date of Patented Invention Not a Factor in Determining Level of Ordinary Skill [New Topic]

Simultaneous development "may or may not be indicative of obviousness."[56] Evidence of contemporaneous development that occurs after the

[53] Custom Accessories, Inc. v. Jeffrey-Allan Indus., Inc., 807 F.2d 955, 962, 1 USPQ 2d 1196, 1201 (Fed. Cir. 1986).

[54] WMS Gaming Inc. v. International Game Tech., 184 F.3d 1339, 51 USPQ 2d 1385 (Fed. Cir. 1999).

[55] *Id.*, 51 USPQ 2d at 1398–99.

[56] Lindemann Maschinenfabrik GMBH v. American Hoist & Derrick Co., 730 F.2d 1452, 1460, 221 USPQ 487 (Fed. Cir. 1984).

Main volume footnote updates begin on page 223.

date of the patented invention will almost never be probative of the ultimate conclusion of obviousness.[57]

For example, in *Ransomes, Inc. v. Great Dane Power Equipment, Inc.*,[58] Ransome owned a patent related to a lawn mower control device. The patent generally described lawn mower controls consisting of two or more control levers, which were coupled to the drive means so that a forward pushing movement applied by the operator resulted in forward movement of the mower, and, when the mower was in reverse gear, a pulling force caused reverse driving of the mower. Ransomes filed suit against Great Dane, alleging that its mowers infringed the patent. Great Dane admitted that the mowers infringed the patent, but counter-claimed that the patent was invalid based on obviousness.

On appeal, Ransomes argued that the district court erred when it relied on evidence of independent development of lawn mower controls containing all of the elements of the claim. Before the district court, Great Dane submitted evidence that a third party, Rich, developed this mower control by 1994, about one year after the filing date of the Ransomes patent. The district court held that this independent development "strengthened" the conclusion that the asserted claim in the patent was obvious, because it "was probative of the knowledge of one skilled in the art."[59]

The Federal Circuit, however, disagreed. The Federal Circuit did not consider the submitted evidence as probative of the knowledge of one skilled in the art because Rich's alleged independent development was simply too late to be probative of whether the invention would have been obvious at the time the invention was made. Put another way, Rich's alleged development of the mower controls approximately one year after the filing date of the patent did not demonstrate that Rich would have known to select and combine the relevant prior art at the time the claimed invention was made, about one year earlier.[60]

The Federal Circuit noted that although some cases have said that simultaneous development might be indicative of obviousness, evidence of development that occurs after the date of the patented in-

---

[57]*See* Hybritech Inc. v. Monoclonal Antibodies, Inc., 802 F.2d 1367, 1380 n. 4, 231 USPQ 81, 91 n. 4 (Fed. Cir. 1986) (contemporaneous development more than a year after the filing date of patent is "of little probative value"); *Lindemann*, 730 F.2d at 1461, 221 USPQ at 487 (independent development more than five years after the invention was made is not relevant to obviousness determination). *See also* Environmental Designs, Ltd. v. Union Oil Co. of Cal., 713 F.2d 693, 698 n. 7, 218 USPQ 865, 869 n. 7 (Fed. Cir. 1983) ("the virtually simultaneous making of the same invention does not in itself preclude patentability of that invention.").

[58]Ransomes, Inc. v. Great Dane Power Equip., Inc., Civ. App. No. 98-1504, (Fed. Cir. Apr. 4, 2000) (unpublished).

[59]*Id.*, slip op. at 7.

[60]*Id.*

Main volume footnote updates begin on page 223.

vention will almost never be probative of the ultimate conclusion of obviousness. For this reason, the district court's reliance on the evidence that Rich developed his mower controls using the same prior art as confronted the inventor of the patent when he invented his control mechanism was an error.

III. Rebutting the Prima Facie Case of Obviousness

A. Rebutting Prima Facie Obviousness With Evidence

[Insert prior to the paragraph containing footnote 238.]

This objective evidence of nonobviousness, typically called secondary considerations, is also an essential component of the obviousness determination.[61] This objective evidence of nonobviousness includes copying, long-felt but unsolved need, failure of others,[62] commercial success,[63] unexpected results created by the claimed invention, unexpected properties of the claimed invention,[64] licenses showing industry respect for the invention,[65] and skepticism of skilled artisans before the invention.[66] In addition, secondary considerations may include success of a potentially infringing product, i.e., a product manufactured by a third party.[67]

B. Preparing Persuasive Affidavit Evidence

2. *Affidavit Used to Explain Secondary Considerations*

[Delete the paragraph following footnote 286 and replace with the following.]

Tec Air, Inc. v. Denso Manufacturing Michigan Inc.[68] involved a patentee that successfully presented evidence of commercial success

---

[61]*In re* Emert, 124 F.3d 1458, 1462, 44 USPQ 2d 1149, 1153 (Fed. Cir. 1997) ("Without Emert providing rebuttal evidence, this prima facie case of obviousness must stand.").

[62]*See* Graham v. John Deere Co., 383 U.S. 1, 17–18, 148 USPQ 459, 467 (1966).

[63]*In re* Huang, 100 F.3d 135, 139–40, 40 USPQ 2d 1685, 1689–90 (Fed. Cir. 1996).

[64]*In re* Mayne, 104 F.3d 1339, 1342, 41 USPQ 2d 1451, 1454 (Fed. Cir. 1997); *In re* Woodruff, 919 F.2d 1575, 1578, 16 USPQ 2d 1934, 1936–37 (Fed. Cir. 1990).

[65]Arkie Lures, Inc. v. Gene Larew Tackle, Inc., 119 F.3d 953, 957, 43 USPQ 2d 1294, 1297 (Fed. Cir. 1997); Pentec, Inc. v. Graphic Controls Corp., 776 F.2d 309, 316, 227 USPQ 766, 771 (Fed. Cir. 1985).

[66]*In re* Dow Chem. Co., 837 F.2d 469, 473, 5 USPQ 2d 1529, 1532 (Fed. Cir. 1988).

[67]*See* Brown & Williamson Tobacco Corp. v. Philip Morris Inc., 229 F.3d 1120, 56 USPQ 2d 1456, 1464 (Fed. Cir. 2000) (evidence of infringing product in patent infringement action considered in secondary considerations).

[68]Tec Air, Inc. v. Denso Mfg. Mich. Inc., 192 F.3d 1353, 52 USPQ 2d 1294 (Fed. Cir. 1999).

Main volume footnote updates begin on page 223.

to maintain the validity of the patent in the context of civil litigation. The invention related to a method of and a device for making properly balanced, injected-molded fans. The invention inserted adjustable screws into hollowed-out sections of the mold insert that was used to form the fan hub. These screws were accessible from the front or cavity side of the mold.

Tec Air sued Denso for infringement because it manufactured radiator and condenser assemblies that included fans balanced according to the claimed method. Denso argued that the invention would have been obvious based on a combination of prior art references. Tec Air introduced evidence of commercial success of the patented invention to show nonobviousness. The district court determined that Tec Air presented sufficient objective evidence of nonobviousness.

On appeal, the Federal Circuit affirmed the holding of nonobviousness. Denso argued that the court should have granted its motion for judgment as a matter of law because the invention of the claims would have been obvious over U.S. Patent No. 3,136,001 (the Gelbard patent) in combination with a prior art brass plug method. The Gelbard patent taught using adjustable screws to create balance lugs on the blade tips of a molded fan. Unlike the screws of Tec Air's patent, these screws were accessible from the rear of the mold. Because, in the brass plug method, the operator drilled the brass plugs from the cavity side of the mold, Denso argued that combining this method with the teachings of the Gelbard patent resulted in cavity-side accessible screws.

The Federal Circuit rejected this argument because Tec Air introduced sufficient evidence of commercial success to show nonobviousness. Tec Air presented evidence that millions of fans were sold by both Tec Air and Denso, and that the patented method eliminated the tedious, haphazard, and expensive process of drilling the surface of the mold cavity. Based on Tec Air's sales evidence, the Federal Circuit noted that a jury reasonably could have found that the invention enjoyed commercial success.

Denso argued that this evidence was insufficient because Tec Air failed to provide market share data. Although sales figures coupled with market data provide stronger evidence of commercial success, the Federal Circuit emphasized that sales figures alone are also evidence of commercial success.[69]

---

[69]*Id.*, 52 USPQ 2d at 1299 (citing *In re* Huang, 100 F.3d 135, 140, 40 USPQ 2d 1685, 1689 (Fed. Cir. 1996) ("This court has noted in the past that evidence related solely to the number of units sold provides a very weak showing of commercial success, if any."); Gambro Lundia AB v. Baxter Healthcare Corp., 110 F.3d 1573, 1579, 42 USPQ 2d 1378, 1384 (Fed. Cir. 1997) ("The record contains significant evidence of the commercial success of [the] invention. The record shows that [a competitor] sold over 14,800 dialysis machines allegedly incorporating the [claimed] invention since 1987."); J.T. Eaton & Co. v. Atlantic Paste & Glue Co., 106 F.3d 1563, 1566, 1572, 41 USPQ 2d 1641, 1643, 1648 (Fed. Cir. 1997) (affirming a finding that "sales evidence . . . shows [strong commercial] success," where the "sales evidence" consisted solely of the patentee's "$17 million of sales from 1979 through 1984, and its $4 million of annual sales from 1985 through 1989")).

Main volume footnote updates begin on page 223.

Tec Air also offered testimony that there was a long-felt but unmet need to create a more efficient method to achieve fan balance prior to the Swin patents. Tec Air also provided testimony from the inventor Swin, Sr., that Tec Air used several unsatisfactory balancing techniques before adopting the patented one. Testimony also showed that the industry experienced problems with the prior art machining methods. Moreover, after Denso ceased infringing the Swin patents, it had to resort to less effective methods of balancing the fans. Based on this evidence, the Federal Circuit reasoned that the jury could reasonably have found there was a long-felt but unmet need in the prior art for an improved balancing method, which the patent satisfied.[70]

[Insert at the end of the section.]

Proper submission of commercial success may be determinative in a finding that the invention is nonobvious, particularly when other factors indicating nonobviousness are also present. For example, in *Carlisle Plastics, Inc. v. Spotless Enterprises, Inc.*[71] the Federal Circuit stated the following:

> We agree with the district court that the commercial success of the embodiment of the invention and the failure of anyone (including Carlisle's predecessor) to combine the prior art elements before the inventor did so provide significant support for the conclusion that the invention was not obvious, notwithstanding that combining the elements in the prior art would seem, with the considerable benefit of hindsight, to be fairly elementary.[72]

One final cautionary note: This discussion relates to the current *Patent Office* and Federal Circuit requirements for establishing commercial success during ex parte prosecution. Because of the varying standards of the nexus requirement between ex parte prosecution and civil court litigation, applicants should submit affidavit evidence complying with both standards whenever possible.

4. One of Ordinary Skill as Affiant

[Insert before the paragraph containing footnote 299.]

For example, in *Union Carbide Corp. v. American Can Co.*,[73] the Federal Circuit stated the following:

> Appellant is correct that the district court gave little weight to the Fischer affidavit. The court first noted that Fischer's background and training,

[70] *Id.*

[71] Carlisle Plastics, Inc. v. Spotless Enters, Inc., Civ. App. 98-1170 (Fed. Cir. Jan. 26, 1999) (unpublished).

[72] *Id.*, slip op. at 4.

[73] Union Carbide Corp. v. American Can Co., 724 F.2d 1567, 220 USPQ 584 (Fed. Cir. 1984).

Main volume footnote updates begin on page 223.

apart from preparation to be a witness in this litigation, gave him no "expertise as to the scope of the field of endeavor of the inventions of the patents in suit or as to what other fields are analogous art," citing *In re Deters*, 515 F.2d 1152, 1155, 185 USPQ 644, 647 (C.C.P.A. 1975), and *In re Altenpohl*, 500 F.2d 1151, 1158, 183 USPQ 38, 44 (C.C.P.A. 1974), as authority for discounting the testimony of one who fails to show skill in the relevant art or whose opinion is without factual support.[74]

On the other hand, when the expert had solved the problem in a similar manner as the inventor, courts have accorded significant weight to the expert testimony. For example, in *Whitley v. Road Corp.*,[75] the Fifth Circuit stated:

> [W]e must determine whether the device in question would have been obvious to a hypothetical individual possessing an ordinary level of skill in the relevant prior art. . . . Our hypothetical boat-trailer manufacturer would have an intimate knowledge of all the features contained in boat trailers produced since the 1930s. We conjure up this hypothetical figure needlessly for we have him in the flesh in the person of Mr. Meloon, president of Correct Craft and active in the field since 1925. He testified at great length on the development of boat trailers in this century. Mr. Meloon recalled trailers produced by his own company which performed the same functions and achieved the same results as appellants' Float-On trailer. We are convinced that the hypothetical person, schooled in the art, would find the Float-On trailer "obvious." A real person did so and had the pictures to prove it.[76]

Courts have also been quite persuaded when an expert has formulated an opinion on the prior art prior to the making of the invention. For example, in *In re Carroll*,[77] the CCPA stated:

> Normally little weight is given to an expert's opinion on an ultimate legal question. . . . In this case, however, we consider Dr. Merkal's opinion, as to what the prior art taught, deserving of considerable deference. Unlike the usual expert opinion, prepared either by the applicant himself, or on his behalf after the controversy has arisen, Dr. Merkal's opinion was formulated prior to the making of the claimed invention. It was therefore completely untainted by either hindsight or bias.[78]

C. Selected Decisions in Rebutting a Prima Facie Case

4. Commercial Success Combined With Copying Provided Strong Evidence of Secondary Considerations [New Topic]

A combination of commercial success and copying by the infringer may provide strong evidence of secondary considerations supporting a

---

[74] *Id.* at 1572, 220 USPQ at 588.

[75] Whitley v. Road Corp., 624 F.2d 698, 207 USPQ 369 (5th Cir. 1980).

[76] *Id.* at 701, 207 USPQ at 371.

[77] *In re* Carroll, 601 F.2d 1184, 202 USPQ 571 (C.C.P.A. 1979).

[78] *Id.* at 1186, 202 USPQ at 573 (citing *In re* Lindell, 385 F.2d 453, 456, 155 USPQ 521, 523–24 (C.C.P.A. 1967); *In re* Chilowsky, 306 F.2d 908, 916, 134 USPQ 515, 521 (C.C.P.A. 1962)).

Main volume footnote updates begin on page 223.

decision of nonobviousness. For example, in *Heidelberg Harris, Inc. v. Mitsubishi Heavy Industries, Ltd.*,[79] the Heidelberg invention related to offset printing presses, which had plate cylinders and blanket cylinders. The plate cylinder carried a printing plate bearing the image to be printed. After the printing plate was inked, it transferred its inked image onto a printing blanket carried by the blanket cylinder. The printing blanket, in turn, transferred the image onto the paper. A multi-layer gapless blanket was used to eliminate standing waves at the nip and thereby reduce slippage. Like the claimed invention, the accused presses employed gapless blankets, but gapped the plates. The accused presses also used a conventional drive, as opposed to a harmonic drive. According to Mitsubishi, its presses employed an increased surface speed differential between the printing plate and the printing blanket (i.e., slippage) to produce superior print quality.

Mitsubishi contended that the subject matter of the patents would have been obvious in view of four primary references:

(1)U.S. Patent No. 3,002,451 (the Shrimpton patent);
(2)U.S. Patent No. 2,949,851 (the Ghormley patent);
(3)U.S. Patent No. 3,568,286 (the Ross patent); and
(4)U.S. Patent No. 4,913,048 (the Tittgemeyer patent).

Mitsubishi alleged that one of ordinary skill in the art would have been motivated to combine these references to achieve the claimed invention. Mitsubishi asserted that the Shrimpton patent, for example, taught that a compressible layer will prevent blurring caused by a small standing wave in the blanket printing surface adjacent to the nip. Mitsubishi also characterized the Ross patent as teaching that a single-layer gapless blanket will experience speed variations through the nip. Additionally, Mitsubishi noted that the Tittgemeyer patent disclosed a gapless press design to "overcome vibratory stresses." Finally, Mitsubishi characterized the testimony of one of the named inventors of the two asserted patents as conceding that eliminating the blanket gap to reduce vibration would have been obvious. Mitsubishi concluded that one of ordinary skill in the art, confronted with the need to eliminate standing waves and speed variations at the nip, would have been motivated to combine the Tittgemeyer, Ross, and Shrimpton patents with the Ghormley patent to achieve the inventions claimed by the patents.

The district court held the invention nonobvious, refusing to accept Mitsubishi's argument that one of ordinary skill would have been motivated to make the combination. The district court relied on

[79] Heidelberg Harris, Inc. v. Mitsubishi Heavy Indus., Ltd., Civ. App. No. 99-1100 (Fed. Cir. Sept. 18, 2000) (unpublished)

Main volume footnote updates begin on page 223.

Heidelberg's evidence of secondary consideration in its holding of nonobviousness. On appeal, the Federal Circuit affirmed.

Mitsubishi argued that Heidelberg's proof of secondary considerations was legally insufficient. The Federal Circuit responded that substantial evidence supported Heidelberg's demonstration of these factors. The commercial success of the invention was supported not only by Heidelberg's sales of $800 million in only five years, but also by Heidelberg's achievement in breaking into the Japanese market. Heidelberg offered overwhelming evidence to support its allegation of industry tribute and acquiescence, including excerpts from the Encyclopedia Britannica's Book of the Year praising the Sunday Press and Heidelberg's receipt of the 1994 Intertech Award for its Sunday Press technology.

The Federal Circuit also held that Heidelberg demonstrated that the invention solved a long-felt but unmet need by developing its Sunday Press via Mitsubishi's own advertisements, which declared "[t]he need for gapless technology [to have] long been recognized" and a Mitsubishi technical report that stated the Heidelberg blanket design was "completely novel with regard to structure and actual results, so we cannot use conventional technology and know-how."[80] Finally, Heidelberg offered strong evidence of copying, including Mitsubishi memoranda and reports indicating that Mitsubishi followed Heidelberg's design in developing its accused presses.

Accepting as established facts the limited teachings of the prior art, the absence of any motivation to combine the references, and the secondary considerations of nonobviousness, the Federal Circuit held that the invention of the asserted claims would not have been obvious to one of ordinary skill in the art. According to the Federal Circuit:

> We are particularly persuaded of the legal sufficiency of the nonobviousness conclusion by Heidelberg's strong evidence of secondary considerations of non-obviousness, such as the Sunday Press's commercial success, its widespread industry acclaim, and the fact that Mitsubishi heavily relied upon the Heidelberg press in developing its own press. Mitsubishi documents even admit that Heidelberg's design was "unique." Consequently, we discern no error in the magistrate judge's entry of judgment that the [invention was] not invalid as obvious.[81]

XII. Special Topic: Means-Plus-Function or Step-Plus-Function Claims

[Insert after footnote 483.]

[80] *Id.*, slip op. at 21.

[81] *Id.* at 22–23.

Main volume footnote updates begin on page 223.

The function serves as the touchstone for identifying the disclosed, corresponding structure or acts that are recited by the means-plus-function or step-plus-function claim limitations.[82]

After identifying the function of the means-plus-function element, the court looks to the written description to identify the structure corresponding to that function. Identification of corresponding structure may embrace more than the preferred embodiment. A means-plus-function claim encompasses all structure in the specification corresponding to that element and equivalent structures.[83]

When multiple embodiments in the specification correspond to the claimed function, proper application of Section 112, sixth paragraph generally reads the claim element to embrace each of those embodiments.[84]

Interim supplemental examination guidelines for determining the applicability of 35 U.S.C. Section 112, sixth paragraph are provided in Appendix D, and the final supplemental examination guidelines are provided in Appendix C.

A. Claim Limitations That Fall Under Section 112, Sixth Paragraph

[Insert after footnote 490.]

The Federal Circuit has subsequently delineated several rules for claim drafters to invoke the strictures of 35 U.S.C. Section 112, sixth paragraph. Specifically, if the word "means" appears in a claim element in combination with a function, it is presumed to be a means-plus-function element to which Section 112, sixth paragraph applies.[85] Nevertheless, according to its express terms, Section 112, sixth paragraph governs only claim elements that do not recite sufficient structural limitations.[86] Therefore, the presumption that Section 112, sixth

[82] See, e.g., Smiths Indus. Med. Sys., Inc. v. Vital Signs, Inc., 183 F.3d 1347, 51 USPQ 2d 1415, 1421 (Fed. Cir. 1999):

> The court erred in the next step of the claim construction process by interpreting the claim language "means for supplying gas" to require a means for supplying gas under pressure. It is improper to import the limitation "under pressure" from the written description into the claim because the claim language is clear on its face. . . . Instead, the function recited by the means-plus-function claim limitation is simply the function of "supplying gas," and it is this function alone that serves as the touchstone for identifying the disclosed, corresponding structure that is recited by the means-plus-function claim limitation.

[83] Micro Chem., Inc. v. Great Plains Chem. Co., 194 F.3d 1250, 52 USPQ 2d 1258, 1263 (Fed. Cir. 1999).

[84] *Id.*, 52 USPQ 2d at 1264 (citing Serrano v. Telular Corp., 111 F.3d 1578, 1583, 42 USPQ 2d 1538, 1542 (Fed. Cir. 1997)).

[85] Sage Prods., Inc. v. Devon Indus., Inc., 126 F.3d 1420, 1427, 44 USPQ 2d 1103, 1109 (Fed. Cir. 1997); Greenberg v. Ethicon Endo-Surgery, Inc., 91 F.3d 1580, 1583, 39 USPQ 2d 1783, 1785 (Fed. Cir. 1996).

[86] Al-Site Corp. v. VSI Int'l, Inc., 174 F.3d 1308, 50 USPQ 2d 1161, 1166 (Fed. Cir. 1999).

Main volume footnote updates begin on page 223.

paragraph applies is overcome if the claim itself recites sufficient structure or material for performing the claimed function.[87]

Although use of the phrase "means for" (or "step for") is not the only way to invoke Section 112, sixth paragraph, that terminology typically invokes it, while other formulations generally do not.[88] Therefore, when an element of a claim does not use the term "means," treatment as a means-plus-function claim element is generally not appropriate.[89] However, when it is apparent that the element invokes purely functional terms, without the additional recital of specific structure or material for performing that function, the claim element may be a means-plus-function element despite the lack of express means-plus-function language.[90]

[Insert headings after footnote 490.]

1. *Examples of Claim Language With Respect to Means-Plus-Function Elements [New Topic]*

a. *"Double-Drive Mechanism" Held Not Means-Plus-Function Element [New Topic]*

[Insert heading prior to paragraph containing footnote 494.]

b. *"Detent Mechanism" Held Not Means-Plus-Function Element [New Topic]*

[Insert heading after footnote 498.]

c. *"Closure Means Being Selectively Movable" Held Means-Plus-Function Element [New Topic]*

[Insert heading after footnote 500.]

d. *"Lever Moving Element for Moving" and "Movable Link Member for Holding" Held Means-Plus-Function Elements [New Topic]*

[Insert heading after footnote 505.]

---

[87] York Prods., Inc. v. Central Tractor Farm & Family Ctr., 99 F.3d 1568, 1574, 40 USPQ 2d 1619, 1623 (Fed. Cir. 1996); Cole v. Kimberly-Clark Corp., 102 F.3d 524, 531, 41 USPQ 2d 1001, 1006 (Fed. Cir. 1996).

[88] Al-Site Corp. v. VSI Int'l, Inc., 174 F.3d 1308, 50 USPQ 2d 1161, 1166 (Fed. Cir. 1999).

[89] *See* Mas-Hamilton Group v. LaGard, Inc., 156 F.3d 1206, 1213–15, 48 USPQ 2d 1010, 1016–18 (Fed. Cir. 1998).

[90] *Id.*

Main volume footnote updates begin on page 223.

e. "Settable Control Module" Held Means-Plus-Function Element [New Topic]

[Insert heading after footnote 509.]

f. "Jet Driving Device" Held Means-Plus-Function Element [New Topic]

[Insert before paragraph containing footnote 513.]

g. "Plate Means" and "Wing Means" Held Not Means-Plus-Function Elements [New Topic]

[Insert before the paragraph containing footnote 515.]

h. "Means Formed on the Sidewall Portions Including Ridge Members" Held Not Means-Plus-Function Element [New Topic]

[Insert after footnote 519.]

i. "Battery Means" and "Lamp Means" Held Not Means-Plus-Function Elements [New Topic]

[Insert after footnote 522.]

j. "Perforation Means" Held Not Means-Plus-Function Element [New Topic]

[Insert before the paragraph containing footnote 527.]

k. "Probe Tip Means" Held Not Means-Plus-Function Element [New Topic]

[Insert before the paragraph containing footnote 529.]

l. "Digital Detector for Receiving" Held Not Means-Plus-Function Element [New Topic]

[Insert after footnote 530.]

m. "Positioning Means" Held Not Means-Plus-Function Element [New Topic]

In *Rodime PLC v. Seagate Technology, Inc.*,[91] the invention related to computer hard-disk drives. Generally, the invention was

[91] Rodime PLC v. Seagate Tech., Inc., 174 F.3d 1294, 50 USPQ 2d 1429 (Fed. Cir. 1999), *cert. denied*, 528 U.S. 1115 (2000).

Main volume footnote updates begin on page 223.

directed to the miniaturization of hard-drive technology from 5-¼ inches to 3-½ inches, a size particularly suited for use in portable computers, and problems incident thereto. The demand for correct positioning of the hard drive introduced numerous problems addressed by the invention. Variations in temperature can significantly affect the positioning mechanism of the disk drive.

To solve this problem, the invention included a thermal compensation scheme. Thermal compensation accounts for different expansion and contraction rates of a disk drive's components. In the embodiment disclosed in the patent, the thermal compensation system was built into the "positioning mechanism"—the mechanism responsible for moving the heads between tracks.[92] Specifically, the patent described constructing the positioning mechanism from appropriate materials to automatically compensate for any mispositioning between the transducer and a track caused by thermal effects. The patent claim recited, for example, the following:

> positioning means for moving said first and second transducer means between the concentrically adjacent tracks on said micro hard-disks, said positioning means including a positioning arm disposed within the sealed housing, a pivot shaft coupled to one end of said positioning arm and supporting said positioning arm for rotational movement relative to said micro hard-disks, four support arms, each supporting one of said heads at one end and each connected to said positioning arm at its other end, a stepper motor having a shaft extending into said sealed housing and means for operating said stepper motor in step increments, each increment causing said read/write heads to move from one track to the next adjacent track on said micro hard-disks.[93]

The district court held that this limitation was in means-plus function format, and Rodime appealed.

On appeal, the Federal Circuit agreed with Rodime and reversed the district court's holding. The Federal Circuit first noted that Section 112, sixth paragraph presumptively applied to the "positioning means" in the asserted claims because that element employed traditional "means" language.[94] In addition, the Federal Circuit noted that the claim language linked the means with a function, namely, moving the transducer between tracks on the hard disk. Accordingly, the Federal Circuit found that the claim element would appear to fall within Section 112, sixth paragraph.

The Federal Circuit, however, noted that the final step in the analysis requires the court to determine whether the claim nevertheless recites sufficient structure for performing the moving function to take it outside the bounds of that provision. The Federal Circuit commented as follows:

---

[92] *Id.*, 50 USPQ 2d at 1431.

[93] *Id.* at 1432.

[94] *Id.* at 1435.

Main volume footnote updates begin on page 223.

> In addition to the recited structure, these claims also recite the interconnection of the structural components and their location with respect to other elements of the claimed combination. For example, the positioning arm is "disposed within the sealed housing." The pivot shaft is "coupled to one end of said positioning arm" and supports "said positioning arm for rotational movement relative to said micro hard-disks." . . . [T]his detailed recitation of structure for performing the moving function removes this element from the purview of Section 112, Para. 6.[95]

The Federal Circuit noted that in reaching the opposite conclusion, the district court appeared concerned that the claim did not recite every last detail of structure disclosed in the specification for performing the claimed moving function. The Federal Circuit said, however, that an exhaustive recitation of structure is not required to avoid Section 112, sixth paragraph. "Instead, the claim need only recite 'sufficient' structure to perform entirely the claimed function."[96]

The Federal Circuit reasoned that based on the structure disclosed in the specification for performing the moving function, the claims recited nearly all (if not all) of the structural components of the positioning mechanism. In any case, the Federal Circuit emphasized that the claims clearly recited more than sufficient structure for moving the transducer from track to track and reversed the district court.[97]

n. "Means Defining an Air Collecting Space" Held Not Means-Plus-Function Element [New Topic]

In *Brita Wasser-Filter-Systeme, Gmbh v. Recovery Engineering, Inc.*,[98] the invention related to water filtration pitchers with filter cartridge inserts. A water filtration pitcher consists of a pitcher, a funnel seated within the pitcher, and a sleeve attached to the funnel in which a water filter sits. Untreated water is poured into the funnel, flows through the filter, which removes impurities, and finally flows into the pitcher. The invention disclosed in the Brita patent provided a filter and sleeve design that was capable of exhausting air bubbles from the sleeve. Thus, the claimed invention comprised a filter (referred to as the "insert") which had an air collecting space that collected and ex-

---

[95] *Id.* at 1436.

[96] *Id.*

[97] *Id. See also* Star Tech. Group, Inc. v. Testerion, Inc., Civ. App. No. 99-1168, slip op. at 6 (Fed. Cir. Sept. 7, 1999) (unpublished):

> The district court held, and neither party disputes, that this element should not be interpreted under 35 U.S.C. 112, 6. The district court's holding in that regard was based on the disclosure of: (1) the claimed structure to perform the function of alignment, (2) the structure's claimed location in the apparatus, and (3) the claimed physical properties of the elastic plate. We agree with the district court that the claim recites definite structure for performing the claimed function and that therefore it should not be interpreted under section 112, 6.

[98] Brita Wasser-Filter-Systeme, Gmbh v. Recovery Eng'g, Inc., Civ. App. No. 99-1322 (Fed. Cir. Sept. 21, 2000) (unpublished).

Main volume footnote updates begin on page 223.

hausted air upwardly and ultimately out of an opening in the sleeve. Claim 1, the only claim at issue, recited:

> 1. A water purification device comprising:
>
> an intake funnel,
>
> a sleeve wherein said sleeve is sealingly connected to said funnel at an upper end of said sleeve, said sleeve further having an opening formed therein,
>
> an insert having approximately cylindrical side walls, a filter cover and a filter bottom for accommodating a granulate filter agent therein with means defining an air collecting space, located in at least a portion of the filter bottom, said means defining the air collecting space extending upwardly at least partially towards the side wall and to the opening in said sleeve, with said filter bottom having opening means to allow the passage of filtrate therethrough, and with said filter cover having opening means whereby fluid can be passed into the insert.[99]

The district court held that "means defining an air collecting space" was a means-plus-function limitation, governed by 35 U.S.C. Section 112, paragraph six. The district court determined that the function claimed was "gathering and removing bubbles from the filter bottom," and the structure corresponding to this function was a space in the filter having a vertical and horizontal component as described in the specification.

On appeal, the Federal Circuit reversed the district court holding that the "means defining an air collecting space" was a means-plus-function limitation. The Federal Circuit noted that although the claim language at issue did not utilize the traditional "means for" predicate before claiming a function, the claim did contain the term "means" followed by the function of defining an air collecting space. Thus, the presumption of Section 112, sixth paragraph treatment was raised. However, the Federal Circuit held that this presumption was overcome by the sufficiently definite structural parameters found in the claim regarding the air collecting space. That is, the claim language itself structurally defined the air collecting space as a component of the insert, i.e., the claim recited "an insert having approximately cylindrical sidewalls, a filter cover and a filter bottom, . . . with means defining an air collecting space."[100] The claim further recited that the air collecting space was "located in at least a portion of the filter bottom" and "extend[s] at least partially towards the side wall and to the opening in said sleeve."[101]

In other words, the Federal Circuit explained, the air collecting space was a void that was formed as part of the insert, and was located at the bottom of the insert (the filter bottom), and extended upwardly along the side walls of the insert and to the opening of the sleeve in

[99] *Id.*, slip op. at 2.

[100] *Id.* at 7.

[101] *Id.*

which the insert sat. Because this structural recitation sufficiently performed the function of "defining an air collecting space," the Federal Circuit held that Section 112, sixth paragraph treatment was not proper.

o. *"Second Baffle Means" Held Not Means-Plus-Function Element [New Topic]*

In *Envirco Corp. v. Clestra Cleanroom, Inc.*,[102] the invention related to a compact fan and filter assembly for use in a clean room. The claimed invention had a housing, a blower fan, a first baffle, a second baffle, and a high efficiency particulate arresting filter. Claim 1 of the patent recited:

> 1. A compact air purification apparatus for providing clean airflow to a clean air enclosure comprising a primary housing having first and second end portions and substantially closed sidewall portions, inlet and discharge openings disposed through said first and second end portions, respectively, a blower means mounted through said inlet opening so as to extend inwardly of said primary housing, said blower means having a motor drivingly connected to a centrifugal fan means, said centrifugal fan being disposed within said primary housing so as to discharge air radially outwardly with respect to said inlet opening, said centrifugal fan including a plurality of radially extending blade means, a filter means mounted within said primary housing adjacent said discharge opening so that all airflow outwardly of said primary housing through said discharge opening passes through said filter means, a first baffle means disposed adjacent said centrifugal fan means and between said centrifugal fan means and said filter means, said first baffle means having outwardly extending wall portions which extend outwardly of said centrifugal fan means toward said sidewalls of said primary housing so as to create an airflow space radially of said centrifugal fan means between said first baffle means and said sidewalls of said primary housing, second baffle means disposed radially outwardly of said centrifugal fan means and said first baffle means, said second baffle means having inner surfaces for directing the airflow from said centrifugal fan means inwardly of said primary housing and between said first baffle means and said filter means whereby air being introduced into said housing by said centrifugal fan means will be directed radially outwardly of said centrifugal fan means and guided by said first baffle means towards said second baffle means and thereafter by said second baffle means between said first baffle means and said air filter means.[103]

Clestra made the accused infringing product, the Fantom fan. The parties agreed that the Fantom had a blower fan, a first baffle, a housing, and a filter covered by the claims in the patent. At issue was whether the sound dampening material of the Fantom constituted, or

[102] Envirco Corp. v. Clestra Cleanroom, Inc., 209 F.3d 1360, 54 USPQ 2d 1449 (Fed. Cir. 2000).

[103] *Id.*, 54 USPQ 2d at 1450–51.

Main volume footnote updates begin on page 223.

was equivalent to, the second baffle means of the asserted patent claims.

The district court construed the term "second baffle means" of the asserted claims of the patent as a means-plus-function claim element under 35 U.S.C. Section 112, paragraph six. Because the district court held that the second baffle means was a means-plus-function claim element, it looked to the specification for the corresponding structure. The district court focused its attention on one of the disclosed preferred embodiments, which included a second baffle having "continuous arcuate surfaces."[104] Therefore, the district court limited the second baffle means to only arcuate, or curved surfaces. However, the district court overlooked other disclosed embodiments, which both contained angular baffles.

Under this claim construction, the district court performed its infringement analysis, comparing the accused. Fantom product to the claims of the patent. The district court granted Clestra's summary judgment motion, and held that the Fantom did not infringe because the L-shaped material in the Fantom was not arcuate. The district court also held the claims of the patent not infringed under the doctrine of equivalents. Envirco appealed.

On appeal, the Federal Circuit reversed the district court's holding that the "second baffle means" invoked Section 112, sixth paragraph. The Federal Circuit noted that use of the word "means" invoked a "presumption" that Section 112, sixth paragraph governed the second baffle claim element. However, the Federal Circuit explained that the district court did not complete the triggering analysis for Section 112, sixth paragraph, and should have determined whether the claims recited sufficient structure for performing the claimed function.[105]

The Federal Circuit reasoned that although using the word "means" to describe the second baffle, the claims also recited sufficient structure to rebut the presumption that the term was in means-plus-function form. The term "baffle" itself, according to the Federal Circuit was a structural term. The dictionary definition of the word "baffle" is "a device (as a plate, wall or screen) to deflect, check, or regulate flow."[106] Because the term "baffle" itself imparted structure, meaning a surface which deflects air, the Federal Circuit held that its use in the claims rebutted the presumption that Section 112, sixth paragraph applied.

---

[104] *Id.* at 1451.

[105] *Id.* at 1452 (citing Sage Prods., Inc. v. Devon Indus., Inc., 126 F.3d 1420, 1427–28, 44 USPQ 2d 1103, 1109 (Fed. Cir. 1997) ("[W]here a claim recites a function, but then goes on to elaborate sufficient structure, material or acts within the claim itself to perform entirely the recited function, the claim is not in means-plus-function format.")).

[106] *Id.* (quoting Webster's Ninth New Collegiate Dictionary 124 (1990)).

Main volume footnote updates begin on page 223.

Further, the Federal Circuit reasoned that the claims described the particular structure of this particular baffle as "having inner surfaces for directing airflow . . . radially outward . . . and thereafter . . . between said first baffle means and said air filter means".[107] In this case, the Federal Circuit held that the claims recited sufficient structure (i.e., a baffle disposed radially outward from the centrifugal fan, with inner surfaces for directing airflow). Therefore, the second baffle limitation was not a means-plus-function claim element. Because the claims recited sufficient structure, including details about the location and formational details about the second baffle, the Federal Circuit held that the district court erred in construing the "second baffle means" as a means-plus-function claim element under Section 112, sixth paragraph.

p. Functional Statement "Sealingly Connected" Not Means-Plus-Function Element [New Topic]

In *Watts v. XL Systems Inc.*,[108] the invention was directed toward connecting sections of pipe together with a primary use in the oil well industry in which miles of pipe may need to be dropped into a hole. Such a pipe consists of a large number of sections, called joints, which are typically 40 feet long and 20 inches wide and are connected together. The joints are commonly connected together in one of two ways. The first uses an integral connection in which the joints themselves have mating threads allowing the joints to be connected directly to each other. The second uses a coupling connection in which the joints still have threads, but are connected to a coupling is disposed between two successive joints. Claim 18, which was representative, read as follows:

> 18. A high efficiency connection for joints of oilwell tubing or the like, comprising: at least two pipes joined together and forming joints of pipe, each joints of pipe having a first end with no increase in wall thickness relative to the average pipe wall thickness and formed with tapered internal threads; the joints each having a second end formed with tapered external threads dimensioned such that one such joint may be sealingly connected directly with another such joint; the threads being of sufficient length and taper such that the pipe wall strength of the first end in the area of the smallest diameter of thread engagement is at least three-fourths of the average pipe wall strength of the joints of pipe.[109]

The district court construed the statement "the joints each having a second end formed with tapered external threads dimensioned such that one such joint may be sealingly connected directly with an-

[107] *Id.*

[108] Watts v. XL Sys. Inc., 232 F.3d 877, 56 USPQ 2d 1836 (Fed. Cir. 2000).

[109] *Id.*, 56 USPQ 2d at 1837.

Main volume footnote updates begin on page 223.

other such joint" to be a means-plus-function limitation and held that they were limited to the disclosed embodiments. Based on its claim construction and the stipulations, the district court held that XL did not infringe any of the claims at issue. Watts appealed the district court's judgment. On appeal, the Federal Circuit reversed the district court's decision regarding whether the claim limitation was a means-plus-function limitation.

Watts argued that the district court was wrong, contending first that because the sealingly connected limitation did not use the word "means," it was presumptively not a means-plus-function limitation. Next, Watts argued that the sealingly connected limitation was not purely functional because the claim described a precise structure by reciting tapered internal and external threads. XL responded that the sealingly connected limitation was a means-plus-function limitation because it did not include structure capable of entirely performing the recited function. XL maintained that the tapered internal and external threads did not seal, but merely provided the location of the seal, and that the seal was created by misaligned taper angles.

On appeal, the Federal Circuit reversed and held XL's arguments to be unavailing. According to the Federal Circuit, the threads represented the sole structural configuration effecting the seal and clearly were not mere indicators of the location of the seal as XL had argued. Although the use of misaligned taper angles, as well as a variety of other mechanisms, may increase the strength of the seal, the Federal Circuit reasoned that the claimed sealing function was accomplished by the claimed threads, and, therefore, the limitations were not purely functional.[110]

Thus, the Federal Circuit held that the "sealingly connected" limitations were not means-plus-function limitations, since the limitations did not recite the word "means," and thus raised the presumption that they were not in means-plus-function form. In addition, the "sealingly connected" term was reasonably well understood in the pertinent art as a name for a structure, performed the function of sealing, and the threads were the sole structural configuration effecting the seal, and not merely indicators of the location of the seal.

q. Data Block Not Means-Plus-Function Limitation When Recited in "Means to Sequentially Display Data Block Inquiries" [New Topic]

In *IMS Technology, Inc. v. Haas Automation, Inc.*,[111] the invention related to the control of a machine tool, such as a milling machine, which was used to cut or remove material from an object, referred to

[110] *Id.* at 1839.

[111] IMS Tech., Inc. v. Haas Automation, Inc., 206 F.3d 1422, 54 USPQ 2d 1129 (Fed. Cir.), *cert. dismissed*, 530 U.S. 1299 (2000).

Main volume footnote updates begin on page 223.

as a workpiece, through a machining operation. Numerical control (NC), which runs a program containing a series of numerical instructions and converts the instructions to electrical control signals, was at issue. These control signals are applied to, for example, servo motors that control the movement of the machine tool.

The invention claimed in the patent permitted interactive programming of the machine tool on the machine shop floor. The machine tool operator created a program by using a keyboard to respond to nested inquiries displayed on a CRT screen. In general, the program contained data blocks, each of which corresponded to one operational step of the machine tool. When the machine tool operator selected an operation, the control system prompted him for additional parameters to be included in the data block for that operational step.

Haas manufactured and sold machine tools with numerical controls. The accused Haas controls also provided interactive programming capability of machine tools on the machine shop floor. Some Haas controls had a floppy disk drive for storing programs; others had only an RS-232 data port which could be connected to a storage device, such as a personal computer, for storing programs in ASCII format. The Haas controls stored programs in G- and M-code format. During execution of programs, the Haas controls translated G-code into a binary format, which was converted into electrical signals delivered to the machine tool for directing its operation.

IMS filed suit against Haas alleging that Haas infringed its patent. Claim 1 was representative, and recited:

> 1. A programmable microcomputer control apparatus for controlling the relative motion between a tool and a workplace comprising:
>
> indicator means for providing at an output digital signals indicative of the relative position between the tool and the workpiece;
>
> an alterable memory operable to retain a control program and control parameters;
>
> a microprocessor unit coupled to the output of the indicator means and to the memory and operable to produce control signals dependent upon said indicator means output and said control parameters according to said control program;
>
> control means for directing said control signals from the microprocessor unit to appropriate motion-providing means;
>
> interface means for transferring a control program and control parameters from an external medium into said alterable memory and for recording the control parameter contents of said memory onto an external medium;
>
> data entry means for loading control parameters into said memory through externally accessible data inputs independently of said interface means; and
>
> display means for displaying control parameters, said control program being operable to display control parameter inquiries on the display

> means, whereby an operator may load control parameters into said memory through said data entry means in response to the inquiries, said apparatus including means to sequentially display data block inquiries and to display, in response to the loading of certain control parameters into said memory relating to the data block inquiries, separate displays of additional control parameter inquiries relating to information used in the data block which was the subject of the previous inquiry, whereby the sequential display of inquiries and direct loading of control parameters as to an operation can be used to make the use of the device simpler and more responsive to the operator.[112]

The district court construed the term "data block," which appeared in the display means limitation of claim 1, as limited to the specific set of variables disclosed in the written description and the disclosed sequence of inquiries regarding those variables. The district court reasoned that the term "data block" was written in means-plus-function format, and therefore, should be limited to the embodiments described in the specification, and equivalents thereof.

On appeal, the Federal Circuit reversed the district court's holding that the term "data block" was written in means-plus-function format. Haas contended that the district court correctly held that Section 112, sixth paragraph applied to limit the meaning of the term "data block" to the variables and sequence disclosed in the written description. The Federal Circuit disagreed and held that the district court misinterpreted Section 112, sixth paragraph. According to the Federal Circuit, Section 112, sixth paragraph does not limit all terms in a means-plus-function or step-plus-function clause to what is disclosed in the written description and equivalents thereof. Rather, "Section 112, sixth paragraph applies only to interpretation of the means or step that performs a recited function when a claim recites insufficient structure or acts for performing the function."[113]

In claim 1, the Federal Circuit reasoned, the display means included a "means to sequentially display data block inquiries."[114] The recited function consisted of sequentially displaying data block inquiries, and the claim recited no structure supporting the means for performing that function. Therefore, in accordance with Section 112, sixth paragraph, the means was construed to cover the disclosed structure, i.e., a CRT, and its equivalents. Accordingly, the Federal Circuit held that the "data block" was not the means that caused the sequential display, and was therefore not subject to construction under Section 112, sixth paragraph.

[Insert after footnote 530.]

---

[112] *Id.*, 54 USPQ 2d at 1131.

[113] *Id.* at 1135.

[114] *Id.*

2. *Examples of Claim Language With Respect to Step-Plus-Function Elements [New Topic]*

The Federal Circuit has attempted to further define the criteria of when a claimed process will be considered a step-plus-function element under Section 112, sixth paragraph. In a concurring opinion, Judge Rader provided the following procedure for determining whether a process claim is to be interpreted as a step-plus-function claim under Section 112, sixth paragraph:

> The correlation between means-plus-function and step-plus-function claim elements assists the difficult process of identifying step-plus-function claim elements. This court has set forth a structured analysis for determining whether the elements of a claim are in means-plus-function form. Specifically, if the word "means" appears in the claim element, there is a presumption that it is a means-plus-function element to which § 112, ¶ 6 applies. . . . This presumption is overcome if the claim itself recites sufficient structure or material for performing the claimed function or when it fails to recite a function associated with the means. . . .
>
> When an element of a claim does not use the term "means," treatment as a means-plus-function claim element is generally not appropriate. . . . However, when it is apparent that the element invokes purely functional terms, without the additional recital of specific structure or material for performing that function, the claim element may be a means-plus-function element, despite the lack of express "means" language. . . .
>
> Given the parallel format of the statute, a similar analysis applies to step-plus-function claim elements. Certain phrases trigger a presumption that § 112, ¶ 6 applies, but other aspects of the element, such as the recitation of a specific act, may overcome that presumption. The difficulty of distinguishing acts from functions in step-plus-function claim elements, however, makes identifying step-plus-function claims inherently more problematic. This difficulty places a significant burden on the claim drafter to choose language with a definite and clear meaning. To invoke a presumption of § 112, ¶ 6 application, a claim drafter must use language that expressly signals the recitation of a function as distinguished from an act.
>
> As used in § 112, ¶ 6, "step" is the generic term for "acts" in the same sense that "means" is the generic term for "structure" and "material." . . . The word "step," however, may introduce either an act or a function depending on context within the claim. Therefore, use of the word "step," by itself, does not invoke a presumption that § 112, ¶ 6 applies. For example, method claim elements may begin with the phrase "steps of" without invoking application of § 112, ¶ 6. . . . The phrase "steps of" colloquially signals the introduction of specific acts, rather than functions, and should therefore not presumptively invoke application of § 112, ¶ 6.
>
> Unlike "of," the preposition "for" colloquially signals the recitation of a function. Accordingly, the phrase "step for" generally introduces functional claim language falling under § 112, ¶ 6. . . . Thus, the phrase "step for" in a method claim raises a presumption that § 112, ¶ 6 applies. This presumption gives legal effect to the commonly understood meanings of "of"—introducing specific materials, structure or acts—and "for"—introducing a function.

Main volume footnote updates begin on page 223.

Even when a claim element uses language that generally falls under the step-plus-function format, however, § 112, ¶ 6 still does not apply when the claim limitation itself recites sufficient acts for performing the specified function.

As this court explained in *O.I. Corp.*:

Of course, [§ 112, ¶ 6] is implicated only when means plus function without definite structure are present, and that is similarly true with respect to steps, that the paragraph is implicated only when steps plus function without acts are present. The statute thus in effect provides that an element in a combination method or process claim may be recited as a step for performing a specified function without the recital of acts in support of the function.

. . . Therefore, when the claim language includes sufficient acts for performing the recited function, § 112, ¶ 6 does not apply.

Again similar to a means-plus-function analysis, the absence of the phrase "step for" from the language of a claim tends to show that the claim element is not in step-plus-function form. However, claim elements without express step-plus-function language may nevertheless fall within § 112, ¶ 6 if they merely claim the underlying function without recitation of acts for performing that function. Unfortunately, method claim elements often recite phrases susceptible to interpretation as either a function or as an act for performing a function. Both acts and functions are often stated using verbs ending in "ing." For instance, if the method claim element at issue in this case had merely recited the "step of" "spreading an adhesive tack coating," it would not have been clear solely from this hypothetical claim language whether "spreading" was a function or an act. In such circumstances, claim interpretation requires careful analysis of the limitation in the context of the overall claim and the specification.

In general terms, the "underlying function" of a method claim element corresponds to what that element ultimately accomplishes in relationship to what the other elements of the claim and the claim as a whole accomplish. "Acts," on the other hand, correspond to how the function is accomplished. Therefore, claim interpretation focuses on what the claim limitation accomplishes, i.e., its underlying function, in relation to what is accomplished by the other limitations and the claim as a whole. If a claim element recites only an underlying function without acts for performing it, then § 112, ¶ 6 applies even without express step-plus-function language.

In sum, similar to means-plus-function claims, this court employs a straightforward analysis for identifying a step-plus-function claim. If the claim element uses the phrase "step for," then § 112, ¶ 6 is presumed to apply. Because the phrasing "step for" would appear to claim every possible act for performing the recited function, in keeping with § 112, ¶ 6, such a claim covers only the specific acts recited in the specification for performing that function, and equivalent acts. On the other hand, the term "step" alone and the phrase "steps of" tend to show that § 112, ¶ 6 does not govern that limitation. Accordingly, this court has similarly denied step-plus-function treatment to method claims which use the conventional "steps of" language.[115]

---

[115] Seal-Flex, Inc. v. Athletic Track & Court Constr., 172 F.3d 836, 50 USPQ 2d 1225, 1233–34 (Fed. Cir. 1999) (Rader, J., concurring) (quoting O.I. Corp. v. Tekmar Co., 115 F.3d 1576, 1583, 42 USPQ 2d 1777, 1782 (Fed. Cir. 1997)).

Main volume footnote updates begin on page 223.

a. "Passing the Alanalyte Slug Through a Passage" Held Not Step-Plus-Function Element [New Topic]

[Insert before the paragraph containing footnote 539.]

b. "Automatically Determining at Least the Last-Dialed Number" Held Not Step-Plus-Function Element [New Topic]

[Insert after footnote 540.]

3. Claim That Recites Some Structure Does Not Necessarily Convert Element Drafted in Means-Plus-Function Format to Non-Means-Plus-Function Format [New Topic]

A claim that recites specific structure does not necessarily convert that element drafted in means-plus-function format to non-means-plus-function format. For example, in *Al-Site Corp. v. VSI International, Inc.*,[116] the invention related to specific hangers for displaying nonprescription eyeglasses. The invention allowed consumers to try on eyeglasses and return them to the rack without removing them from their display hangers. The patent recited the combination of an eyeglass display member and an eyeglass hanger member. The combination included a display member with cantilever support means, and an eyeglass hanger member for mounting a pair of eyeglasses. The claims defined the structure of the eyeglass hanger member as either made from flat sheet material and having an opening means formed below its upper edge, or an attaching portion attachable to a portion of an eyeglasses frame to enable the temples of the frame to be opened and closed.

The district court interpreted the eyeglass hanger member as under the purview of Section 112, sixth paragraph, and VSI appealed the interpretation. On appeal, the Federal Circuit reversed the district court's interpretation of the eyeglass hanger element under Section 112, sixth paragraph. According to the Federal Circuit:

> Under this established analytical framework, the "eyeglass hanger member" elements in the claims . . . do not invoke § 112, ¶ 6. In the first place, these elements are not in traditional means-plus-function format. The word "means" does not appear within these elements. Moreover, although these claim elements include a function, namely, "mounting a pair of eyeglasses," the claims themselves contain sufficient structural limitations for performing those functions. . . . [and] precludes treatment as a means-plus-function claim element. The district court therefore improperly restricted the "eyeglass hanger member" in these

[116] Al-Site Corp. v. VSI Int'l, Inc., 174 F.3d 1308, 50 USPQ 2d 1161 (Fed. Cir. 1999).

Main volume footnote updates begin on page 223.

claims to the structural embodiments in the specification and their equivalents.[117]

Similarly, in *Unidynamics Corp. v. Automatic Products International Ltd.*,[118] the Federal Circuit held that the claim element of "spring means tending to keep the door closed" was under the purview of Section 112, sixth paragraph even though it included some structural recitation.[119] According to the Federal Circuit:

> We disagree with the district court, however, that the recitation of "spring," which is structural language, takes the limitation out of the ambit of the construction dictate of § 112, ¶ 6. . . . The recitation of the word "spring" does not vitiate the patentee's choice.[120]

In *Nagle Industries, Inc. v. Ford Motor Co.*,[121] the Federal Circuit held that the claim element of "slack adjustment means" was also a means-plus-function element interpreted under Section 112, sixth paragraph. As stated by the Federal Circuit:

> The claim phrase "slack adjustment means" is defined by the functional language "for adjusting slack in said strand means." The only structural recitation of attaching the slack adjustment means to the end of the strand means involves the placement of the slack adjustment means within the claimed cable assembly. This recitation of structure does not specify what the slack adjustment means is structurally. . . . Therefore, the claim does not recite "sufficient structure to perform entirely the claimed function." . . . We agree with the district court that the claim limitation "slack adjusting means" is written in means-plus-function language because it recites a means for performing a specified function without the recital of specific structure to carry out that function.[122]

B. Prior Art References as Equivalents Under Section 112, Sixth Paragraph

10. Selected Decisions

s. Not Storing Loop Identification Codes Not Equivalent to Not Storing Duplicate Transmitter Identification Codes [New Topic]

In *Interactive Technologies, Inc. v. Pittway Corp.*,[123] the invention related to "wireless" home security systems. Such systems were pro-

---

[117] *Id.*, 50 USPQ 2d at 1166–67.

[118] Unidynamics Corp. v. Automatic Prods. Int'l Ltd., 157 F.3d 1311, 48 USPQ 2d 1099 (Fed. Cir. 1998).

[119] *Id.*, 48 USPQ 2d at 1101, 1104.

[120] *Id.* at 1104.

[121] Nagle Indus., Inc. v. Ford Motor Co., Civ. App. 97-1449 (Fed. Cir. June 22, 1999) (unpublished).

[122] *Id.*, slip op. at 9 (quoting Rodime PLC v. Seagate Tech., Inc., 174 F.3d 1294, 50 USPQ 2d 1429, 1436 (Fed. Cir. 1999), *cert. denied*, 528 U.S. 1115 (2000)).

[123] Interactive Techs., Inc. v. Pittway Corp., Civ. App. No. 98-1464 (Fed. Cir. June 1, 1999) (unpublished), *cert. denied*, 528 U.S. 1046 (1999).

Main volume footnote updates begin on page 223.

duced by Interactive and Pittway and included a central processing unit (CPU) and remote sensors to sense an intrusion, fire, or other emergency conditions. In wireless systems, the sensors are connected to transmitters, which send radio signals to the CPU.

The invention of Interactive's patent, entitled "Learn Mode Transmitter," attempted to counter various problems by not using house codes and zone numbers, but instead assigned different identification codes to each transmitter. Each transmitter code was randomly programmed at the factory from an essentially infinite pool of numbers, which code was thereafter transmitted with each transmission. By drawing the identification code from such an essentially infinite pool of numbers, the risk of crosstalk was made extremely improbable. Upon installation into the home, a learning or programming phase was undertaken whereby the local CPU upon hearing each transmitter's identity code for the first time wrote the code into a storage location in its memory that was thereafter accessed prior to responding to any later-received transmissions.

To prevent the CPU from learning a code from a sensor transmitter that was sending signals from another home during the learning phase, the invention required that part of the signal include additional codes that described predetermined or detectable conditions. The purpose of using this additional code was that, although a neighboring home might be transmitting signals during the learning phase, such signals were unlikely to include tamper signals, and thus, the requirement of the additional code prevented the CPU learning the identification codes of these stray signals.

Depending on the particular system, Pittway's system (the 5800 system) required that the loop identity code be transmitted either two or four times during its learning mode. In the systems that required only two transmissions, the CPU compared the loop identity code to those codes already in its table of codes. If the loop identity code was not already in the table, the CPU recorded it there. If it was already present, the CPU discarded it. In the four-transmission system, the CPU matched the 20-digit transmitter identification codes from the first two transmissions and then determined from which two-digit sensor the transmissions emanated. Then, if the 22-digit loop identity codes from the last two transmissions matched those of the first two transmissions, the CPU wrote the loop identity code into the table. However, as with the two-transmission system, if the loop identity code was already written into the table, the CPU will discard the incoming code.

The district court held that Pittway's system infringed Interactive's patent as an equivalent system, and Pittway appealed. On appeal, the Federal Circuit reversed. The Federal Circuit emphasized that even though the feature of not storing duplicate loop identification codes performed in Pittway's system might be interchangeable with not storing duplicate transmitter identification codes of Interactive's patent, it was functionally distinct and thus not equivalent as a matter of law. According to the Federal Circuit:

> In the instant case, the function of claim 1, step (f) of writing a transmitter identification code into a code table "if not located" as already in the code table cannot be met equivalently by the 5800's function of storing duplicate transmitter identification codes. This limitation, which appears in various forms in all asserted claims of the ′713 patent, functions to ensure that all stored transmitter identification codes are different. The 5800, by contrast, clearly permits the storage of duplicate transmitter identification codes. While the 5800 does not permit the storage of duplicate loop identification codes, this feature does not "function" to ensure that duplicate transmitter identification codes are not stored. Rather, the function of not storing duplicate transmitter identification codes is altogether missing from the 5800. . . . [W]hile the feature of not storing duplicate loop identification codes might be interchangeable with not storing duplicate transmitter identification codes, it is functionally distinct and thus not equivalent as a matter of law.[124]

t. Disrupting Signal Path Not Equivalent to Bypassing Signal Path [New Topic]

In *General Electric Co. v. Nintendo Co.*,[125] the Federal Circuit held that an invention that bypassed a signal path was not infringed by equivalents by a system that disrupted the signal path. The invention related to a switch that allowed the user of a television monitor to switch between video information received from an antenna and other sources of video information, for example, a video record player, when the user turned on or off the power to the alternative source. The switch directed RF signals (signals in the radio frequency range) from the video record player to the television receiver, while disrupting the flow of broadcast signals from the antenna to the television receiver, when the video record player was on.

The alleged infringing Nintendo products did not disrupt the signal path. The accused systems controlled the signal flow through three transistors. When the Nintendo systems were turned on, the transistors entered saturation, passing the signal from the antenna to ground. When the Nintendo systems were turned off, the transistors left saturation, and the signal passed from the antenna, past the transistors, to the television.

GE filed a patent infringement action alleging Nintendo's infringement of its patent, by Nintendo's video game systems (specifically the Nintendo Entertainment System (NES), the Super Nintendo Entertainment System (SNES), and the Gameboy). Nintendo argued

---

[124] *Id.*, slip op. at 11–12.

[125] General Elec. Co. v. Nintendo Co., 179 F.3d 1350, 50 USPQ 2d 1910 (Fed. Cir. 1999).

Main volume footnote updates begin on page 223.

that its systems did not infringe, literally or by equivalents. The district court agreed with Nintendo and GE appealed.

On appeal, the Federal Circuit affirmed the holding of nonequivalence and, therefore, noninfringement. According to the Federal Circuit:

> The accused systems can, however, infringe the . . . patent, under the doctrine of equivalents, if, inter alia, they perform an equivalent function to the disruption function claimed in the last means-plus-function limitation. . . . However, disrupting the signal path results in an alteration of the signal path, whereas bypassing the signal path does not. We, therefore, agree with the district court, that no reasonable jury could find that an equivalent function (substantially similar or substantially the same function) is performed in the accused systems.[126]

u. *Separately Mounted to Base Not Equivalent to Defined by Base Claim Limitation [New Topic]*

In *Rival Co. v. Sunbeam Corp.*,[127] the Federal Circuit held that a reservoir that was separately mounted to a base was not equivalent to a claim limitation reciting that the reservoir was defined by the base. The invention related to a food steaming device including a heater at the bottom of a reservoir where the water was boiled. The steam escaped through openings between the top of the reservoir and the food tray, circulated around the food tray, and cooked the food. Steam that condensed on the food drained into a separate condensate trough. In holding that the accused device was not an equivalent to the claimed reservoir defined by the base limitation, the Federal Circuit stated the following:

> As we determined above, the accused products clearly do not meet the "boiling water reservoir defined by the base" limitation. The products' drain tube and flow-through heater elements are in no sense "defined by the base"; they are separately mounted to the base with brackets. Rival's equivalence argument would thus render the distinction between claim 1's "defined by the base" and "mounted in the base" limitations meaningless. . . . Because the accused products do not possess the equivalent of a "boiling water reservoir defined by the base," we conclude that the district court correctly granted summary judgment that Sunbeam's products do not infringe claims 1 or 2 of the ′412 patent under the doctrine of equivalents.[128]

v. *Blade Contact Not Equivalent to Cylindrical Contact [New Topic]*

In *Independent Technologies, Inc. v. Siemon Co.*,[129] the Federal Circuit held that a blade contact was not equivalent to a cylindrical

---

[126] *Id.*, 50 USPQ 2d at 1914.

[127] Rival Co. v. Sunbeam Corp., Civ. App. No. 98-1198 (Fed. Cir. Feb. 23, 1999) (unpublished).

[128] *Id.*, slip op. at 15.

[129] Independent Techs., Inc. v. Siemon Co., Civ. App. No. 98-1256 (Fed. Cir. Jan. 29, 1999) (unpublished).

Main volume footnote updates begin on page 223.

contact. Independent Technologies' invention related to a telecommunications adapter designed to interface with a 110-type terminal block. The 110-type terminal block has an array of split-finger contacts, which are known in the industry as insulation displacement contacts (IDCs). The inventive adapter disclosed in the patent comprised a modular, bent-wire jack that was connected via a printed circuit board (PCB) to a plurality of metal blades. The inserted blades provide both electrical contacts and friction-fit stability to the connection.

Siemon's accused device was an adapter designed to interface with 110-type terminal blocks. Like the device disclosed in the patent, Siemon's adapter comprised a modular, bent-wire jack connected via a PCB to electrical contacts. The electrical contacts in the Siemon device, however, were spring loaded and cylindrical. The cylindrical contacts did not insert into the IDCs, but merely touched the IDCs at the IDCs' outermost edges. Siemon's adapter included small, vertically aligned, nonconductive fins that extended outward from the PCB above and below each of the cylindrical contacts.

Independent Technologies sued Siemon for infringing the patent under the doctrine of equivalents, and Siemon argued that no such infringement existed. The district court held that the Siemon adapter did not infringe by equivalents, and Independent Technologies appealed.

On appeal, the Federal Circuit affirmed the holding of noninfringement. According to the Federal Circuit:

> [W]e reject ITI's argument that Siemon's cylindrical contacts, together with their nonconductive fins, are substantially similar to the "conductive blades" and "blade contacts" recited in the asserted claims. . . . The "blade" elements in the claims provide an electrical connection by insertion into 110-type IDCs, resulting in physical metal-to-metal connections over a large portion of the blades' surface area. The evidence before the district court indicated, however, that the cylindrical contacts of the accused device provide an electrical connection without insertion into the IDCs. Specifically, they provide physical metal-to-metal connections over a relatively small portion of the contacts' surface area near their tips.[130]

w. On/Off Conducting State Not Equivalent to Continuous Low-Level Conductive Connection [New Topic]

In *Interlink Electronics v. Incontrol Solutions, Inc.*,[131] the invention related to a switch or transducer that controlled cursor movement. The specification of the patent described a pair of conductive elements comprising a normally open circuit available for connection to an external lead and, thus, a nonconducting relationship between

[130] *Id.*, slip op. at 5.

[131] Interlink Elecs. v. Incontrol Solutions, Inc., Civ. App. No. 98-1567 (Fed. Cir. Aug. 24, 1999) (unpublished).

contacts. Incontrol Solutions' products, however, provided a low-level conductive connection at all times. In affirming the district court's holding of nonequivalence, the Federal Circuit stated the following:

> The district court correctly held that, because Interlink's claims require a non-conducting relationship between the contacts, the accused products cannot infringe under the doctrine of equivalents. Interlink's claims describe a circuit that is either in an off (non-conducting) or on (conducting) electrical state. In contrast, the accused devices provide a low-level conductive connection at all times. They also use a shunt to maintain a parallel connection that decreases the variation in conductivity when an external force is applied. This dampening allows InControl's products to regulate cursor movements with much more precision than Interlink's "on or off" circuit. Thus, there is a substantial difference in the way the devices operate, which precludes infringement under the doctrine of equivalents.[132]

x. Spring Adjustment Device Not Equivalent to Manual Adjustment Device [New Topic]

In *Nagle Industries, Inc. v. Ford Motor Co.*,[133] the Federal Circuit held that a spring adjustment device was not equivalent to a manual adjustment device. The invention related to a pull-pull cable assembly for temperature control systems in automobiles. The claim recited "slack adjustment means" interpreted under Section 112, sixth paragraph that corresponded to the function of adjusting the tension in each of the strands located in a large pulley. The structure associated with that function was either a passageway, a channel with teeth spaced by grooves, a retainer member with a pair of outward-extending tangs that engage the teeth in the channel, and springs or a pair of parallel T-shaped arms, the free ends of which contained a channel and teeth spaced by grooves, and a single spring with C-shaped ends that projected outward and engaged the teeth. In both embodiments, a tool such as a screwdriver is used to adjust the slack manually.

The district court held that the Ford pull-pull cable assembly did not literally infringe any asserted claim of the '281 patent. More specifically, the district court stated:

> It is undisputed that the accused Ford device uses a single spring that works by itself to continuously and automatically eliminate slack and keep the strands taut. Unlike the claimed device, the accused Ford device does not have additional structures, like teeth and an engaging mechanism, that work together with the spring and allow manual adjustments of slack in the strands after installation.[134]

---

[132] *Id.*, slip op. at 4.

[133] Nagle Indus., Inc. v. Ford Motor Co., Civ. App. 97-1449 (Fed. Cir. June 22, 1999) (unpublished).

[134] *Id.*, slip op. at 4.

Main volume footnote updates begin on page 223.

The district court also held that Nagle had presented no genuine issue of material fact as to whether Ford infringed its patent under the doctrine of equivalents. To be equivalent, the district court found, there must be some mechanical device separate and apart from a spring that would allow adjustments to be made in the slack, which was lacking in the Ford device.

On appeal, the Federal Circuit affirmed. According to the Federal Circuit:

> To determine whether a specific structure in an accused device is equivalent under 112, 6, the question is whether the differences between the structure in the accused device and any disclosed in the written description are insubstantial or offer nothing of significance to the structure. . . . We agree with the district court that, as a matter of law, a spring (or two springs) alone cannot be deemed equivalent to either of the two manual adjustment structures disclosed in the written description.[135]

y. *Timing Circuit Not Equivalent to Spring Switch [New Topic]*

In *Orlaford Ltd. v. BBC International, Ltd.*,[136] the Federal Circuit held that a timing circuit was not equivalent to a spring switch. The invention related to footwear and circuitry that caused the footwear to light up and flash when the footwear was moved. Orlaford's patent used a timing circuit in the lighting circuitry. The timing circuit disconnected the battery from the light source a predetermined time after the switch—which alternated between "on" and "off" depending on the motion of the footwear—turned "on" and caused the light source to illuminate.

In BBC's accused devices, illumination was initiated when the spring switch closed (the "on" state) and the LEDs lit up. When the switch opened (the "off" state), the LEDs went through a flashing or fading sequence. It was the action of the spring switch that disconnected the power source from the light source. There was no separate timing circuit that disconnected the power source from the light source a predetermined time after illumination was initiated.

In holding that the spring switch was not an equivalent of the claimed timing circuit, the Federal Circuit stated the following:

> The timing circuit as claimed and described is a group of electronic components connected in such a way as to initially send power from a power source to a light source when a switch transitions from an "off" to an "on" state. After a predetermined amount of time, the timing circuit cuts off power from the power source to the light source, independent of the state of the switch. The spring switch functions in a different way. The amount

---

[135] *Id.* at 14.

[136] Orlaford Ltd. v. BBC Int'l, Ltd., Civ. App. 98-1332 (May 20, 1999) (unpublished).

Main volume footnote updates begin on page 223.

> of time it remains in the "on" state, connecting the power source to the light source, is variable, depending on the impact to the shoe. The spring switch does not automatically terminate power from the battery to the light source, creating a very different result from the timing circuit of [Orlaford's] patent if the spring were somehow stuck in the "on" position. No reasonable jury could find that the new modules contain an equivalent to the timing circuit claimed in the '009 patent.[137]

z. Patent Containing Lower Concentration Not Equivalent to One With Higher Concentration [New Topic]

In *Evans Medical Ltd. v. American Cyanamid Co.*,[138] the Federal Circuit held that an accused protein derived from the whooping cough-causing bacterium having a concentration of only four percent B. pertussis antigen did not infringe a patent claiming over 50 percent of the same antigen. The claims referred to the molecular weight of the antigen—approximately 69 kilodaltons (kD)—as one of its principal distinguishing characteristics. The art has referred to the antigen as the "69kD" antigen. The 69kD antigen is a protein embedded in the outer membranes of B. pertussis, making it somewhat difficult to extract. The 69kD antigen is prepared in the first instance by extracting B. pertussis bacteria overnight in an acidic glycine-hydrochloric acid solution with an isolation step using a monoclonal antibody.

A monoclonal antibody is a protein produced by an organism such as a mouse in response to a challenge to the organism's immune system with a foreign material (often a protein), or "antigen," such as a B. pertussis antigen. The monoclonal antibody so produced is able to form a complex with the challenging antigen that can be readily observed through standard procedures in the art, thus making monoclonal antibody technology a convenient method to identify and isolate antigens.

It was undisputed that American Cyanamid's vaccine accused by Evans Medical of infringing the patents contained only approximately four percent of the 69kD antigen. In affirming the holding of no equivalence, the Federal Circuit stated the following:

> Because it is undisputed that Defendants' antigen product contains no more than four percent of the 69kD antigen, we agree with the district court that there can be no literal infringement. . . . It is equally clear that under the circumstances there can be no infringement under the doctrine of equivalents, for a product cannot be found to be insubstantially different from a claimed one if arriving at such a finding would require vitiation of an essential claim element.[139]

---

[137] *Id.*, slip op. at 15–16.

[138] Evans Med. Ltd. v. American Cyanamid Co., 52 USPQ 2d 1455 (Fed. Cir. 1999) (unpublished).

[139] *Id.* at 1460.

Main volume footnote updates begin on page 223.

aa. Weight Member Attached Solely to Rear Wall Not Equivalent to Weight Member Attached to Rear Wall and Peripheral Mass [New Topic]

In *Antonious v. Spalding & Evenflo Cos.*,[140] the invention related to iron-type golf club heads. The invention was directed to a club head design incorporating a cavity back bar weight mass configuration that was described as increasing golf club performance during a golf swing. Antonious sued Spalding, claiming that Spalding's Top-Flite Tour and Tour Edition irons infringed the patent.

The district court interpreted the phrase "formed on and attached solely to said rear wall within said cavity" to mean that the weight member must be attached solely (i.e., only) to the rear wall (back side of the striking surface) and not attached also to the peripheral mass within the cavity.[141] The district court held that the peripheral mass was not properly considered to be part of the rear wall, and therefore the Spalding golf clubs were not equivalent.

On appeal, the Federal Circuit affirmed the district court. The Federal Circuit noted that because the peripheral mass was defined by the claim as being separate from, albeit located on, the rear wall, the plain meaning of "a single weight member formed on and attached solely to said rear wall" did not include a weight member fastened to the peripheral mass.[142]

In affirming the district court holding that the weight member attached solely to rear wall was not equivalent to weight member attached to rear wall and peripheral mass, the Federal Circuit stated the following:

> We have interpreted the literal scope of the claim limitation "a single weight member formed on and attached solely to said rear wall" to mean that the weight member cannot be connected to any structure other than the rear wall, and that the rear wall does not comprise the peripheral mass. Thus, application of the doctrine of equivalents to expand the scope of the claim to include an iron-type golf club head with a weight member attached to both the rear wall and the peripheral mass would impermissibly eliminate that limitation. . . . Therefore, since the weight member in the accused clubs is attached to both the rear wall and the peripheral mass, no reasonable jury could determine that the "attached solely to said rear wall" limitation is met in the accused clubs by an equivalent.[143]

---

[140] Antonious v. Spalding & Evenflo Cos., Civ. App. No. 98-1478 (Fed. Cir. Aug. 31, 1999) (unpublished).

[141] *Id.*, slip op. at 3.

[142] *Id.* at 6–7.

[143] *Id.* at 12–13.

Main volume footnote updates begin on page 223.

bb. Software Switch Possible Equivalent to Mechanical Switch [New Topic]

In *Overhead Door Corp. v. Chamberlain Group, Inc.*,[144] the invention in Chamberlain's patent related to remote control garage door opener systems. Remote control garage door opener systems typically include hand-held, portable transmitters and a stationary garage door opening motor with a processing unit and receiver. To open or close a garage door, a user presses a button on the transmitter to send a signal to the receiver. The receiver relays the signal to a processing unit that directs the door motor to open or close the garage door. The invention eliminated manual code switches in garage door transmitters, and enabled a garage door opener to learn the identities of and respond to multiple transmitters with different codes. An embodiment of the invention included two or more transmitters with lengthy, factory-programmed codes. The microprocessor in the receiver switched between "program" and "operate" modes.

Like the invention claimed in Chamberlain's patent, Overhead's system featured "program" and "operate" modes, and stored transmitter codes in selected memory locations during the learning process. Overhead's system, however, did not use a manual, mechanical memory selection switch. Rather, Overhead's system featured software that determined the memory location for each new code. A microprocessor, under control of the software, identified unused locations in memory and automatically stored a new code in an unused and available location.

Overhead Door filed a declaratory judgment action, seeking a judgment that its system did not infringe Chamberlain's patent, literally or by equivalents. The district court found that Overhead's system selected memory locations with software rather than a manual switch, and concluded that Overhead's system did not literally infringe Chamberlain's patent. The district court also found that Overhead's system did not infringe Chamberlain's patent under the doctrine of equivalents because Overhead's system included a microprocessor that used software to automatically select memory locations. The district court therefore granted Overhead's summary judgment motion of noninfringement. Chamberlain appealed.

On appeal, the Federal Circuit reversed the summary judgment of no infringement under the doctrine of equivalents. The Federal Circuit indicated that material issues of fact were in dispute as to whether a software-implemented switch could be an equivalent of the claimed mechanical switch. The Federal Circuit commented that the claim language and written description identified the "memory selec-

[144] Overhead Door Corp. v. Chamberlain Group, Inc., 194 F.3d 1261, 52 USPQ 2d 1321 (Fed. Cir. 1999).

Main volume footnote updates begin on page 223.

tion switch" as a mechanical device.[145] The Federal Circuit interpreted "memory selection switch" to mean a mechanical switch with different positions, each position corresponding to a different location in memory, thus enabling the garage door operator to store codes in different memory locations.[146]

The Federal Circuit noted that the record contained considerable evidence, including several reports and declarations by Chamberlain's expert, Dr. Rhyne, that one of ordinary skill in the art would find Overhead's software-driven memory selection system insubstantially different from the hardware switch of Chamberlain's patent. The expert, Dr. Rhyne, averred in his report that "[it is a] fundamental and well understood tenet of the computing art [that] . . . 'any software process can be transformed into an equivalent hardware process, and any hardware process can be transformed into an equivalent software process.'"[147] Dr. Rhyne also stated that this "dualistic transformation," known as the "hardware/software" trade-off, effectively means that the selection of a software pointer for a microprocessor versus a hardware switch to control a microprocessor-based system is simply a matter of design choice.[148] Drawing all reasonable inferences in favor of Chamberlain, as required in reviewing the grant of summary judgment of noninfringement, the Federal Circuit concluded that Dr. Rhyne's statements and supporting citations to computer science literature showed a genuine issue of material fact precluding summary judgment.

The Federal Circuit noted the following:

> In discerning this genuine factual issue, this court also considered the district court's interpretation that a mechanical switch would necessarily require a human operator. In operation of a mechanical switch, a human operator would indeed set the memory selection switch to one of five positions. This "user operated" characteristic of a mechanical switch, however, would not necessarily preclude a finding that software performs equivalently without human operation. Indeed in other contexts, this court has noted the interchangeability of hardware and software.[149]

cc. Foldover Flap Not Equivalent to Dual Flap Structure [New Topic]

In *Kemco Sales, Inc. v. Control Papers Co.*,[150] the invention related to plastic security envelopes that were tamper-evident, i.e., they

---

[145] *Id.*, 52 USPQ 2d at 1326.

[146] *Id.*

[147] *Id.* (citing Ed Klingler, Microprocessor Systems Design 5 (1977)).

[148] *Id.*

[149] *Id.* (citing Pennwalt Corp. v. Durand-Wayland, Inc., 833 F.2d 931, 935, 4 USPQ 2d 1737, 1740 (Fed. Cir. 1987) (en banc) ("If . . . the accused devices differ only in substituting a computer for hard-wired circuitry, [the patentee] might have a stronger position for arguing that the accused devices infringe the claims.")).

[150] Kemco Sales, Inc. v. Control Papers Co., 208 F.3d 1352, 54 USPQ 2d 1308 (Fed. Cir. 2000).

Main volume footnote updates begin on page 223.

indicated when a thief had breached the integrity of the envelope. The security afforded by prior art tamper-evident envelopes using adhesive-type materials was easily circumvented by applying low temperatures to the adhesive region, thereby causing the seal to separate from the envelope. Once the valuables were removed, the envelope eventually resealed on its own, leaving no evidence of tampering. The claimed invention solved this problem by employing two sealing means, one of which served as the primary closing mechanism of the envelope, the other of which indicated an improper attempt to open the envelope. The tamper-evident sealing means was comprised of fragile, temperature-sensitive adhesive and backing material. Claim 27, the only claim at issue, recited the following:

> 27. A tamper-evident sealing system for an envelope made at least partially of plastic material comprising:
>
> [an] envelope pocket having an opening therein through which contents can be placed into the pocket before the opening is closed;
>
> [a] plastic envelope closing means secured to the plastic envelope material to close the opening and to form a closed pocket, the closing means having at least one transverse edge;
>
> [a] first, adhesive, sealing means between the closing means and plastic envelope material for sealing the closing means to the plastic envelope material; and
>
> [a] second, tamper-evident, sealing means secured to both the closing means and the envelope extending substantially along the length of and over the transverse edge which becomes visibly distorted, broken apart, or of disrupted continuity if attempts are made to reopen the second, tamper-evident, sealing means whereby tamper-evidency is provided even if the first, adhesive, sealing means can be reopened and reclosed without visual detection thereof.[151]

The accused device, Control Papers' TripLok envelope, was structurally similar to the claimed invention, and also utilized two adhesive layers. As in the claimed invention, one layer was principally responsible for sealing the envelope, and the other indicated any evidence of tampering. Unlike the claimed invention, the TripLok envelope was closed by way of a dual-lip structure that sealed together via an internal adhesive.

Kemco sued Control Papers, alleging infringement of its patent. Control Papers moved for partial summary judgment of noninfringement, and Kemco cross-moved for summary judgment that claim 27 was literally infringed by the TripLok envelope. Based on its claim construction, the district court held that no reasonable jury could find that the TripLok literally infringed claim 27, as the dual-lip structure that closed the TripLok was not identical to the fold-over flap. The district court further held that no reasonable jury could find that the TripLok envelope infringed under the doctrine of equivalents. Kemco appealed.

---

[151] *Id.*, 54 USPQ 2d at 1309.

Main volume footnote updates begin on page 223.

On appeal, the Federal Circuit affirmed. The Federal Circuit noted that unlike the disclosed flap in Kemco's patent, which closed by folding over the envelope, Control Papers' dual-lip structure closed the accused envelope in a different way by meeting together and binding via the internal adhesive. The accused structure's different way of closing also yielded a substantially different result. The first and second sealing means in the disclosed structure were ultimately attached to the outside of the envelope. In contrast, the first sealing means in the TripLok envelope was internally attached to the two lips of the dual-lip structure, thereby sealing the envelope.[152]

Based on this analysis, the Federal Circuit held that it was clear that Control Papers did not infringe under the doctrine of equivalents. According to the Federal Circuit, the dual-lip structure was not an equivalent of a fold-over flap because the "way" and "result" were substantially different.[153]

dd. Manual Initiation of Maneuver Not Equivalent to Automatic Initiation [New Topic]

In *Space Systems/Loral, Inc. v. Lockheed Martin Corp.*,[154] the invention related to control systems for communication satellites. Communication satellites typically operate in a geosynchronous equatorial orbit, circling the earth once every 24 hours in the equatorial plane, thereby maintaining the same position relative to the earth's surface. Such positioning enables the satellite to maintain a consistent relationship with the ground transmitters from which it receives radio signals.

While orbiting the earth, satellites are subject to various destabilizing forces, such as the gravitational forces of the sun or moon, that can cause the satellite to drift behind or move ahead in its orbit (east-west drift), or drift out of its equatorial orbit and into an inclined orbit (north-south drift). In order to maintain a satellite's "pointing accuracy," i.e., its ability to receive radio signals from a particular ground transmitter and relay them to a specific target area, a satellite's position and attitude must be periodically adjusted.

The patent, i.e., the Chan patent, was directed to an apparatus for autonomously performing maneuvers for three-axis stabilized spacecraft such as geosynchronous satellites. The claimed apparatus included means for performing desaturation of the momentum wheel "while simultaneously accomplishing a preselected compensation of the spacecraft's east-west orbital position."[155] In other words, the claimed apparatus "automatically compensates for . . . east-west drift,

[152] *Id.*

[153] *Id.*

[154] Space Sys./Loral, Inc. v. Lockheed Martin Corp., Civ. App. No. 99-1255 (Fed. Cir. Aug. 23, 2000) (unpublished).

[155] *Id.*, slip op. at 4.

Main volume footnote updates begin on page 223.

while simultaneously allowing for desaturation of the wheels."[156] The written description states that one of the advantages of the claimed apparatus is that "[a]ll manual east-west stationkeeping maneuvers are eliminated."[157] Claim 1, the only claim in the Chan patent at issue, read as follows:

> 1. Apparatus for controlling a 3-axis stabilized spacecraft, comprising:
>
> [a] at least one momentum/reaction wheel mounted on board the spacecraft's attitude with respect to an axis;
>
> [b] a set of thrusters mounted about the periphery of the spacecraft for desaturating the momentum/reaction wheel and for accomplishing change in velocity maneuvers;
>
> [c] coupled to the momentum/reaction wheel, means for determining when the momentum/reaction wheel reaches saturation; and
>
> [d] coupled to the determining means, means for performing any desired desaturation of the momentum/reaction wheel while automatically and simultaneously accomplishing a preselected compensation of the spacecraft's east-west position.[158]

Lockheed manufactured and sold three-axis stabilized, geosynchronous communication satellites that utilized thrusters and momentum wheels to maintain their position and attitude. The satellites were capable of performing momentum wheel desaturation while simultaneously performing stationkeeping maneuvers initiated by a ground operator.

Space Systems/Loral (SSL) sued Lockheed, alleging that Lockheed's satellites infringed claim 1 of the Chan patent. Lockheed filed motions for summary judgment of noninfringement, which the district court granted. SSL appealed, and the Federal Circuit affirmed the holding of noninfringement.

Lockheed emphasized that the accused satellites required a ground operator to initiate maneuvers. Lockheed contended that the Chan patent did not disclose manually initiated maneuvers, and instead disclosed maneuvers initiated by the satellite itself, not by a ground operator.

The Federal Circuit observed that the accused satellites required a ground operator, rather than an automatic means, to select which thrusters to fire in order to perform an east-west change in position. Moreover, it was undisputed that Lockheed's satellites required manual initiation by the ground operator each time the maneuver was required.

SSL argued that claim 1 did not preclude manual initiation of simultaneous stationkeeping and desaturation maneuvers. However, the Federal Circuit agreed with Lockheed that manual initiation was

---

[156] *Id.*

[157] *Id.*

[158] *Id.*

Main volume footnote updates begin on page 223.

antithetical to the concept of being automatic.[159] Moreover, examination of the specification of the Chan patent showed that manual initiation of such maneuvers was neither disclosed nor contemplated.

Thus, while a ground operator determined the frequency of thruster firings and the duration of the firing period, the ground operator did not manually initiate the simultaneous stationkeeping and desaturation maneuvers. Instead, desaturation (as well as simultaneous stationkeeping) was initiated automatically, not by a ground operator. Moreover, the Federal Circuit noted, manual initiation of maneuvers was directly contrary to the stated objective of eliminating all manual east-west stationkeeping maneuvers. Accordingly, the Federal Circuit held that Lockheed's satellites did not literally infringe claim 1. While the Federal Circuit did not make a specific finding regarding equivalency because SSL failed to submit any evidence on that issue, this decision is instructive particularly because of the strong language the Federal Circuit used that automatically initiated maneuvers were "antithetical" to manual-initated maneuvers.[160]

ee. *Majority of Lengths Limitation Not Equivalent to Minority of Lengths Limitation [New Topic]*

In *Moore U.S.A. Inc. v. Standard Register Co.*,[161] the invention related to a C-fold mailer-type business form with an integral return envelope. The integral return envelope was created as part of the mailer during the folding and sealing process. The recipient opened the mailer by removing stubs on the left and right edges. After reading the information printed on the mailer, the user could remove a remittance stub from the top panel, insert the stub into the integral return envelope, detach the envelope from the rest of the mailer, and then seal and mail the envelope. Independent claim 1 recited:

> A mailer type business form intermediate, comprising:
>
> a sheet of paper having a first face, adapted to provide the majority of the interior of the mailer when constructed, and a second face, adapted to provide the majority of the exterior of the mailer when constructed;
>
> said sheet having first and second opposite, parallel longitudinal edges extending the entire length thereof, and opposite ends;
>
> first and second longitudinal lines of weakness formed in said sheet parallel to and adjacent, but spaced from, said first and second longitudinal edges, respectively, said lines of weakness defining, with said longitudinal edges, longitudinal marginal portions;

---

[159] *Id.*, slip op. at 12.

[160] *Id.*

[161] Moore U.S.A. Inc. v. Standard Register Co., 229 F.3d 1091, 56 USPQ 2d 1225 (Fed. Cir. 2000), *cert. denied*, 121 S. Ct. 1734 (2001).

Main volume footnote updates begin on page 223.

> first and second longitudinal strips of adhesive disposed in said first and second longitudinal marginal portions, respectively, of said first face, extending the majority of the lengths of said longitudinal marginal portions, and parallel to said first and second longitudinal edges;
>
> third and fourth longitudinal strips of adhesive disposed parallel to said first and second strips, and disposed adjacent said first and second lines of weakness on the opposite side thereof from said first and second strips, on said first face, said third and fourth longitudinal strips disposed closer to one end of said ends than the other, and extending a distance substantially less than the extent of said first and second strips;
>
> fifth and sixth longitudinal strips of adhesive parallel to said first and second longitudinal edges and disposed in said first and second marginal portions, respectively, on said second face, said fifth and sixth strips located adjacent the same end of said sheet as said third and fourth strips, and having a longitudinal extent at the most equal to said and fourth strips;
>
> means defining a transverse adhesive strip on said first face, perpendicular to said third and fourth strips, longitudinally spaced from said third and fourth strips; and
>
> means defining a line of weakness adjacent said transverse strip, on the opposite side thereof from said third and fourth strips, to allow ready separation of the paper at that line.[162]

The accused mailer by Standard Register, Form 8140C04, was a C-fold mailer with an integral return envelope. Although the accused form was somewhat similar to the patented mailer of Moore, Moore did not dispute that the accused mailer could not literally satisfy claim 1's requirement that the "first and second longitudinal strips of adhesive . . . extend[ ] the majority of the lengths of said longitudinal marginal portions."[163]

With respect to claim 1, the district court held that, because the first and second longitudinal strips of adhesive on the accused form extended less than the majority of the lengths of the longitudinal marginal portions, the accused form could not infringe claim 1 under the doctrine of equivalents. Applying the doctrine of equivalents to the accused form, the district court reasoned, would "remove entirely the 'majority of the lengths' limitation of Claim 1."[164]

Moore contended that the longitudinal strips of the accused form, which extended only a minority of the length of its longitudinal margins, were equivalent to the claimed strips, which extended a majority of the lengths of the longitudinal margins of the patented form. Moore argued that the "majority of the lengths" limitation of claim 1, by contrast, simply involved a matter of degree, not structure. Moore further contended that its desired scope of equivalents for claim 1 would not vitiate the "majority of the lengths" limitation. Moore characterized the critical issue as whether the first and second longitudi-

---

[162] *Id.*, 56 USPQ 2d at 1227.

[163] *Id.* at 1229.

[164] *Id.*

Main volume footnote updates begin on page 223.

nal strips of adhesive that extended "about 48%" of the length of the longitudinal margins were insubstantially different from strips that extended "50.001%" of the length of such margins.

The Federal Circuit disagreed. It held that Moore's use of the term "majority" was not entitled to a scope of equivalents covering a minority for at least two reasons. First, to allow what was undisputedly a minority (i.e., 47.8%) to be equivalent to a majority would vitiate the requirement that the "first and second longitudinal strips of adhesive . . . extend the majority of the lengths of said longitudinal marginal portions."[165] If a minority could be equivalent to a majority, this limitation would hardly be necessary, since the immediately preceding requirement of a "first and second longitudinal strips of adhesive disposed in said first and second longitudinal marginal portions, respectively, of said first face" would suffice.[166] Second, the Federal Circuit reasoned, "it would defy logic to conclude that a minority—the very antithesis of a majority—could be insubstantially different from a claim limitation requiring a majority, and no reasonable juror could find otherwise."[167]

Accordingly, the Federal Circuit held in *Moore*, a patent claim for mailer-type business form with the limitation that first and second longitudinal strips of adhesive extend the majority of the lengths of the longitudinal marginal portions of the form was not infringed, under doctrine of equivalents, by an accused form with longitudinal strips that extended only a minority of the length of its longitudinal margins.

ff. Rubber Grommet Not Equivalent to Threaded Connection [New Topic]

In *Cortland Line Co. v. Orvis Co.*,[168] the invention covered a fishing reel with an interchangeable cartridge spool. Traditionally, fishermen had great difficulty changing fishing lines in response to varying fishing conditions, since to change fishing lines, a fisherman had to remove the entire reel spool from the pole and substitute another reel spool. In addition, owning multiple spare reel spools with different fishing lines was an expensive proposition for most fishermen. The invention solved this problem by providing a fishing reel with an easily interchangeable cartridge spool that mounted onto the reel spool. Claim 1, the only independent claim, recited:

> 1. A fishing reel that provides for an interchangeable line bearing cartridge spool comprising:

---

[165] *Id.* at 1235.

[166] *Id.*

[167] *Id.*

[168] Cortland Line Co. v. Orvis Co., 203 F.3d 1351, 53 USPQ 2d 1734 (Fed. Cir. 2000).

Main volume footnote updates begin on page 223.

> a housing, said housing including a flat wall, said housing having a rigid first spool receiving shaft affixed thereto and protruding away from said wall;
>
> a cartridge spool;
>
> first spool means for mounting said cartridge spool, said first spool means comprising a first end plate, a first spool axle attached rigidly to said first end plate, a second end plate, and means for connecting said second end plate to said first spool axle, said first spool axle having a hollow aperture which is fitted over said first spool receiving shaft;
>
> means attached to said first spool means for manually rotating said first spool means;
>
> said cartridge spool comprising two end plates and a central cartridge spool axle unitarily connected therebetween, said cartridge spool axle being fitted over and mounted upon said first spool axle, said cartridge spool carrying a supply of fishing line, whereby said cartridge spool can be installed on or removed from said first spool.[169]

Orvis sold the accused fishing reel, marketed as Rocky Mountain Reels, having an interchangeable cartridge spool for quick and inexpensive changing of fly line. Cortland sued Orvis alleging infringement of its patent. The district court granted summary judgment of no patent infringement. The district court determined that the Rocky Mountain Reel has no second end plate equivalently. On appeal, the Federal Circuit affirmed the holding of no equivalent infringement.

Cortland asserted that the means for connecting recited in the claim was the interference fit of the rubber grommet to the hollow spool axle. However, the Federal Circuit held that a mere interference fit does not "connect" in substantially the same way, i.e., threadably lock. Moreover, the Federal Circuit reasoned, a mere interference fit would not obtain the result obtained by threaded connectors, which was the reventing of rotation in the center of cylindrical axle of the spool as described in the specification. Accordingly, the Federal Circuit reasoned that the accused fishing reel having the rubber grommet was substantially different from the disclosed threaded connectors of the invention, and therefore, was not a structural equivalent.[170]

According to the Federal Circuit, the rubber grommet did not fasten or lock as did the threaded connector in Cortland's patent. In other words, whereas in the Rocky Mountain Reel, the removable cartridge into which the flanged rubber grommet was fitted separated from the cartridge mounting axle when a moderate amount of force was applied to it, the threaded connector in the Cortland patent did not permit such a separation.[171]

Thus, in *Cortland Line Co.*, the Federal Circuit held that an accused fishing reel did not infringe the asserted claim of the patent-

---

[169] *Id.*, 53 USPQ 2d at 1735.

[170] *Id.* at 1739.

[171] *Id.*

Main volume footnote updates begin on page 223.

in-suit under the doctrine of equivalents, since the rubber grommet in accused device was not an equivalent of the rubber grommet means for connecting the end plate to the spool axle, as required by claim.

gg. *One-Fourth of Impeller Length Not Equivalent to Approximately One-Half Its Length [New Topic]*

In *Toro Co. v. Ariens Co.*,[172] the invention related to single-stage snowthrowers, i.e., snowthrowers that use an impeller both to pick up and to throw snow from the snowthrower. While single-stage snowthrowers are typically lighter and less costly than two-stage snowthrowers, which use different instruments to pick up and to throw the snow, two-stage snowthrowers throw snow farther and control the direction of that snow more effectively than their single-stage analogs. In an attempt to combine the advantages of both types of snowthrowers, the inventors of the patent designed a single-stage snowthrower with an improved impeller and an improved impeller/housing combination. Exemplary claim 24 recited:

> 24. An improved single stage snowthrower, which comprises:
>
> (a) a housing having a front portion which engages the snow and which includes a rear wall and spaced side walls, wherein the rear wall comprises an arcuate lower portion and an upper portion that extends upwardly relative to the lower portion;
>
> (b) a rotatable impeller located on the housing in front of the rear wall thereof and having a predetermined length between the side walls wherein the rotation of the impeller describes a cylinder that is bounded along the rear thereof by the arcuate lower portion of the rear wall and by at least a lower section of the upper portion of the rear wall, wherein the impeller includes an outwardly extending paddle having a curved central snowthrowing section for throwing upwardly away therefrom at approximately the juncture between the lower and upper portions of the rear wall a snow stream which has a width as it departs the snowthrowing section of at least approximately one-half the impeller's predetermined length and in which axially outermost portions of the snow stream have a component of motion that is directed axially inwardly; and
>
> (c) upwardly extending collecting means located on at least the lower section of the upper portion of the rear wall for receiving the snow stream from the impeller and for conducting that snow stream vertically upwardly, wherein the collecting means includes a trough means which tapers inwardly from side-to-side as it rises, and wherein the trough means at its lower end has a width which is at least approximately one-half the impeller's predetermined length.[173]

Ariens' single-stage snowthrower contained a somewhat similar impeller, however, the central portion of its impeller lacked the cur-

[172] Toro Co. v. Ariens Co., Civ. App. No. 99-1285 (Fed. Cir. Apr. 27, 2000) (unpublished).

[173] *Id.*, slip op. at 3–4.

Main volume footnote updates begin on page 223.

vature of the impeller depicted in Toro's patent. The two paddle portions of Arien's accused impeller contained a flat, central section bounded on both sides by curved transition sections.

Toro sued Ariens, alleging that Ariens willfully infringed the patent by making, using, and/or selling snowthrower products covered by that patent. Ariens denied infringement. The district court held in favor of Ariens, concluding that there was no genuine issue of material fact that the claims were not infringed by equivalents. On appeal, the Federal Circuit affirmed.

Toro argued that the district court erred in holding that the claims were not infringed. Ariens responded that the district court properly granted its motion for summary judgment of noninfringement because the accused impeller did not meet the disputed "throwing means" limitation in that claim. Ariens pointed out that the "throwing means" of its accused impeller was only three-to-four inches long, and much less than "approximately one-half of the impeller means' total length" of 18 inches recited in the claim.[174]

The Federal Circuit noted that the district court observed, and Toro did not dispute, that the flat, central section of the accused impeller was approximately three-to-four inches long, and that the total length of the impeller was approximately 18 inches. On this basis, the Federal Circuit did not have any difficulty in affirming the district court's conclusion that Ariens' device did not infringe under the doctrine of equivalents as a matter of law. The Federal Circuit reasoned that even assuming that the accused central snowthrowing section was four inches, it was still less than one-fourth of the total length of the impeller. According to the Federal Circuit, it was beyond argument that one-fourth of the impeller's length was not insubstantially different from "approximately one-half" of its length.[175] Thus, the Federal Circuit held that Arien's snowthrower was not an equivalent to the claimed snowthrower in Toro's patent.

hh. Connection With Single Piece of Metal Not Equivalent to Engagement Between Two Separate Pieces [New Topic]

In *Stairmaster Sports / Medical Products, Inc. v. Groupe Procycle, Inc.*,[176] the invention covered stair-climbing exercise machines with four basic components: pedals, a drive system assembly, a speed-increasing transmission, and a brake that resisted the motion of the drive assembly. The claims required connections between these components. When

---

[174] *Id.* at 14.

[175] *Id.* at 16.

[176] Stairmaster Sports/Medical Prods., Inc. v. Groupe Procycle, Inc., Civ. App. No. 99-1149 (Fed. Cir. Mar. 15, 2000) (unpublished).

Main volume footnote updates begin on page 223.

a user stepped on the pedals of the device, that movement drove the rotation of the drive shaft, which rotation was in turn transferred to the transmission input, and so forth through the other connected components of the patented invention. The claims recited that the connection between the transmission output and the brake, as the "brake being engaged with the transmission output," or as "means for engaging said transmission output and said dynamic brake means."[177]

Procycle manufactured and sold four models of stair-climbers that only had three main components: pedals, a drive shaft, and a brake wheel. When a user depressed the right or left pedal, that motion drove the rotation of an axle and of a large pulley wheel mounted upon that axle. The rotary motion of this large pulley was transferred by a belt to a small pulley-shaped portion of a single piece of metal which formed the brake wheel. The parties disputed whether this single integrally-molded brake was read on by the "brake engaged with a transmission output" and "means for engaging transmission output and brake" language of the claims.[178]

Stairmaster filed suit against Procycle, alleging that certain claims of the patent were infringed under the doctrine of equivalents by all of the Procycle steppers. The district court construed the terms "engaged" and "engaging" in the claims to mean "any type of mechanical engagement capable of coming into contact, interlocking, or meshing [two separate components]."[179] The district court granted Procycle's motion for summary judgment that the Procycle devices did not infringe the claims under the doctrine of equivalents. On appeal, the Federal Circuit affirmed.

The Federal Circuit noted that because the single integrally-molded brake wheel of the Procycle steppers did not engage the transmission output and the brake input, or perform the identical function of engaging those components, the district court correctly concluded that the accused Procycle steppers did not literally infringe the claims of Stairmaster's patent. The Federal Circuit also agreed with the district court that no reasonable jury could find that the molecular interactions between the sub-portions of the brake wheel of Procycle's steppers performed substantially the same function in the same way to achieve the same result as the mechanical engagements of the patent. As stated by the Federal Circuit, "[p]ut another way, no reasonable jury could find that the 'connections' within a single piece of metal perform substantially the same function as an engagement between two separate pieces."[180] Accordingly, the Federal Circuit affirmed

[177] *Id.*, slip op. at 2.

[178] *Id.* at 3.

[179] *Id.*

[180] *Id.* at 6.

Main volume footnote updates begin on page 223.

the grant of summary judgment of noninfringement under the doctrine of equivalents.

ii. Function of Collecting Carbon from Filter Not Equivalent to Function of Trapping Air Bubbles in Filter [New Topic]

In *Brita Wasser-Filter-Systeme, Gmbh v. Recovery Engineering, Inc.*,[181] the invention related to water filtration pitchers with filter cartridge inserts. A water filtration pitcher consists of a pitcher, a funnel seated within the pitcher, and a sleeve attached to the funnel in which a water filter sits. Untreated water is poured into the funnel, flows through the filter, which removes impurities, and finally flows into the pitcher. According to the Brita patent, prior art systems experienced air bubble accumulation in the sleeve during the filtration process due to the rising water level of the pitcher and the chemical reaction that takes place in the filter. This accumulation was undesirable because it impeded the flow of water through the filter. The invention disclosed in the Brita patent sought to address this problem by providing a filter and sleeve design that was capable of exhausting air bubbles from the sleeve. Thus, the claimed invention comprised a filter (referred to as the "insert") with a space that collected and exhausted air upwardly and ultimately out of an opening in the sleeve. Claim 1, the only claim at issue, read as follows:

> 1. A water purification device comprising:
>
> an intake funnel,
>
> a sleeve wherein said sleeve is sealingly connected to said funnel at an upper end of said sleeve, said sleeve further having an opening formed therein,
>
> an insert having approximately cylindrical side walls, a filter cover and a filter bottom for accommodating a granulate filter agent therein with means defining an air collecting space, located in at least a portion of the filter bottom, said means defining the air collecting space extending upwardly at least partially towards the side wall and to the opening in said sleeve, with said filter bottom having opening means to allow the passage of filtrate therethrough, and with said filter cover having opening means whereby fluid can be passed into the insert.[182]

First, the district court held that "means defining an air collecting space" was a means-plus-function limitation, governed by 35 U.S.C. Section 112, paragraph six. The district court determined that the function claimed was "gathering and removing bubbles from the filter bottom," and the structure corresponding to this function was a space

---

[181] Brita Wasser-Filter-Systeme, Gmbh v. Recovery Eng'g, Inc., Civ. App. No. 99-1322 (Fed. Cir. Sept. 21, 2000) (unpublished).

[182] *Id.*, slip op. at 2.

Main volume footnote updates begin on page 223.

in the filter having a vertical and horizontal component as described in the specification. Having construed the claims, the district court granted summary judgment of non-infringement in favor of Recovery. The district court determined that the Recovery device did not meet the means defining an air collecting space limitation, because the Recovery device did not use the structure disclosed in Brita's patent or an equivalent thereof.

The district court determined that the Recovery system did not have a sleeve, as claimed in the patent, because the Recovery "sleeve" was in two pieces that were not continuous, had only one open end, and did not have an opening. Further, the district court determined that because the Recovery sleeve performed a different function in a different way from the claimed sleeve, no genuine issue of material fact existed regarding infringement under the doctrine of equivalents. Therefore, the district court granted summary judgment of non-infringement in favor of Recovery.

On appeal, the Federal Circuit affirmed the holding of non-equivalency, albeit with a revised claim interpretation. The Federal Circuit noted that although the claim language at issue did not utilize the traditional "means for" predicate before claiming a function, the claim contained the term "means" followed by the function of defining an air collecting space. Thus, the presumption of Section 112, sixth paragraph treatment was raised. However, the Federal Circuit held that this presumption was overcome by the sufficiently definite structural parameters found in the claim regarding the air collecting space. That is, the claim language itself structurally defined the air collecting space as a component of the insert, i.e., the claim recited "an insert having approximately cylindrical sidewalls, a filter cover and a filter bottom, . . . with means defining an air collecting space."[183] The claim further recited that the air collecting space was "located in at least a portion of the filter bottom" and "extend[s] at least partially towards the side wall and to the opening in said sleeve."[184] In other words, the air collecting space was a void that was formed as part of the insert, and was located at the bottom of the insert (the filter bottom), and extended upwardly along the side walls of the insert and to the opening of the sleeve in which the insert sat. Because this structural recitation sufficiently performed the function of "defining an air collecting space," the Federal Circuit held that Section 112, sixth paragraph treatment was not proper.

Having determined that this limitation was not governed by Section 112, sixth paragraph, the Federal Circuit interpreted the air collecting space as a void that was structurally defined as part of the

---

[183] *Id.* at 7.

[184] *Id.*

Main volume footnote updates begin on page 223.

insert, formed at the bottom of the insert and extending upwardly along the side walls and to the opening in the sleeve. The claimed sleeve had several functions, such as effecting a sealing connection with the funnel, and providing a place for the insert to sit. In addition, the sleeve functioned to close off the air collecting space formed in the insert so that air bubbles could escape to the opening in the sleeve. As stated in the patent, the "sleeve walls embrace the insert . . . so that the air which occurs in the lower area in the region of the filter bottom can actually be collected in the chimney-like half-tube of the air collecting space."[185]

According to the Federal Circuit, the filter cap of the accused device could not meet the sleeve limitation equivalently because it did not perform the function of facilitating the exhaustion of air bubbles. In contrast, the function of the filter cap of the accused device was to collect carbon fines from the filter so that these fines did not fall into the bottom of the pitcher. Furthermore, the filter cap functioned to keep the filter wet and slow the flow-rate of water going through the pitcher.

XIV. Special Topic: Effect of Dimensional or Range Limitations on Obviousness

[Insert after footnote 685.]

"When unexpected results are used as evidence of nonobviousness, the results must be shown to be unexpected compared with the closest prior art."[186]

[Insert after footnote 705.]

A. Invention Held Obvious Where Showing of Unexpected Results Was Not Compared to Closest Prior Art [New Topic]

"When unexpected results are used as evidence of nonobviousness, the results must be shown to be unexpected compared with the closest prior art."[187] For example, in *In re Case*,[188] the applicant failed to show nonobviousness of the claimed invention because the applicant failed to compare the invention to the closest prior art. The invention related

[185] *Id.* at 16.

[186] *In re* Baxter Travenol Labs., 952 F.2d 388, 392, 21 USPQ 2d 1281, 1285 (Fed. Cir. 1991).

[187] *In re* Baxter Travenol Labs., 952 F.2d 388, 392, 21 USPQ 2d 1281, 1285 (Fed. Cir. 1991).

[188] *In re* Case, Civ. App. No. 98-1531 (Fed. Cir. Aug. 31, 1999) (unpublished).

Main volume footnote updates begin on page 223.

to reducing sidestream smoke from smoking articles, such as cigarettes. Sidestream smoke is the smoke that passes through cigarette paper when a lit cigarette is not being smoked, for example, when the cigarette is sitting in an ashtray.

The patent application claimed a cigarette paper with a total filler content of "about 20% by weight or less," of which "about 4% to about 14%" was magnesium hydroxide or reactive grade magnesium oxide (magnesium oxide).[189] Such a cigarette paper Case asserted unexpectedly improved sidestream smoke reduction. The Examiner rejected the claims as obvious over U.S. Patent No. 4,231,377 (Cline patent) in view of U.S. Patent No. 4,805,644 (Hampl patent). Claims 9–11 were rejected over Cline in view of Hampl and U.S. Patent No. 4,942,888 (Montoya). The Examiner did not reject the claims that recited the closed-end range of the magnesium oxide filler as being "4% to 14%," but did reject the claims that recited the range of "*about* 4% to *about* 14%."[190]

Case appealed to the Board, which sustained the rejections after concluding that the prior art cited by the Examiner established the obviousness of the appealed claims and that the evidence of nonobviousness supplied by Case failed to outweigh the evidence of obviousness established by the prior art. Case then appealed to the Federal Circuit, which affirmed the rejection.

The Federal Circuit noted that the Board found that the Cline patent disclosed the use of magnesium oxide as the sole filler in the disclosed cigarette paper, with the amount being as little as 15 percent by weight of the paper. The Board determined that Cline rendered the claims obvious because Case made no compelling arguments that the difference between "about 14%" and "at least 15%" produced any unexpected results.

The Board also considered, but found unpersuasive, an affidavit prepared by Case. The Case affidavit showed a comparison between cigarettes utilizing papers in accordance with the claimed invention and those of Cline. The Board found that the comparisons did not, as required, compare the claimed invention to the closest prior art because Case "(1) selected embodiments of Cline that were extremely far away from, rather than selecting Cline's embodiments that were much closer to, that of the claimed invention and (2) thereafter selected embodiments of Case that were in the middle of the claimed range, rather than selecting Case's embodiments within the claimed range that were much closer to those disclosed by Cline."[191]

While acknowledging that Cline was the closest prior art reference, Case argued that Cline lacked any suggestion or motivation to

[189] *Id.*, slip op. at 2.

[190] *Id.* at 3 (emphasis added).

[191] *Id.* at 5.

Main volume footnote updates begin on page 223.

create a cigarette wrapper with low total filler levels in combination with low levels of magnesium oxide. The Federal Circuit disagreed with Case, reasoning that, "[b]ecause the ranges of magnesium oxide in Cline and the claimed invention at the very least abut each other, some evidence of unexpected results is necessary to show claims 1 and 17 should be patentable."[192]

The government, on behalf of the Patent Office, contended that because the claimed range of magnesium oxide overlapped the prior art range in Cline, it was incumbent upon Case to show evidence of unexpected results. The government also argued that the Case affidavit did not speak to the closest prior art, mainly because it used magnesium oxide in percentages greatly varied from 15 percent.

The Federal Circuit agreed with the government that the affidavit supplied by Case was insufficient to rebut the prima facie case of obviousness. The Federal Circuit noted that the Board did not err in concluding that the Case affidavit did not compare the closest prior art, which was the Cline patent embodiment where the magnesium oxide was used as the sole filler in an amount as little as 15 percent by weight of the paper. Rather, Case selected embodiments of the Cline patent with magnesium oxide in the amounts of 22.2 percent and 23 percent, and embodiments of the claimed invention with magnesium oxide in the amounts of 10.8 percent and 11 percent.

With respect to additional evidence that Case provided to rebut the prima facie obviousness holding, the Federal Circuit stated the following:

> In its brief and at oral argument Case presented a graph that appears to be compelling evidence of unexpected results. . . . Although superficially compelling, the graph is flawed in a critical respect: the graph does not compare the claimed invention to the closest prior art. The graph is based upon data points selected from Cline and the '779 application. Each of the papers to which these data points relate contain calcium carbonate. As discussed above, the Board's determination that Cline teaches a cigarette paper using 15% magnesium oxide as the sole filler is supported by substantial evidence. Therefore, the closest prior art is a cigarette paper containing magnesium oxide and no calcium carbonate. Since Case has failed to make such a comparison, this graph fails to rebut the prima facie case of obviousness.[193]

For the above reasons, the Federal Circuit affirmed the decision of the Board that Case had not provided sufficient evidence to rebut

---

[192] *Id.* at 10 (citing *In re* Woodruff, 919 F.2d 1575, 1578, 16 USPQ 2d 1934, 1936 (Fed. Cir. 1990) (holding that patentability cannot be found in the difference in ranges between the prior art and the claimed invention unless the applicant shows "that the claimed range achieves unexpected results relative to the prior art range")).

[193] *Id.* at 13–15.

Main volume footnote updates begin on page 223.

the prima facie case of obviousness. Thus, *Case* illustrates that when the prior art is close to the claimed invention, evidence rebutting obviousness must consider the closest prior art.

XV. Special Topic: Combination of Old Elements

[Insert after footnote 707.]

The Federal Circuit has further explained:

> Combination claims can consist of new combinations of old elements or combinations of new and old elements. . . . Because old elements are part of these combination claims, claim limitations may, and often do, read on the prior art. . . . It is well established in patent law that a claim may consist of all old elements, such as the rigid-conduit system, for it may be that the combination of the old elements is novel and patentable. Similarly, it is well established that a claim may consist of all old elements and one new element, thereby being patentable.[194]

In addition, the Federal Circuit has stated:

> Most if not all inventions arise from a combination of old elements. . . . Thus, every element of a claimed invention may often be found in the prior art. . . . However, identification in the prior art of each individual part claimed is insufficient to defeat patentability of the whole claimed invention. . . . Rather, to establish obviousness based on a combination of the elements disclosed in the prior art, there must be some motivation, suggestion or teaching of the desirability of making the specific combination that was made by the applicant.[195]

XVI. Special Topic: Obviousness and Common Assignee

[Insert at the end of the section.]

In 1999, the Intellectual Property and Communications Omnibus Reform Act of 1999 was passed, which loosened the rules of when prior art owned by a common assignee can be used in an obviousness rejection.[196] Section 4807 of the Act, entitled "Prior Art Exclusion for Certain Commonly Assigned Patents," states:

---

[194] Clearstream Wastewater Sys., Inc. v. Hydro-Action, Inc., 206 F.3d 1440, 54 USPQ 2d 1185 (Fed. Cir. 2000) (citing Intel Corp. v. U.S. Int'l Trade Comm'n, 946 F.2d 821, 842, 20 USPQ 2d 1161, 1179 (Fed. Cir. 1991); Panduit Corp. v. Dennison Mfg., 810 F.2d 1561, 1575, 1 USPQ 2d 1593, 1603 (Fed. Cir. 1987)).

[195] *In re* Kotzab, 217 F.3d 1365, 55 USPQ 2d 1313, 1317 (Fed. Cir. 2000).

[196] Intellectual Property and Communications Omnibus Reform Act of 1999, Pub. L. No. 106–113, 4807, Nov. 29, 1999.

Main volume footnote updates begin on page 223.

> (a) PRIOR ART EXCLUSION—Section 103(c) of title 35, United States Code, is amended by striking "subsection (f) or (g)" and inserting "one or more of subsections (e), (f), and (g)".
>
> (b) EFFECTIVE DATE—The amendment made by this section shall apply to any application for patent filed on or after the date of the enactment of this Act.[197]

Thus, Section 103(c) of Title 35, United States Code, now states:

> Subject matter developed by another person, which qualifies as prior art only under one or more of subsections (e), (f) and (g) of section 102 of this title, shall not preclude patentability under this section where the subject matter and the claimed invention were, at the time the invention was made, owned by the same person or subject to an obligation of assignment to the same person.[198]

Thus, this last sentence of Section 103 now creates a safe harbor provision by exempting from prior art technical information that has developed within an organization that falls under Sections 102(e), (f), or (g). Therefore an Examiner may not base a rejection on Sections 102(e), (f), or (g) if the prior art subject matter and the claimed invention were commonly owned at the time the invention was made. The effective date of this amendment is for any application for patent filed on or after November 29, 1999.

Even though it is improper for an Examiner to reject a claim based on obviousness when the prior art subject matter falls under Sections 102(e), (f), or (g), an obviousness rejection may be predicated on subject matter that falls under Sections 102(a) or (b) that was developed by the same organization. This amendment to Section 103(c), therefore, effectively overrules *In re Land*.

Rule 130 has also been amended to incorporate this amendment, as well as the ability to utilize Rule 130 in connection with U.S. published patent applications, and recites the following:

> (a) When any claim of an application or a patent under reexamination is rejected under 35 U.S.C. 103 in view of a U.S. patent or a U.S. patent application publication which is not prior art under 35 U.S.C. 102(b), and the inventions defined by the claims in the application or patent under reexamination and by the claims in the patent or published application are not identical but are not patentably distinct, and the inventions are owned by the same party, the applicant or owner of the patent under reexamination may disqualify the patent or patent application publication as prior art. The patent or patent application publication can be disqualified as prior art by submission of:
>
> (1) A terminal disclaimer in accordance with § 1.321(c), and
>
> (2) An oath or declaration stating that the application or patent under reexamination and the patent or published application are currently owned by the same party, and that the inventor named in the applica-

[197] *Id.* at 4807.

[198] To be codified at 35 U.S.C. § 103(c).

Main volume footnote updates begin on page 223.

tion or patent under reexamination is the prior inventor under 35 U.S.C. 104.[199]

Subsection (a) provides that when any claim of an application or a patent under reexamination is rejected as obvious based on a U.S. patent or U.S. patent application publication to another or others that are not prior art more than one year from the filing date of the application, and the inventions defined by the claims in the application or patent under reexamination and by the claims in the patent or published application are patentably indistinct but not identical, and the inventions are owned by the same party, the applicant or owner of the patent under reexamination may disqualify the patent or published patent application as prior art.

Subsection (a) specifically provides that the patent or published application can be disqualified as prior art by submission of (1) a terminal disclaimer in accordance with Section 1.321(c) and (2) an oath or declaration stating that the application or patent under reexamination and the patent or published patent application are currently owned by the same party, and that the inventor named in the application or patent under reexamination is the prior inventor under 35 U.S.C. Section 104. Thus, Subsection (a) requires the applicant to indicate that the prior art patent or published patent application that is being relied on by the Examiner was in fact invented by the same inventor or inventorship entity of the application that has been rejected thereby.

Subsection (a) also requires an oath or declaration because the assignee information in the terminal disclaimer or recorded assignments may not be current, and the applicant is in the best position to verify that the application or patent under reexamination and the patent or published patent application are currently owned by the same party.[200] The assignment records maintained by the U.S. Patent Office do not generally supply the necessary evidence for the time requirement under Section 103(c), and the assignment records are not required to have such information to be recordable. Thus, the Patent Office has indicated that the following evidence is sufficient to provide proof of common ownership by, or subject to an obligation of assignment to, the same person at the time the invention was made as required under Section 103(c):

For recorded assignments, the applicant provides the following:

1. A statement of the location of the assignments recorded in the Patent Office in accordance with 37 C.F.R. Section 3.11 which convey the entire rights in the application and the reference to the same person(s) or organization(s), and

2. A statement from applicant(s) or their registered practitioner that the application for patent and the "prior art" reference applied against the application were commonly owned by, or subject to an obligation of

[199] Fed. Reg., Vol. 65, No. 183, 57056–57 (Sept. 20, 2000).

[200] *Id.* at 57033.

Main volume footnote updates begin on page 223.

assignment to, the same person, at the time the invention in the application for patent was made; . . .

For unrecorded assignments, the applicant provides the following:

1. Copies of unrecorded assignments which convey the entire rights in the application and the reference to the same person(s) or organization(s), and

2. A statement from applicant(s) or their registered practitioner that the application for patent and the "prior art" reference applied against the application were commonly owned by, or subject to an obligation of assignment to, the same person, at the time the invention in the application for patent was made; or

Applicant provides an affidavit or declaration by the common owner stating:

1. There was common ownership by, or an obligation of assignment to, the same person for the application and the "prior art" reference at the time the invention was made, and

2. Why the applicant believes there was common ownership; or

3. Applicant provides other evidence that established common ownership by, or an obligation of assignment to, same person for the application and the "prior art" reference at the time the invention was made, e.g., a court decision determining the owner.[201]

In circumstances where the common owner is a corporation or other organization, an affidavit or declaration averring ownership may be signed by an official of the corporation or organization empowered to act on behalf of the corporation or organization. A copy of the Patent Office rules setting forth the policy concerning evidence of common ownership is provided in Appendix C.

XVII. Special Topic: Obviousness and On-Sale/Public Use Prior Art

[Insert at the end of the section.]

Comfort Silkie Co. v. Seifert[202] is an example of a case in which two separate public uses were combined to support a holding of invalidity of a patent based on nonobviousness. The patented invention was a baby blanket whose two sides, one made of satin and the other of flannel, slid when rubbed between a child's thumb and finger. Cheryl Porcaro, a nonparty, had made a baby blanket whose two sides, respectively, made of satin and flannel, slid when rubbed be-

[201] See Appendix C, Guidelines Concerning the Implementation of Changes to 35 USC 102(g) and 103(c) and the Interpretation of the Term "Original Application" in the American Inventors Protection Act of 1999.

[202] Comfort Silkie Co. v. Seifert, Civ. App. No. 98-1476 (Fed. Cir. July 16, 1999) (unpublished), *cert. denied*, 529 U.S. 1019 (2000).

Main volume footnote updates begin on page 223.

tween thumb and finger. Evidence was introduced in the form of photographs, depositions, and affidavits that Porcaro had been making these blankets for more than a year before the filing date of the application that issued as the patent owned by Comfort Silkie.

Comfort Silkie argued that there was insufficient evidence to prove that the blankets were used publicly more than a year before the filing date. That is, Comfort Silkie argued that any use before the critical date of the baby blankets was not a public use. Seifert placed one of Porcaro's actual blankets into evidence, and six photographs of various blankets, which Porcaro testified were taken more than a year before the Comfort Silkie's patent application was submitted. It was undisputed that these blankets were taken into public places, as could be seen from the photographs, like airports, public parks, and restaurants with no expectation of privacy or confidentiality.

Comfort Silkie argued that a baby blanket could not be considered to have been in public use because it was within the baby's realm of privacy and could not be touched by strangers. The Federal Circuit quickly disposed of this argument, noting that "if the Supreme Court has held that a woman wearing a corset stay, under her clothes, is a public use, then a fortiori, a baby playing with a blanket in public locations observable by others is a public use."[203]

The only issue that remained was that the blankets that were used in public were not of the same size as the size limitations in claims 5 and 11 of Comfort Silkie's patent, which recited "dimensions of 14 inches by 18 inches or less."[204] The Federal Circuit agreed that the prior public use of the blankets could not alone anticipate claims 5 and 11 of the patent. However, the Federal Circuit noted that a bunny rabbit cloth toy that was sold by Fisher-Price, when combined with Pocaro's blanket, rendered Comfort Silkie's patent obvious. As stated by the Federal Circuit:

> However, Fisher-Price has made, since 1979, a cloth rabbit toy under the mark SECURITY BUNNY, in which the body of the rabbit toy is made of a single ply of blanket-type material with a satin binding. When laid as flatly as possible, the toy, although not itself rectangular, could be circumscribed within a rectangular envelope of the order of 14 inches by 18 inches. The Security Bunny is clearly analogous art, and when combined with the Porcaro blanket, we agree that the size limitation in claims 5 and 11 of the '285 patent would have been a matter of routine variation and therefore the blankets of these two claims were obvious under 35 U.S.C. § 103.[205]

Accordingly, the Federal Circuit held, as a matter of law, that claims 5 and 11 were invalid as being obvious in view of the combination of two public uses.

---

[203] *Id.*, slip op. at 4 (citing Egbert v. Lippmann, 104 U.S. 333 (1881)).

[204] *Id.*

[205] *Id.*

Main volume footnote updates begin on page 223.

MAIN VOLUME FOOTNOTE UPDATES

[43]**[Add the following to the end of footnote 43.]** *See also* Cabinet Vision v. Cabnetware, Civ. App. No. 99-1050, slip op. at 13–14 (Fed. Cir. Feb. 14, 2000) (unpublished) ("More specifically, Cornwell declared during prosecution of the '207 patent that '[b]eginning in 1986, I sold a computer-based program that permitted the user to design one cabinet at a time, and then to display a series of cabinets in an elevational view on a wall. The user assembled the series of cabinets with computer assistance in the display.' Thus, the inventor admits selling a computer design program with many or all of the features of the claimed invention before the critical date of June 16, 1987.").

[78]**[Add the following to the end of footnote 78.]** *See also In re* Greene, Civ. App. No. 99-1317, slip op. at 10 (Fed. Cir. Dec. 6, 1999) (unpublished) (quoting *In re* Heck, 699 F.2d 1331, 1333, 216 USPQ 1038, 1039 (Fed. Cir. 1983) ("Whether a prior art reference 'enables' a claimed use is not essential to a conclusion of obviousness. Nor is use of a patent as a reference limited to what is described in the patent or to the problem that the cited patent is designed to address. Rather, references are 'relevant for all they contain.'")).

[106]**[Replace the S. Ct. cite with the following.]** 521 U.S. 1122.

[134]**[Replace the S. Ct. cite with the following.]** 519 U.S. 822.

[173]**[Replace the existing footnote with the following.]** Armament Sys. & Procedures, Inc. v. Monadnock Lifetime Prods, Inc., Civ. App. 97-1174, slip op. at 12 (Fed. Cir. Aug. 7, 1998) (unpublished).

[188]**[Replace the S. Ct. cite with the following.]** 516 U.S. 990.

[191]**[Replace the existing footnote with the following.]** Armament Sys. & Procedures, Inc. v. Monadnock Lifetime Prods, Inc., Civ. App. 97-1174 (Fed. Cir. Aug. 7, 1998) (unpublished).

[194]**[Replace the S. Ct. cite with the following.]** 524 U.S. 927.

[205]**[Replace existing footnote 205 with the following.]** *In re* Zurko, 111 F.3d 887, 42 USPQ 2d 1476, 1479 (Fed. Cir.), *rev'd on other grounds*, 527 U.S. 150, 50 USPQ 2d 1930 (1999) (citing *In re* Sponnable, 405 F.2d 578, 585, 160 USPQ 237, 243 (C.C.P.A. 1969) ("[A] patentable invention may lie in the discovery of the source of a problem even though the remedy may be obvious once the source of the problem is identified.")).

[261]**[Replace the S. Ct. cite with the following.]** 524 U.S. 927.

[359]**[Delete the cite to the Atlantic Thermoplastics slip opinion and substitute the following.]** 974 F.2d 1279, 23 USPQ 2d 1801, 1803 (Fed. Cir. 1992).

[373]**[Delete the cite to the Atlantic Thermoplastics slip opinion and substitute the following.]** 974 F.2d 1279, 23 USPQ 2d 1801, 1805 (Fed. Cir. 1992).

[443]**[Replace the S. Ct. cite with the following.]** 622 U.S. 1147.

[458]**[Replace existing footnote 458 with the following.]** *In re* Zurko, 111 F.3d 887, 42 USPQ 2d 1476 (Fed. Cir. 1997), *rev'd on other grounds*, 527 U.S. 150, 50 USPQ 2d 1930 (1999).

[472]**[Insert at the end of the footnote.]** *See also* Heidelberg Harris, Inc. v. Mitsubishi Heavy Indus., Ltd., Civ. App. No. 99-1100, slip op. at 12–13 (Fed. Cir. Sept. 18, 2000) (unpublished):

> While the phrase "for reducing vibrations and slippage" was originally added to the body of the '048 claims in the context of means-plus-function language, which indisputably would have acted to limit the claimed inventions, its movement to the preamble of the newly-added claims did not create a similar effect.

> The only relevance of the phrase "reducing vibrations and slippage" is to illustrate the intended purpose of the invention. See Pitney Bowes, Inc. v. Hewlett-Packard Co., 182 F.3d 1298, 1305, 51 USPQ 2d 1161, 1165–66 (Fed. Cir. 1999). The phrase is plainly not "necessary to give life, meaning, and vitality to the claim." Kropa v. Robie, 187 F.2d 150, 152, 88 USPQ 478, 480–81 (C.C.P.A. 1951). It does not, for example, provide an antecedent basis for terms later used in the body of the claim. See Gerber Garment Tech., Inc. v. Lectra Sys., Inc., 916 F.2d 683, 688–89, 16 USPQ 2d 1436, 1441 (Fed. Cir. 1990). Nor could such an expression of the intended use and function of the offset press have distinguished over the prior art. See In re Lechene, 277 F.2d 173, 176, 125 USPQ 2d 396, 399 (C.C.P.A. 1960). Consequently, we hold that the phrase "reducing vibrations and slippage" is not a claim limitation.

[476]**[Change "35 U.S.C. § 112, § 2 (1988)" to "35 U.S.C. § 112, ¶ 2 (1988)."]**

[550]**[Replace "*cert. filed* (Nov. 6, 1995)" with "*rev'd and remanded on other grounds*, 520 U.S. 17, 41 USPQ 2d 1865 (1997)."]**

[553]**[Replace 117 S. Ct. 1040 with the following.]**, 520 U.S. 17, 41 USPQ 2d 1865 (1997).

[557]**[Replace the S. Ct. cite for Pall Corp. v. Micron Separations, Inc. with the following.]** 520 U.S. 1115.

[559]**[Replace "*petition for cert. filed,* (Dec. 16, 1996)" with the following.]** *cert denied,* 520 U.S. 1228 (1997).

[562]**[Replace the S. Ct. cite with the following.]** 522 U.S. 908.

[579]**[Replace the S. Ct. cite with the following.]**, 520 U.S. 17, 41 USPQ 2d 1865 (1997).

[581]**[Replace the S. Ct. cite with the following.]** 520 U.S. 17.

[594]**[Replace the S. Ct. cite with the following.]** 520 U.S. 1155.

[639]**[Replace the S. Ct. cite with the following.]** 522 U.S. 818.

[647]**[Replace the S. Ct. cite with the following.]** 525 U.S. 875.

[729]**[Replace existing footnote 729 with the following.]** Pfaff v. Wells Elecs., Inc., 124 F.3d 1429, 43 USPQ 2d 1928 (Fed. Cir. 1997), *aff'd*, 525 U.S. 55, 48 USPQ 2d 1641 (1998).

8

Disclosure Under 35 U.S.C. Section 112, First Paragraph

II. Enablement: How to Make and Use the Invention

B. Alternative 1: Attacking Prima Facie Case of Nonenablement

[Insert after footnote 19.]

As explained by the Federal Circuit:

> Requiring inclusion in the patent of known scientific/technological information would add an imprecise and open-ended criterion to the content of patent specifications, could greatly enlarge the content of patent specifications and unnecessarily increase the cost of preparing and prosecuting patent applications, and could tend to obfuscate rather than highlight the contribution to which the patent is directed. A patent is not a scientific treatise, but a document that presumes a readership skilled in the field of the invention.[1]

[1]Ajinomoto Co., Inc. v. Archer-Daniels-Midland Co., 228 F.3d 1338, 56 USPQ 2d 1332, 1336 (Fed. Cir. 2000), *cert. denied*, 121 S. Ct. 1957 (2001) (citing W.L. Gore & Associates, Inc. v. Garlock, Inc., 721 F.2d 1540, 1556, 220 USPQ 303, 315 (Fed. Cir. 1983) ("Patents, however, are written to enable those skilled in the art to practice the invention, not the public.")).

Main volume footnote updates begin on page 264.

[Insert after footnote 20.]

Whether claims are sufficiently enabled by a disclosure in a specification is determined as of the date that the patent application was first filed.[2] As stated by the Federal Circuit, "an enablement determination is made retrospectively, i.e., by looking back to the filing date of the patent application and determining whether undue experimentation would have been required to make and use the claimed invention at that time."[3] There is no "prediction" occurring as to whether undue experimentation "would be" required to practice the claimed invention.[4]

1. Element 1: Rational Basis Nonenabling

b. Theoretical Possibility May Be Insufficient to Enable Invention Claiming Theory [New Topic]

The disclosure of the "theoretical possibility" in making and using the invention, with no evidence or examples in support thereof, will generally be insufficient to enable invention when the patent application or patent specifically claims the theory.

For example, in *National Recovery Technologies, Inc. v. Magnetic Separation Systems, Inc.*,[5] the invention, owned by National Recovery Technology (NRT), addressed the problem of separating recyclable plastic materials that were virtually indistinguishable to the human eye by using penetrating electromagnetic radiation. In the separation process, containers to be sorted were advanced along a conveyor wide enough to accommodate several containers. Each container was irradiated with a sheet-like beam of electromagnetic radiation as it progressed along the conveyor. A number of detectors spanning the width of the conveyor were positioned below the containers to measure the intensity level of electromagnetic radiation that passed through each of the containers. The process then used a microprocessor to compare the detected values to preset thresholds to classify the container as being made of one type of plastic or another.

The invention specifically addressed the problem of misclassification due to irregularities in container thickness. However, given the

---

[2] Hybritech, Inc. v. Monoclonal Antibodies, Inc., 802 F.2d 1367, 1384, 231 USPQ 81, 94 (Fed. Cir. 1986).

[3] Enzo Biochem, Inc. v. Calgene, Inc., 188 F.3d 1362, 52 USPQ 2d 1129, 1136 (Fed. Cir. 1999).

[4] *Id.*

[5] National Recovery Techs., Inc. v. Magnetic Separation Sys., Inc., 166 F.3d 1190, 49 USPQ 2d 1671 (Fed. Cir. 1999).

Main volume footnote updates begin on page 264.

unpredictability of container orientation and possible damage to a container's "regular" portions, results of this process were not completely accurate in distinguishing between containers of differing materials. The ideal solution, therefore, was to ensure that only the regular portions of the container were measured and to use only these measurements in classifying the container. Claim 1 of the patent recited the following:

> A method of distinguishing and separating material items having different levels of absorption of penetrating electromagnetic radiation, comprising the steps of:
>
> (a) conveying a plurality of said material items in a random manner simultaneously and longitudinally along an elongated feed path;
>
> (b) establishing a transverse region across said feed path irradiated by a sheet of penetrating electromagnetic radiation;
>
> (c) irradiating said plurality of material items in said transverse region with said penetrating electromagnetic radiation;
>
> (d) simultaneously measuring the amount of penetrating electromagnetic radiation passing through each material item in said transverse region at any instant of time as said items are continuously conveyed longitudinally through said transverse region to generate process signals; wherein more than one process signal is generated for each of said material items, each process signal being commensurate with the amount of penetrating electromagnetic radiation passing through a portion of each material item which is different from any other portion of said material item, and selecting for processing those of said process signals which do not pass through irregularities in the bodies of said material items; and
>
> (e) simultaneously analyzing said process signals to cause said process signals to actuate means for directing said items to a different destination commensurate with the amount of said penetrating electromagnetic radiation passing through each of said corresponding material items.[6]

NRT filed a complaint against Magnetic Separation Systems, Inc. (MSS), that MSS infringed NRT's patents related to this technology. MSS defended by arguing that the patents at issue were invalid under 35 U.S.C. Section 112 for lack of enablement.

The district court granted MSS's motion for summary judgment that claim 1 of the patent was invalid for lack of enablement. The district court held that the written description did not explain how to distinguish between signals that passed through irregular portions of the container and those that did not. The district court concluded that the specification merely instructed one of ordinary skill in the art to select those signals with the highest transmission measurements, not to select those signals that did not pass through irregularities as required by claim 1. NRT appealed.

On appeal, the Federal Circuit affirmed the holding of nonenablement. NRT argued that the district court erred because it required the disclosed embodiment to work perfectly under all circumstances. The

---

[6] *Id.*, 49 USPQ 2d at 1674.

Main volume footnote updates begin on page 264.

Federal Circuit disagreed, reasoning that the specification of the patent first acknowledged the problem: sometimes radiation intensity readings are misleading because the radiation has passed through abnormally thick portions of the scanned container. The ideal solution to this problem was clear: discard intensity measurements taken through irregularities and use only those measurements taken through the regular portions of the container. Claim 1 claimed and thereby required this ideal solution in the step of "selecting for processing those of said process signals which do not pass through irregularities in the bodies of said material items."[7] However, the Federal Circuit noted, the specification of the patent did not describe how to perform this ideal selection step. Rather, the specification instructed one of ordinary skill in the art to "use only those measurements of highest transmission rate through the item. . . ."[8]

The Federal Circuit emphasized that the specification was clear that in order to obtain the most reliable measurements, a good proxy for intensity measurements that did not pass through irregularities were those measurements with the highest transmission rates. However, the Federal Circuit commented, "enabling a proxy for the claimed invention is not the same as enabling the claimed invention itself."[9] According to the Federal Circuit:

> While the written description does enable one of ordinary skill in the art to approximate the claimed function, this is not the same as enabling one of ordinary skill in the art to perform the actual selection step of claim 1 for which NRT claims patent protection. The written description does not at all purport to enable one of ordinary skill in the art to determine where irregularities exist in the containers.[10]

NRT argued that while as a theoretical possibility it might be feasible to construct a system that ignored every single perturbation and flaw in virtually all the items processed, the patent disclosed and claimed a workable, practical system, not a theoretical possibility. The Federal Circuit disagreed, saying:

> [A]s we have explained above, claim 1 broadly claims exactly this theoretical possibility that NRT admits is not disclosed in the specification of the . . . patent. . . . The most that NRT can be credited with is promising the ideal result in claim 1, even though the specification does not completely deliver on this promise.[11]

Thus, *National Recovery Technologies* explains that even though an inventor need not know the theory behind the invention, the inventor must adequately describe how to make and use the invention. The disclosure of the theoretical possibility in making and using the inven-

---

[7] *Id.* at 1676.

[8] *Id.*

[9] *Id.* at 1677.

[10] *Id.*

[11] *Id.*

Main volume footnote updates begin on page 264.

tion may therefore be insufficient to enable invention when the theory is specifically claimed therein.

c. Inventor's Beliefs Insufficient to Enable Invention [New Topic]

In re Cortright[12] is an example of a case in which an inventor's beliefs on the operation of the claimed invention were insufficient for enablement. The invention related to a method of treating baldness by applying Bag Balm, a commercially available product used to soften cow udders, to human scalp. Claim 15 recited a method of "offsetting the effects of lower levels of a male hormone being supplied by arteries to the papilla of scalp hair follicles with the active agent 8-hydroxy-quinoline sulfate to cause hair to grow again on the scalp, comprising rubbing into the scalp the ointment having the active agent 8-hydroxy-quinoline sulfate 0.3% carried in a petrolatum and lanolin base so that the active agent reaches the papilla."[13]

The Board found that Cortright's written description did not teach those of ordinary skill in the art how to make and use the claimed invention without undue experimentation because it failed to provide any teachings as to the administration of Bag Balm in a manner that offset the effects of lower levels of male hormone being supplied by arteries to the papilla of scalp hair follicles. The Board found that the written description "merely surmises that the active ingredient, 8-hydroxy-quinoline sulfate, even reaches the papilla," which would not enable one of ordinary skill to use the claimed method.[14] Cortright appealed.

On appeal, the Federal Circuit affirmed the rejection for non-enablement. The Federal Circuit noted that generally the statements in the patent application relating to observations that salves applied to the scalp penetrate the skin and reach the papilla or that chemicals affect hormones do not run counter to generally accepted scientific norms. Therefore, the Federal Circuit reasoned, a disclosure that the active agent, 8-hydroxy-quinoline sulfate, reached the papilla and offset lower levels of male hormones was not inherently suspect.[15] Nevertheless, the Federal Circuit affirmed the rejection of claim 15 because the written description failed to disclose that the active ingredient reached the papilla or that offsetting occurred. According to the Federal Circuit:

> Here, although the written description states that people observed hair growth after applying Bag Balm to the scalp, it does not disclose that anyone observed the active ingredient reach the papilla and offset the effects of lower levels of male hormones. It states, rather, that "it is believed that the rubbed-in ointment offsets the effects of lower levels of male hormones in the papilla and/or provides an antimicrobial effect on

[12] *In re* Cortright, 165 F.3d 1353, 49 USPQ 2d 1464 (Fed. Cir. 1999).

[13] *Id.*, 49 USPQ 2d at 1465.

[14] *Id.* at 1465.

[15] *Id.* at 1469.

Main volume footnote updates begin on page 264.

> infection," and that "Applicant surmises that the active antimicrobial agent, 8-hydroxy-quinoline sulfate, reaches the papilla, and is effective to off-set the male hormones such as testosterone and/or androsterone, and/or kill or seriously weaken any bacteria about or in the papilla . . . ." These statements reflect no actual observations. Moreover, we have not been shown that one of ordinary skill would necessarily conclude from the information expressly disclosed by the written description that the active ingredient reaches the papilla or that off-setting occurs.[16]

On this basis, the Federal Circuit held that claim 15 did not satisfy the how-to-use requirement of Section 112, first paragraph.

2. *Element 2: Manner and Process of Making and Using Invention*

[Insert at the end of the section.]

"It is not a requirement of patentability that an inventor correctly set forth, or even know, how or why the invention works."[17] Statements that a physiological phenomenon was observed are not inherently suspect simply because the underlying basis for the observation cannot be predicted or explained.[18]

[Insert at the end of the section.]

b. Inoperatively Described Invention Will Not Generally Be Enabling [New Topic]

When an impossible limitation, such as a nonsensical method of operation, is clearly embodied within the claim, the claimed invention must be held invalid.[19] While an otherwise valid patent covering a meritorious invention should not be struck down simply because of the patentee's misconceptions about scientific principles concerning the invention,[20] when "the claimed subject matter is inoperable, the patent may indeed be invalid for failure to meet the utility requirement of 101 and the enablement requirement of 112."[21]

---

[16] *Id.*

[17] Newman v. Quigg, 877 F.2d 1575, 1581, 11 USPQ 2d 1340, 1345 (Fed. Cir. 1989); Fromson v. Advance Offset Plate, Inc., 720 F.2d 1565, 1570, 219 USPQ 1137, 1140 (Fed. Cir. 1983) ("It is axiomatic that an inventor need not comprehend the scientific principles on which the practical effectiveness of his invention rests.").

[18] *In re* Cortright, 165 F.3d 1353, 49 USPQ 2d 1464, 1469 (Fed. Cir. 1999).

[19] Process Control Corp. v. HydReclaim Corp., 190 F.3d 1350, 52 USPQ 2d 1029, 1035 (Fed. Cir. 1999).

[20] Fromson v. Advance Offset Plate, Inc., 720 F.2d 1565, 1570, 219 USPQ 1137, 1140 (Fed. Cir. 1983).

[21] Brooktree Corp. v. Advanced Micro Devices, Inc., 977 F.2d 1555, 1571, 24 USPQ 2d 1401, 1412 (Fed. Cir. 1992) (citing Raytheon Co. v. Roper Corp., 724 F.2d 951, 956, 220 USPQ 592, 596 (Fed. Cir. 1983)).

Main volume footnote updates begin on page 264.

The Federal Circuit has held certain process claims invalid, stating:

> [B]ecause it is for the invention as claimed that enablement must clearly exist, and because the impossible cannot be enabled, a claim containing a limitation impossible to meet may be held invalid under 112. Moreover, when a claim requires a means for accomplishing an unattainable result, the claimed invention must be considered inoperative as claimed and the claim must be held invalid under either 101 or 112 of 35 U.S.C.[22]

Process Control Corp. v. HydReclaim Corp.[23] is an example where the invention being claimed recited a mathematical impossibility resulting in the claim being held inoperative and invalid. HydReclaim is the owner of U.S. Patent No. 5,148,943 (the '943 patent) directed to continuous gravimetric blenders used in the plastics industry. These blenders mixed multiple solid ingredients in appropriate proportions based on weight and fed the mixture to a weighed common hopper. The invention described in the '943 patent measured the weight, rather than the volume, of the material in the common hopper, and maintained that weight in the common hopper at a constant value.

Process Control filed a declaratory judgment action asserting the invalidity of the '943 patent. The district court construed the claims as urged by HydReclaim, sustained the validity of the '943 patent, and found that Process Control had willfully infringed claims.

On appeal, the Federal Circuit reversed. The Federal Circuit noted that it was undisputed by both HydReclaim and Process Control that a consistent definition of "discharge rate" in clauses (b) and (d) of claim 1 lead to a nonsensical conclusion. Due to the principle of conservation of mass, the material processing rate of the processing machine must necessarily be equal to the discharge rate of the material from the common hopper to the processing machine in a steady-state process. However, Clause (d) of claim 1 read:

> (d) determining the material processing rate of the processing machine from the sum of the material discharge rates of the ingredients to the common hopper and the discharge rate of the material from the common hopper to the processing machine.[24]

Clause (d) embodied an inoperable method that violated the principle of conservation of mass. According to the Federal Circuit:

> In other words, clause (d) requires determining a quantity from the sum of that exact same quantity and something else, or symbolically, A = A + B, which is impossible, where, as here, B is not equal to zero. Accordingly, we hold that the correctly construed claims are invalid because they are inoperative, and thus the claims fail to comply with the utility and enablement requirements of 35 U.S.C. §§ 101 and 112, 1, respectively.[25]

---

[22] *Raytheon*, 724 F.2d at 956, 220 USPQ at 596.

[23] Process Control Corp. v. HydReclaim Corp., 190 F.3d 1350, 52 USPQ 2d 1029 (Fed. Cir. 1999).

[24] *Id.*, 52 USPQ 2d at 1035.

[25] *Id.*

Main volume footnote updates begin on page 264.

On this basis, the Federal Circuit held that claim 1 was invalid for failure to enable the claimed invention.

4. *Element 4: One of Ordinary Skill in the Pertinent Technology*

[Insert at the beginning of the section.]

The specification need not describe or enable the invention to a lay person. Rather, the specification need only describe the invention to one of ordinary skill in the art.[26] As explained by the Federal Circuit:

> Requiring inclusion in the patent of known scientific/technological information would add an imprecise and open-ended criterion to the content of patent specifications, could greatly enlarge the content of patent specifications and unnecessarily increase the cost of preparing and prosecuting patent applications, and could tend to obfuscate rather than highlight the contribution to which the patent is directed. A patent is not a scientific treatise, but a document that presumes a readership skilled in the field of the invention.[27]

[Insert at the end of the section.]

Enzo Biochem, Inc. v. Calgene, Inc.[28] is an example of a case in which the determination of the skill in the art was important in determining whether the experimentation needed was undue. The invention related to genetic antisense technology that provides a powerful methodology for controlling gene expression in a particular organism. Gene expression is the process by which information encoded in an organism's DNA is interpreted and processed to give rise to the various proteins that characterize that organism, thereby creating that organism's particular traits. A gene is a double-stranded DNA molecule that contains the information necessary to generate all or part of a particular protein. One DNA strand codes for the protein of interest, and is thus referred to as the "coding" or "sense" strand. The opposing, complementary strand is referred to as the "template" or "antisense" strand.

During the transcription step of gene expression, an enzyme, RNA polymerase, locates and binds to a promoter site (a sequence of nucleotides indicated schematically by "Xs"), which triggers the RNA polymerase to begin transcription. The RNA polymerase unwinds the DNA duplex and transcribes the template strand, thereby making a

---

[26] General Elec. Co. v. Brenner, 407 F 2d 1258, 159 USPQ 335, 337 (D.C. Cir. 1968).

[27] Ajinomoto Co., Inc. v. Archer-Daniels-Midland Co., 228 F.3d 1338, 56 USPQ 2d 1332, 1336 (Fed. Cir. 2000), *cert. denied*, 121 S. Ct. 1957 (2001) (citing W.L. Gore & Assoc., Inc. v. Garlock, Inc., 721 F.2d 1540, 1556, 220 USPQ 303, 315 (Fed. Cir. 1983) ("Patents, however are written to enable those skilled in the art to practice the invention, not the public.")).

[28] Enzo Biochem, Inc. v. Calgene, Inc., 188 F.3d 1362, 52 USPQ 2d 1129 (Fed. Cir. 1999).

Main volume footnote updates begin on page 264.

complementary RNA strand, known as messenger RNA (mRNA). Antisense technology aims to control the expression of a particular gene by blocking the translation of the mRNA produced by the transcription of that gene.

The patent taught the application of antisense technology in regulating three genes in the prokaryote E. coli, using the lpp (lipoprotein), ompC (outer membrane protein C), and ompA (outer membrane protein A) genes. Despite this limited disclosure, inventor Masayori Inouye broadly asserted:

> The practices of this invention are generally applicable with respect to any organism containing genetic material which is capable of being expressed. Suitable organisms include the prokaryotic and eukaryotic organisms, such as bacteria, yeast, and other cellular organisms. The practices of this invention are also applicable to viruses, particularly where the viruses are incorporated into the organism.[29]

The claims of the three patents were likewise drafted to encompass application of antisense methodology in a broad range of organisms.

Enzo sued Calgene, alleging that its patents were infringed, and Calgene counterclaimed, seeking a declaratory judgment that the Enzo's patents were invalid for lack of enablement. The district court held that the claims at issue were invalid as not enabled because undue experimentation was necessary to practice antisense technology in cells other than E. coli.

On appeal, the Federal Circuit affirmed and noted that the district court determined that a person of ordinary skill in the art would be a junior faculty member with one or two years of relevant experience or a postdoctoral student with several years of experience. Even though the level of skill in the art was rather high, the patent was still considered nonenabled.

Enzo argued that the level of skill should be even higher due to the specialized nature of the field of genetics. However, the Federal Circuit disagreed, particularly because Enzo asserted that the level of ordinary skill should be higher than the skill of the research associates of the inventor, Inouye. The Federal Circuit recognized that the field of genetics is highly specialized, and further acknowledged the well-established rule that "when an invention, in its different aspects, involves distinct arts, that specification is adequate which enables the adepts of each art, those who have the best chance of being enabled, to carry out the aspect proper to their specialty."[30] The Federal Circuit disagreed, however, with Enzo's contention that the district court erred in its determination of the appropriate level of skill in the art by not accounting for all of the specialized fields to which the invention pertains. According to the Federal Circuit:

---

[29] *Id.*, 52 USPQ 2d at 1133.

[30] *Id.* at 1137 (quoting *In re* Naquin, 398 F.2d 863, 866, 158 USPQ 317, 319 (C.C.P.A. 1968)).

Main volume footnote updates begin on page 264.

> [T]he "research associates" who conducted the failed experiments, all of whom possessed the requisite level of skill in the art, could hardly be characterized as mere laboratory technicians. We do not think it unreasonable that these highly trained researchers were found to have possessed a sufficient level of expertise to conduct experiments in organisms other than E. coli. Indeed, it defies common sense that Inouye would waste valuable resources conducting experiments in other organisms had he not believed that his research associates possessed sufficient skill to perform them. We also note that three of the failures indicated above were attempts to achieve antisense regulation in three genes in E. coli, the very organism in which Inouye's laboratory specialized.[31]

The Federal Circuit, therefore, concluded that the district court did not err in its assessment of the level of skill in the art, or in relying on Inouye's failed attempts, which were performed by those of the appropriate level of skill following the methodology disclosed in the specifications. Therefore, the district court did not clearly err in finding that the quantity of experimentation required to practice Enzo's antisense was quite high.

a. *Prior Art May Assist in Determining What One of Ordinary Skill Would Understand [New Topic]*

Although the Patent Office must give claims their broadest reasonable interpretation, this interpretation must be consistent with the one that those skilled in the art would reach.[32] Prior art references may be "indicative of what all those skilled in the art generally believe a certain term means . . . [and] can often help to demonstrate how a disputed term is used by those skilled in the art."[33] Accordingly, the interpretation of claim terms should not be so broad that it conflicts with the meaning given to identical terms in other patents from analogous art under analogous situations.[34] Therefore, the interpretation of the same or similar claim terminology in the prior art may be used in determining what one of ordinary skill in the art would have understood the patent disclosure to teach with respect to the enablement requirement.

In re Cortright[35] is an example of a case in which the prior art understanding of terminology used in the patent claims was used in

---

[31] *Id.* at 1137–38.

[32] *See In re* Morris, 127 F.3d 1048, 1054, 44 USPQ 2d 1023, 1027 (Fed. Cir. 1997) ("The PTO applies to the verbiage of the proposed claims the broadest reasonable meaning of the words in their ordinary usage as they would be understood by one of ordinary skill in the art . . . . "); *In re* Bond, 910 F.2d 831, 833, 15 USPQ 2d 1566, 1567 (Fed. Cir. 1990) ("It is axiomatic that, in proceedings before the PTO, claims in an application are to be given their broadest reasonable interpretation consistent with the specification, . . . and that claim language should be read in light of the specification as it would be interpreted by one of ordinary skill in the art."). *See also* M.P.E.P. § 2111.01 ("The words of a claim . . . must be read as they would be interpreted by those of ordinary skill in the art").

[33] Vitronics Corp. v. Conceptronic, Inc., 90 F.3d 1576, 1584, 39 USPQ 2d 1573, 1578–79 (Fed. Cir. 1996).

[34] *In re* Cortright, 165 F.3d 1353, 49 USPQ 2d 1464, 1467 (Fed. Cir. 1999).

[35] *In re* Cortright, 165 F.3d 1353, 49 USPQ 2d 1464 (Fed. Cir. 1999).

Main volume footnote updates begin on page 264.

determining that the claimed invention was in fact enabled by the patent application disclosure. The invention related to a method of treating baldness by applying Bag Balm, a commercially available product used to soften cow udders, to human scalp. Claim 1 recited a method of "treating scalp baldness with an antimicrobial to restore hair growth, which comprises rubbing into the scalp the ointment wherein the active ingredient 8-hydroxy-quinoline sulfate 0.3% is carried in a petrolatum and lanolin base."[36]

The Board found that Cortright's written description did not teach those of ordinary skill in the art how to make and use the claimed invention without undue experimentation because it failed to provide any teachings as to the administration of Bag Balm in a manner that restored hair growth. The Board explained that Example 1 of the patent specification did not show that applying a teaspoon of Bag Balm to the scalp daily for about one month "restored hair growth," and that Examples 2 and 3 did not disclose the amount of Bag Balm to apply or how to restore hair growth. The Board explained that claim 1 was not enabled because it claimed "restoring hair growth," which the Board interpreted as requiring the user's hair "to return to its original state," that is, a full head of hair.[37] Cortright appealed.

On appeal, the Federal Circuit reversed. The Federal Circuit noted that the Patent Office may establish a reason to doubt an invention's asserted utility when the written description "suggests an inherently unbelievable undertaking or involves implausible scientific principles."[38] The Federal Circuit, however, noted that treatments for baldness have gained acceptance, including Rogaine (minoxidil) and Propecia, which are recognized as effective in treating baldness. The Federal Circuit also noted that the Patent Office has granted approximately 100 patents on methods of treating baldness. Some of these patents disclosed applying an electric current to the scalp, whereas others taught ingesting substances orally or applying a salve of some kind to the scalp. Some patents disclosed the active ingredient in chemical terms. Other patents, however, disclosed baldness remedies made from more mundane materials, such as Dead Sea mud, emu oil, potato peelings and lantana leaves, and vitamin D3 and aloe.

The Federal Circuit also focused on the Patent Office's construction of "restore hair growth," which the Federal Circuit indicated was inconsistent with the Patent Office's previous definitions. The Federal Circuit emphasized that one of ordinary skill would not construe "restoring hair growth" to mean "returning the user's hair to its original state," as the Board required.

---

[36] *Id.*, 49 USPQ 2d at 1465.

[37] *Id.* at 1465.

[38] *Id.* (quoting *In re* Brana, 51 F.3d 1560, 1566, 34 USPQ 2d 1436, 1441 (Fed. Cir. 1995)).

Main volume footnote updates begin on page 264.

> To the contrary, consistent with Cortright's disclosure and that of other references, one of ordinary skill would construe this phrase as meaning that the claimed method increases the amount of hair grown on the scalp but does not necessarily produce a full head of hair. Properly construed, claim 1 is amply supported by the written description because Example 1 discloses the amount of Bag Balm to apply (about one teaspoon daily) and the amount of time (about one month) in which to expect results. These dosing instructions enable one of ordinary skill to practice the claimed invention without the need for any experimentation. Therefore, we reverse the board's rejection of claim 1.[39]

5. *Element 5: Without Undue Experimentation*

[Insert before the paragraph containing footnote 55.]

Similarly, a claim is not invalid for lack of enablement or operability simply because the invention does not work perfectly under all conditions.[40] While the necessity of some experimentation does not preclude enablement, the experimentation must not be unduly extensive.[41] Whether making and using the claimed invention would have required undue experimentation is a legal conclusion based upon underlying facts.[42]

[Insert at the end of the first sentence in the paragraph beginning "It is not necessary . . ." on p. 701.]

The above factors "are illustrative, not mandatory. What is relevant depends on the facts."[43]

C. Alternative 2: Rebutting Prima Facie Case of Nonenablement

1. Rule 132 Affidavits

[Insert after the second sentence in the paragraph beginning "The affidavit should be . . ." on p. 713.]

---

[39] *Id.* at 1468.

[40] Hildreth v. Mastoras, 257 U.S. 27, 34 (1921) ("The machine patented may be imperfect in its operation; but if it embodies the general principle and works . . . it is enough."); Decca, Ltd. v. United States, 544 F.2d 1070, 191 USPQ 439, 444 (Ct. Cl. 1976) ("The mere fact that the system has some drawbacks, or that under certain postulated conditions it may not work . . . does not detract from the operability of the disclosed equipment to perform its described function.").

[41] PPG Indus., Inc. v. Guardian Indus. Corp., 75 F.3d 1558, 1564, 37 USPQ 2d 1618, 1623 (Fed. Cir. 1996).

[42] *See* Genentech, Inc. v. Novo Nordisk A/S, 108 F.3d 1361, 1365, 42 USPQ 2d 1001, 1004 (Fed. Cir. 1997) (citing *In re* Wands, 858 F.2d 731, 735, 736–37, 8 USPQ 2d 1400, 1402, 1404 (Fed. Cir. 1988)).

[43] Amgen, Inc. v. Chugai Pharm. Co., 927 F.2d 1200, 1213, 18 USPQ 2d 1016, 1027 (Fed. Cir. 1991).

Main volume footnote updates begin on page 264.

A party who wishes to submit evidence that the claims of a patent are in fact enabled to make the disclosed invention should preferably show that the patent's disclosure was substantially followed, if possible.[44]

F. Special Topic: Enablement and Biological Inventions

[Insert at the end of the section.]

Enzo Biochem, Inc. v. Calgene, Inc.[45] is an example of a case in which the invention was not considered enabled by the patent specification, which only provided a "plan" or "invitation" for those skilled in the art to experiment with the disclosure of the application. The invention related to genetic antisense technology that provided a powerful methodology for controlling gene expression in a particular organism. The patent taught the application of antisense technology in regulating three genes in the prokaryote E. coli, using the lpp (lipoprotein), ompC (outer membrane protein C), and ompA (outer membrane protein A) genes. Despite this limited disclosure, inventor Masayori Inouye broadly asserted:

> The practices of this invention are generally applicable with respect to any organism containing genetic material which is capable of being expressed. Suitable organisms include the prokaryotic and eukaryotic organisms, such as bacteria, yeast, and other cellular organisms. The practices of this invention are also applicable to viruses, particularly where the viruses are incorporated into the organism.[46]

The claims of the three patents were likewise drafted to encompass application of antisense methodology in a broad range of organisms.

Enzo sued Calgene, alleging that its patents were infringed, and Calgene counterclaimed, seeking a declaratory judgment that Enzo's patents were invalid for lack of enablement. The district court held that the claims at issue were invalid as not enabled because the specifications provided little guidance or direction as to the practice of antisense in cells other than E. coli, and that the disclosure constituted no more than a plan or invitation to practice antisense in other cells.

On appeal, the Federal Circuit affirmed. The Federal Circuit noted that the district court found that the amount of direction presented and the number of working examples provided in the specifications were very narrow, despite the wide breadth of the claims at issue, the unpredictability of antisense technology, and the high quantity of experimentation necessary to practice antisense in cells outside

---

[44] Johns Hopkins Univ. v. Cellpro, Inc., 152 F.3d 1342, 1360, 47 USPQ 2d 1705, 1718 (Fed. Cir. 1998).

[45] Enzo Biochem, Inc. v. Calgene, Inc., 188 F.3d 1362, 52 USPQ 2d 1129 (Fed. Cir. 1999).

[46] *Id.*, 52 USPQ 2d at 1133.

Main volume footnote updates begin on page 264.

of E. coli.[47] Outside of the three genes regulated in E. coli, virtually no guidance, direction, or working examples were provided for practicing the invention in eukaryotes, or even any prokaryote other than E. coli, noted the Federal Circuit. In addressing a similar case involving limited disclosure, the Federal Circuit commented:

> It is well settled that patent applicants are not required to disclose every species encompassed by their claims, even in an unpredictable art. However, there must be sufficient disclosure, either through illustrative examples or terminology, to teach those of ordinary skill how to make and use the invention as broadly as it is claimed.[48]

Here, however, the Federal Circuit emphasized, the teachings set forth in the specifications provided no more than a "plan" or "invitation" for those of skill in the art to experiment practicing antisense in eukaryotic cells; the teachings in the specification did not provide sufficient guidance or specificity as to how to execute that plan.[49] On this basis, the Federal Circuit affirmed the holding of invalidity based on the specification not enabling the claimed invention.

I. Relationship Between Enablement and Utility

[Insert after footnote 166.]

If the written description fails to illuminate a credible utility, the Patent Office will make both a Section 112, first paragraph rejection for failure to teach how to use the invention and a Section 101 rejection for lack of utility.[50] This dual rejection occurs because "the how to use prong of section 112 incorporates as a matter of law the requirement of 35 U.S.C. 101 that the specification disclose as a matter of fact a practical utility for the invention."[51] Thus, an applicant's failure to disclose how to use an invention may support a rejection under either Section 112, first paragraph for lack of enablement as a result of "the specification's . . . failure to disclose adequately to one ordinarily skilled in the art 'how to use' the invention without undue experimentation," or Section 101 for lack of utility "when there is a complete absence of data supporting the statements which set forth the desired results of the claimed invention."[52]

---

[47] *Id.* at 1138.

[48] *Id.* (quoting *In re* Vaeck, 947 F.2d 488, 496 & n.23, 20 USPQ 2d 1438, 1445 & n.23 (Fed. Cir. 1991)).

[49] *Id.*

[50] *In re* Cortright, 165 F.3d 1353, 49 USPQ 2d 1464, 1466 (Fed. Cir. 1999).

[51] *In re* Ziegler, 992 F.2d 1197, 1200, 26 USPQ 2d 1600, 1603 (Fed. Cir. 1993).

[52] Envirotech Corp. v. Al George, Inc., 730 F.2d 753, 762, 221 USPQ 473, 480 (Fed. Cir. 1984); *In re* Brana, 51 F.3d 1560, 1564 n. 12, 34 USPQ 2d 1436, 1439 n.12 (Fed. Cir. 1995) ("absence of utility can be the basis of a rejection under both 35 U.S.C. Section 101 and Section 112 Para. 1"); *In re* Fouche, 439 F.2d 1237, 1243, 169 USPQ 429, 434 (C.C.P.A. 1971) ("If [certain] compositions are in fact useless, appellant's specification cannot have taught how to use them.").

Main volume footnote updates begin on page 264.

The Patent Office cannot make this type of rejection, however, unless it has reason to doubt the objective truth of the statements contained in the written description.[53] The Patent Office may establish a reason to doubt an invention's asserted utility when the written description "suggests an inherently unbelievable undertaking or involves implausible scientific principles."[54]

[Insert after footnote 173.]

The Federal Circuit, however, has commented on the differences between the utility requirement as follows:

> Whether a patented device or process is operable is a different inquiry than whether a particular claim is enabled by the specification. In order to satisfy the enablement requirement of 112, paragraph 1, the specification must enable one of ordinary skill in the art to practice the claimed invention without undue experimentation. Thus, with respect to enablement the relevant inquiry lies in the relationship between the specification, the claims, and the knowledge of one of ordinary skill in the art. If, by following the steps set forth in the specification, one of ordinary skill in the art is not able to replicate the claimed invention without undue experimentation, the claim has not been enabled as required by 112, paragraph 1.[55]

III. Written Description

B. Alternative 1: Attacking Prima Facie Case of No Written Description

[Replace the last paragraph of the section with the following.]

The Patent Office has issued revised guidelines describing the written description requirement. These guidelines are reproduced in Appendix C.

---

[53] *See Brana*, 51 F.3d at 1566, 34 USPQ 2d at 1441 ("The PTO has the initial burden of challenging a presumptively correct assertion of utility in the disclosure. Only after the PTO provides evidence showing that one of ordinary skill in the art would reasonably doubt the asserted utility does the burden shift to the applicant to provide rebuttal evidence sufficient to convince such a person of the invention's asserted utility.") (citations omitted); *In re* Marzocchi, 439 F.2d 220, 223, 169 USPQ 367, 369 (C.C.P.A. 1971) ("[A] specification disclosure which contains a teaching of the manner and process of making and using the invention in terms which correspond in scope to those used in describing and defining the subject matter sought to be patented must be taken as in compliance with the enabling requirement of the first paragraph of 112 unless there is reason to doubt the objective truth of the statements contained therein which must be relied on for enabling support.").

[54] *Brana*, 51 F.3d at 1566, 34 USPQ 2d at 1441; *In re* Eltgroth, 419 F.2d 918, 164 USPQ 221, 223–24 (C.C.P.A. 1970) (control of aging process).

[55] National Recovery Techs., Inc. v. Magnetic Separation Sys., Inc., 166 F.3d 1190, 49 USPQ 2d 1671, 1676 (Fed. Cir. 1999).

Main volume footnote updates begin on page 264.

2. *Element 2: One of Ordinary Skill in the Art*

[Insert after footnote 232.]

Thus, the specification need only describe the invention to one of ordinary skill in the art.[56] As explained by the Federal Circuit:

> Requiring inclusion in the patent of known scientific/technological information would add an imprecise and open-ended criterion to the content of patent specifications, could greatly enlarge the content of patent specifications and unnecessarily increase the cost of preparing and prosecuting patent applications, and could tend to obfuscate rather than highlight the contribution to which the patent is directed. A patent is not a scientific treatise, but a document that presumes a readership skilled in the field of the invention.[57]

4. *Element 4: Claimed Invention*

b. *Narrow Written Description May Unnecessarily Limit Scope of Patent Claims*

[Insert after footnote 246.]

The Federal Circuit has become increasingly reluctant to provide a claim interpretation of broader scope covering an alternative embodiment of the invention when the patent specification provides no appreciation of a potential alternative embodiment as understood by one of ordinary skill.[58] The Federal Circuit, however, has cautioned

---

[56] General Elec. Co. v. Brenner, 407 F.2d 1258, 159 USPQ 335, 337 (D.C. Cir. 1968).

[57] Ajinomoto Co. v. Archer-Daniels-Midland Co., 228 F.3d 1338, 56 USPQ 2d 1332, 1336 (Fed. Cir. 2000), *cert. denied*, 121 S. Ct. 1957 (2001) (citing W.L. Gore & Assoc., Inc. v. Garlock, Inc., 721 F.2d 1540, 1556, 220 USPQ 303, 315 (Fed. Cir. 1983) ("Patents, however, are written to enable those skilled in the art to practice the invention, not the public.")).

[58] Wang Labs., Inc. v. America Online, Inc., 197 F.3d 1377, 53 USPQ 2d 1161, 1165 (Fed. Cir. 1999):

> The usage "preferred" does not of itself broaden the claims beyond their support in the specification. . . . General American Transportation Corp. v. Cryo-Trans, Inc., 93 F.3d 766, 770, 772, 39 USPQ 2d 1801, 1803, 1805–06 (Fed. Cir. 1996) (the teaching in the specification was "not just the preferred embodiment of the invention; it is the only one described"). The only embodiment described in the '669 patent specification is the character-based protocol, and the claims were correctly interpreted as limited thereto.

Mitek Surgical Prods., Inc. v. Arthrex, Inc., Civ. App. No. 99-1004, slip op. at 4–5 (Fed. Cir. Feb. 22, 2000) (unpublished):

> Mitek admits that the specification only discloses the structure of a means for securing that contains a retention disk attached to the means. . . . Mitek misses the focus of means-plus-function claim construction. There was no error in the district court's construction of "means for securing" because section 112 ¶ 6 expressly restricts coverage of a means-plus-function claim to the structure disclosed in the specification and the equivalents of that structure. The internal retention disk is the only means for securing structure disclosed in the specification.

Main volume footnote updates begin on page 264.

against limiting broad claim language to the specific disclosure of the patent application. According to the Federal Circuit:

> When presented with relatively unrestricted claim language, however, a trial court must use care in checking the specification for a special meaning. Unless the applicant unambiguously narrowed the scope of broad claim terms in the rest of the patent, the construing court runs the risk of importing unintended limitations from the specification. . . . Indeed this court has cautioned against limiting broad claim language to the preferred embodiments or specific examples in the specification.[59]

The prior art may assist in interpreting the scope of the patent claim. In general, the prior art will restrict or limit the scope of patent claims, particularly those claims drafted in means-plus-function format.[60] However, when the invention is a combination of old elements, and the specification specifically references or describes alternative prior art components, the patent claims will be interpreted broadly to encompass those alternatives, as well as other alternatives that one of ordinary skill in the art would understand from the specification. For example, combination claims can be drafted as a new combination of old elements or combinations of new and old elements.[61]

[Insert after footnote 263.]

However, a carefully drafted patent specification may, in some circumstances, provide a broader scope of interpretation for means-plus-function claims than non-means-plus-function claims.[62] For example, when multiple embodiments in the specification correspond to the claimed function, proper application of Section 112, sixth para-

---

[59] Magnivision, Inc. v. Bonneau Co., Civ. App. No. 99-1093, slip op. at 10–11 (Fed. Cir. July 24, 2000) (unpublished) (citing Transmatic, Inc. v. Gulton Indus. Inc., 53 F.3d 1270, 1277, 35 USPQ 2d 1035, 1041 (Fed. Cir. 1995); Texas Instruments, Inc. v. United States Int'l Trade Comm'n, 805 F.2d 1558, 1563, 231 USPQ 833, 835 (Fed. Cir. 1986)).

[60] Mitek Surgical Prods., Inc. v. Arthrex, Inc., Civ. App. No. 99-1004, slip op. at 5 (Fed. Cir. Feb. 22, 2000) (unpublished):

> The internal retention disk is the only means for securing structure disclosed in the specification. Mitek argues that alternative embodiments of means for securing are disclosed in the prior art. These embodiments are irrelevant when attempting to outwardly expand claim scope as here. Structure in the prior art may be used to limit, but not broaden the scope of means-plus-function structures. See Biodex Corp. v. Loredan Biomedical, Inc., 946 F.2d 850, 863, 20 USPQ 2d 1252, 1262 (Fed. Cir.1991) (stating that prosecution history may be used to limit scope of means-plus-function claims).

[61] Clearstream Wastewater Sys., Inc. v. Hydro-Action, Inc., 206 F.3d 1440, 54 USPQ 2d 1185, 1189 (Fed. Cir. 2000); Intel Corp. v. U.S. Int'l Trade Comm'n, 946 F.2d 821, 842, 20 USPQ 2d 1161, 1179 (Fed. Cir. 1991); Panduit Corp. v. Dennison Mfg., 810 F.2d 1561, 1575, 1 USPQ 2d 1593, 1603 (Fed. Cir. 1987).

[62] *See* Overhead Door Corp. v. Chamberlain Group, Inc., 194 F.3d 1261, 52 USPQ 2d 1321, 1327–28 (Fed. Cir. 1999):

> The claim language and the specification explain that the "memory selection switch" functions to select memory locations. This claim element accomplishes its function by way of a mechanical switch. . . . As properly construed, the "memory selection switch" means a mechanical switch for selecting memory locations. . . .

Main volume footnote updates begin on page 264.

graph generally reads the claim element to embrace each of those embodiments.[63]

[Insert at the end of the section.]

In *Evans Medical Ltd. v. American Cyanamid Co.*,[64] the invention related to a particular protein, or antigen, derived from the whooping cough-causing bacterium, Bordetella pertussis. The antigen was useful as an acellular vaccine against whooping cough. The art has referred to the antigen as the "69kD" antigen. The 69kD antigen is a protein embedded in the outer membranes of B. pertussis, making it somewhat difficult to extract. The 69kD antigen is prepared in the first instance by extracting B. pertussis bacteria overnight in an acidic glycine-hydrochloric acid solution with an isolation step using a monoclonal antibody.

A monoclonal antibody is a protein produced by an organism such as a mouse in response to a challenge to the organism's immune system with a foreign material (often a protein), or "antigen," such as a B. pertussis antigen. The monoclonal antibody so produced is able to form a complex with the challenging antigen that can be readily observed through standard procedures in the art, thus making monoclonal antibody technology a convenient method to identify and isolate antigens.

An exemplary claim recited the following:

> 1. A purified Bordetella pertussis antigen characterized by the following features:
>
> a relative molecular weight of between 67,000 to 73,000 as determined by 12% (w/w) polyacrylamide gel electrophoresis;
>
> a ratio of proline to glutamic acid of substantially 1:1 as determined by amino acid analysis.[65]

In attempting to interpret the term "purified," the Federal Circuit noted that this is a term of degree that inherently requires an

---

Although software operations do not fall within the literal scope of the "memory selection switch" in claim 1, the reissue prosecution history also discloses a broader reading for the "switch means" of claim 5. First, the patentees' representation to the Patent and Trademark Office in its November 29, 1989 sworn declaration indicated their intent to include the algorithm of Figure 3 as a "corresponding structure" for the switch means. . . . While this statement weighs against construing claim 1 to include software operations, it gives a broader reading to claim 5. This statement evinces the patentees' use of the term "switch means" to include microprocessor operations driven by software, i.e., "electronic" switches, as opposed to a mechanical switch of Figure 2. The patentees' use in claim 5 of the term "switch means" rather than "switch" and "being adapted to select" rather than "setable" and "set," to describe software operations, further support a broader construction.

[63] *Id.*, 52 USPQ 2d at 1264 (citing Serrano v. Telular Corp., 111 F.3d 1578, 1583, 42 USPQ 2d 1538, 1542 (Fed. Cir. 1997)).

[64] Evans Med. Ltd. v. American Cyanamid Co., 52 USPQ 2d 1455 (Fed. Cir. 1999) (unpublished).

[65] *Id.*, 52 USPQ 2d at 1457.

Main volume footnote updates begin on page 264.

evaluation of that degree in order to be defined precisely. The Federal Circuit determined that based on an independent review of the record, no consensus emerged on the plain meaning of the term "purified" to one of ordinary skill in the art. In view of the lack of consensus, the Federal Circuit concluded that the term "purified" as used in the claims required clarification. For such clarification, the Federal Circuit noted, the written description needed to be consulted.[66]

In consulting the written description, the Federal Circuit interpreted the term "purified" as being limited to antigen preparations that are greater than 50 percent pure. According to the Federal Circuit:

> We agree with the district court that the written description compels a construction of "purified" requiring that the claimed antigen comprise greater than fifty percent 69kD antigen. The written description states that the 69kD antigen preparation contemplated as the invention for use in vaccines "may, if desired, contain minor quantities of other antigenic compounds." We think it clear that this statement, by its own terms, clearly does not permit "other components" to comprise more than fifty percent of the contemplated 69kD antigenic preparation as used in a vaccine—thus setting a lower bound on the amount of 69kD antigen required by the claims. . . . Thus, while our construction of "purified" does not require that the claimed antigen be "substantially free" of other components—as would be the result of employing all of the purification steps described—that the aim of the invention, as conveyed by the written description, is to enrich for the 69kD antigen, further supports our construction of "purified" as being limited to antigen preparations that are greater than fifty percent pure.[67]

In *Toro Co. v. Ariens Co.*,[68] the invention related to single-stage snowthrowers, i.e., snowthrowers that use an impeller both to pick up and to throw snow from the snowthrower. While single-stage snowthrowers are typically lighter and less costly than two-stage snowthrowers, which use different instruments to pick up and to throw the snow, two-stage snowthrowers throw snow further and control the direction of that snow more effectively than their single-stage analogs. In an attempt to combine the advantages of both types of snowthrowers, the inventors of the patent designed a single-stage snowthrower with an improved impeller and an improved impeller/housing combination. Exemplary claim 24 of the original claims recited:

> 24. An improved single stage snowthrower, which comprises:
>
> (a) a housing having a front portion which engages the snow and which includes a rear wall and spaced side walls, wherein the rear wall com-

---

[66] *Id.* at 1459 (Renishaw PLC v. Marposs Societa' Per Azioni, 158 F.3d 1243, 1248, 48 USPQ 2d 1117, 1120 (Fed. Cir. 1998) ("[A] claim must explicitly recite a term in need of definition before a definition may enter the claim from the written description.")).

[67] *Id. See also* Modine Mfg. Co. v. United States Int'l Trade Comm'n, 75 F.3d 1545, 1551, 37 USPQ 2d 1609, 1612 (Fed. Cir. 1996) ("when the preferred embodiment is described in the specification as the invention itself, the claims are not necessarily entitled to a scope broader than that embodiment").

[68] Toro Co. v. Ariens Co., Civ. App. No. 99-1285 (Fed. Cir. Apr. 27, 2000) (unpublished).

Main volume footnote updates begin on page 264.

prises an arcuate lower portion and an upper portion that extends upwardly relative to the lower portion;

(b) a rotatable impeller located on the housing in front of the rear wall thereof and having a predetermined length between the side walls wherein the rotation of the impeller describes a cylinder that is bounded along the rear thereof by the arcuate lower portion of the rear wall and by at least a lower section of the upper portion of the rear wall, wherein the impeller includes an outwardly extending paddle having a curved central snowthrowing section for throwing upwardly away therefrom at approximately the juncture between the lower and upper portions of the rear wall a snow stream which has a width as it departs the snowthrowing section of at least approximately one-half the impeller's predetermined length and in which axially outermost portions of the snow stream have a component of motion that is directed axially inwardly; and

(c) upwardly extending collecting means located on at least the lower section of the upper portion of the rear wall for receiving the snow stream from the impeller and for conducting that snow stream vertically upwardly, wherein the collecting means includes a trough means which tapers inwardly from side-to-side as it rises, and wherein the trough means at its lower end has a width which is at least approximately one-half the impeller's predetermined length.[69]

Ariens' single-stage snowthrower contained a somewhat similar impeller; however, the central portion of its impeller lacked the curvature of the impeller depicted in Toro's patent. The two paddle portions of Arien's accused impeller contained a flat, central section bounded on both sides by curved transition sections.

Toro sued Ariens, alleging that Ariens willfully infringed the patent by making, using, and/or selling snowthrower products covered by that patent. Ariens argued the claims were invalid for failing to comply with the written description requirement under Section 112, first paragraph. The district court held in favor of Toro. On appeal, the Federal Circuit reversed.

Ariens argued that the district court erred in denying its motion for summary judgment that claims 36–41, that removed the requirement that the impeller be curved from original claim 24, were invalid under Section 112, first paragraph for failure to comply with the written description requirement. Ariens contended that Toro was only in possession of snowthrowers with a curved impeller, and that the patent's narrow written description did not support claims directed to a snowthrower without such an impeller. Toro responded that the district court correctly held that claims 36–41 were not invalid as a matter of law, and that the written description did support the claims at issue.

The Federal Circuit agreed with Ariens that claims 36–41 did not satisfy Section 112, first paragraph. According to the Federal Circuit, Toro broadened the claims beyond what the original claims claimed and the written description disclosed. The Federal Circuit explained that

[69] *Id.*, slip op. at 3–4.

Main volume footnote updates begin on page 264.

the written description in the patent disclosed that the only type of impeller to be used in the claimed snowthrowers was a curved one. In fact, the written description disclosed that in the construction of the impeller of the claimed snowthrower, the curved shape is a built-in feature.

According to the Federal Circuit, the written description identified curved impellers as the only impellers to be used in the claimed invention and made no mention of any other possible design to be used in the claimed snowthrowers. Clearly, the Federal Circuit concluded, the reissue claims exceeded what the inventors had possession of when they filed the patent application.[70]

The Federal Circuit therefore concluded that claims 36–41 were invalid under Section 112, first paragraph as a matter of law, because none of these claims were limited to a curved impeller, and the written description failed to support the claims in which a snowthrower contained an impeller that was anything other than curved. According to the Federal Circuit, "Toro . . . impermissibly obtain[ed] claims that were unsupported by the narrow disclosure in the written description."[71]

In *Toro Co. v. White Consolidated Industries, Inc.*,[72] the patent described and claimed a hand-held convertible vacuum/blower. The vacuum/blower could be used both as a vacuum cleaner for collecting leaves and other debris, and as a blower for dispersing the same. In both modes, a centrifugal fan (called an impeller) rotating in a housing moved air through the device in a constant direction, sucking air in through an air inlet, and blowing air out through an air outlet or exhaust. The patent emphasized that by attaching the air flow restriction ring to the air inlet cover, the ring will always be located precisely where it is needed to automatically restrict the air flow when the air inlet cover was in place.

White, a manufacturer of similar devices, upon Toro's introduction of its improved model embodying the patented structure, attempted to design around the patent. In White's design, the air inlet was also restricted by a ring that was present during operation as a blower and absent in vacuum mode, as in Toro's patent. But unlike Toro's vacuum/blower, White's restriction ring was not attached as part of the air inlet cover, but was a separate part. White's ring was manually inserted into the air inlet opening under the cover during blower operation, and removed along with the cover for vacuum operation. White's restriction ring was not automatically removed with White's cover, but had to be separately lifted out. In addition, White's cover was not completely separable from the housing, but swung open on a hinge.

Toro charged White with infringement of the patent. White argued that its overall design did not incorporate the invention of the

---

[70] *Id.* at 11.

[71] *Id.*

[72] Toro Co. v. White Consol. Indus., Inc., 199 F.3d 1295, 53 USPQ 2d 1065 (Fed. Cir. 1999).

Main volume footnote updates begin on page 264.

patent and constituted a successful attempt to design around its claims. Claim 16 recited, for example:

> 16. A convertible vacuum-blower comprising: a housing having an air inlet and an air outlet;
>
> a motor supported in said housing;
>
> an impeller having a plurality of impeller blades supported for rotary motion in said housing, in fluid communication with said air inlet and said air outlet, and rotatably driven by said motor;
>
> a removable air inlet cover for covering said air inlet, said air inlet cover having apertures for passage of air through the cover;
>
> attachment means for removably securing said air inlet cover to said housing; and
>
> said cover including means for increasing the pressure developed by said vacuum-blower during operation as a blower when air is being supplied to said impeller through said apertured cover.[73]

The Federal Circuit noted that the specification and drawings showed the restriction ring as "part of" and permanently attached to the cover. No other structure was illustrated or described. The specification described the restriction ring as built as part of the air inlet cover, and did not suggest that the cover and the ring may be two distinct components to be inserted and removed separately. To the contrary, the Federal Circuit emphasized that the specification described the advantages of the unitary structure as important to the invention.

In limiting the claim interpretation to the specific embodiment described in Toro's specification the Federal Circuit reasoned:

> The specification shows only a structure whereby the restriction ring is "part of" the cover, in permanent attachment. This is not simply the preferred embodiment; it is the only embodiment. Thus although Toro argues that it is irrelevant whether the ring and the cover are one part or two, in the specification Toro stressed that they are one. . . . The specification does not describe an invention broader than this description of the cover and the restriction ring "automatically" inserted and removed together. Nowhere in the specification, including its twenty-one drawings, is the cover shown without the restriction ring attached to it. Nor is the restriction ring shown other than attached to the cover. The specification states that the restricting ring is automatically inserted and removed by the cover to which it is attached, and illustrates only this structure in the drawings. . . . No other, broader concept was described as embodying the applicant's invention, or shown in any of the drawings, or presented for examination. . . .
>
> Instead, the invention is described throughout the specification as it is claimed, whereby the cover "includes" the ring, so that the ring is inserted by closing the cover and removed by opening the cover, "automatically."[74]

---

[73] *Id.*, 53 USPQ 2d at 1067.

[74] *Id.* at 1069–70.

Main volume footnote updates begin on page 264.

Accordingly, the Federal Circuit held that there was no basis for construing "including" the ring to mean not including the ring, as asserted by Toro.

The Federal Circuit has similarly limited claim interpretation and not permitted the written description to be broadened for means-plus-function claims. For example, in *Cortland Line Co. v. Orvis Co.*,[75] the invention covered a fishing reel with an interchangeable cartridge spool. Traditionally, fishermen had great difficulty changing fishing lines in response to varying fishing conditions. To change fishing lines, a fisherman had to remove the entire reel spool from the pole and substitute another reel spool. In addition, owning multiple spare reel spools with different fishing lines was an expensive proposition for most fishermen. The invention solved this problem by providing a fishing reel with an easily interchangeable cartridge spool that mounted onto the reel spool. Claim 1, the only independent claim, recited:

> 1. A fishing reel that provides for an interchangeable line bearing cartridge spool comprising:
>
> a housing, said housing including a flat wall, said housing having a rigid first spool receiving shaft affixed thereto and protruding away from said wall;
>
> a cartridge spool;
>
> first spool means for mounting said cartridge spool, said first spool means comprising a first end plate, a first spool axle attached rigidly to said first end plate, a second end plate, and means for connecting said second end plate to said first spool axle, said first spool axle having a hollow aperture which is fitted over said first spool receiving shaft;
>
> means attached to said first spool means for manually rotating said first spool means;
>
> said cartridge spool comprising two end plates and a central cartridge spool axle unitarily connected therebetween, said cartridge spool axle being fitted over and mounted upon said first spool axle, said cartridge spool carrying a supply of fishing line, whereby said cartridge spool can be installed on or removed from said first spool.[76]

Orvis sold the accused fishing reel, marketed as Rocky Mountain Reels, having an interchangeable cartridge spool for quick and inexpensive changing of fly line. Cortland sued Orvis alleging infringement of its patent. The district court granted summary judgment of no patent infringement based on its interpretation of the claims limited to the specific embodiment disclosed in the specification. On appeal, the Federal Circuit affirmed the the district court's claim interpretation.

The Federal Circuit noted that the only disputed element of claim 1, the first spool means, contained four components including

---

[75] Cortland Line Co. v. Orvis Co., 203 F.3d 1351, 53 USPQ 2d 1734 (Fed. Cir. 2000).

[76] *Id.*, 53 USPQ 2d at 1735.

a second end plate. The Federal Circuit noted that the written description of the patent described the end plate as a structure that could accommodate "frictional contact" with a cartridge spool to resist relative rotation between the cartridge spool and the end plates. Indeed, the Federal Circuit observed, figure 1 of the specification illustrated the "only" embodiment of the claimed invention.[77] In figure 1, the second end plate is a disk-like structure of sufficient diameter that is separate from the cartridge spool and abuts the end face of the cartridge spool. Thus, the Federal Circuit reasoned that the specification supported the conventional meaning of the word "plate" as a broad, flat disc.

In *Watts v. XL Systems Inc.*,[78] the invention was directed toward connecting sections of pipe together with a primary use in the oil well industry in which miles of pipe may need to be dropped into a hole. Such a pipe consisted of a large number of sections, called joints, which were typically 40 feet long and 20 inches wide and connected together. The joints were commonly connected together in one of two ways. The first used an integral connection in which the joints themselves had mating threads allowing the joints to be connected directly to each other. The second used a coupling connection in which the joints still had threads, but were connected to a coupling disposed between two successive joints. Claim 18, which was representative, read as follows:

> 18. A high efficiency connection for joints of oilwell tubing or the like, comprising: at least two pipes joined together and forming joints of pipe, each joints of pipe having a first end with no increase in wall thickness relative to the average pipe wall thickness and formed with tapered internal threads; the joints each having a second end formed with tapered external threads dimensioned such that one such joint may be sealingly connected directly with another such joint; the threads being of sufficient length and taper such that the pipe wall strength of the first end in the area of the smallest diameter of thread engagement is at least three-fourths of the average pipe wall strength of the joints of pipe.[79]

The district court construed the statement "the joints each having a second end formed with tapered external threads dimensioned such that one such joint may be sealingly connected directly with another such joint" to be limited to the disclosed embodiments. Based on its claim construction, the district court held that XL did not infringe any of the claims at issue. Watts appealed the district court's judgment. On appeal, the Federal Circuit reversed the district court's decision regarding whether the claim limitation was a means-plus-function limitation.

Watts argued that the district court was wrong, contending that the sealingly connected limitation should not be limited to the disclosed embodiments. On appeal, the Federal Circuit reversed and held

[77] *Id.* at 1737.

[78] Watts v. XL Sys. Inc., 232 F.3d 877, 56 USPQ 2d 1836 (Fed. Cir. 2000).

[79] *Id.*, 56 USPQ 2d at 1837.

Main volume footnote updates begin on page 264.

XL's arguments to be unavailing. According to the Federal Circuit, the threads represented the sole structural configuration effecting the seal and clearly were not mere indicators of the location of the seal as XL had argued. Although the use of misaligned taper angles, as well as a variety of other mechanisms, may increase the strength of the seal, the Federal Circuit reasoned that the claimed sealing function was accomplished by the claimed threads, and therefore, the limitations were not purely functional.[80]

The Federal Circuit held that the "sealingly connected" limitation was reasonably well understood in the pertinent art as a name for the structure, performed the function of sealing, and the threads were the sole structural configuration effecting the seal, and not merely indicators of the location of the seal. Accordingly, the Federal Circuit interpreted the "sealingly connected" limitation in the claims of the patent for oil well tubing connections as limited to structures utilizing misaligned taper angles for pipe threads that effect sealing connection. This interpretation was based on the specification, which disclosed only one method by which tapered internal and external threads were "dimensioned" for the sealing connection. Accordingly, the specification actually limited the invention to structures that utilized misaligned taper angles.[81]

c. *Liberal Written Description Will Not Narrow Scope of Patent Claims [New Topic]*

On the other hand, in *Total Containment, Inc. v. Intelpro Corp.*,[82] the written description of the invention included multiple embodiments that were used to interpret the claims to cover more than just a single embodiment of the invention. The invention related to secondarily contained flexible piping systems that included a flexible inner supply pipe and an outer secondary containment pipe. These systems used flexible piping to greatly reduce the required number of pipe joints, potential sources of leaks in prior art rigid piping systems.

In holding that the claimed invention was not limited to a removable inner pipe, the Federal Circuit stated the following:

> Environ principally argues that the . . . specification describes the invention as having a removable inner pipe and that even if the claim does not specify the removability of the inner pipe, each and every embodiment provided in the specification requires the inner pipe to be removable. . . . [W]e do not agree with Environ that the . . . specification is limited to removable inner pipe systems. The Summary of the Invention states that "the present invention provides a piping system for conveying fluid from

[80] *Id.* at 1839.

[81] *Id.*

[82] Total Containment, Inc. v. Intelpro Corp., Civ. App. No. 99-1059 (Fed. Cir. Sept. 15, 1999) (unpublished), *cert. denied*, 529 U.S. 1108 (2000).

Main volume footnote updates begin on page 264.

> the outlet port of a pump to the inlet port of a fluid dispenser." . . . The system is further described in the specification as having a "primary pipe of flexible material" and a "secondary pipe of flexible material generally surrounding the primary pipe." . . . We will not, however, in the absence of any other support, read a limitation into a claim, particularly when the claim has no verbal hook upon which to hang the limitation, simply because the inventor stated that it was an advantage.[83]

Similarly, patent claims have not been limited to the preferred embodiment, when the specification makes clear that the embodiment disclosed in the specification is not the only embodiment of the invention. The general rule is that the claims of a patent are not limited to the preferred embodiment, unless by their own language.[84] The Federal Circuit has stated in this connection, "[i]t is well settled that device claims are not limited to devices which operate precisely as the embodiments described in detail in the patent."[85]

For example, in *Karlin Technology Inc. v. Surgical Dynamics, Inc.*,[86] the invention related to a threaded spinal implant for stabilizing adjacent spinal vertebrae. The invention generally included a hollow cylinder with external threads along, and holes through, the cylindrical surface. The hollow portion of the implant was filled with bone or other osteogenic material so that, while the affected vertebrae were initially stabilized by the implants themselves, bone growth through the holes in the implants eventually fused the vertebrae together.

Surgical Dynamics argued that the invention should be limited to the specialized threads described in the specification based on language in the written description stating that the "present invention" included the highly specialized threads.[87] Karlin argued that this language described the inventor's preferred embodiment, and that "series of threads" should not be construed as limited to the preferred embodiment.

In holding that the patent claims were not to be limited to the specialized threads described in the specification, the Federal Circuit stated:

> Although Figure 4 is expressly stated to show the "present invention," and Figures 4A and 4B refer to "one preferred embodiment," the same spinal implant is shown in each of the figures. The remainder of the written description has similarly mixed references to "present invention" and "preferred embodiment." We therefore conclude that the written description uses the terms "present invention" and "preferred embodiment"

[83] *Id.*, slip op. at 17–18.

[84] Karlin Tech. Inc. v. Surgical Dynamics, Inc., 177 F.3d 968, 50 USPQ 2d 1465, 1469 (Fed. Cir. 1999).

[85] Virginia Panel Corp. v. MAC Panel Co., 133 F.3d 860, 866, 45 USPQ 2d 1225, 1229 (Fed. Cir. 1997), *cert. denied*, 525 U.S. 815 (1998).

[86] Karlin Tech. Inc. v. Surgical Dynamics, Inc., 177 F.3d 968, 50 USPQ 2d 1465 (Fed. Cir. 1999).

[87] *Id.*, 50 USPQ 2d at 1469.

Main volume footnote updates begin on page 264.

> interchangeably. Given this, it is clear that only the preferred embodiment is described as having highly specialized threads. The general rule, of course, is that the claims of a patent are not limited to the preferred embodiment, unless by their own language. . . . There is nothing in this case that warrants departing from the general rule. Thus, the written description does not narrow the ordinary meaning of "series of threads."[88]

Thus, *Karlin Technology* illustrates that claims will not be limited to the written description when the written description does not indicate that the embodiment or embodiments disclosed therein are the only embodiment or embodiments of the invention.

Similarly, in *Lampi Corp. v. American Power Products, Inc.*,[89] the Federal Circuit interpreted the word "having" broadly based on a written description that broadly defined the invention. According to the Federal Circuit:

> Lampi argues on appeal that the term "having" is used in an open sense in the context of the claim limitation at issue, and thus the inclusion of additional components, such as the end caps and translucent cover of the 5544 model, do not render the device non-infringing. . . . We agree with Lampi. . . . The specification in this case indicates that the patentee intended the word "having" in claim 11 to be open. The patent states that "the housing preferably consists of two separable half-shells." . . . This language makes clear that it is merely a preferred embodiment of the invention that the housing be made of only two half-shells, "[s]o that the housing can be easily assembled, the fluorescent lamp tube easily replaced, the wiring required to operate the fluorescent lamp installed during fabrication, and . . . repaired if necessary[.]" . . . Thus, the specification indicates that the housing must have at least two half-shells, but that it may have other parts as well.[90]

G. Special Topic: Written Description of Range Limitations in Claims

[Insert at the end of the Section.]

In *Union Oil Co. of California v. Atlantic Richfield Co.*,[91] the invention related to automotive gasoline compositions that reduced automobile tailpipe emissions. The inventors sought to reduce the levels of carbon monoxide (CO), nitrous oxide (NOx), and hydrocarbons (HC)

---

[88] *Id.*

[89] Lampi Corp. v. American Power Prods., Inc., 228 F.3d 1365, 56 USPQ 2d 1445 (Fed. Cir. 2000).

[90] *Id.*, 56 USPQ 2d at 1453 (citing Genentech, Inc. v. Chiron Corp., 112 F.3d 495, 501, 42 USPQ 2d 1608, 1613 (Fed. Cir. 1997) (explaining that open term "means that the named elements are essential, but other elements may be added and still form a construct within the scope of the claim")).

[91] Union Oil Co. of Cal. v. Atlantic Richfield Co., 208 F.3d 989, 54 USPQ 2d 1227 (Fed. Cir. 2000), *cert. denied*, 121 S. Ct. 1167 (2001).

Main volume footnote updates begin on page 264.

emitted from automobile tailpipes. After considerable experimentation, the inventors discovered relationships between the various petroleum characteristics described above and tailpipe emissions.

Atlantic Richfield originally sued Unocal in district court, seeking a declaratory judgment to invalidate the patent. Unocal counterclaimed, alleging willful infringement of the patent. The district court then construed the claims of the patent, and limited the claims to automotive fuels. As an example, dependent claim 117 recited, when placed in independent form:

> 117. [An unleaded gasoline fuel suitable for combustion in an automotive engine, said fuel having a Reid Vapor pressure no greater than 7.0 psi, and a 50% D-86 distillation point no greater than 200 degrees F., and a 90% D-86 distillation point no greater than 300 degrees F., and a paraffin content greater than 85 volume percent, and an olefin content less than 4 volume percent] wherein the maximum 10% distillation point is 158 degrees F (70 degrees C.).[92]

The patent taught the effects of varying the properties of automotive gasolines to reduce harmful tailpipe emissions. In the art of gasoline production, skilled refiners obtain raw petroleum products and mix them together to achieve a desired product. Each product is the mixture of many chemicals in varying proportions. The patent taught that changes in the proportions of different hydrocarbon-containing streams mixed to produce gasoline with specific properties reduces the amount of NOx, CO, and hydrocarbons emitted from an automobile engine. Varying one or more properties in turn affects other properties of a gasoline product. Therefore, the patent claimed its inventive products in terms of ranges of chemical properties, which work in combination with ranges of other chemical properties to produce a gasoline that reduces emissions, reflecting the way oil refiners formulate gasoline. The claims did not describe each gasoline product in terms of molecular structures or lists of ingredients.

Atlantic Richfield asserted that the specification did not describe the exact chemical component of each combination that fell within the range claims of the patent. However, the Federal Circuit noted that neither the Patent Act nor the case law required such detailed disclosure. According to the Federal Circuit, the written description requirement does not require the applicant to describe exactly the subject matter claimed. Instead, the description must clearly allow persons of ordinary skill in the art to recognize that he or she invented what is claimed.[93] In other words, Section 112, first paragraph requires only sufficient description to show one of skill in the refining art that the inventor possessed the claimed invention at the time of filing.

---

[92] *Id.*, 54 USPQ 2d at 1228.

[93] *Id.* at 1232 (citing *In re* Gosteli, 872 F.2d 1008, 1012, 10 USPQ 2d 1614, 1618 (Fed. Cir. 1989)).

Main volume footnote updates begin on page 264.

The Federal Circuit reasoned that Drs. Jessup and Croudace described their invention in terms of ranges. That form of description does not offend Section 112, first paragraph. In fact, the Federal Circuit emphasized that the invention lent itself to description in terms of ranges and variance of those ranges to achieve particular properties of the gasoline products. The inquiry for adequate written description simply does not depend on a particular claim format, but rather on whether the patent's description would show those of ordinary skill in the petroleum refining art that the inventors possessed the claimed invention at the time of filing.

The Federal Circuit also explained that the patent taught one of ordinary skill that reducing, for example, T50 progressively reduced CO and hydrocarbons; reducing olefins progressively reduced NOx and hydrocarbons; increasing paraffins progressively reduced CO and NOx; and so forth with several other relationships. In addition, the patent claimed ranges for these properties that provided cleaner gasoline emissions. According to the Federal Circuit, the patent unmistakably informed skilled refiners to increase or decrease the various components to arrive at preferred combinations. In fact, the Federal Circuit noted that the written description labeled both preferred and most preferred levels within each range. In sum, the record showed that the inventors possessed the claimed invention at the time of filing in the assessment of those of ordinary skill in the petroleum refining art.

Accordingly, the Federal Circuit held that Union Oil's patent for automotive gasoline compositions, which claimed its inventive products in terms of ranges of chemical properties that worked in combination with ranges of other chemical properties to produce gasolines that reduced emissions, was supported by an adequate written description. This was so even though the specification did not describe exact chemical components of each combination that fell within the claimed ranges, since the specification thoroughly discussed claimed ranges and combinations of multiple properties, and guided the skilled artisan in combining these properties.[94]

H. Relationship Between Written Description Requirement and Related Applications

1. Claiming Priority From a U.S. Application

[On page 762, change the first sentence in the last paragraph to the following.]

---

[94] *Id.* at 1235. *But see* Purdue Pharma L.P. v. Faulding Inc., 230 F.3d 1320, 56 USPQ 2d 1481 (Fed. Cir. 2000) (requiring the specification to "emphasize," "motivate," or describe the "importance" of the invention) (emphasis added):

Main volume footnote updates begin on page 264.

A U.S. application may generally claim the benefit of priority from an earlier U.S. application if the subject matter claimed in the later application fulfills the requirements of Section 112, including containing an adequate written description in the earlier parent application. As stated by the Federal Circuit:

> Although Section 120 incorporates the requirements of Section 112 Para. 1, these requirements and the statutory mechanism allowing the benefit of an earlier filing date are separate provisions with distinct consequences. In accordance with Section 120, claims to subject matter in a later-filed application not supported by an ancestor application in terms of Section 112 Para. 1 are not invalidated; they simply do not receive the benefit of the earlier application's filing date.[95]

V. Best Mode

B. Alternative 1: Attacking Prima Facie Case of No Best Mode

[Insert after footnote 437.]

As explained by the Federal Circuit:

> As we have repeatedly held, the contours of the best mode requirement are defined by the scope of the claimed invention. . . . This consistent body of law postulates that the first task in any best mode analysis is to define the invention at hand. The definition of the invention, like the interpretation of the patent claims, is a legal exercise, wherein the ordinary principles of claim construction apply. . . . We begin, as always, with the language of the claim itself. . . . Claim language is given its ordinary and accustomed meaning except where a different meaning is clearly set forth in the specification or where the accustomed meaning would deprive the claim of clarity. . . .
>
> When the invention is defined, the best mode inquiry moves to determining whether a best mode of carrying out that invention was held by the inventor. If so, that best mode must be disclosed.[96]

Although the examples provide the data from which one can piece together the C submax /C sub24 limitation, neither the text accompanying the examples, nor the data, nor anything else in the specification in any way *emphasizes* the C submax /C sub24 ratio. The district court therefore reasonably concluded that one of ordinary skill in the art would not be directed to the C submax /C sub24 ratio as an aspect of the invention. . . . In the case of the '360 patent, there is nothing in the written description of Examples 1 and 3 that would suggest to one skilled in the art that the C submax /C sub24 ratio is an *important* defining quality of the formulation, nor does the disclosure even *motivate* one to calculate the ratio.

[95] Reiffin v. Microsoft Corp., 214 F.3d 1342, 54 USPQ 2d 1915, 1918 (Fed. Cir. 2000) (citing Hyatt v. Boone, 146 F.3d 1348, 1352, 47 USPQ 2d 1128, 1130 (Fed. Cir. 1998)).

[96] Northern Telecom Ltd. v. Samsung Elecs. Co., 215 F.3d 1281, 55 USPQ 2d 1065, 1068–69 (Fed. Cir. 2000) (citing Engel Indus., Inc. v. Lockformer Co., 946 F.2d 1528, 1531, 20 USPQ 2d 1300, 1302 (Fed. Cir. 1991) ("The best mode inquiry is directed to what the applicant regards as

Main volume footnote updates begin on page 264.

Unclaimed subject matter that is not unrelated to the operation of the claimed invention does not trigger the best mode requirement.[97] Accordingly, the extent of information that an inventor must disclose depends on the scope of the claimed invention.[98] Thus, an inventor need not disclose a mode for obtaining unclaimed subject matter unless the subject matter is novel and essential for carrying out the best mode of the invention.[99] The best mode requirement does not extend to production details that do not concern the quality or nature of the claimed invention, such as equipment on hand, suppliers, expected volume of production, and the like.[100] Routine details may implicate the quality and nature of the invention, but their disclosure is unnecessary because they are readily apparent to one of ordinary skill in the art.[101] As stated by the Federal Circuit, "[i]t logically follows that a patentee's failure to disclose an unclaimed, preferred mode for accomplishing a routine detail does not violate the best mode requirement because one skilled in the art is aware of alternative means for accomplishing the routine detail that would still produce the best mode of the claimed invention."[102]

[Insert at the end of the section.]

Northern Telecom Ltd. v. Samsung Electronics Co.,[103] is another example of a case in which the best mode requirement was not violated. The invention related to aluminum etching used in the manufacture of integrated circuit semiconductor devices to create conductive lines of aluminum between various electronic devices on a silicon substrate. A

---

the invention, which in turn is measured by the claims. Unclaimed subject matter is not subject to the disclosure requirements of Section 112."); Chemcast Corp. v. Arco Indus. Corp., 913 F.2d 923, 927, 16 USPQ 2d 1033, 1037 (Fed. Cir. 1990) (an "objective limitation on the extent of the disclosure required to comply with the best mode requirement is, of course, the scope of the claimed invention"); Randomex, Inc. v. Scopus Corp., 849 F.2d 585, 588, 7 USPQ 2d 1050, 1053 (Fed. Cir. 1988) ("It is concealment of the best mode of practicing the claimed invention that section 112 Para. 1 is designed to prohibit."); Zygo Corp. v. Wyko Corp., 79 F.3d 1563, 1567, 38 USPQ 2d 1281, 1284 (Fed. Cir. 1996) ("The focus of a section 112 inquiry is not what a particular user decides to make and sell or even in what field the invention is most likely to find success. Rather, in keeping with the statutory mandate, our precedent is clear that the parameters of a section 112 inquiry are set by the claims.")).

[97] *Id.*, 55 USPQ 2d 1070.

[98] Eli Lilly & Co. v. Barr Labs., 251 F.3d 955, 58 USPQ 2d 1865, 1874 (Fed. Cir. 2001); Engel Indus., Inc. v. Lockformer Co., 946 F.2d 1528, 1531, 20 USPQ 2d 1300, 1302 (Fed. Cir. 1991).

[99] Eli Lilly & Co. v. Barr Labs., 251 F.3d 955, 58 USPQ 2d 1865, 1875 (Fed. Cir. 2001); Applied Med. Resources Corp. v. United States Surgical Corp., 147 F.3d 1374, 1377, 47 USPQ 2d 1289, 1291 (Fed. Cir. 1998).

[100] Young Dental Mfg. Co., Inc. v. Q3 Special Prods. Inc., 112 F.3d 1137, 1143, 42 USPQ 2d 1589, 1594–95 (Fed. Cir. 1997).

[101] *Id.*

[102] Eli Lilly & Co. v. Barr Labs., 251 F.3d 955, 58 USPQ 2d 1865, 1877 (Fed. Cir. 2001).

[103] Northern Telecom Ltd. v. Samsung Elecs. Co., 215 F.3d 1281, 55 USPQ 2d 1065 (Fed. Cir. 2000).

Main volume footnote updates begin on page 264.

typical manufacturing process begins with a silicon wafer coated with a conductive layer of aluminum or aluminum alloy. The manufacturer first covers the conductive layer with a mask of nonetchable material. Next, an aluminum etching process is applied to remove portions of the conductive film not protected by the mask. Finally, the manufacturer removes the masking material, leaving the desired pattern on the surface of the semiconductor substrate.

The final step in manufacturing an integrated circuit semiconductor device is typically to heat or "sinter" the etched product at temperatures above 400 degrees C. Sintering improves the contact between the conductive lines and the silicon substrate. However, during sintering, a phenomenon known as "spearing" may occur, which results in tiny metal protrusions extending downward from the bottom of the aluminum layer into the silicon substrate. Spearing occurs because elevated temperatures cause silicon to diffuse upward into the aluminum layer, allowing aluminum to fill the spaces vacated by the silicon. Spearing is undesirable because it may cause short circuits between multiple conductive layers in an integrated circuit semiconductor device.

One solution to the spearing problem was to use an aluminum silicon alloy as the metallic layer rather than pure aluminum. If the silicon content of the aluminum alloy exceeded the solid solubility limit for silicon in aluminum at the sintering temperature, then no diffusion of silicon from the substrate would occur and, thus, spearing would be prevented.

The inventors of the Northern Telecom patent discovered that certain etch gases—specifically boron trihalides—would remove the oxide layer and permit etching of the aluminum underneath. The use of boron trihalides in plasma etching enabled etching of aluminum line widths below 2 microns, a significant advance in the miniaturization of semiconductor devices. It was undisputed that the inventors of the patent knew that aluminum silicon alloy could be used in this manner and, indeed, believed that the use of aluminum silicon alloy was necessary to manufacture semiconductors below two microns.

Both Northern Telecom and Samsung agreed that the primary use of the patent was in the manufacture of semiconductor devices. Also undisputed was the fact that fine line etching—that is, etching of lines of less than two microns was preferred for improved semiconductor devices. With those facts in hand, the district court concluded that the best mode of carrying out the invention was to achieve fine line etching. Since the use of aluminum silicon alloy was necessary to preclude a certain spearing phenomenon during the sintering phase, which occurred after the plasma etching phase, the district court held that disclosure of aluminum silicon alloy was required to satisfy the best mode requirement of 35 U.S.C. Section 112. Because the inventors knew that aluminum silicon alloy was necessary to prevent spearing,

Main volume footnote updates begin on page 264.

and since the alloy was not disclosed, the patent was held invalid by the district court.

On appeal, the Federal Circuit reversed. The Federal Circuit noted that Northern Telecom admitted that the best mode of manufacturing fine line semiconductor devices required use of aluminum silicon alloy. However, Northern Telecom contended that this admission was irrelevant to the best mode inquiry since its patent was not drawn to a process for manufacturing fine line semiconductor devices. Northern Telecom pointed out that its claimed process was advantageous in the manufacture of semiconductor devices, without regard to line width, because of the many uncontested advantages of gaseous plasma etching over wet chemical processes that were made possible by plasma etching in the presence of a gaseous trihalide.

The Federal Circuit agreed and explained that the district court misunderstood the invention. According to the Federal Circuit, what was claimed was a process for plasma etching of aluminum and aluminum oxide in the presence of a gaseous trihalide. Fine line etching was simply not part of the claimed invention. However, the best mode alleged by Samsung was the use of aluminum silicon alloy instead of pure aluminum as the interconnect layer in manufacturing integrated circuits with conductive lines of less than two microns. The Federal Circuit reasoned that the claims were not limited to the use of gas plasma etching to produce semiconductor devices with fine conductive lines. Instead, the claims were directed to a general process for plasma etching of aluminum and aluminum oxide in the presence of a gaseous trihalide. Accordingly, the inventors of the process were not required, under 35 U.S.C. Section 112, to disclose the best mode of achieving fine line etching—only the best mode of carrying out the claimed method of plasma etching aluminum and aluminum oxide with a gaseous trihalide. Since it was undisputed that this requirement was satisfied in the specification, the Federal Circuit reversed the district court.

2. *Subjective Intent of Inventor*

[Insert after footnote 444.]

This part of the test in determining compliance with the best mode requirement is wholly subjective,[104] and involves determining "whether, at the time the inventor filed his patent application, he knew of a mode of practicing his claimed invention that he considered to be better than any other."[105]

---

[104] Calabrese v. Square D Co., Civ. App. No. 98-1550, slip op. at 3 (Fed. Cir. Sept. 13, 1999) (unpublished).

[105] Chemcast Corp. v. Arco Indus. Corp., 913 F.2d 923, 927–28, 16 USPQ 2d 1033, 1036 (Fed. Cir. 1990).

Main volume footnote updates begin on page 264.

6. Lack of Requirement of Production Specification

[Insert after footnote 465.]

Similarly, the Federal Circuit has also stated:

> The best mode requirement does not require that every mode for producing the patented invention be disclosed. Nor does it require disclosure of the best method of mass producing the invention. . . . The inventor is only required to disclose his or her own best mode contemplated of practicing the claimed invention at the time the application for the patent was filed. . . . To require disclosure of methods of mass production . . . would "turn a patent specification into a detailed production schedule, which is not its function."[106]

As explained in further detail by the Federal Circuit:

> Requiring inclusion in the patent of known scientific/technological information would add an imprecise and open-ended criterion to the content of patent specifications, could greatly enlarge the content of patent specifications and unnecessarily increase the cost of preparing and prosecuting patent applications, and could tend to obfuscate rather than highlight the contribution to which the patent is directed. A patent is not a scientific treatise, but a document that presumes a readership skilled in the field of the invention.[107]

E. Updating Best Mode on Subsequently Filed Application

[Insert at the end of the section.]

The Federal Circuit had the opportunity to further explore the issue of when the best mode needs to be updated in a continuing application in *Magnivision, Inc. v. Bonneau Co.*[108] The invention related to a hanger for store display of eyeglasses. The hanger's advantage was that it did not have to be removed and replaced when a consumer tried the glasses on and returned them to the display. Magnivision and Bonneau both sold non-prescription eyeglasses. Magnivision sued Bonneau for infringing its patent, and Bonneau argued that the patent was invalid for failure to disclose and update the best mode of practicing the invention in the continuation-in-part application. The district court granted summary judgment in favor of Magnivision on

---

[106] Ricoh Co. v. Nashua Corp., Civ. App. No. 97-1344, slip op. at 10 (Fed. Cir. Feb. 18, 1999) (unpublished), *cert. denied*, 528 U.S. 815 (1999) (quoting Wahl Instruments, Inc. v. Acvious, Inc., 950 F.2d 1575, 1581, 21 USPQ 2d 1123, 1128 (Fed. Cir. 1991)).

[107] Ajinomoto Co. v. Archer-Daniels-Midland Co., 228 F.3d 1338, 56 USPQ 2d 1332, 1336 (Fed. Cir. 2000), *cert. denied*, 121 S. Ct. 1957 (2001) (citing W.L. Gore & Assoc. Inc. v. Garlock, Inc., 721 F.2d 1540, 1556, 220 USPQ 303, 315 (Fed. Cir. 1983) ("Patents, however, are written to enable those skilled in the art to practice the invention, not the public.").

[108] Magnivision, Inc. v. Bonneau Co., Civ. App. No. 99-1093 (Fed. Cir. July 24, 2000) (unpublished).

Main volume footnote updates begin on page 264.

Bonneau's affirmative defense that the patent was invalid for failure to disclose the best mode of practicing the invention, i.e., the district court held that Bonneau had failed to prove that the patent did not in fact disclose the best mode.

On appeal, the Federal Circuit agreed with the district court that Magnivision's patent did comply with the best mode requirement.

The Federal Circuit observed that the best mode issue depended on the timing of the inventor's knowledge of a best mode. Magnivision admitted that the inventor learned in mid-1988 of a better plastic material for the hanger than he had specified in his original January 19, 1988 application. Magnivision's patent described "a relatively stiff resilient plastic material, typically a polythene," or "a moderately stiff yet flexible plastic material."[109] The disputed claim 5 of the patent, i.e., U.S. Patent 5,144,345, referred only to a "flat sheet material."[110] At the time the inventor disclosed this "resilient plastic material" in his original filing, he did not know of a better mode. However, the Federal Circuit noted that at the time the inventor filed the continuation-in-part (CIP) application on December 1, 1988, which issued as the patent, the inventor knew of the better mode.

Citing *Transco v. Performance Contracting*, the Federal Circuit explained the overall inquiry to be made when determining whether the best mode need be updated in a continuing application:

> If the material in a continuation application is "common subject matter" with that of the original application, the inventor need not have updated his best mode disclosure in the continuation application. . . . An inventor only has the obligation to disclose a best mode in a continuation application if the claim feature associated with that best mode first appeared or first received adequate written description in the continuation.[111]

To determine whether the best mode needed to updated, the Federal Circuit indicated that it must determine whether the continuation application first introduced or first supplied written support for the "retaining member for securing a portion of said frame" associated with the better plastic hanger material. The Federal Circuit indicated that the later filed CIP application that led to the issued patent added Figures 4–7 and the text that described these figures. Therefore, the Federal Circuit reasoned, if figures 1–3, which appeared in the original filing, supplied adequate support for the "retaining member" recited in the patent (i.e., claim 5), then the inventor possessed that aspect of the invention at the time of the original filing. In that event, the Federal Circuit concluded, the inventor had no obligation to supply a best mode past that original filing date of the earlier filed application.

---

[109] *Id.*, slip op. at 17.

[110] *Id.*

[111] *Id.* at 17–18 (citing Transco v. Performance Contracting, 38 F.3d 551, 557, 32 USPQ 2d 1077, 1082 (Fed. Cir. 1994)).

Main volume footnote updates begin on page 264.

The Federal Circuit compared figures 1–3 of the earlier and CIP applications with figures 4–7 of the CIP application, and concluded that the CIP application only added information about the fastening means that held the extension to the main body of the hanger when the extension was wrapped around the bridge of the eyeglasses. For the fastening means, the original application disclosed a rivet, while the CIP added a molded-in button. Thus, the Federal Circuit held that the district court correctly concluded that the original application disclosed and supported the disputed element of "a retaining member for securing a portion of said frame," and the inventor had no obligation to disclose a later-learned best mode.[112]

---

[112] *Id.* at 19.

Main volume footnote updates begin on page 264.

MAIN VOLUME FOOTNOTE UPDATES

[100]**[Replace the LEXIS cite with the following.]** 525 U.S. 1141.

[106]**[Replace the LEXIS cite with the following.]** 525 U.S. 1141.

[139]**[Replace the S. Ct. cite with the following.]** 522 U.S. 963.

[250]**[Add at the end of footnote 250.]**, *cert. denied,* 523 U.S. 1089 (1998).

[252]**[Replace the LEXIS cite with the following.]** 525 U.S. 1141.

[277]**[Replace the S. Ct. cite with the following.]** 523 U.S. 1089.

[301]**[In Hyatt v. Boone, replace the LEXIS cite with the following.]** 525 U.S. 1141.

[317]**[Replace the LEXIS cite with the following.]** 525 U.S. 1141.

[396]**[Replace the L. Ed. cite with the following.]** 516 U.S. 988.

[409]**[In Glaxo Inc. v. Novopharm. Ltd., replace the L. Ed. cite with the following.]** 516 U.S. 988.

[409]**[In Transco Prods. Inc. v. Performance Contracting, Inc., replace the S. Ct. cite with the following.]** 513 U.S. 1151.

[437]**[Replace the L. Ed. cite with the following.]** 525 U.S. 1104 (1999).

[443]**[Insert at the end of the footnote.]** *See also* Eli Lilly & Co. v. Barr Labs., 222 F.3d 973, 55 USPQ 2d 1609, 1616 (Fed. Cir. 2000):

> Here, the patents disclose that the best mode of the claimed invention is fluoxetine hydrochloride that is purified through recrystallization. The patents, however, do not claim a process for purifying fluoxetine hydrochloride that is purified through recrystallization or a solvent for performing the recrystallization. Thus, failure to disclose a preferred solvent does not equate to a best mode violation because the patents simply do not claim a recrystallization process or recrystallization solvent.

[450]**[Replace the S. Ct. cite with the following.]** 513 U.S. 1151.

[477]**[Replace the S. Ct. cite with the following.]** 525 U.S. 876.

[481]**[Replace the S. Ct. cite with the following.]** 513 U.S. 1151.

[485]**[Replace the S. Ct. cite with the following.]** 513 U.S. 1151.

[489]**[Replace the S. Ct. cite with the following.]** 522 U.S. 908.

[497]**[Replace the S. Ct. cite with the following.]** 513 U.S. 1151.

[508]**[Replace the S. Ct. cite with the following.]** 513 U.S. 1151.

[519]**[Add to the cite for Transco Prods. Inc. v. Performance Contracting, Inc.]**, *cert. denied*, 513 U.S. 1151 (1995).

[527]**[Replace the L. Ed. cite with the following.]** 516 U.S. 988.

[547]**[Replace the S. Ct. cite with the following.]** 522 U.S. 908.

[557]**[Replace the S. Ct. cite with the following.]** 513 U.S. 1151.

9

Definite Claims Under 35 U.S.C. Section 112, Second Paragraph

II. Alternative 1: Attacking Prima Facie Case of Indefiniteness

A. Element 1: Claims Read in View of Specification

2. *Absence of Limitations Cited in the Specification*

[Insert after footnote 51.]

A claim need not claim every function of a working device. Rather, a claim may specify improvements in one function without claiming the entire machine with its many functions.[1]

4. *Claims Interpreted According to Ordinary Meaning Unless Special Meaning Provided in Specification*

[Insert at the beginning of the section.]

Claim interpretation begins with the language of the claims.[2] The general rule is that terms in the claim are to be given their ordinary

---

[1]Rodime PLC v. Seagate Tech., Inc., 174 F.3d 1294, 50 USPQ 2d 1429, 1435 (Fed. Cir. 1999), *cert. denied*, 528 U.S. 1115 (2000).

[2]Renishaw PLC v. Marposs Societa' Per Azioni, 158 F.3d 1243, 1248, 48 USPQ 2d 1117, 1120 (Fed. Cir. 1998); Abtox, Inc. v. Exitron Corp., 122 F.3d 1019, 1023, 43 USPQ 2d 1545, 1548 (Fed. Cir. 1997); Bell Communications Research, Inc. v. Vitalink Communications Corp., 55 F.3d 615, 619–20, 34 USPQ 2d 1816, 1819 (Fed. Cir. 1995).

Main volume footnote updates begin on page 306.

and accustomed meaning.[3] General descriptive terms will ordinarily be given their full meaning; modifiers will not be added to broad terms standing alone.[4]

In determining the proper meaning of the claims, "we first consider the so-called intrinsic evidence, i.e., the claims, the written description, and, if in evidence, the prosecution history."[5] Moreover, "if upon examination of this intrinsic evidence the meaning of the claim language is sufficiently clear, resort to extrinsic evidence, such as treatises and technical references, as well as expert testimony when appropriate, should not be necessary."[6]

Unambiguous intrinsic evidence in turn provides input to the rules of claim construction, in particular, the rule that explicit statements made by a patent applicant during prosecution to distinguish a claimed invention over prior art may serve to narrow the scope of a claim.[7] That explicit arguments made during prosecution to overcome prior art can lead to narrow claim interpretations makes sense, because "the public has a right to rely on such definitive statements made during prosecution."[8] Indeed, "by distinguishing the claimed invention over the prior art, an applicant is indicating what the claims do not cover."[9] Therefore, a patentee, after relinquishing subject matter to distinguish a prior art reference asserted by the PTO during prosecution, "cannot during subsequent litigation escape reliance [by the defendant] upon this unambiguous surrender of subject matter."[10] Accordingly, claims may not be interpreted one way in order to obtain their allowance and in a different way against accused infringers.[11]

---

[3] *See Renishaw*, 158 F.3d at 1249, 48 USPQ 2d at 1121; York Prods., Inc. v. Central Tractor Farm & Family Ctr., 99 F.3d 1568, 1572, 40 USPQ 2d 1619, 1622 (Fed. Cir. 1996).

[4] *See, e.g.*, Virginia Panel Corp. v. MAC Panel Co., 133 F.3d 860, 865–66, 45 USPQ 2d 1225, 1229 (Fed. Cir. 1997), *cert. denied*, 525 U.S. 815 (1998) (unmodified term "reciprocating" not limited to linear reciprocation); *Bell Communications*, 55 F.3d at 621–22, 34 USPQ 2d at 1821 (unmodified term "associating" not limited to explicit association); Specialty Composites v. Cabot Corp., 845 F.2d 981, 987, 6 USPQ 2d 1601, 1606 (Fed. Cir. 1988) (unmodified term "plasticizer" given full range of ordinary and accustomed meaning).

[5] Digital Biometrics, Inc. v. Identix, Inc., 149 F.3d 1335, 1347, 47 USPQ 2d 1418, 1424 (Fed. Cir. 1998).

[6] *Id.*

[7] *See* Southwall Techs. Inc. v. Cardinal IG Co., 54 F.3d 1570, 1576, 34 USPQ 2d 1673, 1676 (Fed. Cir. 1995) ("The prosecution history limits the interpretation of claim terms so as to exclude any interpretation that was disclaimed during prosecution.").

[8] *Digital Biometrics*, 149 F.3d at 1347, 47 USPQ 2d at 1427.

[9] Ekchian v. Home Depot, Inc., 104 F.3d 1299, 1304, 41 USPQ 2d 1364, 1368 (Fed. Cir. 1997).

[10] *Southwall*, 54 F.3d at 1581, 34 USPQ 2d at 1681.

[11] Spectrum Int'l, Inc. v. Sterilite Corp., 164 F.3d 1372, 49 USPQ 2d 1065, 1069 (Fed. Cir. 1998); Alpex Computer Corp. v. Nintendo Co., 102 F.3d 1214, 1221, 40 USPQ 2d 1667, 1672 (Fed. Cir. 1996), *cert. denied*, 521 U.S. 1104 (1997).

Main volume footnote updates begin on page 306.

C. Element 3: Claim Language Not Reasonably Defined

3. Functional Limitations

[Insert after footnote 144.]

In *Ex parte Bivens*,[12] the invention related to a two-cycle diesel engine derived from the prior art Detroit Diesel Series 92 Turbo Charged Engine. The differences between the two engines involve structural modifications which were said to contribute to advantageous timing characteristics in the Bivens engine. The timing characteristics of the prior art engine were embodied in the timing sequence chart set forth on page 11 of the specification and in the circle diagram depicted in Figure 9A, while the timing characteristics of the engine were embodied in the timing sequence chart set forth on page 12 of the specification and in the circle diagram depicted in Figure 9B. The rejected claims, claims 10–13, made use of these charts and diagrams to define what the applicant Bivens regarded as his invention.

In holding the claims definite, the Board noted that although these timing characteristics were functional in nature in that they defined the prior art engine and the Bivens engine by what they did rather than by what they were, it was well settled that there was nothing intrinsically wrong with the use of such a technique in drafting patent claims.[13] The Board also noted that the limitations in claims 10 and 12 drawn to the chart and diagram relating to the prior art engine amounted to product-by-process limitations used to define the engine. "Such product-by-process limitations do not inherently conflict with the second paragraph of Section 112."[14]

[Insert at the end of the section.]

In *Moore U.S.A. Inc. v. Standard Register Co.*,[15] the Federal Circuit held that the functional language "distance sufficient" was nevertheless definite. The invention related to a C-fold mailer-type business form with an integral return envelope. The integral return envelope was created as part of the mailer during the folding and sealing process. The recipient opened the mailer by removing stubs on the left and right edges. After reading the information printed on the mailer, the user could remove a remittance stub from the top panel, insert the stub into the integral return envelope, detach the envelope from the rest of the mailer, and then seal and mail the envelope.

---

[12] *Ex parte* Bivens, 53 USPQ 2d 1045 (B.P.A.I. 1999) (unpublished).

[13] *Id.* at 1046.

[14] *Id.* (citing *In re* Brown, 459 F.2d 531, 535, 173 USPQ 685, 688 (C.C.P.A. 1972)).

[15] Moore U.S.A. Inc. v. Standard Register Co., 229 F.3d 1091, 56 USPQ 2d 1225 (Fed. Cir. 2000), *cert. denied*, 121 S. Ct. 1734 (2001).

Main volume footnote updates begin on page 306.

Independent claim 1 recited:

A mailer type business form processed by a printer having rollers, and operated to occasionally pause, the mailer comprising:

a folded paper sheet having first and second faces, first and second opposite longitudinal edges, and first and second transverse fold lines defining first, second and third sections of said sheet;

first and second longitudinal lines of weakness forming with said longitudinal edges first and second longitudinal marginal portions;

a first transverse edge and a second transverse edge, both parallel to said first and second fold lines;

longitudinal patterns of adhesive disposed in said longitudinal marginal portions for holding said marginal portions of said first through third sections together;

a first transverse pattern of adhesive disposed adjacent said first transverse edge on said first face and first section; and

said first transverse pattern of adhesive being spaced from its associated transverse edge a distance sufficient to insure that the adhesive does not interfere with rollers of a printer used to process the mailer during pausing of the printer.[16]

The Examiner's initial indefiniteness rejection with respect to the "distance sufficient" limitation in the phrase "said first transverse pattern of adhesive being spaced from its associated transverse edge a distance sufficient to insure that the adhesive does not interfere with rollers of a printer," was based on the Examiner's belief that the limitation was not restricted to any particular printer.[17] However, the Examiner subsequently withdrew the rejection, acknowledging that such functional language was proper and definite. As explained by the Federal Circuit, "there is nothing wrong with defining the dimensions of a device in terms of the environment in which it is to be used."[18]

In *K-2 Corp. v. Salomon S.A.*,[19] the Federal Circuit acknowledged that the phrase "permanently affixed" was functional, and nevertheless considered the phrase presumptively definite. The invention was generally directed to an in-line skate having a soft, pliable inner bootie or shoe surrounded in certain areas by molded plastic or straps affixed to the base of the skate. This arrangement allowed the wearer's foot to breathe and offered a substantially lighter skate while retaining structural stiffness required for performance.

Claim 1 recited the following:

1. In an in-line roller skate having

an upper shoe portion and a lower frame portion . . .

---

[16]*Id.*, 56 USPQ 2d at 1230.

[17]*Id.* at 1239.

[18]*Id.* (citing Orthokinetics, Inc. v. Safety Travel Chairs, Inc., 806 F.2d 1565, 1575–76, 1 USPQ 2d 1081, 1087–88 (Fed. Cir. 1986) (holding that the limitation that the claimed wheelchair have a "front leg portion . . . so dimensioned as to be insertable through the space between the doorframe of an automobile and one of the seats thereof" was not indefinite)).

[19]K-2 Corp. v. Salomon S.A., 191 F.3d 1356, 52 USPQ 2d 1001 (Fed. Cir. 1999).

Main volume footnote updates begin on page 306.

> a non-rigid shoe portion adapted to receive and substantially enclose the entire foot of the skater . . .
>
> support means positioned adjacent selected areas of said non-rigid shoe portion for providing support to aid the skater in maintaining said in-line roller skate in a substantially vertical position . . . and a base portion, . . .
>
> said non-rigid shoe portion being permanently affixed to said base portion at least at said toe area and said heel area for substantially preventing movement therebetween at least in a horizontal plane, wherein at least a portion of said non-rigid shoe portion extends continuously from said base portion to at least the top of said ankle support cuff.[20]

K-2 sued Salomon for infringement of the patent. On cross-motions for summary judgment, the district court rejected K-2's arguments that the disputed "permanently affixed" claim limitation should be construed to be synonymous with "affixed," "secured," or "firmly held," and instead held that the ordinary meaning of "permanently affixed" could not encompass the removable screw used in the heel area of the skate.

On appeal by K-2, the Federal Circuit affirmed. The Federal Circuit noted that the functional language is, of course, an additional limitation in the claim.[21] The Federal Circuit commented that the functional language required that the attachment prevent the bootie from sliding around on top of the base. According to the Federal Circuit:

> [T]he functional language tells us something about the structural requirements of the attachment between the bootie and the base; it speaks not at all, however, about whether that attachment is permanent, something less than permanent, or entirely removable. The only answer to that question, of course, is the specific claim limitation that the bootie be "permanently affixed" to the base. K-2 reads the functional language in a way that would effectively expunge the term "permanently" from the claim language. . . . A more natural construction reads the two clauses as complementary, recognizing that "permanently affixed" requires an unremovable attachment, while the functional language requires that the attachment prevent sliding.[22]

Thus, the functional language "permanently affixed" in *K-2 Corp. v. Salomon S.A.* was presumed to be definite.

[Insert before Section III.]

5. *More Than One Definition for the Same Claim Term May Be Used and the Claims Nevertheless Considered Definite [New Topic]*

---

[20] *Id.*, 52 USPQ 2d at 1002–03.

[21] *Id.* at 1004 (citing Wright Med. Tech., Inc. v. Osteonics Corp., 122 F.3d 1440, 1443–44, 43 USPQ 2d 1837, 1840 (Fed. Cir. 1997) (functional language analyzed as a claim limitation)).

[22] *Id.* at 1005.

Main volume footnote updates begin on page 306.

As a general principle, "the same word appearing in the same claim should be interpreted consistently."[23] However, in circumstances where the patent specification is sufficient to put a reader on notice of the different uses of a term, and where those uses are further apparent from publicly available documents referenced in the patent file, the same claim term may be interpreted differently and still be definite.[24]

Pitney Bowes Inc. v. Hewlett-Packard Co.[25] is an example of a case in which the same claim term received different interpretations in different claims of the same patent, but nevertheless was presumed to be definite. In *Pitney Bowes*, the district court placed significant weight on Pitney Bowes' concession that in 42 out of 44 uses of the term "spot" in the written description, that usage referred to the spots of light generated by the beam of light and not the spots of discharged area on the photo-receptor. Pitney Bowes, however, argued that the term "spot" should be interpreted to mean a spot of discharged area on the photoreceptor.

On appeal, the Federal Circuit agreed with Pitney Bowes, noting that the usage of the term "spot" was noticeably different in the earlier portions of the written description. These earlier uses of the term referred to a "spot" in the sense of a moving spot such as a spot of light produced by the beam. The Federal Circuit also noted that the two uses of the term "spot" in the later part of the written description did not refer to "spot" in the context of a moving spot, but rather in the context of the "spot size" to be employed to avoid roughed edges and improve character formation.[26] This usage of the term was quite distinct from the dynamic spot referred to earlier in the written description, according to the Federal Circuit.

The Federal Circuit then held the following:

> In circumstances such as this, where the language of the written description is sufficient to put a reader on notice of the different uses of a term, and where those uses are further apparent from publicly-available documents referenced in the patent file, it is appropriate to depart from the normal rule of construing seemingly identical terms in the same manner. . . . Parsing the written description, in the context of the prosecution history, puts the reader on notice that the term "spot" has different meanings in the written description depending on its context. . . . [T]he term must be read to correspond to the only plausible meaning in each context. In light of the prosecution history, the only plausible mean-

[23] Digital Biometrics, Inc. v. Identix, Inc., 149 F.3d 1335, 1345, 47 USPQ 2d 1418, 1425 (Fed. Cir. 1998); Fonar Corp. v. Johnson & Johnson, 821 F.2d 627, 632, 3 USPQ 2d 1109, 1113 (Fed. Cir. 1987).

[24] Genentech, Inc. v. Wellcome Found., Ltd., 29 F.3d 1555, 1564, 31 USPQ 2d 1161, 1167 (Fed. Cir. 1994) ("there are at least four possible definitions of the phrase set forth in the specification . . . [and] avoid those definitions upon which the PTO could not reasonably have relied when it issued the patent").

[25] Pitney Bowes Inc. v. Hewlett-Packard Co., 182 F.3d 1298, 51 USPQ 2d 1161 (Fed. Cir. 1999).

[26] *Id.*, 51 USPQ 2d at 1170.

Main volume footnote updates begin on page 306.

ing of the term "spot size," as used in the disputed part of the written description, is the area of discharge on the photoreceptor.[27]

The Federal Circuit therefore presumed that the claims were definite even though the same claim term was defined differently for different claims in the same patent.

6. *Claims May Include Charts/Diagrams [New Topic]*

There is no specific prohibition with respect to the requirements that claims particularly point out and distinctly claim the invention that prevents claims from including charts or diagrams. For example, in *Ex parte Bivens*,[28] the invention related to a two-cycle diesel engine derived from the prior art Detroit Diesel Series 92 Turbo Charged Engine. The differences between the two engines involved structural modifications which were said to contribute to advantageous timing characteristics in the Bivens engine. The timing characteristics of the prior art engine were embodied in the timing sequence chart set forth on page 11 of the specification and in the circle diagram depicted in Figure 9A, while the timing characteristics of the engine were embodied in the timing sequence chart set forth on page 12 of the specification and in the circle diagram depicted in Figure 9B. The rejected claims, claims 10–13, made use of these charts and diagrams to define what the applicant Bivens regarded as his invention.

The Examiner rejected the claims as being indefinite due to the mere inclusion therein of the aforementioned charts and diagrams. On appeal, the Board reversed. The Board indicated that it was not apparent, nor did the Examiner cogently explain, why the inclusion in a claim of the sort of charts and diagrams at issue necessarily violates the definiteness requirement. As for the content of the particular charts and diagrams contained in the appealed claims, the Board also did not understand, nor had the Examiner cogently explained, why the timing characteristics embodied therein were unclear.

According to the Board, although these timing characteristics were functional in nature in that they defined the prior art engine and the Bivens engine by what they did rather than by what they were, it was well settled that there was nothing intrinsically wrong with the use of such a technique in drafting patent claims.[29] The Board also noted that the limitations in claims 10 and 12 drawn to the chart and diagram relating to the prior art engine amounted to product-by-process limitations used to define the engine. "Such product-by-process

---

[27] *Id.*

[28] *Ex parte* Bivens, 53 USPQ 2d 1045 (B.P.A.I. 1999) (unpublished).

[29] *Id.* at 1046.

Main volume footnote updates begin on page 306.

limitations do not inherently conflict with the second paragraph of Section 112."[30]

In light of the foregoing, and notwithstanding the somewhat unconventional claim format employed by Bivens, the Board held that the Examiner had not made out a prima facie case that claims 10 through 13 failed to set out and circumscribe a particular area with a reasonable degree of precision and particularity. Therefore, the rejection was reversed, and the claims were held to be definite under Section 112, second paragraph.[31]

IV. Common Claim Language and Definiteness

B. Numerical Ranges and Amounts

[Insert at the end of the section.]

Interpretation of claims reciting numerical ranges may be governed by the modifiers used in connection with the claimed numerical ranges. For example, in *Jeneric / Pentron, Inc. v. Dillon Co.*,[32] the invention covered a two-phase porcelain composition comprising a leucite crystallite phase dispersed in a glass phase. Porcelain compositions are useful in the preparation and repair of dental restorations such as porcelain-fused-to metal restorations, all-ceramic restorations, inlays, onlays, and veneers. Jeneric sued Dillon for infringing its patent. Dillon argued that the patent was not infringed based on a limiting interpretation of the composition ranges claimed in the patent. For example, claim 1 recited:

> 1. A two-phase porcelain composition comprising a leucite crystallite phase dispersed in a feldspathic glass matrix, a maturing temperature of from about 750 degrees to about 1050 degrees C. and a coefficient of thermal expansion of from about 12 × 10 super-6 -6/ degrees C. to about 17.5 to about 17.5 × 10 super-6 -6/ degrees C. (room temperature to 450 degrees C.), said porcelain composition comprising:

Component	*Amount (wt. %)*
SiO_2	57–66
Al_2O_2	7–15
K_2O	7–15
Na_2O	7–12
Li_2O	.5–3
CaO	0–3
MgO	0–7
F	0–4
CeO_2	0–1

[30] *Id.* (citing *In re* Brown, 459 F.2d 531, 535, 173 USPQ 685, 688 (C.C.P.A. 1972)).

[31] *Id.*

[32] Jeneric/Pentron, Inc. v. Dillon Co., 205 F.3d 1377, 54 USPQ 2d 1086 (Fed. Cir. 2000).

Main volume footnote updates begin on page 306.

> wherein the leucite crystallites possess diameters not exceeding about 10 microns and represent from about 5 to about 65 weight percent of the two-phase porcelain composition.[33]

The district court construed the claims of the patent by reviewing the specification, prosecution history, and extrinsic evidence. In so doing, the court rejected Jeneric's proposed construction that the dental porcelain composition ranges of the table in claim 1 could vary from the recited values. Instead, the district court construed claim 1 as limiting the ranges of compositions to the exact weight percentage ranges. On appeal, the Federal Circuit agreed. The Federal Circuit commented that the district court correctly stated that the claim language "indicates that the invention's chemical components should be limited to the precise ranges set forth therein."[34]

According to the Federal Circuit, the district court's claim interpretation was supported by claim construction principles enunciated by the Federal Circuit in other cases. In general, "[a] term such as 'about' is not subject to a precise construction . . . but is dependent on the factual situation presented."[35] However, the ranges recited in the table of claim 1 did not include the use of the term "about," whereas other numerical ranges, such as the coefficient of thermal expansion, did include the use of the term "about."[36] The Federal Circuit reasoned that without broadening words that ordinarily receive some leeway, the precise weight ranges of claim 1 for the claimed components did not "avoid a strict numerical boundary to the specified parameter."[37]

The Federal Circuit also added, that this construction, assigning numerical precision to composition ranges, was particularly appropriate when other variables in the same claims explicitly used qualifying language. Thus, claim 1 contained a mixture of imprecise and precise claim limitations. Specifically, claim 1 used the word "about" to qualify the values of many variables: the range of the maturing temperature, the coefficient of thermal expansion, the leucite crystallite sizes, and the weight percentage of leucite crystals. In contrast, claim 1 recited precise ranges for the weight of dental compositions. Under these circumstances, the district court correctly limited the weight ranges to those recited precisely in the table of claim 1.[38]

Thus, the *Jeneric/Pentron* decision teaches that if the patent drafter does not use qualifying or broadening language when reciting ranges in a patent claim, the scope of protection may be limited to ex-

---

[33]*Id.*, 54 USPQ 2d at 1088–89.

[34]*Id.* at 1089.

[35]*Id.* (quoting W.L. Gore & Assocs., Inc. v. Garlock, Inc., 842 F.2d 1275, 1280, 6 USPQ 2d 1277, 1282 (Fed. Cir. 1988)).

[36]*Id.*

[37]*Id.* (quoting Pall Corp. v. Micron Separations, Inc., 66 F.3d 1211, 1217, 36 USPQ 2d 1225, 1229 (Fed. Cir. 1995), and citing Modine Mfg. Co. v. United States Int'l Trade Comm'n, 75 F.3d 1545, 1554, 37 USPQ 2d 1609, 1615 (Fed. Cir. 1996)).

[38]*Id.*

Main volume footnote updates begin on page 306.

actly those ranges, particularly where other ranges in the claim include qualifying language.

J. Specific Phrases

1. A

[Insert after footnote 297.]

On the other hand, in *Elkay Manufacturing Co. v. Ebco Manufacturing Co.*,[39] the Federal Circuit interpreted the claim phrase of "an upstanding feed tube" as not limited to a single feed tube. The invention was directed to no-spill adapters for bottled water coolers that permit jugs of water to be inserted into coolers with the cap still on the bottle, thereby eliminating the potential problems of spilling or contaminating water when, for example, a bottle is inserted into a cooler.

The claim recited "an upstanding feed probe . . . to provide a hygienic flow path for delivering liquid from . . . and for admitting air . . . into said container."[40]

Ebco asserted that the normal, accepted meaning of the use of the articles "a" and "an" requires that the above-quoted limitation be construed as describing a single feed tube with a single path for both air and water. The Federal Circuit disagreed and noted that while the articles "a" or "an" may suggest "one," "a" or "an" can mean "one" or "more than one," depending on the context in which the article is used.[41]

In interpreting the articles "a" and "an" to not be limited to a single feed tube, the Federal Circuit stated the following:

> The use of the articles "an" and "a" when referring to "feed tube" and "flow path," respectively, suggest a single feed tube with a single flow path for liquid and air. Other language in the claim similarly suggests a single flow path for both fluids. . . . The asserted claims, however, use the open term "comprising" in their transition phrases. We therefore hold that the plain meaning of "an upstanding feed tube . . . to provide a hygienic flow path for delivering liquid from . . . and for admitting air . . . into said container" is not necessarily limited to a single feed tube with a single flow path for both liquid and air.[42]

In *KCJ Corp. v. Kinetic Concepts, Inc.*,[43] KCJ's invention related to therapeutic mattresses for preventing bedsores. These mattresses evenly distributed the weight of the body without the necessity of inter-

[39] Elkay Mfg. Co. v. Ebco Mfg. Co., 192 F.3d 973, 52 USPQ 2d 1109 (Fed. Cir. 1999), *cert. denied*, 529 U.S. 1066 (2000).

[40] *Id.*, 52 USPQ 2d at 1111.

[41] *Id.* at 1112 (citing Abtox, Inc. v. Exitron Corp., 122 F.3d 1019, 1023, 43 USPQ 2d 1545, 1548 (Fed. Cir. 1997) ("The article 'a' suggests a single chamber. However, patent claim parlance also recognizes that an article can carry the meaning of 'one or more,' for example in a claim using the transitional phrase 'comprising.'")).

[42] *Id.*

[43] KCJ Corp. v. Kinetic Concepts, Inc., 223 F.3d 1351, 55 USPQ 2d 1835 (Fed. Cir. 2000).

Main volume footnote updates begin on page 306.

nal spines or other patient-contacting solid supports, and permitted airflow to all areas of the skin to absorb moisture and prevent heat accumulation. Claim 1 recited:

> 1. An air flotation, ventilated mattress apparatus comprising:
>
> means defining a lower, continuous, inflatable chamber having an air-permeable, flexible upper wall portion, said upper wall portion being constructed for substantially uniform airflow therethrough over substantially the entire plan surface area of said upper wall portion;
>
> air-permeable secondary wall means above said chamber upper wall portion and operably coupled with said chamber-defining means, said secondary wall means being constructed for substantially uniform passage of air therethrough over substantially the entire plan surface area of said secondary wall means, said secondary wall means and upper wall cooperatively defining therebetween an inflatable compartment above said chamber; and
>
> means for continuously introducing positive pressure air into said chamber in order to continuously maintain positive air pressure conditions throughout the entirety of said chamber during the entirety of operation of said mattress apparatus and to inflate both said chamber and compartment by passage of said air into said chamber and thence through said upper wall portion and thereby maintain positive air pressure conditions in said compartment, and to cause said continuous passage of air through said secondary wall means, said mattress apparatus being free of solid internal support structure for supporting a patient, said air introduction means, upper wall portion and secondary wall means being cooperatively configured and arranged for continuous passage of sufficient positive pressure airflow through the chamber, upper wall portion, compartment, and secondary wall means for even, substantially uniform flow of air from said mattress apparatus so that a person lying atop the secondary wall means is supported by said pressurized air without the presence of weight-supporting structure within said mattress apparatus.[44]

The disputed claim construction on appeal involved the limitations of "a . . . continuous . . . chamber."[45] At the heart of the dispute over this limitation was the meaning of the article "a." Specifically, the issue was whether the article "a" limited the number of chambers to only one or did it cover one or more chambers? The district court limited the clause to only one non-interrupted inflatable chamber. The district court stated that "the concept of multiple chambers is at fundamental odds with the concept of continuity, and discrete multiple chambers cannot be read into the patent without sacrificing the concept of continuity."[46] Thus, the district court had little hesitation in concluding that the claim meant exactly what it said: one continuous chamber. Based on that construction, the district court held as a matter of law that claim 1 did not read on Kinetic's accused devices having multiple continuous chambers.

---

[44] *Id.*, 55 USPQ 2d at 1836–37 (bracketed notations removed).

[45] *Id.*

[46] *Id.* at 1839.

Main volume footnote updates begin on page 306.

In reversing the district court's claim interpretation in this regard, the Federal Circuit noted that it:

> has repeatedly emphasized that an indefinite article "a" or "an" in patent parlance carries the meaning of "one or more" in open-ended claims containing the transitional phrase "comprising." . . . Unless the claim is specific as to the number of elements, the article "a" receives a singular interpretation only in rare circumstances when the patentee evinces a clear intent to so limit the article. . . . Under this conventional rule, the claim limitation "a," without more, requires at least one.[47]

The Federal Circuit indicated that it has uniformly applied a general rule for indefinite articles. For instance, the Federal Circuit applied the rule and amplified:

> "The written description supplies additional context for understanding whether the claim language limits the patent scope to a single unitary [element] or extends to encompass a device with multiple [elements]." . . . Moreover, standing alone, a disclosure of a preferred or exemplary embodiment encompassing a singular element does not disclaim a plural embodiment. "[A]lthough the specifications may well indicate that certain embodiments are preferred, particular embodiments appearing in a specification will not be read into the claims when the claim language is broader than such embodiments." . . . Thus, as the rule dictates, when the claim language or context calls for further inquiry, this court consults the written description for a clear intent to limit the invention to a singular embodiment.[48]

The Federal Circuit noted the prosecution history also may assist in the claim interpretation. Indeed, prosecution history "limits the interpretation of claims so as to exclude any interpretation that may have been disclaimed or disavowed during prosecution in order to obtain claim allowance."[49] Accordingly, the Federal Circuit commented that an applicant may disclaim before the Patent Office a plural interpretation and thus lose the benefit of the customary meaning of indefinite articles in patent claims.[50] In view of the use of an indefinite article "a" in the claim language without numerical qualifiers and the absence of disclaimers in the written description and the prosecution history, the Federal Circuit held that the phrase "a . . . continuous . . . chamber" covered one or more continuous chambers.

Accordingly, the Federal Circuit held that the indefinite articles "a" or "an" in patent parlance carried the meaning of "one or more" in open-ended claims that recited the transitional phrase "comprising." Unless the claim specifically recites a specific number of elements,

---

[47] *Id.*

[48] *Id.* (quoting AbTox, Inc. v. Exitron Corp., 122 F.3d 1019, 1024, 43 USPQ 2d 1545, 1548 (Fed. Cir. 1997); Electro Med. Sys., S.A. v. Cooper Life Sciences, Inc., 34 F.3d 1048, 1054, 32 USPQ 2d 1017, 1021 (Fed. Cir. 1994)).

[49] *Id.* (quoting Standard Oil Co. v. American Cyanamid Co., 774 F.2d 448, 452, 227 USPQ 293, 296 (Fed. Cir. 1985)).

[50] *Id.* (citing Alpex Computer Corp. v. Nintendo Co., 102 F.3d 1214, 1220–21, 40 USPQ 2d 1667, 1671–72 (Fed. Cir. 1996)).

Main volume footnote updates begin on page 306.

the article "a" receives a singular interpretation only in rare circumstances when patentee evinces clear intent to so limit the articles "a" or "an."

17. Connected to, Joined, Secured

[Replace heading 17 with the following.]

17. Connected to, Joined, Secured, Coupled

[Insert at the end of the section.]

The unmodified term "coupled" generically describes a connection and does not require or is not limited to a mechanical or physical coupling.[51]

35. Permanently Affixed [New Topic]

In *K-2 Corp. v. Salomon S.A.*,[52] the Federal Circuit interpreted the phrase "permanently affixed" to mean that the fastening be unremovable. The invention was generally directed to an in-line skate having a soft, pliable inner bootie or shoe surrounded in certain areas by molded plastic or straps affixed to the base of the skate. This arrangement allows the wearer's foot to breathe and offers a substantially lighter skate while retaining structural stiffness required for performance. Claim 1 recited the following:

> 1. In an in-line roller skate having
>
> an upper shoe portion and a lower frame portion . . .
>
> a non-rigid shoe portion adapted to receive and substantially enclose the entire foot of the skater . . .
>
> support means positioned adjacent selected areas of said non-rigid shoe portion for providing support to aid the skater in maintaining said in-line roller skate in a substantially vertical position . . . and
>
> a base portion, . . .
>
> said non-rigid shoe portion being permanently affixed to said base portion at least at said toe area and said heel area for substantially preventing movement therebetween at least in a horizontal plane, wherein at least a portion of said non-rigid shoe portion extends continuously from said base portion to at least the top of said ankle support cuff.[53]

---

[51] Johnson Worldwide Assocs., Inc. v. Zebco Corp., 175 F.3d 985, 50 USPQ 2d 1607, 1612 (Fed. Cir. 1999).

[52] K-2 Corp. v. Salomon S.A., 191 F.3d 1356, 52 USPQ 2d 1001 (Fed. Cir. 1999).

[53] *Id.*, 52 USPQ 2d at 1002–03.

Main volume footnote updates begin on page 306.

K-2 sued Salomon for infringement of the patent. On cross-motions for summary judgment, the district court rejected K-2's arguments that the disputed "permanently affixed" claim limitation should be construed to be synonymous with "affixed," "secured," or "firmly held," and instead held that the ordinary meaning of "permanently affixed" could not encompass the removable screw used in the heel area of the skate.

On appeal by K-2, the Federal Circuit affirmed. According to the Federal Circuit:

> Here the critical claim language is "permanently affixed." . . . Thus, our analysis begins with the ordinary and accustomed meaning of the term "permanently" in the phrase "permanently affixed." The ordinary and accustomed meaning of this phrase, . . . does not encompass affixation via removable screw. That is, the ordinary and accustomed meaning of "permanently affixed" in this context requires that the fastening be unremovable.[54]

36. Defined [New Topic]

In *Rival Co. v. Sunbeam Corp.*,[55] the Federal Circuit interpreted the word "defined" to create or form the outline of a shape. The invention related to a food-steaming device including a heater at the bottom of a reservoir where the water was boiled. The steam escaped through openings between the top of the reservoir and the food tray, circulated around the food tray, and cooked the food. Steam that condensed on the food drained into a separate condensate trough.

Claim 1 recited both a boiling water reservoir and a condensate trough that was defined by the base. Rival asserted that this limitation was improperly interpreted to mean that the base created or formed the outline of the shape of the boiling water reservoir and the condensate trough. Rival contended that the expression defined by the base meant contained within or encompassed by the base.[56] Sunbeam countered that the construction was correct because the patent consistently used the term "defined by" to convey a relationship in which one element of the product formed the shape of another element.

The Federal Circuit agreed with Sunbeam that the correct interpretation of the expression "defined by the base" meant that the base "creates or forms the outline of the shape of" both the condensate trough and the boiling water reservoir.[57]

---

[54] *Id.* at 1004.

[55] Rival Co. v. Sunbeam Corp., Civ. App. 98-1198 (Fed. Cir. Feb. 23, 1999) (unpublished).

[56] *Id.*, slip op. at 9.

[57] *Id.* at 10.

Main volume footnote updates begin on page 306.

37. Blade Contact [New Topic]

In *Independent Technologies, Inc. v. Siemon Co.,*[58] the Federal Circuit interpreted the term "blade contact" as a solid contact with rectangular cross section. Independent Technologies' invention related to a telecommunications adapter designed to interface with a 110-type terminal block. The 110-type terminal block had an array of split-finger contacts, known in the industry as insulation displacement contacts (IDCs). The inventive adapter disclosed in the patent comprised a modular, bent-wire jack that was connected via a printed circuit board (PCB) to a plurality of metal blades. The inserted blades provide both electrical contacts and friction-fit stability to the connection.

In affirming the district court interpretation of the term "blade contact," the Federal Circuit stated:

> The technical dictionary cited by Siemon's expert defines "blade contact" as "a solid contact with rectangular cross section, usually with a chamfered mating edge," a definition that accords with the more general definition found in the dictionary cited by the district court, which defined "blade" as "a flat, thin part or section."[59]

38. Metallization [New Topic]

The term "metallization" has been construed to mean a deposited metallic material. For example, in *Sextant Avionique, S.A., v. Analog Devices, Inc.,*[60] the invention related to accelerometers, small devices capable of detecting acceleration used in avionic and automotive applications. When a device is subject to an accelerative force in a particular direction, the test body of the accelerometer sways like a pendulum within the fixed part and thus varies the distance between the capacitor plates. This variation corresponds electrically to a change in the capacitance of the capacitors, which can be detected by circuitry residing elsewhere on the fixed part. These signals can travel from the metallized edges of the test body to the detection circuitry by metallizing the edges of flexible blades in the accelerometer.

The claim at issue recited "wherein electrical connections between the test body and the fixed part of the pendular structure are formed by metallizations formed on the thin faces of said flexible blades."[61] The district court construed the term "metallization" to mean a deposited metallic material. Because Analog did not use a de-

---

[58] Independent Techs., Inc. v. Siemon Co., Civ. App. No. 98-1256 (Fed. Cir. Jan. 29, 1999) (unpublished).

[59] *Id.*, slip op. at 3.

[60] Sextant Avionique, S.A., v. Analog Devices, Inc., 172 F.3d 817, 49 USPQ 2d 1865 (Fed. Cir. 1999).

[61] *Id.*, 49 USPQ 2d at 1866.

Main volume footnote updates begin on page 306.

posited metallic layer, but instead used a doped polycrystalline silicon layer, the district court held that Analog's device did not literally infringe any claim of Sextant's patent.

On appeal, the Federal Circuit affirmed. Sextant argued that the district court erred in its construction of the term metallization, but the Federal Circuit disagreed. According to the Federal Circuit, "[t]he term metallization certainly connotes the use of a metallic material. . . . The [Sextant patent] specification discloses only the deposition of metallic materials, . . . and does not otherwise suggest that the term metallization can include conductive materials generally or materials made conductive by doping."[62] Accordingly, the Federal Circuit held that the district court did not err in its construction of the term metallization, and it therefore did not err in granting summary judgment that Analog's device, which used doped polysilicon, did not literally infringe any of the claims.

39. Enlarged [New Topic]

The Federal Circuit has interpreted the term "enlarged" in accordance with its ordinary meaning, which is something that is larger or greater than that formerly, usually, or normally present. For example, in *Carlisle Plastics, Inc. v. Spotless Enterprises,*[63] the invention related to clothes hangers. The hanger included an enlarged display portion extending from the hanger hook so that it projected above the top contour of the hook, and an indicating device having a hollow body that received at least a portion of the display portion.

The district court construed the term "enlarged display portion" in accordance with the dictionary definition of the term "enlarged," to mean a display portion that is "larger or greater than that formerly, usually, or normally present."[64] The court rejected Spotless' proposed definition of the term "enlarged display portion," which did not require that the display portion be "enlarged" in the usual sense of that word, but required only (1) that the display portion be "large enough to display the indicator" and to "restrain against undesirable movement" by the indicator, and (2) that the display portion be "received in the hollow body of an indicator in a releasable manner but yet restrained against undesirable movement."[65]

On appeal, the Federal Circuit affirmed the district court's claim interpretation:

---

[62]*Id.* at 1870.

[63]Carlisle Plastics, Inc. v. Spotless Enters., Inc., Civ. App. 98-1170 (Fed. Cir. Jan. 26, 1999) (unpublished).

[64]*Id.*, slip op. at 5.

[65]*Id.* at 6.

Main volume footnote updates begin on page 306.

> The district court's claim construction was correct. Although, as the district court noted, Spotless's proposed construction of the term "enlarged display portion" is "inventive," it does not comport with the ordinary meaning of the term, nor does it find any support in the language of the patent or its prosecution history. "Enlarged" is a relative term; to be "enlarged" means that the "enlarged" object must be larger than some reference object. Spotless's definition of "enlarged display portion" does not come to terms with this basic point. . .; indeed, Spotless's definition could even cover a display portion that was significantly smaller than the normal size of the hook. The district court properly rejected Spotless's definition in favor of the definition suggested by common usage of the term "enlarged."[66]

40. Timing Circuit [New Topic]

The Federal Circuit has interpreted the phrase "timing circuit" as an assemblage of electronic components that cuts off the power to a light source a predetermined time after a switch transitions between the "off" to the "on" state.

For example, in *Orlaford Ltd. v. BBC International, Ltd.*,[67] the invention related to footwear and circuitry that caused the footwear to light up and flash when the footwear was moved. Orlaford's patent used a timing circuit in the lighting circuitry. The timing circuit disconnected the battery from the light source a predetermined time after the switch—which alternated between "on" and "off" depending on the motion of the footwear—turned "on" and caused the light source to illuminate. According to the Federal Circuit:

> [W]e interpret "timing circuit" within the context of [Orlaford's] patent to be an assemblage of electronic components that cuts off the power to the light source a predetermined time after a switch, responsive to the motion of the footwear, transitions between the "off" to the "on" state. The timing circuit cuts off the power to the light source regardless of the position of the switch, i.e., if the switch remains in the "on" position, the light source will be disconnected from the power source, preventing battery exhaustion.[68]

41. Select [New Topic]

The Federal Circuit has interpreted the term "select" to mean a choice based on some special, unique, or discrete quality. For example, in *National Recovery Technologies, Inc. v. Magnetic Separation Systems, Inc.*,[69] the invention, owned by National Recovery Technol-

---

[66] *Id.* at 6–7.

[67] Orlaford Ltd. v. BBC Int'l, Ltd., Civ. App. 98-1332 (Fed. Cir. May 20, 1999) (unpublished).

[68] *Id.*, slip op. at 11.

[69] National Recovery Techs., Inc. v. Magnetic Separation Sys., Inc., 166 F.3d 1190, 49 USPQ 2d 1671 (Fed. Cir. 1999).

Main volume footnote updates begin on page 306.

ogy (NRT), addressed the problem of separating recyclable plastic materials that were virtually indistinguishable to the human eye by using penetrating electromagnetic radiation. In the separation process, containers to be sorted were advanced along a conveyor wide enough to accommodate several containers. Each container was irradiated with a sheet-like beam of electromagnetic radiation as it progressed along the conveyor. A number of detectors spanning the width of the conveyor were positioned below the containers to measure the intensity level of electromagnetic radiation that passed through each of the containers. The process then used a microprocessor to compare the detected values to preset thresholds to classify the container as being made of one type of plastic or another.

The patent claim recited "selecting for processing those of said process signals which do not pass through irregularities in the bodies of said material items."[70] NRT argued that the term "select" means that only those signals that do not pass through irregularities are to be preferred to those signals that do. According to NRT, the term "select" did not require absolute perfection in separating signals that passed through an irregularity from those that did not.

In rejecting NRT's proffered interpretation, the Federal Circuit stated the following:

> The plain meaning of the term "select," including the dictionary meaning agreed upon by the parties, implies that some signals are to be picked or chosen and others are to be excluded based upon some special, unique or discrete quality. A specific choice is being made. Both claim 1 and the specification of the '576 patent make clear that those signals that do not pass through irregularities are to be chosen for processing to the exclusion of those signals that do pass through irregularities. Nothing in the plain and ordinary meaning of the term "select" indicates that only a preference for signals that do not pass through irregularities is required. Furthermore, nothing in claim 1 indicates that signals are to be picked based on any other characteristic than penetrating a "normal" or regular portion of a container. Claim 1 clearly indicates that the "special quality" for which a signal is selected is whether or not that signal has passed through an irregularity. There is no indication in the plain meaning of the limitation, or from the claim as a whole, that this selection criterion is to apply only some of the time.[71]

On the other hand, in one decision, the Federal Circuit held that the phrase "selected orientation" required consultation of the specification and prosecution history, and that the ordinary or plain meaning was insufficiently clear. In *Magnivision, Inc. v. Bonneau Co.*,[72] the invention related to a hanger for store display of eyeglasses. The hanger's advantage was that it did not have to be removed and re-

---

[70]*Id.*, 49 USPQ 2d at 1674.

[71]*Id.* at 1675.

[72]Magnivision, Inc. v. Bonneau Co., Civ. App. No. 99-1093 (Fed. Cir. July 24, 2000) (unpublished).

Main volume footnote updates begin on page 306.

placed when a consumer tried the glasses on and returned them to the display. Magnivision and Bonneau both sold non-prescription eyeglasses. Magnivision sued Bonneau for infringing its patent, and Bonneau argued that under the correct interpretation of the patent claim, it could not infringe the patent.

The district court found that the phrase "selected orientation" in the patent meant the specific orientation set forth in the patent—horizontal. The Federal Circuit commented that in this instance, the claim language was quite broad, suggesting any orientation selected for a particular purpose. The phrase "selected orientation," therefore, required consultation of the specification and prosecution history to determine whether the applicant confined the invention to a particular purpose and thus a particular orientation. After all, reasoned the Federal Circuit, the applicant would not have specified a "selected" orientation if it meant to claim every orientation.[73]

After consulting the specification and the prosecution history, the Federal Circuit agreed with the district court that the claims required a horizontal orientation and that the ordinary meaning did not apply. Accordingly, without a horizontal display, the accused device would lack the "selected orientation" as recited in the claims.

42. Series of Threads [New Topic]

In *Karlin Technology Inc. v. Surgical Dynamics, Inc.*,[74] the invention related to a threaded spinal implant for stabilizing adjacent spinal vertebrae. The invention generally included a hollow cylinder with external threads along, and holes through, the cylindrical surface. The hollow portion of the implant was filled with bone or other osteogenic material so that, while the affected vertebrae were initially stabilized by the implants themselves, bone growth through the holes in the implants eventually fused the vertebrae together. The claim recited "a fusion implant comprising a cylindrical member having an outside diameter larger than the space between the two adjacent vertebrae to be fused and a series of threads on the exterior of the cylindrical member for engaging said vertebrae to maintain said implant in place."[75]

The Federal Circuit interpreted the phrase "series of threads" to mean a continuous threading with a plurality of turns. According to the Federal Circuit:

> The relevant definition of "series" is "a number of things or events of the same class coming one after the other in spatial or temporal succession."

[73] *Id.*, slip op. at 13.

[74] Karlin Tech. Inc. v. Surgical Dynamics, Inc., 177 F.3d 968, 50 USPQ 2d 1465 (Fed. Cir. 1999).

[75] *Id.*, 50 USPQ 2d at 1467.

Main volume footnote updates begin on page 306.

> Webster's Ninth New Collegiate Dictionary 1160 (1986). That is what the threads on screws do. "Thread" is defined as a "*continuous* helical rib, as on a screw or pipe." McGraw-Hill Dictionary of Scientific and Technical Terms 2024–25 (5th ed. 1994) (emphasis added). At the same time, it is common to speak of each turn as "a thread," as when referring to the number of threads per inch. See A. Parrish, Mechanical Engineer's Reference Book 4-2 to 4-63 (11th ed. 1973). We therefore conclude that the ordinary meaning of "series of threads" to one of skill in the art, or even according to common knowledge, is continuous threading with a plurality of turns, as found on an ordinary screw or bolt.[76]

43. Uniformly [New Topic]

In *Tekmax, Inc. v. Exide Corp.*,[77] the invention related to a battery plate feeder apparatus with a rotating cylindrical carrier that takes a single battery plate from a stack and places it on its flat side for further processing. The claim recited:

> continuously sealing the overlapping edges of the sheet by compressing the edges into one another between the sealing wheels, the compressive force being applied uniformly along the entire extent of said overlapping edges and being within the range of the plastic flow of the material.[78]

In interpreting the term "uniformly" as along the entire length, the Federal Circuit stated "[a]pplying this 'compressive force' uniformly 'along the entire extent of said overlapping edges' as required by claim 1 necessitates such force application at every point along the seal."[79]

44. Predetermined [New Topic]

The Federal Circuit has interpreted the term "predetermined" to be set previously. For example, in *Essilor International v. Nidek Co.*,[80] the invention related to a machine for automatically grinding a bevel on the edge of an eyeglass lens. The claim recited "means for comparing first and second reference paths with the collection of predetermined paths."[81] In interpreting the word "predetermined," the Federal Circuit stated "[w]e agree with the district court's claim construction. Contrary to Essilor's assertions, the plain meaning of a predetermined bevelling path is a beveling path that has been set previously."[82]

---

[76] *Id.* at 1468.

[77] Tekmax, Inc. v. Exide Corp., Civ. App. No. 97-1386 (Fed. Cir. Jan. 27, 1999) (unpublished).

[78] *Id.*, slip op. at 15.

[79] *Id.* at 20.

[80] Essilor Int'l v. Nidek Co., Civ. App. No. 98-1558 (Fed. Cir. Oct. 29, 1999) (unpublished).

[81] *Id.*, slip op. at 2.

[82] *Id.* at 3.

Main volume footnote updates begin on page 306.

45. At Least One [New Topic]

The Federal Circuit has interpreted the phrase "at least one" to mean that there could be only one or more than one. For example, in *Kistler Instrumente AG v. United States*,[83] "[a]nyone with even the most rudimentary understanding of the English language understands 'at least one piezo-electric crystal means lodged within said component means,' to mean one or more crystals."[84] Similarly, in *Rhine v. Casio, Inc.*,[85] the Federal Circuit stated the following:

> To give meaning to the phrase "at least one light source," we must construe claim 1 to cover a device that has only one light source or a device that has more than one light source, assuming that the "device" is a "flashlight," as that term is used in the claim.[86]

46. Located Between [New Topic]

In *Zelinski v. Brunswick Corp.*,[87] the Federal Circuit interpreted the phrase "located between" to mean wholly or partially between two objects. The invention related to a bowling ball that was intended to "hook" or migrate into the bowling pin "pocket" in a predictable manner after it was thrown. This provided maximum pin displacement with minimum pin deflection. The claim recited "another elongate section having an axis of symmetry extending in a direction generally transverse of the first elongate section and extending from the intermediate portion and located between the center of the spherical mass and the first elongate section."[88]

The district court construed the claim to require that the second elongate section be located entirely between the center of the spherical mass and the first elongate section. Thus, in the context of the claim, the second elongate section must be located only between the center of the spherical mass and the first elongate section.

On appeal, the Federal Circuit disagreed with the district court's interpretation. The Federal Circuit noted that this case turned upon the meaning of the phrase "located between." Zelinski argued that the district court erred by reading the phrase too narrowly. Zelinski argued that its interpretation of "located between" included any weight that was in whole or in part between the center of the spherical mass and the first elongate section. The Federal Circuit agreed and inter-

---

[83] Kistler Instrumente AG v. United States, 628 F.2d 1303, 1318, 211 USPQ 920 (Ct. Cl. 1980).

[84] *Id.*, 211 USPQ at 920.

[85] Rhine v. Casio, Inc., 183 F.3d 1342, 51 USPQ 2d 1377 (Fed. Cir. 1999).

[86] *Id.*, 51 USPQ 2d at 1379.

[87] Zelinski v. Brunswick Corp., 185 F.3d 1311, 51 USPQ 2d 1590 (Fed. Cir. 1999).

[88] *Id.*, 51 USPQ 2d at 1593.

Main volume footnote updates begin on page 306.

preted the phrase "located between" to mean wholly or partially between two objects.[89]

47. Selecting One of [New Topic]

The Federal Circuit has interpreted the phrase "selecting one of" as selecting a single item and not a combination of items. For example, in *WMS Gaming Inc. v. International Game Technology*,[90] the invention related to a slot machine that was capable of decreasing the probability of winning while maintaining the external appearance of a standard mechanical slot machine. Each time the machine was played, the control circuitry randomly determined the stop position of each reel and then stopped the reels at the randomly determined positions. The reels only served the function of displaying the randomly chosen result. To decrease the probability of certain symbols appearing, the control circuitry randomly chose a number from a range greater than the number of stop positions.

In interpreting the function of "randomly selecting one of said plurality of assigned numbers," the Federal Circuit stated the following:

> The plain meaning of "selecting one of said . . . numbers" is selecting a single number, not a combination of numbers. . . . Nothing in the written description, drawings, or prosecution history indicates that the phrases "one of said . . . numbers" or "said selected number" should be given anything other than their ordinary meaning.[91]

48. Continually [New Topic]

The Federal Circuit has interpreted the phrase "continually" to mean "at all times." For example, in *C.R. Bard, Inc. v. Boston Scientific Corp.*,[92] the invention related to balloon catheters. Boston Scientific argued that the district court improperly construed the claim term "continually." The claim at issue stated that "when the balloon is not inflated, the wire will apply continually a longitudinal tension to the balloon, thereby tensioning the balloon in its fluted configuration, ..."[93]

The Federal Circuit held, however, that the district court properly construed the term "continually" to mean "at all times,"[94] and in the context of the invention, at all times after the manufacturing process of the balloon was completed and when the balloon was not inflated.

---

[89] *Id.*

[90] WMS Gaming Inc. v. International Game Tech., 184 F.3d 1339, 51 USPQ 2d 1385 (Fed. Cir. 1999).

[91] *Id.*, 51 USPQ 2d at 1392.

[92] C.R. Bard, Inc. v. Boston Scientific Corp., Civ. App. No. 99-1304 (Fed. Cir. Aug. 28, 2000) (unpublished).

[93] *Id.* slip op. at 3.

[94] *Id.* at 4.

Main volume footnote updates begin on page 306.

49. Data Block [New Topic]

The Federal Circuit has interpreted the phrase "data block" in accordance with its ordinary meaning as a computer data structure containing information used to instruct a computer in performing an operation. For example, in *IMS Technology, Inc. v. Haas Automation, Inc.*,[95] the invention related to the control of a machine tool, such as a milling machine, which was used to cut or remove material from an object, referred to as a workpiece, through a machining operation. Numerical control ("NC"), which runs a program containing a series of numerical instructions and converts the instructions to electrical control signals, was at issue. These control signals were applied to, for example, servo motors that control the movement of the machine tool.

The invention claimed in the patent permitted interactive programming of the machine tool on the machine shop floor. The machine tool operator created a program by using a keyboard to respond to nested inquiries displayed on a CRT screen. In general, the program contained data blocks, each of which corresponded to one operational step of the machine tool. When the machine tool operator selected an operation, the control system prompted him for additional parameters to be included in the data block for that operational step.

Haas manufactured and sold machine tools with numerical controls. The accused Haas controls also provided interactive programming capability of machine tools on the machine shop floor. Some Haas controls had a floppy disk drive for storing programs; others had only an RS-232 data port that could be connected to a storage device, such as a personal computer, for storing programs in ASCII format. The Haas controls stored programs in G- and M-code format. During execution of programs, the Haas controls translated G-code into a binary format, which was converted into electrical signals delivered to the machine tool for directing its operation.

IMS filed suit against Haas alleging that Haas infringed its patent. Claim 1 was representative, and recited:

> 1. A programmable microcomputer control apparatus for controlling the relative motion between a tool and a workpiece comprising:
>
> indicator means for providing at an output digital signals indicative of the relative position between the tool and the workpiece;
>
> an alterable memory operable to retain a control program and control parameters;
>
> a microprocessor unit coupled to the output of the indicator means and to the memory and operable to produce control signals dependent upon said indicator means output and said control parameters according to said control program;

[95] IMS Tech., Inc. v. Haas Automation, Inc., 206 F.3d 1422, 54 USPQ 2d 1129 (Fed. Cir. 2000), *cert. dismissed*, 530 U.S. 1299 (2000).

Main volume footnote updates begin on page 306.

> control means for directing said control signals from the microprocessor unit to appropriate motion-providing means;
>
> interface means for transferring a control program and control parameters from an external medium into said alterable memory and for recording the control parameter contents of said memory onto an external medium;
>
> data entry means for loading control parameters into said memory through externally accessible data inputs independently of said interface means; and
>
> display means for displaying control parameters, said control program being operable to display control parameter inquiries on the display means, whereby an operator may load control parameters into said memory through said data entry means in response to the inquiries, said apparatus including means to sequentially display data block inquiries and to display, in response to the loading of certain control parameters into said memory relating to the data block inquiries, separate displays of additional control parameter inquiries relating to information used in the data block which was the subject of the previous inquiry, whereby the sequential display of inquiries and direct loading of control parameters as to an operation can be used to make the use of the device simpler and more responsive to the operator.[96]

The district court construed the term "data block," which appeared in the display means limitation of claim 1, as limited to the specific set of variables disclosed in the written description and the disclosed sequence of inquiries regarding those variables.

On appeal, the Federal Circuit reversed the district court's interpretation of "data block." Haas contended that the district court correctly limited the meaning of the term "data block" to the variables and sequence disclosed in the written description. The Federal Circuit disagreed. According to the Federal Circuit, the ordinary and customary meaning of "data block" in the context of programmable machine tools is a computer data structure containing the information needed by a machine tool to perform a single machining operation. Haas contended, however, that the ordinary meaning did not apply because the patentee gave the term "data block" a special meaning by describing the preferred embodiment in the patent as follows: "The sequence of inquiries on the CRT screen for a data block follows the sequence: data block number, machine mode, control mode, X dimension, Y dimension, Z dimension, feed rate, pack rate and tool number."[97] The Federal Circuit found nothing in the written description, however, that indicated this was the patentee's specialized definition of "data block." Rather, the written description merely described the preferred embodiment, and to limit "data block" to the sequence of variables disclosed would be to impermissibly read a particular embodiment into the claim.

In sum, the Federal Circuit concluded that the proper construction of the term "data block" was a computer data structure contain-

[96] *Id.*, 54 USPQ 2d at 1131.

[97] *Id.* at 1136.

Main volume footnote updates begin on page 306.

ing the information needed by a machine tool to perform a single machining operation. As properly construed, a "data block" was not limited to the specific set of variables and display sequence disclosed in the written description.[98]

V. Definiteness and Special Claim Issues

A. Interpreting the Preamble

[Insert after footnote 440.]

As the Federal Circuit stated:

> Indeed, when discussing the "claim" in such a circumstance, there is no meaningful distinction to be drawn between the claim preamble and the rest of the claim, for only together do they comprise the "claim." If, however, the body of the claim fully and intrinsically sets forth the complete invention, including all of its limitations, and the preamble offers no distinct definition of any of the claimed invention's limitations, but rather merely states, for example, the purpose or intended use of the invention, then the preamble is of no significance to claim construction because it cannot be said to constitute or explain a claim limitation.[99]

Thus, if the claim preamble, when read in the context of the entire claim, recites limitations of the claim, or, if the claim preamble is "necessary to give life, meaning, and vitality" to the claim, then the claim preamble should be construed as if in the balance of the claim.[100] For example, preamble phrases have been considered to recite limitations that afford patentable weight when the preamble phrase provides an antecedent basis for terms used later in the body of the claim.[101]

E. Process-of-Use Claims

[Insert after footnote 474.]

Similarly, there is no specific prohibition with respect to the requirement that claims particularly point out and distinctly claim the invention that prevents claims from being in a product-by-process for-

---

[98] *Id.*

[99] Pitney Bowes Inc. v. Hewlett-Packard Co., 182 F.3d 1298, 51 USPQ 2d 1161, 1166 (Fed. Cir. 1999).

[100] Kropa v. Robie, 187 F.2d 150, 152, 88 USPQ 478, 480–81 (C.C.P.A. 1951); Rowe v. Dror, 112 F.3d 473, 478, 42 USPQ 2d 1550, 1553 (Fed. Cir. 1997); Corning Glass Works v. Sumitomo Elec. U.S.A., Inc., 868 F.2d 1251, 1257, 9 USPQ 2d 1962, 1966 (Fed. Cir. 1989).

[101] Gerber Garment Tech., Inc. v. Lectra Sys., Inc., 916 F.2d 683, 688–89, 16 USPQ 2d 1436, 1441 (Fed. Cir. 1990); Heidelberg Harris, Inc. v. Mitsubishi Heavy Indus., Ltd., Civ. App. No. 1100 (Fed. Cir. Sept. 18, 2000) (unpublished).

Main volume footnote updates begin on page 306.

mat. For example, in *Ex parte Bivens*,[102] the invention related to a two-cycle diesel engine derived from the prior art Detroit Diesel Series 92 Turbo Charged Engine. The differences between the two engines involved structural modifications that were said to contribute to advantageous timing characteristics in the Bivens engine. The timing characteristics of the prior art engine were embodied in the timing sequence chart set forth on page 11 of the specification and in the circle diagram depicted in Figure 9A, while the timing characteristics of the engine were embodied in the timing sequence chart set forth on page 12 of the specification and in the circle diagram depicted in Figure 9B. The rejected claims, claims 10–13, made use of these charts and diagrams to define what the applicant Bivens regarded as his invention.

The Examiner rejected the claims as being indefinite due to the mere inclusion therein of the aforementioned charts and diagrams. On appeal, the Board reversed. The Board indicated that it was not apparent, nor had the Examiner cogently explained, why the inclusion in a claim of the sort of charts and diagrams at issue necessarily violates the definiteness requirement. As for the content of the particular charts and diagrams contained in the appealed claims, the Board also did not understand, nor had the Examiner cogently explained, why the timing characteristics embodied therein were unclear.

According to the Board, although these timing characteristics were functional in nature in that they defined the prior art engine and the Bivens engine by what they did rather than by what they were, it was well settled that there was nothing intrinsically wrong with the use of such a technique in drafting patent claims.[103] The Board also noted that the limitations in claims 10 and 12 drawn to the chart and diagram relating to the prior art engine amounted to product-by-process limitations used to define the engine. "Such product-by-process limitations do not inherently conflict with the second paragraph of Section 112."[104]

I. Interpreting Transitional Phrases

[Insert after footnote 491.]

However, the term "comprising" may not be used to broaden the scope claim interpretation to cover embodiments found in the prior art. "That is, 'comprising' is not a weasel word with which to abrogate claim limitations."[105]

---

[102] *Ex parte* Bivens, 53 USPQ 2d 1045 (B.P.A.I. 1999) (unpublished).

[103] *Id.* at 1046.

[104] *Id.* (citing *In re* Brown, 459 F.2d 531, 535, 173 USPQ 685, 688 (C.C.P.A. 1972)).

[105] Spectrum Int'l, Inc. v. Sterilite Corp., 164 F.3d 1372, 49 USPQ 2d 1065, 1070 (Fed. Cir. 1998).

Main volume footnote updates begin on page 306.

VII. Relationship Between Second and Sixth Paragraphs of Section 112

[Insert after footnote 515.]

The Federal Circuit has further elaborated the differences between Section 112, first, second, and sixth paragraphs as follows:

> For the sake of clarity, we first set out in one place the provisions of Section 112, Paragraphs 1, 2, and 6.
>
> Section 112. Specification
>
> > [Para. 1] The specification shall contain a written description of the invention, and of the manner and process of making and using it, in such full, clear, concise, and exact terms as to enable any person skilled in the art to which it pertains, or with which it is most nearly connected, to make and use the same, and shall set forth the best mode contemplated by the inventor of carrying out his invention.
> >
> > [Para. 2] The specification shall conclude with one or more claims particularly pointing out and distinctly claiming the subject matter which the applicant regards as his invention.
> >
> > [Para. 6] An element in a claim for a combination may be expressed as a means or step for performing a specified function without the recital of structure, material, or acts in support thereof, and such claim shall be construed to cover the corresponding structure, material, or acts described in the specification and equivalents thereof.
>
> 35 U.S.C. Section 112, Paragraphs 1, 2, and 6 (1994).
>
> Paragraph 1 is, inter alia, an enablement provision requiring that an inventor set forth in the patent specification how to make and use his or her invention. Paragraph 2 requires claims that particularly and distinctly indicate the subject matter that the inventor considers to be his or her invention. Paragraph 6 also addresses claim language, but refers to the specification for its meaning. In doing so, it specifically refers to "structure . . . described in the specification and equivalents thereof." . . . This provision represents a quid pro quo by permitting inventors to use a generic means expression for a claim limitation provided that the specification indicates what structure(s) constitute(s) the means. . . . The language indicates that means-plus-function clauses comprise not only the language of the claims, but also the structure corresponding to that means that is disclosed in the written description portion of the specification (and equivalents thereof). Thus, in order for a claim to meet the particularity requirement of Para. 2, the corresponding structure(s) of a means-plus-function limitation must be disclosed in the written description in such a manner that one skilled in the art will know and understand what structure corresponds to the means limitation. Otherwise, one does not know what the claim means.
>
> Fulfillment of the Section 112, Para. 6 tradeoff cannot be satisfied when there is a total omission of structure. There must be structure in the specification. This conclusion is not inconsistent with the fact that the knowledge of one skilled in the particular art may be used to under-

stand what structure(s) the specification discloses, or that even a dictionary or other documentary source may be resorted to for such assistance, because such resources may only be employed in relation to structure that is disclosed in the specification. Paragraph 6 does not contemplate the kind of open-ended reference to extrinsic works that Para. 1, the enablement provision, does.

Paragraph 1 permits resort to material outside of the specification in order to satisfy the enablement portion of the statute because it makes no sense to encumber the specification of a patent with all the knowledge of the past concerning how to make and use the claimed invention. One skilled in the art knows how to make and use a bolt, a wheel, a gear, a transistor, or a known chemical starting material. The specification would be of enormous and unnecessary length if one had to literally reinvent and describe the wheel.

Section 112, Para. 6, however, does not have the expansive purpose of Para. 1. It sets forth a simple requirement, a quid pro quo, in order to utilize a generic means expression. All one needs to do in order to obtain the benefit of that claiming device is to recite some structure corresponding to the means in the specification, as the statute states, so that one can readily ascertain what the claim means and comply with the particularity requirement of Para. 2. The requirement of specific structure in Section 112, Para. 6 thus does not raise the specter of an unending disclosure of what everyone in the field knows that such a requirement in Section 112, Para. 1 would entail. If our interpretation of the statute results in a slight amount of additional written description appearing in patent specifications compared with total omission of structure, that is the trade-off necessitated by an applicant's use of the statute's permissive generic means term.[106]

[Insert after footnote 518.]

In determining whether sufficient structure has been disclosed to support a means-plus-function limitation, the vantage point is from one of ordinary skill in the art, particularly in view of the close relationship between claim construction and Section 112, second paragraph.[107] That is, Section 112, second paragraph is inextricably intertwined with claim construction, and in the context of Section 112, sixth paragraph, a determination of the structure that corresponds to a particular means-plus-function limitation is a matter of claim construction.[108] Since it is well-established that claims are to be construed in view of the understanding of one skilled in the art,[109] the Federal Circuit has held that the closely related issue concerning whether sufficient structure has in

[106]Atmel Corp. v. Information Storage Devices Inc., 198 F.3d 1374, 53 USPQ 2d 1225, 1230–31 (Fed. Cir. 1999).

[107]Atmel Corp. v. Information Storage Devices Inc., 198 F.3d 1374, 53 USPQ 2d 1225, 1228 (Fed. Cir. 1999).

[108]*See* Chiuminatta Concrete Concepts, Inc. v. Cardinal Indus., Inc., 145 F.3d 1303, 1308, 46 USPQ 2d 1752, 1756 (Fed. Cir. 1998).

[109]K-2 Corp. v. Salomon S.A., 191 F.3d 1356, 1365, 52 USPQ 2d 1001, 1006 (Fed. Cir. 1999) (noting that "claim construction is firmly anchored in reality by the understanding of those of ordinary skill in the art").

Main volume footnote updates begin on page 306.

fact been disclosed to support a means-plus-function limitation should be analyzed under the same standard.[110]

[Insert after footnote 519.]

The specification does not have to describe the structure corresponding to a means-plus-function limitation in explicit detail.[111] For example, in *In re Dossel*,[112] the Federal Circuit held that the specification adequately described the structure corresponding to the means for reconstructing data when it recited a device that received digital data from memory and from a user. The fact that the specification did not recite the term "computer" or quote computer code that may be used in the invention did not render the means clause invalid under Section 112, second paragraph.[113] However, even though the specification does not have to describe the structure in explicit detail, there must be adequate structure disclosed as understood by one of ordinary skill in the art.[114] As stated by the Federal Circuit, "the inquiry asks first whether structure is described in specification, and, if so, whether one skilled in the art would identify the structure from that description."[115]

[Insert at the end of the section.]

For a detailed discussion on when claim terms or phrases are and are not interpreted under Section 112, sixth paragraph, see Chapter 7, Section XII.A.

B. Interpreting Claims Under Section 112, Sixth Paragraph

[Insert after footnote 556.]

The function serves as the touchstone for identifying the disclosed, corresponding structure or acts that are recited by the means-plus-function or step-plus-function claim limitations.[116]

---

[110] Atmel Corp. v. Information Storage Devices Inc., 198 F.3d 1374, 53 USPQ 2d 1225, 1228 (Fed. Cir. 1999).

[111] Essilor Int'l v. Nidek Co., Civ. App. No. 98-1558, slip op. at 8 (Fed. Cir. Oct. 29, 1999) (unpublished).

[112] *In re* Dossel, 115 F.3d 942, 42 USPQ 2d 1881 (Fed. Cir. 1997).

[113] *Id.* at 946–47, 42 USPQ 2d at 1885.

[114] Atmel Corp. v. Information Storage Devices Inc., 198 F.3d 1374, 53 USPQ 2d 1225, 1229 (Fed. Cir. 1999).

[115] *Id.*, 53 USPQ 2d at 1230.

[116] *See, e.g.*, Smiths Indus. Med. Sys., Inc. v. Vital Signs, Inc., 183 F.3d 1347, 51 USPQ 2d 1415, 1421 (Fed. Cir. 1999):

> The court erred in the next step of the claim construction process by interpreting the claim language "means for supplying gas" to require a means for supplying gas under pressure. It is improper to import the limitation "under pressure" from the written description into the claim because the claim language is clear on its face. . . . Instead, the function recited by the means-plus-function claim limitation is simply the function of "supplying gas," and it is this function alone that serves as the touchstone for identifying the disclosed, corresponding structure that is recited by the means-plus-function claim limitation.

Main volume footnote updates begin on page 306.

After identifying the function of the means-plus-function element, the court looks to the written description to identify the structure corresponding to that function. Identification of corresponding structure may embrace more than the preferred embodiment. A means-plus-function claim encompasses all structure in the specification corresponding to that element and equivalent structures.[117]

When multiple embodiments in the specification correspond to the claimed function, proper application of Section 112, sixth paragraph generally reads the claim element to embrace each of those embodiments.[118]

1. Interpreting Means-Plus-Function Claims When Disclosed Structure Is a General Purpose Computer [New Topic]

In a means-plus-function claim in which the disclosed structure is a computer, or microprocessor, programmed to carry out an algorithm, the disclosed structure is not the general purpose computer, but rather the special purpose computer programmed to perform the disclosed algorithm.[119] The structure of a microprocessor programmed to carry out an algorithm is limited by the disclosed algorithm.[120] A general purpose computer, or microprocessor, programmed to carry out an algorithm creates "a new machine, because a general purpose computer in effect becomes a special purpose computer once it is programmed to perform particular functions pursuant to instructions from program software."[121] The instructions of the software program that carry out the algorithm electrically change the general purpose computer by creating electrical paths within the device. These electrical paths create a special purpose machine for carrying out the particular algorithm.

For example, in *WMS Gaming Inc. v. International Game Technology*,[122] the invention related to a slot machine that was capable of decreasing the probability of winning while maintaining the external appearance of a standard mechanical slot machine. Each time the machine was played, the control circuitry randomly determined the stop

---

[117] Micro Chem., Inc. v. Great Plains Chem. Co., 194 F.3d 1250, 52 USPQ 2d 1258, 1263 (Fed. Cir. 1999).

[118] *Id.*, 52 USPQ 2d at 1264 (citing Serrano v. Telular Corp., 111 F.3d 1578, 1583, 42 USPQ 2d 1538, 1542 (Fed. Cir. 1997)).

[119] WMS Gaming Inc. v. International Game Tech., 184 F.3d 1339, 51 USPQ 2d 1385, 1391 (Fed. Cir. 1999); *In re* Alappat, 33 F.3d 1526, 1545, 31 USPQ 2d 1545, 1558 (Fed. Cir. 1994) (en banc).

[120] *WMS Gaming Inc.*, 51 USPQ 2d at 1391.

[121] *Alappat*, 33 F.3d at 1545, 31 USPQ 2d at 1558; *In re* Bernhart, 417 F.2d 1395, 1399–1400, 163 USPQ 611, 615–16 (C.C.P.A. 1969) ("If a machine is programmed in a certain new and unobvious way, it is physically different from the machine without that program; its memory elements are differently arranged.").

[122] WMS Gaming Inc. v. International Game Tech., 184 F.3d 1339, 51 USPQ 2d 1385 (Fed. Cir. 1999).

Main volume footnote updates begin on page 306.

position of each reel and then stopped the reels at the randomly determined positions. The reels only served the function of displaying the randomly chosen result. To decrease the probability of certain symbols appearing, the control circuitry randomly chose a number from a range greater than the number of stop positions.

In interpreting the phrase "means for assigning a plurality of numbers representing said angular positions of said reel," the Federal Circuit stated the following:

> The district court determined that the structure disclosed in the specification to perform the claimed function was "an algorithm executed by a computer." While this finding accurately reflected the parties' stipulation, the court erred by failing to limit the claim to the algorithm disclosed in the specification. The structure of a microprocessor programmed to carry out an algorithm is limited by the disclosed algorithm. . . .
>
> In a means-plus-function claim in which the disclosed structure is a computer, or microprocessor, programmed to carry out an algorithm, the disclosed structure is not the general purpose computer, but rather the special purpose computer programmed to perform the disclosed algorithm. . . . Accordingly, the structure disclosed for the "means for assigning" limitation of claim 1 of the Telnaes patent is a microprocessor programmed to perform the algorithm illustrated in Figure 6. In other words, the disclosed structure is a microprocessor programmed to assign a plurality of single numbers to stop positions such that: 1) the number of single numbers exceeds the number of stop positions; 2) each single number is assigned to only one stop position; 3) each stop position is assigned at least one single number; and 4) at least one stop position is assigned more than one single number.[123]

2. *Specification Must Disclose Some Structure—Mere Incorporation-By-Reference Insufficient [New Topic]*

Section 112, sixth paragraph sets forth a simple requirement, a quid pro quo, in order to utilize a generic means expression. All one needs to do in order to obtain the benefit of that claiming device is to recite some structure corresponding to the means in the specification, as the statute states, so that one can readily ascertain what the claim means and comply with the particularity requirement of Section 112, second paragraph.

Just what constitutes a recital of structure was considered in *Atmel Corp. v. Information Storage Devices Inc.*[124] The invention related to an improved charge pump circuit that was able to boost the voltage applied to, for example, a word line in a memory array during a programming operation without excessive current leakage. Claim 1, the sole claim of the patent, read as follows:

---

[123] *Id.*, 51 USPQ 2d at 1391–92.

[124] Atmel Corp. v. Information Storage Devices Inc., 198 F.3d 1374, 53 USPQ 2d 1225 (Fed. Cir. 1999).

Main volume footnote updates begin on page 306.

1. An apparatus for selectively increasing the voltage on one or more of a plurality of conductive lines having inherent distributed capacitance disposed in a semiconductor circuit comprising:

means disposed on said semiconductor circuit for selecting one or more of said conductive lines;

high voltage generating means disposed on said semiconductor circuit for generating a high voltage from a lower voltage power supply connected to said semiconductor circuit;

voltage pulse generating means disposed on said semiconductor circuit for generating voltage pulses;

means for capacitively coupling voltage pulses from said voltage pulse generating means to a voltage node in said semiconductor circuit;

transfer means responsive to said selecting means and connected to said voltage node for transferring increments of charge from said high voltage generating means to the inherent distributed capacitance in selected ones of said conductive lines in response to said voltage pulses;

said transfer means including switching means cooperating with said selecting means for blocking substantially all of the flow of current through and transfer of charge from said high voltage generating means to said conductive lines which are unselected.[125]

The district court observed that the portion of the specification that pertained to the structural component of this means-plus-function limitation disclosed that:

> [T]he present invention may include high-voltage generator circuit 34. Known Circuit techniques are used to implement high-voltage circuit 34. See On-Chip High Voltage Generation in NMOS Integrated Circuits Using an Improved Voltage Multiplier Technique, IEEE Journal of Solid State Circuits, Vol [.] SC-11, No. 3, June 1976 [the "Dickson article"].[126]

The district court also noted that Figures 2 and 4 of the patent only depicted the high-voltage generator circuit as a black box, and provided no detail as to what electrical components, e.g., transistors, resistors, or capacitors, comprised that circuit. The district court then held that, based on the language in the written description, the structure corresponding to the high voltage generating means could not be any circuits beyond those described in the Dickson article.

For the district court, the issue was whether it was possible to incorporate structures corresponding to the high-voltage means limitation recited in the claim by reference to material not in the specification. The district court concluded that the patent improperly incorporated structure corresponding to the high-voltage means limitation by reference to the Dickson article. Accordingly, the district court disregarded the structures disclosed in the Dickson article. The district court held that the resulting absence of any structure in the specification corresponding to the disputed limitation rendered the claim invalid as indefinite under 35 U.S.C. Section 112, second paragraph.

---

[125] *Id.*, 53 USPQ 2d at 1226.

[126] *Id.*

Main volume footnote updates begin on page 306.

Atmel appealed the district court's grant of summary judgment of indefiniteness. On appeal, the Federal Circuit reversed. The Federal Circuit agreed with Atmel that the district court should have determined whether sufficient structure was disclosed in the specification based on the understanding of one skilled in the art. The Federal Circuit noted, however, that consideration of the understanding of one skilled in the art in no way relieves the patentee of adequately disclosing sufficient structure in the specification.[127]

The Federal Circuit agreed with the district court that structure supporting a means-plus-function claim under Section 112, sixth paragraph must appear in the specification. The Federal Circuit disagreed with the district court, however, that an inquiry under Section 112, second paragraph turns on whether a patentee has "incorporated by reference" material into the specification relating to structure. Instead, the inquiry asks first whether structure is described in the specification, and, if so, whether one skilled in the art would identify the structure from that description.[128]

Atmel argued that even though the text of the Dickson article was not in the specification, sufficient structure was nevertheless disclosed in the specification, and that the district court erred in limiting possible structures corresponding to the high-voltage generating means to those structures included in the Dickson article. While the Federal Circuit agreed with Information Storage Devices that the district court properly held that the Dickson article may not take the place of structure that does not appear in the specification, the specification plainly stated that "[k]nown Circuit techniques are used to implement high-voltage circuit 34. See On-Chip High Voltage Generation in NMOS Integrated Circuits Using an Improved Voltage Multiplier Technique, IEEE Journal of Solid State Circuits. . . ."[129]

The Federal Circuit noted that Atmel's expert testified that this title alone was sufficient to indicate to one skilled in the art the precise structure of the means recited in the specification. Based on this unrebutted testimony, the Federal Circuit concluded that summary judgment was improperly granted invalidating the patent for indefiniteness under Section 112, second paragraph.

Thus, *Atmel Corp.* teaches that the specification must include a description of the structure corresponding to the means, and the use of the incorporation-by-reference rule does not appear to assist in this inquiry. However, in *Atmel Corp.* the Federal Circuit did not require a substantial or significant description to satisfy the requirement of "corresponding structure" under Section 112, sixth paragraph. The *Atmel Corp.* decision is troublesome with respect to its reluctance to

---

[127] *Id.* at 1229.

[128] *Id.* at 1230.

[129] *Id.* at 1231.

Main volume footnote updates begin on page 306.

utilize the incorporation-by-reference rule to recite corresponding structure, particularly since this rule has been around for many years, including prior to the enactment of Section 112, sixth paragraph.[130] "As the expression itself implies, the purpose of 'incorporation by reference' is to make one document become a part of another document by referring to the former in the latter in such a manner that it is apparent that the cited document is part of the referencing document as if it were fully set out therein."[131]

Therefore, unless Congress deviated from this accepted norm, material is "in" the specification if it is incorporated by reference.[132] Hopefully, the Federal Circuit will have the opportunity to reconsider this issue in the future.

VIII. Relationship Between *Definiteness* and *Regards* Requirements Under Section 112, Second Paragraph

[Insert at the end of the section.]

During the prosecution of a patent application, a claim's compliance with Section 112, second paragraph may be analyzed by consideration of evidence beyond the patent specification, including an inventor's statements to the Patent Office.[133] The Federal Circuit has stated that it is not inappropriate for the PTO or a reviewing tribunal to consider such evidence extrinsic to the patent application in light of the goals of the examination process and the fact that pending claims can be freely amended to comport with those goals.[134] As the Federal Circuit explained in *In re Zletz*:

---

[130] *See In re* Hawkins, 486 F.2d 569, 573, 179 USPQ 157, 161 (C.C.P.A. 1973) (practice of incorporation by reference has "longstanding basis in the law"); General Elec. Co. v. Brenner, 407 F.2d 1258, 1261–62, 159 USPQ 335, 337–38 (D.C. Cir. 1968).

[131] *In re* Lund, 376 F.2d 982, 989, 153 USPQ 625, 631 (C.C.P.A. 1967) (emphasis added); Interstate Consol. St. Ry. v. Massachusetts, 207 U.S. 79, 84 (1907) ("If the charter, instead of writing out the requirements of Rev. Laws, 112, Section 72, referred specifically to another document expressing them, and purported to incorporate it, of course the charter would have the same effect as if it itself contained the words."); Black's Law Dictionary 907 (4th ed. 1968) (defining "incorporate" as "[t]o declare that another document shall be taken as part of the document in which the declaration is made as much as if it were set out at length therein").

[132] Atmel Corp. v. Information Storage Devices, Inc., 198 F.3d 1374, 1378, 53 USPQ 2d 1225, 1227 (Fed. Cir. 1999) (Mayer, J., dissenting).

[133] Solomon v. Kimberly-Clark Corp., 216 F.3d 1372, 55 USPQ 2d 1279, 1282 (Fed. Cir. 2000); *In re* Conley, 490 F.2d 972, 976, 180 USPQ 454, 456–57 (C.C.P.A. 1974) (noting that the phrase "which the applicant regards as his invention" in the second portion of Section 112, paragraph 2, "has been relied upon in cases where some material submitted by applicant, other than his specification, shows that a claim does not correspond in scope with what he regards as his invention."); *In re* Moore, 439 F.2d 1232, 1235, 169 USPQ 236, 238 (C.C.P.A. 1971) ("[T]he definiteness of the language employed must be analyzed—not in a vacuum, but always in light of the teachings of the prior art and of the particular application disclosure as it would be interpreted by one possessing the ordinary level of skill in the pertinent art.").

[134] Solomon v. Kimberly-Clark Corp., 216 F.3d 1372, 55 USPQ 2d 1279, 1282 (Fed. Cir. 2000).

Main volume footnote updates begin on page 306.

> During patent examination the pending claims must be interpreted as broadly as their terms reasonably allow. When the applicant states the meaning that the claim terms are intended to have, the claims are examined with that meaning, in order to achieve a complete exploration of the applicant's invention and its relation to the prior art. The reason is simply that during patent prosecution when claims can be amended, ambiguities should be recognized, scope and breadth of language explored, and clarification imposed. . . . An essential purpose of patent examination is to fashion claims that are precise, clear, correct, and unambiguous. Only in this way can uncertainties of claim scope be removed, as much as possible, during the administrative process.[135]

Thus, in the more fluid environment of patent examination, an inventor's statements are relevant to determining compliance with the statute. However, it should be kept in mind that just as an inventor is able to shift the focus of the claimed invention during the prosecution process, the inventor should also be able to explain or shift statements similarly made during the prosecution process. For example, the Federal Circuit has acknowledged that an inventor is not competent to construe patent claims for the following reasons:

> [C]ommonly the claims are drafted by the inventor's patent solicitor and they may even be drafted by the patent examiner in an examiner's amendment (subject to the approval of the inventor's solicitor). While presumably the inventor has approved any changes to the claim scope that have occurred via amendment during the prosecution process, it is not unusual for there to be a significant difference between what an inventor thinks his patented invention is and what the ultimate scope of the claims is after allowance by the PTO.[136]

Thus, due to the complexities of the prosecution process, it is not unusual for the inventor to be unable to effectively communicate the scope of protection that was ultimately afforded during prosecution, or for that matter, the scope of protection that has been shifted or changed via the negotiation process.

E. Subjective Intent May Be Relevant to What Applicant Regards as Invention During Prosecution, But Never During Litigation [New Topic]

The subjective intent of the inventor may be relevant to what the "applicant regards as invention" requirement under Section 112, second paragraph during prosecution, but it is never relevant during litigation. For example, in *Solomon v. Kimberly-Clark Corp.*[137] Sandra Southwell (now Sandra Solomon) was the named inventor on the

---

[135] *In re* Zletz, 893 F.2d 319, 321–22, 13 USPQ 2d 1320, 1322 (Fed. Cir. 1989) (citation omitted); *In re* Prater, 415 F.2d 1393, 1404–05, 162 USPQ 541, 550–51 (C.C.P.A. 1969).

[136] Markman v. Westview Instruments, Inc., 52 F.3d 967, 985, 34 USPQ 2d 1321, 1335 (Fed. Cir. 1995) (en banc), aff'd, 517 U.S. 370, 38 USPQ 2d 1461 (1996) (citation omitted).

[137] Solomon v. Kimberly-Clark Corp., 216 F.3d 1372, 55 USPQ 2d 1279 (Fed. Cir. 2000).

Main volume footnote updates begin on page 306.

patent, which was directed to disposable panties and panty liners for use during a woman's menstrual cycle. Independent claim 1, which was representative of the claims at issue, read as follows:

> 1. A disposable woman's protective menstrual panty for holding a feminine napkin comprising:
>
> a relatively thick layer of disposable absorbent material; and
>
> a depression means in said relatively thick layer of disposable absorbent material, said depression means including a substantially thinner layer of disposable absorbent material operably disposed longitudially [sic] in the crotch area of said panty and extending at least partially upward thereof in both front and rear areas, said depression means being dimensioned for receiving said feminine napkin therein for positioning same during use.[138]

Solomon sued Kimberly-Clark, alleging that its "Personals" panty infringed all 59 claims of the patent. Kimberly-Clark moved for summary judgment, alleging that the patent was invalid under 35 U.S.C. Section 112, second paragraph, because Solomon failed to claim the subject matter that she regarded as her invention. Kimberly-Clark based its allegations in part on Solomon's deposition testimony, in which she allegedly stated on several occasions that the depression limitation in the claimed invention was made of material having a uniform, rather than varying, thickness. Kimberly-Clark contended that those statements were contrary to what was claimed in the patent, based on the interpretation of the claim limitation "depression" to mean a portion of the panty "formed by surrounding a region of substantially thinner material with a region of thicker material."[139]

The district court concluded, however, that Solomon's deposition testimony revealed that her patent did not accurately depict her invention, and thus held that there was no genuine issue of material fact that the patent was invalid under Section 112, second paragraph, for failure to claim the subject matter that the applicant regarded as his or her invention.

On appeal, the Federal Circuit reversed. Solomon argued that the district court erred in invalidating the claims of the patent under Section 112, second paragraph, asserting that a court evaluates compliance with that provision by comparing the claims to the disclosure in the specification, not by comparing the claims to an inventor's deposition testimony. Kimberly-Clark responded that the language of Section 112, second paragraph, plainly states that patent claims must specify what the applicant regards as his or her invention, and that, therefore, claims may be invalid if the inventor's testimony conflicts with the recitations of the claims.

The Federal Circuit first noted that during the prosecution of a patent application, a claim's compliance with both portions of Section

---

[138] *Id.*, 55 USPQ 2d at 1280.

[139] *Id.* at 1281.

Main volume footnote updates begin on page 306.

112, second paragraph, may be analyzed by consideration of evidence beyond the patent specification, including an inventor's statements to the Patent Office.[140] Thus, the Federal Circuit reasoned, in the more fluid environment of patent examination, an inventor's statements are relevant to determining compliance with the statute. On the other hand, when a court analyzes whether issued claims comply with Section 112, second paragraph, the evidence considered in that analysis should be more limited. The Federal Circuit noted that, as for the "definiteness" portion of Section 112, second paragraph, it is well settled that a court will typically limit its inquiry to the way one of skill in the art would interpret the claims in view of the written description portion of the specification.[141]

The Federal Circuit acknowledged that it had not specifically addressed the types of evidence that may be considered in analyzing whether a claim complies with the "which the applicant regards as his invention" portion of that statute. However, the Federal Circuit saw no reason for a different standard to apply, as the rationale for reviewing a limited range of evidence under either portion of the statute is the same, i.e., the way one of skill in the art would interpret the claims in view of the written description portion of the specification to determine whether the applicant claimed what he or she regarded as the invention.

However, the Federal Circuit indicated that a more limited range of evidence should be considered in evaluating validity as opposed to patentability under either portion of Section 112, second paragraph, because the language of issued claims is generally fixed (subject to the limited possibilities of reissue and reexamination), the claims are no longer construed as broadly as is reasonably possible, and what the patentee subjectively intended his or her claims to mean is largely irrelevant to the claim's objective meaning and scope.[142] As has been noted in the context of definiteness, the inquiry under Section 112, second paragraph, focuses on whether the claims, as interpreted in view of the written description, adequately perform their function of notifying the public of the patentee's right to exclude.

Accordingly, the Federal Circuit reasoned that it is particularly inappropriate to consider inventor testimony obtained in the context of

---

[140] *Id.* at 1282. *see also In re* Conley, 490 F.2d 972, 976, 180 USPQ 454, 456–57 (C.C.P.A. 1974) (noting that the phrase "which the applicant regards as his invention" in the second portion of Section 112, paragraph 2, "has been relied upon in cases where some material submitted by applicant, other than his specification, shows that a claim does not correspond in scope with what he regards as his invention."); *In re* Moore, 439 F.2d 1232, 1235, 169 USPQ 236, 238 (C.C.P.A. 1971) ("[T]he definiteness of the language employed must be analyzed—not in a vacuum, but always in light of the teachings of the prior art and of the particular application disclosure as it would be interpreted by one possessing the ordinary level of skill in the pertinent art.").

[141] *Id.*

[142] *Id.*, 55 USPQ 2d at 1283 (citing Markman v. Westview Instruments, Inc., 52 F.3d 967, 985–86, 34 USPQ 2d 1321, 1334–35 (Fed. Cir. 1995) (*en banc*), *aff'd*, 517 U.S. 370, 38 USPQ 2d 1461 (1996)).

Main volume footnote updates begin on page 306.

litigation in assessing validity under Section 112, second paragraph, in view of the absence of probative value of such testimony.[143] The Federal Circuit recognized that "which the applicant regards as his invention" is subjective language. However, once the patent issues, the claims and written description must be viewed objectively, from the standpoint of a person of skill in the art.[144]

Thus, the Federal Circuit concluded that inventor testimony, obtained in the context of litigation, should not be used to invalidate issued claims under Section 112, second paragraph. The Federal Circuit agreed with Solomon that the district court erred in using her deposition testimony to invalidate the claims of the patent under Section 112, second paragraph.

---

[143] *Id. See also* Markman v. Westview Instruments, Inc., 52 F.3d 967, 985, 34 USPQ 2d 1321, 1332–33 (Fed. Cir. 1995) (en banc), aff'd, 517 U.S. 370, 38 USPQ 2d 1461 (1996) ("[t]he subjective intent of the inventor when he used a particular term is of little or no probative weight in determining the scope of a claim (except as documented in the prosecution history)."); Bell & Howell Document Mgmt. v. Altek Sys., 132 F.3d 701, 706, 45 USPQ 2d 1033, 1038 (Fed. Cir. 1997) ("The testimony of an inventor and his attorney concerning claim construction is thus entitled to little or no consideration. The testimony of an inventor is often a self-serving, after-the-fact attempt to state what should have been part of his or her patent application. . . ."); Roton Barrier, Inc. v. Stanley Works, 79 F.3d 1112, 1126, 37 USPQ 2d 1816, 1826 (Fed. Cir. 1996) ("We have previously stated that an inventor's after-the-fact testimony is of little weight compared to the clear import of the patent disclosure itself.").

[144] *Solomon*, 55 USPQ 2d at 1284.

Main volume footnote updates begin on page 306.

MAIN VOLUME FOOTNOTE UPDATES

[168]**[Replace the L. Ed. cite with the following.]** 518 U.S. 1005.

[330]**[Add the following at the end of footnote 330.]** (unpublished)

[365]**[Delete the cite to the National Advanced Systems slip opinion and substitute the following.]** 26 F.3d 1107, 1112 (Fed. Cir. 1994).

[394]**[Add the following to the end of existing footnote 394.]** *See also* Interlink Elecs. v. Incontrol Solutions, Inc., Civ. App. No. 98-1567, slip op. at 2 (Fed. Cir. Aug. 24, 1999) (unpublished) ("'contract' and 'conductor' as 'conductive elements [in a nonconductive relationship] available for connection to an external circuit'").

[411]**[Add at the end of the footnote.]** (unpublished).

[418]**[Replace existing footnote 418 with the following.]** R.A.C.C. Indus., Inc. v. Stun-Tech, Inc., 49 USPQ 2d 1793 (Fed. Cir. 1998) (unpublished) *cert. denied*, 526 U.S. 1098 (1999).

[419]**[Replace existing footnote 419 with the following.]** *Id.* at 1795.

[420]**[Replace existing footnote 420 with the following.]** *Id.* at 1796–97. *See also* Berg Tech., Inc. v. Foxconn Int'l, Inc., Civ. App. No. 98-1324, slip op. at 6 (Fed. Cir. Feb. 23, 1999) (unpublished) ("The term 'adapted to' is often used in claim drafting to indicate 'capable of.'").

[545]**[Add the following to the end of existing footnote 545.]** *See also* Essilor Int'l v. Nidek Co., Civ. App. No. 98-1558, slip op. at 9 (Fed. Cir. Oct. 29, 1999) (unpublished):

> In our case, the patent discloses a "control unit" as the structure that performs the function of storing, comparing and selecting the bevel path. . . . The patent further states that the control unit is composed of a central storage and computation unit and that the construction of a control unit is within the capabilities of a person skilled in the art. . . . The district court found that it would have been clear to one of ordinary skill what structure must perform the function recited in the means-plus-function limitation. The district court found that the necessary elements of the control unit which would perform these functions were described in the patent and that the functions described in the specification could be accomplished using computer programs. We agree with the district court.

10

Related Application and Priority Issues

II. Original U.S. Applications

[Insert at the end of the section.]

35 U.S.C. Section 111 was amended under the American Inventors Protection Act with respect to the above quoted provisions to change the title of the Commissioner to Director of the U.S. Patent and Trademark Office.[1]

III. Provisional U.S. Applications

[On page 944, change the quotation of 35 U.S.C. Section 111 to read as follows.]

(b) PROVISIONAL APPLICATION—

(1) AUTHORIZATION—A provisional application for patent shall be made or authorized to be made by the inventor, except as otherwise provided in this title, in writing to the Director. Such application shall include—

(A) a specification as prescribed by the first paragraph of section 112 of this title; and

(B) a drawing as prescribed by section 113 of this title.

(2) CLAIM—A claim, as required by the second through fifth paragraphs of section 112, shall not be required in a provisional application.

(3) FEE—

[1] 35 U.S.C. § 111 (Supp. 2000).

Main volume footnote updates begin on page 336.

(A) The application must be accompanied by the fee required by law.

(B) The fee may be submitted after the specification and any required drawing are submitted, within such period and under such conditions, including the payment of a surcharge, as may be prescribed by the Director.

(C) Upon failure to submit the fee within such prescribed period, the application shall be regarded as abandoned, unless it is shown to the satisfaction of the Director that the delay in submitting the fee was unavoidable or unintentional.

(4) FILING DATE—The filing date of a provisional application shall be the date on which the specification and any required drawing are received in the Patent and Trademark Office.

(5) ABANDONMENT—Notwithstanding the absence of a claim, upon timely request and as prescribed by the Director, a provisional application may be treated as an application filed under subsection (a). Subject to section 119(e)(3) of this title, if no such request is made, the provisional application shall be regarded as abandoned 12 months after the filing date of such application and shall not be subject to revival after such 12-month period.

(6) OTHER BASIS FOR PROVISIONAL APPLICATION—Subject to all the conditions in this subsection and section 119(e) of this title, and as prescribed by the Director, an application for patent filed under subsection (a) may be treated as a provisional application for patent.

(7) NO RIGHT OF PRIORITY OR BENEFIT OF EARLIEST FILING DATE—A provisional application shall not be entitled to the right of priority of any other application under section 119 or 365(a) of this title or to the benefit of an earlier filing date in the United States under section 120, 121, or 365(c) of this title.[2]

The period of pendency of a provisional application, however, will extend beyond the 12 months to the next succeeding secular business day if the 12-month period expires on a holiday observed in the District of Columbia.[3] Accordingly, there is no co-pendency requirement for a provisional application and either a national or Patent Cooperation Treaty (PCT) application, for the provisional application to be relied upon in any proceeding in the Patent Office.[4]

IV. Foreign Priority Applications

A. Claiming Benefit of Foreign Priority

[On page 946, replace the quotation of 35 U.S.C. Section 119 to read as follows.]

---

[2] 35 U.S.C. § 111 (Supp. 2000).

[3] 35 USC § 119(e) (Supp. 2000).

[4] *Id.*

Main volume footnote updates begin on page 336.

(a) An application for patent for an invention filed in this country by any person who has, or whose legal representatives or assigns have, previously regularly filed an application for a patent for the same invention in a foreign country which affords similar privileges in the case of applications filed in the United States or to citizens of the United States, or in a WTO member country, shall have the same effect as the same application would have if filed in this country on the date on which the application for patent for the same invention was first filed in such foreign country, if the application in this country is filed within twelve months from the earliest date on which such foreign application was filed; but no patent shall be granted on any application for patent for an invention which had been patented or described in a printed publication in any country more than one year before the date of the actual filing of the application in this country, or which had been in public use or on sale in this country more than one year prior to such filing.

(b) (1) No application for patent shall be entitled to this right of priority unless a claim is filed in the Patent and Trademark Office, identifying the foreign application by specifying the application number on that foreign application, the intellectual property authority or country in or for which the application was filed, and the date of filing the application, at such time during the pendency of the application as required by the Director.

(2) The Director may consider the failure of the applicant to file a timely claim for priority as a waiver of any such claim. The Director may establish procedures, including the payment of a surcharge, to accept an unintentionally delayed claim under this section.

(3) The Director may require a certified copy of the original foreign application, specification, and drawings upon which it is based, a translation if not in the English language, and such other information as the Director considers necessary. Any such certification shall be made by the foreign intellectual property authority in which the foreign application was filed and show the date of the application and of the filing of the specification and other papers.[5]

[Change the quote at footnote 15 as follows, and delete footnote 15.]

"affords similar privileges in the case of applications filed in the United States or to citizens of the United States, or in a WTO member country."[6]

[Change the quote ending in footnote 32 as follows.]

An applicant in a nonprovisional application may claim the benefit of the filing date of one or more prior foreign applications under the conditions specified in 35 U.S.C. Sections 119(a) through (d) and (f), 172, and 365(a) and (b).

(1) (i) In an original application filed under 35 U.S.C. 111(a), the claim for priority must be presented during the pendency of the application, and within the later of four months from the actual filing date of the applica-

[5] 35 U.S.C. § 119 (Supp. 2000).

[6] *Id.*

Main volume footnote updates begin on page 336.

> tion or sixteen months from the filing date of the prior foreign application. The time period is not extendable. The claim must identify the foreign application for which priority is claimed, as well as any foreign application for the same subject matter and having a filing date before that of the application for which priority is claimed, by specifying the application number, country (or intellectual property authority), day, month, and year of its filing. . . . The claim for priority and the certified copy of the foreign application specified in 35 U.S.C. 119(b) or PCT Rule 17 must, in any event, be filed before the patent is granted.[7]

A special procedure applies when claiming priority to an international application under the Patent Cooperation Treaty (PCT). In this situation, the first sentence of the specification must also include an indication of whether the international application was published under PCT Article 21(2) in English, regardless of whether the benefit to such application is claimed in the application data sheet.[8]

[Insert at the end of the section.]

Courts have allowed a patentee to correct procedural defects such as a defective claim of foreign priority. For example, where a patentee failed to file a certified copy of a foreign application before the required deadline, and thus failed to obtain the priority date of that application, the court allowed the patentee to correct the claim to foreign priority through a reissue application.[9] The U.S. District Court for the District of Columbia set forth the reasoning for allowing reissue for the purpose of correcting a claim to priority as follows:

> In light of the foregoing discussion, the Court concludes that the phrase "claim in the patent" as used in Section 251 includes a claim to a right of priority on the basis of a foreign filing date and is not limited to claims defining the invention; that a patent may be reissued for the purpose of establishing a claim to priority which was not asserted, or which was not perfected during the prosecution of the original application; and that, accordingly, the plaintiff is entitled to a reissue of its patent.[10]

The courts have gone so far as to allow amendments to abandoned applications to include technical information relating to the claim to priority as well.[11] Where the oath or declaration filed in a parent application is sufficient to satisfy the statutory requirements for a subsequent continuation application, it is unnecessary to make another claim of priority, domestic under Section 120 or foreign under Section 119, in the later application which is identical to and filed during the pendency of the parent application.[12]

---

[7] 37 C.F.R. § 1.55(a) (2000).

[8] 37 C.F.R. § 1.78(a)(2) (2000).

[9] Israel v. Brenner, 273 F. Supp. 714, 155 USPQ 486, 488 (D.D.C. 1967).

[10] *Id.*, 155 USPQ at 488.

[11] Sampson v. Commissioner, 195 USPQ 136, 137 (D.D.C. 1976).

[12] *In re* Van Esdonk, 187 USPQ 671, 671 (Comm'r Pat. 1975).

Main volume footnote updates begin on page 336.

V. U.S. PRIORITY/CONTINUING APPLICATIONS

B. CIP Applications

[Insert after footnote 49.]

The Federal Circuit has similarly stated:

> A CIP application contains subject matter from a prior application and may also contain additional matter not disclosed in the prior application. . . . Different claims of such an application may therefore receive different effective filing dates. . . . Subject matter that arises for the first time in the CIP application does not receive the benefit of the filing date of the parent application. . . . Thus, the decision on the proper priority date—the parent application date or the CIP application date—for subject matter claimed in a CIP application depends on when that subject matter first appeared in the patent disclosures. To decide this question, a court must examine whether the "disclosure of the application relied upon reasonably conveys to the artisan that the inventor had possession at that time of the later claimed subject matter."[13]

[Replace footnote 50 with the following.]

See generally 35 U.S.C. § 120 (Supp. 2000); 37 C.F.R. § 1.53 (2000).

C. Divisional Applications

[Insert after footnote 52.]

35 U.S.C. Section 121 was amended under the American Inventors Protection Act with respect to the above quoted provisions to change the title of the Commissioner to Director of the U.S. Patent and Trademark Office.[14]

[Replace footnote 53 with the following.]

See generally 35 U.S.C. § 120 (Supp. 2000); 37 C.F.R. § 1.53 (2000).

D. Claiming Benefit of U.S. Priority

[Change the text ending in footnote 55 as follows.]

[A]ny nonprovisional application claiming the benefit of one or more prior filed copending nonprovisional applications or interna-

[13] Augustine Med., Inc. v. Gaymar Indus., Inc., 181 F.3d 1291, 50 USPQ 2d 1900, 1908 (Fed. Cir. 1999) (quoting Waldemar Link v. Osteonics Corp., 32 F.3d 556, 558, 31 USPQ 2d 1855, 1857 (Fed. Cir. 1994)).

[14] 35 U.S.C. § 121 (Supp. 2000).

Main volume footnote updates begin on page 336.

tional applications designating the United States of America must contain a reference to each such prior application, identifying it by application number . . . and indicating the relationship of the applications. This reference must be submitted during the pendency of the application, and within the later of four months from the actual filing date of the application or sixteen months from the filing date of the prior foreign application. The time period is not extendable. Unless the reference required by this paragraph is included in an application data sheet (§ 1.76), the specification must contain or be amended to contain such reference in the first sentence following the title.[15]

[Insert after footnote 62.]

The Federal Circuit has similarly stated:

> A CIP application contains subject matter from a prior application and may also contain additional matter not disclosed in the prior application. . . . Different claims of such an application may therefore receive different effective filing dates. . . . Subject matter that arises for the first time in the CIP application does not receive the benefit of the filing date of the parent application. . . . Thus, the decision on the proper priority date—the parent application date or the CIP application date—for subject matter claimed in a CIP application depends on when that subject matter first appeared in the patent disclosures. To decide this question, a court must examine whether the "disclosure of the application relied upon reasonably conveys to the artisan that the inventor had possession at that time of the later claimed subject matter."[16]

[Insert after footnote 65.]

Although Section 120 incorporates the requirements of Section 112 Para. 1, these requirements and the statutory mechanism allowing the benefit of an earlier filing date are separate provisions with distinct consequences. In accordance with Section 120, claims to subject matter in a later-filed application not supported by an ancestor application in terms of Section 112 Para. 1 are not invalidated; they simply do not receive the benefit of the earlier application's filing date.[17]

[Insert after footnote 76.]

Courts have allowed a patentee to correct procedural defects such as defective claims of foreign priority. For example, where a patentee

---

[15] 37 C.F.R. § 1.78(a) (2000).

[16] Augustine Med., Inc. v. Gaymar Indus., Inc., 181 F.3d 1291, 50 USPQ 2d 1900, 1908 (Fed. Cir. 1999) (quoting Waldemar Link v. Osteonics Corp., 32 F.3d 556, 558, 31 USPQ 2d 1855, 1857 (Fed. Cir. 1994)).

[17] Reiffin v. Microsoft Corp., 214 F.3d 1342, 54 USPQ 2d 1915, 1918 (Fed. Cir. 2000) (citing Hyatt v. Boone, 146 F.3d 1348, 1352, 47 USPQ 2d 1128, 1130 (Fed. Cir. 1998)).

Main volume footnote updates begin on page 336.

failed to file a certified copy of a foreign application before the required deadline, and thus failed to obtain the priority date of that application, the court allowed the patentee to correct the claim to foreign priority through a reissue application.[18] Similarly, the Patent Office has held that a reissue application may be filed for the purpose of correcting a claim to domestic priority under 35 U.S.C. Section 120, particularly where the patentee had previously substantially complied with the requirements for claiming priority.[19] The courts have gone so far as to allow amendments to abandoned applications to include technical information relating to the claim to priority as well.[20]

Where the oath or declaration filed in a parent application is sufficient to satisfy the statutory requirements for a subsequent continuation application, it is unnecessary to make another claim of priority, domestic under Section 120 or foreign under Section 119, in the later application which is identical to and filed during the pendency of the parent application.[21]

VI. Continuing Applications and Estoppel Issues

C. Statements Made in Related Continuing Applications

[Insert at the end of the section.]

When the earlier and later applications share the same claim terminology and/or arguments, an estoppel with respect to an earlier application will generally apply to one or more later applications, and particularly when an applicant links the two or more applications during prosecution. For example, the Federal Circuit stated the following in *Elkay Manufacturing Co. v. Ebco Manufacturing Co.*:[22]

> When multiple patents derive from the same initial application, the prosecution history regarding a claim limitation in any patent that has issued applies with equal force to subsequently issued patents that contain the same claim limitation. . . . The facts in the present case are even more compelling than in Jonsson for applying the prosecution history of the first issued patent to the second issued patent. Here, Elkay added new claims 26–28 during the prosecution of the '639 application, which issued as claims 1–3, respectively, in the '855 patent. In describing the claims, *Elkay stated that "new claim 26 is patterned after a combination of claims 1,3 and 5 of [the '531 patent] with the "feed tube" changed to—*

[18]Israel v. Brenner, 273 F. Supp. 714, 155 USPQ 486, 488 (D.D.C. 1967).

[19]Sampson v. Commissioner, 195 USPQ 136, 137–38 (D.D.C. 1976) (reissue applicant who substantially complied with 35 U.S.C. Section 120 is entitled to have amendments entered to include filing dates of prior abandoned applications in chain).

[20]*Id.* at 137.

[21]*In re* Van Esdonk, 187 USPQ 671, 671 (Comm'r Pat. 1975).

[22]Elkay Mfg. Co. v. Ebco Mfg. Co., 192 F.3d 973, 52 USPQ 2d 1109 (Fed. Cir. 1999), *cert. denied*, 529 U.S. 1066 (2000).

Main volume footnote updates begin on page 336.

feed probe—. . . ." By making this statement, Elkay affirmatively linked the meaning of claim 26 of the '639 application to claims 1, 3, and 5 of the '531 patent. Because Elkay's statement put competitors on clear notice of that *linkage* and because the '531 and '855 patents stem from the same genus, it is proper to consider the prosecution history of claim 1 of the '855 patent to be an amalgam of the prosecution histories of both patents.[23]

1. Estoppels in Earlier Application Will Not Extend to Broader Claims in Later Application [New Topic]

Estoppels relating to an applicant's amendments/arguments in earlier applications will not generally extend to broader claims allowed in later applications.[24] This is contrary to the usual rule that the entire prosecution history, including parent and grandparent applications, must be analyzed in interpreting a claim.[25]

For example, in *Princeton Biochemicals, Inc. v. Beckman Instruments, Inc.*,[26] the invention related to an apparatus for use in the process of capillary electrophoresis whereby molecules and proteins are separated from fluid samples as a result of application of an electrical charge. Princeton sued Beckman for patent infringement, asserting that Beckman infringed claim 32 of U.S. Patent No. 5,045,172 (the '172 patent). The parties disputed whether the claim covered only the embodiment where the holder and the capillary tube moved vertically toward a stationary sample cup and table, or also the alternative embodiment in which the sample cup and table moved vertically toward a stationary holder and capillary tube as in the accused devices.

Princeton argued that the district court erred in construing the "holder limitation" of claim 32. In particular, Princeton asserted that the district court erred by requiring a "vertically moving" holder, as no such limitation was present in the asserted claim. Nor, argued Princeton, were any arguments made during the prosecution of the application that resulted in the '172 patent and directed at claim 32 that would support reading a vertical movement limitation into that claim.

On appeal, the Federal Circuit agreed, stating that "[a] careful review of the prosecution history reveals that Princeton is correct."[27] The Federal Circuit noted that a continuation-in-part (CIP) application

[23] *Id.*, 52 USPQ 2d at 1114 (emphasis added).

[24] Princeton Biochemicals, Inc. v. Beckman Instruments, Inc., Civ. App. No. 98-1525, slip op. at 10 (Fed. Cir. Aug. 19, 1999) (unpublished).

[25] Mark I Mktg. Corp. v. Donnelley & Sons Co., 66 F.3d 285, 291, 36 USPQ 2d 1095, 1100 (Fed. Cir. 1995).

[26] Princeton Biochemicals, Inc. v. Beckman Instruments, Inc., Civ. App. No. 98-1525 (Fed. Cir. Aug. 19, 1999) (unpublished).

[27] *Id.*, slip op. at 9.

Main volume footnote updates begin on page 336.

was filed in which claim 32 (claim 1 as originally filed) was returned to its original, unamended form. Thereafter, claim 32 was rejected as obvious over prior art. However, claim 32 was not subsequently amended to include any requirement of vertical movement and in fact was not amended to distinguish over the cited prior art. The Examiner thus allowed the combined claim to issue as claim 32 without any amendment being made or any argument being espoused that would limit the holder limitation to the embodiment where the holder/capillary was vertically moving in relation to a stationary sample cup/table.

On this basis the Federal Circuit held the following:

> We hold that the prosecution history does not limit the holder limitation of claim 32 to only vertically movable holders. Although the applicant amended claim 1 to include a vertical movement requirement of the holder in the original application, the subsequent filing of the CIP application and the return of claim 1 to its original, unamended form, counsels against applying the usual rule that the entire prosecution history, including parent and grandparent applications, be analyzed in interpreting a claim.[28]

Thus, *Princeton Biochemicals* teaches that estoppels relating to an applicant's amendments/arguments in earlier applications will not generally extend to broader claims allowed in later applications that do not include those specific limitations.

A similar situation occurred in *Al-Site Corp. v. VSI International, Inc.*,[29] wherein the Federal Circuit stated the following:

> In a further attempt to overturn the jury verdict of infringement under the doctrine of equivalents with respect to the '345, '726, and '911 patents, VSI relies on prosecution history estoppel. This court has reviewed VSI's prosecution history estoppel argument and finds it unpersuasive. To overcome prior art objections by the Examiner, Magnivision amended what became claim 8 of the '532 patent to require that the extension project from the bottom edge portion of the hanger tag. . . . VSI argues that because all of Magnivision's patents arose from related applications, the same prosecution history estoppel applies to them as well. VSI therefore contends that because the arms of its Version 2 hanger tag extend from the sides of the body of the tag, it cannot infringe the claims of these patents under the doctrine of equivalents as restricted by prosecution history estoppel. While in some cases, the prosecution history of a related application may limit application of the doctrine of equivalents in a later filed patent, in this case the specific limitation added in the claims of an earlier issued patent is not present in the claims of the later issued patents. The '345, '726, and '911 patents all have limitations not found in the '532 patent and did not necessarily require the specific limitation added to the claims of the '532 patent to be patentable. The specific limitations added to gain allowance of the '532 patent are not included in and are therefore not relevant to determining the scope of the claims of the later issued patents.[30]

---

[28] *Id.* at 10.

[29] Al-Site Corp. v. VSI Int'l, Inc., 174 F.3d 1308, 50 USPQ 2d 1161 (Fed. Cir. 1999).

[30] *Id.*, 50 USPQ 2d at 1170.

Main volume footnote updates begin on page 336.

2. *Amendments/Arguments With Respect to Claims in One Patent May Create an Estoppel for Claims in Another Patent Having Similar Language [New Topic]*

The prosecution history of a parent application may limit the scope of a later application using the same claim term.[31] For example, in *Augustine Medical, Inc. v. Gaymar Industries, Inc.*,[32] the invention related to convective thermal blankets. During prosecution, Augustine Medical amended the claims to recite the limitation that the blankets were "self-erecting" and also argued this feature.[33] Augustine Medical sued Gaymar, and Gaymar argued that the claims were not infringed, literally or by equivalents, because its blankets did not satisfy the "self-erecting" limitation.

On appeal, the Federal Circuit agreed with Augustine Medical. The Federal Circuit noted:

> The prosecution histories of the Augustine patents show that the applicant expressly surrendered coverage of any forced-air blanket other than a "self-erecting" convective thermal blanket which stands off of a patient when in operation. During prosecution of application No. 07/227,189 (the '189 application), a parent application to later applications resulting in the '102, '320 and '371 patents, Augustine Medical canceled or amended all of the original claims in favor of new claims containing the "self-erecting" limitation. Augustine Medical made these amendments in response to the examiner's rejections over the prior art.[34]

Because the prosecution history of a parent application may limit the scope of a later application using the same claim term, the Federal Circuit held that the claim amendments "self-erecting" and underlying arguments restricted the scope of the claims in each of the later issued patents containing the "self-erecting" limitation.[35]

F. No Time Limit for Submitting Broadened Claims in Continuation Applications [New Topic]

Section 120 of 35 U.S.C., governing continuation applications, does not contain any time limit on an applicant seeking broadened claims.[36] In contrast, 35 U.S.C. Section 251, governing reissue proceedings, does contain a specific time limit of two years.[37] Moreover, Congress specifically provided for intervening rights in Section 252 of the reissue statute, whereas Congress made no such provision for in-

[31] Jonsson v. Stanley Works, 903 F.2d 812, 818, 14 USPQ 2d 1863, 1870 (Fed. Cir. 1990).

[32] Augustine Med., Inc. v. Gaymar Indus., Inc., 181 F.3d 1291, 50 USPQ 2d 1900 (Fed. Cir. 1999).

[33] *Id.*, 50 USPQ 2d at 1906.

[34] *Id.*

[35] *Id.* at 1907.

[36] *See* 35 U.S.C. § 120 (1994).

[37] 35 U.S.C. § 251 (1994).

Main volume footnote updates begin on page 336.

tervening rights in the context of continuation applications.[38] In this connection, the CCPA has commented that "a limit upon continuing applications [i.e., similar to the two-year limit in reissue proceedings] is a matter of policy for Congress, not for us."[39]

Similarly, the Federal Circuit has recognized the practice of filing continuation applications containing claims broader than those in a parent application, subject to double patenting objections, in order to encompass a competitor's product.[40]

In *Ricoh Co. v. Nashua Corp.*,[41] the Federal Circuit confirmed that the two-year broadening rule for reissue applications does not apply to continuation applications. In this connection, the Federal Circuit stated:

> Nashua contends that it is entitled to intervening rights for the products it developed during the pendency of the '626 application because the '603 patent broadened the claims of the '730 patent over two years after the issuance of the parent patent by using a continuation application, thus impermissibly circumventing the statutory mandates of a reissue proceeding. . . . [A]bsent congressional indication that intervening rights are to be applied in the context of continuation applications, we reject Nashua's argument that we should judicially adopt equitable safeguards, in contravention of established precedent, when Congress itself has declined to do so.[42]

VII. Continuing Applications and Best Mode Issues

A. Updating Best Mode for Continuing Applications

[Insert at the end of the section.]

The Federal Circuit had the opportunity to further explore this issue of when the best mode needs to be updated in a continuing application in *Magnivision, Inc. v. Bonneau Co.*[43] The invention related to a hanger for store display of eyeglasses. The hanger's advantage was that it did not have to be removed and replaced when a consumer tried the glasses on and returned them to the display. Magnivision and Bonneau both sold non-prescription eyeglasses. Magnivision sued Bonneau for infringing its patent, and Bonneau argued that the patent was invalid for failure to disclose and update the best mode of practicing the invention in the continuation-in-part application. The

[38] 35 U.S.C. §§ 120, 252 (1994).

[39] *In re* Hogan, 559 F.2d 595, 604 n.13, 194 USPQ 527, 536 n.13 (C.C.P.A. 1977).

[40] Texas Instruments, Inc. v. United States Int'l Trade Comm'n, 871 F.2d 1054, 1065, 10 USPQ 2d 1257, 1265 (Fed. Cir. 1989).

[41] Ricoh Co. v. Nashua Corp., Civ. App. No. 97-1344 (Fed. Cir. Feb. 18, 1999) (unpublished), *cert. denied*, 528 U.S. 815 (1999).

[42] *Id.*, slip op. at 5–6.

[43] Magnivision, Inc. v. Bonneau Co., Civ. App. No. 99-1093 (Fed. Cir. July 24, 2000) (unpublished).

Main volume footnote updates begin on page 336.

district court granted summary judgment in favor of Magnivision on Bonneau's affirmative defense that the patent was invalid for failure to disclose the best mode of practicing the invention, i.e., the district court held that Bonneau had failed to prove that the patent did not in fact disclose the best mode.

On appeal, the Federal Circuit agreed with the district court that Magnivision's patent did comply with the best mode requirement.

The Federal Circuit observed that the best mode issue depended on the timing of the inventor's knowledge of a best mode. Magnivision admitted that the inventor learned in mid-1988 of a better plastic material for the hanger than he had specified in his original January 19, 1988 application. Magnivision's patent described "a relatively stiff resilient plastic material, typically a polythene," or "a moderately stiff yet flexible plastic material."[44] The disputed claim 5 of the patent, i.e., U.S. Patent 5,144,345, referred only to a "flat sheet material."[45] At the time the inventor disclosed this "resilient plastic material" in his original filing, he did not know of a better mode. However, the Federal Circuit noted that at the time the inventor filed the continuation-in-part (CIP) application on December 1, 1988, which issued as the patent, the inventor knew of the better mode.

Citing *Transco v. Performance Contracting*, the Federal Circuit explained the overall inquiry to be made when determining whether the best mode need be updated in a continuing application:

> If the material in a continuation application is "common subject matter" with that of the original application, the inventor need not have updated his best mode disclosure in the continuation application. . . . An inventor only has the obligation to disclose a best mode in a continuation application if the claim feature associated with that best mode first appeared or first received adequate written description in the continuation.[46]

To determine whether the best mode needed to be updated, the Federal Circuit indicated that it must determine whether the continuation application first introduced or first supplied written support for the "retaining member for securing a portion of said frame" associated with the better plastic hanger material. The Federal Circuit indicated that the later-filed CIP application that led to the issued patent added Figures 4–7 and the text that described these figures. Therefore, the Federal Circuit reasoned, if figures 1–3, which appeared in the original filing, supplied adequate support for the "retaining member" recited in the patent (i.e., claim 5), then the inventor possessed that aspect of the invention at the time of the original filing. In that event, the Federal Circuit concluded, the inventor had no obligation to supply a best mode past the original filing date of the earlier-filed application.

---

[44] *Id.*, slip op. at 17.

[45] *Id.*

[46] *Id.*, slip op. at 17–18 (citing Transco v. Performance Contracting, 38 F.3d 551, 557, 32 USPQ 2d 1077, 1082 (Fed. Cir. 1994), *cert. denied*, 513 U.S. 1151 (1995)).

Main volume footnote updates begin on page 336.

The Federal Circuit compared figures 1–3 in the earlier and CIP applications with figures 4–7 of the CIP application, and concluded that the CIP application only added information about the fastening means that held the extension to the main body of the hanger when the extension was wrapped around the bridge of the eyeglasses. For the fastening means, the original application disclosed a rivet, while the CIP added a molded-in button. Thus, the Federal Circuit held that the district court correctly concluded that the original application disclosed and supported the disputed element of "a retaining member for securing a portion of said frame," and the inventor had no obligation to disclose a later-learned best mode.[47]

VIII. Double Patenting Rejections

[Insert at the end of the section.]

A. Same-Invention Double Patenting

Accordingly, through a statutorily prescribed term, Congress limits the duration of a patentee's right to exclude others from practicing a claimed invention.[48]

35 U.S.C. § 101 states "Whoever invents or discovers any new and useful process, machine, manufacture, or composition of matter, or any new and useful improvement thereof, may obtain a patent therefor . . ." The prohibition of double patenting of the same invention is based on 35 U.S.C. § 101.[49] By "same invention," the court means "identical subject matter."[50] A good test, and probably the only objective test, for "same invention," is whether one of the claims would be literally infringed without literally infringing the other. If it could be, the claims do not define identically the same invention.[51] All types of double patenting which are not "same invention" double patenting have come to be referred to as "obviousness-type" double patenting.[52]

---

[47] *Id.*, slip op. at 19.

[48] *See* 35 U.S.C. § 154(a)(2) (Supp. 2000) (discussing the length of a patent term).

[49] *In re* Goodman, 11 F.3d 1046, 1052, 29 USPQ 2d 2010, 2015 (Fed. Cir. 1993); *In re* Longi, 759 F.2d 887, 892, 225 USPQ 645, 648 (Fed. Cir. 1985).

[50] *Longi*, 759 F.2d at 892, 225 USPQ at 648; *In re* Vogel, 422 F.2d 438, 441, 164 USPQ 619, 621 (C.C.P.A. 1970).

[51] *Vogel*, 422 F.2d at 441, 164 USPQ at 621–22 (halogen is not the "same" as chlorine; meat is not the "same" as pork).

[52] *In re* Van Ornum, 686 F.2d 937, 942–43, 214 USPQ 761, 766 (C.C.P.A. 1982) (discussing cases leading to Vogel's restatement of the law of double patenting, numerous cases were considered in which application claims were directed to mere obvious modifications of, or improvements on, inventions defined in the claims of patents already issued to the same inventors, or to common assignees, subsequently being classified as "obviousness type double patenting.").

Main volume footnote updates begin on page 336.

The judicially-created doctrine of obviousness-type double patenting secures that legislative limitation by prohibiting a party from obtaining an extension of exclusive rights through claims in a later patent that are not patentably distinct from claims in an earlier patent.[53] As the Court of Customs and Patent Appeals (CCPA) explained, "[t]he fundamental reason for the rule [of obviousness-type double patenting] is to prevent unjustified timewise extension of the right to exclude granted by a patent no matter how the extension is brought about."[54]

Obviousness-type double patenting entails a two-step analysis. First, as a matter of law, the court construes the claim in the earlier patent and the claim in the later patent, and it overlays the later claim on the earlier claim to determine whether the later claim encompasses subject matter previously claimed.[55] Second, the court determines whether the differences in subject matter between the two claims is such that the claims are patentably distinct.[56]

Same invention double patenting is a legal doctrine that forbids an inventor from obtaining a second valid patent for either the same invention or an obvious modification of the same invention claimed in that inventor's first patent.[57] The basic concept of double patenting is that the same invention cannot be patented more than once since to do so would result in a second patent that would expire some time after the first patent expired and extend the protection timewise.[58]

"Obviousness-type" double patenting extends the fundamental legal doctrine to preclude "obvious variants" of what has already been patented.[59] "Obviousness-type" double patenting precludes issuance where there is no "patentable difference" or no "patentable distinction"

---

[53]*In re* Braat, 937 F.2d 589, 592, 19 USPQ 2d 1289, 1291–92 (Fed. Cir. 1991); *In re* Longi, 759 F.2d 887, 892, 225 USPQ 645, 648 (Fed. Cir. 1985) (explaining that, even though no explicit statutory basis exists for obviousness-type double patenting, the doctrine is necessary to prevent a patent term extension through claims in a second patent that are not patentably distinct from those in the first patent).

[54]*In re* Van Ornum, 686 F.2d 937, 943–44, 214 USPQ 761, 766 (C.C.P.A. 1982) (quoting *In re* Schneller, 397 F.2d 350, 158 USPQ 210, 214 (C.C.P.A. 1968)).

[55]*See* Georgia-Pacific Corp. v. United States Gypsum Co., 195 F.3d 1322, 1326, 52 USPQ 2d 1590, 1593 (Fed. Cir. 1999), *cert. denied*, 121 S. Ct. 54 (2000) (stating that "analysis of the claims is the first step" in an obviousness-type double patenting inquiry); General Foods Corp. v. Studiengesellschaft Kohle, 972 F.2d 1272, 1279, 23 USPQ 2d 1839, 1844 (Fed. Cir. 1992).

[56]*Georgia-Pacific*, 195 F.3d at 1327, 52 USPQ 2d at 1595 (proceeding to determine whether differences between the two claims are patentably distinct after construing the claims); *General Foods*, 972 F.2d at 1279, 23 USPQ 2d at 1844 (explaining that the terms "patentably distinguishable," "patentable distinctions," and obvious variations are equivalent for analytical purposes).

[57]*In re* Longi, 759 F.2d 887, 892, 225 USPQ 645, 648 (Fed. Cir. 1985).

[58]General Foods Corp. v. Studiengesellschaft Kohle mbH, 972 F.2d 1272, 1279–80, 23 USPQ 2d 1839, 1845 (Fed. Cir. 1992); *In re* Kaplan, 789 F.2d 1574, 1579–80, 229 USPQ 678, 683 (Fed. Cir. 1986).

[59]*In re* Berg, 140 F.3d 1428, 1432, 46 USPQ 2d 1226, 1229 (Fed. Cir. 1998); *In re* Goodman, 11 F.3d 1046, 1052, 29 USPQ 2d 2010, 2015 (Fed. Cir. 1993); General Foods Corp. v. Studiengesellschaft Kohle mbH, 972 F.2d 1272, 1280, 23 USPQ 2d 1839, 1845 (Fed. Cir. 1992).

Main volume footnote updates begin on page 336.

between the two claims.[60] This allows the public to practice obvious variations of the first patented invention after the first patent expires.[61] The courts adopted the doctrine out of necessity where claims in two applications by the same inventor were so much alike that to allow the latter would effectively extend the life of the first patent.[62] In order to overcome an "obviousness-type" double patenting rejection, an applicant may file a "terminal disclaimer," foregoing that portion of the term of the second patent that extends beyond the term of the first patent.[63]

Thus, if a claim sought in the application is not identical to, yet not patentably distinct from, a claim in an inventor's earlier patent, then the claim must be rejected under "obviousness-type" double patenting rejection.[64] In determining whether a claim sought in the application is patentably distinct from the claims in an inventor's earlier patent, a variety of tests have been utilized. Under the "one-way" test, the Examiner asks whether the application claims are obvious over the patent claims.[65] In a modified test, similar to the "one-way" test, the Examiner asks whether the application claims are generic to any species set forth in the patent claims.[66] Under the "two-way" test, the Examiner asks whether the application claims are obvious over the patent claims and also asks whether the patent claims are obvious over the application claims.[67]

B. Nonstatutory-Type Double Patenting

[Insert at the end of the section.]

3. *"Comprising" of Different Scope Than "Consisting," but Not Patentably Distinct [New Topic]*

The Federal Circuit has held that the use of the term "comprising" in one claim of a first patent and "consisting of" in a second claim

[60] *Goodman*, 11 F.3d at 1052, 29 USPQ2d at 2015; *General Foods*, 972 F.2d at 1278–79, 23 USPQ 2d at 1844.

[61] *In re* Longi, 759 F.2d 887, 892–93, 225 USPQ 645, 648 (Fed. Cir. 1985).

[62] Gerber Garment Tech., Inc. v. Lectra Sys., 916 F.2d 683, 686, 16 USPQ 2d 1436, 1439 (Fed. Cir. 1990); *In re* Thorington, 418 F.2d 528, 534, 163 USPQ 644, 648 (C.C.P.A. 1969), *cert. denied*, 397 U.S. 1038, 165 USPQ 290 (1970).

[63] *In re* Berg, 140 F.3d 1428, 1431–32, 46 USPQ 2d 1226, 1229 (Fed. Cir. 1998).

[64] *Berg*, 140 F.3d at 1431, 46 USPQ 2d at 1229; *In re* Braat, 937 F.2d 589, 592, 19 USPQ 2d 1289, 1291–92 (Fed. Cir. 1991); *In re* Goodman, 11 F.3d 1046, 1052, 29 USPQ 2d 2010, 2015 (Fed. Cir. 1993); *In re* Vogel, 422 F.2d 438, 441, 164 USPQ 619, 622 (C.C.P.A. 1970).

[65] *In re* Berg, 140 F.3d 1428, 1433–34, 46 USPQ 2d 1226, 1230–31 (Fed. Cir. 1998); *In re* Emert, 124 F.3d 1458, 1461–62, 44 USPQ 2d 1149, 1152 (Fed. Cir. 1997).

[66] *In re* Goodman, 11 F.3d 1046, 1052–53, 29 USPQ 2d 2010, 2015–16 (Fed. Cir. 1993); *In re* Van Ornum, 686 F.2d 937, 942–43, 214 USPQ 761, 766–67 (C.C.P.A. 1982).

[67] *In re* Dembiczak, 175 F.3d 994, 1002, 50 USPQ 2d 1614, 1619–20 (Fed. Cir. 1999); *In re* Braat, 937 F.2d 589, 593–94, 19 USPQ 2d 1289, 1292–93 (Fed. Cir. 1991).

Main volume footnote updates begin on page 336.

in another patent renders the scope of the two claims different, but is not generally sufficient to render the claims patentably distinct from each other, thereby requiring a terminal disclaimer to overcome any obviousness-type double patenting issues.

For example, in *Georgia-Pacific Corp. v. United States Gypsum Co.*,[68] the two patents at issue related to fiberglass mat-reinforced gypsum boards and the use of such boards in exterior insulation systems. Georgia-Pacific Corporation sued United States Gypsum Co. (USG) for infringing U.S. Patent No. 4,647,496 (the '496 patent) and U.S. Patent No. 5,371,989 (the '989 patent). USG contended that the '989 patent was invalid for obviousness-type double patenting over the claims of a third patent, U.S. Patent No. 4,810,569 (the '569 patent). Georgia-Pacific, however, asserted that there were patentable distinctions between the claims of these patents.

Georgia Pacific specifically argued that the terms "comprise" and "consist" have different meanings as used in the patents and were, therefore, not invalid for obviousness-type double patenting. On appeal, the Federal Circuit disagreed and held that the claims in the '989 patent were invalid over the claims in the '569 patent for obviousness-type double patenting. The Federal Circuit noted that the MPEP explains the difference between "comprise" and "consist" in patent law as follows:

> The transitional term "comprising" . . . is inclusive or open-ended and does not exclude additional, unrecited elements or method steps.
>
> The transitional phrase "consisting of" excludes any element step, or ingredient not specified in the claim.[69]

From these definitions, the Federal Circuit reasoned, it is clear that "comprise" is a broader term than "consist." Accordingly, the set of mats that were "comprised" of glass fibers included the subset of mats that "consist" of glass fibers and also included mats made up of glass fibers and other substances, whereas mats that "consist" of glass fibers were made up of glass fibers and nothing else. The Federal Circuit commented that claim 1 of the earlier '569 patent used the broader term "comprise," while claim 1 of the later '989 patent used the narrower term "consist." Thus, any mat that met the "consist" requirement of the '989 patent would also meet the "comprise" requirement of the '569 patent. In effect, the Federal Circuit reasoned, the invention claimed in the '989 patent was, with respect to the glass mats, merely a subset of the invention claimed in the '569 patent.

After analyzing the language of the claims, the Federal Circuit held that claim 1 of the '989 patent was merely an obvious variation of claim 1 of the '569 patent. While claim 1 of the '989 patent was slightly

---

[68] Georgia-Pacific Corp. v. United States Gypsum Co., 195 F.3d 1322, 52 USPQ 2d 1590 (Fed. Cir. 1999), *cert. denied*, 121 S. Ct. 54 (2000).

[69] *Id.*, 52 USPQ 2d at 1595 (quoting M.P.E.P. § 2111.03 (6th ed. 1997)).

Main volume footnote updates begin on page 336.

broader than claim 1 of the '569 patent with respect to the outer surfaces of the board, this difference was not enough to distinguish the two claims. With respect to the composition of the glass mats, the language and the disclosure of the '989 patent not only failed to distinguish it from the '569 patent, but indicated that it was merely a subset of the '569 patent. These differences were not sufficient to render the claims patentably distinct, and, therefore, claim 1 of the '989 patent was held invalid. According to the Federal Circuit:

> Except for the use of "comprising" in the '569 patent and "consisting of" in the '989 patent, the "said" clause in both is identical, and the clause "randomly distributed glass fibers" denotes a non-woven glass mat, so with regard to the structure of the mat, the two claims are identical. The use of the term "comprising" in the '569 patent and "consisting of" in the '989 patent renders the scope of the two claims different, but the difference is not sufficient to render claim 17 of the '989 patent nonobvious in light of claim 1 of the '569 patent, because it would have been obvious to construct the mat only out of glass fibers and adhesive, rather than out of glass fibers and adhesive and other unspecified substances.[70]

4. *Obviousness-Type Double Patenting Between Design and Utility Patents [New Topic]*

The law provides that, in some very rare cases, obviousness-type double patenting may be found between design and utility patents.[71] Double patenting between a design and utility patent is possible "if the features producing the novel aesthetic effect of a design patent or application are the same as those recited in the claims of a utility patent or application as producing a novel structure."[72] In these cases, a "two-way" test for determining obviousness-type double patenting is generally applicable.[73] Under this test, the obviousness-type double patenting rejection is appropriate only if the claims of the two patents cross-read, meaning that "the test is whether the subject matter of the claims of the patent sought to be invalidated would have been obvious from the subject matter of the claims of the other patent, and vice versa."[74]

In re Dembiczak[75] is an example of a case in which a textual description in claims of a utility patent was not sufficient to invalidate a design patent for obviousness-type double patenting. The invention re-

[70] *Id.* at 1596.

[71] Carman Indus., Inc. v. Wahl, 724 F.2d 932, 939–40, 220 USPQ 481, 487 (Fed. Cir. 1983) (noting that, while theoretically possible, "double patenting is rare in the context of utility versus design patents").

[72] *In re* Thorington, 418 F.2d 528, 536–37, 163 USPQ 644, 650 (C.C.P.A. 1969); *In re* Hargraves, 53 F.2d 900, 11 USPQ 240, 241 (C.C.P.A. 1931).

[73] *See Carman*, 724 F.2d at 940, 220 USPQ at 487.

[74] *Id.*, 220 USPQ at 487; *In re* Braat, 937 F.2d 589, 593, 19 USPQ 2d 1289, 1292 (Fed. Cir. 1991) (explaining two-way test).

[75] *In re* Dembiczak, 175 F.3d 994, 50 USPQ 2d 1614 (Fed. Cir. 1999).

Main volume footnote updates begin on page 336.

lated to a large trash bag made of orange plastic and decorated with lines and facial features, allowing the bag, when filled with trash or leaves, to resemble a Halloween-style pumpkin, or Jack-o'-lantern. As the inventors, Anita Dembiczak and Benson Zinbarg (collectively, "Dembiczak") noted, the invention solved the long-standing problem of unsightly trash bags placed on the curbs of America, and, by fortuitous happenstance, allowed users to express their whimsical or festive nature while properly storing garbage, leaves, or other household debris awaiting collection.

The patent application at issue included claims directed to various embodiments of the pumpkin bag. Though the claims varied, independent claim 74 was representative:

> 74. A decorative bag for use by a user with trash filling material, the bag simulating the general outer appearance of an outer surface of a pumpkin having facial indicia thereon, comprising:
>
> a flexible waterproof plastic trash or leaf bag having an outer surface which is premanufactured orange in color for the user to simulate the general appearance of the outer skin of a pumpkin, and having facial indicia including at least two of an eye, a nose and a mouth on the orange color outer surface for forming a face pattern on said orange color outer surface to simulate the general outer appearance of a decorative pumpkin with a face thereon,
>
> said trash or leaf bag having first and second opposite ends, at least said second end having an opening extending substantially across the full width of said trash or leaf bag for receiving the trash filling material,
>
> wherein when said trash or leaf bag is filled with trash filling material and closed, said trash or leaf bag takes the form and general appearance of a pumpkin with a face thereon.[76]

The Board affirmed the Examiner's obviousness-type double patenting rejection in light of the two design patents to Dembiczak. The Board held that the design patents depicted a generally rounded bag with Jack-o'-lantern facial indicia and that the Holiday reference supplied the missing limitations, such as the "thin, flexible material" of manufacture, the orange color, the initially open upper end, and the trash-filling material. Using a two-way test for obviousness-type double patenting, the Board held that the claims of the Dembiczak design patents did not exclude the additional structural limitations of the pending utility claims, and thus the design patents were merely obvious variations of the subject matter disclosed in the utility claims.

Acknowledging that the two-way test was to be applied, the Board concluded that "the design claimed in each of appellants' design patents does not exclude the features pertaining to the construction and color of the bag, the use of a plastic material for making the bag, the size or thickness of the bag . . . or the use of various types of filling material. . . . The particular details of the facial indicia would have

[76] *Id.*, 50 USPQ 2d at 1615.

Main volume footnote updates begin on page 336.

been a matter of design choice as evidenced by the Holiday handbook." Therefore, according to the Board, in view of Holiday, the claims of the design patents were obvious variants of the pending utility patent claims.[77]

On appeal, the Federal Circuit reversed. The Federal Circuit initially noted that in order for a design to be unpatentable because of obviousness, there must first be a basic design reference in the prior art, the design characteristics of which are "basically the same as the claimed design."[78] The phrase "having facial indicia thereon" found in the claims of the pending utility application is not a design reference that is "basically the same as the claimed design."[79] In fact, the Federal Circuit emphasized that this phrase described almost nothing with respect to design characteristics. The Federal Circuit also commented that the Board's suggestion that the design details were simply "a matter of design choice" evinces a misapprehension of the subject matter of design patents.[80] According to the Federal Circuit:

> The position adopted by the Board—that a textual description of facial indicia found in the claims of the utility patent application makes obvious the specific designs claimed in the (patentably distinct) Dembiczak design patents—would presumably render obvious, or even anticipate, all design patents where a face was depicted on a bag. But this, of course, is not the law; the textual description cannot be said to be a reference "basically the same as the claimed design," of the design patents at issue here. . . . The Board's conclusion of obviousness is incorrect.[81]

On this basis, the Federal Circuit found that the Board erred in concluding that the design patents were obvious variants of the pending utility claims and, therefore, reversed the double patenting rejections.

5. *Double Patenting Violated When Species Claimed in Later Patent is by Same Party that Claimed Genus in Earlier Patent [New Topic]*

Obviousness-type double patenting has been found where a genus is claimed in an earlier patent and then the same party claims a species of that genus in a later patent. The contention that the genus claim of the earlier patent covers thousands of possible pharmaceutical compounds does not preclude a finding that a species claim in a later

---

[77] *Id.* at 1616.

[78] *Id.* at 1619 (quoting *In re* Borden, 90 F.3d 1570, 1574, 39 USPQ 2d 1524, 1526 (Fed. Cir. 1996); *In re* Rosen, 673 F.2d 388, 391, 213 USPQ 347, 350 (C.C.P.A. 1982)).

[79] *Id.* (quoting *Borden*, 90 F.3d at 1574, 39 USPQ 2d at 1526).

[80] *Id.* at 1620 (citing *Carman*, 724 F.2d at 939 n.13, 220 USPQ at 486 n.13 ("Utility patents afford protection for the mechanical structure and function of an invention whereas design patent protection concerns the ornamental or aesthetic features of a design.")).

[81] *Id.*

Main volume footnote updates begin on page 336.

application is invalid for obviousness-type double patenting. According to the Federal Circuit, the double patenting analysis is not concerned with what one skilled in art would be aware of from reading the claims, but with what inventions the claims define.[82]

For example, in Eli Lilly & Co. v. Barr Laboratories,[83] the invention related to fluoxetine hydrochloride which is the active ingredient in Eli Lilly and Company's (Lilly's) antidepressant drug Prozac. The patent covered the administration of fluoxetine hydrochloride to inhibit serotonin uptake in an animal's brain neurons. Lilly, on April 10, 1996, brought an infringement action alleging that Barr infringed claim 7 of U.S. Patent No. 4,626,549 (the ′549 patent). Barr argued that claim 7 of the ′549 patent was invalid for double patenting. The district court summarily held in favor of Lilly, concluding that claim 7 was not invalid based on double patenting.

Barr appealed the district court's summary judgment ruling. The Federal Circuit reversed and held that claim 7 of the ′549 patent was invalid for obviousness-type double patenting.

Claim 7 of the ′549 patent, which depends on claim 4, related to blocking the uptake of the monoamine serotonin in an animal's brain neurons through administration of the compound N-methyl-3-(p-trifluoromethylphenoxy)-3-phenylpropylamine hydrochloride, commonly referred to as fluoxetine hydrochloride.

U.S. Patent No. 4,590,213 (the ′213 patent) issued earlier than the ′549 patent, and claimed a method of treating humans suffering from anxiety which comprised the administration of a pharmaceutical compound within a class of claimed compounds. Thus, according to the Federal Circuit, the ′213 patent covered the administration of fluoxetine hydrochloride to treat depression.[84] The ′895 patent expired in April 1994.

The Federal Circuit emphasized that claim 1 of the ′213 patent, which had expired, already covered the administration of fluoxetine hydrochloride for treating anxiety. The Federal Circuit also stated that "a later genus claim limitation is anticipated by, and therefore not patentably distinct from, an earlier species claim."[85] The Federal Circuit, in dicta, appears to have created a per se rule regarding double patenting with respect to a later genus claim covered by an earlier species claim.

However, the Federal Circuit also went on to determine whether the claims were patentably distinct under the typical obviousness-type double patenting analysis. The Federal Circuit reasoned that the only discernible difference between claim 1 of the ′213 patent and

---

[82]*In re* Sarett, 327 F.2d 100, 1013, 140 USPQ 474, 481 (C.C.P.A. 1964).

[83]Eli Lilly & Co. v. Barr Labs., 251 F.3d 955, 58 USPQ 2d 1865 (Fed. Cir. 2001).

[84]*Id.*, 58 USPQ 2d at 1881.

[85]*Id.* at 1880.

Main volume footnote updates begin on page 336.

claim 7 of the '549 patent was that claim 1 only addressed the treatment of anxiety in humans while claim 7 addressed the treatment of serotonin uptake in animals. The Federal Circuit held that claim 7 of the '549 patent was invalid based on obviousness-type double patenting over claim 1 of the '213 patent.

Accordingly, the Federal Circuit held in *Eli Lilly*, that claim 7 in the '549 patent for a method of administering fluoxetine hydrochloride to inhibit serotonin uptake covered subject matter previously claimed in claim 1 of the expired '213 patent, pertaining to method of treating anxiety in humans by administering a compound within a certain class of compounds, and was invalid for obviousness-type double patenting over claim 1.

6. Double Patenting Not Found Where Examiner Did Not Provide Sufficient Evidence to Support Prima Facie Case [New Topic]

A double patenting violation will not be found where the Examiner does not provide sufficient evidence to support a prima facie case of double patenting. For example, in *Ex parte Davis*,[86] the invention related to a cartridge loading apparatus for use with a disk drive. Claims 1 and 21 to 27 were rejected under the judicially created doctrine of nonstatutory (i.e., obviousness-type) double patenting over claim 1 of U.S. Patent No. 5,684,776, claim 1 of U.S. Patent No. 5,703,857, and claim 1 of U.S. Patent No. 5,724,331. The Examiner argued that the claims at issue were not patentably distinct from the inventions claimed in the above mentioned patents.

On appeal, the Board reversed the rejection. Based upon a review of the claims under appeal and the claims in the issued patents, the Board held that absent the presence of additional evidence not before it on appeal, claims 1 and 21–27 under appeal were patentably distinct from the claims in the issued patents. The Board reasoned that it was quite clear that only the claims in the present application recited a cartridge loading apparatus having a bias coil arm including a bias coil assembly and a lever arm engageable with a notch formed in one of the first or second sliders as set forth in, for example, claim 1. Thus, claim 1 and claims 21 to 27 dependent thereon were patentably distinct from the claims in the issued patents, in the absence of any evidence establishing that the claimed bias coil arm was known in the art in such a combination.

The Board observed that while the Examiner stated that subcomponents, such as the bias coil assembly, door links, cartridge receiver latch, and parking arm, were known in the art, the Examiner did not produce any evidence that the claimed bias coil arm was known in the

[86]*Ex parte* Davis, 56 USPQ 2d 1434 (B.P.A.I. 2000) (unpublished).

Main volume footnote updates begin on page 336.

art, much less that it would have been obvious to add such a bias coil assembly to the inventor's previously claimed subject matter.

In summary, the Board held that the Examiner failed to establish that the claims under appeal were not patentably distinct from the other patents, and reversed the rejection.

D. Terminal Disclaimers

[Replace the quote ending with footnote 245 with the following.]

> (a) When any claim of an application or a patent under reexamination is rejected under 35 U.S.C. 103 in view of a U.S. patent or a U.S. patent application publication which is not prior art under 35 U.S.C. 102(b), and the inventions defined by the claims in the application or patent under reexamination and by the claims in the patent or published application are not identical but are not patentably distinct, and the inventions are owned by the same party, the applicant or owner of the patent under reexamination may disqualify the patent or patent application publication as prior art. The patent or patent application publication can be disqualified as prior art by submission of:
>
> (1) A terminal disclaimer in accordance with § 1.321(c), and
>
> (2) An oath or declaration stating that the application or patent under reexamination and the patent or published application are currently owned by the same party, and that the inventor named in the application or patent under reexamination is the prior inventor under 35 U.S.C. 104.
>
> (b) When an application or a patent under reexamination claims an invention which is not patentably distinct from an invention claimed in a commonly owned patent with the same or a different inventive entity, a double patenting rejection will be made in the application or a patent under reexamination. A judicially created double patenting rejection may be obviated by filing a terminal disclaimer in accordance with 1.321(c).[87]

IX. Restriction Requirement Practice

A. Restriction Between Different Inventions

4. *Estoppel May Arise by Failure to Prosecute Claims in Divisional Application in Face of Prior Art Rejection [New Topic]*

Limiting a claim because of a restriction requirement does not necessarily invoke prosecution history estoppel.[88] However, an estop-

[87] Fed. Reg., Vol 65, No. 183, 57057 (Sept. 20, 2000).

[88] Bayer Aktiengesellschaft v. Duphar Int'l Research B. V., 738 F.2d 1237, 1243, 222 USPQ 649, 653 (Fed. Cir. 1984).

Main volume footnote updates begin on page 336.

pel may arise by failure to prosecute claims in a divisional application in the face of a prior art rejection. The determination of whether an amendment was made for purposes of patentability on grounds of obviousness is adjudged from the viewpoint of a person of skill in the field of the invention, and when the issue includes consideration of formalities of patent practice, experience in patent law and procedures is presumed.[89] The court must determine what such a person would conclude from the prosecution record.[90]

Merck & Co. v. Mylan Pharmaceuticals, Inc.[91] involved an estoppel finding when the applicant Merck failed to prosecute claims in a divisional application in the face of a prior art rejection. The invention was directed to a controlled release formulation of a combination of the drugs levodopa and carbidopa, used to treat Parkinson's disease. The desired controlled release was achieved by delivering these drugs in a polymer vehicle, the specific composition of which was the issue in this dispute.

The district court ruled that Merck had surrendered coverage of a HPC/HPMC polymer vehicle during prosecution, by amending and narrowing the claims in response to the Examiner's rejection of Merck's broad claims on the ground of obviousness in view of certain prior art. Merck argued to the district court that it was compelled by the Examiner to elect a species from the proposed Markush genus, and that it amended its claims for this reason and not because the claims were unpatentable under § 103. Merck further argued that it simply complied with the Examiner's formal requirement of an examination expedient, and did not yield anything in response to the rejection on obviousness. According to Merck, once it had elected a species, the Examiner's rejection based on the prior art simply became irrelevant to the prosecution. Thus, Merck argued that its election to prosecute a claim covering its commercial formulation when the Examiner required an election of species did not affect an estoppel against equivalent polymer combinations.

The district court found that Merck limited its claims to the particular polymer species in response to the Examiner's obviousness rejection, notwithstanding that the Examiner had also imposed a restriction requirement and, therefore, an estoppel occurred.

On appeal, the Federal Circuit affirmed the district court decision. According to the Federal Circuit:

> Although Merck carried the Markush-group polymers into the divisional application, upon rejection under § 103 and the formal requirement for

---

[89] Merck & Co. v. Mylan Pharms., Inc., 190 F.3d 1335, 51 USPQ 2d 1954, 1958 (Fed. Cir. 1999).

[90] EMI Group N. Am., Inc. v. Intel Corp., 157 F.3d 887, 898, 48 USPQ 2d 1181, 1189 (Fed. Cir. 1998), *cert. denied*, 526 U.S. 1112 (1999); Modine Mfg. Co. v. United States Int'l Trade Comm'n, 75 F.3d 1545, 1555–56, 37 USPQ 2d 1609, 1616 (Fed. Cir. 1996).

[91] Merck & Co. v. Mylan Pharm., Inc., 190 F.3d 1335, 51 USPQ 2d 1954 (Fed. Cir. 1999).

Main volume footnote updates begin on page 336.

> an election of species Merck again elected the HPC/PVACA combination. Although this action also resolved the requirement of an election of species, we conclude that the controlling fact is that Merck no longer sought to claim any of the several other polymer vehicles. . . . We therefore conclude that the most reasonable reading of the prosecution history is that Merck's actions in limiting all of the claims of both patents to a single species of combined polymer vehicle, without further pursuit of the broader polymer claims, were primarily in consideration of the patentability rejection. . . . Thus we conclude that prosecution history estoppel arises.[92]

5. *Restriction Requirement in Application Does Not Have Any Bearing on Enablement of Prior Art Reference [New Topic]*

The Patent Office's determination or opinion regarding an application under examination has no general relevance or bearing with respect to the suitableness or enablement of a prior art reference. For example, the fact that a restriction requirement is issued in an application between the method claims and the system claims, thereby indicating that the claimed method may be performed by systems other than the claimed system, does not have any bearing on enablement of a prior art reference that describes a different system used to implement the claimed method.

For example, in *Helifix Ltd. v. Blok-Lok, Ltd.*,[93] the invention was directed to a method of securing layers of masonry (wythes), such as an exterior brick wall and an interior concrete wall, by means of ties. The typical tie was described as spiral-shaped, seven-to eight-inches long, and made of solid stainless steel. In January 1993, representatives of Helifix attended the World of Concrete trade show in Las Vegas, Nevada, where they displayed and distributed a brochure (the '93 brochure). The '93 brochure described Helifix stainless steel ties and their use in masonry refacing and new construction, including methods of construction.

During initial prosecution, the grandparent application of the Helifix patent was filed with claim 1 directed to a method of securing wythes with a helical tie, claim 2 directed to a tool for driving a helical tie into a wall, and claims 3 and 4 directed to helical ties. The Patent Office issued a restriction requirement between the method, tool, and tie claims. With respect to the method and tool claims, the Patent Office asserted that the tool was not required to insert the tie. Helifix elected to pursue the method claim. In due course, the grandparent application was abandoned in favor of the parent application of the Helifix patent.

---

[92] *Id.*, 51 USPQ 2d at 1958.

[93] Helifix Ltd. v. Blok-Lok, Ltd., 208 F.3d 1339, 54 USPQ 2d 1299 (Fed. Cir. 2000).

Main volume footnote updates begin on page 336.

The parent application was filed with claim 1 directed to the method, claims 2 and 5–7 directed to the tool, and claims 3 and 4 directed to the helical tie. The Patent Office again issued a restriction requirement along the same lines as the restriction requirement issued in the grandparent application, asserting that the tool was not required to insert the tie. Helifix did not present any substantive arguments in response to this restriction requirement, and elected to pursue the tool claims.

The Helifix patent application was filed with the same claims as the parent application; however, the tool and tie claims were subsequently canceled, leaving only method claim 1. This claim of the Helifix patent recited:

> 1. A method of securing two or more wythes in a building structure utilizing a helical tie member having longitudinal helical flutes terminating at a cutting end at one end and terminating at a remote end opposite the cutting end comprising the steps of:
>
> drilling a first wythe to a diameter less than a diameter of the flutes on the tie to be inserted,
>
> drilling a pilot hole in a second wythe to a predetermined depth,
>
> inserting the remote end of the tie into a tool which impactingly drives the tie and rotatably permits the same to rotate as a helical bed is developed in the first wythe due to penetration by the tie,
>
> passing the flutes into the second wythe and continuing to impactingly drive the tie to a base of the pilot hole,
>
> removing the driving tool from the remote end of the tie,
>
> and thereafter finishing the remote end of the tie in accordance with mandates of the site.[94]

Helifix filed suit against Blok-Lok, alleging that Blok-Lok was infringing its patent. Blok-Lok filed a counterclaim which included a request for a declaratory judgment of patent invalidity. Blok-Lok asserted that the '93 brochure described the method claimed in the Helifix patent and that the claimed method was on sale at the January 1993 World of Concrete trade show. Because the earliest United States priority date of the Helifix patent was more than one year after the brochure was publicly distributed and more than one year after the trade show, Blok-Lok asserted that the method was unpatentable under 35 U.S.C. Section 102(b).

The district court construed claim 1 of the patent, focusing on the tool recited in the claim. The district court concluded that the claim was not limited to the specific tool described in the patent specification. The district court then determined that the patent was anticipated by the '93 brochure under 35 U.S.C. Section 102(b), and that activities at the World of Concrete trade show in January 1993 amounted to an on-sale bar under 35 U.S.C. Section 102(b). Although

---

[94] *Id.*, 54 USPQ 2d at 1300–01.

Main volume footnote updates begin on page 336.

the '93 brochure did not describe the tool used to perform the claimed method, the district court determined that such a tool was enabled because the Patent Office had issued a restriction requirement between the claimed method and the specific tool described in the specification. Accordingly, the district court assumed that the restriction requirement indicated that any tool could perform the claimed method, and therefore, the fact that the '93 brochure did not specifically describe a tool that could implement the claimed method was irrelevant to the enablement of the '93 brochure. The district court therefore granted Blok-Lok's motion for summary judgment of patent invalidity.

On appeal, the Federal Circuit reversed, holding that the '93 brochure was not enabling, and therefore, was not an anticipatory reference under Section 102. Helifix argued that the '93 brochure did not enable a tool capable of practicing the method recited in the patent and that such a tool was not available at the time of the World of Concrete trade show. The Federal Circuit concluded that Blok-Lok failed to provide clear and convincing evidence that the '93 brochure enabled a person of ordinary skill in the art to practice the claimed method. In particular, Blok-Lok did not present any evidence indicating that a person of ordinary skill in the art could have made or obtained a tool capable of being used in the claimed method without an undue amount of experimentation.[95]

The Federal Circuit explained that the Patent Office can issue a restriction requirement if it finds that two or more inventions claimed in a patent application are "independent and distinct."[96] A process and apparatus (tool) for its practice can be restricted if either "the process as claimed can be practiced by another materially different apparatus or by hand" or "the apparatus as claimed can be used to practice another and materially different process."[97] In response to a restriction requirement, an applicant must elect one invention for examination.[98] Claims to the non-elected invention(s) are withdrawn from consideration and must be canceled before the application is allowed to issue as a patent.[99]

The Federal Circuit rejected Block-Lok's argument that the Patent Office's repeated assertions that the tool claimed in the patent applications was not required to insert the tie demonstrated that the '93 brochure need not describe the tool to enable the claimed method. According to the Federal Circuit:

---

[95] *Id.* at 1304 (citing *In re* Sheppard, 339 F.2d 238, 242, 144 USPQ 42, 45 (C.C.P.A. 1981) (reversing a rejection under 35 U.S.C. Section 102(b) where the asserted prior art reference did not permit someone skilled in the art to possess the claimed invention without an undue amount of experimentation)).

[96] *Id.* (Citing 35 U.S.C. § 121 (1994)).

[97] *Id.* (Citing M.P.E.P. § 806.05(e) (7th ed. 1998)).

[98] *Id.* (Citing 37 C.F.R. § 1.142(a) (1999)).

[99] *Id.* (Citing 37 C.F.R. § 1.142(b) (1999)).

Main volume footnote updates begin on page 336.

> Both Block-Lok and the district court, however, have read too much into the restriction requirements in this case. The restriction requirements at issue merely reflect the Patent Office's conclusions that claim 1, by its terms, is not limited to a method using the tool recited in claim 2. Accordingly, the restriction requirements between the method claimed in the [Helifix] patent and the specific tool described in the specification in no way bear on the enablement of a different tool.[100]

Accordingly, the Federal Circuit held that the action of the U.S. Patent Office in issuing restriction requirements between the claimed method and a tool described in the specification of the patent to implement the method does not reflect the Patent Office's determination that other tools could be devised to practice claimed method, and thus did not bear in any way on enablement of a prior art reference.

---

[100] *Id.*

Main volume footnote updates begin on page 336.

MAIN VOLUME FOOTNOTE UPDATES

[57]**[Replace the S. Ct. cite with the following.]** 513 U.S. 1151.

[87]**[Replace the LEXIS cite with the following.]** 525 U.S. 1141.

[138]**[Replace the S. Ct. cite with the following.]** 513 U.S. 1151.

[245]**[Add the following to the end of footnote 245.]** *See also* 37 C.F.R. § 1.130 (1999).

[248]**[Add the following to the end of footnote 248.]** *See also* Sash Controls, Inc. v. Talon, L.L.C., Civ. App. No. 98-1152, slip. op. at 6–7 (Fed. Cir. Jan. 27, 1999) (unpublished).

11

Design Patent Requirements

II. Avoiding Statutory Subject Matter Rejections Under 35 U.S.C. Section 101

A. Ornamental Design for an Article of Manufacture

[Insert after footnote 7.]

The "ornamental" requirement of the design statute means that the design must not be governed solely by function, i.e., that this is not the only possible form of the article that could perform its function.[1] A design patent is for a useful article, but patentability is based on the design of the article, not the use. The design may contribute distinctiveness or consumer recognition to the design, but an absence of artistic merit does not mean that the design is purely functional.[2]

B. Ornamental Design Hidden in Normal Use of Object

[Insert at the end of the section.]

On the other hand, the validity of a design patent does not require that the article be visible throughout its use; it requires only that the design be of an article of manufacture and that the design meets the requirements of Title 35.[3] Thus, an article that is not exposed to view during use can be the subject of a design patent. Further, the design may contribute distinctiveness or consumer recognition to the design, but an absence of artistic merit does not mean that the design is purely functional.[4]

C. Primarily Ornamental Versus Primarily Functional

[Insert at the end of the section.]

1. Arguments During Prosecution May Be Used to Support Functionality Rejection [New Topic]

Arguments made during prosecution of a design patent may be used to support functionality rejection where the claimed design was

---

[1] L.A. Gear, Inc. v. Thom McAn Shoe Co., 988 F.2d 1117, 1123, 25 USPQ 2d 1913, 1917 (Fed. Cir. 1993).

[2] Seiko Epson Corp. v. Nu-Kote Int'l, Inc., 190 F.3d 1360, 52 USPQ 2d 1011, 1017–18 (Fed. Cir. 1999).

[3] Keystone Retaining Wall Sys., Inc. v. Westrock, Inc., 997 F.2d 1444, 27 USPQ 2d 1297 (Fed. Cir. 1993) (design patent for wall blocks, much of which are not visible after installation); *In re* Webb, 916 F.2d 1553, 16 USPQ 2d 1433 (Fed. Cir. 1990) (design patent for a hip prosthesis that is not in view after implantation in patient).

[4] Seiko Epson Corp. v. Nu-Kote Int'l, Inc., 190 F.3d 1360, 52 USPQ 2d 1011, 1017–18 (Fed. Cir. 1999).

distinguished from the prior art on the ground of features that are described in a related utility patent as functional. For example, in *Berry Sterling Corp. v. Pescor Plastics, Inc.*,[5] Berry designed a cup for a promotional program of the Coca Cola Company, called the "Coke to Go" program. Coca Cola wanted a design for a cup that could be used by vendors to sell Coca Cola products to drive-through or take-out customers. Coca Cola wanted a cup that would fit in a variety of car cup holders, that would stack well, and that could be manufactured inexpensively.

Pescor Plastics, Inc. began selling cups that Berry alleged were copies of the design claimed in its application. Berry filed an infringement suit against Pescor for infringing its design patent. The court held that the patent was invalid as functional.

On appeal, the Federal Circuit affirmed. Berry asserted that its claimed design was ornamental and not functional because there were many alternative designs that performed the same function, that of a container made to fit a vehicle receptor. The Federal Circuit disagreed. The Federal Circuit noted that substantial evidence supported the jury's verdict that the patent was invalid because the claimed design was functional. Significantly, the Federal Circuit referred to statements Berry made during prosecution to distinguish the claimed design over the prior art:

> During the prosecution of the . . . patent, the claimed design was distinguished from the prior art on the ground that the upper portion and lower fluted body portion of the cup form a single area joined by a shoulder. . . . These features of the cup—that serve to distinguish the claimed design from the prior art—are described as functional in the utility patent granted on the same article, U.S. Patent No. 5,427,269 ('269 patent).[6]

The Federal Circuit emphasized that the '269 patent recited that these features were functional:

> The shoulder aids the container in securely nesting in the vehicle container receptacle.
>
> In order to strengthen the sidewalls of the lower body portion and to facilitate material flow in manufacture of the upper body portion, the lower body portion of the container is formed of a series of fluted sides that provide support to the lower body portion.[7]

The '269 patent also stated that "the reduced thickness of the upper body portion allows the rim of the container to be reduced in size, and thus provides more compact nesting of the container."[8]

On this basis, the Federal Circuit held that the claimed design was functional and, therefore, not patentable. According to the Federal Circuit:

---

[5] Berry Sterling Corp. v. Pescor Plastics, Inc., Civ. App. No. 98-1381 (Fed. Cir. Aug. 30, 1999) (unpublished).

[6] *Id.*, slip op. at 11.

[7] *Id.* at 11–12.

[8] *Id.* at 12.

In this case, each of the features that create the overall appearance of the design are dictated by functional considerations. The rim, the tapered upper and lower body portions, the transitional shoulder, and the fluted bottom and their arrangement are all dictated by functional considerations. In short, the overall appearance of the design is dictated by the use of the article and is not primarily ornamental.[9]

D. Obviousness-Type Double Patenting Between Design and Utility Patents [New Topic]

The law provides that, in some very rare cases, obviousness-type double patenting may be found between design and utility patents.[10] Double patenting, generally prohibited under 35 U.S.C. Section 101 between utility patents, is also possible between a design and utility patent "if the features producing the novel aesthetic effect of a design patent or application are the same as those recited in the claims of a utility patent or application as producing a novel structure."[11] In these cases, a "two-way" test for determining obviousness-type double patenting is generally applicable.[12] Under this test, the obviousness-type double patenting rejection is appropriate only if the claims of the two patents cross-read, meaning that "the test is whether the subject matter of the claims of the patent sought to be invalidated would have been obvious from the subject matter of the claims of the other patent, and vice versa."[13]

In re Dembiczak[14] is an example where a textual description in claims of a utility patent was not sufficient to invalidate a design patent for obviousness-type double patenting. The invention related to a large trash bag made of orange plastic and decorated with lines and facial features, allowing the bag, when filled with trash or leaves, to resemble a Halloween-style pumpkin, or Jack-o'-lantern. As the inventors, Anita Dembiczak and Benson Zimbarg (collectively, Dembiczak) noted, the invention solved the long-standing problem of unsightly trash bags placed on the curbs of America, and, by fortuitous happenstance, allowed users to express their whimsical or festive nature while properly storing garbage, leaves, or other household debris awaiting collection.

---

[9] *Id.*

[10] Carman Indus., Inc. v. Wahl, 724 F.2d 932, 939–40, 220 USPQ 481, 487 (Fed. Cir. 1983) (noting that, while theoretically possible, "double patenting is rare in the context of utility versus design patents").

[11] *In re* Thorington, 418 F.2d 528, 536–37, 163 USPQ 644, 650 (C.C.P.A. 1969); *In re* Phelan, 205 F.2d 183, 98 USPQ 156, 157 (C.C.P.A. 1953); *In re* Barber, 81 F.2d 231, 28 USPQ 187, 188 (C.C.P.A. 1936); *In re* Hargraves, 53 F.2d 900, 11 USPQ 240, 241 (C.C.P.A. 1931).

[12] *See Carman*, 724 F.2d at 940, 220 USPQ at 487.

[13] *Id.*, 220 USPQ at 487; *In re* Braat, 937 F.2d 589, 593, 19 USPQ 2d 1289, 1292 (Fed. Cir. 1991) (explaining two-way test).

[14] *In re* Dembiczak, 175 F.3d 994, 50 USPQ 2d 1614 (Fed. Cir. 1999).

The patent application at issue included claims directed to various embodiments of the pumpkin bag. Though the claims varied, independent claim 74 was representative:

> 74. A decorative bag for use by a user with trash filling material, the bag simulating the general outer appearance of an outer surface of a pumpkin having facial indicia thereon, comprising:
>
> a flexible waterproof plastic trash or leaf bag having an outer surface which is premanufactured orange in color for the user to simulate the general appearance of the outer skin of a pumpkin, and having facial indicia including at least two of an eye, a nose and a mouth on the orange color outer surface for forming a face pattern on said orange color outer surface to simulate the general outer appearance of a decorative pumpkin with a face thereon,
>
> said trash or leaf bag having first and second opposite ends, at least said second end having an opening extending substantially across the full width of said trash or leaf bag for receiving the trash filling material,
>
> wherein when said trash or leaf bag is filled with trash filling material and closed, said trash or leaf bag takes the form and general appearance of a pumpkin with a face thereon.[15]

The Board affirmed the Examiner's obviousness-type double patenting rejection in light of the two design patents to Dembiczak. The Board held that the design patents depicted a generally rounded bag with Jack-o'-lantern facial indicia, and that the Holiday reference supplied the missing limitations, such as the "thin, flexible material" of manufacture, the orange color, the initially open upper end, and the trash filling material. Using a two-way test for obviousness-type double patenting, the Board held that the claims of the Dembiczak design patents did not exclude the additional structural limitations of the pending utility claims, and thus the design patents were merely obvious variations of the subject matter disclosed in the utility claims.

Acknowledging that the two-way test was to be applied, the Board concluded that "the design claimed in each of appellants' design patents does not exclude the features pertaining to the construction and color of the bag, the use of a plastic material for making the bag, the size or thickness of the bag . . . or the use of various types of filling material . . . . The particular details of the facial indicia would have been a matter of design choice as evidenced by the Holiday handbook." Therefore, according to the Board, in view of Holiday, the claims of the design patents were obvious variants of the pending utility patent claims.[16]

On appeal, the Federal Circuit reversed. The Federal Circuit initially noted that in order for a design to be unpatentable because of obviousness, there must first be a basic design reference in the prior

[15] *Id.*, 50 USPQ 2d at 1615.

[16] *Id.*, 50 USPQ 2d at 1616.

art, the design characteristics of which are "basically the same as the claimed design."[17] The phrase "having facial indicia thereon" found in the claims of the pending utility application is not a design reference that is "basically the same as the claimed design."[18] In fact, the Federal Circuit emphasized that such statement described almost nothing with respect to design characteristics. The Federal Circuit also commented that the Board's suggestion that the design details were simply "a matter of design choice" evinces a misapprehension of the subject matter of design patents.[19]

According to the Federal Circuit:

> The position adopted by the Board—that a textual description of facial indicia found in the claims of the utility patent application makes obvious the specific designs claimed in the (patentably distinct) Dembiczak design patents—would presumably render obvious, or even anticipate, all design patents where a face was depicted on a bag. But this, of course, is not the law; the textual description cannot be said to be a reference "basically the same as the claimed design," of the design patents at issue here. . . . The Board's conclusion of obviousness is incorrect.[20]

On this basis, the Federal Circuit found that the Board erred in concluding that the design patents were obvious variants of the pending utility claims and, therefore, reversed the double patenting rejections.

III. Complying with the Requirements of 35 U.S.C. Section 112

A. Drawings

[Insert after footnote 45.]

Inconsistent drawings in a design patent may support a holding of nonenablement only if the inconsistent drawings describe more than one design. For example, in *Antonious v. Spalding & Evenflo Cos.*,[21] the invention related to iron-type golf club heads. The invention was directed to a club head design incorporating a cavity back bar weight mass configuration that was described as increasing golf club performance during a golf swing. Antonious sued Spalding, claiming that

---

[17] *Id.* at 1619 (quoting *In re* Borden, 90 F.3d 1570, 1574, 39 USPQ 2d 1524, 1526 (Fed. Cir. 1996); *In re* Rosen, 673 F.2d 388, 391, 213 USPQ 347, 350 (C.C.P.A. 1982)).

[18] *Id.* (quoting *Borden*, 90 F.3d at 1574, 39 USPQ 2d at 1526).

[19] *Id.* at 1620 (citing *Carman*, 724 F.2d at 939 n. 13, 220 USPQ at 486 n. 13 ("Utility patents afford protection for the mechanical structure and function of an invention whereas design patent protection concerns the ornamental or aesthetic features of a design.")).

[20] *Id.*

[21] Antonious v. Spalding & Evenflo Cos., Inc., Civ. App. No. 98-1478 (Fed. Cir. Aug. 31, 1999) (unpublished).

Spalding's Top-Flite Tour and Tour Edition irons infringed the design patent.

The district court held both design patents of Antonious invalid pursuant to Section 112, first paragraph, on the ground that each showed two materially different designs. The district court focused its analysis on apparent differences between Figure 4 and Figures 2 and 3 in each patent.

Specifically, the court observed that Figure 4 showed neither of the two points of novelty that the court found in Figures 2 and 3 (i.e., a weight bar that was thicker at the bottom than at the top, and, in Figure 2 of the '056 patent, a triangular top ridge), and that Figure 4 showed a flat or "squashed" appearance compared to the corresponding club heads shown in Figures 2 and 3.

On appeal, the Federal Circuit reversed. The primary validity issue described by the Federal Circuit was whether the design patents each disclosed one embodiment of one design, more than one embodiment of one design, or more than one design. The Federal Circuit commented that the "squashed" appearance of Figure 4 compared to the corresponding Figures 2 and 3 in each patent was due to the perspective used in drawing the figure. That perspective also accounted for the failure of Figure 4 to indicate the triangular top ridge shown in Figure 2 of that patent.

The Federal Circuit noted that the apparent differences in the thickness profile of the weight bar shown in the figures could be a potential source of a substantially different overall appearance that could justify holding the patents invalid for attempting to claim more than one design. However, the Federal Circuit did not consider this sufficient to invalidate the patents. According to the Federal Circuit:

> We agree with the district court that Figure 4 of each patent appears to show a constant-thickness weight bar. We cannot tell, though, whether this is due to a drawing error, the perspective used in drawing the figures, or if Antonious intended to claim an embodiment of the golf club head design with a constant-thickness weight bar. However, Figures 2 and 3 plainly show a tapered weight bar. We conclude that a person of skill in the art would primarily look to Figures 2 and 3 to determine the shape of the weight bar, and any associated discrepancies in Figure 4 would not be sufficient to preclude such a person from gaining an overall understanding of the total substance of the designs. Thus, we conclude that the figures in each of the design patents disclose at most different embodiments of one design per patent.[22]

Thus, the Federal Circuit was satisfied that the figures in each patent did not disclose more than one design. Therefore, the patents were not invalid for being indefinite.

---

[22] *Id.*, slip op. at 17.

IV. Overcoming a Novelty Rejection Under 35 U.S.C. Section 102

[Insert before Section A.]

Design patents must meet the same novelty requirements as utility patents.[23]

V. Overcoming an Obviousness Rejection Under 35 U.S.C. Section 103

A. Scope and Content of the Prior Art

[Insert after footnote 130.]

Sash Controls, Inc. v. Talon, L.L.C.[24] is an example of a case in which two prior art references were considered to be within the analogous art of a design application. The design patent owned by Sash (Sash patent) related to sliding glass door handles involving a handle connected by risers to an escutcheon plate, which in turn attached the handle to the door. Talon argued that the district court properly found that the claimed design of the patent was obvious in light of the teachings of a related patent, U.S. Des. No. 320,334 to Clancy (Clancy patent), and a second reference to Baldwin (Baldwin reference). Although the Baldwin reference pictured a handle for a pivoting door and not a sliding glass door, Talon argued that it was analogous art.

The Federal Circuit noted that the principal difference between the prior art design of the Clancy patent and the design of the Sash patent was the rounding of the ends of the escutcheon plate. The Baldwin reference taught such rounding for an escutcheon plate. Sash argued, however, that a designer of patio door handles would not look to Baldwin because it related to a swing door handle requiring a twisting action, whereas a patio door handle of the Sash patent required a pulling action.

In holding that the Baldwin reference was analogous to the design in the Sash patent, the Federal Circuit stated the following:

> The Baldwin reference, however, provides a teaching of the rounding of the corners of the escutcheon plate, not a teaching involving the door

[23] *See* Avia Group Int'l v. L.A. Gear Cal., Inc., 853 F.2d 1557, 1563, 7 USPQ 2d 1548, 1553 (Fed. Cir. 1988); Sash Controls, Inc. v. Talon, L.L.C., Civ. App. No. 98-1152, slip op. at 7 (Fed. Cir. Jan. 27, 1999) (unpublished).

[24] Sash Controls, Inc. v. Talon, L.L.C., Civ. App. No. 98-1152 (Fed. Cir. Jan. 27, 1999) (unpublished).

> handle itself. . . . Both a patio door handle and a swing door handle require the mounting escutcheon plate. We find that the designer of ordinary capability of patio door handles would look to swing door handle art for such common features as the escutcheon plate. Therefore, Baldwin is analogous art and provides the missing teaching of the rounding of the corners of the escutcheon plate.[25]

[25] *Id.*, slip op. at 8.

12

Post-Issuance Actions: Reissue, Reexamination, Certificates of Correction, and Maintenance Fees [New]

I. Introduction to Post-Issuance Actions

The prosecution of a patent application does not end when the Patent Office issues a patent. The patentee may discover an error in the patent and may therefore need to correct the error. The patentee may also discover that the claims of the patent are too narrow or too broad, or that they otherwise fail to protect the full scope of the invention. In certain circumstances, a third party may challenge the patentability of an invention after the patent is issued. Finally, even if a patent is without error, adequately protects the invention, and is not the subject of challenge, the patentee will be required to pay certain maintenance fees during the life of the patent in order to keep the patent in force during its entire term.

Reissue, reexaminations, and issuances of Certificates of Correction have many similarities and are generally treated similarly with respect to judicial review.[1] Examples of the similarities between the provisions include: all three provisions are located within Title 35, Chapter 25 of the United States Code; the Patent Statute makes clear that the effect of a reissued patent, a reexamined patent, and a patent for which a Certificate of Correction has been granted are the same: all have the full force and effect of the original issued patent; and all three proceedings are conducted, with limited exceptions, *ex parte* in the Patent Office. Since the three types of proceedings are so similar in their purpose and effect, logic dictates the conclusion that Congress intended the same framework for judicial review to apply under all three provisions.[2] This is true even though the reexamination and reissue sections of the Patent Statute are comprehensive and implicitly preclude judicial review, whereas the Certificate of Correction section is more general and completely silent on the issue of judicial review.[3]

This chapter discusses the correction of errors and the amendment of a patent through reissue, reexamination, and Certificates of Correction. It also describes the maintenance fees and due dates that a patent holder must know in order to keep a patent in force.

II. Reissue

A. Statutory Authority

The reissue process allows a patentee to correct errors in the patent that arose without deceptive intent. The Supreme Court articulated the fundamental elements of the reissue process some time ago in *Topliff v. Topliff*:[4]

> To hold that a patent can never be reissued for an enlarged claim would be not only to override the obvious intent of the statute, but would operate in many cases with great hardship upon the patentee. The specification and claims of a patent, particularly if the invention be at all

[1] Hallmark Cards Inc. v. Lehman, 959 F. Supp. 539, 42 USPQ 2d 1134, 1138 (D.D.C. 1997).

[2] *Id.*, 42 USPQ 2d at 1138.

[3] Participation by third parties in reissue proceedings is limited to the protest provision, from which there is no appeal. 37 C.F.R. § 1.291. Participation in reexamination proceedings is limited to a request for reexamination and a reply to the patent owner's statement. 37 C.F.R. §§ 1.510, 1.535. The requester may not actively participate further and may not appeal. 37 C.F.R. § 1.552(e); Syntex (U.S.A.) Inc. v. United States Patent and Trademark Office, 882 F.2d 1570, 11 USPQ 2d 1866, 1870–71 (Fed. Cir. 1989).

[4] Topliff v. Topliff, 145 U.S. 156 (1892).

> complicated, constitute one of the most difficult legal instruments to draw with accuracy, and in view of the fact that valuable inventions are often placed in the hands of inexperienced persons to prepare such specifications and claims, it is no matter of surprise that the latter frequently fail to describe with requisite certainty the exact invention of the patentee, and err either in claiming that which the patentee had not in fact invented, or in omitting some element which was a valuable or essential part of his actual invention. Under such circumstances, it would be manifestly unjust to deny him the benefit of a reissue to secure to him his actual invention, provided it is evident that there has been a mistake and he had been guilty of no want of reasonable diligence in discovering it, and no third persons have in the meantime acquired the right to manufacture or sell what he had failed to claim. The object of the patent law is to secure to inventors a monopoly of what they have actually invented or discovered, and it ought not to be defeated by a too strict and technical adherence to the letter of the statute, or by the application of artificial rules of interpretation.[5]

The statutory authority for the reissue procedure is 35 U.S.C. Section 251. Section 251 states:

> Whenever any patent is, through error without any deceptive intention, deemed wholly or partly inoperative or invalid, by reason of a defective specification or drawing, or by reason of the patentee claiming more or less than he had a right to claim in the patent, the Director shall, on the surrender of such patent and the payment of the fee required by law, reissue the patent for the invention disclosed in the original patent, and in accordance with a new and amended application, for the unexpired part of the term of the original patent. No new matter shall be introduced into the application for reissue.
>
> The Director may issue several reissued patents for distinct and separate parts of the thing patented, upon demand of the applicant, and upon payment of the required fee for a reissue for each of such reissued patents.
>
> The provisions of this title relating to applications for patent shall be applicable to applications for reissue of a patent, except that application for reissue may be made and sworn to by the assignee of the entire interest if the application does not seek to enlarge the scope of the claims of the original patent.
>
> No reissued patent shall be granted enlarging the scope of the claims of the original patent unless applied for within two years from the grant of the original patent.[6]

B. Requirements for Reissue

Section 251 describes five elements that a patentee must satisfy in order to obtain the reissue of a patent. These elements that comprise the prima facie case entitling the patentee to reissue are:

1. The patent must be invalid or inoperative.
2. The defect must have arisen through error and without deceptive intent.
3. There must be no new matter in the reissue application.

---

[5] *Id.* at 171.

[6] 35 U.S.C. § 251 (1994).

4. If the reissue application seeks to enlarge the scope of the claims, the reissue application must be filed within two years of the date of the original patent grant.
5. The subject matter claimed in the reissue application must be patentable.

Accordingly, an applicant who is unable to demonstrate that these five elements are satisfied likely will not obtain a reissue of the patent. Each element is discussed in further detail in the following subsections.

1. Element 1: The Patent Must Be Invalid or Inoperative

A patentee may seek reissue of a patent to correct an error or a defect in the patent. Courts liberally interpret the "error" to which reissue may apply.[7] Such errors can include claims that are too narrow, claims that are too broad, a disclosure that contains inaccuracies, or an application that fails to or incorrectly claims foreign priority or other priority.

The error may be discovered by persons other than the patentee, such as the Examiner.[8]

That the error was discovered by another (in this case the Examiner) does not diminish the assertion in the supplemental reissue declaration that the original patent is wholly or partly inoperative or invalid because of the ambiguity, or the assertion that the error arose without any deceptive intention.[9]

A patent attorney's or patent agent's failure to appreciate the scope of the invention is "one of the most common sources of defects" for which reissue is sought.[10] As stated by the Federal Circuit:

> One of the most commonly asserted "errors" in support of a broadening reissue is the failure of the patentee's attorney to appreciate the full scope of the invention during the prosecution of the original patent application. . . . This form of error has generally been accepted as sufficient to satisfy the "error" requirement of 251.[11]

For example, if the inventor's attorney failed to appreciate the scope of the invention and thus drafted claims that are too narrow, the inventor may seek correction through reissue.[12] Similarly, if the attorney failed to correctly understand the scope of the prior art, that "error" may also be corrected via the reissue process. For example, in *In re Wilder*,[13] the Federal Circuit stated the following:

---

[7] *See* Mentor Corp. v. Coloplast, Inc., 998 F.2d 992, 27 USPQ 2d 1521, 1524 (Fed. Cir. 1993).

[8] *In re* Altenpohl, 500 F.2d 1151, 183 USPQ 38, 43 (C.C.P.A. 1974).

[9] *Id.*

[10] Hester Indus., Inc. v. Stein, Inc., 142 F.3d 1472, 46 USPQ 2d 1641, 1647 (Fed. Cir.), *cert. denied,* 525 U.S. 947 (1998); *Mentor,* 27 USPQ 2d at 1524.

[11] *Hester*, 46 USPQ 2d at 1647.

[12] *In re* Wilder, 736 F.2d 1516, 222 USPQ 369, 371–72 (Fed. Cir. 1984), *cert. denied*, 469 U.S. 1209 (1985).

[13] *In re* Wilder, 736 F.2d 1516, 222 USPQ 369 (Fed. Cir. 1984), *cert. denied*, 469 U.S. 1209 (1985).

> These statements in the declarations accompanying the reissue application show that the error relied upon is the attorney's failure to appreciate the full scope of the invention. That error arose because the attorney assumed the presence of features in the prior art that were not there. The board concluded this is not error that may be corrected through reissue because the defect could have been discovered during prosecution of the original patent. The board said, "there may have been a lack of prescience of the existence of a genus but such lack of prescience does not constitute an error in the sense of section 251." . . . An attorney's failure to appreciate the full scope of the invention is one of the most common sources of defects in patents. The fact that the error could have been discovered at the time of prosecution with a more thorough patentability search or with improved communication between the inventors and the attorney does not, by itself, preclude a patent owner from correcting defects through reissue. . . . Under these circumstances, the attorney's explanation of his error in misunderstanding the scope of the invention is sufficient to satisfy the error requirement of 35 U.S.C. 251. We accordingly reverse the board's rejection for failure to allege error correctable through reissue.[14]

Courts have also permitted the use of reissue to correct other defects in claims. For example, in *In re Altenpohl*,[15] the patentee used the phrase "said support post" in a dependent claim without providing an antecedent basis for the support post in the corresponding independent claim. The error remained in the issued patent, and the court held that reissue may be used to cure such an ambiguity by adding the antecedent basis to the independent claim.[16] As stated by the CCPA:

> Lack of antecedent basis in a claim could render it invalid under 35 USC 112, second paragraph, and correction of such a defect by reissue should not have to depend on difference in scope of the claim. Inasmuch as 35 USC 251 is a remedial provision, which should be liberally construed, a patentee should be allowed to correct an error or ambiguity in a claim without having to rely on implication or litigation.[17]

Reissue may also be used to correct inaccuracies in the specification or drawings. For example, in *In re Oda*,[18] an error had occurred in the translation of a Japanese specification into English. The error resulted in the term "nitric acid" appearing in the specification as "nitrous acid." The court allowed the patentee to correct the mistake through reissue.

Courts have even allowed a patentee to correct procedural defects such as claims of foreign priority or the failure to join all inventors. For example, where a patentee failed to file a certified copy of a foreign application before the required deadline, and thus failed to obtain the priority date of that application, the court allowed the patentee to correct the claim to foreign priority through a reissue application.[19] The

---

[14] *Id.*, 222 USPQ at 371–72.

[15] *In re* Altenpohl, 500 F.2d 1151, 183 USPQ 38 (C.C.P.A. 1974).

[16] *Id.*, 183 USPQ at 43.

[17] *Id.*

[18] *In re* Oda, 443 F.2d 1200, 170 USPQ 268 (C.C.P.A. 1971).

[19] Israel v. Brenner, 273 F. Supp. 714, 155 USPQ 486, 488 (D.D.C. 1967).

U.S. District Court for the District of Columbia set forth the reasoning for allowing reissue for the purpose of correcting a claim to priority as follows:

> In light of the foregoing discussion, the Court concludes that the phrase "claim in the patent" as used in Section 251 includes a claim to a right of priority on the basis of a foreign filing date and is not limited to claims defining the invention; that a patent may be reissued for the purpose of establishing a claim to priority which was not asserted, or which was not perfected during the prosecution of the original application; and that, accordingly, the plaintiff is entitled to a reissue of its patent.[20]

Similarly, the Patent Office has held that a reissue application may be filed for the purpose of correcting a claim to domestic priority under 35 U.S.C. Section 120, particularly where the patentee had previously substantially complied with the requirements for claiming priority.[21] The courts have gone so far as to allow amendments to abandoned applications to include technical information relating to the claim to priority as well.[22]

In another case, where it was discovered that one of several joint inventors was the sole inventor of some of the claimed subject matter in a patent that was issued to the joint inventors, the sole inventor was permitted to obtain a reissue patent naming him as the sole inventor of the subject matter of which he was the sole inventor.[23]

However, if a patentee files a reissue application without seeking any change in the specification or claims, the application will be dismissed. For example, in a case where a patentee filed a reissue application merely to argue that the Patent Office erred by failing to declare an interference between two copending applications, the court upheld the Patent Office's rejection of the application because it did not include a request to change the specification or claim.[24] Further, reissue does not provide a patentee with "a second opportunity to prosecute *de novo* his original application."[25]

a. The Recapture Rule

The recapture of subject matter that the patentee deliberately canceled or withdrew in order to obtain issuance in the prosecution of an original application is not generally an "error" upon which reissue may be granted.[26] This prohibition, which is known as the "recapture rule," prohibits a patentee from adding or amending claims that are the

---

[20] *Id.*

[21] Sampson v. Commissioner, 195 USPQ 136, 137–38 (D.D.C. 1976) (reissue applicant who substantially complied with 35 U.S.C. Section 120 is entitled to have amendments entered to include filing dates of prior abandoned applications in chain).

[22] *Id.* at 137.

[23] *Ex parte* Scudder, 169 USPQ 814, 815 (B.P.A.I. 1971).

[24] *In re* Keil, 808 F.2d 830, 1 USPQ 2d 1427, 1428 (Fed. Cir. 1987).

[25] *In re* Weiler, 790 F.2d 1576, 229 USPQ 673, 677 (Fed. Cir. 1986).

[26] *In re* Willingham, 282 F.2d 353, 127 USPQ 211, 215 (C.C.P.A. 1960).

same or of broader scope than those deliberately canceled or narrowed during prosecution of the original patent in order to obtain allowance of the original claims.[27] In essence, the recapture rule prevents a patentee from obtaining a patent on a claim that the patentee has admitted was not in fact patentable.[28] As stated by the Federal Circuit:

> If a patentee tries to recapture what he or she previously surrendered in order to obtain allowance of original patent claims, that "deliberate withdrawal or amendment . . . cannot be said to involve the inadvertence or mistake contemplated by 35 U.S.C. 251, and is not an error of the kind which will justify the granting of a reissue patent which includes the matter withdrawn." . . . "The recapture rule bars the patentee from acquiring, through reissue, claims that are of the same or of broader scope than those claims that were cancelled from the original application." . . . The recapture rule does not apply where there is no evidence that amendment of the originally filed claims was in any sense an admission that the scope of that claim was not in fact patentable.[29]

The Federal Circuit has established a four-step analysis for determining whether reissue claims are invalid for violating the recapture rule. This four-step analysis is:

- whether and in what aspect the reissue claims are broader than the claims of the original patent;
- whether the broader aspects of the reissue claims relate to surrendered subject matter;
- whether the surrendered subject matter has crept back into the reissue claim; and
- whether the reissue claims, although broadened, were materially narrowed in other ways so as to avoid the recapture rule.[30]

The recapture rule prevents a patentee from using reissue to prosecute de novo the original application.[31] It also serves effectively as an estoppel to ensure that competitors who rely on prosecution history do not later become infringers.

In judging whether the recapture rule applies, the Federal Circuit has explained:

> [T]he following principles flow: (1) if the reissue claim is as broad as or broader than the canceled or amended claim in all aspects, the recapture rule bars the claim; (2) if it is narrower in all aspects, the recapture rule does not apply, but other rejections are possible; (3) if the reissue claim is broader in some aspects, but narrower in others, then: (a) if the reissue claim is as broad as or broader in an aspect germane to a prior art rejec-

[27] *In re* Clement, 131 F.3d 1467, 45 USPQ 2d 1161, 1164 (Fed. Cir. 1997); Haliczer v. United States, 356 F.2d 541, 148 USPQ 565, 569 (Ct. Cl. 1966); Mentor Corp. v. Coloplast, Inc., 998 F.2d 992, 27 USPQ 2d 1521, 1524 (Fed. Cir. 1993).

[28] *See* Seattle Box Co. v. Industrial Crating & Packing, Inc., 731 F.2d 818, 221 USPQ 568, 574 (Fed. Cir. 1984).

[29] Mentor Corp. v. Coloplast, Inc., 998 F.2d 992, 27 USPQ 2d 1521, 1525 (Fed. Cir. 1993) (quoting Haliczer v. United States, 356 F.2d 541, 545, 148 USPQ 565, 569 (Ct. Cl. 1966); Ball Corp. v. United States, 729 F.2d 1429, 1436, 221 USPQ 289, 295 (Fed. Cir. 1984)).

[30] *See Clement*, 45 USPQ 2d at 1163–65.

[31] *In re* Weiler, 790 F.2d 1576, 229 USPQ 673, 677 (Fed. Cir. 1986).

> tion, but narrower in another aspect completely unrelated to the rejection, the recapture rule bars the claim; (b) if the reissue claim is narrower in an aspect germane to prior art rejection, and broader in an aspect unrelated to the rejection, the recapture rule does not bar the claim, but other rejections are possible.[32]

In determining whether there was a surrender of claimed material, the prosecution history of the patent will be examined for evidence of an admission regarding patentability by the applicant.[33] It is also notable that a surrender can occur through argument alone.[34]

Claim amendments are particularly relevant to the recapture rule because "an amendment to overcome a prior art rejection evidences an admission that the claim was not patentable."[35] Thus, an amendment that removes a limitation that was specifically introduced into the claim during prosecution can trigger the prohibition of the recapture rule. In addition, a claim "by the inclusion of an additional limitation [has] exactly the same effect as if the claim as originally presented had been canceled and replaced by a new claim including that limitation."[36] Because the recapture rule bars a reissue claim that is the same as a deliberately canceled claim, it also bars a reissue claim that differs from the canceled claim only by being broader.[37] Further, the recapture rule may also apply to disclaimed claims.[38] For example, the Federal Circuit has stated the following:

> Arguments made to overcome prior art can equally evidence an admission sufficient to give rise to a finding of surrender. . . . Logically, this is true even when the arguments are made in the absence of any claim amendment. Amendment of a claim is not the only permissible predicate for establishing a surrender.[39]

The recapture rule is similar to prosecution history estoppel, which prevents the application of the doctrine of equivalents in a manner contrary to the patent's prosecution history. Like the recapture rule, prosecution history estoppel prevents a patentee from regaining subject matter surrendered during prosecution in support of patentability.[40]

The deliberate cancellation of a claim of an original application in order to secure a patent cannot ordinarily be said to be an "error" and will in most cases prevent the applicant from obtaining the canceled claim by reissue. The extent to which it may also prevent him or her from obtaining other claims differing in form or substance from that

---

[32] *In re* Clement, 131 F.3d 1467, 45 USPQ 2d 1161, 1165 (Fed. Cir. 1997).

[33] Hester Indus., Inc. v. Stein, Inc., 142 F.3d 1472, 46 USPQ 2d 1641, 1648 (Fed. Cir.), *cert. denied*, 525 U.S. 947 (1998).

[34] *Id.*

[35] *Id.*

[36] *In re* Byers, 230 F.2d 451, 109 USPQ 53, 55 (C.C.P.A. 1956).

[37] *Id.*, 109 USPQ at 56.

[38] Vectra Fitness, Inc. v. TNWK Corp., 162 F.3d 1379, 49 USPQ 2d 1144, 1148 (Fed. Cir. 1998).

[39] Hester Indus., Inc. v. Stein, Inc., 142 F.3d 1472, 46 USPQ 2d 1641, 1648 (Fed. Cir.), *cert. denied*, 525 U.S. 947 (1998).

[40] *Id.*, 46 USPQ 2d at 1649.

canceled claim necessarily depends upon the facts in each case and particularly on the reasons for the cancellation.[41]

For example, in *In re Clement*,[42] the application related to a method for treating waste paper, and the originally issued claims included limitations requiring, among other things, that (1) force used in the process be greater than 50 kilowatt-hours per ton, and (2) process conditions include a pH of at least nine. During prosecution of the original application, the applicant specifically argued that the force and pH limitations were necessary to overcome the Examiner's rejection that the original claims (without the limitations) were anticipated by prior art. During reissue, the Examiner rejected the reissue claims that both added new limitations and sought to omit the force and pH conditions. The ground for the rejection was that the reissue sought to recapture deliberately canceled subject matter, even though the claims also introduced new limitations that narrowed the claims. The Board of Patent Appeals and Interferences (Board) affirmed the Examiner's decision, holding that the claims violated the recapture rule.

On appeal, the Federal Circuit affirmed the Board's decision, even though the reissue application introduced new limitations into the reissue claims, because the claims were "broader than they [were] narrower in a manner directly pertinent to the subject matter that [the applicant] surrendered during prosecution."[43]

As another example, in *Mentor Corp. v. Coloplast, Inc.*,[44] during prosecution of the claims of a patent covering a condom catheter, the patentee narrowed claims by adding a requirement that adhesive on the catheter be transferred from the outer to the inner surface as the catheter was unrolled. The amendment was made to overcome a rejection that was based on prior art. During reissue, the patentee sought to add reissue claims that did not include the adhesive requirement. The Federal Circuit, however, held that the attempt to add such claims was an impermissible recapture of surrendered material.[45]

However, if a reissue claim is broadened in a way that does not attempt to reclaim what was surrendered earlier, the recapture rule does not apply.[46] For example, in certain situations, limitations added during original prosecution *can* be removed during reissue. "Deliberately canceling or amending a claim in an effort to overcome a reference strongly suggests that the applicant admits that the scope of the claim before the cancellation or amendment is unpatentable, but it is not dispositive because other evidence in the prosecution history may indicate the contrary."[47]

---

[41]Mentor Corp. v. Coloplast, Inc., 998 F.2d 992, 995–96, 27 USPQ 2d 1521, 1524 (Fed. Cir. 1993).

[42]*In re* Clement, 131 F.3d 1467, 45 USPQ 2d 1161 (Fed. Cir. 1997).

[43]*Id.*, 45 USPQ 2d at 1161.

[44]Mentor Corp. v. Coloplast, Inc., 998 F.2d 992, 27 USPQ 2d 1521 (Fed. Cir. 1993).

[45]*Id.*, 27 USPQ 2d at 1526.

[46]*Id.* at 1525.

[47]*In re* Clement, 131 F.3d 1467, 45 USPQ 2d 1161, 1165 (Fed. Cir. 1997).

For example, in *Seattle Box Co. v. Industrial Crating & Packing, Inc.*,[48] the patent related to a system for bundling pipes that included a spacer block. During prosecution of the original application, the applicant's attorney amended claim 1 to specify that the spacer block must have a height that is greater than the diameter of the pipe that was being bundled. Soon after the amendment, the Patent Office issued the patent. The applicant subsequently applied for a reissue patent that included a claim that deleted the limitation relating to the size of the spacer block, arguing that the limitation was unnecessary and arose only through inadvertence by counsel. The Patent Office issued the reissue patent with the broadened claim. Later, in an infringement action, a third party argued that the reissue violated the recapture rule. The Federal Circuit, however, rejected the argument, stating that there was no evidence that the amendment of the originally filed claim was an admission that the scope of the original claim was unpatentable.[49]

As another example, in *Ball Corp. v. United States*,[50] the invention related to an antenna assembly that included a number of conductive "feedlines." During prosecution of the original application, the applicant added a limitation calling for a plurality of feedlines in order to overcome prior art. The original prosecution also included an amendment that required a "substantially cylindrical conductor," but that limitation was unrelated to the prior art rejection, and it was not argued to distinguish the claims from a prior art reference. On reissue, the patentee removed the "cylindrical" limitation from the claim, and the reissue patent subsequently issued. In a later infringement action, the reissue patent was challenged on the basis of, among other things, the recapture rule. The Federal Circuit, however, held that the recapture rule was inapplicable because the patentee was not attempting to recapture subject matter that was deliberately canceled in order to obtain the original patent.[51]

Courts have declined to apply the recapture rule in several other situations. For example, in *In re Willingham*,[52] the patent application included a claim relating to a deep hole drill comprising a drill tip secured to a hollow shank, the drill tip and shank having a plurality of flutes. The applicant amended the application to delete the claim and substitute a claim that required the flutes to be "straight" and "equally spaced." In a reissue application, the patentee sought a claim that removed the "straight" and "equally spaced" limitations. Because the Examiner had not rejected the original claim, and the record did not indicate that the claim was narrowed in order to overcome a prior art

[48] Seattle Box Co. v. Industrial Crating & Packing, Inc., 731 F.2d 818, 221 USPQ 568 (Fed. Cir. 1984).

[49] *Id.*, 221 USPQ at 574.

[50] Ball Corp. v. United States, 729 F.2d 1429, 221 USPQ 289 (Fed. Cir. 1984).

[51] *Id.*, 221 USPQ at 295; *see also In re* Clement, 131 F.3d 1467, 45 USPQ 2d 1161, 1166 (Fed. Cir. 1997).

[52] *In re* Willingham, 282 F.2d 353, 127 USPQ 211 (C.C.P.A. 1960).

rejection, the court held that the limitations were an error and that reissue was proper.[53]

Appendix C includes guidelines published by the U.S. Patent Office applying the recapture rule to reissue applications.

2. *Element 2: Defect Arose Through Error and Without Deceptive Intent*

The error must have arisen without deceptive intent, or else a reissue application will be denied. "Deceptive intent" means actual fraud or other forms of inequitable conduct. Inequitable conduct "requires a finding of an intent to mislead or deceive" the Patent Office, usually through inference from circumstantial evidence.[54]

Regarding "intent to mislead," the Federal Circuit stated the following in *In re Weiler*:[55]

> References to "intent to claim" in our cases, though occasionally including § 112 considerations, resolve ultimately into the question of error. "Determining what protection [an inventor] intended to secure by [an] original patent for the purposes of § 251 is an essentially factual inquiry confined to the *objective* intent manifested by the original patent." *In re Rowand*, 526 F.2d 558, 560, 187 USPQ 487, 489 (C.C.P.A. 1975) (emphasis in original). As explained in a later decision, *Rowand*'s test of "intent to claim" was not one of "intent" per se, but looked to "objective indicia of intent." *In re Mead*, 581 F.2d 251, 256, 198 USPQ 412, 417 (C.C.P.A. 1978). . . .
>
> This court has recently moved the "intent to claim" approach toward closer conformity with the statute, describing it as merely one factor "that sheds light upon whether the claims of the reissue application are directed to the same invention as the original patent *and the reissue would correct an inadvertent error in the original patent*." *In re Hounsfield*, 669 F.2d 1320, 1323, 216 USPQ 1045, 1048 (Fed. Cir. 1982) (emphasis added).

The Federal Circuit further stated in *Hester Industries, Inc. v. Stein, Inc.*:[56]

> This court squarely addressed the issue in *Amos*, 953 F.2d at 616, 21 USPQ 2d at 1273. The *Amos* court held that § 251 does not include a separate requirement of an objective intent to claim. . . . Rather, the court concluded: "the essential inquiry under the 'original patent' clause of § 251 . . . is whether one skilled in the art, reading the specification, would identify the subject matter of the new claims as invented and disclosed by the patentees." *Id.* at 618, 21 USPQ 2d at 1275. The court noted that this inquiry is analogous to the "written description" requirement of 35 U.S.C. § 112 ¶1 (1994). *Id.* The court further stated that, to the extent the construct of an objective intent to claim is useful,

[53] *Id.*, 127 USPQ at 215.

[54] *See* Hewlett-Packard Co. v. Bausch & Lomb, Inc., 882 F.2d 1556, 11 USPQ 2d 1750, 1755 (Fed. Cir. 1989), *cert. denied*, 493 U.S. 1076 (1990).

[55] *In re* Weiler, 790 F.2d 1576, 229 USPQ 673, 676–77 (Fed. Cir. 1986).

[56] Hester Indus., Inc. v. Stein, Inc., 142 F.3d 1472, 46 USPQ 2d 1641, 1651 (Fed. Cir.), *cert. denied*, 525 U.S. 947 (1998).

it is "only one factor that sheds light" on whether the "original patent" clause of § 251 is satisfied.

In a case where an applicant offered an amendment to a claim and gave the Examiner the option to either accept the amendment or retain the preamendment claim language, the court refused to find deceptive intent on the part of either the applicant or the Examiner. Rather, the court viewed the applicant's reliance on the Examiner's discretion as the applicant's good faith appreciation of the Examiner's competency.[57]

The "intent to claim" requirement constitutes judicial shorthand denoting whether the requirement of the reissue statute, 35 U.S.C. Section 251, for "error" has been established, and objective indicia of intent must be evaluated in determining "intent to claim."[58] The filing of the reissue application to legitimately attempt to limit the claims simply as a hedge against possible invalidity of the original claims has been considered to fall within a category of error for which the reissue statute applies.[59]

For example, in *Ex parte Larkin*,[60] the invention related to a packaged foodstuff comprising a food grade vinyl halide polymer stabilized with a particular monoalkyltin compound. The claims were rejected under 35 U.S.C. Section 251 as lacking statutory basis for reissue. The rationale underpinning the Examiner's rejection was that the applicant Larkin's failure to claim a packaged foodstuff in the application upon which the patent issued did not constitute an "error" within the meaning of 35 U.S.C. Section 251, since there was no intent to claim the packaged foodstuff in the original application.

On appeal, the Board reversed. The Board noted that the reissue statute is remedial in nature and based upon fundamental principles of equity and fairness. Accordingly, the reissue statute is to be construed liberally.[61] However, the Board also emphasized that the reissue statute was not intended as a panacea for any problem that arose during patent prosecution or to afford a patentee the opportunity to prosecute an application a second time de novo.[62]

The Board explained that, based upon a review of the patent for which Larkin sought reissue, it was abundantly clear that the entire thrust of the invention was an improvement in food packaging by utilizing a particular monoalkyltin stabilizer. The Board further noted that Larkin pointed out objective support in the patent for the conclusion that the essence of the disclosed invention was an improvement in

---

[57]*In re*, Willingham, 282 F.2d 353, 127 USPQ 211, 215 (C.C.P.A. 1960).

[58]*In re* Mead, 581 F.2d 251, 256, 198 USPQ 412, 417 (C.C.P.A. 1978).

[59]*In re* Handel, 312 F.2d 943, 136 USPQ 460, 464 (C.C.P.A. 1963) ("Yet the whole purpose of the [reissue] statute, so far as claims are concerned, is to permit limitations to be added to claims that are too broad or to be taken from claims that are too narrow.").

[60]*Ex parte* Larkin, 9 USPQd 2d 1078 (B.P.A.I. 1988).

[61]*Id.* at 1079 (citing *In re* Bennett, 766 F.2d 524, 226 USPQ 413, 416 (Fed. Cir. 1985) (en banc)).

[62]*Id.* at 1080.

food packaging. In addition, the preamble of claim 1 of the patent characterized the stabilizer as "A food grade liquid organotin stabilizer for polyvinyl chloride . . ."[63] The Board also noted that the only disclosed utility of the stabilizer in the patent was for food packaging material.

Under the facts of this particular case, it was the Board's opinion that the food grade monoalkyltin stabilizer previously claimed was inextricably linked to the later claimed packaged foodstuff comprising a food grade vinyl halide polymer stabilized with that particular monoalkyltin compound in the reissue application. Accordingly, the Board held that Larkin's failure to claim the packaged foodstuff in the original application constituted the "error" capable of being remedied by the reissue statute.[64]

Thus, the Board in *Larkin* held that an applicant's failure to claim, in original application, claim limitations added by reissue that were inextricably linked to the originally claimed invention constituted "error" capable of being remedied by the reissue statute, and such reissue application was a legitimate attempt to limit the claims as a hedge against the possible invalidity of the original claims.

3. Element 3: No New Matter

A patentee may not add new matter to the specification or claims of a patent through reissue. "Where a patent is fatally defective, e.g., invalid for inadequate disclosure, such a defect cannot be cured by reissue seeking to put into the specification something required to be there when the patent application was originally filed."[65] Thus, a patentee may not use reissue to correct, for example, the failure to disclose a best mode. Rather, reissue merely allows a patentee to modify the claims or the disclosure, based on what the patentee has already disclosed.

For example, in *In re Hay*,[66] the original patent related to an electrical resistor that was embedded in a plastic housing. However, in an infringement suit, the patent was held to be invalid because it failed to disclose the only type of plastic that the patentee found would work. In reissue, the patentee sought to add to the specification a sentence describing that type of plastic. However, the addition was prohibited because it comprised new matter.[67]

Because a patentee cannot add new matter to the specification through reissue, the reissue claims must be for the same general invention as was claimed in the original patent.[68] The "same general

---

[63] *Id.*

[64] *Id.*

[65] *In re* Hay, 534 F.2d 917, 189 USPQ 790, 792 (C.C.P.A.), *cert. denied*, 429 U.S. 977 (1976).

[66] *In re* Hay, 534 F.2d 917, 189 USPQ 790 (C.C.P.A.), *cert. denied*, 429 U.S. 977 (1976).

[67] *Id.*, 189 USPQ at 792.

[68] 35 U.S.C. § 251.

invention" can, in some cases, include items not expressly disclosed in the original application. For example, in *In re Peters & Anderson*,[69] the original patent specification disclosed and claimed a flat panel television display device comprised of, among other things, tapered metal tips. The patentee sought a reissue patent that would remove the limitation that required the tips to be tapered. The Federal Circuit found that one skilled in the art "would readily understand that in practicing the invention it is unimportant whether the tips were tapered."[70] The court thus held that the reissue application was allowable because the applicant merely sought to remove an unnecessary limitation.[71]

A patentee should take care that material incorporated by reference is properly incorporated in the original application, or else later inclusion of the improperly incorporated material could be viewed as an attempt to capture new matter. For example, where a patent application refers to a parent application (e.g., a continuation, continuation-in-part, or division), unless the application is a continued prosecution application, the application must expressly state that it incorporates the parent application by reference. Otherwise, all material in the parent application is not necessarily a part of the surviving application, and the applicant will be required to provide additional information to show that the application includes other information showing the applicant intended to incorporate by reference the parent application.[72]

In certain cases, courts have found that the simple broadening of a claim by removing a claim limitation comprised the addition of "new matter" to a patent. For example, in *Ballew v. Watson*,[73] the patent claimed a magnetic fishing tool having a basket feature. The specification emphasized the basket feature in several places, noting that the basket feature provided a significant advantage over prior art magnetic fishing tools. After the patent issued, the patentee filed a reissue application that included a claim that omitted the basket feature. The district court held that the removal of the limitation would "create newness" or new matter because a different invention would result that was not disclosed in the original application.[74]

At least one court has stated that the term "new matter" has "never been clearly defined for it cannot be."[75] Rather, it is determined on a case-by-case basis. Just because something is inserted into the application that was not there before does not necessarily mean that it is new matter.[76] For example, where commonly owned applications were incorporated by reference into the original application, the reissue could include specific matter taken from the applications that were incorpo-

---

[69] *In re* Peters & Anderson, 723 F.2d 891, 221 USPQ 952 (Fed. Cir. 1983).

[70] *Id.*, 221 USPQ at 953.

[71] *Id.*

[72] *See In re* de Seversky, 474 F.2d 671, 177 USPQ 144, 146–47 (C.C.P.A. 1973).

[73] Ballew v. Watson, 290 F.2d 353, 129 USPQ 48 (D.C. Cir. 1959).

[74] *Id.*, 129 USPQ at 50.

[75] *In re* Oda, 443 F.2d 1200, 170 USPQ 268 (C.C.P.A. 1971).

[76] *Id.*

rated by reference.[77] Further, a change of wording to correct an error (such as an error in translation of a foreign specification) is not new matter if one skilled in the art would appreciate not only the existence of the error in the specification but also what the error is.[78] For a more detailed discussion on new matter, see Chapter 8, Section IV.

4. Element 4: Reissue Seeking to Enlarge Scope of Claims

Reissue can be a very valuable tool for a patentee because it allows a patentee to broaden the scope of a patent's claims after the patent has issued. As noted above, an attorney's failure to appreciate the full scope of the invention is a common type of error that is correctable through reissue.[79] Thus, in certain circumstances, a patent holder can correct the attorney's error by broadening the scope of the claims in a reissue patent application.

However, this ability to broaden a patent's claims is not without limitation. Specifically, broadening reissue is only available for the limited period of two years from the date of the patent grant. The two-year limit serves as a balance by providing a patentee with the opportunity to correct errors while ensuring that the public will know, with certainty after the two-year period, what is protected by a patent and what remains available to the public.[80] After the two-year period, subject matter disclosed in the specification but not claimed is dedicated to the public.[81] For this reason, competitors should not truly rely on the claims in a patent until two years after the patent grant. There is no time limit to file a reissue application if the claims will not be broadened.

A claim in a reissue application is broader than a claim in the original patent if the reissue claim "contains within its scope any conceivable apparatus or process which would not have infringed the original patent."[82] In other words, a claim is broadened with respect to the two-year limitation if it is broader in any respect, even if it is narrowed in other respects.[83] In addition, a claim is broader if it omits any limitation that was present in the original patent claims.[84] The two-year limit from the date of the patent grant also applies to claims that may have been disclaimed after the patent issued.[85]

---

[77] *In re* Goodwin, 43 USPQ 2d 1856, 1857 (Comm'r Pat. 1997).

[78] *Ex parte* Brodbeck, 199 USPQ 230, 231 (B.P.A.I. 1977); *see also In re* Oda, 443 F.2d 1200, 170 USPQ 268, 272 (C.C.P.A. 1971).

[79] Mentor Corp. v. Coloplast, Inc., 998 F.2d 992, 27 USPQ 2d 1521, 1524 (Fed. Cir. 1993).

[80] *In re* Graff, 111 F.3d 874, 42 USPQ 2d 1471, 1474 (Fed. Cir. 1997); *In re* Fotland, 779 F.2d 31, 228 USPQ 2d 193, 194 (Fed. Cir. 1985).

[81] *See* Maxwell v. J. Baker Inc., 86 F.3d 1098, 39 USPQ 2d 1001, 1006 (Fed. Cir. 1996), *cert. denied*, 520 U.S. 1115 (1997).

[82] Tillotson, Ltd. v. Walbro Corp., 831 F.2d 1033, 4 USPQ 2d 1450, 1453 n.2 (Fed. Cir. 1987).

[83] *Id.*

[84] Hester Indus., Inc. v. Stein, Inc., 142 F.3d 1472, 46 USPQ 2d 1641, 1649 (Fed. Cir.), *cert. denied*, 525 U.S. 947 (1998).

[85] Vectra Fitness, Inc. v. TNWK Corp., 162 F.3d 1379, 49 USPQ 2d 1144, 1148 (Fed. Cir. 1998).

A reissue applicant should note that the mere filing of a reissue application within the two-year period is not, in itself, enough to guarantee the availability of broadening reissue. Rather, the proposed broadened claims must also be filed within the two-year period.[86]

5. *Element 5: Subject Matter Claimed in Reissue Application Must Be Patentable*

A reissue application is examined in the same manner as an original application. Therefore, as with claims in an original application, claims in a reissue application must be patentable. The reissue claims must satisfy all typical requirements as claims in original applications, including utility, novelty, nonobviousness, enablement, written description, best mode, and definiteness. For example, the reissue claims will be rejected if not adequately supported by the disclosure of the original specification.[87] In *Hickory Springs Manufacturing Co. v. Fredman Bros. Furniture Co.*,[88] the specification described a combination bed assembly and stated that a superior result was achieved by the assembly's unique rail design. A reissue application sought to claim different rail designs. Because the rail designs were not supported by the specification, the reissue claims were rejected.[89]

C. Reissue Procedures

The first step in the reissue process is that the applicant must prepare and file the reissue application. Like original applications, a reissue application must contain a disclosure, any necessary drawings, and claims.[90] The specification of the reissue application must include the entire specification and claims of the original patent.[91] Any additions to the original specification or original claims must be underlined, and any deletions must be enclosed in square brackets.[92] No new drawings or amended drawings are permitted in a reissue application if such new drawings will introduce new matter into the reissue application. Rather, the reissue application may only use the drawings that were used in the original patent.[93]

A reissue oath or declaration is required.[94] All inventors and assignees must consent to the reissue, although the assignee can make

---

[86] *See In re* Graff, 111 F.3d 874, 42 USPQ 2d 1471, 1474 (Fed. Cir. 1997).

[87] *See In re* Doyle, 482 F.2d 1385, 179 USPQ 227, 232 (C.C.P.A. 1973), *cert. denied*, 416 U.S. 935 (1974).

[88] Hickory Springs Mfg. Co. v. Fredman Bros. Furniture Co., 338 F. Supp. 636, 173 USPQ 339 (S.D. Ill. 1972), *aff'd*, 509 F.2d 55, 184 USPQ 459 (7th Cir. 1975).

[89] *Id.*, 173 USPQ at 340.

[90] 37 C.F.R. § 1.171.

[91] 37 C.F.R. § 1.173.

[92] *Id.*

[93] 37 C.F.R. § 1.174(a).

[94] 37 C.F.R. §§ 1.172 and 1.175.

the oath or declaration alone if there is no broadening of claims.[95] The oath or declaration must state that the applicant believes the patent to be wholly or partially inoperative or invalid by reason of a defective specification or drawing, or by reason that the patentee claimed more or less than he or she had a right to claim.[96] The reissue declaration must also describe at least one error being relied on as the basis for reissue.[97] Further, it must state that the error arose without any deceptive intention on the part of the applicant.[98]

Prior to regulatory amendments that took effect in 1997, applicants were also required to make a factual showing of how the error arose in order to demonstrate a lack of deceptive intent.[99] However, current regulations only require a statement that there is no deceptive intent, as the Patent Office normally conducts no investigation and accepts such a statement on its face.[100] Additional information may be provided in the original declaration or in a supplemental declaration, as appropriate.[101]

The reissue application must include the original patent or an offer to surrender the patent.[102] If the original patent is lost, the applicant must include a declaration or affidavit explaining the loss.[103] If the applicant supplies the original patent and the Patent Office refuses reissue, the applicant may request that the Patent Office return the original patent.[104]

The applicant must also claim foreign priority, if applicable, as foreign priority claims in an original application do not carry through to a reissue.[105] The applicant must also include an information disclosure statement supplying prior art to be considered with respect to patentability, as the duty to disclose applies to reissue applications.[106] Of course, a filing fee will also apply.[107]

The provisions of the patent statutes generally relating to applications also apply to applications for reissue patents, and there may be more than one reissue patent for distinct and separate parts of the

---

[95] 37 C.F.R. § 1.172; *see also* Baker Hughes Inc. v. Kirk, 921 F. Supp. 801, 38 USPQ 2d 1885, 1892 (D.D.C. 1995).

[96] 37 C.F.R. § 1.175(a)(1).

[97] *Id.*

[98] 37 C.F.R. § 1.175(a)(2).

[99] Nupla Corp. v. IXL Mfg. Co., 114 F.3d 191, 42 USPQ 2d 1711, 1715 (Fed. Cir. 1997); *In re* Constant, 827 F.2d 728, 3 USPQ 2d 1479, 1480 (Fed. Cir.), *cert. denied*, 484 U.S. 894 (1987).

[100] 37 C.F.R. § 1.175(b)(1); 62 Fed. Reg. 53,132, 53,165–66 (Oct. 10, 1997).

[101] 37 C.F.R. § 1.175(b)(1).

[102] 37 C.F.R. § 1.178.

[103] *Id.*

[104] *Id.*

[105] M.P.E.P. § 1417.

[106] M.P.E.P. § 1429.

[107] 37 C.F.R. § 1.19(b)(4).

invention being patented.[108] Thus, continuation and divisional applications may be filed claiming priority to a reissue application.[109]

The two-year limitation on asserting claims broader than those in the original patent remains in effect with respect to divisional or continuation reissue applications.[110] In other words, an applicant may not submit broadened claims for the first time more than two years after the issuance of the original patent; the two-year limitation does not begin each time a subsequent application is filed.[111] In *In re Graff*,[112] the Federal Circuit considered this exact issue and reached the following conclusion:

> On [sic] this case, the public had no public notice that broadening was being sought until after the two-year period. We discern no justification for imposing this degree of uncertainty upon the public.[113]

As indicated above, the Patent Office will examine a reissue application in the same manner as an original application.[114] Notice of reissue will be published in the *Official Gazette*, and examination will not begin sooner than two months after publication of the notice.[115] Further, the reissue prosecution file is open to the public, and, therefore, the public will be able to obtain copies of all communications between the Patent Office and the reissue applicant.[116] The Patent Office will examine all claims de novo.[117]

D. Effect of Reissue

If the Examiner grants the reissue application, the reissue patent will have the same legal effect as the original patent. For example, the reissue will not change the term of the original patent. Further, to the extent that the original patent claims and reissue patent claims are identical, the reissue will not extinguish pending causes of action relating to the original patent.[118]

Section 252 of the Patent Act describes the full scope of the rights of a person who practices an invention prior to reissue. If, after the issuance of the original patent but before the issuance of the reissue, a third party made, purchased, or used an item or process covered by the

---

[108] 35 U.S.C. § 251 (1994); *In re* Graff, 111 F.3d 874, 42 USPQ 2d 1471, 1473 (Fed. Cir. 1997).

[109] *See Graff*, 42 USPQ 2d at 1473.

[110] *Id.*

[111] *Id.*

[112] *In re* Graff, 111 F.3d 874, 42 USPQ 2d 1471 (Fed. Cir. 1997).

[113] *Id.*, 42 USPQ 2d at 1474.

[114] *See* 37 C.F.R. § 1.176.

[115] *Id.*

[116] 37 C.F.R. § 1.11(b).

[117] 37 C.F.R. § 1.176.

[118] 35 U.S.C. § 252; Kaufman Co. v. Lantech Inc., 807 F.2d 970, 1 USPQ 2d 1202, 1206–07 (Fed. Cir. 1986).

claims of the reissue patent but not covered by the claims of the original patent, the third party will have an intervening right to continue to make, purchase, or use the invention and will not be prohibited from doing so in the future.[119] However, for claims having a scope identical to the original claims, liability can exist for infringing activities that occurred before the reissue date.[120] In addition, the third party will be allowed to slightly modify the invention covered by the intervening right so long as the modifications are essentially repairs and do not transform the invention.[121]

Reissue can be a useful mechanism by which a patentee may prepare a patent for litigation. For example, if the patentee sees potential problems with existing claim language, the patentee may be able to revise the language through reissue before initiating an infringement action. Reissue can also be used to narrow claims to avoid newly discovered references, or to broaden claims to capture a third-party action that barely avoids literal infringement.

The filing of a reissue application may also give a patentee a mechanism to provoke an interference. The Patent Office has no authority to declare an interference between two issued patents.[122] However, the Patent Office may declare an interference between an issued patent and a pending application, including a reissue application.[123]

The reissue patent will not issue until the patentee provides the Examiner with a surrender of the original patent grant.[124] The reissue patent will be printed in a manner that shows the changes from the original patent. Thus, all original patent claims, including canceled claims (in brackets), will be reprinted in a reissue patent.

E. Potential Pitfalls of Reissue

A patentee who seeks reissue should consider the effects that reissue may have on the claims of the original patent. All claims in a reissue application, including claims identical to those in the patent, are subject to review and possible rejection.[125] "Reissue is essentially a reprosecution of all claims."[126] It does not matter that a rejection was not made, or was made and dropped, during prosecution of the original application. For example, in *L.E.A. Dynatech Inc. v. Allina*,[127] the plaintiff sought a declaratory judgment of noninfringement and unenforceabil-

---

[119]*Kaufman,* 1 USPQ 2d at 1206–07.

[120]Laitram Corp. v. NEC Corp., 952 F.2d 1357, 21 USPQ 2d 1276, 1278 (Fed. Cir. 1991).

[121]*Id.*; Cohen v. United States, 487 F.2d 525, 179 USPQ 859, 861 (Ct. Cl. 1973).

[122]35 U.S.C. § 135.

[123]Slip Track Sys., Inc. v. Metal Lite, Inc., 159 F.3d 1337, 48 USPQ 2d 1055, 1056 (Fed. Cir. 1998).

[124]37 C.F.R. § 1.178.

[125]M.P.E.P. § 1445.

[126]Hewlett-Packard Co. v. Bausch & Lomb, Inc., 882 F.2d 1556, 11 USPQ 2d 1750, 1756 (Fed. Cir. 1989), *cert. denied*, 493 U.S. 1076 (1990).

[127]L.E.A. Dynatech Inc. v. Allina, 49 F.3d 1527, 33 USPQ 2d 1840 (Fed. Cir. 1995).

ity of five patents, while the patentee counterclaimed on the basis of infringement of one of the patents. While the suit was pending, the patentee filed a reissue application on the patent that was the subject of the counterclaim without informing the court or the plaintiff. After reviewing the reissue application, the Patent Office rejected all claims that were set forth in the application, including the claims that the Patent Office had previously issued in the patent. Therefore, the district court dismissed all claims and counterclaims in the action (with respect to all patents) with prejudice.[128]

As another example, in *In re Graff*,[129] the patentee filed a reissue application, declaring that the error was that a figure in the patent as issued did not match the figure as filed. The patentee proposed no change in the claims. However, in accordance with Patent Office practice for reissue applications, the Examiner conducted a new prior art search. The Examiner discovered a new reference and rejected all the claims on the ground of obviousness.[130]

Further, as noted above, if the claims in the original and reissue patent are not identical, the patentee may only enforce the claims from the date of the reissue.[131] Therefore, existing infringement claims could be extinguished as a result of the reissue.

The prosecution files of a reissue application are open to the public.[132] Therefore, a reissue applicant should consider the possible effects of public view of the files. For example, if an infringement proceeding is pending, the defendant could review the file and use statements made during prosecution, or the defendant could also bring prior art to the Patent Office in an attempt to defend the claims.[133]

III. Ex Parte Reexamination

A. Introduction to Ex Parte Reexamination

In general, after a patent issues, the Patent Office has no further authority to examine the patentability of the subject invention. However, in 1980, Congress passed the reexamination statute,[134] which permits the Patent Office to review issued patents for substantial new questions of patentability in certain situations. The reexamination process effectively serves as a "quality control" mechanism to cure defects in government action. Unlike reissue, which has been part of the

[128] *Id.*, 33 USPQ 2d at 1841.

[129] *In re* Graff, 111 F.3d 874, 42 USPQ 2d 1471 (Fed. Cir. 1997).

[130] *Id.*, 42 USPQ 2d at 1472.

[131] 35 U.S.C. § 252; Kaufman Co. v. Lantech Inc., 807 F.2d 970, 1 USPQ 2d 1202, 1206–07 (Fed. Cir. 1986).

[132] 37 C.F.R. § 1.11(b).

[133] *See* 35 U.S.C. § 301 (1994).

[134] Pub. L. No. 96-517, 94 Stat. 3015 (1980).

Patent Act and subject to judicial application for over a century, reexamination has only been available since the reexamination statute took effect on July 1, 1981.

The reexamination statute is codified at 35 U.S.C. Sections 301–307. Section 302 sets forth the basic availability of the reexamination procedure as follows:

> Any person at any time may file a request for reexamination by the Office of any claim of a patent on the basis of any prior art cited under the provisions of section 301 of this title. The request must be in writing and must be accompanied by payment of a reexamination fee established by the Director of Patents pursuant to the provisions of section 41 of this title. The request must set forth the pertinency and manner of applying cited prior art to every claim for which reexamination is requested. Unless the requesting person is the owner of the patent, the Director promptly will send a copy of the request to the owner of record of the patent.[135]

Within three months of receiving such a request, the Director determines whether the prior art raises a "substantial new question of patentability."[136] If the Director determines that it does, he or she must order reexamination of the patent. If he or she determines that the cited prior art raises no substantial new question of patentability, the request for reexamination is denied.[137] The "determination . . . that no substantial new question of patentability has been raised will be final and nonappealable."[138] The statute contains no provision for appeal or review of a determination that a substantial new question has been raised.

The Director's threshold determination merely triggers the reexamination proceeding; it does not affect the validity of the patent. As to the larger question of whether the cited patents and printed publications render the claims of the challenged patent unpatentable on the merits, the statute confers a right of appeal and court review.[139] A patent owner cannot avoid reexamination by seeking immediate judicial review, because at this stage there is no final agency action.[140] The legislative scheme of the reexamination statutes leave the Director's initial determination of whether a substantial new question of patentability exists entirely to the Director's discretion and not subject to judicial review.[141]

The reexamination statute was an important part of a larger effort to revive the United States' competitive vitality by restoring confidence in the validity of patents issued by the PTO.[142] Congressman Robert Kastenmeier described the reexamination proposal as "an effort to re-

---

[135] 35 U.S.C. § 302 (Supp. 2000) (changing title of Commissioner to Director).

[136] 35 U.S.C. § 303(a).

[137] 35 U.S.C. § 304.

[138] 35 U.S.C. § 303(c).

[139] 35 U.S.C. § 306.

[140] Patlex Corp. v. Quigg, 680 F. Supp. 33, 6 USPQ 2d 1296, 1298 (D.D.C. 1988).

[141] *Id.*

[142] Patlex Corp. v. Mossinghoff, 758 F.2d 594, 601, 225 USPQ 243, 248, *aff'd on reh'g*, 771 F.2d 480, 226 USPQ 985 (Fed. Cir. 1985).

verse the current decline in U.S. productivity by strengthening the patent and copyright systems to improve investor confidence in new technology."[143]

The proponents of reexamination anticipated three principal benefits. First, reexamination based on references that were not previously included in the patentability examination could resolve validity disputes more quickly and less expensively than litigation. Second, courts would benefit from the expertise of the PTO for prior art that was not previously of record. Third, reexamination would strengthen confidence in patents whose validity was clouded because pertinent prior art had not previously been considered by the PTO.[144] These benefits are achieved by authorizing the PTO to correct errors in the prior examination:

> The reexamination statute's purpose is to correct errors made by the government, to remedy defective governmental (not private) action, and if need be to remove patents that never should have been granted. . . . A defectively examined and therefore erroneously granted patent must yield to the reasonable Congressional purpose of facilitating the correction of governmental mistakes.[145]

However, Congress recognized that this broad purpose must be balanced against the potential for abuse, whereby unwarranted reexaminations can harass the patentee and waste the patent life. The legislative record and the record of the interested public reflect a serious concern that reexamination not create new opportunities for abusive tactics and burdensome procedures.[146] Thus, reexamination as enacted was carefully limited to new prior art, that is, "new information about preexisting technology which may have escaped review at the time of the initial examination of the application."[147] No grounds for reexamination were to be permitted other than based on new prior art and Sections 102 and 103. As explained in the legislative history, matters that were decided in the original examination would be barred from reexamination:

> This "substantial new question" requirement would protect patentees from having to respond to, or participate in unjustified reexaminations. Further, it would act to bar reconsideration of any argument already decided by the Office, whether during the original examination or an earlier reexamination.[148]

Thus, the statute guarded against simply repeating the prior examination on the same issues and arguments. Commissioner Diamond explained the importance of this safeguard:

---

[143] 126 Cong. Rec. 29,895 (1980).

[144] *Patlex*, 758 F.2d at 602, 225 USPQ at 248–49.

[145] *Patlex*, 758 F.2d at 604, 225 USPQ at 250.

[146] *In re* Recreative Techs. Corp., 83 F.3d 1394, 38 USPQ 2d 1776, 1777–78 (Fed. Cir. 1996).

[147] H.R. Rep. No. 96-1307, 96th Cong., 2d Sess. 3 (1980), *reprinted in* 1980 U.S.C.C.A.N. 6460, 6462.

[148] *Id.* at 7, *reprinted in* 1980 U.S.C.C.A.N. at 6466.

> [The proposed statute] carefully protects patent owners from reexamination proceedings brought for harassment or spite. The possibility of harassing patent holders is a classic criticism of some foreign reexamination systems and we made sure it would not happen here.[149]

The Federal Circuit has held that (1) the reexamination statute is constitutional,[150] (2) there is no presumption of validity of a patent in reexamination proceedings,[151] (3) Patent Office practice that does not permit a patent owner to oppose a request for reexamination prior to the decision to order reexamination is constitutional,[152] and (4) Patent Office practice resolving doubt in favor of ordering reexamination is void.[153]

The Director will grant a request for reexamination if the Director finds that the cited prior art raises "a substantial new question of patentability affecting any claim of the patent."[154] Thus, the reexamination statute requires the following three elements to set forth the applicant's prima facie case entitling the applicant to reexamination: (1) the inclusion of one or more prior art references; (2) identification of the claim or claims for which reexamination is required; and (3) an explanation of why the cited prior art presents a substantial new question of patentability of the relevant claim.

1. *Subject of Ex Parte Reexamination*

Ex parte reexamination is a procedure that allows the Patent Office to address substantial new questions of patentability.[155] Patentees can confuse the reissue and reexamination processes. The basic difference between the two procedures is that reexamination is used to correct patents that are defective or invalid because the Patent Office failed to consider relevant prior art during prosecution of the original application, while reissue is used to correct errors made by the patentee.[156] Further, unlike reissue, reexamination cannot be used to broaden the scope of the claims.[157]

---

[149] *Industrial Innovation & Patent & Copyright Law Amendments: Hearings on H.R. 6933, 6934, 3806 & 214 Before the Subcomm. on Courts, Civil Liberties and the Administration of Justice of the House Comm. on the Judiciary*, 96th Cong., 2d Sess. 594 (1980) (statement of Sidney Diamond, Commissioner of Patents & Trademarks).

[150] Patlex Corp. v. Mossinghoff, 758 F.2d 594, 599–606, 225 USPQ 243, 246–252 (Fed. Cir. 1985).

[151] *Id.* at 605, 225 USPQ at 251.

[152] *Id.* at 607, 225 USPQ at 253.

[153] Patlex Corp. v. Mossinghoff, 771 F.2d 480, 486–87, 226 USPQ 985, 989–90 (Fed. Cir. 1985).

[154] 35 U.S.C. § 303(a).

[155] 35 U.S.C. § 302.

[156] *See* Patlex Corp. v. Mossinghoff, 758 F.2d 594, 605, 225 USPQ 243, 250 (Fed. Cir. 1985). However, if a minor error is discovered during reexamination, it may be corrected during reexamination, and a separate reissue proceeding is not required. Kaufman Co. v. Lantech Inc., 807 F.2d 970, 1 USPQ 2d 1202, 1208 (Fed. Cir. 1986).

[157] *See* Quantum Corp. v. Rodime, PLC, 65 F.3d 1577, 36 USPQ 2d 1162, 1165 (Fed. Cir. 1995), *cert. denied*, 517 U.S. 1167 (1996); Anderson v. International Eng'g & Mfg., Inc., 160 F.3d 1345, 48 USPQ 2d 1631, 1634 (Fed. Cir. 1998).

Thus reexamination as enacted was carefully limited to new prior art, that is, "new information about preexisting technology which may have escaped review at the time of the initial examination of the application."[158] The reexamination statute limits the scope of the reexamination to patents and printed publications.[159] A written statement describing the prior art is insufficient alone to be considered for the reexamination request. On the other hand, a declaration or oath explaining other prior art publications may be considered. However, Patent Office procedure must be observed. Accordingly, a statement that does not satisfy the Patent Office requirements for submission will not be considered in the reexamination.[160]

Consequently, the Director may not on reexamination consider whether the specification of a patent being reexamined contains an enabling disclosure for the already issued patent claims. The PTO's Manual of Patent Examining Procedure (MPEP) provides:

> Where new claims are presented or where any part of the disclosure is amended, the claims of the reexamination proceeding, are to be examined for compliance with 35 U.S.C. § 112. Consideration of 35 U.S.C. § 112 issues should be limited to the amendatory (i.e., new language) matter. For example, a claim which is amended or a new claim which is presented containing a limitation not found in the original patent claim should be considered for compliance under 35 U.S.C. § 112 only with respect to that limitation. To go further would be inconsistent with the statute to the extent that 35 U.S.C. § 112 issues would be raised as to matter in the original patent claim.[161]

The reexamination statute does not contemplate a "reexamination" of the sufficiency of a disclosure. Rather, it is limited to reexamination of patentability based on prior art patents and publications. Accordingly, the Patent Office lacks jurisdiction to reexamine the sufficiency of the specification of a priority application when this issue has been decided previously by the Examiner.[162] In *Patlex Corp. v. Quigg*,[163] the U.S. District Court for the District of Columbia refused to decide, however, whether the Director has jurisdiction in a reexamination to inquire into the sufficiency of the specification of a "parent" application where the sufficiency of the "parent" application vis-a-vis the claims of the patent being reexamined was not previously determined by the Patent Office.[164]

Thus, the statute guards against simply repeating the prior examination on the same issues and arguments. Commissioner Diamond explained the importance of this safeguard:

---

[158] H.R. Rep. No. 96-1307, 96th Cong., 2d Sess. 3 (1980), *reprinted in* 1980 U.S.C.C.A.N. 6460, 6462.

[159] 35 U.S.C. §§ 301–302.

[160] *In re* Ductmate Indus., Inc. Re. 90/004,369, p.3 (Comm'r Pat. Feb. 12, 1997).

[161] M.P.E.P. § 2258 (7th ed. Rev. Feb. 1, 2000).

[162] Patlex Corp. v. Quigg, 680 F. Supp. 33, 6 USPQ 2d 1296, 1299 (D.D.C. 1988).

[163] Patlex Corp. v. Quigg, 680 F. Supp. 33, 6 USPQ 2d 1296 (D.D.C. 1988).

[164] *Id.*, 6 USPQ 2d at 1300.

> [The proposed statute] carefully protects patent owners from reexamination proceedings brought for harassment or spite. The possibility of harassing patent holders is a classic criticism of some foreign reexamination systems and we made sure it would not happen here.[165]

2. *Persons Eligible to Request Ex Parte Reexamination*

Any person can request reexamination at any time during the enforceability of a patent.[166] For example, a third party may file a reexamination request in order to challenge the validity of a patent. Because reexamination proceedings are typically less costly than defending an infringement action, an accused infringer may also wish to file a reexamination request in order to prove that the patent is not valid.[167] Requests may even be filed anonymously, although the Patent Office provides no assurance that a requestor's identity will remain confidential.[168] Therefore, a requestor who wants to remain anonymous should either submit the request through an attorney[169] or not submit any identifying information with the request for reexamination. The Patent Office may also seek reexamination on its own initiative, without a third-party request.[170] If the requestor is not the patentee, the Patent Office will send a copy of the request, as well as any subsequent communication if the request is granted, to the patentee.[171]

3. *Presumption of Validity*

Section 282 of the Patent Act sets forth a presumption that issued patents are valid.[172] The availability of reexamination proceedings, however, may appear to contradict the presumption because a reexamination proceeding is a mechanism to challenge a patent's validity. Although the Patent Act does not state whether the Section 282 presumption applies during reexamination proceedings, the Federal Circuit has held that the presumption does *not* apply in reexamination.[173] Rather, because the purpose of reexamination is to "start over" in the Patent Office, a patent is reexamined as if it were an originally filed application.[174]

---

[165] *Industrial Innovation & Patent & Copyright Law Amendments: Hearings on H.R. 6933, 6934, 3806 & 214 Before the Subcomm. on Courts, Civil Liberties and the Administration of Justice of the House Comm. on the Judiciary*, 96th Cong., 2d Sess. 594 (1980) (statement of Sidney Diamond, Commissioner of Patents & Trademarks).

[166] 35 U.S.C. § 302.

[167] *See* Kaufman Co. v. Lantech Inc., 807 F.2d 970, 1 USPQ 2d 1202, 1206 (Fed. Cir. 1986).

[168] M.P.E.P. 2203.

[169] *See* Syntex (U.S.A.) Inc. v. United States Patent & Trademark Office, 882 F.2d 1570, 11 USPQ 2d 1866, 1868 (Fed. Cir. 1989).

[170] 35 U.S.C. § 304.

[171] 35 U.S.C. § 302.

[172] 35 U.S.C. § 282.

[173] *In re* Etter, 756 F.2d 852, 225 USPQ 1, 5–6 (Fed. Cir.), *cert. denied*, 464 U.S. 828 (1985).

[174] *Id.*

B. Elements of Ex Parte Reexamination Request

The first step in the reexamination procedure is the filing of the request for reexamination. The request must include six elements:[175]

1. The request must raise a substantial new question of patentability.
2. The request must identify each claim for which reexamination is requested, and it must include a detailed explanation applying the cited prior art to the claim.
3. The request must include a copy of each cited or relied-upon prior art patent or printed publication.
4. The request must include a cut-up and mounted copy of the entire specification of the subject patent where each column of the patent occupies or is placed on one side of a separate sheet of paper.
5. If the request was filed by someone other than the patent owner, the request must include a certification that a copy of the request was served upon the patent owner.
6. As with any Patent Office filing, the request must include a filing fee.

1. *Substantial New Question of Patentability*

Reexamination is a procedure that allows the Patent Office to address substantial new questions of patentability relating to prior art and printed publications.[176] The question of patentability is not a "new question" if the prior art was considered in the original prosecution.[177] As stated by the Federal Circuit:

> The statutory instruction that a new question of patentability must be raised is explicit in 35 U.S.C. § 303. Reexamination is barred for questions of patentability that were decided in the original examination. That power can not be acquired by internal rule of procedure or practice. The policy balance reflected in the reexamination statute's provisions can not be unilaterally realigned by the agency.[178]

In *In re Portola Packaging Inc.*,[179] the Federal Circuit defined "substantial new question of patentability" as follows:

> We also reject the Commissioner's argument that the amendments made during reexamination created a substantial new question of patentability. That the claims were amended by Portola does not mean that a new examination of the amended claims involved substantial new issues of patentability. It is clear that the scope of a patent claim may not be enlarged by amendment during reexamination.... Thus, after the reexamination amendment, the claim could not cover subject matter broader than the scope of the claim that was originally allowed.... It naturally follows

[175] 37 C.F.R. § 1.510(b).

[176] 37 C.F.R. § 1510(b)(1).

[177] *In re* Recreative Techs. Corp., 83 F.3d 1394, 38 USPQ 2d 1776, 1779 (Fed. Cir. 1996).

[178] *Id.*, 83 F.3d 1394, 38 USPQ 2d 1776, 1779 (Fed. Cir. 1996).

[179] *In re* Portola Packaging Inc., 110 F.3d 786, 42 USPQ 2d 1295 (Fed. Cir. 1997).

> then that when the original examiner examined the original claims in light of the cited prior art, the subject matter of the narrower, amended claims was necessarily considered in relation to the cited prior art.[180]

The Patent Office currently defines a new question of patentability broadly to include prior art that was submitted to the Examiner during prosecution of the original application, but not specifically applied in a rejection, or not applied in a manner for which the reexamination is based. This currently controversial definition is based on the Patent Office's interpretation of *In re Portola Packaging, Inc.*[181] A copy of the Patent Office guidelines for reexamination is included in Appendix C. In addition, fraud, inequitable conduct, or prior public use or sale will not be considered in a reexamination proceeding.[182] The Patent Office has changed its procedure for when a prior art reference is considered by an Examiner for purposes of reexamination. In particular, the Patent Office has stated:

> The entry of such a submission does not mean that the patents or printed publications contained in the submission will be necessarily considered and cited by the examiner. If the examiner considers a patent or printed publication contained in the submission to be pertinent in determining patentability, the examiner will initial that patent or printed publication on the listing of the patents or publication submitted for consideration by the Office. Unless, however, a patent or publication in a submission under § 1.99 is discussed during prosecution, the patent or publication will not be deemed to have been "considered" pursuant to the Office's *Portola* guidelines.[183]

This change in procedure is troubling in view of public policy favoring the issuance of valid patents. The burden of doing so falls on the Patent Office, and this change in procedure appears to represent an attempt to shift that burden. It is to be hoped that the Federal Circuit will require the Patent Office to carry out its responsibilities in considering prior art references actually submitted by an applicant during prosecution.

There is no specific requirement that the Examiner review each submitted prior art reference independently or compare each new prior art reference to the claims as a whole in order to determine whether a substantial new question of patentability is present. For example, one way that has been used by the Patent Office to show whether or not a substantial new question of patentability exists is to compare the previous prior art cited or applied in the original patent prosecution with the new prior art cited in the reexamination request.[184] According to the Patent Office, to state that certain teachings in newly cited prior art are

---

[180] *Id.*, 42 USPQ 2d at 1299–1300.

[181] *In re* Portola Packaging Inc., 110 F.3d 786, 42 USPQ 2d 1295 (Fed. Cir. 1997).

[182] *See In re* Lanham, 1 USPQ 2d 1877, 1878 (Comm'r Pat. 1986).

[183] Fed. Reg., Vol. 65, No. 183,57032 (Sept. 20, 2000) (citing Guidelines for Reexamination of Cases in View of In re Portola Packaging, Inc., 110 F.3d 786, 42 USPQ 2d 1295 (Fed. Cir. 1997), Notice, 64 FR 15346 (Mar. 31, 1999), 1223 Off. Gaz. Pat. Office 124 (June 22, 1999)).

[184] *In re* Rief, Re. 90/004,654, p.2 (Comm'r Pat. Sept. 19, 1997).

substantially equivalent to teachings in prior art of record is perfectly logical, reasonable, and proper.[185] In addition, it is the Patent Office's view that there is no requirement in the reexamination statutes or rules that an Examiner must perform a typical anticipation or obviousness analysis of each piece of prior art cited in a reexamination request.[186]

Significantly, the source of the substantial new question related to patentability is limited to prior art patents or printed publications.[187] Thus, reexamination is not allowed if the prior art was merely on sale, offered for sale, or displayed in public.[188] Other prior art references, such as trade show demonstrations or other items, are also not proper subjects for reexamination requests. Reexamination requests based on double patenting, however, are permitted since double patenting is based on a printed publication, i.e., the claims of another patent.[189] For example, the Federal Circuit has stated:

> Since the statute in other places refers to prior art in relation to reexamination, . . . it seems apparent that Congress intended that the phrases "patents and publications" and "other patents or printed publications" in section 303(a) not be limited to prior art patents or printed publications. . . . A patent is clearly the type of evidence that Congress intended the PTO to consider during reexamination, and the cost of examination is not significantly increased by having the PTO consider the ground of double patenting, as it involves issues of claim identity and obviousness, well within the PTO's everyday expertise. . . . Thus, we conclude that the PTO was authorized during reexamination to consider the question of double patenting based upon the '762 patent.[190]

The Patent Office may find a significant new question of patentability for *any* claim in the patent, not just the claim or claims pointed out by the requester.[191]

2. *Fee*

The cost of filing a request for reexamination is not small. A request filed by the patent owner in 2000 required a fee of approximately $2,520.[192] However, anyone seriously considering filing a reexamination request should contact the Patent Office for the most current fee information. If the Patent Office does not find a substantial question of patentability, the Patent Office will only refund approximately one-third of the fee to the requester.[193]

---

[185] *Id.* at 3.

[186] *Id.* at 2.

[187] 35 U.S.C. § 301.

[188] M.P.E.P. § 2258.

[189] *See In re* Lonardo, 119 F.3d 960, 964, 43 USPQ 2d 1262, 1266 (Fed. Cir. 1997), *cert. denied.* 522 U.S. 1147 (1998); *Ex Parte* Obiaya, 227 USPQ 58, 61 (B.P.A.I. 1985).

[190] *In re* Lonardo, 119 F.3d 960, 43 USPQ 2d 1262, 1266 (Fed. Cir. 1997), *cert. denied*, 522 U.S. 1147 (1998).

[191] 37 C.F.R. § 1.515(a).

[192] 37 C.F.R. § 1.20(c).

[193] 37 C.F.R. § 1.26(c).

C. Ex Parte Reexamination Proceedings

Under 35 U.S.C. Section 301, any person may cite to the PTO prior art, consisting of patents and printed publications, that may affect the patentability of any claim of a patent.[194] Section 302 of the statute authorizes any person to request reexamination of a patent based on that "prior art." Within three months of receiving such a request, the Director determines whether the prior art raises a "substantial new question of patentability."[195] If the Director determines that it does, he or she must order reexamination of the patent.[196] If he or she determines that the cited prior art raises no substantial new question of patentability, the request for reexamination is denied. The "determination . . . that no substantial new question of patentability has been raised will be final and nonappealable."[197] The statute contains no provision for appeal or review of a determination that a substantial new question has been raised. The Director's threshold determination merely triggers the reexamination proceeding; it does not affect the validity of the patent. As to the larger question of whether the cited patents and printed publications render the claims of the challenged patent unpatentable on the merits, the statute confers a right of appeal and court review.[198]

The Patent Office must determine whether a substantial new question of patentability exists, and thus grant or deny a reexamination request, within three months of the filing of the request.[199] As stated previously, the determination is not subject to appeal or reconsideration.[200]

1. Submissions by Patent Owner

If the Patent Office orders reexamination, whether on its own initiative or after a third-party request, the patent owner may file a statement on the new question of patentability within two months from the order.[201] The statement must clearly describe why the patent owner believes the claimed subject matter to be patentable over the prior art.[202] The statement may include proposed amendments to the patent.[203] Proposed amendments to the claims must include the entire text of each subject claim (unless the claim is being canceled), and each new

---

[194] Patlex Corp. v. Quigg, 680 F. Supp. 33, 6 USPQ 2d 1296, 1298 (D.D.C. 1988).

[195] 35 U.S.C. § 303(a).

[196] 35 U.S.C. § 304.

[197] 35 U.S.C. § 303(c).

[198] 35 U.S.C. § 306.

[199] 37 C.F.R. § 1.515(a).

[200] M.P.E.P. § 2246; Patlex Corp. v. Quigg, 680 F. Supp. 33, 6 USPQ 2d 1296, 1298 (D.D.C. 1988).

[201] 37 C.F.R. § 1.530(b).

[202] 37 C.F.R. § 1.530(c).

[203] 37 C.F.R. § 1.530(b).

claim or addition must include underlining below the new subject matter.[204] Deletions must be in brackets.[205] Each amendment must be accompanied by an explanation of the support in the disclosure for the amendment.[206]

2. *Prohibition Against Broadening*

No amendment may introduce new matter or enlarge the scope of the claims.[207] A claim has been enlarged if it includes within its scope any subject matter that would not have infringed the original patent. For example, in *Quantum Corp. v. Rodime, PLC*,[208] the original patent claimed a hard disk drive system having a track density of "at least 600 dpi." During reexamination, the patentee broadened the claim to encompass systems having a track density of "at least *approximately* 600 dpi."[209] The Federal Circuit held that the addition of the word "approximately" to the claim broadened the claim after reexamination because it eliminated the absolute lowest range of 600 dpi.[210]

The determination of whether a claim has been broadened is a matter of claim construction that is treated as a question of law.[211] Claims that are impermissibly broadened will be held to be invalid.[212]

3. *Submissions by Third-Party Requester*

The requester may file a reply to the patent owner's statement within two months of the date of the service of the statement.[213] However, if the patent owner does not file a statement, the requester may not file a reply or any other document.[214] In an ordinary reexamination proceeding, the active participation of the requester ends with the reply, and the requester also has no opportunity to participate in any interviews with the Examiner, although the requester will receive copies of any documents filed in the proceeding.[215]

Amendments to the Patent Act in 1999 granted third parties a greater opportunity to participate in reexamination proceedings. The

---

[204] 37 C.F.R. § 1.530(d)(2).

[205] 37 C.F.R. § 1.530(d)(2)(i)(C).

[206] 37 C.F.R. § 1.530(d)(2)(iii).

[207] 35 U.S.C. § 305; 37 C.F.R. § 1.530(d)(3).

[208] Quantum Corp. v. Rodime, PLC, 65 F.3d 1577, 36 USPQ 2d 1162 (Fed. Cir. 1995), *cert. denied*, 517 U.S. 1167 (1996).

[209] *Id.*, 36 USPQ 2d at 1163.

[210] *Id.* at 1165–66.

[211] Giese v. Pierce Chem. Co., 43 F. Supp. 2d 98, 50 USPQ 2d 1810, 1813 (D. Mass. 1999); *In re* Freeman, 30 F.3d 1459, 31 USPQ 2d 1444, 1447 (Fed. Cir. 1994).

[212] *Giese*, 50 USPQ 2d at 1813.

[213] 37 C.F.R. §§ 1.530(c) and 1.535.

[214] 37 C.F.R. § 1.535.

[215] 37 C.F.R. § 1.550(a)(1).

Intellectual Property and Communications Omnibus Reform Act of 1999 added Sections 311 through 318 to the Patent Act.[216] If a third-party requester requests reexamination under these provisions, the third party will have an opportunity to file written comments to any response filed by the patent owner.[217] The comments must be filed within 30 days from the date of service of the owner's response, and the comments may only address issues raised by the Office Action or the patent owner's response thereto.[218] After an inter partes reexamination proceeding, the third-party requester may appeal any final decision favorable to patentability, and the requester may also be a party to any appeal taken by the patent owner.[219] However, the third party whose request for inter partes reexamination is granted may not, in any subsequent civil action, assert the invalidity of any claim on any ground that the requester raised, or could have raised, in the reexamination proceeding.[220] A copy of the amended statutory provisions is provided in Appendix C; a copy of the current Patent Office final rules is included in Appendix C; and the previous proposals to implement the third-party reexamination statute are included in Appendix D. A detailed discussion of inter partes reexamination is included in Section IV below.

4. *Ex Parte Reexamination Procedures*

Reexamination is performed by the Examiner in the Patent Office on the basis of the prior art patents or printed publications.[221] During the reexamination process, the Examiner may consider *any* prior art, not just that submitted by the requestor.[222] The patent owner will be given 30 days to respond to any Office Action, and each response may include further arguments or proposed amendments or new claims to place the patent in a patentable condition.[223] The patent owner may also request an extension of time to file any document due in a reexamination proceeding, but the request must show sufficient cause why the extension is necessary, and it must specify a reasonable period of time.[224] The patent owner and/or the attorney or agent of record may also participate in interviews with the Examiner.[225]

---

[216] Intellectual Property and Communications Omnibus Reform Act of 1999, Pub. L. No. 106-113, Nov. 29, 1999 to be codified as 35 U.S.C. §§ 311–318.

[217] 35 U.S.C. § 313(b)(3).

[218] *Id.*

[219] 35 U.S.C. § 315(b).

[220] 35 U.S.C. § 315(c).

[221] 37 C.F.R. §§ 1.550(a) and 1.552(a).

[222] M.P.E.P. § 2258.

[223] 37 C.F.R. § 1.550(b).

[224] 37 C.F.R. § 1.550(c).

[225] 37 C.F.R. § 1.560.

The patent owner is required to advise the Patent Office of any concurrent proceedings relating to the patent.[226] If a patent in the process of reexamination becomes involved in litigation, or if a reissue application is pending, the Patent Office has the discretion to stay the reexamination proceeding.[227] The Patent Office may also merge copending reexamination proceedings, or copending reissue and reexamination proceedings, relating to the same patent.[228]

At the end of a reexamination proceeding, the Examiner will issue a reexamination certificate. The certificate will state the results of the reexamination proceeding and set forth the content of the patent following the proceeding.[229] A notice of the certificate's issuance will be published in the *Official Gazette*.[230]

The patent owner may appeal any decision adverse to the patentability of any original, amended, or new claim of the patent.[231] On the other hand, participation by third parties in reissue proceedings is limited to the protest provision, from which there is no appeal.[232] Participation in reexamination proceedings is limited to a request for reexamination and a reply to the patent owner's statement.[233] The requester may not actively participate further and may not appeal.[234] A patent owner is limited to appealing the decision of the Board to the Federal Circuit, and has no right of appeal to the district court.[235]

The Patent Office will generally assign the reexamination request to an Examiner different from the Examiner who previously examined the original application. In addition, a patentability review conference is conducted with the Examiner assigned to the reexamination to principally review patentability issues to enhance the objective analysis and quality of the ex parte reexamination proceedings. A copy of the Patent Office guidelines implementing this procedure is included in Appendix C.

D. Result of Ex Parte Reexamination

At the end of the reexamination proceeding, the Examiner will issue a reexamination certificate. This certificate may be a certificate indicating patentability, a certificate of unpatentability, or a certificate to claim cancellation.[236] Any claims surviving reexamination may be

---

[226] 37 C.F.R. § 1.565(a).

[227] 37 C.F.R. § 1.565(b).

[228] 37 C.F.R. § 1.565(c)–(d).

[229] 37 C.F.R. § 1.570(a).

[230] 37 C.F.R. § 1.570(f).

[231] 35 U.S.C. § 306.

[232] 37 C.F.R. § 1.291.

[233] 37 C.F.R. §§ 1.510, 1.535.

[234] 37 C.F.R. § 1.552(e); Syntex (U.S.A.) Inc. v. United States Patent & Trademark Office, 882 F.2d 1570, 11 USPQ 2d 1866, 1870–71 (Fed. Cir. 1989).

[235] 35 U.S.C. §§ 134, 145 (Supp. 2000).

[236] 35 U.S.C. § 307.

viewed by a reviewing court as having an even greater presumption of validity, as they have been "twice blessed" by the Patent Office.[237] The patentee can also receive new claims, although reexamination cannot be used to enlarge the scope of any claim.[238]

Claims amended during reexamination are entitled to the date of the original patent so long as they are generally identical to the claims of the original patent and have no substantive change.[239] "Identical" does not necessarily mean that the claims must be a word-for-word match. Rather, "identical" means "without substantive change."[240] For example, in a claim that included the element of a "wall" that the specification indicated was always a bottom wall, an amendment during reexamination to insert the word "bottom" before the word "wall" resulted in an identical claim.[241] If the claims are not "identical," the patentee has no right to recover damages for infringing any nonidentical claim before the date that the reexamination certificate was issued.[242]

IV. Optional Inter Partes Reexamination Procedures

A. Overview of Inter Partes Reexamination

Under the Intellectual Property and Communications Omnibus Reform Act of 1999, Congress drafted legislation to permit inter partes reexamination, or third party participation in reexamination, of issued patents.[243] On November 29, 1999, Public Law 106-113 was signed into law as the Optional *Inter Partes* Reexamination Procedure in a newly created Chapter 31 of Title 35 of the United States Code.[244] The statutes introducing inter partes procedures in the reexamination process are independent of the existing ex parte reexamination procedures, as is evident from the use of the word "optional" in the title of the new law. Accordingly, ex parte reexamination remains intact, and can still be used by those who do not wish to utilize this optional inter partes reexamination procedure.

---

[237] *See* Transmatic, Inc. v. Gulton Indus., Inc., 53 F.3d 1270, 35 USPQ 2d 1035, 1038–39 (Fed. Cir. 1995).

[238] 35 U.S.C. § 305.

[239] 35 U.S.C. § 307(b); Tennant Co. v. Hako Minuteman, Inc., 878 F.2d 1413, 11 USPQ 2d 1303, 1306 (Fed. Cir. 1989); *see also* Kaufman Co. v. Lantech Inc., 807 F.2d 970, 1 USPQ 2d 1202, 1206–07 (Fed. Cir. 1986).

[240] *Tennant*, 11 USPQ 2d at 1306.

[241] *Id.*

[242] *Id.*; Fortel Corp. v. Phone-Mate, Inc., 825 F.2d 1577, 3 USPQ 2d 1991, 1994 (Fed. Cir. 1987).

[243] Intellectual Property and Communications Omnibus Reform Act of 1999, Public Law 106-113, Title IV §§ 4601–4608 (1999).

[244] 35 U.S.C. §§ 311–318 (Supp. 2000).

The effective date of the optional inter partes reexamination procedure "shall apply to any patent that issues from an original application filed in the United States on or after [the date of enactment, November 29, 1999]."[245] Exactly what is meant by "original application" is not entirely clear. For example, a Continued Prosecution Application under 37 C.F.R. Section 1.53(d) or Divisional application under 37 C.F.R. Section 1.53 (b) might not be considered an original application eligible for the inter partes reexamination procedure. Similarly, it is not clear whether a continuation-in-part application filed under 37 C.F.R. Section 1.53(b) is also considered an original application. In the final rules, the Patent Office has defined "original application" to be any application filed on or after November 29, 1999, including continuation applications, divisional applications, continuation-in-part applications, continued prosecution applications, design applications, plant applications, and national stage applications of international applications under the Patent Cooperation Treaty (PCT).[246] However, requests for continued prosecution are not considered original applications by the U.S. Patent Office.

Inter partes reexamination was created in order to "reduce expensive patent litigation in U.S. district courts by giving third-party requesters, in addition to the existing ex parte reexamination in Chapter 30 of title 35, the option of inter partes reexamination proceedings in the USPTO."[247] While the existing ex parte reexamination procedure was also created to be an alternative to costly patent litigation, the lack of third-party participation has resulted in some criticism of the process as being too favorable toward patentees. In addition, patent owners asserted harassment at the hands of third parties who filed multiple reexamination requests for the same patent. Third-party requesters resorted to this strategy to prevent the patent owner from presenting what the requesters considered a one-sided view of the prior art to the Examiner. Hence, the new legislation seeks to overcome these perceived problems in the ex parte reexamination procedures by allowing third-party participation and limiting the number of inter partes reexaminations.

Specifically, 35 U.S.C. Sections 314 and 315 create three important new rights for the third-party requester: (1) the right to file written comments addressing issues raised by an action on the merits from the Patent Office and issues raised by the patent owner's response thereto;[248] (2) the right to appeal, within the Patent Office, any final decision favorable to the patentability of an original, amended, or new claim of

[245] Intellectual Property and Communications Omnibus Reform Act of 1999, Public Law 106–113, Title IV § 4608 (1999).

[246] Fed. Reg. Vol. 65, No. 236, 76757 (Dec. 7, 2000).

[247] 145 Cong. Rec. S14,696-03, 14,720 (Daily ed. Nov. 17, 1999).

[248] 35 U.S.C. § 314 (Supp. 2000).

the patent;[249] and (3) the right to be a party to any appeal taken by the patent owner to the Board.[250]

Disclosure of the identity of the real party in interest is required.[251] More importantly, various estoppels against the third-party requester are generally intended to be created for the right of initiating an inter partes reexamination.[252] While the right to appeal an adverse decision finding claims patentable has now been provided to the third-party requester, the right of appeal is limited to the Board.[253] The third-party requester has no right to appeal an adverse decision of the Board to the Federal Circuit.[254] The filing of simultaneous multiple inter partes reexamination requests is precluded by anyone involved in a previous inter partes request.[255] Finally, while the third-party requester is now permitted the opportunity to participate in the reexamination process, a short 30-day time limit has been set for the third-party requester to prevent the inter partes reexamination being used as a delay tactic.[256] A copy of the proposed rules for inter partes reexamination is included in Appendix D; a copy of the final rules implemented by the Patent Office is included in Appendix C.

B. Request for Reexamination

The first three sections of Chapter 31 are similar to Sections 302 through 304 of Chapter 30 relating to the existing ex parte reexamination statute. Like Section 302, Section 311 says that any person at any time may file a request for reexamination of a patent on the basis of any prior art cited under the provisions of Section 301. However, a request must specifically indicate that it is for inter partes reexamination. The request must be in writing, accompanied by the applicable fee, and set forth the pertinency and manner of applying cited art to every claim for which reexamination is requested.[257] The Director is responsible for forwarding the request to the patent owner, if the request is made by a third party. Unlike the ex parte procedure, however, the request must "include the identity of the real party in interest . . . ."[258] Thus, a request for reexamination under the new laws should largely resemble requests submitted under prior practice, with the exception that the request for inter partes reexamination needs to be specifically stated and the real party in interest must be identified.

---

[249] 35 U.S.C. § 315 (Supp. 2000).

[250] 35 U.S.C. § 315 (Supp. 2000).

[251] 35 U.S.C. § 311 (Supp. 2000).

[252] 35 U.S.C. §§ 315–316 (Supp. 2000).

[253] 35 U.S.C. § 134 (Supp. 2000).

[254] 35 U.S.C. § 134 (Supp. 2000).

[255] 35 U.S.C. § 317 (Supp. 2000).

[256] 35 U.S.C. § 314 (Supp. 2000).

[257] 35 U.S.C. § 311 (Supp. 2000).

[258] 35 U.S.C. § 311 (Supp. 2000).

Once the request for inter partes reexamination has been filed, the Director has three months from the filing of the request to "determine whether a substantial new question of patentability affecting any claim of the patent concerned is raised by the request, with or without consideration of other patents or printed publications."[259] The Director also has the right to make this determination on his or her own initiative.[260] This decision is made of record and supplied to the patent owner and any third-party requester.[261] This decision is final, and not appealable under either ex parte or inter partes practice. However, a finding that there is no substantial new question of patentability can be reviewed by petition of the third-party requester within one month of the mailing date of the decision refusing reexamination.[262]

Both the existing ex parte reexamination procedures and the new inter partes reexamination procedures rely on the finding of a substantial new question of patentability as the basis for ordering reexamination. A substantial new question of patentability and the basis for finding such are the same under both reexamination procedures, that is, the determination is based solely on prior art patents and publications.[263] Issues such as fraud, prior invention, public use, or offers for sale cannot be the basis for a request for reexamination under either the ex parte or inter partes reexamination laws.

Once a determination that a substantial new question of patentability exists has been made, inter partes reexamination shall be ordered. A first action on the merits may accompany an order for inter partes reexamination.

C. Inter Partes Reexamination Procedures

Once the reexamination has been ordered and an action on the merits issues, the patent is examined in a manner similar to that in an initial examination of original application, with some limited exceptions.[264] For example, claims from the issued patent may not be reexamined for compliance with the requirements under Section 112, while new claims or amended claims are subject to such review.[265] Further, similar to ex parte reexamination, no claim amendments or new claims may enlarge the scope of the patent.[266]

Any papers filed by the patent owner or the third-party requester must be served on the other, and the Patent Office is responsible for

---

[259] 35 U.S.C. § 312 (Supp. 2000).

[260] 35 U.S.C. § 312 (Supp. 2000).

[261] 35 U.S.C. § 312 (Supp. 2000).

[262] 37 C.F.R. § 1.927 (Supp. 2000).

[263] 35 U.S.C. § 312 (Supp. 2000).

[264] *See* 35 U.S.C. § 314(a) (Supp. 2000).

[265] Patlex Corp. v. Quigg, 680 F. Supp. 33, 6 USPQ 2d 1296, 1299 (D.D.C. 1988); M.P.E.P. § 2258.

[266] 35 U.S.C. § 314(a) (Supp. 2000).

providing the third party with any communications it sends. Each time a patent owner files a response to an action on the merits, "the third-party requester shall have one opportunity to file written comments addressing issues raised by the action of the Office or the patent owner's response thereto . . . ."[267] The third-party requester has 30 days from the date of service of the patent owner's response to get those written comments to the Patent Office. Since this 30-day time limit is established by statute, the Patent Office will not permit any extensions of time, for any reason.[268] This very short time for response by the third-party requester may be sufficient reason to avoid the new inter partes procedure due to the possibility that an inadequate response might result. No interviews are permitted in inter partes reexamination.[269] Since the inter partes reexamination creates various estoppels under the statute, an inadequate response might have devastating consequences for the third-party requester. The various estoppels are discussed below.

D. Appeals

Under the ex parte reexamination provisions, a third-party requester could submit additional views regarding the positions taken by the Patent Office or the patent owner by filing multiple reexamination requests.[270] While this mechanism provided another bite at the apple for the third party, once the reexamination proceeded to the appeal stage, no communications would be accepted from the third party. Further, once the Office found the claims patentable or allowable, there was little the third party could do to counteract such a finding.

In addition to the participation before the Examiner, the third party can appeal to the Board of Patent Appeals and Interferences (Board) any decision adverse to its position, i.e., "any final decision favorable to the patentability of any original or proposed amended or new claim of the patent."[271] Moreover, the third party has the right to participate in any appeal taken by the patent owner to the Board.

However, the enacted legislation does not permit the third party an appeal to the Federal Circuit of a decision adverse to its interests or to participate in an appeal taken by the patent owner to the Federal Circuit. As stated in newly amended Section 134, "[t]he third-party requester may not appeal the decision of the Board of Patent Appeals and Interferences."[272]

---

[267] 35 U.S.C. § 314(b)(3) (Supp. 2000).

[268] *See* M.P.E.P. § 2251 (stating that statutory time periods will not be extended, in the context of the two-month period provided in § 304 for the third-party requester's reply to the patent owner's statement).

[269] Fed. Reg. Vol. 65, No. 236, 76768 (Dec. 7, 2000); 37 C.F.R. § 1.955 (Supp. 2000).

[270] *See* M.P.E.P. § 2240.

[271] 35 U.S.C. §§ 134, 315(b)(1) (Supp. 2000).

[272] 35 U.S.C. § 134 (Supp. 2000).

As under the ex parte procedures, the patent owner has the right to appeal to the Board as well as to the Federal Circuit. However, the new legislation has not provided the right to bring a civil action in the U.S. District Court for the District of Columbia.[273] Such a right no longer exists under the ex parte reexamination statute as well.[274]

E. Reexamination Certificate

After reexamination proceedings have terminated, either by the completion of the appellate process or the expiration of the time for appeal, the Director shall issue a certificate either canceling claims found unpatentable, confirming the patentability of claims determined to be patentable, or adding any proposed amended or new claim determined to be patentable.[275] Newly amended or added claims are subject to the provisions of intervening rights when the claims of the original patent and the reissued patent are not substantially identical.[276]

F. Multiple Reexaminations Prohibited

The ex parte reexamination procedures did not specifically prohibit simultaneous reexamination proceedings for the same patent, and provided for consolidation of reexamination proceedings.[277] In contrast, with respect to inter partes reexamination, even though third parties may participate in the reexamination process, the filing of a subsequent request for inter partes reexamination by the patent owner, the third-party requester, or privies of either, is prohibited until an inter partes reexamination certificate is issued and published.[278] The Patent Office has not defined what exactly constitutes privies of the third-party requester, and intends this definition to be necessary in only limited situations. The reason is that all that the additional third-party requester need do is file a certification that the estoppel provisions prohibit the filing of the inter partes reexamination.[279] The Patent Office does not intend looking beyond the required certification unless the patent owner objects.[280]

G. Stay of Litigation

While stays of co-pending litigation involving the patent undergoing reexamination were and are possible under the ex parte reexamination procedures, they were not expressly required. In contrast, the

---

[273] 35 U.S.C. §§ 134, 145 (Supp. 2000).

[274] *Id.*

[275] 35 U.S.C. § 316 (Supp. 2000).

[276] *See* 35 U.S.C. § 252 (Supp. 2000).

[277] 37 C.F.R. § 1.565 (Supp. 2000).

[278] 35 U.S.C. § 317 (Supp. 2000).

[279] Fed. Reg. Vol. 65, No. 236, 76759 (Dec. 7, 2000); 37 C.F.R. § 1.915(b)(7) (Supp. 2000).

[280] *Id.*

inter partes reexamination proceedings expressly provide that litigation "may" be stayed at the request of the patent owner, if the pending litigation involves an issue of patentability of any claim of the patent which is the subject of the inter partes reexamination order.[281] According to Section 318, the stay should only be denied if the court determines that a stay would not serve the interests of justice.[282]

Thus, in contrast with the ex parte procedures, inter partes reexamination favors the staying of a co-pending litigation, which would be consistent with the intent to reduce costly and time-consuming litigation.

H. Effects of Inter Partes Reexamination — Estoppels

As a consequence of providing the third-party requester with the right to participate in the reexamination, the third party risks the possibility of three different types of estoppels.

First, a third-party requester whose request for an inter partes reexamination results in an order for reexamination is:

> estopped from asserting at a later time, in any civil action arising in whole or in part under section 1338 of title 28, United States Code, the invalidity of any claim finally determined to be valid and patentable on any ground which the third-party requester raised or could have raised during the inter partes reexamination proceedings. This subsection does not prevent the assertion of invalidity based on newly discovered prior art unavailable to the third-party requester and the Patent and Trademark Office at the time of the inter partes reexamination proceedings.[283]

Second, when a final decision has been entered against a party to a civil action arising in whole or in part under Section 1338 finding that the party has not proved the invalidity of any patent claim in suit, or if a final decision in inter partes reexamination is favorable to the patentability of any original claim or new or amended claim of the patent, then:

> Once a final decision has been entered against a party in a civil action arising in whole or in part under section 1338 of title 28, United States Code, that the party has not sustained its burden of proving the invalidity of any patent claim in suit or if a final decision in an inter partes reexamination proceeding instituted by a third-party requester is favorable to the patentability of any original or proposed amended or new claim of the patent, then neither that party nor its privies may thereafter request an inter partes reexamination of any such patent claim on the basis of issues which that party or its privies raised or could have raised in such civil action or inter partes reexamination proceeding, and an inter partes reexamination requested by that party or its privies on the basis of such issues may not thereafter be maintained by the Office, notwithstanding any other provision of this chapter. This subsection does not prevent the

---

[281] 35 U.S.C. § 318 (Supp. 2000).

[282] 35 U.S.C. § 318 (Supp. 2000).

[283] 35 U.S.C. § 315(c) (Supp. 2000).

assertion of invalidity based on newly discovered prior art unavailable to the third-party requester and the Patent and Trademark Office at the time of the inter partes reexamination proceedings.[284]

Finally, Section 4607, entitled "Estoppel Effect of Reexamination," provides that the third-party requester is "estopped from challenging at a later time, in any civil action, any fact determined during the process of such reexamination."[285] Determinations of fact "later proved to be erroneous based on information unavailable at the time of the inter partes reexamination decision" are excepted from this estoppel.[286]

All three of these estoppels create practical issues for a third party considering requesting inter partes reexamination.

The second estoppel appears to be the least difficult of the three estoppel-creating sections. This estoppel prevents the filing of a subsequent inter partes, but not ex parte, reexamination request. In addition, while a substantial new question of patentability can generally be found based on the addition of teachings from an unconsidered reference together with the teachings of already available references in ex parte reexamination, a subsequent inter partes reexamination is only allowed if the reference was newly discovered prior art unavailable to the third-party requester and the Patent Office during the prior inter partes reexamination proceedings. Accordingly, if the third-party requester fails in the inter partes reexamination, there is no additional chance to bring a subsequent inter partes reexamination, unless the prior art was not available at the time of the request.

The first and the third estoppels pose further difficulties for the third-party requester. The first estoppel prevents a third party from raising a ground for invalidity in a civil action that was raised or could have been raised during the inter partes reexamination. The third estoppel prevents a third party from later challenging any fact determined during the inter partes reexamination proceeding. The only "out" from the first estoppel is based on newly discovered prior art. The "out" for the third estoppel is based on "information unavailable at the time of the inter partes reexamination decision." Section 4607 does not specifically state to whom the information was "unavailable."

Interestingly, while the second estoppel, Section 317(b), prohibits a third-party requester *and its privies* from requesting a subsequent reexamination on grounds which could have been raised in the first *inter partes* reexamination, the first estoppel, Section 315(c), limits only the third party itself, not its privies. Thus, cooperating entities with a common interest in invalidating a patent would not appear to be estopped from later raising the same issues in a court proceeding.

---

[284] 35 U.S.C. § 317(b) (Supp. 2000).

[285] Intellectual Property and Communication Omnibus Reform Act of 1999, tit. IV(F) § 4607 (1999).

[286] *Id.* It is unclear why this estoppel was not specifically codified in Title 31 of the inter partes reexamination statutes.

The requirement for the *inter partes* reexamination request to name the real party in interest would seem to preclude naming a straw man to avoid the estoppel effect of Section 315(c). Independent members of the public, i.e., "good Samaritans," acting in concert to some degree to challenge the validity of a patent, are not estopped under Section 315(c) so long as they are not considered real parties in interest. Thus, if the party with the smallest liability can be induced to "volunteer" to be the requester, the others may be insulated from the first estoppel of Section 315(c).

Thus, while granting the right to participate in the reexamination process, the new law, in Section 317(a), explicitly prohibits the filing of a subsequent request for inter partes reexamination by the patent owner, the third-party requester, or privies of either, until an inter partes reexamination certificate is issued and published pursuant to Section 316.[287] The Patent Office has not defined what exactly constitutes privies of the third-party requester, and intends this definition to be necessary in only limited situations. The reason is that all that the additional third-party requester need do is file a certification that the estoppel provisions prohibit the filing of the inter partes reexamination.[288] The Patent Office does not intend looking beyond the required certification.[289]

V. Certificates of Correction

A. Basis for a Certificate of Correction

Like the reissue process, a Certificate of Correction is a mechanism that allows a patentee to correct errors that exist in a patent and that arose in good faith. The Patent Act describes three situations wherein a patentee may obtain a Certificate of Correction: (1) where the Patent Office made a mistake in printing the patent;[290] (2) where the applicant made a typographical or other minor mistake;[291] and (3) where there is an erroneously named inventor or inventors in a patent.[292]

1. *Correction of Patent Office Mistake*

The Patent Act allows a patentee to request a Certificate of Correction "[w]henever a mistake in a patent, incurred through the fault of the Patent and Trademark Office, is clearly disclosed by the records of the

[287] 35 U.S.C. § 317(a).

[288] Fed. Reg. Vol. 65, No. 236, 76759 (Dec. 7, 2000); 37 C.F.R. § 1.915(b)(7) (Supp. 2000).

[289] *Id.*

[290] 35 U.S.C. § 254.

[291] 35 U.S.C. § 255.

[292] 35 U.S.C. § 256.

Office."[293] If the mistake is of such a nature that the intended meaning of the patent is obvious from the context, the Patent Office may decline to issue a Certificate of Correction and instead may simply place the patent holder's request in the patent file to serve as notice in case questions should arise in the future.[294] No fee is required to request a Certificate to correct a mistake made by the Patent Office.[295]

2. Correction of Applicant's Mistake

The Patent Act also allows a patentee to request a Certificate of Correction "[w]henever a mistake of a clerical or typographical nature, or of minor character, which was not the fault of the Patent and Trademark Office, appears in a patent."[296] The request must demonstrate that the mistake occurred in good faith, and it must be accompanied by a fee.[297] For example, the Patent Office may issue a Certificate of Correction to correct an obvious typographical error, such as the applicant's use of the word "motor" in a specification where it was obvious from the context that the applicant meant to say "rotor."[298] The Patent Office may also issue a certificate to correct an improper claim of priority to a prior co-pending application.[299]

The Patent Office will not, however, issue a Certificate of Correction to correct an applicant's mistake where the correction would result in the addition of new matter to the patent, if the correction would materially affect the scope or meaning of the patent, or if the correction would require reexamination.[300] For example, a Certificate of Correction may not expand the scope of the claims of a patent.[301] In *In re Arnott*,[302] the patentee obtained a reissue patent that omitted one of the claims from the original patent. The omission resulted in one of the dependent claims in the reissue patent improperly referencing the independent claim upon which it was to depend. The patentee requested a Certificate of Correction and asserted that the improper reference was the result of the patentee's clerical mistake. The court, however, noted that the change was not one of minor character but instead would change the scope of the claim. Thus, the court held that the Patent Act's provisions relating to reissue were controlling, and

---

[293] 35 U.S.C. § 254.

[294] M.P.E.P. § 1480.

[295] 35 U.S.C. § 254

[296] 35 U.S.C. § 255.

[297] *Id.*

[298] Sargent-Welch Scientific Co. v. U/B Indus. Inc., 496 F. Supp. 972, 210 USPQ 948, 954 (N.D. Ill. 1980); *see also* 37 C.F.R. § 1.78.

[299] *See In re* Lambrech, 202 USPQ 620, 621 (Comm'r Pat. § 1976).

[300] *Id.*; M.P.E.P. § 1481.

[301] Eagle Iron Works v. McLanahan Corp., 429 F.2d 1375, 166 USPQ 225, 231 (3d Cir. 1970).

[302] *In re* Arnott, 19 USPQ 2d 1049 (Comm'r Pat. 1991).

that those relating to Certificates of Correction were not available to correct the error.[303]

3. Correction of Named Inventor

The Patent Act provides that "[w]henever through error a person is named in an issued patent as the inventor, or through error an inventor is not named in an issued patent and such error arose without deceptive intent on his part, the Director may, upon application of all of the parties and assignees, with proof of the facts and such other requirements as may be imposed, issue a certificate correcting such error."[304] A certificate to correct inventorship may also be ordered by a court after notice to and a hearing of all parties concerned.[305] The Certificate of Correction is generally submitted with, or after, papers that are filed to correct inventorship under 35 U.S.C. Section 256,[306] as described below.

B. Certificate of Correction Procedures and Effects

1. The Application Process

A patent holder may request a Certificate of Correction by filing a petition with the Patent Office.[307] The petition must *expressly* request the certificate, as a mere letter calling attention to an error in a patent will not be acknowledged by the Patent Office, even if the patent holder requests that the letter be made of record in the patent file.[308] If the request is to correct an applicant's mistake or to correct a named inventor, a fee must accompany the request.[309]

In the case of a petition to correct a named inventor, the petition must include statements from each person being added as an inventor and each person being deleted as an inventor that the error in naming inventors arose without any deceptive intent on his or her part.[310] A simple statement indicating that "the error arose without deceptive intent" will satisfy this requirement.[311] In addition, all named inventors who are not being added or deleted must submit a statement either agreeing to the change or stating that they have no disagreement relating to the change.[312] Further, all assignees must submit a statement

---

[303] *Id.* at 1052–54.

[304] 35 U.S.C. § 256.

[305] *Id.*

[306] *Id.*

[307] 37 C.F.R. §§ 1.322–1.324.

[308] M.P.E.P. § 1480.

[309] 37 C.F.R. §§ 1.323 and 1.324(b)(4).

[310] 37 C.F.R. § 1.324(b)(1).

[311] M.P.E.P. § 1481.

[312] 37 C.F.R. § 1.324(b)(2).

agreeing to the change.[313] For a detailed explanation of correcting inventorship post patent grant, see Chapter 3, Section VI.B.

In the case of a petition to correct an applicant's mistake in claiming priority to a prior co-pending application, all of the statutory and regulatory requirements for claiming priority must have been satisfied.[314] In addition, it must be apparent from the record of the patent and the parent that the priority claim is appropriate.[315] For a detailed explanation of the requirements for domestic and/or foreign priority, see Chapter 10, Sections III–V.

Only those persons having an ownership interest in a patent may request a Certificate of Correction. Third parties have no right to request or participate in the request for a Certificate of Correction. Further, a third party has no right to appeal the Patent Office's decision as to whether or not to issue a Certificate of Correction.[316] That is, the Congressional framework precludes the right of third parties to file civil actions in cases involving the issuance of a Certificate of Correction; the third party's recourse for the alleged error made by the Patent Office is to raise the issue as a defense in an infringement suit.[317]

Third parties do not have standing to demand that the Patent Office issue, or refuse to issue, a Certificate of Correction.[318] However, a Certificate of Correction may be issued based on information supplied by a third party.[319] The Patent Office has no obligation to act on or respond to submissions of information or requests to issue Certificates of Correction by a third party.[320] A paper submitted by a third party will not be made of record in the file that it relates to nor will it retained by the Patent Office.[321] The Patent Office, however, will review such a paper to determine whether the Patent Office wishes to proceed with a Certificate of Correction based on the information supplied in such a paper.[322] The Patent Office intends to retain its discretion in issuing Certificates of Correction, and may not issue a Certificate of Correction even if a mistake is identified, particularly if the identified mistake is not a significant one that would justify the cost and time of issuing a Certificate of Correction even if requested by the patentee or patentee's assignee.

When information about mistakes in patents is received by the Patent Office, the Patent Office does not intend to correspond with

---

[313] 37 C.F.R. § 1.324(b)(3).

[314] M.P.E.P. § 1481.

[315] *Id.*

[316] Hallmark Cards Inc. v. Lehman, 959 F. Supp. 539, 42 USPQ 2d 1134, 1138 (D.D.C. 1997).

[317] *Id.*

[318] Hallmark Cards, Inc. v. Lehman, 959 F. Supp. 539, 543–44, 42 USPQ 2d 1134, 1138 (D.D.C. 1997).

[319] 37 C.F.R. § 1.322(a)(1)(iii) (Supp. 2000).

[320] 37 C.F.R. § 1.322(a)(2)(i) (Supp. 2000).

[321] 37 C.F.R. § 1.322(a)(2)(ii) (Supp. 2000).

[322] *Id.*

third parties about the information they submitted, either to inform the third parties of whether it intends to issue a Certificate of Correction or to issue a denial of any request for issuance of a Certificate of Correction that may accompany the information. The Patent Office will confirm to the party submitting such information that such information has in fact been received by the Patent Office if a stamped, self-addressed post card has been submitted.[323]

2. *Issuance and Effect*

When the Patent Office issues a Certificate of Correction, the Certificate of Correction will be attached to the patent and recorded in the patent file.[324] A patent that received a Certificate of Correction has the same effect and operation in law as if the patent were originally issued in its corrected form.[325] Each week, the Patent Office publishes a notice listing all patents for which a Certificate of Correction was issued during the applicable week.[326]

The Certificate of Correction is only effective for causes of action arising after it was issued. This interpretation of Section 254 is based upon the language of the statute, which requires that, for causes arising after the Patent Office issues a Certificate of Correction, the Certificate of Correction is to be treated as part of the original patent, i.e., as if the certificate had been issued along with the original patent. By necessary implication, for causes arising before its issuance, the Certificate of Correction is not effective.[327]

Where a claim is invalid on its face without the Certificate of Correction, it is illogical to allow the patent holder, once the Certificate of Correction has issued, to sue an alleged infringer for activities that occurred before the issuance of the Certificate of Correction.[328] Moreover, the Federal Circuit has indicated that it does not seem to be asking too much to expect a patentee to check a patent when it is issued in order to determine whether it contains any errors that require the issuance of a Certificate of Correction.[329] For example, a Certificate of Correction that added a missing appendix to the patent-in-suit in order to correct an omission by the Patent Office was not be given effect in an action that arose before the certificate was issued.[330]

On the other hand, to the extent that the correction via the certificate is of a minor character, the Certificate of Correction may not

---

[323] 37 C.F.R. § 1.322 (Supp. 2000).

[324] 35 U.S.C. § 254.

[325] 35 U.S.C. §§ 254–256.

[326] M.P.E.P. 1480.

[327] Southwest Software Inc. v. Harlequin Inc., 226 F.3d 1280, 56 USPQ 2d 1161, 1172 (Fed. Cir. 2000).

[328] *Id.*, 56 USPQ 2d at 1173.

[329] *Id.*

[330] *Id.*

create any intervening rights that would have precluded the patentee from obtaining damages prior to the correction.

Intervening rights do not arise if a correction makes no change in the scope of a patent.[331] A correction for the purpose of perfecting a claim for priority under 35 U.S.C. Section 120 does not change the scope of a patent and has been held to be a correction of minor character.[332] Where the correction has been made by reissue, intervening rights have been denied.[333] The courts have refused to recognize intervening rights advanced on the ground that the correction antedated prior art that would otherwise invalidate patent claims. As stated by the Patent Office:

> Assuming that intervening rights might be recognized in some circumstances where a patent is corrected by certificate of correction, the recognition of such rights cannot reasonably be expected where the correction simply adds an omitted claim for priority under 35 USC § 120.[334]

For example, where the oath or declaration filed in a parent application is sufficient to satisfy the statutory requirements for a subsequent continuation application, it is unnecessary to make another claim of priority, domestic under Section 120 or foreign under Section 119, in the later application which is identical to and filed during the pendency of the parent application.[335]

VI. Maintenance Fees

A. Introduction to Maintenance Fees

Patents filed before June 8, 1995, have a term equal to the greater of 20 years from filing or 17 years from issue.[336] Patents filed after June 8, 1995, have a term equal to 20 years from the filing date of the application.[337] However, a patent will prematurely expire before the end of its term if the patent holder fails to submit certain fees, known as "maintenance fees," to the Patent Office at specific times during the life of the patent. The maintenance fee requirement was added to the Patent Act in 1980, and it requires that the owner of almost any patent based on an application that was filed on or after December 12, 1980

---

[331] Eagle Iron Works v. McLanahan Corp., 429 F.2d 1375, 166 USPQ 225, 231 (3d Cir. 1970).

[332] *See* Fontijn v. Okamoto, 518 F.2d 610, 186 USPQ 97, 108 (C.C.P.A. 1975); Stricker Indus. Supply Corp. v. Blaw-Knox Co., 321 F. Supp. 876, 167 USPQ 442, 445–46 (N.D. Ill. 1970).

[333] Kelley Mfg. Co. v. Lilliston Corp., 636 F.2d 919, 213 USPQ 29, 30 (4th Cir. 1980), *cert. denied*, 449 U.S. 874 (1980).

[334] *In re* Schuurs and Van Weemen, 218 USPQ 443, 444 (Comm'r Pat. 1983). *See also In re* Lambrech, 202 USPQ 620, 622 (Comm'r Pat. 1976).

[335] *In re* Van Esdonk, 187 USPQ 671, 671 (Comm'r Pat. 1975).

[336] *See* 35 U.S.C. § 154.

[337] *Id.*

submit fees to the Patent Office on or before the following milestone dates:

- 3 years and 6 months after the date of the patent grant;
- 7 years and 6 months after the date of the patent grant; and
- 11 years and 6 months after the date of the patent grant.[338]

The fee amounts (which are halved for small entities) are set forth in the Patent Act and in Patent Office regulations.[339] Maintenance fee requirements do not apply to design patents or plant patents.[340]

B. Timing, Effect of Failure to Pay, and Surcharges

Patent Office regulations provide that maintenance fees may be paid without an additional surcharge at any time during the six-month period prior to and including the due date. For example, the first maintenance fee is due during the period from three years through three years and six months from the date of the patent grant. Similarly, the second maintenance fee is due during the period from seven years through seven years and six months from the date of the patent grant, and the third maintenance fee is due during the period from 11 years through 11 years and six months from the date of the patent grant.[341]

Maintenance fees also may be paid during a six-month grace period after each due date. However, any maintenance fees paid during the grace period must include a surcharge.[342] If the patentee fails to pay the maintenance fee before the end of the grace period, the patent will expire at the end of the grace period.[343]

If a patent expires due to a failure to pay the maintenance fee, the patentee may file a petition to reinstate the patent. Such a petition must be accompanied by the appropriate fee and a surcharge, and it must demonstrate that the delay in payment of the fee was either unavoidable or unintentional.[344] A delay is unavoidable if "reasonable care was taken to ensure that the maintenance fee would be paid timely."[345] An example of an "unintentional" delay is where the patentee reasonably relied on patent counsel's docketing system, but the patent counsel's employee erroneously entered an incorrect due date in the counsel's docketing system.[346] The Patent Office's determination of

[338] 35 U.S.C. § 41(b).

[339] *Id.*; 37 C.F.R. § 1.20(e)–(g).

[340] 35 U.S.C. § 41(b).

[341] 37 C.F.R. § 1.362(d).

[342] 35 U.S.C. § 41(b); 37 C.F.R. § 1.362(e).

[343] 35 U.S.C. § 41(b); M.P.E.P. § 2506.

[344] 37 C.F.R. § 1.378.

[345] 37 C.F.R. § 1.378(b)(3).

[346] Laerdal Med. Corp. v. Ambu Inc., 877 F. Supp. 255, 259, 34 USPQ 2d 1140, 1144 (D. Md. 1995); *see also* California Med. Prods., Inc. v. Tecnol Med. Prods., Inc., 921 F. Supp. 1219, 1259–60 (D. Del. 1995); *compare* Smith v. Mossinghoff, 671 F.2d 533, 213 USPQ 977 (D.C. Cir. 1982) (attorney's failure to monitor docketing system due to preoccupation with depositions, trial, and relocation of residence is not unavoidable delay).

whether a delay is unavoidable or unintentional is subject to great deference.[347] When filing a petition for revival based on unavoidable or unintentional delay, the petition need not include a detailed explanation if it was filed within three months of discovery of when the patent became abandoned, as the Patent Office does not generally question the delay when filing occurs within such a period.[348]

35 U.S.C. Section 41(c)(1) gives the Director of the Patent Office authority to accept maintenance fee payments (and thus revive patents) that are over 30 months late if the delay is shown to have been unavoidable.[349] Whether or not a delay is unavoidable is decided on a case-by-case basis, taking all of the facts and circumstances into account.[350] The burden of showing that the cause of the delay was unavoidable is on the person seeking to revive the patent.[351] Pursuant to PTO regulations, a showing that the delay in paying a maintenance fee was unavoidable can be made when:

> reasonable care was taken to ensure that the maintenance fee would be paid timely and that the petition was filed promptly after the patentee was notified of, or otherwise became aware of, the expiration of the patent. The showing must enumerate the steps taken to ensure timely payment of the maintenance fee, the date and the manner in which the patentee became aware of the expiration of the patent, and the steps taken to file the petition promptly.[352]

Decisions on reinstating a lapsed patent are made by applying the "reasonably prudent person" standard.[353] The test of whether the delay is unavoidable "is applicable to ordinary human affairs, and requires no more or greater care or diligence that is generally used and observed by prudent and careful men in relation to their most important business."[354]

1. *Reliance On Assignor to Pay Maintenance Fee Not Sufficient to Be Considered Unavoidable Delay [New Topic]*

A patent owner's reliance on the assignor to pay the maintenance fee is not considered unavoidable delay. For example, in *R.R. Donnelley & Sons Co. v. Dickinson*,[355] Donnelley brought suit against Q. Todd Dickinson, Under Secretary of Commerce for Intellectual Property and Director of the U.S. Patent Office, to appeal his denial of Donnelley's repeated attempts to have its patent reinstated. The parties did not

---

347 Rydeen v. Quigg, 748 F. Supp. 900, 905, 16 USPQ 2d 1876, 1879–80 (D.D.C. 1990), *aff'd*, 937 F.2d 623 (Fed. Cir. 1991), *cert. denied*, 502 U.S. 1075 (1992).

348 M.P.E.P. § 711.03(c).

349 35 U.S.C. § 41(c)(1) (1994).

350 Smith v. Mossinghoff, 671 F.2d 533, 538, 213 USPQ 977, 982 (D.C. Cir. 1982).

351 R.R. Donnelley & Sons Co. v. Dickinson, 57 USPQ 2d 1244, 1247 (N.D. Ill. 2000).

352 37 C.F.R. § 1.378(b)(3).

353 Ray v. Lehman, 55 F.3d 606, 608–09 34 USPQ 2d 1786, 1787 (Fed. Cir. 1995).

354 *In re* Mattullath, 38 App. D.C. 497, 514 (1912).

355 R.R. Donnelley & Sons Co. v. Dickinson, 57 USPQ 2d 1244 (N.D. Ill. 2000).

dispute that the patent lapsed due to the nonpayment of the second maintenance fee required by 35 U.S.C. Section 41. The disagreement was whether the Director's decision not to revive the patent was arbitrary, capricious, an abuse of discretion, or otherwise not in accordance with law. Donnelley contended that it was; Director Dickinson maintained that it was not.

The Director based the determination of failure to show unavoidable delay on Donnelley's failure to put forth any effort to personally monitor the payment of the maintenance fees and failure to hire or otherwise arrange for someone else to monitor the payment of the maintenance fees. Instead, Donnelley left the payment of the maintenance fees to the assignor of the patent. Donnelley argued that the Director erred in placing the onus of reasonable care on Donnelley instead of on the third parties. Donnelley pointed out that when a patentee relies on a third party or counsel to pay its maintenance fees, the Patent Office's focus should shift to determine whether the third party acted reasonably and prudently.

However, the Director disagreed in this case because the assignor had given up all legal rights to the patent, and therefore, could not insist that anyone make the maintenance payments. Donnelley also failed to provide evidence that the assignor understood its obligation in this matter and that it was being relied upon by Donnelley to attend to payment of the maintenance fees.

Donnelley also argued that the Patent Office has revived patents for lesser cause than that demonstrated in the instant case, such as its decision to revive a patent in *Laerdal Medical Corp. v. Ambu Inc.*,[356] due to a docketing error. However, *Laerdal* was distinguished from the instant case, since the patentee in *Laerdal* personally hired a patent attorney to handle matters related to the patent. Conversely, in the instant case, Donnelley left the payment of maintenance fees to the assignor and made no effort to ensure that the maintenance fees were being paid. Thus, the district court agreed with the Director that Donnelley's delay in paying the maintenance fees on the patent did not fit within the limits of "unavoidable". Accordingly, the district court found that Donnelley failed to establish that the Director's reasoning or conclusion was in any way "arbitrary, capricious, an abuse of discretion, or otherwise not in accordance with law."[357]

C. Maintenance Fee Payment Procedures

Patentees should carefully maintain an appropriate docketing system to track maintenance fee due dates, as the Patent Office has no duty to notify patentees when their maintenance fees are due.[358] The

---

[356] Laerdal Med. Corp. v. Ambu Inc., 877 F. Supp. 255, 259, 34 USPQ 2d 1140 (D. Md. 1995).

[357] *R.R. Donnelley*, 57 USPQ 2d at 1248.

[358] Rydeen v. Quigg, 748 F. Supp. 900, 905, 16 USPQ 2d 1876, 1882 (D.D.C. 1990), *aff'd*, 937 F.2d 623 (Fed. Cir. 1991), *cert. denied,* 502 U.S. 1075 (1992).

Patent Office publishes a notice in the *Official Gazette* of all patent numbers for which maintenance fees are due, and it may also send a reminder notice to the patentee's address of record if the maintenance fee has not been paid during the grace period.[359] However, a patentee should not rely on such notices, as it is ultimately the patent holder's responsibility to keep track of maintenance fee due dates.

The patentee, or any other person or entity on behalf of the patentee, may pay maintenance fees.[360] The fee submitter should pay the maintenance fee directly to the Patent Office in U.S. cash, Treasury notes, national bank notes, post office money orders, or certified checks, or through deduction from a Patent Office deposit account.[361] The maintenance fee submission must be accompanied by an identification of the patent or patents for which maintenance fees are being paid, and it must reference *both* the patent number and the application number of the patent.[362] The submission should also identify the fee year, the amount of the fee including any surcharge being submitted, any assigned customer number, and whether small entity status is being claimed.[363]

---

[359] M.P.E.P. § 2575.

[360] 37 C.F.R. § 1.366(a).

[361] M.P.E.P. § 1522; 37 C.F.R. § 1.366(b).

[362] 37 C.F.R. § 1.366(c).

[363] 37 C.F.R. § 1.366(d).

Appendix B

Sample Patent Prosecution and Appeal Documents

Appendix B-1h

PTO/SB/101 (Rev. 5-95). Approved through 9/30/98. OMB 0651-0032. Patent and Trademark Office: U.S. DEPARTMENT OF COMMERCE.
Under the Paperwork Reduction Act of 1995, no persons are required to respond to a collection of information unless it contains a valid OMB control number.

Declaration and Power of Attorney for Patent Application

專利申請聲明及委託書

Chinese Language Declaration

中文聲明

作為下述發明者，我在此宣告：

As a below named inventor, I hereby declare that:

我的住址、郵局地址和國籍均列在我名下，

My residence, post office address and citizenship are as stated next to my name.

我相信我是首創的、第一個和唯一的發明者(如只列出一人姓名)或是首創的、首位共同發明者(如列出數人姓名)・我提出作為專利申請權利要求的題目如下

I believe I am the original, first and sole inventor (if only one name is listed below) or an original, first and joint inventor (if plural names are listed below) of the subject matter which is claimed and for which a patent is sought on the invention entitled

____

____

如不在下面小方格中打叉則須將說明書附此：

the specification of which is attached hereto unless the following box is checked:

☐ 以美國申請號碼或PCT國際申請號碼 __________
立案于 ____________________
修正于(如適用) ____________________

☐ was filed on ____________________
as United States Application Number or PCT International Application Number
__________ and was amended on
__________ (if applicable).

我在此聲明我已閱畢并理解上述說明書的內容，包括上述任何修正案所修正的權利要求・

I hereby state that I have reviewed and understand the contents of the above identified specification, including the claims, as amended by any amendment referred to above.

按照聯邦法規第三十七節第一・五六條，我有責任提供支持專利權的實質性資料。

I acknowledge the duty to disclose information which is material to patentability as defined in Title 37, Code of Federal Regulations, § 1.56.

Burden Hour Statement: This form is estimated to take 0.4 hours to complete. Time will vary depending upon the needs of the individual case. Any comments on the Amount of time you are required to complete this form should be sent to the Chief Information Officer, Patent and Trademark Office, Washington, DC 20231. DO NOT SEND FEES OR COMPLETED FORMS TO THIS ADDRESS. SEND TO: Assistant Commissioner for Patents, Washington, DC 20231.

PTO/SB/101 (Rev. 5-95). Approved through 9/30/98. OMB 0651-0032. Patent and Trademark Office: U.S. DEPARTMENT OF COMMERCE.

Chinese Language Declaration

我申請享受按照美國法規第三十五節第一百一十九條(a)-(d)項或第365條(b)項列出的以下任何外國專利申請書或發明者證書或第365條(a)項列出任何PCT國際申請指定至少在美國以外的任何一個國家的外國優先權，並確認下列方格內打記號，具有優先權申請前立案日期的、任何外國專利申請書或發明者證書或是PCT國際申請書。

I hereby claim foreign priority under Title 35, United States Code, § 119(a)-(d) or § 365(b) of any foreign application(s) for patent or inventor's certificate, or § 365(a) of any PCT International application which designated at least one country other than the United States, listed below and have also identified below, by checking the box, any foreign application for patent or inventor's certificate, or PCT International application having a filing date before that of the application on which priority is claimed.

國外優先申請書

(號碼) (Number)	(國名) (Country)	(申請日/月/年) (Day/Month/Year Filed)	不要求優先權 Priority Not Claimed
			☐
			☐
			☐

我申請享受被美國法規第35節119(e)列出的以下任何美國臨時申請書的利益。

I hereby claim the benefit under Title 35, United States Code, § 119(e) of any United States provisional application(s) listed below.

(申請順序號碼) (Application No.)	(申請日期) (Filing Date)

我申請享受按照美國法規第三十五節一百二十條或365條(c)項列出任何PCT國際申請所指定的美國列出的以下任何美國申請書的利益，如果此申請書中提出的每項權利要求的題目未按美國法規或是PCT國際申請第三十五節第一百二十條第一段的要求在以前的美國申請書中披露，則我有責任按照聯邦法規第三十七節第一・五六(甲)條提供支持專利權的實質性資料，這一法規條文生效于以前申請的立案日期之後，但在美國或PCT 國際申請立案日期之前。

I hereby claim the benefit under Title 35, United States Code, § 120 of any United States application(s), or § 365(c) of any PCT International application designating the United States, listed below and, insofar as the subject matter of each of the claims of this application is not disclosed in the prior United States or PCT International application in the manner provided by the first paragraph of Title 35, United States Code, § 112, I acknowledge the duty to disclose information which is material to patentability as defined in Title 37, Code of Federal Regulations, § 1.56 which became available between the filing date of the prior application and the national or PCT International filing date of this application.

(申請順序號碼) (Application No.)	(申請日期) (Filing Date)	(狀況) (已獲專利權、申請中、取消) (Status) (patented, pending, abandoned)

我在此聲明根據我所知而作的所有聲明都真實無誤，所有有關資料和信息的聲明也真實無誤：我還知道，按照美國法規第十八節第一千零一項，任何蓄意偽造的聲明都將受到罰款或監禁，或同時受到兩種懲罰。這類蓄意偽造的聲明將危及此申請書或任何已頒發專利的效力。

I hereby declare that all statements made herein of my own knowledge are true and that all statements made on information and belief are believed to be true; and further that these statements were made with the knowledge that willful false statements and the like so made are punishable by fine or imprisonment, or both, under Section 1001 of Title 18 of the United States Code and that such willful false statements may jeopardize the validity of the application or any patent issued thereon.

PTO/SB/101 (Rev. 5-95). Approved through 9/30/98. OMB 0651-0032. Patent and Trademark Office: U.S. DEPARTMENT OF COMMERCE.
Under the Paperwork Reduction Act of 1995, no persons are required to respond to a collection of information unless it contains a valid OMB control number.

Chinese Language Declaration

委託書：
以列名發明者的身份，我在此指定下列律師和/或代理人執行此申請並從事與專利商標公署有關的所有業務(列出姓名和註冊號碼)：

POWER OF ATTORNEY: As a named inventor, I hereby appoint the following attorney(s) and/or agent(s) to prosecute this application and transact all business in the Patent and Trademark Office connected therewith: *(list name and registration number)*

通訊地址 | Send Correspondence to:

直撥電話(姓名及電話號碼) | Direct Telephone Calls to: *(name and telephone number)*

第一個或唯一的發明者全名	Full name of sole or first inventor
發明者簽字 日期	Inventor's signature Date
地址	Residence
國籍	Citizenship
郵局地址	Post Office Address
第二個共同發明者全名(如有)	Full name of second joint inventor, if any
第二個發明者簽字 日期	Second Inventor's signature Date
住址	Residence
國籍	Citizenship
郵局地址	Post Office Address

(第三個和其他共同發明者需提供同樣資料和簽字。) (Supply information and signature for third and subsequent joint inventors.)

Appendix B-1i

PTO/SB/110 (Rev. 5-95). Approved through 9/30/98. OMB 0651-0032. Patent and Trademark Office: U.S. DEPARTMENT OF COMMERCE.
Under the Paperwork Reduction Act of 1995, no persons are required to respond to a collection of information unless it contains a valid OMB control number.

Declaration and Power of Attorney for Patent Application

특허 출원 관련 선언 및 위임권

Korean Language Declaration

아래 지명된 발명자로서, 본인은 하기 사항을 선언합니다.

As a below named inventor, I hereby declare that:

본인의 거주지, 우송 주소 및 국적은 본인의 성명 아래에 기재된 것과 동일합니다.

My residence, post office address and citizenship are as stated next to my name.

본인은 하기 명시된 발명에 대한 특허를 청구하는 주제의 최초 원래 단독 발명자이거나 (아래에 한 이름만이 기재된 경우) 또는 최초 원래 공동 발명자임을 (아래에 여러 이름이 기재된 경우) 확인합니다.

____

____

I believe I am the original, first and sole inventor (if only one name is listed below) or an original, first and joint inventor (if plural names are listed below) of the subject matter which is claimed and for which a patent is sought on the invention entitled

____

____

다음 난이 체크되어 있지 않으면 본 발명의 명세서가 여기에 첨부됩니다.

☐ 미합중국 출원번호 또는 PCT 국제 출원번호는
______________________ 로
______________________ 일에 출원되었고
______________________ 일에 개정되었음
(해당 경우).

the specification of which is attached hereto unless the following box is checked:

☐ was filed on ______________________
as United States Application Number or PCT International Application Number
______________ and was amended on
______________ (if applicable).

본인은 상기 개정에 의해 수정된 상기 명세서는 물론 특허 청구의 내용을 검사했으며 이해했음을 확인합니다.

I hereby state that I have reviewed and understand the contents of the above identified specification, including the claims, as amended by any amendment referred to above.

본인은 연방 규정 코드인 제37장의 제1.56항에 의거하여 특허 자격에 관한 자료 정보를 공개할 의무를 인정합니다.

I acknowledge the duty to disclose information which is material to patentability as defined in Title 37, Code of Federal Regulations, § 1.56.

Burden Hour Statement: This form is estimated to take 0.4 hours to complete. Time will vary depending upon the needs of the individual case. Any comments on the amount of time you are required to complete this form should be sent to the Chief Information Officer, Patent and Trademark Office, Washington, DC 20231. DO NOT SEND FEES OR COMPLETED FORMS TO THIS ADDRESS. SEND TO: Assistant Commissioner for Patents, Washington, DC 20231.

Korean Language Declaration

본인은 외국인 특허 출원(들)이나 발명자의 증명서 관련 경우에는 미합중국 코드인 제35장의 제17.9(a)-(d)항이나 제365(b)항에 의거하여 또는 미합중국 이외에 적어도 한 국가를 지정하는 PCT 국제 출원의 경우에는 제365(a)항에 의거하여 하기 명시된 특허 출원의 외국 우선권을 주장하며, 외국인 특허 출원, 발명자 증명서 또는 우선권이 주장되는 출원일 이전에 제출된 PCT 국제 출원도 또한 아래에 해당란을 체크함으로서 확인하였습니다.

I hereby claim foreign priority under Title 35, United States Code, § 119(a)-(d) or § 365(b) of any foreign application(s) for patent or inventor's certificate, or § 365(a) of any PCT International application which designated at least one country other than the United States, listed below and have also identified below, by checking the box, any foreign application for patent or inventor's certificate, or PCT International application having a filing date before that of the application on which priority is claimed.

(Number) (번호)	(Country) (국가)	(Day/Month/Year Filed) (출원일자 일/월/년)	Priority Not Claimed 우선권 주장 않음
			☐
			☐

본인은 미합중국 코드인 제35장 제119항(e)에 명시된 바와 같이 하기 미합중국 가출원에 관련된 특권을 요구합니다.

I hereby claim the benefit under Title 35, United States Code, § 119(e) of any United States provisional application(s) listed below.

(Application No.) (출원 번호)	(Filing Date) (출원일자)

본언은 미합중국 코드인 제35장의 미국인 출원(들) 관련 제120항에 명시된 바와 같이 또는 미합중국을 지정하는 PCT 국제 출원 관련 제365(c)항에 명시된 바와 같이 하기 출원의 특권을 요구합니다. 이 출원서에 있는 각 특허 청구의 내용이 미합중국 코드인 제35장 제112항의 첫번째 절에서 명시된 바와 같이 종전의 미국 또는 PCT 국제 출원에 발표되지 않았으면 본언은 연방 규정 코드인 제37장 제1.56항에 명시된 바와 같이 종전 출원일자와 이 출원서의 국내 또는 PCT 국제 출원일자 사이에 특허 자격에 대한 자료 정보를 공개할 의무를 인정합니다.

I hereby claim the benefit under Title 35, United States Code, § 120 of any United States application(s), or § 365(c) of any PCT International application designating the United States, listed below and, insofar as the subject matter of each of the claims of this application is not disclosed in the prior United States or PCT International application in the manner provided by the first paragraph of Title 35, United States Code, § 112, I acknowledge the duty to disclose information which is material to patentability as defined in Title 37, Code of Federal Regulations, § 1.56 which became available between the filing date of the prior application and the national or PCT International filing date of this application.

(Application No.) (출원 번호)	(Filing Date) (출원일자)	(Status) (patented, pending, abandoned) (현황)(특허 획득, 출원중, 포기)

본인이 아는 한도 내에서 여기에 제공된 모든 내용이 사실이고, 제공된 정보나 소신이 모두 사실임을 확인하며, 더나아가 미합중국 코드 제18장의 제1001절에 명시된 바와 같이 고의의 허위 진술 및 이와 유사한 행위는 벌금이나 투옥으로 처벌 받거나 벌금과 감옥형을 모두 받을 수 있고 이러한 고의의 허위 진술은 특허 출원이나 후에 발급된 특허의 유효성을 위태롭게 함을 인지하면서 여기에 진술함을 선언합니다.

I hereby declare that all statements made herein of my own knowledge are true and that all statements made on information and belief are believed to be true; and further that these statements were made with the knowledge that willful false statements and the like so made are punishable by fine or imprisonment, or both, under Section 1001 of Title 18 of the United States Code and that such willful false statements may jeopardize the validity of the application of any patent issued thereon.

PTO/SB/110 (Rev. 5-95). Approved through 9/30/98. OMB 0651-0032. Patent and Trademark Office: U.S. DEPARTMENT OF COMMERCE.
Under the Paperwork Reduction Act of 1995, no persons are required to respond to a collection of information unless it contains a valid OMB control number.

Korean Language Declaration

위임권: 지명된 발명자로서 본인은 이 특허를 출원하고 이와 관련하여 특허 및 상표청이 요구하는 실무를 처리하기 위해서 하기 변호사(들) 및/또는 대리인(들)을 임명합니다. (*성명 및 등록번호 기입*)	**POWER OF ATTORNEY: As a named inventor, I hereby appoint the following attorney(s) and/or agent(s) to prosecute this application and transact all business in the Patent and Trademark Office connected therewith: (*list name and registration number*)**
서신 수신자	Send Correspondence to:
직통 전화 수신자: (*성명 및 전화번호*)	Direct Telephone Calls to: (*name and telephone number*)

단독 또는 첫번째 발명자의 성명	Full name of sole or first inventor
발명자의 서명 일자	Inventor's signature Date
거주지	Residence
국적	Citizenship
우송 주소	Post Office Address
만약 있으면 두번째 공동 발명자의 이름	Full name of second joint inventor, if any
두번째 발명자의 서명 일자	Second Inventor's signature Date
거주지	Residence
국적	Citizenship
우송 주소	Post Office Address

(세번째 그리고 차후의 공동 발명자들에 대한 유사한 정보와 그들의 서명을 제공할 것.)

(Supply information and signature for third and subsequent joint inventors.)

Appendix B-1j

PTO/SB/107 (5-96)
Approved for use through 9/30/98 OMB 0651-0032
Patent and Trademark Office: U.S. DEPARTMENT OF COMMERCE
Under the Paperwork Reduction Act of 1995, no persons are required to respond to a collection of information unless it displays a valid OMB control number.

Declaration and Power of Attorney for Patent Application

Заявление о подаче заявки на патент и доверенность поверенному

Заявление на русском языке

Russian Language Declaration

Я, нижеупомянутый изобретатель, настоящим подтверждаю, что:

As a below named inventor, I hereby declare that:

Мое местожительство, почтовый адрес и гражданство действительно таковы, как указано ниже, непосредственно после моего имени.

My residence, post office address and citizenship are as stated next to my name.

Я убежден, что я являюсь первоначальным, первым и единственным изобретателем (если ниже указано только одно имя), или одним из первоначальных и первых со-авторов (если ниже указаны несколько имен) заявляемого изобретения, на которое запрашивается патент и которое называется:

____

____

I believe I am the original, first and sole inventor (if only one name is listed below) or an original, first and joint inventor (if plural names are listed below) of the subject matter which is claimed and for which a patent is sought on the invention entitled

____

____

Описание изобретения приложено к сему (если в расположенной ниже клетке нет отметки):

the specification of which is attached hereto unless the following box is checked:

☐ было подано /дата/__________________ как заявка США номер или международный РСТ №
__________ с изменениями, внесенными /дата/
__________ (если требуется).

☐ was filed on __________________
as United States Application Number or PCT International Application Number
__________ and was amended on
__________ (if applicable).

Настоящим я заявляю, что я изучил и понимаю содержание вышеназванного описания, включая формулу изобретения со всеми поправками, указанными выше.

I hereby state that I have reviewed and understand the contents of the above identified specification, including the claims, as amended by any amendment referred to above.

Я признаю обязанность сообщить информацию, необходимую для патентования в соответствии с §1.56 раздела 37 Кодекса Федеральных Правил.

I acknowledge the duty to disclose information which is material to patentability as defined in Title 37, Code of Federal Regulations, § 1.56.

Настоящим я предъявляю иностранные преимущественные права приоритета в соответствии с §119 (a)-(d) или §365 (b) раздела 35 Кодекса Соединенных Штатов на любую(ые) иностранную(ые) заявку(и) на патент или авторское свидетельство, или с §365 (a) на любую международную заявку РСТ, назначившую одну или больше стран кроме Соединенных Штатов, перечисленную(ые) ниже, а также указал ниже с расположением отметки в клетке все иностранные заявки на патент или авторское свидетельство или международную заявку РСТ, поданные ранее, чем заявка, на которую предъявлено притязание на приоритет.

I hereby claim foreign priority under Title 35, United States Code, § 119(a)-(d) or § 365(b) of any foreign application(s) for patent or inventor's certificate, or § 365(a) of any PCT International application which designated at least one country other than the United States, listed below and have also identified below, by checking the box, any foreign application for patent or inventor's certificate, or PCT International application having a filing date before that of the application on which priority is claimed.

Burden Hour Statement: This form is estimated to take 0.4 hours to complete. Time will vary depending upon the needs of the individual case. Any comments on the amount of time you are required to complete this form should be sent to the Chief Information Officer, Patent and Trademark Office, Washington, DC 20231. DO NOT SEND FEES OR COMPLETED FORMS TO THIS ADDRESS. SEND TO: Assistant Commissioner for Patents, Washington, DC 20231.

PTO/SB/107 (5-96)
Approved for use through 9/30/98 OMB 0651-0032
Patent and Trademark Office: U.S. DEPARTMENT OF COMMERCE
Under the Paperwork Reduction Act of 1995, no persons are required to respond to a collection of information unless it displays a valid OMB control number.

Prior Foreign Application(s)
Прежняя(ие) иностранная(ые) заявка(и)

Притязание на приоритет не предъявляется

Priority Not Claimed

Номер (Number) Страна (Country)	День/Месяц/Год подачи (Day/Month/Year Filed)	☐
Номер (Number) Страна (Country)	День/Месяц/Год подачи (Day/Month/Year Filed)	☐
Номер (Number) Страна (Country)	День/Месяц/Год подачи (Day/Month/Year Filed)	☐

Настоящим я предъявляю иностранные преимущественные права приоритета в соответствии с § 119 (е) раздела 35 Кодекса Соединенных Штатов на любую(ые) предварительную(ые) заявку(и), перечисленную(ые) ниже.

I hereby claim the benefit under Title 35, United States Code, § 119(e) of any United States provisional application(s) listed below.

(Заявка №) (Application No.) — (Дата подачи заяки) (Filing Date)

(Заявка №) (Application No.) — (Дата подачи заяки) (Filing Date)

Настоящим я заявляю претензию на выгоду, в соответствии с § 120 раздела 35 Кодекса Соединенных Штатов, от всех нижеперечисленных заявок(ки) США или с § 365 (с) от любой международной заявки PCT, назначившей Соединенные Штаты, в той мере, в которой предмет изобретения в каждом пункте, на который заявлен приоритет, не был раскрыт в поданной ранее заявке США или международной заявке PCT, как это предусмотрено в первом абзаце § 112 раздела 35 Кодекса Соединенных Штатов. Я признаю обязанность раскрыть информацию, которая является вещественной для патентоспособности, как это предусмотрено в § 1.56 раздела 37 Кодекса Федеральных Правил, которая стала доступна за период времени между подачей предшествующей заявки и датой подачи национальной или международной заяки PCT.

I hereby claim the benefit under Title 35, United States Code, § 120 of any United States application(s), or § 365(c) of any PCT International application designating the United States, listed below and, insofar as the subject matter of each of the claims of this application is not disclosed in the prior United States or PCT International application in the manner provided by the first paragraph of Title 35, United States Code, § 112, I acknowledge the duty to disclose information which is material to patentability as defined in Title 37, Code of Federal Regulations, § 1.56 which became available between the filing date of the prior application and the national or PCT International filing date of this application.

PTO/SB/107 (5-96)
Approved for use through 9/30/98 OMB 0651-0032
Patent and Trademark Office: U.S. DEPARTMENT OF COMMERCE
Under the Paperwork Reduction Act of 1996, no persons are required to respond to a collection of information unless it displays a valid OMB control number.

(Заявка №)	(Дата подачи заявки)	(Статус - запатентовано, рассматривается, заявитель отказался)
(Application No.)	(Filing Date)	(Status - patented, pending, abandoned)
(Заявка №)	(Дата подачи заявки)	(Статус - запатентовано, рассматривается, заявитель отказался)
(Application No.)	(Filing Date)	(Status - patented, pending, abandoned)

Настоящим подтверждаю, что все заявления, сделанные здесь на основе моих знаний, являются правдой, и я также верю в достоверность всех заявлений, основанных на доступной мне информации и убеждениях; кроме того, эти заявления были сделаны со знанием того, что умышленно ложные заявления и подобные им действия караются штрафом, или тюремным заключением, или тем и другим, в соответствии со статьей 1001 раздела 18 Кодекса Соединенных Штатов, и что такие ложные сведения могут сделать недействительной как эту заявку, так и любой патент, по ней выданный.

I hereby declare that all statements made herein of my own knowledge are true and that all statements made on information and belief are believed to be true; and further that these statements were made with the knowledge that willful false statements and the like so made are punishable by fine or imprisonment, or both, under Section 1001 of Title 18 of the United States Code and that such willful false statements may jeopardize the validity of the application or any patent issued thereon.

ДОВЕРЕННОСТЬ ПОВЕРЕННОМУ: В качестве названного здесь изобретателя, я уполномачиваю следующего(их) поверенного(ых) и/или агента(ов) подать эту заявку и осуществлять все операции с ней связанные в Ведомстве по Патентам и Торговым Знакам (далее идет имя и регистрационный номер).

POWER OF ATTORNEY: As a named inventor, I hereby appoint the following attorney(s) and/or agent(s) to prosecute this application and transact all business in the Patent and Trademark Office connected therewith: (*list name and registration number*)

Корреспонденцию посылать по адресу:

Send Correspondence to:

По телефону обращаться к:
(имя и номер телефона)

Direct Telephone Calls to: (*name and telephone number*)

PTO/SB/107 (5-96)
Approved for use through 9/30/98 OMB 0651-0032
Patent and Trademark Office: U.S. DEPARTMENT OF COMMERCE
Under the Paperwork Reduction Act of 1995, no persons are required to respond to a collection of information unless it displays a valid OMB control number.

Полное имя единственного или первого автора изобретения		Full name of sole or first inventor	
Подпись автора изобретения	Дата	Inventor's signature	Date
Местожительство		Residence	
Гражданство		Citizenship	
Почтовый адрес		Post Office Address	
Полное имя второго автора изобретения (если имеется)		Full name of second joint inventor, if any	
Подпись автора изобретения	Дата	Second Inventor's signature	Date
Местожительство		Residence	
Гражданство		Citizenship	
Почтовый адрес		Post Office Address	
(Аналогичная информация о третьем и последующих авторах изобретения должна быть представлена, а также их подписи)		(Supply information and signature for third and subsequent joint inventors.)	

Appendix B-6

Utility and Continuation Application

[Replaces Appendix B-6 in the main volume.]

PTO/SB/05 (03-01)
Approved for use through 10/31/2002. OMB 0651-0032
U.S. Patent and Trademark Office; U.S. DEPARTMENT OF COMMERCE

Please type a plus sign (+) inside this box → ☐

Under the Paperwork Reduction Act of 1995, no persons are required to respond to a collection of information unless it displays a valid OMB control number.

UTILITY PATENT APPLICATION TRANSMITTAL

(Only for new nonprovisional applications under 37 CFR 1.53(b))

Attorney Docket No.	
First Inventor	
Title	
Express Mail Label No.	

APPLICATION ELEMENTS

See MPEP chapter 600 concerning utility patent application contents.

ADDRESS TO: Assistant Commissioner for Patents
Box Patent Application
Washington, DC 20231

1. ☐ Fee Transmittal Form (e.g., PTO/SB/17) *(Submit an original and a duplicate for fee processing)*
2. ☐ Applicant claims small entity status. See 37 CFR 1.27.
3. ☐ Specification [*Total Pages* ☐] *(preferred arrangement set forth below)*
   - Descriptive title of the invention
   - Cross Reference to Related Applications
   - Statement Regarding Fed sponsored R & D
   - Reference to sequence listing, a table, or a computer program listing appendix
   - Background of the Invention
   - Brief Summary of the Invention
   - Brief Description of the Drawings *(if filed)*
   - Detailed Description
   - Claim(s)
   - Abstract of the Disclosure
4. ☐ Drawing(s) *(35 U.S.C. 113)* [*Total Sheets* ☐]
5. Oath or Declaration [*Total Pages* ☐]
   a. ☐ Newly executed (original or copy)
   b. ☐ Copy from a prior application (37 CFR 1.63 (d)) *(for continuation/divisional with Box 18 completed)*
      i. ☐ DELETION OF INVENTOR(S)
      Signed statement attached deleting inventor(s) named in the prior application, see 37 CFR 1.63(d)(2) and 1.33(b).
6. ☐ Application Data Sheet. See 37 CFR 1.76
7. ☐ CD-ROM or CD-R in duplicate, large table or Computer Program *(Appendix)*
8. Nucleotide and/or Amino Acid Sequence Submission *(if applicable, all necessary)*
   a. ☐ Computer Readable Form (CRF)
   b. Specification Sequence Listing on:
      i. ☐ CD-ROM or CD-R (2 copies); or
      ii. ☐ paper
   c. ☐ Statements verifying identity of above copies

ACCOMPANYING APPLICATION PARTS

9. ☐ Assignment Papers (cover sheet & document(s))
10. ☐ 37 CFR 3.73(b) Statement *(when there is an assignee)* ☐ Power of Attorney
11. ☐ English Translation Document *(if applicable)*
12. ☐ Information Disclosure Statement (IDS)/PTO-1449 ☐ Copies of IDS Citations
13. ☐ Preliminary Amendment
14. ☐ Return Receipt Postcard (MPEP 503) *(Should be specifically itemized)*
15. ☐ Certified Copy of Priority Document(s) *(if foreign priority is claimed)*
16. ☐ Nonpublication Request under 35 U.S.C. 122 (b)(2)(B)(i). Applicant must attach form PTO/SB/35 or its equivalent.
17. ☐ Other: ....

18. If a CONTINUING APPLICATION, *check appropriate box, and supply the requisite information below and in a preliminary amendment, or in an Application Data Sheet under 37 CFR 1.76:*

☐ Continuation ☐ Divisional ☐ Continuation-in-part (CIP) of prior application No.:________/________________

Prior application information: *Examiner* ________________ *Group Art Unit:* ________________

For CONTINUATION OR DIVISIONAL APPS only: The entire disclosure of the prior application, from which an oath or declaration is supplied under Box 5b, is considered a part of the disclosure of the accompanying continuation or divisional application and is hereby incorporated by reference. The incorporation <u>can only</u> be relied upon when a portion has been inadvertently omitted from the submitted application parts.

19. CORRESPONDENCE ADDRESS

☐ *Customer Number or Bar Code Label* *(Insert Customer No. or Attach bar code label here)* or ☐ *Correspondence address below*

Name					
Address					
City		*State*		*Zip Code*	
Country		*Telephone*		*Fax*	

Name (Print/Type)		*Registration No. (Attorney/Agent)*	
Signature		*Date*	

Burden Hour Statement: This form is estimated to take 0.2 hours to complete. Time will vary depending upon the needs of the individual case. Any comments on the amount of time you are required to complete this form should be sent to the Chief Information Officer, U.S. Patent and Trademark Office, Washington, DC 20231. DO NOT SEND FEES OR COMPLETED FORMS TO THIS ADDRESS. SEND TO: Assistant Commissioner for Patents, Box Patent Application, Washington, DC 20231.

PTO/SB/17 (11-00)
Approved for use through 10/31/2002. OMB 0651-0032
U.S. Patent and Trademark Office; U.S. DEPARTMENT OF COMMERCE
Under the Paperwork Reduction Act of 1995, no persons are required to respond to a collection of information unless it displays a valid OMB control number.

FEE TRANSMITTAL for FY 2001

Patent fees are subject to annual revision.

TOTAL AMOUNT OF PAYMENT ($)

Complete if Known	
Application Number	
Filing Date	
First Named Inventor	
Examiner Name	
Group Art Unit	
Attorney Docket No.	

METHOD OF PAYMENT

1. ☐ The Commissioner is hereby authorized to charge indicated fees and credit any overpayments to:

Deposit Account Number

Deposit Account Name

☐ Charge Any Additional Fee Required Under 37 CFR 1.16 and 1.17

☐ Applicant claims small entity status. See 37 CFR 1.27

2. ☐ **Payment Enclosed:**

☐ Check ☐ Credit card ☐ Money Order ☐ Other

FEE CALCULATION

1. BASIC FILING FEE

Large Entity Fee Code	Large Entity Fee ($)	Small Entity Fee Code	Small Entity Fee ($)	Fee Description	Fee Paid
101	710	201	355	Utility filing fee	
106	320	206	160	Design filing fee	
107	490	207	245	Plant filing fee	
108	710	208	355	Reissue filing fee	
114	150	214	75	Provisional filing fee	

SUBTOTAL (1) ($)

2. EXTRA CLAIM FEES

			Extra Claims		Fee from below		Fee Paid
Total Claims		-20** =		X		=	
Independent Claims		- 3** =		X		=	
Multiple Dependent						=	

Large Entity Fee Code	Large Entity Fee ($)	Small Entity Fee Code	Small Entity Fee ($)	Fee Description
103	18	203	9	Claims in excess of 20
102	80	202	40	Independent claims in excess of 3
104	270	204	135	Multiple dependent claim, if not paid
109	80	209	40	** Reissue independent claims over original patent
110	18	210	9	** Reissue claims in excess of 20 and over original patent

SUBTOTAL (2) ($)

**or number previously paid, if greater; For Reissues, see above

FEE CALCULATION (continued)

3. ADDITIONAL FEES

Large Entity Fee Code	Large Entity Fee ($)	Small Entity Fee Code	Small Entity Fee ($)	Fee Description	Fee Paid
105	130	205	65	Surcharge - late filing fee or oath	
127	50	227	25	Surcharge - late provisional filing fee or cover sheet	
139	130	139	130	Non-English specification	
147	2,520	147	2,520	For filing a request for *ex parte* reexamination	
112	920*	112	920*	Requesting publication of SIR prior to Examiner action	
113	1,840*	113	1,840*	Requesting publication of SIR after Examiner action	
115	110	215	55	Extension for reply within first month	
116	390	216	195	Extension for reply within second month	
117	890	217	445	Extension for reply within third month	
118	1,390	218	695	Extension for reply within fourth month	
128	1,890	228	945	Extension for reply within fifth month	
119	310	219	155	Notice of Appeal	
120	310	220	155	Filing a brief in support of an appeal	
121	270	221	135	Request for oral hearing	
138	1,510	138	1,510	Petition to institute a public use proceeding	
140	110	240	55	Petition to revive - unavoidable	
141	1,240	241	620	Petition to revive - unintentional	
142	1,240	242	620	Utility issue fee (or reissue)	
143	440	243	220	Design issue fee	
144	600	244	300	Plant issue fee	
122	130	122	130	Petitions to the Commissioner	
123	50	123	50	Processing fee under 37 CFR 1.17(q)	
126	180	126	180	Submission of Information Disclosure Stmt	
581	40	581	40	Recording each patent assignment per property (times number of properties)	
146	710	246	355	Filing a submission after final rejection (37 CFR § 1.129(a))	
149	710	249	355	For each additional invention to be examined (37 CFR § 1.129(b))	
179	710	279	355	Request for Continued Examination (RCE)	
169	900	169	900	Request for expedited examination of a design application	

Other fee (specify) ______________________________

*Reduced by Basic Filing Fee Paid

SUBTOTAL (3) ($)

SUBMITTED BY				Complete *(if applicable)*	
Name (Print/Type)		*Registration No. (Attorney/Agent)*		*Telephone*	
Signature				*Date*	

WARNING: Information on this form may become public. Credit card information should not be included on this form. Provide credit card information and authorization on PTO-2038.

Burden Hour Statement: This form is estimated to take 0.2 hours to complete. Time will vary depending upon the needs of the individual case. Any comments on the amount of time you are required to complete this form should be sent to the Chief Information Officer, U.S. Patent and Trademark Office, Washington, DC 20231. DO NOT SEND FEES OR COMPLETED FORMS TO THIS ADDRESS. SEND TO: Assistant Commissioner for Patents, Washington, DC 20231.

Appendix B-7

Continued Prosecution Application (CPA)

[Replaces Appendix B-7 in the main volume.]

PTO/SB/29 (10-00)
Approved for use through 10/31/2002. OMB 0651-0032
U.S. Patent and Trademark Office; U.S. DEPARTMENT OF COMMERCE
Under the Paperwork Reduction Act of 1995, no persons are required to respond to a collection of information unless it displays a valid OMB control number.

CONTINUED PROSECUTION APPLICATION (CPA)
REQUEST TRANSMITTAL
Submit an original, and a duplicate for fee processing.
(Only for Continuation or Divisional applications under 37 CFR 1.53(d))

CHECK BOX, if applicable: ☐ DUPLICATE

Address to: **Assistant Commissioner for Patents Box CPA Washington, DC 20231**	*Attorney Docket No. of Prior Application*	
	First Named Inventor	
	Examiner Name	
	Group Art Unit	
	Express Mail Label No.	

This is a request for a ☐ continuation or ☐ divisional application under 37 CFR 1.53(d), (continued prosecution application (CPA)) of prior application number _______/____________________ , filed on________________, entitled____.

NOTES

FILING QUALIFICATIONS: *The prior application identified above must be a nonprovisional application that is either: (1) complete as defined by 37 CFR 1.51(b), or (2) the national stage of an international application in compliance with 35 U.S.C. 371. Effective May 29, 2000, a CPA may only be filed in a utility or a plant application if the prior nonprovisional application was filed before May 29, 2000. A CPA may be filed in a design application regardless of the filing date of the prior application. See "Request for Continued Examination Practice changes to and Provisional Application Practice,"* Final Rule, *65 Fed. Reg. 50092 (Aug. 16, 2000); Interim Rule, 65 Fed. Reg.14865 (Mar. 20, 2000), 1233 Off. Gaz. Pat. Office (Apr. 11, 2000).*

C-I-P NOT PERMITTED: *A continuation-in-part application cannot be filed as a CPA under 37 CFR 1.53(d), but must be filed under 37 CFR 1.53(b).*

EXPRESS ABANDONMENT OF PRIOR APPLICATION: *The filing of this CPA is a request to expressly abandon the prior application as of the filing date of the request for a CPA. 37 CFR 1.53(b) must be used to file a continuation, divisional, or continuation-in-part of an application that is not to be abandoned.*

ACCESS TO PRIOR APPLICATION: *The filing of this CPA will be construed to include a waiver of confidentiality by the applicant under 35 U.S.C. 122 to the extent that any member of the public who is entitled under the provisions of 37 CFR 1.14 to access to, copies of, or information concerning, the prior application may be given similar access to, copies of, or similar information concerning, the other application or applications in the file jacket.*

35 U.S.C. 120 STATEMENT: *In a CPA, no reference to the prior application is needed in the first sentence of the specification and none should be submitted. If a sentence referencing the prior application is submitted, it will not be entered. A request for a CPA is the specific reference required by 35 U.S.C. 120 and to every application assigned the application number identified in such request, 37 CFR 1.78(a).*

WARNING: Information on this form may become public. Credit card information should not be included on this form. Provide credit card information and authorization on PTO-2038.

1. ☐ Enter the unentered amendment previously filed on ______________________ under 37 CFR 1.116 in the prior nonprovisional application.
2. ☐ A preliminary amendment is enclosed.
3. This application is filed by fewer than all the inventors named in the prior application, 37 CFR 1.53(d)(4).
   a. ☐ ***DELETE*** the following inventor(s) named in the prior nonprovisional application:
   ....
   ....
   b. ☐ The inventor(s) to be deleted are set forth on a separate sheet attached hereto.
4. ☐ A new power of attorney or authorization of agent (PTO/SB/81) is enclosed.
5. Information Disclosure Statement (IDS) is enclosed:
   a. ☐ PTO-1449
   b. ☐ Copies of IDS Citations

[Page 1 of 2]

Burden Hour Statement: This form is estimated to take 0.4 hours to complete. Time will vary depending upon the needs of the individual case. Any comments on the amount of time you are required to complete this form should be sent to the Chief Information Officer, U.S. Patent and Trademark Office, Washington, DC 20231. DO NOT SEND FEES OR COMPLETED FORMS TO THIS ADDRESS. SEND TO: Assistant Commissioner for Patents, Box CPA, Washington, DC 20231.

PTO/SB/29 (10-00)
Approved for use through 10/31/2002. OMB 0651-0032
U.S. Patent and Trademark Office; U.S. DEPARTMENT OF COMMERCE
Under the Paperwork Reduction Act of 1995, no persons are required to respond to a collection of information unless it displays a valid OMB control number.

CLAIMS	(1) FOR	(2) NUMBER FILED	(3) NUMBER EXTRA	(4) RATE	(5) CALCULATIONS
	TOTAL CLAIMS (37 CFR 1.16(c) or (j))	-20* =		x $_______ =	$
	INDEPENDENT CLAIMS (37 CFR 1.16(b) or (i))	-3** =		x $_______ =	
	MULTIPLE DEPENDENT CLAIMS (if applicable) (37 CFR 1.16(d))			+ $_______ =	
				BASIC FEE (37 CFR 1.16)	
				Total of above Calculations =	
	Reduction by 50% for filing by small entity (Note 37 CFR 1.27).				
	* Reissue claims in excess of 20 and over original patent. ** Reissue independent claims over original patent.			TOTAL =	

6. ☐ Small entity status: Applicant claims small entity status. See 37 CFR 1.27.
7. The Commissioner is hereby authorized to credit overpayments or charge the following fees to Deposit Account No. ______-______________:
   a. ☐ Fees required under 37 CFR 1.16.
   b. ☐ Fees required under 37 CFR 1.17.
   c. ☐ Fees required under 37 CFR 1.18.
8. ☐ A check in the amount of $______________ is enclosed.
9. ☐ Payment by credit card. Form PTO-2038 is attached.
10. ☐ Applicant requests suspension of action under 37 CFR 1.103(b) for a period of _________months (not to exceed 3 months) and the fee under 37 CFR 1.17(i) is enclosed.
11. ☐ New Attorney Docket Number, if desired ___________________________
    [Prior application Attorney Docket Number will carryover to this CPA unless a new Attorney Docket Number has been provided herein.]
12. a. ☐ Receipt For Facsimile Transmitted CPA (PTO/SB/29A)
    b. ☐ Return Receipt Postcard (Should be specifically itemized, See MPEP 503)
13. ☐ Other: ....

NOTE: ***The prior application's correspondence address will carry over to this CPA UNLESS a new correspondence address is provided below.***

14. NEW CORRESPONDENCE ADDRESS

☐ *Customer Number or Bar Code Label* *(Insert Customer No. or Attach bar code label here)* *or* ☐ *New correspondence address below*

Name					
Address					
City		*State*		*Zip Code*	
Country		*Telephone*		*Fax*	

15. SIGNATURE OF APPLICANT, ATTORNEY, OR AGENT REQUIRED

Name (Print /Type)	
Signature	
Registration No. (Attorney/Agent)	
Date	

[Page 2 of 2]

PTO/SB/29A (08-00)
Approved for use through 10/31/2002. OMB 0651-0032
U.S. Patent and Trademark Office; U.S. DEPARTMENT OF COMMERCE
Under the Paperwork Reduction Act of 1995, no persons are required to respond to a collection of information unless it displays a valid OMB control number.

If this RECEIPT is included with a request for a CPA filed by facsimile transmission, it will be date stamped and mailed to the ADDRESS in item 1.

RECEIPT FOR FACSIMILE TRANSMITTED CPA

(To accompany a request for a Continued Prosecution Application (CPA) under 37 CFR 1.53(d) filed by facsimile transmission)

1. ADDRESS — *Applicant's Mailing Address for this receipt must be CLEARLY PRINTED or TYPED in the box below.*

NOTE: By this receipt, the USPTO (a) acknowledges that a request for a CPA was filed by facsimile transmission on the date stamped below by the USPTO and (b) verifies only that the application number provided by the applicant on this receipt is the same as the application number provided on the accompanying request for a CPA. This receipt CANNOT be used to acknowledge receipt of any paper(s) other than the request for a CPA.

2. APPLICATION IDENTIFICATION:
(Provide at least enough information to identify the application)

a. For prior application

Application No.: ....
Filing Date: ....
Title: ....
Attorney Docket No.: ....
First Named Inventor: ....

b. For instant CPA application

New Attorney Docket No.: ....
(if applicable)

The USPTO date stamp, which appears in the box to the right, is an acknowledgement by the USPTO of receipt of a request for a CPA filed by facsimile transmission on the date indicated below.

(THIS AREA FOR PTO DATE STAMP USE)

USPTO HANDLING INSTRUCTIONS:

Please stamp area to the right with the date the complete transmission of the request for a CPA was received in the USPTO and also include the USPTO organization name that provided the date stamp (stamp may include both items). Verify that the application number provided by applicant on this receipt is the same as the application number provided by applicant on the request for a CPA accompanying this receipt. If there is an inconsistency between the application number provided on this receipt and the request for a CPA, strike through the inconsistent application number provided on this receipt and insert the correct application number, if possible. Then place in a window envelope and mail.

Burden Hour Statement: This form is estimated to take 0.4 hours to complete. Time will vary depending upon the needs of the individual case. Any comments on the amount of time you are required to complete this form should be sent to the Chief Information Officer, U.S. Patent and Trademark Office, Washington, DC 20231. DO NOT SEND FEES OR COMPLETED FORMS TO THIS ADDRESS. SEND TO: Assistant Commissioner for Patents, Box Patent Application, Washington, DC 20231.

Appendix B-10

Request for Deferral of Examination 37 CFR 1.103(d)

PTO/SB/37 (01-01)
Approved for use through XX/XX/XXXX. OMB 0651-0031
U.S. Patent and Trademark Office; U.S. DEPARTMENT OF COMMERCE
Under the Paperwork Reduction Act of 1995, no persons are required to respond to a collection of information unless it displays a valid OMB control number.

Request for Deferral of Examination 37 CFR 1.103(d)

Application Number		Group Art Unit	
Filing Date		Examiner Name	
First Named Inventor		Attorney Docket Number	

Address to: Assistant Commissioner for Patents
Washington, D.C. 20231

I hereby request deferral of examination under 37 CFR 1.103(d) for the above-identified (non-reissue) utility or plant application filed under 37 CFR 1.53(b) for a period of ____________ months (maximum 3 years), from the earliest filing date for which a benefit is claimed. Deferral of Examination under 37 CFR 1.103(d) is suspension of action. As a result, any patent term adjustment may be reduced. See 37 CFR 1.704(c)(1).

__Note:__ The request will not be granted unless the application is in condition for publication as provided in 37 CFR 1.211(c) and the Office has not issued either an Office action under 35 U.S.C. 132 or a notice of allowance under 35 U.S.C. 151.

☐ If the application is filed prior to November 29, 2000:

I hereby request voluntary publication of the above-identified application under 37 CFR 1.221. A copy of the application in compliance with the Office's electronic filing system requirements has been submitted and the confirmation number is ________________.

__Note:__ A request for voluntary publication under 37 CFR 1.221 requires a copy of the application in compliance with the Office's electronic filing system requirements (EFS) as set forth in the USPTO Electronic Business Center Web Page at www.uspto.gov/ebc, the publication fee set forth in 37 CFR 1.18(d), and the processing fee for the voluntary publication set forth in 37 CFR 1.17(i).

☐ If applicant previously filed a nonpublication request under 37 CFR 1.213(a):

I hereby **rescind** under 37 CFR 1.213(b) the previous filed request that the above-identified application not be published under 35 U.S.C. 122(b).

__Note:__ Application will be scheduled for publication at 18 months from the earliest claimed filing date for which a benefit is claimed.

Fees

a. ☐ The Commissioner is hereby authorized to charge the following fees, or credit any overpayment, to Deposit Account No.____________________.

- i. ☐ Processing fee set forth in 37 CFR 1.17(i) for request for deferral of examination.
- ii. ☐ Publication fee set forth in 37 CFR 1.18(d).
- iii. ☐ Processing fee set forth in 37 CFR 1.17(i) for voluntary publication.
- iv. ☐ Other____.

b. ☐ Check in the amount of $________________________________ is enclosed.

c. ☐ Payment by credit card *(Form PTO-2038 enclosed).*

__Note:__ The publication fee set forth in 37 CFR 1.18(d) and the processing fee in 37 CFR 1.17(i) for deferral of examination are required when the request of deferral of examination is filed.

Signature of Applicant, Attorney, or Agent in Compliance with 37 CFR 1.33(b) Required			
Name (Print/Type)		*Registration Number (Attorney/Agent)*	
Signature		*Date*	
__Note:__ Signatures of all the inventors or assignees of record of the entire interest or their representative(s) are required. Submit multiple forms for more than one signature, see below.*			
☐ *Total of ________forms are submitted.			

Burden Hour Statement: This form is estimated to take 0.2 hours to complete. Time will vary depending upon the needs of the individual case. Any comments on the amount of time you are required to complete this form should be sent to the Chief Information Officer, U.S. Patent and Trademark Office, Washington, DC 20231. DO NOT SEND FEES OR COMPLETED FORMS TO THIS ADDRESS. SEND Fees and Completed Forms to the following address: Assistant Commissioner for Patents, Washington, DC 20231.

Appendix B-11

Nonpublication Request Under 35 U.S.C. 122(b)(2)(B)(i)

PTO/SB/35 (11-00)
Approved for use through 10/31/2002. OMB 0651-0031
U.S. Patent and Trademark Office; U. S. DEPARTMENT OF COMMERCE
Under the Paperwork Reduction Act of 1995, no persons are required to respond to a collection of information unless it displays a valid OMB control number.

NONPUBLICATION REQUEST UNDER 35 U.S.C. 122(b)(2)(B)(i)	First Named Inventor	
	Title	
	Atty Docket Number	

I hereby certify that the invention disclosed in the attached application **has not and will not be** the subject of an application filed in another country, or under a multilateral agreement, that requires publication at eighteen months after filing.

I hereby request that the attached application not be published under 35 U.S.C. 122(b).

Date

Signature

Typed or printed name

This request must be signed in compliance with 37 CFR 1.33(b) and submitted with the application **upon filing.**

Applicant may rescind this nonpublication request at any time. If applicant rescinds a request that an application not be published under 35 U.S.C. 122(b), the application will be scheduled for publication at eighteen months from the earliest claimed filing date for which a benefit is claimed.

If applicant subsequently files an application directed to the invention disclosed in the attached application in another country, or under a multilateral international agreement, that requires publication of applications eighteen months after filing, the applicant **must** notify the United States Patent and Trademark Office of such filing within forty-five (45) days after the date of the filing of such foreign or international application. **Failure to do so will result in abandonment of this application (35 U.S.C. 122(b)(2)(B)(iii)).**

Burden Hour Statement: This collection of information is required by 37 CFR 1.213(a). The information is used by the public to request that an application not be published under 35 U.S.C. 122(b) (and the PTO to process that request). Confidentiality is governed by 35 U.S.C. 122 and 37 CFR 1.14. This form is estimated to take 6 minutes to complete. Time will vary depending upon the needs of the individual case. Any comments on the amount of time you are required to complete this form should be sent to the Chief Information Officer, U.S. Patent and Trademark Office, Washington, DC 20231. DO NOT SEND FEES OR COMPLETED FORMS TO THIS ADDRESS. SEND TO: Assistant Commissioner for Patents, Washington, DC 20231.

Appendix B-12

Request to Rescind Previous Nonpublication Request

PTO/SB/36 (4-01)
Approved for use through 10/31/2002. OMB 0651-0031
U.S. Patent and Trademark Office; U.S. DEPARTMENT OF COMMERCE
Under the Paperwork Reduction Act of 1995, no persons are required to respond to a collection of information unless it displays a valid OMB control number.

REQUEST TO RESCIND PREVIOUS NONPUBLICATION REQUEST 35 U.S.C. 122(b)(2)(B)(ii)		
	Application Number	
	Filing Date	
	First Named Inventor	
	Title	
	Atty Docket Number	
	Group Art Unit	
	Examiner	

I hereby **rescind** the previous request that the above-identified application not be published under 35 U.S.C. 122(b).

Date

Signature

Typed or printed name

This request must be signed in compliance with 37 CFR 1.33(b).

Note: Filing this rescission of a previous nonpublication request is considered the notice of a subsequent foreign or International filling required by 35 USC 122(b)(2)(B)(iii) and 37 CFR 1.213(c) if this rescission is filed no later than forty-five days (45) days after the date of filing of such foreign or international application. See 37 CFR 1.137(f) if a notice of subsequent foreign or International filling required by 35 USC 122(b)(2)(B)(iii) and 37 CFR 1.213(c) is **not** filed within forty-five days (45) days after the date of filing of the foreign or international application.

CERTIFICATE OF MAILING OR TRANSMISSION

I hereby certify that this correspondence is being deposited with the United States Postal Service with sufficient postage as first class mail in an envelope addressed to: Commissioner For Patents, Box RCE, Washington, DC 20231, or facsimile transmitted to the U.S. Patent and Trademark Office on:

Name (Print/Type)

Signature | *Date*

Burden Hour Statement: This collection of information is required by 37 CFR 1.213(b). The information is used by the public to rescind a previously filed request that an application not be published under 35 U.S.C. 122(b) (and the PTO to process that rescission). Confidentiality is governed by 35 U.S.C. 122 and 37 CFR 1.14. This form is estimated to take 6 minutes to complete. Time will vary depending upon the needs of the individual case. Any comments on the amount of time you are required to complete this form should be sent to the Chief Information Officer, U.S. Patent and Trademark Office, Washington, DC 20231. DO NOT SEND FEES OR COMPLETED FORMS TO THIS ADDRESS. SEND TO: Assistant Commissioner for Patents, Washington, DC 20231.

Appendix B-13

Request for Continued Examination (RCE) Transmittal

PTO/SB/30 (08-00)
Approved for use through 10/31/2002. OMB 0651-0031
U.S. Patent and Trademark Office: U.S. DEPARTMENT OF COMMERCE
Under the Paperwork Reduction Act of 1995, no persons are required to respond to a collection of information unless it displays a valid OMB control number.

REQUEST FOR CONTINUED EXAMINATION (RCE) TRANSMITTAL

Subsection (b) of 35 U.S.C. § 132, effective on May 29, 2000, provides for continued examination of an utility or plant application filed on or after June 8, 1995.
See The American Inventors Protection Act of 1999 (AIPA).

Application Number	
Filing Date	
First Named Inventor	
Group Art Unit	
Examiner Name	
Attorney Docket Number	

This is a Request for Continued Examination (RCE) under 37 C.F.R. § 1.114 of the above-identified application.

NOTE: *37 C.F.R. § 1.114 is effective on May 29, 2000. If the above-identified application was filed prior to May 29, 2000, applicant may wish to consider filing a continued prosecution application (CPA) under 37 C.F.R. § 1.53 (d) (PTO/SB/29) instead of a RCE to be eligible for the patent term adjustment provisions of the AIPA. See Changes to Application Examination and Provisional Application Practice*, Final Rule, 65 *Fed. Reg.* 50092 (Aug. 16, 2000); Interim Rule, 65 *Fed. Reg.* 14865 (Mar. 20, 2000), 1233 *Off. Gaz. Pat. Office* 47 (Apr. 11, 2000), which established RCE practice.

1. Submission required under 37 C.F.R. § 1.114
   - a. ☐ Previously submitted
     - i. ☐ Consider the amendment(s)/reply under 37 C.F.R. § 1.116 previously filed on ____________________ (Any unentered amendment(s) referred to above will be entered).
     - ii. ☐ Consider the arguments in the Appeal Brief or Reply Brief previously filed on ____________________
     - iii. ☐ Other ______________________________
   - b. ☐ Enclosed
     - i. ☐ Amendment/Reply
     - ii. ☐ Affidavit(s)/Declaration(s)
     - iii. ☐ Information Disclosure Statement (IDS)
     - iv. ☐ Other ______________________________
2. Miscellaneous
   - a. ☐ Suspension of action on the above-identified application is requested under 37 C.F.R. § 1.103(c) for a period of _________ months. (Period of suspension shall not exceed 3 months; Fee under 37 C.F.R. § 1.17(i) **required**)
   - b. ☐ Other ______________________________
3. Fees The RCE fee under 37 C.F.R. § 1.17(e) is required by 37 C.F.R. § 1.114 when the RCE is filed.
   - a. ☐ The Director is hereby authorized to charge the following fees, or credit any overpayments, to Deposit Account No.____________________________
     - i. ☐ RCE fee required under 37 C.F.R. § 1.17(e)
     - ii. ☐ Extension of time fee (37 C.F.R. §§ 1.136 and 1.17)
     - iii. ☐ Other ______________________________
   - b. ☐ Check in the amount of $__________________ enclosed
   - c. ☐ Payment by credit card (Form PTO-2038 enclosed)

SIGNATURE OF APPLICANT, ATTORNEY, OR AGENT REQUIRED

Name *(Print /Type)*		*Registration No. (Attorney/Agent)*	
Signature		*Date*	

CERTIFICATE OF MAILING OR TRANSMISSION

I hereby certify that this correspondence is being deposited with the United States Postal Service with sufficient postage as first class mail in an envelope addressed to: Commissioner For Patents, Box RCE, Washington, DC 20231, or facsimile transmitted to the U.S. Patent and Trademark Office on:

Name *(Print/Type)*			
Signature		*Date*	

Burden Hour Statement: This form is estimated to take 6 minutes to complete. Time will vary depending upon the needs of the individual case. Any comments on the amount of time you are required to complete this form should be sent to the Chief Information Officer, U.S. Patent and Trademark Office, Washington, DC 20231. DO NOT SEND FEES OR COMPLETED FORMS TO THIS ADDRESS. SEND TO: Assistant Commissioner for Patents, Box RCE, Washington, DC 20231.

Appendix B-14

Request for Statutory Invention Registration

PTO/SB/94 (10-00)
Approved for use through 03/31/2003. OMB 0651-0036
U.S. Patent and Trademark Office; U.S. DEPARTMENT OF COMMERCE
Under the Paperwork Reduction Act of 1995, no persons are required to respond to a collection of information unless it displays a valid OMB control number.

Request for Statutory Invention Registration

Application Number________________________, or ☐ attached hereto

Filed: ________________________________

Title: ____

Applicant(s): ____

A. In the above identified patent application, I hereby:

1. Request and authorize the Commissioner of Patents and Trademarks to publish the above identified regularly filed patent application as a Statutory Invention Registration. (35 U.S.C. 157)
2. Waive the right to receive a United States patent on the same invention claimed in the above identified patent application. These rights, which are waived, include those specified in 35 U.S.C. 183 and 271 through 289 as well as all attributes specified for patents in any other provisions of law other than title 35, United States Code. The waiver includes, but is not limited to, the remedies under 19 U.S.C. 1337 and 1337a, 22 U.S.C. 2356 and 28 U.S.C. 1498. (35 U.S.C. 157(c))
3. Understand that the above waiver will be effective pursuant to 37 CFR 1.293 upon publication of the Statutory Invention Registration to waive the inventor's right to receive a United States patent on the invention claimed in the Statutory Invention Registration. (37 CFR 1.293(b)(1))
4. State that, in my opinion, the disclosure and claims of the above identified patent application meet the requirements of 35 U.S.C. 112. (37 CFR 1.293(b)(3))
5. State that, in my opinion, the above identified patent application complies with the requirements for printing as set forth in the Rules of Practice for Patent Cases, 37 CFR Part 1. (37 CFR 1.293(b)(4))
6. Enclose the fee* set forth in 37 CFR 1.17(n) or (o) for requesting publication of a Statutory Invention Registration:

☐ A first Office Action <u>has not been mailed</u> in the above application, 37 CFR 1.17(n)........... $______

☐ A first Office Action <u>has been mailed</u> in the above application, 37 CFR 1.17(o)................ $______

Request fee $ ______

<u>MINUS BASIC FILING FEE, IF PREVIOUSLY PAID</u>

☐ Basic filing fee for utility patent application set forth in 37 CFR 1.16(a); or

☐ Basic filing fee for design patent application set forth in 37 CFR 1.16(f); or

☐ Basic filing fee for plant patent application set forth in 37 CFR 1.16(g)
Minus basic filing fee $________ Amount due $ ______

Payment charged to credit card _______________. Form PTO-2038 is attached.
Amount enclosed by check or money order __________________.
Please charge Deposit Account No. __________________the amount of $ ____________________.
If payment of any additional fee is required for publication of the Statutory Invention Registration, charge such amount to Deposit Account No. __________________.

* Where this request is submitted at the time the application is filed, the filing fee is included in the fee.

[Page 1 of 2]

This collection of information is required by 35 USC 157. This information is used by the public to request (and by the U.S. PTO to process) a statutory invention registration. Confidentiality is governed by 35 U.S.C. 122 and 37 CFR 1.14. This form is estimated to take 24 minutes to complete, including gathering, preparing, and submitting the statutory invention registration. Time will vary depending on the individual case. Any comments on the amount of time you require to complete this form and/or suggestions for reducing this burden should be sent to the Chief Information Officer, U.S. Patent and Trademark Office, U.S. Department of Commerce, Washington, DC 20231. DO NOT SEND FEES OR COMPLETED FORMS TO THIS ADDRESS. SEND TO: Assistant Commissioner for Patents, Washington, D.C. 20231.

PTO/SB/94 (10-00)
Approved for use through 03/31/2003. OMB 0651-0036
U.S. Patent and Trademark Office; U.S. DEPARTMENT OF COMMERCE

B. For printing of the Statutory Invention Registration front page, if desired, list below the name(s) of not more than 3 registered patent attorneys and agents OR alternatively, the name of a firm having as a member a registered patent attorney or agent. If no name is listed below, no name will be printed on the Statutory Invention Registration.

____

____.

C. Name of assignee, it any, for printing on the Statutory Invention Registration ___________________.
Address (City and State or Country)____.
State of incorporation, if assignee is a corporation ____________________________________.

WARNING: Information on this form may become public. Credit card information should not be included on this form. Provide credit card information and authorization on PTO-2038.

____
Signature(s) (37 CFR 1.293(a))
☐ attorney or agent of record ☐ applicant(s) and any assignee

Appendix C

Rules and Guidelines

Appendix C-8a

Revised Utility Examination Guidelines; Request for Comments

64 FR 71440
Department of Commerce
Patent and Trademark Office
[Docket No. 991027289-9289-01]
RIN 0651-AB09

Revised Utility Examination Guidelines;
Request for Comments

Agency: Patent and Trademark Office, Commerce.

Action: Notice and request for public comments.

Summary: The Patent and Trademark Office (PTO) requests comments from any interested member of the public on the following Revised Utility Examination Guidelines. The PTO is publishing a revised version of guidelines to be used by Office personnel in their review of patent applications for compliance with the utility requirement based on comments received in response to the Request for Comments on Interim Guidelines for Examination of Patent Applications. Under the 35 U.S.C. 112, para. 1 "Written Description" Requirement; Extension of Comment Period and Notice of Hearing. 63 FR 50887 (September 23, 1998). These Revised Utility Guidelines will be used by PTO personnel in their review of patent applications for compliance with the "utility" requirement of 35 U.S.C. 101. This revision supersedes the Utility Examination Guidelines that were published at 60 FR 36263 (1995) and at 1177 O.G. 146 (1995).

Dates: Written comments on the Revised Utility Examination Guidelines will be accepted by the PTO until March 22, 2000.

Addresses: Written comments should be addressed to Box 8, Commissioner of Patents and Trademarks, Washington, DC 20231, marked to the attention of Mark Nagumo, or to Box Comments, Assistant Commissioner for Patents, Washington, DC 20231, marked to the attention of Linda S. Therkorn. Alternatively, comments may be submitted to Mark Nagumo via facsimile at (703) 305-9373 or by electronic mail addressed to "mark.nagumo@uspto.gov"; or to Linda Therkorn via facsimile at (703) 305-8825 or by electronic mail addressed to "linda.therkorn@uspto.gov."

For Further Information Contact: Mark Nagumo by telephone at (703) 305-8666, by facsimile at (703) 305-9373, by electronic mail "mark. nagumo@uspto.gov," or by mail marked to his attention addressed to the Commissioner of Patents and Trademarks, Box 8, Washington, DC 20231; or Linda Therkorn by telephone at (703) 305-9323, by facsimile at (703) 305-8825, by electronic mail at "linda. therkorn@uspto. gov," or by mail marked to her attention addressed to Box Comments, Assistant Commissioner of Patents and Trademarks, Washington, DC 20231.

Supplementary Information: The PTO requests comments from any interested member of the public on the following Revised Utility Examination Guidelines. As of the publication date of this notice, this revision will be used by PTO personnel in their review of patent applications for compliance with the "utility" requirement of 35 U.S.C. 101. Because this revision governs internal practices, it is exempt from notice and comment rulemaking under 5 U.S.C. 553(b)(A).

Written comments should include the following information: (1) Name and affiliation of the individual responding, and (2) an indication of whether the comments offered represent views of the respondent's organization or are respondent's personal views.

Parties presenting written comments are requested, where possible, to provide their comments in machine-readable format in addition to a paper copy. Such submissions may be provided by electronic mail messages sent over the Internet, or on a 3.5″ floppy disk formatted for use in a Macintosh, Windows, Windows for Workgroups, Windows 95, Windows 98, Windows NT, or MS-DOS based computer.

Written comments will be available for public inspection on or about April 19, 2000, in Suite 918, Crystal Park 2, 2121 Crystal Drive, Arlington, Virginia. In addition, comments provided in machine readable format will be available through the PTO's Website at http://www. uspto.gov.

I. Discussion of Public Comments

Comments received by the Office in response to the request for public comment on the Interim Written Description Guidelines regarding the patentability of expressed sequence tags (ESTs) suggested the need for revision or clarification of the final Utility Examination Guidelines as published at 60 FR 36263 (1995) and 1177 O.G. 146 (1995). All comments have been carefully considered. Many comments stated that sufficient patentable utility has not been shown when the sole disclosed use of an EST is to identify other nucleic acids whose utility was not known, and the function of the corresponding gene is not known. Moreover, several comments opined that ESTs are genomic research tools that should be available for unencumbered research to advance the public good. One comment stated that asserted utilities for ESTs, such as mapping the genome or tissue typing, would probably not satisfy the requirements of 35 U.S.C. 101 if the length of the attached DNA sequence were greatly extended. Other comments stated that the disclosure of a DNA sequence alone is insufficient to enable scientists to use ESTs for mapping or tissue typing. Some comments suggested that PTO examination procedures would result in granting patents based on nonspecific and nonsubstantial utilities, contrary to established case law. See Brenner v. Manson, 383 U.S. 519, 534–35, 148 USPQ 689, 695 (1966) (requiring disclosure of "specific utility," and of "substantial utility," "where specific benefit exists in currently available form"); accord, In re Ziegler, 992 F.2d 1197, 1201, 26 USPQ 2d 1600, 1603 (Fed. Cir. 1996) (requiring that a specific and substantial or practical utility for the invention be disclosed as a condition of meeting the practical utility requirement of Sec. 101). Consequently, a number of changes have been made to the Utility Examination Guidelines to clarify the position of the Patent and Trademark Office. Updated training material will be developed in the examination corps to address technology-specific issues.

II. Guidelines for Examination of Applications for Compliance With the Utility Requirement

A. Introduction

The following guidelines establish the policies and procedures to be followed by Office personnel in the evaluation of any patent application for compliance with the utility requirements of 35 U.S.C. 101 and 112. These guidelines have been promulgated to assist Office personnel in their review of applications for compliance with the utility requirement. The guidelines do not alter the substantive requirements of 35 U.S.C. 101 and 112, nor are they designed to obviate the examiner's review of applications for compliance with all other statutory requirements for patentability.

B. Examination Guidelines for the Utility Requirement

Office personnel are to adhere to the following procedures when reviewing patent applications for compliance with the "useful invention" ("utility") requirement of 35 U.S.C. 101 and 112, first paragraph.

1. Read the claims and the supporting written description.
   (a) Determine what the applicant has claimed, noting any specific embodiments of the invention.
   (b) Ensure that the claims define statutory subject matter (i.e., a process, machine, manufacture, composition of matter, or improvement thereof).
2. Review the claims and the supporting written description to determine if the applicant has asserted for the claimed invention any specific and substantial utility that is credible.
   (a) If the invention has a well-established utility, regardless of any assertion made by the applicant, do not impose a rejection based on lack of utility. An invention has a well-established utility if a person of ordinary skill in the art would immediately appreciate why the invention is useful based on the characteristics of the invention (e.g., properties or applications of a product or process).
   (b) If the applicant has asserted that the claimed invention is useful for any particular practical purpose (i.e., it has a "specific and substantial utility") and the assertion would be considered credible by a person of ordinary skill in the art, do not impose a rejection based on lack of utility.
      (1) A claimed invention must have a specific and substantial utility. This requirement excludes "throw-away," "insubstantial," or "nonspecific" utilities, such as the use of a complex invention as landfill, as a way of satisfying the utility requirement of 35 U.S.C. 101.
      (2) Credibility is assessed from the perspective of one of ordinary skill in the art in view of the disclosure and any other evidence of record (e.g., test data, affidavits or declarations from experts in the art, patents or printed publications) that is probative of the applicant's assertions. An applicant need only provide one credible assertion of specific and substantial utility for each claimed invention to satisfy the utility requirement.
   (c) If no assertion of specific and substantial utility for the claimed invention made by the applicant is credible, and the claimed invention does not have a well-established utility, reject the claim(s) under section 101 on the grounds that the invention as claimed lacks utility. Also reject the claims under Sec. 112, first paragraph, on the basis that the disclosure fails to teach how to use the invention as claimed. The section 112, first paragraph, rejection imposed in conjunction with a section 101 rejection should incorporate by reference the grounds of the corresponding section 101 rejection.
   (d) If the applicant has not asserted any specific and substantial utility for the claimed invention and it does not have a well-established utility, impose a rejection under section 101, emphasizing that the applicant has not disclosed a specific and substantial utility for the invention. Also impose a separate

rejection under section 112, first paragraph, on the basis that the applicant has not disclosed how to use the invention due to the lack of a specific and substantial utility. The sections 101 and 112 rejections shift the burden of coming forward with evidence to the applicant to:

(1) Explicitly identify a specific and substantial utility for the claimed invention; and

(2) Provide evidence that one of ordinary skill in the art would have recognized that the identified specific and substantial utility was well established at the time of filing. The examiner should review any subsequently submitted evidence of utility using the criteria outlined above. The examiner should also ensure that there is an adequate nexus between the showing and the application as filed.

3. Any rejection based on lack of utility should include a detailed explanation why the claimed invention has no specific and substantial credible utility. Whenever possible, the examiner should provide documentary evidence (e.g., scientific or technical journals, excerpts from treatises or books, or U.S. or foreign patents) to support the factual basis for the prima facie showing of no specific and substantial credible utility. If documentary evidence is not available, the examiner should specifically explain the scientific basis for his or her factual conclusions.

(a) Where the asserted specific and substantial utility is not credible, a prima facie showing of no specific and substantial credible utility must establish that it is more likely than not that a person skilled in the art would not consider credible any specific and substantial utility asserted by the applicant for the claimed invention.

The prima facie showing must contain the following elements:

(1) An explanation that clearly sets forth the reasoning used in concluding that the asserted specific and substantial utility is not credible;

(2) Support for factual findings relied upon in reaching this conclusion; and

(3) An evaluation of all relevant evidence of record.

(b) Where no specific and substantial utility is disclosed or known, a prima facie showing of no specific and substantial utility must establish that it is more likely than not that a person skilled in the art would not be aware of any well-established credible utility that is both specific and substantial.

The prima facie showing must contain the following elements:

(1) An explanation that clearly sets forth the reasoning used in concluding that there is no known well established utility for the claimed invention that is both specific and substantial;

(2) Support for factual findings relied upon in reaching this conclusion; and

(3) An evaluation of all relevant evidence of record.

4. A rejection based on lack of utility should not be maintained if an asserted utility for the claimed invention would be considered specific, substantial, and credible by a person of ordinary skill in the art in view of all evidence of record.

Office personnel are reminded that they must treat as true a statement of fact made by an applicant in relation to an asserted utility, unless countervailing evidence can be provided that shows that one of ordinary skill in the art would have a legitimate basis to doubt the credibility of such a statement. Similarly, Office personnel must accept an opinion from a qualified expert that is based upon relevant facts whose accuracy is not being questioned; it is improper to disregard the opinion solely because of a disagreement over the significance or meaning of the facts offered.

Once a prima facie showing of no specific and substantial credible utility has been properly established, the applicant bears the burden of rebutting it. The applicant can do this by amending the claims, by providing reasoning or arguments, or by providing evidence in the form of a declaration under 37 CFR 1.132 or a printed publication that rebuts the basis or logic of the prima facie showing. If the applicant responds to the prima facie rejection, the Office personnel should review the original disclosure, any evidence relied upon in establishing the prima facie showing, any claim amendments, and any new reasoning or evidence provided by the applicant in support of an asserted specific and substantial credible utility. It is essential for Office personnel to recognize, fully consider and respond to each substantive element of any response to a rejection based on lack of utility. Only where the totality of the record continues to show that the asserted utility is not specific, substantial, and credible should a rejection based on lack of utility be maintained.

If the applicant satisfactorily rebuts a prima facie rejection based on lack of utility under section 101, withdraw the Sec. 101 rejection and the corresponding rejection imposed under section 112, first paragraph.

Dated: December 16, 1999.

Q. Todd Dickinson
Assistant Secretary of Commerce and Commissioner of Patents and Trademarks.
[FR Doc. 99-33054 Filed 12-20-99; 8:45 am]

Appendix C-12a

Interim Supplemental Examination Guidelines for Determining the Applicability of 35 U.S.C. 112 para. 6

64 FR 41392
Department of Commerce
Patent and Trademark Office
[Docket No. 990406087-9087-01]
RIN 0651-ZA03

Interim Supplemental Examination Guidelines for Determining the Applicability of 35 U.S.C. 112 para. 6

Agency: Patent and Trademark Office, Commerce.

Action: Notice.

Summary: The Patent and Trademark Office (PTO) requests comments from the public regarding interim supplemental examination guidelines to be used by office personnel in their review of patent applications to determine when 35 U.S.C. 112 para. 6 should be applied to a given claim limitation.

Dates: The interim supplemental examination guidelines are effective July 30, 1999.

Written comments on the interim supplemental examination guidelines will be accepted by the PTO until September 28, 1999.

Addresses: Written comments should be addressed to the attention of Magdalen Greenlief, Box Comments, Assistant Commissioner for Patents, Washington, DC 20231 or to Ray Chen, Office of the Solicitor, P.O. Box 15667, Arlington, Virginia 22215, or by facsimile transmission to (703) 305-8825, or by electronic mail at magdalen.greenlief@uspto.gov or ray.chen@uspto.gov.

Written comments will be made available for public inspection in Suite 910, Crystal Park 2, 2121 Crystal Drive, Arlington, Virginia 22202. In addition, comments provided in machine readable format will be available through the PTO's Website at http://www.uspto.gov.

For Further Information Contact: Magdalen Greenlief, Box Comments, Assistant Commissioner for Patents, Washington, DC 20231 or Ray Chen, Office of the Solicitor, P.O. Box 15667, Arlington, Virginia 22215, or by facsimile transmission to (703) 305-8825, or by electronic mail at magdalen.greenlief@uspto.gov or ray.chen@uspto.gov.

Supplementary Information: The following interim supplemental examination guidelines are being published for public comment. In May 1994, the PTO issued guidelines implementing the change in examination practice necessitated by the Federal Circuit's decision in In re Donaldson Co., 16 F.3d 1189, 29 USPQ 2d 1845 (Fed. Cir. 1994) (en banc). Since Donaldson, several decisions by the Federal Circuit have analyzed: (1) When a particular claim limitation invokes 35 U.S.C. 112 para. 6; and (2) the duty of the applicant to describe the corresponding structure, material, or acts that perform the function recited in a means-plus-function limitation. In order to clarify these issues, the PTO is issuing these interim supplemental examination guidelines to assist PTO personnel in the examination of patent applications to determine: (1) Whether a claim limitation invokes 35 U.S.C. 112 para. 6; and (2) whether the written description adequately describes the corresponding structure, material, or acts needed to support a claim limitation under 35 U.S.C. 112 para. 6.

It has been determined that these interim supplemental examination guidelines are not a significant rule for purposes of Executive Order 12866. Because these supplemental examination guidelines are interpretive rules and general statements of policy, they are exempt from notice and comment rulemaking under 5 U.S.C. 553(b)(A). The collection of information for the filing and processing of a patent application has been reviewed and previously approved by the Office of Management and Budget under the following control numbers: 0651-0031 and 0651-0032. These supplemental examination guidelines involve no additional collection of information subject to the Paperwork Reduction Act, 44 U.S.C. ch. 35. Notwithstanding any other provision of law, no person is required to respond nor shall a person be subject to a penalty for failure to comply with a collection of information subject to the requirements of the Paperwork Reduction Act unless that collection of information displays a currently valid OMB Control Number.

Members of the public may present written comments on these supplemental examination guidelines. Written comments should include the following information:

—Name and affiliation of the individual responding; and
—An indication of whether the comments offered represent views of the respondent's organization or are the respondent's personal views.

The PTO is particularly interested in comments relating to the 3-prong analysis as to when a claim limitation will be interpreted by PTO personnel to invoke 35 U.S.C. 112 para. 6. The PTO is also interested in comments relating to the analysis as to when a "means-" (or "step-") plus-function claim limitation satisfies the requirements of 35 U.S.C. Sec. 112 para. 2.

I. Interim Supplemental Examination Guidelines for Claims Subject to 35 U.S.C. 112 para. 6

In February 1994, the Court of Appeals for the Federal Circuit (Federal Circuit) held in an en banc decision that "the 'broadest reasonable interpretation' that an examiner may give means-plus-function language is that statutorily mandated in [35 U.S.C. 112 para. 6] * * * [T]he PTO may not disregard the structure disclosed in the specification corresponding to such language when rendering a patentability determination." In re Donaldson Co., 16 F.3d 1189, 1194–95, 29 USPQ 2d 1845, 1850 (Fed. Cir. 1994) (en banc). In May 1994, the PTO issued guidelines implementing changes in examination practice in response to Donaldson. See Means or Step Plus Function Limitation Under 35 U.S.C. Sec. 112, para. 6; Notice, 1162 Off. Gaz. Pat. Office 59 (May 17, 1994) ("1994 Guidelines").

The 1994 Guidelines note that there is no "magic" language that invokes 35 U.S.C. 112 para. 6.[1] However, to establish uniformity to the extent possible, in view of the recent case law, and to make the prosecution record clear, these interim guidelines

[1]See 1994 Guidelines at 59.

supplement the 1994 Guidelines in assisting examiners to determine when 35 U.S.C. 112 para. 6 should be applied. To the extent these supplemental guidelines are inconsistent with the 1994 Guidelines, the supplemental guidelines are controlling.

The PTO must apply 35 U.S.C. 112 para. 6 in appropriate cases, and give claims their broadest reasonable interpretation, in light of and consistent with the written description of the invention in the application.[2] Thus, a claim limitation will be interpreted to invoke 35 U.S.C. 112 para. 6 if it meets the following 3-prong analysis:

(1) the claim limitations must use the phrase "means for" or "step for";[3]
(2) the "means for" or "step for" must be modified by functional language;[4] and
(3) the phrase "means for" or "step for" must not be modified by structure, material or acts for achieving the specified function.[5]

With respect to the first prong of this analysis, a claim element that does not include the phrase "means for" or "step for" will not be considered to invoke 35 U.S.C. 112 para. 6. If an applicant wishes to have the claim limitation treated under 35 U.S.C. 112

---

[2] See In re Donaldson Co., 16 F.3d 1189, 1194, 29 USPQ 2d 1845, 1850 (Fed. Cir. 1994) (en banc) (stating that 35 U.S.C. 112 para. 6 "merely sets a limit on how broadly the PTO may construe means-plus-function language under the rubric of 'reasonable interpretation' "). The Federal Circuit has held that applicants (and reexamination patentees) before the PTO have the opportunity and the obligation to define their inventions precisely during proceedings before the PTO. See In re Morris, 127 F.3d 1048, 1056–57, 44 USPQ 2d 1023, 1029–30 (Fed. Cir. 1997) (35 U.S.C. 112 para. 2 places the burden of precise claim drafting on the applicant); In re Zletz, 893 F.2d 319, 322, 13 USPQ 2d 1320, 1322 (Fed. Cir. 1989) (manner of claim interpretation that is used by courts in litigation is not the manner of claim interpretation that is applicable during prosecution of a pending application before the PTO); Sage Products Inc. v. Devon Industries Inc., 126 F.3d 1420, 1425, 44 USPQ 2d 1103, 1107 (Fed. Cir. 1997) (patentee who had a clear opportunity to negotiate broader claims during prosecution but did not do so, may not seek to expand the claims through the doctrine of equivalents, for it is the patentee, not the public, who must bear the cost of its failure to seek protection for this foreseeable alteration of its claimed structure). Thus, applicants and reexamination patentees before the PTO have an opportunity and obligation to specify, consistent with these supplemental guidelines, when a claim limitation invokes 35 U.S.C. 112 para. 6.

[3] Cf. Seal-Flex, Inc. v. Athletic Track and Court Construction, 172 F.3d 836, 849–50, 50 USPQ 2d 1225, 1233–34 (Fed. Cir. 1999) (Radar, J., concurring) (use of the phrase "step for" in a method claim raises a presumption that 35 U.S.C. 112 para. 6 applies, whereas, use of the word "step" by itself or the phrase "step of" does not invoke a presumption that 35 U.S.C. 112 para. 6 applies); Ethicon, Inc. v. United States Surgical Corp., 135 F.3d 1456, 1463, 45 USPQ 2d 1545, 1550 (Fed. Cir. 1998) ("use of the word 'means' gives rise to 'a presumption that the inventor used the term advisedly to invoke the statutory mandates for means-plus-function clauses'"); O.I. Corp. v. Tekmar, 115 F.3d 1576, 1583, 42 USPQ 2d 1777, 1782 (Fed. Cir. 1997) (method claim that paralleled means-plus-function apparatus claim but lacked "step for" language did not invoke 35 U.S.C. 112 para. 6). Thus, absent an express recitation of "means for" or "step for" in the limitation, the broadest reasonable interpretation will not be limited to "corresponding structure * * * and equivalents thereof." Cf. Morris, 127 F.3d at 1055, 44 USPQ 2d at 1028 ("no comparable mandate in the patent statute that relates the claim scope of non-Sec. 112 para. 6 claims to particular matter found in the specification").

[4] See York Prod., Inc. v. Central Tractor Farm & Family Center, 99 F.3d 1568, 1574, 40 USPQ 2d 1619, 1624 (Fed. Cir. 1996) (holding that a claim limitation containing the term "means" does not invoke 35 U.S.C. 112 para. 6 if the claim limitation does not link the term "means" to a specific function).

[5] See Seal-Flex, 172 F.3d at 849, 50 USPQ 2d at 1234 (Rader, J., concurring) ("Even when a claim element uses language that generally falls under the step-plus-function format, however, 112 para. 6 still does not apply when the claim limitation itself recites sufficient acts for performing the specified function"). Cf. Rodime PLC v. Seagate Technology, Inc., 174 F.3d 1294, 1303–04, 50 USPQ 2d 1429, 1435–36 (Fed. Cir. 1999) (holding "positioning means for moving" does not invoke 35 U.S.C. 112, para. 6 because the claim further provides a list of the structure underlying the means and the detailed recitation of the structure for performing the moving function removes this element from the purview of 35 U.S.C. 112, para. 6); Cole v. Kimberly-Clark Corp., 102 F.3d 524, 531, 41 USPQ 2d 1001, 1006 (Fed. Cir. 1996) (holding "perforation

para. 6, applicant must either: (1) Amend the claim to include the phrase "means for" or "step for" in accordance with these interim guidelines; or (2) show that even though the phrase "means for" or "step for" is not used, the claim limitation is written as a function to be performed and does not provide any structure, material, or acts which would preclude application of 35 U.S.C. 112 para. 6.[6]

Accordingly, these interim guidelines provide applicants with the opportunity to either invoke or not invoke 35 U.S.C. 112 para. 6 based upon a clear and simple set of criteria.

II. Procedures for Determining Whether the Written Description Adequately Describes the Corresponding Structure, Material, or Acts Necessary To Support a Claim Limitation Which Invokes 35 U.S.C. 112 para. 6

If a claim limitation invokes 35 U.S.C. 112 para. 6, it must be interpreted to cover the corresponding structure, materials, or acts in the specification and "equivalents thereof."[7] If the written description fails to set forth the supporting structure, material or acts corresponding to the means- (or step-) plus-function, the claim may not meet the requirement of 35 U.S.C. 112 p ara. 2:

Although [35 U.S.C. 112 para. 6] statutorily provides that one may use means-plus-function language in a claim, one is still subject to the requirement that a claim "particularly point out and distinctly claim" the invention. Therefore, if one employs means-plus-function language in a claim, one must set forth in the specification an adequate disclosure showing what is meant by that language. If an applicant fails to

---

means * * * for tearing" does not invoke 35 U.S.C. 112 para. 6 because the claim describes the structure supporting the tearing function (i.e., perforation)). In other cases, the Federal Circuit has held otherwise. See Unidynamics Corp. v. Automatic Prod. Int'l, 157 F.3d 1311, 1319, 48 USPQ 2d 1099, 1104 (Fed. Cir. 1998) (holding "spring means" does invoke 35 U.S.C. 112 para. 6). During examination, however, applicants have the opportunity and the obligation to define their inventions precisely, including whether a claim limitation invokes 35 U.S.C. 112 para. 6. Thus, if the phrase "means for" or "step for" is modified by structure, material or acts for achieving the specified function, the PTO will not apply 35 U.S.C. 112 para. 6 until such modifying language is deleted from the claim limitation. See also supra note 1.

[6] While traditional "means for" or "step for" language does not automatically make an element a means- (or step-) plus-function element, conversely, lack of such language does not prevent a limitation from being construed as a means- (or step-) plus-function limitation. See Signtech USA, Ltd. v. Vutek, Inc., 174 F.3d 1352, 1356, 50 USPQ 2d 1372, 1374–75 (Fed. Cir. 1999) ("ink delivery means positioned on * * *" invokes 35 U.S.C. 112 para. 6 since the phrase "ink delivery means" is equivalent to "means for ink delivery"); Al-Site Corp. v. VSI International Inc., 174 F.3d 1308, 1318, 50 USPQ 2d 1161, 1166–67 (Fed. Cir. 1999) (although the claim elements "eyeglass hanger member" and "eyeglass contacting member" include a function, these claim elements do not invoke 35 U.S.C. 112 para. 6 because the claims themselves contain sufficient structural limitations for performing those functions); Seal-Flex, 172 F.3d at 849, 50 USPQ 2d at 1234 (Radar, J., concurring) ("claim elements without express step-plus-function language may nevertheless fall within 112 para. 6 if they merely claim the underlying function without recitation of acts for performing that function * * * In general terms, the 'underlying function' of a method claim element corresponds to what that element ultimately accomplishes in relationship to what the other elements of the claim and the claim as a whole accomplish. 'Acts,' on the other hand, correspond to how the function is accomplished."); Personalized Media Communications LLC v. ITC, 161 F.3d 696, 703–04, 48 USPQ 2d 1880, 1886–87 (Fed. Cir. 1998); Mas-Hamilton Group v. LaGard Inc., 156 F.3d 1206, 1213, 48 USPQ 2d 1010, 1016 (Fed. Cir. 1998) ("lever moving element for moving the lever" and "movable link member for holding the lever * * * and for releasing the lever" were construed as means-plus-function limitations invoking 35 U.S.C. 112 para. 6 since the claimed limitations were described in terms of their function not their mechanical structure).

[7] See 35 U.S.C. 112 para. 6. See also B. Braun Medical, Inc. v. Abbott Lab., 124 F.3d 1419, 1424, 43 USPQ 2d 1896, 1899 (Fed. Cir. 1997).

set forth an adequate disclosure, the applicant has in effect failed to particularly point out and distinctly claim the invention as required by [35 U.S.C. 112 para. 2].[8]

Whether a claim reciting an element in means- (or step-) plus-function language fails to comply with 35 U.S.C. 112 para. 2 because the specification does not disclose adequate structure (or material or acts) for performing the recited function is closely related to the question of whether the specification meets the description requirement in 35 U.S.C. 112 para. 1.[9] However, 35 U.S.C. 112 para. 6 does not impose any requirements in addition to those imposed by 35 U.S.C. 112 para. 1.[10] Conversely, the invocation of 35 U.S.C. 112 para. 6 does not exempt an applicant from compliance with 35 U.S.C. 112 Paras. 1 and 2.[11]

The written description does not have to explicitly describe the structure (or material or acts) corresponding to a means- (or step-) plus-function limitation to particularly point out and distinctly claim the invention as required by 35 U.S.C. 112 para. 2.[12] Rather, disclosure of structure corresponding to a means-plus-function limitation may be implicit in the written description if it would have been clear to those skilled in the art what structure must perform the function recited in the means-plus-function limitation.[13] However, the claims must still be analyzed to determine whether there exists corresponding adequate support for such claim under 35 U.S.C. 112 para. 1.[14]

Therefore, a means- (or step-) plus-function claim limitation satisfies 35 U.S.C. 112 para. 2 if: (1) The written description links or associates particular structure, materials, or acts to the function recited in a means- (or step-) plus-function claim limitation; or (2) it is clear based on the facts of the application that one skilled in the art would have known what structure, materials, or acts perform the function recited in a means- (or step-) plus-function limitation.

37 CFR 1.75(d)(1) provides, in part, that "the terms and phrases used in the claims must find clear support or antecedent basis in the description so that the meaning of the terms in the claims may be ascertainable by reference to the description." In the situation in which the written description only implicitly or inherently sets forth the structure, materials, or acts corresponding to a means- (or step-) plus-function, and the examiner concludes that one skilled in the art would recognize what structure, materials, or acts perform the function recited in a means- (or step-) plus-function, the examiner should either: (1) Have the applicant clarify the record by amending the

---

[8] See Donaldson, 16 F.3d at 1195, 29 USPQ 2d at 1850; see also B. Braun Medical, 124 F.3d at 1425, 43 USPQ 2d at 1900; and In re Dossel, 115 F.3d 942, 946, 42 USPQ2d 1881, 1884–85 (Fed. Cir. 1997).

[9] See In re Noll, 545 F.2d 141, 149, 191 USPQ 721, 727 (CCPA 1976) (unless the means-plus-function language is itself unclear, a claim limitation written in means-plus-function language meets the definiteness requirement in 35 U.S.C. 112 para. 2 so long as the specification meets the written description requirement in 35 U.S.C. 112 para. 1).

[10] See In re Knowlton, 481 F.2d 1357, 1366, 178 USPQ 486, 492–93 (CCPA 1973).

[11] See Donaldson, 16 F.3d at 1195, 29 USPQ 2d at 1850; Knowlton, 481 F.2d at 1366, 178 USPQ at 493.

[12] See Dossel, 115 F.3d at 946, 42 USPQ 2d at 1885. Under proper circumstances, drawings may provide a written description of an invention as required by 35 U.S.C. para. 112. Vas-Cath, Inc. v. Mahurkar, 935 F.2d 1555, 1565, 19 USPQ 2d 1111, 1118 (Fed. Cir. 1991).

[13] See Dossel, 115 F.3d at 946–47, 42 USPQ 2d at 1885 ("Clearly, a unit which receives digital data, performs complex mathematical computations and outputs the results to a display must be implemented by or on a general or special purpose computer (although it is not clear why the written description does not simply state 'computer' or some equivalent phrase.)").

[14] In considering whether there is 35 U.S.C. 112 para. 1 support for the claim limitation, the examiner must consider not only the original disclosure contained in the summary and detailed description of the invention portions of the specification, but also the original claims, abstract, and drawings. See In re Mott, 539 F.2d 1291, 1299, 190 USPQ 536, 542–43 (CCPA 1976) (claims); In re Anderson, 471 F.2d 1237, 1240, 176 USPQ 331, 333 (CCPA 1973) (claims); In re Armbruster, 512 F.2d 676, 678–79, 185 USPQ 152, 153–54 (CCPA 1975) (abstract); Anderson, 471 F.2d at 1240, 176 USPQ at 333 (abstract); Vas-Cath Inc. v. Mahurkar, 935 F.2d at 1564, 19 USPQ 2d at 1117 (drawings); In re Wolfensperger, 302 F.2d 950, 955–57, 133 USPQ 537, 541–43 (CCPA 1962) (drawings).

written description such that it expressly recites what structure, materials, or acts perform the function recited in the claim element;[15] or (2) state on the record what structure, materials, or acts perform the function recited in the means- (or step-) plus-function limitation.

In implementing the change in examination practice necessitated by Donaldson, the PTO set forth a two-step process for making a prima facie case of equivalence of a prior art element during ex parte examination. First, the examiner must find that the prior art element performs the function specified in the claim element, and, second, the examiner must find that the prior art element is not excluded by any explicit definition provided in the specification for an equivalent.[16] This two-step process is not superseded by these interim supplemental guidelines, and is consistent with the requirement that the PTO give claims their broadest reasonable interpretation.[17] The specification need not describe the equivalents of the structures, materials, or acts corresponding to the means- (or step-) plus-function claim element.[18] Where, however, the specification is silent as to what constitutes equivalents, the burden is placed upon the applicant to show that a prior art element which performs the claimed function is not an equivalent of the structure, material, or acts disclosed in the specification.[19]

Dated: July 21, 1999.

Q. Todd Dickinson,
Acting Assistant Secretary of Commerce and Acting Commissioner of Patents and Trademarks.
[FR Doc. 99-19368 Filed 7-29-99; 8:45 am]

---

[15] Even if the disclosure implicitly sets forth the structure, materials, or acts corresponding to a means- (or step-) plus-function claim element in compliance with 35 U.S.C. 112 Paras. 1 and 2, the PTO may still require the applicant to amend the specification pursuant to 37 CFR 1.75(d) and MPEP 608.01(o) to explicitly state, with reference to the terms and phrases of the claim element, what structure, materials, or acts perform the function recited in the claim element. See 35 U.S.C. 112 para. 6 ("An element in a claim for a combination may be expressed as a means or step for performing a specified function without the recital of structure, material, or acts in support thereof, and such claim shall be construed to cover the corresponding structure, material, or acts described in the specification and equivalents thereof." (emphasis added)); see also B. Braun Medical, 124 F.3d at 1424, 43 USPQ 2d at 1900 (holding that "pursuant to this provision [35 U.S.C. 112 para. 6], structure disclosed in the specification is 'corresponding' structure only if the specification or prosecution history clearly links or associates that structure to the function recited in the claim. This duty to link or associate structure to function is the quid pro quo for the convenience of employing 112, paragraph 6."); Wolfensperger, 302 F.2d at 955, 133 USPQ at 542 (just because the disclosure provides support for a claim element does not mean that the PTO cannot enforce its requirement that the terms and phrases used in the claims find clear support or antecedent basis in the written description).

[16] See Means or Step Plus Function Limitation Under 35 U.S.C. 112, para. 6; 1162 Off. Gaz. Pat. Office at 59–60.

[17] See Donaldson, 16 F.3d at 1194, 29 USPQ 2d at 1850 (stating that 35 U.S.C. 112 para. 6 "merely sets a limit on how broadly the PTO may construe means-plus-function language under the rubric of 'reasonable interpretation'").

[18] See Noll, 545 F.2d at 149–50, 191 USPQ at 727 (the meaning of equivalents is well understood in patent law, and an applicant need not describe in his specification the full range of equivalents of his invention) (citation omitted). Cf. Hybritech Incorporated v. Monoclonal Antibodies, Inc., 802 F.2d 1367, 1384, 231 USPQ 81, 94 (Fed. Cir. 1986) ("a patent need not teach, and preferably omits, what is well known in the art").

[19] See 1994 Guidelines at 60; see also In re Mulder, 716 F.2d 1542, 1549, 219 USPQ 189, 196 (Fed. Cir. 1983).

Appendix C-15a

Revised Interim Guidelines for Examination of Patent Applications Under the 35 U.S.C. Sec. 112, para. 1 "Written Description" Requirement; Request for Comments

64 FR 71427
Department of Commerce
Patent and Trademark Office
[Docket No. 991027288-9288-01]
RIN 0651-AB10

Revised Interim Guidelines for Examination of Patent Applications Under the 35 U.S.C. Sec. 112, para. 1 "Written Description" Requirement; Request for Comments

Agency: Patent and Trademark Office, Commerce.

Action: Notice and request for public comments.

Summary: The Patent and Trademark Office (PTO) requests comments from any interested member of the public on the following Revised Interim Guidelines for Examination of Patent Applications Under the 35 U.S.C. 112, para. 1 "Written Description" Requirement (Revised Interim Guidelines). These Revised Interim Guidelines will be used by PTO personnel in their review of patent applications for compliance with the "written description" requirement of 35 U.S.C. Sec. 112, para. 1. This revision supersedes the Interim Written Description Guidelines which were published contemporaneously in both the Federal Register and Official Gazette at 63 FR 32,639 (June 15, 1998) and 1212 O.G. 15 (July 7, 1998), respectively. This revision reflects the current understanding of the PTO regarding the written description requirement of 35 U.S.C. 112, para. 1 and is applicable to all technologies.

Dates: Written comments on the Revised Interim Guidelines will be accepted by the PTO until March 22, 2000.

Addresses: Written comments should be addressed to Box 8, Commissioner of Patents and Trademarks, Washington, DC 20231, marked to the attention of Stephen Walsh, or to Box Comments, Assistant Commissioner for Patents, Washington, DC 20231, marked to the attention of Linda S. Therkorn. Alternatively, comments may be submitted to Stephen Walsh via facsimile at (703) 305-9373 or by electronic mail addressed to "stephen.walsh@uspto.gov" or to Linda Therkorn via facsimile at (703) 305-8825 or by electronic mail addressed to "linda.therkorn@uspto.gov."

For Further Information Contact: Stephen Walsh by telephone at (703) 305-9035, by facsimile at (703) 305-9373, by mail to his attention addressed to Box 8, Commissioner of Patents and Trademarks, Washington, DC 20231, or by electronic mail at "stephen. walsh@uspto.gov'; or Linda Therkorn by telephone at (703) 305-8800, by facsimile at (703) 305-8825, by mail addressed to Box Comments, Assistant Commissioner for Patents, Washington, DC 20231, or by electronic mail at "linda.therkorn@uspto.gov."

Supplementary Information: The PTO requests comments from any interested member of the public on the following Revised Interim Guidelines. As of the publication date of this notice, this revision will be used by PTO personnel in their review of patent applications for compliance with the "written description" requirement of 35 U.S.C. 112, para. 1. Because this revision governs internal practices, it is exempt from notice and comment rulemaking under 5 U.S.C. 553 (b)(A).

Written comments should include the following information: (1) Name and affiliation of the individual responding, and (2) an indication of whether the comments offered represent views of the respondent's organization or are respondent's personal views. If you believe the PTO should further amend these revised interim guidelines before they are made final, you should include the following information in your comments: (1) The rationale supporting the proposal, including the identification of applicable legal authority; and (2) a description of the potential benefits and drawbacks of adopting the proposal. The PTO is particularly interested in comments relating to the following topics: (1) The accuracy of the methodology, (2) the legal analysis in the guidelines, and (3) relevant factors to consider in determining whether the written description requirement is satisfied.

Parties presenting written comments are requested, where possible, to provide their comments in machine-readable format in addition to a paper copy. Such submissions may be provided by electronic mail messages sent over the Internet, or on a 3.5" floppy disk formatted for use in a Macintosh, Windows, Windows for Workgroups, Windows 95, Windows 98, Windows NT, or MS-DOS based computer.

Written comments will be available for public inspection on or about April 19, 2000, in Suite 918, Crystal Park 2, 2121 Crystal Drive, Arlington, Virginia. In addition, comments provided in machine readable format will be available through the PTO's Website at http://www.uspto.gov.

Discussion of Public Comments

Comments were received from 13 individuals and 16 organizations in response to the Request for Comments on the Interim Guidelines for the Examination of Patent Applications Under the 35 U.S.C. 112, para. 1 "Written Description" Requirement published contemporaneously in the Federal Register and Official Gazette at 63 FR 32,639 (June 15, 1998) and 1212 O.G. 15 (July 7, 1998), respectively; and the Extension of Comment Period and Notice of Hearing published at 63 FR 50887 (September 23, 1998) and 1214 O.G. 180 (September 29, 1998). The written comments and the testimony at the public hearing have been carefully considered.

Overview of Comments

The majority of comments favored issuance of written description guidelines, with revisions. Several major issues arose in the oral testimony and written comments submitted in response to the Interim Guidelines on the Written Description

Requirement with respect to the scope of the Guidelines, the method of analysis, and the content of the examples. In view of the comments and testimony received, the Guidelines have been rewritten in a technology neutral manner which is broadly applicable to all areas of technology and to all types of claims (original, new, or amended, and product, process, or product-by-process). Furthermore, the examples have been removed from the Guidelines and examples addressing a broad range of technologies will be incorporated into examiner training materials. Revised Interim Guidelines are being issued for a second round of Notice and Comment because the form and content of the Guidelines are sufficiently different from the previous Guidelines that additional public comment is desired.

The Extension of Comment Period and Notice of Hearing published at 63 FR 50887 (September 23, 1998) and 1214 O.G. 180 (September 29, 1998) asked for comments regarding the patentability of Expressed Sequence Tags (ESTs). Many comments took this opportunity to heavily criticize the patentability of ESTs, grounding their arguments in fairness and policy issues. Many comments also expressed the opinion that ESTs lacked the utility, enablement, and written description necessary to satisfy title 35 of the U.S. Code. The Revised Interim Guidelines are not the appropriate vehicle to fully address the patentability of ESTs. In view of comments and testimony with respect to ESTs and the enablement and utility requirements, the Office is revising the Utility Guidelines as published at 60 FR 36263 (July 14, 1995), and will also be revising the examiner training material with regard to both the utility and enablement requirements. Comments pertaining to the utility and enablement requirements will be addressed in the notice revising the Utility Guidelines. Responses to the comments germane to the written description requirement are set forth below.

Responses to Specific Comments

(1) *Comment:* Several comments criticized the Guidelines for failing to set out a general, systematic examination of the case law on written description. Comments mentioned Vas-Cath, Inc. v. Mahurkar, 935 F.2d 1555, 19 USPQ 2d 1111 (Fed. Cir. 1991), in particular as important for summarizing the state of the law as the Federal Circuit sees it. Other comments particularly urged a general analysis of case law as it pertains to written description for chemical compounds, and criticized the fact that the Guidelines relied heavily on only three recent cases. *Response:* The suggestion to provide a general, systematic legal analysis has been adopted. The Revised Interim Guidelines are grounded more broadly than the three cases heavily relied upon in the original Interim Guidelines, and cases dealing with a variety of arts are relied upon.

(2) *Comment:* The comments were equally divided with respect to the issue of whether the Guidelines should be broadly applicable to all technologies or limited to biotechnology, DNA claims, or unpredictable arts. Two of the comments urging broad applicability stated that the law should be articulated in a clear and technology neutral fashion, and several comments urged that examples and training materials should illustrate application of the Guidelines in a diverse range of technologies. One comment suggested that applications in which written description problems are likely to arise should be identified generically, rather than requiring a written description analysis in each application. *Response:* The suggestion to cover all technologies and to articulate the law in a clear and technology neutral fashion has been adopted. While a written description analysis is required in each case, the Revised Interim Guidelines clearly specify when a written description issue is most likely to arise, and—for most applications—the Revised Interim Guidelines will quickly lead the examiner to determine that, at least for original claims, the written description requirement has been met. The Revised Interim Guidelines avoid narrowing the application of the written description requirement to a single art, and the examiner training materials will illustrate application of the revision in various technologies.

(3) *Comment:* While the majority of comments supported the Interim Guidelines, eight comments opposed their issuance. Some of those opposing the guidelines argued that the decision in Regents of the University of California v. Eli Lilly, 119

F.3d 1559, 43 USPQ 2d 1398 (Fed. Cir. 1997), cert. denied, 523 U.S. 1089 (1998), is a drastic departure from legal precedent and PTO practice. In particular, two comments suggested that the Interim Guidelines should be replaced by Revised Interim Guidelines, and one comment recommended that final Guidelines be deferred until the U.S. Court of Appeals for the Federal Circuit or the U.S. Supreme Court hands down decisions that elaborate, construe, modify, or overrule Eli Lilly and/or decide related issues not dealt with by that case. See Comments (5) and (9) for more opposing comments. *Response:* This revision is based on the Office's current understanding of the law and is believed to be fully consistent with binding precedent of the U.S. Supreme Court and the U.S. Court of Appeals for the Federal Circuit. Guidelines are necessary in this area to promote uniformity and consistency in the examination process. The suggestion to issue Revised Interim Guidelines for a second round of Notice and Comment has been adopted. The revision is written in a technology neutral manner, and the form is sufficiently different from the previous guidelines that additional public comment is desired.

(4) *Comment:* Six comments were in favor of including process and product-by-process claims in the analysis, whereas one comment was opposed. One comment criticized the Guidelines for failing to acknowledge the "safe harbor" product-by-process type claim noted in Fiers v. Revel, 984 F.2d 1164, 25 USPQ 2d 1601 (Fed. Cir. 1993), and Amgen Inc. v. Chugai Pharmaceutical Co., 927 F.2d 1200, 18 USPQ 2d 1016 (Fed. Cir. 1991). One comment observed that process and product-by-process claims tend not to implicate many written description issues, and it may be useful to point out possible enablement deficiencies for such claims. Two comments suggested that the Guidelines should distinguish between claims to processes whose patentability depends on the compositions used in them, as opposed to those where patentability rests in the steps of the process itself. *Response:* The suggestion to address process and product-by-process claims has been adopted. Furthermore, the training materials will analyze claims wherein the patentability depends on the compositions used therein, as well as those where the patentability rests in the process steps themselves. Enablement issues raised by process and product-by-process claims are outside the scope of these Revised Interim Guidelines.

(5) *Comment:* While one comment stated that the Guidelines correctly present the relationship between written description and enablement, a number of comments dispute that the statute actually has a written description requirement distinct from the enablement requirement. One comment requested that the PTO refrain from issuing any Guidelines in this area until the U.S. Supreme Court rules on the Federal Circuit's present position on written description. Several comments urged the PTO to announce that it will not follow the court decisions applying the separate written description requirement, while others observed that the PTO and the practitioners must nevertheless follow the case law. Some of these comments urged the PTO to withdraw the Guidelines on the grounds that they are premature because the case law has not developed sufficiently. Others urged the PTO to limit application of the Guidelines to the narrow subject matter of the Fiers, Amgen, and Eli Lilly cases. *Response:* A separate written description requirement has long been a part of the U.S. patent law. See, e.g., In re Ruschig, 379 F.2d 990, 154 USPQ 118 (CCPA 1967). The Federal Circuit has recognized the distinct and separable nature of this requirement. See Vas-Cath. Although the interpretation of the law is always evolving, the PTO is obliged to follow the law as currently interpreted by the court. As noted above, the suggestion to limit the application of the Revised Interim Guidelines to certain subject matter has not been adopted.

(6) *Comment:* While several of the comments stated that the Guideline's explanation of the purpose of the written description requirement is accurate, a number of comments suggested that the concept of "possession" should be more fully explained or developed. One comment urged that the meaning of "possession of the invention" is different for written description than enablement, whereas another observed that an "in possession of the invention" test for compliance with the written description requirement does not appear in 35 U.S.C. 112, and its definition and application are not clearly stated in the Federal Circuit cases to date. Another comment urged that de-

scriptive attributes which provide proof of written description should include evidence typically provided to prove a complete and enabling conception. One comment stated that the meaning of "has invented" is unclear and queried if actual reduction to practice is required. The same comment asked for clarification on what kind of description equates with possession of a claimed species. One comment stated that a question left unanswered in the Guidelines is that if one has "made" an invention, is one necessarily in possession of it, or are there some further criteria? Two comments observed that physical possession is not necessary: one must have complete conception of the invention in mind. These comments suggested that the possession analysis incorporate the Supreme Court's statements in Pfaff v. Wells Electronics, Inc., 525 U.S. 55, 48 USPQ 2d 1641 (1998) (the word "invention" must refer to a concept that is complete: one can prove that an invention is complete and ready for patenting before it has been reduced to practice). One of these comments elaborated that the doctrine of simultaneous conception and reduction to practice should remain applicable to only a very small number of cases, including biotechnology cases. *Response:* The Revised Interim Guidelines expand the explanation of possession by discussing decisions that offer some guidance as to how possession may be shown. The concepts in Pfaff v. Wells Electronics that are pertinent to an analysis of compliance with the written description requirement have been incorporated in this revision. At this time, the Federal Circuit has not indicated that reduction to practice is necessary for conception or written description of a biotechnological invention. The Office does not intend to impose a written description requirement that is more robust than that set forth by the courts. Accordingly, the Revised Interim Guidelines do not impose a per se requirement for reduction to practice in any technology to satisfy the written description requirement. However, the Federal Circuit has recognized that in some instances an inventor may only be able to establish a conception (and therefore possession) by pointing to a reduction to practice through a successful experiment. See Amgen Inc. v. Chugai Pharmaceutical Co., 927 F.2d at 1206, 18 USPQ 2d at 1021. In such instances, the alleged conception fails not merely because the field is unpredictable or because of the general uncertainty surrounding experimental sciences, but because the conception is incomplete due to factual uncertainty that undermines the specificity of the inventor's idea of the invention. Burroughs Wellcome Co. v. Barr Laboratories Inc., 40 F.3d 1223, 1229, 32 USPQ 2d 1915, 1920 (Fed. Cir. 1994). Reduction to practice in effect provides the only evidence to corroborate conception (and therefore possession) of the invention. Id.

(7) *Comment:* Other comments on "possession" urged that possession is to be evaluated by looking to the claims; that the possession question is to be assessed as set forth in In re Alton, 76 F.3d 1168, 1176, 37 USPQ 2d 1578, 1584 (Fed. Cir. 1996); and that compliance must be assessed on a case-by-case basis given that the question of compliance with the written description requirement is one of fact. One comment stated that the test should be whether the inventor had envisioned the embodiments, not that one of skill in the art can now envision the embodiments. Another comment stated that the Guidelines should take a position with regard to their application to the analysis of declarations submitted under 37 CFR 1.131. *Response:* The Revised Interim Guidelines require the examiner to determine whether there is sufficient written description to inform a skilled artisan that the applicant was in possession of the claimed invention as a whole at the time the application was filed. The revision also indicates that compliance with the written description requirement is a question of fact which must be resolved on a case-by-case basis. While this revision addresses the analysis of possession only in the context of the written description requirement, similar principles apply in determining whether an inventor has met his or her burden of demonstrating possession of the claimed invention in an affidavit or declaration submitted under 37 CFR 1.131.

(8) *Comment:* Several comments suggested that the Guidelines should address questions of support for claims added or amended by the applicant during prosecution (or during an interference). Two comments suggested that the Guidelines should address the "omitted element" prong of the written description requirement. One comment indicated the Guidelines should harmonize chemical and nonchemical case

law on when an applicant may amend to broaden or change a definition based on an original disclosure. Another comment stated that the Guidelines should acknowledge that it is proper to amend the claims to excise prior art. *Response:* The suggestions to address questions of support for new or amended claims and to address the "omitted element" test have been adopted.

(9) *Comment:* Several comments indicated that case law such as In re Koller, 613 F.2d 819, 204 USPQ 702 (CCPA 1980), hold that original claims constitute their own written description, or that a statement in ipsis verbis is a sufficient description, and that those cases should be adhered to. Three comments pointed out that the Guidelines fail to distinguish between original claims and added/amended claims, arguing that the original claim doctrine should exempt originally filed claims from further requirements. *Response:* The Revised Interim Guidelines emphasize that a description as filed is presumed to be adequate, unless or until the examiner introduces sufficient evidence or technical reasoning to the contrary. The original claim doctrine continues to be viable, but the court has indicated that every claim must be supported by sufficient evidence of possession, and that, under certain circumstances, claim language may not provide an adequate written description of itself. There are no per se rules, since the analysis must be done on a case-by-case basis. While original claims have an initial presumption of descriptive support, the applicant should show support for new or amended claims. See, e.g., Manual of Patent Examining Procedure (MPEP) Secs. 714.02 and 2163.06 (7th Ed., July 1998) ("Applicant should * * * specifically point out the support for any amendments made to the disclosure.").

(10) *Comment:* One comment indicated that written description problems may arise where there is an inadequate description or demonstration of possession of a genus or where there is an improper genus (no common structure and function that is linked to the practical utility disclosed by the specification). Another comment stated that the Guidelines should address the informational nature of nucleic acid sequences and amino acid sequences. One comment urged that "[a] written description of a genus is sufficient when it is described in enough detail that possession is understood," and that the number of species relates more to enablement. *Response:* The Revised Interim Guidelines indicate that the written description requirement for a claimed genus may be satisfied through sufficient description of a representative number of species. The revision does not require a particular number of species to support a genus, but rather requires that the species adequately described be representative of the claimed genus.

(11) *Comment:* A comment urged that the Guidelines should explicitly state that the maturation of the technology will increase the understanding of one skilled in the art, and ease the predictable scope of the claimed invention beyond the exemplified embodiments, as recognized in the applicant's specification. *Response:* The Revised Interim Guidelines emphasize that in a mature art with a high level of knowledge and skill, less evidence of possession is required.

(12) *Comment:* One comment objected to the requirement for an assessment of predictability as a touchstone for written description. The comment described this inquiry as new and lacking case law support. Several comments stated that predictability is an inquiry relating to the enablement requirement, but not to the written description requirement. Others commented generally that the Guidelines conflate what should be separate enablement and written description analyses. On the other hand, at least one comment stated that the distinctions between these elements converge when lack of enablement results from undue breadth of claims. One comment stated that a review of the application is insufficient to establish the level of predictability in an art. Another queried if the review is to be done after a search in the art and assessment of the art. Another comment stated that the lack of guidance for distinguishing between predictable and unpredictable areas within the field of biotechnology leads to confusion. *Response:* The Revised Interim Guidelines reduce the emphasis on predictability because of the confusion with enablement. Instead, the Guidelines emphasize the knowledge in the art and the skill of the practitioner considered in the totality of the circumstances. With respect to the comment regarding biotechnology, this sliding scale will permit broader claims as the knowledge and skill

in this art improve. The Guidelines discuss how the general knowledge in the art may be relied on as evidence of how much description may be needed in particular cases.

(13) *Comment:* Several comments criticized the methodology of the Guidelines because the analytic steps set out by the court in In re Moore, 439 F.2d 1232, 169 USPQ 236 (CCPA 1971) (first determine what the claims cover, then review the specification for support) were reversed. *Response:* The Revised Interim Guidelines restate the analytic sequence so it is clearly consistent with In re Moore. The revision also makes it clear that each claim must be separately analyzed and given its broadest reasonable interpretation in light of and consistent with the written description. See, e.g., In re Morris, 127 F.3d 1048, 1054, 44 USPQ 2d 1023, 1027 (Fed. Cir. 1997).

(14) *Comment:* One comment suggested that the Guidelines should provide more instruction on the different amount of description needed to support an essential feature of an invention in contrast to a nonessential feature. The comment explained that contrasting the amount of description needed to support a novel or nonobvious feature of an invention with the amount of description needed for features of an invention that were known in the prior art would be helpful. *Response:* The Revised Interim Guidelines distinguish between novel and old elements in a claim to clarify that the amount of written support needed in an application can vary depending on the general knowledge that was readily available in a particular art.

(15) *Comment:* One comment criticized the analysis for setting out conclusions before the analytic method and for distorting or bypassing the analysis. The same comment said that some of the examples yield illogical results. *Response:* The examples have been deleted from the Guidelines, and the analytical method has been clarified.

(16) *Comment:* The Guidelines were heavily criticized in ten comments for overemphasizing the importance of the preamble and for indicating that generic preamble terms such as "nucleic acid" would need less descriptive support than narrow terms such as "cDNA." One comment objected to the proposition that one may have an adequate written description of a genus of DNA when one does not disclose what gene product the DNA encodes and what that gene product does. This comment recommended deletion of the example bridging F.R. 32640–41 ("a gene comprising SEQ ID NO: 1") as inconsistent with the rest of the Guidelines. *Response:* The Revised Interim Guidelines clarify that the examiner must consider the claim as a whole and that the preamble may be a limitation of the claim. Preamble language is discussed in the context of determining what the claim as a whole encompasses within its scope. However, the Revised Interim Guidelines maintain that any term may trigger a need for more descriptive support because of usage or context. The revision clarifies that during examination claim terms are given their broadest reasonable interpretation consistent with the specification. See In re Morris, 127 F.3d 1048, 44 USPQ 2d 1023 (Fed. Cir. 1997). The examples have been removed from the text of the revision.

(17) *Comment:* Four comments objected to the Guidelines' definitions for the terms gene, mRNA, and cDNA, stating that the art often refers only to the coding portion of the molecules and does not necessarily imply the presence of regulatory elements or recite specific structures. One comment further indicated that adoption of the PTO's new definition of these terms for purposes of written description considerations could potentially destabilize the economic infrastructure of the biotechnology community because innumerable patents have issued claiming such molecules without regard to the PTO's new interpretation of claim language. The Guidelines were said to use two inconsistent meanings for the term gene that differed in scope and confused the distinction between genus and species. *Response:* The Revised Interim Guidelines no longer define the term "gene."

(18) *Comment:* One comment indicated that the PTO has the opportunity to emphasize the written description requirement as an anti-submarine patent device; this comment and another observed that two parties could obtain claims which would be almost identical in scope in hindsight, based on completely different paths to the claim. *Response:* In Hyatt v. Boone, 146 F.3d 1348, 1353, 47 USPQ 2d 1128, 1131 (Fed. Cir. 1998), the Federal Circuit addressed the submarine patent issue in finding that the appellant's parent application lacked written descriptive support for a later added claim. When an explicit limitation in a claim "is not present in the written description

whose benefit is sought it must be shown that a person of ordinary skill would have understood, at the time the patent application was filed, that the description requires that limitation." Id.

(19) *Comment:* A comment stated that the Guidelines give too much emphasis to claim structure, as if the claim is the sole source of the written description. Another comment had a different view, stating that the Guidelines fail to focus on the invention being claimed, and noting that in some circumstances, failure to provide the structure of a gene, enzyme, etc. should not result in finding that a claim containing it fails to meet the written description requirement. *Response:* The Office gives a claim its broadest reasonable interpretation during examination. If the claim taken as a whole requires a limitation not set forth in the original disclosure it may raise an issue of lack of proper written description. As noted in In re Hiniker Co., 150 F.3d 1362, 1369, 47 USPQ2d 1523, 1529 (Fed. Cir. 1998), "the name of the game is the claim."

(20) *Comment:* One comment indicated that there was not enough emphasis on transitional phrases and their impact on the adequacy of the written description. *Response:* As with the preamble, the transitional phrase is discussed in the context of the scope of the claimed invention as a whole.

(21) *Comment:* The Extension of Comment Period and Notice of Hearing requested comments as to how the transition terms "having" and "consisting essentially of" should be treated within the context of nucleotide and amino acid sequence claims. Two comments observed that transitional phrases in the context of nucleotide and amino acid sequence claims should have the same treatment as in chemical cases. Another comment stated that "consisting essentially of" language in DNA or vector claims should not be rejected as per se improper under 35 U.S.C. 112, para. 2. Two comments stated that lacking an art-accepted meaning or a definition in the specification, "having" would imply an open claim format; another comment stated that "having" is understood to mean "comprising." The term "consisting essentially of" was defined by one comment as a closed claim format that is essentially limited to the compound or composition defined explicitly following the transitional phrase, and by two other comments as having the stated sequence and excluding any alterations which materially change the structure and/or function of the specified sequence. One comment opined that "A DNA consisting essentially of SEQ ID NO: 1" would be limited to DNAs having the nucleotide sequence set forth in SEQ ID NO: 1 plus minor additions at the 5′—and/or 3′—ends of the recited sequence. Another comment observed that the meaning of "consisting essentially of" depends on how the specification defines its usage. *Response:* During examination, the claim as a whole is given the broadest reasonable interpretation consistent with the specification. Transitional phrases should be given the same treatment in all cases. The Revised Interim Guidelines set forth legally recognized definitions for transition language in an endnote. "Consisting essentially of" is acceptable transition language in nucleic acid and protein claims. The impact of the transition language on enablement and practical utility will not be dealt with in this forum.

(22) *Comment:* One comment criticized the use of the taxonomic terms "genus" and "species." The comment explained that because the terminology is well established in biology, it should not be applied to chemical compounds. Two comments described the Guidelines as deficient in analyzing the proper relationship of preamble, transitional phrase and claim body for distinguishing genus from species claims. According to another comment, the Guidelines confuse genus and species claims. *Response:* The Revised Interim Guidelines refer to the terms "genus" and "species" in their well accepted legal sense as widely used patent terms of art that are recognized as distinct from their use as taxonomic terms. The revision clarifies what is meant by genus and species.

(23) *Comment:* Several comments found the explanations for the examples deficient because they do not clarify what would constitute a sufficient disclosure. One comment urged that there is no guidance provided as to what would constitute sufficient identifying characteristics, and the Guidelines do not set forth the number of the examples needed for sufficient written description. Another comment urged that structure, or function plus partial structure, or function plus "some characteristics"

(e.g., 2 or more), is sufficient to meet the written description requirement. Yet another comment urged that uncertainties and potential problems exist because it is unclear how "relevant" or "sufficient" identifying characteristics are established; that it is unclear how functional properties fit into the analysis; and that problems exist with the level of uncertainty when the complete structure is not disclosed or the structure is not disclosed and only a few identifying characteristics are disclosed. Another comment urged that the methodology is incomplete as to how many identifying characteristics are required and what characteristics are relevant for description of a species. This comment applied the same reasoning to the number of species required for describing a genus. One comment urged that functional characteristics in combination with certain objectively defined physical characteristics can serve to characterize the compound sufficiently to establish possession, even in less developed arts. One comment urged that the ability to predict structure from function is given as a standard for the written description requirement without any citation to authority. *Response:* The Revised Interim Guidelines do not include examples within the text. The test for whether sufficient identifying characteristics have been disclosed is not a bright-line test, but rather requires weighing various factors including the level of skill and knowledge in the art, and the extent to which relevant identifying characteristics are described. The revision provides more guidance to the examiners by citing as examples cases involving mature arts with a high level of skill and knowledge (e.g., Pfaff v. Wells Electronics, Fonar Corp. v. General Electric Co., 107 F.3d 1543, 1549, 41 USPQ 2d 1801, 1805 (Fed. Cir. 1997) and Vas-Cath v. Mahurkar), as well as cases in emerging technologies where more description is necessary (e.g., Eli Lilly, Amgen v. Chugai, and Fiers v. Revel). The test remains whether one of skill in the art, provided with the disclosure, would recognize that the applicant was in possession of the claimed subject matter when the application was filed.

(24) *Comment:* The Extension of Comment Period and Notice of Hearing requested comments on how the final Guidelines should address the deposit of a biological material made under 37 CFR 1.801, and comments on the extent to which a deposit of biological material may be relied upon to support the addition or correction of sequence information. Several comments expressed the opinion that deposit of a compound or biological material can be one means of demonstrating possession of a specifically claimed compound that has not otherwise been described in a complete manner in the specification. One comment stated that if a gene were cloned but not sequenced, and the vector in question were deposited, the sequence is an inherent property of the deposited vector and hence the description requirement would be satisfied if the claim referred to the deposit. One comment urged that the description requirement may be satisfied by the inherent properties of a disclosed structure, citing Kennecott Corp. v. Kyocera Int'l Inc., 835 F.2d 1419, 5 USPQ 2d 1194 (Fed. Cir. 1987). As for the later addition or correction of information, several comments indicated that actual possession established through a deposit with a partial characterization (i.e., to correlate the physical description to the material that has been deposited, such as molecular weight, partial sequence) should be sufficient to avoid problems with new matter where the information added to a disclosure is an inherent characteristic of the compound or composition. One comment indicated that correcting a sequence based on more accurate sequencing of deposited material does not introduce new matter. One comment stated that present genus-species concepts should prevent an applicant from obtaining an unfair advantage by depositing a large amount of material and then relying on inherency; if a variety of materials are deposited in a single host, the specification must adequately describe how to isolate the intended molecule(s). Two comments expressly stated "no comment" with regard to the issue of adding a substantial amount of sequence information. One comment opined that the date of deposit is not controlling with regard to the issue of whether the written description requirement is met, and a second comment observed that In re Lundak, 773 F.2d 1216, 227 USPQ 90 (Fed. Cir. 1985), cannot be limited by rule. *Response:* The Revised Interim Guidelines indicate that a deposit of a claimed biological material in accordance with the requirements of 37 CFR 1.801 et seq. is evidence of actual reduction to practice of the biological material. However, a deposit is not a substitute for a written

description of the claimed invention. The Revised Interim Guidelines also address the issue of when a deposit can be relied upon to correct minor sequencing errors. However, addition of sequence information based on a deposit is not specifically addressed; these circumstances create issues yet to be resolved by the courts, and will be resolved on a case-by-case basis in the PTO. See, e.g., In re Fisher, 427 F.2d 833, 836, 166 USPQ 18, 21 (CCPA 1970).

(25) *Comment:* One comment explained that associating taxonomic groupings with gene sequences is a dated concept because genes are not distinguishable as to origin. The generic term "mammal gene" was said to be meaningless, absent an implied process limitation that the gene was obtained from a mammal. *Response:* The examples have been removed from the revision. However, the training materials will permit applicants to use taxonomic modifiers such as "mammalian" because the usage is ubiquitous in the literature and in patents and generally has an accepted meaning in the art.

(26) *Comment:* One comment urged that broad functional claims lacking defining structure should not be granted on the basis of a "not easily generalizable disclosure." A different comment stated that functional characteristics can be appropriate in all arts. Comments differed on hybridization, where some held it is a proper defining characteristic, and another stated it is insufficient. *Response:* The Revised Interim Guidelines do not establish per se rules regarding functional language. When used appropriately, functional language may provide an adequate written description of the claims invention as discussed in the Revised Interim Guidelines.

(27) *Comment:* Several comments indicated that the Guidelines present inadequate guidance with respect to analyzing written description support for genus claims. One comment stated that the Guidelines provide inadequate criteria for selection of appropriate genuses. Another comment stated that the Guidelines do not provide adequate guidance to determine whether an applicant has presented a properly formed genus, and suggested that "a genus designation should be strictly tied to the disclosed properties of the structures being claimed." Another comment stated that the Guidelines should clarify that the genus/species distinction is determined by the transitional phrase and body of the claim, not the preamble. Another comment stated that the Guidelines provide inadequate guidance as to the number of species required to meet the written description requirement for a genus. One comment urged that a relevant factor to consider is whether the claims cover embodiments broader than the essential elements of the embodiments described in the specification as in Gentry Gallery Inc. v. Berkline, 134 F.3d 1473, 45 USPQ 2d 1498 (Fed. Cir. 1998). According to this comment, species rarely, if ever, constitute sufficient support for generic claims unless accompanied by a general disclosure that is commensurate in scope with the claims. *Response:* The Revised Interim Guidelines follow Federal Circuit case law which requires a representative number of species to satisfy the written description requirement for a genus. Written description is a question of fact, and what constitutes a representative number for a genus is a factual determination left to a case-by-case analysis by the examiner.

(28) *Comment:* One comment urged that general allegations of "unpredictability in the art" are insufficient to support a case against the applicant, and that examiners should be instructed to weigh applicant's evidence of what the description provides to one of skill in the art. *Response:* The suggestion to clarify that a general allegation of "unpredictability in the art" is insufficient to support a rejection has been adopted. A disclosure as filed is prima facie adequate. To support a rejection, the PTO has the burden of showing why the applicant's evidence is insufficient. In any case where lack of written description is found, the PTO should cite documentary evidence in support of the finding. Where documentary evidence is not available, technical reasoning, as distinguished from legal reasoning, may support the finding when the technical line of reasoning relates to fact finding regarding possession of the invention.

(29) *Comment:* One comment indicated that rejections based on the enablement and written description requirements of 35 U.S.C. 112 should be made separately, and the rejections should not mix standards. *Response:* Examiners are directed to make separate rejections based on the enablement and written description require-

ments of 35 U.S.C. 112. See, e.g., MPEP Sec. 706.03(c) (explaining when it is appropriate to use a particular form paragraph for rejecting claims under 35 U.S.C. 112, para.1) and MPEP Sec. 2164 ("limitations must be analyzed for both enablement and description using their separate and distinct criteria").

(30) *Comment:* One comment observed that the Guidelines do not guide examiners in how to suggest amendments to bring the claims into compliance. The comment also observed that examiners may be ill-equipped to deal with evaluating the sufficiency of applicant's efforts. *Response:* The training materials will provide guidance as to how rejections for lack of an adequate written description can be overcome.

(31) *Comment:* One comment stated that the Guidelines should instruct examiners to pay due regard to the scientific and commercial realities of each individual invention, such that the scope of the claims is a fair reflection of the applicant's contribution to te art. *Response:* The scientific and commercial realities of each invention are considered to the extent that they impact analysis of a claimed invention for compliance with Title 35 of the U.S. Code. The Office is bound to follow the law and cannot make judgment calls as to what is "a fair reflection of the applicant's contribution to the art."

(32) *Comment:* While two comments observed that the Guidelines should not have a significant impact on patents or pending or newly filed applications because they are only Guidelines which are not binding on the Board or examiners, three comments were of the opinion that the Guidelines would impact pending and newly filed cases by limiting the scope of patent protection. One comment was of the opinion that the Guidelines should have no impact on issued cases except reissues, whereas another expected many issued patents to be declared invalid (more as a result of Eli Lilly than the Guidelines). Another comment observed that the Guidelines should not impose significant new burdens on patent applicants in the biotechnology arts or give rise to a new "anti-patenting" posture in the biotechnology examination group; however, the PTO should not be misled into adapting "customer-friendly" examination standards that do not subject applications to a thorough and rigorous examination. One comment opined that the Guidelines will result in a great increase in the number of appeals until the Federal Circuit makes clear that the law is quite different, thus delaying commercialization of potentially life improving and life saving inventions. According to this comment, universities and small inventors do not have the financial support to provide the exhaustive kind of work the Guidelines can require for meaningful coverage; this will mean that many biotechnology inventions will not be commercialized. One comment stated that the Commissioner indicates that meaningful patent coverage is required for commercial exploitation of biotechnological inventions, yet the PTO continues to take a position that leads away from what the Commissioner espouses. Another comment felt that the scope of allowed claims would be dependent on the examiner; a potential applicant would not know what sort of claims could be obtained based on a particular disclosure. One comment opined that applications filed after publication of the Guidelines will probably be much more detailed and longer in length. *Response:* The Revised Interim Guidelines clarify that a written description issue should rarely arise for an original claim because such a claim is presumed to have adequate descriptive support. The burden is on the examiner to provide evidence or reasoning in support of any rejection. Such an approach would not be expected to increase the number of appeals, nor should it require exhaustive work for meaningful coverage. The Revised Interim Guidelines are intended to promote uniformity, not diminish it.

(33) *Comment:* One comment indicated it is premature to instruct examiners in the proposed Guidelines since they may change dramatically as a result of public comment. Three comments stated that the Guidelines should not be applied until final Guidelines have been approved; two of these indicated that the Guidelines should only be applied to applications filed after implementation. One comment suggested preparing separate guidance for currently pending applications. *Response:* Separate guidance is not required for pending applications and applications filed after implementation of any final Guidelines; the Guidelines do not establish new law or rules or impose any additional requirements on applicants.

(34) *Comment:* One comment requested that the PTO address the issue of open-claim language for EST claims in the final Guidelines because of their importance to the biotechnology industry. Several comments stated that permitting open-ended language with respect to an EST claim contradicts the written description requirement because the common structural features of the EST do not constitute a "substantial portion of the genus" as required by the Eli Lilly case. According to these commentators, a claim such as "a DNA comprising SEQ. ID. NO: 1" would lack written description when SEQ. ID. NO: 1 was a gene fragment. *Response:* The Revised Interim Guidelines maintain the view that use of such terms as "gene" in the preamble of an EST claim may raise a written description issue if one skilled in the art would understand that a "gene" requires elements which are not sufficiently described. However, claims to "a DNA comprising SEQ. ID. NO: 1" are unlikely to raise a written description issue. The comments do not explain why there is a written description problem for a claim such as "a DNA comprising SEQ. ID. 1" when SEQ. ID. 1 is an EST, while there is no problem when SEQ. ID. 1 is a whole gene or a gene promoter. The only difference seems to be the utility of the DNA fragment.

(35) *Comment:* One comment asserted that the scope and level of unpredictability of the structure is so large that the person skilled in the art could not envisage sufficient species to place the genus in possession of the inventor at the time of filing, and that it should be a rare disclosure that supports EST claims broader than the specific SEQ. ID, even for claims such as "a DNA comprising the EST of SEQ. ID. NO: 1." The comment also suggested that claim language that supports the introduction of an infinite amount of random sequence would require an immense number of exemplary species. Several commentators advanced the position that disclosure of only a small fragment does not convey that the inventor was in possession of all of the possible molecules or that the inventor was in possession of the fragment wherever it occurs. *Response:* A claim such as "a DNA comprising the EST of SEQ. ID. NO: 1" or "a gene comprising the EST of SEQ. ID. NO: 1" will be analyzed for compliance with the written description requirement by determining whether the partial structure in combination with any other disclosed relevant identifying characteristics are sufficient to show that a skilled artisan would recognize that the applicant was in possession of the claimed invention as a whole. The Office does not agree with the comment that the scope of such an EST claim is necessarily too large to satisfy the written description requirement. The PTO has issued numerous patents in the past directed to nucleic acids that use open-ended language. Although an applicant presenting an original claim to an EST using open-ended claim language with disclosure of only the EST sequence is not in possession of any arbitrary specific possible molecule that contains the EST, the applicant may be in possession of a broad genus of DNA where the EST is in any random nucleic acid sequence. The comment's statement to the contrary would preclude open-ended claims incorporating any DNA sequence such as gene or promoter. In fact, such a view would appear to preclude open-ended language for any other polymer. However, such open-ended EST claims may not comply with the utility and scope of enablement requirements of 35 U.S.C. 101 and 112.

Revised Interim Guidelines for the Examination of Patent Applications Under the 35 U.S.C. Sec. 112, para. 1 "Written Description" Requirement

These revised interim "Written Description Guidelines" are intended to assist Office personnel in the examination of patent applications for compliance with the written description requirement of 35 U.S.C. 112, para. 1. This revision is based on the Office's current understanding of the law and public comments received in response to the PTO's previous request for public comments on its Interim Written Description Guidelines and is believed to be fully consistent with binding precedent of the U.S. Supreme Court, as well as the U.S. Court of Appeals for the Federal Circuit and its predecessor courts.

This revision does not constitute substantive rulemaking and hence does not have the force and effect of law. It is designed to assist Office personnel in analyzing claimed subject matter for compliance with substantive law. Rejections will be based upon the substantive law, and it is these rejections which are appealable. Consequently, any perceived failure by Office personnel to follow the Revised Interim Guidelines is neither appealable nor petitionable.

These Revised Interim Guidelines are intended to form part of the normal examination process. Thus, where Office personnel establish a prima facie case of lack of written description for a claim, a thorough review of the prior art and examination on the merits for compliance with the other statutory requirements, including those of 35 U.S.C. 101, 102, 103, and 112, is to be conducted prior to completing an Office action which includes a rejection for lack of written description. Office personnel are to rely on this revision of the guidelines in the event of any inconsistent treatment of issues involving the written description requirement between these Revised Interim Guidelines and any earlier guidance provided from the Office.

I. General Principles Governing Compliance With the "Written Description" Requirement for Applications

The first paragraph of 35 U.S.C. 112 requires that the "specification shall contain a written description of the invention. * * *" This requirement is separate and distinct from the enablement requirement.[1] The written description requirement has several policy objectives. "[T]he 'essential goal' of the description of the invention requirement is to clearly convey the information that an applicant has invented the subject matter which is claimed."[2] Another objective is to put the public in possession of what the applicant claims as the invention. The written description requirement of the Patent Act promotes the progress of the useful arts by ensuring that patentees adequately describe their inventions in their patent specifications in exchange for the right to exclude others from practicing the invention for the duration of the patent's term.[3]

To satisfy the written description requirement, a patent specification must describe the claimed invention in sufficient detail that one skilled in the art can reasonably conclude that the inventor had possession of the claimed invention.[4] An

---

[1] See, e.g., Vas-Cath, Inc. v. Mahurkar, 935 F.2d 1555, 1560, 19 USPQ2d 1111, 1114 (Fed. Cir. 1991).

[2] In re Barker, 559 F.2d 588, 592 n.4, 194 USPQ 470, 473 n.4 (CCPA 1977).

[3] See Regents of the University of California v. Eli Lilly, 119 F.3d 1559, 1566, 43 USPQ 2d 1398, 1404 (Fed. Cir. 1997), cert. denied, 523 U.S. 1089 (1998).

[4] See, e.g., Vas-Cath, Inc. v. Mahurkar, 935 F.2d at 1563, 19 USPQ 2d at 1116. Much of the written description case law addresses whether the specification as originally filed supports claims not originally in the application. The issue raised in the cases is most often phrased as whether the original application provides "adequate support" for the claims at issue or whether the material added to the specification incorporates "new matter" in violation of 35 U.S.C. Sec. 132. The "written description" question similarly arises in the interference context, where the issue is whether the specification of one party to the interference can support the newly added claims corresponding to the count at issue, i.e., whether that party can "make the claim" corresponding to the interference count. E.g., see Martin v. Mayer, 823 F.2d 500, 502, 3 USPQ 2d 1333, 1335 (Fed. Cir. 1987).

In addition, early opinions suggest the Patent and Trademark Office was unwilling to find written descriptive support when the only description was found in the claims; however, this viewpoint was rejected. See In re Koller, 613 F.2d 819, 204 USPQ 702 (CCPA 1980) (original claims constitute their own description); In re Gardner, 475 F.2d 1389, 177 USPQ 396 (CCPA 1973) (accord); In re Wertheim, 541 F.2d 257, 191 USPQ 90 (CCPA 1976) (accord). It is now well accepted that a satisfactory description may be in the claims or any other portion of the originally filed specification.

These early opinions did not address the quality or specificity of particularity that was required in the description, i.e., how much description is enough.

applicant shows possession of the claimed invention by describing the claimed invention with all of its limitations.[5] Possession may be shown by actual reduction to practice,[6] or by showing that the invention was "ready for patenting" such as by the disclosure of drawings or other descriptions of the invention that are sufficiently specific to enable a person skilled in the art to practice the invention.[7] A question as to whether a specification provides an adequate written description may arise in the context of an original claim which is not described sufficiently, a new or amended claim wherein a claim limitation has been added or removed, or a claim to entitlement of an earlier priority date or effective filing date under 35 U.S.C. 119, 120, or 365(c).[8] Compliance with the written description requirement is a question of fact which must be resolved on a case-by-case basis.[9]

A. Original Claims

There is a strong presumption that an adequate written description of the claimed invention is present when the application is filed.[10] However, the issue of a lack of adequate written description may arise even for an original claim when an aspect of the claimed invention has not been described with sufficient particularity such that one skilled in the art would recognize that the applicant had possession of the claimed invention.[11] The claimed invention as a whole may not be adequately described if the claims require an essential or critical element which is not adequately described in the specification and which is not conventional in the art.[12] This problem

---

[5]Lockwood v. American Airlines, Inc., 107 F.3d 1565, 1572, 41 USPQ 2d 1961, 1966 (Fed. Cir. 1997).

[6]An application specification may show actual reduction to practice by describing testing of the claimed invention or, in the case of biological materials, by specifically describing a deposit made in accordance with 37 CFR 1.801 et seq. 37 CFR 1.804, 1.809. See also Deposit of Biological Materials for Patent Purposes, Final Rule, 54 FR 34,864 (August 22, 1989) ("The requirement for a specific identification is consistent with the description requirement of the first paragraph of 35 U.S.C. 112, and to provide an antecedent basis for the biological material which either has been or will be deposited before the patent is granted." Id. at 34876. "[T]he description must be sufficient to permit verification that the deposited biological material is in fact that disclosed. Once the patent issues, the description must be sufficient to aid in the resolution of questions of infringement." Id. at 34,880.). Such a deposit is not a substitute for a written description of the claimed invention. The written description of the deposited material needs to be as complete as possible because the examination for patentability proceeds solely on the basis of the written description. See, e.g., In re Lundak, 773 F.2d 1216, 227 USPQ 90 (Fed. Cir. 1985). See also 54 FR at 34,880 ("As a general rule, the more information that is provided about a particular deposited biological material, the better the examiner will be able to compare the identity and characteristics of the deposited biological material with the prior art.").

[7]Pfaff v. Wells Electronics, Inc., 525 U.S. 55, ______, 119 S.Ct. 304, 312, 48 USPQ 2d 1641, 1647 (1998).

[8]A description requirement issue can arise for original claims (see, e.g., Eli Lilly, 119 F.3d 1559, 43 USPQ 2d 1398) as well as new or amended claims. Most typically, the issue will arise in the context of determining whether new or amended claims are supported by the description of the invention in the application as filed (see, e.g., In re Wright, 866 F.2d 422, 9 USPQ 2d 1649 (Fed. Cir. 1989)), whether a claimed invention is entitled to the benefit of an earlier priority date or effective filing date under 35 U.S.C. 119, 120, or 365(c) (see, e.g., Tronzo v. Biomet, Inc., 156 F.3d 1154, 47 USPQ 2d 1829 (Fed. Cir. 1998); Fiers v. Revel, 984 F.2d 1164, 25 USPQ 2d 1601 (Fed. Cir. 1993); In re Ziegler, 992 F.2d 1197, 1200, 26 USPQ 2d 1600, 1603 (Fed. Cir. 1993)), or whether a specification provides support for a claim corresponding to a count in an interference (see, e.g., Fields v. Conover, 443 F.2d 1386, 170 USPQ 276 (CCPA 1970)).

[9]Vas-Cath, Inc. v. Mahurkar, 935 F.2d at 1563, 19 USPQ 2d at 1116 (Fed. Cir. 1991).

[10]In re Wertheim, 541 F.2d at 262, 191 USPQ at 96.

[11]See note 4.

[12]For example, consider the claim "A gene comprising SEQ ID NO: 1." A determination of what the claim as a whole covers may result in a conclusion that specific structures such as a

may arise where an invention is described solely in terms of a method of its making coupled with its function and there is no described or art recognized correlation or relationship between the structure of the invention and its function.[13] A lack of adequate written description problem also arises if the knowledge and level of skill in the art would not permit one skilled in the art to immediately envisage the product claimed from the disclosed process.[14]

B. New or Amended Claims

The proscription against the introduction of new matter in a patent application[15] serves to prevent an applicant from adding information that goes beyond the subject matter originally filed.[16] Thus, the written description requirement prevents an applicant from claiming subject matter that was not adequately described in the specification as filed. New or amended claims which introduce elements or limitations

---

promoter, a coding region, or other elements are included. Although all genes encompassed by this claim share the characteristic of comprising SEQ ID NO: 1, there may be insufficient description of those specific structures (e.g., promoters, enhancers, coding regions, and other regulatory elements) which are also included.

[13]A biomolecule sequence described only by a functional characteristic, without any known or disclosed correlation between that function and the structure of the sequence, normally is not a sufficient identifying characteristic for written description purposes, even when accompanied by a method of obtaining the claimed sequence. For example, even though a genetic code table would correlate a known amino acid sequence with a genus of coding nucleic acids, the same table cannot predict the native, naturally occurring nucleic acid sequence of a naturally occurring mRNA or its corresponding cDNA. Cf. In re Bell, 991 F.2d 781, 26 USPQ 2d 1529 (Fed. Cir. 1993), and In re Deuel, 51 F.3d 1552, 34 USPQ 2d 1210 (Fed. Cir. 1995) (holding that a process could not render the product of that process obvious under 35 U.S.C. 103). The Federal Circuit has pointed out that under United States law, a description that does not render a claimed invention obvious cannot sufficiently describe the invention for the purposes of the written description requirement of 35 U.S.C. 112. Eli Lilly, 119 F.3d at 1567, 43 USPQ 2d at 1405. The fact that a great deal more than just a process is necessary to render a product invention obvious means that a great deal more than just a process is necessary to provide written description for a product invention.

Compare Fonar Corp. v. General Electric Co., 107 F.3d 1543, 1549, 41 USPQ 2d 1801, 1805 (Fed. Cir. 1997) ("As a general rule, where software constitutes part of a best mode of carrying out an invention, description of such a best mode is satisfied by a disclosure of the functions of the software. This is because, normally, writing code for such software is within the skill of the art, not requiring undue experimentation, once its functions have been disclosed * * *. Thus, flow charts or source code listings are not a requirement for adequately disclosing the functions of software.").

[14]See, e.g., Fujikawa v. Wattanasin, 93 F.3d 1559, 1571, 39 USPQ 2d 1895, 1905 (Fed. Cir. 1996) (a "laundry list" disclosure of every possible moiety does not constitute a written description of every species in a genus because it would not "reasonably lead" those skilled in the art to any particular species); In re Ruschig, 379 F.2d 990, 995, 154 USPQ 118, 122–23 (CCPA 1967) ("If n-propylamine had been used in making the compound instead of n-butylamine, the compound of claim 13 would have resulted. Appellants submit to us, as they did to the board, an imaginary specific example patterned on specific example 6 by which the above butyl compound is made so that we can see what a simple change would have resulted in a specific supporting disclosure being present in the present specification. The trouble is that there is no such disclosure, easy though it is to imagine it.").

[15]35 U.S.C. 132 and 251. See also In re Rasmussen, 650 F.2d 1212, 1214, 211 USPQ 323, 326 (CCPA 1981). See Manual of Patent Examining Procedure (MPEP) Secs. 2163.06–2163.07 (7th Ed., July 1998) for a more detailed discussion of the written description requirement and its relationship to new matter.

[16]The claims as filed in the original specification are part of the disclosure and therefore, if an application as originally filed contains a claim disclosing material not found in the remainder of the specification, the applicant may amend the specification to include the claimed subject matter. In re Benno, 768 F.2d 1340, 226 USPQ 683 (Fed. Cir. 1985).

which are not supported by the as-filed disclosure violate the written description requirement.[17] While there is no in haec verba requirement, newly added claim limitations must be supported in the specification through express, implicit, or inherent disclosure. An amendment to correct an obvious error does not constitute new matter where one skilled in the art would not only recognize the existence of the error in the specification, but also the appropriate correction.[18]

Under certain circumstances, omission of a limitation can raise an issue regarding whether the inventor had possession of a broader, more generic invention.[19] A claim that omits an element which applicant describes as an essential or critical feature of the invention originally disclosed does not comply with the written description requirement.[20]

The fundamental factual inquiry is whether the specification conveys with reasonable clarity to those skilled in the art that, as of the filing date sought, applicant was in possession of the invention as now claimed.[21]

---

[17] See, e.g., In re Lukach, 442 F.2d 967, 169 USPQ 795 (CCPA 1971) (subgenus range was not supported by generic disclosure and specific example within the subgenus range); In re Smith, 458 F.2d 1389, 1395, 173 USPQ 679, 683 (CCPA 1972) (a subgenus is not necessarily described by a genus encompassing it and a species upon which it reads).

[18] In re Oda, 443 F.2d 1200, 170 USPQ 260 (CCPA 1971). With respect to the correction of sequencing errors in applications disclosing nucleic acid and/or amino acid sequences, it is well known that sequencing errors are a common problem in molecular biology. See, e.g., Richterich, Peter, "Estimation of Errors in 'Raw' DNA Sequences: A Validation Study," Genome Research, 8:251–259 (1998). If an application as filed includes sequence information and references a deposit of the sequenced material made in accordance with the requirements of 37 CFR 1.801 et seq., corrections of minor errors in the sequence may be possible based on the argument that one of skill in the art would have resequenced the deposited material and would have immediately recognized the minor error. Deposits made after the filing date can only be relied upon to provide support for the correction of sequence information if applicant submits a statement in compliance with 37 CFR 1.804 stating that the biological material which is deposited is a biological material specifically defined in the application as filed.

[19] See, e.g., Gentry Gallery, Inc. v. Berkline Corp., 134 F.3d 1473, 45 USPQ 2d 1498 (Fed. Cir. 1998) (claims to a section sofa comprising, inter alia, a console and a control means were held invalid for failing to satisfy the written description requirement where the claims were broadened by removing the location of the control means.); Johnson Worldwide Associates Inc. v. Zebco Corp., 175 F.3d 985, 993, 50 USPQ 2d 1607, 1613 (Fed. Cir. 1999) (In Gentry Gallery, the "court's determination that the patent disclosure did not support a broad meaning for the disputed claim terms was premised on clear statements in the written description that described the location of a claim element—the 'control means'—as 'the only possible location' and that variations were 'outside the stated purpose of the invention.' Gentry Gallery, 134 F.3d at 1479, 45 USPQ 2d at 1503. Gentry Gallery, then, considers the situation where the patent's disclosure makes crystal clear that a particular (i.e., narrow) understanding of a claim term is an 'essential element of [the inventor's] invention.'"); Tronzo v. Biomet, Inc., 156 F.3d 1154, 1159, 47 USPQ 2d 1829, 1833 (Fed. Cir. 1998) (claims to generic cup shape were not entitled to filing date of parent application which disclosed "conical cup" in view of the disclosure of the parent application stating the advantages and importance of the conical shape.).

[20] See Gentry Gallery, 134 F.3d at 1480, 45 USPQ 2d at 1503; In re Sus, 306 F.2d 494, 134 USPQ 301 (CCPA 1962) ("[O]ne skilled in this art would not be taught by the written description of the invention in the specification that any 'aryl or substituted aryl radical' would be suitable for the purposes of the invention but rather that only certain aryl radicals and certain specifically substituted aryl radicals [i.e., aryl azides] would be suitable for such purposes."). A claim which omits matter disclosed to be essential to the invention as described in the specification or in other statements of record may also be subject to rejection under 35 U.S.C. Sec. 112, para. 1 as not enabling, or under 35 U.S.C. 112, para. 2. See In re Mayhew, 527 F.2d 1229, 188 USPQ 356 (CCPA 1976); In re Venezia, 530 F.2d 956, 189 USPQ 149 (CCPA 1976); and In re Collier, 397 F.2d 1003, 158 USPQ 266 (CCPA 1968). See also Reiffin v. Microsoft Corp., 48 USPQ 2d 1274, 1277 (N.D. Cal. 1998) and MPEP Sec. 2172.01.

[21] See, e.g., Vas-Cath, Inc., 935 F.2d at 1563–64, 19 USPQ 2d at 1117.

II. Methodology for Determining Adequacy of Written Description

A. Read and Analyze the Specification for Compliance With 35 U.S.C. 112, para. 1

Office personnel should adhere to the following procedures when reviewing patent applications for compliance with the written description requirement of 35 U.S.C. 112, para. 1. The examiner has the initial burden, after a thorough reading and evaluation of the content of the application, of presenting evidence or reasons why a person skilled in the art would not recognize that the written description of the invention provides support for the claims. There is a strong presumption that an adequate written description of the claimed invention is present in the specification as filed;[22] however, with respect to newly added or amended claims, applicant should show support in the original disclosure for the new or amended claims.[23] Consequently, rejection of an original claim for lack of written description should be rare. The inquiry into whether the description requirement is met is a question of fact that must be determined on a case-by-case basis.[24]

1. For Each Claim, Determine What the Claim as a Whole Covers

Claim construction is an essential part of the examination process. Each claim must be separately analyzed and given its broadest reasonable interpretation in light of and consistent with the written description.[25] The entire claim must be considered, including the preamble language[26] and the transitional phrase.[27] The claim as a whole,

---

[22] Wertheim, 541 F.2d at 262, 191 USPQ at 96.

[23] See MPEP Secs. 714.02 and 2163.06 ("Applicant should * * * specifically point out the support for any amendments made to the disclosure."); and MPEP Sec. 2163.04 ("If applicant amends the claims and points out where and/or how the originally filed disclosure supports the amendment(s), and the examiner finds that the disclosure does not reasonably convey that the inventor had possession of the subject matter of the amendment at the time of the filing of the application, the examiner has the initial burden of presenting evidence or reasoning to explain why persons skilled in the art would not recognize in the disclosure a description of the invention defined by the claims.").

[24] See In re Smith, 458 F.2d 1389, 1395, 173 USPQ 679, 683 (CCPA 1972) ("Precisely how close [to the claimed invention] the description must come to comply with Sec. 112 must be left to case-by-case development."); In re Wertheim, 541 F.2d at 262, 191 USPQ at 96 (inquiry is primarily factual and depends on the nature of the invention and the amount of knowledge imparted to those skilled in the art by the disclosure).

[25] See, e.g., In re Morris, 127 F.3d 1048, 1053–54, 44 USPQ 2d 1023, 1027 (Fed. Cir. 1997).

[26] "Preamble language" is that language in a claim appearing before the transitional phase, e.g., before "comprising," "consisting essentially of," or "consisting of."

[27] The transitional term "comprising" (and other comparable terms, e.g., "containing," "including," and "having") is "open-ended—it covers the expressly recited subject matter, alone or in combination with unrecited subject matter. See, e.g., Ex parte Davis, 80 USPQ 448, 450 (Bd. App. 1948) ("comprising" leaves the "claim open for the inclusion of unspecified ingredients even in major amounts"), quoted with approval in Moleculon Research Corp v. CBS, Inc., 793 F.2d 1261, 1271, 229 USPQ 805, 812 (Fed. Cir. 1986). "By using the term 'consisting essentially of,' the drafter signals that the invention necessarily includes the listed ingredients and is open to unlisted ingredients that do not materially affect the basic and novel properties of the invention. A 'consisting essentially of' claim occupies a middle ground between closed claims that are written in a 'consisting of' format and fully open claims that are drafted in a 'comprising' format." PPG Industries v. Guardian Industries, 156 F.3d 1351, 1354, 48 USPQ 2d 1351, 1353–54 (Fed. Cir. 1998). For search and examination purposes, absent a clear indication in the specification of what the basic and novel characteristics actually are, 'consisting essentially of' will be construed as equivalent to "comprising." See, e.g., PPG, 156 F.3d at 1355, 48 USPQ at 1355 ("PPG could have defined the scope of the phrase 'consisting essentially of' for purposes of its patent by making clear in its specification what it regarded as constituting a material change in the basic and novel characteristics of the invention.").

including all limitations found in the preamble,[28] the transitional phrase, and the body of the claim, must be sufficiently described in the specification to satisfy the written description requirement.[29]

The examiner should evaluate each claim to determine if sufficient structures, acts, or functions are recited to make clear the scope and meaning of the claim, including the weight to be given the preamble.[30] The absence of definitions or details for well-established terms or procedures should not be the basis of a rejection under 35 U.S.C. 112, para. 1, for lack of adequate written description. Limitations may not, however, be imported into the claims from the specification.

2. *Review the Entire Application to Understand What Applicant Has Described as the Essential Features of the Invention*

Prior to determining whether the disclosure satisfies the written description requirement for the claimed subject matter, the examiner should review the claims and the entire specification, including the specific embodiments, figures, and sequence listings, to understand what applicant has identified as the essential distinguishing characteristics of the invention. The analysis of whether the specification complies with the written description requirement requires the examiner to determine the correspondence between what applicant has described as the essential identifying characteristic features of the invention, i.e., what the applicant has demonstrated possession of, and what applicant has claimed. Such a review is conducted from the standpoint of one of skill in the art at the time the application was filed,[31] and should include a determination of the field of the invention and the level of skill and knowledge in the art. Generally, there is an inverse correlation between the level of skill and knowledge in the art and the specificity of disclosure necessary to satisfy the written description requirement. Information which is well known in the art does not have to be described in detail in the specification.[32]

3. *Determine Whether There is Sufficient Written Description To Inform a Skilled Artisan That Applicant Was in Possession of the Claimed Invention as a Whole at the Time the Application Was Filed*

a. Original claims.—Possession may be shown in any number of ways. Possession may be shown by actual reduction to practice, by a clear depiction of the invention in detailed drawings which permit a person skilled in the art to clearly recognize that applicant had possession of the claimed invention, or by a written description of the invention describing sufficient relevant identifying character-

---

[28] See Pac-Tec Inc. v. Amerace Corp., 903 F.2d 796, 801, 14 USPQ 2d 1871, 1876 (Fed. Cir. 1990) (determining that preamble language that constitutes a structural limitation is actually part of the claimed invention).

[29] An applicant shows possession of the claimed invention by describing the claimed invention with all of its essential novel elements. Lockwood, 107 F.3d at 1572, 41 USPQ 2d at 1966.

[30] See, e.g., Bell Communications Research, Inc. v. Vitalink Communications Corp., 55 F.3d 615, 620, 34 USPQ 2d 1816, 1820 (Fed. Cir. 1995) ("[A] claim preamble has the import that the claim as a whole suggests for it."); Corning Glass Works v. Sumitomo Elec. U.S.A., Inc., 868 F.2d 1251, 1257, 9 USPQ 2d 1962, 1966 (Fed. Cir. 1989) (The determination of whether preamble recitations are structural limitations can be resolved only on review of the entirety of the application "to gain an understanding of what the inventors actually invented and intended to encompass by the claim.").

[31] See, e.g., Wang Labs. v. Toshiba Corp., 993 F.2d 858, 865, 26 USPQ 2d 1767, 1774 (Fed. Cir. 1993).

[32] See, e.g., Hybritech Inc. v. Monoclonal Antibodies, Inc., 802 F.2d 1367, 1379–80, 231 USPQ 81, 90 (Fed. Cir. 1986).

istics such that a person skilled in the art would recognize that the inventor had possession of the claimed invention.[33]

A specification may show actual reduction to practice by showing that the inventor constructed an embodiment or performed a process that met all the limitations of the claim, and determined that the invention would work for its intended purpose.[34] Actual reduction to practice of a biological material may be shown by specifically describing a deposit made in accordance with the requirements of 37 C.F.R. Sec. 1.801 et seq.[35]

An applicant may show possession of an invention by disclosure of drawings that are sufficiently detailed to show that applicant was in possession of the claimed invention as a whole.[36] The description need only describe in detail that which is new or not conventional.[37] This is equally true whether the claimed invention is directed to a product or a process. Normally a reduction to drawings will adequately describe the claimed invention.[38]

An applicant may also show that an invention is complete by disclosure of sufficiently detailed relevant identifying characteristics which provide evidence that applicant was in possession of the claimed invention,[39] i.e., complete or partial structure,

---

[33] Pfaff v. Wells Electronics, Inc., 119 S.Ct. at 311, 48 USPQ 2d at 1646 ("The word 'invention' must refer to a concept that is complete, rather than merely one that is 'substantially complete.' It is true that reduction to practice ordinarily provides the best evidence that an invention is complete. But just because reduction to practice is sufficient evidence of completion, it does not follow that proof of reduction to practice is necessary in every case. Indeed, both the facts of the Telephone Cases and the facts of this case demonstrate that one can prove that an invention is complete and ready for patenting before it has actually been reduced to practice.").

[34] Cooper v. Goldfarb, 154 F.3d 1321, 1327, 47 USPQ 2d 1896, 1901 (Fed. Cir. 1998). See also UMC Elecs. Co. v. United States, 816 F.2d 647, 652, 2 USPQ 2d 1465, 1468 (Fed. Cir. 1987) ("[T]here cannot be a reduction to practice of the invention * * * without a physical embodiment which includes all limitations of the claim."); Estee Lauder Inc. v. L'Oreal S.A., 129 F.3d 588, 593, 44 USPQ 2d 1610, 1614 (Fed. Cir. 1997) ("[A] reduction to practice does not occur until the inventor has determined that the invention will work for its intended purpose."); Mahurkar v. C.R. Bard Inc., 79 F.3d 1572, 1578, 38 USPQ 2d 1288, 1291 (Fed. Cir. 1996) (determining that the invention will work for its intended purpose may require testing depending on the character of the invention and the problem it solves).

[35] 37 CFR Secs. 1.804, 1.809. See also note 6.

[36] See, e.g., Vas-Cath, 935 F.2d at 1565, 19 USPQ 2d at 1118 ("drawings alone may provide a 'written description' of an invention as required by Sec. 112"); In re Wolfensperger, 302 F.2d 950, 133 USPQ 537 (CCPA 1962) (the drawings of applicant's specification provided sufficient written descriptive support for the claim limitation at issue); Autogiro Co. of America v. United States, 384 F.2d 391, 398, 155 USPQ 697, 703 (Ct. Cl. 1967) ("[I]n those instances where a visual representation can flesh out words, drawings may be used in the same manner and with the same limitations as the specification.").

[37] See Hybritech v. Monoclonal Antibodies, 802 F.2d at 1384, 231 USPQ at 94; Fonar Corp. v. General Electric Co., 107 F.3d at 1549, 41 USPQ 2d at 1805 (source code description not required).

[38] This is especially true for the mechanical and electrical arts. See, e.g., Pfaff v. Wells Electronics, 119 S.Ct. at 312, 48 USPQ 2d at 1647.

[39] For example, the presence of a restriction enzyme map of a gene may be relevant to a statement that the gene has been isolated. One skilled in the art may be able to determine when the gene disclosed is the same as or different from a gene isolated by another by comparing the restriction enzyme map. In contrast, evidence that the gene could be digested with a nuclease would not normally represent a relevant characteristic since any gene would be digested with a nuclease. Similarly, isolation of an mRNA and its expression to produce the protein of interest is strong evidence of possession of an mRNA for the protein.

Examples of identifying characteristics include a sequence, structure, binding affinity, binding specificity, molecular weight, and length. Although structural formulas provide a convenient method of demonstrating possession of specific molecules, other identifying characteristics or

other physical and/or chemical properties, functional characteristics when coupled with a known or disclosed correlation between function and structure, or some combination of such characteristics.[40] What is conventional or well known to one skilled in the art need not be disclosed in detail.[41] If a skilled artisan would have understood the inventor to be in possession of the claimed invention at the time of filing, even if every nuance of the claims is not explicitly described in the specification, then the adequate description requirement is met.[42]

(1) For each claim drawn to a single embodiment or species:[43]
   (a) Determine whether the application describes an actual reduction to practice of the claimed invention.
   (b) If the application does not describe an actual reduction to practice, determine whether the invention is complete as evidenced by a reduction to drawings.
   (c) If the application does not describe an actual reduction to practice or reduction to drawings, determine whether the invention has been set forth in terms of distinguishing identifying characteristics as evidenced by other descriptions of the invention that are sufficiently detailed to show that applicant was in possession of the claimed invention.
      (i) Determine whether the application as filed describes the complete structure (or acts of a process) of the claimed invention as a whole. The complete structure of a species or embodiment typically satisfies the requirement that the description be set forth "in such full, clear, concise, and exact

---

combinations of characteristics may demonstrate the requisite possession. For example, unique cleavage by particular enzymes, isoelectric points of fragments, detailed restriction enzyme maps, a comparison of enzymatic activities, or antibody cross-reactivity may be sufficient to show possession of the claimed invention to one of skill in the art. See Lockwood, 107 F.3d at 1572, 41 USPQ 2d at 1966 ("written description" requirement may be satisfied by using "such descriptive means as words, structures, figures, diagrams, formulas, etc., that fully set forth the claimed invention").

However, a definition by function alone "does not suffice" to sufficiently describe a coding sequence "because it is only an indication of what the gene does, rather than what it is." Eli Lilly, 119 F.3d at 1568, 43 USPQ 2d at 1406. See also Fiers, 984 F.2d at 1169–71, 25 USPQ 2d at 1605–06 (discussing Amgen Inc. v. Chugai Pharmaceutical Co., 927 F.2d 1200, 18 USPQ 2d 1016 (Fed. Cir. 1991)).

[40] If a claim limitation invokes 35 U.S.C. Sec. 112, para. 6, it must be interpreted to cover the corresponding structure, materials, or acts in the specification and "equivalents thereof." See 35 U.S.C. 112, para. 6. See also B. Braun Medical, Inc. v. Abbott Lab., 124 F.3d 1419, 1424, 43 USPQ 2d 1896, 1899 (Fed. Cir. 1997). If the written description fails to set forth the supporting structure, material or acts corresponding to the means- (or step-) plus-function, the claim may not meet the requirement of 35 U.S.C. 112, para. 1. A means- (or step-) plus-function claim limitation satisfies 35 U.S.C. 112, para. 1 if: (1) The written description links or associates particular structure, materials, or acts to the function recited in a means- (or step-) plus-function claim limitation; or (2) it is clear based on the facts of the application that one skilled in the art would have known what structure, materials, or acts perform the function recited in a means- (or step-) plus-function limitation. In considering whether there is 35 U.S.C. Sec. 112, para. 1 support for the claim limitation, the examiner must consider not only the original disclosure contained in the summary and detailed description of the invention portions of the specification, but also the original claims, abstract, and drawings. See the Interim Supplemental Examination Guidelines for Determining the Applicability of 35 U.S.C. 112 para. 6, 64 FR 41392 (July 30, 1999).

[41] See Hybritech Inc. v. Monoclonal Antibodies, Inc., 802 F.2d at 1384, 231 USPQ at 94.

[42] See, e.g., Vas-Cath, 935 F.2d at 1563, 19 USPQ 2d at 1116; Martin v. Johnson, 454 F.2d 746, 751, 172 USPQ 391, 395 (CCPA 1972) (stating "the description need not be in ipsis verbis [i.e., 'in the same words'] to be sufficient").

[43] A claim which is limited to a single disclosed embodiment or species is analyzed as a claim drawn to a single embodiment or species, whereas a claim which encompasses two or more embodiments or species within the scope of the claim is analyzed as a claim drawn to a genus. See also MPEP Sec. 806.04(e).

terms" to show possession of the claimed invention.[44] If a complete structure is disclosed, the written description requirement is satisfied for that species or embodiment, and a rejection under 35 U.S.C. 112, para. 1 for lack of written description must not be made.

(ii) If the application as filed does not disclose the complete structure (or acts of a process) of the claimed invention as a whole, determine whether the specification discloses other relevant identifying characteristics sufficient to describe the claimed invention in such full, clear, concise, and exact terms that a skilled artisan would recognize applicant was in possession of the claimed invention.[45] Whether the specification shows that applicant was in possession of the claimed invention is not a single, simple factual determination, but rather is a conclusion reached by weighing many factual considerations. Factors to be considered in determining whether there is sufficient evidence of possession include the level of skill and knowledge in the art, partial structure, physical and/or chemical properties, functional characteristics alone or coupled with a known or disclosed correlation between structure and function, and the method of making the claimed invention. Disclosure of any combination of such identifying characteristics that distinguish the claimed invention from other materials and would lead one of skill in the art to the conclusion that the applicant was in possession of the claimed species is sufficient. Patents and printed publications in the art should be relied upon to determine whether an art is mature and what the level of knowledge and skill is in the art. In most technologies which are mature, and wherein the knowledge and level of skill in the art is high, a written description question should not be raised for original claims even if the specification discloses only a method of making the invention and the function of the invention.[46] In contrast, in emerging and unpredictable technologies, more evidence is required to show possession. For example, disclosure of only a method of making the invention and the function may not be

---

[44] 35 U.S.C. 112, para. 1. Cf. Fields v. Conover, 443 F.2d 1386, 1392, 170 USPQ 276, 280 (CCPA 1971) (finding a lack of written description because the specification lacked the "full, clear, concise, and exact written description" which is necessary to support the claimed invention).

[45] For example, if the art has established a strong correlation between structure and function, one skilled in the art would be able to predict with a reasonable degree of confidence the structure of the claimed invention from a recitation of its function. Thus, the written description requirement may be satisfied through disclosure of function and minimal structure when there is a well-established correlation between structure and function. In contrast, without such a correlation, the capability to recognize or understand the structure from the mere recitation of function and minimal structure is highly unlikely. In this latter case, disclosure of function alone is little more than a wish for possession; it does not satisfy the written description requirement. See Eli Lilly, 119 F.3d at 1568, 43 USPQ 2d at 1406 (written description requirement not satisfied by merely providing "a result that one might achieve if one made that invention"); In re Wilder, 736 F.2d 1516, 1521, 222 USPQ 369, 372–73 (Fed. Cir. 1984) (affirming a rejection for lack of written description because the specification does "little more than outline goals appellants hope the claimed invention achieves and the problems the invention will hopefully ameliorate"). Compare Fonar, 107 F.3d at 1549, 41 USPQ 2d at 1805 (disclosure of software function adequate in that art).

[46] See, e.g., In re Hayes Microcomputer Products Inc. Patent Litigation, 982 F.2d 1527, 1534–35, 25 USPQ 2d 1241, 1246 (Fed. Cir. 1992) ("One skilled in the art would know how to program a microprocessor to perform the necessary steps described in the specification. Thus, an inventor is not required to describe every detail of his invention. An applicant's disclosure obligation varies according to the art to which the invention pertains. Disclosing a microprocessor capable of performing certain functions is sufficient to satisfy the requirement of section 112, first paragraph, when one skilled in the relevant art would understand what is intended and know how to carry it out.").

sufficient to support a product claim other than a product-by-process claim.[47] Furthermore, disclosure of partial structure without additional characterization of the product may not be sufficient to evidence possession of the claimed invention.[48]

Any claim to a species that does not meet the test described under at least one of (a), (b), or (c) must be rejected as lacking adequate written description under 35 U.S.C. 112, para. 1.

(2) For each claim drawn to a genus:

The written description requirement for a claimed genus may be satisfied through sufficient description of a representative number of species by actual reduction practice (see (1)(a), above), reduction to drawings (see (1)(b), above), or by disclosure of relevant identifying characteristics, i.e., structure or other physical and/or chemical properties, by functional characteristics coupled with a known or disclosed correlation between function and structure, or by a combination of such identifying characteristics, sufficient to show the applicant was in possession of the claimed genus (see (1)(c), above).[49]

A "representative number of species" means that the species which are adequately described are representative of the entire genus. Thus, when there is substantial variation within the genus, one must describe a sufficient variety of species to reflect the variation within the genus. What constitutes a "representative number" is an inverse function of the skill and knowledge in the art. Satisfactory disclosure of a "representative number" depends on whether one of skill in the art would recognize that the applicant was in possession of the necessary common attributes or features of the elements possessed by the members of the genus in view of the species disclosed. In an unpredictable art, adequate written description of a genus which embraces widely variant species cannot be achieved by disclosing only one species within the genus.[50] Description of a representative number of species does not require the description to be of such specificity that it

---

[47] See, e.g., Fiers v. Revel, 984 F.2d at 1169, 25 USPQ 2d at 1605; Amgen Inc. v. Chugai Pharmaceutical Co., 927 F.2d 1200, 1206, 18 USPQ 2d 1016, 1021 (Fed. Cir. 1991). Where the process has actually been used to produce the product, the written description requirement for a product-by-process claim is clearly satisfied; however, the requirement may not be satisfied where it is not clear that the acts set forth in the specification can be performed, or that the product is produced by that process.

[48] See, e.g., Amgen Inc. v. Chugai Pharmaceutical Co., 927 F.2d 1200, 1206, 18 USPQ 2d 1016, 1021 (Fed. Cir. 1991) ("A gene is a chemical compound, albeit a complex one, and it is well established in our law that conception of a chemical compound requires that the inventor be able to define it so as to distinguish it from other materials, and to describe how to obtain it. Conception does not occur unless one has a mental picture of the structure of the chemical, or is able to define it by its method of preparation, its physical or chemical properties, or whatever characteristics sufficiently distinguish it. It is not sufficient to define it solely by its principal biological property, e.g., encoding human erythropoietin, because an alleged conception having no more specificity than that is simply a wish to know the identity of any material with that biological property. We hold that when an inventor is unable to envision the detailed constitution of a gene so as to distinguish it from other materials, as well as a method for obtaining it, conception has not been achieved until reduction to practice has occurred, i.e., until after the gene has been isolated.") (citations omitted). In such instances the alleged conception fails not merely because the field is unpredictable or because of the general uncertainty surrounding experimental sciences, but because the conception is incomplete due to factual uncertainty that undermines the specificity of the inventor's idea of the invention. Burroughs Wellcome Co. v. Barr Laboratories Inc., 40 F.3d 1223, 1229, 32 USPQ 2d 1915, 1920 (Fed. Cir. 1994). Reduction to practice in effect provides the only evidence to corroborate conception (and therefore possession) of the invention. Id.

[49] See Eli Lilly, 119 F.3d at 1568, 43 USPQ 2d at 1406.

[50] See, e.g., Eli Lilly.

would provide individual support for each species that the genus embraces.[51] If a representative number of adequately described species are not disclosed for a genus, the claim to that genus must be rejected as lacking adequate written description under 35 U.S.C. 112, para. 1.

b. New claims, amended claims, or claims asserting entitlement to the benefit of an earlier priority date or filing date under 35 U.S.C. Secs. 119, 120, or 365(c).—The examiner has the initial burden of presenting evidence or reasoning to explain why persons skilled in the art would not recognize in the original disclosure a description of the invention defined by the claims.[52] However, when filing an amendment an applicant should show support in the original disclosure for new or amended claims.[53] To comply with the written description requirement of 35 U.S.C. 112, para. 1, or to be entitled to an earlier priority date or filing date under 35 U.S.C. 119, 120, or 365(c), each claim limitation must be expressly,[54] implicitly,[55] or inherently[56] supported in the originally filed disclosure.[57] Furthermore, each claim must include all elements which applicant has described as essential.[58]

If the originally filed disclosure does not provide support for each claim limitation, or if an element which applicant describes as essential or critical is not claimed, a new or amended claim must be rejected under 35 U.S.C. 112, para. 1, as lacking adequate written description, or in the case of a claim for priority under 35 U.S.C. 119, 120, or 365(c), the claim for priority must be denied.

---

[51] For example, in the genetics arts, it is unnecessary for an applicant to provide enough different species that the disclosure will permit one of skill to determine the nucleic acid or amino acid sequence of another species from the application alone. The stochastic nature of gene evolution would make such a predictability nearly impossible. Thus, the Federal Circuit could not have intended that representative number requires predictability of sequences.

[52] See Wertheim, 541 F.2d at 263, 191 USPQ at 97 ("[T]he PTO has the initial burden of presenting evidence or reasons why persons skilled in the art would not recognize in the disclosure a description of the invention defined by the claims."). See also MPEP Sec. 2163.05.

[53] See MPEP Secs. 714.02 and 2163.06 ("Applicant should * * * specifically point out the support for any amendments made to the disclosure.").

[54] See, e.g., In re Wright, 866 F.2d 422, 425, 9 USPQ 2d 1649, 1651 (Fed. Cir. 1989) (Original specification for method of forming images using photosensitive microcapsules which describes removal of microcapsules from surface and warns that capsules not be disturbed prior to formation of image, unequivocally teaches absence of permanently fixed microcapsules and supports amended language of claims requiring that microcapsules be "not permanently fixed" to underlying surface, and therefore meets description requirement of 35 U.S.C. 112.).

[55] See, e.g., In re Robins, 429 F.2d 452, 456–57, 166 USPQ 552, 555 (CCPA 1970) ("[W]here no explicit description of a generic invention is to be found in the specification * * * mention of representative compounds may provide an implicit description upon which to base generic claim language."); In re Smith, 458 F.2d 1389, 1395, 173 USPQ 679, 683 (CCPA 1972) (a subgenus is not necessarily implicitly described by a genus encompassing it and a species upon which it reads).

[56] See, e.g., In re Robertson, 169 F.3d 743, 745, 49 USPQ 2d 1949, 1950–51 (Fed. Cir. 1999) ("To establish inherency, the extrinsic evidence 'must make clear that the missing descriptive matter is necessarily present in the thing described in the reference, and that it would be so recognized by persons of ordinary skill. Inherency, however, may not be established by probabilities or possibilities. The mere fact that a certain thing may result from a given set of circumstances is not sufficient.'") (citations omitted).

[57] When an explicit limitation in a claim "is not present in the written description whose benefit is sought it must be shown that a person of ordinary skill would have understood, at the time the patent application was filed, that the description requires that limitation." Hyatt v. Boone, 146 F.3d 1348, 1353, 47 USPQ 2d 1128, 1131 (Fed. Cir. 1998).

[58] See, e.g., Johnson Worldwide Associates Inc. v. Zebco Corp., 175 F.3d at 993, 50 USPQ 2d at 1613; Gentry Gallery, Inc. v. Berkline Corp., 134 F.3d at 1479, 45 USPQ 2d at 1503; Tronzo v. Biomet, Inc., 156 F.3d at 1159, 47 USPQ 2d at 1833; and Reiffin v. Microsoft Corp., 48 USPQ 2d at 1277.

III. Complete Patentability Determination Under All Statutory Requirements and Clearly Communicate Findings, Conclusions and Their Bases

The above only describes how to determine whether the written description requirement of 35 U.S.C. 112, para. 1 is satisfied. Regardless of the outcome of that determination, Office personnel must complete the patentability determination under all the relevant statutory provisions of Title 35 of the U.S. Code.

Once Office personnel have concluded analysis of the claimed invention under all the statutory provisions, including 35 U.S.C. 101, 112, 102, and 103, they should review all the proposed rejections and their bases to confirm their correctness. Only then should any rejection be imposed in an Office action. The Office action should clearly communicate the findings, conclusions, and reasons which support them. When possible, the Office action should offer helpful suggestions on how to overcome rejections.

A. For Each Claim Lacking Written Description Support, Reject the Claim Under Section 112, para. 1, for Lack of Adequate Written Description

A description as **filed** is presumed to be adequate, unless or until sufficient evidence or reasoning to the contrary has been presented by the examiner to rebut the presumption.[59] The examiner, therefore, must have a reasonable basis to challenge the adequacy of the written description. The examiner has the initial burden of presenting by a preponderance of evidence why a person skilled in the art would not recognize in an applicant's disclosure a description of the invention defined by the claims.[60] In rejecting a claim, the examiner must set forth express findings of fact regarding the above analysis which support the lack of written description conclusion. These findings should:

(1) identify the claim limitation at issue; and
(2) establish a prima facie case by providing reasons why a person skilled in the art at the time the application was filed would not have recognized that the inventor was in possession of the invention as claimed in view of the disclosure of the application as filed. A general allegation of "unpredictability in the art" is not a sufficient reason to support a rejection for lack of adequate written description.

When appropriate, suggest amendments to the claims which can be supported by the application's written description, being mindful of the prohibition against the addition of new matter in the claims or description.[61]

B. Upon Reply By Applicant, Again Determine the Patentability of the Claimed Invention, Including Whether the Written Description Requirement is Satisfied by Reperforming the Analysis Described Above in View of the Whole Record

Upon reply by applicant, before repeating any rejection under 35 U.S.C. 112, para. 1 for lack of written description, review the basis for the rejection in view of the record as a whole, including amendments, arguments, and any evidence submitted by applicant. If the whole record now demonstrates that the written description requirement is satisfied, do not repeat the rejection in the next Office action. If the

---

[59] See, e.g., In re Marzocchi, 439 F.2d 220, 224, 169 USPQ 367, 370 (CCPA 1971).

[60] Wertheim, 541 F.2d at 262, 191 USPQ at 96.

[61] See In re Rasmussen, 650 F.2d at 1214, 211 USPQ at 326.

record still does not demonstrate that written description is adequate to support the claim(s), repeat the rejection under 35 U.S.C. 112, para. 1, fully respond to applicant's rebuttal arguments, and properly treat any further showings submitted by applicant in the reply. Any affidavits, including those relevant to the 112, para. 1, written description requirement,[62] must be thoroughly analyzed and discussed in the next Office action.

Dated: December 16, 1999.

Q. Todd Dickinson,
Assistant Secretary of Commerce and Commissioner of Patents and Trademarks.
[FR Doc. 99-33053 Filed 12-20-99; 8:45 am]

---

[62] See In re Alton, 76 F.3d 1168, 1176, 37 USPQ 2d 1578, 1584 (Fed. Cir. 1996).

Appendix C-21

Calculation of Term of a U.S. Patent

I. A patent which issues based on an application filed prior to June 8, 1995 will have a term that is the longer of 17 years from the date of issue or 20 years from the filing date of the application.

II. A patent which issues based on an application filed on or after June 8, 1995 will have a mandatory term of 20 years from the filing date.

III. A patent which issues based on an application filed on or after June 8, 1995, which application is a continuation or divisional of an application(s) filed prior to June 8, 1995, will have a mandatory term of 20 years from the first application filed in U.S.[1]

IV. A patent which issues based on a PCT application filed on or after June 8, 1995 will have a term of 20 years from the PCT filing date, regardless of whether the continuation route or national stage entry is selected.

V. A patent which issues from a national stage application based on a PCT application filed prior to June 8, 1995, designating the United States (filed under 371 (c) in the U.S.), will have a term that is the longer of 17 years from the date of issue or 20 years from the filing date of the PCT application.

VI. A patent which issues from a U.S. application filed on or after June 8, 1995, which is a continuation of a PCT application filed prior to June 8, 1995, will have a mandatory term of 20 years from the PCT filing date.

35 U.S.C. 154 (a–c); 35 U.S.C. 365 (a–c); 37 C.F.R. 1.129 (a).

Appendix C-22

A Guide to Filing a Utility Patent Application

Introduction

The U.S. Patent and Trademark Office (PTO) is the government agency responsible for examining patent applications and issuing patents. A patent is a type of property right. It gives the patent holder the right, for a limited time, to exclude others from making, using, or selling the subject matter that is within the scope of protection granted by the patent. The PTO determines whether a patent should be granted in a particular case. However, it is up to the patent holder to enforce his or her own rights if the PTO does grant a patent.

The purpose of this guide is to provide you with basic information about filing a utility patent application. A patent application is a complex legal document, best prepared by one trained to prepare such documents. Thus, after reviewing this guide, you may wish to consult with a patent attorney or agent. Additional information is available:

- by calling the PTO's General Information Services at 800-PTO-9199 or 7033084357,
- from the PTO's Web site at **www.uspto.gov,** and
- at your nearest Patent and Trademark Depository Library (PTDL). You will find information regarding the nearest PTDL at the end of this guide.

There are various types of patents—utility, design, and plant. There are also two types of utility patent application—provisional and nonprovisional. Each year the PTO receives approximately 200,000 patent applications. Most of these are for nonprovisional utility patents.

This guide contains information to assist you in filing your nonprovisional utility patent application. It discusses the required parts of the utility patent application and includes samples of some of the forms you may use. This information is generally derived from the Patent Act, found at Title 35 of the *United States Code* (U.S.C.), and Title 37 of the *Code of Federal Regulations* (CFR). These materials are available at PTDLs and at most law libraries.

If you have questions about:

- other types of patent applications,
- locating a patent attorney or agent,
- obtaining the most up-to-date *Fee Schedule*, or
- obtaining copies of other PTO publications,

please contact General Information Services, the PTO's Web site, or a PTDL.

Nonprovisional Utility Patent Application Requirements

A nonprovisional utility patent application must be in the English language or be accompanied by a verified translation in the English language and a fee set forth in 37 CFR §1.17(k) [Non-English Specification Fee Code 139].

All papers which are to become part of the permanent records of the PTO must be typewritten or produced by a mechanical (or computer) printer. The text must be in permanent black ink or its equivalent; on but one side of the paper; in portrait orientation; on white paper that is all of the same size, flexible, strong, smooth, non-shiny, durable, and without holes. The paper size must be either:

- 21.6 cm. by 27.9 cm. (8½ by 11 inches), or
- 21.0 cm. by 29.7 cm. (DIN size A4).

There must be a left margin of at least 2.5 cm. (1 inch) and top, right, and bottom margins of at least 2.0 cm. (¾ inch). Drawing page requirements are discussed separately below.

A nonprovisional utility patent application *must* include a specification, including a claim or claims; drawings, when necessary; an oath or declaration; and the prescribed filing fee. A complete nonprovisional utility patent application *should* contain the elements listed below, arranged in the order shown.

- Utility Patent Application Transmittal Form or Transmittal Letter
- Fee Transmittal Form and Appropriate Fee
- Specification
- Drawings (when necessary)
- Oath or Declaration
- Sequence Listing (when necessary)

These elements are further described as follows:

Utility Patent Application Transmittal Form or Transmittal Letter

A Utility Patent Application Transmittal form (Form PTO/SB/05) or a transmittal letter should be filed with every patent application to instruct the PTO on the services desired in the processing of the application. It identifies the name of the applicant, the type of application, the title of the invention, the contents of the application, and any accompanying enclosures. (Form PTO/SB/21 is to be used for all correspondence after initial filing.)

Fee Transmittal Form and Appropriate Fee

The Fee Transmittal form (Form PTO/SB/17) should be used to calculate the prescribed fee and indicate the method of payment.

Fees for a patent application should be submitted with the application and must be made payable to the "Commissioner of Patents and Trademarks." If an application is filed without the basic filing fee, the applicant will be notified and will be required to submit the filing fee along with a surcharge within the time period set in the notice. Fees are subject to change and the applicant should consult the current *Fee Schedule* before filing.

Please note that two sets of fees exist, one for small entities and one for other than small entities. If you qualify as a small entity for patent fee purposes, you must file the appropriate small entity statement (Form PTO/SB/09, PTO/SB/10, PTO/SB/11, or PTO/SB/12) to claim your entitlement to reduced fees.

Specification

The specification is a written description of the invention and of the manner and process of making and using the same. The specification must be in such full, clear, concise, and exact terms as to enable any person skilled in the art or science to which the invention pertains to make and use the same.

Computer program listings, when required to be submitted as part of the specification, must be direct printouts (not copies) from the computer's printer with dark, solid black letters not less than 0.21 cm. (0.08 inch) high (elite type), on white, unshaded and unlined paper; and the sheets should be submitted in a protective cover.

The pages of the specification (but not the transmittal letter sheets or other forms), including claims and abstract, should be numbered consecutively, starting with 1. The page numbers should be centrally located preferably below the text. The lines of the specification must be 1.5 or double spaced (lines of text not comprising the specification need not be 1.5 or double spaced). It is desirable to include an indentation at the beginning of each new paragraph.

It is preferable to use all of the section headings described below to represent the parts of the specification. Section headings should be in upper case without underlining or bold type. If the section contains no text, the phrase "Not Applicable" should follow the section heading.

TITLE OF INVENTION

The title of the invention (or an introductory portion stating the name, citizenship, residence of each applicant, and the title of the invention) should appear as the heading on the first page of the specification. The title should be brief but technically accurate and descriptive. It is preferred that the title not exceed 280 typewritten spaces.

CROSS-REFERENCE TO RELATED APPLICATIONS

Any nonprovisional utility patent application claiming the benefit of one or more prior filed copending nonprovisional applications (or international applications designating the United States of America) must contain in the first sentence of the specification following the title, a reference to each such prior application, identifying it by the application number (consisting of the series code and serial number) or international application number and international filing date, and indicating the relationship of the applications. Cross-references to other related patent applications may be made when appropriate.

STATEMENT REGARDING FEDERALLY SPONSORED RESEARCH OR DEVELOPMENT

The application should contain a statement as to rights to inventions made under federally sponsored research and development (if any).

REFERENCE TO A MICROFICHE APPENDIX

If a computer program listing printout is required and is 11 or more pages long, you must submit such listing in the form of microfiche which will not be part of the printed patent. The total number of microfiche and total number of frames should be specified.

BACKGROUND OF THE INVENTION

This section should include a statement of the field of endeavor to which the invention pertains. This section may also include a paraphrasing of the applicable U.S. patent *Classification Definitions* or the subject matter of the claimed invention. In the past, this part of this section may have been titled "Field of Invention" or "Technical Field."

This section should also contain a description of information known to you, including references to specific documents, which are related to your invention. It should contain, if applicable, references to specific problems involved in the prior art (or state of technology) which are solved by your invention. In the past, this section may have been titled "Description of the Related Art" or "Description of Prior Art."

BRIEF SUMMARY OF THE INVENTION

This section should present the substance or general idea of the claimed invention in summarized form. The summary may point out the advantages of the invention and how it solves previously existing problems, preferably those problems identified in the BACKGROUND OF THE INVENTION. A statement of the object of the invention may also be included.

BRIEF DESCRIPTION OF THE SEVERAL VIEWS OF THE DRAWING

Where there are drawings, you must include a listing of all figures by number and with corresponding statements explaining what each figure depicts.

DETAILED DESCRIPTION OF THE INVENTION

In this section, the invention must be explained along with the process of making and using the invention in full, clear, concise, and exact terms. This section should distinguish the invention from other inventions and from what is old; and describe completely the process, machine, manufacture, composition of matter, or improvement invented. In the case of an improvement, the description should be confined to the specific improvement and to the parts which necessarily cooperate with it or which are necessary to completely understand the invention.

It is required that the description be sufficient so that any person of ordinary skill in the pertinent art, science, or area could make and use the invention without extensive experimentation. The best mode contemplated by you of carrying out your invention must be set forth in the description. Each element in the drawings should be mentioned in the description. This section has often, in the past, been titled "Description of the Preferred Embodiment."

CLAIM OR CLAIMS

The claim or claims must particularly point out and distinctly claim the subject matter which you regard as the invention. The claims define the scope of the protection of the patent. Whether a patent will be granted is determined, in large measure, by the choice of wording of the claims.

A nonprovisional application for a utility patent must contain at least one claim. The claim or claims section must begin on a separate sheet. If there are several claims, they shall be numbered consecutively in Arabic numerals, with the least restrictive claim presented as claim number 1.

The claims section must begin with a statement such as "What I claim as my invention is: . . ." or "I (We) claim: . . ." followed by the recitation of the particular matter which you regard as your invention.

One or more claims may be presented in dependent form, referring back to and further limiting another claim or claims in the same application. All dependent claims should be grouped together with the claim or claims to which they refer to the extent practicable. Any dependent claim which refers to more than one other claim ("a multiple dependent claim") shall refer to such other claims in the alternative only. Each claim should be a single sentence, and where a claim sets forth a number of elements or steps, each element or step of the claim should be separated by a line indentation.

The fee required to be submitted with a nonprovisional utility patent application is, in part, determined by the number of claims, independent claims, and dependent claims.

ABSTRACT OF THE DISCLOSURE

The purpose of the abstract is to enable the PTO and the public to determine quickly the nature of the technical disclosures of your invention. The abstract points out what is new in the art to which your invention pertains; however, it will not be used for interpreting the scope of the claim(s). It should be in narrative form and generally limited to a single paragraph, and it must begin on a separate page.

Drawings (when necessary)

A patent application is required to contain drawings if drawings are necessary for the understanding of the subject matter sought to be patented. The drawings must show every feature of the invention as specified in the claims. Omission of drawings may cause an application to be considered incomplete. Please see the detailed discussion of drawing requirements.

Oath Or Declaration

The oath or declaration (Forms PTO/SB/01, PTO/SB/02A, PTO/SB/02B, and PTO/SB/02C) must identify the application with which it is associated, and must give the name, city and either state or country of residence, country of citizenship, and post office address of each inventor. It must state whether the inventor is a sole or joint inventor of the invention claimed. Additionally, designation of a correspondence address is needed on the oath or declaration. Providing a correspondence address will help to ensure prompt delivery of all notices, official letters, and other communications.

The oath or declaration must be signed by all of the actual inventors. An oath may be administered by any person within the United States, or by a diplomatic or consular officer of a foreign country, who is authorized by the United States to administer oaths. A declaration does not require any witness or person to administer or verify its signing. Thus, use of a declaration is preferable.

The oath or declaration must be in a language which you understand. If you comprehend the English language, you should preferably use an English language oath or declaration. If you cannot comprehend English, any oath or declaration must be in a language which you can comprehend and shall state that you understand the content of any documents to which the oath or declaration relates. If the oath or declaration used is in a language other than English, the oath or declaration must either be (1) accompanied by a verified English translation, or (2) in a form provided or approved by the Patent and Trademark Office.

If the person making the oath or declaration is not the inventor, the oath or declaration shall state the relationship of that person to the inventor, upon information and belief, the facts which the inventor would have been required to state, and the circumstances which render the inventor unable to sign, namely death, insanity or legal incapacity or unavailability/refusal to sign. (See 37 CFR §§1.42, 1.43, and 1.47.)

Sequence Listing (when necessary)

This section, for the disclosure of a nucleotide and/or amino acid sequence, should contain a listing of the sequence complying with 37 CFR §1.821 through 37 CFR §1.825.

Obtaining A Receipt for Documents Mailed to the PTO

A receipt for documents mailed to the PTO can be obtained by attaching a stamped, self-addressed postcard to the first page of the documents. The postcard should contain a detailed list that identifies each type of document and the number of pages of each document. Upon receipt at PTO, the detailed list on the postcard will be compared to the actual contents of the delivery. Any discrepancies between the detailed list and the actual contents will be noted on the postcard. The postcard will be initialed and date stamped by the person at PTO who received the delivery. The postcard will be returned by mail to the addressee whose name appears on the postcard.

The returned postcard serves as evidence of receipt in the PTO of all items listed on the postcard, unless otherwise noted by PTO on the postcard. That is, if the postcard receipt has been annotated to indicate that a particular paper was not received, the postcard receipt will not serve as evidence of receipt of that paper in the PTO. Likewise, the postcard receipt will not serve as evidence of receipt of papers which are not adequately itemized.

When preparing the detailed list of documents identified on the postcard, it is important to include the following identifying information:

- the application number (if known)
- the filing date of the application (if known)
- the title of the invention
- the name of the inventor or inventors

The postcard should also include a detailed list of every document type and the number of pages of each document that are included in the delivery. If the postcard is submitted with a patent application, the detailed listing should include the following items:

- the title and number of pages of each PTO form
- the number of pages of specification (excluding claims)
- the number of claims and the number of claims pages
- the number of figures of drawing and the number of sheets of drawing
- whether oath or declaration statement is included
- the type and number of other documents that are included
- the amount of payment and the method of payment (i.e., check, money order, deposit account)

It is important that the postcard itemize each component of the application. For example, a general statement such as "complete application" or "patent application" or "drawings" will not show that each of the required components of an application was included if one of the items is later found to be missing by PTO.

When the self-addressed postcard is submitted with a utility patent application, the PTO will stamp the postcard being returned to the addressee with both the receipt date and the application number before placing it in the outgoing mail.

Upon receipt of the returned postcard, the addressee should promptly review the postcard to ensure that all documents and all pages were received by PTO.

Drawing Requirements

Information on drawing requirements is based substantially on Title 37, Code of Federal Regulations, (CFR) §1.84. There are two acceptable categories for presenting drawings in utility patent applications: black ink (black and white) and color.

Black and white drawings are normally required. India ink, or its equivalent that secures black solid lines, must be used for drawings. Drawings made by computer printer must be originals, not photocopies.

On rare occasions, color drawings may be necessary as the only practical medium by which the subject matter sought to be patented in a utility patent application is disclosed. The PTO will accept color drawings in utility patent applications and statutory invention registrations only after granting a petition explaining why the color drawings are necessary. Any such petition must include the following:

- the appropriate fee set forth in 37 CFR §1.17(i) [or Patent Petition Fee Code 122];
- three (3) sets of color drawings; and
- the following language as the first paragraph in that portion of the specification relating to the BRIEF DESCRIPTION OF THE SEVERAL VIEWS OF THE DRAWING. If the language is not in the specification, a proposed amendment to insert the language must accompany the petition.

"The file of this patent contains at least one drawing executed in color. Copies of this patent with color drawing(s) will be provided by the Patent and Trademark Office upon request and payment of the necessary fee."

Photographs are not ordinarily permitted in utility patent applications. However, the PTO will accept photographs in utility patent applications only after granting a petition filed by the applicant which requests that photographs be accepted. Any such petition must include the following:

- the appropriate fee set forth in 37 CFR §1.17(i) [or Patent Petition Fee Code 122]; and
- three (3) sets of photographs.

Photographs must either be developed on double weight photographic paper or be permanently mounted on Bristol board. The photographs must be of sufficient quality so that all details in the drawing are reproducible in the printed patent.

Color photographs will be accepted in utility patent applications if the conditions for accepting color drawings have been satisfied.

Identification of Drawings

Identifying indicia, if provided, should include the application number or the title of the invention, your name, docket number (if any), and the name and telephone number of a person to call if the PTO is unable to match the drawings to the proper application. This information should be placed on the back of each sheet of drawings a minimum distance of 1.5 cm. (⅝ inch) down from the top of the page. In addition, a reference to the application number (or, if an application number has not been assigned, your name) may be included in the left hand corner of the drawing sheet, provided that reference appears within 1.5 cm. (⅝ inch) from the top of the sheet.

Graphic Forms in Drawings

Chemical or mathematical formulas, tables, computer program listings, and waveforms may be submitted as drawings and are subject to the same requirements as drawings. Each chemical or mathematical formula must be labeled as a separate figure, using brackets when necessary, to show that information is properly integrated. Each group of waveforms must be presented as a single figure, using a common vertical axis with time extending along the horizontal axis. Each individual waveform discussed in the specification must be identified with a separate letter designation adjacent to the vertical axis. These may be placed in a landscape orientation if they cannot be presented satisfactorily in a portrait orientation. Typewritten characters used in such formulas and tables must be chosen from a block (nonscript) type font or lettering style having capital letters which are at least 0.21 cm. (0.08 inch) high (elite type). A space at least 0.64 cm. (¼ inch) high should be provided between complex formulas or tables and the text.

Paper

Drawings submitted to the PTO must be made on paper which is flexible, strong, white, smooth, nonshiny, and durable. All sheets must be free from cracks, creases, and folds. Only one side of the sheet shall be used for the drawing. Each sheet must be reasonably free from erasures and must be free from alterations, overwritings, and interlineations. Photographs must either be developed on double weight photographic paper or be permanently mounted on Bristol broad.

All drawings sheets in an application must be the same size. One of the shorter sides of the sheet is regarded as its top. The size of the sheets on which drawings are made must be:

- 21.6 cm. by 27.9 cm. (8½ by 11 inches), or
- 21.0 cm. by 29.7 cm. (DIN size A4).

The sheets must not contain frames around the sight (the usable surface), but should have scan target points (cross hairs) printed on two catercorner margin corners. The following margins are required:

- On 21.6 cm. by 27.9 cm. (8½ by 11 inch) drawing sheets, each sheet must include a top margin of at least 2.5 cm. (1 inch), a left side margin of at least 2.5 cm. (1 inch), a right side margin of at least 1.5 cm. (⅝ inch), and a bottom margin of at least 1.0 cm. (⅜ inch) from the edges, thereby leaving a sight no greater than 17.6 cm. by 24.4 cm. 6^15^⁄16 by 9⅝ inches).

- On 21.0 cm. by 29.7 cm. (DIN size A4) drawing sheets, each sheet must include a top margin of at least 2.5 cm. (1 inch), a left side margin of at least 2.5 cm. (1 inch), a right side margin of at least 1.5 cm (⅝ inch), and a bottom margin of at least 1.0 cm. (⅜ inch) from the edges, thereby leaving a sight no greater than 17.0 cm. by 26.2 cm.

Views

The drawing must contain as many views as necessary to show the invention. The views may be plan, elevation, section, or perspective views. Detail views of portions of elements, on a larger scale if necessary, may also be used. All views of the drawing must be grouped together and arranged on the sheet(s) without wasting space, preferably in an upright position, clearly separated from one another, and must not be included in the sheets containing the specifications, claims, or abstract. Views must not be connected by projection lines and must not contain center lines. Waveforms of electrical signals may be connected by dashed lines to show the relative timing of the waveforms.

EXPLODED VIEWS

Exploded views, with the separated parts embraced by a bracket, to show the relationship or order of assembly of various parts are permissible. When an exploded view is shown in a figure which is on the same sheet as another figure, the exploded view should be placed in brackets.

PARTIAL VIEWS

When necessary, a view of a large machine or device in its entirety may be broken into partial views on a single sheet, or extended over several sheets if there is no loss in facility of understanding the view. Partial views drawn on separate sheets must always be capable of being linked edge to edge so that no partial view contains parts of another partial view. A smaller scale view should be included showing the whole formed by the partial views and indicating the positions of the parts shown. When a portion of a view is enlarged for magnification purposes, the view and the enlarged view must each be labeled as separate views.

Where views on two or more sheets form, in effect, a single complete view, the views on the several sheets must be so arranged that the complete figure can be assembled without concealing any part of any of the views appearing on the various sheets.

A very long view may be divided into several parts placed one above the other on a single sheet. However, the relationship between the different parts must be clear and unambiguous.

SECTIONAL VIEWS

The plane upon which a sectional view is taken should be indicated on the view from which the section is cut by a broken line. The ends of the broken line should be designated by Arabic or Roman numerals corresponding to the view number of the sectional view, and should have arrows to indicate the direction of sight. Hatching must be used to indicate section portions of an object, and must be made by regularly spaced oblique parallel lines spaced sufficiently apart to enable the lines to be distinguished without difficulty. Hatching should not impede the clear reading of the reference characters and lead lines. If it is not possible to place reference characters outside the hatched area, the hatching may be broken off wherever reference characters are inserted. Hatching must be at a substantial angle to the surrounding axes or principal lines, preferably 45°.

A cross section must be set out and drawn to show all of the materials as they are shown in the view from which the cross section was taken. The parts in cross section must show proper material(s) by hatching with regularly spaced parallel oblique strokes; the space between strokes being chosen on the basis of the total area to be hatched. The various parts of a cross section of the same item should be hatched in the same manner and should accurately and graphically indicate the nature of the material(s) illustrated in cross section.

The hatching of juxtaposed different elements must be angled in a different way. In the case of large areas, hatching may be confined to an edging drawn around the entire inside of the outline of the area to be hatched. Different types of hatching should have different conventional meanings as regards the nature of a material seen in cross section.

ALTERNATE POSITION

A moved position may be shown by a broken line superimposed upon a suitable view if this can be done without crowding; otherwise, a separate view must be used for this purpose.

MODIFIED FORMS

Modified forms of construction must be shown in separate views.

Arrangement of Views

One view must not be placed upon another or within the outline of another. All views on the same sheet should stand in the same direction and, if possible, stand so that they can be read with the sheet held in an upright position. If views wider than the width of the sheet are necessary for the clearest illustration of the invention, the sheet may be turned on its side so that the top of the sheet is on the right-hand side, with the appropriate top margin used as the heading space. Words must appear in a horizontal, left-to-right fashion when the page is either upright or turned so that the top becomes the right side, except for graphs utilizing standard scientific convention to denote the axis of abscissas (of X) and the axis of ordinates (of Y).

View for the Official Gazette

One of the views should be suitable for publication in the *Official Gazette* as the illustration of the invention.

Scale

The scale to which a drawing is made must be large enough to show the mechanism without crowding when the drawing is reduced in size to two-thirds in reproduction. Views of portions of the mechanism on a larger scale should be used when necessary to show details clearly. Two or more sheets may be used if one does not give sufficient room. The number of sheets should be kept to a minimum.

When approved by the examiner, the scale of the drawing may be graphically represented. Indications such as "actual size" or "scale ½" are not permitted on the drawings since these lose their meaning with reproduction in a different format.

Elements of the same view must be in proportion to each other, unless a difference in proportion is indispensable for the clarity of the view. Instead of showing elements in different proportion, a supplementary view may be added giving a larger-scale illustration of the element of the initial view. The enlarged element shown in the second view should be surrounded by a finely drawn or "dot-dash" circle in the first view indicating its location without obscuring the view.

Character of Lines, Numbers, and Letters

All drawings must be made by a process which will give them satisfactory reproduction characteristics. Every line, number, and letter must be durable, clean, black (except for color drawings), sufficiently dense and dark, and uniformly thick and well-defined. The weight of all lines and letters must be heavy enough to permit adequate reproduction. This requirement applies to all lines however fine, to shading, and to lines representing cut surfaces in sectional views. Lines and strokes of different thicknesses may be used in the same drawing where different thicknesses have a different meaning.

Shading

The use of shading in views is encouraged if it aids in understanding the invention and if it does not reduce legibility. Shading is used to indicate the surface or shape of spherical, cylindrical, and conical elements of an object. Flat parts may also be lightly shaded. Such shading is preferred in the case of parts shown in perspective, but not for cross sections. See discussion of sectional views above. Spaced lines for shading are preferred. These lines must be thin, as few in number as practicable, and they must contrast with the rest of the drawings. As a substitute for shading, heavy lines on the shade side of objects can be used except where they superimpose on each other or obscure reference characters. Light should come from the upper left corner at an angle of 45°. Surface delineations should preferably be shown by proper shading. Solid black shading areas are not permitted, except when used to represent bar graphs or color.

Symbols

Graphical drawing symbols may be used for conventional elements when appropriate. The elements for which such symbols and labeled representations are used must be adequately identified in the specification. Known devices should be illustrated by symbols which have a universally recognized conventional meaning and are generally accepted in the art. Other symbols which are not universally recognized may be used, subject to approval by the PTO, if they are not likely to be confused with existing conventional symbols, and if they are readily identifiable.

Legends

Suitable descriptive legends may be used, or may be required by the examiner, where necessary for understanding of the drawing subject to approval by the PTO. They should contain as few words as possible.

Numbers, Letters, and Reference Characters

The English alphabet must be used for letters, except where another alphabet is customarily used, such as the Greek alphabet to indicate angles, wavelengths, and mathematical formulas.

Reference characters (numerals are preferred), sheet numbers, and view numbers must be plain and legible, and must not be used in association with brackets or inverted commas, or enclosed within outlines (encircled). They must be oriented in the same direction as the view so as to avoid having to rotate the sheet. Reference characters should be arranged to follow the profile of the object depicted.

Numbers, letters, and reference characters must measure at least 0.32 cm. (⅛ inch) in height. They should not be placed in the drawing so as to interfere with its comprehension. Therefore, they should not cross or mingle with the lines. They should not be placed upon hatched or shaded surfaces. When necessary, such as indicating a surface or cross section, a reference character may be underlined and a blank space may be left in the hatching or shading where the character occurs so that it appears distinct.

The same part of an invention appearing in more than one view of the drawing must always be designated by the same reference character, and the same reference character must never be used to designate different parts.

Reference characters not mentioned in the description shall not appear in the drawings. Reference characters mentioned in the description must appear in the drawings.

Lead Lines and Arrows

Lead lines are those lines between the reference characters and the details to which they refer. Such lines may be straight or curved and should be as short as possible. They must originate in the immediate proximity of the reference character and extend to the feature indicated. Lead lines must not cross each other. Lead lines are required for each reference character except for those which indicate the surface or cross section on which they are placed. Such a reference character must be underlined to make it clear that a lead line has not been left out by mistake. Lead lines must be executed in the same way as lines in the drawing.

Arrows may be used at the ends of lines, provided that their meaning is clear, as follows:

- on a lead line, a freestanding arrow to indicate the entire section towards which it points;
- on a lead line, an arrow touching a line to indicate the surface shown by the line looking along the direction of the arrow; or
- to show the direction of movement.

Copyright or Mask Work Notice

A copyright or mask work notice may appear in the drawing, but must be placed within the sight of the drawing immediately below the figure representing the copyright or mask work material and be limited to letters having a print size of 0.32 cm. to 0.64 cm. (⅛ to ¼ inches) high. The content of the notice must be limited to only those elements provided for by law. For example, "©1983 John Doe" (17 U.S.C. 401) and "*M* John Doe" (17 U.S.C. 909) would be properly limited and, under current statutes, legally sufficient notices of copyright and mask work, respectively. Inclusion of a copyright or mask work notice will be permitted only if the authorization language set forth in 37 CFR §1.71(e) is included at the beginning (preferably as the first paragraph) of the specification.

Numbering of Sheets of Drawings and Views

The sheets of drawings should be numbered in consecutive Arabic numerals, starting with 1, within the sight (the usable surface). These numbers, if present, must be placed in the middle of the top of the sheet, but not in the margin. The numbers can be placed on the right-hand side if the drawing extends too close to the middle of the top edge of the usable surface. The drawing sheet numbering must be clear and larger than the numbers used as reference characters to avoid confusion. The number of each sheet should be shown by two Arabic numerals placed on either side of an oblique line, with the first being the sheet number and the second being the total number of sheets of drawings, with no other marking.

The different views must be numbered in consecutive Arabic numerals, starting with 1, independent of the numbering of the sheets and, if possible, in the order in which they appear on the drawing sheet(s). Partial views intended to form one complete view, on one or several sheets, must be identified by the same number followed by a capital letter. View numbers must be preceded by the abbreviation **FIG.** Where only a single view is used in an application to illustrate the claimed invention, it must not be numbered and the abbreviation **FIG.** must not appear.

Numbers and letters identifying the views must be simple and clear and must not be used in association with brackets, circles, or inverted commas. The view numbers must be larger than the numbers used for reference characters.

Security Markings

Authorized security markings may be placed on the drawings provided they are outside the sight, preferably centered in the top margin.

Corrections

Any corrections on drawings submitted to the PTO must be durable and permanent.

Holes

No holes should be made by the applicant in the drawing sheets.

Patent and Trademark Depository Library (PTDL) LIST

The **Patent and Trademark Depository Library Program** is comprised of a network of Patent and Trademark Depository Libraries (PTDLs) located in the 50 states, the District of Columbia, and Puerto Rico which provide access to many of the same products and services offered at the PTO search facilities in Arlington, VA. The scope of PTDL collections, hours of operation, services, and fees (where applicable) vary depending on PTDL location. Users are advised to call ahead to determine products and services available at a particular PTDL. PTDLs also offer automated access to patent and trademark information. All PTDLs offer free access to the *Cassis* CD-ROM series search tools to assist patrons in the use of patent and trademark collections.

Last Modified: 9/3/98

Appendix C-23

Change in Procedure Relating to an Application Filing Date

Department of Commerce
Patent and Trademark Office
[Docket No. 951019254-6136-02]
RIN 0651-XX05

Change in Procedure Relating to an Application Filing Date

Agency: Patent and Trademark Office, Commerce.

Action: Notice of Change in Procedure.

Summary: The Patent and Trademark Office (PTO) is implementing a change in procedure relating to the treatment of applications filed without all the pages of the specification or without all of the figures of the drawings. Under this new procedure, the PTO will accord a filing date to any application that contains something that can be construed as a written description, any necessary drawing, and, in a nonprovisional application, at least one claim, regardless of whether the application is filed without all the pages of the specification or without all of the figures of the drawings. Applications filed without all the pages of the specification or without all of the figures of the drawings will be treated by mailing a notice indicating that the application has been accorded a filing date, but is missing pages of the specification or figures of drawings. The notice will indicate that failure to timely (37 CFR 1.181(f)) file a petition under 37 CFR 1.53(c) or 1.182 in response to such notice will result in the PTO treating the original application papers (the original disclosure of the invention) as including only those application papers present in the PTO on the date of deposit.

Effective Date: July 22, 1996.

For Further Information Contact: Robert W. Bahr by telephone at (703) 305-9285, by facsimile at (703) 308-6916, or Jeffrey V. Nase by telephone at (703) 305-9285, or by mail addressed to Box Comments-Patents, Assistant Commissioner for Patents, Washington, D.C. 20231.

Supplementary Information

The PTO is implementing a change in procedure relating to the treatment of applications filed without all the pages of the specification (Section 608.01 of the

Manual of Patent Examining Procedure (MPEP)) (e.g., with page numbering revealing that page(s) are missing), or without all of the figures of the drawings (MPEP 608.02) (e.g., without drawing figures that are mentioned in the specification). The procedure set forth in this notice will be incorporated into the next revision of the MPEP.

The current treatment of applications that fail to identify the names of the actual inventor(s) (e.g., an application naming the inventorship only as "Jane Doe et al.") as required by 37 CFR 1.41(a) and 1.53(b) is not affected by the adoption of the procedure set forth in this notice.

In a Notice entitled "Proposed Changes in Procedures Relating to an Application Filing Date" (Filing Date Notice), published in the Federal Register at 60 FR 56982–84 (November 13, 1995), and in the PTO Official Gazette at 1181 Off. Gaz. Pat. Office 12–13 (December 5, 1995), the PTO proposed a change in procedure relating to the treatment of applications filed without all the pages of the specification or without all of the figures of the drawings. In view of the comments received in response to the Filing Date Notice, the PTO is adopting the proposed change.

The adopted procedure for the treatment of applications filed without all the pages of the specification or without all of the figures of the drawings is set forth below.

Applications Filed Without All Pages of Specification

The Initial Application Examination Division reviews application papers to determine whether all of the pages of the specification are present in the application. If the application is filed without all of the page(s) of the specification, but containing something that can be construed as a written description, at least one drawing figure, if necessary under 35 U.S.C. 113, the names of all the inventors, and, in a nonprovisional application, at least one claim, the Initial Application Examination Division will mail a "Notice of Omitted Items" indicating that the application papers so deposited have been accorded a filing date, but are lacking some page(s) of the specification.

The mailing of a "Notice of Omitted Items" will permit the applicant to either: (1) promptly establish prior receipt in the PTO of the page(s) at issue (generally by way of a date-stamped postcard receipt (MPEP 503)), or (2) promptly submit the omitted page(s) in a nonprovisional application and accept the date of such submission as the application filing date. An applicant asserting that the page(s) was in fact deposited in the PTO with the application papers must file a petition under 37 CFR 1.53(c) (and the petition fee under 37 CFR 1.17(i) (37 CFR 1.17(q) in a provisional application), which will be refunded if it is determined that the page(s) was in fact received by the PTO with the application papers deposited on filing) with evidence of such deposit within two months of the date of the "Notice of Omitted Items" (37 CFR 1.181(f)). An applicant desiring to submit the omitted page(s) in a nonprovisional application and accept the date of such submission as the application filing date must file any omitted page(s) with an oath or declaration in compliance with 37 CFR 1.63 and 1.64 referring to such page(s) and a petition under 37 CFR 1.182 (with the petition fee under 37 CFR 1.17(h)) requesting the later filing date within two months of the date of the "Notice of Omitted Items" (37 CFR 1.181(f)).

An applicant willing to accept the application as deposited in the PTO need not respond to the "Notice of Omitted Items," and the failure to file a petition under 37 CFR 1.53(c) or 1.182 (and the requisite petition fee) as discussed above within two months of the date of the "Notice of Omitted Items" (37 CFR 1.181(f)) will be treated as constructive acceptance by the applicant of the application as deposited in the PTO. Amendment of the specification is required in a nonprovisional application to renumber the pages consecutively and cancel any incomplete sentences caused by the absence of the omitted pages. Such amendment should be by way of preliminary amendment submitted prior to the first Office action to avoid delays in the prosecution of the application.

If the application does not contain anything that can be construed as a written description, the Initial Application Examination Division will mail a Notice of Incomplete Application (PTO-1123) indicating that the application lacks the specification required by 35 U.S.C. 112. The applicant may file a petition under 37 CFR 1.53(c) (and the petition fee under 37 CFR 1.17(i) (37 CFR 1.17(q) in a provisional application)) asserting that: (1) the missing specification was submitted, or (2) the application papers as deposited contain an adequate written description under 35 U.S.C. 112. The petition under 37 CFR 1.53(c) must be accompanied by sufficient evidence (37 CFR 1.181(b)) to establish the applicant's entitlement to the requested filing date (e.g., a date-stamped postcard receipt (MPEP 503) to establish prior receipt in the PTO of the missing specification). Alternatively, the applicant may submit the omitted specification, including at least one claim in a nonprovisional application, accompanied by an oath or declaration in compliance with 37 CFR 1.63 and 1.64 referring to the specification being submitted and accept the date of such submission as the application filing date.

Original claims form part of the original disclosure and provide their own written description. See In re Anderson, 471 F.2d 1237, 176 USPQ 331 (CCPA 1973). As such, an application that contains at least one claim, but does not contain anything which can be construed as a written description of such claim(s), would be unusual.

Nonprovisional Applications Filed Without at Least One Claim

35 U.S.C. 111(a)(2) requires that an application for patent include, inter alia, "a specification as prescribed by section 112 of this title," and 35 U.S.C. 111(a)(4) provides that the "filing date of an application shall be the date on which the specification and any required drawing are received in the Patent and Trademark Office." 35 U.S.C. 112, first paragraph, provides, in part, that "[t]he specification shall contain a written description of the invention," and 35 U.S.C. 112, second paragraph, provides that "[t]he specification shall conclude with one or more claims particularly pointing out and distinctly claiming the subject matter which the applicant regards as his invention." Also, the Court of Appeals for the Federal Circuit stated in Litton Systems, Inc. v. Whirlpool Corp.:

> Both statute, 35 U.S.C. 111 [(a)], and federal regulations, 37 CFR 1.51 [(a)(1)], make clear the requirement that an application for a patent must include . . . a specification and claims. . . . The omission of any one of these component parts makes a patent application incomplete and thus not entitled to a filing date.

728 F.2d 1423, 1437, 221 USPQ 97, 105 (Fed. Cir. 1984) (citing Gearon v. United States, 121 F. Supp 652, 654, 101 USPQ 460, 461 (Ct. Cl. 1954), cert. denied, 348 U.S. 942, 104 USPQ 409 (1955)) (emphasis in the original).

Therefore, in an application filed under 35 U.S.C. 111(a), a claim is a statutory requirement for according a filing date to the application. 35 U.S.C. 162 and 171 make 35 U.S.C. 112 applicable to plant and design applications, and 35 U.S.C. 162 specifically requires the specification in a plant patent application to contain a claim. 35 U.S.C. 111(b)(2), however, provides that "[a] claim, as required by the second through fifth paragraphs of section 112, shall not be required in a provisional application." Thus, with the exception of provisional applications filed under 35 U.S.C. 111(b), any application filed without at least one claim is incomplete and not entitled to a filing date.

If a nonprovisional application does not contain at least one claim, a "Notice of Incomplete Application" will be mailed to the applicant(s) indicating that no filing date has been granted and setting a period for submitting a claim. The filing date will be the date of receipt of at least one claim. See In re Mattson, 208 USPQ 168 (Comm'r Pats. 1980).

As 37 CFR 1.53(b)(2)(ii) permits the conversion of an application filed under 35 U.S.C. 111(a) to an application under 35 U.S.C. 111(b), an applicant in an application, other than for a design patent, filed under 35 U.S.C. 111(a) on or after June 8, 1995, without at least one claim has the alternative of filing a petition under 37 CFR 1.53(b)(2)(ii) to convert such application into an application under 35 U.S.C. 111(b), which does not require a claim to be entitled to its date of deposit as a filing date. Such a petition, however, must be filed prior to the expiration of twelve months after the date of deposit of the application under 35 U.S.C. 111(a), and comply with the other requirements of 37 CFR 1.53(b)(2)(ii).

Applications Filed Without Any Drawings

35 U.S.C. 111(a)(2)(B) and 111(b)(2)(B) each provide, in part, that an "application shall include . . . a drawing as prescribed by section 113 of this title" and 35 U.S.C. 111(a)(4) and 111(b)(4) each provide, in part, that the "filing date . . . shall be the date on which . . . any required drawing are received in the Patent and Trademark Office." 35 U.S.C. 113 in turn provides that an "applicant shall furnish a drawing where necessary for the understanding of the subject matter sought to be patented."

Applications filed without drawings are initially inspected to determine whether a drawing is referred to in the specification, and if not, whether a drawing is necessary for an understanding of the invention. 35 U.S.C. 113.

In general, it has been PTO practice to treat an application that contains at least one process or method claim as an application for which a drawing is not necessary for an understanding of the invention under 35 U.S.C. 113. The same practice has been followed in composition applications. Other situations in which drawings are usually not considered necessary for an understanding of the invention under 35 U.S.C. 113 are:

I. Coated articles or products: where the invention resides solely in coating or impregnating a conventional sheet (e.g., paper or cloth, or an article of known and conventional character with a particular composition), unless significant details of structure or arrangement are involved in the article claims;

II. Articles made from a particular material or composition: where the invention consists in making an article of a particular material or composition, unless significant details of structure or arrangement are involved in the article claims;

III. Laminated Structures: where the claimed invention involves only laminations of sheets (and coatings) of specified material unless significant details of structure or arrangement (other than the mere order of the layers) are involved in the article claims; or

IV. Articles, apparatus or systems where sole distinguishing feature is presence of a particular material: where the invention resides solely in the use of a particular material in an otherwise old article, apparatus or system recited broadly in the claims, for example:
   a. A hydraulic system distinguished solely by the use therein of a particular hydraulic fluid;
   b. Packaged sutures wherein the structure and arrangement of the package are conventional and the only distinguishing feature is the use of a particular material.

A nonprovisional application having at least one claim, or a provisional application having at least some disclosure, directed to the subject matter discussed above for which a drawing is usually not considered essential for a filing date, not describing drawing figures in the specification, and filed without drawings will usually be processed for examination, so long as the application contains something that can be construed as a written description and the names of all the inventors. A nonprovisional application having at least one claim, or a provisional application having at least some disclosure, directed to the subject matter discussed above for which a drawing is usually not considered essential for a filing date, describing drawing figure(s) in the specification, but filed without drawings will be treated as an application filed without all of the drawing figures referred to in the specification as discussed below, so long as the application contains something that can be construed as a written description and the names of all the inventors. In a situation in which the appropriate examining group determines that drawings are necessary under 35 U.S.C. 113 the filing date issue will be reconsidered on reference from the examining group.

If a nonprovisional application does not have at least one claim, or a provisional application does not have at least some disclosure, directed to the subject matter discussed above for which a drawing is usually not considered essential for a filing date, and is filed without drawings, the Initial Application Examination Division will mail a "Notice of Incomplete Application" indicating that the application lacks drawings and that 35 U.S.C. 113 requires a drawing where necessary for the understanding of the subject matter sought to be patented.

The applicant may file a petition under 37 CFR 1.53(c) (and the petition fee under 37 CFR 1.17(i) (37 CFR 1.17(q) in a provisional application)) asserting that (1) the drawing(s) at issue was submitted, or (2) the drawing(s) is not necessary under 35 U.S.C. 113 for a filing date. The petition must be accompanied by sufficient evidence to establish the applicant's entitlement to the requested filing date (e.g., a date-stamped postcard receipt (MPEP 503) to establish prior receipt in the PTO of the drawing(s) at issue). Alternatively, the applicant may submit drawing(s) accompanied by an oath or declaration in compliance with 37 CFR 1.63 and 1.64 referring to the drawing(s) being submitted and accept the date of such submission as the application filing date.

In design applications, the Initial Application Examination Division will mail a "Notice of Incomplete Application" indicating that the application lacks the drawings required under 35 U.S.C. 113. The applicant may: (1) promptly file a petition under 37 CFR 1.53(c) (and the petition fee under 37 CFR 1.17(i)) asserting that the missing drawing(s) was submitted, or (2) promptly submit drawing(s) accompanied by an oath or declaration in compliance with 37 CFR 1.63 and 1.64 and accept the date of such submission as the application filing date. 37 CFR 1.154(a) provides that the claim in a design application "shall be in formal terms to the ornamental design for the article (specifying name) as shown, or as shown and described." As such, petitions under 37 CFR 1.53(c) asserting that drawings are unnecessary under 35 U.S.C. 113 for a filing date in a design application will not be found persuasive.

Applications Filed Without All Figures of Drawings

The Initial Application Examination Division reviews application papers to determine whether all mentioned drawing figures in the specification are present in the application. If the application is filed without all of the drawing figure(s) referred to in the specification, and the application contains something that can be construed as a written description, at least one drawing, if necessary under 35 U.S.C. 113, the names of all the inventors, and, in a nonprovisional application, at least one claim, the Initial Application Examination Division will mail a "Notice of Omitted Items" indicating that the application papers so deposited have been accorded a filing date, but are lacking some of the drawings described in the specification.

The mailing of a "Notice of Omitted Items" will permit the applicant to either: (1) promptly establish prior receipt in the PTO of the drawing(s) at issue (generally by way of a date-stamped postcard receipt (MPEP 503)), or (2) promptly submit the omitted drawing(s) in a nonprovisional application and accept the date of such submission as the application filing date. An applicant asserting that the drawing(s) was in fact deposited in the PTO with the application papers must file a petition under 37 CFR 1.53(c) (and the petition fee under 37 CFR 1.17(i) (37 CFR 1.17(q) in a provisional application), which will be refunded if it is determined that the drawing(s) was in fact received by the PTO with the application papers deposited on filing) with evidence of such deposit within two months of the date of the "Notice of Omitted Items" (37 CFR 1.181(f)). An applicant desiring to submit the omitted drawings in a nonprovisional application and accept the date of such submission as the application filing date must file any omitted drawing(s) with an oath or declaration in compliance with 37 CFR 1.63 and 1.64 referring to such drawing(s) and a petition under 37 CFR 1.182 (with the petition fee under 37 CFR 1.17(h)) requesting the later filing date within two months of the date of the "Notice of Omitted Items" (37 CFR 1.181(f)).

An applicant willing to accept the application as deposited in the PTO need not respond to the "Notice of Omitted Items," and the failure to file a petition under 37 CFR 1.53(c) or 1.182 (and the requisite petition fee) as discussed above within two months of the date of the "Notice of Omitted Items" (37 CFR 1.181(f)) will be treated as constructive acceptance by the applicant of the application as deposited in the PTO. Amendment of the specification is required in a nonprovisional application to cancel all references to the omitted drawing, both in the brief and detailed descriptions of the drawings and including any reference numerals shown only in the omitted drawings. In addition, a separate letter is required in a nonprovisional application to renumber the drawing figures consecutively (showing the proposed changes in red ink), if necessary, and amendment of the specification is required to correct the references to the drawing figures to correspond with any relabelled drawing figures, both in the brief and detailed descriptions of the drawings. Such amendment and correction to the drawing figures, if necessary, should be by way of preliminary amendment submitted prior to the first Office action to avoid delays in the prosecution of the application.

Subsequent Treatment of Application

In instances in which a "Notice of Incomplete Application" has been mailed, further action by the applicant is necessary for the application to be accorded a filing date. As such, the application will be retained in the Initial Application Examination Division to await such action. Unless the applicant either completes the application or files a petition under 37 CFR 1.53(c) (and the petition fee under 37 CFR 1.17(i) or 1.17(q)) within the period set in the "Notice of Incomplete Application," the application will be processed as an incomplete application under 37 CFR 1.53(c).

In instances in which a "Notice of Omitted Items" has been mailed, the application will be retained in the Initial Application Examination Division for a period of two months from the mailing date of "Notice of Omitted Items" to permit the applicant to either: (1) establish prior receipt in the PTO of the page(s) or drawing(s) at issue, or (2) promptly submit the omitted page(s) or drawing(s) in a nonprovisional application and accept the date of such submission as the application filing date. Extensions of time under 37 CFR 1.136 will not be applicable to this two-month time period.

The grant of a petition under 37 CFR 1.182 to accept the omitted page(s) or drawing(s) in a nonprovisional application and accord the date of such submission as the application filing date will be indicated by the issuance of a new filing receipt indicating the filing date accorded the application.

Unless the applicant timely files a petition under 37 CFR 1.53(c) or 1.182 (and the requisite petition fee), the application will maintain the filing date as of the date of deposit of the application papers in the PTO, and the original application papers (i.e., the original disclosure of the invention) will include only those application papers present in the PTO on the date of deposit. Nonprovisional applications that are complete under 35 CFR 1.51(a)(1) will then be forwarded to the appropriate examining group for examination of the application. Provisional applications that are complete under 35 CFR 1.51(a)(2) will then be forwarded to Files Repository. The current practice for treating applications that are not complete under 37 CFR 1.51(a) will remain unchanged (37 CFR 1.53(d)).

Any petition under 37 CFR 1.53(c) or 1.182 not filed within this two-month period may be dismissed as untimely. 37 CFR 1.181(f). Under the adopted procedure, the PTO may strictly adhere to the two-month period set forth in 37 CFR 1.181(f), and dismiss as untimely any petition not filed within this two-month period. This strict adherence to the two-month period set forth in 37 CFR 1.181(f) is justified as such applications will now be forwarded for examination at the end of this two-month period. It is further justified in instances in which the applicant seeks to submit the omitted page(s) or drawing(s) in a nonprovisional application and request the date of such submission as the application filing date since: (1) according the application a filing date later than the date of deposit may affect the date of expiration of any patent issuing on the application due to the changes to 35 U.S.C. 154 contained in Public Law 103-465, § 532, 108 Stat. 4809 (1994), and (2) the filing of a continuation-in-part application is a sufficiently equivalent mechanism for adding additional subject matter to avoid the loss of patent rights.

The submission of omitted page(s) or drawing(s) in a nonprovisional application and acceptance of the date of such submission as the application filing date is tantamount to simply filing a new application. Thus, applicants should consider filing a new application as an alternative to submitting a petition under 37 CFR 1.182 (with the petition fee under 37 CFR 1.17(h)) with any omitted page(s) or drawing(s), which is a cost-effective alternative in instances in which an nonprovisional application is deposited without filing fees. Likewise, in view of the relatively low filing fee for provisional applications, and the PTO's desire to minimize the processing of provisional applications, the PTO will not grant petitions under 37 CFR 1.182 to accept omitted page(s) or drawing(s) and accord an application filing date as of the date of such submission. Instead, the applicant should simply refile the complete provisional application.

Response to Comments

Thirteen comments were received in response to the Filing Date Notice. Nine comments expressly supported the proposed change, while the remaining four comments simply made additional comments or suggested additional changes, but did not oppose the proposed change. The written comments have been analyzed, and responses to the comments follow.

(1): One comment suggested that the PTO should, by rulemaking, permit the addition of subject matter in a foreign application for which priority is claimed.

Response: Where an application includes in the papers deposited on filing with the application a certified copy of a foreign application for which priority is claimed, the PTO will grant a timely petition under 37 CFR 1.182 requesting that: (1) the corresponding sheets of drawings in the foreign priority application be accepted for any omitted sheets of drawings in the application, or (2) the foreign priority application be accepted as the application as filed, which may result in the treatment of the foreign priority application as an application filed in a non-English language (37 CFR 1.52(d)).

In instances in which the foreign priority application was not present among the papers deposited on filing with the application, any addition of subject matter from the foreign priority application into the application must be considered as new matter under 35 U.S.C. 132 (and, as such, will not be permitted by petition), unless the application-as-filed specifically incorporates the foreign priority application by reference.

Drawing figures do not require translation of the subject matter shown therein and individual drawing figures are sufficiently segregated that it is considered appropriate to permit, by petition under 37 CFR 1.182, the acceptance of the corresponding sheets of drawings in the foreign priority application for any omitted sheets of drawings in the application. The specification of a foreign priority application, however, is generally subject to translation and revision prior to its filing in the PTO as the specification of an application. As such, it is considered appropriate to permit, by petition under 37 CFR 1.182, the acceptance of a foreign priority application as the application as filed, but it is not considered acceptable to permit the acceptance of a translation of portions of the foreign priority application for omitted pages of the specification.

Finally, the occurrence of situations in which it is necessary for an applicant to request that the corresponding sheets of drawings in the foreign priority application be accepted for any omitted sheets of drawings in the application, or the foreign priority application be accepted as the application as filed is relatively rare. In addition, the treatment of these few applications on an ad hoc basis pursuant to 37 CFR 1.182 and 1.183 has proven acceptable.

(2): One comment suggested that the PTO should consider requiring a declaration from the attorney averring that the omitted matter was inadvertently omitted.

Response: First, in view of a registered practitioner's responsibilities as set forth in 37 CFR Part 10, the PTO does not generally require verification of statements by registered practitioners. See, e.g., 37 CFR 1.125 and 1.137. Second, as there is no apparent benefit to omitting material from an application as deposited in the PTO, there appears to be little justification for requiring even a statement that the omitted matter was inadvertently omitted.

(3): One comment questioned whether the change would be applicable to applications filed under 37 CFR 1.60 or 1.62.

Response: The adopted procedure applies to applications filed under 37 CFR 1.53.

37 CFR 1.60 requires, inter alia, that the application be a true copy of the prior application (37 CFR 1.60(b)(2)), and a copy that omits pages of specification or sheets of drawings from the prior application is not a true copy of the prior application. As such, a copy that omits pages of specification or sheets of drawings from the prior application is an improper application under 37 CFR 1.60, and cannot be accorded a filing date as an application under 37 CFR 1.60 until the filing error is corrected.

The PTO considers 37 CFR 1.60 to be unnecessary in view of changes to 37 CFR 1.4(d), and a trap for the unwary. The PTO has previously proposed to eliminate 37 CFR 1.60 (See notice of proposed rulemaking entitled "Changes to Implement 20-Year Patent Term and Provisional Application" (20-Year Term Notice of Proposed Rulemaking) published in the Federal Register at 59 FR 63951 (December 12, 1994), and in the Patent and Trademark Office Official Gazette at 1170 Off. Gaz. Pat. Office 377 (January 3, 1995)), and will again propose to eliminate 37 CFR 1.60, as well as 37 CFR 1.62, in an impending rulemaking to implement the Administration's regulatory reform initiative.

A continuation or divisional application may be filed under 35 U.S.C. 111(a) using the procedures set forth in 37 CFR 1.53(b)(1), by providing a copy of the prior application, including a copy of the oath or declaration in such prior application, as filed. The patent statutes and rules of practice do not require that an oath or declaration include a recent date of execution, and the Examining Corps has been directed not to object to an oath or declaration as lacking either a recent date of execution or any date of execution. This change in examining practice will appear in the next revision of the MPEP. As is currently the situation under 37 CFR 1.60 and 1.62, the applicant's duty of candor and good faith including compliance with the duty of disclosure requirements of § 1.56 is continuous and applies to the continuation or divisional application, notwithstanding the lack of a newly executed oath or declaration.

37 CFR 1.60(b)(4) and 1.62(a) currently permit the filing of a continuation or divisional application by less than all of the inventors named in a prior application without a newly executed oath or declaration. The oath or declaration in an application filed under 37 CFR 1.53(b), however, must identify the inventorship of such application. Thus, unless it is necessary to file a continuation or divisional application under 37 CFR 1.60 to name less than all of the inventors named in a prior application, applicants are encouraged to file continuing applications under 37 CFR 1.53(b) (i.e., omit any reference to 37 CFR 1.60 in the application papers) to avoid an inadvertent failure to comply with all of the requirements of 37 CFR 1.60.

An application under 37 CFR 1.62 uses the content of the prior application, and is itself only a request for an application under 37 CFR 1.62. As such, there is no concern that an application under 37 CFR 1.62 will be filed without all the pages of the specification or without all of the figures of the drawings.

(4): One comment questioned whether a filing date would be accorded if the name of an inventor were omitted.

Response: 37 CFR 1.41 and 1.53 currently require that an application be filed in the name of the actual inventor or inventors, and this notice does not involve changes to the rules of practice. The PTO will propose to eliminate this requirement in 37 CFR 1.41 and 1.53 in the rulemaking to implement the Administration's regulatory reform initiative.

(5): One comment suggested that the notices be mailed out as soon as possible to avoid a loss of rights for those applicants who require completion or refiling of the application. Another comment suggested that the decision as to whether an application is "incomplete" should be made by the Examining Corps, rather than on a formalistic basis by the Initial Application Examination Division.

Response: The efficient pre-examination processing of applications is in the mutual interest of the PTO and applicants. The PTO is currently in the process of modifying its pre-examination processing procedures to avoid any unnecessary delay. This new procedure will not impact the pre-examination processing of applications, in that the Initial Application Examination Division will mail a "Notice of Incomplete Application," "Notice of Omitted Items," and "Notice to File Missing Parts" under this new procedure at the time the "Notice of Incomplete Application" and "Notice to File Missing Parts" are currently mailed.

The adopted procedure replaces formalistic procedures with procedures based upon the requirements for a filing date as set forth in 35 U.S.C. 111, 112, and 113. Filing date issues are ultimately decided by the Office of Petitions in the Office of the Deputy Assistant Commissioner for Patent Policy and Projects (MPEP 1002.02(b)(35)) on the basis of whether and when the application meets the requirements for a filing date as set forth in 35 U.S.C. 111, 112, and 113, and not on the basis of who made the initial decision not to accord a filing date to the application.

It should be recognized that there is tension between the comments objecting to any review of the entitlement of an application to a filing date by the Initial Application Examination Division (arguing that this issue should be considered only by the Examining Corps) and the desire for speedy notification to the applicant that a portion of the application appears to have been omitted. To defer all review of the entitlement of an application to a filing date until the application is picked-up for examination would cause a significant delay in any such notification to the applicant.

(6): One comment noted that 35 U.S.C. 111(b) does not require a claim for a provisional application. Several comments suggested that the PTO automatically treat any nonprovisional application filed without at least one claim as a provisional application, if such application is otherwise entitled to a filing date as a provisional application.

Response: A provisional application does not require a claim to be entitled to a filing date. As discussed supra, an applicant in an application, other than for a design patent, filed under 35 U.S.C. 111(a) on or after June 8, 1995, without at least one claim has the alternative of filing a petition under 37 CFR 1.53(b)(2)(ii) to convert such application into an application under 35 U.S.C. 111(b). The PTO does not consider it appropriate to "automatically" consider an application filed under 35 U.S.C. 111(a) without a claim to be an application under 35 U.S.C. 111(b) (a provisional application), since the applicant may not desire an application under 35 U.S.C. 111(b), and may desire to file a claim to obtain an application filing date as of the date of submission of such claim.

(7): One comment suggested that the MPEP should clearly indicate that applications filed without all the pages of specification or all the figures of drawings described in the specification cannot automatically be treated as defective under 35 U.S.C. 112, but must be considered for compliance with 35 U.S.C. 112 by the subject matter that is present in the application papers.

Response: In an effort to improve the examination of applications, chapter 2100 of the MPEP has been revised to set forth specific guidelines for rejections under 35 U.S.C. 101, 102, 103, and 112. MPEP 2161 et seq. set forth the guidelines for rejections under 35 U.S.C. 112, first and second paragraphs, and do not authorize a rejection under 35 U.S.C. 112 based merely upon the fact that pages of specification or figures of drawing were omitted.

(8): One comment questioned whether the proposed procedure for the treatment of applications filed without all the pages of specification or all the figures of drawings described in the specification is applicable to provisional applications, noting that 35 U.S.C. 111(b) provides that a claim is not required in a provisional application.

Response: The adopted procedure applies to applications (both provisional and nonprovisional) filed under 37 CFR 1.53. The procedure recognizes that 35 U.S.C. 111(b) does not require a claim in a provisional application.

(9): One comment suggested that the two-month period for taking action would be unfair in instances in which the PTO prepares and enters the notice into the

Patent Application Locating and Monitoring (PALM) system but fails to mail the notice or mails the notice to an incorrect correspondence address.

Response: The "Notice of Omitted Items" is not an action within the meaning of 35 U.S.C. 133 to which a response is required to avoid abandonment. An applicant simply has the opportunity to file a petition, but need not take action, in response to a "Notice of Omitted Items." Thus, the timeliness of any such petition is governed by 37 CFR 1.181(f). 37 CFR 1.181(f) provides that any petition not filed within two months from the action complained of may be dismissed as untimely.

Establishing prior receipt in the PTO of the page(s) or drawing(s) at issue or submitting the omitted page(s) or drawing(s) and accepting the date of such submission as the application filing date would result in an addition to the papers constituting the original disclosure of the application, and submitting the omitted page(s) or drawing(s) and accepting the date of such submission as the application filing date would result in a change in application filing date. As a change in either the original disclosure or filing date of an application would interfere with the examination of the application for compliance with 35 U.S.C. 102, 103, and 112, the PTO will not forward an application in which a "Notice of Omitted Items" has been mailed for examination until it is apparent that the applicant has not responded to the "Notice of Omitted Items." Thus, a nonprovisional application will not be processed for examination, and the examination of the application will be delayed, until the expiration of two months from the mailing date of "Notice of Omitted Items." The two-month period set forth in 37 CFR 1.181(f) is considered an appropriate balance between providing an applicant sufficient time to take action in response to a "Notice of Omitted Items" and avoiding unnecessary delays in the examination of the application, which would be undesirable in view of 35 U.S.C. 154 as amended by Public Law 103-465. While an applicant willing to accept a nonprovisional application as deposited in the PTO need not respond to the "Notice of Omitted Items," the filing of an express communication to that effect would permit the PTO to proceed with the processing of the application for examination, and, as such, may reduce the delay in the examination of the application.

While a "Notice of Omitted Items" is not an action within the meaning of 35 U.S.C. 133, the principles regarding nonreceipt or delayed receipt of a "Notice of Omitted Items," due either to a failure on the part of the PTO to properly mail such notice or a failure on the part of the U.S. Postal Service to deliver such notice to the correspondence address in a timely manner, are applicable to the nonreceipt or delayed receipt of a "Notice of Omitted Items." Applicants are directed to the Notice entitled "Withdrawing the Holding of Abandonment When Office Actions Are Not Received," published in the PTO Official Gazette at 1156 Off. Gaz. Pat. Office 53 (November 16, 1993), for the evidence necessary to establish nonreceipt of a "Notice of Omitted Items," and the Notice entitled "Procedures For Restarting Response Periods," published in the PTO Official Gazette at 1160 Off. Gaz. Pat. Office 14 (March 1, 1994), for the evidence necessary to establish delayed receipt of a "Notice of Omitted Items."

(10): One comment suggested that while the proposed procedure is an improvement, it still conflicts with 35 U.S.C. 112 and 113. The comment specifically argues that the sufficiency of an application is a matter for determination by an examiner skilled in the subject matter of the application, in that Congress did not intend that the sufficiency of an application be determined by the Initial Patent Examination Division.

Response: The adopted procedure will accord a filing date to any application that contains something that can be construed as a written description, any necessary drawing, and, in a nonprovisional application, at least one claim. This procedure is consistent with the requirements for a filing date as set forth in 35 U.S.C. 111, 112, and 113. 35 U.S.C. 113, second sentence, contemplates that drawings may be filed after the filing date of an application. 35 U.S.C. 113, however, provides that an "applicant shall furnish a drawing where necessary for the understanding of the subject matter sought to be patented," and 35 U.S.C. 111(a)(4) and 111(b)(4) each provide, in part, that the "filing date . . . shall be the date on which . . . any required drawing are received in the Patent and Trademark Office." As such, the PTO has the statutory authority, and responsibility, to determine whether a drawing is necessary under 35 U.S.C. 113 in an application filed without drawings prior to according a filing date to that application.

There is nothing in 35 U.S.C. 111, 112, or 113 that limits the authority of the Commissioner to delegate the determination of whether or when any application meets the requirements for a filing date as set forth in 35 U.S.C. 111, 112, and 113. In any event, filing date issues are, as discussed supra, ultimately decided by Office of the Deputy Assistant Commissioner for Patent Policy and Projects on the basis of whether and when the application meets the requirements for a filing date as set forth in 35 U.S.C. 111, 112, and 113, and not on the basis of who made the initial decision not to accord a filing date to the application.

(11): One comment suggested that the proposed procedure be adopted by rulemaking. Another comment suggested that the proposed procedure either be adopted by rulemaking or clearly set forth in the MPEP.

Response: 37 CFR 1.53(b)(1) provides that the "filing date of an application for patent filed under this section, except for a provisional application, is the date on which: a specification containing a description pursuant to § 1.71 and at least one claim pursuant to § 1.75; and any drawing required by § 1.81(a), are filed in the Patent and Trademark Office in the name of the actual inventor or inventors as required by § 1.41." 37 CFR 1.53(b)(2) provides that the "filing date of a provisional application is the date on which: a specification as prescribed by 35 U.S.C. 112, first paragraph; and any drawing required by § 1.81(a), are filed in the Patent and Trademark Office in the name of the actual inventor or inventors as required by § 1.41." Thus, no change to the rules of practice is necessary to adopt the procedure set forth in this notice.

It should be noted that the MPEP 608.01 sets forth the former procedure for treating an application filed without all of the pages of specification or filed under 35 U.S.C. 111(a) without at least one claim. Likewise, MPEP 608.02 sets forth the former procedure for treating an application filed without drawings or all of the figures of drawings.

The next revision of the MPEP will incorporate the change in procedure set forth in this notice.

Date:__________

Bruce A. Lehman
Assistant Secretary of Commerce and
Commissioner of Patents and Trademarks

Appendix C-24

Provisional Application for Patent

November 29, 2000

Background

Since June 8, 1995, the United States Patent and Trademark Office (USPTO) has offered inventors the option of filing a provisional application for patent which was designed to provide a lower-cost first patent filing in the United States and to give U.S. applicants parity with foreign applicants under the GATT Uruguay Round Agreements.

A provisional application for patent is a U.S. national application for patent filed in the USPTO under 35 U.S.C. §111(b). It allows filing without a formal patent claim, oath or declaration, or any information disclosure (prior art) statement. It provides the means to establish an early effective filing date in a non-provisional patent application filed under 35 U.S.C. §111(a). It also allows the term "Patent Pending" to be applied.

A provisional application for patent (provisional application) has a pendency lasting 12 months from the date the provisional application is filed. **The 12-month pendency period cannot be extended.** Therefore, an applicant who files a provisional application <u>must</u> file a corresponding non-provisional application for patent (non-provisional application) during the 12-month pendency period of the provisional application in order to benefit from the earlier filing of the provisional application. In accordance with 35 U.S.C. §119(e), the corresponding non-provisional application must contain or be amended to contain a specific reference to the provisional application.

Once a provisional application is filed, an alternative to filing a corresponding non-provisional application is to convert the provisional application to a non-provisional application by filing a grantable petition under 37 CFR §1.53(c)(3) requesting such a conversion within 12 months of the provisional application filing date.

However, converting a provisional application to a non-provisional application (versus filing a non-provisional application claiming the benefit of the provisional application) will have a negative impact on patent term. The term of a patent issuing from a non-provisional application resulting from the conversion of a provisional application will be measured from the original filing date of the provisional application.

By filing a provisional application first, and then filing a corresponding non-provisional application that references the provisional application within the 12-month provisional application pendency period, a patent term endpoint may be extended by as much as 12 months.

Provisional Application for Patent Filing Date Requirements

The provisional application must be made in the name(s) of all of the inventor(s). It can be filed up to one year following the date of first sale, offer for sale, public use, or publication of the invention. (These pre-filing disclosures, although protected in the United States, may preclude patenting in foreign countries.)

A filing date will be accorded to a provisional application only when it contains:

- a written description of the invention, complying with all requirements of 35 U.S.C. §112 ¶ 1 and
- any drawings necessary to understand the invention, complying with 35 U.S.C. §113.

If either of these items are missing or incomplete, no filing date will be accorded to the provisional application. To be complete, a provisional application must also include the filing fee as set forth in 37 C.F.R. 1.16(k) and a cover sheet identifying:

- the application as a provisional application for patent;
- the name(s) of all inventors;
- inventor residence(s);
- title of the invention;
- name and registration number of attorney or agent and docket number (if applicable);
- correspondence address; and
- any US Government agency that has a property interest in the application.

A sample cover sheet may be obtained from the USPTO.

The information in this brochure is general in nature and is not meant to substitute for advice provided by a patent practitioner. Applicants unfamiliar with the requirements of US patent law and procedures should consult an attorney or agent registered to practice before the USPTO.

A list of attorneys and agents can be searched at the USPTO Web site at http://www.uspto.gov and examined without charge at Patent and Trademark Depository Libraries (PTDLs). A printed list is available from the US Government Printing Office at:

Superintendent of Documents (SuDocs)
P.O. Box 371954
Pittsburgh, PA 15250-7954

For information or to order by telephone call 202-512-1800. The SuDocs Web site is at http://www.access.gpo.gov/su_docs/.

Cautions

- Provisional applications are not examined on their merits.
- The benefits of the provisional application cannot be claimed if the one-year deadline for filing a non-provisional application has expired.
- Provisional applications cannot claim the benefit of a previously-filed application, either foreign or domestic.
- It is recommended that the disclosure of the invention in the provisional application be as complete as possible. In order to obtain the benefit of the filing date of a provisional application the claimed subject matter in the later filed non-provisional application must have support in the provisional application.
- If there are multiple inventors, each inventor must be named in the application.
- The inventor(s) named in the provisional application must have made a contribution to the invention as described. If multiple inventors are named, each inventor named must have made a contribution individually or jointly to the subject matter disclosed in the application.

- The non-provisional application must have one inventor in common with the inventor(s) named in the provisional application to claim benefit of the provisional application filing date.
- A provisional application must be entitled to a filing date and include the basic filing fee in order for a non-provisional application to claim benefit of that provisional application.
- There is a surcharge for filing the basic filing fee or the cover sheet on a date later than filing the provisional application.
- Provisional applications for patent may not be filed for design inventions.
- Amendments are not permitted in provisional applications after filing, other than those to make the provisional application comply with applicable regulations.
- No information disclosure statement may be filed in a provisional application.
- A provisional application cannot result in a U.S. patent unless one of the following two events occur within 12 months of the provisional application filing date:
  1. a corresponding non-provisional application for patent entitled to a filing date is filed that claims the benefit of the earlier filed provisional application; or
  2. a grantable petition under 37 CFR 1.53(c)(3) to convert the provisional application into a non-provisional application is filed.

Fee

The current fee for a provisional application can be found on the fee page. [A small entity applicant must file a small entity statement.] Payment by check or money order must be made payable to "Commissioner of Patents." Mail the provisional application and filing fee to:

Box Provisional Patent Application
Commissioner for Patents
Washington, DC 20231

Features

- provides simplified filing with a lower initial investment with one full year to assess the invention's commercial potential before committing to the higher cost of filing and prosecuting a non-provisional application for patent;
- establishes an official United States patent application filing date for the invention;
- permits one year's authorization to use "Patent Pending" notice in connection with the invention;
- begins the Paris Convention priority year;
- enables immediate commercial promotion of the invention with greater security against having the invention stolen;
- preserves application in confidence without publication in accordance with 35 U.S.C. 122(b), effective November 29, 2000;
- permits applicant to obtain USPTO certified copies;
- allows for the filing of multiple provisional applications for patent and for consolidating them in a single §111(a) non-provisional application for patent;
- provides for submission of additional inventor names by petition if omission occurred without deceptive intent (deletions are also possible by petition).

Warnings

A provisional application automatically becomes abandoned when its pendency expires 12 months after the provisional application filing date by operation of law. Applicants <u>must</u> file a non-provisional application claiming benefit of the earlier provisional application filing date in the USPTO before

the provisional application pendency period expires in order to preserve any benefit from the provisional-application filing.

Beware that an applicant whose invention is "in use" or "on sale" (see 35 U.S.C. §102(b)) in the United States during the one-year provisional-application pendency period may lose more than the benefit of the provisional application filing date if the one-year provisional-application pendency period expires before a corresponding non-provisional application is filed. Such an applicant may also lose the right to ever patent the invention (see 35 U.S.C. §102(b)).

Effective November 29, 2000, a claim under 35 U.S.C. 119(e) for the benefit of a prior provisional application must be filed during the pendency of the non-provisional application, and within four months of the non-provisional application filing date or within sixteen months of the provisional application filing date (whichever is later). See 37 CFR 1.78 as amended effective November 29, 2000.

Independent inventors should fully understand that a provisional application will not mature into a granted patent without further submissions by the inventor. Some invention promotion firms misuse the provisional application process leaving the inventor with no patent.

Contacts

Direct questions regarding regulations or procedures to the Office of the Deputy Commissioner for Patent Examination Policy.

Telephone: 703-305-9285

Fax: 703-308-6916

Direct questions regarding legislative changes to the Office of Legislative and International Affairs.

Telephone: 703-305-9300
Fax: 703-305-8885

The Office of Independent Inventor Programs provides a point of contact to the independent inventor community.

Write:

Director - United States Patent and Trademark Office
Office of Independent Inventor Programs
Box 24
Washington, DC 20231

Telephone: 703-306-5568
Fax: 703-306-5570
E-mail: independentinventor@uspto.gov

For additional copies of this brochure, or for further information, contact the USPTO General Information Services Division.

Telephone: 800-PTO-9199
Fax: 703-305-7786
TTY: 703-305-7785
or access USPTO's Internet site at http://www.uspto.gov/.

Last Modified: Thursday, November 30, 2000

Appendix C-25

Memorandum: Applying the Recapture Rule to Reissue Applications

MEMORANDUM

Date: September 21, 1999

To: Patent Examining Corps

From: Stephen G. Kunin
Deputy Assistant Commissioner for Patent Policy and Projects
UNITED STATES DEPARTMENT OF COMMERCE
Patent and Trademark Office

Subject: Applying the Recapture Rule to Reissue Applications

The following material provides guidance to the patent examining corps in applying the recapture rule to reissue applications. The substance of the material will be incorporated into Chapter 1400 of the MPEP in the next revision.

Recapture of Surrendered Subject Matter

A reissue will not be granted to "recapture" claimed subject matter which was surrendered in an application to obtain the original patent- *Hester Industries, Inc. v. Stein, Inc.*, 142 F.3d 1472, 46 USPQ 2d 1641 (Fed. Cir. 1998); *In re Clement,* 131 F.3d 1464, 45 USPQ 2d 1161 (Fed. Cir. 1997); *Ball Corp. v. United States*, 729 F.2d 1429, 1436, 221 USPQ 289, 295 (Fed. Cir. 1984); *In re Wadlinger*, 496 F.2d 1200, 181 USPQ 826 (CCPA 1974); *In re Richman*, 409 F.2d 269, 276, 161 USPQ 359, 363–364 (CCPA 1969); *In re Willingham*, 282 F.2d 353, 127 USPQ 211 (CCPA 1960).

Two Step Test for Recapture:

In *Clement*, 131 F.3d at 1468–69, 45 USPQ 2d at 1164, the Court of Appeals for the Federal Circuit set forth guidance for recapture as follows:

> The first step in applying the recapture rule is to determine whether and in what aspect the reissue claims are broader than the patent claims. For example, a reissue claim that deletes a limitation or element from the patent claims is broader in that limitation's aspect. . . . Under *Mentor* [*Mentor Corp. v. Coloplast, Inc.*, 998 F.2d 992, 994, 27 USPQ 2d 1521, 1524

(Fed. Cir. 1993)], courts must determine in which aspects the reissue claim is broader, which includes broadening as a result of an omitted limitation. . . .

The second step is to determine whether the broader aspects of the reissue claims relate to surrendered subject matter. To determine whether an applicant surrendered particular subject matter, we look to the prosecution history for arguments and changes to the claims made in an effort to overcome a prior art rejection. *See Mentor*, 998 F.2d at 995–96, 27 USPQ 2d at 1524–25; *Ball Corp. v. United States*, 729 F.2d 1429, 1436, 221 USPQ 289, 294–95 (Fed. Cir. 1984).

In every reissue application, the examiner must first review each claim for the presence of broadening, as compared with the scope of the claims of the patent to be reissued. A reissue claim is broadened where some limitation of the patent claims is no longer required in the reissue claim; *see* MPEP § 1412.03 for guidance as to the nature of a "broadening claim."

Where a claim in a reissue application is in fact broadened, the examiner must next determine whether the broader aspects of that reissue claim relate to subject matter that applicant previously surrendered during the prosecution of the original application (which became the patent to be reissued). Each limitation of the patent claims, which is omitted or broadened in the reissue claim, must be reviewed for this determination.

It is noted that the facts in *Hester* and *Clement* (and the other cases cited above) were directed to subject matter surrendered in response to art rejections. The question as to whether other rejections may also give rise to recapture, however, remains unsettled in the case law.

Criteria for Determining That Subject Matter Has Been Surrendered:

If the limitation now being omitted or broadened in the present reissue was originally presented/argued/stated in the original application to make the claims allowable over a rejection or objection made in the original application, the omitted limitation relates to subject matter previously surrendered by applicant, and impermissible recapture exists.

The examiner should review the prosecution history of the original application file (of the patent to be reissued) for recapture. The prosecution history includes the rejections and applicant's arguments made therein. The record of the original application must show that the broadening aspect (the omitted/broadened limitation(s)) relates to subject matter that applicant previously surrendered. For example:

1) A limitation of the patent claims is omitted in the reissue claims. This omission provides a broadening aspect in the reissue claims, as compared to the claims of the patent. The omitted limitation was originally **argued** in the original application to make the application claims allowable over a rejection or objection made in the application. Thus, the omitted limitation relates to subject matter previously surrendered, in the original application.

Note: The argument that the claim limitation defined over the rejection must have been specific as to the limitation; rather than a general statement regarding the claims as a whole. In other words, a general "boiler plate" sentence will not be sufficient to establish recapture. An example of one such "boiler plate" sentence is:

"In closing, it is argued that the limitations of claims 1–7 distinguish the claims from the teachings of the prior art, and claims 1–7 are thus patentable."

This general "argument" will not, by itself, be sufficient to establish surrender and recapture.

2) The limitation omitted in the reissue was added in the original application claims for the purpose of making the claims allowable over a rejection or objection made

in the application. Even though applicant made no argument on the record that the limitation was added to obviate the rejection, the nature of the addition to the claim can show that the limitation was added in direct reply to the rejection. This too will establish the omitted limitation as relating to subject matter previously surrendered. To illustrate this, note the following example:

The original application claims recite limitations A+B+C, and the Office action rejection combines two references to show A+B+C. In the amendment replying to the Office action, applicant adds limitation D to A+B+C in the claims, but makes no argument as to that addition. The examiner then allows the claims. Even though there is no argument as to the addition of limitation D, it must be presumed that the D limitation was added to obviate the rejection. The subsequent deletion of (omission of) limitation D in the reissue claims would be presumed to be a broadening in an aspect of the reissue claims related to surrendered subject matter.

3) The limitation A omitted in the reissue claims was present in the claims of the original application. The examiner's reasons for allowance in the original application stated that it was that limitation A which distinguished over a potential combination of references X and Y. Applicant did not present on the record a counter statement or comment as to the examiner's reasons for allowance, and permitted the claims to issue. The omitted limitation is thus established as relating to subject matter previously surrendered.

Argument (Without Amendment to the Claims) in the Original Application May Be Sufficient to Establish Recapture:

In *Clement*, the recapture was directed to subject matter surrendered in the original application by **changes** made to the claims (i.e., amendment of the claims) in an effort to overcome a prior art rejection. The *Clement* Court, however, also stated that "[t]o determine whether an applicant surrendered particular subject matter, we look to the prosecution history for **arguments** and changes to the claims made in an effort to overcome a prior art rejection." [Emphasis added] 131 F.3d at 1469, 45 USPQ 2d at 1164. This statement in *Clement* was subsequently discussed in *Hester Industries, Inc. v. Stein, Inc., supra*, where the Court observed that surrender of claimed subject matter may occur by *arguments* made during the prosecution of the original patent application *even where there was no claim change made.* The Court in *Hester* held that the surrender which forms the basis for impermissible recapture "can occur through arguments alone." 142 F.3d at 1482, 46 USPQ 2d at 1649. Accordingly, where claims are broadened in a reissue application, the examiner should review the prosecution history of the original patent file for recapture, even where the claims were never amended during the prosecution of the application which resulted in the patent.

Reissue Claims Are Same or Broader in Scope in All Aspects:

The recapture rule bars the patentee from acquiring through reissue claims that are, in all aspects, of the same scope as, or are broader in scope than, those claims canceled from the original application to obtain a patent. *Ball*, 729 F.2d at 1436, 221 USPQ at 295.

Reissue Claims Are Narrower in Scope in All Aspects:

The patentee is free to acquire, through reissue, claims that are narrower in scope in all aspects than claims canceled from the original application to obtain a patent. If the reissue claims are narrower than the claims canceled from the original application, yet broader than the original patent claims, reissue must be sought within 2 years after the grant of the original patent. *Ball*, 729 F.2d at 1436, 221 USPQ at 295. See MPEP § 1412.03 as to broadening claims.

Reissue Claims are Broader in Some Aspects, But Narrower in Others:

Reissue claims that are broader in certain aspects and narrower in others *vis-à-vis* claims canceled from the original application to obtain a patent may avoid the effect of the recapture rule if the claims are broader in a way that does not attempt to reclaim what was surrendered earlier. *Mentor Corp. v. Coloplast, Inc.*, 998 F.2d 992, 994, 27 USPQ 2d 1521, 1525 (Fed. Cir. 1993). "[I]f the reissue claim is as broad as or broader in an aspect germane to a prior art rejection, but narrower in another aspect completely unrelated to the rejection, the recapture rule bars the claim; [] if the reissue claim is narrower in an aspect germane to [a] prior art rejection, and broader in an aspect unrelated to the rejection, the recapture rule does not bar the claim, but other rejections are possible." *Clement*, 131 F.3d at 1470, 45 USPQ 2d at 1165.

If the broadening aspect of the reissue claim relates to subject matter previously surrendered, the examiner must determine whether the newly added narrowing limitation in the reissue claim modifies the claim such that the scope of the claim no longer results in a recapture of the surrendered subject matter. If the narrowing limitation modifies the claim in such a manner that the scope of the claim no longer results in a recapture of the surrendered subject matter, then there is no recapture. In this situation, even though a rejection based on recapture is not made, the examiner should make of record the reason(s) why, as a result of the narrowing limitation, there is no recapture.

Reissue to Take Advantage of 35 U.S.C. 103(b):

A patentee may file a reissue application to permit consideration of process claims which qualify for 35 U.S.C. 103(b) treatment if a patent is granted on an application entitled to the benefit of 35 U.S.C. 103(b), without an election having been made as a result of error without deceptive intent. See MPEP § 706.02(n). **This is not to be considered a recapture.** The addition of process claims, however, will generally be considered to be a *broadening* of the invention (*Ex Parte Wikdahl*, 10 USPQ 2d 1546 (Bd. Pat. App. & Inter. 1989)), and such addition must be applied for within two years of the grant of the original patent. See also MPEP § 1412.03 as to broadened claims.

Reissue for Article Claims Which Are Functional Descriptive Material Stored on a Computer-Readable Medium:

A patentee may file a reissue application to permit consideration of article of manufacture claims which are functional descriptive material stored on a computer-readable medium, where these article claims correspond to the process or machine claims which have been patented. The error in not presenting claims to this statutory category of invention (the "article" claims) must have been made as a result of error without deceptive intent. The addition of these "article" claims will generally be considered to be a *broadening* of the invention (*Ex Parte Wikdahl*, 10 USPQ 2d 1546 (Bd. Pat. App. & Inter. 1989)), and such addition must be applied for within two years of the grant of the original patent. See also MPEP § 1412.03 as to broadened claims.

Rejection Based Upon Recapture:

Reissue claims which recapture surrendered subject matter should be rejected using form paragraph 14.17 as follows. **< Note: the MPEFP has not yet been revised to include this version of 14.17 >**

¶ 14.17 Rejection, 35 U.S.C. 251, Recapture

Claim **[1]** rejected under 35 U.S.C. 251 as being an improper recapture of broadened claimed subject matter surrendered in the application for the patent upon which the present reissue is based. *See Hester Industries, Inc. v. Stein, Inc.*, 142 F.3d 1472, 46 USPQ 2d 1641 (Fed. Cir. 1998); *In re Clement,* 131 F.3d 1464, 45 USPQ 2d 1161 (Fed.

Cir. 1997); *Ball Corp. v. United States*, 729 F.2d 1429, 1436, 221 USPQ 289, 295 (Fed. Cir. 1984). A broadening aspect is present in the reissue which was not present in the application for patent. The record of the application for the patent shows that the broadening aspect (in the reissue) relates to subject matter that applicant previously surrendered during the prosecution of the application. Accordingly, the narrow scope of the claims in the patent was not an error within the meaning of 35 U.S.C. 251, and the broader scope surrendered in the application for the patent cannot be recaptured by the filing of the present reissue application.

[2]

Examiner Note: In bracket 2, the examiner should explain the specifics of why recapture exists, including an identification of the omitted/broadened claim limitations in the reissue which provide the "broadening aspect" to the claim(s), and where in the original application the narrowed claim scope was presented/argued to obviate a rejection/objection. See MPEP 1412.02.

Examples:

The following examples illustrate recurring fact situations presenting recapture issues and their resolution. It should be noted that each recapture issue should be decided on a case-by-case basis.

Bread compositions and bread making are used in the examples for ease of comparison, and so that the reader need not adjust to a very different fact pattern for different examples.

Example 1 - Recapture based on claim limitations added in original application to overcome prior art:

Original prosecution:

An application was filed containing only one claim reciting:

Claim 1: A bread containing chocolate, pepper, and tomatoes, which provide a unique taste to the bread.

During the original prosecution, the examiner issued an Office action rejecting claim 1 based upon references X and Y which together teach a bread having chocolate, pepper, and tomatoes.

In an amendment replying to the Office action, applicant added (from the specification) "orange peels" to claim 1 and argued that the amendment overcame the rejection based on references X and Y. The claim, as amended, recited:

Claim 1 (once amended): A bread containing chocolate, pepper, tomatoes and **orange peels**, which provide a unique taste to the bread.

The examiner allowed the claim and passed the application to issue. A patent then issued on the application.

Reissue proceedings:

In a reissue application, new claim 2 is presented for a bread containing chocolate, pepper, and tomatoes, which provide a unique taste to the bread. Because of market place developments which now show the need to claim a bread without "orange peels," new claim 2 does not include the limitation of "orange peels" that defined over references X and Y in the original application.

The reissue oath points out that the original presentation (in the patent) of only a claim which included "orange peels" was "error" upon which reissue may be based; thus, claim 2 which omits "orange peels" is added in the reissue. The oath points out that the error arose because applicant's attorney incorrectly assumed that the manufacture of the bread without orange peels was not commercially feasible due to the consistency of the resulting bread.

A "commercial success" affidavit is newly presented in the reissue application to show that claim 2 is patentable over references X and Y even without "orange peels," and the examiner deems the affidavit to be persuasive. Accordingly, the examiner determines that claim 2 defines over references X and Y and the remainder of the art.

Resolution of the recapture issue:

Claim 2 would be barred by recapture. The limitation omitted in the reissue is "orange peels." This provides a broadening aspect to the reissue claim that was clearly argued in the original application to overcome the rejection based on references X and Y. Thus, omission of "orange peels" is related to subject matter surrendered in the original application. This is the fundamental case of recapture. Since recapture exists, claim 2 should be rejected under 35 U.S.C. 251 based on recapture in the manner set forth above under the heading "Rejection based upon recapture:".

In this example, applicant narrowed the claims for the purpose of obtaining allowance in the original prosecution, and applicant is now precluded from recapturing subject matter previously surrendered. See also *Mentor Corp. v. Coloplast, Inc.*, 998 F.2d 992, 994, 27 USPQ 2d 1521, 1524 (Fed. Cir. 1993) with respect to this example. (In *Mentor*, there were narrowing limitations added to the reissue claims that did not serve to materially narrow the claims in a manner effective to avoid a recapture bar; however, those narrowing limitations are not included in this example of fundamental recapture.)

Example 2 - Recapture based upon applicant's statement made during the original prosecution:

Original prosecution:

An application was filed containing only one claim reciting:

Claim 1: A bread baking oven for baking bread using only steam comprising:

a chamber;

means passing a continuously running conveyor belt through the chamber to expose bread in the chamber only to steam as the sole baking medium;

and means providing two sources of steam to bake the bread:

> one being a source of steam comprising a pool of water within the chamber with heating means for boiling the water to create steam,
>
> and the other a steam generator supplying supplemental steam into the chamber to maintain the atmosphere, together with the first steam source, at near 100% humidity, 100 degrees C. and a pressure above atmospheric.

During the prosecution of the original patent, the examiner repeatedly rejected claim 1 based upon prior art references X and Y which together teach the claimed oven. Applicant repeatedly replied with the argument that **baking solely with steam** and the **two sources of steam** limitations distinguished claim 1 from references X and Y, and that each of these limitations are critical to patentability. Applicant did not amend the claim, and ultimately applicant appealed to the Board of Patent Appeals and Interferences. In the appeal, applicant again relied upon the argument of baking solely with steam and the two sources of steam. The Board reversed the examiner, and the examiner passed the application to issue. A patent issued on the application.

Reissue proceedings:

In a reissue application, claim 2 is newly presented containing the same language as in claim 1 except that it does not contain the requirement that **the baking be solely with steam**, and does not require that the steam be generated via **two sources of steam.**

The reissue oath points out that the presentation of only a claim which included these two limitations was "error" by the attorney in failing to recognize the full scope of the invention.

During the prosecution of the reissue application, the examiner is persuaded that claim 2 defines over the prior art.

Resolution of the recapture issue:

Claim 2 is barred by recapture.

In this example, reissue claim 2 is broader than patent claim 1 by the omission of two limitations, baking solely with steam and steam generation via two sources of steam. Applicant surrendered the claim scope for a bread baking apparatus which omits these two limitations because applicant repeatedly argued during prosecution of the original application (including on appeal) that these two limitations distinguished original claim 1 from references X and Y and that each of the limitations was critical to patentability. These repeated arguments constitute an admission by applicant that the two limitations were necessary to overcome the prior art. Thus, claim 2 is broader than the original application claim in an aspect relevant to prior art rejection and related to the surrendered subject matter. Accordingly, impermissible recapture exists, and claim 2 should be rejected under 35 U.S.C. 251, based upon recapture.

Impermissible recapture exists in this example even though applicant never amended the original application claim to add baking solely with steam and steam generation via two sources of steam; the two limitations were present in the originally presented claim of the application. Subject matter can be surrendered by way of arguments *or* by claim amendment made during the prosecution of the original patent application. In the present example, applicant's argument provided the basis for a finding of surrender of subject matter.

A similar situation arose in *Hester Industries, Inc. v. Stein, Inc.*, 142 F.3d 1472, 46 USPQ 2d 1641 (Fed. Cir. 1998). In *Hester*, however, the reissue claims also included narrowing limitations added via the reissue that did not serve to materially narrow the claims in a manner effective to avoid a recapture bar; those limitations are not included (presented) in this example, since they are not directed to the focus of the example.

Example 3 - Reissue broadens, but the broadening is not related to the prior art rejection-No recapture:

Original prosecution:

As in Example 1, an application was filed containing only one claim reciting:

Claim 1: A bread containing chocolate, pepper, and tomatoes, which provide a unique taste to the bread.

During the prosecution, the examiner issued an Office action rejecting claim 1 based upon references X and Y which together teach a bread having chocolate, pepper, and tomatoes.

In an amendment replying to the Office action, applicant added (from the specification) "orange peels" to claim 1 and argued that this amendment overcame the rejection based on references X and Y, in that it provided a sweetness to the bread. The amended claim recited:

Claim 1 (once amended): A bread containing chocolate, pepper, tomatoes and **orange peels**, which provide a unique taste to the bread.

The examiner allowed the claim and passed the application to issue. A patent issued on the application.

Reissue proceedings:

In a reissue application, new claim 2 is presented.

Claim 2: A bread containing chocolate, tomatoes and orange peels, which provide a unique taste to the bread.

New claim 2 does not include the "pepper" of claim 1 of the original application. The reissue oath points out that limiting the bread to a pepper-containing bread (in the patent) was "error" upon which reissue may be based; thus, claim 2 which omits "pepper" is added in the reissue application. The oath points out that the error arose because applicant's attorney incorrectly assumed that read with pepper was the only thing applicant was interested in producing.

The examiner determines that claim 2 defines over references X and Y and the remainder of the art, even without the pepper limitation.

Resolution of the recapture issue:

Claim 2 would be not barred by recapture. The limitation omitted in the reissue is "pepper." This provides a broadening aspect to the reissue claim that was never argued in the original application to overcome the rejection based on references X and Y. Thus, omission of "pepper" is not related to subject matter surrendered in the original application; a bread omitting pepper was never surrendered.

Regarding this example, see *Ball Corp. v. United States*, 729 F.2d 1429, 1436, 221 USPQ 289, 295 (Fed. Cir. 1984).

Example 4(a) - Reissue narrows & broadens, where the broadening is related to the prior art rejection and the narrowing is not- Yes recapture:

Original prosecution:

As in Examples 1 and 3, an application is filed containing only one claim reciting:

Claim 1: A bread containing chocolate, pepper, and tomatoes, which provide a unique taste to the bread.

During the prosecution, the examiner issues an Office action rejecting claim 1 based upon references X and Y which together teach a bread having chocolate, pepper, and tomatoes.

In an amendment replying to the Office action, applicant added (from the specification) "orange peels" to claim 1 and argued that the amendment overcame the rejection based on references X and Y. The claim now recites:

Claim 1 (once amended): A bread containing chocolate, pepper, tomatoes and **orange peels**, which provide a unique taste to the bread.

The examiner allowed the claim and passed the application to issue. A patent issued on the application.

Reissue proceedings:

In a reissue application, a new claim (i.e., claim 2) is presented for a bread containing chocolate, **diced green bell peppers** and tomatoes, which provide a unique taste to the bread. This reissue claim does not contain the "orange peels" that defined over references X and Y in the application. It does, however, require that the pepper be "diced green bell peppers" (unlike the case of example 1). The "diced green bell" limitation of the "pepper" is a limitation which was overlooked in the prosecution of the patent, and as such, constitutes "error" upon which reissue may be based. The examiner determines that newly presented claim 2 defines over references X and Y and the remainder of the art, based upon the "diced green bell peppers."

Resolution of the recapture issue:

Claim 2 would be barred by recapture. The limitation omitted in the reissue is "orange peels." This provides a broadening aspect to the reissue claim that was clearly argued in the original application to overcome the rejection based on references

X and Y. Thus, omission of "orange peels" is related to subject matter surrendered in the original application. A narrowing limitation was also provided in reissue claim 2; i.e., a limitation that limits the "pepper" to "diced green bell peppers." This narrowing limitation, however, is not at all related to the "orange peels" and the manner in which it defined over the art. Since the narrowing is **not** related to the prior art rejection and **not** related to the subject matter surrendered in the original application (omission of orange peels), recapture exists and claim 2 should rejected under 35 U.S.C. 251.

See *In re Clement,* 131 F.3d 1464, 45 USPQ 2d 1161 (Fed. Cir. 1997).

Example 4(b) - Reissue narrows & broadens where both are related to prior art rejections (different ones)-Yes recapture:

Original prosecution:

An application was filed containing only one claim reciting:

Claim 1: A method of treating bread dough to remove seed contaminants contained therein, which comprises:

(a) forming a flowing dough;

(b) irradiating the dough to soften the seeds at a temperature above room temperature; and

(c) adhering the softened seeds to a membrane at a temperature below room temperature and then recovering the dough.

During the prosecution, the examiner issued an Office action rejecting claim 1 based upon references X and Y which together teach steps (a)–(c). Claim 1 was also rejected based upon reference Z which teaches steps (a)–(c) in a somewhat different manner (than references X and Y do).

In an amendment replying to the action, applicant added **"101 and 115° C."** to step (b) of claim 1, and **5–15° C.** to step (c), in place of "a temperature above room temperature" and "a temperature below room temperature," respectively. Applicant argued that the temperature additions define the claim over references X and Y. Applicant also added new step (d) to claim 1, reciting the collecting of the seed-free dough while mixing and irradiating it. Applicant argued this addition to define the claim over reference Z.

The claim now recites:

Claim 1 (once amended): A method of treating a bread dough to remove seed contaminants contained therein, which comprises:

(a) forming a flowing dough at room temperature;

(b) irradiating the dough to soften the seeds while heating the dough to between **101 and 115° C.**;

(c) adhering the softened seeds to a membrane at a temperature of **5–15° C.** and then recovering the dough; and

(d) **collecting the seed-free dough while mixing and irradiating the dough.**

The examiner allowed the claim and passed the application to issue; a patent then issued on the application.

Reissue proceedings:

In a reissue application, claim 2 is now presented containing the same language as in claim 1 except that it does not contain the **"101 and 115° C,"** and **5–15° C."** limitations that defined over references X and Y in the application. Added to claim 2 step (d) is the limitation "in a vacuum," so that step (d) now recites-

(d) collecting the seed-free dough **in a vacuum** while mixing and irradiating the dough.

The reissue oath points out that the presentation (in the patent) of only a claim which included the two temperature limitations was "error" upon which reissue may be based; thus, claim 2 which is free of the temperature limitations is added in the reissue. The reissue oath additionally points out that "in a vacuum" is added because it further defines over reference Z.

The examiner determines that claim 2 defines over references X, Y and Z and the remainder of the art.

Resolution of the recapture issue:

Claim 2 would be barred by recapture:

In this example, reissue claim 2 is both broader and narrower than patent claim 1 in areas relevant to the prior art rejections.

Comparing reissue claim 2 with patent claim 1, claim 2 is narrower in one aspect, namely, the step (d) dough collection **"in a vacuum."** This narrowing relates to a prior art rejection because, during the prosecution of the patent, applicant added step (d) to overcome reference Z.

Reissue claim 2 is broader in that it eliminates the "**101 and 115° C.**" and **5–15° C."** temperature limitations. This provides a broadening aspect to the reissue claim to exclude the temperature limitations that were clearly argued in the original application to overcome the rejection based on references X and Y.

Reissue claim 2 is broader in a manner *directly pertinent to the subject matter that applicant surrendered* during the prosecution (i.e., the method of treating the bread dough to remove seed contaminants, absent the "**101 and 115° C.**" and **5–15° C.**" temperature limitations).

The narrowing aspect of reissue claim 2 (requiring a "**vacuum**") relates to a prior art rejection because, during the prosecution of the patent, applicant added the dough collection limitation (d) in an effort to overcome reference Z. The narrowing does not, however, relate to the prior art rejection which applicant dealt with in the original prosecution by adding the "**101 and 115° C.**" and **5–15° C.**" temperature limitations (thereby making the temperature limitation surrender). Accordingly, the narrowing limitation cannot save claim 2 from the recapture doctrine.

Since recapture exists, claim 2 should be rejected under 35 U.S.C. 251 as being a recapture.

See *In re Clement,* 131 F.3d 1464, 45 USPQ 2d 1161 (Fed. Cir. 1997).

Example 5 - The reissue both broadens and narrows by newly presenting a separate species-Yes recapture

Original prosecution:

The original application claim recited:

> Claim 1: A bread containing chocolate, pepper, and tomatoes, which provide a unique taste to the bread.

The specification disclosed that citrus fruit peels provide added texture to the bread. Examples were provided in the specification where "orange peel" and "lemon peel" are used for texture. Note, however, that citrus fruit peels were not included as a component of the only claim in the case.

In the amendment replying to the Office action, applicant added "orange peels" to claim 1. Applicant argued that "orange peels" define the claim over references X and Y, because the orange peels make the bread sweeter. The amended claim recited:

> Claim 1 (once amended): A bread containing chocolate, pepper, tomatoes and **orange peel,** which provide a unique taste to the bread.

Reissue proceedings:

In a reissue application, new claim 2 is presented for a bread containing chocolate, pepper, **lemon peel** and tomatoes, which provide a unique taste to the bread. The lemon peel is argued to provide softness to the bread. This reissue claim (claim 2) does not contain the "orange peel" that defined over references X and Y in the application. It does, however, require "lemon peel." Both "orange peel" and "lemon peel" are disclosed species of "citrus fruit peel," and the inclusion of a claim to the second disclosed species (the "lemon peel") was overlooked in the prosecution of the patent. Such constitutes "error" upon which reissue may be based. The examiner determines that newly presented claim 2 defines over references X and Y, and the remainder of the art, based upon the "lemon peel."

Resolution of the recapture issue:

Claim 2 is barred by recapture. The limitation omitted in the reissue is "orange peel," and omission of "orange peel" is related to subject matter surrendered in the original application. The presence of the "orange peel" limitation and the resultant sweetness argued in the original application became an integral part of the claim, and a bread absent the "orange peel" limitation and the resultant sweetness has been surrendered. Claim 2 has the alternative species "lemon peel," but it omits the "orange peel" limitation with its resultant sweetness. Accordingly, even though claim 2 is narrower in that it requires the lemon peel limitation, there is impermissible recapture, and claim 2 should be rejected under 35 U.S.C. 251, as such.

Consulting T.C. Spre in Case of Doubt

The above examples provide guidance in common fact situations involving recapture issues which may arise. Where variants of these fact situations arise for which the examiner is unsure of their resolution, the Special Program Examiner(s) of the Technology Centers should be consulted.

Cc: Nicholas P. Godici
Edward R. Kazenske
Bruce Kisliuk

Appendix C-26

Guidelines for Reexamination of Cases in View of *In re Portola Packaging, Inc.*

1223 OG 124
June 22, 1999
Department of Commerce
Patent and Trademark Office

DEPARTMENT OF COMMERCE

Patent and Trademark Office

Guidelines for Reexamination of Cases in View of
***In re Portola Packaging, Inc.*,**
110 F.3d 786, 42 USPQ2d 1295 (Fed. Cir. 1997)

Agency: Patent and Trademark Office, Commerce.

Action: Notice

Summary: The Patent and Trademark Office (PTO) is publishing the final version of guidelines to be used by Office personnel in their review of requests for reexaminations and ongoing reexaminations for compliance with the decision in *In re Portola Packaging, Inc.*, 110 F.3d 786, 42 USPQ2d 1295 (Fed. Cir. 1997). Because these guidelines govern internal practices. they are exempt from notice and comment under 5 U.S.C. § 553(b)(A).

Dates: The guidelines are effective as of publication in the FEDERAL REGISTER.

For Further Information Contact: John M. Whealan by telephone at (703) 305-9035; by facsimile at (703) 305-9373; by mail addressed to Box 8, Commissioner of Patents and Trademarks, Washington, D.C. 20231; or by electronic mail at "john.whealan@uspto.gov".

SUPPLEMENTAL INFORMATION:

I. Discussion of Public Comments

Comments were received by the PTO from eight individuals and one bar association in response to the Request for Comments on Interim Guidelines for Reexamination of Cases in View of *In re Portola Packaging, Inc.,* 110 F.3d 786, 42 USPQ2d 1295 (Fed. Cir. 1997), published June 15, 1998 (63 Fed. Reg. 32646). In general, six of the eight individual comments were critical of the guidelines; one individual comment was partially supportive of the guidelines and one suggested a legislative change; the comments from the bar association were in complete support of the guidelines. All of the comments have been carefully considered.

A. Below is a listing of comments along with a corresponding Office response explaining why each has not been adopted:

(1) Comment: Most of the critical comments suggest the Office is misinterpreting the "holding" of *Portola Packaging.* These comments believe *Portola Packaging* held that (i) the Office may not initiate a reexamination proceeding based solely on prior art previously cited during prosecution of the application which matured into the patent, regardless of whether that art was discussed, and (ii) no rejection can be made during a subsequent reexamination based solely on prior art cited during prosecution of the application which matured into the patent, even if that prior an was not previously discussed. Response: The Office views these positions as dicta and not the "holding" of *Portola Packaging.*

The Federal Circuit recently explained the difference between the holding of a case and dicta. *See In re McGrew,* 120 F.3d 1236, 1238–39, 43 USPQ2d 1632, 1635 (Fed. Cir. 1997). The Court explained that dicta consists of the statements in an opinion "upon a point or points not necessary to the decision of the case." *Id.* at 1238, 43 USPQ2d at 1635. The Court further explained that since "dictum is not authoritative," it need not be followed. *Id.*

The Office considers the portions of the *Portola Packaging* opinion relied on by the critical commenters as dicta and not the holding of the case. In *Portola Packaging,* the prior art relied upon in the reexamination (that was found by the Court to be improperly used) was not only cited, but it was also discussed and applied to reject claims during prosecution of the application which matured into the patent. Thus, *Portola Packaging* holds that a rejection in a reexamination proceeding may not be based solely on prior art that was previously applied to reject claims during prosecution of the application which matured into the patent. *Portola Packaging* does not, however, hold (as suggested by the commenters) that prior art in the record of the application that matured into the patent, which was not discussed, may never form the sole basis for a rejection during a subsequent reexamination proceeding. Such a broad reading of *Portola Packaging* would encourage the practice of applicants citing numerous references during prosecution of an application to preclude subsequent reexamination based on those references. This practice of flooding the Office with references during prosecution of an application in order to prevent their subsequent use in reexamination could overwhelm the examination process and limit the effectiveness of reexamination.

(2) Comment: One comment went further and suggested that *Portola Packaging* precluded reexamination based on any reference which is not new art. Response: The Office disagrees with this comment in view of the interpretation of the holding of *Portola Packaging* set forth in the preceding paragraph.

(3) Comment: One comment suggested the elimination of the unusual fact pattern situations exemplified in Part E, since in their opinion, *Portola Packaging* holds that previously cited art may never be relied on in a reexamination. Response: Once again, the Office views this position as dictum and not the holding of the case.

(4) Comment: One comment suggested the Office should seek a legislative overruling of the "holding" of *Portola Packaging.* Response: As the Office is following the holding of the case (as set forth above), the case need not be overruled. However, changes regarding the type of prior art that may be considered in reexamination proceedings may be proposed in upcoming legislation.

(5) Comment: One comment suggested that the form notices set forth in Section F may prompt an applicant to file a reissue application to resolve any issues that are precluded from resolution during reexamination. Response: The form notices in Section F have been modified to indicate that no patentability determination has been made in the reexamination (over prior art precluded by *Portola Packaging*). The notices do not suggest the filing of a reissue application. This of course would be an option open to the patent owner as *Portola Packaging* does not apply to reissue applications.

(6) Comment: One comment suggested that the practice of an examiner placing his initials next to a reference on an information disclosure statement (IDS), citation form PTOL-1449, or its equivalent, is sufficient to indicate that an examiner has considered the reference. Response: Where the IDS citations are submitted but not described, the examiner is only responsible for cursorily reviewing the references. The initials of the examiner on the PTOL-1449 indicate only that degree of review unless the reference is either applied against the claims, or discussed by the examiner as pertinent art of interest, in a subsequent office action.

As noted in (1) above, the prior art relied upon in the reexamination in *Portola Packaging* was not merely cited and initialed, but it was discussed and applied to reject claims in the application that matured into the patent. *Portola Packaging* does not hold that prior art that was of record but not discussed may not form the sole basis of a rejection of the claims. Accordingly, under *Portola Packaging* the mere presence of the examiner's initials next to a reference on an IDS citation does not preclude consideration of the reference in a subsequent reexamination proceeding.

(7) Comment: One comment suggested that the guidelines were inconsistent with *In re Hiniker Co.*, 150 F.3d 1362, 47 USPQ2d 1523 (Fed. Cir. 1998). Response: In *Hiniker*, the Federal Circuit affirmed a rejection in a reexamination proceeding which was based, in part, on new prior art. *See* 150 F.3d at 1367, 47 USPQ2d at 1527. *Hiniker*, therefore, does not preclude a rejection in a reexamination proceeding based on prior art that was cited but never discussed during the prosecution of the application which matured into the patent, since such a situation was not presented to the Court.

In *Hiniker*, the Court did state that *Portola Packaging* "held that prior art that was before the original examiner could not support a reexamination proceeding despite the fact that it was *not the basis of a rejection in the original prosecution;* as long as the art was before the original examiner, it would be considered 'old art.'" 150 F.3d at 1365–66, 47 USPQ2d at 1526 (citing *Portola Packaging*) (emphasis added). It is undisputed, however, that the prior art relied on to reject the claims in the reexamination proceeding in *Portola Packaging* was the same prior art that was relied on to reject claims during the prosecution of the application which matured into the patent. *See Portola Packaging*, 110 F.3d at 787, 42 USPQ2d at 1296–97. Accordingly, the *Hiniker* panel was not addressing the issue of prior art that was not discussed when it characterized the holding of *Portola Packaging* since it is clear that an "old art" rejection was at issue in *Portola Packaging*, whereas a "new art" rejection was at issue in *Hiniker*.

(8) Comment: One comment suggested that reexaminations should be the same as all other examinations. Response: Reexamination is based on patents and printed publications. Thus the scope of reexamination is narrower than that involved in the examination of a patent application. Certain issues of patentability that may be considered during prosecution of the application may not be considered during reexamination of the patent. If the patent owner desires consideration of questions of patentability not appropriate for reexamination, those issues can only be addressed in a reissue application filed under 35 U.S.C. § 251.

(9) Comment: One comment queried whether applicants will now be required to discuss all references listed on an IDS statement. Response: There is no such requirement in the current rules. Under the guidelines set forth herein, however, references that are not discussed during the prosecution of an application which matures into a patent will not be precluded from consideration in a subsequent reexamination proceeding.

B. The following comments have been adopted to the extent indicated in the corresponding Office response:

(1) Comment: Two comments suggested that the statements in Section F to be used in denying or terminating a reexamination were misleading and could cast a shadow on the validity of the patent. One comment further proposed changing the language to, "No new patentability determination has been made in this reexamination proceeding." Response: The Office has considered these suggestions, and in an attempt to be more clear, has modified the language in Section F to be used in denying or terminating a reexamination proceeding.

C. The following comments supported the interim guidelines and suggested no changes:

(1) Comment: The comments from the bar association supported the guidelines as consistent with *Portola Packaging* and the legislative intent of the reexamination process to resolve validity questions efficiently and economically. In addition, the bar association felt the guidelines were consistent with the Federal Circuit decision in *In re Lonardo* 119 F.3d 960.43 USPQ2d 1262 (Fed. Cir. 1997), *cert. denied*, 118 S. Ct. 1164 (1998).

(2) The bar association also commented that the guidelines (and in particular the unusual fact patterns set forth in Section E) are consistent with the rebuttable presumption of administrative correctness relied on by the Court in *Portola Packaging*. Courts presume that Government officials have properly discharged their duties, absent clear evidence to the contrary. Thus, since the presumption of administrative correctness is rebuttable, the guidelines properly provide for reexamination based on a previously considered reference where the evidence clearly shows that the examiner did not appreciate the issue raised in the reexamination request during the prosecution of the application that matured into the patent.

II. Guidelines for Reexamination of Cases in View of *In re Portola Packaging, Inc.*, 110 F.3d 786, 42 USPQ2d 1295 (Fed. Cir. 1997)

The following guidelines have been developed to assist Patent and Trademark Office (PTO) personnel in determining whether to order a reexamination or terminate an ongoing reexamination in view of the United States Court of Appeals for the Federal Circuit's decision in *In re Portola Packaging, Inc.*[1] These guidelines supersede and supplement any previous guidelines issued by the PTO with respect to reexamination. These guidelines apply to all reexaminations regardless of whether they are initiated by the Commissioner, requested by the patentee, or requested by a third party. These guidelines will be incorporated into Chapter 2200 of the Manual of Patent Examining Procedure (MPEP).

A. Explanation of *Portola Packaging*

In order for the PTO to conduct reexamination, prior art must raise a substantial new question of patentability."[2] In *Portola Packaging*, the Federal Circuit held that a combination of two references that were relied upon individually to reject claims during the prosecution of the application which matured into the patent does not raise a substantial new question of patentability in a subsequent reexamination of the patent.[3]

---

[1] 110 F.3d 786.42 USPQ2d 1295 (Fed. Cir.) *reh'g in banc denied,* 122 F.3d 1473.44 USPQ2d 1060 (1997).

[2] 35 U.S.C. § 304.

[3] During the original prosecution of the application which led to the patent, the PTO had rejected the claims separately based upon the Hunter and Faulstich references. The PTO never applied the references in combination. During reexamination, Portola Packaging amended the

The Federal Circuit also held that an amendment of the claims during reexamination does not justify using old prior art to raise a substantial new question of patentability.[4] The Court explained that "a rejection made during reexamination does not raise a substantial new question of patentability if it is supported only by prior art previously considered by the PTO."[5]

B. General Principles Governing Compliance with *Portola Packaging*

If prior art was previously relied upon to reject a claim in a prior related PTO proceeding,[6] the PTO will not order or conduct reexamination based *only* on such prior art, regardless of whether that prior art is to be relied upon to reject the same or different claims in the reexamination.

If prior art was *not* relied upon to reject a claim, but was cited in the record of a prior related PTO proceeding, and *its relevance to the patentability of any claim was actually discussed on the record,*[7] the PTO will *not order or conduct reexamination based only* on such prior art.

In contrast, the PTO *may* order and conduct reexamination based on prior art that was cited but whose relevance to patentability of the claims was *not discussed* in any prior related PTO proceeding.

C. Procedures for Determining Whether a Reexamination May be *Ordered* in Compliance with *Portola Packaging*

PTO personnel must adhere to the following procedures when determining whether a reexamination may be *ordered* in compliance with the Federal Circuit's decision in *Portola Packaging:*

1. Read the reexamination request to identify the prior art on which the request is based.
2. Conduct any necessary search of the prior art relevant to the subject matter of the patent for which reexamination was requested.[8]

---

patent claims, and for the first time the PTO rejected the amended patent claims based upon the Hunter and Faulstich references in combination. Despite these facts, the Federal Circuit determined that the PTO was precluded from conducting reexamination on those references, 110 F.3d at 790, 42 USPQ2d at 1299.

[4] 110 F.3d at 791, 42 USPQ2d at 1299.

[5] 110 F.3d at 791, 42 USPQ2d at 1300.

[6] Prior related PTO proceedings include the application which matured into the patent that is being reexamined, any reissue application for the patent, and any reexamination proceeding for the patent.

[7] The relevance of the prior art to patentability may be discussed by either the applicant, patentee, examiner, or any third party. However, 37 C.F.R. § 1.2 requires that all PTO business be transacted in writing. Thus, the PTO cannot presume that a prior art reference was previously relied upon to reject or discussed in a prior PTO proceeding if there is no basis in the written record to so conclude other than the examiner's initials or a check mark on a PTO 1449 form, or equivalent, submitted with an information disclosure statement. Thus, any discussion of prior art must appear on the record of a prior related PTO proceeding. Examples of generalized statements in a prior related PTO proceeding that would not preclude reexamination include statements that prior art is "cited to show the state of the art," "cited to show the background of the invention," or "cited of interest."

[8] *See* 35 U.S.C. § 303 ("On his own initiative, and *any time,* the Commissioner may determine whether a substantial new question of patentability is raised by patents and publication discovered by him . . ."); *see also* MPEP § 2244 ("If the examiner believes that additional prior art patents and publications can be readily obtained by searching to supply any deficiencies in the prior art cited in the request, the examiner can perform such an additional search.").

3. Read the prosecution histories of all prior related PTO proceedings.

4. Determine if the prior art in the reexamination request and the prior art found in any search was:

   (a) relied upon to reject any claim in a prior related PTO proceeding; or

   (b) cited *and* its relevance to patentability of any claim discussed in a prior related PTO proceeding.

5. *Deny* the reexamination request if the decision to order reexamination would be based *only* on prior art that was, in a prior related PTO proceeding, (a) relied upon to reject any claim, and/or (b) cited and its relevance to patentability of any claim discussed.[9]

6. *Order* reexamination if the decision to order reexamination would be based at least in part on prior art that was, in a prior related PTO proceeding, neither (a) relied upon to reject any claim, nor (b) cited and its relevance to patentability of any claim discussed and a substantial new question of patentability is raised with respect to any claim of the patent.[10]

D. Procedures for Determining Whether an Ongoing Reexamination Must be Terminated in Compliance with *Portola Packaging*

PTO personnel must adhere to the following procedures when determining whether any *current* or *future ongoing* reexamination should be terminated in compliance with the Federal Circuit's decision in *Portola Packaging:*

1. Prior to making any rejection in an ongoing reexamination, determine for any prior related PTO proceeding what prior art was (a) relied upon to reject any claim or (b) cited *and* discussed.

2. Base any and all rejections of the patent claims under reexamination *at least in part* on prior art that was, in any prior related PTO proceeding, neither (a) relied upon to reject any claim, nor (b) cited and its relevance to patentability of any claim discussed.

3. Withdraw any rejections based only on prior art that was, in any prior related PTO proceeding, previously either (a) relied upon to reject any claim, or (b) cited and its relevance to patentability of any claim discussed.

4. Terminate reexaminations in which the *only* remaining rejections are *entirely* based on prior art that was, in any prior related PTO proceeding, previously (a) relied upon to reject any claim, and/or (b) cited and its relevance to patentability of a claim discussed.[11]

---

[9] *See Portola Packaging, Inc.,* 110 F.3d at 790, 42 USPQ2d at 1299 (examiner presumed to have done his job). There may be unusual fact patterns and evidence which suggest that the examiner did not consider the prior art that was discussed in the prior PTO proceeding. These cases should be brought to the attention of the Group Director. For a discussion of the treatment of such cases, see section E above.

[10] If not specified, a reexamination generally includes all claims. However, reexamination may be limited to specific claims. *See* 35 U.S.C. § 304 (authorizing the power to grant reexamination for determination of a "substantial new question of patentability affecting *any claim* of a patent.") (emphasis added). Thus, the Commissioner may order reexamination confined to specific claims. However, reexamination is not necessarily limited to those questions set forth in the reexamination order. *See* 37 C.F.R. § 1.104(a) ("The examination shall be complete with respect both to compliance of the application or patent under reexamination with the applicable statutes and rules and to the patentability of the invention as claimed . . .").

[11] The Commissioner may conduct a search for new art prior to determining whether a substantial new question of patentability exists prior to terminating any ongoing reexamination proceeding. *See* 35 U.S.C. § 303. *See also* 35 U.S.C. § 305 (indicating that "reexamination will be conducted according to the procedures established for initial examination," thereby suggesting that the Commissioner may conduct a search during an ongoing reexamination proceeding).

E. Application of *Portola Packaging* to Unusual Fact Patterns

The PTO recognizes that each case must be decided on its particular facts and that cases with unusual fact patterns will occur. In such a case, the reexamination should be brought to the attention of the Group Director who will then determine the appropriate action to be taken.

Unusual fact patterns may appear in cases in which prior art was relied upon to reject any claim or cited and discussed with respect to the patentability of a claim in a prior related PTO proceeding, but other evidence clearly shows that the examiner did not appreciate the issues raised in the reexamination request or the ongoing reexamination with respect to that art. Such other evidence may appear in the reexamination request, in the nature of the prior art, in the prosecution history of the prior examination, or in an admission by the patent owner, applicant, or inventor.[12]

For example, if a textbook was cited during prosecution of the application which matured into the patent, the record of that examination may show that only select information from the textbook was discussed with respect to the patentability of the claims.[13] If a subsequent reexamination request relied upon other information in the textbook that actually teaches what is required by the claims, it may be appropriate to rely on this other information in the textbook to order and/or conduct reexamination.[14]

Another example involves the situation where an examiner discussed a reference in a prior PTO proceeding, but did not either reject a claim based upon the reference or maintain the rejection based on the mistaken belief that the reference did not qualify as prior art.[15] If the reexamination request were to explain how and why the reference actually does qualify, as prior art, it may be appropriate to rely on the reference to order and/or conduct reexamination.[16]

Another example involves foreign language prior art references. If a foreign language prior art reference was cited and discussed in any prior PTO proceeding, *Portola Packaging* may not prohibit reexamination over a complete and accurate translation of that foreign language prior art reference. Specifically, if a reexamination request were to explain why a more complete and accurate translation of that same foreign language prior art reference actually teaches what is required by the patent claims, it may be appropriate to rely on the foreign language prior art reference to order and/or conduct reexamination.

Another example of an unusual fact pattern involves cumulative references. To the extent that a cumulative reference is repetitive of a prior art reference that was previously applied or discussed, *Portola Packaging* may prohibit reexamination of the patent claims based only on the repetitive reference.[17] However, it is expected that a

---

[12]*See* 37 C.F.R. § 1.104(c)(3).

[13]The file history of the prior PTO proceeding should indicate which portion of the textbook was previously considered. *See* 37 C.F.R. § 1.98(a)(2)(ii) (an information disclosure statement must include a copy of each "publication or that *portion* which caused it to be listed") (emphasis added).

[14]However, a reexamination request that merely provides a new interpretation of a reference already previously relied upon or actually discussed by the PTO does not create a substantial new question of patentability.

[15]For example, the examiner may not have believed that the reference qualified as prior art because: (i) the reference was undated or was believed to have a bad date; (ii) the applicant submitted a declaration believed to be sufficient to antedate the reference under 37 C.F.R. § 1.131; or (iii) the examiner attributed an incorrect filing date to the claimed invention.

[16]For example, the request could: (i) verify the date of the reference; (ii) undermine the sufficiency of the declaration filed under 37 C.F.R. § 1.131; or (iii) explain the correct filing date accorded a claim.

[17]For purposes of reexamination, a cumulative reference that is repetitive is one that substantially reiterates verbatim the teachings of a reference that was either previously relied upon or discussed in a prior PTO proceeding even though the title or the citation of the reference may be different.

repetitive reference which cannot be considered by the PTO during reexamination will be a rare occurrence since most references teach additional information or present information in a different way than other references, even though the references might address the same general subject matter.

F. Notices Regarding Compliance with *Portola Packaging*

1. If a request for reexamination is denied under C.5 above in order to comply with the Federal Circuit's decision in *Portola Packaging,* the notice of reexamination denial should state: "This reexamination request is denied based on *In re Portola Packaging, Inc.*, 110 F.3d 786, 42 USPQ2d 1295 (Fed. Cir. 1997). No patentability determination has been made in this reexamination proceeding."

2. If an ongoing reexamination is terminated under D.4 above in order to comply with the Federal Circuit's decision in *Portola Packaging,* the Notice of Intent to Issue a Reexamination Certificate should state: "This reexamination is terminated based on *In re Portola Packaging, Inc.*, 110 F.3d 786, 42 USPQ2d 1295 (Fed. Cir. 1997). No patentability determination has been made in this reexamination proceeding."

3. If a rejection in the reexamination has previously issued and that rejection is withdrawn under D.3 above in order to comply with the Federal Circuit's decision in *Portola Packaging,* the Office action withdrawing such rejection should state: "The rejection is withdrawn in view of *In re Portola Packaging, Inc.,* 110 F.3d 786, 42 USPQ2d 1295 (Fed. Cir. 1997). No patentability determination of the claims of the patent in view of such prior art has been made in this reexamination proceeding." If multiple rejections have been made, the Office action should clarify which rejections are being withdrawn.

Q. TODD DICKINSON
Acting Assistant Secretary of Commerce and
Acting Commissioner of Patents and Trademarks

Appendix C-27

S. 1948, Intellectual Property and Communications Omnibus Reform Act of 1999, Titles I Through IV*

106th CONGRESS
1st Session

S. 1948

To amend the provisions of title 17, United States Code, and the Communications Act of 1934, relating to copyright licensing and carriage of broadcast signals by satellite.

IN THE SENATE OF THE UNITED STATES

NOVEMBER 17, 1999

Mr. LOTT introduced the following bill; which was read twice and referred to the Committee on the Judiciary

---

A BILL

To amend the provisions of title 17, United States Code, and the Communications Act of 1934, relating to copyright licensing and carriage of broadcast signals by satellite.

Be it enacted by the Senate and House of Representatives of the United States of America in Congress assembled,

---

*Titles V and VI do not relate to patents.

SECTION I. SHORT TITLE; TABLE OF CONTENTS

(a) SHORT TITLE.—This Act may be cited as the "Intellectual Property and Communications Omnibus Reform Act of 1999".

(b) TABLE OF CONTENTS.—The table of contents of this Act is as follows:

* * *

TITLE I—SATELLITE HOME VIEWER IMPROVEMENT

SEC. 1001. SHORT TITLE.

This title may be cited as the "Satellite Home Viewer Improvement Act of 1999".

TITLE IV—INVENTOR PROTECTION

SEC. 4001. SHORT TITLE.

This title may be cited as the "American Inventors Protection Act of 1999".

Subtitle A—Inventors' Rights

SEC. 4101. SHORT TITLE.

This subtitle may be cited as the "Inventors' Rights Act of 1999".

SEC. 4102. INTEGRITY IN INVENTION PROMOTION SERVICES.

(a) IN GENERAL.—Chapter 29 of title 35, United States Code, is amended by adding at the end the following new section:

"§ 297. Improper and deceptive invention promotion

"(a) In General.—An invention promoter shall have a duty to disclose the following information to a customer in writing, prior to entering into a contract for invention promotion services:

"(1) the total number of inventions evaluated by the invention promoter for commercial potential in the past 5 years, as well as the number of those inventions that received positive evaluations, and the number of those inventions that received negative evaluations;

"(2) the total number of customers who have contracted with the invention promoter in the past 5 years, not including customers who have purchased trade show services, research, advertising, or other nonmarketing services from the invention promoter, or who have defaulted in their payment to the invention promoter;

"(3) the total number of customers known by the invention promoter to have received a net financial profit as a direct result of the invention promotion services provided by such invention promoter;

"(4) the total number of customers known by the invention promoter to have received license agreements for their inventions as a direct result of the invention promotion services provided by such invention promoter; and

"(5) the names and addresses of all previous invention promotion companies with which the invention promoter or its officers have collectively or individually been affiliated in the previous 10 years.

"(b) Civil Action.—(1) Any customer who enters into a contract with an invention promoter and who is found by a court to have been injured by any material false or fraudulent statement or representation, or any omission of material fact, by that invention promoter (or any agent, employee, director, officer, partner, or independent contractor of such invention promoter), or by the failure of that invention promoter to disclose such information as required under subsection (a), may recover in a civil action against the invention promoter (or the officers, directors, or partners of such invention promoter), in addition to reasonable costs and attorneys' fees—

"(A) the amount of actual damages incurred by the customer; or

"(B) at the election of the customer at any time before final judgment is rendered, statutory damages in a sum of not more than $5,000, as the court considers just.

"(2) Notwithstanding paragraph (1), in a case where the customer sustains the burden of proof, and the court finds, that the invention promoter intentionally misrepresented or omitted a material fact to such customer, or willfully failed to disclose such information as required under subsection (a), with the purpose of deceiving that customer, the court may increase damages to not more than three times the amount awarded, taking into account past complaints made against the invention promoter that resulted in regulatory sanctions or other corrective actions based on those records compiled by the Commissioner of Patents under subsection (d).

"(c) Definitions.—For purposes of this section—

"(1) a 'contract for invention promotion services' means a contract by which an invention promoter undertakes invention promotion services for a customer;

"(2) a 'customer' is any individual who enters into a contract with an invention promoter for invention promotion services;

"(3) the term 'invention promoter' means any person, firm, partnership, corporation, or other entity who offers to perform or performs invention promotion services for, or on behalf of, a customer, and who holds itself out through advertising in any mass media as providing such services, but does not include—

"(A) any department or agency of the Federal Government or of a State or local government;

"(B) any nonprofit, charitable, scientific, or educational organization, qualified under applicable State law or described under section 170(b)(1)(A) of the Internal Revenue Code of 1986;

"(C) any person or entity involved in the evaluation to determine commercial potential of, or offering to license or sell, a utility patent or a previously filed nonprovisional utility patent application;

"(D) any party participating in a transaction involving the sale of the stock or assets of a business; or

"(E) any party who directly engages in the business of retail sales of products or the distribution of products; and

"(4) the term 'invention promotion services' means the procurement or attempted procurement for a customer of a firm, corporation, or other entity to develop and market products or services that include the invention of the customer.

"(d) RECORDS OF COMPLAINTS.—

"(1) RELEASE OF COMPLAINTS.—The Commissioner of Patents shall make all complaints received by the Patent and Trademark Office involving invention promoters publicly available, together with any response of the invention promoters. The Commissioner of Patents shall notify the invention promoter of a complaint and provide a reasonable opportunity to reply prior to making such complaint publicly available.

"(2) REQUEST FOR COMPLAINTS.—The Commissioner of Patents may request complaints relating to invention promotion services from any Federal or State agency and include such complaints in the records maintained under paragraph (1), together with any response of the invention promoters.".

(b) CONFORMING AMENDMENT.—The table of sections at the beginning of chapter 29 of title 35, United States Code, is amended by adding at the end the following new item:

"297. Improper and deceptive invention promotion.".

SEC. 4103. EFFECTIVE DATE.

This subtitle and the amendments made by this subtitle shall take effect 60 days after the date of the enactment of this Act.

Subtitle B—Patent and Trademark Fee Fairness

SEC. 4201. SHORT TITLE.

This subtitle may be cited as the "Patent and Trademark Fee Fairness Act of 1999".

SEC. 4202. ADJUSTMENT OF PATENT FEES.

(a) ORIGINAL FILING FEE.—Section 41(a)(1)(A) of title 35, United States Code, relating to the fee for filing an original patent application, is amended by striking "$760" and inserting "$690".

(b) REISSUE FEE.—Section 41(a)(4)(A) of title 35, United States Code, relating to the fee for filing for a reissue of a patent, is amended by striking "$760" and inserting "$690".

(c) NATIONAL FEE FOR CERTAIN INTERNATIONAL APPLICATIONS.—Section 41(a)(10) of title 35, United States Code, relating to the national fee for certain international applications, is amended by striking "$760" and inserting "$690".

(d) MAINTENANCE FEES.—Section 41(b)(1) of title 35, United States Code, relating to certain maintenance fees, is amended by striking "$940" and inserting "$830".

SEC. 4203. ADJUSTMENT OF TRADEMARK FEES.

Notwithstanding the second sentence of section 31(a) of the Trademark Act of 1946 (15 U.S.C. 111(a)), the Under Secretary of Commerce for Intellectual Property and Director of the United States Patent and Trademark Office is authorized in fiscal year 2000 to adjust trademark fees without regard to fluctuations in the Consumer Price Index during the preceding 12 months.

SEC. 4204. STUDY ON ALTERNATIVE FEE STRUCTURES.

The Under Secretary of Commerce for Intellectual Property and Director of the United States Patent and Trademark Office shall conduct a study of alternative fee structures that could be adopted by the United States Patent and Trademark Office to encourage maximum participation by the inventor community in the United States. The Director shall submit such study to the Committees on the Judiciary of the House of Representatives and the Senate not later than 1 year after the date of the enactment of this Act.

SEC. 4205. PATENT AND TRADEMARK OFFICE FUNDING.

Section 42(c) of title 35, United States Code, is amended in the second sentence—

(1) by striking "Fees available" and inserting "All fees available"; and

(2) by striking "may" and inserting "shall".

SEC. 4206. EFFECTIVE DATE.

(a) IN GENERAL.—Except as provided in subsection (b), the amendments made by this subtitle shall take effect on the date of the enactment of this Act.

(b) SECTION 4202.—The amendments made by section 4202 of this subtitle shall take effect 30 days after the date of the enactment of this Act.

Subtitle C—First Inventor Defense

SEC. 4301. SHORT TITLE.

This subtitle may be cited as the "First Inventor Defense Act of 1999".

SEC. 4302. DEFENSE TO PATENT INFRINGEMENT BASED ON EARLIER INVENTOR.

(a) DEFENSE.—Chapter 28 of title 35, United States Code, is amended by adding at the end the following new section:

"§ 273. Defense to infringement based on earlier inventor

"(a) DEFINITIONS.—For purposes of this section—

"(1) the terms 'commercially used' and 'commercial use' mean use of a method in the United States, so long as such use is in connection with an internal commercial use or an actual arm's-length sale or other arm's-length commercial transfer of a useful end result, whether or not the subject matter at issue is accessible to or otherwise known to the public, except that the subject matter for which commercial marketing or use is subject to a premarketing regulatory review period during which the safety or efficacy of the subject matter is established, including any period specified in section 156(g), shall be deemed 'commercially used' and in 'commercial use' during such regulatory review period;

"(2) in the case of activities performed by a nonprofit research laboratory, or nonprofit entity such as a university, research center, or hospital, a use for which the public is the intended beneficiary shall be considered to be a use described in paragraph (1), except that the use—

"(A) may be asserted as a defense under this section only for continued use by and in the laboratory or nonprofit entity; and

"(B) may not be asserted as a defense with respect to any subsequent commercialization or use outside such laboratory or nonprofit entity;

"(3) the term 'method' means a method of doing or conducting business; and

"(4) the 'effective filing date' of a patent is the earlier of the actual filing date of the application for the patent or the filing date of any earlier United States, foreign, or international application to which the subject matter at issue is entitled under section 119, 120, or 365 of this title.

"(b) DEFENSE TO INFRINGEMENT.—

"(1) IN GENERAL.—It shall be a defense to an action for infringement under section 271 of this title with respect to any subject matter that would otherwise infringe one or more claims for a method in the patent being asserted against a person, if such person had, acting in good faith, actually reduced the subject matter to practice at least 1 year before the effective filing date of such patent, and commercially used the subject matter before the effective filing date of such patent.

"(2) EXHAUSTION OF RIGHT.—The sale or other disposition of a useful end product produced by a patented method, by a person entitled to assert a defense under this section with respect to that useful end result shall exhaust the patent owner's rights under the patent to the extent such rights would have been exhausted had such sale or other disposition been made by the patent owner.

"(3) LIMITATIONS AND QUALIFICATIONS OF DE FENSE.—The defense to infringement under this section is subject to the following:

"(A) PATENT.—A person may not assert the defense under this section unless the invention for which the defense is asserted is for a method.

"(B) DERIVATION.—A person may not assert the defense under this section if the subject matter on which the defense is based was derived from the patentee or persons in privity with the patentee.

"(C) NOT A GENERAL LICENSE.—The defense asserted by a person under this section is not a general license under all claims of the patent at issue, but extends only to the specific subject matter claimed in the patent with respect to which the person can assert a defense under this chapter, except that the defense shall also extend to variations in the quantity or volume of use of the claimed subject matter, and to improvements in the claimed subject matter that do not infringe additional specifically claimed subject matter of the patent.

"(4) BURDEN OF PROOF.—A person asserting the defense under this section shall have the burden of establishing the defense by clear and convincing evidence.

"(5) ABANDONMENT OF USE.—A person who has abandoned commercial use of subject matter may not rely on activities performed before the date of such abandonment in establishing a defense under this section with respect to actions taken after the date of such abandonment.

"(6) PERSONAL DEFENSE.—The defense under this section may be asserted only by the person who performed the acts necessary to establish the defense and, except for any transfer to the patent owner, the right to assert the defense shall not be licensed or assigned or transferred to another person except as an ancillary and subordinate part of a good faith assignment or transfer for other reasons of the entire enterprise or line of business to which the defense relates.

"(7) LIMITATION ON SITES.—A defense under this section, when acquired as part of a good faith assignment or transfer of an entire enterprise or line of business to which the defense relates, may only be asserted for uses at sites where the subject matter that would otherwise infringe one or more of the claims is in use before the later of the effective filing date of the patent or the date of the assignment or transfer of such enterprise or line of business.

"(8) UNSUCCESSFUL ASSERTION OF DEFENSE.—If the defense under this section is pleaded by a person who is found to infringe the patent and who subsequently fails to demonstrate a reasonable basis for asserting the defense, the court shall find the case exceptional for the purpose of awarding attorney fees under section 285 of this title.

"(9) INVALIDITY.—A patent shall not be deemed to be invalid under section 102 or 103 of this title solely because a defense is raised or established under this section.".

(b) CONFORMING AMENDMENT.—The table of sections at the beginning of chapter 28 of title 35, United States Code, is amended by adding at the end the following new item:

"273. Defense to infringement based on earlier inventor.".

SEC. 4303. EFFECTIVE DATE AND APPLICABILITY.

This subtitle and the amendments made by this subtitle shall take effect on the date of the enactment of this Act, but shall not apply to any action for infringement that is pending on such date of enactment or with respect to any subject matter for which an adjudication of infringement, including a consent judgment, has been made before such date of enactment.

Subtitle D—Patent Term Guarantee

SEC. 4401. SHORT TITLE.

This subtitle may be cited as the "Patent Term Guarantee Act of 1999".

SEC. 4402. PATENT TERM GUARANTEE AUTHORITY.

(a) ADJUSTMENT OF PATENT TERM.—Section 154(b) of title 35, United States Code, is amended to read as follows:

"(b) ADJUSTMENT OF PATENT TERM.—

"(1) PATENT TERM GUARANTEES.—

"(A) GUARANTEE OF PROMPT PATENT AND TRADEMARK OFFICE RESPONSES.—Subject to the limitations under paragraph (2), if the issue of an original patent is delayed due to the failure of the Patent and Trademark Office to—

"(i) provide at least one of the notifications under section 132 of this title or a notice of allowance under section 151 of this title not later than 14 months after—

"(I) the date on which an application was filed under section 111(a) of this title; or

"(II) the date on which an international application fulfilled the requirements of section 371 of this title;

"(ii) respond to a reply under section 132, or to an appeal taken under section 134, within 4 months after the date on which the reply was filed or the appeal was taken;

"(iii) act on an application within 4 months after the date of a decision by the Board of Patent Appeals and Interferences under section 134 or 135 or a decision by a Federal court under section 141, 145, or 146 in a case in which allowable claims remain in the application; or

"(iv) issue a patent within 4 months after the date on which the issue fee was paid under section 151 and all outstanding requirements were satisfied,

the term of the patent shall be extended 1 day for each day after the end of the period specified in clause (i), (ii), (iii), or (iv), as the case may be, until the action described in such clause is taken.

"(B) GUARANTEE OF NO MORE THAN 3-YEAR APPLICATION PENDENCY.—Subject to the limitations under paragraph (2), if the issue of an original patent is delayed due to the failure of the United States Patent and Trademark Office to issue a patent within 3 years after the actual filing date of the application in the United States, not including—

"(i) any time consumed by continued examination of the application requested by the applicant under section 132(b);

"(ii) any time consumed by a proceeding under section 135(a), any time consumed by the imposition of an order under section 181, or any time consumed by appellate review by the Board of Patent Appeals and Interferences or by a Federal court; or

"(iii) any delay in the processing of the application by the United States Patent and Trademark Office requested by the applicant except as permitted by paragraph (3)(C), the term of the patent shall be extended 1 day for each day after the end of that 3-year period until the patent is issued.

"(C) GUARANTEE OR ADJUSTMENTS FOR DELAYS DUE TO INTERFERENCES, SECRECY ORDERS, AND APPEALS.—Subject to the limitations under paragraph (2), if the issue of an original patent is delayed due to—

"(i) a proceeding under section 135(a);

"(ii) the imposition of an order under section 181; or

"(iii) appellate review by the Board of Patent Appeals and Interferences or by a Federal court in a case in which the patent was issued under a decision in the review reversing an adverse determination of patentability,

the term of the patent shall be extended 1 day for each day of the pendency of the proceeding, order, or review, as the case may be.

"(2) LIMITATIONS.—

"(A) IN GENERAL.—To the extent that periods of delay attributable to grounds specified in paragraph (1) overlap, the period of any adjustment granted under this subsection shall not exceed the actual number of days the issuance of the patent was delayed.

"(B) DISCLAIMED TERM.—No patent the term of which has been disclaimed beyond a specified date may be adjusted under this section beyond the expiration date specified in the disclaimer.

"(C) REDUCTION OF PERIOD OF ADJUSTMENT.—

"(i) The period of adjustment of the term of a patent under paragraph (1) shall be reduced by a period equal to the period of time during which the applicant failed to engage in reasonable efforts to conclude prosecution of the application.

"(ii) With respect to adjustments to patent term made under the authority of paragraph (1)(B), an applicant shall be deemed to have failed to engage in reasonable efforts to conclude processing or examination of an application for the cumulative total of any periods of time in excess of 3 months that are taken to respond to a notice from the Office making any rejection, objection, argument, or other request, measuring such 3-month period from the date the notice was given or mailed to the applicant.

"(iii) The Director shall prescribe regulations establishing the circumstances that constitute a failure of an applicant to engage in reasonable efforts to conclude processing or examination of an application.

"(3) PROCEDURES FOR PATENT TERM ADJUSTMENT DETERMINATION.—

"(A) The Director shall prescribe regulations establishing procedures for the application for and determination of patent term adjustments under this subsection.

"(B) Under the procedures established under subparagraph (A), the Director shall—

"(i) make a determination of the period of any patent term adjustment under this subsection, and shall transmit a notice of that determination with the written notice of allowance of the application under section 151; and

"(ii) provide the applicant one opportunity to request reconsideration of any patent term adjustment determination made by the Director.

"(C) The Director shall reinstate all or part of the cumulative period of time of an adjustment under paragraph (2)(C) if the applicant, prior to the issuance of the patent, makes a showing that, in spite of all due care, the applicant was unable to respond within the 3-month period, but in no case shall more than three additional months for each such response beyond the original 3-month period be reinstated.

"(D) The Director shall proceed to grant the patent after completion of the Director's determination of a patent term adjustment under the procedures established under this subsection, notwithstanding any appeal taken by the applicant of such determination.

"(4) APPEAL OF PATENT TERM ADJUSTMENT DETERMINATION.—

"(A) An applicant dissatisfied with a determination made by the Director under paragraph (3) shall have remedy by a civil action against the Director filed in the United States District Court for the District of Columbia within 180 days after the grant of the patent. Chapter 7 of title 5, United States Code, shall apply to such action. Any final judgment resulting in a change to the period of adjustment of the patent term shall be served on the Director, and the Director shall thereafter alter the term of the patent to reflect such change.

"(B) The determination of a patent term adjustment under this subsection shall not be subject to appeal or challenge by a third party prior to the grant of the patent.".

(b) CONFORMING AMENDMENTS.—

(1) Section 282 of title 35, United States Code, is amended in the fourth paragraph by striking "156 of this title" and inserting "154(b) or 156 of this title".

(2) Section 1295(a)(4)(C) of title 28, United States Code, is amended by striking "145 or 146" and inserting "145, 146, or 154(b)".

SEC. 4403. CONTINUED EXAMINATION OF PATENT APPLICATIONS.

Section 132 of title 35, United States Code, is amended—

(1) in the first sentence by striking "Whenever" and inserting "(a) Whenever"; and

(2) by adding at the end the following:

"(b) The Director shall prescribe regulations to provide for the continued examination of applications for patent at the request of the applicant. The Director may establish appropriate fees for such continued examination and shall provide a 50 percent reduction in such fees for small entities that qualify for reduced fees under section 41(h)(1) of this title.".

SEC. 4404. TECHNICAL CLARIFICATION.

Section 156(a) of title 35, United States Code, is amended in the matter preceding paragraph (1) by inserting ", which shall include any patent term adjustment granted under section 154(b)," after "the original expiration date of the patent".

SEC. 4405. EFFECTIVE DATE.

(a) AMENDMENTS MADE BY SECTIONS 4402 AND 4404.—The amendments made by sections 4402 and 4404 shall take effect on the date that is 6 months after the date of the enactment of this Act and, except for a design patent application filed under chapter 16 of title 35, United States Code, shall apply to any application filed on or after the date that is 6 months after the date of the enactment of this Act.

(b) AMENDMENTS MADE BY SECTION 4403.—The amendments made by section 4403—

(1) shall take effect on the date that is 6 months after the date of the enactment of this Act, and shall apply to all applications filed under section 111(a) of title 35, United States Code, on or after June 8, 1995, and all applications complying with section 371 of title 35, United States Code, that resulted from international applications filed on or after June 8, 1995; and

(2) do not apply to applications for design patents under chapter 16 of title 35, United States Code.

Subtitle E—Domestic Publication of Patent Applications Published Abroad

SEC. 4501. SHORT TITLE.

This subtitle may be cited as the "Domestic Publication of Foreign Filed Patent Applications Act of 1999".

SEC. 4502. PUBLICATION.

(a) PUBLICATION.—Section 122 of title 35, United States Code, is amended to read as follows:

"§ 122. Confidential status of applications; publication of patent applications

"(a) CONFIDENTIALITY.—Except as provided in subsection (b), applications for patents shall be kept in confidence by the Patent and Trademark Office and no information concerning the same given without authority of the applicant or owner unless necessary to carry out the provisions of an Act of Congress or in such special circumstances as may be determined by the Director.

"(b) PUBLICATION.—

"(1) IN GENERAL.—(A) Subject to paragraph (2), each application for a patent shall be published, in accordance with procedures determined by the Director, promptly after the expiration of a period of 18 months from the earliest filing date for which a benefit is sought under this title. At the request of the applicant, an application may be published earlier than the end of such 18-month period.

"(B) No information concerning published patent applications shall be made available to the public except as the Director determines.

"(C) Notwithstanding any other provision of law, a determination by the Director to release or not to release information concerning a published patent application shall be final and nonreviewable.

"(2) EXCEPTIONS.—(A) An application shall not be published if that application is—

"(i) no longer pending;

"(ii) subject to a secrecy order under section 181 of this title;

"(iii) a provisional application filed under section 111(b) of this title; or

"(iv) an application for a design patent filed under chapter 16 of this title.

"(B)(i) If an applicant makes a request upon filing, certifying that the invention disclosed in the application has not and will not be the subject of an application filed in another country, or under a multilateral international agreement, that requires publication of applications 18 months after filing, the application shall not be published as provided in paragraph (1).

"(ii) An applicant may rescind a request made under clause (i) at any time.

"(iii) An applicant who has made a request under clause (i) but who subsequently files, in a foreign country or under a multilateral international agreement specified in clause (i), an application directed to the invention disclosed in the application filed in the Patent and Trademark Office, shall notify the Director of such filing not later than 45 days after the date of the filing of such foreign or international application. A failure of the applicant to provide such notice within the prescribed period shall result in the application being regarded as abandoned, unless it is shown to the satisfaction of the Director that the delay in submitting the notice was unintentional.

"(iv) If an applicant rescinds a request made under clause (i) or notifies the Director that an application was filed in a foreign country or under a multilateral international agreement specified in clause (i), the application shall be published in accordance with the provisions of paragraph (1) on or as soon as is practical after the date that is specified in clause (i).

"(v) If an applicant has filed applications in one or more foreign countries, directly or through a multilateral international agreement, and such foreign filed applications corresponding to an application filed in the Patent and Trademark Office or the description of the invention in such foreign filed applications is less extensive than the application or description of the invention in the application filed in the Patent and Trademark Office, the applicant may submit a redacted copy of the application filed in the Patent and Trademark Office eliminating any part or description of the invention in such application that is not also contained in any of the corresponding applications filed in a foreign country. The Director may only publish the redacted copy of the application unless the redacted copy of the application is not received within 16 months after the earliest effective filing date for which a benefit is sought under this title. The provisions of section 154(d) shall not apply to a claim if the description of the invention published in the redacted application filed under this clause with respect to the claim does not enable a person skilled in the art to make and use the subject matter of the claim.

"(c) PROTEST AND PRE-ISSUANCE OPPOSITION.—The Director shall establish appropriate procedures to ensure that no protest or other form of pre-issuance opposition to the grant of a patent on an application may be initiated after publication of the application without the express written consent of the applicant.

"(d) NATIONAL SECURITY.—No application for patent shall be published under subsection (b)(1) if the publication or disclosure of such invention would be detrimental to the national security. The Director shall establish appropriate procedures to ensure that such applications are promptly identified and the secrecy of such inventions is maintained in accordance with chapter 17 of this title.".

(b) STUDY.—

(1) IN GENERAL.—The Comptroller General shall conduct a 3-year study of the applicants who file only in the United States on or after the effective date of this subtitle and shall provide the results of such study to the Judiciary Committees of the House of Representatives and the Senate.

(2) CONTENTS.—The study conducted under paragraph (1) shall—

(A) consider the number of such applicants in relation to the number of applicants who file in the United States and outside of the United States;

(B) examine how many domestic-only filers request at the time of filing not to be published;

(C) examine how many such filers rescind that request or later choose to file abroad;

(D) examine the status of the entity seeking an application and any correlation that may exist between such status and the publication of patent applications; and

(E) examine the abandonment/issuance ratios and length of application pendency before patent issuance or abandonment for published versus unpublished applications.

SEC. 4503. TIME FOR CLAIMING BENEFIT OF EARLIER FILING DATE.

(a) IN A FOREIGN COUNTRY.—Section 119(b) of title 35, United States Code, is amended to read as follows:

"(b)(1) No application for patent shall be entitled to this right of priority unless a claim is filed in the Patent and Trademark Office, identifying the foreign application by specifying the application number on that foreign application, the intellectual property authority or country in or for which the application was filed, and the date of filing the application, at such time during the pendency of the application as required by the Director.

"(2) The Director may consider the failure of the applicant to file a timely claim for priority as a waiver of any such claim. The Director may establish procedures, including the payment of a surcharge, to accept an unintentionally delayed claim under this section.

"(3) The Director may require a certified copy of the original foreign application, specification, and drawings upon which it is based, a translation if not in the English language, and such other information as the Director considers necessary. Any such certification shall be made by the foreign intellectual property authority in which the foreign application was filed and show the date of the application and of the filing of the specification and other papers.".

(b) IN THE UNITED STATES.—

(1) IN GENERAL.—Section 120 of title 35, United States Code, is amended by adding at the end the following: "No application shall be entitled to the benefit of an earlier filed application under this section unless an amendment containing the specific reference to the earlier filed application is submitted at such time during the pendency of the application as required by the Director. The Director may consider the failure to submit such an amendment within that time period as a waiver of any benefit under this section. The Director may establish procedures, including the payment of a surcharge, to accept an unintentionally delayed submission of an amendment under this section.".

(2) RIGHT OF PRIORITY.—Section 119(e)(1) of title 35, United States Code, is amended by adding at the end the following: "No application shall be entitled to the benefit of an earlier filed provisional application under this subsection unless an amendment containing the specific reference to the earlier filed provisional application is submitted at such time during the pendency of the application as required by the Director. The Director may consider the failure to submit such an amendment within that time period as a waiver of any benefit under this subsection. The Director may establish procedures, including the payment of a surcharge, to accept an unintentionally delayed submission of an amendment under this subsection during the pendency of the application.".

SEC. 4504. PROVISIONAL RIGHTS.

Section 154 of title 35, United States Code, is amended—

(1) in the section caption by inserting "**; provisional rights**" after "**patent**"; and

(2) by adding at the end the following new subsection:

"(d) PROVISIONAL RIGHTS.—

"(1) IN GENERAL.—In addition to other rights provided by this section, a patent shall include the right to obtain a reasonable royalty from any person who, during the period beginning on the date of publication of the application for such patent under section 122(b), or in the case of an international application filed under the treaty defined in section 351(a) designating the United States under Article 21(2)(a) of such treaty, the date of publication of the application, and ending on the date the patent is issued—

"(A)(i) makes, uses, offers for sale, or sells in the United States the invention as claimed in the published patent application or imports such an invention into the United States; or

"(ii) if the invention as claimed in the published patent application is a process, uses, offers for sale, or sells in the United States or imports into the United States products made by that process as claimed in the published patent application; and

"(B) had actual notice of the published patent application and, in a case in which the right arising under this paragraph is based upon an international application designating the United States that is published in a language other than English, had a translation of the international application into the English language.

"(2) RIGHT BASED ON SUBSTANTIALLY IDENTICAL INVENTIONS.—The right under paragraph (1) to obtain a reasonable royalty shall not be available under this subsection unless the invention as claimed in the patent is substantially identical to the invention as claimed in the published patent application.

"(3) TIME LIMITATION ON OBTAINING A REASONABLE ROYALTY.—The right under paragraph (1) to obtain a reasonable royalty shall be available only in an action brought not later than 6 years after the patent is issued. The right under paragraph (1) to obtain a reasonable royalty shall not be affected by the duration of the period described in paragraph (1).

"(4) REQUIREMENTS FOR INTERNATIONAL APPLICATIONS.—

"(A) EFFECTIVE DATE.—The right under paragraph (1) to obtain a reasonable royalty based upon the publication under the treaty defined in section 351(a) of an international application designating the United States shall commence on the date on which the Patent and Trademark Office receives a copy of the publication under the treaty of the international application, or, if the publication under the treaty of the international application is in a language other than English, on the date on which the Patent and Trademark Office receives a translation of the international application in the English language.

"(B) COPIES.—The Director may require the applicant to provide a copy of the international application and a translation thereof.".

SEC. 4505. PRIOR ART EFFECT OF PUBLISHED APPLICATIONS.

Section 102(e) of title 35, United States Code, is amended to read as follows:

"(e) The invention was described in—

"(1) an application for patent, published under section 122(b), by another filed in the United States before the invention by the applicant for patent, except that an international application filed under the treaty defined in section 351(a) shall have the effect under this subsection of a national application published under section 122(b) only if the international application designating the United States was published under Article 21(2)(a) of such treaty in the English language; or

"(2) a patent granted on an application for patent by another filed in the United States before the invention by the applicant for patent, except that a patent shall not be deemed filed in the United States for the purposes of this subsection based on the filing of an international application filed under the treaty defined in section 351(a); or".

SEC. 4506. COST RECOVERY FOR PUBLICATION.

The Under Secretary of Commerce for Intellectual Property and Director of the United States Patent and Trademark Office shall recover the cost of early publication required by the amendment made by section 4502 by charging a separate publication fee after notice of allowance is given under section 151 of title 35, United States Code.

SEC. 4507. CONFORMING AMENDMENTS.

The following provisions of title 35, United States Code, are amended:

(1) Section 11 is amended in paragraph 1 of subsection (a) by inserting "and published applications for patents" after "Patents".

(2) Section 12 is amended—

(A) in the section caption by inserting "**and applications**" after "**patents**"; and

(B) by inserting "and published applications for patents" after "patents".

(3) Section 13 is amended—

(A) in the section caption by inserting "**and applications**" after "**patents**"; and

(B) by inserting "and published applications for patents" after "patents".

(4) The items relating to sections 12 and 13 in the table of sections for chapter 1 are each amended by inserting "and applications" after "patents".

(5) The item relating to section 122 in the table of sections for chapter 11 is amended by inserting "; publication of patent applications" after "applications".

(6) The item relating to section 154 in the table of sections for chapter 14 is amended by inserting "; provisional rights" after "patent".

(7) Section 181 is amended—

(A) in the first undesignated paragraph—

(i) by inserting "by the publication of an application or" after "disclosure"; and

(ii) by inserting "the publication of the application or" after "withhold";

(B) in the second undesignated paragraph by inserting "by the publication of an application or" after "disclosure of an invention";

(C) in the third undesignated paragraph—

(i) by inserting "by the publication of the application or" after "disclosure of the invention"; and

(ii) by inserting "the publication of the application or" after "withhold"; and

(D) in the fourth undesignated paragraph by inserting "the publication of an application or" after "and" in the first sentence.

(8) Section 252 is amended in the first undesignated paragraph by inserting "substantially" before "identical" each place it appears.

(9) Section 284 is amended by adding at the end of the second undesignated paragraph the following: "Increased damages under this paragraph shall not apply to provisional rights under section 154(d) of this title.".

(10) Section 374 is amended to read as follows:

"§ 374. Publication of international application

"The publication under the treaty defined in section 351(a) of this title, of an international application designating the United States shall confer the same rights and shall have the same effect under this title as an application for patent published under section 122(b), except as provided in sections 102(e) and 154(d) of this title.".

(11) Section 135(b) is amended—

(A) by inserting "(1)" after "(b)"; and

(B) by adding at the end the following:

"(2) A claim which is the same as, or for the same or substantially the same subject matter as, a claim of an application published under section 122(b) of this title may be made in an application filed after the application is published only if the claim is made before 1 year after the date on which the application is published.".

SEC. 4508. EFFECTIVE DATE.

Sections 4502 through 4507, and the amendments made by such sections, shall take effect on the date that is 1 year after the date of the enactment of this Act and shall apply to all applications filed under section 111 of title 35, United States Code, on or after that date, and all applications complying with section 371 of title 35, United States Code, that resulted from international applications filed on or after that date. The amendments made by sections 4504 and 4505 shall apply to any such application voluntarily published by the applicant under procedures established under this subtitle that is pending on the date that is 1 year after the date of the enactment of this Act. The amendment made by section 4504 shall also apply to international applications designating the United States that are filed on or after the date that is 1 year after the date of the enactment of this Act.

Subtitle F—Optional Inter Partes Reexamination Procedure

SEC. 4601. SHORT TITLE.

This subtitle may be cited as the "Optional Inter Partes Reexamination Procedure Act of 1999".

SEC. 4602. EX PARTE REEXAMINATION OF PATENTS.

The chapter heading for chapter 30 of title 35, United States Code, is amended by inserting "**EX PARTE**" before "**REEXAMINATION OF PATENTS**".

SEC. 4603. DEFINITIONS.

Section 100 of title 35, United States Code, is amended by adding at the end the following new subsection:

"(e) The term 'third-party requester' means a person requesting ex parte reexamination under section 302 or inter partes reexamination under section 311 who is not the patent owner.".

SEC. 4604. OPTIONAL INTER PARTES REEXAMINATION PROCEDURES.

(a) IN GENERAL.—Part 3 of title 35, United States Code, is amended by adding after chapter 30 the following new chapter:

"CHAPTER 31—OPTIONAL INTER PARTES REEXAMINATION PROCEDURES

"§ 311. Request for inter partes reexamination

"(a) IN GENERAL.—Any person at any time may file a request for inter partes reexamination by the Office of a patent on the basis of any prior art cited under the provisions of section 301.

"(b) REQUIREMENTS.—The request shall—

"(1) be in writing, include the identity of the real party in interest, and be accompanied by payment of an inter partes reexamination fee established by the Director under section 41; and

"(2) set forth the pertinency and manner of applying cited prior art to every claim for which reexamination is requested.

"(c) COPY.—Unless the requesting person is the owner of the patent, the Director promptly shall send a copy of the request to the owner of record of the patent.

"§ 312. Determination of issue by Director

"(a) REEXAMINATION.—Not later than 3 months after the filing of a request for inter partes reexamination under section 311, the Director shall determine whether a substantial new question of patentability affecting any claim of the patent concerned is raised by the request, with or without consideration of other patents or printed publications. On the Director's initiative, and at any time, the Director may determine whether a substantial new question of patentability is raised by patents and publications.

"(b) RECORD.—A record of the Director's determination under subsection (a) shall be placed in the official file of the patent, and a copy shall be promptly given or mailed to the owner of record of the patent and to the third-party requester, if any.

"(c) FINAL DECISION.—A determination by the Director under subsection (a) shall be final and non-appealable. Upon a determination that no substantial new question of patentability has been raised, the Director may refund a portion of the inter partes reexamination fee required under section 311.

"§ 313. Inter partes reexamination order by Director

"If, in a determination made under section 312(a), the Director finds that a substantial new question of patentability affecting a claim of a patent is raised, the determination shall include an order for inter partes reexamination of the patent for resolution of the question. The order may be accompanied by the initial action of the Patent and Trademark Office on the merits of the inter partes reexamination conducted in accordance with section 314.

"§ 314. Conduct of inter partes reexamination proceedings

"(a) In General.—Except as otherwise provided in this section, reexamination shall be conducted according to the procedures established for initial examination under the provisions of sections 132 and 133. In any inter partes reexamination proceeding under this chapter, the patent owner shall be permitted to propose any amendment to the patent and a new claim or claims, except that no proposed amended or new claim enlarging the scope of the claims of the patent shall be permitted.

"(b) Response.—(1) This subsection shall apply to any inter partes reexamination proceeding in which the order for inter partes reexamination is based upon a request by a third-party requester.

"(2) With the exception of the inter partes reexamination request, any document filed by either the patent owner or the third-party requester shall be served on the other party. In addition, the third-party requester shall receive a copy of any communication sent by the Office to the patent owner concerning the patent subject to the inter partes reexamination proceeding.

"(3) Each time that the patent owner files a response to an action on the merits from the Patent and Trademark Office, the third-party requester shall have one opportunity to file written comments addressing issues raised by the action of the Office or the patent owner's response thereto, if those written comments are received by the Office within 30 days after the date of service of the patent owner's response.

"(c) Special Dispatch.—Unless otherwise provided by the Director for good cause, all inter partes reexamination proceedings under this section, including any appeal to the Board of Patent Appeals and Interferences, shall be conducted with special dispatch within the Office.

"§ 315. Appeal

"(a) Patent Owner.—The patent owner involved in an inter partes reexamination proceeding under this chapter—

"(1) may appeal under the provisions of section 134 and may appeal under the provisions of sections 141 through 144, with respect to any decision adverse to the patentability of any original or proposed amended or new claim of the patent; and

"(2) may be a party to any appeal taken by a third-party requester under subsection (b).

"(b) Third-Party Requester.—A third-party requester may—

"(1) appeal under the provisions of section 134 with respect to any final decision favorable to the patentability of any original or proposed amended or new claim of the patent; or

"(2) be a party to any appeal taken by the patent owner under the provisions of section 134, subject to subsection (c).

"(c) Civil Action.—A third-party requester whose request for an inter partes reexamination results in an order under section 313 is estopped from asserting at a later time, in any civil action arising in whole or in part under section 1338 of title 28, United States Code, the invalidity of any claim finally determined to be valid and patentable on any ground which the third-party requester raised or could have raised during the inter partes reexamination proceedings. This subsection does not prevent the assertion of invalidity based on newly discovered prior art unavailable to the third-party requester and the Patent and Trademark Office at the time of the inter partes reexamination proceedings.

"§316. Certificate of patentability, unpatentability, and claim cancellation

"(a) In General.—In an inter partes reexamination proceeding under this chapter, when the time for appeal has expired or any appeal proceeding has terminated, the Director shall issue and publish a certificate canceling any claim of the patent finally determined to be unpatentable, confirming any claim of the patent determined to be patentable, and incorporating in the patent any proposed amended or new claim determined to be patentable.

"(b) AMENDED OR NEW CLAIM.—Any proposed amended or new claim determined to be patentable and incorporated into a patent following an inter partes reexamination proceeding shall have the same effect as that specified in section 252 of this title for reissued patents on the right of any person who made, purchased, or used within the United States, or imported into the United States, anything patented by such proposed amended or new claim, or who made substantial preparation therefor, prior to issuance of a certificate under the provisions of subsection (a) of this section.

"§ 317. Inter partes reexamination prohibited

"(a) ORDER FOR REEXAMINATION.—Notwithstanding any provision of this chapter, once an order for inter partes reexamination of a patent has been issued under section 313, neither the patent owner nor the third-party requester, if any, nor privies of either, may file a subsequent request for inter partes reexamination of the patent until an inter partes reexamination certificate is issued and published under section 316, unless authorized by the Director.

"(b) FINAL DECISION.—Once a final decision has been entered against a party in a civil action arising in whole or in part under section 1338 of title 28, United States Code, that the party has not sustained its burden of proving the invalidity of any patent claim in suit or if a final decision in an inter partes reexamination proceeding instituted by a third-party requester is favorable to the patentability of any original or proposed amended or new claim of the patent, then neither that party nor its privies may thereafter request an inter partes reexamination of any such patent claim on the basis of issues which that party or its privies raised or could have raised in such civil action or inter partes reexamination proceeding, and an inter partes reexamination requested by that party or its privies on the basis of such issues may not thereafter be maintained by the Office, notwithstanding any other provision of this chapter. This subsection does not prevent the assertion of invalidity based on newly discovered prior art unavailable to the third-party requester and the Patent and Trademark Office at the time of the inter partes reexamination proceedings.

"§ 318. Stay of litigation

"Once an order for inter partes reexamination of a patent has been issued under section 313, the patent owner may obtain a stay of any pending litigation which involves an issue of patentability of any claims of the patent which are the subject of the inter partes reexamination order, unless the court before which such litigation is pending determines that a stay would not serve the interests of justice.".

(b) CONFORMING AMENDMENT.—The table of chapters for part III of title 25, United States Code, is amended by striking the item relating to chapter 30 and inserting the following:

"30. Prior Art Citations to Office and Ex Parte Reexamination of Patents .... **301.**
"31. Optional Inter Partes Reexamination of Patents .... **311".**

SEC. 4605. CONFORMING AMENDMENTS.

(a) PATENT FEES; PATENT SEARCH SYSTEMS.—Section 41(a)(7) of title 35, United States Code, is amended to read as follows:

"(7) On filing each petition for the revival of an unintentionally abandoned application for a patent, for the unintentionally delayed payment of the fee for issuing each patent, or for an unintentionally delayed response by the patent owner in any reexamination proceeding, $1,210, unless the petition is filed under section 133 or 151 of this title, in which case the fee shall be $110.".

(b) APPEAL TO THE BOARD OF PATENTS APPEALS AND INTERFERENCES.—Section 134 of title 35, United States Code, is amended to read as follows:

"§ 134. Appeal to the Board of Patent Appeals and Interferences

"(a) PATENT APPLICANT.—An applicant for a patent, any of whose claims has been twice rejected, may appeal from the decision of the administrative patent judge to the Board of Patent Appeals and Interferences, having once paid the fee for such appeal.

"(b) PATENT OWNER.—A patent owner in any reexamination proceeding may appeal from the final rejection of any claim by the administrative patent judge to the Board of Patent Appeals and Interferences, having once paid the fee for such appeal.

"(c) THIRD-PARTY.—A third-party requester in an inter partes proceeding may appeal to the Board of Patent Appeals and Interferences from the final decision of the administrative patent judge favorable to the patentability of any original or proposed amended or new claim of a patent, having once paid the fee for such appeal. The third-party requester may not appeal the decision of the Board of Patent Appeals and Interferences.".

(c) APPEAL TO COURT OF APPEALS FOR THE FEDERAL CIRCUIT.—Section 141 of title 35, United States Code, is amended by adding the following after the second sentence: "A patent owner in any reexamination proceeding dissatisfied with the final decision in an appeal to the Board of Patent Appeals and Interferences under section 134 may appeal the decision only to the United States Court of Appeals for the Federal Circuit.".

(d) PROCEEDINGS ON APPEAL.—Section 143 of title 35, United States Code, is amended by amending the third sentence to read as follows: "In any reexamination case, the Director shall submit to the court in writing the grounds for the decision of the Patent and Trademark Office, addressing all the issues involved in the appeal.".

(e) CIVIL ACTION TO OBTAIN PATENT.—Section 145 of title 35, United States Code, is amended in the first sentence by inserting "(a)" after "section 134".

SEC. 4606. REPORT TO CONGRESS.

Not later than 5 years after the date of the enactment of this Act, the Under Secretary of Commerce for Intellectual Property and Director of the United States Patent and Trademark Office shall submit to the Congress a report evaluating whether the inter partes reexamination proceedings established under the amendments made by this subtitle are inequitable to any of the parties in interest and, if so, the report shall contain recommendations for changes to the amendments made by this subtitle to remove such inequity.

SEC. 4607. ESTOPPEL EFFECT OF REEXAMINATION.

Any party who requests an inter partes reexamination under section 311 of title 35, United States Code, is estopped from challenging at a later time, in any civil action, any fact determined during the process of such reexamination, except with respect to a fact determination later proved to be erroneous based on information unavailable at the time of the inter partes reexamination decision. If this section is held to be unenforceable, the enforceability of the remainder of this subtitle or of this title shall not be denied as a result.

SEC. 4608. EFFECTIVE DATE.

(a) IN GENERAL.—Subject to subsection (b), this subtitle and the amendments made by this subtitle shall take effect on the date of the enactment of this Act and shall apply to any patent that issues from an original application filed in the United States on or after that date.

(b) SECTION 4605(a).—The amendments made by section 4605(a) shall take effect on the date that is 1 year after the date of the enactment of this Act.

[Note: Subtitle G, Patent and Trademark Office, has little to do with patent prosecution and has been omitted.]

Subtitle H—Miscellaneous Patent Provisions

SEC. 4801. PROVISIONAL APPLICATIONS.

(a) ABANDONMENT.—Section 111(b)(5) of title 35, United States Code, is amended to read as follows:

"(5) ABANDONMENT.—Notwithstanding the absence of a claim, upon timely request and as prescribed by the Director, a provisional application may be treated as an application filed under subsection (a). Subject to section 119(e)(3) of this title, if no such request is made, the provisional application shall be regarded as abandoned 12 months after the filing date of such application and shall not be subject to revival after such 12-month period.".

(b) TECHNICAL AMENDMENT RELATING TO WEEKENDS AND HOLIDAYS.—Section 119(e) of title 35, United States Code, is amended by adding at the end the following:

"(3) If the day that is 12 months after the filing date of a provisional application falls on a Saturday, Sunday, or Federal holiday within the District of Columbia, the period of pendency of the provisional application shall be extended to the next succeeding secular or business day.".

(c) ELIMINATION OF COPENDENCY REQUIREMENT.—Section 119(e)(2) of title 35, United States Code, is amended by striking "and the provisional application was pending on the filing date of the application for patent under section 111(a) or section 363 of this title".

(d) EFFECTIVE DATE.—The amendments made by this section shall take effect on the date of the enactment of this Act and shall apply to any provisional application filed on or after June 8, 1995, except that the amendments made by subsections (b) and (c) shall have no effect with respect to any patent which is the subject of litigation in an action commenced before such date of enactment.

SEC. 4802. INTERNATIONAL APPLICATIONS.

Section 119 of title 35, United States Code, is amended as follows:

(1) In subsection (a), insert "or in a WTO member country," after "or citizens of the United States,".

(2) At the end of section 119 add the following new subsections:

"(f) Applications for plant breeder's rights filed in a WTO member country (or in a foreign UPOV Contracting Party) shall have the same effect for the purpose of the right of priority under subsections (a) through (c) of this section as applications for patents, subject to the same conditions and requirements of this section as apply to applications for patents.

"(g) As used in this section—

"(1) the term 'WTO member country' has the same meaning as the term is defined in section 104(b)(2) of this title; and

"(2) the term 'UPOV Contracting Party' means a member of the International Convention for the Protection of New Varieties of Plants.".

SEC. 4803. CERTAIN LIMITATIONS ON DAMAGES FOR PATENT INFRINGEMENT NOT APPLICABLE.

Section 287(c)(4) of title 35, United States Code, is amended by striking "before the date of enactment of this subsection" and inserting "based on an application the earliest effective filing date of which is prior to September 30, 1996".

SEC. 4804. ELECTRONIC FILING AND PUBLICATIONS.

(a) PRINTING OF PAPERS FILED.—Section 22 of title 35, United States Code, is amended by striking "printed or typewritten" and inserting "printed, typewritten, or on an electronic medium".

(b) PUBLICATIONS.—Section 11(a) of title 35, United States Code, is amended by amending the matter preceding paragraph 1 to read as follows:

"(a) The Director may publish in printed, type-written, or electronic form, the following:".

(c) COPIES OF PATENTS FOR PUBLIC LIBRARIES.— Section 13 of title 35, United States Code, is amended by striking "printed copies of specifications and drawings of patents" and inserting "copies of specifications and drawings of patents in printed or electronic form".

(d) MAINTENANCE OF COLLECTIONS.—

(1) ELECTRONIC COLLECTIONS.—Section 41(i)(1) of title 35, United States Code, is amended by striking "paper or microform" and inserting "paper, microform, or electronic".

(2) CONTINUATION OF MAINTENANCE.—The Under Secretary of Commerce for Intellectual Property and Director of the United States Patent and Trademark Office shall not, pursuant to the amendment made by paragraph (1), cease to maintain, for use by the public, paper or microform collections of United States patents, foreign patent documents, and United States trademark registrations, except pursuant to notice and opportunity for public comment and except that the Director shall first submit a report to the Committees on the Judiciary of the Senate and the House of Representatives detailing such plan, including a description of the mechanisms in place to ensure the integrity of such collections and the data contained therein, as well as to ensure prompt public access to the most current available information, and certifying that the implementation of such plan will not negatively impact the public.

SEC. 4805. STUDY AND REPORT ON BIOLOGICAL DEPOSITS IN SUPPORT OF BIOTECHNOLOGY PATENTS.

(a) IN GENERAL.—Not later than 6 months after the date of the enactment of this Act, the Comptroller General of the United States, in consultation with the Under Secretary of Commerce for Intellectual Property and Director of the United States Patent and Trademark Office, shall conduct a study and submit a report to Congress on the potential risks to the United States biotechnology industry relating to biological deposits in support of biotechnology patents.

(b) CONTENTS.—The study conducted under this section shall include—

(1) an examination of the risk of export and the risk of transfers to third parties of biological deposits, and the risks posed by the change to 18-month publication requirements made by this subtitle;

(2) an analysis of comparative legal and regulatory regimes; and

(3) any related recommendations.

(c) CONSIDERATION OF REPORT.—In drafting regulations affecting biological deposits (including any modification of title 37, Code of Federal Regulations, section 1.801 et seq.), the United States Patent and Trademark Office shall consider the recommendations of the study conducted under this section.

SEC. 4806. PRIOR INVENTION.

Section 102(g) of title 35, United States Code, is amended to read as follows:

"(g)(1) during the course of an interference conducted under section 135 or section 291, another inventor involved therein establishes, to the extent permitted in section 104, that before such person's invention thereof the invention was made by such other inventor and not abandoned, suppressed, or concealed, or (2) before such person's invention thereof, the invention was made in this country by another inventor who had not abandoned, suppressed, or concealed it. In determining priority of invention under this subsection, there shall be considered not only the respective dates of conception and reduction to practice of the invention, but also the reasonable diligence of one who was first to conceive and last to reduce to practice, from a time prior to conception by the other.".

SEC. 4807. PRIOR ART EXCLUSION FOR CERTAIN COMMONLY ASSIGNED PATENTS.

(a) PRIOR ART EXCLUSION.—Section 103(c) of title 35, United States Code, is amended by striking "subsection (f) or (g)" and inserting "one or more of subsections (e), (f), and (g)".

(b) EFFECTIVE DATE.—The amendment made by this section shall apply to any application for patent filed on or after the date of the enactment of this Act.

SEC. 4808. EXCHANGE OF COPIES OF PATENTS WITH FOREIGN COUNTRIES.

Section 12 of title 35, United States Code, is amended by adding at the end the following: "The Director shall not enter into an agreement to provide such copies of specifications and drawings of United States patents and applications to a foreign country, other than a NAFTA country or a WTO member country, without the express authorization of the Secretary of Commerce. For purposes of this section, the terms 'NAFTA country' and 'WTO member country' have the meanings given those terms in section 104(b).".

* * *

Appendix C-28

Changes to Implement Patent Term Adjustment Under Twenty-Year Patent Term; Final Rule

65 FR 56366
Department of Commerce
Patent and Trademark Office
37 CFR Part 1
RIN 0651 — AB06

Agency: United States Patent and Trademark Office, Commerce

Action: Final Rule

* * *

Dates: Effective Dates: Sections 1.702 through 1.705 and the amendment to §1.701 are effective October 18, 2000. The amendment to §1.18 is effective November 17, 2000.

Applicability Date: Section 1.701 applies to original (non-reissue) patents issued on applications (other than for a design patent) filed on or after June 8, 1995, and before May 29, 2000. Sections 1.702 through 1.705 apply to original applications (other than for a design patent) filed on or after May 29, 2000, and to patents issued on such applications.

* * *

PART 1—RULES OF PRACTICE IN PATENT CASES

1. The authority citation for 37 CFR part 1 continues to read as follows:

Authority: 35 U.S.C. 2(b)(2).

2. Section 1.18 is amended by revising its heading and adding paragraphs (d), (e) and (f) to read as follows:

§1.18 Patent post allowance (including issue) fees.

* * * * *

(d) [Reserved]

(e) For filing an application for patent term adjustment under §1.705: $200.00.

(f) For filing a request for reinstatement of all or part of the term reduced pursuant to §1.704(b) in an application for patent term adjustment under §1.705: $400.00.

3. The heading for Subpart F of part 1 is revised to read as follows:

Subpart F—Adjustment and Extension of Patent Term

4. The authority citation for Subpart F of part 1 is revised to read as follows:

Authority: 35 U.S.C. 2(b)(2), 154, and 156.

5. A new, undesignated center heading is added to Subpart F before §1.701 to read as follows:

Adjustment of Patent Term Due to Examination Delay

6. Section 1.701 is amended by revising its heading and adding a new paragraph (e) to read as follows:

§1.701 Extension of patent term due to examination delay under the Uruguay Round Agreements Act (original applications, other than designs, filed on or after June 8, 1995, and before May 29, 2000).

* * * * *

(e) The provisions of this section apply only to original patents, except for design patents, issued on applications filed on or after June 8, 1995, and before May 29, 2000.

7. New §§1.702 through 1.705 are added to read as follows:

§1.702 Grounds for adjustment of patent term due to examination delay under the Patent Term Guarantee Act of 1999 (original applications, other than designs, filed on or after May 29, 2000).

(a) *Failure to take certain actions within specified time frames.* Subject to the provisions of 35 U.S.C. 154(b) and this subpart, the term of an original patent shall be adjusted if the issuance of the patent was delayed due to the failure of the Office to:

(1) Mail at least one of a notification under 35 U.S.C. 132 or a notice of allowance under 35 U.S.C. 151 not later than fourteen months after the date on which the application was filed under 35 U.S.C. 111(a) or fulfilled the requirements of 35 U.S.C. 371 in an international application;

(2) Respond to a reply under 35 U.S.C. 132 or to an appeal taken under 35 U.S.C. 134 not later than four months after the date on which the reply was filed or the appeal was taken;

(3) Act on an application not later than four months after the date of a decision by the Board of Patent Appeals and Interferences under 35 U.S.C. 134 or 135 or a decision by a Federal court under 35 U.S.C. 141, 145, or 146 where at least one allowable claim remains in the application; or

(4) Issue a patent not later than four months after the date on which the issue fee was paid under 35 U.S.C. 151 and all outstanding requirements were satisfied.

(b) *Failure to issue a patent within three years of the actual filing date of the application.* Subject to the provisions of 35 U.S.C. 154(b) and this subpart, the term of an original patent shall be adjusted if the issuance of the patent was delayed due to the failure of the Office to issue a patent within three years after the date on which the application was filed under 35 U.S.C. 111(a) or the national stage commenced under 35 U.S.C. 371(b) or (f) in an international application, but not including:

(1) Any time consumed by continued examination of the application under 35 U.S.C. 132(b);

(2) Any time consumed by an interference proceeding under 35 U.S.C. 135(a);

(3) Any time consumed by the imposition of a secrecy order under 35 U.S.C. 181;

(4) Any time consumed by review by the Board of Patent Appeals and Interferences or a Federal court; or

(5) Any delay in the processing of the application by the Office that was requested by the applicant.

(c) *Delays caused by interference proceedings.* Subject to the provisions of 35 U.S.C. 154(b) and this subpart, the term of an original patent shall be adjusted if the issuance of the patent was delayed due to interference proceedings under 35 U.S.C. 135(a).

(d) *Delays caused by secrecy order.* Subject to the provisions of 35 U.S.C. 154(b) and this subpart, the term of an original patent shall be adjusted if the issuance of the patent was delayed due to the application being placed under a secrecy order under 35 U.S.C. 181.

(e) *Delays caused by successful appellate review.* Subject to the provisions of 35 U.S.C. 154(b) and this subpart, the term of an original patent shall be adjusted if the issuance of the patent was delayed due to review by the Board of Patent Appeals and Interferences under 35 U.S.C. 134 or by a Federal court under 35 U.S.C. 141 or 145, if the patent was issued pursuant to a decision reversing an adverse determination of patentability.

(f) The provisions of this section and §§1.703 through 1.705 apply only to original applications, except applications for a design patent, filed on or after May 29, 2000, and patents issued on such applications.

§1.703 Period of adjustment of patent term due to examination delay.

(a) The period of adjustment under §1.702(a) is the sum of the following periods:

(1) The number of days, if any, in the period beginning on the day after the date that is fourteen months after the date on which the application was filed under 35 U.S.C. 111(a) or fulfilled the requirements of 35 U.S.C. 371 and ending on the date of mailing of either an action under 35 U.S.C. 132, or a notice of allowance under 35 U.S.C. 151, whichever occurs first;

(2) The number of days, if any, in the period beginning on the day after the date that is four months after the date a reply under §1.111 was filed and ending on the date of mailing of either an action under 35 U.S.C. 132, or a notice of allowance under 35 U.S.C. 151, whichever occurs first;

(3) The number of days, if any, in the period beginning on the day after the date that is four months after the date a reply in compliance with §1.113(c) was filed and ending on the date of mailing of either an action under 35 U.S.C. 132, or a notice of allowance under 35 U.S.C. 151, whichever occurs first;

(4) The number of days, if any, in the period beginning on the day after the date that is four months after the date an appeal brief in compliance with §1.192 was filed and ending on the date of mailing of any of an examiner's answer under §1.193, an action under 35 U.S.C. 132, or a notice of allowance under 35 U.S.C. 151, whichever occurs first;

(5) The number of days, if any, in the period beginning on the day after the date that is four months after the date of a final decision by the Board of Patent Appeals and Interferences or by a Federal court in an appeal under 35 U.S.C. 141 or

a civil action under 35 U.S.C. 145 or 146 where at least one allowable claim remains in the application and ending on the date of mailing of either an action under 35 U.S.C. 132 or a notice of allowance under 35 U.S.C. 151, whichever occurs first; and

(6) The number of days, if any, in the period beginning on the day after the date that is four months after the date the issue fee was paid and all outstanding requirements were satisfied and ending on the date a patent was issued.

(b) The period of adjustment under §1.702(b) is the number of days, if any, in the period beginning on the day after the date that is three years after the date on which the application was filed under 35 U.S.C. 111(a) or the national stage commenced under 35 U.S.C. 371(b) or (f) in an international application and ending on the date a patent was issued, but not including the sum of the following periods:

(1) The number of days, if any, in the period beginning on the date on which a request for continued examination of the application under 35 U.S.C. 132(b) was filed and ending on the date the patent was issued;

(2) (i) The number of days, if any, in the period beginning on the date an interference was declared or redeclared to involve the application in the interference and ending on the date that the interference was terminated with respect to the application; and

(ii) The number of days, if any, in the period beginning on the date prosecution in the application was suspended by the Office due to interference proceedings under 35 U.S.C. 135(a) not involving the application and ending on the date of the termination of the suspension;

(3) (i) The number of days, if any, the application was maintained in a sealed condition under 35 U.S.C. 181;

(ii) The number of days, if any, in the period beginning on the date of mailing of an examiner's answer under §1.193 in the application under secrecy order and ending on the date the secrecy order was removed;

(iii) The number of days, if any, in the period beginning on the date applicant was notified that an interference would be declared but for the secrecy order and ending on the date the secrecy order was removed; and

(iv) The number of days, if any, in the period beginning on the date of notification under §5.3(c) of this chapter and ending on the date of mailing of the notice of allowance under 35 U.S.C. 151; and,

(4) The number of days, if any, in the period beginning on the date on which a notice of appeal to the Board of Patent Appeals and Interferences was filed under 35 U.S.C. 134 and §1.191 and ending on the date of the last decision by the Board of Patent Appeals and Interferences or by a Federal court in an appeal under 35 U.S.C. 141 or a civil action under 35 U.S.C. 145, or on the date of mailing of either an action under 35 U.S.C. 132, or a notice of allowance under 35 U.S.C. 151, whichever occurs first, if the appeal did not result in a decision by the Board of Patent Appeals and Interferences.

(c) The period of adjustment under §1.702(c) is the sum of the following periods, to the extent that the periods are not overlapping:

(1) The number of days, if any, in the period beginning on the date an interference was declared or redeclared to involve the application in the interference and ending on the date that the interference was terminated with respect to the application; and

(2) The number of days, if any, in the period beginning on the date prosecution in the application was suspended by the Office due to interference proceedings under 35 U.S.C. 135(a) not involving the application and ending on the date of the termination of the suspension.

(d) The period of adjustment under §1.702(d) is the sum of the following periods, to the extent that the periods are not overlapping:

(1) The number of days, if any, the application was maintained in a sealed condition under 35 U.S.C. 181;

(2) The number of days, if any, in the period beginning on the date of mailing of an examiner's answer under §1.193 in the application under secrecy order and ending on the date the secrecy order was removed;

(3) The number of days, if any, in the period beginning on the date applicant was notified that an interference would be declared but for the secrecy order and ending on the date the secrecy order was removed; and

(4) The number of days, if any, in the period beginning on the date of notification under §5.3(c) of this chapter and ending on the date of mailing of the notice of allowance under 35 U.S.C. 151.

(e) The period of adjustment under §1.702(e) is the sum of the number of days, if any, in the period beginning on the date on which a notice of appeal to the Board of Patent Appeals and Interferences was filed under 35 U.S.C. 134 and §1.191 and ending on the date of a final decision in favor of the applicant by the Board of Patent Appeals and Interferences or by a Federal court in an appeal under 35 U.S.C. 141 or a civil action under 35 U.S.C. 145.

(f) The adjustment will run from the expiration date of the patent as set forth in 35 U.S.C. 154(a)(2). To the extent that periods of adjustment attributable to the grounds specified in §1.702 overlap, the period of adjustment granted under this section shall not exceed the actual number of days the issuance of the patent was delayed. The term of a patent entitled to adjustment under §1.702 and this section shall be adjusted for the sum of the periods calculated under paragraphs (a) through (e) of this section, to the extent that such periods are not overlapping, less the sum of the periods calculated under §1.704. The date indicated on any certificate of mailing or transmission under §1.8 shall not be taken into account in this calculation.

(g) No patent, the term of which has been disclaimed beyond a specified date, shall be adjusted under §1.702 and this section beyond the expiration date specified in the disclaimer.

§1.704 Reduction of period of adjustment of patent term.

(a) The period of adjustment of the term of a patent under §§1.703(a) through (e) shall be reduced by a period equal to the period of time during which the applicant failed to engage in reasonable efforts to conclude prosecution (processing or examination) of the application.

(b) With respect to the grounds for adjustment set forth in §§1.702(a) through (e), and in particular the ground of adjustment set forth in §1.702(b), an applicant shall be deemed to have failed to engage in reasonable efforts to conclude processing or examination of an application for the cumulative total of any periods of time in excess of three months that are taken to reply to any notice or action by the Office making any rejection, objection, argument, or other request, measuring such three-month period from the date the notice or action was mailed or given to the applicant, in which case the period of adjustment set forth in §1.703 shall be reduced by the number of days, if any, beginning on the day after the date that is three months after the date of mailing or transmission of the Office communication notifying the applicant of the rejection, objection, argument, or other request and ending on the date the reply was filed. The period, or shortened statutory period, for reply that is set in the Office action or notice has no effect on the three-month period set forth in this paragraph.

(c) Circumstances that constitute a failure of the applicant to engage in reasonable efforts to conclude processing or examination of an application also include the following circumstances, which will result in the following reduction of the period of adjustment set forth in §1.703 to the extent that the periods are not overlapping:

(1) Suspension of action under §1.103 at the applicant's request, in which case the period of adjustment set forth in §1.703 shall be reduced by the number of days, if any, beginning on the date a request for suspension of action under §1.103 was filed and ending on the date of the termination of the suspension;

(2) Deferral of issuance of a patent under §1.314, in which case the period of adjustment set forth in §1.703 shall be reduced by the number of days, if any, beginning on the date a request for deferral of issuance of a patent under §1.314 was filed and ending on the date the patent was issued;

(3) Abandonment of the application or late payment of the issue fee, in which case the period of adjustment set forth in §1.703 shall be reduced by the number

of days, if any, beginning on the date of abandonment or the date after the date the issue fee was due and ending on the earlier of:

(i) The date of mailing of the decision reviving the application or accepting late payment of the issue fee; or

(ii) The date that is four months after the date the grantable petition to revive the application or accept late payment of the issue fee was filed;

(4) Failure to file a petition to withdraw the holding of abandonment or to revive an application within two months from the mailing date of a notice of abandonment, in which case the period of adjustment set forth in §1.703 shall be reduced by the number of days, if any, beginning on the day after the date two months from the mailing date of a notice of abandonment and ending on the date a petition to withdraw the holding of abandonment or to revive the application was filed;

(5) Conversion of a provisional application under 35 U.S.C. 111(b) to a nonprovisional application under 35 U.S.C. 111(a) pursuant to 35 U.S.C. 111(b)(5), in which case the period of adjustment set forth in §1.703 shall be reduced by the number of days, if any, beginning on the date the application was filed under 35 U.S.C. 111(b) and ending on the date a request in compliance with §1.53(c)(3) to convert the provisional application into a nonprovisional application was filed;

(6) Submission of a preliminary amendment or other preliminary paper less than one month before the mailing of an Office action under 35 U.S.C. 132 or notice of allowance under 35 U.S.C. 151 that requires the mailing of a supplemental Office action or notice of allowance, in which case the period of adjustment set forth in §1.703 shall be reduced by the lesser of:

(i) The number of days, if any, beginning on the day after the mailing date of the original Office action or notice of allowance and ending on the date of mailing of the supplemental Office action or notice of allowance; or

(ii) Four months;

(7) Submission of a reply having an omission (§1.135(c)), in which case the period of adjustment set forth in §1.703 shall be reduced by the number of days, if any, beginning on the day after the date the reply having an omission was filed and ending on the date that the reply or other paper correcting the omission was filed;

(8) Submission of a supplemental reply or other paper, other than a supplemental reply or other paper expressly requested by the examiner, after a reply has been filed, in which case the period of adjustment set forth in §1.703 shall be reduced by the number of days, if any, beginning on the day after the date the initial reply was filed and ending on the date that the supplemental reply or other such paper was filed;

(9) Submission of an amendment or other paper after a decision by the Board of Patent Appeals and Interferences, other than a decision designated as containing a new ground of rejection under §1.196(b) or statement under §1.196(c), or a decision by a Federal court, less than one month before the mailing of an Office action under 35 U.S.C. 132 or notice of allowance under 35 U.S.C. 151 that requires the mailing of a supplemental Office action or supplemental notice of allowance, in which case the period of adjustment set forth in §1.703 shall be reduced by the lesser of:

(i) The number of days, if any, beginning on the day after the mailing date of the original Office action or notice of allowance and ending on the mailing date of the supplemental Office action or notice of allowance; or

(ii) Four months;

(10) Submission of an amendment under §1.312 or other paper after a notice of allowance has been given or mailed, in which case the period of adjustment set forth in §1.703 shall be reduced by the lesser of:

(i) The number of days, if any, beginning on the date the amendment under §1.312 or other paper was filed and ending on the mailing date of the Office action or notice in response to the amendment under §1.312 or such other paper; or

(ii) Four months; and

(11) Further prosecution via a continuing application, in which case the period of adjustment set forth in §1.703 shall not include any period that is prior to the actual filing date of the application that resulted in the patent.

(d) A paper containing only an information disclosure statement in compliance with §§1.97 and 1.98 will not be considered a failure to engage in reasonable efforts to conclude prosecution (processing or examination) of the application under paragraphs (c)(6), (c)(8), (c)(9), or (c)(10) of this section if it is accompanied by a statement that each item of information contained in the information disclosure statement was cited in a communication from a foreign patent office in a counterpart application and that this communication was not received by any individual designated in §1.56(c) more than thirty days prior to the filing of the information disclosure statement. This thirty-day period is not extendable.

(e) Submission of an application for patent term adjustment under §1.705(b) (with or without request under §1.705(c) for reinstatement of reduced patent term adjustment) will not be considered a failure to engage in reasonable efforts to conclude prosecution (processing or examination) of the application under paragraph (c)(10) of this section.

§1.705 Patent term adjustment determination.

(a) The notice of allowance will include notification of any patent term adjustment under 35 U.S.C. 154(b).

(b) Any request for reconsideration of the patent term adjustment indicated in the notice of allowance, except as provided in paragraph (d) of this section, and any request for reinstatement of all or part of the term reduced pursuant to §1.704(b) must be by way of an application for patent term adjustment. An application for patent term adjustment under this section must be filed no later than the payment of the issue fee but may not be filed earlier than the date of mailing of the notice of allowance. An application for patent term adjustment under this section must be accompanied by:

(1) The fee set forth in §1.18(e); and

(2) A statement of the facts involved, specifying:

(i) The correct patent term adjustment and the basis or bases under §1.702 for the adjustment;

(ii) The relevant dates as specified in §§1.703(a) through (e) for which an adjustment is sought and the adjustment as specified in §1.703(f) to which the patent is entitled;

(iii) Whether the patent is subject to a terminal disclaimer and any expiration date specified in the terminal disclaimer; and

(iv) (A) Any circumstances during the prosecution of the application resulting in the patent that constitute a failure to engage in reasonable efforts to conclude processing or examination of such application as set forth in §1.704; or

(B) That there were no circumstances constituting a failure to engage in reasonable efforts to conclude processing or examination of such application as set forth in §1.704.

(c) Any application for patent term adjustment under this section that requests reinstatement of all or part of the period of adjustment reduced pursuant to §1.704(b) for failing to reply to a rejection, objection, argument, or other request within three months of the date of mailing of the Office communication notifying the applicant of the rejection, objection, argument, or other request must also be accompanied by:

(1) The fee set forth in §1.18(f); and

(2) A showing to the satisfaction of the Commissioner that, in spite of all due care, the applicant was unable to reply to the rejection, objection, argument, or other request within three months of the date of mailing of the Office communication notifying the applicant of the rejection, objection, argument, or other request. The Office shall not grant any request for reinstatement for more than three additional months for each reply beyond three months from the date of

mailing of the Office communication notifying the applicant of the rejection, objection, argument, or other request.

(d) If the patent is issued on a date other than the projected date of issue and this change necessitates a revision of the patent term adjustment indicated in the notice of allowance, the patent will indicate the revised patent term adjustment. If the patent indicates a revised patent term adjustment due to the patent being issued on a date other than the projected date of issue, any request for reconsideration of the patent term adjustment indicated in the patent must be filed within thirty days of the date the patent issued and must comply with the requirements of paragraphs (b)(1) and (b)(2) of this section.

(e) The periods set forth in this section are not extendable.

(f) No submission or petition on behalf of a third party concerning patent term adjustment under 35 U.S.C. 154(b) will be considered by the Office. Any such submission or petition will be returned to the third party, or otherwise disposed of, at the convenience of the Office.

8. A new, undesignated center heading is added to Subpart F before §1.710 to read as follows:

Extension of Patent Term Due to Regulatory Review

Dated: September 5, 2000.

Q. Todd Dickinson,

Under Secretary of Commerce for Intellectual Property and Director of the United States Patent and Trademark Office.
[FR Doc. 00-23263 Filed 9-15-00; 8:45 am]

Appendix C-29

Substantive Changes in Title 35 of the United States Code Made by Pub. L. No. 106-113

[Note: The following comparison is based on a compilation prepared by the U.S. Patent and Trademark Office dated January 18, 2000. The comparison has been edited to show only substantive changes effected by Pub. L. No. 106-113. Language containing only minor changes, such as the substitution of "Director" for "Commissioner," has been omitted, as have legislative histories. Readers who wish to see all changes made in Title 35 by Pub. L. No. 106-113 should consult the original compilation on the PTO website at <http://www.uspto.gov/web/offices/dcom/olia/35amend2.pdf>.

Language added by Pub. L. No. 106–113 is shown in *italics*. Sections included in this comparison are shown in *italics* in the table of contents below.]

PART I - THE UNITED STATES PATENT AND TRADEMARK OFFICE

CHAPTER 1 - ESTABLISHMENT, OFFICERS AND EMPLOYEES, FUNCTIONS

Sec.

1. *Establishment.*
2. *Powers and duties.*
3. *Officers and employees.*
4. Restrictions on officers and employees as to interests in patents.
5. *Patent and Trademark Office Public Advisory Committees.*
6. *Board of Patent Appeals and Interferences.*
7. Library.
8. Classification of patents.
9. Certified copies of records.
10. *Publications*
11. *Exchange of copies of patents and applications with foreign countries.*
12. *Copies of patents and applications for public libraries.*
13. *Annual report to Congress.*

CHAPTER 2 - PROCEEDINGS IN THE PATENT AND TRADEMARK OFFICE

21. Filing date and day for taking action.
22. Printing of papers filed.
23. Testimony in Patent and Trademark Office cases.
24. Subpoenas; witnesses.
25. Declaration in lieu of oath.
26. Effect of defective execution.

CHAPTER 3 - PRACTICE BEFORE PATENT AND TRADEMARK OFFICE

31. Regulations for agents and attorneys.
32. *Suspension or exclusion from practice.*
33. Unauthorized representation as practitioner.

CHAPTER 4 - PATENT FEES' FUNDING, SEARCH SYSTEMS

41. Patent fees; patent and trademark search systems.
42. *Patent and Trademark Office funding.*

PART II - PATENTABILITY OF INVENTIONS AND GRANT OF PATENTS

CHAPTER 10 - PATENTABILITY OF INVENTIONS

100. *Definitions.*
101. Inventions patentable.
102. *Conditions for patentability; novelty and loss of right to patent.*
103. Conditions for patentability; non-obvious subject matter.
104. Invention made abroad.
105. Inventions in outer space.

CHAPTER 11 - APPLICATION FOR PATENT

111. *Application.*
112. Specification.
113. Drawings.
114. Models, specimens.
115. Oath of applicant.
116. Inventors.
117. Death or incapacity of inventor.
118. Filing by other than inventor.
119. *Benefit of earlier filing date; right of priority.*

120. *Benefit of earlier filing date in the United States.*
121. Divisional applications
122. *Confidential status of applications; publication of patent applications.*

CHAPTER 12 - EXAMINATION OF APPLICATION

131. Examination of application.
132. *Notice of rejection; reexamination.*
133. Time for prosecuting application.
134. *Appeal to the Board of Patent Appeals and Interferences.*
135. *Interferences.*

CHAPTER 13 - REVIEW OF PATENT AND TRADEMARK OFFICE DECISION

141. *Appeal to Court of Appeals for the Federal Circuit.*
142. Notice of appeal.
143. Proceedings on appeal.
144. Decision on appeal.
145. Civil action to obtain a patent.
146. Civil action in case of interference.

CHAPTER 14 - ISSUE OF PATENT

151. Issue of patent.
152. Issue of patent to assignee.
153. How issued.
154. *Contents and term of patent; provisional rights.*
155. Patent term extension.
155A A patent term restoration.
156. Extension of patent term.
157. Statutory invention registration.

CHAPTER 15 - PLANT PATENTS

161. Patents for plants.
162. Description, claim.
163. Grant.
164. Assistance of the Department of Agriculture.

CHAPTER 16 - DESIGNS

171. Patents for designs.
172. Right of priority.
173. Term of design patent.

CHAPTER 17 - SECRECY OF CERTAIN INVENTIONS AND FILING APPLICATIONS IN FOREIGN COUNTRIES

181. *Secrecy of certain inventions and withholding of patent.*
182. Abandonment of invention for unauthorized disclosure.
183. Right to compensation.
184. Filing of application in foreign country.
185. Patent barred for filing without license.
186. Penalty.
187. Non-applicability to certain persons.
188. Rules and regulations, delegation of power.

CHAPTER 18 - PATENT RIGHTS IN INVENTIONS MADE WITH FEDERAL ASSISTANCE

200. Policy and objective.
201. Definitions.
202. Disposition of rights.
203. March-in rights.

204. Preference for United States industry.
205. Confidentiality.
206. Uniform clauses and regulations.
207. Domestic and foreign protection of federally owned inventions.
208. Regulations governing Federal licensing.
209. Restrictions on licensing of federally owned inventions.
210. Precedence of chapter.
211. Relationship to antitrust laws.
212. Disposition of rights in educational awards.

PART III - PATENTS AND PROTECTION OF PATENT RIGHTS

CHAPTER 25 - AMENDMENT AND CORRECTION OF PATENTS

251. Reissue of defective patents.
252. Effect of reissue.
253. Disclaimer.
254. Certificate of correction of Patent and Trademark Office mistake.
255. Certificate of correction of applicant's mistake.
256. Correction of named inventor.

CHAPTER 26 - OWNERSHIP AND ASSIGNMENT

261. Ownership; assignment.
262. Joint owners.

CHAPTER 27 - GOVERNMENT INTERESTS IN PATENTS

266. [Repealed.]
267. Time for taking action in Government applications.
268. [Reserved]
269. [Reserved]
270. [Reserved]

CHAPTER 28 - INFRINGEMENT OF PATENTS

271. Infringement of patent.
272. Temporary presence in the United States.
273. *Defense to infringement based on earlier invention.*

CHAPTER 29 - REMEDIES FOR INFRINGEMENT OF PATENT, AND OTHER ACTIONS

281. Remedy for infringement of patent.
282. *Presumption of validity; defenses.*
283. Injunction.
284. *Damages.*
285. Attorney fees.
286. Time limitation on damages.
287. *Limitation on damages and other remedies; marking and notice.*
288. Action for infringement of a patent containing an invalid claim.
289. Additional remedy for infringement of design patent.
290. Notice of patent suits.
291. Interfering patents.
292. False marking.
293. Nonresident patentee; service and notice.
294. Voluntary arbitration.
295. Presumptions: Product made by patented process.
296. Liability of States, instrumentalities of States, and State officials for infringement of patents.
297. *Improper and deceptive invention promotion.*

CHAPTER 30 - PRIOR ART CITATIONS TO OFFICE AND *EX PARTE* REEXAMINATION OF PATENTS

301. Citation of prior art.
302. Request for reexamination.
303. Determination of issue by Director.
304. Reexamination order by Director.
305. Conduct of reexamination proceedings.
306. Appeal.
307. Certificate of patentability, unpatentability, and claim cancellation.

CHAPTER 31 - OPTIONAL *INTER PARTES* REEXAMINATION PROCEDURES

311. *Request for* inter partes *reexamination.*
312. *Determination of issue by Director.*
313. Inter partes *reexamination order by Director.*
314. *Conduct of* inter partes *reexamination proceedings.*
315. *Appeal.*
316. *Certificate of patentability, unpatentability, and claim cancellation.*
317. Inter partes *reexamination prohibited.*
318. *Stay of litigation.*

PART IV - PATENT COOPERATION TREATY

CHAPTER 35 - DEFINITIONS

351. Definitions.

CHAPTER 36 - INTERNATIONAL STAGE

361. Receiving Office.
362. International Searching Authority and International Preliminary Examining Authority.
363. International application designating the United States: Effect.
364. International stage: Procedure.
365. Right of priority; benefit of the filing date of a prior application.
366. Withdrawn international application.
367. Actions of other authorities: Review.
368. Secrecy of certain inventions; filing international applications in foreign countries.

CHAPTER 37 - NATIONAL STAGE

371. National stage: Commencement.
372. National stage: Requirements and procedure.
373. Improper applicant.
374. *Publication of international application: Effect.*
375. Patent issued on international application: Effect.
376. Fees.

§1 Establishment

(a) *ESTABLISHMENT. The United States Patent and Trademark Office is established as an agency of the United States, within the Department of Commerce. In carrying out its functions, the United States Patent and Trademark Office shall be subject to the policy direction of the Secretary of Commerce, but otherwise shall retain responsibility for decisions regarding the management and administration of its operations and shall exercise independent control of its budget allocations and expenditures, personnel decisions and processes, procurements, and other administrative and management functions in accordance with this title and applicable provisions of law. Those operations designed to grant and issue patents and those operations which are designed to facilitate the registration of trademarks shall be treated as separate operating units within the Office.*

(b) *OFFICES. The United States Patent and Trademark Office shall maintain its principal office in the metropolitan Washington, D.C., area, for the service of process and papers and for the purpose of carrying out its functions. The United States Patent and Trademark Office shall be deemed, for purposes of venue in civil actions, to be a resident of the district in which its principal office is located, except where jurisdiction is otherwise provided by law. The United States Patent and Trademark Office may establish satellite offices in such other places in the United States as it considers necessary and appropriate in the conduct of its business.*

(c) *REFERENCE. For purposes of this title, the United States Patent and Trademark Office shall also be referred to as the 'Office' and the 'Patent and Trademark Office'.*

§2 *Powers and duties*

(a) *In General. The United States Patent and Trademark Office, subject to the policy direction of the Secretary of Commerce*

(1) *shall be responsible for the granting and issuing of patents and the registration of trademarks; and*

(2) *shall be responsible for disseminating to the public information with respect to patents and trademarks.*

(b) *Specific Powers. The Office—*

(1) *shall adopt and use a seal of the Office, which shall be judicially noticed and with which letters patent, certificates of trademark registrations, and papers issued by the Office shall be authenticated;*

(2) *may establish regulations, not inconsistent with law, which*

(A) *shall govern the conduct of proceedings in the Office;*

(B) *shall be made in accordance with section 553 of title 5, United States Code;*

(C) *shall facilitate and expedite the processing of patent applications, particularly those which can be filed, stored, processed, searched, and retrieved electronically, subject to the provisions of section 122 relating to the confidential status of applications;*

(D) *may govern the recognition and conduct of agents, attorneys, or other persons representing applicants or other parties before the Office, and may require them, before being recognized as representatives of applicants or other persons, to show that they are of good moral character and reputation and are possessed of the necessary qualifications to render to applicants or other persons valuable service, advice, and assistance in the presentation or prosecution of their applications or other business before the Office;*

(E) *shall recognize the public interest in continuing to safeguard broad access to the United States patent system through the reduced fee structure for small entities under section 41(h) (1) of this title; and*

(F) *provide for the development of a performance-based process that includes quantitative and qualitative measures and standards for evaluating cost-effectiveness and is consistent with the principles of impartiality and competitiveness;*

(3) *may acquire, construct, purchase, lease, hold, manage, operate, improve, alter, and renovate any real, personal, or mixed property, or any interest therein, as it considers necessary to carry out its functions;*

(4) (A) *may make such purchases, contracts for the construction, maintenance, or management and operation of facilities, and contracts for supplies or services, without regard to the provisions of the Federal Property and Administrative Services Act of 1949 (40 U.S.C. 471 et seq.), the Public Buildings Act (40 U.S.C. 601 et seq.), and the Stewart B. McKinney Homeless Assistance Act (42 U.S.C. 11301 et seq.); and*

(B) *may enter into and perform such purchases and contracts for printing services, including the process of composition, platemaking, presswork, silk screen processes, binding, microform, and the products of such processes, as it considers necessary to carry out the functions of the Office, without regard to sections 501 through 517 and 1101 through 1123 of title 44, United States Code;*

(5) *may use, with their consent, services, equipment, personnel, and facilities of other departments, agencies, and instrumentalities of the Federal Government, on a reimbursable basis, and cooperate with such other departments, agencies, and instrumentalities in the establishment and use of services, equipment, and facilities of the Office;*

(6) *may, when the Director determines that it is practicable, efficient, and cost-effective to do so, use, with the consent of the United States and the agency, instrumentality, Patent and Trademark Office, or international organization concerned, the services, records, facilities, or personnel of any State or local government agency or instrumentality or foreign patent and trademark office or international organization to perform functions on its behalf;*

(7) *may retain and use all of its revenues and receipts, including revenues from the sale, lease, or disposal of any real, personal, or mixed property, or any interest therein, of the Office;*

(8) *shall advise the President, through the Secretary of Commerce, on national and certain international intellectual property policy issues;*

(9) *shall advise Federal departments and agencies on matters of intellectual property policy in the United States and intellectual property protection in other countries;*

(10) *shall provide guidance, as appropriate, with respect to proposals by agencies to assist foreign governments and international intergovernmental organizations on matters of intellectual property protection;*

(11) *may conduct programs, studies, or exchanges of items or services regarding domestic and international intellectual property law and the effectiveness of intellectual property protection domestically and throughout the world;*

(12) (A) *shall advise the Secretary of Commerce on programs and studies relating to intellectual property policy that are conducted, or authorized to be conducted, cooperatively with foreign intellectual property offices and international intergovernmental organizations; and*

(B) *may conduct programs and studies described in subparagraph (A); and*

(13) (A) *in coordination with the Department of State, may conduct programs and studies cooperatively with foreign intellectual property offices and international intergovernmental organizations; and*

(B) *with the concurrence of the Secretary of State, may authorize the transfer of not to exceed $100,000 in any year to the Department of State for the purpose of making special payments to international intergovernmental organizations for studies and programs for advancing international cooperation concerning patents, trademarks, and other matters.*

(c) (1) *Clarification of Specific Powers. The special payments under subsection (b)(13)(B) shall be in addition to any other payments or contributions to international organizations described in subsection (b)(13)(B) and shall not be subject to any limitations imposed by law on the amounts of such other payments or contributions by the United States Government.*

(2) *Nothing in subsection (b) shall derogate from the duties of the Secretary of State or from the duties of the United States Trade Representative as set forth in section 141 of the Trade Act of 1974 (19 U.S.C. 2171).*

(3) *Nothing in subsection (b) shall derogate from the duties and functions of the Register of Copyrights or otherwise alter current authorities relating to copyright matters.*

(4) *In exercising the Director's powers under paragraphs (3) and (4)(A) of subsection (b), the Director shall consult with the Administrator of General Services.*

(5) *In exercising the Director's powers and duties under this section, the Director shall consult with the Register of Copyrights on all copyright and related matters.*

(d) *Construction. Nothing in this section shall be construed to nullify, void, cancel, or interrupt any pending request-for-proposal let or contract issued by the General Services Administration for the specific purpose of relocating or leasing space to the United States Patent and Trademark Office.*

§3 Officers and employees

(a) *Under Secretary and Director.*

(1) *In general. The powers and duties of the United States Patent and Trademark Office shall be vested in an Under Secretary of Commerce for Intellectual Property and Director of the United States Patent and Trademark Office (in this title referred to as the "Director"), who shall be a citizen of the United States and who shall be appointed by the President, by and with the advice and consent of the Senate. The Director shall be a person who has a professional background and experience in patent or trademark law.*

(2) *Duties.*

(A) *In general. The Director shall be responsible for providing policy direction and management supervision for the Office and for the issuance of patents and the register of trademarks. The Director shall perform these duties in a fair, impartial, and equitable manner.*

(B) *Consulting with the public advisory committees. The Director shall consult with the Patent Public Advisory Committee established in section 5 on a regular basis on matters relating to the patent operations of the Office, shall consult with the Trademark Public Advisory Committee established in section 5 on a regular basis on matters relating to the trademark operations of the Office, and shall consult with the respective Public Advisory Committee before submitting budgetary proposals to the Office of Management and Budget or changing or proposing to change patent or trademark user fees or patent or trademark regulations which are subject to the requirement to provide notice and opportunity for public comment under section 553 of title 5, United States Code, as the case may be.*

(3) *Oath. The Director shall, before taking office, take an oath to discharge faithfully the duties of the Office.*

(4) *Removal. The Director may be removed from office by the President. The President shall provide notification of any such removal to both Houses of Congress.*

(b) *Officers and Employees of the Office*

(1) *Deputy Under Secretary and Deputy Director. The Secretary of Commerce, upon nomination by the Director, shall appoint a Deputy Under Secretary of Commerce for Intellectual Property and Deputy Director of the United States Patent and Trademark Office who shall be vested with the authority to act in the capacity of Director in the event of the absence or incapacity of the Director. The Deputy Director shall be a citizen of the United States who has a professional background and experience in patent or trademark law.*

(2) *Commissioners*

(A) *Appointment and duties. The Secretary of Commerce shall appoint a Commissioner for Patents and a Commissioner for Trademarks without re-*

gard to chapter 33, 51, or 53 of title 5, United States Code. The Commissioner for Patents shall be a citizen of the United States with demonstrated management ability and professional background and experience in patent law and serve for a term of 5 years. The Commissioner for Trademarks shall be a citizen of the United States with demonstrated management ability and professional background and experience in trademark law and serve for a term of 5 years. The Commissioner for Patents and the Commissioner for Trademarks shall serve as the chief operating officers for the operations of the Office relating to patents and trademarks, respectively, and shall be responsible for the management and direction of all aspects of the activities of the Office that affect the administration of patent and trademark operations, respectively. The Secretary may reappoint a Commissioner to subsequent terms of 5 years as long as the performance of the Commissioner as set forth in the performance agreement in subparagraph (B) is satisfactory.

(B) *Salary and performance agreement. The Commissioners shall be paid an annual rate of basic pay not to exceed the maximum rate of basic pay for the Senior Executive Service established under section 5382 of title 5, United States Code, including any applicable locality-based comparability payment that may be authorized under section 5304(h)(2)(C) of title 5, United States Code. The compensation of the Commissioners shall be considered, for purposes of section 207(c)(2)(A) of title 18, United States Code, to be the equivalent of that described under clause (ii) of section 207(c)(2)(A) of title 18, United States Code. In addition, the Commissioners may receive a bonus in an amount of up to, but not in excess of, 50 percent of the Commissioners' annual rate of basic pay, based upon an evaluation by the Secretary of Commerce, acting through the Director, of the Commissioners' performance as defined in an annual performance agreement between the Commissioners and the Secretary. The annual performance agreements shall incorporate measurable organization and individual goals in key operational areas as delineated in an annual performance plan agreed to by the Commissioners and the Secretary. Payment of a bonus under this subparagraph may be made to the Commissioners only to the extent that such payment does not cause the Commissioners' total aggregate compensation in a calendar year to equal or exceed the amount of the salary of the Vice President under section 104 of title 3, United States Code.*

(C) *Removal. The Commissioners may be removed from office by the Secretary for misconduct or nonsatisfactory performance under the performance agreement described in subparagraph (B), without regard to the provisions of title 5, United States Code. The Secretary shall provide notification of any such removal to both Houses of Congress.*

(3) *Other officers and employees. The Director shall—*

(A) *appoint such officers, employees (including attorneys), and agents of the Office as the Director considers necessary to carry out the functions of the Office; and*

(B) *define the title, authority, and duties of such officers and employees and delegate to them such of the powers vested in the Office as the Director may determine.*

The Office shall not be subject to any administratively or statutorily imposed limitation on positions or personnel, and no positions or personnel of the Office shall be taken into account for purposes of applying any such limitation.

(4) *Training of examiners. The Office shall submit to the Congress a proposal to provide an incentive program to retain as employees patent and trademark examiners of the primary examiner grade or higher who are eligible for retirement, for the sole purpose of training patent and trademark examiners.*

(5) *National security positions. The Director, in consultation with the Director of the Office of Personnel Management, shall maintain a program for identifying*

national security positions and providing for appropriate security clearances, in order to maintain the secrecy of certain inventions, as described in section 181, and to prevent disclosure of sensitive and strategic information in the interest of national security.

(c) *Continued Applicability of Title 5, United States Code. Officers and employees of the Office shall be subject to the provisions of title 5, United States Code, relating to Federal employees.*

(d) *Adoption of Existing Labor Agreements. The Office shall adopt all labor agreements which are in effect, as of the day before the effective date of the Patent and Trademark Office Efficiency Act, with respect to such Office (as then in effect).*

(e) *Carryover of Personnel.*

(1) *From PTO. Effective as of the effective date of the Patent and Trademark Office Efficiency Act, all officers and employees of the Patent and Trademark Office on the day before such effective date shall become officers and employees of the Office, without a break in service.*

(2) *Other personnel. Any individual who, on the day before the effective date of the Patent and Trademark Office Efficiency Act, is an officer or employee of the Department of Commerce (other than an officer or employee under paragraph (1)) shall be transferred to the Office, as necessary to carry out the purposes of this Act, if*

(A) *such individual serves in a position for which a major function is the performance of work reimbursed by the Patent and Trademark Office, as determined by the Secretary of Commerce;*

(B) *such individual serves in a position that performed work in support of the Patent and Trademark Office during at least half of the incumbent's work time, as determined by the Secretary of Commerce; or*

(C) *such transfer would be in the interest of the Office, as determined by the Secretary of Commerce in consultation with the Director.*

Any transfer under this paragraph shall be effective as of the same effective date as referred to in paragraph (1), and shall be made without a break in service.

(f) *Transition Provisions.*

(1) *Interim appointment of Director. On or after the effective date of the Patent and Trademark Office Efficiency Act, the President shall appoint an individual to serve as the Director until the date on which a Director qualifies under subsection (a). The President shall not make more than one such appointment under this subsection.*

(2) *Continuation in office of certain officers. (A) The individual service as the Assistant Commissioner for Patents on the day before the effective date of the Patent and Trademark Office Efficiency Act may serve as the Commissioner for Patents until the date on which a Commissioner of Patents is appointed under subsection (b).*

(B) *The individual serving as the Assistant Commissioner for Trademarks on the day before the effective date of the Patent and Trademark Office Efficiency Act may serve as the Commissioner for Trademarks until the date on which a Commissioner for Trademarks is appointed under subsection (b).*

§5 *Patent and Trademark Office Public Advisory Committees*

(a) *Establishment of Public Advisory Committees.*

(1) *The United States Patent and Trademark Office shall have a Patent Public Advisory Committee and a Trademark Public Advisory Committee, each of which shall have nine voting members who shall be appointed by the Secretary of Commerce and serve at the pleasure of the Secretary of Commerce. Members of each Public Advisory Committee shall be appointed for a term of 3 years, except that of the members first appointed, three shall be appointed for a term of 1 year, three shall be appointed for a term of 2 years. In making appointments to each Committee, the Secretary of Commerce shall consider the risk of loss of com-*

petitive advantage in international commerce or other harm to United States companies as a result of such appointments.

(2) *Chair. The Secretary shall designate a chair of each Advisory Committee, whose term as chair shall be for 3 years.*

(3) *Timing of appointments. Initial appointments to each Advisory Committee shall be made within 3 months after the effective date of the Patent and Trademark Office Efficiency Act. Vacancies shall be filled within 3 months after they occur.*

(b) *Basis for Appointments. Members of each Advisory Committee-*

(1) *shall be citizens of the United States who shall be chosen so as to represent the interests of diverse users of the United States Patent and Trademark Office with respect to patents, in the case of the Patent Public Advisory Committee, and with respect to trademarks, in the case of the Trademark Public Advisory Committee;*

(2) *shall include members who represent small and large entity applicants located in the United States in proportion to the number of applications filed by such applicants, but in no case shall members who represent small entity patent applicants, including small business concerns, independent inventors, and nonprofit organizations, constitute less than 25 percent of the members of the Patent Public Advisory Committee, and such members shall include at least one independent inventor; and*

(3) *shall include individuals with substantial background and achievement in finance, management, labor relations, science, technology, and office automation.*

In addition to the voting members, each Advisory Committee shall include a representative of each labor organization recognized by the United States Patent and Trademark Office. Such representatives shall be nonvoting members of the Advisory Committee to which they are appointed.

(c) *Meetings. Each Advisory Committee shall meet at the call of the chair to consider an agenda set by the chair.*

(d) *Duties. Each Advisory Committee shall-*

(1) *review the policies, goals, performance, budget, and user fees of the United States Patent and Trademark Office with respect to patents, in the case of the Patent Public Advisory Committee, and with respect to trademarks, in the case of the Trademark Public Advisory Committee, and advise the Director on these matters;*

(2) *within 60 days after the end of each fiscal year-*

(A) *prepare an annual report on the matters referred to in paragraph (1);*

(B) *transmit the report to the Secretary of Commerce, the President, and the Committees on the Judiciary of the Senate and the House of Representatives; and*

(C) *publish the report in the Official Gazette of the United States Patent and Trademark Office.*

(e) *Compensation. Each member of each Advisory Committee shall be compensated for each day (including travel time) during which such member is attending meetings or conferences of that Advisory Committee or otherwise engaged in the business of that Advisory Committee, at the rate which is the daily equivalent of the annual rate of basic pay in effect for level III of the Executive Schedule under section 5314 of title 5, United States Code. While away from such member's home or regular place of business such member shall be allowed travel expenses, including per diem in lieu of subsistence, as authorized by section 3703 of title 5, United States Code.*

(f) *Access to Information. Members of each Advisory Committee shall be provided access to records and information in the United States Patent and Trademark Office, except for personnel or other privileged information and information concerning patent applications required to be kept in confidence by section 122.*

(g) *Applicability of Certain Ethics Laws. Members of each Advisory Committee shall be special Government employees within the meaning of section 202 of title 18, United States Code.*

(h) *Inapplicability of Federal Advisory Committee Act. The Federal Advisory Committee Act (5 U.S.C. App.) shall not apply to each Advisory Committee.*

(i) *Open Meetings. The meetings of each Advisory Committee shall be open to the public, except that each Advisory Committee may by majority vote meet in executive session when considering personnel or other confidential information.*

§6 *Board of Patent Appeals and Interferences*

(a) *Establishment and Composition. There shall be in the United States Patent and Trademark Office a Board of Patent Appeals and Interferences. The Director, the Commissioner for Patents, the Commissioner for Trademarks, and the administrative patent judges shall constitute the Board. The administrative patent judges shall be persons of competent legal knowledge and scientific ability who are appointed by the Director.*

(b) *Duties. The Board of Patent Appeals and Interferences shall, on written appeal of an applicant, review adverse decisions of examiners upon applications for patents and shall determine priority and patentability of invention in interferences declared under section 135(a). Each appeal and interference shall be heard by at least three members of the Board, who shall be designated to the Director. Only the Board of Patent Appeals and Interferences may grant rehearings.*

§*10* Publications

(a) The *Director* may *publish in printed, typewritten, or electronic form,* the following:

1. Patents *and published applications for patents,* including specifications and drawings, together with copies of the same. The Patent and Trademark Office may print the headings of the drawings for patents for the purpose of photolithography.

* * *

§*11* Exchange of copies of patents *and applications* with foreign countries

The *Director* may exchange copies of specifications and drawings of United States patents *and published applications for patents* for those of foreign countries. *The Director shall not enter into an agreement to provide such copies of specifications and drawings of United States patents and applications to a foreign country, other than a NAFTA country or a WTO member country, without the express authorization of the Secretary of Commerce. For purposes of this section, the terms "NAFTA country" and "WTO member country" have the meanings given those terms in section 104(b).*

§*12* Copies of patents *and applications* for public libraries

The *Director* may supply *copies of specifications and drawings of patents in printed or electronic form and published applications for patents* to public libraries in the United States which shall maintain such copies for the use of the public, at the rate for each year's issue established for this purpose in section 41(d) of this title.

§*13* Annual report to Congress

The Director shall report to the Congress, not later than 180 days after the end of each fiscal year, the moneys received and expended by the Office, the purposes for which the moneys were spent, the quality and quantity of the work of the Office, the nature of training provided to examiners, the evaluation of the Commissioner of Patents and the Commissioner of Trademarks by the Secretary of Commerce, the compensation of the Commissioners, and other information relating to the Office.

§32 Suspension or exclusion from practice

The *Director* may, after notice and opportunity for a hearing suspend or exclude, either generally or in any particular case, from further practice before the Patent and

Trademark Office, any person, agent, or attorney shown to be incompetent or disreputable, or guilty of gross misconduct, or who does not comply with the regulations established under section 31 of this title, or who shall, by word, circular, letter, or advertising, with intent to defraud in any manner, deceive, mislead, or threaten any applicant or prospective applicant, or other person having immediate or prospective business before the Office. The reasons for any such suspension or exclusion shall be duly recorded. *The Director shall have the discretion to designate any attorney who is an officer or employee of the United States Patent and Trademark Office to conduct the hearing required by this section.* The United States District Court for the District of Columbia, under such conditions and upon such proceedings as it by its rules determines, may review the action of the *Director* upon the petition of the person so refused recognition or so suspended or excluded.

§42 Patent and Trademark Office funding *(Changes effective on the date of enactment (November 29, 1999))*

* * *

(c) To the extent and in the amounts provided in advance in appropriations Acts, fees authorized in this title or any other Act to be charged or established by the *Director* shall be collected by and shall be available to the *Director* to carry out the activities of the Patent and Trademark Office. *All fees available* to the *Director* under section 31 of the Trademark Act of 1946 [*15 USCS §1113*] *shall* be used only for the processing of trademark registrations and for other activities, services, and materials relating to trademarks and to cover a proportionate share of the administrative costs of the Patent and Trademark Office.

* * *

§100 Definitions

When used in this title unless the context otherwise indicates—

* * *

(e) *The term "third-party requester" means a person requesting* ex parte *reexamination under section 302 or* inter partes *reexamination under section 311 who is not the patent owner.*

§102 Conditions for patentability; novelty and loss of right to patent

A person shall be entitled to a patent unless—

(a) the invention was known or used by others in this country, or patented or described in a printed publication in this or a foreign country, before the invention thereof by the applicant for patent, or

(b) the invention was patented or described in a printed publication in this or a foreign country or in public use or on sale in this country, more than one year prior to the date of the application for patent in the United States, or

(c) he has abandoned the invention, or

(d) the invention was first patented or caused to be patented, or was the subject of an inventor's certificate, by the applicant or his legal representatives or assigns in a foreign country prior to the date of the application for patent in this country on an application for patent or inventor's certificate filed more than twelve months before the filing of the application in the United States, or

(e) the invention was described in

(1) *an application for patent, published under section 122(b), by another filed in the United States before the invention by the applicant for patent, except that an international application filed under the treaty defined in section 351(a) shall have the effect under this subsection of a national application published under section 122(b) only if the international application designating the United States was published under Article 21(2)(a) of such treaty in the English language; or*

(2) *a patent granted on an application for patent by another filed in the United States before the invention by the applicant for patent, except that a patent shall not be deemed filed in the United States for the purposes of this subsection based on the filing of an international application filed under the treaty defined in section 351(a); or*

(f) he did not himself invent the subject matter sought to be patented, or

(g) *(1) during the course of an interference conducted under section 135 or section 291, another inventor involved therein establishes, to the extent permitted in section 104, that before such person's invention thereof the invention was made by such other inventor and not abandoned, suppressed, or concealed, or (2) before such person's* invention thereof, the invention was made in this country by another *inventor* who had not abandoned, suppressed, or concealed it. In determining priority of invention *under this subsection,* there shall be considered not only the respective dates of conception and reduction to practice of the invention, but also the reasonable diligence of one who was first to conceive and last to reduce to practice, from a time prior to conception by the other.

§103 Conditions for patentability; non-obvious subject matter

* * *

(c) Subject matter developed by another person, which qualifies as prior art only under subsection *(e),* (f)*, and* (g) of section 102 of this title, shall not preclude patentability under this section where the subject matter and the claimed invention were, at the time the invention was made, owned by the same person or subject to an obligation of assignment to the same person.

§111 Application

* * *

(b) Provisional application.

* * *

(5) Abandonment. *Notwithstanding the absence of a claim, upon timely request and as prescribed by the Director, a provisional application may be treated as an application filed under subsection (a). Subject to section 119(e)(3) of this title, if no such request is made, the provisional application shall be regarded as abandoned 12 months after the filing date of such application and shall not be subject to revival after such 12-month period.*

§119 Benefit of earlier filing date; right of priority

(a) An application for patent for an invention filed in this country by any person who has, or whose legal representatives or assigns have, previously regularly filed an application for a patent for the same invention in a foreign country which affords similar privileges in the case of applications filed in the United States or to citizens of the United States *or in a WTO Member country,* shall have the same effect as the same application would have if filed in this country on the date on which the application for patent for the same invention was first filed in such foreign country, if the application in this country is filed within twelve months from the earliest date on which such foreign application was filed; but no patent shall be granted on any application for patent for an invention which had been patented or described in a printed publication in any country more than one year before the date of the actual filing of the application in this country, or which had been in public use or on sale in this country more than one year prior to such filing.

(b) (1) *No application for patent shall be entitled to this right of priority unless a claim is filed in the Patent and Trademark Office, identifying the foreign application by specifying the application number on that foreign application, the intellectual property authority or country in or for which the application was filed, and the date of filing the application, at such time during the pendency of the application as required by the Director.*

(2) *The Director may consider the failure of the applicant to file a timely claim for priority as a waiver of any such claim. The Director may establish procedures, including the payment of a surcharge, to accept an unintentionally delayed claim under this section.*

(3) *The Director may require a certified copy of the original foreign application, specification, and drawings upon which it is based, a translation if not in the English language, and such other information as the Director considers necessary. Any such certification shall be made by the foreign intellectual property authority in which the foreign application was filed and show the date of the application and of the filing of the specification and other papers.*

(c) In like manner and subject to the same conditions and requirements, the right provided in this section may be based upon a subsequent regularly filed application in the same foreign country instead of the first filed foreign application, provided that any foreign application filed prior to such subsequent application has been withdrawn, abandoned, or otherwise disposed of, without having been laid open to public inspection and without leaving any rights outstanding, and has not served, nor thereafter shall serve, as a basis for claiming a right of priority.

(d) Applications for inventors' certificates filed in a foreign country in which applicants have a right to apply, at their discretion, either for a patent or for an inventor's certificate shall be treated in this country in the same manner and have the same effect for purpose of the right of priority under this section as applications for patents, subject to the same conditions and requirements of this section as apply to applications for patents, provided such applicants are entitled to the benefits of the Stockholm Revision of the Paris Convention at the time of such filing.

(e) (1) An application for patent filed under section 111(a) or section 363 of this title for an invention disclosed in the manner provided by the first paragraph of section 112 of this title in a provisional application filed under section 111(b) of this title, by an inventor or inventors named in the provisional application, shall have the same effect, as to such invention, as though filed on the date of the provisional application filed under section 111(b) of this title, if the application for patent filed under section 111(a) or section 363 of this title is filed not later than 12 months after the date on which the provisional application was filed and if it contains or is amended to contain a specific reference to the provisional application. *No application shall be entitled to the benefit of an earlier filed provisional application under this subsection unless an amendment containing the specific reference to the earlier filed provisional application is submitted at such time during the pendency of the application as required by the Director. The Director may consider the failure to submit such an amendment within that time period as a waiver of any benefit under this subsection. The Director may establish procedures, including the payment of a surcharge, to accept an unintentionally delayed submission of an amendment under this subsection during the pendency of the application.*

(2) A provisional application filed under section 11(b) of this title may not be relied upon in any proceeding in the Patent and Trademark Office unless the fee set forth in subparagraph (A) or (C) of section 41(a)(1) of this title has been paid.

(3) *If the day that is 12 months after the filing date of a provisional application falls on a Saturday, Sunday, or Federal holiday within the District of Columbia, the period of pendency of the provisional application shall be extended to the next succeeding secular or business day.*

(f) Applications for plant breeder's rights filed in a WTO Member country (or in a foreign UPOV Contracting Party) shall have the same effect for the purpose of the right of priority under subsections (a) through (c) of this section as applications for patents, subject to the same conditions and requirements of this section as apply to applications for patents.

(g) *As used in this section—*

(1) *the term "WTO member country" has the same meaning as the term is defined in section 104(b)(2) of this title; and*

(2) *the term "UPOV Contracting Party" means a member of the International Convention for the Protection of New Varieties of Plants.*

§120 Benefit of earlier filing date in the United States

An application for patent for an invention disclosed in the manner provided by the first paragraph of section 112 of this title in an application previously filed in the United States, or as provided by section 363 of this title, which is filed by an inventor or inventors named in the previously filed application shall have the same effect, as to such invention, as though filed on the date of the prior application, if filed before the patenting or abandonment of or termination of proceedings on the first application or on an application similarly entitled to the benefit of the filing date of the first application and if it contains or is amended to contain a specific reference to the earlier filed application. *No application shall be entitled to the benefit of an earlier filed application under this section unless an amendment containing the specific reference to the earlier filed application is submitted at such time during the pendency of the application as required by the Director. The Director may consider the failure to submit such an amendment within that time period as a waiver of any benefit under this section. The Director may establish procedures, including the payment of a surcharge, to accept an unintentionally delayed submission of an amendment under this section.*

§122 Confidential status of applications; *publication of patent applications*

(Effective 1 year after the date of enactment (November 29, 1999) and applies to all applications filed under section 111 on or after that date and to all applications complying with section 371 that resulted from international applications filed on or after that date.)

(*a*) *Confidentiality. Except as provided in subsection* (*b*), applications for patents shall be kept in confidence by the Patent and Trademark Office and no information concerning the same given without authority of the applicant or owner unless necessary to carry out the provisions of any Act of Congress or in such special circumstances as may be determined by the *Director.*

(*b*) *Publication.*

(1) *In general. (A) Subject to paragraph (2), each application for a patent shall be published, in accordance with procedures determined by the Director, promptly after the expiration of a period of 18 months from the earliest filing date for which a benefit is sought under this title. At the request of the applicant, an application may be published earlier than the end of such 18-month period.*

(B) No information concerning published patent applications shall be made available to the public except as the Director determines.

(C) Notwithstanding any other provision of law, a determination by the Director to release or not to release information concerning a published patent application shall be final and nonreviewable.

(2) *(A) Exceptions. An application shall not be published if that application is*

(i) *no longer pending;*

(ii) *subject to a secrecy order under section 181 of this title;*

(iii) *a provisional application filed under section 111(b) of this title; or*

(iv) *an application for a design patent filed under chapter 16 of this title.*

(B) (i) If an applicant makes a request upon filing, certifying that the invention disclosed in the application has not and will not be the subject of an application filed in another country, or under a multilateral international agreement, that requires publication of applications 18 months after filing, the application shall not be published as provided in paragraph (1).

(ii) An applicant may rescind a request made under clause (i) at any time.

(iii) An applicant who has made a request under clause (i) but who subsequently files, in a foreign country or under a multilateral international agreement specified in clause (i), an application directed to the invention dis-

closed in the application filed in the Patent and Trademark Office, shall notify the Director of such filing not later than 45 days after the date of the filing of such foreign or international application. A failure of the applicant to provide such notice within the prescribed period shall result in the application being regarded as abandoned, unless it is shown to the satisfaction of the Director that the delay in submitting the notice was unintentional.

(*iv*) *If an applicant rescinds a request made under clause (i) or notifies the Director that an application was filed in a foreign country or under a multilateral international agreement specified in clause (i), the application shall be published in accordance with the provisions of paragraph (1) on or as soon as practical after the date that is specified in clause (i).*

(v) *If an applicant has filed applications in one or more foreign countries, directly or through a multilateral international agreement, and such foreign filed applications corresponding to an application filed in the Patent and Trademark Office or the description of the invention in such foreign filed applications is less extensive than the application or description of the invention in the application filed in the Patent and Trademark Office, the applicant may submit a redacted copy of the application filed in the Patent and Trademark Office eliminating any part or description of the invention in such application that is not also contained in any of the corresponding applications filed in a foreign country. The Director may only publish the redacted copy of the application unless the redacted copy of the application is not received within 16 months after the earliest effective filing date for which a benefit is sought under this title. The provisions of section 154(d) shall not apply to a claim if the description of the invention published in the redacted application filed under this clause with respect to the claim does not enable a person skilled in the art to make and use the subject matter of the claim.*

(*c*) *Protest and Pre-Issuance Opposition. The Director shall establish appropriate procedures to ensure that no protest or other form of pre-issuance opposition to the grant of a patent on an application may be initiated after publication of the application without the express written consent of the applicant.*

(*d*) *National Security. No application for patent shall be published under subsection (b)(1) if the publication or disclosure of such invention would be detrimental to the national security. The Director shall establish appropriate procedures to ensure that such applications are promptly identified and the secrecy of such inventions is maintained in accordance with chapter 17 of this title.*

§132 Notice of rejection; reexamination

(*a*) Whenever, on examination, any claim for a patent is rejected, or any objection or requirement made, the *Director* shall notify the applicant thereof, stating the reasons for such rejection, or objection or requirement, together with such information and references as may be useful in judging of the propriety of continuing the prosecution of his application; and if after receiving such notice, the applicant persists in his claim for a patent, with or without amendment, the application shall be reexamined. No amendment shall introduce new matter into the disclosure of the invention.

(*b*) *The Director shall prescribe regulations to provide for the continued examination of applications for patent at the request of the applicant. The Director may establish appropriate fees for such continued examination and shall provide a 50 percent reduction in such fees for small entities that qualify for reduced fees under section 41(h)(1) of this title.* (*Effective 6 months after the date of enactment (November 29, 1999) and applies to all applications filed under section 111(a) on or after June 8, 1995 and all applications complying with section 371 of title 35 that resulted from international applications filed on or after June 8, 1995.*)

§134 Appeal to the Board of Patent Appeals and Interferences

(*a*) *Patent Applicant.* An applicant for a patent, any of whose claims has been twice rejected, may appeal from the decision of *the administrative patent judge* to the Board of Patent Appeals and Interferences, having once paid the fee for such appeal.

(*b*) *Patent Owner.* A patent owner in any reexamination proceeding may appeal from the final rejection of any claim by the administrative patent judge to the Board of Patent Appeals and Interferences, having once paid the fee for such appeal.

(*c*) *Third-Party. A third-party requester in an* inter partes *proceeding may appeal to the Board of Patent Appeals and Interferences from the final decision of the administrative patent judge favorable to the patentability of any original or proposed amended or new claim of a patent, having once paid the fee for such appeal. The third-party requester may not appeal the decision of the Board of Patent Appeals and Interferences.*

§135 Interferences

* * *

(b) (*1*) A claim which is the same as, or for the same or substantially the same subject matter as, a claim of an issued patent may not be made in any application unless such a claim is made prior to one year from the date on which the patent was granted.

(*2*) *A claim which is the same as, or for the same or substantially the same subject matter as, a claim of an application published under section 122(b) of this title may be made in an application filed after the application is published only if the claim is made before 1 year after the date on which the application is published.*

* * *

§141 Appeal to Court of Appeals for the Federal Circuit

An applicant dissatisfied with the decision in an appeal to the Board of Patent Appeals and Interferences under section 134 of this title may appeal the decision to the United States Court Appeals for the Federal Circuit. By filing such an appeal the applicant waives his or her right to proceed under section 145 of this title. A party to an interference dissatisfied with the decision of the Board of Patent Appeals and Interferences on the interference may appeal the decision to the United States Court of Appeals for the Federal Circuit, but such appeal shall be dismissed if any adverse party to such interference, within twenty days after the appellant has filed notice of appeal in accordance with section 142 of this title, files notice with the Commissioner that the party elects to have all further proceedings conducted as provided in section 146 of this title. *In any reexamination case, the Director shall submit to the court in writing the grounds for the decision of the Patent and Trademark Office, addressing all the issues involved in the appeal.* If the appellant does not, within thirty days after the filing of such notice by the adverse party, file a civil action under section 146, the decision appealed from shall govern the further proceedings in the case.

§154 Contents and term of patent; *provisional rights*

* * *

(b) *Adjustment of patent term.* (*Effective 6 months after the date of enactment (November 29, 1999) and applies to patent applications, other than design patent applications, filed on or after the date that is 6 months after the date of enactment.*)

(1) *Patent term guarantees.*

(A) *Guarantee of prompt Patent and Trademark Office responses. Subject to the limitations under paragraph (2), if the issue of an original patent is delayed due to the failure of the Patent and Trademark Office to*

(i) *provide at least one of the notifications under section 132 of this title or a notice of allowance under section 151 of this title not later than 14 months after*

(I) *the date on which an application was filed under section 111(a) of this title; or*

(II) *the date on which an international application fulfilled the requirements of section 371 of this title*

(ii) *responds to a reply under section 132, or to an appeal taken under section 134, within 4 months after the date on which the reply was filed or the appeal was taken;*

(iii) *act on an application within 4 months after the date of a decision by the Board of Patent Appeals and Interferences under section 134 or 135 or a decision by a Federal court under section 141, 145, or 146 in a case in which allowable claims remain in the application; or*

(iv) *issue a patent within 4 months after the date on which the issue fee was paid under section 151 and all outstanding requirements were satisfied,*

the term of the patent shall be extended 1 day for each day after the end of the period specified in clause (i), (ii), (iii), or (iv), as the case may be, until the action described in such clause is taken.

(B) *Guarantee of no more than 3-year application pendency. Subject to the limitations under paragraph (2), if the issue of an original patent is delayed due to the failure of the United States Patent and Trademark Office to issue a patent within 3 years after the actual filing date of the application in the United States, not including*

(i) *any time consumed by continued examination of the application requested by the applicant under section 132(b);*

(ii) *any time consumed by a proceeding under section 135(a), any time consumed by the imposition of an order under section 181, or any time consumed by appellate review by the Board of Patent Appeals and Interferences or by a Federal court; or*

(iii) *any delay in the processing of the application by the United States Patent and Trademark Office requested by the applicant except as permitted by paragraph (3)(C),*

the term of the patent shall be extended 1 day for each day after the end of that 3-year period until the patent is issued.

(C) *Guarantee or adjustments for delays due to interferences, secrecy orders, and appeals. Subject to the limitations under paragraph (2), if the issue of an original patent is delayed due to*

(i) *a proceeding under section 135(a);*

(ii) *the imposition of an order under section 181; or*

(iii) *appellate review by the Board of Patent Appeals and Interferences or by a Federal court in a case in which the patent was issued under a decision in the review reversing an adverse determination of patentability,*

the term of the patent shall be extended 1 day for each day of the pendency of the proceeding, order, or review, as the case may be.

(2) *Limitations.*

(A) *In general. To the extent that periods of delay attributable to grounds specified in paragraph (1) overlap, the period of any adjustment granted under this subsection shall not exceed the actual number of days the issuance of the patent was delayed.*

(B) *Disclaimed term. No patent the term of which has been disclaimed beyond a specified date may be adjusted under this section beyond the expiration date specified in the disclaimer.*

(C) *Reduction of period of adjustment.*

(i) *The period of adjustment of the term of a patent under paragraph (1) shall be reduced by a period equal to the period of time during which the applicant failed to engage in reasonable efforts to conclude prosecution of the application.*

(ii) *With respect to adjustments to patent term made under the authority of paragraph (1)(B), an applicant shall be deemed to have failed to engage in reasonable efforts to conclude processing or examination of an application for the cumulative total of any periods of time in excess of 3 months that are taken to respond to a notice from the Office making any rejection, objection, argument, or other request, measuring such 3-month period from the date the notice was given or mailed to the applicant.*

(iii) *The Director shall prescribe regulations establishing the circumstances that constitute a failure of an applicant to engage in reasonable efforts to conclude processing or examination of an application.*

(3) *Procedures for patent term adjustment determination.*

(A) *The Director shall prescribe regulations establishing procedures for the application for and determination of patent term adjustments under this subsection.*

(B) *Under the procedures established under paragraph (A), the Director shall*

(i) *make a determination of the period of any patent term adjustment under this subsection, and shall transmit a notice of that determination with the written notice of that determination with the written notice of allowance of the application under section 151; and*

(ii) *provide the applicant one opportunity to request reconsideration of any patent term adjustment determination made by the Director.*

(C) *The Director shall reinstate all or part of the cumulative period of time of an adjustment under paragraph (2)(C) if the applicant, prior to the issuance of the patent, makes a showing that, in spite of all due care, the applicant was unable to respond within the 3-month period, but in no case shall more than three additional months for each such response beyond the original 3-month period be reinstated.*

(D) *The Director shall proceed to grant the patent after completion of the Director's determination of a patent term adjustment under the procedures established under this subsection, notwithstanding any appeal taken by the applicant of such determination.*

(4) *Appeal of patent term adjustment determination.*

(A) *An applicant dissatisfied with a determination made by the Director under paragraph (3) shall have remedy by a civil action against the Director filed in the United States District Court for the District of Columbia within 180 days after the grant of the patent. Chapter 7 of title 5, United States Code, shall apply to such action. Any final judgment resulting in a change to the period of adjustment of the patent term shall be served on the Director, and the Director shall thereafter alter the term of the patent to reflect such change.*

(B) *The determination of a patent term adjustment under this subsection shall not be subject to appeal or challenge by a third party prior to the grant of the patent.*

(d) *Provisional Rights.*

(1) *In general. In addition to other rights provided by this section, a patent shall include the right to obtain a reasonable royalty from any person who, during the period beginning on the date of publication of the application for such patent under section 112(b), or in the case of an international application filed under the treaty defined in section 351(a) designating the United States under Article 21(2)(a) of such treaty, the date of publication of the application, and ending on the date the patent is issued*

(A) (*i*) *makes, uses, offers for sale, or sells in the United States the invention as claimed in the published patent application or imports such an invention into the United States; or*

(ii) *if the invention as claimed in the published patent application is a process, uses, offers for sale, or sells in the United States or imports into the United States products made by that process as claimed in the published patent application, and*

(B) *had actual notice of the published patent application and, in a case in which the right arising under this paragraph is based upon an international application designating the United States that is published in a language other than English, had a translation of the international application into the English language.*

(2) *Right based on substantially identical inventions. The right under paragraph (1) to obtain a reasonable royalty shall not be available under this subsection unless the invention as claimed in the patent is substantially identical to the invention as claimed in the published patent application.*

(3) *Time limitation on obtaining a reasonable royalty. The right under paragraph (1) to obtain a reasonable royalty shall not be affected by the duration of the period described in paragraph (1).*

(4) *Requirements for international applications.*

(A) *Effective date. The right under paragraph (1) to obtain a reasonable royalty based upon the publication under the treaty defined in section 351(a) of an international application designating the United States shall commence on the date on which the Patent and Trademark Office receives a copy of the publication under the treaty of the international application, or, if the publication under the treaty of the international application is in a language other than English, on the date on which the Patent and Trademark Office receives a translation of the international application in the English language.*

(B) *Copies. The Director may require the applicant to provide a copy of the international application and a translation thereof.*

§156 Extension of patent term

(a) The term of a patent which claims a product, a method of using a product, or a method of manufacturing a product shall be extended in accordance with this section from the original expiration date of the patent, *which shall include any patent term adjustment granted under section 154(b), if—*

(1) the term of the patent has not expired before an application is submitted under subsection (d)(1) for its extension;

(2) the term of the patent has never been extended under subsection (e)(1) of this section;

(3) an application for extension is submitted by the owner of record of the patent or its agent and in accordance with the requirements of paragraphs (1) through (4) of subsection (d);

(4) the product has been subject to a regulatory review period before it's commercial marketing or use;

(5) (A) except as provided in subparagraph (B) or (C), the permission for the commercial marketing or use of the product after such regulatory review period is the first permitted commercial marketing or use of the product under the provision of law under which such regulatory review period occurred;

(B) in the case of a patent which claims a method of manufacturing the product which primarily uses recombinant DNA technology in the manufacture of the product, the permission for the commercial marketing or use of the product after such regulatory review period is the first permitted commercial marketing or use of a product manufactured under the process claimed in the patent; or

(C) for purposes of subparagraph (A), in the case of a patent which—

(i) claims a new animal drug or a veterinary biological product which (I) is not covered by the claims in any other patent which has been extended, and (II) has received permission for the commercial marketing or use in non-food-producing animals and in food-producing animals, and

(ii) was not extended on the basis of the regulatory review period for use in non-food-producing animals, the permission for the commercial marketing or use of the drug or product after the regulatory review period for use in food-producing animals is the first permitted commercial marketing or use of the drug or product for administration to a food-producing animal.

The product referred to in paragraphs (4) and (5) is hereinafter in this section referred to as the "approved product".

* * *

§181 Secrecy of certain inventions and withholding of patent

Whenever publication or disclosure *by the publication of an application or* by the grant of a patent on an invention in which the Government has a property interest might, in the opinion of the head of the interested Government agency, be detrimental to the national security, the Commissioner *of Patents* upon being so notified shall order that the invention be kept secret and shall withhold *the publication of the application or* the grant of a patent therefor under the conditions set forth hereinafter.

Whenever the publication or disclosure of an invention *by publication of an application* or by the granting of a patent, in which the Government does not have a property interest, might, in the opinion of the Commissioner *of Patents,* be detrimental to the national security, he shall make the application for patent in which such invention is disclosed available for inspection to the Atomic Energy Commission, the Secretary of Defense, and the chief officer of any other department or agency of the Government designated by the President as a defense agency of the United States.

Each individual to whom the application is disclosed shall sign a dated acknowledgement thereof, which acknowledgment shall be entered in the file of the application. If, in the opinion of the Atomic Energy Commission, the Secretary of a Defense Department, or the chief officer of another department or agency so designated, the publication or disclosure of the invention *by the publication of the application* or by the granting of a patent therefor would be detrimental to the national security, the Atomic Energy Commission, the Secretary of a Defense Department, or such other chief officer shall notify the Commissioner and the Commissioner of *Patents* shall order that the invention be kept secret and shall withhold *the publication of the application* or the grant of a patent for such period as the national interest requires, and notify the applicant thereof. Upon proper showing by the head of the department or agency who caused the secrecy order to be issued that the examination of the application might jeopardize the national interest, the Commissioner *of Patents* shall thereupon maintain the application in a sealed condition and notify the applicant thereof. The owner of an application which has been placed under a secrecy order shall have a right to appeal from the order to the Secretary of Commerce under rules prescribed by him.

An invention shall not be ordered kept secret and *the publication of an application or* the grant of a patent withheld for a period of more than one year. The Commissioner *of Patents* shall renew the order at the end thereof, or at the end of any renewal period, for additional periods of one year upon notification by the head of the department or the chief officer of the agency who caused the order to be issued that an affirmative determination has been made that the national interest continues so to require. An order in effect, or issued, during a time when the United States is at war, shall remain in effect for the duration of hostilities and one year following cessation of hostilities. An order in effect, or issued, during a national emergency declared by the President shall remain in effect for the duration of the national emergency and six months thereafter. The Commissioner *of Patents* may rescind any order upon notification by the heads of the departments and the chief officers of the agencies who caused the order to be issued that the publication or disclosure of the invention is no longer deemed detrimental to the national security.

§273 *Defense to infringement based on earlier inventor (Effective on the date of enactment, but only to actions occurring thereafter.)*

(a) *DEFINITIONS. For purposes of this section*

(1) *the terms "commercially used" and "commercial use" mean use of a method in the United States, so long as such use is in connection with an internal commercial use or an actual arm's-length sale or other arm's-length commercial transfer of a useful end result, whether or not the subject matter at issue is accessible to or otherwise known to the public, except that the subject matter for which commercial marketing or use is subject to a premarketing regulatory review period during which the safety or efficacy of the subject matter is established, including any period specified in section 156(g), shall be deemed "commercially used" and in "commercial use" during such regulatory review period;*

(2) *in the case of activities performed by a nonprofit research laboratory, or nonprofit entity such as a university, research center, or hospital, a use for which the public is the intended beneficiary shall be considered to be a use described in paragraph (1), except that the use*

(A) *may be asserted as a defense under this section only for continued use by and in the laboratory or nonprofit entity; and*

(B) *may not be asserted as a defense with respect to any subsequent commercialization or use outside such laboratory or nonprofit entity;*

(3) *the term "method" means a method of doing or conducting business; and*

(4) *the "effective filing date" of a patent is the earlier of the actual filing date of the application for the patent or the filing date of any earlier United States, foreign, or international application to which the subject matter at issue is entitled under section 119, 120, or 365 of this title.*

(b) *DEFENSE TO INFRINGEMENT*

(1) *IN GENERAL. It shall be a defense to an action for infringement under section 271 of this title with respect to any subject matter that would otherwise infringe one or more claims for a method in the patent being asserted against a person, if such person had, acting in good faith, actually reduced the subject matter to practice at least 1 year before the effective filing date of such patent, and commercially used the subject matter before the effective filing date of such patent.*

(2) *EXHAUSTION OF RIGHT. The sale or other disposition of a useful end product produced by a patented method, by a person entitled to assert a defense under this section with respect to that useful end result shall exhaust the patent owner's rights under the patent to the extent such rights would have been exhausted had such sale or other disposition been made by the patent owner.*

(3) *LIMITATIONS AND QUALIFICATION OF DEFENSE. The defense to infringement under this section is subject to the following:*

(A) *PATENT. A person may not assert the defense under this section unless the invention for which the defense is asserted is for a method.*

(B) *DERIVATION. A person may not assert the defense under this section if the subject matter on which the defense is based was derived from the patentee or persons in privity with the patentee.*

(C) *NOT A GENERAL LICENSEE. The defense asserted by a person under this section is not a general license under all claims of the patent at issue, but extends only to the specific subject matter claimed in the patent with respect to which the person can assert a defense under this chapter, except that the defense shall also extend to variations in the quantity or volume of use of the claimed subject matter, and to improvements in the claimed subject matter that do not infringe additional specifically claimed subject matter of the patent.*

(4) *BURDEN OF PROOF. A person asserting the defense under this section shall have the burden of establishing the defense by clear and convincing evidence.*

(5) *ABANDONMENT OF USE. A person who has abandoned commercial use of subject matter may not rely on activities performed before the date of such abandonment in establishing a defense under this section with respect to actions taken after the date of such abandonment.*

(6) *PERSONAL DEFENSE. The defense under this section may be asserted only by the person who performed the acts necessary to establish the defense and except for any transfer to the patent owner, the right to assert the defense shall not be licensed or assigned or transferred to another person except as an ancillary and subordinate part of a good faith assignment or transfer for other reasons of the entire enterprise or line of business to which the defense relates.*

(7) *LIMITATION ON SITES. A defense under this section, when acquired as part of a good faith assignment or transfer of an entire enterprise or line of business to which the defense relates, may only be asserted for uses at sites where the subject matter that would otherwise infringe one or more of the claims is in use before the later of the effective filing date of the patent or the date of the assignment or transfer of such enterprise or line of business.*

(8) *UNSUCCESSFUL ASSERTION OF DEFENSE. If the defense under this section is pleaded by a person who is found to infringe the patent and who subsequently fails to demonstrate a reasonable basis for asserting the defense, the court shall find the case exceptional for the purpose of awarding attorney fees under section 285 of this title.*

(9) *INVALIDITY. A patent shall not be deemed to be invalid under section 102 or 103 of this title solely because a defense is raised or established under this section.*

§282 Presumption of validity; defenses

* * *

Invalidity of the extension of a patent term or any portion thereof under section *154(b) or* 156 of this title because of the material failure—

(1) by the applicant for the extension, or

(2) by the *Director,*

to comply with the requirements of such section shall be a defense in any action involving the infringement of a patent during the period of the extension of its term and shall be pleaded. A due diligence determination under section 156(d)(2) is not subject to review in such an action.

§284 Damages

* * *

When the damages are not found by a jury, the court shall assess them. In either event the court may increase the damages up to three times the amount found or assessed. *Increased damages under this paragraph shall not apply to provisional rights under section 154(d) of this title.*

* * *

§287 Limitation on damages and other remedies; marking and notice

* * *

(4) This subsection shall not apply to any patent issued *based on an application the earliest effective filing date of which is prior to September 30, 1996.*

§297 Improper and deceptive invention promotion (Effective 60 days after the date of enactment (November 29, 1999))

(a) *IN GENERAL. An invention promoter shall have a duty to disclose the following information to a customer in writing, prior to entering into a contract for invention promotion services:*

(1) *the total number of inventions evaluated by the invention promoter for commercial potential in the past 5 years, as well as the number of those inventions that received negative evaluations;*

(2) *the total number of customers who have contracted with the invention promoter in the past 5 years, not including customers who have purchased trade show services, research, advertising or other nonmarketing services from the invention promoter, or who have defaulted in their payment to the invention promoter;*

(3) *the total number of customers known by the invention promoter to have received a net financial profit as a direct result of the invention promotion services provided by such invention promoter;*

(4) *the total number of customers known by the invention promoter to have received license agreements for their inventions as a direct result of the invention promotion services provided by such invention promoter; and*

(5) *the names and addresses of all previous invention promotion companies with which the invention promoter or its officers have collectively or individually been affiliated in the previous 10 years.*

(b) *CIVIL ACTION (1) Any customer who enters into a contract with an invention promoter and who is found by a court to have been injured by any material false or fraudulent statement or representation, or any omission of material fact, by that invention promoter (or any agent, employee, director, officer, partner, or independent contractor of such invention promoter), or by the failure of that invention promoter to disclose such information as required under subsection (a), may recover in a civil action against the invention promoter (or the officers, directors, or partners of such invention promoter), in addition to reasonable costs and attorneys' fees*

(A) *the amount of actual damages incurred by the customer; or*

(B) *at the election of the customer at any time before final judgment is rendered, statutory damages in a sum of not more than $5,000, as the court considers just.*

(2) *Notwithstanding paragraph (1), in a case where the customer sustains the burden of proof, and the court finds, that the invention promoter intentionally misrepresented or omitted a material fact to such customer, or willfully failed to disclose such information as required under subsection (a), with the purpose of deceiving that customer, the court may increase damages to not more than three times the amount awarded, taking into account past complaints made against the invention promoter that resulted in regulatory sanctions or other corrective actions based on those records compiled by the Commissioner of Patents under subsection (d).*

(c) *DEFINITIONS. For purposes of this section*

(1) *a "contract for invention promotion services" means a contract by which an invention promoter undertakes invention promotion services for a customer;*

(2) *a "customer" is any individual who enters into a contract with an invention promoter for invention promotion services;*

(3) *the term "invention promoter" means any person, firm, partnership, corporation, or other entity who offers to perform or performs invention promotion services for, or on behalf of, a customer, and who holds itself out through advertising in any mass media as providing such services, but does not include*

(A) *any department or agency of the Federal Government or of a State or local government;*

(B) *any nonprofit, charitable, scientific, or educational organization, qualified under applicable State law or described under section 170(b)(1)(A) of the Internal Revenue Code of 1986;*

(C) *any person or entity involved in the evaluation to determine commercial potential of, or offering to license or sell, a utility patent or a previously filed nonprovisional utility patent application;*

(D) *any party participating in a transaction involving the sale of the stock or assets of a business; or*

(E) *any party who directly engages in the business of retail sales of products or the distribution of products; and*

(4) *the term "invention promotion services" means the procurement or attempted procurement for a customer of a firm, corporation, or other entity to develop and market products or services that include the invention of the customer.*

(d) *RECORDS OF COMPLAINTS*

(1) *RELEASE OF COMPLAINTS. The Commissioner of Patents shall make all complaints received by the Patent and Trademark Office involving invention promoters publicly available, together with any response of the invention promoters. The Commissioner of Patents shall notify the invention promoter of a complaint and provide a reasonable opportunity to reply prior to making such complaint publicly available.*

(2) *REQUEST FOR COMPLAINTS. The Commissioner of Patents may request complaints relating to invention promotion services from any Federal or State agency and include such complaints in the records maintained under paragraph (1), together with any response of the invention promoters.*

§311 Request for **inter partes** *reexamination*

(a) *In General. Any person at any time may file a request for* inter partes *reexamination by the Office of a patent on the basis of any prior art cited under the provisions of section 301.*

(b) *Requirements. The request shall*

(1) *be in writing, include the identity of the real party in interest, and be accompanied by payment of an* inter partes *reexamination fee established by the Director under section 41; and*

(2) *set forth the pertinency and manner of applying cited prior art to every claim for which reexamination is requested.*

(c) *Copy. Unless the requesting person is the owner of the patent, the Director promptly shall send a copy of the request to the owner of record of the patent.*

§312 Determination of issue by Director

(a) *Reexamination. Not later than 3 months after the filing of a request for* inter partes *reexamination under section 311, the Director shall determine whether a substantial new question of patentability affecting any claim of the patent concerned is raised by the request, with or without consideration of other patents or printed publications. On the Director's initiative, and at any time, the Director may determine whether a substantial new question of patentability is raised by patents and publications.*

(b) *Record. A record of the Director's determination under subsection (a) shall be placed in the official file of the patent, and a copy shall be promptly given or mailed to the owner of record of the patent and to the third-party requester, if any.*

(c) *Final Decision. A determination by the Director under subsection (a) shall be final and non-appealable. Upon a determination that no substantial new question of patentability has been raised, the Director may refund a portion of the* inter partes *reexamination fee required under section 311.*

§313 **Inter partes** *reexamination order by Director*

If, in a determination made under section 312(a), the Director finds that a substantial new question of patentability affecting a claim of a patent is raised, the determination shall include an order for inter partes *reexamination of the patent for resolution of the question. The order may be accompanied by the initial action of the Patent and Trademark Office on the merits of the* inter partes *reexamination conducted in accordance with section 314.*

§314 Conduct of **inter partes** *reexamination proceedings*

(a) *In General. Except as otherwise provided in this section, reexamination shall be conducted according to the procedures established for initial examination under the provisions of sections 132 and 133. In any* inter partes *reexamination proceeding under this chapter, the patent owner shall be permitted to propose any amendment to the patent and a new claim or claims, except that no proposed amended or new claim enlarging the scope of the claims of the patent shall be permitted.*

(b) *Response. (1) This subsection shall apply to any* inter partes *reexamination proceeding in which the order for* inter partes *reexamination is based upon a request by a third-party requester.*

(2) With the exception of the inter partes *reexamination request, any document filed by either the patent owner or the third-party requester shall be served on the other party. In addition, the third-party requester shall receive a copy of any communication sent by the Office to the patent owner concerning the patent subject to the* inter partes *reexamination proceeding.*

(3) *Each time that the patent owner files a response to an action on the merits from the Patent and Trademark Office, the third-party requester shall have one opportunity to file written comments addressing issues raised by the action of the Office or the patent owner's response thereto, if those written comments are received by the Office within 30 days after the date of service of the patent owner's response.*

(c) *Special Dispatch. Unless otherwise provided by the Director for good cause, all* inter partes *reexamination proceedings under this section, including any appeal to the Board of Patent Appeals and Interferences, shall be conducted with special dispatch within the Office.*

§315 Appeal

(a) *Patent Owner. The patent owner involved in an* inter partes *reexamination proceeding under this chapter*

(1) *may appeal under the provisions of section 134 and may appeal under the provisions of sections 141 through 144, with respect to any decision adverse to the patentability of any original or proposed amended or new claim of the patent; and*

(2) *may be a party to any appeal taken by a third-party requester under subsection (b).*

(b) *Third-Party Requester. A third-party requester may*

(1) *appeal under the provisions of section 134 with respect to any final decision favorable to the patentability of any original or proposed amended or new claim of the patent; or*

(2) *be a party to any appeal taken by the patent owner under the provisions of section 134, subject to subsection (c).*

(c) *Civil Action. A third-party requester whose request for an* inter partes *reexamination results in an order under section 313 is estopped from asserting at a later time, in any civil action arising in whole or in part under section 1338 of title 28, United States Code, the invalidity of any claim finally determined to be valid and patentable on any ground which the third-party requester raised or could have raised during the* inter partes *reexamination proceedings. This subsection does not prevent the assertion of invalidity based on newly discovered prior art unavailable to the third-party requester and the Patent and Trademark Office at the time of the* interpartes *reexamination proceedings.*

§316 Certificate of patentability, unpatentability, and claim cancellation

(a) *In General. In an* inter partes *reexamination proceeding under this chapter, when the time for appeal has expired or any appeal proceeding has terminated, the Director shall issue and publish a certificate canceling any claim of the patent finally determined to be unpatentable, confirming any claim of the patent determined to be patentable, and incorporating in the patent any proposed amended or new claim determined to be patentable.*

(b) *Amended or New Claim. Any proposed amended or new claim determined to be patentable and incorporated into a patent following an* inter partes *reexamination proceeding shall have the same effect as that specified in section 252 of this title for reissued patents on the right of any person who made, purchased, or used within the United States, or imported into the United States, anything patented by such proposed amended or new claim, or who made substantial preparation therefor, prior to issuance of a certificate under the provisions of subsection (a) of this section.*

§317 Inter partes *reexamination prohibited*

(a) *Order for Reexamination. Notwithstanding any provision of this chapter, once an order for* inter partes *reexamination of a patent has been issued under section 313, neither the patent owner nor the third-party requester, if any, nor privies of either, may file a subsequent request for* inter partes *reexamination of the patent until an* inter partes *reexamination certificate is issued and published under section 316, unless authorized by the Director.*

(b) *Final Decision. Once a final decision has been entered against a party in a civil action arising in whole or in part under section 1338 of title 28, United States Code, that the party has not sustained its burden of proving the invalidity of any patent claim in suit or if a final decision in an* inter partes *reexamination proceeding instituted by a third-party requester is favorable to the patentability of any original or proposed amended or new claim of the patent, then neither that party nor its privies may thereafter request an* inter partes *reexamination of any such patent claim on the basis of issues which that party or its privies raised or could have raised in such civil action or* inter partes *reexamination proceeding, and an* inter partes *reexamination requested by that party or its privies on the basis of such issues may not thereafter be maintained by the Office, notwithstanding any other provision of this chapter. This subsection does not prevent the assertion of invalidity based on newly discovered prior art unavailable to the third-party requester and the Patent and Trademark Office at the time of the* inter partes *reexamination proceedings.*

§318 Stay of litigation

Once an order for inter partes *reexamination of a patent has been issued under section 313, the patent owner may obtain a stay of any pending litigation which involves an issue of patentability of any claims of the patent which are the subject of the* inter partes *reexamination order, unless the court before which such litigation is pending determines that a stay would not serve the interests of justice.*

§374 Publication of international application

The publication under the treaty *defined in section 351(a) of this title,* of an international application *designating the United States* shall confer *the same* rights and shall have *the same* effect under this title *as an application for patent published under section 122(b), except as provided in sections 102(e) and 154(d) of this title.*

Appendix C-30

Changes to Implement Eighteen-Month Publication of Patent Applications; Final Rule

65 FR 57024
Department of Commerce
Patent and Trademark Office
37 CFR Parts 1 and 5
RIN 0651—AB05

Agency: United States Patent and Trademark Office, Commerce

Action: Final Rule

* * *

Dates: Effective Date: November 29, 2000.

Applicability Date: Sections 1.103(d), 1.211, 1.213, 1.215, 1.217, 1.219, and 1.221, and the changes to §§1.14, 1.55, 1.72, 1.78, 1.85, 1.99, 1.137, 1.138, and 1.311, apply to any patent application filed on or after November 29, 2000, and to any patent application in which applicant requests voluntary publication.

* * *

PART 1—RULES OF PRACTICE IN PATENT CASES

1. The authority citation for 37 CFR Part 1 continues to read as follows:

Authority: 35 U.S.C. 2(b)(2).

2. Section 1.9 is amended by revising paragraph (c) to read as follows:

§1.9 Definitions.

* * * * *

(c) A published application as used in this chapter means an application for patent which has been published under 35 U.S.C. 122(b).

* * * * *

3. Section 1.11 is amended by revising paragraph (a) to read as follows:

§1.11 Files open to the public.

(a) The specification, drawings, and all papers relating to the file of an abandoned published application, except if a redacted copy of the application was used for the patent application publication, a patent, or a statutory invention registration are open to inspection by the public, and copies may be obtained upon the payment of the fee set forth in §1.19(b)(2). See §2.27 for trademark files.

* * * * *

4. Section 1.12 is amended by revising paragraphs (a)(1) and (b) to read as follows:

§1.12 Assignment records open to public inspection.

(a)(1) Separate assignment records are maintained in the United States Patent and Trademark Office for patents and trademarks. The assignment records, relating to original or reissue patents, including digests and indexes (for assignments recorded on or after May 1, 1957), published patent applications, and assignment records relating to pending or abandoned trademark applications and to trademark registrations (for assignments recorded on or after January 1, 1955), are open to public inspection at the United States Patent and Trademark Office, and copies of those assignment records may be obtained upon request and payment of the fee set forth in §1.19 and §2.6 of this chapter.

* * * * *

(b) Assignment records, digests, and indexes relating to any pending or abandoned patent application which has not been published under 35 U.S.C. 122(b) are not available to the public. Copies of any such assignment records and related information shall be obtainable only upon written authority of the applicant or applicant's assignee or attorney or agent or upon a showing that the person seeking such information is a *bona fide* prospective or actual purchaser, mortgagee, or licensee of such application, unless it shall be necessary to the proper conduct of business before the Office or as provided in this part.

* * * * *

5. Section 1.13 is revised to read as follows:

§1.13 Copies and certified copies.

(a) Non-certified copies of patents, patent application publications, and trademark registrations and of any records, books, papers, or drawings within the jurisdiction of the United States Patent and Trademark Office and open to the public, will be furnished by the United States Patent and Trademark Office to any person, and copies of other records or papers will be furnished to persons entitled thereto, upon payment of the appropriate fee.

(b) Certified copies of patents, patent application publications, and trademark registrations and of any records, books, papers, or drawings within the jurisdiction of the United States Patent and Trademark Office and open to the public or persons entitled thereto will be authenticated by the seal of the United States Patent and Trademark Office and certified by the Commissioner, or in his or her name attested by an officer of the United States Patent and Trademark Office authorized by the Commissioner, upon payment of the fee for the certified copy.

6. Section §1.14 is amended by revising paragraphs (a), (b), (c), (e), (i) and (j) to read as follows:

§1.14 Patent applications preserved in confidence.

(a) *Confidentiality of patent application information.* Patent applications that have not been published under 35 U.S.C. 122(b) are generally preserved in confidence pursuant to 35 U.S.C. 122(a). Information concerning the filing, pendency, or subject matter of an application for patent, including status information, and access to the application, will only be given to the public as set forth in §1.11 or in this section.

(1) *Status information* is:

(i) Whether the application is pending, abandoned, or patented;

(ii) Whether the application has been published under 35 U.S.C. 122(b); and

(iii) The application "numerical identifier" which may be:

(A) The eight-digit application number (the two-digit series code plus the six-digit serial number); or

(B) The six-digit serial number plus any one of the filing date of the national application, the international filing date, or date of entry into the national stage.

(2) Access is defined as providing the application file for review and copying of any material in the application file.

(b) *When status information may be supplied.* Status information of an application may be supplied by the Office to the public if any of the following apply:

(1) Access to the application is available pursuant to paragraph (e) of this section;

(2) The application is referred to by its numerical identifier in a published patent document (*e.g.*, a U.S. patent, a U.S. patent application publication, or an international application publication), or in a U.S. application open to public inspection (§1.11(b), or paragraph (e)(2)(i) or (e)(2)(ii) of this section);

(3) The application is a published international application in which the United States of America has been indicated as a designated state; or

(4) The application claims the benefit of the filing date of an application for which status information may be provided pursuant to paragraphs (b)(1) through (b)(3) of this section.

(c) *When copies may be supplied.* A copy of an application-as-filed or a file wrapper and contents may be supplied by the Office to the public[, subject to paragraph (i) of this section (which addresses international applications),] if any of the following apply:

(1) *Application-as-filed.*

(i) If a U.S. patent application publication or patent incorporates by reference, or includes a specific reference under 35 U.S.C. 119(e) or 120 to, a pending or abandoned application, a copy of that application-as-filed may be provided to any person upon written request including the fee set forth in §1.19(b)(1); or

(ii) If an international application, which designates the U.S. and which has been published in accordance with PCT Article 21(2), incorporates by reference or claims priority under PCT Article 8 to a pending or abandoned U.S. application, a copy of that application-as-filed may be provided to any person upon written request including a showing that the publication of the application in accordance with PCT Article 21(2) has occurred and that the U.S. was designated, and upon payment of the appropriate fee set forth in §1.19(b)(1).

(2) *File wrapper and contents.* A copy of the specification, drawings, and all papers relating to the file of an abandoned or pending published application may be provided to any person upon written request, including the fee set forth in §1.19(b)(2). If a redacted copy of the application was used for the patent application publication, the copy of the specification, drawings, and papers may be limited to a redacted copy.

* * * * *

(e) *Public access to a pending or abandoned application.* Access to an application may be provided to any person[, subject to paragraph (i) of this section,] if a written request for access is submitted, the application file is available, and any of the following apply:

(1) The application is open to public inspection pursuant to §1.11(b); or

(2) The application is abandoned, it is not within the file jacket of a pending application under §1.53(d), and it is referred to:

(i) In a U.S. patent application publication or patent;

(ii) In another U.S. application which is open to public inspection either pursuant to §1.11(b) or paragraph (e)(2)(i) of this section; or

(iii) In an international application which designates the U.S. and is published in accordance with PCT Article 21(2).

* * * * *

(i) *International applications.*

(1) Copies of international application files for international applications which designate the U.S. and which have been published in accordance with PCT Article 21(2), or copies of a document in such application files, will be furnished in accordance with PCT Articles 30 and 38 and PCT Rules 94.2 and 94.3, upon written request including a showing that the publication of the application has occurred and that the U.S. was designated, and upon payment of the appropriate fee (see §1.19(b)(2) or 1.19(b)(3)), if:

(i) With respect to the Home Copy, the international application was filed with the U.S. Receiving Office;

(ii) With respect to the Search Copy, the U.S. acted as the International Searching Authority; or

(iii) With respect to the Examination Copy, the United States acted as the International Preliminary Examining Authority, an International Preliminary Examination Report has issued, and the United States was elected.

(2) A copy of an English language translation of an international application which has been filed in the United States Patent and Trademark Office pursuant to 35 U.S.C. 154(2)(d)(4) will be furnished upon written request including a showing that the publication of the application in accordance with PCT Article 21(2) has occurred and that the U.S. was designated, and upon payment of the appropriate fee (§1.19(b)(2) or §1.19(b)(3)).

(3) Access to international application files for international applications which designate the U.S. and which have been published in accordance with PCT Article 21(2), or copies of a document in such application files, will be furnished in accordance with PCT Articles 30 and 38 and PCT Rules 94.2 and 94.3, upon written request including a showing that the publication of the application has occurred and that the U.S. was designated.

(4) In accordance with PCT Article 30, copies of an international application-as-filed under paragraph (c)(1) of this section will not be provided prior to the international publication of the application pursuant to PCT Article 21(2).

(5) Access to international application files under paragraphs (e) and (i)(3) of this section will not be permitted with respect to the Examination Copy in accordance with PCT Article 38.

(j) *Access or copies in other circumstances.* The Office, either *sua sponte* or on petition, may also provide access or copies of all or part of an application if necessary to carry out an Act of Congress or if warranted by other special circumstances. Any petition by a member of the public seeking access to, or copies of, all or part of any pending or abandoned application preserved in confidence pursuant to paragraph (a) of this section, or any related papers, must include:

(1) The fee set forth in §1.17(h); and

(2) A showing that access to the application is necessary to carry out an Act of Congress or that special circumstances exist which warrant petitioner being granted access to all or part of the application.

7. Section 1.17 is amended by revising the section heading and paragraphs (h), (i), (l), (m) and (p) and adding paragraph (t) to read as follows:

§1.17 Patent application and reexamination processing fees.

* * * * *

(h) For filing a petition under one of the following sections which refers to this paragraph: $130.00.

§1.12—for access to an assignment record.
§1.14—for access to an application.
§1.47—for filing by other than all the inventors or a person not the inventor.
§1.53(e)—to accord a filing date.
§1.59—for expungement and return of information.
§1.84—for accepting color drawings or photographs.

§1.91—for entry of a model or exhibit.

§1.102—to make an application special.

§1.103(a)—to suspend action in an application.

§1.138(c)—to expressly abandon an application to avoid publication.

§1.182—for decision on a question not specifically provided for.

§1.183—to suspend the rules.

§1.295—for review of refusal to publish a statutory invention registration.

§1.313—to withdraw an application from issue.

§1.314—to defer issuance of a patent.

§1.377—for review of decision refusing to accept and record payment of a maintenance fee filed prior to expiration of a patent.

§1.378(e)—for reconsideration of decision on petition refusing to accept delayed payment of maintenance fee in an expired patent.

§1.644(e)—for petition in an interference.

§1.644(f)—for request for reconsideration of a decision on petition in an interference.

§1.666(b)—for access to an interference settlement agreement.

§1.666(c)—for late filing of interference settlement agreement.

§1.741(b)—to accord a filing date to an application under §1.740 for extension of a patent term.

§5.12—for expedited handling of a foreign filing license.

§5.15—for changing the scope of a license.

§5.25—for retroactive license.

(i) Processing fee for taking action under one of the following sections which refers to this paragraph: $130.00.

§1.28(c)(3)—for processing a non-itemized fee deficiency based on an error in small entity status.

§1.41—for supplying the name or names of the inventor or inventors after the filing date without an oath or declaration as prescribed by §1.63, except in provisional applications.

§1.48—for correcting inventorship, except in provisional applications.

§1.52(d)—for processing a nonprovisional application filed with a specification in a language other than English.

§1.53(b)(3)—to convert a provisional application filed under §1.53(c) into a nonprovisional application under §1.53(b).

§1.55—for entry of late priority papers.

§1.99(e)—for processing a belated submission under §1.99.

§1.103(b)—for requesting limited suspension of action, continued prosecution application (§1.53(d)).

§1.103(c)—for requesting limited suspension of action, request for continued examination (§1.114).

§1.103(d)—for requesting deferred examination of an application.

§1.217—for processing a redacted copy of a paper submitted in the file of an application in which a redacted copy was submitted for the patent application publication.

§1.221—for requesting voluntary publication or republication of an application.

§1.497(d)—for filing an oath or declaration pursuant to 35 U.S.C. 371(c)(4) naming an inventive entity different from the inventive entity set forth in the international stage.

§3.81—for a patent to issue to assignee, assignment submitted after payment of the issue fee.

* * * * *

(l) For filing a petition for the revival of an unavoidably abandoned application under 35 U.S.C. 111, 133, 364, or 371, for the unavoidably delayed payment of the issue fee under 35 U.S.C. 151, or for the revival of an unavoidably terminated reexamination proceeding under 35 U.S.C. 133 (§1.137(a)):

By a small entity (§1.27(a)): $55.00.
By other than a small entity: $110.00.

(m) For filing a petition for revival of an unintentionally abandoned application, for the unintentionally delayed payment of the fee for issuing a patent, or for the revival of an unintentionally terminated reexamination proceeding under 35 U.S.C. 41(a)(7) (§1.137(b)):

By a small entity (§1.27(a)): $620.00.
By other than a small entity: $1,240.00.

* * * * *

(p) For an information disclosure statement under §1.97(c) or (d) or a submission under §1.99: $180.00.

* * * * *

(t) For the acceptance of an unintentionally delayed claim for priority under 35 U.S.C. 119, 120, 121, or 365(a) or (c) (§§1.55 and 1.78): $1,240.00.

8. Section 1.18 is amended by adding paragraph (d) to read as follows:

§1.18 Patent post-allowance (including issue) fees.

* * * * *

Publication fee .... $300.00.

* * * * *

9. Section 1.19 is amended by revising paragraph (a) to read as follows:

§1.19 Document supply fees.

* * * * *

(a) Uncertified copies of patent application publications and patents:

(1) Printed copy of the paper portion of a patent application publication or patent, including a design patent, statutory invention registration, or defensive publication document:

(i) Regular service, which includes preparation of copies by the Office within two to three business days and delivery by United States Postal Service or to an Office Box; and preparation of copies by the Office within one business day of receipt and delivery by electronic means (*e.g.*, facsimile, electronic mail) ....$3.00.

(ii) Next business day delivery to Office Box ....$6.00.

(iii) Expedited delivery by commercial delivery service...............$25.00.

(2) Printed copy of a plant patent in color:..$15.00.

(3) Color copy of a patent (other than a plant patent) or statutory invention registration containing a color drawing ....$25.00.

* * * * *

10. Section 1.24 is removed and reserved.

§1.24 [Removed and Reserved]

11. Section 1.52 is amended by revising paragraph (d) to read as follows:

§1.52 Language, paper, writing, margins, compact disc specifications.

* * * * *

(d) A nonprovisional or provisional application may be filed in a language other than English.

(1) *Nonprovisional application.* If a nonprovisional application is filed in a language other than English, an English language translation of the non-English language application, a statement that the translation is accurate, and the pro-

cessing fee set forth in §1.17(i) are required. If these items are not filed with the application, applicant will be notified and given a period of time within which they must be filed in order to avoid abandonment.

(2) *Provisional application.* If a provisional application is filed in a language other than English, an English language translation of the non-English language provisional application will not be required in the provisional application. See §1.78(a) for the requirements for claiming the benefit of such provisional application in a nonprovisional application.

* * * * *

12. Section 1.55 is amended by revising paragraph (a) and adding paragraph (c) to read as follows:

§1.55 Claim for foreign priority.

(a) An applicant in a nonprovisional application may claim the benefit of the filing date of one or more prior foreign applications under the conditions specified in 35 U.S.C. 119(a) through (d), 172, and 365(a).

(1)(i) In an original application filed under 35 U.S.C. 111(a), the claim for priority must be presented during the pendency of the application, and within the later of four months from the actual filing date of the application or sixteen months from the filing date of the prior foreign application. This time period is not extendable. The claim must identify the foreign application for which priority is claimed, as well as any foreign application for the same subject matter and having a filing date before that of the application for which priority is claimed, by specifying the application number, country (or intellectual property authority), day, month, and year of its filing. The time period in this paragraph does not apply to an application for a design patent.

(ii) In an application that entered the national stage from an international application after compliance with 35 U.S.C. 371, the claim for priority must be made during the pendency of the application and within the time limit set forth in the PCT and the Regulations under the PCT.

(2) The claim for priority and the certified copy of the foreign application specified in 35 U.S.C. 119(b) or PCT Rule 17 must, in any event, be filed before the patent is granted. If the claim for priority or the certified copy of the foreign application is filed after the date the issue fee is paid, it must be accompanied by the processing fee set forth in §1.17(i), but the patent will not include the priority claim unless corrected by a certificate of correction under 35 U.S.C. 255 and §1.323.

(3) When the application becomes involved in an interference (§1.630), when necessary to overcome the date of a reference relied upon by the examiner, or when deemed necessary by the examiner, the Office may require that the claim for priority and the certified copy of the foreign application be filed earlier than provided in paragraphs (a)(1) or (a)(2) of this section.

(4) An English language translation of a non-English language foreign application is not required except when the application is involved in an interference (§1.630), when necessary to overcome the date of a reference relied upon by the examiner, or when specifically required by the examiner. If an English language translation is required, it must be filed together with a statement that the translation of the certified copy is accurate.

* * * * *

(c) Unless such claim is accepted in accordance with the provisions of this paragraph, any claim for priority under 35 U.S.C. 119(a)–(d) or 365(a) not presented within the time period provided by paragraph (a) of this section is considered to have been waived. If a claim for priority under 35 U.S.C. 119(a)–(d) or 365(a) is presented after the time period provided by paragraph (a) of this section, the claim may be accepted if the claim identifying the prior foreign application by specifying its application number, country (or intellectual property authority), and the day, month, and year of its filing was unintentionally delayed. A petition to accept a delayed claim for priority under 35 U.S.C. 119(a)–(d) or 365(a) must be accompanied by:

(1) The surcharge set forth in §1.17(t); and

(2) A statement that the entire delay between the date the claim was due under paragraph (a)(1) of this section and the date the claim was filed was unintentional. The Commissioner may require additional information where there is a question whether the delay was unintentional.

13. Section 1.72 is amended by revising paragraph (a) to read as follows:

§1.72 Title and abstract.

(a) The title of the invention may not exceed 500 characters in length and must be as short and specific as possible. Characters that cannot be captured and recorded in the Office's automated information systems may not be reflected in the Office's records in such systems or in documents created by the Office. Unless the title is supplied in an application data sheet (§1.76), the title of the invention should appear as a heading on the first page of the specification.

* * * * *

14. Section 1.76 is amended by adding a new paragraph (b)(7) to read as follows:

§1.76 Application data sheet.

* * * * *

(b) * * *

(7) *Assignee information.* This information includes the name (either person or juristic entity) and address of the assignee of the entire right, title, and interest in an application. Providing this information in the application data sheet does not substitute for compliance with any requirement of part 3 of this chapter to have an assignment recorded by the Office.

* * * * *

15. Section 1.78 is amended by revising paragraphs (a)(2), (a)(3), and (a)(4), and adding new paragraphs (a)(5) and (a)(6) to read as follows:

§1.78 Claiming benefit of earlier filing date and cross references to other applications.

(a)(1) * * *

(2) Except for a continued prosecution application filed under §1.53(d), any nonprovisional application claiming the benefit of one or more prior filed copending nonprovisional applications or international applications designating the United States of America must contain a reference to each such prior application, identifying it by application number (consisting of the series code and serial number) or international application number and international filing date and indicating the relationship of the applications. This reference must be submitted during the pendency of the application, and within the later of four months from the actual filing date of the application or sixteen months from the filing date of the prior application. This time period is not extendable. Unless the reference required by this paragraph is included in an application data sheet (§1.76), the specification must contain or be amended to contain such reference in the first sentence following the title. If the application claims the benefit of an international application, the first sentence of the specification must include an indication of whether the international application was published under PCT Article 21(2) in English (regardless of whether benefit for such application is claimed in the application data sheet). The request for a continued prosecution application under §1.53(d) is the specific reference required by 35 U.S.C. 120 to the prior application. The identification of an application by application number under this section is the specific reference required by 35 U.S.C. 120 to every application assigned that application number. Cross references to other related applications may be made when ap-

propriate (see §1.14). Except as provided in paragraph (a)(3) of this section, the failure to timely submit the reference required by 35 U.S.C. 120 and this paragraph is considered a waiver of any benefit under 35 U.S.C. 120, 121, or 365(c) to such prior application. The time period set forth in this paragraph does not apply to an application for a design patent.

(3) If the reference required by 35 U.S.C. 120 and paragraph (a)(2) of this section is presented in a nonprovisional application after the time period provided by paragraph (a)(2) of this section, the claim under 35 U.S.C. 120, 121, or 365(c) for the benefit of a prior filed copending nonprovisional application or international application designating the United States of America may be accepted if the reference identifying the prior application by application number or international application number and international filing date was unintentionally delayed. A petition to accept an unintentionally delayed claim under 35 U.S.C. 120, 121, or 365(c) for the benefit of a prior filed application must be accompanied by:

(i) The surcharge set forth in §1.17(t); and

(ii) A statement that the entire delay between the date the claim was due under paragraph (a)(2) of this section and the date the claim was filed was unintentional. The Commissioner may require additional information where there is a question whether the delay was unintentional.

(4) A nonprovisional application other than for a design patent may claim an invention disclosed in one or more prior filed provisional applications. In order for a nonprovisional application to claim the benefit of one or more prior filed provisional applications, each prior provisional application must name as an inventor at least one inventor named in the later filed nonprovisional application and disclose the named inventor's invention claimed in at least one claim of the later filed nonprovisional application in the manner provided by the first paragraph of 35 U.S.C. 112. In addition, each prior provisional application must be entitled to a filing date as set forth in §1.53(c), and the basic filing fee set forth in §1.16(k) must be paid within the time period set forth in §1.53(g).

(5) Any nonprovisional application claiming the benefit of one or more prior filed copending provisional applications must contain a reference to each such prior provisional application, identifying it as a provisional application, and including the provisional application number (consisting of series code and serial number), and, if the provisional application is filed in a language other than English, an English language translation of the non-English language provisional application and a statement that the translation is accurate. This reference and English language translation of a non-English language provisional application must be submitted during the pendency of the nonprovisional application, and within the later of four months from the actual filing date of the nonprovisional application or sixteen months from the filing date of the prior provisional application. This time period is not extendable. Unless the reference required by this paragraph is included in an application data sheet (§1.76), the specification must contain or be amended to contain such reference in the first sentence following the title. Except as provided in paragraph (a)(6) of this section, the failure to timely submit the reference and English language translation of a non-English language provisional application required by 35 U.S.C. 119(e) and this paragraph is considered a waiver of any benefit under 35 U.S.C. 119(e) to such prior provisional application.

(6) If the reference or English language translation of a non-English language provisional application required by 35 U.S.C. 119(e) and paragraph (a)(5) of this section is presented in a nonprovisional application after the time period provided by paragraph (a)(5) of this section, the claim under 35 U.S.C. 119(e) for the benefit of a prior filed provisional application may be accepted during the pendency of the nonprovisional application if the reference identifying the prior application by provisional application number and any English language translation of a non-English language provisional application were unintentionally delayed. A petition to accept an unintentionally delayed claim under 35 U.S.C. 119(e) for the benefit of a prior filed provisional application must be accompanied by:

(i) The surcharge set forth in §1.17(t); and

(ii) A statement that the entire delay between the date the claim was due under paragraph (a)(5) of this section and the date the claim was filed was unintentional. The Commissioner may require additional information where there is a question whether the delay was unintentional.

* * * * *

16. Section 1.84 is amended by revising paragraphs (a)(2), (e), and (j) to read as follows:

§1.84 Standards for drawings.

(a) * * *

(2) *Color.* On rare occasions, color drawings may be necessary as the only practical medium by which to disclose the subject matter sought to be patented in a utility or design patent application or the subject matter of a statutory invention registration. The color drawings must be of sufficient quality such that all details in the drawings are reproducible in black and white in the printed patent. Color drawings are not permitted in international applications (see PCT Rule 11.13), or in an application, or copy thereof, submitted under the Office electronic filing system. The Office will accept color drawings in utility or design patent applications and statutory invention registrations only after granting a petition filed under this paragraph explaining why the color drawings are necessary. Any such petition must include the following:

(i) The fee set forth in §1.17(h);

(ii) Three (3) sets of color drawings;

(iii) A black and white photocopy that accurately depicts, to the extent possible, the subject matter shown in the color drawing; and

(iv) An amendment to the specification to insert (unless the specification contains or has been previously amended to contain) the following language as the first paragraph of the brief description of the drawings:

> The patent or application file contains at least one drawing executed in color. Copies of this patent or patent application publication with color drawing(s) will be provided by the Office upon request and payment of the necessary fee.

* * * * *

(e) *Type of paper.* Drawings submitted to the Office must be made on paper which is flexible, strong, white, smooth, non-shiny, and durable. All sheets must be reasonably free from cracks, creases, and folds. Only one side of the sheet may be used for the drawing. Each sheet must be reasonably free from erasures and must be free from alterations, overwritings, and interlineations. Photographs must be developed on paper meeting the sheet-size requirements of paragraph (f) of this section and the margin requirements of paragraph (g) of this section. See paragraph (b) of this section for other requirements for photographs.

* * * * *

(j) *Front page view.* The drawing must contain as many views as necessary to show the invention. One of the views should be suitable for inclusion on the front page of the patent application publication and patent as the illustration of the invention. Views must not be connected by projection lines and must not contain center lines. Applicant may suggest a single view (by figure number) for inclusion on the front page of the patent application publication and patent.

* * * * *

17. Section 1.85 is amended by revising paragraph (a) to read as follows:

§1.85 Corrections to drawings.

(a) A utility or plant application will not be placed on the files for examination until objections to the drawings have been corrected. Except as provided in §1.215(c), any patent application publication will not include drawings filed after the application has been placed on the files for examination. Unless applicant is otherwise notified in an Office action, objections to the drawings in a utility or plant application will not be held in abeyance, and a request to hold objections to the drawings in abeyance will not be considered a *bona fide* attempt to advance the application to final action (§1.135(c)). If a drawing in a design application meets the requirements of §1.84(e), (f), and (g) and is suitable for reproduction, but is not otherwise in compliance with §1.84, the drawing may be admitted for examination.

* * * * *

18. Section 1.98 is amended by revising paragraphs (a)(2) and (b) to read as follows:

§1.98 Content of information disclosure statement.

(a) * * *

(2) A legible copy of:

(i) Each U.S. patent application publication and U.S. and foreign patent;

(ii) Each publication or that portion which caused it to be listed;

(iii) For each cited pending U.S. application, the application specification including the claims, and any drawing of the application, or that portion of the application which caused it to be listed including any claims directed to that portion; and

(iv) All other information or that portion which caused it to be listed; and

* * * * *

(b)(1) Each U.S. patent listed in an information disclosure statement must be identified by inventor, patent number, and issue date.

(2) Each U.S. patent application publication listed in an information disclosure statement shall be identified by applicant, patent application publication number, and publication date.

(3) Each U.S. application listed in an information disclosure statement must be identified by the inventor, application number, and filing date.

(4) Each foreign patent or published foreign patent application listed in an information disclosure statement must be identified by the country or patent office which issued the patent or published the application, an appropriate document number, and the publication date indicated on the patent or published application.

(5) Each publication listed in an information disclosure statement must be identified by publisher, author (if any), title, relevant pages of the publication, date, and place of publication.

* * * * *

19. A new §1.99 is added to read as follows:

§1.99 Third-party submission in published application.

(a) A submission by a member of the public of patents or publications relevant to a pending published application may be entered in the application file if the submission complies with the requirements of this section and the application is still pending when the submission and application file are brought before the examiner.

(b) A submission under this section must identify the application to which it is directed by application number and include:

(1) The fee set forth in §1.17(p);

(2) A list of the patents or publications submitted for consideration by the Office, including the date of publication of each patent or publication;

(3) A copy of each listed patent or publication in written form or at least the pertinent portions; and

(4) An English language translation of all the necessary and pertinent parts of any non-English language patent or publication in written form relied upon.

(c) The submission under this section must be served upon the applicant in accordance with §1.248.

(d) A submission under this section shall not include any explanation of the patents or publications, or any other information. The Office will dispose of such explanation or information if included in a submission under this section. A submission under this section is also limited to ten total patents or publications.

(e) A submission under this section must be filed within two months from the date of publication of the application (§1.215(a)) or prior to the mailing of a notice of allowance (§1.311), whichever is earlier. Any submission under this section not filed within this period is permitted only when the patents or publications could not have been submitted to the Office earlier, and must also be accompanied by the processing fee set forth in §1.17(i). A submission by a member of the public to a pending published application that does not comply with the requirements of this section will be returned or discarded.

(f) A member of the public may include a self-addressed postcard with a submission to receive an acknowledgment by the Office that the submission has been received. A member of the public filing a submission under this section will not receive any communications from the Office relating to the submission other than the return of a self-addressed postcard. In the absence of a request by the Office, an applicant has no duty to, and need not, reply to a submission under this section. No further submission on behalf of the member of the public will be considered, unless such submission raises new issues which could not have been earlier presented.

20. Section 1.103 is amended by redesignating paragraphs (d) through (f) as (e) through (g) and adding a new paragraph (d) to read as follows:

§1.103 Suspension of action by the Office.

* * * * *

(d) *Deferral of examination.* On request of the applicant, the Office may grant a deferral of examination under the conditions specified in this paragraph for a period not extending beyond three years from the earliest filing date for which a benefit is claimed under title 35, United States Code. A request for deferral of examination under this paragraph must include the publication fee set forth in §1.18(d) and the processing fee set forth in §1.17(i). A request for deferral of examination under this paragraph will not be granted unless:

(1) The application is an original utility or plant application filed under §1.53(b) or resulting from entry of an international application into the national stage after compliance with §1.494 or §1.495;

(2) The applicant has not filed a nonpublication request under §1.213(a), or has filed a request under §1.213(b) to rescind a previously filed nonpublication request;

(3) The application is in condition for publication as provided in §1.211(c); and

(4) The Office has not issued either an Office action under 35 U.S.C. 132 or a notice of allowance under 35 U.S.C. 151.

* * * * *

21. Section 1.104 is amended by removing paragraph (a)(5) and revising paragraph (d)(1) to read as follows:

§1.104 Nature of Examination.

* * * * *

(d) *Citation of references.*

(1) If domestic patents are cited by the examiner, their numbers and dates, and the names of the patentees will be stated. If domestic patent application publications are cited by the examiner, their publication number, publication date, and the names of the applicants will be stated. If foreign published applications or patents are cited, their nationality or country, numbers and dates, and the names of the patentees will be stated, and such other data will be furnished as

may be necessary to enable the applicant, or in the case of a reexamination proceeding, the patent owner, to identify the published applications or patents cited. In citing foreign published applications or patents, in case only a part of the document is involved, the particular pages and sheets containing the parts relied upon will be identified. If printed publications are cited, the author (if any), title, date, pages or plates, and place of publication, or place where a copy can be found, will be given.

* * * * *

22. Section 1.130 is amended by revising the section heading and paragraph (a) to read as follows:

§1.130 Affidavit or declaration to disqualify commonly owned patent or published application as prior art.

(a) When any claim of an application or a patent under reexamination is rejected under 35 U.S.C. 103 on a U.S. patent or U.S. patent application publication which is not prior art under 35 U.S.C. 102(b), and the inventions defined by the claims in the application or patent under reexamination and by the claims in the patent or published application are not identical but are not patentably distinct, and the inventions are owned by the same party, the applicant or owner of the patent under reexamination may disqualify the patent or patent application publication as prior art. The patent or patent application publication can be disqualified as prior art by submission of:

(1) A terminal disclaimer in accordance with §1.321(c); and

(2) An oath or declaration stating that the application or patent under reexamination and patent or published application are currently owned by the same party, and that the inventor named in the application or patent under reexamination is the prior inventor under 35 U.S.C. 104.

* * * * *

23. Section 1.131 is amended by revising paragraph (a) to read as follows:

§1.131 Affidavit or declaration of prior invention.

(a) When any claim of an application or a patent under reexamination is rejected, the inventor of the subject matter of the rejected claim, the owner of the patent under reexamination, or the party qualified under §§1.42, 1.43, or 1.47, may submit an appropriate oath or declaration to establish invention of the subject matter of the rejected claim prior to the effective date of the reference or activity on which the rejection is based. The effective date of a U.S. patent, U.S. patent application publication, or international application publication under PCT Article 21(2) is the earlier of its publication date or date that it is effective as a reference under 35 U.S.C. 102(e). Prior invention may not be established under this section in any country other than the United States, a NAFTA country, or a WTO member country. Prior invention may not be established under this section before December 8, 1993, in a NAFTA country other than the United States, or before January 1, 1996, in a WTO member country other than a NAFTA country. Prior invention may not be established under this section if either:

(1) The rejection is based upon a U.S. patent or U.S. patent application publication of a pending or patented application to another or others which claims the same patentable invention as defined in §1.601(n); or

(2) The rejection is based upon a statutory bar.

* * * * *

24. Section 1.132 is revised to read as follows:

§1.132 Affidavits or declarations traversing rejections or objections.

When any claim of an application or a patent under reexamination is rejected or objected to, any evidence submitted to traverse the rejection or objection on a basis not otherwise provided for must be by way of an oath or declaration under this section.

25. Section 1.137 is revised to read as follows:

§1.137 Revival of abandoned application, terminated reexamination proceeding, or lapsed patent.

(a) *Unavoidable.* If the delay in reply by applicant or patent owner was unavoidable, a petition may be filed pursuant to this paragraph to revive an abandoned application, a reexamination proceeding terminated under §§1.550(d) or 1.957(b) or (c), or a lapsed patent. A grantable petition pursuant to this paragraph must be accompanied by:

(1) The reply required to the outstanding Office action or notice, unless previously filed;

(2) The petition fee as set forth in §1.17(l);

(3) A showing to the satisfaction of the Commissioner that the entire delay in filing the required reply from the due date for the reply until the filing of a grantable petition pursuant to this paragraph was unavoidable; and

(4) Any terminal disclaimer (and fee as set forth in §1.20(d)) required pursuant to paragraph (d) of this section.

(b) *Unintentional.* If the delay in reply by applicant or patent owner was unintentional, a petition may be filed pursuant to this paragraph to revive an abandoned application, a reexamination proceeding terminated under §§1.550(d) or 1.957(b) or (c), or a lapsed patent. A grantable petition pursuant to this paragraph must be accompanied by:

(1) The reply required to the outstanding Office action or notice, unless previously filed;

(2) The petition fee as set forth in §1.17(m);

(3) A statement that the entire delay in filing the required reply from the due date for the reply until the filing of a grantable petition pursuant to this paragraph was unintentional. The Commissioner may require additional information where there is a question whether the delay was unintentional; and

(4) Any terminal disclaimer (and fee as set forth in §1.20(d)) required pursuant to paragraph (d) of this section.

(c) *Reply.* In a nonprovisional application abandoned for failure to prosecute, the required reply may be met by the filing of a continuing application. In a nonprovisional utility or plant application filed on or after June 8, 1995, and abandoned for failure to prosecute, the required reply may also be met by the filing of a request for continued examination in compliance with §1.114. In an application or patent, abandoned or lapsed for failure to pay the issue fee or any portion thereof, the required reply must include payment of the issue fee or any outstanding balance. In an application, abandoned for failure to pay the publication fee, the required reply must include payment of the publication fee.

(d) *Terminal disclaimer.* (1) Any petition to revive pursuant to this section in a design application must be accompanied by a terminal disclaimer and fee as set forth in §1.321 dedicating to the public a terminal part of the term of any patent granted thereon equivalent to the period of abandonment of the application. Any petition to revive pursuant to this section in either a utility or plant application filed before June 8, 1995, must be accompanied by a terminal disclaimer and fee as set forth in §1.321 dedicating to the public a terminal part of the term of any patent granted thereon equivalent to the lesser of:

(i) The period of abandonment of the application; or

(ii) The period extending beyond twenty years from the date on which the application for the patent was filed in the United States or, if the application contains a specific reference to an earlier filed application(s) under 35 U.S.C. 120, 121, or 365(c), from the date on which the earliest such application was filed.

(2) Any terminal disclaimer pursuant to paragraph (d)(1) of this section must also apply to any patent granted on a continuing utility or plant application filed before June 8, 1995, or a continuing design application, that contains a specific reference under 35 U.S.C. 120, 121, or 365(c) to the application for which revival is sought.

(3) The provisions of paragraph (d)(1) of this section do not apply to applications for which revival is sought solely for purposes of copendency with a util-

ity or plant application filed on or after June 8, 1995, to lapsed patents, or to reexamination proceedings.

(e) *Request for reconsideration.* Any request for reconsideration or review of a decision refusing to revive an abandoned application, a terminated reexamination proceeding, or lapsed patent upon petition filed pursuant to this section, to be considered timely, must be filed within two months of the decision refusing to revive or within such time as set in the decision. Unless a decision indicates otherwise, this time period may be extended under:

(1) The provisions of §1.136 for an abandoned application or lapsed patent;

(2) The provisions of §1.550(c) for a terminated *ex parte* reexamination proceeding filed under §1.510; or

(3) The provisions of §1.956 for a terminated *inter partes* reexamination proceeding filed under §1.913.

(f) *Abandonment for failure to notify the Office of a foreign filing:* A nonprovisional application abandoned pursuant to 35 U.S.C. 122(b)(2)(B)(iii) for failure to timely notify the Office of the filing of an application in a foreign country or under a multinational treaty that requires publication of applications eighteen months after filing, may be revived only pursuant to paragraph (b) of this section. The reply requirement of paragraph (c) of this section is met by the notification of such filing in a foreign country or under a multinational treaty, but the filing of a petition under this section will not operate to stay any period for reply that may be running against the application.

(g) *Provisional applications.* A provisional application, abandoned for failure to timely respond to an Office requirement, may be revived pursuant to this section. Subject to the provisions of 35 U.S.C. 119(e)(3) and §1.7(b), a provisional application will not be regarded as pending after twelve months from its filing date under any circumstances.

26. Section 1.138 is amended by revising paragraph (a) and adding paragraph (c) to read as follows:

§1.138 Express abandonment.

(a) An application may be expressly abandoned by filing a written declaration of abandonment identifying the application in the United States Patent and Trademark Office. Express abandonment of the application may not be recognized by the Office before the date of issue or publication unless it is actually received by appropriate officials in time to act.

* * * * *

(c) An applicant seeking to abandon an application to avoid publication of the application (see §1.211(a)(1)) must submit a declaration of express abandonment by way of a petition under this section including the fee set forth in §1.17(h) in sufficient time to permit the appropriate officials to recognize the abandonment and remove the application from the publication process. Applicant should expect that the petition will not be granted and the application will be published in regular course unless such declaration of express abandonment and petition are received by the appropriate officials more than four weeks prior to the projected date of publication.

27. Section 1.165 is amended by revising paragraph (b) to read as follows:

§1.165 Plant drawings.

* * * * *

(b) The drawings may be in color. The drawing must be in color if color is a distinguishing characteristic of the new variety. Two copies of color drawings or photographs and a black and white photocopy that accurately depicts, to the extent possible, the subject matter shown in the color drawing or photograph must be submitted.

28. A new, undesignated center heading and new §§1.211, 1.213, 1.215, 1.217, 1.219, and 1.221 are added to Subpart B-National Processing Provisions to read as follows:

Publication of Applications

§1.211 Publication of applications.

(a) Each U.S. national application for patent filed in the Office under 35 U.S.C. 111(a) and each international application in compliance with 35 U.S.C. 371 will be published promptly after the expiration of a period of eighteen months from the earliest filing date for which a benefit is sought under title 35, United States Code, unless:

(1) The application is recognized by the Office as no longer pending;

(2) The application is national security classified (see §5.2(c)), subject to a secrecy order under 35 U.S.C. 181, or under national security review;

(3) The application has issued as a patent in sufficient time to be removed from the publication process; or

(4) The application was filed with a nonpublication request in compliance with §1.213(a).

(b) Provisional applications under 35 U.S.C. 111(b) shall not be published, and design applications under 35 U.S.C. chapter 16 and reissue applications under 35 U.S.C. chapter 25 shall not be published under this section.

(c) An application filed under 35 U.S.C. 111(a) will not be published until it includes the basic filing fee (§1.16(a) or 1.16(g)), any English translation required by §1.52(d), and an executed oath or declaration under §1.63. The Office may delay publishing any application until it includes a specification having papers in compliance with §1.52 and an abstract (§1.72(b)), drawings in compliance with §1.84, and a sequence listing in compliance with §§1.821 through 1.825 (if applicable), and until any petition under §1.47 is granted.

(d) The Office may refuse to publish an application, or to include a portion of an application in the patent application publication (§1.215), if publication of the application or portion thereof would violate Federal or state law, or if the application or portion thereof contains offensive or disparaging material.

(e) The publication fee set forth in §1.18(d) must be paid in each application published under this section before the patent will be granted. If an application is subject to publication under this section, the sum specified in the notice of allowance under §1.311 will also include the publication fee which must be paid within three months from the date of mailing of the notice of allowance to avoid abandonment of the application. This three-month period is not extendable. If the application is not published under this section, the publication fee (if paid) will be refunded.

§1.213 Nonpublication request.

(a) If the invention disclosed in an application has not been and will not be the subject of an application filed in another country, or under a multilateral international agreement, that requires publication of applications eighteen months after filing, the application will not be published under 35 U.S.C. 122(b) and §1.211 provided:

(1) A request (nonpublication request) is submitted with the application upon filing;

(2) The request states in a conspicuous manner that the application is not to be published under 35 U.S.C. 122(b);

(3) The request contains a certification that the invention disclosed in the application has not been and will not be the subject of an application filed in another country, or under a multilateral international agreement, that requires publication at eighteen months after filing; and

(4) The request is signed in compliance with §1.33(b).

(b) The applicant may rescind a nonpublication request at any time. A request to rescind a nonpublication request under paragraph (a) of this section must:

(1) Identify the application to which it is directed;

(2) State in a conspicuous manner that the request that the application is not to be published under 35 U.S.C. 122(b) is rescinded; and

(3) Be signed in compliance with §1.33(b).

(c) If an applicant who has submitted a nonpublication request under paragraph (a) of this section subsequently files an application directed to the invention disclosed in the application in which the nonpublication request was submitted in another country, or under a multilateral international agreement, that requires publication of applications eighteen months after filing, the applicant must notify the Office of such filing within forty-five days after the date of the filing of such foreign or international application. The failure to timely notify the Office of the filing of such foreign or international application shall result in abandonment of the application in which the nonpublication request was submitted (35 U.S.C. 122(b)(2)(B)(iii)).

§1.215 Patent application publication.

(a) The publication of an application under 35 U.S.C. 122(b) shall include a patent application publication. The date of publication shall be indicated on the patent application publication. The patent application publication will be based upon the application papers deposited on the filing date of the application, as well as the executed oath or declaration submitted to complete the application, and any application papers or drawings submitted in reply to a preexamination notice requiring a title and abstract in compliance with §1.72, application papers in compliance with §1.52, drawings in compliance with §1.84, or a sequence listing in compliance with §§1.821 through 1.825, except as otherwise provided in this section. The patent application publication will not include any amendments, including preliminary amendments, unless applicant supplies a copy of the application containing the amendment pursuant to paragraph (c) of this section.

(b) If applicant wants the patent application publication to include assignee information, the applicant must include the assignee information on the application transmittal sheet or the application data sheet (§1.76). Assignee information may not be included on the patent application publication unless this information is provided on the application transmittal sheet or application data sheet included with the application on filing. Providing this information on the application transmittal sheet or the application data sheet does not substitute for compliance with any requirement of part 3 of this chapter to have an assignment recorded by the Office.

(c) At applicant's option, the patent application publication will be based upon the copy of the application (specification, drawings, and oath or declaration) as amended during examination, provided that applicant supplies such a copy in compliance with the Office electronic filing system requirements within one month of the actual filing date of the application or fourteen months of the earliest filing date for which a benefit is sought under title 35, United States Code, whichever is later.

(d) If the copy of the application submitted pursuant to paragraph (c) of this section does not comply with the Office electronic filing system requirements, the Office will publish the application as provided in paragraph (a) of this section. If, however, the Office has not started the publication process, the Office may use an untimely filed copy of the application supplied by the applicant under paragraph (c) of this section in creating the patent application publication.

§1.217 Publication of a redacted copy of an application.

(a) If an applicant has filed applications in one or more foreign countries, directly or through a multilateral international agreement, and such foreign-filed applications or the description of the invention in such foreign-filed applications is less extensive than the application or description of the invention in the application filed in the Office, the applicant may submit a redacted copy of the application filed in the Office for publication, eliminating any part or description of the invention that is not also contained in any of the corresponding applications filed in a foreign country. The Office will publish the application as provided in §1.215(a) unless the applicant files a redacted copy of the application in compliance with this section within sixteen months after the earliest filing date for which a benefit is sought under title 35, United States Code.

(b) The redacted copy of the application must be submitted in compliance with the Office electronic filing system requirements. The title of the invention in the redacted copy of the application must correspond to the title of the application at the time the redacted copy of the application is submitted to the Office. If the redacted copy of the application does not comply with the Office electronic filing system requirements, the Office will publish the application as provided in §1.215(a).

(c) The applicant must also concurrently submit in paper (§1.52(a)) to be filed in the application:

(1) A certified copy of each foreign-filed application that corresponds to the application for which a redacted copy is submitted;

(2) A translation of each such foreign-filed application that is in a language other than English, and a statement that the translation is accurate;

(3) A marked-up copy of the application showing the redactions in brackets; and

(4) A certification that the redacted copy of the application eliminates only the part or description of the invention that is not contained in any application filed in a foreign country, directly or through a multilateral international agreement, that corresponds to the application filed in the Office.

(d) The Office will provide a copy of the complete file wrapper and contents of an application for which a redacted copy was submitted under this section to any person upon written request pursuant to §1.14(c)(2), unless applicant complies with the requirements of paragraphs (d)(1), (d)(2), and (d)(3) of this section.

(1) Applicant must accompany the submission required by paragraph (c) of this section with the following:

(i) A copy of any Office correspondence previously received by applicant including any desired redactions, and a second copy of all Office correspondence previously received by applicant showing the redacted material in brackets; and

(ii) A copy of each submission previously filed by the applicant including any desired redactions, and a second copy of each submission previously filed by the applicant showing the redacted material in brackets.

(2) In addition to providing the submission required by paragraphs (c) and (d)(1) of this section, applicant must:

(i) Within one month of the date of mailing of any correspondence from the Office, file a copy of such Office correspondence including any desired redactions, and a second copy of such Office correspondence showing the redacted material in brackets; and

(ii) With each submission by the applicant, include a copy of such submission including any desired redactions, and a second copy of such submission showing the redacted material in brackets.

(3) Each submission under paragraph (d)(1) or (d)(2) of this paragraph must also be accompanied by the processing fee set forth in §1.17(i) and a certification that the redactions are limited to the elimination of material that is relevant only to the part or description of the invention that was not contained in the redacted copy of the application submitted for publication.

(e) The provisions of §1.8 do not apply to the time periods set forth in this section.

§1.219 Early publication.

(a) Applications that will be published under §1.211 may be published earlier than as set forth in §1.211(a) at the request of the applicant. Any request for early publication must be accompanied by the publication fee set forth in §1.18(d). If the applicant does not submit a copy of the application in compliance with the Office electronic filing system requirements pursuant to §1.215(c), the Office will publish the application as provided in §1.215(a). No consideration will be given to requests for publication on a certain date, and such requests will be treated as a request for publication as soon as possible.

§1.221 Voluntary publication or republication of patent application publication.

(a) Any request for publication of an application filed before, but pending on, November 29, 2000, and any request for republication of an application previously published under §1.211, must include a copy of the application in compliance with the Office electronic filing system requirements and be accompanied by the publication fee set forth in §1.18(d) and the processing fee set forth in §1.17(i). If the request does not comply with the requirements of this paragraph or the copy of the application does not comply with the Office electronic filing system requirements, the Office will not publish the application and will refund the publication fee.

(b) The Office will grant a request for a corrected or revised patent application publication other than as provided in paragraph (a) of this section only when the Office makes a material mistake which is apparent from Office records. Any request for a corrected or revised patent application publication other than as provided in paragraph (a) of this section must be filed within two months from the date of the patent application publication. This period is not extendable.

29. Section 1.291 is amended by revising paragraph (a)(1) to read as follows:

§1.291 Protests by the public against pending applications.

(a) * * *

(1) The protest is submitted prior to the date the application was published or the mailing of a notice of allowance under §1.311, whichever occurs first; and

* * * * *

30. Section 1.292 is amended by revising paragraph (b)(3) to read as follows:

§1.292 Public use proceedings.

* * * * *

(b) * * *

(3) The petition is submitted prior to the date the application was published or the mailing of a notice of allowance under §1.311, whichever occurs first.

* * * * *

31. Section 1.311 is revised to read as follows:

§1.311 Notice of allowance.

(a) If, on examination, it appears that the applicant is entitled to a patent under the law, a notice of allowance will be sent to the applicant at the correspondence address indicated in §1.33. The notice of allowance shall specify a sum constituting the issue fee which must be paid within three months from the date of mailing of the notice of allowance to avoid abandonment of the application. The sum specified in the notice of allowance may also include the publication fee, in which case the issue fee and publication fee (§1.211(f)) must both be paid within three months from the date of mailing of the notice of allowance to avoid abandonment of the application. This three-month period is not extendable.

(b) An authorization to charge the issue or other post-allowance fees set forth in §1.18 to a deposit account may be filed in an individual application only after mailing of the notice of allowance. The submission of either of the following after the mailing of a notice of allowance will operate as a request to charge the correct issue fee to any deposit account identified in a previously filed authorization to charge fees:

(1) An incorrect issue fee; or

(2) A completed Office-provided issue fee transmittal form (where no issue fee has been submitted).

32. A new §1.417 is added to read as follows:

§1.417 Submission of translation of international application.

The submission of the international publication or an English language translation of an international application pursuant to 35 U.S.C. 154(d)(4) must clearly identify the international application to which it pertains (§1.5(a)) and, unless it is being submitted pursuant to §1.494 or §1.495, be clearly identified as a submission pursuant to 35 U.S.C. 154(d)(4). Otherwise, the submission will be treated as a filing under 35 U.S.C. 111(a). Such submissions should be marked "Box PCT."

33. Section 1.494 is amended by revising paragraph (f) to read as follows:

§1.494 Entering the national stage in the United States of America as a Designated Office.

* * * * *

(f) The documents and fees submitted under paragraphs (b) and (c) of this section must, except for a copy of the international publication or translation of the international application that is identified as provided in §1.417, be clearly identified as a submission to enter the national stage under 35 U.S.C. 371. Otherwise, the submission will be considered as being made under 35 U.S.C. 111(a).

* * * * *

34. Section 1.495 is amended by revising paragraph (g) to read as follows:

§1.495 Entering the national stage in the United States of America as an Elected Office.

* * * * *

(g) The documents and fees submitted under paragraphs (b) and (c) of this section must, except for a copy of the international publication or translation of the international application that is identified as provided in §1.417, be clearly identified as a submission to enter the national stage under 35 U.S.C. 371. Otherwise, the submission will be considered as being made under 35 U.S.C. 111(a).

* * * * *

PART 5—SECRECY OF CERTAIN INVENTIONS AND LICENSES TO EXPORT AND FILE APPLICATIONS IN FOREIGN COUNTRIES

35. The authority citation for 37 CFR part 5 is revised to read as follows:

Authority: 35 U.S.C. 2(b)(2), 41, 181–188, as amended by the Patent Law Foreign Filing Amendments Act of 1988, Pub. L. 100-418, 102 Stat. 1567; the Arms Export Control Act, as amended, 22 U.S.C. 2751 *et seq.*; the Atomic Energy Act of 1954, as amended, 42 U.S.C. 2011 *et seq.*; the Nuclear Non Proliferation Act of 1978, 22 U.S.C. 3201 *et seq.*; and the delegations in the regulations under these Acts to the Commissioner (15 CFR 370.10(j), 22 CFR 125.04, and 10 CFR 810.7).

36. Section 5.1 is amended by revising paragraph (e) to read as follows:

§5.1 Applications and correspondence involving national security.

* * * * *

(e) An application will not be published under §1.211 of this chapter or allowed under §1.311 of this chapter if publication or disclosure of the application would be detrimental to national security. An application under national security review will not be published at least until six months from its filing date or three months from the date the application was referred to a defense agency, whichever is later. A national security classified patent application will not be published under §1.211 of this chapter or allowed under §1.311 of this chapter until the application is declassified and any secrecy order under §5.2(a) has been rescinded.

Dated: September 12, 2000.

Q. Todd Dickinson,
Under Secretary of Commerce for Intellectual Property and Director of the United States Patent and Trademark Office.
[FR Doc. 00-23822 Filed 9-19-00; 8:45 am]

Appendix C-31

Changes to Application Examination and Provisional Application Practice

65 FR 14865
Department of Commerce
Patent and Trademark Office
37 CFR Part 1
RIN 0651-AB13

Agency: United States Patent and Trademark Office, Commerce

Action: Interim rule

* * *

Dates: Effective Date: May 29, 2000

* * *

PART 1—RULES OF PRACTICE IN PATENT CASES

1. The authority citation for 37 CFR Part 1 is revised to read as follows:

Authority: 35 U.S.C. 2(b)(2), unless otherwise noted.

2. Section 1.7 is revised to read as follows:

§1.7 Times for taking action; Expiration on Saturday, Sunday or Federal holiday.

(a) Whenever periods of time are specified in this part in days, calendar days are intended. When the day, or the last day fixed by statute or by or under this part for taking any action or paying any fee in the United States Patent and Trademark Office falls on Saturday, Sunday, or on a Federal holiday within the District of Columbia, the action may be taken, or the fee paid, on the next succeeding business day which is not a Saturday, Sunday, or a Federal holiday. See §1.304 for time for appeal or for commencing civil action.

(b) If the day that is twelve months after the filing date of a provisional application under 35 U.S.C. 111(b) and §1.53(c) falls on Saturday, Sunday, or on a Federal holiday within the District of Columbia, the period of pendency shall be extended to the next succeeding secular or business day which is not a Saturday, Sunday, or a Federal holiday.

3. Section 1.17 is amended by adding paragraph (e) and revising paragraph (i) to read as follows:

§1.17 Patent application processing fees.

* * * * *

(e) To request continued examination pursuant to §1.114:
By a small entity 345.00
By other than a small entity 690.00

* * * * *

(i) For filing a petition to the Commissioner under one of the following sections which refers to this paragraph 130.00

§1.12—for access to an assignment record.
§1.14—for access to an application.
§1.41—to supply the name or names of the inventor or inventors after the filing date without an oath or declaration as prescribed by §1.63, except in provisional applications.
§1.47—for filing by other than all the inventors or a person not the inventor.
§1.48—for correction of inventorship, except in provisional applications.
§1.53—to accord a filing date, except in provisional applications.
§1.53(c)—to convert a provisional application filed under §1.53(c) to a nonprovisional application under §1.53(b).
§1.55—for entry of late priority papers.
§1.59—for expungement and return of information.
§1.84—for accepting color drawings or photographs.
§1.91—for entry of a model or exhibit.
§1.97(d)—to consider an information disclosure statement.
§1.102—to make an application special.
§1.103—to suspend action in application.
§1.177—for divisional reissues to issue separately.
§1.313—to withdraw an application from issue.
§1.314—to defer issuance of a patent.
§1.666(b)—for access to an interference settlement agreement.
§3.81—for a patent to issue to assignee, assignment submitted after payment of the issue fee.

* * * * *

4. Section 1.53 is amended by redesignating paragraph (c)(3) as paragraph (c)(4), adding a new paragraph (c)(3), and revising paragraph (d)(1) to read as follows:

§1.53 Application number, filing date, and completion of application.

* * * * *

(c) * * *

(3) A provisional application filed under paragraph (c) of this section may be converted to a nonprovisional application filed under paragraph (b) of this section and accorded the original filing date of the provisional application. The conversion of a provisional application to a nonprovisional application will not result in either the refund of any fee properly paid in the provisional application or the application of any such fee to the filing fee, or any other fee, for the nonprovisional application. A request to convert a provisional application to a nonprovisional application must be accompanied by the fee set forth in §1.17(i) and an amendment including at least one claim as prescribed by the second paragraph of 35 U.S.C. 112, unless the provisional application under paragraph (c) of this section otherwise contains at least one claim as prescribed by the second paragraph of 35 U.S.C. 112. A request to convert a provisional application to a nonprovisional application must also be filed prior to the earliest of:

(i) Abandonment of the provisional application filed under paragraph (c) of this section; or

(ii) Expiration of twelve months after the filing date of the provisional application filed under paragraph (c) of this section.

* * * * *

(d) * * *

(1) A continuation or divisional application (but not a continuation-in-part) of a prior nonprovisional application may be filed as a continued prosecution application under this paragraph, provided that:

(i) The prior nonprovisional application is:

(A) A utility or plant application that was filed under 35 U.S.C. 111(a) before May 29, 2000, and is complete as defined by §1.51(b);

(B) A design application that is complete as defined by §1.51(b); or

(C) The national stage of an international application that was filed under 35 U.S.C. 363 before May 29, 2000, and is in compliance with 35 U.S.C. 371; and

(ii) The application under this paragraph is filed before the earliest of:

(A) Payment of the issue fee on the prior application, unless a petition under §1.313(c) is granted in the prior application;

(B) Abandonment of the prior application; or

(C) Termination of proceedings on the prior application.

* * * * *

Section 1.78 is amended by revising paragraph (a)(3) to read as follows:

§1.78 Claiming benefit of earlier filing date and cross-references to other applications.

(a) * * *

(3) A nonprovisional application other than for a design patent may claim an invention disclosed in one or more prior filed provisional applications. In order for a nonprovisional application to claim the benefit of one or more prior filed provisional applications, each prior provisional application must name as an inventor at least one inventor named in the later filed nonprovisional application and disclose the named inventor's invention claimed in at least one claim of the later filed nonprovisional application in the manner provided by the first paragraph of 35 U.S.C. 112. In addition, each prior provisional application must be entitled to a filing date as set forth in §1.53(c), have any required English-language translation filed therein within the time period set forth in §1.52(d), and have paid therein the basic filing fee set forth in §1.16(k) within the time period set forth in §1.53(g).

* * * * *

5. Section 1.97 is amended by revising paragraph (b) to read as follows:

§1.97 Filing of information disclosure statement.

* * * * *

(b) An information disclosure statement shall be considered by the Office if filed by the applicant within any one of the following time periods:

(1) Within three months of the filing date of a national application;

(2) Within three months of the date of entry of the national stage as set forth in §1.491 in an international application;

(3) Before the mailing of a first Office action on the merits; or

(4) Before the mailing of a first Office action after the filing of a request for continued examination under §1.114.

* * * * *

6. Section 1.104 is amended by revising paragraph (c)(4) to read as follows:

§1.104 Nature of examination.

* * * * *

(c) * * *

(4) Subject matter which is developed by another person which qualifies as prior art only under 35 U.S.C. 102(e), (f) or (g) may be used as prior art under 35 U.S.C. 103 against a claimed invention unless the entire rights to the subject matter and the claimed invention were commonly owned by the same person or organization or subject to an obligation of assignment to the same person or organization at the time the claimed invention was made.

* * * * *

7. Section 1.113 is revised to read as follows:

§1.113 Final rejection or action.

(a) On the second or any subsequent examination or consideration by the examiner the rejection or other action may be made final, whereupon applicant's or patent owner's reply is limited to appeal in the case of rejection of any claim (§1.191), or to amendment as specified in §1.114 or §1.116. Petition may be taken to the Commissioner in the case of objections or requirements not involved in the rejection of any claim (§1.181). Reply to a final rejection or action must comply with §1.114 or paragraph (c) of this section.

(b) In making such final rejection, the examiner shall repeat or state all grounds of rejection then considered applicable to the claims in the application, clearly stating the reasons in support thereof.

(c) Reply to a final rejection or action must include cancellation of, or appeal from the rejection of, each rejected claim. If any claim stands allowed, the reply to a final rejection or action must comply with any requirements or objections as to form.

8. Section 1.114 is added immediately following §1.113 to read as follows:

§1.114 Request for continued examination.

(a) An applicant may request continued examination of the application by filing a submission and the fee set forth in §1.17(e) prior to the earliest of:

(1) Payment of the issue fee, unless a petition under §1.313 is granted;

(2) Abandonment of the application; or

(3) The filing of a notice of appeal to the U.S. Court of Appeals for the Federal Circuit under 35 U.S.C. 141, or the commencement of a civil action under 35 U.S.C. 145 or 146, unless the appeal or civil action is terminated.

(b) A submission as used in this section includes, but is not limited to, an information disclosure statement, an amendment to the written description, claims, or drawings, new arguments, or new evidence in support of patentability. If reply to an Office action under 35 U.S.C. 132 is outstanding, the submission must meet the reply requirements of §1.111.

(c) If an applicant timely files a submission and fee set forth in §1.17(e), the Office will withdraw the finality of any Office action and the submission will be entered and considered. If an applicant files a request for continued examination under this section after appeal, but prior to a decision on the appeal, it will be treated as a request to withdraw the appeal and to reopen prosecution of the application before the examiner. An appeal brief under §1.192 or a reply brief under §1.193(b), or related papers, will not be considered a submission under this section.

(d) The provisions of this section do not apply in any application in which the Office has not mailed at least one of an Office action under 35 U.S.C. 132 or a notice of allowance under 35 U.S.C. 151. The provisions of this section also do not apply to:

(1) A provisional application;

(2) An application for a utility or plant patent filed under 35 U.S.C. 111(a) before June 8, 1995;

(3) An international application filed under 35 U.S.C. 363 before June 8, 1995;

(4) An application for a design patent; or

(5) A patent under reexamination.

9. Section 1.116 is revised to read as follows:

§1.116 Amendments after final action or appeal.

(a) An amendment after final action or appeal must comply with §1.114 or this section.

(b) After a final rejection or other final action (§1.113), amendments may be made canceling claims or complying with any requirement of form expressly set forth in a previous Office action. Amendments presenting rejected claims in better form for consideration on appeal may be admitted. The admission of, or refusal to admit, any amendment after final rejection, and any related proceedings, will not operate to relieve the application or patent under reexamination from its condition as subject to appeal or to save the application from abandonment under §1.135.

(c) If amendments touching the merits of the application or patent under reexamination are presented after final rejection, or after appeal has been taken, or when such amendment might not otherwise be proper, they may be admitted upon a showing of good and sufficient reasons why they are necessary and were not earlier presented.

(d) No amendment can be made as a matter of right in appealed cases. After decision on appeal, amendments can only be made as provided in §1.198, or to carry into effect a recommendation under §1.196.

10. Section 1.198 is revised to read as follows:

§1.198 Reopening after decision.

Cases which have been decided by the Board of Patent Appeals and Interferences will not be reopened or reconsidered by the primary examiner except under the provisions of §1.114 or §1.196 without the written authority of the Commissioner, and then only for the consideration of matters not already adjudicated, sufficient cause being shown.

11. Section 1.312 is revised to read as follows:

§1.312 Amendments after allowance.

No amendment may be made as a matter of right in an application after the mailing of the notice of allowance. Any amendment filed pursuant to this section must be filed before or with the payment of the issue fee, and may be entered on the recommendation of the primary examiner, approved by the Commissioner, without withdrawing the application from issue.

12. Section 1.313 is revised to read as follows:

§1.313 Withdrawal from issue.

(a) Applications may be withdrawn from issue for further action at the initiative of the Office or upon petition by the applicant. To request that the Office withdraw an application from issue, applicant must file a petition under this section including the fee set forth in §1.17(i) and a showing of good and sufficient reasons why withdrawal of the application is necessary. If the Office withdraws the application from issue, the Office will issue a new notice of allowance if the Office again allows the application.

(b) Once the issue fee has been paid, the Office will not withdraw the application from issue at its own initiative for any reason except:

(1) A mistake on the part of the Office;

(2) A violation of §1.56 or illegality in the application;

(3) Unpatentability of one or more claims; or

(4) For interference.

(c) Once the issue fee has been paid, the application will not be withdrawn from issue upon petition by the applicant for any reason except:

(1) Unpatentability of one or more claims, which petition must be accompanied by an unequivocal statement that one or more claims are unpatentable, an amendment to such claim or claims, and an explanation as to how the amendment causes such claim or claims to be patentable;

(2) Consideration of a submission pursuant to §1.114; or

(3) Express abandonment of the application. Such express abandonment may be in favor of a continuing application.

(d) A petition under this section will not be effective to withdraw the application from issue unless it is actually received and granted by the appropriate officials before the date of issue. Withdrawal of an application from issue after payment of the issue fee may not be effective to avoid publication of application information.

Dated: March 10, 2000.

Q. Todd Dickinson,
Assistant Secretary of Commerce and Commissioner of Patents and Trademarks.
[FR Doc. 00-6514 Filed 3-17-00; 8:45 am]

Appendix C-32

Request for Continued Examination Practice and Changes to Provisional Application Practice; Final Rule

65 FR 50092
Department of Commerce
Patent and Trademark Office
37 CFR Part 1
RIN 0651-AB13

Agency: United States Patent and Trademark Office, Commerce

Action: Final rule

* * *

Effective Date: August 16, 2000

* * *

PART 1—RULES OF PRACTICE IN PATENT CASES

1. The authority citation for 37 CFR Part 1 continues to read as follows:

Authority: 35 U.S.C. 2(b)(2).

2. Section 1.53 is amended by revising paragraph (c)(3) to read as follows:

§1.53 Application number, filing date, and completion of application.

* * * * *

(c) * * *

(3) A provisional application filed under paragraph (c) of this section may be converted to a nonprovisional application filed under paragraph (b) of this section and accorded the original filing date of the provisional application. The conversion of a provisional application to a nonprovisional application will not result in either the refund of any fee properly paid in the provisional application or the application of any such fee to the filing fee, or any other fee, for the nonprovisional application. Conversion of a

provisional application to a nonprovisional application under this paragraph will result in the term of any patent to issue from the application being measured from at least the filing date of the provisional application for which conversion is requested. Thus, applicants should consider avoiding this adverse patent term impact by filing a nonprovisional application claiming the benefit of the provisional application under 35 U.S.C. 119(e) (rather than converting the provisional application into a nonprovisional application pursuant to this paragraph). A request to convert a provisional application to a nonprovisional application must be accompanied by the fee set forth in §1.17(i) and an amendment including at least one claim as prescribed by the second paragraph of 35 U.S.C. 112, unless the provisional application under paragraph (c) of this section otherwise contains at least one claim as prescribed by the second paragraph of 35 U.S.C. 112. The nonprovisional application resulting from conversion of a provisional application must also include the filing fee for a nonprovisional application, an oath or declaration by the applicant pursuant to §§1.63, 1.162, or 1.175, and the surcharge required by §1.16(e) if either the basic filing fee for a nonprovisional application or the oath or declaration was not present on the filing date accorded the resulting nonprovisional application (*i.e.*, the filing date of the original provisional application). A request to convert a provisional application to a nonprovisional application must also be filed prior to the earliest of:

(i) Abandonment of the provisional application filed under paragraph (c) of this section; or

(ii) Expiration of twelve months after the filing date of the provisional application filed under this paragraph (c).

* * * * *

3. Section 1.103 is revised to read as follows:

§1.103 Suspension of action by the Office.

(a) *Suspension for cause.* On request of the applicant, the Office may grant a suspension of action by the Office under this paragraph for good and sufficient cause. The Office will not suspend action if a reply by applicant to an Office action is outstanding. Any petition for suspension of action under this paragraph must specify a period of suspension not exceeding six months. Any petition for suspension of action under this paragraph must also include:

(1) A showing of good and sufficient cause for suspension of action; and

(2) The fee set forth in §1.17(h), unless such cause is the fault of the Office.

(b) *Limited suspension of action in a continued prosecution application (CPA) filed under §1.53(d).* On request of the applicant, the Office may grant a suspension of action by the Office under this paragraph in a continued prosecution application filed under §1.53(d) for a period not exceeding three months. Any request for suspension of action under this paragraph must be filed with the request for an application filed under §1.53(d), specify the period of suspension, and include the processing fee set forth in §1.17(i).

(c) *Limited suspension of action after a request for continued examination (RCE) under §1.114.* On request of the applicant, the Office may grant a suspension of action by the Office under this paragraph after the filing of a request for continued examination in compliance with §1.114 for a period not exceeding three months. Any request for suspension of action under this paragraph must be filed with the request for continued examination under §1.114, specify the period of suspension, and include the processing fee set forth in §1.17(i).

(d) *Notice of suspension on initiative of the Office.* The Office will notify applicant if the Office suspends action by the Office on an application on its own initiative.

(e) *Suspension of action for public safety or defense.* The Office may suspend action by the Office by order of the Commissioner if the following conditions are met:

(1) The application is owned by the United States;

(2) Publication of the invention may be detrimental to the public safety or defense; and

(3) The appropriate department or agency requests such suspension.

(f) *Statutory invention registration.* The Office will suspend action by the Office for the entire pendency of an application if the Office has accepted a request to publish a statutory invention registration in the application, except for purposes relating to patent interference proceedings under Subpart E of this part.

4. Section 1.114 is revised to read as follows:

§1.114 Request for continued examination.

(a) If prosecution in an application is closed, an applicant may request continued examination of the application by filing a submission and the fee set forth in §1.17(e) prior to the earliest of:

(1) Payment of the issue fee, unless a petition under §1.313 is granted;

(2) Abandonment of the application; or

(3) The filing of a notice of appeal to the U.S. Court of Appeals for the Federal Circuit under 35 U.S.C. 141, or the commencement of a civil action under 35 U.S.C. 145 or 146, unless the appeal or civil action is terminated.

(b) Prosecution in an application is closed as used in this section means that the application is under appeal, or that the last Office action is a final action (§1.113), a notice of allowance (§1.311), or an action that otherwise closes prosecution in the application.

(c) A submission as used in this section includes, but is not limited to, an information disclosure statement, an amendment to the written description, claims, or drawings, new arguments, or new evidence in support of patentability. If reply to an Office action under 35 U.S.C. 132 is outstanding, the submission must meet the reply requirements of §1.111.

(d) If an applicant timely files a submission and fee set forth in §1.17(e), the Office will withdraw the finality of any Office action and the submission will be entered and considered. If an applicant files a request for continued examination under this section after appeal, but prior to a decision on the appeal, it will be treated as a request to withdraw the appeal and to reopen prosecution of the application before the examiner. An appeal brief under §1.192 or a reply brief under §1.193(b), or related papers, will not be considered a submission under this section.

(e) The provisions of this section do not apply to:

(1) A provisional application;

(2) An application for a utility or plant patent filed under 35 U.S.C. 111(a) before June 8, 1995;

(3) An international application filed under 35 U.S.C. 363 before June 8, 1995;

(4) An application for a design patent; or

(5) A patent under reexamination.

5. Section 1.313 is amended by revising paragraphs (a) and (c)(2) to read as follows:

§1.313 Withdrawal from issue.

(a) Applications may be withdrawn from issue for further action at the initiative of the Office or upon petition by the applicant. To request that the Office withdraw an application from issue, applicant must file a petition under this section including the fee set forth in §1.17(h) and a showing of good and sufficient reasons why withdrawal of the application from issue is necessary. A petition under this section is not required if a request for continued examination under §1.114 is filed prior to payment of the issue fee. If the Office withdraws the application from issue, the Office will issue a new notice of allowance if the Office again allows the application.

* * * * *

(c) * * *

(2) Consideration of a request for continued examination in compliance with §1.114; or

* * * * *

Dated: August 9, 2000.

Q. Todd Dickinson,
Under Secretary of Commerce for Intellectual Property and Director of the United States Patent and Trademark Office.
[FR Doc. 00-20744 Filed 8-15-00; 8:45 am]

Appendix C-33

Changes to Implement the Patent Business Goals

[The following sections of 37 CFR Parts 1, 3, 5, and 10 have been changed to implement the Patent Business Goals. The relevant changes were published in the Federal Register at 65 FR 54604 on September 8, 2000 (Final Rule), 65 FR 78958 on December 18, 2000 (Final Rule and Corrections to Implement Final Rule), and 65 FR 80755 on December 22, 2000 (Final Rule; correction).

The language reproduced here is taken from BNA's *Patent, Trademark, and Copyright Regulations* (James D. Crowne, ed.), and is current as of May 14, 2001. Asterisk ellipses (* * *) indicate the omission of subsections unaltered by the Patent Business Goals rulemaking.]

§1.4 Nature of correspondence and signing requirements.

* * *

(b) Since each file must be complete in itself, a separate copy of every paper to be filed in a patent or trademark application, patent file, trademark registration file, or other proceeding must be furnished for each file to which the paper pertains, even though the contents of the papers filed in two or more files may be identical. The filing of duplicate copies of correspondence in the file of an application, patent, trademark registration file, or other proceeding should be avoided, except in situations in which the Office requires the filing of duplicate copies. The Office may dispose of duplicate copies of correspondence in the file of an application, patent, trademark registration file, or other proceeding.

(c) Since different matters may be considered by different branches or sections of the United States Patent and Trademark Office, each distinct subject, inquiry or order must be contained in a separate paper to avoid confusion and delay in answering papers dealing with different subjects.

* * *

§1.6 Receipt of correspondence.

* * *

(d)(9) Correspondence to be filed in an interference proceeding which consists of a preliminary statement under §1.621; a transcript of a deposition under §1.676 or of interrogatories, or cross-interrogatories; or an evidentiary record and exhibits under §1.653.

* * *

§1.9 Definitions.

* * *

(i) National security classified as used in this chapter means specifically authorized under criteria established by an Act of Congress or Executive Order to be kept secret in the interest of national defense or foreign policy and, in fact, properly classified pursuant to such Act of Congress or Executive Order.

§1.12 Assignment records open to public inspection.

* * *

(c) Any request by a member of the public seeking copies of any assignment records of any pending or abandoned patent application preserved in confidence under §1.14, or any information with respect thereto, must:

(1) Be in the form of a petition including the fee set forth in §1.17(h); or

* * *

§1.14 Patent applications preserved in confidence.

(a) *Confidentiality of patent application information.* Patent applications that have not been published under 35 U.S.C. 122(b) are generally preserved in confidence pursuant to 35 U.S.C. 122(a). Information concerning the filing, pendency, or subject matter of an application for patent, including status information, and access to the application, will only be given to the public as set forth in §1.11 or in this section.

(1) Status information is:

(i) Whether the application is pending, abandoned, or patented;

(ii) Whether the application has been published under 35 U.S.C. 122(b); and

(iii) The application "numerical identifier" which may be:

(A) The eight-digit application number (the two-digit series code plus the six-digit serial number); or

(B) The six-digit serial number plus any one of the filing date of the national application, the international filing date, or date of entry into the national stage.

(2) Access is defined as providing the application file for review and copying of any material in the application file.

(b) *When status information may be supplied.* Status information of an application may be supplied by the Office to the public if any of the following apply:

(1) Access to the application is available pursuant to paragraph (e) of this section;

(2) The application is referred to by its numerical identifier in a published patent document (e.g., a U.S. patent, a U.S. patent application publication, or an international application publication), or in a U.S. application open to public inspection (§1.11(b), or paragraph (e)(2)(i) or (e)(2)(ii) of this section);

(3) The application is a published international application in which the United States of America has been indicated as a designated state; or

(4) The application claims the benefit of the filing date of an application for which status information may be provided pursuant to paragraphs (b)(1) through (b)(3) of this section.

(c) *When copies may be supplied.* A copy of an application-as-filed or a file wrapper and contents may be supplied by the Office to the public, subject to paragraph (i) of this section (which addresses international applications), if any of the following apply:

(1) *Application-as-filed.*

(i) If a U.S. patent application publication or patent incorporates by reference, or includes a specific reference under 35 U.S.C. 119(e) or 120 to, a pending or abandoned application, a copy of that application-as-filed may be provided to any person upon written request including the fee set forth in §1.19(b)(1); or

(ii) If an international application, which designates the U.S. and which has been published in accordance with PCT Article 21(2), incorporates by reference or claims priority under PCT Article 8 to a pending or abandoned U.S. application, a copy of that application-as-filed may be provided to any person upon written request including a showing that the publication of the application in accordance with PCT Article 21(2) has occurred and that the U.S. was designated, and upon payment of the appropriate fee set forth in §1.19(b)(1).

(2) *File wrapper and contents.* A copy of the specification, drawings, and all papers relating to the file of an abandoned or pending published application may be provided to any person upon written request, including the fee set forth in §1.19(b)(2). If a redacted copy of the application was used for the patent application publication, the copy of the specification, drawings, and papers may be limited to a redacted copy.

(b) *When status information may be supplied.* Status information of an application may be supplied by the Office to the public if any of the following apply:

(1) Access to the application is available pursuant to paragraph (e) of this section;

(2) The application is referred to by its numerical identifier in a published patent document (e.g., a U.S. patent or a foreign application or patent publication) or in a U.S. application open to public inspection (§1.11(b) or paragraph (e)(2)(i) of this section); or

(3) The application is a published international application in which the United States of America has been indicated as a designated state.

(4) The application claims the benefit of the filing date of an application for which status information may be provided pursuant to paragraphs (b)(1) through (b)(3) of this section.

(c) *Copy of application-as-filed.* If a U.S. patent incorporates by reference a pending or abandoned application, a copy of that application-as-filed may be provided to any person upon written request accompanied by the fee set forth in §1.19(b)(1).

(d) *Power to inspect a pending or abandoned application.* Access to an application may be provided to any person if the application file is available, and the application contains written authority (e.g., a power to inspect) granting access to such person. The written authority must be signed by:

(1) An applicant;

(2) An attorney or agent of record;

(3) An authorized official of an assignee of record (made of record pursuant to §3.71 of this chapter); or

(4) A registered attorney or agent named in the papers accompanying the application papers filed under §1.53 or the national stage documents filed under §1.494 or §1.495, if an executed oath or declaration pursuant to §1.63 or §1.497 has not been filed.

(e) *Public access to a pending or abandoned application.* Access to an application may be provided to any person, subject to paragraph (i) of this section, if a written request for access is submitted, the application file is available, and any of the following apply:

(1) The application is open to public inspection pursuant to §1.11(b); or

(2) The application is abandoned, it is not within the file jacket of a pending application under §1.53(d), and it is referred to:

(i) In a U.S. patent application publication or patent;

(ii) In another U.S. application which is open to public inspection either pursuant to §1.11(b) or paragraph (e)(2)(i) of this section; or

(iii) In an international application which designates the U.S. and is published in accordance with PCT Article 21(2).

(f) *Applications reported to Department of Energy.* Applications for patents which appear to disclose, purport to disclose or do disclose inventions or discoveries relating to atomic energy are reported to the Department of Energy, which Department will be given access to the applications. Such reporting does not constitute a determination that the subject matter of each application so reported is in fact useful or is an invention or discovery, or that such application in fact discloses subject matter in categories specified by 42 U.S.C. 2181(c) and (d).

(g) *Decisions by the Commissioner or the Board of Patent Appeals and Interferences.* Any decision by the Commissioner or the Board of Patent Appeals and Interferences which would not otherwise be open to public inspection may be published or made available for public inspection if:

(1) The Commissioner believes the decision involves an interpretation of patent laws or regulations that would be of precedential value; and

(2) The applicant, or a party involved in an interference for which a decision was rendered, is given notice and an opportunity to object in writing within two months on the ground that the decision discloses a trade secret or other confidential information. Any objection must identify the deletions in the text of the decision considered necessary to protect the information, or explain why the entire decision must be withheld from the public to protect such information. An applicant or party will be given time, not less than twenty days, to request reconsideration and seek court review before any portions of a decision are made public under this paragraph over his or her objection.

(h) *Publication pursuant to §1.47.* Information as to the filing of an application will be published in the Official Gazette in accordance with §1.47(c).

(i) *International applications.*

(1) Copies of international application files for international applications which designate the U.S. and which have been published in accordance with PCT Article 21(2), or copies of a document in such application files, will be furnished in accordance with PCT Articles 30 and 38 and PCT Rules 94.2 and 94.3, upon written request including a showing that the publication of the application has occurred and that the U.S. was designated, and upon payment of the appropriate fee (see §1.19(b)(2) or 1.19(b)(3)), if:

(i) With respect to the Home Copy, the international application was filed with the U.S. Receiving Office;

(ii) With respect to the Search Copy, the U.S. acted as the International Searching Authority; or

(iii) With respect to the Examination Copy, the United States acted as the International Preliminary Examining Authority, an International Preliminary Examination Report has issued, and the United States was elected.

(2) A copy of an English language translation of an international application which has been filed in the United States Patent and Trademark Office pursuant to 35 U.S.C. 154(2)(d)(4) will be furnished upon written request including a showing that the publication of the application in accordance with PCT Article 21(2) has occurred and that the U.S. was designated, and upon payment of the appropriate fee (§1.19(b)(2) or §1.19(b)(3)).

(3) Access to international application files for international applications which designate the U.S. and which have been published in accordance with PCT Article 21(2), or copies of a document in such application files, will be furnished in accordance with PCT Articles 30 and 38 and PCT Rules 94.2 and 94.3, upon written request including a showing that the publication of the application has occurred and that the U.S. was designated.

(4) In accordance with PCT Article 30, copies of an international application-as-filed under paragraph (c)(1) of this section will not be provided prior to the international publication of the application pursuant to PCT Article 21(2).

(5) Access to international application files under paragraphs (e) and (i)(3) of this section will not be permitted with respect to the Examination Copy in accordance with PCT Article 38.

(j) *Access or copies in other circumstances.* The Office, either sua sponte or on petition, may also provide access or copies of all or part of an application if necessary to carry out an Act of Congress or if warranted by other special circumstances. Any petition by a member of the public seeking access to, or copies of, all or part of any pending or abandoned application preserved in confidence pursuant to paragraph (a) of this section, or any related papers, must include:

(1) The fee set forth in §1.17(h); and

(2) A showing that access to the application is necessary to carry out an Act of Congress or that special circumstances exist which warrant petitioner being granted access to all or part of the application.

Note: See §1.612(a) for access by an interference party to a pending or abandoned application.

§1.16 National application filing fees.

(a) Basic fee for filing each application for an original patent, except provisional, design or plant applications:

By a small entity (§1.27(a)) $355.00
By other than a small entity $710.00

(b) In addition to the basic filing fee in an original application, except provisional applications, for filing or later presentation of each independent claim in excess of 3:

By a small entity (§1.27(a)) $40.00
By other than a small entity $80.00

(c) In addition to the basic filing fee in an original application, except provisional applications, for filing or later presentation of each claim (whether independent or dependent) in excess of 20 (Note that §1.75(c) indicates how multiple dependent claims are considered for fee calculation purposes.):

By a small entity (§1.27(a)) $9.00
By other than a small entity $18.00

(d) In addition to the basic filing fee in an original application, except provisional applications, if the application contains, or is amended to contain, a multiple dependent claim(s), per application:

By a small entity (§1.27(a)) $135.00
By other than a small entity $270.00

(If the additional fees required by paragraphs (b), (c), and (d) of this section are not paid on filing or on later presentation of the claims for which the additional fees are due, they must be paid or the claims canceled by amendment, prior to the expiration of the time period set for response by the Office in any notice of fee deficiency.)

(e) Surcharge for filing the basic filing fee or oath or declaration on a date later than the filing date of the application, except provisional applications:

By a small entity (§1.27(a)) $65.00
By other than a small entity $130.00

(f) Basic fee for filing each design application:

By a small entity (§1.27(a)) $160.00
By other than a small entity $320.00

(g) Basic fee for filing each plant application, except provisional applications:

By a small entity (§1.27(a)) $245.00
By other than a small entity $490.00

(h) Basic fee for filing each reissue application:

By a small entity (§1.27(a)) $355.00
By other than a small entity $710.00

(i) In addition to the basic filing fee in a reissue application, for filing or later presentation of each independent claim which is in excess of the number of independent claims in the original patent:

By a small entity (§1.27(a)) $40.00
By other than a small entity $80.00

(j) In addition to the basic filing fee in a reissue application, for filing or later presentation of each claim (whether independent or dependent) in excess of 20 and also in excess of the number of claims in the original patent. (Note that §1.75(c) indicates how multiple dependent claims are considered for fee calculation purposes):

By a small entity (§1.27(a)) $9.00
By other than a small entity $18.00

(Note, see §1.445, 1.482 and 1.492 for international application filing and processing fees.)

(k) Basic fee for filing each provisional application:
By a small entity (§1.27(a)) $75.00
By other than a small entity $150.00

(l) Surcharge for filing the basic filing fee or cover sheet (§1.51(a)(2)(i)) on a date later than the filing date of the provisional application:
By a small entity (§1.27(a)) $25.00
By other than a small entity $50.00

* * *

§1.17 Patent application and reexamination processing fees.

(a) Extension fees pursuant to §1.136(a):
(1) For reply within first month:
By a small entity (§1.27(a)) $55.00
By other than a small entity $110.00
(2) For reply within second month:
By a small entity (§1.27(a)) $195.00
By other than a small entity $390.00
(3) For reply within third month:
By a small entity (§1.27(a)) $445.00
By other than a small entity $890.00
(4) For reply within fourth month:
By a small entity (§1.27(a)) $695.00
By other than a small entity $1,390.00
(5) For reply within fifth month:
By a small entity (§1.27(a)) $945.00
By other than a small entity $1,890.00

(b) For filing a notice of appeal from the examiner to the Board of Patent Appeals and Interferences:
By a small entity (§1.27(a)) $155.00
By other than a small entity $310.00

(c) In addition to the fee for filing a notice of appeal, for filing a brief in support of an appeal:
By a small entity (§1.27(a)) $155.00
By other than a small entity $310.00

(d) For filing a request for an oral hearing before the Board of Patent Appeals and Interferences in an appeal under 35 U.S.C. 134:
By a small entity (§1.27(a)) $135.00
By other than a small entity $270.00

(e) To request continued examination pursuant to §1.114:
By a small entity (§1.27(a)) $355.00
By other than a small entity $710.00

(f) [Reserved]

(g) [Reserved]

(h) For filing a petition under one of the following sections which refers to this paragraph $130.00
§1.12—for access to an assignment record.
§1.14—for access to an application.
§1.47—for filing by other than all the inventors or a person not the inventor.
§1.53(e)—to accord a filing date.
§1.59—for expungement and return of information.
§1.84—for accepting color drawings or photographs.
§1.91—for entry of a model or exhibit.
§1.102—to make an application special.
§1.103(a)—to suspend action in an application.
§1.138(c)—to expressly abandon an application to avoid publication.
§1.182—for decision on a question not specifically provided for.

§1.183—to suspend the rules.

§1.295—for review of refusal to publish a statutory invention registration.

§1.313—to withdraw an application from issue.

§1.314—to defer issuance of a patent.

§1.377—for review of decision refusing to accept and record payment of a maintenance fee filed prior to expiration of a patent.

§1.378(e)—for reconsideration of decision on petition refusing to accept delayed payment of maintenance fee in an expired patent.

§1.644(e)—for petition in an interference.

§1.644(f)—for request for reconsideration of a decision on petition in an interference.

§1.666(b)—for access to an interference settlement agreement.

§1.666(c)—for late filing of interference settlement agreement.

§1.741(b)—to accord a filing date to an application under §1.740 for extension of a patent term.

§5.12—for expedited handling of a foreign filing license.

§5.15—for changing the scope of a license.

§5.25—for retroactive license.

(i) Processing fee for taking action under one of the following sections which refers to this paragraph $130.00

§1.28(c)(3)—for processing a non-itemized fee deficiency based on an error in small entity status.

§1.41—for supplying the name or names of the inventor or inventors after the filing date without an oath or declaration as prescribed by §1.63, except in provisional applications.

§1.48—for correcting inventorship, except in provisional applications.

§1.52(d)—for processing a nonprovisional application filed with a specification in a language other than English.

§1.53(b)(3)—to convert a provisional application filed under §1.53(c) to a nonprovisional application under §1.53(b).

§1.55—for entry of late priority papers.

§1.99(e)—for processing a belated submission under §1.99.

§1.103(b)—for requesting limited suspension of action, continued prosecution application (§1.53(d)).

§1.103(c)—for requesting limited suspension of action, request for continued examination (§1.114).

§1.103(d)—for requesting deferred examination of an application.

§1.217—for processing a redacted copy of a paper submitted in the file of an application in which a redacted copy was submitted for the patent application publication.

§1.221—for requesting voluntary publication or republication of an application.

§1.497(d)—for filing an oath or declaration pursuant to 35 U.S.C. 371(c)(4) naming an inventive entity different from the inventive entity set forth in the international stage.

§3.81—for a patent to issue to assignee, assignment submitted after payment of the issue fee.

(j) For filing a petition to institute a public use proceeding under §1.292 . . . . $1,510.00

(k) For filing a request for expedited examination under §1.155(a) $900.00

(l) For filing a petition for the revival of an unavoidably abandoned application under 35 U.S.C. 111, 133, 364, or 371, for the unavoidably delayed payment of the issue fee under 35 U.S.C. 151, or for the revival of an unavoidably terminated reexamination proceeding under 35 U.S.C. 133 (§1.137(a)):

By a small entity (§1.27(a)) $55.00

By other than a small entity $110.00

(m) For filing a petition for revival of an unintentionally abandoned application, for the unintentionally delayed payment of the fee for issuing a patent, or for the revival of an unintentionally terminated reexamination proceeding under 35 U.S.C. 41(a)(7) (§1.137(b)):

By a small entity (§1.27(a)) $620.00
By other than a small entity $1,240.00

(n) For requesting publication of a statutory invention registration prior to the mailing of the first examiner's action pursuant to §1.104—$920.00 reduced by the amount of the application basic filing fee paid.

(o) For requesting publication of a statutory invention registration after the mailing of the first examiner's action pursuant to §1.104—$1,840.00 reduced by the amount of the application basic filing fee paid.

(p) For submission of an information disclosure statement under §1.97(c) or (d) or a submission under §1.99 . . . . $180.00

(q) Processing fee for taking action under one of the following sections which refers to this paragraph $50.00

§1.41—to supply the name or names of the inventor or inventors after the filing date without a cover sheet as prescribed by §1.51(c)(1) in a provisional application.

§1.48—for correction of inventorship in a provisional application.

§1.53(c)(2)—to convert a nonprovisional application filed under §1.53(b) to a provisional application under §1.53(c).

(r) For entry of a submission after final rejection under §1.129(a):
By a small entity (§1.27(a)) $355.00
By other than a small entity $710.00

(s) For each additional invention requested to be examined under §1.129(b):
By a small entity (§1.27(a)) $355.00
By other than a small entity $710.00

* * *

§1.18 Patent post allowance (including issue) fees.

(a) Issue fee for issuing each original or reissue patent, except a design or plant patent:
By a small entity (§1.27(a)) $620.00
By other than a small entity $1,240.00

(b) Issue fee for issuing a design patent:
By a small entity (§1.27(a)) $220.00
By other than a small entity $440.00

(c) Issue fee for issuing a plant patent:
By a small entity (§1.27(a)) $300.00
By other than a small entity $600.00

* * *

§1.19 Document supply fees.

The United States Patent and Trademark Office will supply copies of the following documents upon payment of the fees indicated. The copies will be in black and white unless the original document is in color, a color copy is requested and the fee for a color copy is paid.

(a) Uncertified copies of patent application publications and patents:

(1) Printed copy of the paper portion of a patent application publication or patent, including a design patent, statutory invention registration, or defensive publication document:

(i) Regular service, which includes preparation of copies by the Office within two to three business days and delivery by United States Postal Service or to an Office Box; and preparation of copies by the Office within one business day of receipt and delivery by electronic means (e.g., facsimile, electronic mail) $3.00

(ii) Next business day delivery to Office Box $6.00

(iii) Expedited delivery by commercial delivery service $25.00

(2) Printed copy of a plant patent in color $15.00

(3) Color copy of a patent (other than a plant patent) or statutory invention registration containing a color drawing $25.00

(b) Certified and uncertified copies of Office documents:

(1) Certified or uncertified copy of the paper portion of patent application as filed:

(i) Regular service $15.00

(ii) Expedited regular service $30.00

(2) Certified or uncertified copy of paper portion of patent-related file wrapper and contents:

(i) File wrapper and paper contents of 400 or fewer pages $200.00

(ii) Additional fee for each additional 100 pages or portion thereof $40.00

(iii) Additional fee for certification $25.00

(iv) Expedited regular service $30.00

(3) Certified or uncertified copy on compact disc of patent-related file-wrapper contents that were submitted on compact disc:

(i) First compact disc in a single order $30.00

(ii) Each additional compact disc in the single order of paragraph (b)(3)(i) of this section $15.00

(4) Certified or uncertified copy of Office records, per document except as otherwise provided in this section $25.00

(5) For assignment records, abstract of title and certification, per patent $25.00

* * *

(g) [Removed and reserved]

(h) [Removed and reserved]

§1.20 Post-issuance fees and reexamination fees.

* * *

(b) Processing for correction of inventorship in a patent (§1.324) . . . $130.00

* * *

(d) For filing each statutory disclaimer (§1.321):

By a small entity (§1.27(a)) $55.00

By other than a small entity $110.00

(e) For maintaining an original or reissue patent, except a design or plant patent, based on an application filed on or after December 12, 1980, in force beyond four years; the fee is due by three years and six months after the original grant:

By a small entity (§1.27(a)) $425.00

By other than a small entity $850.00

(f) For maintaining an original or reissue patent, except a design or plant patent, based on an application filed on or after December 12, 1980, in force beyond eight years; the fee is due by seven years and six months after the original grant:

By a small entity (§1.27(a)) $975.00

By other than a small entity $1,950.00

(g) For maintaining an original or reissue patent, except a design or plant patent, based on an application filed on or after December 12, 1980, in force beyond twelve years; the fee is due by eleven years and six months after the original grant:

By a small entity (§1.27(a)) $1,495.00

By other than a small entity $2,990.00

(h) Surcharge for paying a maintenance fee during the six-month grace period following the expiration of three years and six months, seven years and six months, and eleven years and six months after the date of the original grant of a patent based on an application filed on or after December 12, 1980:

By a small entity (§1.27(a)) $65.00

By other than a small entity $130.00

* * *

§1.22 Fees payable in advance.

* * *

(b) All fees paid to the United States Patent and Trademark Office must be itemized in each individual application, patent, trademark registration file, or other proceeding in such a manner that it is clear for which purpose the fees are paid. The Office may return fees that are not itemized as required by this paragraph. The provisions of §1.5(a) do not apply to the resubmission of fees returned pursuant to this paragraph.

§1.25 Deposit accounts.

* * *

(b) Filing, issue, appeal, international-type search report, international application processing, petition, and post-issuance fees may be charged against these accounts if sufficient funds are on deposit to cover such fees. A general authorization to charge all fees, or only certain fees, set forth in §§1.16 to 1.18 to a deposit account containing sufficient funds may be filed in an individual application, either for the entire pendency of the application or with a particular paper filed. An authorization to charge a fee to a deposit account will not be considered payment of the fee on the date the authorization to charge the fee is effective as to the particular fee to be charged unless sufficient funds are present in the account to cover the fee. An authorization to charge fees under §1.16 in an application submitted under §1.494 or §1.495 will be treated as an authorization to charge fees under §1.492. An authorization to charge fees set forth in §1.18 to a deposit account is subject to the provisions of §1.311(b). An authorization to charge to a deposit account the fee for a request for reexamination pursuant to §1.510 or §1.913 and any other fees required in a reexamination proceeding in a patent may also be filed with the request for reexamination.

§1.26 Refunds.

(a) The Commissioner may refund any fee paid by mistake or in excess of that required. A change of purpose after the payment of a fee, such as when a party desires to withdraw a patent or trademark filing for which the fee was paid, including an application, an appeal, or a request for an oral hearing, will not entitle a party to a refund of such fee. The Office will not refund amounts of twenty-five dollars or less unless a refund is specifically requested, and will not notify the payor of such amounts. If a party paying a fee or requesting a refund does not provide the banking information necessary for making refunds by electronic funds transfer (31 U.S.C. 3332 and 31 CFR part 208), or instruct the Office that refunds are to be credited to a deposit account, the Commissioner may require such information, or use the banking information on the payment instrument to make a refund. Any refund of a fee paid by credit card will be by a credit to the credit card account to which the fee was charged.

(b) Any request for refund must be filed within two years from the date the fee was paid, except as otherwise provided in this paragraph or in §1.28(a). If the Office charges a deposit account by an amount other than an amount specifically indicated in an authorization (§1.25(b)), any request for refund based upon such charge must be filed within two years from the date of the deposit account statement indicating such charge, and include a copy of that deposit account statement. The time periods set forth in this paragraph are not extendable.

* * *

§1.27 Definition of small entities and establishing status as a small entity to permit payment of small entity fees; when a determination of entitlement to small entity status and notification of loss of entitlement to small entity status are required; fraud on the Office.

(a) *Definition of small entities.* A small entity as used in this chapter means any party (person, small business concern, or nonprofit organization) under paragraphs (a)(1) through (a)(3) of this section.

(1) *Person.* A person, as used in paragraph (c) of this section, means any inventor or other individual (e.g., an individual to whom an inventor has transferred some rights in the invention), who has not assigned, granted, conveyed, or licensed, and is under no obligation under contract or law to assign, grant, convey, or license, any rights in the invention. An inventor or other individual who has transferred some rights, or is under an obligation to transfer some rights in the invention to one or more parties, can also qualify for small entity status if all the parties who have had rights in the invention transferred to them also qualify for small entity status either as a person, small business concern, or nonprofit organization under this section.

(2) *Small business concern.* A small business concern, as used in paragraph (c) of this section, means any business concern that:

(i) Has not assigned, granted, conveyed, or licensed, and is under no obligation under contract or law to assign, grant, convey, or license, any rights in the invention to any person, concern, or organization which would not qualify for small entity status as a person, small business concern, or nonprofit organization.

(ii) Meets the standards set forth in 13 CFR part 121 to be eligible for reduced patent fees. Questions related to standards for a small business concern may be directed to: Small Business Administration, Size Standards Staff, 409 Third Street, S.W., Washington, D.C. 20416.

(3) *Nonprofit Organization.* A nonprofit organization, as used in paragraph (c) of this section, means any nonprofit organization that:

(i) Has not assigned, granted, conveyed, or licensed, and is under no obligation under contract or law to assign, grant, convey, or license, any rights in the invention to any person, concern, or organization which would not qualify as a person, small business concern, or a nonprofit organization, and

(ii) Is either:

(A) A university or other institution of higher education located in any country;

(B) An organization of the type described in section 501(c)(3) of the Internal Revenue Code of 1986 (26 U.S.C. 501(c)(3)) and exempt from taxation under section 501(a) of the Internal Revenue Code (26 U.S.C. 501(a));

(C) Any nonprofit scientific or educational organization qualified under a nonprofit organization statute of a state of this country (35 U.S.C. 201(i)); or

(D) Any nonprofit organization located in a foreign country which would qualify as a nonprofit organization under paragraphs (a)(3)(ii)(B) of this section or (a)(3)(ii)(C) of this section if it were located in this country.

(4) *License to a Federal agency.*

(i) For persons under paragraph (a)(1) of this section, a license to the Government resulting from a rights determination under Executive Order 10096 does not constitute a license so as to prohibit claiming small entity status.

(ii) For small business concerns and nonprofit organizations under paragraphs (a)(2) and (a)(3) of this section, a license to a Federal agency resulting from a funding agreement with that agency pursuant to 35 U.S.C. 202(c)(4) does not constitute a license for the purposes of paragraphs (a)(2)(i) and (a)(3)(i) of this section.

(b) *Establishment of small entity status permits payment of reduced fees.* A small entity, as defined in paragraph (a) of this section, who has properly asserted entitlement to small entity status pursuant to paragraph (c) of this section will be accorded small entity status by the Office in the particular application or patent in which entitlement to small entity status was asserted. Establishment of small entity status allows the payment of certain reduced patent fees pursuant to 35 U.S.C. 41(h).

(c) *Assertion of small entity status.* Any party (person, small business concern or nonprofit organization) should make a determination, pursuant to paragraph (f) of this section, of entitlement to be accorded small entity status based on the definitions set forth in paragraph (a) of this section, and must, in order to establish small entity status for the purpose of paying small entity fees, actually make an assertion of entitlement to small entity status, in the manner set forth in paragraphs (c)(1) or (c)(3) of this section, in the application or patent in which such small entity fees are to be paid.

(1) *Assertion by writing.* Small entity status may be established by a written assertion of entitlement to small entity status. A written assertion must:

(i) Be clearly identifiable;

(ii) Be signed (see paragraph (c)(2) of this section); and

(iii) Convey the concept of entitlement to small entity status, such as by stating that applicant is a small entity, or that small entity status is entitled to be asserted for the application or patent. While no specific words or wording are required to assert small entity status, the intent to assert small entity status must be clearly indicated in order to comply with the assertion requirement.

(2) *Parties who can sign and file the written assertion.* The written assertion can be signed by:

(i) One of the parties identified in §1.33(b) (e.g., an attorney or agent registered with the Office), §3.73(b) of this chapter notwithstanding, who can also file the written assertion;

(ii) At least one of the individuals identified as an inventor (even though a §1.63 executed oath or declaration has not been submitted), notwithstanding §1.33(b)(4), who can also file the written assertion pursuant to the exception under §1.33(b) of this part; or

(iii) An assignee of an undivided part interest, notwithstanding §§1.33(b)(3) and 3.73(b) of this chapter, but the partial assignee cannot file the assertion without resort to a party identified under §1.33(b) of this part.

(3) *Assertion by payment of the small entity basic filing or basic national fee.* The payment, by any party, of the exact amount of one of the small entity basic filing fees set forth in §§1.16(a), (f), (g), (h), or (k), or one of the small entity basic national fees set forth in §§1.492(a)(1), (a)(2), (a)(3), (a)(4), or (a)(5), will be treated as a written assertion of entitlement to small entity status even if the type of basic filing or basic national fee is inadvertently selected in error.

(i) If the Office accords small entity status based on payment of a small entity basic filing or basic national fee under paragraph (c)(3) of this section that is not applicable to that application, any balance of the small entity fee that is applicable to that application will be due along with the appropriate surcharge set forth in §1.16(e), or §1.16(l).

(ii) The payment of any small entity fee other than those set forth in paragraph (c)(3) of this section (whether in the exact fee amount or not) will not be treated as a written assertion of entitlement to small entity status and will not be sufficient to establish small entity status in an application or a patent.

(4) *Assertion required in related, continuing, and reissue applications.* Status as a small entity must be specifically established by an assertion in each related, continuing and reissue application in which status is appropriate and desired. Status as a small entity in one application or patent does not affect the status of any other application or patent, regardless of the relationship of the applications or patents. The refiling of an application under §1.53 as a continuation, divisional, or continuation-in-part application (including a continued prosecution application under §1.53(d)), or the filing of a reissue application, requires a new assertion as to continued entitlement to small entity status for the continuing or reissue application.

(d) *When small entity fees can be paid.* Any fee, other than the small entity basic filing fees and the small entity national fees of paragraph (c)(3) of this section, can be paid in the small entity amount only if it is submitted with, or subsequent to, the submission of a written assertion of entitlement to small entity status, except when refunds are permitted by §1.28(a).

(e) *Only one assertion required.*

(1) An assertion of small entity status need only be filed once in an application or patent. Small entity status, once established, remains in effect until changed

pursuant to paragraph (g)(1) of this section. Where an assignment of rights or an obligation to assign rights to other parties who are small entities occurs subsequent to an assertion of small entity status, a second assertion is not required.

(2) Once small entity status is withdrawn pursuant to paragraph (g)(2) of this section, a new written assertion is required to again obtain small entity status.

(f) *Assertion requires a determination of entitlement to pay small entity fees.* Prior to submitting an assertion of entitlement to small entity status in an application, including a related, continuing, or reissue application, a determination of such entitlement should be made pursuant to the requirements of paragraph (a) of this section. It should be determined that all parties holding rights in the invention qualify for small entity status. The Office will generally not question any assertion of small entity status that is made in accordance with the requirements of this section, but note paragraph (h) of this section.

(g)(1) *New determination of entitlement to small entity status is needed when issue and maintenance fees are due.* Once status as a small entity has been established in an application or patent, fees as a small entity may thereafter be paid in that application or patent without regard to a change in status until the issue fee is due or any maintenance fee is due.

(2) *Notification of loss of entitlement to small entity status is required when issue and maintenance fees are due.* Notification of a loss of entitlement to small entity status must be filed in the application or patent prior to paying, or at the time of paying, the earliest of the issue fee or any maintenance fee due after the date on which status as a small entity as defined in paragraph (a) of this section is no longer appropriate. The notification that small entity status is no longer appropriate must be signed by a party identified in §1.33(b). Payment of a fee in other than the small entity amount is not sufficient notification that small entity status is no longer appropriate.

(h) *Fraud attempted or practiced on the Office.*

(1) Any attempt to fraudulently establish status as a small entity, or pay fees as a small entity, shall be considered as a fraud practiced or attempted on the Office.

(2) Improperly, and with intent to deceive, establishing status as a small entity, or paying fees as a small entity, shall be considered as a fraud practiced or attempted on the Office.

§1.28 Refunds when small entity status is later established; how errors in small entity status are excused.

(a) *Refunds based on later establishment of small entity status.* A refund pursuant to §1.26, based on establishment of small entity status, of a portion of fees timely paid in full prior to establishing status as a small entity may only be obtained if an assertion under §1.27(c) and a request for a refund of the excess amount are filed within three months of the date of the timely payment of the full fee. The three-month time period is not extendable under §1.136. Status as a small entity is waived for any fee by the failure to establish the status prior to paying, at the time of paying, or within three months of the date of payment of, the full fee.

(b) *Date of payment.*

(1) The three-month period for requesting a refund, pursuant to paragraph (a) of this section, starts on the date that a full fee has been paid;

(2) The date when a deficiency payment is paid in full determines the amount of deficiency that is due, pursuant to paragraph (c) of this section.

(c) *How errors in small entity status are excused.* If status as a small entity is established in good faith, and fees as a small entity are paid in good faith, in any application or patent, and it is later discovered that such status as a small entity was established in error, or that through error the Office was not notified of a loss of entitlement to small entity status as required by §1.27(g)(2), the error will be excused upon: compliance with the separate submission and itemization requirements of paragraphs (c)(1) and (c)(2) of this section, and the deficiency payment requirement of paragraph (c)(2) of this section:

(1) *Separate submission required for each application or patent.* Any paper submitted under this paragraph must be limited to the deficiency payment (all fees paid in error), required by paragraph (c)(2) of this section, for one application or one patent. Where more than one application or patent is involved, separate submissions of deficiency payments (e.g., checks) and itemizations are required for each application or patent. See §1.4(b).

(2) *Payment of deficiency owed.* The deficiency owed, resulting from the previous erroneous payment of small entity fees, must be paid.

(i) *Calculation of the deficiency owed.* The deficiency owed for each previous fee erroneously paid as a small entity is the difference between the current fee amount (for other than a small entity) on the date the deficiency is paid in full and the amount of the previous erroneous (small entity) fee payment. The total deficiency payment owed is the sum of the individual deficiency owed amounts for each fee amount previously erroneously paid as a small entity. Where a fee paid in error as a small entity was subject to a fee decrease between the time the fee was paid in error and the time the deficiency is paid in full, the deficiency owed is equal to the amount (previously) paid in error;

(ii) *Itemization of the deficiency payment.* An itemization of the total deficiency payment is required. The itemization must include the following information:

(A) Each particular type of fee that was erroneously paid as a small entity (e.g., basic statutory filing fee, two-month extension of time fee), along with the current fee amount for a non-small entity;

(B) The small entity fee actually paid, and when. This will permit the Office to differentiate, for example, between two one-month extension of time fees erroneously paid as a small entity but on different dates;

(C) The deficiency owed amount (for each fee erroneously paid); and

(D) The total deficiency payment owed, which is the sum or total of the individual deficiency owed amounts set forth in paragraph (c)(2)(ii)(C) of this section.

(3) *Failure to comply with requirements.* If the requirements of paragraphs (c)(1) and (c)(2) of this section are not complied with, such failure will either: be treated as an authorization for the Office to process the deficiency payment and charge the processing fee set forth in §1.17(i), or result in a requirement for compliance within a one-month non-extendable time period under §1.136(a) to avoid the return of the fee deficiency paper, at the option of the Office.

(d) *Payment of deficiency operates as notification of loss of status.* Any deficiency payment (based on a previous erroneous payment of a small entity fee) submitted under paragraph (c) of this section will be treated under §1.27(g)(2) as a notification of a loss of entitlement to small entity status.

§1.33 Correspondence respecting patent applications, reexamination proceedings, and other proceedings.

(a) *Correspondence address and daytime telephone number.* When filing an application, a correspondence address must be set forth in either an application data sheet (§1.76), or elsewhere, in a clearly identifiable manner, in any paper submitted with an application filing. If no correspondence address is specified, the Office may treat the mailing address of the first named inventor (if provided, see §§1.76(b)(1) and 1.63(c)(2)) as the correspondence address. The Office will direct all notices, official letters, and other communications relating to the application to the correspondence address. The Office will not engage in double correspondence with an applicant and a registered attorney or agent, or with more than one registered attorney or agent except as deemed necessary by the Commissioner. If more than one correspondence address is specified, the Office will establish one as the correspondence address. For the party to whom correspondence is to be addressed, a daytime telephone number should be supplied in a clearly identifiable manner and may be changed by any party who may change the correspondence address. The correspondence address may be changed as follows:

(1) *Prior to filing of a §1.63 oath or declaration by any of the inventors.* If a §1.63 oath or declaration has not been filed by any of the inventors, the correspondence address may be changed by the party who filed the application. If the application was filed by a registered attorney or agent, any other registered practitioner named in the transmittal papers may also change the correspondence address. Thus, the inventor(s), any registered practitioner named in the transmittal papers accompanying the original application, or a party that will be the assignee who filed the application, may change the correspondence address in that application under this paragraph.

(2) *Where a §1.63 oath or declaration has been filed by any of the inventors.* If a §1.63 oath or declaration has been filed, or is filed concurrent with the filing of an application, by any of the inventors, the correspondence address may be changed by the parties set forth in paragraph (b) of this section, except for paragraph (b)(2).

(b) *Amendments and other papers.* Amendments and other papers, except for written assertions pursuant to §1.27(c)(2)(ii) of this part, filed in the application must be signed by:

(1) A registered attorney or agent of record appointed in compliance with §1.34(b);

(2) A registered attorney or agent not of record who acts in a representative capacity under the provisions of §1.34(a);

(3) An assignee as provided for under §3.71(b) of this chapter; or

(4) All of the applicants (§1.41(b)) for patent, unless there is an assignee of the entire interest and such assignee has taken action in the application in accordance with §3.71 of this chapter.

* * *

§1.34 Recognition for representation.

(a) When a registered attorney or agent acting in a representative capacity, pursuant to §1.31, appears in person or signs a paper in practice before the United States Patent and Trademark Office in a patent case, his or her personal appearance or signature shall constitute a representation to the United States Patent and Trademark Office that under the provisions of this subchapter and the law, he or she is authorized to represent the particular party in whose behalf he or she acts. In filing such a paper, the registered attorney or agent should specify his or her registration number with his or her signature. Further proof of authority to act in a representative capacity may be required.

(b) When a registered attorney or agent shall have filed his or her power of attorney, or authorization, duly executed by the person or persons entitled to prosecute an application or a patent involved in a reexamination proceeding, pursuant to §1.31, he or she is a principal registered attorney or agent of record in the case. A principal registered attorney or agent, so appointed, may appoint an associate registered attorney or agent who shall also then be of record.

§1.36 Revocation of power of attorney or authorization; withdrawal of registered attorney or agent.

A power of attorney or authorization of agent, pursuant to §1.31, may be revoked at any stage in the proceedings of a case, and a registered attorney or agent may withdraw, upon application to and approval by the Commissioner. A registered attorney or agent, except an associate registered attorney or agent whose address is the same as that of the principal registered attorney or agent, will be notified of the revocation of the power of attorney or authorization, and the applicant or patent owner will be notified of the withdrawal of the registered attorney or agent. An assignment will not of itself operate as a revocation of a power or authorization previously given, but the assignee of the entire interest may revoke previous powers and be represented by a registered attorney or agent of the assignee's own selection. See §1.613(d) for withdrawal in an interference.

§1.41 Applicant for patent.

(a) A patent is applied for in the name or names of the actual inventor or inventors.

(1) The inventorship of a nonprovisional application is that inventorship set forth in the oath or declaration as prescribed by §1.63, except as provided for in §§1.53(d)(4) and 1.63(d). If an oath or declaration as prescribed by §1.63 is not filed during the pendency of a nonprovisional application, the inventorship is that inventorship set forth in the application papers filed pursuant to §1.53(b), unless applicant files a paper, including the processing fee set forth in §1.17(i), supplying or changing the name or names of the inventor or inventors.

(2) The inventorship of a provisional application is that inventorship set forth in the cover sheet as prescribed by §1.51(c)(1). If a cover sheet as prescribed by §1.51(c)(1) is not filed during the pendency of a provisional application, the inventorship is that inventorship set forth in the application papers filed pursuant to §1.53(c), unless applicant files a paper including the processing fee set forth in §1.17(q), supplying or changing the name or names of the inventor or inventors.

(3) In a nonprovisional application filed without an oath or declaration as prescribed by §1.63 or a provisional application filed without a cover sheet as prescribed by §1.51(c)(1), the name, residence, and citizenship of each person believed to be an actual inventor should be provided when the application papers pursuant to §1.53(b) or §1.53(c) are filed.

(4) The inventors who submitted an application under §1.494 or §1.495 are the inventors in the international application designating the United States (§1.48(f)(1) does not apply to applications entering the national stage).

* * *

(c) Any person authorized by the applicant may physically or electronically deliver an application for patent to the Office on behalf of the inventor or inventors, but an oath or declaration for the application (§1.63) can only be made in accordance with §1.64.

* * *

§1.44 [Removed and Reserved]

§1.47 Filing when an inventor refuses to sign or cannot be reached.

(a) If a joint inventor refuses to join in an application for patent or cannot be found or reached after diligent effort, the application may be made by the other inventor on behalf of himself or herself and the nonsigning inventor. The oath or declaration in such an application must be accompanied by a petition including proof of the pertinent facts, the fee set forth in §1.17(h), and the last known address of the nonsigning inventor. The nonsigning inventor may subsequently join in the application by filing an oath or declaration complying with §1.63.

(b) Whenever all of the inventors refuse to execute an application for patent, or cannot be found or reached after diligent effort, a person to whom an inventor has assigned or agreed in writing to assign the invention, or who otherwise shows sufficient proprietary interest in the matter justifying such action, may make application for patent on behalf of and as agent for all the inventors. The oath or declaration in such an application must be accompanied by a petition including proof of the pertinent facts, a showing that such action is necessary to preserve the rights of the parties or to prevent irreparable damage, the fee set forth in §1.17(h), and the last known address of all of the inventors. An inventor may subsequently join in the application by filing an oath or declaration complying with §1.63.

(c) The Office will send notice of the filing of the application to all inventors who have not joined in the application at the address(es) provided in the petition under this section, and publish notice of the filing of the application in the Official Gazette. The Office may dispense with this notice provision in a continuation or divisional application, if notice regarding the filing of the prior application was given to the nonsigning inventor(s).

(35 U.S.C. 6, Pub. L. 97-247)
[48 FR 2709, Jan. 20, 1983; 62 FR 53132, Oct. 10, 1997; 65 FR 54603, Sept. 8, 2000]

§1.48 Correction of inventorship in a patent application, other than a reissue application, pursuant to 35 U.S.C. 116.

(a) *Nonprovisional application after oath / declaration filed.* If the inventive entity is set forth in error in an executed §1.63 oath or declaration in a nonprovisional application, and such error arose without any deceptive intention on the part of the person named as an inventor in error or on the part of the person who through error was not named as an inventor, the inventorship of the nonprovisional application may be amended to name only the actual inventor or inventors. If the nonprovisional application is involved in an interference, the amendment must comply with the requirements of this section and must be accompanied by a motion under §1.634. Amendment of the inventorship requires:

(1) A request to correct the inventorship that sets forth the desired inventorship change;

(2) A statement from each person being added as an inventor and from each person being deleted as an inventor that the error in inventorship occurred without deceptive intention on his or her part;

(3) An oath or declaration by the actual inventor or inventors as required by §1.63 or as permitted by §§1.42, 1.43 or §1.47;

(4) The processing fee set forth in §1.17(i); and

(5) If an assignment has been executed by any of the original named inventors, the written consent of the assignee (see §3.73(b) of this chapter).

(b) *Nonprovisional application—fewer inventors due to amendment or cancellation of claims.* If the correct inventors are named in a nonprovisional application, and the prosecution of the nonprovisional application results in the amendment or cancellation of claims so that fewer than all of the currently named inventors are the actual inventors of the invention being claimed in the nonprovisional application, an amendment must be filed requesting deletion of the name or names of the person or persons who are not inventors of the invention being claimed. If the application is involved in an interference, the amendment must comply with the requirements of this section and must be accompanied by a motion under §1.634. Amendment of the inventorship requires:

(1) A request, signed by a party set forth in §1.33(b), to correct the inventorship that identifies the named inventor or inventors being deleted and acknowledges that the inventor's invention is no longer being claimed in the nonprovisional application; and

(2) The processing fee set forth in §1.17(i).

(c) *Nonprovisional application—inventors added for claims to previously unclaimed subject matter.* If a nonprovisional application discloses unclaimed subject matter by an inventor or inventors not named in the application, the application may be amended to add claims to the subject matter and name the correct inventors for the application. If the application is involved in an interference, the amendment must comply with the requirements of this section and must be accompanied by a motion under §1.634. Amendment of the inventorship requires:

(1) A request to correct the inventorship that sets forth the desired inventorship change;

(2) A statement from each person being added as an inventor that the addition is necessitated by amendment of the claims and that the inventorship error occurred without deceptive intention on his or her part;

(3) An oath or declaration by the actual inventors as required by §1.63 or as permitted by §§1.42, 1.43, or §1.47;

(4) The processing fee set forth in §1.17(i); and

(5) If an assignment has been executed by any of the original named inventors, the written consent of the assignee (see §3.73(b) of this chapter).

(d) *Provisional application—adding omitted inventors.* If the name or names of an inventor or inventors were omitted in a provisional application through error without any deceptive intention on the part of the omitted inventor or inventors, the provisional application may be amended to add the name or names of the omitted inventor or inventors. Amendment of the inventorship requires:

(1) A request, signed by a party set forth in §1.33(b), to correct the inventorship that identifies the inventor or inventors being added and states that the inventorship error occurred without deceptive intention on the part of the omitted inventor or inventors; and

(2) The processing fee set forth in §1.17(q).

(e) *Provisional application—deleting the name or names of the inventor or inventors.* If a person or persons were named as an inventor or inventors in a provisional application through error without any deceptive intention on the part of such person or persons, an amendment may be filed in the provisional application deleting the name or names of the person or persons who were erroneously named. Amendment of the inventorship requires:

(1) A request to correct the inventorship that sets forth the desired inventorship change;

(2) A statement by the person or persons whose name or names are being deleted that the inventorship error occurred without deceptive intention on the part of such person or persons;

(3) The processing fee set forth in §1.17(q); and

(4) If an assignment has been executed by any of the original named inventors, the written consent of the assignee (see §3.73(b) of this chapter).

(f)(1) *Nonprovisional application—filing executed oath/declaration corrects inventorship.* If the correct inventor or inventors are not named on filing a nonprovisional application under §1.53(b) without an executed oath or declaration under §1.63 by any of the inventors, the first submission of an executed oath or declaration under §1.63 by any of the inventors during the pendency of the application will act to correct the earlier identification of inventorship. See §§1.41(a)(4) and 1.497(d) for submission of an executed oath or declaration to enter the national stage under 35 U.S.C. 371 and §1.494 or §1.495 naming an inventive entity different from the inventive entity set forth in the international stage.

(2) *Provisional application—filing cover sheet corrects inventorship.* If the correct inventor or inventors are not named on filing a provisional application without a cover sheet under §1.51(c)(1), the later submission of a cover sheet under §1.51(c)(1) during the pendency of the application will act to correct the earlier identification of inventorship.

(g) *Additional information may be required.* The Office may require such other information as may be deemed appropriate under the particular circumstances surrounding the correction of inventorship.

(h) *Reissue applications not covered.* The provisions of this section do not apply to reissue applications. See §§1.171 and 1.175 for correction of inventorship in a patent via a reissue application.

(i) *Correction of inventorship in patent or interference.* See §1.324 for correction of inventorship in a patent, and §1.634 for correction of inventorship in an interference.

§1.51 General requisites of an application.

* * *

(b) A complete application filed under §1.53(b) or §1.53(d) comprises:

(1) A specification as prescribed by 35 U.S.C. 112, including a claim or claims, see §§1.71 to 1.77;

(2) An oath or declaration, see §§1.63 and 1.68;

(3) Drawings, when necessary, see §§1.81 to 1.85; and

(4) The prescribed filing fee, see §1.16.

* * *

§1.52 Language, paper, writing, margins, compact disc specifications.

(a) *Papers that are to become a part of the permanent United States Patent and Trademark Office records in the file of a patent application or a reexamination proceeding.*

(1) All papers, other than drawings, that are to become a part of the permanent United States Patent and Trademark Office records in the file of a patent

application or reexamination proceeding must be on sheets of paper that are the same size, and:

(i) Flexible, strong, smooth, non-shiny, durable, and white;

(ii) Either 21.0 cm by 29.7 cm (DIN size A4) or 21.6 cm by 27.9 cm (8½ by 11 inches), with each sheet including a top margin of at least 2.0 cm (¾ inch), a left side margin of at least 25 cm (1 inch), a right side margin of at least 2.0 cm (¾ inch), and a bottom margin of at least 2.0 cm (¾ inch);

(iii) Written on only one side in portrait orientation;

(iv) Plainly and legibly written either by a typewriter or machine printer in permanent dark ink or its equivalent; and

(v) Presented in a form having sufficient clarity and contrast between the paper and the writing thereon to permit the direct reproduction of readily legible copies in any number by use of photographic, electrostatic, photo-offset, and microfilming processes and electronic capture by use of digital imaging and optical character recognition.

(2) All papers that are to become a part of the permanent records of the United States Patent and Trademark Office should have no holes in the sheets as submitted.

(3) The provisions of this paragraph and paragraph (b) of this section do not apply to the pre-printed information on forms provided by the Office, or to the copy of the patent submitted in double column format as the specification in a reissue application or request for reexamination.

(4) See §1.58 for chemical and mathematical formulae and tables, and §1.84 for drawings.

(5) If papers that do not comply with paragraph (a)(1) of this section are submitted as part of the permanent record, other than the drawings, applicant, or the patent owner, or the requester in a reexamination proceeding, will be notified and must provide substitute papers that comply with paragraph (a)(1) of this section within a set time period.

(b) *The application (specification, including the claims, drawings, and oath or declaration) or reexamination proceeding and any amendments or corrections to the application or reexamination proceeding.*

(1) The application or proceeding and any amendments or corrections to the application (including any translation submitted pursuant to paragraph (d) of this section) or proceeding, except as provided for in §1.69 and paragraph (d) of this section, must:

(i) Comply with the requirements of paragraph (a) of this section; and

(ii) Be in the English language or be accompanied by a translation of the application and a translation of any corrections or amendments into the English language together with a statement that the translation is accurate.

(2) The specification (including the abstract and claims) for other than reissue applications and reexamination proceedings, and any amendments for applications (including reissue applications) and reexamination proceedings to the specification, except as provided for in §§1.821 through 1.825, must have:

(i) Lines that are 1½ or double spaced;

(ii) Text written in a nonscript type font (e.g., Arial, Times Roman, or Courier) lettering style having capital letters which are at least 0.21 cm (0.08 inch) high; and

(iii) Only a single column of text.

(3) The claim or claims must commence on a separate sheet (§1.75(h)).

(4) The abstract must commence on a separate sheet or be submitted as the first page of the patent in a reissue application or reexamination proceeding (§1.72(b)).

(5) Other than in a reissue application or reexamination proceeding, the pages of the specification including claims and abstract must be numbered consecutively, starting with 1, the numbers being centrally located above or preferably, below, the text.

(6) Other than in a reissue application or reexamination proceeding, the paragraphs of the specification, other than in the claims or abstract, may be numbered at the time the application is filed, and should be individually and consecutively numbered using Arabic numerals, so as to unambiguously identify each paragraph. The number should consist of at least four numerals enclosed in square brackets, including leading zeros (e.g., [0001]). The numbers and enclosing brackets should appear to the right of the left margin as the first item in each paragraph, before the first word of the paragraph, and should be highlighted in bold. A gap, equivalent to approximately four spaces, should follow the number. Nontext elements (e.g., tables, mathematical or chemical formulae, chemical structures, and sequence data) are considered part of the numbered paragraph around or above the elements, and should not be independently numbered. If a nontext element extends to the left margin, it should not be numbered as a separate and independent paragraph. A list is also treated as part of the paragraph around or above the list, and should not be independently numbered. Paragraph or section headers (titles), whether abutting the left margin or centered on the page, are not considered paragraphs and should not be numbered.

(7) If papers that do not comply with paragraphs (b)(1) through (b)(5) of this section are submitted as part of the application, applicant, or patent owner, or requester in a reexamination proceeding, will be notified and the applicant, patent owner or requester in a reexamination proceeding must provide substitute papers that comply with paragraphs (b)(1) through (b)(5) of this section within a set time period.

(c) (1) Any interlineation, erasure, cancellation or other alteration of the application papers filed must be made before the signing of any accompanying oath or declaration pursuant to §1.63 referring to those application papers and should be dated and initialed or signed by the applicant on the same sheet of paper. Application papers containing alterations made after the signing of an oath or declaration referring to those application papers must be supported by a supplemental oath or declaration under §1.67. In either situation, a substitute specification (§1.125) is required if the application papers do not comply with paragraphs (a) and (b) of this section.

(2) After the signing of the oath or declaration referring to the application papers, amendments may only be made in the manner provided by §1.121.

(3) Notwithstanding the provisions of this paragraph, if an oath or declaration is a copy of the oath or declaration from a prior application, the application for which such copy is submitted may contain alterations that do not introduce matter that would have been new matter in the prior application.

* * *

(e) *Electronic documents that are to become part of the permanent United States Patent and Trademark Office records in the file of a patent application or reexamination proceeding.*

(1) The following documents may be submitted to the Office on a compact disc in compliance with this paragraph:

(i) A computer program listing (see §1.96);

(ii) A "Sequence Listing" (submitted under §1.821(c)); or

(iii) A table (see §1.58) that has more than 50 pages of text.

(2) A compact disc as used in this part means a Compact Disc-Read Only Memory (CD-ROM) or a Compact Disc-Recordable (CD-R) in compliance with this paragraph. A CD-ROM is a "read-only" medium on which the data is pressed into the disc so that it cannot be changed or erased. A CD-R is a "write once" medium on which once the data is recorded, it is permanent and cannot be changed or erased.

(3) (i) Each compact disc must conform to the International Standards Organization (ISO) 9660 standard, and the contents of each compact disc must be in compliance with the American Standard Code for Information Interchange (ASCII).

(ii) Each compact disc must be enclosed in a hard compact disc case within an unsealed padded and protective mailing envelope and accompanied by a transmittal letter on paper in accordance with paragraph (a) of this section. The transmittal letter must list for each compact disc the machine format (e.g., IBM-PC, Macintosh), the operating system compatibility (e.g., MS-DOS, MS-Windows, Macintosh, Unix), a list of files contained on the compact disc including their names, sizes in bytes, and dates of creation, plus any other special information that is necessary to identify, maintain, and interpret the information on the compact disc. Compact discs submitted to the Office will not be returned to the applicant.

(4) Any compact disc must be submitted in duplicate unless it contains only the "Sequence Listing" in computer readable form required by §1.821(e). The compact disc and duplicate copy must be labeled "Copy 1" and "Copy 2," respectively. The transmittal letter which accompanies the compact disc must include a statement that the two compact discs are identical. In the event that the two compact discs are not identical, the Office will use the compact disc labeled "Copy 1" for further processing. Any amendment to the information on a compact disc must be by way of a replacement compact disc in compliance with this paragraph containing the substitute information, and must be accompanied by a statement that the replacement compact disc contains no new matter. The compact disc and copy must be labeled "COPY 1 REPLACEMENT MM/DD/YYYY" (with the month, day and year of creation indicated), and "COPY 2 REPLACEMENT MM/DD/YYYY," respectively.

(5) The specification must contain an incorporation-by-reference of the material on the compact disc in a separate paragraph (§1.77(b)(4)), identifying each compact disc by the names of the files contained on each of the compact discs, their date of creation and their sizes in bytes. The Office may require applicant to amend the specification to include in the paper portion any part of the specification previously submitted on compact disc.

(6) A compact disc must also be labeled with the following information:

(i) The name of each inventor (if known);

(ii) Title of the invention;

(iii) The docket number, or application number if known, used by the person filing the application to identify the application; and

(iv) A creation date of the compact disc.

(v) If multiple compact discs are submitted, the label shall indicate their order (e.g. "1 of X").

(vi) An indication that the disk is "Copy 1" or "Copy 2" of the submission. See paragraph (b)(4) of this section.

(7) If a file is unreadable on both copies of the disc, the unreadable file will be treated as not having been submitted. A file is unreadable if, for example, it is of a format that does not comply with the requirements of paragraph (e)(3) of this section, it is corrupted by a computer virus, or it is written onto a defective compact disc.

§1.53 Application number, filing date, and completion of application.

* * *

(c) *Application filing requirements—Provisional application.* The filing date of a provisional application is the date on which a specification as prescribed by the first paragraph of 35 U.S.C. 112, and any drawing required by §1.81(a) are filed in the Patent and Trademark Office. No amendment, other than to make the provisional application comply with the patent statute and all applicable regulations, may be made to the provisional application after the filing date of the provisional application.

(1) A provisional application must also include the cover sheet required by §1.51(c)(1), which may be an application data sheet (§1.76), or a cover letter identifying the application as a provisional application. Otherwise, the application will be treated as an application filed under paragraph (b) of this section.

(2) An application for patent filed under paragraph (b) of this section may be converted to a provisional application and be accorded the original filing date of

the application filed under paragraph (b) of this section. The grant of such a request for conversion will not entitle applicant to a refund of the fees that were properly paid in the application filed under paragraph (b) of this section. Such a request for conversion must be accompanied by the processing fee set forth in §1.17(q) and be filed prior to the earliest of:

(i) Abandonment of the application filed under paragraph (b) of this section;

(ii) Payment of the issue fee on the application filed under paragraph (b) of this section;

(iii) Expiration of twelve months after the filing date of the application filed under paragraph (b) of this section; or

(iv) The filing of a request for a statutory invention registration under §1.293 in the application filed under paragraph (b) of this section.

* * *

(4) A provisional application is not entitled to the right of priority under 35 U.S.C. 119 or 365(a) or §1.55, or to the benefit of an earlier filing date under 35 U.S.C. 120, 121 or 365(c) or §1.78 of any other application. No claim for priority under 35 U.S.C. 119(e) or §1.78(a)(4) may be made in a design application based on a provisional application. No request under §1.293 for a statutory invention registration may be filed in a provisional application. The requirements of §§1.821 through 1.825 regarding application disclosures containing nucleotide and/or amino acid sequences are not mandatory for provisional applications.

(d) *Application filing requirements—Continued prosecution (nonprovisional) application.*

* * *

(4) An application filed under this paragraph may be filed by fewer than all the inventors named in the prior application, provided that the request for an application under this paragraph when filed is accompanied by a statement requesting deletion of the name or names of the person or persons who are not inventors of the invention being claimed in the new application. No person may be named as an inventor in an application filed under this paragraph who was not named as an inventor in the prior application on the date the application under this paragraph was filed, except by way of correction of inventorship under §1.48.

* * *

(10) See §1.103(b) for requesting a limited suspension of action in an application filed under this paragraph.

(e) *Failure to meet filing date requirements.*

* * *

(2) Any request for review of a notification pursuant to paragraph (e)(1) of this section, or a notification that the original application papers lack a portion of the specification or drawing(s), must be by way of a petition pursuant to this paragraph accompanied by the fee set forth in §1.17(h). In the absence of a timely (§1.181(f)) petition pursuant to this paragraph, the filing date of an application in which the applicant was notified of a filing error pursuant to paragraph (e)(1) of this section will be the date the filing error is corrected.

* * *

(f) *Completion of application subsequent to filing—Nonprovisional (including continued prosecution or reissue) application.*

(1) If an application which has been accorded a filing date pursuant to paragraph (b) or (d) of this section does not include the basic filing fee, or if an application which has been accorded a filing date pursuant to paragraph (b) of this section does not include an oath or declaration by the applicant pursuant to §§1.63, 1.162 or §1.175, and applicant has provided a correspondence address (§1.33(a)), appli-

cant will be notified and given a period of time within which to pay the filing fee, file an oath or declaration in an application under paragraph (b) of this section, and pay the surcharge required by §1.16(e) to avoid abandonment.

(2) If an application which has been accorded a filing date pursuant to paragraph (b) of this section does not include the basic filing fee or an oath or declaration by the applicant pursuant to §§1.63, 1.162 or §1.175, and applicant has not provided a correspondence address (§1.33(a)), applicant has two months from the filing date of the application within which to pay the basic filing fee, file an oath or declaration, and pay the surcharge required by §1.16(e) to avoid abandonment.

(3) This paragraph applies to continuation or divisional applications under paragraphs (b) or (d) of this section and to continuation-in-part applications under paragraph (b) of this section.

(4) See §1.63(d) concerning the submission of a copy of the oath or declaration from the prior application for a continuation or divisional application under paragraph (b) of this section.

(5) If applicant does not pay one of the basic filing or the processing and retention fees (§1.21(l)) during the pendency of the application, the Office may dispose of the application.

(g) *Completion of application subsequent to filing—provisional application.*

(1) If a provisional application which has been accorded a filing date pursuant to paragraph (c) of this section does not include the cover sheet required by §1.51(c)(1) or the basic filing fee (§1.16(k)), and applicant has provided a correspondence address (§1.33(a)), applicant will be notified and given a period of time within which to pay the basic filing fee, file a cover sheet (§1.51(c)(1)), and pay the surcharge required by §1.16(l) to avoid abandonment.

(2) If a provisional application which has been accorded a filing date pursuant to paragraph (c) of this section does not include the cover sheet required by §1.51(c)(1) or the basic filing fee (§1.16(k)), and applicant has not provided a correspondence address (§1.33(a)), applicant has two months from the filing date of the application within which to pay the basic filing fee, file a cover sheet (§1.51(c)(1)), and pay the surcharge required by §1.16(l) to avoid abandonment.

(3) If applicant does not pay the basic filing fee during the pendency of the application, the Office may dispose of the application.

§1.55 Claim for foreign priority.

(a) An applicant in a nonprovisional application may claim the benefit of the filing date of one or more prior foreign applications under the conditions specified in 35 U.S.C. 119(a) through (d) and (f), 172, and 365(a) and (b).

(1)(i) In an original application filed under 35 U.S.C. 111(a), the claim for priority must be presented during the pendency of the application, and within the later of four months from the actual filing date of the application or sixteen months from the filing date of the prior foreign application. This time period is not extendable. The claim must identify the foreign application for which priority is claimed, as well as any foreign application for the same subject matter and having a filing date before that of the application for which priority is claimed, by specifying the application number, country (or intellectual property authority), day, month, and year of its filing. The time period in this paragraph does not apply to an application for a design patent.

(ii) In an application that entered the national stage from an international application after compliance with 35 U.S.C. 371, the claim for priority must be made during the pendency of the application and within the time limit set forth in the PCT and the Regulations under the PCT.

(2) The claim for priority and the certified copy of the foreign application specified in 35 U.S.C. 119(b) or PCT Rule 17 must, in any event, be filed before the patent is granted. If the claim for priority or the certified copy of the foreign application is filed after the date the issue fee is paid, it must be accompanied by the processing fee set forth in Sec. 1.17(i), but the patent will not include the priority claim unless corrected by a certificate of correction under 35 U.S.C. 255 and Sec. 1.323.

(3) When the application becomes involved in an interference (Sec. 1.630), when necessary to overcome the date of a reference relied upon by the examiner, or when deemed necessary by the examiner, the Office may require that the claim for priority and the certified copy of the foreign application be filed earlier than provided in paragraphs (a)(1) or (a)(2) of this section.

(4) An English language translation of a non-English language foreign application is not required except when the application is involved in an interference (Sec. 1.630), when necessary to overcome the date of a reference relied upon by the examiner, or when specifically required by the examiner. If an English language translation is required, it must be filed together with a statement that the translation of the certified copy is accurate.

* * *

§1.56 Duty to disclose information material to patentability.

* * *

(e) In any continuation-in-part application, the duty under this section includes the duty to disclose to the Office all information known to the person to be material to patentability, as defined in paragraph (b) of this section, which became available between the filing date of the prior application and the national or PCT international filing date of the continuation-in-part application.

§1.58 Chemical and mathematical formulae and tables.

* * *

(b) Tables that are submitted in electronic form (§§1.96(c) and 1.821(c)) must maintain the spatial relationships (e.g., columns and rows) of the table elements and preserve the information they convey. Chemical and mathematical formulae must be encoded to maintain the proper positioning of their characters when displayed in order to preserve their intended meaning.

* * *

§1.59 Expungement of information or copy of papers in application file.

* * *

(b) An applicant may request that the Office expunge and return information, other than what is excluded by paragraph (a)(2) of this section, by filing a petition under this paragraph. Any petition to expunge and return information from an application must include the fee set forth in §1.17(h) and establish to the satisfaction of the Commissioner that the return of the information is appropriate.

* * *

§1.63 Oath or declaration.

(a) An oath or declaration filed under §1.51(b)(2) as a part of a nonprovisional application must:

(1) Be executed, i.e., signed, in accordance with either §1.66 or §1.68. There is no minimum age for a person to be qualified to sign, but the person must be competent to sign, i.e., understand the document that the person is signing;

(2) Identify each inventor by full name, including the family name, and at least one given name without abbreviation together with any other given name or initial;

(3) Identify the country of citizenship of each inventor; and

(4) State that the person making the oath or declaration believes the named inventor or inventors to be the original and first inventor or inventors of the subject matter which is claimed and for which a patent is sought.

(b) In addition to meeting the requirements of paragraph (a) of this section, the oath or declaration must also:

(1) Identify the application to which it is directed;

(2) State that the person making the oath or declaration has reviewed and understands the contents of the application, including the claims, as amended by any amendment specifically referred to in the oath or declaration; and

(3) State that the person making the oath or declaration acknowledges the duty to disclose to the Office all information known to the person to be material to patentability as defined in §1.56.

(c) Unless such information is supplied on an application data sheet in accordance with §1.76, the oath or declaration must also identify:

(1) The mailing address, and the residence if an inventor lives at a location which is different from where the inventor customarily receives mail, of each inventor; and

(2) Any foreign application for patent (or inventor's certificate) for which a claim for priority is made pursuant to §1.55, and any foreign application having a filing date before that of the application on which priority is claimed, by specifying the application number, country, day, month, and year of its filing.

* * *

(e) A newly executed oath or declaration must be filed in any continuation-in-part application, which application may name all, more, or fewer than all of the inventors named in the prior application.

§1.64 Person making oath or declaration.

(a) The oath or declaration (§1.63), including any supplemental oath or declaration (§1.67), must be made by all of the actual inventors except as provided for in §§1.42, 1.43, 1.47, or §1.67.

(b) If the person making the oath or declaration or any supplemental oath or declaration is not the inventor (§§1.42, 1.43, 1.47, or §1.67), the oath or declaration shall state the relationship of the person to the inventor, and, upon information and belief, the facts which the inventor is required to state. If the person signing the oath or declaration is the legal representative of a deceased inventor, the oath or declaration shall also state that the person is a legal representative and the citizenship, residence, and mailing address of the legal representative.

§1.67 Supplemental oath or declaration.

(a) The Office may require, or inventors and applicants may submit, a supplemental oath or declaration meeting the requirements of §1.63 or §1.162 to correct any deficiencies or inaccuracies present in the earlier filed oath or declaration.

(1) Deficiencies or inaccuracies relating to all the inventors or applicants (§§1.42, 1.43, or §1.47) may be corrected with a supplemental oath or declaration signed by all the inventors or applicants.

(2) Deficiencies or inaccuracies relating to fewer than all of the inventor(s) or applicant(s) (§§1.42, 1.43 or §1.47) may be corrected with a supplemental oath or declaration identifying the entire inventive entity but signed only by the inventor(s) or applicant(s) to whom the error or deficiency relates.

(3) Deficiencies or inaccuracies due to the failure to meet the requirements of §1.63(c) (e.g., to correct the omission of a mailing address of an inventor) in an oath or declaration may be corrected with an application data sheet in accordance with §1.76.

(4) Submission of a supplemental oath or declaration or an application data sheet (§1.76), as opposed to who must sign the supplemental oath or declaration or an application data sheet, is governed by §1.33(a)(2) and paragraph (b) of this section.

* * *

(c) [Removed and reserved]

§1.72 Title and abstract.

(a) The title of the invention may not exceed 500 characters in length and must be as short and specific as possible. Characters that cannot be captured and recorded in the Office's automated information systems may not be reflected in the Office's records in such systems or in documents created by the Office. Unless the title is supplied in an application data sheet (§1.76), the title of the invention should appear as a heading on the first page of the specification.

(b) A brief abstract of the technical disclosure in the specification must commence on a separate sheet, preferably following the claims, under the heading "Abstract" or "Abstract of the Disclosure." The abstract in an application filed under 35 U.S.C. 111 may not exceed 150 words in length. The purpose of the abstract is to enable the United States Patent and Trademark Office and the public generally to determine quickly from a cursory inspection the nature and gist of the technical disclosure. The abstract will not be used for interpreting the scope of the claims.

§1.76 Application data sheet.

(a) *Application data sheet.* An application data sheet is a sheet or sheets, that may be voluntarily submitted in either provisional or nonprovisional applications, which contains bibliographic data, arranged in a format specified by the Office. If an application data sheet is provided, the application data sheet is part of the provisional or nonprovisional application for which it has been submitted.

(b) *Bibliographic data.* Bibliographic data as used in paragraph (a) of this section includes:

(1) *Applicant information.* This information includes the name, residence, mailing address, and citizenship of each applicant (§1.41(b)). The name of each applicant must include the family name, and at least one given name without abbreviation together with any other given name or initial. If the applicant is not an inventor, this information also includes the applicant's authority (§§1.42, 1.43, and 1.47) to apply for the patent on behalf of the inventor.

(2) *Correspondence information.* This information includes the correspondence address, which may be indicated by reference to a customer number, to which correspondence is to be directed (see §1.33(a)).

(3) *Application information.* This information includes the title of the invention, a suggested classification, by class and subclass, the Technology Center to which the subject matter of the invention is assigned, the total number of drawing sheets, a suggested drawing figure for publication (in a nonprovisional application), any docket number assigned to the application, the type of application (e.g., utility, plant, design, reissue, provisional), whether the application discloses any significant part of the subject matter of an application under a secrecy order pursuant to §5.2 of this chapter (see §5.2(c)), and, for plant applications, the Latin name of the genus and species of the plant claimed, as well as the variety denomination. The suggested classification and Technology Center information should be supplied for provisional applications whether or not claims are present. If claims are not present in a provisional application, the suggested classification and Technology Center should be based upon the disclosure.

(4) *Representative information.* This information includes the registration number of each practitioner having a power of attorney or authorization of agent in the application (preferably by reference to a customer number). Providing this information in the application data sheet does not constitute a power of attorney or authorization of agent in the application (see §1.34(b)).

(5) *Domestic priority information.* This information includes the application number, the filing date, the status (including patent number if available), and relationship of each application for which a benefit is claimed under 35 U.S.C. 119(e), 120, 121, or 365(c). Providing this information in the application data sheet constitutes the specific reference required by 35 U.S.C. 119(e) or 120, and §1.78(a)(2) or §1.78(a)(4), and need not otherwise be made part of the specification.

(6) *Foreign priority information.* This information includes the application number, country, and filing date of each foreign application for which priority is claimed, as well as any foreign application having a filing date before that of the application for which priority is claimed. Providing this information in the ap-

plication data sheet constitutes the claim for priority as required by 35 U.S.C. 119(b) and §1.55(a).

(7) *Assignee information.* This information includes the name (either person or juristic entity) and address of the assignee of the entire right, title, and interest in an application. Providing this information in the application data sheet does not substitute for compliance with any requirement of part 3 of this chapter to have an assignment recorded by the Office.

(c) *Supplemental application data sheets.* Supplemental application data sheets:

(1) May be subsequently supplied prior to payment of the issue fee either to correct or update information in a previously submitted application data sheet, or an oath or declaration under §1.63 or §1.67, except that inventorship changes are governed by §1.48, correspondence changes are governed by §1.33(a), and citizenship changes are governed by §1.63 or §1.67; and

(2) Should identify the information that is being changed (added, deleted, or modified) and therefore need not contain all the previously submitted information that has not changed.

(d) *Inconsistencies between application data sheet and oath or declaration.* For inconsistencies between information that is supplied by both an application data sheet under this section and by an oath or declaration under §§1.63 and 1.67:

(1) The latest submitted information will govern notwithstanding whether supplied by an application data sheet, or by a §1.63 or §1.67 oath or declaration, except as provided by paragraph (d)(3) of this section;

(2) The information in the application data sheet will govern when the inconsistent information is supplied at the same time by a §1.63 or §1.67 oath or declaration, except as provided by paragraph (d)(3) of this section;

(3) The oath or declaration under §1.63 or §1.67 governs inconsistencies with the application data sheet in the naming of inventors (§1.41(a)(1)) and setting forth their citizenship (35 U.S.C. 115);

(4) The Office will initially capture bibliographic information from the application data sheet (notwithstanding whether an oath or declaration governs the information). Thus, the Office shall generally not look to an oath or declaration under §1.63 to see if the bibliographic information contained therein is consistent with the bibliographic information captured from an application data sheet (whether the oath or declaration is submitted prior to or subsequent to the application data sheet). Captured bibliographic information derived from an application data sheet containing errors may be recaptured by a request therefor and the submission of a supplemental application data sheet, an oath or declaration under §1.63 or §1.67, or a letter pursuant to §1.33(b).

§1.77 Arrangement of application elements.

(a) The elements of the application, if applicable, should appear in the following order:

(1) Utility Application Transmittal Form.
(2) Fee Transmittal Form.
(3) Application data sheet (See §1.76).
(4) Specification.
(5) Drawings.
(6) Executed oath or declaration.

(b) The specification should include the following sections in order:

(1) Title of the invention, which may be accompanied by an introductory portion stating the name, citizenship, and residence of the applicant (unless included in the application data sheet).

(2) Cross-reference to related applications (unless included in the application data sheet).

(3) Statement regarding federally sponsored research or development.

(4) Reference to a "Sequence Listing," a table, or a computer program listing appendix submitted on a compact disc and an incorporation-by-reference of the

material on the compact disc (see §1.52(e)(5)). The total number of compact discs including duplicates and the files on each compact disc shall be specified.

(5) Background of the invention.

(6) Brief summary of the invention.

(7) Brief description of the several views of the drawing.

(8) Detailed description of the invention.

(9) A claim or claims.

(10) Abstract of the disclosure.

(11) "Sequence Listing," if on paper (see §§1.821 through 1.825).

(c) The text of the specification sections defined in paragraphs (b)(1) through (b)(11) of this section, if applicable, should be preceded by a section heading in uppercase and without underlining or bold type.

§1.78 Claiming benefit of earlier filing date and cross-references to other applications.

(a)

* * *

(2) Except for a continued prosecution application filed under §1.53(d), any nonprovisional application claiming the benefit of one or more prior filed copending nonprovisional applications or international applications designating the United States of America must contain a reference to each such prior application, identifying it by application number (consisting of the series code and serial number) or international application number and international filing date and indicating the relationship of the applications. This reference must be submitted during the pendency of the application, and within the later of four months from the actual filing date of the application or sixteen months from the filing date of the prior application. This time period is not extendable. Unless the reference required by this paragraph is included in an application data sheet (§1.76), the specification must contain or be amended to contain such reference in the first sentence following the title. If the application claims the benefit of an international application, the first sentence of the specification must include an indication of whether the international application was published under PCT Article 21(2) in English (regardless of whether benefit for such application is claimed in the application data sheet). The request for a continued prosecution application under §1.53(d) is the specific reference required by 35 U.S.C. 120 to the prior application. The identification of an application by application number under this section is the specific reference required by 35 U.S.C. 120 to every application assigned that application number. Cross references to other related applications may be made when appropriate (see §1.14). Except as provided in paragraph (a)(3) of this section, the failure to timely submit the reference required by 35 U.S.C. 120 and this paragraph is considered a waiver of any benefit under 35 U.S.C. 120, 121, or 365(c) to such prior application. The time period set forth in this paragraph does not apply to an application for a design patent.

* * *

(4) A nonprovisional application other than for a design patent may claim an invention disclosed in one or more prior filed provisional applications. In order for a nonprovisional application to claim the benefit of one or more prior filed provisional applications, each prior provisional application must name as an inventor at least one inventor named in the later filed nonprovisional application and disclose the named inventor's invention claimed in at least one claim of the later filed nonprovisional application in the manner provided by the first paragraph of 35 U.S.C. 112. In addition, each prior provisional application must be entitled to a filing date as set forth in §1.53(c), and the basic filing fee set forth in §1.16(k) must be paid within the time period set forth in §1.53(g).

* * *

(c) If an application or a patent under reexamination and at least one other application naming different inventors are owned by the same party and contain conflicting claims, and there is no statement of record indicating that the claimed inventions were commonly owned or subject to an obligation of assignment to the same person at the time the later invention was made, the Office may require the assignee to state whether the claimed inventions were commonly owned or subject to an obligation of assignment to the same person at the time the later invention was made, and, if not, indicate which named inventor is the prior inventor.

* * *

§1.84 Standards for drawings.

(a) *Drawings.* There are two acceptable categories for presenting drawings in utility and design patent applications:

(1) *Black ink.* Black and white drawings are normally required. India ink, or its equivalent that secures solid black lines, must be used for drawings; or

(2) *Color.* On rare occasions, color drawings may be necessary as the only practical medium by which to disclose the subject matter sought to be patented in a utility or design patent application or the subject matter of a statutory invention registration. The color drawings must be of sufficient quality such that all details in the drawings are reproducible in black and white in the printed patent. Color drawings are not permitted in international applications (see PCT Rule 11.13), or in an application, or copy thereof, submitted under the Office electronic filing system. The Office will accept color drawings in utility or design patent applications and statutory invention registrations only after granting a petition filed under this paragraph explaining why the color drawings are necessary. Any such petition must include the following:

(i) The fee set forth in Sec. 1.17(h);

(ii) Three (3) sets of color drawings;

(iii) A black and white photocopy that accurately depicts, to the extent possible, the subject matter shown in the color drawing; and

(iv) An amendment to the specification to insert (unless the specification contains or has been previously amended to contain) the following language as the first paragraph of the brief description of the drawings:

"The patent or application file contains at least one drawing executed in color. Copies of this patent or patent application publication with color drawing(s) will be provided by the Office upon request and payment of the necessary fee."

(b) *Photographs.*

(1) *Black and white.* Photographs, including photocopies of photographs, are not ordinarily permitted in utility and design patent applications. The Office will accept photographs in utility and design patent applications, however, if photographs are the only practicable medium for illustrating the claimed invention. For example, photographs or photomicrographs of: electrophoresis gels, blots (e.g., immunological, western, Southern, and northern), autoradiographs, cell cultures (stained and unstained), histological tissue cross sections (stained and unstained), animals, plants, in vivo imaging, thin layer chromatography plates, crystalline structures, and, in a design patent application, ornamental effects, are acceptable. If the subject matter of the application admits of illustration by a drawing, the examiner may require a drawing in place of the photograph. The photographs must be of sufficient quality so that all details in the photographs are reproducible in the printed patent.

(2) *Color photographs.* Color photographs will be accepted in utility and design patent applications if the conditions for accepting color drawings and black and white photographs have been satisfied. See paragraphs (a)(2) and (b)(1) of this section.

(c) *Identification of drawings.* Identifying indicia, if provided, should include the title of the invention, inventor's name, and application number, or docket number (if any) if an application number has not been assigned to the application. If this information is provided, it must be placed on the front of each sheet and centered within the top margin.

* * *

(j) *Front page view.* The drawing must contain as many views as necessary to show the invention. One of the views should be suitable for inclusion on the front page of the patent application publication and patent as the illustration of the invention. Views must not be connected by projection lines and must not contain center lines. Applicant may suggest a single view (by figure number) for inclusion on the front page of the patent application publication and patent.

(k) *Scale.* The scale to which a drawing is made must be large enough to show the mechanism without crowding when the drawing is reduced in size to two-thirds in reproduction. Indications such as "actual size" or "scale ½" on the drawings are not permitted since these lose their meaning with reproduction in a different format.

* * *

(o) *Legends.* Suitable descriptive legends may be used subject to approval by the Office, or may be required by the examiner where necessary for understanding of the drawing. They should contain as few words as possible.

* * *

(x) *Holes.* No holes should be made by applicant in the drawing sheets.

(y) *Types of drawings.* See §1.152 for design drawings, §1.165 for plant drawings, and §1.174 for reissue drawings.

§1.185 Corrections to drawings.

(a) A utility or plant application will not be placed on the files for examination until objections to the drawings have been corrected. Except as provided in §1.215(c), any patent application publication will not include drawings filed after the application has been placed on the files for examination. Unless applicant is otherwise notified in an Office action, objections to the drawings in a utility or plant application will not be held in abeyance, and a request to hold objections to the drawings in abeyance will not be considered a bona fide attempt to advance the application to final action (§1.135(c)). If a drawing in a design application meets the requirements of §1.84(e), (f), and (g) and is suitable for reproduction, but is not otherwise in compliance with §1.84, the drawing may be admitted for examination.

(b) The Office will not release drawings for purposes of correction. If corrections are necessary, new corrected drawings must be submitted within the time set by the Office.

(c) If a corrected drawing is required or if a drawing does not comply with §1.84 at the time an application is allowed, the Office may notify the applicant and set a three month period of time from the mail date of the notice of allowability within which the applicant must file a corrected or formal drawing in compliance with §1.84 to avoid abandonment. This time period is not extendable under §1.136(a) or §1.136(b).

§1.91 Models or exhibits not generally admitted as part of application or patent.

(a) A model or exhibit will not be admitted as part of the record of an application unless it:

* * *

(3) Is filed with a petition under this section including:

(i) The petition fee as set forth in §1.17(h); and

* * *

§1.96 Submission of computer program listings.

* * *

(b) *Material which will be printed in the patent:* If the computer program listing is contained in 300 lines or fewer, with each line of 72 characters or fewer, it may be submitted either as drawings or as part of the specification.

(1) *Drawings.* If the listing is submitted as drawings, it must be submitted in the manner and complying with the requirements for drawings as provided in §1.84. At least one figure numeral is required on each sheet of drawing.

(2) *Specification.*

(i) If the listing is submitted as part of the specification, it must be submitted in accordance with the provisions of §1.52.

(ii) Any listing having more than 60 lines of code that is submitted as part of the specification must be positioned at the end of the description but before the claims. Any amendment must be made by way of submission of a substitute sheet.

(c) *As an appendix which will not be printed:* Any computer program listing may, and any computer program listing having over 300 lines (up to 72 characters per line) must, be submitted on a compact disc in compliance with §1.52(e). A compact disc containing such a computer program listing is to be referred to as a "computer program listing appendix." The "computer program listing appendix" will not be part of the printed patent. The specification must include a reference to the "computer program listing appendix" at the location indicated in §1.77(b)(4).

(1) Multiple computer program listings for a single application may be placed on a single compact disc. Multiple compact discs may be submitted for a single application if necessary. A separate compact disc is required for each application containing a computer program listing that must be submitted on a "computer program listing appendix."

(2) The "computer program listing appendix" must be submitted on a compact disc that complies with §1.52(e) and the following specifications (no other format shall be allowed):

(i) *Computer Compatibility:* IBM PC/XT/AT, or compatibles, or Apple Macintosh;

(ii) *Operating System Compatibility:* MS-DOS, MS-Windows, Unix, or Macintosh;

(iii) *Line Terminator:* ASCII Carriage Return plus ASCII Line Feed;

(iv) *Control Codes:* the data must not be dependent on control characters or codes which are not defined in the ASCII character set; and

(v) *Compression:* uncompressed data.

§1.97 Filing of information disclosure statement.

(a) In order for an applicant for a patent or for a reissue of a patent to have an information disclosure statement in compliance with §1.98 considered by the Office during the pendency of the application, the information disclosure statement must satisfy one of paragraphs (b), (c), or (d) of this section.

(b) An information disclosure statement shall be considered by the Office if filed by the applicant within any one of the following time periods:

(1) Within three months of the filing date of a national application other than a continued prosecution application under §1.53(d);

(2) Within three months of the date of entry of the national stage as set forth in §1.491 in an international application;

(3) Before the mailing of a first Office action on the merits; or

(4) Before the mailing of a first Office action after the filing of a request for continued examination under §1.114.

(c) An information disclosure statement shall be considered by the Office if filed after the period specified in paragraph (b) of this section, provided that the information disclosure statement is filed before the mailing date of any of a final action under §1.113, a notice of allowance under §1.311, or an action that otherwise closes prosecution in the application, and it is accompanied by one of:

(1) The statement specified in paragraph (e) of this section; or

(2) The fee set forth in §1.17(p).

(d) An information disclosure statement shall be considered by the Office if filed by the applicant after the period specified in paragraph (c) of this section, provided that the information disclosure statement is filed on or before payment of the issue fee and is accompanied by:

(1) The statement specified in paragraph (e) of this section; and

(2) The fee set forth in §1.17(p).

(e) A statement under this section must state either:

(1) That each item of information contained in the information disclosure statement was first cited in any communication from a foreign patent office in a counterpart foreign application not more than three months prior to the filing of the information disclosure statement; or

(2) That no item of information contained in the information disclosure statement was cited in a communication from a foreign patent office in a counterpart foreign application, and, to the knowledge of the person signing the certification after making reasonable inquiry, no item of information contained in the information disclosure statement was known to any individual designated in §1.56(c) more than three months prior to the filing of the information disclosure statement.

* * *

(i) If an information disclosure statement does not comply with either this section or §1.98, it will be placed in the file but will not be considered by the Office.

§1.98 Content of information disclosure statement.

(a) Any information disclosure statement filed under §1.97 shall include:

(1) A list of all patents, publications, applications, or other information submitted for consideration by the Office;

(2) legible copy of:

(i) Each U.S. patent application publication and U.S. and foreign patent;

(ii) Each publication or that portion which caused it to be listed;

(iii) For each cited pending U.S. application, the application specification including the claims, and any drawing of the application, or that portion of the application which caused it to be listed including any claims directed to that portion; and

(iv) All other information or that portion which caused it to be listed; and

(3)(i) A concise explanation of the relevance, as it is presently understood by the individual designated in §1.56(c) most knowledgeable about the content of the information, of each patent, publication, or other information listed that is not in the English language. The concise explanation may be either separate from applicant's specification or incorporated therein.

(ii) A copy of the translation if a written English-language translation of a non-English-language document, or portion thereof, is within the possession, custody, or control of, or is readily available to any individual designated in §1.56(c).

(b)(1) Each U.S. patent listed in an information disclosure statement must be identified by inventor, patent number, and issue date.

(2) Each U.S. patent application publication listed in an information disclosure statement shall be identified by applicant, patent application publication number, and publication date.

(3) Each U.S. application listed in an information disclosure statement must be identified by the inventor, application number, and filing date.

(4) Each foreign patent or published foreign patent application listed in an information disclosure statement must be identified by the country or patent office which issued the patent or published the application, an appropriate document number, and the publication date indicated on the patent or published application.

(5) Each publication listed in an information disclosure statement must be identified by publisher, author (if any), title, relevant pages of the publication, date, and place of publication.

(c) When the disclosures of two or more patents or publications listed in an information disclosure statement are substantively cumulative, a copy of one of the patents or publications may be submitted without copies of the other patents or publications, provided that it is stated that these other patents or publications are cumulative.

(d) A copy of any patent, publication, pending U.S. application or other information, as specified in paragraph (a) of this section, listed in an information disclosure statement is required to be provided, even if the patent, publication, pending U.S. application or other information was previously submitted to, or cited by, the Office in an earlier application, unless:

(1) The earlier application is properly identified in the information disclosure statement and is relied on for an earlier effective filing date under 35 U.S.C. 120; and

(2) The information disclosure statement submitted in the earlier application complies with paragraphs (a) through (c) of this section.

§1.102 Advancement of examination.

* * *

(d) A petition to make an application special on grounds other than those referred to in paragraph (c) of this section must be accompanied by the fee set forth in §1.17(h).

§1.104 Nature of examination.

(a) *Examiner's action.*

* * *

(2) The applicant, or in the case of a reexamination proceeding, both the patent owner and the requester, will be notified of the examiner's action. The reasons for any adverse action or any objection or requirement will be stated in an Office action and such information or references will be given as may be useful in aiding the applicant, or in the case of a reexamination proceeding the patent owner, to judge the propriety of continuing the prosecution.

* * *

(e) *Reasons for allowance.* If the examiner believes that the record of the prosecution as a whole does not make clear his or her reasons for allowing a claim or claims, the examiner may set forth such reasoning. The reasons shall be incorporated into an Office action rejecting other claims of the application or patent under reexamination or be the subject of a separate communication to the applicant or patent owner. The applicant or patent owner may file a statement commenting on the reasons for allowance within such time as may be specified by the examiner. Failure by the examiner to respond to any statement commenting on reasons for allowance does not give rise to any implication.

§1.105 Requirements for information.

(a)(1) In the course of examining or treating a matter in a pending or abandoned application filed under 35 U.S.C. 111 or 371 (including a reissue application), in a patent, or in a reexamination proceeding, the examiner or other Office employee may require the submission, from individuals identified under §1.56(c), or any assignee, of such information as may be reasonably necessary to properly examine or treat the matter, for example:

(i) *Commercial databases:* The existence of any particularly relevant commercial database known to any of the inventors that could be searched for a particular aspect of the invention.

(ii) *Search:* Whether a search of the prior art was made, and if so, what was searched.

(iii) *Related information:* A copy of any non-patent literature, published application, or patent (U.S. or foreign), by any of the inventors, that relates to the claimed invention.

(iv) *Information used to draft application:* A copy of any non-patent literature, published application, or patent (U.S. or foreign) that was used to draft the application.

(v) *Information used in invention process:* A copy of any non-patent literature, published application, or patent (U.S. or foreign) that was used in the invention process, such as by designing around or providing a solution to accomplish an invention result.

(vi) *Improvements:* Where the claimed invention is an improvement, identification of what is being improved.

(vii) *In use:* Identification of any use of the claimed invention known to any of the inventors at the time the application was filed notwithstanding the date of the use.

(2) Where an assignee has asserted its right to prosecute pursuant to §3.71(a) of this chapter, matters such as paragraphs (a)(1)(i), (iii), and (vii) of this section may also be applied to such assignee.

(3) Any reply that states that the information required to be submitted is unknown and/or is not readily available to the party or parties from which it was requested will be accepted as a complete reply.

(b) The requirement for information of paragraph (a)(1) of this section may be included in an Office action, or sent separately.

(c) A reply, or a failure to reply, to a requirement for information under this section will be governed by §§1.135 and 1.136.

§1.111 Reply by applicant or patent owner to a non-final Office action.

(a)(1) If the Office action after the first examination (§1.104) is adverse in any respect, the applicant or patent owner, if he or she persists in his or her application for a patent or reexamination proceeding, must reply and request reconsideration or further examination, with or without amendment. See §§1.135 and 1.136 for time for reply to avoid abandonment.

(2) A second (or subsequent) supplemental reply will be entered unless disapproved by the Commissioner. A second (or subsequent) supplemental reply may be disapproved if the second (or subsequent) supplemental reply unduly interferes with an Office action being prepared in response to the previous reply. Factors that will be considered in disapproving a second (or subsequent) supplemental reply include:

(i) The state of preparation of an Office action responsive to the previous reply as of the date of receipt (§1.6) of the second (or subsequent) supplemental reply by the Office; and

(ii) The nature of any changes to the specification or claims that would result from entry of the second (or subsequent) supplemental reply.

* * *

(c) In amending in reply to a rejection of claims in an application or patent under reexamination, the applicant or patent owner must clearly point out the patentable novelty which he or she thinks the claims present in view of the state of the art disclosed by the references cited or the objections made. The applicant or patent owner must also show how the amendments avoid such references or objections.

§1.112 Reconsideration before final action.

After reply by applicant or patent owner (§1.111 or §1.945) to a non-final action and any comments by an inter partes reexamination requester (§1.947), the application or the patent under reexamination will be reconsidered and again examined. The applicant, or in the case of a reexamination proceeding the patent owner and any third party requester, will be notified if claims are rejected, objections or requirements made, or decisions favorable to patentability are made, in the same manner as after the first examination (§1.104). Applicant or patent owner may reply to such Office action in the same manner provided in §1.111 or §1.945, with or without amendment, unless such

Office action indicates that it is made final (§1.113) or an appeal (§1.191) has been taken (§1.116), or in an inter partes reexamination, that it is an action closing prosecution (§1.949) or a right of appeal notice (§1.953).

§1.115 Preliminary amendments.

(a) A preliminary amendment is an amendment that is received in the Office (§1.6) on or before the mail date of the first Office action under §1.104.

(b)(1) A preliminary amendment will be entered unless disapproved by the Commissioner. A preliminary amendment may be disapproved if the preliminary amendment unduly interferes with the preparation of a first Office action in an application. Factors that will be considered in disapproving a preliminary amendment include:

(i) The state of preparation of a first Office action as of the date of receipt (§1.6) of the preliminary amendment by the Office; and

(ii) The nature of any changes to the specification or claims that would result from entry of the preliminary amendment.

(2) A preliminary amendment will not be disapproved if it is filed no later than:

(i) Three months from the filing date of an application under §1.53(b);

(ii) The filing date of a continued prosecution application under §1.53(d); or

(iii) Three months from the date the national stage is entered as set forth in §1.491 in an international application.

(c) The time periods specified in paragraph (b)(2) of this section are not extendable.

§1.121 Manner of making amendments.

(a) *Amendments in applications, other than reissue applications.* Amendments in applications, other than reissue applications, are made by filing a paper, in compliance with §1.52, directing that specified amendments be made.

(b) *Specification other than the claims and listings provided for elsewhere (§§1.96 and 1.825).*

(1) *Amendment by instruction to delete, replace, or add a paragraph.* Amendments to the specification, other than the claims and listings provided for elsewhere (§§1.96 and 1.825), may be made by submitting:

(i) An instruction, which unambiguously identifies the location, to delete one or more paragraphs of the specification, replace a deleted paragraph with one or more replacement paragraphs, or add one or more paragraphs;

(ii) Any replacement or added paragraph(s) in clean form, that is, without markings to indicate the changes that have been made; and

(iii) Another version of any replacement paragraph(s), on one or more pages separate from the amendment, marked up to show all the changes relative to the previous version of the paragraph(s). The changes may be shown by brackets (for deleted matter) or underlining (for added matter), or by any equivalent marking system. A marked up version does not have to be supplied for an added paragraph or a deleted paragraph as it is sufficient to state that a particular paragraph has been added, or deleted.

(2) *Amendment by replacement section.* If the sections of the specification contain section headings as provided in §§1.77(b), 1.154(b), or §1.163(c), amendments to the specification, other than the claims, may be made by submitting:

(i) A reference to the section heading along with an instruction to delete that section of the specification and to replace such deleted section with a replacement section;

(ii) A replacement section in clean form, that is, without markings to indicate the changes that have been made; and

(iii) Another version of the replacement section, on one or more pages separate from the amendment, marked up to show all changes relative to the previous version of the section. The changes may be shown by brackets (for deleted matter) or underlining (for added matter), or by any equivalent marking system.

(3) *Amendment by substitute specification.* The specification, other than the claims, may also be amended by submitting:

(i) An instruction to replace the specification;

(ii) A substitute specification in compliance with §1.125(b); and

(iii) Another version of the substitute specification, separate from the substitute specification, marked up to show all changes relative to the previous version of the specification. The changes may be shown by brackets (for deleted matter), or underlining (for added matter), or by any equivalent marking system.

(4) *Reinstatement:* Deleted matter may be reinstated only by a subsequent amendment presenting the previously deleted matter.

(c) *Claims.*

(1) *Amendment by rewriting, directions to cancel or add:* Amendments to a claim must be made by rewriting such claim with all changes (e.g., additions, deletions, modifications) included. The rewriting of a claim (with the same number) will be construed as directing the cancellation of the previous version of that claim. A claim may also be canceled by an instruction.

(i) A rewritten or newly added claim must be in clean form, that is, without markings to indicate the changes that have been made. A parenthetical expression should follow the claim number indicating the status of the claim as amended or newly added (e.g., "amended," "twice amended," or "new").

(ii) If a claim is amended by rewriting such claim with the same number, the amendment must be accompanied by another version of the rewritten claim, on one or more pages separate from the amendment, marked up to show all the changes relative to the previous version of that claim. A parenthetical expression should follow the claim number indicating the status of the claim, e.g., "amended," "twice amended," etc. The parenthetical expression "amended," "twice amended," etc. should be the same for both the clean version of the claim under paragraph (c)(1)(i) of this section and the marked up version under this paragraph. The changes may be shown by brackets (for deleted matter) or underlining (for added matter), or by any equivalent marking system. A marked up version does not have to be supplied for an added claim or a canceled claim as it is sufficient to state that a particular claim has been added, or canceled.

(2) A claim canceled by amendment (deleted in its entirety) may be reinstated only by a subsequent amendment presenting the claim as a new claim with a new claim number.

(3) A clean version of the entire set of pending claims may be submitted in a single amendment paper. Such a submission shall be construed as directing the cancellation of all previous versions of any pending claims. A marked up version is required only for claims being changed by the current amendment (see paragraph (c)(1)(ii) of this section). Any claim not accompanied by a marked up version will constitute an assertion that it has not been changed relative to the immediate prior version.

(d) *Drawings.* Application drawings are amended in the following manner: Any change to the application drawings must be submitted on a separate paper showing the proposed changes in red for approval by the examiner. Upon approval by the examiner, new drawings in compliance with §1.84 including the changes must be filed.

(e) *Disclosure consistency.* The disclosure must be amended, when required by the Office, to correct inaccuracies of description and definition, and to secure substantial correspondence between the claims, the remainder of the specification, and the drawings.

(f) *No new matter.* No amendment may introduce new matter into the disclosure of an application.

(g) *Exception for examiner's amendments.* Changes to the specification, including the claims, of an application made by the Office in an examiner's amendment may be made by specific instructions to insert or delete subject matter set forth in the examiner's amendment by identifying the precise point in the specification or the claim(s) where the insertion or deletion is to be made. Compliance with paragraphs (b)(1), (b)(2) or (c)(1) of this section is not required.

(h) *Amendments in reissue applications.* Any amendment to the description and claims in reissue applications must be made in accordance with §1.173.

(i) *Amendments in reexamination proceedings.* Any proposed amendment to the description and claims in patents involved in reexamination proceedings in both ex parte reexaminations filed under §1.510 and inter partes reexaminations filed under §1.913 must be made in accordance with §1.530(d)–(j).

(j) *Amendments in provisional applications.* Amendments in provisional applications are not normally made. If an amendment is made to a provisional application, however, it must comply with the provisions of this section. Any amendments to a provisional application shall be placed in the provisional application file but may not be entered.

§1.125 Substitute specification.

* * *

(b) A substitute specification, excluding the claims, may be filed at any point up to payment of the issue fee if it is accompanied by:

* * *

> (2) A marked up version of the substitute specification showing all the changes (including the matter being added to and the matter being deleted from) to the specification of record. Numbering the paragraphs of the specification of record is not considered a change that must be shown pursuant to this paragraph.

(c) A substitute specification submitted under this section must be submitted in clean form without markings as to amended material. The paragraphs of any substitute specification, other than the claims, should be individually numbered in Arabic numerals so that any amendment to the specification may be made by replacement paragraph in accordance with §1.121(b)(1).

§1.131 Affidavit or declaration of prior invention.

(a) When any claim of an application or a patent under reexamination is rejected, the inventor of the subject matter of the rejected claim, the owner of the patent under reexamination, or the party qualified under §§1.42, 1.43, or 1.47, may submit an appropriate oath or declaration to establish invention of the subject matter of the rejected claim prior to the effective date of the reference or activity on which the rejection is based. The effective date of a U.S. patent, U.S. patent application publication, or international application publication under PCT Article 21(2) is the earlier of its publication date or date that it is effective as a reference under 35 U.S.C. 102(e). Prior invention may not be established under this section in any country other than the United States, a NAFTA country, or a WTO member country. Prior invention may not be established under this section before December 8, 1993, in a NAFTA country other than the United States, or before January 1, 1996, in a WTO member country other than a NAFTA country. Prior invention may not be established under this section if either:

> (1) The rejection is based upon a U.S. patent or U.S. patent application publication of a pending or patented application to another or others which claims the same patentable invention as defined in Sec. 1.601(n); or
>
> (2) The rejection is based upon a statutory bar.

* * *

§1.132 Affidavits or declarations traversing rejections or objections.

When any claim of an application or a patent under reexamination is rejected or objected to, any evidence submitted to traverse the rejection or objection on a basis not otherwise provided for must be by way of an oath or declaration under this section.

§1.133 Interviews.

(a)(1) Interviews with examiners concerning applications and other matters pending before the Office must be conducted on Office premises and within Office hours, as the respective examiners may designate. Interviews will not be permitted at any other time or place without the authority of the Commissioner.

(2) An interview for the discussion of the patentability of a pending application will not occur before the first Office action, unless the application is a continuing or substitute application.

(3) The examiner may require that an interview be scheduled in advance.

* * *

§1.136 Extensions of time.

* * *

(c) If an applicant is notified in a "Notice of Allowability" that an application is otherwise in condition for allowance, the following time periods are not extendable if set in the "Notice of Allowability" or in an Office action having a mail date on or after the mail date of the "Notice of Allowability":

(1) The period for submitting an oath or declaration in compliance with §1.63; and

(2) The period for submitting formal drawings set under §1.85(c).

(3) The period for making a deposit set under §1.809(c).

§1.137 Revival of abandoned application, terminated reexamination proceeding, or lapsed patent.

* * *

(d) *Terminal disclaimer.*

(1) Any petition to revive pursuant to this section in a design application must be accompanied by a terminal disclaimer and fee as set forth in §1.321 dedicating to the public a terminal part of the term of any patent granted thereon equivalent to the period of abandonment of the application. Any petition to revive pursuant to this section in either a utility or plant application filed before June 8, 1995, must be accompanied by a terminal disclaimer and fee as set forth in §1.321 dedicating to the public a terminal part of the term of any patent granted thereon equivalent to the lesser of:

(i) The period of abandonment of the application; or

(ii) The period extending beyond twenty years from the date on which the application for the patent was filed in the United States or, if the application contains a specific reference to an earlier filed application(s) under 35 U.S.C. 120, 121, or 365(c), from the date on which the earliest such application was filed.

(2) Any terminal disclaimer pursuant to paragraph (d)(1) of this section must also apply to any patent granted on a continuing utility or plant application filed before June 8, 1995, or a continuing design application, that contains a specific reference under 35 U.S.C. 120, 121, or 365(c) to the application for which revival is sought.

(3) The provisions of paragraph (d)(1) of this section do not apply to applications for which revival is sought solely for purposes of copendency with a utility or plant application filed on or after June 8, 1995, to lapsed patents, or to reexamination proceedings.

* * *

§1.138 Express abandonment.

(a) An application may be expressly abandoned by filing a written declaration of abandonment identifying the application in the United States Patent and Trademark Office. Express abandonment of the application may not be recognized by the Office before the date of issue or publication unless it is actually received by appropriate officials in time to act.

(b) A written declaration of abandonment must be signed by a party authorized under §1.33(b)(1), (b)(3), or (b)(4) to sign a paper in the application, except as otherwise provided in this paragraph. A registered attorney or agent, not of record, who acts in a representative capacity under the provisions of §1.34(a) when filing a continuing application, may expressly abandon the prior application as of the filing date granted to the continuing application.

(c) An applicant seeking to abandon an application to avoid publication of the application (see §1.211(a)(1)) must submit a declaration of express abandonment by way of a petition under this section including the fee set forth in §1.17(h) in sufficient time to permit the appropriate officials to recognize the abandonment and remove the application from the publication process. Applicant should expect that the petition will not be granted and the application will be published in regular course unless such declaration of express abandonment and petition are received by the appropriate officials more than four weeks prior to the projected date of publication.

§1.152 Design drawings.

The design must be represented by a drawing that complies with the requirements of §1.84 and must contain a sufficient number of views to constitute a complete disclosure of the appearance of the design. Appropriate and adequate surface shading should be used to show the character or contour of the surfaces represented. Solid black surface shading is not permitted except when used to represent the color black as well as color contrast. Broken lines may be used to show visible environmental structure, but may not be used to show hidden planes and surfaces that cannot be seen through opaque materials. Alternate positions of a design component, illustrated by full and broken lines in the same view are not permitted in a design drawing. Photographs and ink drawings are not permitted to be combined as formal drawings in one application. Photographs submitted in lieu of ink drawings in design patent applications must not disclose environmental structure but must be limited to the design claimed for the article.

§1.154 Arrangement of application elements in a design application.

(a) The elements of the design application, if applicable, should appear in the following order:

(1) Design application transmittal form.
(2) Fee transmittal form.
(3) Application data sheet (see §1.76).
(4) Specification.
(5) Drawings or photographs.
(6) Executed oath or declaration (see §1.153(b)).

(b) The specification should include the following sections in order:

(1) Preamble, stating the name of the applicant, title of the design, and a brief description of the nature and intended use of the article in which the design is embodied.

(2) Cross-reference to related applications (unless included in the application data sheet).

(3) Statement regarding federally sponsored research or development.
(4) Description of the figure or figures of the drawing.
(5) Feature description.
(6) A single claim.

(c) The text of the specification sections defined in paragraph (b) of this section, if applicable, should be preceded by a section heading in uppercase letters without underlining or bold type.

§1.155 Expedited examination of design applications.

(a) The applicant may request that the Office expedite the examination of a design application. To qualify for expedited examination:

(1) The application must include drawings in compliance with §1.84;
(2) The applicant must have conducted a preexamination search; and
(3) The applicant must file a request for expedited examination including:
(i) The fee set forth in §1.17(k); and

(ii) A statement that a preexamination search was conducted. The statement must also indicate the field of search and include an information disclosure statement in compliance with §1.98.

(b) The Office will not examine an application that is not in condition for examination (e.g., missing basic filing fee) even if the applicant files a request for expedited examination under this section.

§1.163 Specification and arrangement of application elements in a plant application.

(a) The specification must contain as full and complete a disclosure as possible of the plant and the characteristics thereof that distinguish the same over related known varieties, and its antecedents, and must particularly point out where and in what manner the variety of plant has been asexually reproduced. For a newly found plant, the specification must particularly point out the location and character of the area where the plant was discovered.

(b) The elements of the plant application, if applicable, should appear in the following order:

(1) Plant application transmittal form.
(2) Fee transmittal form.
(3) Application data sheet (see §1.76).
(4) Specification.
(5) Drawings (in duplicate).
(6) Executed oath or declaration (§1.162).

(c) The specification should include the following sections in order:

(1) Title of the invention, which may include an introductory portion stating the name, citizenship, and residence of the applicant.
(2) Cross-reference to related applications (unless included in the application data sheet).
(3) Statement regarding federally sponsored research or development.
(4) Latin name of the genus and species of the plant claimed.
(5) Variety denomination.
(6) Background of the invention.
(7) Brief summary of the invention.
(8) Brief description of the drawing.
(9) Detailed botanical description.
(10) A single claim.
(11) Abstract of the disclosure.

(d) The text of the specification or sections defined in paragraph (c) of this section, if applicable, should be preceded by a section heading in upper case, without underlining or bold type.

§1.173 Reissue specification, drawings, and amendments.

(a) *Contents of a reissue application.* An application for reissue must contain the entire specification, including the claims, and the drawings of the patent. No new matter shall be introduced into the application. No reissue patent shall be granted enlarging the scope of the claims of the original patent unless applied for within two years from the grant of the original patent, pursuant to 35 U.S.C. 251.

(1) *Specification, including claims.* The entire specification, including the claims, of the patent for which reissue is requested must be furnished in the form of a copy of the printed patent, in double column format, each page on only one side of a single sheet of paper. If an amendment of the reissue application is to be included, it must be made pursuant to paragraph (b) of this section. The formal requirements for papers making up the reissue application other than those set forth in this section are set out in §1.52. Additionally, a copy of any disclaimer (§1.321), certificate of correction (§§1.322 through 1.324), or reexamination certificate (§1.570) issued in the patent must be included. (See also §1.178.)

(2) *Drawings.* Applicant must submit a clean copy of each drawing sheet of the printed patent at the time the reissue application is filed. If such copy com-

plies with §1.84, no further drawings will be required. Where a drawing of the reissue application is to include any changes relative to the patent being reissued, the changes to the drawing must be made in accordance with paragraph (b)(3) of this section. The Office will not transfer the drawings from the patent file to the reissue application.

(b) *Making amendments in a reissue application.* An amendment in a reissue application is made either by physically incorporating the changes into the specification when the application is filed, or by a separate amendment paper. If amendment is made by incorporation, markings pursuant to paragraph (d) of this section must be used. If amendment is made by an amendment paper, the paper must direct that specified changes be made.

(1) *Specification other than the claims.* Changes to the specification, other than to the claims, must be made by submission of the entire text of an added or rewritten paragraph, including markings pursuant to paragraph (d) of this section, except that an entire paragraph may be deleted by a statement deleting the paragraph without presentation of the text of the paragraph. The precise point in the specification must be identified where any added or rewritten paragraph is located. This paragraph applies whether the amendment is submitted on paper or compact disc (see §§1.52(e)(1) and 1.821(c), but not for discs submitted under §1.821(e)).

(2) *Claims.* An amendment paper must include the entire text of each claim being changed by such amendment paper and of each claim being added by such amendment paper. For any claim changed by the amendment paper, a parenthetical expression "amended," "twice amended," etc., should follow the claim number. Each changed patent claim and each added claim must include markings pursuant to paragraph (d) of this section, except that a patent claim or added claim should be canceled by a statement canceling the claim without presentation of the text of the claim.

(3) *Drawings.* Any change to the patent drawings must be submitted as a sketch on a separate paper showing the proposed changes in red for approval by the examiner. Upon approval by the examiner, new drawings in compliance with §1.84 including the approved changes must be filed. Amended figures must be identified as "Amended," and any added figure must be identified as "New." In the event that a figure is canceled, the figure must be surrounded by brackets and identified as "Canceled."

(c) *Status of claims and support for claim changes.* Whenever there is an amendment to the claims pursuant to paragraph (b) of this section, there must also be supplied, on pages separate from the pages containing the changes, the status (i.e., pending or canceled), as of the date of the amendment, of all patent claims and of all added claims, and an explanation of the support in the disclosure of the patent for the changes made to the claims.

(d) *Changes shown by markings.* Any changes relative to the patent being reissued which are made to the specification, including the claims, upon filing, or by an amendment paper in the reissue application, must include the following markings:

(1) The matter to be omitted by reissue must be enclosed in brackets; and

(2) The matter to be added by reissue must be underlined, except for amendments submitted on compact discs (§§1.96 and 1.821(c)). Matter added by reissue on compact discs must be preceded with "U>" and end with "/U>" to properly identify the material being added.

(e) *Numbering of patent claims preserved.* Patent claims may not be renumbered. The numbering of any claim added in the reissue application must follow the number of the highest numbered patent claim.

(f) *Amendment of disclosure may be required.* The disclosure must be amended, when required by the Office, to correct inaccuracies of description and definition, and to secure substantial correspondence between the claims, the remainder of the specification, and the drawings.

(g) *Amendments made relative to the patent.* All amendments must be made relative to the patent specification, including the claims, and drawings, which are in effect as of the date of filing of the reissue application.

[65 FR 54603, Sept. 8, 2000]

§1.174 [Reserved]

§1.176 Examination of reissue.

(a) A reissue application will be examined in the same manner as a non-reissue, non-provisional application, and will be subject to all the requirements of the rules related to non-reissue applications. Applications for reissue will be acted on by the examiner in advance of other applications.

(b) Restriction between subject matter of the original patent claims and previously unclaimed subject matter may be required (restriction involving only subject matter of the original patent claims will not be required). If restriction is required, the subject matter of the original patent claims will be held to be constructively elected unless a disclaimer of all the patent claims is filed in the reissue application, which disclaimer cannot be withdrawn by applicant.

§1.177 Issuance of multiple reissue patents.

(a) The Office may reissue a patent as multiple reissue patents. If applicant files more than one application for the reissue of a single patent, each such application must contain or be amended to contain in the first sentence of the specification a notice stating that more than one reissue application has been filed and identifying each of the reissue applications by relationship, application number and filing date. The Office may correct by certificate of correction under §1.322 any reissue patent resulting from an application to which this paragraph applies that does not contain the required notice.

(b) If applicant files more than one application for the reissue of a single patent, each claim of the patent being reissued must be presented in each of the reissue applications as an amended, unamended, or canceled (shown in brackets) claim, with each such claim bearing the same number as in the patent being reissued. The same claim of the patent being reissued may not be presented in its original unamended form for examination in more than one of such multiple reissue applications. The numbering of any added claims in any of the multiple reissue applications must follow the number of the highest numbered original patent claim.

(c) If any one of the several reissue applications by itself fails to correct an error in the original patent as required by 35 U.S.C. 251 but is otherwise in condition for allowance, the Office may suspend action in the allowable application until all issues are resolved as to at least one of the remaining reissue applications. The Office may also merge two or more of the multiple reissue applications into a single reissue application. No reissue application containing only unamended patent claims and not correcting an error in the original patent will be passed to issue by itself.

§1.178 Original patent; continuing duty of applicant.

(a) The application for a reissue should be accompanied by either an offer to surrender the original patent, or the original patent itself, or if the original is lost or inaccessible, by a statement to that effect. The application may be accepted for examination in the absence of the original patent or the statement, but one or the other must be supplied before the application is allowed. If a reissue application is refused, the original patent, if surrendered, will be returned to applicant upon request.

(b) In any reissue application before the Office, the applicant must call to the attention of the Office any prior or concurrent proceedings in which the patent (for which reissue is requested) is or was involved, such as interferences, reissues, reexaminations, or litigations and the results of such proceedings (see also §1.173(a)(1)).

§1.181 Petition to the Commissioner.

* * *

(f) The mere filing of a petition will not stay any period for reply that may be running against the application, nor act as a stay of other proceedings. Any petition under this part not filed within two months of the mailing date of the action or notice from which relief is requested may be dismissed as untimely, except as otherwise provided. This two-month period is not extendable.

* * *

§1.193 Examiner's answer and reply brief.

* * *

(b)(1) Appellant may file a reply brief to an examiner's answer or a supplemental examiner's answer within two months from the date of such examiner's answer or supplemental examiner's answer. See §1.136(b) for extensions of time for filing a reply brief in a patent application and §1.550(c) for extensions of time for filing a reply brief in a reexamination proceeding. The primary examiner must either acknowledge receipt and entry of the reply brief or withdraw the final rejection and reopen prosecution to respond to the reply brief. A supplemental examiner's answer is not permitted, unless the application has been remanded by the Board of Patent Appeals and Interferences for such purpose.

* * *

§1.303 Civil action under 35 U.S.C. 145, 146, 306.

(a) Any applicant or any owner of a patent involved in an ex parte reexamination proceeding filed under §1.510 for a patent that issues from an original application filed in the United States before November 29, 1999, dissatisfied with the decision of the Board of Patent Appeals and Interferences, and any party to an interference dissatisfied with the decision of the Board of Patent Appeals and Interferences may, instead of appealing to the U.S. Court of Appeals for the Federal Circuit (§1.301), have remedy by civil action under 35 U.S.C. 145 or 146, as appropriate. Such civil action must be commenced within the time specified in §1.304.

* * *

§1.311 Notice of allowance.

* * *

(b) An authorization to charge the issue or other post-allowance fees set forth in §1.18 to a deposit account may be filed in an individual application only after mailing of the notice of allowance. The submission of either of the following after the mailing of a notice of allowance will operate as a request to charge the correct issue fee to any deposit account identified in a previously filed authorization to charge fees:

(1) An incorrect issue fee; or

(2) A completed Office-provided issue fee transmittal form (where no issue fee has been submitted).

§1.314 Issuance of patent.

If applicant timely pays the issue fee, the Office will issue the patent in regular course unless the application is withdrawn from issue (§1.313) or the Office defers issuance of the patent. To request that the Office defer issuance of a patent, applicant must file a petition under this section including the fee set forth in §1.17(h) and a showing of good and sufficient reasons why it is necessary to defer issuance of the patent.

§1.322 Certificate of correction of Office mistake.

(a)(1) The Commissioner may issue a certificate of correction pursuant to 35 U.S.C. 254 to correct a mistake in a patent, incurred through the fault of the Office, which mistake is clearly disclosed in the records of the Office:

(i) At the request of the patentee or the patentee's assignee;

(ii) Acting sua sponte for mistakes that the Office discovers; or

(iii) Acting on information about a mistake supplied by a third party.

(2)(i) There is no obligation on the Office to act on or respond to a submission of information or request to issue a certificate of correction by a third party under paragraph (a)(1)(iii) of this section.

(ii) Papers submitted by a third party under this section will not be made of record in the file that they relate to nor be retained by the Office.

(3) If the request relates to a patent involved in an interference, the request must comply with the requirements of this section and be accompanied by a motion under §1.635.

(4) The Office will not issue a certificate of correction under this section without first notifying the patentee (including any assignee of record) at the correspondence address of record as specified in §1.33(a) and affording the patentee or an assignee an opportunity to be heard.

* * *

§1.323 Certificate of correction of applicant's mistake.

The Office may issue a certificate of correction under the conditions specified in 35 U.S.C. 255 at the request of the patentee or the patentee's assignee, upon payment of the fee set forth in §1.20(a). If the request relates to a patent involved in an interference, the request must comply with the requirements of this section and be accompanied by a motion under §1.635.
[49 FR 48454, Dec. 12, 1984; 65 FR 54603, Sept. 8, 2000]

§1.324 Correction of inventorship in patent, pursuant to 35 U.S.C. 256.

* * *

(b) Any petition pursuant to paragraph (a) of this section must be accompanied by:
(1) Where one or more persons are being added, a statement from each person who is being added as an inventor that the inventorship error occurred without any deceptive intention on his or her part;

* * *

(c) For correction of inventorship in an application see §§1.48 and 1.497, and in an interference see §1.634.

§1.366 Submission of maintenance fees.

* * *

(c) In submitting maintenance fees and any necessary surcharges, identification of the patents for which maintenance fees are being paid must include the patent number, and the application number of the United States application for the patent on which the maintenance fee is being paid. If the payment includes identification of only the patent number (i.e., does not identify the application number of the United States application for the patent on which the maintenance fee is being paid), the Office may apply the payment to the patent identified by patent number in the payment or may return the payment.

* * *

(f) Notification of any change in status resulting in loss of entitlement to small entity status must be filed in a patent prior to paying, or at the time of paying, the earliest maintenance fee due after the date on which status as a small entity is no longer appropriate. See §1.28(g).

* * *

§1.446 Refund of international application filing and processing fees.

(a) Money paid for international application fees, where paid by actual mistake or in excess, such as a payment not required by law or treaty and its regulations, may be refunded. A mere change of purpose after the payment of a fee will not entitle a party to a refund of such fee. The Office will not refund amounts of twenty-five dollars or less unless a refund is specifically requested and will not notify the payor of such amounts. If the payor or party requesting a refund does not provide the banking information necessary for making refunds by electronic funds transfer, the Office may use the banking information provided on the payment instrument to make any refund by electronic funds transfer.

(b) Any request for refund under paragraph (a) of this section must be filed within two years from the date the fee was paid. If the Office charges a deposit account by an amount other than an amount specifically indicated in an authorization under §1.25(b), any request for refund based upon such charge must be filed within two years from the date of the deposit account statement indicating such charge and include a copy of that deposit account statement. The time periods set forth in this paragraph are not extendable.

* * *

§1.497 Oath or declaration under 35 U.S.C. 371(c)(4).

* * *

(b) * * *

(2) If the person making the oath or declaration or any supplemental oath or declaration is not the inventor (§§1.42, 1.43, or §1.47), the oath or declaration shall state the relationship of the person to the inventor, and, upon information and belief, the facts which the inventor would have been required to state. If the person signing the oath or declaration is the legal representative of a deceased inventor, the oath or declaration shall also state that the person is a legal representative and the citizenship, residence and mailing address of the legal representative.

* * *

(d) If the oath or declaration filed pursuant to 35 U.S.C. 371(c)(4) and this section names an inventive entity different from the inventive entity set forth in the international application, or a change to the inventive entity has been effected under PCT Rule 92, subsequent to the execution of any declaration which was filed under PCT Rule 4.17(iv), the oath or declaration must be accompanied by:

(1) A statement from each person being added as an inventor and from each person being deleted as an inventor that any error in inventorship in the international application occurred without deceptive intention on his or her part;

(2) The processing fee set forth in §1.17(i); and

(3) If an assignment has been executed by any of the original named inventors, the written consent of the assignee (see §3.73(b) of this chapter).

(e) The Office may require such other information as may be deemed appropriate under the particular circumstances surrounding the correction of inventorship.

* * *

§1.510 Request for ex parte reexamination.

* * *

(b) Any request for reexamination must include the following parts:

* * *

(4) A copy of the entire patent including the front face, drawings, and specification/ claims (in double column format) for which reexamination is requested, and a copy of any disclaimer, certificate of correction, or reexamination certificate issued in the patent. All copies must have each page plainly written on only one side of a sheet of paper.

* * *

(e) A request filed by the patent owner may include a proposed amendment in accordance with §1.530.

* * *

§1.530 Statement by patent owner in ex parte reexamination; amendment by patent owner in ex parte or inter partes reexamination; inventorship change in ex parte or inter partes reexamination.

* * *

(d) *Making amendments in a reexamination proceeding.* A proposed amendment in an ex parte or an inter partes reexamination proceeding is made by filing a paper directing that proposed specified changes be made to the patent specification, including the claims, or to the drawings. An amendment paper directing that proposed specified changes be made in a reexamination proceeding may be submitted as an accompaniment to a request filed by the patent owner in accordance with §1.510(e), as part of a patent owner statement in accordance with paragraph (b) of this section, or, where permitted, during the prosecution of the reexamination proceeding pursuant to §1.550(a) or §1.937.

(1) *Specification other than the claims.* Changes to the specification, other than to the claims, must be made by submission of the entire text of an added or rewritten paragraph including markings pursuant to paragraph (f) of this section, except that an entire paragraph may be deleted by a statement deleting the paragraph, without presentation of the text of the paragraph. The precise point in the specification must be identified where any added or rewritten paragraph is located. This paragraph applies whether the amendment is submitted on paper or compact disc (see §§1.96 and 1.825).

(2) *Claims.* An amendment paper must include the entire text of each patent claim which is being proposed to be changed by such amendment paper and of each new claim being proposed to be added by such amendment paper. For any claim changed by the amendment paper, a parenthetical expression "amended," "twice amended," etc., should follow the claim number. Each patent claim proposed to be changed and each proposed added claim must include markings pursuant to paragraph (f) of this section, except that a patent claim or proposed added claim should be canceled by a statement canceling the claim, without presentation of the text of the claim.

(3) *Drawings.* Any change to the patent drawings must be submitted as a sketch on a separate paper showing the proposed changes in red for approval by the examiner. Upon approval of the changes by the examiner, only new sheets of drawings including the changes and in compliance with §1.84 must be filed. Amended figures must be identified as "Amended," and any added figure must be identified as "New." In the event a figure is canceled, the figure must be surrounded by brackets and identified as "Canceled."

(4) The formal requirements for papers making up the reexamination proceeding other than those set forth in this section are set out in §1.52.

(e) *Status of claims and support for claim changes.* Whenever there is an amendment to the claims pursuant to paragraph (d) of this section, there must also be supplied, on pages separate from the pages containing the changes, the status (i.e., pending or canceled), as of the date of the amendment, of all patent claims and of all added claims, and an explanation of the support in the disclosure of the patent for the changes to the claims made by the amendment paper.

(f) *Changes shown by markings.* Any changes relative to the patent being reexamined which are made to the specification, including the claims, must include the following markings:

(1) The matter to be omitted by the reexamination proceeding must be enclosed in brackets; and

(2) The matter to be added by the reexamination proceeding must be underlined.

(g) *Numbering of patent claims preserved.* Patent claims may not be renumbered. The numbering of any claims added in the reexamination proceeding must follow the number of the highest numbered patent claim.

(h) *Amendment of disclosure may be required.* The disclosure must be amended, when required by the Office, to correct inaccuracies of description and definition, and to secure substantial correspondence between the claims, the remainder of the specification, and the drawings.

(i) *Amendments made relative to patent.* All amendments must be made relative to the patent specification, including the claims, and drawings, which are in effect as of the date of filing the request for reexamination.

(j) *No enlargement of claim scope.* No amendment may enlarge the scope of the claims of the patent or introduce new matter. No amendment may be proposed for entry in an expired patent. Moreover, no amendment, other than the cancellation of claims, will be incorporated into the patent by a certificate issued after the expiration of the patent.

(k) *Amendments not effective until certificate.* Although the Office actions will treat proposed amendments as though they have been entered, the proposed amendments will not be effective until the reexamination certificate is issued.

(l) *Correction of inventorship in an ex parte or inter partes reexamination proceeding.*

(1) When it appears in a patent being reexamined that the correct inventor or inventors were not named through error without deceptive intention on the part of the actual inventor or inventors, the Commissioner may, on petition of all the parties set forth in §1.324(b)(1)–(3), including the assignees, and satisfactory proof of the facts and payment of the fee set forth in §1.20(b), or on order of a court before which such matter is called in question, include in the reexamination certificate to be issued under §1.570 or §1.977 an amendment naming only the actual inventor or inventors. The petition must be submitted as part of the reexamination proceeding and must satisfy the requirements of §1.324.

(2) Notwithstanding the preceding paragraph (l)(1) of this section, if a petition to correct inventorship satisfying the requirements of §1.324 is filed in a reexamination proceeding, and the reexamination proceeding is terminated other than by a reexamination certificate under §1.570 or §1.977, a certificate of correction indicating the change of inventorship stated in the petition will be issued upon request by the patentee.

§1.550 Conduct of ex parte reexamination proceedings.

(a) All ex parte reexamination proceedings, including any appeals to the Board of Patent Appeals and Interferences, will be conducted with special dispatch within the Office. After issuance of the ex parte reexamination order and expiration of the time for submitting any responses, the examination will be conducted in accordance with §§1.104 through 1.116 and will result in the issuance of an ex parte reexamination certificate under §1.570.

(b) The patent owner in an ex parte reexamination proceeding will be given at least thirty days to respond to any Office action. In response to any rejection, such response may include further statements and/or proposed amendments or new claims to place the patent in a condition where all claims, if amended as proposed, would be patentable.

* * *

§1.565 Concurrent Office proceedings which include an ex parte reexamination proceeding.

(a) In an ex parte reexamination proceeding before the Office, the patent owner must inform the Office of any prior or concurrent proceedings in which the patent is or was involved such as interferences, reissues, ex parte reexaminations, inter partes reexaminations, or litigation and the results of such proceedings. See §1.985 for notification of prior or concurrent proceedings in an inter partes reexamination proceeding.

* * *

§1.666 Filing of interference settlement agreements.

* * *

(b) If any party filing the agreement or understanding under paragraph (a) of this section so requests, the copy will be kept separate from the file of the interference, and made available only to Government agencies on written request, or to any person upon petition accompanied by the fee set forth in §1.17(h) and on a showing of good cause.

* * *

§1.720 Conditions for extension of patent term.

The term of a patent may be extended if:

* * *

(b) The term of the patent has never been previously extended, except for extensions issued pursuant to §§1.701, 1.760, or §1.790;

* * *

(g) The term of the patent, including any interim extension issued pursuant to §1.790, has not expired before the submission of an application in compliance with §1.741; and

* * *

§1.730 Applicant for extension of patent term; signature requirements.

(a) Any application for extension of a patent term must be submitted by the owner of record of the patent or its agent and must comply with the requirements of §1.740.

(b) If the application is submitted by the patent owner, the application must be signed either by:

(1) The patent owner in compliance with §3.73(b) of this chapter; or

(2) A registered practitioner on behalf of the patent owner.

(c) If the application is submitted on behalf of the patent owner by an agent of the patent owner (e.g., a licensee of the patent owner), the application must be signed by a registered practitioner on behalf of the agent. The Office may require proof that the agent is authorized to act on behalf of the patent owner.

(d) If the application is signed by a registered practitioner, the Office may require proof that the practitioner is authorized to act on behalf of the patent owner or agent of the patent owner.

§1.740 Formal requirements for application for extension of patent term; correction of informalities.

(a) An application for extension of patent term must be made in writing to the Commissioner. A formal application for the extension of patent term must include:

(1) A complete identification of the approved product as by appropriate chemical and generic name, physical structure or characteristics;

(2) A complete identification of the Federal statute including the applicable provision of law under which the regulatory review occurred;

(3) An identification of the date on which the product received permission for commercial marketing or use under the provision of law under which the applicable regulatory review period occurred;

(4) In the case of a drug product, an identification of each active ingredient in the product and as to each active ingredient, a statement that it has not been previously approved for commercial marketing or use under the Federal Food, Drug, and Cosmetic Act, the Public Health Service Act, or the Virus-Serum-Toxin Act, or a statement of when the active ingredient was approved for commercial marketing or use (either alone or in combination with other active ingredients), the use for which it was approved, and the provision of law under which it was approved.

(5) A statement that the application is being submitted within the sixty day period permitted for submission pursuant to §1.720(f) and an identification of the date of the last day on which the application could be submitted;

(6) A complete identification of the patent for which an extension is being sought by the name of the inventor, the patent number, the date of issue, and the date of expiration;

(7) A copy of the patent for which an extension is being sought, including the entire specification (including claims) and drawings;

(8) A copy of any disclaimer, certificate of correction, receipt of maintenance fee payment, or reexamination certificate issued in the patent;

(9) A statement that the patent claims the approved product, or a method of using or manufacturing the approved product, and a showing which lists each applicable patent claim and demonstrates the manner in which at least one such patent claim reads on:

(i) The approved product, if the listed claims include any claim to the approved product;

(ii) The method of using the approved product, if the listed claims include any claim to the method of using the approved product; and

(iii) The method of manufacturing the approved product, if the listed claims include any claim to the method of manufacturing the approved product;

(10) A statement beginning on a new page of the relevant dates and information pursuant to 35 U.S.C. 156(g) in order to enable the Secretary of Health and Human Services or the Secretary of Agriculture, as appropriate, to determine the applicable regulatory review period as follows:

(i) For a patent claiming a human drug, antibiotic, or human biological product:

(A) The effective date of the investigational new drug (IND) application and the IND number;

(B) The date on which a new drug application (NDA) or a Product License Application (PLA) was initially submitted and the NDA or PLA number; and

(C) The date on which the NDA was approved or the Product License issued;

(ii) For a patent claiming a new animal drug:

(A) The date a major health or environmental effects test on the drug was initiated, and any available substantiation of that date, or the date of an exemption under subsection (j) of Section 512 of the Federal Food, Drug, and Cosmetic Act became effective for such animal drug;

(B) The date on which a new animal drug application (NADA) was initially submitted and the NADA number; and

(C) The date on which the NADA was approved;

(iii) For a patent claiming a veterinary biological product:

(A) The date the authority to prepare an experimental biological product under the Virus-Serum-Toxin Act became effective;

(B) The date an application for a license was submitted under the Virus-Serum-Toxin Act; and

(C) The date the license issued;

(iv) For a patent claiming a food or color additive:

(A) The date a major health or environmental effects test on the additive was initiated and any available substantiation of that date;

(B) The date on which a petition for product approval under the Federal Food, Drug and Cosmetic Act was initially submitted and the petition number; and

(C) The date on which the FDA published a Federal Register notice listing the additive for use;

(v) For a patent claiming a medical device:

(A) The effective date of the investigational device exemption (IDE) and the IDE number, if applicable, or the date on which the applicant began the first clinical investigation involving the device, if no IDE was submitted, and any available substantiation of that date;

(B) The date on which the application for product approval or notice of completion of a product development protocol under Section 515 of the Federal Food, Drug and Cosmetic Act was initially submitted and the number of the application; and

(C) The date on which the application was approved or the protocol declared to be completed;

(11) A brief description beginning on a new page of the significant activities undertaken by the marketing applicant during the applicable regulatory review period with respect to the approved product and the significant dates applicable to such activities;

(12) A statement beginning on a new page that in the opinion of the applicant the patent is eligible for the extension and a statement as to the length of extension claimed, including how the length of extension was determined;

(13) A statement that applicant acknowledges a duty to disclose to the Commissioner of Patents and Trademarks and the Secretary of Health and Human Services or the Secretary of Agriculture any information which is material to the determination of entitlement to the extension sought (see §1.765);

(14) The prescribed fee for receiving and acting upon the application for extension (see §1.20(j)); and

(15) The name, address, and telephone number of the person to whom inquiries and correspondence relating to the application for patent term extension are to be directed.

(b) The application under this section must be accompanied by two additional copies of such application (for a total of three copies).

(c) If an application for extension of patent term is informal under this section, the Office will so notify the applicant. The applicant has two months from the mail date of the notice, or such time as is set in the notice, within which to correct the informality. Unless the notice indicates otherwise, this time period may be extended under the provisions of §1.136.

§1.741 Complete application given a filing date; petition procedure.

(a) The filing date of an application for extension of a patent term is the date on which a complete application is received in the Office or filed pursuant to the procedures set forth in §1.8 or §1.10. A complete application must include:

* * *

(5) Sufficient information to enable the Commissioner to determine under subsections (a) and (b) of 35 U.S.C. 156 the eligibility of a patent for extension, and the rights that will be derived from the extension, and information to enable the Commissioner and the Secretary of Health and Human Services or the Secretary of Agriculture to determine the length of the regulatory review period; and

* * *

(b) If an application for extension of patent term is incomplete under this section, the Office will so notify the applicant. If applicant requests review of a notice that an application is incomplete, or review of the filing date accorded an application under this section, applicant must file a petition pursuant to this paragraph accompanied by the fee set forth in §1.17(h) within two months of the mail date of the notice that the application is incomplete, or the notice according the filing date complained of. Unless the notice indicates otherwise, this time period may be extended under the provisions of §1.136.

§1.760 Interim extension of patent term under 35 U.S.C. 156(e)(2).

An applicant who has filed a formal application for extension in compliance with §1.740 may request one or more interim extensions for periods of up to one year each pending a final determination on the application pursuant to §1.750. Any such request should be filed at least three months prior to the expiration date of the patent. The Commissioner may issue interim extensions, without a request by the applicant, for periods of up to one year each until a final determination is made. The patent owner or agent will be notified when an interim extension is granted and notice of the extension will be published in the Official Gazette of the United States Patent and Trademark Office. The notice will be recorded in the official file of the patent and will be considered as part of the original patent. In no event will the interim extensions granted under this section be longer than the maximum period for extension to which the applicant would be eligible.

§1.780 Certificate or order of extension of patent term.

If a determination is made pursuant to §1.750 that a patent is eligible for extension and that the term of the patent is to be extended, a certificate of extension, under seal, or an order granting interim extension under 35 U.S.C. 156(d)(5), will be issued to the applicant for the extension of the patent term. Such certificate or order will be recorded in the official file of the patent and will be considered as part of the original patent. Notification of the issuance of the certificate or order of extension will be published in the Official Gazette of the United States Patent and Trademark Office. Notification of the issuance of the order granting an interim extension under 35 U.S.C. 156(d)(5), including the identity of the product currently under regulatory review, will be published in the Official Gazette of the United States Patent and Trademark Office and in the Federal Register. No certificate of, or order granting, an extension will be issued if the term of the patent cannot be extended, even though the patent is otherwise determined to be eligible for extension. In such situations, the final determination made pursuant to §1.750 will indicate that no certificate or order will issue.

§1.821 Nucleotide and/or amino acid sequence disclosures in patent applications.

* * *

(c) Patent applications which contain disclosures of nucleotide and/or amino acid sequences must contain, as a separate part of the disclosure, a paper or compact disc copy (see §1.52(e)) disclosing the nucleotide and/or amino acid sequences and associated information using the symbols and format in accordance with the requirements of §§1.822 and 1.823. This paper or compact disc copy is referred to elsewhere in this subpart as the "Sequence Listing." Each sequence disclosed must appear separately in the "Sequence Listing." Each sequence set forth in the "Sequence Listing" must be assigned a separate sequence identifier. The sequence identifiers must begin with 1 and increase sequentially by integers. If no sequence is present for a sequence identifier, the code "000" must be used in place of the sequence. The response for the numeric identifier <160> must include the total number of SEQ ID NOs, whether followed by a sequence or by the code "000."

* * *

(e) A copy of the "Sequence Listing" referred to in paragraph (c) of this section must also be submitted in computer readable form (CRF) in accordance with the requirements of §1.824. The computer readable form must be a copy of the "Sequence Listing" and may not be retained as a part of the patent application file. If the computer readable form of a new application is to be identical with the computer readable form of another application of the applicant on file in the Office, reference may be made to the other application and computer readable form in lieu of filing a duplicate computer readable form in the new application if the computer readable form in the other application was compliant with all of the requirements of this subpart. The new application must be accompanied by a letter making such reference to the other application and computer readable form, both of which shall be completely identified. In the new application, applicant must also request the use of the compliant computer readable "Sequence Listing" that is already on file for the other application and must state that the paper or compact disc copy of the "Sequence Listing" in the new application is identical to the computer readable copy filed for the other application.

(f) In addition to the paper or compact disc copy required by paragraph (c) of this section and the computer readable form required by paragraph (e) of this section, a statement that the "Sequence Listing" content of the paper or compact disc copy and the computer readable copy are the same must be submitted with the computer readable form, e.g., a statement that "the sequence listing information recorded in computer readable form is identical to the written (on paper or compact disc) sequence listing."

* * *

§1.823 Requirements for nucleotide and/or amino acid sequences as part of the application papers.

(a)(1) *If the "Sequence Listing" required by §1.821(c) is submitted on paper:* The "Sequence Listing," setting forth the nucleotide and/or amino acid sequence and associated information in accordance with paragraph (b) of this section, must begin on a new page and must be titled "Sequence Listing." The pages of the "Sequence Listing" preferably should be numbered independently of the numbering of the remainder of the application. Each page of the "Sequence Listing" shall contain no more than 66 lines and each line shall contain no more than 72 characters. A fixed-width font should be used exclusively throughout the "Sequence Listing."

(2) *If the "Sequence Listing" required by §1.821(c) is submitted on compact disc:* The "Sequence Listing" must be submitted on a compact disc in compliance with §1.52(e). The compact disc may also contain table information if the application contains table information that may be submitted on a compact disc (§1.52(e)(1)(iii)). The specification must contain an incorporation-by-reference of the Sequence Listing as required by §1.52(e)(5). The presentation of the "Sequence Listing" and other materials on compact disc under §1.821(c) does not substitute for the Computer Readable Form that must be submitted on disk, compact disc, or tape in accordance with §1.824.

* * *

§1.824 Form and format for nucleotide and/or amino acid sequence submissions in computer readable form.

(a) The computer readable form required by §1.821(e) shall meet the following requirements:

(1) The computer readable form shall contain a single "Sequence Listing" as either a diskette, series of diskettes, or other permissible media outlined in paragraph (c) of this section.

(2) The "Sequence Listing" in paragraph (a)(1) of this section shall be submitted in American Standard Code for Information Interchange (ASCII) text. No other formats shall be allowed.

(3) The computer readable form may be created by any means, such as word processors, nucleotide/amino acid sequence editors' or other custom computer programs; however, it shall conform to all requirements detailed in this section.

(4) File compression is acceptable when using diskette media, so long as the compressed file is in a self-extracting format that will decompress on one of the systems described in paragraph (b) of this section.

(5) Page numbering must not appear within the computer readable form version of the "Sequence Listing" file.

(6) All computer readable forms must have a label permanently affixed thereto on which has been hand-printed or typed: the name of the applicant, the title of the invention, the date on which the data were recorded on the computer readable form, the operating system used, a reference number, and an application number and filing date, if known. If multiple diskettes are submitted, the diskette labels must indicate their order (e.g., "1 of X").

(b) Computer readable form submissions must meet these format requirements:

(1) *Computer Compatibility*: IBM PC/XT/AT or Apple Macintosh;

(2) *Operating System Compatibility*: MS-DOS, MS-Windows, Unix or Macintosh;

(3) *Line Terminator*: ASCII Carriage Return plus ASCII Line Feed; and

(4) *Pagination*: Continuous file (no "hard page break" codes permitted).

(c) Computer readable form files submitted may be in any of the following media:

(1) *Diskette*: 3.50 inch, 1.44 Mb storage; 3.50 inch, 720 Kb storage; 5.25 inch, 1.2 Mb storage; 5.25 inch, 360 Kb storage.

(2) *Magnetic tape*: 0.5 inch, up to 24000 feet; Density: 1600 or 6250 bits per inch, 9 track; Format: Unix tar command; specify blocking factor (not "block size"); Line Terminator: ASCII Carriage Return plus ASCII Line Feed.

(3) *8mm Data Cartridge: Format*: Unix tar command; specify blocking factor (not "block size"); Line Terminator: ASCII Carriage Return plus ASCII Line Feed.

(4) *Compact disc*: Format: ISO 9660 or High Sierra Format.

(5) *Magneto Optical Disk*: Size/Storage Specifications: 5.25 inch, 640 Mb.

(d) Computer readable forms that are submitted to the Office will not be returned to the applicant.

§1.825 Amendments to or replacement of sequence listing and computer readable copy thereof.

(a) Any amendment to a paper copy of the "Sequence Listing" (§1.821(c)) must be made by the submission of substitute sheets and include a statement that the substitute sheets include no new matter. Any amendment to a compact disc copy of the "Sequence Listing" (§1.821(c)) must be made by the submission of a replacement compact disc (2 copies) in compliance with §1.52(e). Amendments must also be accompanied by a statement that indicates support for the amendment in the application, as filed, and a statement that the replacement compact disc includes no new matter.

(b) Any amendment to the paper or compact disc copy of the "Sequence Listing," in accordance with paragraph (a) of this section, must be accompanied by a substitute copy of the computer readable form (§1.821(e)) including all previously submitted data with the amendment incorporated therein, accompanied by a statement that the copy in computer readable form is the same as the substitute copy of the "Sequence Listing."

* * *

§3.27 Mailing address for submitting documents to be recorded.

Documents and cover sheets to be recorded should be addressed to the Commissioner, United States Patent and Trademark Office, Box Assignment, Washington, D.C. 20231, unless they are filed together with new applications or with a request under §3.81.

§3.71 Prosecution by assignee.

(a) *Patents—conducting of prosecution.* One or more assignees as defined in paragraph (b) of this section may, after becoming of record pursuant to paragraph (c) of this section, conduct prosecution of a national patent application or a reexamination proceeding to the exclusion of either the inventive entity, or the assignee(s) previously entitled to conduct prosecution.

(b) *Patents—Assignee(s) who can prosecute.* The assignee(s) who may conduct either the prosecution of a national application for patent or a reexamination proceeding are:

(1) *A single assignee.* An assignee of the entire right, title and interest in the application or patent being reexamined who is of record, or

(2) *Partial assignee(s) together or with inventor(s).* All partial assignees, or all partial assignees and inventors who have not assigned their right, title and interest in the application or patent being reexamined, who together own the entire right, title and interest in the application or patent being reexamined. A partial assignee is any assignee of record having less than the entire right, title and interest in the application or patent being reexamined.

(c) *Patents—Becoming of record.* An assignee becomes of record either in a national patent application or a reexamination proceeding by filing a statement in compliance with §3.73(b) that is signed by a party who is authorized to act on behalf of the assignee.

(d) *Trademarks.* The assignee of a trademark application or registration may prosecute a trademark application, submit documents to maintain a trademark registration, or file papers against a third party in reliance on the assignee's trademark application or registration, to the exclusion of the original applicant or previous assignee. The assignee must establish ownership in compliance with §3.73(b).

§3.73 Establishing right of assignee to take action.

(a) The inventor is presumed to be the owner of a patent application, and any patent that may issue therefrom, unless there is an assignment. The original applicant is presumed to be the owner of a trademark application or registration, unless there is an assignment.

(b)(1) In order to request or take action in a patent or trademark matter, the assignee must establish its ownership of the patent or trademark property of paragraph (a) of this section to the satisfaction of the Commissioner. The establishment of ownership by the assignee may be combined with the paper that requests or takes the action. Ownership is established by submitting to the Office a signed statement identifying the assignee, accompanied by either:

(i) Documentary evidence of a chain of title from the original owner to the assignee (e.g., copy of an executed assignment). The documents submitted to establish ownership may be required to be recorded pursuant to §3.11 in the assignment records of the Office as a condition to permitting the assignee to take action in a matter pending before the Office; or

(ii) A statement specifying where documentary evidence of a chain of title from the original owner to the assignee is recorded in the assignment records of the Office (e.g., reel and frame number).

(2) The submission establishing ownership must show that the person signing the submission is a person authorized to act on behalf of the assignee by:

(i) Including a statement that the person signing the submission is authorized to act on behalf of the assignee; or

(ii) Being signed by a person having apparent authority to sign on behalf of the assignee, e.g., an officer of the assignee.

(c) For patent matters only:

(1) Establishment of ownership by the assignee must be submitted prior to, or at the same time as, the paper requesting or taking action is submitted.

(2) If the submission under this section is by an assignee of less than the entire right, title and interest, such assignee must indicate the extent (by percentage) of its ownership interest, or the Office may refuse to accept the submission as an establishment of ownership.

§3.81 Issue of patent to assignee.

(a) *With payment of the issue fee:* An application may issue in the name(s) of the assignee(s) consistent with the application's assignment where a request for such issuance is submitted with payment of the issue fee, provided the assignment has been previously recorded in the Office. If the assignment has not been previously recorded, the request should be accompanied by the assignment and either a direction to record the assignment in the Office pursuant to §3.28, or a statement under §3.73(b).

(b) *After payment of the issue fee:* An application may issue in the name(s) of the assignee(s) consistent with the application's assignment where a request for such issuance along with the processing fee set forth in §1.17(i) of this chapter is submitted after the date of payment of the issue fee, but prior to issuance of the patent, provided the assignment has been previously recorded in the Office. If the assignment has not been previously recorded, the request should be accompanied by the assignment and either a direction to record the assignment in the Office pursuant to §3.28, or a statement under §3.73(b).

(c) *Partial assignees.*

(1) If one or more assignee(s) together with one or more inventor(s) hold the entire right, title, and interest in the application, the patent may issue in the names of the assignee(s) and the inventor(s).

(2) If multiple assignees hold the entire right, title, and interest to the exclusion of all the inventors, the patent may issue in the names of the multiple assignees.

§5.1 Applications and correspondence involving national security.

(a) All correspondence in connection with this part, including petitions, should be addressed to "Commissioner for Patents (Attention Licensing and Review), Washington, D.C. 20231."

(b) Application as used in this part includes provisional applications filed under 35 U.S.C. 111(b) (§1.9(a)(2) of this chapter), nonprovisional applications filed under 35 U.S.C. 111(a) or entering the national stage from an international application after compliance with 35 U.S.C. 371 (§1.9(a)(3)), or international applications filed under the Patent Cooperation Treaty prior to entering the national stage of processing (§1.9(b)).

(c) Patent applications and documents relating thereto that are national security classified (see §1.9(i) of this chapter) and contain authorized national security markings (e.g., "Confidential," "Secret" or "Top Secret") are accepted by the Office. National security classified documents filed in the Office must be either hand-carried to Licensing and Review or mailed to the Office in compliance with paragraph (a) of this section.

(d) The applicant in a national security classified patent application must obtain a secrecy order pursuant to §5.2(a). If a national security classified patent application is filed without a notification pursuant to §5.2(a), the Office will set a time period within which either the application must be declassified, or the application must be placed under a secrecy order pursuant to §5.2(a), or the applicant must submit evidence of a good faith effort to obtain a secrecy order pursuant to §5.2(a) from the relevant department or agency in order to prevent abandonment of the application. If evidence of a good faith effort to obtain a secrecy order pursuant to §5.2(a) from the relevant department or agency is submitted by the applicant within the time period set by the Office, but the application has not been declassified or placed under a secrecy order pursuant to §5.2(a), the Office will again set a time period within which either the application must be declassified, or the application must be placed under a secrecy order pursuant to §5.2(a), or the applicant must submit evidence of a good faith effort to again obtain a secrecy order pursuant to §5.2(a) from the relevant department or agency in order to prevent abandonment of the application.

(e) An application will not be published under §1.211 of this chapter or allowed under §1.311 of this chapter if publication or disclosure of the application would be detrimental to national security. An application under national security review will not be published at least until six months from its filing date or three months from the date the application was referred to a defense agency, whichever is later. A national security classified patent application will not be published under §1.211 of this chapter or allowed under §1.311 of this chapter until the application is declassified and any secrecy order under §5.2(a) has been rescinded.

(f) Applications on inventions made outside the United States and on inventions in which a U.S. Government defense agency has a property interest will not be made available to defense agencies.

§5.2 Secrecy order.

* * *

(c) An application disclosing any significant part of the subject matter of an application under a secrecy order pursuant to paragraph (a) of this section also falls within the scope of such secrecy order. Any such application that is pending before the Office must be promptly brought to the attention of Licensing and Review, unless such application is itself under a secrecy order pursuant to paragraph (a) of this section. Any subsequently filed application containing any significant part of the subject matter of an application under a secrecy order pursuant to paragraph (a) of this section must either be hand-carried to Licensing and Review or mailed to the Office in compliance with §5.1(a).

§5.12 Petition for license.

* * *

(b) A petition for license must include the fee set forth in §1.17(h) of this chapter, the petitioner's address, and full instructions for delivery of the requested license when it is to be delivered to other than the petitioner. The petition should be presented in letter form.

§10.23 Misconduct.

* * *

(c) Conduct which constitutes a violation of paragraphs (a) and (b) of this section includes, but is not limited to:

* * *

(11) Except as permitted by §1.52(c) of this chapter, knowingly filing or causing to be filed an application containing any material alteration made in the application papers after the signing of the accompanying oath or declaration without identifying the alteration at the time of filing the application papers.

* * *

Appendix C-34

Patent Application Data Entry Format

Format for the Patent Application Capture and Review System

Patent Application Data Entry Format

Guide for Preparing Bibliographic Data for Electronic Capture

CONTENTS

Paperwork Reduction Act Notice

This information collection is subject to the Paperwork Reduction Act of 1995 (44 U.S.C. § 3501 *et seq.*), and has been reviewed by the Office of Management and Budget (OMB) under OMB control number 0651-0032 and is approved through September 30, 2000. This collection of information is required by 35 U.S.C. §§ 111, 112, 113, 115, 119, and 120. The Patent Application Data Entry Format is used by the public to submit bibliographic information to the PTO. Use of this voluntary format allows the PTO to scan the bibliographic information into its automated electronic information management systems easily and efficiently. This information will be treated confidentially in accordance with 35 U.S.C. § 122 and 37 C.F.R. § 1.14. It is estimated to take twelve minutes to read the user guide and submit the bibliographic information. The time may vary depending upon the needs of the individual case. Any comments on the amount of time you require to complete this format and/or suggestions for reducing this burden, should be sent to the Chief Information Officer, U.S. Patent and Trademark Office, U.S. Department of Commerce, Washington, D.C., 20231. DO NOT SEND FEES OR COMPLETED FORMS TO THIS ADDRESS. SEND TO: Assistant Commissioner for Patents, Washington, D.C., 20231.

Notwithstanding any other provision of law, no person is required to respond to nor shall a person be subject to a penalty for failure to comply with a collection of information subject to the requirements of the Paperwork Reduction Act unless that collection of information displays a currently valid OMB control number.

R E V I S I O N S – Summary of Changes to Version 1

Version 1 of this Guide was widely distributed between April 1998, and October 1998. Based on suggestions and experience of applicants and PTO's review of the effectiveness of the OCR technology to read the Patent Data Entry Format sheets already submitted by applicants, it is prudent to make the modifications summarized here. While these modifications will improve accuracy, **previous Guide version labels will still be read.**

1. Appendix B has been added to explain the nature of the Electronic Mail acknowledgment feature and the applicant permission needed for PTO to send it.

2. Under Inventor Information,
the label **State/Province::**
  has been changed to **State or Province::**
the label **State/Prov. Of Residence::**
  has been changed to **State or Prov. Of Residence::**
the label **Citizenship::**
  has been changed to **Citizenship Country::**

3. Under Correspondence Information,
the label **E-Mail::**
  has been changed to **Electronic Mail::**
the label **State/Province::**
  has been changed to **State or Province::**

4. Under Application Information,
the label **Formal Drawings::**
  has been changed to **Formal Drawings?::**
the label **Licensed - U S Government Agency::**
  has been changed to **Licensed US Govt. Agency::**
the label **Contract Number::**
  has been changed to **Contract or Grant Numbers::**
the label **Grant Number::**
  has been deleted.
the label **Secrecy Order in Parent Application::**
  has been changed to **Secrecy Order in Parent Appl.?::**

5. Under Continuity Information,
data for the label **This Application is a::**
  the data value **Claim benefit of**
    has been changed to **Non Prov. of Provisional**

R E V I S I O N S (continued)

6. In all fields where a "Yes" or "No" answer is required,
   the data values **Y** and **N**
   have been changed to **Yes** and **No**.

7. In Appendix A,
   the Recommended fonts have been changed to
   Courier, Arial, and Univers
   Not Recommended now includes
   Times New Roman, Gothic

THE DATA ENTRY FORMAT

Patent Application Data Entry Format

THE **Patent Application Data Entry Format** was designed to turn a customer's paper document into an electronic PTO data record. Image scanning and optical character recognition equipment promise more accurate data recording than our current method of manual data entry.

Using this format, initial information about a newly filed application may be entered, just as it is presented, directly into PTO information systems.

Customers using the **Patent Application Data Entry Format** can expect two advantages when applying for a patent:

1. Improved accuracy of filing receipts. The need for corrected filing receipts related to PTO errors will be significantly reduced.

2. Accurately recorded application data This will also reduce application prosecution delays.

Use of the format involves typing the "Section Heading," typing a specific "label" followed by a double colon "label delimiter", one or more tabs, and then the data corresponding to the label. *See the Format Diagram below.*

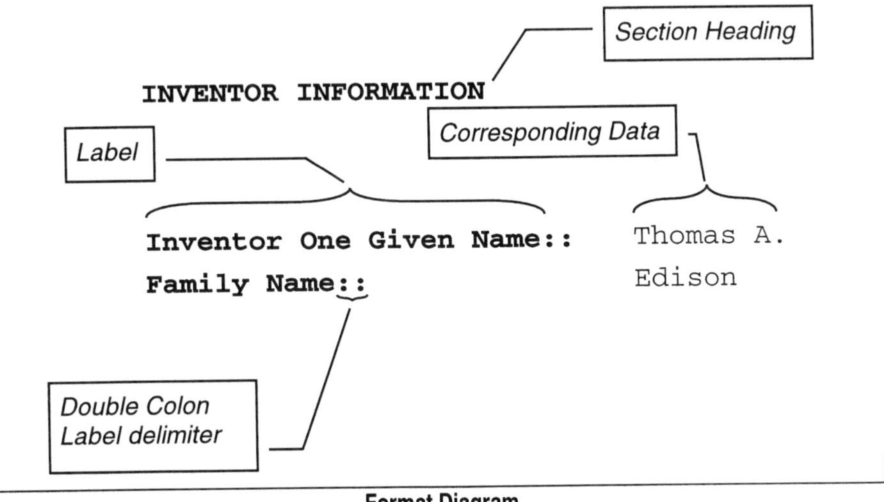

Format Diagram

For bibliographic information, the format includes six section headings:

Inventor Information

Correspondence Information

Application Information

Representative Information

Continuity Information

Prior Foreign Applications

Every applicant must supply the information listed in the first three sections: **Inventor Information**, some **Correspondence Information** and some **Application Information**. In many cases the Patent Data Entry Format will be complete with just this information.

Information identified in the **Representative Information**, **Continuity Information** and **Prior Foreign Applications** sections will not necessarily apply to all applications.

NOTE: Any section or label information which does not apply does not need to be listed.

INSTRUCTIONS

When preparing information in the Patent Application Data Entry Format, keep these points in mind:

- The only section headings and labels that must appear on your data format sheet are those for which you have corresponding data.
- Each section heading must be on a separate line.
- Each label must be on a separate line.
- Each line of information provided must have a label to the left. In other words, if a single piece of information, such as title requires multiple lines, each line must begin with its own label to the left.
- Section headings and labels must be typed exactly as designated in the format.
- Section headings and labels are not case sensitive. (*i.e., All capital letters or initial capitals are permitted.*)
- The corresponding data for each label must be limited to the maximum length stated in this Guide. This limit include spaces and punctuation.
- Typography, Document Format requirements and Paper Characteristics requirements are listed in Appendix A.

The next eight pages explain in detail the format elements and how each should be entered.

Inventor Information

*Identify each Inventor's name with a separate, consecutive number starting with "**One.**" i.e.: **Inventor One ... Inventor Two ...***

*When the inventor is not named in a non-provisional application, an alphanumeric identifier should be entered as the family name of **Inventor One**.*

Inventor One Given Name::	*No more than 50 characters*
Family Name::	*No more than 50 characters*
Name Suffix::	*No more than 10 characters*

*A **Given Name** refers to any or all names except for the last name or surname. Include a middle name or initial on this line, if desired.*

*A **Family Name** is the last name or surname.*

*A **Name Suffix** is an optional generational term added to the last name, such as Jr., Sr., III, etc.*

The postal address requested here is the location where the inventor receives mail. This address might be the same as the correspondence address. However, both are separate pieces of information.

Postal Address Line One::	*No more than 50 characters*
Postal Address Line Two::	*No more than 50 characters*
City::	*No more than 40 characters*
State or Province::	*No more than 50 characters*
Country::	*No more than 50 characters*
Postal or Zip Code::	*No more than 20 characters*

If the inventor receives mail in the U.S. or Canada, type the 2-character State or 3-character Province abbreviation used when mailing a letter. Do not use this field for any other country.

If the inventor receives mail in a country other than the U.S., type the country name. This is not needed for U.S. addressees.

This information needs to be provided ONLY if it is different from the inventor's postal address information.

When these 3 labels are omitted, the inventor's residence will be presumed to be the city, state and country listed in the postal address information.

City of Residence::	*No more than 40 characters*
State or Prov. of Residence::	*No more than 50 characters*
Country of Residence::	*No more than 50 characters*
Citizenship Country::	*No more than 50 characters*

If the inventor receives mail in the U.S. or Canada, type the 2-character State or 3-character province abbreviation used when mailing a letter. Do not use this field for any other

If the inventor is a resident of a country other than the U.S., type the country name. This is not needed for U.S. addresses.

For United States, type US. For countries other than the US, type the country name.

Inventor Information format continued ...

Inventor Information (*continued from page 3*)

When someone other than the inventor is filing the application, the following information must also be provided. This information should immediately follow the inventor information for whom the applicant is filing (outlined on page 3).

*If you are filing the application and you are not the inventor, type your name after the **Given Name of Applicant** and **Family Name** labels. Type one and only one of these three labels followed by your authority code.*

*It is important that the **Applicant** information immediately follow the **Inventor** information on whose behalf the application is being filed.*

*The term **Applicant** as used in this section refers to a person who is not the inventor and is filing the application on behalf of the inventor under 42 U.S.C. 2457(a)(2), or 35 U.S.C. 117 or 35 U.S.C.118.*

Given Name of Applicant::	*No more than 50 characters*
Family Name::	*No more than 50 characters*
Name Suffix::	*No more than 10 characters*
Authority Under 1.42::	*2 numbers only*
or	
Authority Under 1.43::	*2 numbers only*
or	
Authority Under 1.47::	*2 numbers only*
Postal Address Line One::	*No more than 50 characters*
Postal Address Line Two::	*No more than 50 characters*
City::	*No more than 40 characters*
State or Province::	*No more than 50 characters*
Country::	*No more than 50 characters*
Postal or Zip Code::	*No more than 20 characters*
City of Residence::	*No more than 40 characters*
State or Prov. of Residence::	*No more than 50 characters*
Country of Residence::	*No more than 50 characters*
Citizenship Country::	*No more than 50 characters*

*The **Applicant's Authority** is indicated with a two character code. The code is used to identify the authority by which a party, other than the inventor, may file the application.*

Valid Applicant Authority Codes are:

02 - Administrator of NASA
08 - Party of Interest under 35 U.S.C. 118
11 - Legal Representative under 35 U.S.C. 117

 Version 2 12/11/98

Correspondence Information

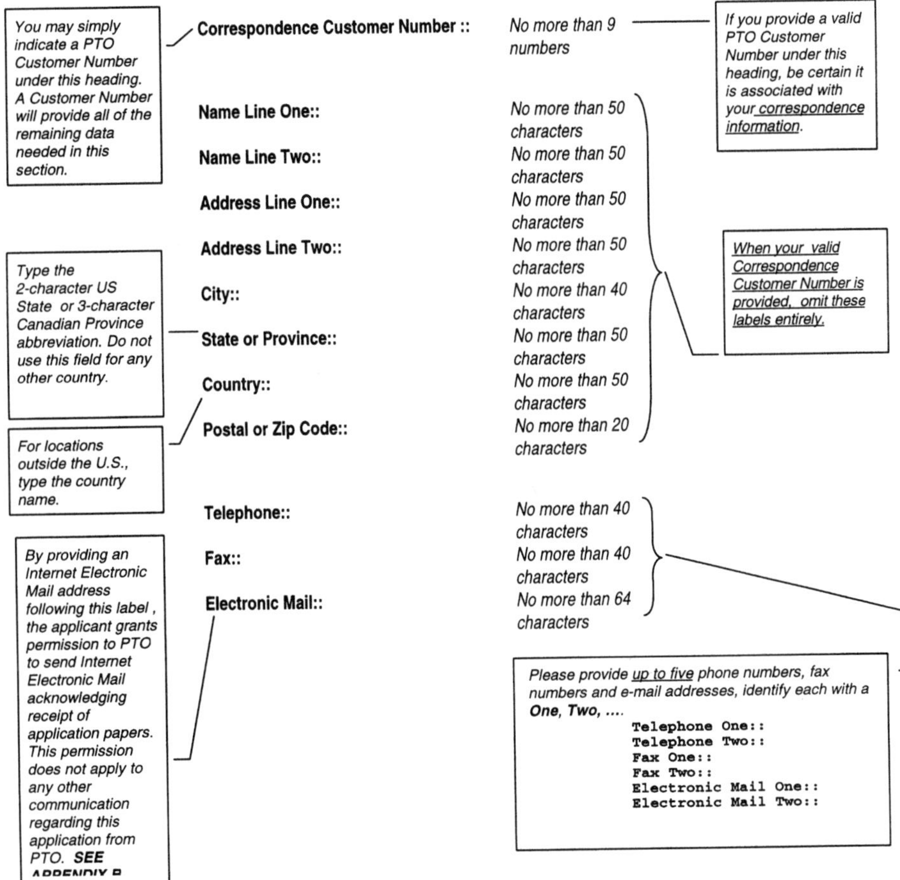

You may simply indicate a PTO Customer Number under this heading. A Customer Number will provide all of the remaining data needed in this section.
Correspondence Customer Number :: *No more than 9 numbers*
If you provide a valid PTO Customer Number under this heading, be certain it is associated with your correspondence information.
Name Line One:: *No more than 50 characters*
Name Line Two:: *No more than 50 characters*
Address Line One:: *No more than 50 characters*
Address Line Two:: *No more than 50 characters*
City:: *No more than 40 characters*
State or Province:: *No more than 50 characters*
Country:: *No more than 50 characters*
Postal or Zip Code:: *No more than 20 characters*
When your valid Correspondence Customer Number is provided, omit these labels entirely.
Type the 2-character US State or 3-character Canadian Province abbreviation. Do not use this field for any other country.
For locations outside the U.S., type the country name.
Telephone:: *No more than 40 characters*
Fax:: *No more than 40 characters*
Electronic Mail:: *No more than 64 characters*
By providing an Internet Electronic Mail address following this label, the applicant grants permission to PTO to send Internet Electronic Mail acknowledging receipt of application papers. This permission does not apply to any other communication regarding this application from PTO. **SEE**
Please provide up to five phone numbers, fax numbers and e-mail addresses, identify each with a **One, Two, ...**
Telephone One::
Telephone Two::
Fax One::
Fax Two::
Electronic Mail One::
Electronic Mail Two::

NOTE: For information concerning the Customer Number practice, see the notice "Extension of the Payor Number Practice (Through Customer Numbers) to matters Involving Pending Patent Applications," published in the *Federal Register* at 61 *Fed. Reg.* 54622 (October 21, 1996), and in the *Official Gazette* at 1191 *Off. Gaz Pat. Office* 187 (October 29, 1996).

Application Information

Type the invention title on up to 7 lines. The PTO system will capture 280 total characters including spaces and punctuation. Label each line as

*Identify each **Title Line** with a separate, consecutive number starting with **"One."** i.e.: **Title Line One::** **Title Line Two::** ...*

Title Line One::	*No more than 40 characters*
Title Line Two::	*No more than 40 characters*
Title Line Three::	*No more than 40 characters*
Title Line Four::	*No more than 40 characters*
Title Line Five::	*No more than 40 characters*
Title Line Six::	*No more than 40 characters*
Title Line Seven::	*No more than 40 characters*
Total Drawing Sheets::	*No more than 4 numbers*
Formal Drawings?::	*No more than 3 characters*
Application Type::	*No more than 40 characters*
Docket Number::	*No more than 12 characters*

Enter the total number of sheets of drawings as a numeral

Type **Yes** *or* **No***. When total number of drawings sheets are given, indicate if they are formal.*

*Identify your application as one of the following **Application Types**:*

- *Utility*
- *Design*
- *Plant*
- *Provisional*

If your Application is a Reissue, type:

- *Utility Reissue*
- *Design Reissue*
- *Plant Reissue*

Do not use this format for Reexamination Applications

***Docket Number** refers to any application identifier not more than 12 characters long, which is assigned by the attorney or agent or the inventor.*

Application Information *(continued from page 6)*

Identify each line of ***Contract or Grant Numbers*** *with a separate, consecutive number starting with "****One****", "****Two****", ... as shown.*

Multiple contract or grant numbers may be entered on each line separated by a " ; ". Do not split contract or grant numbers across 2 lines.

Licensed US Govt. Agency::	*No more than 40 characters*
Contract or Grant Numbers One::	*No more than 40 characters*
Contract or Grant Numbers Two::	*No more than 40 characters*

Where a Government contractor retains U.S. domestic patent rights, the contractor is required to include the name of the U.S. Government agency and the Government contract number or grant number. (See MPEP § 310)

Secrecy Order in Parent Appl.?::	*No more than 3 characters*

Type **Yes** *or* **No**.

Rule 37 C.F.R. 5.2, *states that if an invention has been determined to be a matter of national security, the Commissioner of Patents & Trademarks has the right to keep the invention secret. Under the same rule, applicants are obligated to notify the Office of any related cases which the Commissioner has kept secret.*

Representative Information

*If a Customer Number is not indicated, identify each representative's registration number with separate, consecutive number starting with "**One**". List up to 50 maximum.*

If a Representative Customer Number is supplied, do not provide any individual registration numbers.

Representative Customer Number::	*No more than 9 numbers*
Registration Number One::	*No more than 6 numbers*
Registration Number Two::	*No more than 6 numbers*

Your Customer Number will provide all of the data required under this heading.

If you provide a valid PTO Customer Number here, be certain it is associated with your representative information.

NOTE: For information concerning the Customer Number practice, see the notice "Extension of the Payor Number Practice (Through Customer Numbers) to matters Involving Pending Patent Applications," published in the *Federal Register* at 61 *Fed. Reg.* 54622 (October 21, 1996), and in the *Official Gazette* at 1191 *Off. Gaz Pat. Office* 187 (October 29, 1996).

Continuity Information

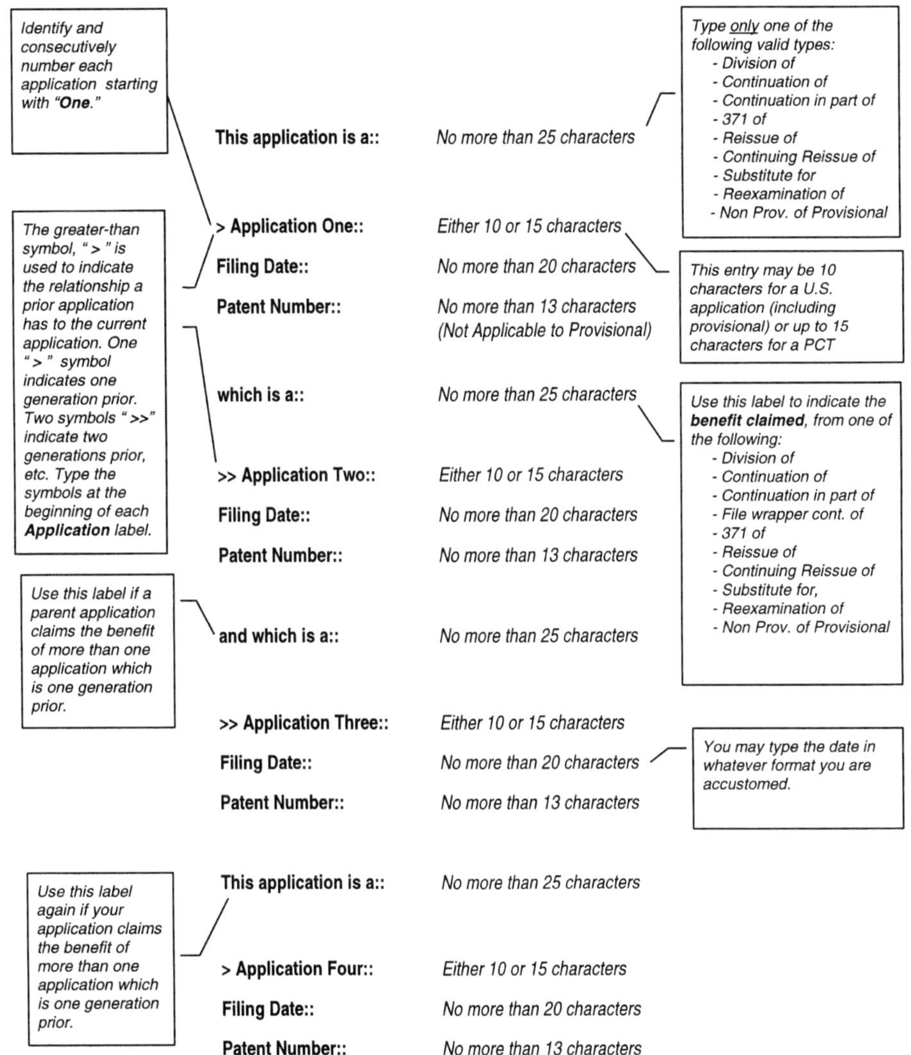

*Identify and consecutively number each application starting with "**One**."*
This application is a::
No more than 25 characters
Type only one of the following valid types:
- Division of
- Continuation of
- Continuation in part of
- 371 of
- Reissue of
- Continuing Reissue of
- Substitute for
- Reexamination of
- Non Prov. of Provisional
*The greater-than symbol, " > " is used to indicate the relationship a prior application has to the current application. One " > " symbol indicates one generation prior. Two symbols " >>" indicate two generations prior, etc. Type the symbols at the beginning of each **Application** label.*
> Application One::
Either 10 or 15 characters
Filing Date::
No more than 20 characters
This entry may be 10 characters for a U.S. application (including provisional) or up to 15 characters for a PCT
Patent Number::
No more than 13 characters (Not Applicable to Provisional)
which is a::
No more than 25 characters
*Use this label to indicate the **benefit claimed**, from one of the following:*
- Division of
- Continuation of
- Continuation in part of
- File wrapper cont. of
- 371 of
- Reissue of
- Continuing Reissue of
- Substitute for,
- Reexamination of
- Non Prov. of Provisional
>> Application Two::
Either 10 or 15 characters
Filing Date::
No more than 20 characters
Patent Number::
No more than 13 characters
Use this label if a parent application claims the benefit of more than one application which is one generation prior.
and which is a::
No more than 25 characters
>> Application Three::
Either 10 or 15 characters
Filing Date::
No more than 20 characters
You may type the date in whatever format you are accustomed.
Patent Number::
No more than 13 characters
Use this label again if your application claims the benefit of more than one application which is one generation prior.
This application is a::
No more than 25 characters
> Application Four::
Either 10 or 15 characters
Filing Date::
No more than 20 characters
Patent Number::
No more than 13 characters

Continuity Information Example

This application is a::	Continuation in Part of
> Application One::	09/456,789
Filing Date::	Aug. 15, 1999
which is a::	Continuation in Part of
>> Application Two::	09/412,345
Filing Date::	April 15, 1999
which is a::	Division of
>>> Application Three::	09/234,567
Filing Date::	December 13, 1989
Patent::	6,456,789
This application is a::	Continuation in Part of
> Application Four::	09/412,348
Filing Date::	March 13,1999
which is a::	Division of
>> Application Five::	09/234,432
Filing Date::	October 22,1998
Patent Number::	6,789,456
and which is a::	Continuation of
>> Application Six::	09/234,100
Filing Date::	June 11,1998

Below is a diagram of the continuity example shown on page 9.

Applications One, Two and Three show one complete line of priority. Application Four begins two additional lines of priority, one completed with Five and the other with Six. Notice that Applications One and Four are linked to the Current Application with the same label, "**This Application is a::**." Notice that Applications Five and Six are linked to Application Four with different labels. Five is linked using "**which is a::**" and Six is linked using "**and which is a::**."

Claiming benefit from a Provisional application is accomplished by indicating Non Prov. of Provisional after the label "**This application is a::**" and indicating the provisional application number following the "**Application _::**" label. An example of claiming priority of a provisional application is included in the attached example 4 below.

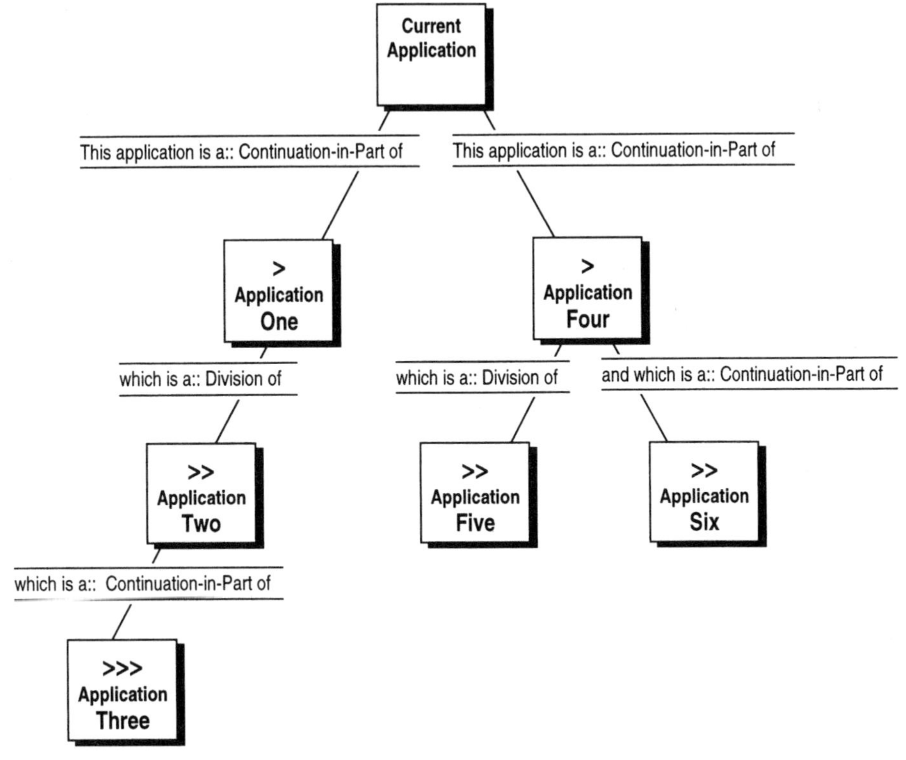

Prior Foreign Applications

*Starting with "**One**" identify each application with separate, consecutive number.*

Foreign Application One::	*No more than 15 characters*
Filing Date::	*No more than 20 characters*
Country::	*No more than 50 characters*
Priority Claimed::	*No more than 3 characters*
Foreign Application Two::	*No more than 15 characters*
Filing Date::	*No more than 20 characters*
Country::	*No more than 50 characters*
Priority Claimed::	*No more than 3 characters*

Type the name of the country.

Type **Yes** *or* **No**.

You may type the date in whatever format you are accustomed.

DATA ENTRY FORMAT EXAMPLES

Initial Information Data Sheet Example 1 (Independent Inventor with Representation)

Inventor Information

Inventor One Given Name::	Maximillian
Family Name::	Katch
Postal Address Line One::	716 My Place
Postal Address Line Two::	Apt. 3
City::	New York
State or Province::	NY
Postal or Zip Code::	10013
Citizenship Country::	USA

Correspondence Information

Name Line One::	Mister Jones & Associates
Address Line One::	875 Busy Avenue
Address Line Two::	Suite 740
City::	New York
State or Province::	NY
Postal or Zip Code::	10012
Telephone::	(212) 555-9283
Fax::	(212) 555-4321

Application Information

Title Line One::	Handling and Eating Utensils for use with
Title Line Two::	Broiled or Sauteed Mussels and other Shellfish
Total Drawing Sheets::	6
Formal Drawings?::	No
Application Type::	Utility

Representative Information

Registration Number One::	99,001
Registration Number Two::	99,412
Registration Number Three::	99,998
Registration Number Four::	99,123

Initial Information Data Sheet Example 2 (Independent Inventors without Representation and one having a different postal address from residence)

```
INVENTOR INFORMATION
Inventor One Given Name::            Mach
Family Name::                        Speed
Name Suffix::                        Sr.
Postal Address Line One::            415 Mappgas St.
City::                               Cleveland
State or Province::                  OH
Postal or Zip Code::                 14343-2363
Citizenship Country::                USA
Inventor Two Given Name::            Ethel
Family Name::                        Propill
Postal Address Line One::            Oberstrasse 17/2a
City::                               Skieff
Country::                            Austria
Postal or Zip Code::                 Zonas 143
City of Residence::                  Akron
State or Prov. Of Residence::        OH
Citizenship Country::                USA

CORRESPONDENCE INFORMATION
Name Line One::                 Mach Speed
Address Line One::              1220 North Long Drag Street
City::                          Cleveland
State or Province::             OH
Postal or Zip Code::            44121
Telephone::                     (123)555-9876
Fax::                           (123)555-1234
Electronic Mail::               gofast.car@post.com

APPLICATION INFORMATION
Title Line One::                Safety belt for a skate board
Total Drawings Sheets::         4
Formal Drawings?::              Yes
Application Type::              utility
Docket Number::                 d-724m/98
```

Initial Information Data Sheet Example 3 (Inventor with Representation)

Inventor Information

Inventor One Given Name:: Les
Family Name:: Brainstrain
Postal Address Line One:: 415 Emcee Square
City:: Lincoln
State or Province:: NE
Postal or Zip Code:: 98765
Citizenship Country:: USA

Correspondence Information

Correspondence Customer Number:: 999,999

Application Information

Title Line One:: Device for Planting and Cultivation of
Title Line Two:: Corn and the Like Type Plants
Total Drawing Sheets:: 14
Formal Drawings?:: Yes
Application Type:: Utility
Docket Number:: 600031-CSC

Representative Information

Registration Number:: 99,221

Continuity Information

This application is a:: Continuation of
>Application One:: 09/912,354
Filing Date:: Jan. 22, 1998

Initial Information Data Sheet Example 4 (Multiple Inventors with Representation, Continuity and Priority)

Inventor Information

Inventor One Given Name:: D. James
Family Name:: Hook
Postal Address Line One:: 1427 Peachpunch Street, N.W.
City:: Atlanta
State or Province:: GA
Postal or Zip Code:: 30329
Citizenship Country:: Canada

Inventor Two Given Name:: Edward
Family Name:: Line
Postal Address Line One:: 427 West Front Street
Postal Address Line Two:: Apartment 32
City:: Detroit
State or Province:: MI
Postal or Zip Code:: 48217
Citizenship Country:: USA

Inventor Three Given Name:: David A. E.
Family Name:: Sinker
Postal Address:: 274 Bradford Lane
City:: Bedford
Country:: England
Postal or Zip Code:: SG19 23B
Citizenship Country:: United Kingdom

Correspondence Information

Name Line One:: Sindey Peck
Name Line Two:: Foghorn & Leghorn
Address Line One:: Suite 400
Address Line Two:: 1062 Featherbrick Street, S.W.
City:: Washington
State or Province:: DC
Postal or Zip Code:: 20013-1694
Telephone One:: (202) 555-6973
Telephone Two:: (301) 555-9283
Fax:: (202) 555-6794
Electronic Mail:: speckLd@eggs.com

Application Information

Title Line One:: Self Regulating Egg Timer Having
Title Line Two:: Continuous Energy Replenishment
Total Drawing Sheets:: 18
Formal Drawings?:: Yes
Application Type:: Utility
Docket Number:: N16

Representative Information

Representative Customer Number:: 999,999

Continuity Information

This application is a:: Non Prov. of Provisional
> Application One:: 60/555,555
Filing Date:: 07-01-97

This application is a:: Continuation-in-Part of
> Application Two:: 09/536,983
Filing Date:: 08-12-97

which is a:: File Wrapper Cont. of
>> Application Three:: 09/346,273
Filing Date:: 04-23-96

which is a:: Divisional of
>>> Application Four:: 09/102,810
Filing Date:: 10-04-1994

Prior Foreign Applications

Foreign Application One:: 4,235,671
Filing Date:: 10-05-93
Country:: Great Britain
Priority Claimed:: Yes

APPENDIX A

Physical Characteristics of Documents Prepared in the Data Entry Format

THE following guidelines have been established to minimize errors in the scanning and text conversion of patent application information.

1. Paper Characteristics

General Requirements

All sheets shall be:

- free from creases and cracks
- not be folded or rolled.
- free from erasures, alterations, and overwriting.
- printed on only one side of each sheet
- originals
- free from staple
- on white, copier or non-impact printer type paper
- printed or typed on in black ink.

Specific Requirements

Paper Size

Required:	8.5 x 11 inch or A4 (210 mm x 297 mm)
Not permitted:	Legal (8.5 x 14 inch) or any other size

2. Typography used in documents

General requirements

The characters should be created with a word processor or typewriter. Hand written characters are not permitted.

Specific requirements

Font/Character size

Recommended: 12 point or larger

Fonts

Recommended: Courier, Arial, Univers

Not Recommended:

OCR-A, OCR-B,

Times New Roman, Gothic

Font Styles and Effects

Permitted: All capitals, upper and lower case, Bold.

Not permitted: Italic, small capitals, single or double underlining, strikeout, no shading or highlighting, reverse or negative printing.

Special Characters

Greek characters, mathematical characters, superscripts and subscripts are not permitted, except in the Title.

NOTE:

- The numeral key "1" should be used for the number "one", and the letter key " l " should be used for the letter "ell."
- The letter key "O" should be used for the letter "O" and the numeral key "0" should be used for the numeric zero.
- The "@" symbol is required in an e-mail address.

3. Document Format

Margins

8.5 x 11 inch paper -
top: 1.25 inch (30 mm)
left side: 1.0 inch (25 mm)
right side: 0.75 inch (20 mm)
bottom: 0.75 inch (20 mm)

A4 paper -
top: 30 mm (1.25 inch)
left side: 25 mm (1.0 inch)
right side: 20 mm (0.75 inch)
bottom: 20 mm (0.75 inch)

Orientation

Required: Portrait - each page will be used in an upright position (i.e., short side at the top and bottom)

Not permitted: Landscape

Line Spacing

No less than single line spacing.

Hyphenation and Word Splitting

Hyphenations are permitted within a line, but not across lines. Word splitting at the end of a line by the use of hyphens is not permitted.

Page Numbering

All sheets shall be numbered in consecutive Arabic numerals. (e.g.: 1, 2, 3) Page numbers shall be located at the bottom center of each page.

Page Justification

All text will be left-justified. Right justification and full justification are not permitted.

4. Other patent data entry sheet guidelines:

- **No** express mail stamps
- **No** extraneous typed or written information
- **No** line numbering
- **No** tables or spreadsheets

APPENDIX B

PTO will send, via Internet Electronic Mail, an acknowledgment letter indicating the Application Number, Mailroom date and Docket Number (if provided) if the e-mail address is indicated on the Data Entry Format sheet. **Note: By providing an Electronic Mail address applicant implicitly authorizes PTO to send the acknowledgment letter but does not authorize PTO to use the Electronic Mail address for any other communication regarding the application.** See the attached example of the acknowledgment letter below.

COURTESY ACKNOWLEDGMENT OF APPLICATION RECEIPT

Application Serial Number: ____________________

Mailroom Date: ____________________

Docket Number: ____________________

Thank you for using the Patent Application Data Entry Format. The above identified application was received by the U.S. Patent and Trademark Office on the above date and has been imaged captured by the Patent Image Capture System. The above date does NOT represent that a filing date has been granted. A filing date receipt will be sent once an initial formalities examination of the application papers has been completed and all required parts of the application needed for granting of a filing date have been found to be present.

Date E-mailed

____

N.B. : This is only a courtesy notice. PTO is under no obligation to send this notice. Failure by PTO to send such notice or non-receipt by applicant(s) shall have NO effect on the rights and/or obligations of either PTO or applicant(s).

Appendix C-35

Guidelines Concerning the Implementation of Changes to 35 U.S.C. 102(g) and 103(c) and the Interpretation of the Term "Original Application" in the American Inventors Protection Act of 1999

On November 29, 1999, the American Inventors Protection Act of 1999 (hereinafter "Act") was enacted.[1] This notice addresses several of the changes created by the Act which do not require rulemaking to implement. First, the Patent and Trademark Office (PTO) is hereby setting forth guidelines to establish its interpretation of the changes made to 35 U.S.C. 102(g) and 103(c). Second, the PTO is hereby setting forth an interpretation of the term "original application" to clarify the application of the Option Inter Partes Reexamination Procedure created in Subtitle F of the Act. Further, this notice instructs patent examiners and the public on how to implement these changes and addresses situations that are anticipated to arise in the future.

An O.G. notice stating the PTO's interpretation of 35 U.S.C. 102(e) as amended by the Act is expected to be published in the near future. The notice will also include guidelines for implementing the amended 102(e) and illustrative examples.

I. Guidelines To Implement Changes in 35 U.S.C. 102(g)

Section 4806 of the Act amended 35 U.S.C. 102(g) to read as follows:

A person shall be entitled to a patent unless-

(g)(1) during the course of an interference conducted under section 135 or section 291, another inventor involved therein establishes, to the extent permitted in section 104, that before such person's invention thereof the invention was made by such other

[1]The American Inventors Protection Act of 1999 is a part of the conference report (H. Rep. 106-479) on H.R. 3194, Consolidated Appropriations Act, Fiscal Year 2000. The text of the American Inventors Protection Act of 1999 is contained in title IV of S. 1948, the Intellectual Property and Communications Omnibus Reform Act of 1999 (Public Law 106-113).

inventor and not abandoned, suppressed or concealed, or (2) before such person's invention thereof, the invention was made in this country by another inventor who had not abandoned, suppressed or concealed it. In determining priority of invention under this subsection, there shall be considered not only the respective dates of conception and reduction to practice of the invention, but also the reasonable diligence of one who was first to conceive and last to reduce to practice, from a time prior to conception by the other.

The effective date of this change to 102(g) is the date of enactment, November 29, 1999. Amended 102(g) will apply to all interference proceedings involving applications pending on November 29, 1999 since this change merely ratifies an existing interpretation of the law. The significant features resulting from this amendment to 102(g) are the following:

(1) Amended 102(g) makes it explicitly clear that a party involved in an interference proceeding under 35 U.S.C. 135 or 291 may establish a date of invention under 104. 35 U.S.C. 104, as amended by GATT (Public Law 103-465, 108 Stat. 4809 (1994)) and NAFTA (Public Law 103-182, 107 Stat. 2057 (1993)), permits a party to establish a date of invention in a NAFTA member country on or after December 8, 1993 or in WTO member country other than a NAFTA member country on or after January 1, 1996.

(2) Apart from interference proceedings under 35 U.S.C. 135(a), and ex parte examination following an interference to enforce the judgment in the interference and the estoppel provisions of 37 CFR 1.658(c) [see also In re Deckler, 977 F.2d 1449, 24 USPQ2d 1448 (Fed. Cir. 1992) (party losing interference is not entitled to claims to same patentable invention as count—based on estoppel) and Ex parte Tytgat, 225 USPQ 907 (Bd. App. 1985) (same)], evidence of a date of invention in a NAFTA or WTO country other than the United States will not be considered prior art under 102(g), as amended.

(3) No change is anticipated in 37 CFR 1.131 practice, which will continue to require diligence until reduction to practice. In re Eickmeyer, 602 F.2d 974, 202 USPQ 655 (CCPA 1979), states that Rule 131 practice is not necessarily controlled by the laws pertaining to interference. In addition, through a Rule 131 affidavit, parties will be able to continue to show evidence of the date of invention in a NAFTA member country and a WTO member country to the extent permitted by 35 U.S.C. 104.

Implementation Steps As to Amended 35 U.S.C. 102(g)

Since the amendment to 102(g) merely ratifies an existing interpretation of the law, no changes in practice are needed.

II. Guidelines To Implement Changes in 35 U.S.C. 103(c)

Section 4807 of the Act amended 35 U.S.C. 103(c) to read as follows:

(c) Subject matter developed by another person, which qualifies as prior art only under one or more of subsections (e), (f), and (g) of section 102 of this title, shall not preclude patentability under this section where the subject matter and the claimed invention were, at the time the invention was made, owned by the same person or subject to an obligation of assignment to the same person.

This change to 103(c) applies to any patent application filed on or after the date of enactment, November 29, 1999. American Inventors Protection Act of 1999, Pub. L. No. 106-113, Sec. 4807(b). This amendment to 103(c) does not apply to any application filed before November 29, 1999, any request for examination under 37 CFR 1.129 of such an application nor any request for continued examination, which is defined in section 4403 of the Act, of such an application. The significant features resulting from this amendment to 103(c) are the following:

(1) Subject matter which was prior art under former 35 U.S.C. 103(c) via 102(e) is now disqualified as prior art against the claimed invention if that subject matter and the claimed invention "were, at the time the invention was made, owned by the same person or subject to an obligation of assignment to the same person."

(2) The mere filing of a continuation application on or after November 29, 1999 will serve to exclude commonly owned 102(e) prior art that was applied, or could have been applied, in a rejection under 103 in the parent application. For reissue applications, the doctrine of recapture may prevent the presentation of claims that were cancelled or amended to overcome such prior art applied in the application which matured into the patent for which reissue is being sought. See (4) below for further explanation.

(3) This amendment applies only to prior art usable in an obviousness rejection under 103. Subject matter that qualifies as anticipatory prior art under 102, including 102(e), is not affected, and may still be used to reject claims as being anticipated.

(4) The recapture doctrine may prevent the presentation of claims in reissue applications that were amended or cancelled from the application which matured into the patent for which reissue is being sought, if the claims were amended or cancelled to distinguish the claimed invention from 102(e)/103 prior art which was commonly owned or assigned at the time the invention was made.

(5) The burden of establishing that subject matter is disqualified as prior art is placed on the patent applicants once the patent examiners have established a prima facie case of obviousness based on the subject matter.

(6) Nonstatutory and statutory double patenting rejections, based on subject matter now disqualified as prior art in amended 103(c), may still be made by patent examiners.

Implementation Steps As to Amended 35 U.S.C. 103(c)

A. Applications To Be Considered.

(1) The amendment of 103(c) "... shall apply to any application for patent filed on or after the date of enactment of this Act," which is November 29, 1999. Therefore, amended 103(c) will be applied to all utility, design and plant patent applications filed on or after November 29, 1999, including continuing applications filed under 37 CFR 1.53(b), continued prosecution applications filed under 37 CFR 1.53(d) and reissues. Reexaminations proceedings are not "any application for patent." Therefore, this amendment to 103(c) does not apply to reexamination proceedings.

(2) Amended 103(c) does not affect any application filed before November 29, 1999, a request for examination under 37 CFR 1.129(a) of such an application nor a request for continued examination (defined in section 4403 of the Act) of such an application.

B. Examination Procedure with respect to amended 103(c).

(1) Examiners are encouraged to check the assignment records, which are available on the Patent Application Locating and Monitoring (PALM) system, for the patents and applications involved in any rejection to see if there is a possible common owner or assignee with the application being examined. Since examiners should always apply potentially commonly owned or assigned prior art, the review of assignment records is only to indicate to the examiner whether making one or more appropriate back up rejections should be considered. The assignment records on PALM show the execution date of any recorded assignment. Since applicants are not required to record assignments, however, these records are not the exclusive means to determine whether there was common ownership at the time the invention was made. In addition, the Office records other papers, such as employment contracts, which are not evidence of common ownership. Therefore, the examiners should be careful to refer to the box labeled "Brief" on the bottom of the PALM screen which provides a brief description of the paper recorded as

stated by the applicant. Examiners should not fail to apply a reference believed to be commonly owned at the time of the invention based only upon the data in PALM. The assignment information in PALM, however, may give an examiner a warning that a reference may be disqualified by the applicant in the future.

(2) Applications and patents will be considered by the examiner to be owned by, or subject to an obligation of assignment to, the same person, at the time the invention was made, if:

(a) the applicant provides evidence that the application and patent files refer to assignments recorded in the PTO in accordance with 37 CFR 3.11 which convey the entire rights in the applications to the same person(s) or organization(s) at the time of the invention;

(b) copies of unrecorded assignments which convey the entire rights in the applications to the same person(s) or organization(s) at the time of the invention are filed in each of the applications and patents;

(c) an affidavit or declaration by the common owner is filed which states that there was common ownership at the time the invention was made and explains why the affiant believes there was common ownership; or

(d) other evidence is submitted which establishes common ownership of the applications and patents at the time the invention was made, e.g., a court decision determining the owner. In circumstances where the common owner is a corporation or other organization, an affidavit or declaration averring ownership may be signed by an official of the corporation or organization empowered to act on behalf of the corporation or organization.

(3) If the application file being examined does not establish that it and the reference patent(s) or application(s) are owned by, or subject to an obligation of assignment to, the same person, at the time the invention was made, the examiner will:

(a) assume the application(s) and patent(s) are not commonly owned;

(b) examine the application on all grounds other than any conflict between the reference patent(s) or application(s) arising from a possible 103 rejection based on 102(e), (f) and/or (g);

(c) consider the applicability of any references under 103 based on 102(e), (f) and/or (g), including provisional rejections under 35 U.S.C. 102(e)/103; and

(d) apply the best references against the claimed invention by making rejections under 102 and 103, including any rejections under 103 based on 102(e), (f) and/or (g), until such time that proof is submitted that the application(s) and patent(s) were commonly owned, at the time the invention was made (see (2) above). When applying any 102(e)/103 references against the claims, the examiner should anticipate that an affidavit (or other adequate proof) averring common ownership at the time the invention was made may disqualify any patent or application applied in a rejection under 103 based on 102(e). If such an affidavit (or other adequate proof) is filed in reply to the 102(e)/103 rejection and the claims are not amended, the examiner may not make the next Office action final if a new rejection is made.

(4) If the application being examined establishes that it and any reference patent or application were owned by, or subject to an obligation of assignment to, the same person, at the time the invention was made, the examiner will:

(a) examine the applications as to all grounds except 102(e), (f) and (g) as they apply through 103, including provisional rejections under 35 U.S.C. 102(e)/103;

(b) examine the applications for double patenting, including statutory and nonstatutory double patenting, and make a provisional rejection, if appropriate; and

(c) invite the applicant to file a terminal disclaimer to overcome any provisional or actual nonstatutory double patenting rejection, if appropriate.

III. Interpretation of the Term "Original Application" to Clarify the Application of the Optional Inter Partes Reexamination Procedure

Section 4608 of the Act states the effective date and applicability of the Optional Inter Partes Reexamination Procedure established by Subtitle F of the Act. Specifically, Section 4608 states that the changes in Subtitle F " . . . shall take effect on the date of enactment of this Act and shall apply to any patent that issues from an original application filed in the United States on or after that date."

The phrase "original application" is interpreted to encompass utility, plant and design applications, including first filed applications, continuations, divisionals, continuations-in-part, continued prosecution applications (CPAs) and the national stage phase of international applications. This interpretation is consistent with the use of the phrase in 35 U.S.C. 251 and the federal rules pertaining to reexamination. In addition, section 201.04(a) of the Manual of Patent Examination and Procedure (MPEP) defines an original application as " . . . an application which is not a reissue application." Section 201.04(a) of the MPEP further states that "[a]n original application may be a first filing or a continuing application." Therefore, the Optional Inter Partes Reexamination Procedure is applicable to patents which issue from all applications (except for reissues) filed on or after November 29, 1999. A patent which issued from an application filed prior to November 29, 1999 with a request for continued examination (defined in section 4403 of the Act) on or after May 29, 2000, however, is not eligible for the Optional Inter Partes Reexamination Procedure. A request for continued examination is not considered a filing of an application.

FOR FURTHER INFORMATION CONTACT: Jeanne Clark or Robert Clarke, Legal Advisors in the Special Program Law Office, by telephone at (703) 305-1622, by fax at (703) 305-1013, or by e-mail addressed to Jeanne.Clarke@USPTO.gov. or Robert.Clarke@USPTO.gov.

Stephen G. Kunin
Deputy Assistant Commissioner
for Patent Policy and Projects

Appendix C-36

Supplemental Examination Guidelines for Determining the Applicability of 35 U.S.C. §112, ¶6

1236 OG 98
July 25, 2000

DEPARTMENT OF COMMERCE

United States Patent and Trademark Office
RIN 0651-AB23

Supplemental Examination Guidelines for Determining the Applicability of 35 U.S.C. §112, ¶6

Agency: United States Patent and Trademark Office, Commerce

Action: Notice

Summary: The U.S. Patent and Trademark Office (USPTO) is publishing the final supplemental examination guidelines to be used by Office personnel in their review of patent applications to determine (1) whether a claim limitation invokes 35 U.S.C. §112, ¶6, and (2) whether the written description describes adequate corresponding structure, material, or acts needed to support a claim limitation under 35 U.S.C. §112, ¶6. Because these supplemental examination guidelines are interpretive rules and general statements of policy, they are exempt from notice and comments rulemaking under 5 U.S.C. §553(b)(A).

Dates: The supplemental examination guidelines are effective June 21, 2000.

For Further Information Contact: Magdalen Greenlief, by mail addressed to Box Comments, Commissioner for Patents, Washington, DC 20231, or Ray Chen, Office of the Solicitor, P.O. Box 15667, Arlington, Virginia 22215, or by facsimile transmission to (703) 305-8825, or by electronic mail at *magdalen.greenlief@uspto.gov* or *ray.chen@uspto.gov*.

Supplementary Information: The USPTO published "Interim Supplemental Examination Guidelines for Determining the Applicability of 35 U.S.C. §112 ¶6" in the Federal Register on July 30, 1999, at 64 FR 41392, requesting comments from the public on the supplemental examination guidelines. The interim supplemental examination guidelines are adopted with modifications as suggested by some of the commentors noted below. In particular, (1) a statement has been added to the supplemental examination guidelines to clearly state that the guidelines do not constitute substantive rulemaking and hence do not have the force and effect of law, (2) the third prong of the 3-prong analysis for determining whether a claim limitation invokes 35 U.S.C. §112, ¶6 has been modified to indicate that the phrase "means for" or "step for" must not be modified by sufficient structure, material, or acts for achieving the specified function, and (3) the last step of the process for making a *prima facie* case of equivalence of a prior art element during *ex parte* examination has been modified to state that where the examiner finds that the prior art element is an equivalent of the means-(or step-) plus-function limitation, the examiner should provide an explanation and rationale as to why the prior art element is an equivalent.

Discussion of Public Comments

Comments were received by the USPTO from three individuals, two bar associations, one law firm and one corporation in response to the request for comments on the interim supplemental examination guidelines. All comments have been fully considered. One comment was directed to Markush-type claims which is not germane to the subject matter addressed in these guidelines and thus, a response has not been included in the discussion below. One comment indicated that the supplemental examination guidelines will work well since under the supplemental examination guidelines applicants can clearly invoke or not invoke 35 U.S.C. §112, ¶6 and examiners can clearly determine whether or not 35 U.S.C. §112, ¶6 has been invoked. Other comments generally supported the 3-prong analysis, but with certain modifications.

Comment 1: One comment indicated that it is not clear whether the guidelines are interpretative and without force of law, or are intended to be rules or regulations (or their equivalent) issued under 35 U.S.C. §6 and having the force of law. The commentor suggested that a specific statement be made as to the intent of the Office.

Response: The suggestion has been adopted. As stated in the "Supplementary Information" portion of the interim supplemental examination guidelines, these supplemental examination guidelines are interpretative rules and general statements of policy, and therefore, are exempt from notice and comment rulemaking under 5 U.S.C. 553(b)(A). The USPTO will further include a statement in the body of the guidelines to clearly state that the guidelines do not constitute substantive rulemaking and hence do not have the force and effect of law.

Comment 2: One comment stated that the proposed guidelines put a great deal of emphasis on form over substance since a "means" is a means whether one uses that word or not.

Response: The Federal Circuit has stated that when an element of a claim does not use the term "means," treatment as a means-plus-function claim element is generally not appropriate. *See Kemco Sales, Inc. v. Control Papers Co.*, 54 USPQ2d 1308, 1313 (Fed. Cir. 2000) ("absence of the word 'means' creates a presumption that section 112, paragraph 6 has not been invoked"), *Al-Site Corp. v. VSI Int'l, Inc.*, 174 F.3d 1308, 1318, 50 USPQ2d 1161, 1166 (Fed. Cir. 1999) ("when an element of a claim does not use the term 'means,' treatment as a means-plus-function claim element is generally not appropriate"), *Mas-Hamilton Group v. LaGard, Inc.*, 156 F.3d 1206, 1213–15, 48 USPQ2d 1010, 1016–18 (Fed. Cir. 1998), and *Greenberg v. Ethicon Endo-Surgery Inc.*, 91 F.3d 1580, 1584, 39 USPQ2d 1783, 1787 (Fed. Cir. 1996) ("use of the term 'means' (particularly as used in the phrase 'means for') generally invokes section 112(6) and that the use of a different formulation generally does not"). Even if the term "means" was used, the Federal Circuit has held, in certain circumstances, that the claim limitation does not invoke 35 U.S.C. §112, ¶6. *See Rodime PLC v. Seagate Tech., Inc.*, 174 F.3d 1294, 1303–04, 50 USPQ2d 1429, 1435–36 (Fed. Cir. 1999) (holding "positioning means for moving" does not invoke 35 U.S.C. §112, ¶6), and *Cole v. Kimberly-Clark Corp.*, 102 F.3d 524, 530–31, 41 USPQ2d 1001, 1006 (Fed. Cir. 1996) (claim limitation "perforation means for tearing" does not invoke 35 U.S.C. §112, ¶6). The supplemental examination guidelines provide applicants with a simple method for clearly stating their intent to invoke 35 U.S.C. §112, ¶6. The specific phraseology used by the applicant in a claim limitation will determine whether the claim limitation invokes 35 U.S.C. §112, ¶6. Furthermore, by following the plain language of the statute, the language employed in the patent claim(s) will place the public on notice whether a claim limitation invokes 35 U.S.C. §112, ¶6.

Comment 3: One comment stated that the guidelines are contrary to statute and to the court interpretations of the statute since the Federal Circuit has expressly held that a claim is to be interpreted as under 35 U.S.C. §112, ¶6 even if the word "means" is not used as long as there is an object disclosed (i.e., a means) coupled with a function (citing *Raytheon Co. v. Roper Corp.*, 724 F.2d 951, 220 USPQ 592 (Fed. Cir. 1983)).

Response: The USPTO believes that the supplemental examination guidelines are consistent with the statute and controlling precedent. As noted by the Federal Circuit in *Ethicon Inc. v. United States Surgical Corp.*, 135 F.3d 1456, 1463, 45 USPQ2d 1545, 1550 (Fed. Cir. 1998), *cert. denied*, 525 U.S. 923 (1998), "use of the word 'means' gives rise to a 'presumption that the inventor used the term advisedly to invoke the statutory mandates for means-plus-function clauses.' " See also J. Rader's concurring opinion in *Seal-Flex. Inc. v. Athletic Track and Court Constr.*, 172 F.3d 836, 849–50, 50 USPQ2d 1225, 1233–34 (Fed. Cir. 1999), stating that use of the phrase "step for" in a method claim raises a presumption that 35 U.S.C. §112, ¶6 applies, whereas, use of the word "step" by itself or the phrase "step of" does not invoke a presumption that 35 U.S.C. §112, ¶6 applies. Because the scope of a claim limitation that invokes 35 U.S.C. §112, ¶6 is actually more limited than a claim limitation stated in structural terms, the Office wants to avoid inadvertent invocations of 35 U.S.C. §112, ¶6. *Cf. Kemco Sales, Inc. v. Control Papers Co.*, 54 USPQ2d 1308, 1316 (Fed. Cir. 2000) (where sealing of a flap inside an envelope pocket was not equivalent to sealing it outside the pocket). If a claim limitation does not include the phrase "means for" or "step for," the examiner will not treat that claim limitation as invoking 35 U.S.C. §112, ¶6. As noted in the supplemental examination guidelines, if applicant wants that claim limitation to be subject to the provisions of 35 U.S.C. §112, ¶6, applicant may do so by following the options set forth in the explanation portion of the first prong of the 3-prong analysis. By providing applicant with the option of making a showing that even though the phrase is not used, the claim limitation should be treated under 35 U.S.C. §112, ¶6 since it is written as a function to be performed and does not recite sufficient structure, material, or acts to perform the claimed function, these supplemental examination guidelines are consistent with the Federal Circuit's interpretation of 35 U.S.C. §112, ¶6.

Comment 4: One comment suggested that to permit a claim drafter who does not use the phrase "means for" or "step for" to make a showing that the claim limitation should still be treated under 35 U.S.C. §112, ¶6, rather than amending the claim to include the "means for" or "step for" phrase, is unwise. The commentor suggested that the USPTO promulgate a rule to always require the use of the phrase "means for" or "step for" if applicant wishes to have a claim limitation be treated under 35 U.S.C. §112, ¶6. The commentor further stated that it is more important to have a clear and unambiguous, easily administered, bright-line rule for claim interpretation than it is to have the rule fine-tuned for tolerating all conceivable caprice in claim drafting.

Response: The suggestion has not been adopted. To promulgate a rule to always require applicant to use the phrase "means for" or "step for" in order to invoke 35 U.S.C. §112, ¶6 without providing applicant with an option to make a showing that even though the phrase is not used, the claim limitation should be treated under 35 U.S.C. §112, ¶6 since it is written as a function to be performed and does not recite sufficient structure, material, or acts to perform the claimed function would be inconsistent with the Federal Circuit's interpretation of 35 U.S.C. §112, ¶6. *See, e.g., Mas-Hamilton Group v. LaGard, Inc.*, 156 F.3d 1206, 1213–14, 48 USPQ2d 1010, 1016–17 (Fed. Cir. 1998) ("lever moving element for moving the lever" and "movable link member for holding the lever and for releasing the lever" were construed as means-plus-function limitations invoking 35 U.S.C. §112, ¶6).

Comment 5: One comment suggested that examiners should be instructed not to require that "means for" or "step for" language be used since applicants should be able to decide what language they choose to use in a claim.

Response: The suggestion has not been adopted. The USPTO wants to provide reasonable certainty that 35 U.S.C. §112, ¶6 is not invoked unless applicant wants the claim limitation to be subject to that provision. To avoid inadvertent invocations of 35 U.S.C. §112, ¶6, the supplemental examination guidelines set forth a 3-prong analysis which must be met before a claim limitation is treated under 35 U.S.C. §112, ¶6. As noted in the supplemental examination guidelines, a claim limitation that does not include the phrase "means for" or "step for" will not be treated by the examiner as invoking the provisions of 35 U.S.C. §112, ¶6. In such a case, the examiner will apply prior art to the claim limitation without the invocation of 35 U.S.C. §112, ¶6. In reply to the examiner's Office action, if applicant wishes to have the claim limitation treated under 35 U.S.C. §112, ¶6, applicant has the option to either amend the claim to include the phrase "means for" or "step for" or to make a showing that even though the phrase "means for" or "step for" is not used, the claim limitation is written as a function to be performed and does not recite sufficient structure, material, or acts to perform the claimed function. If applicant does not wish to use the phrase "means for" or "step for," under the supplemental examination guidelines, applicant must show that even though the phrase "means for" or "step for" is not used, the claim limitation is written as a function to be performed and does not recite sufficient structure, material, or acts for performing those functions. *See Al-Site Corp. v. VSI Int'l, Inc.*, 174 F.3d 1308, 1318, 50 USPQ2d 1161, 1166–67 (Fed. Cir. 1999) (although the claim limitations "eyeglass hanger member" and "eyeglass contacting member" include a function, these claim limitations do not invoke 35 U.S.C. §112, ¶6 because the claims themselves contain sufficient structural limitations for performing those functions).

Comment 6: Two comments indicated that the presence of some structure should not prevent the invocation of the provisions of 35 U.S.C. §112, ¶6. The commentors suggested that the third prong of the 3-prong analysis be modified to read that "the phrase 'means for' or 'step for' must not be modified by sufficient structure, material, or acts for achieving the claimed function," citing *Seal-Flex, Inc. v. Athletic Track and Court Constr.*, 172 F.3d 836, 50 USPQ2d 1225 (Fed. Cir. 1999), and *Unidynamics Corp. v. Automatic Prod. Int'l*, 157 F.3d 1311, 48 USPQ2d 1099 (Fed. Cir. 1998).

Response: A review of the case law indicates that the recitation of some structure in means-(or step-) plus-function element does not preclude the applicability of 35 U.S.C. §112, ¶6 when the structure merely serves to further specify the function of that means. *See Laitram Corp. v. Rexnord, Inc.*, 939 F.2d 1533, 1536, 19 USPQ2d 1367, 1369 (Fed. Cir. 1991). Therefore, the suggestion has been adopted to this extent.

Comment 7: One comment suggested that the guidelines be clarified to indicate what happens if the applicant neither amends the claim to include the phrase "means for" or "step for" nor makes a showing but stands firm on the claim that the applicant initially presented and insists that 35 U.S.C. §112, ¶6 authorizes the claim. The commentor indicated that explanation of this point will benefit the applicants and the examiners.

Response: If a claim limitation does not include the phrase "means for" or "step for," the claim limitation will not be treated by the examiner as invoking the provisions of 35 U.S.C. §112, ¶6. The examiner in such case will apply prior art to the claim limitation without the invocation of 35 U.S.C. §112, ¶6. In reply to the examiner's Office action, if applicant either refuses to amend the claim to include the phrase "means for" or "step for" or refuses to make a showing that even though the phrase "means for" or "step for" is not used, the claim limitation is written as a function to be performed and does not recite sufficient structure, material, or acts to perform the claimed function, the next Office action may be made final in accordance with the practice of making a second or subsequent action final (see MPEP 706.07(a)). Applicant may appeal the examiner's rejection to the Board of Patent Appeals and Interferences pursuant to 35 U.S.C. §134.

Comment 8: One comment suggested that the examining corps should be encouraged, and preferably required, to include a statement regarding 35 U.S.C. §112, ¶6 in all Office actions where appropriate so that applicants may agree with or argue against the examiner's position.

Response: The suggestion is adopted in part. In those instances where a claim limitation meets the 3-prong analysis as set forth in the supplemental examination guidelines and is being treated under 35 U.S.C. §112, ¶6, the examiner will include a statement in the Office action that the claim limitation is being treated under 35 U.S.C. §112, ¶6. However, if a claim limitation does not use the phrase "means for" or "step for," that is, the first prong of the 3-prong analysis is not met, the examiner will not treat such a claim limitation under 35 U.S.C. §112, ¶6. It will not be necessary to state in the Office action that 35 U.S.C. §112, ¶6 has not been invoked, since the presumption is that applicant did not intend to invoke the provisions of 35 U.S.C. §112, ¶6 because applicant did not use the specific phrase "means for" or "step for." If a claim limitation does include the phrase "means for" or "step for," that is, the first prong of the 3-prong analysis is met, but the examiner determines that either the second prong or the third prong of the 3-prong analysis is not met, then in these instances, the examiner must include a statement in the Office action explaining the reasons why a claim limitation which uses the phrase "means for" or "step for" is not being treated under 35 U.S.C. §112, ¶6.

Comment 9: One comment suggested that 35 U.S.C. §112, ¶6 was not intended to address functional language used for mere background and away from the point of novelty and that the Federal Circuit has not directly addressed the use of functional language other than when it occurs at the point of novelty. The commentor stated that examiners need not go through the 3-prong analysis where the functional claiming language is not at the point of novelty since 35 U.S.C. §112, ¶6 does not apply to such claim limitations. The commentor further stated that rejection for failure to use the "means for" or "step for" language of 35 U.S.C. §112, ¶6 would be proper for, and only for, a claim to subject matter that Congress intended 35 U.S.C. §112, ¶6 to address (at the point of novelty). The commentor suggested that the guidelines be modified accordingly.

Response: The suggestion has not been adopted. In a recent decision, *Clearstream Wastewater Sys., Inc. v. Hydro-Action, Inc.*, 54 USPQ2d 1185, 1188–90 (Fed. Cir. 2000), the Federal Circuit held that the district court erred in concluding that the means limitations for the aerating system could only cover new elements of the preferred embodiment. The means-plus-function limitation was "means for aerating." The written description disclosed both a new and inventive flexible-hose structure and a prior art, rigid-conduit structure as corresponding structures for performing the claimed function. The Federal Circuit read the means-plus-function terms for the aerating system in the claims as being capable of covering the old, rigid-conduit system as well as the new, flexible-hose system. Furthermore, it is noted that examiners do not reject a claim for failure to use the "means for" or "step for" language of 35 U.S.C. §112, ¶6. There is no statutory basis for such a rejection. If a claim limitation does not include the phrase "means for" or "step for," the presumption is that applicant did not intend to invoke 35 U.S.C. §112, ¶6 and the examiner will not treat the claim limitation under 35 U.S.C. §112, ¶6.

Comment 10: One comment stated that where the examiner has concluded that one skilled in the art would recognize what structure, material, or acts perform the function, it does not make sense to require that the applicant amend the specification to expressly recite what corresponding structure, material, or acts perform the function recited in a claim element. Furthermore, the commentor finds it even more troubling to have the examiner, at his option, state on the record what structure, material, or acts perform the claimed function since there is a danger of unfairly limiting the scope of the claims.

Response: The USPTO disagrees with the comment. In *B. Braun Medical, Inc. v. Abbott Lab.*, 124 F.3d 1419, 1424, 43 USPQ2d 1896, 1900 (Fed. Cir. 1997) the Federal Circuit stated that "structure disclosed in the specification is 'corresponding' structure only if the specification or prosecution history clearly links or associates that structure to the function recited in the claim. This duty to link or associate structure to function is the quid pro quo for the convenience of employing Section 112, Para. 6." It is important to have a clear prosecution history file record. See *Warner-Jenkinson Co. v. Hilton Davis Chem. Co.*, 520 U.S. 17, 41 USPQ2d 1865 (1997); *York Prods., Inc. v. Central Tractor Farm & Family Ctr.*, 99 F.3d 1568, 1575, 40 USPQ2d 1619, 1624 (Fed. Cir. 1996) ("the record before the Patent and Trademark Office is often of critical significance in determining the meaning of the claims"). 35 U.S.C. §112, ¶6 states that "[a]n element in a claim for a combination may be expressed as a means or step for performing a specified function without the recital of structure, material, or acts in support thereof, and such claim shall be construed to cover the corresponding structure, material, or acts *described in the specification* and equivalents thereof" (emphasis added). If the disclosure implicitly sets forth the structure, material, or acts corresponding to a means-(or step-) plus-function claim limitation and the examiner concludes that one skilled in the art would recognize what structure, material, or acts perform the claimed function, the examiner may still require applicant, pursuant to 37 CFR 1.75 (d)(1), to clarify the record by amending the written description such that it expressly recites what structure, material, or acts perform the claimed function. If applicant chooses not to amend the written description to clarify the record, it is incumbent upon the examiner in exercising his or her responsibility to see that the file history is as complete as is reasonably possible. The examiner may do so by stating on the record what structure, material, or acts perform the function recited in the means-plus-function limitation. If applicant disagrees with the examiner's statement, applicant has the obligation to clarify the record by submitting a reply explaining the reasons why applicant disagrees with the statement made by the examiner.

Comment 11: One comment stated that "[t]o use the convenience of functional claim elements under Section 112(6), an applicant, therefore, must explicitly describe and link structure within the specification with the corresponding functional claim element." The commentor further stated that the USPTO's reliance on the very fact specific decision of *In re Dossel*, to permit applicant to implicitly set forth the structure corresponding to a means-plus-function limitation in the written description, is misplaced. The commentor suggested that the guidelines be modified to state that where the written description only implicitly or inherently sets forth the structure, material, or acts corresponding to a means-(or step-) plus-function, the examiner must require applicant to explicitly describe or link a structure within the specification to the corresponding functional claim element.

Response: The comment has not been adopted. In a recent decision, *Atmel Corp. v. Information Storage Devices Inc.*, 198 F.3d 1374, 1379, 53 USPQ2d 1225, 1228 (Fed. Cir. 1999), the Federal Circuit stated that "the 'one skilled in the art' mode of analysis applies with equal force when determining whether a §112 ¶6 means-plus-function limitation is sufficiently definite under §112 ¶2." The court further stated that the interim supplemental examination guidelines published by the USPTO, which stated that the "disclosure of structure corresponding to a means-plus-function limitation may be implicit in the written description *if it would have been clear to those skilled in the art* what structure must perform the function recited in the means-plus-function limitation," is consistent with the court's holding in the case. In order to make the file record clear, the examiner should, pursuant to 37 CFR 1.75(d)(1), require applicant to amend the written description to expressly recite what structure, material, or acts perform the function recited in the claim or the examiner could state on the record what structure, material, or acts perform the function recited in the claim.

Comment 12: One comment was directed to the process for making a prima facie case of equivalence of a prior art element. The commentor stated that even though this process is not superseded by these interim supplemental guidelines, the commentor is of the opinion that the process is inconsistent with the Federal Circuit ruling in *In re Donaldson*, 16 F.3d 1189, 29 USPQ2d 1845 (Fed. Cir. 1994). In particular, the guidelines state that if the examiner finds that the prior art element performs the claimed function and is not excluded by any explicit definition provided in the specification for an equivalent, the examiner has met the prima facie case of equivalence. The commentor stated that this amounts to ignoring the means disclosed in the specification contrary to *Donaldson*. The commentor suggested that the test for equivalents should be modified to require the examiner to provide a rationale for why the prior art element is an equivalent to the claimed means since such a rationale is necessary in order to make out a *prima facie* case of equivalence.

Response: The comment has been adopted. The supplemental examination guidelines have been modified to state that if the examiner finds that (1) a prior art element performs the claimed function, (2) the prior art element is not excluded by any explicit definition provided in the specification for an equivalent, and (3) the prior art element is an equivalent, the examiner should provide an explanation and rationale in the Office action as to why the prior art element is an equivalent to the claimed means. Factors that will support a conclusion that the prior art element is an equivalent are:

(1) the prior art element performs the identical function specified in the claim in substantially the same way, and produces substantially the same results as the corresponding element disclosed in the specification. *Odetics, Inc. v. Storage Tech. Corp.*, 185 F.3d 1259, 1267, 51 USPQ2d 1225, 1229–30 (Fed. Cir. 1999);

(2) a person of ordinary skill in the art would have recognized the interchangeability of the element shown in the prior art for the corresponding element disclosed in the specification. *Al-Site Corp. v. VSI Int'l, Inc.*, 174 F.3d 1308, 1316, 50 USPQ2d 1161, 1165 (Fed. Cir. 1999); *Chiuminatta Concrete Concepts, Inc. v. Cardinal Indus.*, 145 F.3d 1303, 1309, 46 USPQ2d 1752, 1757 (Fed. Cir. 1998); *Lockheed Aircraft Corp. v. United States*, 553 F.2d 69, 83, 193 USPQ 449, 461 (Ct. Cl. 1977);

(3) there are insubstantial differences between the prior art element and the corresponding element disclosed in the specification. *IMS Tech., Inc. v. Haas Automation, Inc.*, 206 F.3d 1422, 1436, 54 USPQ2d 1129, 1138 (Fed. Cir. 2000); *Valmont Indus. v. Reinke Mfg. Co.*, 983 F.2d 1039, 1043, 25 USPQ2d 1451, 1455 (Fed. Cir. 1993);

(4) the prior art element is a structural equivalent of the corresponding element disclosed in the specification. *In re Bond*, 910 F.2d 831, 833, 15 USPQ2d 1566, 1568 (Fed. Cir. 1990).

A showing of at least one of the above-noted factors by the examiner should be sufficient to support a conclusion that the prior art element is an equivalent of the means-(or step-) plus-function limitation. The examiner should then conclude that the claimed limitation is met by the prior art element. In addition to the conclusion that the prior art element is an equivalent, examiners should also demonstrate, where appropriate, why it would have been obvious to one of ordinary skill in the art at the time of the invention to substitute applicant's described structure, material, or acts for that described in the prior art reference. *See In re Brown*, 459 F.2d 531, 535, 173 USPQ 685, 688 (CCPA 1972). The burden then shifts to applicant to show that the prior art element is not an equivalent of the structure, material, or acts disclosed in the application. *See In re Mulder*, 716 F.2d 1542, 1549, 219 USPQ 189, 196 (Fed. Cir. 1983). This three-step process is consistent with the requirement that the USPTO gives claims their broadest reasonable interpretation. *See In re Donaldson Co.*, 16 F.3d 1189, 1194, 29 USPQ2d 1845, 1850 (Fed. Cir. 1994) (stating that 35 U.S.C. §112, ¶6 "merely sets a limit on how broadly the PTO may construe means-plus-function language under the rubric of 'reasonable interpretation'"). The USPTO believes that this three-step process for making a *prima facie* case of equivalence is consistent with binding precedent of the Federal Circuit.

Comment 13: One comment stated the USPTO does not have the authority to alter substantive law, and thus, the USPTO must either go to the Supreme Court or to Congress to obtain an amendment to 35 U.S.C. §112, ¶6.

Response: The suggestion has not been adopted. As noted in the response to comment 12 above, the USPTO believes that these supplemental examination guidelines are consistent with the Federal Circuit's interpretation of 35 U.S.C. §112, ¶6.

I. Supplemental Examination Guidelines for Claims Subject to 35 U.S.C. §112, ¶6

In February 1994, the Court of Appeals for the Federal Circuit (Federal Circuit) held in an en banc decision that "the 'broadest reasonable interpretation' that an examiner may give means-plus-function language is that statutorily mandated in [35 U.S.C. §112, ¶6] . . . [T]he PTO may not disregard the structure disclosed in the specification corresponding to such language when rendering a patentability determination." *In re Donaldson Co.*, 16 F.3d 1189, 1194–95, 29 USPQ2d 1845, 1850 (Fed. Cir. 1994) (en banc). In May 1994, the United States Patent and Trademark Office (USPTO) issued guidelines implementing changes in examination practice in response to *Donaldson. See Means or Step Plus Function Limitation Under 35 U.S.C. §112, ¶6*; Notice, 1162 *Off. Gaz. Pat. Office* 59 (May 17, 1994) ("1994 Guidelines").

The 1994 Guidelines note that there is no "magic" language that invokes 35 U.S.C. §112, ¶6.[1] However, to establish uniformity to the extent possible, in view of the recent case law, and to make the prosecution record clearer, these guidelines supplement the 1994 Guidelines in assisting examiners to determine when 35 U.S.C. §112, ¶6 should be applied. To the extent these supplemental guidelines are inconsistent with the 1994 Guidelines, the supplemental guidelines are controlling.

These supplemental examination guidelines are based on the Office's current understanding of the law and are believed to be fully consistent with binding precedent of the Supreme Court, the Federal Circuit and the Federal Circuit's predecessor courts. These supplemental examination guidelines do not constitute substantive rulemaking and hence do not have the force and effect of law.

The USPTO must apply 35 U.S.C. §112, ¶6 in appropriate cases, and give claims their broadest reasonable interpretation, in light of and consistent with the written description of the invention in the application.[2] Thus, a claim limitation will be interpreted to invoke 35 U.S.C. §112, ¶6 if it meets the following 3-prong analysis:

---

[1] *See* 1994 Guidelines at 59.

[2] *See In re Donaldson Co.*, 16 F.3d 1189, 1194, 29 USPQ2d 1845, 1850 (Fed. Cir. 1994) (in banc) (stating that 35 U.S.C. §112, ¶6 "merely sets a limit on how broadly the PTO may construe means-plus-function language under the rubric of 'reasonable interpretation'"). The Federal Circuit has held that applicants (and reexamination patentees) before the USPTO have the opportunity and the obligation to define their inventions precisely during proceedings before the PTO. *See In re Morris*, 127 F.3d 1048, 1056–57, 44 USPQ2d 1023, 1029–30 (Fed. Cir. 1997) (35 U.S.C. §112, ¶2 places the burden of precise claim drafting on the applicant); *In re Zletz*, 893 F.2d 319, 322, 13 USPQ2d 1320, 1322 (Fed. Cir. 1989) (manner of claim interpretation that is used by courts in litigation is not the manner of claim interpretation that is applicable during prosecution of a pending application before the PTO); *Sage Prods., Inc. v. Devon Indus., Inc.*, 126 F.3d 1420, 1425, 44 USPQ2d 1103, 1107 (Fed. Cir. 1997) (patentee who had a clear opportunity to negotiate broader claims during prosecution but did not do so, may not seek to expand the claims through the doctrine of equivalents, for it is the patentee, not the public, who must bear the cost of its failure to seek protection for this foreseeable alteration of its claimed structure). Thus, applicants and reexamination patentees before the USPTO have an opportunity and obligation to specify, consistent with these supplemental guidelines, when a claim limitation invokes 35 U.S.C. §112, ¶6.

(1) the claim limitations must use the phrase "means for" or "step for";[3]
(2) the "means for" or "step for" must be modified by functional language;[4] and
(3) the phrase "means for" or "step for" must not be modified by sufficient structure, material, or acts for achieving the specified function.[5]

With respect to the first prong of this analysis, a claim element that does not include the phrase "means for" or "step for" will not be considered to invoke 35 U.S.C. §112, ¶6. If an applicant wishes to have the claim limitation treated under 35 U.S.C. §112, ¶6, applicant must either (1) amend the claim to include the phrase "means for" or "step for" in accordance with these guidelines, or (2) show that even though the phrase "means for" or "step for" is not used, the claim limitation is written as a function to be performed and does not recite sufficient structure, material, or acts which would preclude application of 35 U.S.C. §112, ¶6.[6]

---

[3] *Cf. Seal-Flex, Inc. v. Athletic Track and Court Constr.*, 172 F.3d 836, 849–50, 50 USPQ2d 1225, 1233–34 (Fed. Cir. 1999) (Rader, J., concurring) (use of the phrase "step for" in a method claim raises a presumption that 35 U.S.C. §112, ¶6 applies, whereas, use of the word "step" by itself or the phrase "step of" does not invoke a presumption that 35 U.S.C. §112, ¶6 applies); *Ethicon, Inc. v. United States Surgical Corp.*, 135 F.3d 1456, 1463, 45 USPQ2d 1545, 1550 (Fed. Cir. 1998), *cert. denied*, 525 U.S. 923 (1998) ("use of the word 'means' gives rise to 'a presumption that the inventor used the term advisedly to invoke the statutory mandates for means-plus-function clauses'"); *O.I. Corp. v. Tekmar*, 115 F.3d 1576, 1583, 42 USPQ2d 1777, 1782 (Fed. Cir. 1997) (method claim that paralleled means-plus-function apparatus claim but lacked "step for" language did not invoke 35 U.S.C. §112, ¶6). Thus, absent an express recitation of "means for" or "step for" in the limitation, the broadest reasonable interpretation will not be limited to "corresponding structure . . . and equivalents thereof." *Cf. Morris*, 127 F.3d at 1055, 44 USPQ2d at 1028 ("no comparable mandate in the patent statute that relates the claim scope of non-§112 ¶6 claims to particular matter found in the specification").

[4] *See York Prods., Inc. v. Central Tractor Farm & Family Ctr.*, 99 F.3d 1568, 1574, 40 USPQ2d 1619, 1624 (Fed. Cir. 1996) (holding that a claim limitation containing the term "means" does not invoke 35 U.S.C. §112, ¶6 if the claim limitation does not link the term "means" to a specific function).

[5] *See Seal-Flex*, 172 F.3d at 849, 50 USPQ2d at 1234 (Rader, J., concurring) ("Even when a claim element uses language that generally falls under the step-plus-function format, however, §112 ¶6 still does not apply when the claim limitation itself recites sufficient acts for performing the specified function"). *Cf. Rodime PLC v. Seagate Tech., Inc.*, 174 F.3d 1294, 1303–04, 50 USPQ2d 1429, 1435–36 (Fed. Cir. 1999) (holding "positioning means for moving" does not invoke 35 U.S.C. §112, ¶6 because the claim further provides a list of the structure underlying the means and the detailed recitation of the structure for performing the moving function removes this element from the purview of 35 U.S.C. §112, ¶6); *Cole v. Kimberly-Clark Corp.*, 102 F.3d 524, 531, 41 USPQ2d 1001, 1006 (Fed. Cir. 1996) (holding "perforation means for tearing" does not invoke 35 U.S.C. §112, ¶6 because the claim describes the structure supporting the tearing function (i.e., perforation)). In other cases, the Federal Circuit has held otherwise. *See Unidynamics Corp. v. Automatic Prod. Int'l*, 157 F.3d 1311, 1319, 48 USPQ2d 1099, 1104 (Fed. Cir. 1998) (holding "spring means" does invoke 35 U.S.C. §112, ¶6). During examination, however, applicants have the opportunity and the obligation to define their inventions precisely, including whether a claim limitation invokes 35 U.S.C. §112, ¶6. Thus, if the phrase "means for" or "step for" is modified by sufficient structure, material, or acts for achieving the specified function, the USPTO will not apply 35 U.S.C. §112, ¶6 until such modifying language is deleted from the claim limitation. *See also supra* note 1.

[6] While traditional "means for" or "step for" language does not automatically make an element a means-(or step-) plus-function element, conversely, lack of such language does not necessarily prevent a limitation from being construed as a means-(or step-) plus-function limitation. *See Signtech USA, Ltd. v. Vutek, Inc.*, 174 F.3d 1352, 1356–57, 50 USPQ2d 1372, 1374–75 (Fed. Cir. 1999) ("ink delivery means positioned on." invokes 35 U.S.C. §112, ¶6 since the phrase "ink delivery means" is equivalent to "means for ink delivery"); *Al-Site Corp. v. VSI Int'l, Inc.*, 174 F.3d 1308, 1317–19, 50 USPQ2d 1161, 1166–67 (Fed. Cir. 1999) (although the claim elements "eyeglasses hanger member" and "eyeglass contacting member" include a function, these claim elements do not invoke 35 U.S.C. §112, ¶6 because the claims themselves contain sufficient structural limitations for performing those functions); *Seal-Flex*, 172 F.3d at 849, 50 USPQ2d at 1234 (Rader, J., concurring) ("claim elements without express step-plus-function language may nevertheless fall within §112 ¶6 if they merely claim the underlying function without recitation of acts for performing that function . . . In general terms, the 'underlying function' of a method claim

Accordingly, these supplemental examination guidelines provide applicants with the opportunity to either invoke or not invoke 35 U.S.C. §112, ¶6 based upon a clear and simple set of criteria.

II. Procedures for determining whether the written description adequately describes the corresponding structure, material, or acts necessary to support a claim limitation which invokes 35 U.S.C. §112, ¶6

If a claim limitation invokes 35 U.S.C. §112, ¶6, it must be interpreted to cover the corresponding structure, material, or acts in the specification and "equivalents thereof."[7] If the written description fails to set forth the supporting structure, material or acts corresponding to the means-(or step-) plus-function, the claim may not meet the requirement of 35 U.S.C. §112, ¶2:

Although [35 U.S.C. §112, ¶6] statutorily provides that one may use means-plus-function language in a claim, one is still subject to the requirement that a claim "particularly point out and distinctly claim" the invention. Therefore, if one employs means-plus-function language in a claim, one must set forth in the specification an adequate disclosure showing what is meant by that language. If an applicant fails to set forth an adequate disclosure, the applicant has in effect failed to particularly point out and distinctly claim the invention as required by [35 U.S.C. §112, ¶2].[8]

Whether a claim reciting an element in means-(or step-) plus-function language fails to comply with 35 U.S.C. §112, ¶2 because the specification does not disclose adequate structure (or material or acts) for performing the recited function is closely related to the question of whether the specification meets the description requirement in 35 U.S.C. §112, ¶1.[9] However, 35 U.S.C. §112, ¶6 does not impose any requirements in addition to those imposed by 35 U.S.C. §112, ¶1.[10] Conversely, the invocation of 35 U.S.C. §112, ¶6 does not exempt an applicant from compliance with 35 U.S.C. §112, ¶¶1 and 2.[11]

Under certain limited circumstances, the written description does not have to explicitly describe the structure (or material or acts) corresponding to a means-(or step-) plus-function limitation to particularly point out and distinctly claim the invention as required by 35 U.S.C. §112, ¶2.[12] Rather, disclosure of structure corresponding to a

---

element corresponds to *what* that element ultimately accomplishes in relationship to what the other elements of the claim and the claim as a whole accomplish. 'Acts,' on the other hand, correspond to *how* the function is accomplished."); *Personalized Media Communications LLC v. ITC*, 161 F.3d 696, 703–04, 48 USPQ2d 1880, 1886–87 (Fed. Cir. 1998); *Mas-Hamilton Group v. LaGard, Inc.*, 156 F.3d 1206, 1213, 48 USPQ2d 1010, 1016 (Fed. Cir. 1998) ("lever moving element for moving the lever" and "movable link member for holding the lever and for releasing the lever" were construed as means-plus-function limitations invoking 35 U.S.C. §112, ¶6 since the claimed limitations were described in terms of their function, not their mechanical structure).

[7] *See* 35 U.S.C. §112, ¶6. *See also B. Braun Medical, Inc. v. Abbott Lab.*, 124 F.3d 1419, 1424, 43 USPQ2d 1896, 1899 (Fed. Cir. 1997).

[8] *See Donaldson*, 16 F.3d at 1195, 29 USPQ2d at 1850; *see also B. Braun Medical*, 124 F.3d at 1425, 43 USPQ2d at 1900; and *In re Dossel*, 115 F.3d 942, 946, 42 USPQ2d 1881, 1884–85 (Fed. Cir. 1997).

[9] *See In re Noll*, 545 F.2d 141, 149, 191 USPQ 721, 727 (CCPA 1976) (unless the means-plus-function language is itself unclear, a claim limitation written in means-plus-function language meets the definiteness requirement in 35 U.S.C. §112, ¶2 so long as the specification meets the written description requirement in 35 U.S.C. §112, ¶1).

[10] *See In re Knowlton*, 481 F.2d 1357, 1366, 178 USPQ 486, 492–93 (CCPA 1973).

[11] *See Donaldson*, 16 F.3d at 1195, 29 USPQ2d at 1850; *Knowlton*, 481 F.2d at 1366, 178 USPQ at 493.

[12] *See Dossel*, 115 F.3d at 946, 42 USPQ2d at 1885. Under proper circumstances, drawings may provide a written description of an invention as required by 35 U.S.C. §112. *Vas-Cath, Inc. v. Mahurkar*, 935 F.2d 1555, 1565, 19 USPQ2d 1111, 1118 (Fed. Cir. 1991).

means-plus-function limitation may be implicit in the written description if it would have been clear to those skilled in the art what structure must perform the function recited in the means-plus-function limitation.[13] However, the claims must still be analyzed to determine whether there exists corresponding adequate support for such claim under 35 U.S.C. §112, ¶1.[14]

Therefore, a means-(or step-) plus-function claim limitation satisfies 35 U.S.C. §112, ¶2 if: (1) the written description links or associates particular structure, material, or acts to the function recited in a means-(or step-) plus-function claim limitation; or (2) it is clear based on the disclosure in the application that one skilled in the art would have known what structure, material, or acts perform the function recited in a means-(or step-) plus-function limitation.

37 CFR 1.75(d)(1) provides, in part, that "the terms and phrases used in the claims must find clear support or antecedent basis in the description so that the meaning of the terms in the claims may be ascertainable by reference to the description." In the situation in which the written description only implicitly or inherently sets forth the structure, material, or acts corresponding to a means-(or step-) plus-function, and the examiner concludes that one skilled in the art would recognize what structure, material, or acts perform the function recited in a means-(or step-) plus-function, the examiner should either (1) have the applicant clarify the record by amending the written description such that it expressly recites what structure, material, or acts perform the function recited in the claim element[15] or (2) state on the record what structure, material, or acts perform the function recited in the means-(or step-) plus-function limitation.

---

[13] *See Atmel Corp. v. Information Storage Devices Inc.*, 198 F.3d 1374, 1379, 53 USPQ2d 1225, 1228 (Fed. Cir. 1999) (stating that the "one skilled in the art" analysis should apply in determining whether sufficient structure has been disclosed to support a means-plus-function limitation and that the USPTO's recently issued proposed Supplemental Guidelines are consistent with the court's holding on this point); *Dossel*, 115 F.3d at 946–47, 42 USPQ2d at 1885 ("Clearly, a unit which receives digital data, performs complex mathematical computations and outputs the results to a display must be implemented by or on a general or special purpose computer (although it is not clear why the written description does not simply state 'computer' or some equivalent phrase.)").

[14] In considering whether there is 35 U.S.C. §112, ¶1 support for the claim limitation, the examiner must consider not only the original disclosure contained in the summary and detailed description of the invention portions of the specification, but also the original claims, abstract, and drawings. *See In re Mott*, 539 F.2d 1291, 1299, 190 USPQ 536, 542–43 (CCPA 1976) (claims); *In re Anderson*, 471 F.2d 1237, 1240, 176 USPQ 331, 333 (CCPA 1973) (claims); *Hill-Rom Co. v. Kinetic Concepts, Inc.*, 54 USPQ2d 1437 (Fed. Cir. 2000) (abstract); *In re Armbruster*, 512 F.2d 676, 678–79, 185 USPQ 152, 153–54 (CCPA 1975) (abstract); *Anderson*, 471 F.2d at 1240, 176 USPQ at 333 (abstract); *Vas-Cath Inc. v. Mahurkar*, 935 F.2d 1555, 1564, 19 USPQ2d 1111, 1117 (Fed. Cir. 1991) (drawings); *In re Wolfensperger*, 302 F.2d 950, 955–57, 133 USPQ 537, 541–43 (CCPA 1962) (drawings).

[15] Even if the disclosure implicitly sets forth the structure, material, or acts corresponding to a means-(or step-) plus-function claim element in compliance with 35 U.S.C. §112, ¶¶1 and 2, the USPTO may still require the applicant to amend the specification pursuant to 37 CFR 1.75(d) and MPEP 608.01(o) to explicitly state, with reference to the terms and phrases of the claim element, what structure, material, or acts perform the function recited in the claim element. *See* 35 U.S.C. §112, ¶6 ("An element in a claim for a combination may be expressed as a means or step for performing a specified function without the recital of structure, material, or acts in support thereof, and such claim shall be construed to cover the corresponding structure, material, or acts *described in the specification* and equivalents thereof." (emphasis added)); *see also B. Braun Medical*, 124 F.3d at 1424, 43 USPQ2d at 1900 (holding that "pursuant to this provision [35 U.S.C. §112, ¶6], structure disclosed in the specification is 'corresponding' structure only if the specification or prosecution history clearly links or associates that structure to the function recited in the claim. This duty to link or associate structure to function is the *quid pro quo* for the convenience of employing 112, paragraph 6."); *Wolfensperger*, 302 F.2d at 955, 133 USPQ at 542 (just because the disclosure provides support for a claim element does not mean that the USPTO cannot enforce its requirement that the terms and phrases used in the claims find clear support or antecedent basis in the written description).

III. Making a *Prima Facie* Case of 35 U.S.C. §112, ¶6 Equivalence

If the examiner finds that a prior art element (1) performs the function specified in the claim, (2) is not excluded by any explicit definition provided in the specification for an equivalent, and (3) is an equivalent of the means-(or step-) plus-function limitation, the examiner should provide an explanation and rationale in the Office action as to why the prior art element is an equivalent. Factors that will support a conclusion that the prior art element is an equivalent are:

(1) the prior art element performs the identical function specified in the claim in substantially the same way, and produces substantially the same results as the corresponding element disclosed in the specification;[16]

(2) a person of ordinary skill in the art would have recognized the interchangeability of the element shown in the prior art for the corresponding element disclosed in the specification;[17]

(3) there are insubstantial differences between the prior art element and the corresponding element disclosed in the specification;[18]

(4) the prior art element is a structural equivalent of the corresponding element disclosed in the specification.[19]

A showing of at least one of the above-noted factors by the examiner should be sufficient to support a conclusion that the prior art element is an equivalent. The examiner should then conclude that the claimed limitation is met by the prior art element. In addition to the conclusion that the prior art element is an equivalent, examiners should also demonstrate, where appropriate, why it would have been obvious to one of ordinary skill in the art at the time of the invention to substitute applicant's described structure, material, or acts for that described in the prior art reference. *See In re Brown*, 459 F.2d 531, 535, 173 USPQ 685, 688 (CCPA 1972). The burden then shifts to applicant to show that the prior art element is not an equivalent of the structure, material, or acts disclosed in the application. *See In re Mulder*, 716 F.2d 1542, 1549, 219 USPQ 189, 196 (Fed. Cir. 1983).

To the extent that the three-step process for making a prima facie case of equivalence of a prior art element during *ex parte* examination set forth in these supplemental examination guidelines is inconsistent with the 1994 Guidelines, the supplemental examination guidelines control. The supplemental examination guidelines are consistent with the requirement that the USPTO give claims their broadest reasonable interpretation.[20] The specification need not describe the equivalents of the structures, material, or acts corresponding to the means-(or step-) plus-function claim element.[21] Where, however, the specification is silent as to what constitutes equivalents and the

---

[16] *Kemco Sales, Inc. v. Control Papers Co.*, 54 USPQ2d 1308, 1315 (Fed. Cir. 2000); *Odetics, Inc. v. Storage Tech. Corp.*, 185 F.3d 1259, 1267, 51 USPQ2d 1225, 1229–30 (Fed. Cir. 1999).

[17] *Al-Site Corp. v. VSI Int'l, Inc.*, 174 F.3d 1308, 1316, 50 USPQ2d 1161, 1165 (Fed. Cir. 1999); *Chiuminatta Concrete Concepts, Inc. v. Cardinal Indus., Inc.*, 145 F.3d 1303, 1309, 46 USPQ2d 1752, 1757 (Fed. Cir. 1998); *Lockheed Aircraft Corp. v. United States*, 553 F.2d 69, 83, 193 USPQ 449, 461 (Ct. Cl. 1977).

[18] *IMS Technology, Inc. v. Haas Automation, Inc.*, 206 F.3d 1422, 1436, 54 USPQ2d 1129, 1138 (Fed. Cir. 2000); *Valmont Indus. v. Reinke Mfg. Co.*, 983 F.2d 1039, 1043, 25 USPQ2d 1451, 1455 (Fed. Cir. 1993).

[19] *In re Bond*, 910 F.2d 831, 833, 15 USPQ2d 1566, 1568 (Fed. Cir. 1990).

[20] *See Donaldson*, 16 F.3d at 1194, 29 USPQ2d at 1850 (stating that 35 U.S.C. §112, ¶6 "merely sets a limit on how broadly the USPTO may construe means-plus-function language under the rubric of 'reasonable interpretation'").

[21] *See Noll*, 545 F.2d at 149–50, 191 USPQ at 727 (the meaning of equivalents is well understood in patent law, and an applicant need not describe in his specification the full range of equivalents of his invention) (citation omitted). *Cf. Hybritech Inc. v. Monoclonal Antibodies, Inc.*, 802 F.2d 1367, 1384, 231 USPQ 81, 94 (Fed. Cir. 1986) ("a patent need not teach, and preferably omits, what is well known in the art").

examiner has made out a *prima facie* case of equivalence, the burden is placed upon the applicant to show that a prior art element which performs the claimed function is not an equivalent of the structure, material, or acts disclosed in the specification.[22]

June 15, 2000

Q. TODD DICKINSON
Under Secretary of Commerce for Intellectual Property and Director of the United States Patent and Trademark Office

---

[22] *See* 1994 Guidelines at 60; *see also In re Mulder*, 716 F.2d 1542, 1549, 219 USPQ 189, 196 (Fed. Cir. 1983).

Appendix C-37

Guidelines Setting Forth a Modified Policy Concerning the Evidence of Common Ownership, or an Obligation of Assignment to the Same Person, as Required by 35 U.S.C. 103(c)

I. Summary

An earlier Official Gazette notice set forth the position of the United States Patent and Trademark Office (USPTO) regarding interpretation and implementation of the changes made to 35 U.S.C. 103(c) by the American Inventors Protection Act of 1999 (hereinafter "AIPA").[1] See "Guidelines Concerning the Implementation of Changes to 35 USC 102(g) and 103(c) and the Interpretation of the Term 'Original Application' in the American Inventors Protection Act of 1999," 1233 O.G. 54 (April 11, 2000) (hereinafter "the Guidelines"). The Guidelines suggested several different forms of evidence, based on 37 CFR 1.104(a)(5), to show common ownership or an obligation of assignment to the same person, of the application and the reference at the time the invention was made. In a rule change to implement the eighteen-month publication provisions of the AIPA, 37 CFR 1.104(a)(5) was removed. See "Changes to Implement Eighteen-Month Publication of Patent Applications; Final Rule," 65 FR 57023, 57033, 57056 (September 20, 2000).

This notice sets forth a modified policy concerning evidence of common ownership, or an obligation of assignment to the same person, at the time the invention was made. Henceforth, applications and references (whether patents, patent applications, patent application publications, etc.) will be considered by the examiner to be owned by, or subject to an obligation of assignment to, the same person, at the time the invention was made, if the applicant(s) or the attorney or agent of record makes a statement to

[1] The American Inventors Protection Act of 1999 is a part of the conference report (H. Rep. 106-479) on H.R. 3194, Consolidated Appropriations Act, Fiscal Year 2000. The text of the American Inventors Protection Act of 1999 is contained in title IV of S. 1948, the Intellectual Property and Communications Omnibus Reform Act of 1999 (Public Law 106-113). The American Inventors Protection Act of 1999 was enacted on November 29, 1999.

the effect that the application and the reference were, at the time the invention was made, owned by, or subject to an obligation of assignment to, the same person.

This new (modified) policy will apply when an applicant seeks to exclude a reference available under 35 U.S.C. 102(e), (f) and/or (g) pursuant to 35 U.S.C. 103(c). This policy applies for applications filed on or after November 29, 1999 where a reference available under 35 U.S.C. 102(e) is sought to be excluded, and any application where a reference available under only 35 U.S.C. 102 (f) and/or (g) is sought to be excluded.

A reference excluded under amended 35 U.S.C. 103(c) may continue to serve as the basis of a rejection under 35 USC 102(e), and serve as part of the basis of a double patenting rejection.

II. Background

The AIPA amended 35 U.S.C. 103(c) to add that subject matter that only qualifies as prior art under 35 U.S.C. 102(e) and that was commonly owned, or subject to an obligation of assignment to the same person, at the time the invention was made cannot be applied in a rejection under 35 U.S.C. 103(a). Section 4807 of the AIPA amended 35 U.S.C. 103(c) to read as follows:

> "(c) Subject matter developed by another person, which qualifies as prior art only under one or more of subsections (e), (f), and (g) of section 102 of this title, shall not preclude patentability under this section where the subject matter and the claimed invention were, at the time the invention was made, owned by the same person or subject to an obligation of assignment to the same person."

This change to 103(c) applies to any patent application filed on or after the date of enactment, November 29, 1999. See AIPA 4807(b). This amendment to 103(c) does not apply to any application filed before November 29, 1999, any request for examination under 37 CFR 1.129 of such an application, nor any request for continued examination under 37 CFR 1.114 of such an application.

For the implementation of the change to 35 U.S.C. 103(c), the Guidelines stated that:

> Applications and patents will be considered by the examiner to be owned by, or subject to an obligation of assignment to, the same person, at the time the invention was made, if:
>
> (a) the applicant provides evidence that the application and patent files refer to assignments recorded in the PTO in accordance with 37 CFR 3.11 which convey the entire rights in the applications to the same person(s) or organization(s) at the time of the invention;
> (b) copies of unrecorded assignments which convey the entire rights in the applications to the same person(s) or organization(s) at the time of the invention are filed in each of the applications and patents;
> (c) an affidavit or declaration by the common owner is filed which states that there was common ownership at the time the invention was made and explains why the affiant believes there was common ownership; or
> (d) other evidence is submitted which establishes common ownership of the applications and patents at the time the invention was made, e.g., a court decision determining the owner.

The listing of the above-mentioned types of evidence was based on 37 CFR 1.104(a)(5), which has now been removed. See "Changes to Implement Eighteen-Month Publication of Patent Applications; Final Rule," 65 FR 57023, 57033, 57056 (September 20, 2000).

III. Modified Policy on Evidence to Establish Common Ownership or an Obligation for Assignment to the Same Person

The policy on what evidence is needed to establish common ownership, or an obligation to the same person, set forth in the Guidelines (restated above) is hereby replaced by the following policy:

> Applications and references (whether patents, patent applications, patent application publications, etc.) will be considered by the examiner to be owned by, or subject to an obligation of assignment to the same person, at the time the invention was made, if the applicant(s) or an attorney or agent of record makes a statement to the effect that the application and the reference were, at the time the invention was made, owned by, or subject to an obligation of assignment to, the same person.

This policy is being changed in order to simplify the examination and processing of requests for the exclusion of prior art under 35 U.S.C. 103(c). The applicant(s) or the representative(s) of record have the best knowledge of the ownership of their application(s) and reference(s), and their statement of such is sufficient evidence because of their paramount obligation of candor and good faith to the USPTO.

The statement concerning common ownership should be clear and conspicuous (e.g., on a separate piece of paper or in a separately labeled section) in order to ensure that the examiner quickly notices the statement. Applicants may, but are not required to, submit further evidence, such as assignment records, affidavits or declarations by the common owner, or court decisions, in addition to the above-mentioned statement concerning common ownership.

For example, an attorney or agent of record receives an Office action for Application X in which all the claims are rejected under 35 U.S.C. 103(a) using Patent A in view of Patent B. In her response to the Office action, the attorney or agent of record for Application X states, in a clear and conspicuous manner, that:

> "Application X and Patent A were, at the time the invention of Application X was made, owned by Company Z."

This statement alone is sufficient evidence to disqualify Patent A from being used in a rejection under 35 U.S.C. 103(a) against the claims of Application X.

In rare instances, the examiner may have independent evidence that raises a material doubt as to the accuracy of applicant's representation of either (1) the common ownership of, or (2) the existence of an obligation to commonly assign, the application being examined and the applied US patent or US patent application publication reference. In such cases, the examiner may explain why the accuracy of the representation is doubted, and require objective evidence of common ownership of, or the existence of an obligation to assign, the application being examined and the applied reference as of the date of invention of the application being examined.

IV. The Interpretation of the Phrase "Same Person"

The phrase "same person" includes persons, organization(s) or corporation(s). If an invention claimed in an application is owned by more than one entity and those entities seek to exclude a reference's use under 35 U.S.C. 103, then the reference must be owned by, or subject to an obligation of assignment to, the same entities that owned the application, at the time the invention was made. For example, assume Company A owns twenty percent of patent Application X and Company B owns eighty percent of patent Application X at the time the invention of Application X was made. In addition, assume that Companies A and B seek to exclude Reference Z's use under 35 U.S.C. 103(a). Reference Z must have been co-owned, or been under an obligation of assignment to both companies, on the date the invention was made in order for the exclusion to be properly requested. A statement such as "Application X and Patent Z were, at the time the invention of Application X was made, jointly owned by Companies A and B" would be sufficient evidence of common ownership.

For applications owned by a joint venture of two or more entities, both the application and the reference must have been owned by, or subject to an obligation of assignment to, the joint venture at the time the invention was made. For example, if Company A and Company B formed a joint venture, Company C, both Application X and Reference Z must have been owned by, or subject to an obligation of assignment to, Company C at the time the invention was made in order for Reference Z to be properly excluded as prior art under 35 U.S.C. 103(c). If Company A by itself owned Reference

Z at the time the invention of Application X was made, a request for the exclusion of Reference Z as prior art under 35 U.S.C. 103(c) would not be proper.

V. Implementation and Effective Date of the Modified Policy

As stated above, this new (modified) policy will apply when an applicant seeks to exclude a reference available under 35 U.S.C. 102(e), (f) and/or (g) pursuant to 35 U.S.C. 103(c). This policy applies for applications filed on or after November 29, 1999 where a reference available under 35 U.S.C. 102(e) is sought to be excluded, and any application where a reference available under only 35 U.S.C. 102 (f) and/or (g) is sought to be excluded.

The policy changes made by this notice are effective on the date of publication of this notice, and shall be applied in any Office action mailed on or after that date. If a reply by applicant filed before that date has already been acted on by the Office, and applicant seeks reconsideration in view of this notice, applicant should reassert the evidence, e.g., a statement signed by a registered practitioner or by the applicant, concerning entitlement to prior art exclusion in the previously submitted reply in a timely submitted reply. This may be done by calling attention to the contents of the previous reply or by incorporating the previously submitted evidence in the next reply.

If an Office action includes a non-final rejection to certain claims which is obviated by a reply based on a proper claim of entitlement to the new exclusion, then a subsequent Office action should not be made final if the action relies on newly applied prior art against the same claims.

If a final rejection of certain claims is obviated by a timely reply based on a proper claim of entitlement to the new exclusion, then the Office should acknowledge the reply by modifying the status of the claims. For example, if the only rejection in the final rejection is obviated by evidence demonstrating entitlement to exclude prior art under amended 35 USC 103(c) in the reply, the Office should indicate that the claims are allowable, or prosecution should be reopened should the claims be considered unpatentable in view of newly applied prior art. Applicant's evidence concerning the exclusion is entitled to being considered even after a final rejection has been made, since if the exclusion is established, the propriety of the rejection is obviated as a matter of law. Applicants should be aware, however, that the failure to submit evidence of entitlement to exclude prior art following the first Office action including the use of such prior art in a rejection under 35 U.S.C. 103(a) may be considered by the Office as conduct that is considered to be a failure to engage in reasonable efforts to conclude prosecution if such prior art is thereafter excluded under 35 USC 103(c). See 37 CFR 1.704(c) and see, Discussion of Comment 19, Changes To Implement Patent Term Adjustment Under Twenty-Year Patent Term; Final Rule, 65 F. R. 56365, 79 (September 18, 2000).

FOR FURTHER INFORMATION CONTACT: Jeanne Clark or Robert Clarke, Legal Advisors in the Office of Patent Legal Administration, by telephone at (703) 305-1622, by fax at (703) 305-1013, or by e-mail addressed to Jeanne.Clark@USPTO.gov or Robert.Clarke@USPTO.gov.

Stephen G. Kunin
Deputy Commissioner
for Patent Examination Policy

Appendix C-38

Update on Facsimile Submission of Assigned Documents to the USPTO

1237 OG 81
August 15, 2000

Update on Facsimile Submission of Assignment Documents to the USPTO

As was first announced in the Official Gazette (OG) of January 25, 2000, the United States Patent and Trademark Office (USPTO) now has the capability to accept facsimile (fax) transmissions to record an assignment or other documents affecting title. This process allows customers to submit their assignment documents via fax directly into the automated Patent and Trademark Assignment System (PTAS) and then receive the resulting recordation notice on their fax machine.

Since the inception of this process, the Assignment Services Division has been documenting the types of occurrences which can either delay or prevent the USPTO from receiving and processing fax-transmitted documents. The following questions and answers supplement the information provided in the initial January 25, 2000, OG Notice.

Why are you telling me that my document is "upside down"?

In a routine fax transmission, page orientation (top of the page first into the machine or bottom of the page first) is not critical because the reader can easily flip and arrange the pages to read them top to bottom. However, it is critical to our process that each page is faxed top to bottom with the top margin being fed first into the machine. Once they have been received in PTAS, fax transmitted assignments are processed strictly by electronic means. Although the PTAS software can rotate a document 180 degrees for viewing purposes, when the electronic document is extracted to generate the archival microfilm record, each page is extracted *exactly* as it was first received. Accordingly, a document sent "upside down" would be microfilmed upside down. To further complicate matters, because the system generated recordation and reel and frame markings on the pages would be in the opposite orientation, the resulting document would be difficult to read.

The assignment document I sent you is perfectly proper and valid. What do you mean that my document is an "invalid submission type"?

An "invalid submission" has nothing to do with the validity or legal standing of the document you submitted for recordation. "Invalid submission type" means you have sent us one of several kinds of documents that we cannot process via fax at this time. As first specified in the OG of January 25, 2000, there are six types of documents which we cannot process via fax:

1. Assignments submitted concurrent with newly filed patent applications. These must continue to be sent to the Office of Initial Patent Examination with the application.
2. Documents submitted in accordance with the Trademark Law Treaty where an application or registration number is not identified.
3. Documents with two or more cover sheets, e.g., a single document with one cover sheet to record an assignment, and a second cover sheet to record separately a license relating to the same property.
4. Requests for corrections to documents recorded previously.
5. Requests for "at cost" recordation services.
6. Documents with payment by credit card.

In addition to these documents, our experience with the fax capability over the past several months has added to the list of "invalid document types":

7. Resubmission of a non-recorded assignment.

I am the attorney of record. Why are you sending back my assignment document as non-recorded due to "unauthorized user"?

The person who signs the cover sheet statement must be listed as an "authorized user" in the USPTO Revenue Accounting Management (RAM) system in order for the Assignment Services Division to collect the recordation fee from your firm's deposit account. Customer updates to the "authorized user" list may be faxed to the Office of Finance, Deposit Account Division at (703) 308-6778, and must be signed by an authorized user. If you have questions concerning your current list of individuals authorized to charge your deposit account, you may also contact that division at (703) 305-4632.

Why am I getting back mailed correspondence about documents that I faxed to you?

The principal reasons we have to mail back correspondence to you concerning a faxed document are: (1) no identifying fax number on your document; and (2) an incorrect/unusable fax number associated with your document.

Standard business practice is that your complete fax number, your company or personal name, and the time and date of transmission should be transmitted along with your document. You need to program this sender information (TX Terminal Id) into your fax machine's memory, and then the information will be sent automatically during your fax transmissions. Our software attaches your fax number to the incoming package and allows PTAS to extract the number to electronically process the return of your recorded assignment.

Your fax number must be a dedicated line. Shared lines, or lines going through a switchboard, will terminate the fax transmission. Either a person will answer, or there will be no answer.

How many times will PTAS attempt to fax my return documents?

Currently two attempts, 24 hours apart, are made to fax out your return documents. If the documents cannot be faxed after the second try, they will then be mailed to you.

Why does faxing most often fail to work?

We are seeing four principal reasons why return faxes fail:

1. Phone line problems on the receiving end, which include old and invalid area codes being used. For example, 201 is still a valid area code in Northern New Jersey, but if your fax machine's area code is now in 973, the transmission will fail when we try 201.

2. A person, usually a receptionist or operator, answers the number.
3. The fax line is busy during the transmission attempt.
4. There is no answer at the number.

Each of these conditions would cause an automatic second attempt to fax your return documents.

What is the fax number for the Patent and Trademark Assignment System?

The system's fax number is (703) 306-5995. ***Please do not fax general assignment correspondence or recordation status inquiries to the PTAS fax system. These are not documents to be recorded. Faxing such documents delays our answering your question and causes extra work to delete the images and associated records from PTAS.***

What if I have a question about the fax service or need help?

Assignment Services Division staff are available to assist customers Monday through Friday from 8:30 a.m. to 5:00 p.m. Eastern Time. The telephone number is (703) 308-9723.

July 7, 2000

PATRICK ROWE, *Director*
Office of Public Records

Appendix C-39

Change in Policy of Examiner Assignment in *Ex Parte* Reexamination Proceedings and Establishment of Patentability Review Conferences in *Ex Parte* Reexamination Proceedings

1237 OG 138
August 29, 2000

Change in Policy of Examiner Assignment in *Ex Parte* Reexamination Proceedings and Establishment of Patentability Review Conferences in *Ex Parte* Reexamination Proceedings

Effective immediately, the United States Patent and Trademark Office (USPTO) is implementing the following two changes in *ex parte* reexamination practice:

I. Examiner Assignment Policy: It will be the general policy of the USPTO to assign *ex parte* requests for reexamination of a patent to an examiner different from the examiner(s) who examined the patent application.

II. Patentability Review Conference: A "patentability review conference" will be convened in each *ex parte* reexamination proceeding (1) just prior to issuing a final rejection, and (2) just prior to issuing a Notice of Intent to Issue Reexamination Certificate (NIRC).

These changes in the policy of examiner assignment and the introduction of the patentability review conference are directed specifically to *ex parte* reexamination practice, including an *ex parte* reexamination proceeding merged with a reissue application. They do not apply to proceedings under the newly enacted *inter partes* reexamination statute nor to merged *ex parte-inter partes* reexamination proceedings. Similar policies are, however, being considered for proceedings under the recently enacted *inter partes* reexamination statute, including merged *ex parte-inter partes* reexamination proceedings. *See* Notice of proposed rulemaking, Rules to Implement

Optional Inter Partes Reexamination Proceedings, 65 Fed. Reg. 18154, 18157–58 (2000), 1234 OG 93, 96 (2000). Response to Issue 4. Specific guidance as to policies, practices and procedures as they will apply to *inter partes* reexamination proceedings will be forthcoming in a separate O.G. Notice to be published in conjunction with the final rules on *inter partes* reexamination.

I. Examiner Assignment Policy in *Ex Parte* Reexamination Proceedings

A. Background

After a request for *ex parte* reexamination is received by the USPTO, the reexamination request is forwarded to the appropriate Technology Center (TC) and then to the TC Art Unit in which the reexamination proceeding is to be examined. Normally, the Art Unit that currently examines the class and subclass in which the patent to be reexamined is currently classified will conduct the reexamination. The reexamination request is then assigned by the Supervisory Patent Examiner (SPE) of the Art Unit to an examiner familiar with the claimed subject matter of the patent. That examiner will be referred to as the "examiner in charge" of the reexamination.

Historically, the examiner chosen by the SPE has generally been the original examiner who examined the patent for which reexamination is requested. When the original examiner has been available, he or she has been presumed to be the examiner most familiar with the technology and prosecution history of the patent. Statistics compiled by the USPTO do not support the existence of any significant difference in the rate of reaffirming the patentability of claims, whether the cases are assigned to the original examiner or to a different examiner. The public, however, has voiced complaints that a perception of "original examiner bias" exists.

B. Implementation of New Examiner Assignment Policy in *Ex Parte* Reexamination

In view of the public perception of "original examiner bias," the USPTO is changing its practice for assigning *ex parte* reexamination requests to an examiner. Henceforth, the general policy of the USPTO will be to assign all such *ex parte* requests, which are filed after the date of this notice, to an examiner different from the examiner(s) who examined the patent application.

Exceptions to this general policy include cases where the SPE is the only Primary Examiner in the Art Unit, or where the original examiner is the only examiner with adequate knowledge of the relevant technology. In the unusual case where there is a need to assign the request to the original examiner, the assignment must be approved by the TC Group Director and so indicated in the decision on the request for reexamination order.

C. Consequences of Inadvertent Assignment to an "Original Examiner"

Should a reexamination be inadvertently assigned to an "original examiner," the patent owner or the third party requester who objects must promptly file a paper alerting the USPTO to this fact. Any request challenging the assignment of an examiner to the case must be made within two months of the first Office action or other Office communication indicating the examiner assignment, or reassignment will not be considered. Reassignment of the reexamination to a different examiner will be addressed on a case-by-case basis. In no event will the assignment to the original examiner, by itself, be grounds for vacating any Office decision(s) or action(s) and "restarting" the reexamination.

II. Patentability Review Conferences in *Ex Parte* Reexamination Proceedings

A. Background

Currently, reexaminations are monitored by Special Program Examiners in each Technology Center. Prior to the issuance of the reexamination certificate, all reexamination proceedings are screened for obvious errors and to ensure that the record has been prepared properly. This screening is currently performed in the Office of Patent Legal Administration. In addition, the Office of Patent Quality Review conducts a patentability review in a sample of reexamination proceedings.

Reexaminations often involve patents in litigation, and the outcome for the patent owner and for the patent challenger can be dispositive. The USPTO and the public share the concern that the reexaminations should be conducted at the highest possible level of quality. Accordingly, the USPTO will conduct "patentability review conferences" to enhance the quality of *ex parte* reexamination proceedings. The patentability review conferences will provide substantive review of all the issues before the examiner, thereby enhancing objective analysis and quality in the *ex parte* reexamination proceeding.

B. Implementation of Patentability Review Conference in *Ex Parte* Reexamination

Effective immediately, a "patentability review conference" will be convened in each pending *ex parte* reexamination proceeding (1) just prior to issuing a final rejection, and (2) just prior to issuing a Notice of Intent to Issue a Reexamination Certificate (NIRC). These are the two most critical events in reexamination proceedings. Each conference will provide a forum to consider all issues of patentability as well as procedural issues having an impact on patentability.

C. Make-up of the Patentability Review Conference

The patentability review conference will consist of three members, one of whom may be the SPE. The first member will be the examiner in charge of the proceeding. The SPE will select the other two members, who will be examiner-conferees. The examiner-conferees will be Primary Examiners, or examiners who are knowledgeable in the technology of the invention claimed in the patent being reexamined, and/or who are experienced in reexamination practice. The majority of those present at the conference will be examiners who were not involved in the examination or issuance of the patent. An "original" examiner should be chosen as a conferee only if that examiner is the most knowledgeable in the art, or there is some other specific and justifiable reason to choose an original examiner as a participant in the conference.

The patentability review conference will be similar to the appeal conference presently carried out prior to the issuance of an examiner's answer following the filing of a Notice of Appeal and Brief. See MPEP 1208. A patentability review conference must be held in each instance where a final rejection is about to be issued in a reexamination proceeding. A patentability review conference must be held in each instance where an NIRC is about to be issued, unless the NIRC is being issued: (1) following and consistent with a decision by the Board of Patent Appeals and Interferences on the merits of the proceeding, or (2) as a consequence of the patent owner's failure to respond or take other action where such a response or action is necessary to maintain pendency of the proceeding and, as a result of which failure to respond, all of the claims will be canceled. When the patentability review conference results in the issuance of a final rejection or an NIRC, the two conferees will place their initials, followed by the word "conferee," below the signature of the examiner. The signature of the examiner and initials of the conferees on the resulting Office action will reflect that the patentability review conference has been conducted.

D. Consequences of Failure to Hold Conference

Should the examiner issue a final rejection or NIRC without holding a patentability review conference, the patent owner or the third party requester who wishes to object must promptly file a paper alerting the USPTO of this fact. Any challenge of the failure to hold a patentability review conference must be made within two months of the Office action, or the challenge will not be considered. Convening the conference to reconsider the examiner's decision will be addressed on a case-by-case basis. In no event will the failure to hold a review conference, by itself, be grounds for vacating any Office decision(s) or action(s) and "restarting" the reexamination proceeding.

E. Discussion

Review of the patentability of the claims by more than one Primary Examiner should diminish the perception that the patent owner can disproportionately influence the examiner in charge of the proceeding. The conference will also provide greater assurance that all matters will be addressed appropriately. All issues in the proceeding will be viewed from the perspectives of three examiners. What the examiner in charge of the proceeding might have missed, the other two conference members would likely detect. The conference will provide for a comprehensive discussion of, and finding for, each issue. The present initiative limits the use of the multiple examiner conference review to the two most critical points in the proceeding: (1) where the examiner decides whether to issue a final rejection of claims, and (2) where the examiner decides whether to issue an NIRC to confirm or allow claims. Thus, this initiative provides the advantage that the proceeding will be looked at by three "pairs of eyes" at the most important points in the reexamination, without expending an inordinate amount of resources and without unduly delaying the proceeding.

Incorporation into the Manual of Patent Examining Procedure (MPEP):

The "Examiner Assignment Policy" and "Patentability Review Conference" initiatives, as well as their particulars, will be incorporated into the MPEP in due course.

Inquiries:

Inquiries regarding this matter should be directed to Kenneth M. Schor, Senior Legal Advisor, Office of Patent Legal Administration:

By e-mail: kenneth.schor@uspto.gov
By telephone: (703) 308-6710
By FAX: (703) 872-9408, marked to the attention of Kenneth M. Schor
By mail: United States Patent and Trademark Office
Box Comments—Patents
Commissioner for Patents
Washington, D.C. 20231
Attention: Kenneth M. Schor

August 4, 2000

Q. TODD DICKINSON
Under Secretary of Commerce for Intellectual Property and Director of the United States Patent and Trademark Office

Appendix C-40

Rules to Implement Optional *Inter Partes* Reexamination Proceedings; Final Rule

65 FR 76756
Department of Commerce
United States Patent and Trademark Office
37 CFR Part 1
RIN 0651—AB04

Agency: United States Patent and Trademark Office, Commerce

Action: Final rule

* * *

Effective Date: February 5, 2001

* * *

PART 1—RULES OF PRACTICE IN PATENT CASES

1. The authority citation for 37 CFR part 1 continues to read as follows:

Authority: 35 U.S.C. 2(b)(2), unless otherwise noted.

2. Section 1.4(a)(2) is revised to read as follows:

§1.4 Nature of correspondence and signature requirements.

(a) * * *

(2) Correspondence in and relating to a particular application or other proceeding in the Office. See particularly the rules relating to the filing, processing, or other proceedings of national applications in subpart B, §§1.31 to 1.378; of international applications in subpart C, §§1.401 to 1.499; of *ex parte* reexaminations of patents in subpart D, §§1.501 to 1.570; of interferences in subpart E, §§1.601 to 1.690; of extension of patent term in subpart F, §§1.710 to 1.785; of *inter partes* reexaminations of patents in subpart H, §§1.902 to 1.997; and of trademark applications §§2.11 to 2.189.

* * * * *

3. Section 1.6(d)(5) is revised to read as follows:

§1.6 Receipt of Correspondence.

* * * * *

(d) * * *

(5) A request for reexamination under §1.510 or §1.913;

* * * * *

4. Section 1.20(c) is revised to read as follows:

§1.20 Post-issuance and reexamination fees.

* * * * *

(c) In reexamination proceedings
(1) For filing a request for *ex parte* reexamination (§1.510(a))—$2,520.00
(2) For filing a request for *inter partes* reexamination (§1.915(a))—$8,800.00

* * * * *

5. Section 1.25(b) is revised to read as follows:

§1.25 Deposit accounts.

* * * * *

(b) Filing, issue, appeal, international-type search report, international application processing, petition, and post-issuance fees may be charged against these accounts if sufficient funds are on deposit to cover such fees. A general authorization to charge all fees, or only certain fees, set forth in §§1.16 to 1.18 to a deposit account containing sufficient funds may be filed in an individual application, either for the entire pendency of the application or with a particular paper filed. An authorization to charge a fee to a deposit account will not be considered payment of the fee on the date the authorization to charge the fee is effective as to the particular fee to be charged unless sufficient funds are present in the account to cover the fee. An authorization to charge fees under §1.16 in an application submitted under §1.494 or §1.495 will be treated as an authorization to charge fees under §1.492. An authorization to charge fees set forth in §1.18 to a deposit account is subject to the provisions of §1.311(b). An authorization to charge to a deposit account the fee for a request for reexamination pursuant to §1.510 or §1.913 and any other fees required in a reexamination proceeding in a patent may also be filed with the request for reexamination.

6. Section 1.26(c) is revised to read as follows:

§1.26 Refunds.

* * * * *

(c) If the Commissioner decides not to institute a reexamination proceeding, for *ex parte* reexaminations filed under §1.510, a refund of $1,690 will be made to the reexamination requester. For *inter partes* reexaminations filed under §1.913, a refund of $7,970 will be made to the reexamination requester. The reexamination requester should indicate the form in which any refund should be made (e.g., by check, electronic funds transfer, credit to a deposit account, etc.). Generally, reexamination refunds will be issued in the form that the original payment was provided.

7. Section 1.112 is revised to read as follows:

§1.112 Reconsideration before final action.

After reply by applicant or patent owner (§1.111 or §1.945) to a non-final action and any comments by an *inter partes* reexamination requester (§1.947), the application or the patent under reexamination will be reconsidered and again examined. The applicant, or in the case of a reexamination proceeding the patent owner and any third party requester, will be notified if claims are rejected, objections or requirements made, or decisions favorable to patentability are made, in the same manner as after the first examination (§1.104). Applicant or patent owner may reply to such Office action in the same manner provided in §1.111 or §1.945, with or without amendment, unless such Office action indicates that it is made final (§1.113) or an appeal (§1.191) has been taken (§1.116), or in an *inter partes* reexamination, that it is an action closing prosecution (§1.949) or a right of appeal notice (§1.953).

8. Section 1.113(a) is revised to read as follows:

§1.113 Final rejection or action.

(a) On the second or any subsequent examination or consideration by the examiner the rejection or other action may be made final, whereupon applicant's, or for *ex parte* reexaminations filed under §1.510, patent owner's reply is limited to appeal in the case of rejection of any claim (§1.191), or to amendment as specified in §1.114 or §1.116. Petition may be taken to the Commissioner in the case of objections or requirements not involved in the rejection of any claim (§1.181). Reply to a final rejection or action must comply with §1.114 or paragraph (c) of this section. For final actions in an *inter partes* reexamination filed under §1.913, see §1.953.

* * * * *

9. Sections 1.116(b) and (d) are revised to read as follows:

§1.116 Amendments after final action, action closing prosecution, right of appeal notice, or appeal.

* * * * *

(b) After a final rejection or other final action (§1.113) in an application or in an *ex parte* reexamination filed under §1.510, or an action closing prosecution (§1.949) in an *inter partes* reexamination filed under §1.913, amendments may be made canceling claims or complying with any requirement of form expressly set forth in a previous Office action. Amendments presenting rejected claims in better form for consideration on appeal may be admitted. The admission of, or refusal to admit, any amendment after a final rejection, a final action, an action closing prosecution, or any related proceedings will not operate to relieve the application or patent under reexamination from its condition as subject to appeal or to save the application from abandonment under §1.135, or the reexamination from termination. No amendment can be made in an *inter partes* reexamination proceeding after the right of appeal notice under §1.953 except as provided for in paragraph (d) of this section.

* * * * *

(d) No amendment can be made as a matter of right in appealed cases. After decision on appeal, amendments can only be made as provided in §§1.198 and 1.981, or to carry into effect a recommendation under §1.196 or §1.977.

10. Section 1.121(i) is revised to read as follows:

§1.121 Manner of making amendments.

* * * * *

(i) *Amendments in reexamination proceedings:* Any proposed amendment to the description and claims in patents involved in reexamination proceedings in both *ex parte* reexaminations filed under §1.510 and *inter partes* reexaminations filed under §1.913 must be made in accordance with §1.530(d)–(j).

11. Sections 1.136(a)(2) and (b) are revised to read as follows:

§1.136 Extensions of time.

(a) * * *

(2) The date on which the petition and the fee have been filed is the date for purposes of determining the period of extension and the corresponding amount of

the fee. The expiration of the time period is determined by the amount of the fee paid. A reply must be filed prior to the expiration of the period of extension to avoid abandonment of the application (§1.135), but in no situation may an applicant reply later than the maximum time period set by statute, or be granted an extension of time under paragraph (b) of this section when the provisions of this paragraph are available. See §1.136(b) for extensions of time relating to proceedings pursuant to §§1.193(b), 1.194, 1.196 or 1.197; §1.304 for extensions of time to appeal to the U.S. Court of Appeals for the Federal Circuit or to commence a civil action; §1.550(c) for extensions of time in *ex parte* reexamination proceedings; §1.956 for extensions of time in *inter partes* reexamination proceedings; and §1.645 for extensions of time in interference proceedings.

* * * * *

(b) When a reply cannot be filed within the time period set for such reply and the provisions of paragraph (a) of this section are not available, the period for reply will be extended only for sufficient cause and for a reasonable time specified. Any request for an extension of time under this paragraph must be filed on or before the day on which such reply is due, but the mere filing of such a request will not affect any extension under this paragraph. In no situation can any extension carry the date on which reply is due beyond the maximum time period set by statute. See §1.304 for extensions of time to appeal to the U.S. Court of Appeals for the Federal Circuit or to commence a civil action; §1.645 for extensions of time in interference proceedings; §1.550(c) for extensions of time in *ex parte* reexamination proceedings; and §1.956 for extensions of time in *inter partes* reexamination proceedings.

* * * * *

12. Sections 1.181(a) and (c) are revised to read as follows:

§1.181 Petition to the Commissioner.

(a) Petition may be taken to the Commissioner:

(1) From any action or requirement of any examiner in the *ex parte* prosecution of an application, or in the *ex parte* or *inter partes* prosecution of a reexamination proceeding which is not subject to appeal to the Board of Patent Appeals and Interferences or to the court;

(2) In cases in which a statute or the rules specify that the matter is to be determined directly by or reviewed by the Commissioner; and

(3) To invoke the supervisory authority of the Commissioner in appropriate circumstances. For petitions in interferences, see §1.644.

* * * * *

(c) When a petition is taken from an action or requirement of an examiner in the *ex parte* prosecution of an application, or in the *ex parte* or *inter partes* prosecution of a reexamination proceeding, it may be required that there have been a proper request for reconsideration (§1.111) and a repeated action by the examiner. The examiner may be directed by the Commissioner to furnish a written statement, within a specified time, setting forth the reasons for his or her decision upon the matters averred in the petition, supplying a copy to the petitioner.

* * * * *

13. Section 1.191(a) is revised to read as follows:

§1.191 Appeal to Board of Patent Appeals and Interferences.

(a) Every applicant for a patent or for reissue of a patent, and every owner of a patent under *ex parte* reexamination filed under §1.510 for a patent that issued from an original application filed in the United States before November 29, 1999, any of whose claims has been twice or finally (§1.113) rejected, may appeal from the decision of the examiner to the Board of Patent Appeals and Interferences by filing a notice of appeal and the fee set forth in §1.17(b) within the time period provided under §§1.134 and 1.136 for reply. Notwithstanding the above, for an *ex parte* reexamination proceeding filed under §1.510 for a patent that issued from an original application filed in the United States on or after November 29, 1999, no appeal may be filed until the claims have been finally rejected (§1.113). Appeals to the Board of Patent Appeals and Interferences in *inter partes* reexamination proceedings filed under §1.913 are controlled by §§1.959 through 1.981. Sections 1.191 through 1.198 are not applicable to appeals in *inter partes* reexamination proceedings filed under §1.913.

* * * * *

14. Section 1.301 is revised to read as follows:

§1.301 Appeal to U.S. Court of Appeals for the Federal Circuit.

Any applicant or any owner of a patent involved in any *ex parte* reexamination proceeding filed under §1.510, dissatisfied with the decision of the Board of Patent Appeals and Interferences, and any party to an interference dissatisfied with the decision of the Board of Patent Appeals and Interferences, may appeal to the U.S. Court of Appeals for the Federal Circuit. The appellant must take the following steps in such an appeal: In the U.S. Patent and Trademark Office, file a written notice of appeal directed to the Commissioner (see §§1.302 and 1.304); and in the Court, file a copy of the notice of appeal and pay the fee for appeal as provided by the rules of the Court. For *inter partes* reexamination proceedings filed under §1.913, §1.983 is controlling.

15. Section 1.303 is amended by revising paragraphs (a) and (b) and by adding a new paragraph (d) to read as follows:

§1.303 Civil action under 35 U.S.C. 145, 146, 306.

(a) Any applicant or any owner of a patent involved in an *ex parte* reexamination proceeding filed under §1.510 for a patent that issues from an original application filed in the United States before November 29, 1999, dissatisfied with the decision of the Board of Patent Appeals and Interferences, and any party to an interference dissatisfied with the decision of the Board of Patent Appeals and Interferences may, instead of appealing to the U.S. Court of Appeals for the Federal Circuit (§1.301), have remedy by civil action under 35 U.S.C. 145 or 146, as appropriate. Such civil action must be commenced within the time specified in §1.304.

(b) If an applicant in an *ex parte* case or an owner of a patent involved in an *ex parte* reexamination proceeding filed under §1.510 for a patent that issues from an original application filed in the United States before November 29, 1999, has taken an appeal to the U.S. Court of Appeals for the Federal Circuit, he or she thereby waives his or her right to proceed under 35 U.S.C. 145.

* * * * *

(d) For an *ex parte* reexamination proceeding filed under §1.510 for a patent that issues from an original application filed in the United States on or after November 29, 1999, and for an *inter partes* reexamination proceeding filed under §1.913, no remedy by civil action under 35 U.S.C. 145 is available.

16. Sections 1.304(a)(1) and (a)(2) are revised to read as follows:

§1.304 Time for appeal or civil action.

(a) (1) The time for filing the notice of appeal to the U.S. Court of Appeals for the Federal Circuit (§1.302) or for commencing a civil action (§1.303) is two months from the date of the decision of the Board of Patent Appeals and Interferences. If a request for rehearing or reconsideration of the decision is filed within the time period provided under §1.197(b), §1.658(b), or §1.979(a), the time for filing an appeal or commencing a civil action shall expire two months after action on the request. In interferences the time for filing a cross-appeal or cross-action expires:

(i) Fourteen days after service of the notice of appeal or the summons and complaint; or

(ii) Two months after the date of decision of the Board of Patent Appeals and Interferences, whichever is later.

(2)The time periods set forth in this section are not subject to the provisions of §1.136, §1.550(c), §1.956, or §1.645(a) or (b).

* * * * *

17. The section heading for subpart D is revised to read as follows:

Subpart D—Ex Parte Reexamination of Patents

* * * * *

18. Section 1.501 is amended by revising paragraph (a) to read as follows:

§1.501 Citation of prior art in patent files.

(a) At any time during the period of enforceability of a patent, any person may cite, to the Office in writing, prior art consisting of patents or printed publications which that person states to be pertinent and applicable to the patent and believes to have a bearing on the patentability of any claim of the patent. If the citation is made by the patent owner, the explanation of pertinency and applicability may include an explanation of how the claims differ from the prior art. Such citations shall be entered in the patent file except as set forth in §§1.502 and 1.902.

* * * * *

19. New §1.502 is added to read as follows:

§1.502 Processing of prior art citations during an *ex parte* reexamination proceeding.

Citations by the patent owner under §1.555 and by an *ex parte* reexamination requester under either §1.510 or §1.535 will be entered in the reexamination file during a reexamination proceeding. The entry in the patent file of citations submitted after the date of an order to reexamine pursuant to §1.525 by persons other than the patent owner, or an *ex parte* reexamination requester under either §1.510 or §1.535, will be delayed until the reexamination proceeding has been terminated. See §1.902 for processing of prior art citations in patent and reexamination files during an *inter partes* reexamination proceeding filed under §1.913.

20. The undesignated center heading immediately preceding §1.510 is revised as follows:

Request for *Ex Parte* Reexamination

21. Section 1.510 is amended by revising its heading and paragraph (a) to read as follows:

§1.510 Request for *ex parte* reexamination.

(a) Any person may, at any time during the period of enforceability of a patent, file a request for an *ex parte* reexamination by the Office of any claim of the patent on the basis of prior art patents or printed publications cited under §1.501. The request must be accompanied by the fee for requesting reexamination set in §1.20(c)(1).

* * * * *

22. Section 1.515 is amended by revising its heading and the text to read as follows:

§1.515 Determination of the request for *ex parte* reexamination.

(a) Within three months following the filing date of a request for an *ex parte* reexamination, an examiner will consider the request and determine whether or not a substantial new question of patentability affecting any claim of the patent is raised by the request and the prior art cited therein, with or without consideration of other patents or printed publications. The examiner's determination will be based on the claims in effect at the time of the determination, will become a part of the official file of the patent, and will be mailed to the patent owner at the address as provided for in §1.33(c) and to the person requesting reexamination.

(b) Where no substantial new question of patentability has been found, a refund of a portion of the fee for requesting *ex parte* reexamination will be made to the requester in accordance with §1.26(c).

(c) The requester may seek review by a petition to the Commissioner under §1.181 within one month of the mailing date of the examiner's determination refusing *ex parte* reexamination. Any such petition must comply with §1.181(b). If no petition is timely filed or if the decision on petition affirms that no substantial new question of patentability has been raised, the determination shall be final and nonappealable.

23. Section 1.520 is amended by revising its heading and the text to read as follows:

§1.520 *Ex parte* reexamination at the initiative of the Commissioner.

The Commissioner, at any time during the period of enforceability of a patent, may determine whether or not a substantial new question of patentability is raised by patents or printed publications which have been discovered by the Commissioner or which have been brought to the Commissioner's attention, even though no request for reexamination has been filed in accordance with §1.510 or §1.913. The Commissioner may initiate *ex parte* reexamination without a request for reexamination pursuant to §1.510 or §1.913. Normally requests from outside the Office that the Commissioner undertake reexamination on his own initiative will not be considered. Any determination to initiate *ex parte* reexamination under this section will become a part of the official file of the patent and will be mailed to the patent owner at the address as provided for in §1.33(c).

24. The undesignated center heading following §1.520 is revised to read as follows:

Ex Parte Reexamination

25. Section 1.525 is amended by revising its heading and the text of paragraphs (a) and (b) to read as follows:

§1.525 Order for *ex parte* reexamination.

(a) If a substantial new question of patentability is found pursuant to §1.515 or §1.520, the determination will include an order for *ex parte* reexamination of the patent for resolution of the question. If the order for *ex parte* reexamination resulted from a petition pursuant to §1.515(c), the *ex parte* reexamination will ordinarily be conducted by an examiner other than the examiner responsible for the initial determination under §1.515(a).

(b) The notice published in the *Official Gazette* under §1.11(c) will be considered to be constructive notice and *ex parte* reexamination will proceed.

26. Section 1.530 is amended by revising its heading and paragraphs (a), (b), (c), (d) introductory text, and (l) to read as follows:

§1.530 Statement by patent owner in *ex parte* reexamination; amendment by patent owner in *ex parte* or *inter partes* reexamination; inventorship change in *ex parte* or *inter partes* reexamination.

(a) Except as provided in §1.510(e), no statement or other response by the patent owner in an *ex parte* reexamination proceeding shall be filed prior to the determinations made in accordance with §1.515 or §1.520. If a premature statement or other response is filed by the patent owner, it will not be acknowledged or considered in making the determination.

(b) The order for *ex parte* reexamination will set a period of not less than two months from the date of the order within which the patent owner may file a statement on the new question of patentability, including any proposed amendments the patent owner wishes to make.

(c) Any statement filed by the patent owner shall clearly point out why the subject matter as claimed is not anticipated or rendered obvious by the prior art patents or printed publications, either alone or in any reasonable combinations. Where the reexamination request was filed by a third party requester, any statement filed by the patent owner must be served upon the *ex parte* reexamination requester in accordance with §1.248.

(d) *Making amendments in a reexamination proceeding.* A proposed amendment in an *ex parte* or an *inter partes* reexamination proceeding is made by filing a paper directing that proposed specified changes be made to the patent specification, including the claims, or to the drawings. An amendment paper directing that proposed specified changes be made in a reexamination proceeding may be submitted as an accompaniment to a request filed by the patent owner in accordance with §1.510(e), as part of a patent owner statement in accordance with paragraph (b) of this section, or, where permitted, during the prosecution of the reexamination proceeding pursuant to §1.550(a) or §1.937.

* * * * *

(l) *Correction of inventorship in an ex parte or inter partes reexamination proceeding.*

(1) When it appears in a patent being reexamined that the correct inventor or inventors were not named through error without deceptive intention on the part of the actual inventor or inventors, the Commissioner may, on petition of all the parties set forth in §1.324(b)(1)–(3), including the assignees, and satisfactory proof of the facts and payment of the fee set forth in §1.20(b), or on order of a court before which such matter is called in question, include in the reexamination certificate to be issued under §1.570 or §1.977 an amendment naming only the actual inventor or inventors. The petition must be submitted as part of the reexamination proceeding and must satisfy the requirements of §1.324.

(2) Notwithstanding the preceding paragraph (l)(1) of this section, if a petition to correct inventorship satisfying the requirements of §1.324 is filed in a reexamination proceeding, and the reexamination proceeding is terminated other than by a reexamination certificate under §1.570 or §1.977, a certificate of correction indicating the change of inventorship stated in the petition will be issued upon request by the patentee.

27. Section 1.535 is revised to read as follows:

§1.535 Reply by third party requester in *ex parte* reexamination.

A reply to the patent owner's statement under §1.530 may be filed by the *ex parte* reexamination requester within two months from the date of service of the patent owner's statement. Any reply by the *ex parte* requester must be served upon the patent owner in accordance with §1.248. If the patent owner does not file a statement under §1.530, no reply or other submission from the *ex parte* reexamination requester will be considered.

28. Section 1.540 is revised to read as follows:

§1.540 Consideration of responses in *ex parte* reexamination.

The failure to timely file or serve the documents set forth in §1.530 or in §1.535 may result in their being refused consideration. No submissions other than the statement pursuant to §1.530 and the reply by the *ex parte* reexamination requester pursuant to §1.535 will be considered prior to examination.

29. Section 1.550 is revised to read as follows:

§1.550 Conduct of *ex parte* reexamination proceedings.

(a) All *ex parte* reexamination proceedings, including any appeals to the Board of Patent Appeals and Interferences, will be conducted with special dispatch within the Office. After issuance of the *ex parte* reexamination order and expiration of the time for submitting any responses, the examination will be conducted in accordance with §§1.104 through 1.116 and will result in the issuance of an *ex parte* reexamination certificate under §1.570.

(b) The patent owner in an *ex parte* reexamination proceeding will be given at least thirty days to respond to any Office action. In response to any rejection, such response may include further statements and/or proposed amendments or new claims to place the patent in a condition where all claims, if amended as proposed, would be patentable.

(c) The time for taking any action by a patent owner in an *ex parte* reexamination proceeding will be extended only for sufficient cause and for a reasonable time specified. Any request for such extension must be filed on or before the day on which action by the patent owner is due, but in no case will the mere filing of a request effect any extension. See §1.304(a) for extensions of time for filing a notice of appeal to the U.S. Court of Appeals for the Federal Circuit or for commencing a civil action.

(d) If the patent owner fails to file a timely and appropriate response to any Office action or any written statement of an interview required under §1.560(b), the *ex parte* reexamination proceeding will be terminated, and the Commissioner will proceed to issue a certificate under §1.570 in accordance with the last action of the Office.

(e) If a response by the patent owner is not timely filed in the Office,

(1) The delay in filing such response may be excused if it is shown to the satisfaction of the Commissioner that the delay was unavoidable; a petition to accept an unavoidably delayed response must be filed in compliance with §1.137(a); or

(2) The response may nevertheless be accepted if the delay was unintentional; a petition to accept an unintentionally delayed response must be filed in compliance with §1.137(b).

(f) The reexamination requester will be sent copies of Office actions issued during the *ex parte* reexamination proceeding. After filing of a request for *ex parte* reexamination by a third party requester, any document filed by either the patent owner or the third party requester must be served on the other party in the reexamination proceeding in the manner provided by §1.248. The document must reflect service or the document may be refused consideration by the Office.

(g) The active participation of the *ex parte* reexamination requester ends with the reply pursuant to §1.535, and no further submissions on behalf of the reexamination requester will be acknowledged or considered. Further, no submissions on behalf of any third parties will be acknowledged or considered unless such submissions are:

(1) in accordance with §1.510 or §1.535; or

(2) entered in the patent file prior to the date of the order for *ex parte* reexamination pursuant to §1.525.

(h) Submissions by third parties, filed after the date of the order for *ex parte* reexamination pursuant to §1.525, must meet the requirements of and will be treated in accordance with §1.501(a).

30. Section 1.552 is revised to read as follows:

§1.552 Scope of reexamination in *ex parte* reexamination proceedings.

(a) Claims in an *ex parte* reexamination proceeding will be examined on the basis of patents or printed publications and, with respect to subject matter added or deleted in the reexamination proceeding, on the basis of the requirements of 35 U.S.C. 112.

(b) Claims in an *ex parte* reexamination proceeding will not be permitted to enlarge the scope of the claims of the patent.

(c) Issues other than those indicated in paragraphs (a) and (b) of this section will not be resolved in a reexamination proceeding. If such issues are raised by the patent owner or third party requester during a reexamination proceeding, the existence of such issues will be noted by the examiner in the next Office action, in which case the patent owner may consider the advisability of filing a reissue application to have such issues considered and resolved.

31. Section 1.555 is amended by revising its heading and paragraph (c) to read as follows:

§1.555 Information material to patentability in *ex parte* reexamination and *inter partes* reexamination proceedings.

* * * * *

(c) The responsibility for compliance with this section rests upon the individuals designated in paragraph (a) of this section and no evaluation will be made by the Office in the reexamination proceeding as to compliance with this section. If questions of compliance with this section are raised by the patent owner or the third party requester during a reexamination proceeding, they will be noted as unresolved questions in accordance with §1.552(c).

32. Section 1.560 is revised to read as follows:

§1.560 Interviews in *ex parte* reexamination proceedings.

(a) Interviews in *ex parte* reexamination proceedings pending before the Office between examiners and the owners of such patents or their attorneys or agents of record must be conducted in the Office at such times, within Office hours, as the respective examiners may designate. Interviews will not be permitted at any other time or place without the authority of the Commissioner. Interviews for the discussion of the patentability of claims in patents involved in *ex parte* reexamination proceedings will not be conducted prior to the first official action. Interviews should be arranged in advance. Requests that reexamination requesters participate in interviews with examiners will not be granted.

(b) In every instance of an interview with an examiner in an *ex parte* reexamination proceeding, a complete written statement of the reasons presented at the interview as warranting favorable action must be filed by the patent owner. An interview does not remove the necessity for response to Office actions as specified in §1.111. Patent owner's response to an outstanding Office action after the interview does not remove the necessity for filing the written statement. The written statement must be filed as a separate part of a response to an Office action outstanding at the time of the interview, or as a separate paper within one month from the date of the interview, whichever is later.

33. Section 1.565 is revised to read as follows:

§1.565 Concurrent Office proceedings which include an *ex parte* reexamination proceeding.

(a) In an *ex parte* reexamination proceeding before the Office, the patent owner must inform the Office of any prior or concurrent proceedings in which the patent is or was involved such as interferences, reissues, *ex parte* reexaminations, *inter partes* reexaminations, or litigation and the results of such proceedings. See §1.985 for notification of prior or concurrent proceedings in an *inter partes* reexamination proceeding.

(b) If a patent in the process of *ex parte* reexamination is or becomes involved in litigation, the Commissioner shall determine whether or not to suspend the reexamination. See §1.987 for *inter partes* reexamination proceedings.

(c) If *ex parte* reexamination is ordered while a prior *ex parte* reexamination proceeding is pending and prosecution in the prior *ex parte* reexamination proceeding has not been terminated, the *ex parte* reexamination proceedings will be consolidated and result in the issuance of a single certificate under §1.570. For merger of *inter partes* reexamination proceedings, see §1.989(a). For merger of *ex parte* reexamination and *inter partes* reexamination proceedings, see §1.989(b).

(d) If a reissue application and an *ex parte* reexamination proceeding on which an order pursuant to §1.525 has been mailed are pending concurrently on a patent, a decision will normally be made to merge the two proceedings or to suspend one of the two proceedings. Where merger of a reissue application and an *ex parte* reexamination proceeding is ordered, the merged examination will be conducted in accordance with §§1.171 through 1.179, and the patent owner will be required to place and maintain the same claims in the reissue application and the *ex parte* reexamination proceeding during the pendency of the merged proceeding. The examiner's actions and responses by the patent owner in a merged proceeding will apply to both the reissue application and the *ex parte* reexamination proceeding and be physically entered into both files. Any *ex parte* reexamination proceeding merged with a reissue application shall be terminated by the grant of the reissued patent. For merger of a reissue application and an *inter partes* reexamination, see §1.991.

(e) If a patent in the process of *ex parte* reexamination is or becomes involved in an interference, the Commissioner may suspend the reexamination or the interference. The Commissioner will not consider a request to suspend an interference unless a motion (§1.635) to suspend the interference has been presented to, and denied by, an administrative patent judge, and the request is filed within ten (10) days of a decision by an administrative patent judge denying the motion for suspension or such other time as the administrative patent judge may set. For concurrent *inter partes* reexamination and interference of a patent, see §1.993.

34. The undesignated center heading following §1.565 is revised to read as follows:

Ex Parte Reexamination Certificate

35. Section 1.570 is revised to read as follows:

§1.570 Issuance of *ex parte* reexamination certificate after *ex parte* reexamination proceedings.

(a) Upon the conclusion of *ex parte* reexamination proceedings, the Commissioner will issue an *ex parte* reexamination certificate in accordance with 35 U.S.C. 307 setting forth the results of the *ex parte* reexamination proceeding and the content of the patent following the *ex parte* reexamination proceeding.

(b) An *ex parte* reexamination certificate will be issued in each patent in which an *ex parte* reexamination proceeding has been ordered under §1.525 and has not been merged with any *inter partes* reexamination proceeding pursuant to §1.989(a). Any statutory disclaimer filed by the patent owner will be made part of the *ex parte* reexamination certificate.

(c) The *ex parte* reexamination certificate will be mailed on the day of its date to the patent owner at the address as provided for in §1.33(c). A copy of the *ex parte* reexamination certificate will also be mailed to the requester of the *ex parte* reexamination proceeding.

(d) If an *ex parte* reexamination certificate has been issued which cancels all of the claims of the patent, no further Office proceedings will be conducted with that patent or any reissue applications or any reexamination requests relating thereto.

(e) If the *ex parte* reexamination proceeding is terminated by the grant of a reissued patent as provided in §1.565(d), the reissued patent will constitute the *ex parte* reexamination certificate required by this section and 35 U.S.C. 307.

(f) A notice of the issuance of each *ex parte* reexamination certificate under this section will be published in the *Official Gazette* on its date of issuance.

36. A new subpart H is added to read as follows:

Subpart H—*Inter Partes* Reexamination of Patents That Issued From an Original Application Filed in the United States on or After November 29, 1999

Sec.

Prior Art Citations

1.902 Processing of prior art citations during an *inter partes* reexamination proceeding.

Requirements for *Inter Partes* Reexamination Proceedings

1.903 Service of papers on parties in *inter partes* reexamination.
1.904 Notice of *inter partes* reexamination in Official Gazette.
1.905 Submission of papers by the public in *inter partes* reexamination.
1.906 Scope of reexamination in *inter partes* reexamination proceeding.
1.907 *Inter partes* reexamination prohibited.
1.913 Persons eligible to file request for *inter partes* reexamination.
1.915 Content of request for *inter partes* reexamination.
1.919 Filing date of request for *inter partes* reexamination.
1.923 Examiner's determination on the request for *inter partes* reexamination.
1.925 Partial refund if request for *inter partes* reexamination is not ordered.
1.927 Petition to review refusal to order *inter partes* reexamination.

Inter Partes Reexamination of Patents

1.931 Order for *inter partes* reexamination.

Information Disclosure in *Inter Partes* Reexamination

1.933 Patent owner duty of disclosure in *inter partes* reexamination proceedings.

Office Actions and Responses (Before the Examiner) in *Inter Partes* Reexamination

1.935 Initial Office action usually accompanies order for *inter partes* reexamination.
1.937 Conduct of *inter partes* reexamination.
1.939 Unauthorized papers in *inter partes* reexamination.
1.941 Amendments by patent owner in *inter partes* reexamination.
1.943 Requirements of responses, written comments, and briefs in *inter partes* reexamination.
1.945 Response to Office action by patent owner in *inter partes* reexamination.
1.947 Comments by third party requester to patent owner's response in *inter partes* reexamination.
1.948 Limitations on submission of prior art by third party requester following the order for *inter partes* reexamination.
1.949 Examiner's Office action closing prosecution in *inter partes* reexamination.
1.951 Options after Office action closing prosecution in *inter partes* reexamination.
1.953 Examiner's Right of Appeal Notice in *inter partes* reexamination.

Interviews Prohibited in *Inter Partes* Reexamination

1.955 Interviews prohibited in *inter partes* reexamination proceedings.

Extensions of Time, Termination of Proceedings, and Petitions to Revive in *Inter Partes* Reexamination

1.956 Patent owner extensions of time in *inter partes* reexamination.
1.957 Failure to file a timely, appropriate or complete response or comment in *inter partes* reexamination.
1.958 Petition to revive terminated *inter partes* reexamination or claims terminated for lack of patent owner response.

Appeal to the Board of Patent Appeals and Interferences in *Inter Partes* Reexamination

1.959 Notice of appeal and cross appeal to Board of Patent Appeals and Interferences in *inter partes* reexamination.
1.961 Jurisdiction over appeal in *inter partes* reexamination.
1.962 Appellant and respondent in *inter partes* reexamination defined.
1.963 Time for filing briefs in *inter partes* reexamination.
1.965 Appellant's brief in *inter partes* reexamination.

Subpart H—*Inter Partes* Reexamination of Patents That Issued From an Original Application Filed in the United States on or After November 29, 1999

Prior Art Citations

§1.902 Processing of prior art citations during an *inter partes* reexamination proceeding.

Citations by the patent owner in accordance with §1.933 and by an *inter partes* reexamination third party requester under §1.915 or §1.948 will be entered in the *inter partes* reexamination file. The entry in the patent file of other citations submitted after the date of an order for reexamination pursuant to §1.931 by persons other than the patent owner, or the third party requester under either §1.915 or §1.948, will be delayed until the *inter partes* reexamination proceeding has been terminated. See §1.502 for processing of prior art citations in patent and reexamination files during an *ex parte* reexamination proceeding filed under §1.510.

Requirements for *Inter Partes* Reexamination Proceedings

§1.903 Service of papers on parties in *inter partes* reexamination.

The patent owner and the third party requester will be sent copies of Office actions issued during the *inter partes* reexamination proceeding. After filing of a request for *inter partes* reexamination by a third party requester, any document filed by either the patent owner or the third party requester must be served on every other party in the reexamination proceeding in the manner provided in §1.248. Any document must reflect service or the document may be refused consideration by the Office. The failure of the patent owner or the third party requester to serve documents may result in their being refused consideration.

§1.904 Notice of *inter partes* reexamination in *Official Gazette*.

A notice of the filing of an *inter partes* reexamination request will be published in the *Official Gazette*. The notice published in the *Official Gazette* under §1.11(c) will be considered to be constructive notice of the *inter partes* reexamination proceeding and *inter partes* reexamination will proceed.

§1.905 Submission of papers by the public in *inter partes* reexamination.

Unless specifically provided for, no submissions on behalf of any third parties other than third party requesters as defined in 35 U.S.C. 100(e) will be considered unless such submissions are in accordance with §1.915 or entered in the patent file prior to the date of the order for reexamination pursuant to §1.931. Submissions by third parties, other than third party requesters, filed after the date of the order for reexamination pursuant to §1.931, must meet the requirements of §1.501 and will be treated in accordance with §1.902. Submissions which do not meet the requirements of §1.501 will be returned.

§1.906 Scope of reexamination in *inter partes* reexamination proceeding.

(a) Claims in an *inter partes* reexamination proceeding will be examined on the basis of patents or printed publications and, with respect to subject matter added or deleted in the reexamination proceeding, on the basis of the requirements of 35 U.S.C. 112.

(b) Claims in an *inter partes* reexamination proceeding will not be permitted to enlarge the scope of the claims of the patent.

(c) Issues other than those indicated in paragraphs (a) and (b) of this section will not be resolved in an *inter partes* reexamination proceeding. If such issues are raised by the patent owner or the third party requester during a reexamination proceeding, the existence of such issues will be noted by the examiner in the next Office action, in which case the patent owner may desire to consider the advisability of filing a reissue application to have such issues considered and resolved.

§1.907 *Inter partes* reexamination prohibited.

(a) Once an order to reexamine has been issued under §1.931, neither the third party requester, nor its privies, may file a subsequent request for *inter partes* reexamination of the patent until an *inter partes* reexamination certificate is issued under §1.997, unless authorized by the Commissioner.

(b) Once a final decision has been entered against a party in a civil action arising in whole or in part under 28 U.S.C. 1338 that the party has not sustained its burden of proving invalidity of any patent claim-in-suit, then neither that party nor its privies may thereafter request *inter partes* reexamination of any such patent claim on the basis of issues which that party, or its privies, raised or could have raised in such civil action, and an *inter partes* reexamination requested by that party, or its privies, on the basis of such issues may not thereafter be maintained by the Office.

(c) If a final decision in an *inter partes* reexamination proceeding instituted by a third party requester is favorable to patentability of any original, proposed amended, or new claims of the patent, then neither that party nor its privies may thereafter request *inter partes* reexamination of any such patent claims on the basis of issues which that party, or its privies, raised or could have raised in such *inter partes* reexamination proceeding.

§1.913 Persons eligible to file request for *inter partes* reexamination.

Except as provided for in §1.907, any person may, at any time during the period of enforceability of a patent which issued from an original application filed in the United States on or after November 29, 1999, file a request for *inter partes* reexamination by the Office of any claim of the patent on the basis of prior art patents or printed publications cited under §1.501.

§1.915 Content of request for *inter partes* reexamination.

(a) The request must be accompanied by the fee for requesting *inter partes* reexamination set forth in §1.20(c)(2).

(b) A request for *inter partes* reexamination must include the following parts:

(1) An identification of the patent by patent number and every claim for which reexamination is requested.

(2) A citation of the patents and printed publications which are presented to provide a substantial new question of patentability.

(3) A statement pointing out each substantial new question of patentability based on the cited patents and printed publications, and a detailed explanation of the pertinency and manner of applying the patents and printed publications to every claim for which reexamination is requested.

(4) A copy of every patent or printed publication relied upon or referred to in paragraphs (b)(1) through (3) of this section, accompanied by an English language translation of all the necessary and pertinent parts of any non-English language document.

(5) A copy of the entire patent including the front face, drawings, and specification/claims (in double column format) for which reexamination is requested, and a copy of any disclaimer, certificate of correction, or reexamination certificate issued in the patent. All copies must have each page plainly written on only one side of a sheet of paper.

(6) A certification by the third party requester that a copy of the request has been served in its entirety on the patent owner at the address provided for in §1.33(c). The name and address of the party served must be indicated. If service was not possible, a duplicate copy of the request must be supplied to the Office.

(7) A certification by the third party requester that the estoppel provisions of §1.907 do not prohibit the *inter partes* reexamination.

(8) A statement identifying the real party in interest to the extent necessary for a subsequent person filing an *inter partes* reexamination request to determine whether that person is a privy.

(c) If an *inter partes* request is filed by an attorney or agent identifying another party on whose behalf the request is being filed, the attorney or agent must have a power of attorney from that party or be acting in a representative capacity pursuant to §1.34(a).

(d) If the *inter partes* request does not meet all the requirements of subsection 1.915(b), the person identified as requesting *inter partes* reexamination may be so notified and given an opportunity to complete the formal requirements of the request within a specified time. Failure to comply with the notice may result in the *inter partes* reexamination proceeding being vacated.

§1.919 Filing date of request for *inter partes* reexamination.

(a) The filing date of a request for *inter partes* reexamination is the date on which the request satisfies the fee requirement of §1.915(a).

(b) If the request is not granted a filing date, the request will be placed in the patent file as a citation of prior art if it complies with the requirements of §1.501.

§1.923 Examiner's determination on the request for *inter partes* reexamination.

Within three months following the filing date of a request for *inter partes* reexamination under §1.919, the examiner will consider the request and determine whether or not a substantial new question of patentability affecting any claim of the patent is raised by the request and the prior art citation. The examiner's determination will be based on the claims in effect at the time of the determination, will become a part of the official file of the patent, and will be mailed to the patent owner at the address as provided for in §1.33(c) and to the third party requester. If the examiner determines that no substantial new question of patentability is present, the examiner shall refuse the request and shall not order *inter partes* reexamination.

§1.925 Partial refund if request for *inter partes* reexamination is not ordered.

Where *inter partes* reexamination is not ordered, a refund of a portion of the fee for requesting *inter partes* reexamination will be made to the requester in accordance with §1.26(c).

§1.927 Petition to review refusal to order *inter partes* reexamination.

The third party requester may seek review by a petition to the Commissioner under §1.181 within one month of the mailing date of the examiner's determination refusing to order *inter partes* reexamination. Any such petition must comply with §1.181(b). If no petition is timely filed or if the decision on petition affirms that no substantial new question of patentability has been raised, the determination shall be final and nonappealable.

Inter Partes Reexamination of Patents

§1.931 Order for *inter partes* reexamination.

(a) If a substantial new question of patentability is found, the determination will include an order for *inter partes* reexamination of the patent for resolution of the question.

(b) If the order for *inter partes* reexamination resulted from a petition pursuant to §1.927, the *inter partes* reexamination will ordinarily be conducted by an examiner other than the examiner responsible for the initial determination under §1.923.

Information Disclosure in *Inter Partes* Reexamination

§1.933 Patent owner duty of disclosure in *inter partes* reexamination proceedings.

(a) Each individual associated with the patent owner in an *inter partes* reexamination proceeding has a duty of candor and good faith in dealing with the Office, which includes a duty to disclose to the Office all information known to that individual to be material to patentability in a reexamination proceeding as set forth in §1.555(a) and (b). The duty to disclose all information known to be material to patentability in an *inter partes* reexamination proceeding is deemed to be satisfied by filing a paper in compliance with the requirements set forth in §1.555(a) and (b).

(b) The responsibility for compliance with this section rests upon the individuals designated in paragraph (a) of this section, and no evaluation will be made by the Office in the reexamination proceeding as to compliance with this section. If questions of compliance with this section are raised by the patent owner or the third party requester during a reexamination proceeding, they will be noted as unresolved questions in accordance with §1.906(c).

Office Actions and Responses (Before the Examiner) in *Inter Partes* Reexamination

§1.935 Initial Office action usually accompanies order for *inter partes* reexamination.

The order for *inter partes* reexamination will usually be accompanied by the initial Office action on the merits of the reexamination.

§1.937 Conduct of *inter partes* reexamination.

(a) All *inter partes* reexamination proceedings, including any appeals to the Board of Patent Appeals and Interferences, will be conducted with special dispatch within the Office, unless the Commissioner makes a determination that there is good cause for suspending the reexamination proceeding.

(b) The *inter partes* reexamination proceeding will be conducted in accordance with §§1.104 through 1.116, the sections governing the application examination process, and will result in the issuance of an *inter partes* reexamination certificate under §1.997, except as otherwise provided.

(c) All communications between the Office and the parties to the *inter partes* reexamination which are directed to the merits of the proceeding must be in writing and filed with the Office for entry into the record of the proceeding.

§1.939 Unauthorized papers in *inter partes* reexamination.

(a) If an unauthorized paper is filed by any party at any time during the *inter partes* reexamination proceeding it will not be considered and may be returned.

(b) Unless otherwise authorized, no paper shall be filed prior to the initial Office action on the merits of the *inter partes* reexamination.

§1.941 Amendments by patent owner in *inter partes* reexamination.

Amendments by patent owner in *inter partes* reexamination proceedings are made by filing a paper in compliance with §§1.530(d)–(k) and 1.943.

§1.943 Requirements of responses, written comments, and briefs in *inter partes* reexamination.

(a) The form of responses, written comments, briefs, appendices, and other papers must be in accordance with the requirements of §1.52.

(b) Responses by the patent owner and written comments by the third party requester shall not exceed 50 pages in length, excluding amendments, appendices of claims, and reference materials such as prior art references.

(c) Appellant's briefs filed by the patent owner and the third party requester shall not exceed thirty pages or 14,000 words in length, excluding appendices of claims and reference materials such as prior art references. All other briefs filed by any party shall not exceed fifteen pages in length or 7,000 words. If the page limit for any brief is exceeded, a certificate is required stating the number of words contained in the brief.

§1.945 Response to Office action by patent owner in *inter partes* reexamination.

The patent owner will be given at least thirty days to file a response to any Office action on the merits of the *inter partes* reexamination.

§1.947 Comments by third party requester to patent owner's response in *inter partes* reexamination.

Each time the patent owner files a response to an Office action on the merits pursuant to §1.945, a third party requester may once file written comments within a period of 30 days from the date of service of the patent owner's response. These comments shall be limited to issues raised by the Office action or the patent owner's response. The time for submitting comments by the third party requester may not be extended. For the purpose of filing the written comments by the third party requester, the comments will be considered as having been received in the Office as of the date of deposit specified in the certificate under §1.8.

§1.948 Limitations on submission of prior art by third party requester following the order for *inter partes* reexamination.

(a) After the *inter partes* reexamination order, the third party requester may only cite additional prior art as defined under §1.501 if it is filed as part of a comments submission under §1.947 or §1.951(b) and is limited to prior art:

(1) which is necessary to rebut a finding of fact by the examiner;

(2) which is necessary to rebut a response of the patent owner; or

(3) which for the first time became known or available to the third party requester after the filing of the request for *inter partes* reexamination proceeding. Prior art submitted under paragraph (a)(3) of this section must be accompanied by a statement as to when the prior art first became known or available to the third party requester and must include a discussion of the pertinency of each reference to the patentability of at least one claim.

(b) [Reserved].

§1.949 Examiner's Office action closing prosecution in *inter partes* reexamination.

Upon consideration of the issues a second or subsequent time, or upon a determination of patentability of all claims, the examiner shall issue an Office action treating all claims present in the *inter partes* reexamination, which may be an action closing prosecution. The Office action shall set forth all rejections and determinations not to make a proposed rejection, and the grounds therefor. An Office action will not usually close prosecution if it includes a new ground of rejection which was not previously addressed by the patent owner, unless the new ground was necessitated by an amendment.

§1.951 Options after Office action closing prosecution in *inter partes* reexamination.

(a) After an Office action closing prosecution in an *inter partes* reexamination, the patent owner may once file comments limited to the issues raised in the Office action closing prosecution. The comments can include a proposed amendment to the claims, which amendment will be subject to the criteria of §1.116 as to whether or not it shall be admitted. The comments must be filed within the time set for response in the Office action closing prosecution.

(b) When the patent owner does file comments, a third party requester may once file comments responsive to the patent owner's comments within 30 days from the date of service of patent owner's comments on the third party requester.

§1.953 Examiner's Right of Appeal Notice in *inter partes* reexamination.

(a) Upon considering the comments of the patent owner and the third party requester subsequent to the Office action closing prosecution in an *inter partes* reexamination, or upon expiration of the time for submitting such comments, the examiner shall issue a Right of Appeal Notice, unless the examiner reopens prosecution and issues another Office action on the merits.

(b) *Expedited Right of Appeal Notice:* At any time after the patent owner's response to the initial Office action on the merits in an *inter partes* reexamination, the patent owner and all third party requesters may stipulate that the issues are appropriate for a final action, which would include a final rejection and/or a final determination favorable to patentability, and may request the issuance of a Right of Appeal Notice. The request must have the concurrence of the patent owner and all third party requesters present in the proceeding and must identify all the appealable issues and the positions of the patent owner and all third party requesters on those issues. If the examiner determines that no other issues are present or should be raised, a Right of Appeal Notice limited to the identified issues shall be issued. Any appeal by the parties shall be conducted in accordance with §§1.959–1.983.

(c) The Right of Appeal Notice shall be a final action, which comprises a final rejection setting forth each ground of rejection and/or final decision favorable to patentability including each determination not to make a proposed rejection, an identification of the status of each claim, and the reasons for decisions favorable to patentability and/or the grounds of rejection for each claim. No amendment can be made in response to the Right of Appeal Notice. The Right of Appeal Notice shall set a one-month time period for either party to appeal. If no notice of appeal is filed, the *inter partes* reexamination proceeding will be terminated, and the Commissioner will proceed to issue a certificate under §1.997 in accordance with the Right of Appeal Notice.

Interviews Prohibited in *Inter Partes* Reexamination

§1.955 Interviews prohibited in *inter partes* reexamination proceedings.

There will be no interviews in an *inter partes* reexamination proceeding which discuss the merits of the proceeding.

Extensions of Time, Termination of Proceedings, and Petitions to Revive in *Inter Partes* Reexamination

§1.956 Patent owner extensions of time in *inter partes* reexamination.

The time for taking any action by a patent owner in an *inter partes* reexamination proceeding will be extended only for sufficient cause and for a reasonable time specified. Any request for such extension must be filed on or before the day on which action by the patent owner is due, but in no case will the mere filing of a request effect any extension. See §1.304(a) for extensions of time for filing a notice of appeal to the U.S. Court of Appeals for the Federal Circuit.

§1.957 Failure to file a timely, appropriate or complete response or comment in *inter partes* reexamination.

(a) If the third party requester files an untimely or inappropriate comment, notice of appeal or brief in an *inter partes* reexamination, the paper will be refused consideration.

(b) If no claims are found patentable, and the patent owner fails to file a timely and appropriate response in an *inter partes* reexamination proceeding, the reexamination proceeding will be terminated and the Commissioner will proceed to issue a certificate under §1.997 in accordance with the last action of the Office.

(c) If claims are found patentable and the patent owner fails to file a timely and appropriate response to any Office action in an *inter partes* reexamination proceeding, further prosecution will be limited to the claims found patentable at the time of the failure to respond, and to any claims added thereafter which do not expand the scope of the claims which were found patentable at that time.

(d) When action by the patent owner is a *bona fide* attempt to respond and to advance the prosecution and is substantially a complete response to the Office action, but consideration of some matter or compliance with some requirement has been inadvertently omitted, an opportunity to explain and supply the omission may be given.

§1.958 Petition to revive terminated *inter partes* reexamination or claims terminated for lack of patent owner response.

(a) If a response by the patent owner is not timely filed in the Office, the delay in filing such response may be excused if it is shown to the satisfaction of the Commissioner that the delay was unavoidable. A grantable petition to accept an unavoidably delayed response must be filed in compliance with §1.137(a).

(b) Any response by the patent owner not timely filed in the Office may be accepted if the delay was unintentional. A grantable petition to accept an unintentionally delayed response must be filed in compliance with §1.137(b).

Appeal to the Board of Patent Appeals and Interferences in *Inter Partes* Reexamination

§1.959 Notice of appeal and cross appeal to Board of Patent Appeals and interferences in *inter partes* reexamination.

(a)(1) Upon the issuance of a Right of Appeal Notice under §1.953, the patent owner involved in an *inter partes* reexamination proceeding may appeal to the Board of Patent Appeals and Interferences with respect to the final rejection of any claim of the patent by filing a notice of appeal within the time provided in the Right of Appeal Notice and paying the fee set forth in §1.17(b).

(2) Upon the issuance of a Right of Appeal Notice under §1.953, a third party requester involved in an *inter partes* reexamination proceeding may appeal to the Board of Patent Appeals and Interferences with respect to any final decision favorable to the patentability, including any final determination not to make a proposed rejection, of any original, proposed amended, or new claim of the patent by filing a notice of appeal within the time provided in the Right of Appeal Notice and paying the fee set forth in §1.17(b).

(b)(1) Within fourteen days of service of a third party requester's notice of appeal under paragraph (a)(2) of this section and upon payment of the fee set forth in §1.17(b), a patent owner who has not filed a notice of appeal may file a notice of cross appeal with respect to the final rejection of any claim of the patent.

(2) Within fourteen days of service of a patent owner's notice of appeal under paragraph (a)(1) of this section and upon payment of the fee set forth in §1.17(b), a third party requester who has not filed a notice of appeal may file a notice of cross appeal with respect to any final decision favorable to the patentability, including any final determination not to make a proposed rejection, of any original, proposed amended, or new claim of the patent.

(c) The notice of appeal or cross appeal in an *inter partes* reexamination proceeding must identify the appealed claim(s) and must be signed by the patent owner, the third party requester, or their duly authorized attorney or agent.

(d) An appeal or cross appeal, when taken, must be taken from all the rejections of the claims in a Right of Appeal Notice which the patent owner proposes to contest or from all the determinations favorable to patentability, including any final determination not to make a proposed rejection, in a Right of Appeal Notice which a third party requester proposes to contest. Questions relating to matters not affecting the merits of the invention may be required to be settled before an appeal is decided.

(e) The times for filing a notice of appeal or cross appeal may not be extended.

§1.961 Jurisdiction over appeal in *inter partes* reexamination.

Jurisdiction over the *inter partes* reexamination proceeding passes to the Board of Patent Appeals and Interferences upon transmittal of the file, including all briefs and examiner's answers, to the Board of Patent Appeals and Interferences. Prior to the entry of a decision on the appeal, the Commissioner may *sua sponte* order the *inter partes* reexamination proceeding remanded to the examiner for action consistent with the Commissioner's order.

§1.962 Appellant and respondent in *inter partes* reexamination defined.

For the purposes of *inter partes* reexamination, appellant is any party, whether the patent owner or a third party requester, filing a notice of appeal or cross appeal. If more than one party appeals or cross appeals, each appealing or cross appealing party is an appellant with respect to the claims to which his or her appeal or cross appeal is directed. A respondent is any third party requester responding under §1.967 to the appellant's brief of the patent owner, or the patent owner responding under §1.967 to the appellant's brief of any third party requester. No third party requester may be a respondent to the appellant brief of any other third party requester.

§1.963 Time for filing briefs in *inter partes* reexamination.

(a) An appellant's brief in an *inter partes* reexamination must be filed no later than two months from the latest filing date of the last-filed notice of appeal or cross appeal or, if any party to the *inter partes* reexamination is entitled to file an appeal or cross appeal but fails to timely do so, the expiration of time for filing (by the last party entitled to do so) such notice of appeal or cross appeal. The time for filing an appellant's brief may not be extended.

(b) Once an appellant's brief has been properly filed, any brief must be filed by respondent within one month from the date of service of the appellant's brief. The time for filing a respondent's brief may not be extended.

(c) The examiner will consider both the appellant's and respondent's briefs and may prepare an examiner's answer under §1.969.

(d) Any appellant may file a rebuttal brief under §1.971 within one month of the date of the examiner's answer. The time for filing a rebuttal brief may not be extended.

(e) No further submission will be considered and any such submission will be treated in accordance with §1.939.

§1.965 Appellant's brief in *inter partes* reexamination.

(a) Appellant(s) may once, within time limits for filing set forth in §1.963, file a brief in triplicate and serve the brief on all other parties to the *inter partes* reexamination proceeding in accordance with §1.903. The brief must be signed by the appellant, or the appellant's duly authorized attorney or agent and must be accompanied by the requisite fee set forth in §1.17(c). The brief must set forth the authorities and arguments on which appellant will rely to maintain the appeal. Any arguments or authorities not included in the brief will be refused consideration by the Board of Patent Appeals and Interferences, unless good cause is shown.

(b) A party's appeal shall stand dismissed upon failure of that party to file an appellant's brief, accompanied by the requisite fee, within the time allowed.

(c) The appellant's brief shall contain the following items under appropriate headings and in the order indicated below, unless the brief is filed by a party who is not represented by a registered practitioner. The brief may include an appendix containing only those portions of the record on which reliance has been made.

(1) *Real Party in Interest.* A statement identifying the real party in interest.

(2) *Related Appeals and Interferences.* A statement identifying by number and filing date all other appeals or interferences known to the appellant, the appellant's legal representative, or assignee which will directly affect or be directly affected by or have a bearing on the decision of the Board of Patent Appeals and Interferences in the pending appeal.

(3) *Status of Claims.* A statement of the status of all the claims, pending or canceled. If the appellant is the patent owner, the appellant must also identify the rejected claims whose rejection is being appealed. If the appellant is a third party requester, the appellant must identify the claims that the examiner has made a determination favorable to patentability, which determination is being appealed.

(4) *Status of Amendments.* A statement of the status of any amendment filed subsequent to the close of prosecution.

(5) *Summary of Invention.* A concise explanation of the invention or subject matter defined in the claims involved in the appeal, which shall refer to the specification by column and line number, and to the drawing(s), if any, by reference characters.

(6) *Issues.* A concise statement of the issues presented for review. No new ground of rejection can be proposed by a third party requester appellant.

(7) *Grouping of Claims.* If the appellant is the patent owner, for each ground of rejection in the Right of Appeal Notice which appellant contests and which applies to a group of two or more claims, the Board of Patent Appeals and Interferences shall select a single claim from the group and shall decide the appeal as to the ground of rejection on the basis of that claim alone unless a statement is included that the claims of the group do not stand or fall together; and, in the argument under paragraph (c)(8) of this section, appellant explains why the claims of this group are believed to be separately patentable. Merely pointing out differences in what the claims cover is not an argument as to why the claims are separately patentable.

(8) *Argument.* The contentions of appellant with respect to each of the issues presented for review in paragraph (c)(6) of this section, and the bases therefor, with citations of the authorities, statutes, and parts of the record relied on. Each issue should be treated under a separate, numbered heading.

(i) For each rejection under 35 U.S.C. 112, first paragraph, or for each determination favorable to patentability, including a determination not to make a proposed rejection under 35 U.S.C. 112, first paragraph, which appellant contests, the argument shall specify the errors in the rejection or the determination and how the first paragraph of 35 U.S.C. 112 is complied with, if the appellant is the patent owner, or is not complied with, if the appellant is a third party requester, including, as appropriate, how the specification and drawing(s), if any,

(A) Describe, if the appellant is the patent owner, or fail to describe, if the appellant is a third party requester, the subject matter defined by each of the appealed claims; and

(B) Enable, if the appellant is the patent owner, or fail to enable, if the appellant is a third party requester, any person skilled in the art to make and use the subject matter defined by each of the appealed claims.

(ii) For each rejection under 35 U.S.C. 112, second paragraph, or for each determination favorable to patentability including a determination not to make a proposed rejection under 35 U.S.C. 112, second paragraph, which appellant contests, the argument shall specify the errors in the rejection, if the appellant is the patent owner, or the determination, if the appellant is a third party requester, and how the claims do, if the appellant is the patent owner, or do not, if the appellant is a third party requester, particularly point out and distinctly claim the subject matter which the inventor regards as the invention.

(iii) For each rejection under 35 U.S.C. 102 or for each determination favorable to patentability including a determination not to make a proposed rejection under 35 U.S.C. 102 which appellant contests, the argument shall specify the errors in the rejection, if the appellant is the patent owner, or determination, if the appellant is a third party requester, and why the appealed claims are, if the appellant is the patent owner, or are not, if the appellant is a third party requester, patentable under 35 U.S.C. 102, including any specific limitations in the appealed claims which are or are not described in the prior art.

(iv) For each rejection under 35 U.S.C. 103 or for each determination favorable to patentability, including a determination not to make a proposed rejection under 35 U.S.C. 103 which appellant contests, the argument shall specify the errors in the rejection, if the appellant is the patent owner, or determination, if the appellant is a third party requester. If appropriate, also state the specific limitations in the appealed claims which are or are not described in the prior art and explain how such limitations render the claimed subject matter obvious, if the appellant is a third party requester, or unobvious, if the appellant is the patent owner, over the prior art. If the rejection or determination is based upon a combination of references, the argument shall explain why the references, taken as a whole, do or do not suggest the claimed subject matter. The argument should include, as may be appropriate, an explanation of why features disclosed in one reference may or may not properly be combined with features disclosed in another reference. A general argument that all the limitations are or are not described in a single reference does not satisfy the requirements of this paragraph.

(v) For any rejection other than those referred to in paragraphs (c)(8)(i) to (iv) of this section or for each determination favorable to patentability, including any determination not to make a proposed rejection other than those referred to in paragraphs (c)(8)(i) to (iv) of this section which appellant contests, the argument shall specify the errors in the rejection, if the appellant is the patent owner, or determination, if the appellant is a third party requester, and the specific limitations in the appealed claims, if appropriate, or other reasons, which cause the rejection or determination to be in error.

(9) *Appendix*. An appendix containing a copy of the claims appealed by the appellant.

(10) *Certificate of Service*. A certification that a copy of the brief has been served in its entirety on all other parties to the reexamination proceeding. The names and addresses of the parties served must be indicated.

(d) If a brief is filed which does not comply with all the requirements of paragraph (c) of this section, appellant will be notified of the reasons for non-compliance and provided with a non-extendable period of one month within which to file an amended brief. If the appellant does not file an amended brief during the one-month period, or files an amended brief which does not overcome all the reasons for non-compliance stated in the notification, that appellant's appeal will stand dismissed.

§1.967 Respondent's brief in *inter partes* reexamination.

(a) Respondent(s) in an *inter partes* reexamination appeal may once, within the time limit for filing set forth in §1.963, file a respondent brief in triplicate and serve the brief on all parties in accordance with §1.903. The brief must be signed by the party, or the party's duly authorized attorney or agent, and must be accompanied by the requisite fee set forth in §1.17(c). The brief must state the authorities and arguments on which respondent will rely. Any arguments or authorities not included in the brief will be refused consideration by the Board of Patent Appeals and Interferences, unless good cause is shown. The respondent brief shall be limited to issues raised in the appellant brief to which the respondent brief is directed. A third party respondent brief may not address any brief of any other third party.

(b) The respondent brief shall contain the following items under appropriate headings and in the order here indicated, and may include an appendix containing only those portions of the record on which reliance has been made.

(1) *Real Party in Interest.* A statement identifying the real party in interest.

(2) *Related Appeals and Interferences.* A statement identifying by number and filing date all other appeals or interferences known to the respondent, the respondent's legal representative, or assignee (if any) which will directly affect or be directly affected by or have a bearing on the decision of the Board of Patent Appeals and Interferences in the pending appeal.

(3) *Status of claims.* A statement accepting or disputing appellant's statement of the status of claims. If appellant's statement of the status of claims is disputed, the errors in appellant's statement must be specified with particularity.

(4) *Status of amendments.* A statement accepting or disputing appellant's statement of the status of amendments. If appellant's statement of the status of amendments is disputed, the errors in appellant's statement must be specified with particularity.

(5) *Summary of invention.* A statement accepting or disputing appellant's summary of the invention or subject matter defined in the claims involved in the appeal. If appellant's summary of the invention or subject matter defined in the claims involved in the appeal is disputed, the errors in appellant's summary must be specified.

(6) *Issues.* A statement accepting or disputing appellant's statement of the issues presented for review. If appellant's statement of the issues presented for review is disputed, the errors in appellant's statement must be specified. A counter statement of the issues for review may be made. No new ground of rejection can be proposed by a third party requester respondent.

(7) *Argument.* A statement accepting or disputing the contentions of the appellant with each of the issues. If a contention of the appellant is disputed, the errors in appellant's argument must be specified, stating the basis therefor, with citations of the authorities, statutes, and parts of the record relied on. Each issue should be treated under a separate heading. An argument may be made with each of the issues stated in the counter statement of the issues, with each counter-stated issue being treated under a separate heading. The provisions of §1.965 (c)(8)(iii) and (iv) of these regulations shall apply to any argument raised under 35 U.S.C. 102 or sec. 103.

(8) *Certificate of Service.* A certification that a copy of the respondent brief has been served in its entirety on all other parties to the reexamination proceeding. The names and addresses of the parties served must be indicated.

(c) If a respondent brief is filed which does not comply with all the requirements of paragraph (b) of this section, respondent will be notified of the reasons for non-compliance and provided with a non-extendable period of one month within which to file an amended brief. If the respondent does not file an amended brief during the one-month period, or files an amended brief which does not overcome all the reasons for non-compliance stated in the notification, the respondent brief will not be considered.

§1.969 Examiner's answer in *inter partes* reexamination.

(a) The primary examiner in an *inter partes* reexamination appeal may, within such time as directed by the Commissioner, furnish a written statement in answer to the patent owner's and/or third party requester's appellant brief or respondent brief including, as may be necessary, such explanation of the invention claimed and of the references, the grounds of rejection, and the reasons for patentability, including grounds for not adopting a proposed rejection. A copy of the answer shall be supplied to all parties to the reexamination proceeding. If the primary examiner finds that the appeal is not regular in form or does not relate to an appealable action, he or she shall so state.

(b) An examiner's answer may not include a new ground of rejection.

(c) An examiner's answer may not include a new determination not to make a proposed rejection of a claim.

(d) Any new ground of rejection, or any new determination not to make a proposed rejection, must be made in an Office action reopening prosecution.

§1.971 Rebuttal brief in *inter partes* reexamination.

Within one month of the examiner's answer in an *inter partes* reexamination appeal, any appellant may once file a rebuttal brief in triplicate. The rebuttal brief of the patent owner may be directed to the examiner's answer and/or any respondent brief. The rebuttal brief of any third party requester may be directed to the examiner's answer and/or the respondent brief of the patent owner. The rebuttal brief of a third party requester may not be directed to the respondent brief of any other third party requester. No new ground of rejection can be proposed by a third party requester. The time for filing a rebuttal brief may not be extended. The rebuttal brief must include a certification that a copy of the rebuttal brief has been served in its entirety on all other parties to the reexamination proceeding. The names and addresses of the parties served must be indicated.

§1.973 Oral hearing in *inter partes* reexamination.

(a) An oral hearing in an *inter partes* reexamination appeal should be requested only in those circumstances in which an appellant or a respondent considers such a hearing necessary or desirable for a proper presentation of the appeal. An appeal decided without an oral hearing will receive the same consideration by the Board of Patent Appeals and Interferences as an appeal decided after oral hearing.

(b) If an appellant or a respondent desires an oral hearing, he or she must file a written request for such hearing accompanied by the fee set forth in §1.17(d) within two months after the date of the examiner's answer. The time for requesting an oral hearing may not be extended.

(c) An oral argument may be presented at oral hearing by, or on behalf of, the primary examiner if considered desirable by either the primary examiner or the Board of Patent Appeals and Interferences.

(d) If an appellant or a respondent has requested an oral hearing and has submitted the fee set forth in §1.17(d), a hearing date will be set, and notice given to all parties to the reexamination proceeding, as well as the primary examiner. The notice shall set a non-extendable period within which all requests for oral hearing shall be submitted by any other party to the appeal desiring to participate in the oral hearing. A hearing will be held as stated in the notice, and oral argument will be limited to thirty minutes for each appellant and respondent who has requested an oral hearing, and twenty minutes for the primary examiner unless otherwise ordered before the hearing begins. No appellant or respondent will be permitted to participate in an oral hearing unless he or she has requested an oral hearing and submitted the fee set forth in §1.17(d).

(e) If no request and fee for oral hearing have been timely filed by an appellant or a respondent, the appeal will be assigned for consideration and decision on the written record.

§1.975 Affidavits or declarations after appeal in *inter partes* reexamination.

Affidavits, declarations, or exhibits submitted after the *inter partes* reexamination has been appealed will not be admitted without a showing of good and sufficient reasons why they were not earlier presented.

§1.977 Decision by the Board of Patent Appeals and Interferences; remand to examiner in *inter partes* reexamination.

(a) The Board of Patent Appeals and Interferences, in its decision, may affirm or reverse each decision of the examiner on all issues raised on each appealed claim, or remand the reexamination proceeding to the examiner for further consideration. The reversal of the examiner's determination not to make a rejection proposed by the third party requester constitutes a decision adverse to the patentability of the claims which are subject to that proposed rejection which will be set forth in the decision of the Board of Patent Appeals and Interferences as a new ground of rejection under paragraph (b) of this section. The affirmance of the rejection of a claim on any of the grounds specified constitutes a general affirmance of the decision of the examiner on that claim, except as to any ground specifically reversed.

(b) Should the Board of Patent Appeals and Interferences have knowledge of any grounds not raised in the appeal for rejecting any pending claim, it may include in the decision a statement to that effect with its reasons for so holding, which statement shall constitute a new ground of rejection of the claim. A decision which includes a new ground of rejection shall not be considered final for purposes of judicial review. When the Board of Patent Appeals and Interferences makes a new ground of rejection, the patent owner, within one month from the date of the decision, must exercise one of the following two options with respect to the new ground of rejection to avoid termination of the appeal proceeding as to the rejected claim:

(1) The patent owner may submit an appropriate amendment of the claim so rejected or a showing of facts relating to the claim, or both.

(2) The patent owner may file a request for rehearing of the decision of the Board of Patent Appeals and Interferences under §1.979(a).

(c) Where the patent owner has responded under paragraph (b)(1) of this section, any third party requester, within one month of the date of service of the patent owner response, may once file comments on the response. Such written comments must be limited to the issues raised by the decision of the Board of Patent Appeals and Interferences and the patent owner's response. Any third party requester that had not previously filed an appeal or cross appeal and is seeking under this subsection to file comments or a reply to the comments is subject to the appeal and brief fees under §1.17(b) and (c), respectively, which must accompany the comments or reply.

(d) Following any response by the patent owner under paragraph (b)(1) of this section and any written comments from a third party requester under paragraph (c) of this section, the reexamination proceeding will be remanded to the examiner. The statement of the Board of Patent Appeals and Interferences shall be binding upon the examiner unless an amendment or showing of facts not previously of record be made which, in the opinion of the examiner, overcomes the new ground of rejection. The examiner will consider any response under paragraph (b)(1) of this section and any written comments by a third party requester under paragraph (c) of this section and issue a determination that the rejection should be maintained or has been overcome.

(e) Within one month of the examiner's determination pursuant to paragraph (d) of this section, the patent owner or any third party requester may once submit comments in response to the examiner's determination. Within one month of the date of service of comments in response to the examiner's determination, any party may file a reply to the comments. No third party requester reply may address the comments of any other third party requester reply. Any third party requester that had not previously filed an appeal or cross appeal and is seeking under this subsection to file comments or a reply to the comments is subject to the appeal and brief fees under §1.17(b) and (c), respectively, which must accompany the comments or reply.

(f) After submission of any comments and any reply pursuant to paragraph (e) of this section, or after time has expired, the reexamination proceeding will be returned to the Board of Patent Appeals and Interferences which shall reconsider the matter and issue a new decision. The new decision will incorporate the earlier decision, except for those portions specifically withdrawn.

(g) The time period set forth in paragraph (b) of this section is subject to the extension of time provisions of §1.956. The time periods set forth in paragraphs (c) and (e) of this section may not be extended.

§1.979 Action following decision by the Board of Patent Appeals and Interferences or dismissal of appeal in *inter partes* reexamination.

(a) Parties to the appeal may file a request for rehearing of the decision within one month of the date of:

(1) The original decision of the Board of Patent Appeals and Interferences under §1.977(a),

(2) The original §1.977(b) decision under the provisions of §1.977(b)(2),

(3) The expiration of the time for the patent owner to take action under §1.977(b)(2), or

(4) The new decision of the Board of Patent Appeals and Interferences under §1.977(f).

(b) Within one month of the date of service of any request for rehearing under paragraph (a) of this section, or any further request for rehearing under paragraph (c) of this section, any party to the appeal may once file comments in opposition to the request for rehearing or the further request for rehearing. The comments in opposition must be limited to the issues raised in the request for rehearing or the further request for rehearing.

(c) If a party to an appeal files a request for rehearing under paragraph (a) of this section, or a further request for rehearing under this section, the Board of Patent Appeals and Interferences will issue a decision on rehearing. This decision is deemed to incorporate the earlier decision, except for those portions specifically withdrawn. If the decision on rehearing becomes, in effect, a new decision, and the Board of Patent Appeals and Interferences so states, then any party to the appeal may, within one month of the new decision, file a further request for rehearing of the new decision under this subsection.

(d) Any request for rehearing shall state the points believed to have been misapprehended or overlooked in rendering the decision and also state all other grounds upon which rehearing is sought.

(e) The patent owner may not appeal to the U.S. Court of Appeals for the Federal Circuit under §1.983 until all parties' rights to request rehearing have been exhausted, at which time the decision of the Board of Patent Appeals and Interferences is final and appealable by the patent owner.

(f) An appeal by a third party requester is considered terminated by the dismissal of the third party requester's appeal, the failure of the third party requester to timely request rehearing under §1.979(a) or (c), or a final decision under §1.979(e). The date of such termination is the date on which the appeal is dismissed, the date on which the time for rehearing expires, or the decision of the Board of Patent Appeals and Interferences is final. An appeal by the patent owner is considered terminated by the dismissal of the patent owner's appeal, the failure of the patent owner to timely request rehearing under §1.979(a) or (c), or the failure of the patent owner to timely file an appeal to the U.S. Court of Appeals for the Federal Circuit under §1.983. The date of such termination is the date on which the appeal is dismissed, the date on which the time for rehearing expires, or the date on which the time for the patent owner's appeal to the U.S. Court of Appeals for the Federal Circuit expires. If an appeal to the U.S. Court of Appeals for the Federal Circuit has been filed, the patent owner's appeal is considered terminated when the mandate is received by the Office. Upon termination of an appeal, if no other appeal is present, the reexamination proceeding will be terminated and the Commissioner will issue a certificate under §1.997.

(g) The times for requesting rehearing under paragraph (a) of this section, for requesting further rehearing under paragraph (c) of this section, and for submitting comments under paragraph (b) of this section may not be extended.

§1.981 Reopening after decision by the Board of Patent Appeals and Interferences in *inter partes* reexamination.

Cases which have been decided by the Board of Patent Appeals and Interferences will not be reopened or reconsidered by the primary examiner except under the provisions of §1.977 without the written authority of the Commissioner, and then only for the consideration of matters not already adjudicated, sufficient cause being shown.

Patent Owner Appeal to the United States Court of Appeals for the Federal Circuit in *Inter Partes* Reexamination

§1.983 Patent owner appeal to the United States Court of Appeals for the Federal Circuit in *inter partes* reexamination.

(a) The patent owner in a reexamination proceeding who is dissatisfied with the decision of the Board of Patent Appeals and Interferences may, subject to §1.979(e), appeal to the U.S. Court of Appeals for the Federal Circuit. The appellant must take the following steps in such an appeal:

(1) In the U.S. Patent and Trademark Office, file a timely written notice of appeal directed to the Commissioner in accordance with §§1.302 and 1.304; and

(2) In the Court, file a copy of the notice of appeal and pay the fee, as provided for in the rules of the Court.

Concurrent Proceedings Involving Same Patent in *Inter Partes* Reexamination

§1.985 Notification of prior or concurrent proceedings in *inter partes* reexamination.

(a) In any *inter partes* reexamination proceeding, the patent owner shall call the attention of the Office to any prior or concurrent proceedings in which the patent is or was involved, including but not limited to interference, reissue, reexamination, or litigation and the results of such proceedings.

(b) Notwithstanding any provision of the rules, any person at any time may file a paper in an *inter partes* reexamination proceeding notifying the Office of a prior or concurrent proceedings in which the same patent is or was involved, including but not limited to interference, reissue, reexamination, or litigation and the results of such proceedings. Such paper must be limited to merely providing notice of the other proceeding without discussion of issues of the current *inter partes* reexamination proceeding. Any paper not so limited will be returned to the sender.

§1.987 Suspension of *inter partes* reexamination proceeding due to litigation.

If a patent in the process of *inter partes* reexamination is or becomes involved in litigation, the Commissioner shall determine whether or not to suspend the *inter partes* reexamination proceeding.

§1.989 Merger of concurrent reexamination proceedings.

(a) If any reexamination is ordered while a prior *inter partes* reexamination proceeding is pending for the same patent and prosecution in the prior *inter partes* reexamination proceeding has not been terminated, a decision may be made to merge the two proceedings or to suspend one of the two proceedings. Where merger is ordered, the merged examination will normally result in the issuance of a single reexamination certificate under §1.997.

(b) An *inter partes* reexamination proceeding filed under §1.913 which is merged with an *ex parte* reexamination proceeding filed under §1.510 will result in the merged proceeding being governed by §§1.902 through 1.997, except that the rights of any third party requester of the *ex parte* reexamination shall be governed by §§1.510 through 1.560.

§1.991 Merger of concurrent reissue application and *inter partes* reexamination proceeding.

If a reissue application and an *inter partes* reexamination proceeding on which an order pursuant to §1.931 has been mailed are pending concurrently on a patent, a decision may be made to merge the two proceedings or to suspend one of the two proceedings. Where merger of a reissue application and an *inter partes* reexamination proceeding is ordered, the merged proceeding will be conducted in accordance with §§1.171 through 1.179, and the patent owner will be required to place and maintain the same claims in the reissue application and the *inter partes* reexamination proceeding during the pendency of the merged proceeding. In a merged proceeding the third party requester may participate to the extent provided under §§1.902 through 1.997, except that such participation shall be limited to issues within the scope of *inter partes* reexamination. The examiner's actions and any responses by the patent owner or third party requester in a merged proceeding will apply to both the reissue application and the *inter partes* reexamination proceeding and be physically entered into both files. Any *inter partes* reexamination proceeding merged with a reissue application shall be terminated by the grant of the reissued patent.

§1.993 Suspension of concurrent interference and *inter partes* reexamination proceeding.

If a patent in the process of *inter partes* reexamination is or becomes involved in an interference, the Commissioner may suspend the *inter partes* reexamination or the interference. The Commissioner will not consider a request to suspend an interference unless a motion under §1.635 to suspend the interference has been presented to, and denied by, an administrative patent judge and the request is filed within ten (10) days of a decision by an administrative patent judge denying the motion for suspension or such other time as the administrative patent judge may set.

§1.995 Third party requester's participation rights preserved in merged proceeding.

When a third party requester is involved in one or more proceedings, including an *inter partes* reexamination proceeding, the merger of such proceedings will be accomplished so as to preserve the third party requester's right to participate to the extent specifically provided for in these regulations. In merged proceedings involving different requesters, any paper filed by one party in the merged proceeding shall be served on all other parties of the merged proceeding.

Reexamination Certificate in *Inter Partes* Reexamination

§1.997 Issuance of *inter partes* reexamination certificate.

(a) Upon the conclusion of an *inter partes* reexamination proceeding, the Commissioner will issue a certificate in accordance with 35 U.S.C. 316 setting forth the results of the *inter partes* reexamination proceeding and the content of the patent following the *inter partes* reexamination proceeding.

(b) A certificate will be issued in each patent in which an *inter partes* reexamination proceeding has been ordered under §1.931. Any statutory disclaimer filed by the patent owner will be made part of the certificate.

(c) The certificate will be sent to the patent owner at the address as provided for in §1.33(c). A copy of the certificate will also be sent to the third party requester of the *inter partes* reexamination proceeding.

(d) If a certificate has been issued which cancels all of the claims of the patent, no further Office proceedings will be conducted with that patent or any reissue applications or any reexamination requests relating thereto.

(e) If the *inter partes* reexamination proceeding is terminated by the grant of a reissued patent as provided in §1.991, the reissued patent will constitute the reexamination certificate required by this section and 35 U.S.C. 316.

(f) A notice of the issuance of each certificate under this section will be published in the *Official Gazette*.

Dated: November 21, 2000.

Q. Todd Dickinson,
Under Secretary of Commerce for Intellectual Property and Director of the United States Patent and Trademark Office.
[FR Doc. 00-30425 Filed 12-6-00; 8:45 am]

Appendix D

Proposed Patent Office Guidelines

Appendix D-7

Notice of Proposed Rulemaking (NPR)—Changes to Implement the Patent Business Goals: Executive Summary

Executive Summary

64 FR 53772 (October 4, 1999) 1228 OG 15 (November 2, 1999)

The Federal Register notice may be accessed at:
http://www.uspto.gov/web/offices/com/sol/notices/fr991004.pdf

Below is a listing of the more significant proposals set forth in the Notice of Proposed Rulemaking entitled "Changes to Implement the Patent Business Goals." Only a brief summary of those proposals that would actually change current practice is included in this listing. Conforming amendments in the rules, and those proposals that would merely clarify what current practice requires are not included in this listing. The last item of the listing sets forth all the rules that would be changed independent of the significance of the proposed change.

For further information contact, at (703) 305-9285, either:
Robert J. Spar, Director, or Hiram H. Bernstein or Robert Bahr,
Senior Legal Advisors, Special Program Law Office, D A/C PPP

Brief Summary of the Proposals by Rule Order

1) § 1.4(b) Provides that the Office may dispose of duplicate copies of correspondence (not required to be filed in duplicate).

2) § 1.9(f)(4)(i) Removes bar to small entity status for a person granting a license to the U.S. government from a rights determination under Executive Order 10096.

3) § 1.14 Completely re-written so as to be easier to understand. No longer provides for giving *status* information about any application that claims a priority benefit to a file that status can be given on (currently § 1.14(a)(1)(ii)). No longer provides for *access* to abandoned

	applications which claim priority from the filing date of an application that issued as a patent or an application that is open to public inspection (currently § 1.14 (a)(3)(iv)(C)).
4) § 1.19(b)(2)	New fee for a copy of a patent-related file wrapper, from $150 total to $250 for the first 400 or fewer pages plus $25 for each additional 100 pages over 400.
5) § 1.22(b)	Where a single payment is made that represents more than one fee, a "should" is changed to a "must" for itemization of fees being paid, and where the itemization does not occur, the payment may be returned.
§ 1.22(c)	Defines that the date of payment of a fee, whether it is paid by check or by an authorization to charge a deposit account, is the date the fee paper was filed in the Office. See proposed § 1.28(b).
6) § 1.26(a)	Provides means to facilitate refunds by electronic transfer.
§ 1.26(b)	Replaces a subjective standard of within a "reasonable time" for requesting a refund with an objective two year limit measured from the date of payment as defined by § 1.22(c), or from the date of a deposit account statement where the Office charges an amount other than what was indicated in the authorization.
7) § 1.27(b)(1)	Small entity status can be established by a simple written assertion of entitlement to small entity status without use of a specialized form, or a reference to § 1.9, or actually presenting the averments required by the rule. The Office will liberally construe any written reference to small entity status to be a request for small entity status.
§ 1.27(b)(2)	The parties who can request small entity status are expanded to include a registered practitioner (who need not actually be of record), one of the inventors (instead of all the inventors), or a partial assignee (instead of all the assignees).
§ 1.27(b)(3)	Payment of any exact small entity basic filing or national fee is sufficient to assert and obtain small entity status (even if incorrectly identified for the type of application being filed), which expands the practice from continuing and reissue applications under current § 1.28(a)(2).
8) § 1.28(a)	The period for requesting a refund based on small entity status would be increased to 3 months from 2 months (from the date of payment of the large entity fee).
§ 1.28(b)(1)	The date of payment of a full fee (non-small entity) is defined by reference to proposed §1.22(c) thereby causing full fees paid by authorizations to charge a deposit account to have a date of payment as of the date the fee paper was filed, which is earlier than when the deposit account was actually debited.
§ 1.28(c)(1)	Any paper correcting an error in claiming small entity status where one or more small entity fees were erroneously paid must be limited to the payment error(s) in one application or in one patent file.
§ 1.28(c)(2)	Submissions of deficiency payments for errors in claiming small entity status must be itemized.
§ 1.28(c)(3)	Failure to comply with the separate submission and itemization requirements of § 1.28(c)(1) and (2) will either be treated as

authorization for the Office to process the deficiency payment and charge a processing fee or result in a requirement for compliance with these requirements within a one month non-extendable time period to avoid return of the fee deficiency paper, at the option of the Office.

9) § 1.33(a) The correspondence address must be specified in a clearly identifiable manner or in a newly proposed Application Data Sheet of § 1.76, or correspondence would be forwarded to the first named inventor. A request is added for a daytime telephone number.

§ 1.33(a)(1) Prior to filing a § 1.63 oath/declaration, the correspondence address may be changed by the party filing the application, including those inventors who filed the application (versus all the listed inventors), a party that will be a (full or partial) assignee (as the inventors are only identified and not named until the oath/declaration is filed), the attorney or agent, or any other practitioner named in the application transmittal papers.

10) § 1.44 Reserved. The accompanying proof requirement for the power or authority of the legal representative for a dead inventor (§ 1.42) or an insane or legally incapacitated inventor (§ 1.43) would be deleted. The oath/dec by an identified legal representative would be sufficient.

11) § 1.47(c) The Office may dispense with notice provisions to nonsigning inventors of a prior application upon the filing of a continuation or divisional application.

12) § 1.52(b)(6) Would provide for the option of numbering paragraphs in the specification, not including the claims, abstract, or non-text elements, to support the proposed change to § 1.121 relating to amendment by replacement paragraphs.

§ 1.52(d)(2) Would eliminate the requirement for an English language translation of non-English language provisional applications in the provisional application. If a non-provisional application claims the benefit of the provisional application, an English language translation would only be required if an interference is declared or if the examiner specifically requires one (as a result of finding intervening prior art). The translations are not required in provisional applications as they are not examined.

13) § 1.53(e)(2) The petition fee relating to a notification of failure to meet filing date requirements for a provisional application under § 1.53(c) would be raised to the same level as the petition fee relating to applications under §§ 1.53(b) and (d).

§ 1.53(f)(5) Would replace the current one year period for submitting a retention fee to retain a (prior) application for priority purposes where the filing fee was not submitted with a requirement that the retention fee be submitted while the prior application is still pending (the retention fee that is being substituted for the filing fee would be required to be submitted within the period for submission of the non-submitted filing fee).

14) § 1.55(a) Would no longer permit a petition under § 1.312(b) for entry of a claim for foreign priority *after the issue fee is paid.* A priority claim would be permitted to be filed (along with the processing fee) but it would not be reviewed for compliance with the conditions of 35 U.S.C. 119(a)–(d). The patent would not contain a priority claim,

	but the patentee could file a certificate of correction request under § 1.323.
15) § 1.56(e)	Adds an explicit duty to disclose all information known to be material to patentability as defined under § 1.56(b) which became available between the filing date of the prior application and the national or PCT international filing date of a continuation-in-part application. This change would do away with the need for a separate CIP § 1.63 form that contains the provision that now would be explicitly added to § 1.56(b). Compare current § 1.63(e) with the instant proposed section.
16) § 1.63(c)	Permits certain information (inventor's full name, mailing address and residence, and foreign application information) to be on an Application Data Sheet rather than in the § 1.63 oath/dec. Missing information need not, therefore, be submitted by way of supplemental oath/dec.
17) § 1.67(a)	Supplemental oaths/decs may be submitted by fewer than all the inventors or an applicant other than an inventor to correct deficiencies or inaccuracies if the earlier filed oath/dec complied with § 1.63(a)
18 § 1.72	The word length of the abstract for consistency with PUT would be required not to exceed 150 replacing the MPEP 608.01(b) range of 50–250.
19) [§ 1.75]	[The proposal in the advance notice for placing a limit on the number of claims in an application is NOT carried forward in the NPR.]
20) § 1.76	A new rule that would optionally provide for an "Application Data Sheet" containing bibliographic data in a specified format as a result of deployment of PRINTEFS.
21) § 1.78(a)(2)	Would permit the specific priority reference required by 35 U.S.C. § 120 to be in the Application Data Sheet of § 1.76 rather than in the first sentence in the specification following the title. (This would be used in creating the patent front page.)
22) § 1.84	Drawing standards would be relaxed as the Office will focus on what is needed to reproduce the drawings for printing in the patent and for communicating the invention to the examiner. The standards of paragraphs (d), (h)–(j), (k)(1) and (3), (m), (n), (p), (r),(s), and (x) would be deleted and moved to the MPEP. Would permit color drawings/photographs to be printed in color in the patent without need for a petition. A processing fee would be required. Examiner may require black and white drawing if the subject matter admits of illustration by a black and white drawing.
23) § 1.85(c)	Extensions of time would no longer be permitted to extend the three month period for filing corrected or formal drawings from the Notice of Allowability (in view of 4 week, rather than 16 week, printing from the date the issue fee is paid). See also §§ 1.312(b), 3.81(b).
24) § 1.96	Require computer program listings to be submitted on CD-ROM or CD-R as the official copy and eliminate microfiche submissions. See also § 1.821.

25) [§§ 1.97, 1.98] [Proposals for a statement of personal review of each item cited, unique descriptions, and a limit on the number of citations in the advance notice are NOT carried forward in the NPR.]

§ 1.97(b)(1) Elimination of the current 3 month window for filing an IDS submission in a CPA (§ 1.53(d))—since CPAs are treated as amended applications by examiners and subject to short turnover times.

§ 1.97(c) The limitation "or an action that otherwise closes prosecution" is added.

§ 1.97(d)(2) The $130 petition fee would now be a $240 IDS fee for IDSs submitted between close of prosecution and payment of the issue fee—to reflect Office increased handling costs under new patent printing processes.

§ 1.97(e)(1) Added requirement that the item of information be cited for the "first" time in a communication in a counterpart application from a foreign patent office not more than three months prior to its submission in the U.S. application. (This avoids abuse which occurs when document was first cited in SR, then submitted to Office after it was again cited in ER from same foreign office.)

26) § 1.98(a)(2) Paragraph (iii) would require submission of copies of U.S. patent applications that are being cited in IDS statements. (This will reduce petitions for access to pending application cited in prosecution histories of patents.)

27) § 1.103 On filing of a CPA application, provide for an opportunity to request a three month postponement of a first Office action, which request would require a processing fee. (This will permit applicant time to file a preliminary amendment and avoid a first action FR.)

28) § 1.105 A new rule that would provide explicit authority for an examiner or other Office employee to require the submission of such information as may be reasonably necessary to properly examine an application or treat a matter therein. (So as to prevent abuse, any inquiry from the examiner would have to have some basis in the record.) The requirement for information may be included in an Office action that includes other matters or sent separately. Any reply that states that the information required to be submitted is unknown and/or is not available would be accepted as a complete reply.

29) § 1.111 Commissioner (delegated to Directors) would have the right to disapprove entry of second supplemental replies (a third reply) (where: a significant amount of time had already been spent by the examiner on preparation of an Office action on the previous replies, and substantial rework would be required in view of the second supplemental reply). See also § 1.115

30) § 1.115 A new rule. The right of disapproval of § 1.111 (for second supplemental replies) would also be available for preliminary amendments not filed within three months of non-CPAs, or not filed with CPAs.

31) § 1.121 Amendment made by "clean" copy replacement of entire numbered paragraph, or claim, or section. Where paragraphs of the specification are not numbered, amendment by replacement specification or section would be required as Office would not do

the paragraph numbering. Adding or deleting a paragraph would not require renumbering of other paragraphs. Entire paragraph/claim can be deleted by instruction.

Addition/deletion of specific words or sentences would no longer be permitted.

A marked-up copy of replacement paragraphs/sections for examiner use must be submitted until electronic file wrapper instituted. See also § 1.52(b)(6). When creating paragraph numbers for a previously submitted specification not containing paragraph numbers, the applicant need not show added numbers as changes in the marked-up copy.

32) § 1.131(a) Eliminates the requirement that the section is only applicable to avoid rejections based on a U.S. patent to expand its use, e.g., to include overcoming a rejection based on a prior knowledge or use under 35 U.S.C. 102(a).

33) § 1.132 Expands scope of rule to overcome rejection based on a prior knowledge or use under 35 U.S.C. 102(a).

34) § 1.137(c) For revivals of utility and plant applications filed before June 8, 1995, the period needed to be disclaimed would not be the entire period of abandonment but only the period extending beyond 20 years from the earliest filing date if it is a lesser period than the period of abandonment.

The terminal disclaimer provisions would no longer apply in pre June 8, 1995 applications (except designs) where revival is sought solely for purposes of copendency with a utility or plant application filed on or after June 8, 1995, since the 20 year term of the later application begins from the 35 U.S.C. § 120 benefit date of the earlier application.

35) § 1.152 Would eliminate provisions, currently found in paragraph (b) of § 1.152, relating to the integral nature of indicia disclosed in drawings or photographs filed with a design application to conform to *In re Daniels*, 46 USPQ2d 1788 (Fed. Cir. 1998).

36) § 1.155 The section is redrafted to establish a procedure to create a "rocket docket" for design applications. A preliminary examination search, a statement that the search was made with an indication of the field of search, an IDS, formal drawings in compliance with § 1.84, and a fee would be required (estimated to be $900).

37) § 1.163(c)(4) The Latin name of the genus and species of the plant would be required to be supplied in the plant application to aid in search and examination.

§ 1.163(c)(14) The requirement for a plant color coding sheet would be removed.

38) § 1.173(a)(1) Requires reissue specification and claims to be furnished as a copy of the printed patent in single column format.

§ 1.173(a)(2) Transfer of the drawings from the patent file to the reissue application would no longer be permitted. New drawings, such as copies from the printed patent, will be required.

§ 1.173(c) Requires an explanation of support in the disclosure of the patent for changes to the claims made at filing since the addition of new matter is prohibited.

39) § 1.176(a)	The prohibition against requiring division in reissues would be eliminated, and a provision added to permit restriction between: (a) claims to previously unclaimed subject matter added in a reissue application, and (b) the original patent claims.
40) § 1.177	Eliminates the requirements: a) that divisional reissues be limited to separate and distinct parts of the thing patented, b) that divisional reissues issue simultaneously unless ordered by the Commissioner, c) for a petition to avoid simultaneous issuance, and d) of referral to the Commissioner upon filing of the divisional reissue. The rule would be expanded to include continuations of reissues as well as divisionals, and require that all multiple applications for reissue of a single patent include a cross reference to the other reissue application(s). Where one reissue issues without the appropriate cross reference, the Office would issue a certificate of correction to provide the cross reference. (These are changes consequential to *In re Graff*, 42 USPQ2d 1471 (Fed. Cir. 1997.)
41) § 1.178	Where the original patent is lost or inaccessible and an offer to surrender it in a reissue application cannot therefore be made, a statement rather than an affidavit or declaration would be required to inform the Office of the loss or lack of access. An offer to surrender a patent (that has not been lost or is not inaccessible) would no longer be required to accompany the filing of a reissue application ("must" replaced by "should").
42) [§ 1.191+]	[The 2 proposals in the ANPR (for a pre and a post brief appeal review procedure) are NOT carried forward in the NPR. Instead, the Office will hold an appeal conference as set forth in the MPEP 1208.]
43) § 1.311(b)	Authorizations to charge the issue fee may be filed only after the mailing of the notice of allowance.
44) § 1.312(b)	No amendments would be permitted while keeping the application in the issue process. Thus, amendments (after issue fee paid) *must be accompanied by: a petition to withdraw the application from issue*, an unequivocal statement that at least one claim is unpatentable, and an explanation of how the amendment is necessary to render the claim or claims patentable. See also §§ 1.85, 3.81(b).
45) § 1.313(b)	Applicant would no longer be permitted to withdraw an application from issue on the basis of: mistake on the part of the Office, a violation of § 1.56 or illegality in the application, or for interference. The Office would retain the ability to do so on these grounds. Applicants could still withdraw based on unpatentability or for express abandonment (to refile the application for consideration of an IDS).
46) § 1.324(b)(1)	Eliminate the requirement for a statement from the inventor being deleted from a patent that the inventorship error occurred without deceptive intent to conform to *Stark v. Advanced Magnetics, Inc.*, 43 USPQ2d 1321 (Fed. Cir. 1997).
47) § 1.366(c)	Additionally provide that where the maintenance fee payment only identifies the patent number (and not also the application number) the Office may apply the payment to the identified patent or return the payment.

48) § 1.550(c)(2) Where an untimely response is submitted in a reexamination proceeding, a petition to accept the response would be granted, provided the petition is filed before expiration of the maximum statutory period and is accompanied by: a statement that the delay was unintentional, and the petition fee (§ 1.17(h)) of $130 (the fee is not dependent on the actual amount of time for which the petition was needed).

49) § 1.740(a)(9) Replace requirement for explaining how each applicable claim reads on the categories of approved product, or method of using, or method of manufacturing, with the requirement that the explanation is needed for only one claim in each category.

50) § 1.740(b) The requirement for an oath/dec is deleted.

51) § 1.741(b) Review of a notice that an application for extension of patent term is incomplete, or review of the filing date accorded an application therefor, would now require a petition and petition fee, and the period for filing the petition would now be extendable under § 1.136.

52) § 1.809(c) The three month extendable time period for making a deposit would be replaced with a period not specified in the rule but fixed in an Office action that would not be extendable.

53) § 1.821+ Permit nucleotide and/or amino acid sequence listings submitted on CD- ROM or CD-R to be the official copy. Two computer readable form submissions would be required, one of which must be an archival CD-ROM or CD-R, and paper need not be submitted. See also § 1.96.

54) § 3.71 Revised to provide definitions of a single assignee and partial assignees linked to being of record in the patent application/ proceeding and to set forth how each may become of record and thereby intervene to control prosecution in a patent application/ proceeding.

55) § 3.73 Clarify that the documentary evidence required must include proof of who the assignee is. Clarify that the § 3.73(b) submission is required in addition to (although it may be combined with) the specific action taken (e.g., appointing an attorney) by the assignee. Require that a partial assignee in a patent application/proceeding indicate in the submission the extent of its ownership interest, to help account for the entire ownership interest.

56) § 3.81(b) Eliminate the provision for submission of an assignment after the issue fee is paid. See §§ 1.85, 1.312(b).

57) § 5.12 Requires a petition fee (§ 1.17(h)) for all petitions for a foreign filing license (rather than just expedited petitions) since all such petitions are treated on an expedited basis.

The NPR proposes changes to the following sections of title 37 of the Code of Federal Regulations:

1.4, 1.6, 1.9, 1.12, 1.14, 1.17, 1.19, 1.22, 1.25, 1.26, 1.27, 1.28, 1.33, 1.41, 1.47, 1.48, 1.51, 1.52, 1.53, 1.55, 1.56, 1.59, 1.63, 1.64, 1.67, 1.72, 1.77, 1.78, 1.84, 1.85, 1.91, 1.96, 1.97, 1.98, 1.102, 1.103, 1.111, 1.112, 1.121, 1.125, 1.131, 1.132, 1.133, 1.136, 1.137, 1.138, 1.152, 1.154, 1.155, 1.163, 1.173, 1.176, 1.177, 1.178, 1.193, 1.303, 1.311, 1.312, 1.313, 1.314, 1.322, 1.323, 1.324, 1.366, 1.446, 1.497, 1.510, 1.530, 1.550, 1.666, 1.720, 1.730, 1.740, 1.741, 1.780, 1.809, 1.821, 1.823, 1.825, 3.27, 3.71, 3.73, 3.81, 5.1, 5.2, 5.12, and 10.23.

Additionally, this notice also proposes to amend title 37 of the Code of Federal Regulations by removing §§ 1.44 and 1.174, and adding §§ 1.176, 1.105, and 1.115.

Appendix D-8

Changes to Implement the Patent Business Goals: Notice of Proposed Rulemaking—Overheads

Changes to Implement the Patent Business Goals

Notice of Proposed Rulemaking (NPR)

64 FR 53771 (October 4, 1999),
1228 OG 15 (November 2, 1999)

The Fed. Reg. Notice may be accessed at:
http://www.uspto.gov/web/offices/com/sol/notices/fr991004.pdf

Advance Notice of Proposed Rulemaking (ANPR) - First of Three Steps

- 63 FR 53497-53530 (October 5, 1998)
- 1215 OG 87 (October 27, 1998)
- Comment period closed 12/4/98
  - all comments are available on PTO Web site
    - http://www.uspto.gov/web/offices/pac/dapp/opla/comments/anpr/
  - 10 Intellectual Property Organizations
  - 10 Law firms
  - 9 businesses
  - 60+ other comments

Notice of Proposed Rulemaking (NPR) - Second (Current) Step

- NPR published:
  - 64 FR 53771 (October 4, 1999)
  - 1228 OG 15 (November 2, 1999)
  - Goals:
    - From applicant's perspective: reduce paperwork burdens and simplify processing requirements
    - From PTO's: support Patent Business Goals
  - NPR includes 11 items from ANPR plus other items to provide additional benefits

Comments on NPR; Final Rule

- Submit written comments by: Dec. 3, 1999
  - e-mail: regreform@uspto.gov
  - fax (703) 308-6916,
- For questions, contact Senior Legal Advisors, in Special Program Law Office (703) 305-9285:
  - Hiram Bernstein, or Robert Bahr
- The third step - which is the final rule:
  - will be on a fast track
  - implementation by Spring/Summer 2000
    - public should have sufficient lead time to prepare for compliance

Patent Business Goals

- **Goal 1:** Reduce PTO processing time to 12 months or less for all inventions.
- **Goal 2:** Establish fully-supported and integrated industry sectors.
- **Goal 3:** Receive applications and publish patents electronically.
- **Goal 4:** Exceed our customers' quality expectations, through the competencies and empowerment of our employees.
- **Goal 5:** Assess fees commensurate with resource utilization and customer efficiency.

The Rulemaking Objective

☺ **What did we want to do: make changes that would maximize applicant's patent term:**

- **make submissions easier for applicants**
  - **reduce or simplify requirements**
  - **clarify requirements (make easier to understand)**
    - **took some difficult to understand rules and revised them to make them easier to comply with**
- **studied petitions that are filed to see where problems from applicant's perspective were arising**
- **eliminate processing steps that caused delays in PTO**

The Rulemaking Process

- ☺ **How did we go about doing it:**
  - **went back to basics and reconsidered what <u>formal</u> requirements continue to be necessary and what can be eliminated**
  - **operations from beginning (OIPE) through prosecution (Corps) to end (Publication) were canvassed:**
    - **what is delaying processing of newly filed applications?**
      - **fees related to small entity status, proof under § 1.44**
    - **what is delaying prosecution/examination of applications?**
      - **suspension of action for CPAs to permit IDSs, amdts.**
    - **what is delaying publication of patents?**
      - **drawing informalities, C of Cs caused by red ink amdts.**

ANPR Topics Proposed in NPR

1) Simplifying request for small entity status (Topic 1)
2) Harmonizing standards for patent drawings (Topic 5)
3) Printing patents in color (Topic 6)
4) Reducing time for filing corrected or formal drawings (Topic 7)
5) Permitting electronic submission of voluminous material (Topic 8)
6) Requiring copies of U.S. applications cited in IDS (Topic 9)
7) Imposing limits on preliminary amendments and supplemental replies (Topic 12)
8) Amending by replacement paragraphs/claims (Topic 13)
9) Creating a rocket docket for design applications (Topic 15)
10) Changing multiple reissue application treatment (Topic 17)
11) Eliminating pre-authorization of payment of issue fee (Topic 19)

ANPR Topics Not Proposed in NPR

1) Requiring sep. surcharges and supplying filing receipts (Topic 2)
2) Permitting delayed submission of an oath/dec., and changing time period for submission of the basic filing fee and English translation (Topic 3)
3) Limiting the number of claims in an application (Topic 4)
4) Limit on number of references cited, statement of personal review, and "unique" description requirements (Topic 9)
5) Refusing IDS consideration under certain circumstances (Topic 10)
6) Providing no cause suspension of action (Topic 11)
7) Providing for presumptive elections (Topic 14)
8) Requiring identification of broadening in reissue appl. (Topic 16)
9) Creating alt. review procedures for appl. under appeal (Topic 18)
10) Reevaluating the Disclosure Document Program (Topic 20)
11) Create PTO review service for applicant-created forms (Topic 21)

Plain Language, §§ 1.14, 1.33, 1.173, 3.71, 3.73

☺ Rules completely rewritten to clarify:

- § 1.14: defines and clarifies when "status" information about an application and "access" to an application is available and to whom it is available
- § 1.33: clarifies who may change a correspondence address, see also slide 16
- § 1.173: consolidates reissue requirements for filing spec., including claims, and drawings

Plain Language (cont'd).

- § 3.71: defines single and partial assignees, and how assignee(s), after becoming of record in a proceeding/application, can take action
- § 3.73: relates the taking of action by an assignee under § 3.71 and provides additional requirement under § 3.73 to submit proof of the appropriate assignee to take action, thus making it clear that two requirements are involved: 1) the action to be taken, and 2) proof of the proper assignee (to take the action)

Fees, §§ 1.22(b), 1.22(c), 1.26(b)

☺ Itemization will be required when multiple fees made by a single payment, § 1.22(b)

Will define the "date of payment" as the date of filing of the fee paper, § 1.22(c)

Provides objective standards for seeking a refund:

- treats payments made by check and by authorization to charge a deposit account the same way
- date of payment for authorizations to charge a deposit account will be the date of filing of the fee paper, no longer the date the deposit account is debited
- will define the time period for requesting a refund to be 2 years from date of payment (replacing within a "reasonable time"), § 1.26(b)

Fees (cont'd), §§ 1.19(b)(2), 1.28(a), 1.28(c)

- increase period for requesting refunds based on small entity status to 3 months from 2 months, § 1.28(a)

If small entity fees were paid in error, the deficiency payment submission should be itemized and limited to a single application, § 1.28(c)

New fee for copy of a patent related file wrapper, § 1.19(b)(2): $250 for up to 400 pages plus $25 for each additional 100 pages

Establishing Small Entity Status, § 1.27

☺ Eliminate need for small entity forms!

Small entity status may be established by:

- simple written assertion - no specific words required, e.g., check box on transmittal letter
  - Office will liberally construe written attempts to establish small entity status as an assertion
- paying any exact small entity <u>basic filing fee</u>
  - after filing, only written assertion acceptable

Establishing Small Entity Status, (cont'd). § 1.27

– party who can make assertion expanded to include: registered attorney/agent (need not be of record), one inventor, or a partial assignee

Requirement for good faith investigation to determine if entitled to small entity status is not changed

Correspondence Address, § 1.33(a)(1) (see also slides 10, 20)

☺ Prior to filing of a § 1.63 oath/dec., the correspondence address can be changed by:

(1) the party filing the case, even if filed

– by less than all the inventors

– by a (potential) assignee or a partial one

– by a registered practitioner (without power of attorney), or

(2) registered practitioners identified as a representative by the party filing the application

Proof of Authority of Legal Representative, § 1.44 (Deleted)

☺ Delete current requirement for accompanying proof of power or authority of legal representatives. Sufficient to submit § 1.63 oath/dec by identified legal representative under:

- § 1.42 (dead inventor),
- § 1.43 (insane or legally incapacitated inventor)

– 37 CFR 1.44 reserved

Foreign Priority (35 U.S.C. 119), §§ 1.55(a)

☺ <u>After issue fee</u> is paid, a <u>petition for entry</u> of a claim for foreign priority will no longer be entered in view of faster patent printing, § 1.55(a)(2)(iv), (see also slides 26, 39, and 40):

- while a claim (& cert. copy) could be filed, Office will not review for compliance with conditions of 35 U.S.C. 119 (a)-(d)
  - claim would be of record but not evaluated
- patent would <u>not</u> contain priority claim info.
  - certificate of correction under § 1.323 could be filed

CIP Declarations, § 1.56(e)

☺ Adds an explicit duty to disclose all information known to be material that became available between the filing date of a prior application and a CIP application

- <u>Impact</u> - When a CIP application is filed, the standard § 1.63 declaration form can be used:
  - no longer a need for a separate CIP § 1.63 Dec.

Application Data Sheet, §§ 1.63, 1.76 (new)

- ☺ Optionally, new § 1.76 permits submission of an Application Data Sheet containing bibliographic data in a specified format:
  - – rather then provide info. in oath/dec.
- <u>Impact</u> - Certain missing information need not therefore be submitted by way of a § 1.67 supplemental oath/dec (§ 1.63(c)):
  - – inventor's full name, correspondence address, residence, and foreign application information

Supplemental Oaths/Decs., § 1.67(a)

☺ Supplemental oaths/decs. may be submitted by fewer than all the inventors to correct deficiencies or inaccuracies if the earlier filed oath/declaration complied with § 1.63(a).

Abstracts, § 1.72(b)

☺ The word length for an abstract of the disclosure would be required not to exceed 150 words:

– replaces current MPEP 608.01(b) range of 50-250 words

Priority under 35 U.S.C. 120, § 1.78(a)(2)

☺ Would permit the required priority reference under 35 U.S.C. 120 to be in the Application Data Sheet (ADS) (new § 1.76)

- If in ADS, the domestic priority reference would no longer be required in the first sentence of the specification following the title

Drawing Requirements Liberalized, § 1.84

☺ Drawings will be as easy to file in U.S. national applications as in the PCT, as the Office will focus on what is needed for:

- communication of invention to examiner
- reproduction of drawing for printing in patent

Printing Patents in Color, § 1.84

☺ Print color drawings/photographs in color in the patent if filed as part of the application:

– a processing fee to recover PTO cost of printing/processing shall be imposed

☺ Eliminate the current requirements for a petition and a petition fee to permit color

Time for Filing Formal Drawings, § 1.85

☺ New patent issue procedure in 4 weeks from payment of the issue fee (vs 16 weeks), requires most electronic capture of application before issue fee is paid (see also slides 18, 39, 40), and formal drawings no later than payment of issue fee, thus:

- Time for filing formal drawings will stay the same - at 3 months from Notice of Allowability, **BUT**
  - no extensions of time, not even § 1.136(b) to be permitted
- Uniform reply period for both the issue fee and any requirement for formal or corrected drawings
- See 1221 OG 14 (April 6, 1999)

Electronic Submission of Voluminous Material, §§ 1.96 and 1.821 *et seq.*

- ☺ Permit nucleotide and/or amino acid sequence listing submitted on CD-ROM, or CD-R to be the official copy:
  - Require 2 computer readable form (CRF) submissions, one of which must be an archival CD-ROM, or CD-R
  - No paper copy has to be filed
- ☺ Require computer program listings to be submitted on CD-ROM, or CD-R as the official copy; eliminate microfiche submissions

IDS Submissions, §§ 1.97, 1.98

- **Elimination of three month window for filing an IDS in a CPA application, § 1.97(b)(1)**
- **The $130 petition fee would now be a $240 IDS fee for IDSs submitted between close of prosecution and payment of issue fee, § 1.97(d)(2)**
- **If U.S. patent application is cited in an IDS, copy must be supplied, § 1.98(a)(2)(iii)**

IDS Submissions (cont'd).

☺ **In re Portola Guidelines, 64 FR 15346 (March 31, 1999); 1223 OG 124 (June 22, 1999):**

- **examiner is only responsible for cursory review of IDS citations which are not described**
- **prior art, even though listed on a patent, but whose relevance to the patentability of any claim is not actually discussed on the record, may be used for ordering and conducting a subsequent reexamination proceeding**

Postponement of Action in CPAs, § 1.103

☺ CPA applications were designed to provide two more opportunities for examination of an application without the pre-processing delays associated with the filing of a new application. To preserve the two opportunities, yet retain quick action:

- Applicants may obtain a 3 month postponement of the first action in a CPA application, if request is submitted with the CPA application and accompanied by a processing fee

Preliminary Amendments, and Supplemental Replies, §§ 1.115 (new), 1.111

☺ Commissioner would have the right to disapprove entry of:

- prelim amendments not filed w/i 3 mos. of non-CPAs,
- prelim amendments not filed with CPAs, § 1.115, or
- second supplemental replies (a third reply)

  where:

  - a significant amount of time had already been spent by the examiner on prep. of an Office action, <u>and</u>
  - substantial rework would be required, § 1.111(a)

Amendment by Replacement Paragraphs/Claims, or Sections, § 1.121

☺ Amendments made by "clean" copy replacement of entire numbered paragraph or claim or section

- Marked-up copy showing changes by any compare system must be submitted until electronic file wrapper (EFW) system instituted by Office
- Numbering of all paragraphs:
  - permitted when specification is in paper form, § 1.52(b)
  - not necessary with EFW, will go to substitute spec.
- Adding or deleting a paragraph will not require renumbering of other paragraphs

Amendment by Replacement Paragraphs/Claims, or Sections, § 1.121 (cont'd).

- Deletion of entire paragraph/claim by instruction permitted
- If paragraphs in specification are not numbered, amendment by substitute specification or section (if labeled) would be required
- Addition/Deletion of specific words or sentences would not be permitted
- Office considered but did not propose the making of amendments by:
  - replacement pages (like PCT)

Revivals, § 1.137(c)

☺ For utility and plant applications filed prior to June 8, 1995, the period to be disclaimed:

- no longer has to be the entire period of abandonment
- but only the period extending beyond 20 years from earliest filing date:
  - if this is a lesser period than the period of aband.

- Terminal disclaimers not needed in pre June 8, 1995 applications(except designs) when revival sought solely for copendency with post June 8, 1995 applications

Designs, §§ 1.152, 1.155

☺ Elimination of provisions relating to integral nature of indicia disclosed in drawings or photographs, § 1.152(b)

- Creation of expedited treatment (§ 1.155) if:
  - submission of request with $900 fee (estimated)
  - preliminary search performed
  - statement given as to where search was made
  - IDS submitted
  - formal drawings in compliance with § 1.84

Reissues, §§ 1.173, 1.176,1.177

☺ No transfer of dwgs from patent, § 1.173

- Statement of support for changes made to claims on filing now required, § 1.173(c)
- Permit restriction between original patent claims and claims added toward previously unclaimed subject matter, § 1.176(a)
- Eliminates requirements for independent and distinct parts, and simultaneous issuance of divisional reissues, § 1.177
- Multiple reissues must be x-refer'd, § 1.177

Eliminate Pre-authorization of Payment of the Issue Fee, § 1.311

☺ Only allow authorizations to charge the issue fee to a deposit account in reply to the Notice of Allowance and Issue Fee Due (PTOL-85)

- PTO still waits for return of form PTOL-85(B):
  - for certain data to be printed on patent (e.g., assignee) as well as maintenance fee address
- Thus, pre-authorization to charge the issue fee is of no benefit to Office

Eliminate Pre-authorization Payment of the Issue Fee, § 1.311 (cont'd).

- Delay in issue fee payment is sometimes beneficial as it gives applicant time to:
  - submit a § 1.312(a) amendment
  - submit a § 1.97 IDS
  - file a CPA
  - make business decisions:
    - reevaluating the scope of protection
    - deciding whether to pay the issue fee
- Can have quick issuance of patent if PTOL-85(B) is promptly returned with the issue fee

Amendments After Issue Fee Paid, § 1.312(b)

☺ In view of the recently instituted fast patent publication process (in 4 not 16 weeks from payment of issue fee)(see also slides 18, 26, and 40), amendments after the issue fee has been paid must include:

- a petition to <u>withdraw</u> application from issue!
- an unequivocal statement that at least one claim is unpatentable
- an explanation how amendment is necessary to render claim patentable
- see 1221 OG 14 (April 6, 1999)

Reexams, § 1.550(c)(2), Assignments, § 3.81(b)

- ☺ In a reexam, an untimely response may be accepted if a petition to accept the response, the petition fee per § 1.17(h), and a statement of unintentional delay are filed w/i 6 mos. of mail date of office action
- ☺ No longer can provide an assignment after the date the issue fee is paid in view of faster patent printing. (See also slides 18, 26, and 39)

Thank You

Appendix D-9

Changes to Implement the Patent Business Goals: Proposed Rule

Department of Commerce
Patent and Trademark Office
37 CFR Parts 1, 3, 5, and 10
[Docket No.: 980826226–9185–02]
RIN 0651–AA98

Changes To Implement the Patent Business Goals

Agency: Patent and Trademark Office, Commerce.

Action: Notice of proposed rulemaking.

Summary: The Patent and Trademark Office (Office) has established business goals for the organizations reporting to the Assistant Commissioner for Patents (Patent Business Goals). The focus of the Patent Business Goals is to increase the level of service to the public by raising the efficiency and effectiveness of the Office's business processes. In furtherance of the Patent Business Goals, the Office is proposing changes to the rules of practice to eliminate unnecessary formal requirements, streamline the patent application process, and simplify and clarify their provisions.

Dates: Comment Deadline Date: To be ensured of consideration, written comments must be received on or before December 3, 1999. While comments may be submitted after this date, the Office cannot ensure that consideration will be given to such comments. No public hearing will be held.

Addresses: Comments should be sent by electronic mail message over the Internet addressed to regreform@uspto.gov. Comments may also be submitted by mail addressed to: Box Comments—Patents, Assistant Commissioner for Patents, Washington, D.C. 20231, or by facsimile to (703) 308–6916, marked to the attention of Hiram H. Bernstein. Although comments may be submitted by mail or facsimile, the Office prefers to receive comments via the Internet. Where comments are submitted by mail, the Office would prefer that the comments be submitted on a DOS formatted 3¼ inch disk accompanied by a paper copy.

The comments will be available for public inspection at the Special Program Law Office, Office of the Deputy Assistant Commissioner for Patent Policy and Projects, located at Room 3–C23 of Crystal Plaza 4, 2201 South Clark Place, Arlington, Virginia, and will be available through anonymous file transfer protocol (ftp) via the Internet (address: ftp.uspto.gov). Since comments will be made available for public inspection, information that is not desired to be made public, such as an address or phone number, should not be included in the comments.

For Further Information Contact: Hiram H. Bernstein or Robert W. Bahr, by telephone at (703) 305–9285, or by mail addressed to: Box Comments—Patents, Assistant Commissioner for Patents, Washington, DC 20231, or by facsimile to (703) 308–6916, marked to the attention of Mr. Bernstein.

Supplementary Information: The organizations reporting to the Assistant Commissioner for Patents have established five business goals (Patent Business Goals) to meet the Office's Year 2000 commitments. The Patent Business Goals have been adopted as part of the Fiscal Year 1999 Corporate Plan Submission of the President. The five Patent Business Goals are:

Goal 1: Reduce Office processing time (cycle time) to twelve months or less for all inventions.

Goal 2: Establish fully-supported and integrated Industry Sectors.

Goal 3: Receive applications and publish patents electronically.

Goal 4: Exceed our customers' quality expectations, through the competencies and empowerment of our employees.

Goal 5: Align fees commensurate with resource utilization and customer efficiency.

This rulemaking proposes changes to the regulations to support the Patent Business Goals. A properly reengineered or reinvented system eliminates the redundant or unnecessary steps that slow down processing and frustrate customers. In furtherance of the Patent Business Goals, these proposed changes to the rules of practice take a fresh view of the business end of issuing patents, and continue a process of simplification. Formal requirements of rules that are no longer useful would be eliminated. When the intent of an applicant is understood, the Office would simply go forward with the processing. The essentials are maintained, while formalities are greatly reduced. The object is to focus on the substance of examination and decrease the time that an application for patent is sidelined with unnecessary procedural issues.

Additionally, the Office desires to continue to make its rules more understandable, such as by using plain language instead of legalese. The Office is seeking efficiency by improving the clarity of the wording of the regulations so that applicants and Office employees understand unequivocally what is required at each stage of the prosecution and can get it right on the first try. The Office welcomes comments and suggestions on this effort.

In streamlining this process, the Office will be able to issue a patent in a shorter time by eliminating formal requirements that must be performed by the applicant, his or her representatives and the Office itself. Applicants will benefit from a reduced overall cost to them for receiving patent protection and from a faster receipt of their patents.

Finally, these proposed changes are intended to improve the Office's business processes in the context of the current legal and technological environment. Should these environments change (*e.g.*, by adoption of an international Patent Law Treaty, enactment of patent legislation, or implementation of new automation capabilities), the Office would have to reconsider its business processes and make such further changes to the rules of practice as are necessary.

Advance Notice of Proposed Rulemaking

The Office published an advance notice of proposed rulemaking (Advance Notice) presenting a number of changes to patent practice and procedure under consideration to implement the Patent Business Goals. See Changes to Implement the Patent Business Goals; Advance Notice of Proposed Rulemaking, 63 FR 53497 (October 5, 1998), 1215 Off. Gaz. Pat. Office 87 (October 27, 1998). The Advance Notice set forth twenty-one topics on which the Office specifically requested public input:

Topic (1) Simplifying requests for small entity status;
Topic (2) Requiring separate surcharges and supplying filing receipts;
Topic (3) Permitting delayed submission of an oath or declaration, and changing time period for submission of the basic filing fee and English translation;
Topic (4) Limiting the number of claims in an application;
Topic (5) Harmonizing standards for patent drawings;
Topic (6) Printing patents in color;
Topic (7) Reducing time for filing corrected or formal drawings;
Topic (8) Permitting electronic submission of voluminous material;
Topic (9) Imposing limits/requirements on information disclosure statement submissions;
Topic (10) Refusing information disclosure statement consideration under certain circumstances;
Topic (11) Providing no cause suspension of action;
Topic (12) Requiring a handling fee for preliminary amendments and supplemental replies;
Topic (13) Changing amendment practice to replacement by paragraphs/claims;
Topic (14) Providing for presumptive elections;
Topic (15) Creating a rocket docket for design applications
Topic (16) Requiring identification of broadening in a reissue application;
Topic (17) Changing multiple reissue application treatment;
Topic (18) Creating alternative review procedures for applications under appeal;
Topic (19) Eliminating preauthorization of payment of the issue fee;
Topic (20) Reevaluating the Disclosure Document Program; and
Topic (21) Creating a Patent and Trademark Office review service for applicant-created forms.

See Changes to Implement the Patent Business Goals, 63 FR at 53499, 1215 Off. Gaz. Pat. Office at 89.

Changes Set Forth in the Advance Notice Included in This Notice of Proposed Rulemaking (Notice)

This notice proposes changes to the rules of practice based upon the following topics in the Advance Notice:

(1) Simplifying request for small entity status (Topic 1—§§ 1.9, 1.27, and 1.28);
(2) Harmonizing standards for patent drawings (Topic 5—§ 1.84);
(3) Printing patents in color (Topic 6—§ 1.84);
(4) Reducing time for filing corrected or formal drawings (Topic 7—§§ 1.85 and 1.136);
(5) Permitting electronic submission of voluminous material (Topic 8—§§ 1.96, 1.821, 1.823, and 1.825);
(6) Imposing limits/requirements on information disclosure statement: submissions (Topic 9—§§ 1.97 and 1.98);
(7) Requiring a handling fee for preliminary amendments and supplemental replies (Topic 12—§§ 1.111 and 1.115);
(8) Changing amendment practice to replacement by paragraphs/claims (Topic 13—§§ 1.52 and 1.121);
(9) Creating a rocket docket for design applications (Topic 15—§ 1.155);
(10) Changing multiple reissue application treatment (Topic 17—§ 1.177); and
(11) Eliminating preauthorization of payment of the issue fee (Topic 19—§§ 1.25 and 1.311).

The Office has taken into account the comments submitted in reply to the Advance Notice in arriving at the specific changes to the rules of practice being proposed in this notice. These comments are addressed with the relevant proposed rule change in the section-by-section discussion portion of this notice.

This notice also includes a number of proposed changes to the rules of practice that are not based upon proposals set forth in the Advance Notice. This notice proposes changes to the following sections of title 37 of the Code of Federal Regulations: 1.4, 1.6, 1.9, 1.12, 1.14, 1.17, 1.19, 1.22, 1.25, 1.26, 1.27, 1.28, 1.33, 1.41, 1.47, 1.48, 1.51, 1.52, 1.53, 1.55, 1.56, 1.59, 1.63, 1.64, 1.67, 1.72, 1.77, 1.78, 1.84, 1.85, 1.91, 1.96, 1.97, 1.98, 1.102, 1.103, 1.111, 1.112, 1.121, 1.125, 1.131, 1.132, 1.133, 1.136, 1.137, 1.138, 1.152, 1.154, 1.155, 1.163, 1.173, 1.176, 1.177, 1.178, 1.193, 1.303, 1.311, 1.312, 1.313, 1.314, 1.322, 1.323, 1.324, 1.366, 1.446, 1.497, 1.510, 1.530, 1.550, 1.666, 1.720, 1.730, 1.740, 1.741, 1.780, 1.809, 1.821, 1.823, 1.825, 3.27, 3.71, 3.73, 3.81, 5.1, 5.2, 5.12, and 10.23. Additionally, this notice proposes to amend title 37 of the Code of Federal Regulations by removing §§ 1.44 and 1.174, and adding §§ 1.76, 1.105, and 1.115.

Changes Set Forth in the Advance Notice That Are NOT Included in This Notice

This notice does not include proposed changes to the rules of practice based upon the following topics in the Advance Notice:

(1) Requiring separate surcharges and supplying filing receipts (Topic 2);

(2) Permitting delayed submission of an oath or declaration, and changing the time period for submission of the basic filing fee and English translation (Topic 3);

(3) Limiting the number of claims in an application (Topic 4);

(4) Refusing information disclosure statement consideration under certain circumstances (Topic 10);

(5) Providing no cause suspension of action (Topic 11);

(6) Providing for presumptive elections (Topic 14);

(7) Requiring identification of broadening in a reissue application (Topic 16);

(8) Creating alternative review procedures for applications under appeal (Topic 18);

(9) Reevaluating the Disclosure Document Program (Topic 20); and (10) Creating a Patent and Trademark Office review service for applicant-created forms (Topic 21).

Comments received in response to the Advance Notice on these topics are addressed below.

Requiring Separate Surcharges and Supplying Filing Receipts (Topic 2)

The Office indicated that it was considering charging separate surcharges in a nonprovisional application under 35 U.S.C. 111(a) for (a) the delayed submission of an oath or declaration, and (b) the delayed submission of the basic filing fee. That is, a single surcharge (currently $130) would be required if one of (a) the oath or declaration or (b) the basic filing fee were not present on filing. Two surcharges (totaling $260) would be required if both the oath or declaration and the basic filing fee were not present on filing. Therefore, the absence (on filing) of the oath or declaration or the basic filing fee would have necessitated a separate surcharge. The Office also indicated that it was considering issuing another filing receipt, without charge, to correct any errors or to update filing information, as needed.

While a few comments supported the proposal (indicating that the additional services were worth the additional fees), a majority of comments opposed charging separate surcharges. These included arguments that: (1) the proposal is simply a fee increase with no advantage to applicants; and (2) a separate surcharge should be required only if the oath or declaration and the basic filing fee are submitted separately because there is no additional cost to the Office to process both the oath or declaration and the basic filing fee in the same submission.

Response: This notice does not propose changing § 1.53 to charge separate surcharges in a nonprovisional application under 35 U.S.C. 111(a) for the delayed submission of an oath or declaration, and for the delayed submission of the basic filing fee.

Permitting Delayed Submission of an Oath or Declaration, and Changing the Time Period for Submission of the Basic Filing Fee and English Translation (Topic 3)

The Office indicated that it was considering: (1) Amending § 1.53 to provide that an executed oath or declaration for a nonprovisional application would not be required until the expiration of a period that would be set in a "Notice of Allowability" (PTOL–37); and (2) amending §§ 1.52 and 1.53 to provide that the basic filing fee and an English translation (if necessary) for a nonprovisional application must be submitted within one month (plus any extensions under § 1.136) from the filing date of the application. The Office was specifically considering amending § 1.53 to provide that an executed oath or declaration for a nonprovisional application would not be required until the applicant is notified that it must be submitted within a one-month period that would be set in a "Notice of Allowability," provided that the following are submitted within one month (plus any extensions under § 1.136) from the filing date of the application: (1) The name(s), residence(s), and citizenship(s) of the person(s) believed to be the inventor(s); (2) all foreign priority claims; and (3) a statement submitted by a registered practitioner that: (a) an inventorship inquiry has been made, (b) the practitioner has sent a copy of the application (as filed) to each of the person(s) believed to be the inventor(s), (c) the practitioner believes that the inventorship of the application is as indicated by the practitioner, and (d) the practitioner has given the person(s) believed to be the inventor(s) notice of their obligations under § 1.63(b). The Office was also specifically considering amending §§ 1.52 and 1.53 to provide, by rule, that the basic filing fee and an English translation (if the application was filed in a language other than English) for a nonprovisional application must be submitted within one month (plus any extensions under § 1.136) from the filing date of the application. Applicants would not be given a notice (*e.g.*, a "Notice To File Missing Parts of Application" (PTO–1533)) that the basic filing fee is missing or insufficient, unless the application is filed with an insufficient basic filing fee that at least equals the basic filing fee that was in effect the previous fiscal year. The filing receipt, however, would indicate the amount of filing fee received. Further, the filing receipt would remind applicants that the basic filing fee must be submitted within one month (plus any extensions under § 1.136) from the filing date of the application.

While some comments supported this proposed change, a majority of comments opposed permitting delayed submission of an oath or declaration; and changing the time period for submission of the basic filing fee and English translation.

The reasons given for opposition to the proposed change to permit delayed submission of an oath or declaration included arguments that: (1) The proposed inventorship inquiry and notification requirements for practitioners who submitted an application without an executed oath or declaration would be too onerous; (2) an application should not be examined until inventorship is settled and the inventors have acknowledged their duty of disclosure; (3) the delayed submission of an oath or declaration would cause confusion as to ownership of the application, which would cause confusion as to who is authorized to appoint a representative in the application; (4) the delayed submission of an oath or declaration would increase the difficulty in acquiring the inventor's signatures on an oath or declaration, which would lead to an increase in the number of petitions under § 1.47, as well as an increase in the number of oaths or declarations signed by the legal representatives of deceased inventors; and (5) the delayed submission of an oath or declaration would increase the number of certified copies of an application not having a copy of the executed oath or declaration (considered undesirable). Some comments suggested that the Office seek legislation to eliminate the oath requirement of 35 U.S.C. 115.

The reasons given for opposition to the proposed change to the time period for submission of the basic filing fee and English translation included arguments that: (1) A one-month period for submitting the basic filing fee or English translation is too short because applicants may not know the assigned application number within one month of the application filing date (*i.e.,* this period should be two or three months); (2) the period for submitting the basic filing fee or English translation should be tied to the mail date of the Filing Receipt; and (3) the public relies upon the current Notice to File

Missing Parts of Application practice to inform applicants as to whether the filing fee and the oath or declaration has been received by the Office (*i.e.*, verify whether the Office has received the basic filing fee and oath or declaration), and to inform applicants of the period for reply for supplying the missing basic filing fee and/or oath or declaration.

Response: This notice does not propose changing §§ 1.52 and 1.53 to provide that: (1) An executed oath or declaration for a nonprovisional application would not be required until the expiration of a period that would be set in a "Notice of Allowability" (PTOL–37); or (2) the basic filing fee and an English translation (if necessary) for a nonprovisional application must be submitted within one month (plus any extensions under § 1.136) from the filing date of the application.

Limiting the Number of Claims in an Application (Topic 4)

The Office indicated in the Advance Notice that it was considering a change to § 1.75 to limit the number of total and independent claims that will be examined (at one time) in an application. The Office was specifically considering a change to the rules of practice to: (1) Limit the number of total claims that will be examined (at one time) in an application to forty; and (2) limit the number of independent claims that will be examined (at one time) in an application to six. In the event that an applicant presented more than forty total claims or six independent claims for examination at one time, the Office would withdraw the excess claims from consideration, and require the applicant to cancel the excess claims.

While the comments included sporadic support for this proposed change, the vast majority of comments included strong opposition to placing limits on the number of claims in an application. The reasons given for opposition to the proposed change included arguments that: (1) Decisions by the Court of Appeals for the Federal Circuit (Federal Circuit) leave such uncertainty as to how claims will be interpreted that additional claims are necessary to adequately protect the invention; (2) the applicant (and not the Office) should be permitted to decide how many claims are necessary to adequately protect the invention; (3) there are situations in which an applicant justifiably needs more than six independent and forty total claims to adequately protect an invention; (4) the proposed change exceeds the Commissioner's rule making authority; (5) the change will simply result in more continuing applications and is just a fee raising scheme; (6) the Office currently abuses restriction practice and this change will further that abuse; and (7) since only five percent of all applicants exceed the proposed claim ceiling, there is no problem. Several comments which opposed the proposed change offered the following alternatives: (1) Charge higher fees (or a surcharge) for applications containing an excessive number of claims; (2) charge fees for an application based upon what it costs (*e.g.*, number of claims, pages of specification, technology, IDS citations) to examine the application; and (3) credit examiners based upon the number of claims in the application. Several comments which indicated that the proposed change would be acceptable, placed the following conditions on that indication: (1) That a multiple dependent claim be treated as a single claim for counting against the cap; (2) that a multiple dependent claim be permitted to depend upon a multiple dependent claim; (3) that a Markush claim be treated as a single claim for counting against the cap; (4) that any additional applications are taken up by the same examiner in the same time frame; (5) that allowed dependent claims rewritten in independent form do not count against the independent claim limit; (6) that the Office permit rejoinder of dependent claims upon allowance; and (7) that higher claim limits are used.

Response: This notice does not propose changing § 1.75 to place a limit on the number of claims that will be examined in a single application.

Refusing Information Disclosure Statement Consideration Under Certain Circumstances (Topic 10)

The Office indicated in the Advance Notice that it was considering revising § 1.98 to reserve the Office's authority to not consider submissions of an Information Disclosure Statement (IDS) in unduly burdensome circumstances, even where all the stated requirements of § 1.98 are met. The Office was specifically considering an amendment to § 1.98 to permit the Office to refuse consideration of an unduly burdensome IDS submission (*e.g.*, extremely large documents and compendiums), and give the applicant an opportunity to modify the submission to eliminate the burdensome aspect of the IDS.

While the proposal received support from a significant minority of the comments, the large majority of comments included strong opposition to the proposal to revise § 1.98. The reasons given for opposition to the proposed change included arguments that: (1) The term "unduly burdensome" is not defined objectively; thus, decisions as to whether a submission is too burdensome for consideration will be subjective; (2) without a clear definition of "unduly burdensome" (to provide a standard), the proposal would not pass the Administrative Procedure Act tests of scrutiny; (3) the Office will have to expend time and effort in deciding the petitions and defending, in court, its subjective decisions not to consider "unduly burdensome" IDSs (thus, the proposal will cost the Office time in the long run); (4) the proposal gives the examiner unlimited ability to not consider art submitted due to the ambiguous standard for refusal of an IDS submission coupled with the examiner's discretion to advance the status of the application to a point where the IDS would not be timely even though it is corrected; (5) the Office's refusal to examine unduly burdensome IDS submissions despite compliance with the rules (other than the burdensome aspect) would impose a huge financial and time burden upon applicants to fix what the examiner deems as unduly burdensome; (6) imposing this new financial and time burden would be contrary to the stated purpose of the Office to expedite prosecution and to relieve the burdens on the examination process; (7) burdensome IDS situations exist, and the Office should learn to deal with them as a service to its customers and in order to meet its mission of issuing valid patents (the Office cannot realistically ignore situations where the IDS documents cited are complex or lengthy, and nothing can be done about the complexity or length by applicant); (8) the burdensome IDS problem is not frequent and the rare unduly burdensome IDS submissions should be addressed on a case-by-case basis (thus, no rule change is needed); (9) no data has been presented to show the problem is wide-spread, and more facts are needed to show the extent and nature of the unduly burdensome IDS problem; (10) citations should not be discarded from the record where the unduly burdensome IDS has not been corrected since an original and only copy of the citation (which is submitted so the examiner can more fully appreciate the citation) may be very expensive or even impossible to replace; (11) reducing the size of a citation can make it less valuable, the submitted "relevant portions" (the partial citation) may be taken out-of-context of the entire citation, and the excerpt containing the relevant portion would not provide additional assistance to the examiner as to background, terminology, and alternative subject matter which may bear on the examination.

Response: This notice does not propose changing § 1.98 to reserve the Office's authority to not consider submissions of an IDS in unduly burdensome circumstances, even where all the stated requirements of § 1.98 are met.

Providing No Cause Suspension of Action (Topic 11)

The Office indicated that it was considering adding an additional suspension of action practice, under which an applicant may request deferred examination of an application without a showing of "good and sufficient cause," and for an extended period of time, provided that the applicant waived the confidential status of the application under 35 U.S.C. 122, and agreed to publication of the application. The Office was specifically considering a procedure under which the applicant may (prior to the first Office action) request deferred examination for a period not to exceed three years, provided that: (1) The application is entitled to a filing date; (2) the filing fee has been paid; (3) any needed English-language translation of the application has been filed; and (4) all "outstanding requirements" have been satisfied (except that the oath or declaration need not be submitted if the names of all of the persons believed to be the inventors are identified).

The comments included support and opposition in roughly equal measure to the proposed extended suspension of action procedure. The reasons given for opposition to the proposal included arguments that: (1) The "deferred examination" of application under an extended suspension of action and the publication of an application under such suspension of action would create uncertainty over legal rights; and (2) the publication provisions of such a suspension of action procedure amount to an eighteen-month publication system that is not authorized by 35 U.S.C. 122.

Response: This notice does not propose changing § 1.103 to provide for extended suspension of action.

Providing for Presumptive Elections (Topic 14)

The Office indicated in the Advance Notice that it was considering a change to the restriction practice to eliminate the need for a written restriction requirement and express election in most restriction situations. The Office was specifically considering a change to the restriction practice to provide: (1) That if more than one independent and distinct invention is claimed in an application, the applicant is considered to have constructively elected the invention first presented in the claims; (2) for rejoinder of certain process claims in an application containing allowed product claims; and (3) for rejoinder of certain combination claims in an application containing allowed subcombination claims.

While some comments supported this proposed change, a large majority of comments opposed providing for presumptive elections. The reasons given for opposition to the proposed change included arguments that: (1) The commercially important invention may change (or is not known until) after the application is prepared and filed; (2) the change will increase cost of preparing an application since the order of claims must be carefully considered; (3) examiners aggressively apply restriction, and presumptive elections will increase the number of restrictions; and (4) the loss of the ability to contest improper restrictions prior to examination on the merits will lead to less likelihood of success in persuading examiner to withdraw an improper restriction. Several comments which opposed the proposed change offered as an alternative that the Office adopt the PCT unity of invention standard in considering restriction. Several comments which indicated that the proposed change would be acceptable placed the following conditions on that indication: (1) That any presumptive election practice not apply to an election of species; and (2) that an election by presumption apply only if an attempted telephone restriction requirement is not successful.

Response: This notice does not propose changing § 1.141 *et seq.* to provide for a presumptive election. The Office is considering the impact of applying the "unity of invention" standard of the PCT, rather than the "independent and distinct" standard of 35 U.S.C. 121, in restriction practice. Nevertheless, this change to restriction practice, without a corresponding change to other patent fees, would have a negative impact on the Office's ability to obtain the necessary operating funding.

Requiring Identification of Broadening in a Reissue Application (Topic 16)

The Office indicated in the Advance Notice that it was considering a change to § 1.173 to require reissue applicants to identify all occurrences of broadening of the patent claims in a reissue application. As proposed, reissue applicants would have to point out all occurrences of broadening in the claims as an aid to examiners who should consider issues involving broadening relative to the two-year limit and the recapture doctrine.

While a few comments supported this proposed change, a large majority of comments strongly opposed the concept. A number of those commenting were wary of the consequences in court resulting from their failure to identify all issues of broadening in a reissue application. Several of the commenters expressed concerns that patent owners could have their patent claims put at risk in litigation if they unintentionally failed to identify all occurrences of broadening, which they feared could be a basis for charging patentees with inequitable conduct. Some were concerned about saddling applicants with yet another burden which more properly should be left with the Office and the examiner. Others felt that any unintentional omission of a broadening identification could raise problems for the practitioner, which problems are not offset by any increase in benefits derived by presenting this information to the Office.

Response: This notice does not propose changing § 1.173 to require an identification of all occurrences of broadening in reissue claims. In view of the comments received, the Office will continue to rely on the examiner to identify any occurrences of broadening during the examination of the reissue application, and not impose any additional burden on the reissue applicants. The Office does not wish to undo the benefits of the recently liberalized reissue oath/declaration requirements by proposing additional rule changes which may add burdens as well as possible unforeseen risks.

Creating Alternative Review Procedures for Applications Under Appeal (Topic 18)

The Office indicated in the Advance Notice that it was considering alternative review procedures to reduce the number of appeals forwarded to the Board of Patent Appeals and Interferences. The Office was specifically considering two alternative review procedures to reduce the number of appeals having to be forwarded to the Board of Patent Appeals and Interferences for decision. Both review procedures would have involved a review that would be available upon request and payment of a fee by the appellant, and would have involved review by at least one other Office official. The first review would have occurred after the filing of a notice of appeal but before the filing of an appeal brief and have involved a review of all rejections of a single claim being appealed to see whether any rejection plainly fails to establish a *prima facie* case of unpatentability. The second review would have occurred after the filing of an appeal brief and have involved a review of all rejections on appeal.

The comments were split between supporting and opposing the appeal review procedures under consideration. Most comments opposing the appeal review procedures under consideration supported the concept of screening the tenability of rejections in applications before they are forwarded to the Board of Patent Appeals and Interferences, but argued that: (1) The proposed appeal review amounts to quality control for which the applicant should not be required to pay (appeal fees should be raised if appropriate); (2) an appeal review is meaningless (only advisory) unless the decision is binding on the examiner; (3) the Board of Patent Appeals and Interferences may give undue deference to a rejection that has been through an appeal review; and (4) the proposed appeal review will delay ultimate review by the Board of Patent Appeals and Interferences. Several comments indicated that the proposed change would be acceptable, but included the following conditions with that indication: (1) That the applicant need not pay for either review; (2) that the reviewer be someone outside the normal chain of review for an application being forwarded to the Board of Patent Appeals and Interferences for decision; (3) that the reviewer be someone who has at least full signatory authority; (4) that the report gives a detailed explanation of the results of the appeal review (especially if a position is changed/application allowed); (5) that fees (appeal or appeal review) be refunded if the review results in the allowance of the application; (6) that the pre-brief review involve review of the application by more than one person; (7) that the pre-brief review also determine whether any *prima facie* case of unpatentability has been overcome; and (8) that the appeal process should be revised to model the German Patent Office.

Response: This notice does not propose changing § 1.191 *et seq.* to provide for appeal reviews. The Office intends to increase the use of the current appeal conference procedures as set forth in section 1208 of the Manual of Patent Examining Procedure (7th ed. 1998)(MPEP).

Reevaluating the Disclosure Document Program (Topic 20)

The Office indicated in the Advance Notice that it was reevaluating the Disclosure Document Program (DDP) because this program has been the subject of numerous abuses by so-called "invention development companies" resulting in complaints from individual inventors, and therefore may be *detrimental* to the interests of its customers. At the same time, the distinctly different provisional applications provide a viable alternate route whereby, for the basic small entity filing fee of $75 (§ 1.16(k)), a provisional application may be filed by a small entity. A provisional application does not require a claim in compliance with 35 U.S.C. 112, ¶ 2, or an inventor's oath under 35 U.S.C. 115. Although abandoned after one year, provisional applications are retained by the Office for at least twenty years, or longer if it is referenced in a patent. A provisional application is considered a constructive reduction to practice of an invention as of the filing date accorded the provisional application if it describes the invention in sufficient detail to enable a person of ordinary skill in the art to make and use the invention and discloses the best mode known by the inventor for carrying out the invention. Unlike the DDP, a provisional application may be used under the Paris Convention to establish a priority date for foreign filing. In other words, except for adding the best mode requirement, the disclosure requirements for a provisional application are identical to the disclosure requirements for a Disclosure Document and a provisional application provides users with a filing date without starting the patent term period. Thus, almost any paper filed today as a proper Disclosure Document can now be filed as a provisional application with the necessary cover sheet.

For these reasons, the Office posed in the Advance Notice several questions directed to whether the DDP served a useful function. Only one comment presented evidence of a single instance where a disclosure document was used in conjunction with an interference, but this person was an extensive user of the DDP and cautioned that independent inventors fail to keep records of the date of their invention. The same commenter suggested that if the attorney signing the provisional application could also claim small entity status for his client, this would diminish the need for the DDP. This appears likely to be adopted since, contemporaneously with this proposal, under Topic 1 (relating to the simplification of the request for small entity status), it is being proposed that applicant or applicant's attorney may assert entitlement to small entity status. This proposal will make it easier for both attorneys or applicants to assert small entity status when filing provisional applications. See discussion of proposed changes to §§ 1.9, 1.27 and 1.28 relating to small entity status for further details.

Six commenters felt that the program should be eliminated because there is no value to applicants in light of the provisional application procedure. Some felt that the program creates a dangerous situation in that applicants may assume they are getting some type of patent protection or that the statutory bar provision in 35 U.S.C. 102(b) has been avoided. One commenter characterized the DDP as an "unwitting vehicle and accomplice for fraud and delusion of small inventors by so-called 'invention development companies', or self-delusions of independent inventors, who have been mailing thousands of these 'Disclosure Documents' to the PTO * * *." Another commenter, however, postulated that if the only difference between the DDP and provisional applications was the cost, then the cancellation of the DDP would only result in the abuse of the provisional patent applications at a higher cost to unsuspecting inventors.

Four commenters confused the DDP with defensive publications as their responses wrongfully indicated a belief that the DDP involved publication of the disclosures. One commenter suggested that before the program is eliminated that the Office should engage in an educational program (with a survey) to explain the questionable value of the program and alternative procedures available to the public. The commenter further stated that the education program should focus on those individuals who use the DDP and could include a survey of those individuals to determine the benefit to the public. A second commenter supported the concept of contacting the independent inventors. At least one other comment suggested that elimination might be detrimental to individual inventors.

Response: A review of the comments on this proposal reveals that the independent inventor community submitted only a few of the responses. The Office considers it inappropriate to proceed with this proposal in the absence of greater input from the independent inventor community. Therefore, this notice does not propose changes to the rules of practice concerning the Disclosure Document Program. The Office will continue to study the Disclosure Document Program and seek greater input from the independent inventor community before any further action is taken. In this regard, the matter will be referred to the Office of Independent Inventor Programs, headed by Director Donald Grant Kelly. The Office of Independent Inventor Programs was established on March 15, 1999. Reporting directly to the Commissioner, this new office was established to provide assistance to independent inventors, particularly in terms of improved communications, educational outreach, and Office-based support. In addition, the Office of Independent Inventor Programs will work to establish or strengthen cooperative efforts with the Federal Trade Commission, the Department of Justice, and various Bar Associations to address the growing problem of invention development company marketing scams.

Creating a Patent and Trademark Office Review Service for Applicant-Created Forms (Topic 21)

The Office indicated that it was considering establishing a new service, under which the Office would (for a fee) review applicant-created forms intended to be used for future correspondence to the Office. After the review is completed, the Office would provide a written report, including comments and suggestions (if any), but the Office would not formally "approve" any form. If a (reviewed) form is modified in view of a Office written report, comments and/or suggestion, the revised form could be resubmitted to the Office for a follow up review for an additional charge (roughly estimated at approximately $50). After a form has been reviewed and revised, as may be needed, to comply with the Office's written report, it would be acceptable for the form to indicate if it is a substitute for an Office form, and that it has been "reviewed by the Patent and Trademark Office."

The Office received few comments on this proposal. Of those comments received on this proposal, most supported this new service. The comments included the following specific concerns and suggestions: (1) That the form review service be optional and not mandatory; (2) that there be one fee per form, regardless of the number of submissions needed to have the form reviewed; (3) the service had little value unless the Office would be willing to approve a form; and (4) the time has come to require the use of mandatory forms.

Response: The Office indicated in the Advance Notice that this new service would involve significant start-up costs, and, absent positive feedback on the matter, the Office does not intend to implement this new service. See Changes to Implement the Patent Business Goals, 63 FR at 53530, 1215 Off. Gaz. Pat. Office at 117. In view of the limited interest shown by the comments in this new service, the Office has decided not to proceed with the proposal to provide a review service for applicant-created forms.

Discussion of Specific Rules

Title 37 of the Code of Federal Regulations, Parts 1, 3, 5, and 10, are proposed to be amended as follows:

Part 1

Section 1.4: Section 1.4(b) is proposed to be amended to refer to a patent or trademark application, patent file, trademark registration file, or other proceeding, rather than only an application file. Section 1.4(b) is also proposed to be amended to provide that the filing of duplicate copies of correspondence in a patent or trademark application, patent file, trademark registration file, or other proceeding should be avoided (except in situations in which the Office requires the filing of duplicate copies), and that the Office may dispose of duplicate copies of correspondence in a patent or trademark application, patent file, trademark registration file, or other proceeding. Finally, § 1.4(b) and § 1.4(c) are also proposed to be amended to change "should" to "must" because the Office needs separate copies of papers directed to two or more files, or of papers dealing with different subjects.

Section 1.6: Section 1.6(d)(9) is proposed to be amended to delete the reference to recorded answers under § 1.684(c), as § 1.684(c) has been removed and reserved.

Section 1.9: Section 1.9(f) is proposed to be amended to provide the definition of who can qualify to pay small entity fees, and paragraphs (c) through (e) of § 1.9 are proposed to be removed and reserved.

Paragraph (f) of § 1.9 is proposed to: (1) Be reformatted, (2) define a "person" to include inventors and also noninventors holding rights in the invention, (3) explain that qualification depends on whether any rights in the invention were transferred and to whom, and (4) provide that a license by a person to the Government under certain situations does not bar entitlement to small entity status.

Section 1.9 paragraph (f) is proposed to be reformatted to place the subject matter relating to definitions of small entities: (1) Persons, (2) small business concerns; and (3) nonprofit organizations, in one paragraph rather than as currently in paragraphs (c) through (e). The expression "independent inventor" of current paragraph (c) is proposed to be replaced with the term "person" in paragraph (f)(1) (and other paragraphs of this section). The term "person" in paragraph (f) is proposed to be defined to include individuals who are inventors and also individuals who are not inventors but who have been transferred some right or rights in the invention. This would clarify that individuals who are not inventors but who have rights in the invention are covered by the provisions of §§ 1.9 and 1.27.

Paragraphs (f)(2)(i) and (f)(3)(i) of § 1.9 are proposed to be added to clarify that in order for small entity businesses and nonprofit organizations to remain entitled to small entity status, they must not in some manner transfer or be under an obligation to transfer any rights in the invention to any party that would not qualify for small entity status. Current § 1.27 paragraphs (b), (f)(1)(iii), and (f)(1)(iii) make clear that this rights transfer requirement applies to all parties (independent inventors, small businesses and nonprofit organizations, respectively). The absence of this requirement however, from current § 1.9 paragraphs (d) and (e) (small business and nonprofit organization, respectively), notwithstanding its presence in § 1.9 paragraph (c) (independent inventor), has lead to confusion as to the existence of such a requirement for small businesses and nonprofit organizations. In view of the appearance of the rights transfer requirement in § 1.9, it is proposed to be removed from all paragraphs of § 1.27.

Paragraph (f)(4)(i) of § 1.9 is proposed to be added to provide a new exception relating to the granting of a license to the U.S. Government by a person, that results from a particular rights determination. Such a license would not bar entitlement to small entity status. Similarly paragraph (f)(4)(ii) of § 1.9 is proposed to be added to have transferred to it (from current § 1.27 paragraphs (c)(2) and (d)(2)) the current exceptions relating to a license to a Federal agency by a small business or a nonprofit organization resulting from a particular funding agreement. Again, such a license would not bar entitlement to small entity status.

For additional proposed changes to small entity requirements see §§ 1.27 and 1.28.

Section 1.9(i) is proposed to be added to define "national security classified." Section 1.9(i), as proposed, defines "national security classified" as used in 37 CFR Chapter 1 as meaning "specifically authorized under criteria established by an Act of Congress or Executive order to be kept secret in the interest of national defense or foreign policy and, in fact, properly classified pursuant to Act of Congress or Executive order."

Section 1.12: Section 1.12(c)(1) is proposed to be amended to change the reference to the fee set forth in "§§ 1.17(i)" to the fee set forth in "§ 1.17(h)." This change is for consistency with the changes to § 1.17(h) and § 1.17(i). See discussion of changes to § 1.17(h) and § 1.17(i).

Section 1.14: Section 1.14 is proposed to be amended to make it easier to understand. Section 1.14 is also proposed to be amended to provide that the Office will no longer give status information or access in certain situations where applicants have an expectation of confidentiality.

Section 1.14(a) is proposed to be amended to define "status information" and "access." "Status information" is proposed to be defined as information that the applica-

payable. The provision of § 1.22(c)(1)(ii) would apply, for example, in the following situation: In reply to an Office action setting a three-month shortened statutory period for reply, a paper is filed three and one-half months after the mail date of the Office action without payment of the fee for a one-month extension of time. Thereafter, the applicant discovers the lack of payment and files a second paper including an authorization to charge the appropriate fee for any extension of time required, but the second paper is received in the Office (§ 1.6) four and one-half months from the mail date of the Office action. The fee required for the reply to the Office action to be timely is considered paid when the second paper was received (§ 1.6) in the Office. Section 1.22(c)(1)(iii) is proposed to provide that a fee paid by an authorization to charge such fee to a deposit account containing sufficient funds to cover the applicable fee amount (§ 1.25) is considered paid on the date of the agreement, if the deposit account charge authorization is the result of an agreement between the applicant and an Office employee as long as the agreement is reduced to a writing. That is, the fee is considered paid on the date of the agreement (*e.g.*, the date of the interview), and the date the agreement is subsequently reduced to writing (*e.g.*, the mail date of the interview summary) is not relevant to the date the fee is considered paid.

Section 1.22(c)(2) is proposed to provide that a fee paid other than by an authorization to charge such fee to a deposit account is considered paid on the date the applicable fee amount is received in the Office (§ 1.6). Section 1.22(c)(3) is proposed to provide that the applicable fee amount is determined by the fee in effect on the date such fee is paid in full. When fees change (due to a CPI increase under 35 U.S.C. 41(f) or other legislative change), the Office generally accords fee payments the benefit of the provisions of § 1.8 vis-à-vis the applicable fee amount even though the fee is not considered paid until it is received in the Office (§ 1.6). See Revision of Patent Fees for Fiscal Year 1999, Final Rule Notice, 63 FR 67578, 67578–79 (December 8, 1998), 1217 Off. Gaz. Pat. Office 148, 148 (December 29, 1998). This treatment of fee payments is an "exception" to the provisions of § 1.22(c) as proposed, in that such fee would be not be entitled to any benefit under § 1.8 vis-à-vis the applicable fee amount but for the express exception provided in the fee change rulemaking. Of course, a fee is considered timely if the fee is submitted to the Office under the procedure set forth in § 1.8(a) (unless excluded under § 1.8(a)(2)), even though the fee is not considered paid until it is actually received in the Office (§ 1.6).

Section 1.25: Section 1.25(b) is proposed to be amended to provide that an authorization to charge fees under § 1.16 in an application submitted under § 1.494 or § 1.495 will be treated as an authorization to charge fees under § 1.492. There are many instances in which papers filed for the purpose of entering the national stage under 35 U.S.C. 371 and § 1.494 or § 1.495 include an authorization to charge fees under § 1.16 (rather than fees under § 1.492). In such instances, the Office treats the authorization as an authorization to charge fees under § 1.492 since: (1) Timely payment of the appropriate national fee under § 1.492 is necessary to avoid abandonment of the application as to the United States; and (2) the basic filing fee under § 1.16 is not applicable to such papers or applications. Therefore, the Office is proposing to change § 1.25(b) to place persons filing papers to enter the national stage under 35 U.S.C. 371 and § 1.494 or § 1.495 on notice as to how an authorization to charge fees under § 1.16 will be treated.

Section 1.25(b) is also proposed to be amended to provide that an authorization to charge fees set forth in § 1.18 to a deposit account is subject to the provisions of § 1.311(b).

Section 1.26: The Office is proposing to amend the rules of practice to provide that all requests for refund must be filed within specified time periods. The rules of practice do not (other than in the situation in which a request for refund is based upon subsequent entitlement to small entity status) set any time period (other than "a reasonable time") within which a request for refund must be filed. In the absence of such a time period, Office fee record keeping systems and business planning must account for the possibility that a request for refund may be filed at any time, including many years after payment of the fee at issue.

It is a severe burden on the Office to treat a request for refund filed years after payment of the fee at issue. Since Office fee record keeping systems change over time, the Office must check any system on which fees for the application, patent or trademark registration have been posted to determine what fees were in fact paid. In addition, changes in fee amounts, which usually occur on October 1 of each year, make it difficult to determine with certainty whether a fee paid years ago was the correct fee at the time and under the condition it was paid.

It also causes business planning problems to account for the possibility that a request for refund may be filed years after payment of the fee at issue. Without any set time period within which a request for refund must be filed, the Office must maintain fee records, in any automated fee record keeping system ever used by the Office, in perpetuity. Finally, as the Office can never be absolutely certain that a submitted fee was not paid by mistake or in excess of that required, the absence of such a time period subjects the Office to unending and uncertain financial obligations.

Accordingly, the Office is proposing to amend § 1.26 to provide non-extendable time periods within which any request for refund must be filed to be timely.

Section 1.26(a) is proposed to be amended by dividing its first sentence into two sentences. Section 1.26(a) is further amended for consistency with 35 U.S.C. 42(d) ("[t]he Commissioner may refund a fee paid by mistake or any amount paid in excess of that required"). Under 35 U.S.C. 42(d), the Office may refund: (1) a fee paid when no fee is required (a fee paid by mistake); or (2) any fee paid in excess of the amount of fee that is required. See Ex parte Grady, 59 USPQ 276, 277 (Comm'r Pats. 1943) (the statutory authorization for the refund of fees under the "by mistake" clause is applicable only to a mistake relating to the fee payment). In the situation in which an applicant or patentee takes an action "by mistake" (*e.g.,* files an application or maintains a patent in force "by mistake"), the submission of fees required to take that action (*e.g.,* a filing fee submitted with such application or a maintenance fee submitted for such patent) is not a "fee paid by mistake" within the meaning of 35 U.S.C. 42(d). Section 1.26(a) is also proposed to be amended to revise the "change of purpose" provisions to read "[a] change of purpose after the payment of a fee, as when a party desires to withdraw a patent or trademark filing for which the fee was paid, including an application, an appeal, or a request for an oral hearing, will not entitle a party to a refund of such fee."

Section 1.26(a) is also proposed to be amended to change the sentence "[a]mounts of twenty-five dollars or less will not be returned unless specifically requested within a reasonable time, nor will the payer be notified of such amount; amounts over twenty-five dollars may be returned by check or, if requested, by credit to a deposit account" to "[t]he Office will not refund amounts of twenty-five five dollars or less unless a refund is specifically requested, and will not notify the payor of such amounts." Except as discussed below, the Office intends to continue to review submitted fees to determine that they have not been paid by mistake or in excess of that required, and to *sua sponte* refund fees (of amounts over twenty-five dollars) determined to have been paid by mistake or in excess of that required. Section 1.26(a), however, is proposed to be amended to eliminate language that appears to obligate the Office to *sua sponte* refund fees to be consistent with the provisions of § 1.26(b) which requires that any request for refund be filed within a specified time period.

Section 1.26(a) is also proposed to be amended to facilitate refunds by electronic funds transfer. Section 31001(x) of the Omnibus Consolidated Rescissions and Appropriations Act of 1996, Pub. L. 104–134, 110 Stat. 1321 (1996) (the Debt Collection Improvement Act of 1996), amended 31 U.S.C. 3332 to require that all disbursements by Federal agencies (subject to certain exceptions and waivers) be made by electronic funds transfer. The Department of the Treasury has implemented this legislation at 31 CFR Part 208. See Management of Federal Agency Disbursements, Final Rule Notice, 63 FR 51489 (September 25, 1998). Thus, § 1.26(a) is proposed to be amended to enable the Office to obtain the banking information necessary for making refunds by electronic funds transfer in accordance with 31 U.S.C. 3332 and 31 CFR Part 208.

Specifically, § 1.26(a) is also proposed to be amended such that if a party paying a fee or requesting a refund does not instruct that refunds be credited to a deposit account, the Office will attempt to make any refund by electronic funds transfer. If such party does not provide the banking information necessary for making refunds by electronic funds transfer, the Commissioner may either require such banking information or use the banking information on the payment instrument to make a refund. This provision will authorize the Office to: (1) Use the banking information on the payment instrument (*e.g.*, a personal check is submitted to pay the fee) when making a refund due to an excess payment; or (2) require such banking information in other situations (*e.g.*, a refund is requested or a money order or certified bank check is submitted containing an excess payment). The purpose of this proposed change to § 1.26(a) is to encourage parties to submit the banking information necessary for making refunds by electronic funds transfer (if not on the payment instrument) upfront, and not to add a step (requiring such banking information) to the refund process. If it is not cost-effective to require the banking information necessary for making refunds by electronic funds transfer, the Office may simply issue any refund by treasury check. *See* 31 CFR 208.4(f).

Section 1.26(b) is proposed to be added to provide that any request for refund must be filed within two years from the date the fee was paid, except as otherwise provided in § 1.26(b) or in § 1.28(a). See the discussion of proposed § 1.22(c) concerning the date a fee is considered paid.

Section 1.26(b) is also proposed to provide that if the Office charges a deposit account by an amount other than an amount specifically indicated in an authorization (§ 1.25(b)), any request for refund based upon such charge must be filed within two years from the date of the deposit account statement indicating such charge, and that such request must be accompanied by a copy of that deposit account statement. This provision of § 1.26(b) would apply, for example, in the following types of situations: (1) A deposit account is charged for an extension of time as a result of there being a prior general authorization in the application (§ 1.136(a)(3)); or (2) a deposit account is charged for the outstanding balance of a fee as a result of an insufficient fee being submitted with an authorization to charge the deposit account for any additional fees that are due. In these situations, the party providing the authorization is not in a position to know the exact amount by which the deposit account will be charged until the date of the deposit account statement indicating the amount of the charge.

Finally, § 1.26(b) is proposed to provide that the time periods set forth in § 1.26(b) are not extendable.

Section 1.27: The Office is considering simplifying applicant's request for small entity status under § 1.27. The currently used small entity statement forms are proposed to be eliminated as they would no longer be needed. Some material in § 1.28 is proposed to be reorganized into § 1.27.

Small entity status would be established at any time by a simple assertion of entitlement to small entity status. The currently required statements, which include a formalistic reference to § 1.9, would no longer be required. Payment of an exact small entity basic filing or national fee would also be considered an assertion of small entity status. This would be so even if the wrong exact basic filing or national fee was selected. To establish small entity status after payment of the basic filing fee as a non-small entity, a written assertion of small entity status would be required to be submitted. The parties who could assert small entity status would be liberalized to include one of several inventors or a partial assignee.

Other clarifying changes are proposed to be made including a transfer of material into § 1.27 from § 1.28 drawn towards: (1) Assertions in related, continuing and reissue applications; (2) notification of loss of entitlement to small entity status; and (3) fraud on the Office in regard to establishing small entity status or paying small entity fees.

While there would be no change in the current requirement to make an investigation in order to determine entitlement to small entity status, a recitation would be added noting the need for a determination of entitlement prior to an assertion of status; the Office would only be changing the ease with which small entity status could be claimed once it has been determined that a claim to such status is appropriate.

For additional proposed changes to small entity requirements see §§ 1.9 and 1.28.

Problem and Background

Section 1.27 currently requires that a request for small entity status be accompanied by submission of an appropriate statement that the party seeking small entity status qualifies in accordance with § 1.9. Either a reference to § 1.9 or a specific statement relating to the provisions of § 1.9 is mandatory. For a small business, the small business must either state that exclusive rights remain with the small business, or if not, identify the party to which some rights have been transferred so that the party to which rights have been transferred can submit its own small entity statement (current § 1.27(c)(1)(iii)). This can lead to the submission of multiple small entity statements for each request for small entity status where rights in the invention are split. The request for small entity status and reference/statement may be submitted prior to paying, or, at the latest, at the time of paying, any small entity fee. In part, to ensure that at least the reference to § 1.9 is complied with, the Office has produced four types of small entity statement forms (including ones for the inventors, small businesses and non-profit organizations) that include the required reference to § 1.9 and specific statements as to exclusive rights in the invention. Where an application has not been assigned and there are multiple inventors, each inventor must actually sign a small entity statement, the execution of which must all be coordinated and submitted at the same time. Similarly, coordination of execution and submission of statements is needed where there is more than one assignee. Additionally, the statement forms relating to small businesses and non-profit organizations need to be signed by an appropriate official empowered to act on behalf of the small business or non-profit organization. Refunds of non-small entity fees can only be obtained if a refund is specifically requested within two months of the payment of the full (non-small entity) fee and is supported by all required small entity statements. *See* current § 1.28(a)(1). The current two-month refund window under § 1.28 is not extendable.

The rigid requirements of §§ 1.27 and 1.28 have led to a substantial number of problems. Applicants, particularly *pro se* applicants, do not always recognize that a particular reference to § 1.9 is required in their request to establish small entity status. They believe that all they have to do is pay the small entity fee and state that they are a small entity. Further, the time required to ascertain who are the appropriate officials to sign the statement and to have the statements (referring to § 1.9) signed and collected (where more than one is necessary), results, in many instances, in having to pay the higher non-small entity fees and then seek a refund. These situations result in: (1) Small entity applicants also having to pay additional fees (*e.g.*, surcharges and extension(s) of time fees for the delayed submission of the small entity statement form); (2) additional correspondence with the office to perfect a claim for small entity status; and (3) the filing of petitions with petition fees to revive abandoned applications. This increases the pendency of the prosecution of the application in the Office and, in some cases, results in loss of patent term. For example, under current procedures, if a *pro se* applicant files a new application with small entity fees but without a small entity statement, the office mails a notice to the *pro se* applicant requiring the full basic filing fee of a non-small entity. Even if the applicant timely files a small entity statement, the applicant must still timely pay the small entity surcharge for the delayed submission of the small entity statement to avoid abandonment of the application. A second example is a non-profit organization paying the basic filing fee as a non-small entity because of difficulty in obtaining the non-profit small entity statement form signed by an appropriate official. In this situation, a refund pursuant to § 1.26, based on establishing status as a small entity, may only be obtained if a statement under § 1.27 and the request for a refund of the excess amount are filed within the non-extendable two-month period from the date of the timely payment of the full fee. A third example is an application filed without the basic filing fee on behalf of a small business by a practitioner who includes the standard authorization to pay additional fees. The Office will immediately charge the non-small entity basic filing fee without specific notification thereof at the time of the charge. By the time the deposit account statement is received and reviewed, the two-month period for refund may have expired.

Accordingly, a simpler procedure to establish small entity status would reduce processing time within the Office (Patent Business Goal 1) and would be a tremendous benefit to small entity applicants as it would eliminate the time-consuming and aggravating processing requirements that are mandated by the current rules. Thus, the proposed simplification would help small entity applicants to receive patents sooner with fewer expenditures in fees and resources and the office could issue the patent with fewer resources (Patent Business Goals 4 and 5).

Assertion as to Entitlement to Small Entity Status; Assertion by Writing

The Office is proposing to allow small entity status to be established by the submission of a simple written assertion of entitlement to small entity status. The current formal requirements of § 1.27, which include a reference to either § 1.9, or to the exclusive rights in the invention, would be eliminated.

The written assertion would not be required to be presented in any particular form. Written assertions of small entity status or references to small entity fees would be liberally interpreted to represent the required assertion. The written assertion could be made in any paper filed in or with the application and need be no more than a simple sentence or a box checked on an application transmittal letter or reply cover sheet. It is the intent of the Office to modify its application transmittal forms to provide for such a check box. Accordingly, small entity status could be established without submission of any of the current small entity statement forms (PTO/SB/09–12) that embody and comply with the current requirements of § 1.27 and which are now used to establish small entity status.

Assertion by Payment of Small Entity Basic Filing or National Fee

The payment of an exact small entity basic filing or national fee will also be considered to be a sufficient assertion of entitlement to small entity status. An applicant filing a patent application and paying an exact small entity basic filing or national fee would automatically establish small entity status for the application even without any further written assertion of small entity status. This is so even if an applicant were to inadvertently select the wrong type of small entity basic filing or national fee for the application being filed. If small entity status was not established when the basic filing fee was paid, such as by payment of a large entity basic filing or national fee, a later claim to small entity status would require a written assertion. Payment of a small entity fee other than a small entity basic filing or national fee (*e.g.*, extension of time, or issue fee) without inclusion of a written assertion would not be sufficient.

Even though applicants can assert small entity status by payment of an exact small entity basic filing or national fee, the Office strongly encourages applicants to file a written assertion of small entity status. A written assertion would guarantee the applicant that the application will have small entity status even if applicant fails to pay the exact small entity basic filing or national fee. The limited provision providing for small entity status by payment of an exact small entity basic filing or national fee is only intended to act as a safety net to avoid possible financial loss to inventors or small businesses that can qualify for small entity status.

Caution: Even though small entity status would be accorded where the wrong type of small entity basic filing fee or national fee were selected but the exact amount of the fee were paid, applicant would still need to pay the correct small entity amount for the basic filing or national fee where selection of the wrong type of fee results in a deficiency. While an accompanying *general* authorization to charge any additional fees would suffice to pay the balance due of the proper small entity basic filing or national fee, *specific* authorizations to charge fees under § 1.17 or extension of time fees would not suffice to pay any balance due of the proper small entity basic filing or national fee because they do not actually authorize payment of small entity amounts.

Examples: Applications under 35 U.S.C. 111: If an applicant were to file a utility application under 35 U.S.C. 111 yet only pay the exact small entity amount for a design application (currently the small entity filing fees for utility and design applications are $380 and $155, respectively), small entity status for the utility application would be accorded. See the following examples:

(1) Where the utility application was filed inadvertently with the exact small entity basic filing fee for a design application rather than for a utility application and an authorization to charge the filing fee was not present, the Office would accord small entity status and mail a Notice to File Missing Parts of Application, requiring the $225 difference between the small entity utility application filing fee owed and the small entity design application filing fee actually paid plus a small entity surcharge (of $65) for the late submission of the correct filing fee.

(2) Where the utility application was filed without any filing fee but the $155 exact small entity filing fee for a design application was inadvertently paid in response to a Notice to File Missing Parts of Application, small entity status would be established even though the correct small entity filing fee for a utility application was not fully paid.

While the Office will notify applicant of the remaining amount due, the period for reply to pay the correct small entity utility basic filing fee would, however, continue to run. Small entity extensions of time under § 1.136(a) would be needed for the later submission of the $225 difference between the $380 small entity utility basic filing fee owed and the $155 small entity design filing fee inadvertently paid. If there was an authorization to charge a deposit account in the response to the Notice, the $225 difference would have been charged along with the small entity $65 surcharge and the period for response to the Notice to File Missing Parts of Application would not continue to run.

Applications entering that national stage under 35 U.S.C. 371: Section 1.492(a) sets forth five (5) different basic national fee amounts which apply to different situations. If an applicant pays a basic national fee which is the exact small entity amount for one of the fees set forth in § 1.492(a), but not the particular fee which applies to that application, the applicant will be considered to have made an assertion of small entity status. This is true whether the fee paid is higher or lower than the actual fee required. See the following examples.

(1) An applicant pays $485 (the small entity amount due under § 1.492(a)(3), where the United States was neither the International Searching Authority (ISA) nor the International Preliminary Examining Authority (IPEA) and the search report was not prepared by the European Patent Office (EPO) or Japanese Patent Office (JPO)) when in fact the required small entity fee is $420 under § 1.492(a)(5), because the JPO or EPO prepared the search report. The applicant will be considered to have made the assertion of small entity status. The office will apply $420 to the payment of the basic national fee and refund the overpayment of $65.

(2) An applicant pays $420 (the small entity fee due under § 1.492(a)(5) where the search report was prepared by the EPO or JPO). In fact, the search report was prepared by the Australian Patent Office and no preliminary examination fee was paid to the Patent and Trademark Office. Thus, the required small entity fee is $485 under § 1.492(a)(3). The applicant will be considered to have made the assertion of small entity status. If the applicant has authorized payment of fee deficiencies to a deposit account, the Office will charge the $65 to the deposit account and apply it and the $420 to the basic national fee. If there is no authorization or there are insufficient fees in the deposit account, the basic national fee payment is insufficient. If the balance is not provided before 20 or 30 months from the priority date has expired, the application is abandoned.

If payment is attempted to be made of the proper type of basic filing or national fee, but it is not the exact small entity fee required (an incorrect fee amount is supplied) and a written assertion of small entity status is not present, small entity status would not be accorded. The Office would mail a notice of insufficient basic filing or national fee with a surcharge due as in current practice if an authorization to charge the basic filing or national fee were not present. The Office would not consider a basic filing or national fee submitted in an amount above the correct fee amount, but below the non-small entity fee amount, as a request to establish small entity status unless an additional written assertion is also present. Of course, the submission of a basic filing or national fee below the correct fee amount would not serve to establish small entity status.

Where an application is originally filed by a party, who is in fact a small entity, with an authorization to charge fees (including basic filing or national fees) and there is no indication (assertion) of entitlement to small entity status present, that authorization would not be sufficient to establish small entity status unless the authorization was specifically directed to small entity basic filing or national fees. The general authorization to charge fees would continue to be acted upon immediately and the full (not small entity) basic filing or national fees would be charged with applicant having three months to request a refund by asserting entitlement to *small entity* status. This would be so even if the application were a continuing application where small entity status had been established in the prior application.

Parties Who Could Assert Entitlement to Small Entity Status by Writing

The parties who could submit a written assertion of entitlement to small entity status would be any party permitted by Office regulations, § 1.33(b), to file a paper in an application. This eliminates the additional requirement of obtaining the signature of an appropriate party other than the party prosecuting the application. By way of example, in the case of three *pro se* inventors for a particular application, the three inventors upon filing the application could submit a written assertion of entitlement to small entity status and thereby establish small entity status for the application. For small business concerns and non-profit organizations, the practitioner could supply the assertion rather than the current requirement for an appropriate official of the organization to execute a small entity statement form. In addition, a written assertion of entitlement to small entity status would be able to be made by one of several inventors or a partial assignee. Current practice does not require an assignee asserting small entity status to submit a § 3.73(b) certification, and such certifications would not be required under the proposed revision either for partial assignees or for an assignee of the entire right, title, and interest.

Parties who Could Assert Entitlement to Small Entity Status by Payment of Basic Filing or National Fee

Where small entity status is sought by way of payment of the basic filing or national fee, any party may submit payment, such as by check, and small entity status would be accorded.

Inventors Asserting Small Entity Status

Any inventor would be permitted to submit a written assertion of small entity status, including inventors who are not officially named of record until an executed oath/declaration is submitted. *See* § 1.41(a)(1). Where an application is filed without an executed oath/declaration pursuant to § 1.53(f), the Office will accept the written assertion of an individual who has merely been identified as an inventor on filing of the application (*e.g.*, application transmittal letter) as opposed to being named as an inventor. Sections 1.4(d)(2) and 10.18(b) are seen as sufficient basis to permit any individual to provide a written assertion so long as the individual identifies himself or herself as an inventor. Where a § 1.63 oath or declaration is later filed, any original written assertion as to small entity status will remain unless changed by an appropriate party under § 1.27(f)(2). Where a later filed § 1.63 oath or declaration sets forth an inventive entity that does not include the person who initially was identified as an inventor and who asserted small entity status, small entity status will also remain. Where small entity status is asserted by payment of the small entity basic filing, or national fee any party may submit such fee, including an inventor who was not identified in the application transmittal letter, or a third party.

Caution: The fact that certain parties can execute a written assertion of entitlement to small entity status, such as one of several inventors, or a partial assignee, does not entitle that written assertion to be entered in the Official file record and become an effective paper unless the person submitting the paper is authorized to do so under § 1.33(b). In other words, the fact that one of several inventors can sign a written assertion of entitlement to small entity status does not also imply that the same inventor can submit the paper to the Office and have it entered of record. The written assertion, even though effective once entered in the Official file record, must still be submitted by a party entitled to file a paper under § 1.33(b). Payment of the small entity basic filing or national stage fee would not be subject to such submission requirement and any payment thereof would be accepted and treated as an effective assertion of small entity status.

Policy Considerations

Office policy and procedures already permit establishment of small entity status in certain applications through simplified procedures. For example, small entity status may be established in a continuing or reissue application simply by payment of the small entity basic filing fee if the prior application/patent had small entity status. *See* current § 1.28(a)(2). The instant concept of payment of the small entity basic statutory filing fee to establish small entity status in a new application is merely a logical extension of that practice.

There may be some concern that elimination of the small entity statement forms will result in applicants who are not actually entitled to small entity status requesting such status. On balance, it seems that more errors occur where small entity applicants who are entitled to such status run afoul of procedural hurdles created by the requirements of § 1.27 than the requirements help to prevent status claims for those who are not in fact entitled to such status.

Continued Obligations for Thorough Investigation of Small Entity Status

Applicants should not confuse the fact that the Office is making it easier to qualify for small entity status with the need to do a complete and thorough investigation before an assertion is made that they do, in fact, qualify for small entity status. *It should be clearly understood that, even though it would be much easier to assert and thereby establish small entity status, applicants would continue to need to make a full and complete investigation of all facts and circumstances before making a determination of actual entitlement to small entity status. Where entitlement to small entity status is uncertain it should not be claimed.* See MPEP 509.03. The assertion of small entity status (even by mere payment of the exact small entity basic filing fee) is not appropriate until such an investigation has been completed. Thus, in the previous example of the three *pro se* inventors, before one of the inventors could pay the small entity basic filing or national fee to establish small entity status, the single inventor asserting entitlement to small entity status would need to check with the other two inventors to determine whether small entity status was appropriate.

The intent of § 1.27 is that the person making the assertion of entitlement to small entity status is the person in a position to know the facts about whether or not status as a small entity can be properly established. That person, thus, has a duty to investigate the circumstances surrounding entitlement to small entity status to the fullest extent. Therefore, while the Office is interested in making it easier to claim small entity status, it is important to note that small entity status must not be claimed unless the person or persons can unequivocally make the required self-certification. Section 1.27(g) would recite current provisions in § 1.28(d)(1) and (2) relating to fraud practiced on the Office.

Consistent with § 1.4(d)(2), the payment of a small entity basic filing or national fee, would constitute a certification under § 10.18(b). Thus, a simple payment of the small entity basic filing or national fee, without a specific written assertion, will activate the provisions of § 1.4(d)(2) and, by that, invoke the self-certification requirement set forth in § 10.18(b), regardless of whether the party is a practitioner or non-practitioner.

Clarification of Need for Investigation

Section 1.27 is proposed to be clarified (paragraph (e)) by explicitly providing that a determination "should" be made of entitlement to small entity status according to the requirement set forth in § 1.9 prior to asserting small entity status. The need for such a determination of entitlement to small entity status prior to assertion of small entity status is set forth in terms of that there "should" be such a determination, rather than there "must" be such a determination. In view of the ease with which small entity status would now be obtainable, it is deemed advisable to provide an explicit direction that a determination of entitlement to small entity status pursuant to § 1.9 be made before its assertion. Consideration was given to making the need for a determination a requirement rather than advisory; however, the decision was made to make it advisory, particularly in view of the following possible scenario: One of three inventors submits a written assertion of entitlement to small entity status without making any determination of entitlement to such status, such as by checking with the other two inventors to see if they have assigned any rights in the invention. Small entity status was proper at the time asserted notwithstanding the lack of a proper determination. If the determination is set forth as a requirement ("must"), the lack of such a determination might act to cause an unduly harsh result where small entity status was in fact appropriate and the failure to check prior to assertion was innocent. It is recognized that the use of "should" may cause concern that a cavalier approach to asserting entitlement to small entity status may be taken by encouraging some who are asserting status not to make a complete determination as the determination is not set forth as being mandatory. On balance, it is thought that the use of "should" would lead to more equitable results. The danger of encouraging the assertion of small entity status without a prior determination as to qualification for small entity status is thought to be small, because, should status turn out to be improper, the lack of a prior determination may result in a failure to meet the lack of deceptive intent requirements under § 1.27(g) or § 1.28(c). The Office has noted that any attempt to improperly establish status as a small entity will be viewed as a serious matter. *See* MPEP 509.03.

Removal of Status

Section 1.27 is also proposed to be clarified (paragraph (f)(2)) that once small entity status is established in an application, any change in status from small to large, would also require a specific written assertion to that extent, rather than only payment of a large entity fee, similar to current practice. For example, when paying the issue fee in an application that has previously been accorded small entity status and the required new determination of continued entitlement to small entity status reveals that status has been lost, applicant should not just simply pay the large issue fee or cross out the recitation of small entity status on the returned copy of the notice of allowance (PTOL–85(b)), but submit a separate paper requesting removal of small entity status pursuant to proposed § 1.27(f)(2).

Correction of any inadvertent and incorrect establishment of small entity status would be by way of a paper under proposed § 1.28(c) as in current practice.

Response to Comments

Many comments supported the proposal without qualification. Only two, however, explicitly mentioned the payment option for obtaining small entity status with one recognizing that any error is now easier to correct under § 1.28(c). Others would eliminate the possibility of obtaining small entity status based on payment of the exact small entity basic filing (or national fee) due to possible error in paying an unintended small entity basic filing (or national fee) and being accorded an unwanted small entity status. There was only one total opposition to the proposal as a "bad" idea.

Comment: Several comments supported the proposal as a positive change that is both helpful to applicants and attorneys and one that will reduce the cost of establishing small entity status, particularly where there are multiple forms required due to joint ownership or licensing of multiple rights. It was noted that the proposal eliminates the time-consuming requirement for obtaining a signature of a person, such as an officer of the company, who may not have been involved in the application drafting process. It was also stated that the need to withhold the filing fee on filing an original application would be eliminated where the current small entity statement cannot be signed in time.

Response: The comments were adopted. The proposal from the Advance Notice is being carried forward in the instant notice. The particular parties who may assert entitlement to small entity status is being further liberalized over the Advance Notice to include only one of the inventors or a partial assignee.

Comment: One individual opposed the proposal because the submission of a paper is the only effective way an attorney can be certain that a client is complying with the requirements for small entity status. Eliminating the form removes the incentive of the client to provide the attorney with needed information, particularly with respect to foreign clients.

Response: A copy of §§ 1.9 and 1.27 can be supplied to a client as easily as the form and should be just as effective with foreign clients. It is not seen that the requirement of signing the form would be a more certain means that compliance exists than if the client would have to state to the attorney, either orally or in a letter, that the client complies with the requirements for asserting entitlement to small entity status. The form itself does not provide the underlying factual basis for entitlement to small entity status. It merely recites the requirement of § 1.9 and that the party executing it seeks small entity status. The attorney is not now required to confirm that a client is in compliance once the form is signed by the client and would not be required to make such confirmation under the proposal. It would continue to be up to the client to determine whether it wishes to assume whatever risk there may be should it decide to do the small entity determination by itself rather than rely on the attorney for aid.

Comment: A few comments would eliminate the option of asserting small entity status by payment of the basic filing (or national fee) due to possible errors in fee payments thereby obtaining unwanted small entity status. One comment recognized that the Office's adoption in the last rulemaking of a straightforward approach to correction under § 1.28(c) would make correction of improper status for good faith errors a simple procedure.

Response: The comment seeking elimination of the payment option is not adopted. The comment noting the previous easing of correction for good faith errors so that the possibility of inadvertent errors should not be a bar to the payment option is adopted. It is expected that this would occur very infrequently if at all in that the exact small entity amount must be submitted. Only errors in amounts paid where the error was the exact small entity amount for the basic filing (or national fee) would trigger small entity status. In view of the continued need for an affirmative determination of entitlement to small entity status to be made, the error would mostly occur by a misreading of a fee chart. Such type of error if it inadvertently leads to the establishment of small entity status would be easily correctable by the current § 1.28(c).

Comment: Some comments sought to ensure that the written assertion would be easy to make by adding a check box to provide for an assertion on: Office forms, the § 1.63 declaration, on the application, or on the transmittal sheet.

Response: The comments are adopted to the extent that this is an implementation issue to be addressed when a final rule is issued. The Office intends at this time to at least supply a check box on its application transmittal forms.

Paragraph by Paragraph Analysis

Section 1.27 is proposed to be amended in its title to recognize a new means of establishing small entity status by replacing "statement" with "assertion," to indicate that an assertion of small entity status would permit the payment of small entity fees, and to reflect transfer of subject matter from § 1.28 relating to determination of entitlement to and notification of loss of entitlement to small entity status, and fraud on the Office.

Paragraphs (a) through (d) of § 1.27 is proposed to be reformatted and amended to recite "assertion" as a new means for establishing small entity status to replace "statement", and new paragraphs (e), (f)(1) and (f)(2), and (g) are proposed to be added.

Paragraph (b) of § 1.27 is proposed to be reformatted to add paragraphs (b)(1) through (b)(4) of § 1.27. Paragraph (b) (1) of § 1.27 would permit assertion of small entity status by a writing that is clearly identifiable as present ((b)(1)(i)), signed ((b)(1)(ii)), and convey the concept of small entity status without the need for specific words but with a clear indication of an intent to assert entitlement to small entity status ((b)(1)(iii)). Paragraph (b)(2) of § 1.27 would make submission of a written assertion to obtain small entity status easier in view of increased categories of parties who could submit such a paper. The parties who could sign the written assertion are identified as: one of the parties who can currently submit a paper under § 1.33(b) ((b)(2)(i) of § 1.27), at least one of the inventors ((b)(2)(ii) of § 1.27) rather than all the inventors (applicants) as required by § 1.33(b)(4) for other types of papers, or a partial assignee ((b)(2)(iii) of § 1.27) rather than all the partial assignees and any applicant retaining an interest as required by § 1.33(b)(3) for other types of papers. A § 3.73(b) certification would not be required for an assignee under either paragraphs (b)(2)(i) or (iii). Paragraph (b)(3) of § 1.27 would permit the payment, by any party, of an exact amount of one of the small entity basic filing or national fees set forth in § 1.16(a), (f), (g), (h), or (k), or § 1.492(a)(1) through (a)(5) to be treated as a written assertion of entitlement to small entity status even where an incorrect type of basic filing or national fee is inadvertently selected in error. Paragraph (b)(3)(i) would provide that where small entity status was accorded based on the payment of a wrong type of small entity basic filing or national fee, the correct small entity amount would still be owed. Paragraph (b)(3)(ii) would provide that payment of a small entity fee in its exact amount for a fee other than what is provided for in paragraph (b)(3) would not be sufficient to establish small entity status absent a concomitant written assertion of entitlement to small entity status. After a basic filing or national fee is paid as a large entity, a refund under § 1.28(a) of the large entity portion can only be obtained by establishing small entity status by a written assertion and not by paying a second basic filing or national fee in a small entity amount. Payment of a large entity basic filing or national fee precludes paying a second basic filing or national fee in a small entity amount to establish small entity status. Paragraph (b)(4) of § 1.27 recites material transferred from current § 1.28(a)(2).

Paragraph (c) of § 1.27 is proposed to be amended to provide that fees other than the basic filing and national fees can only be paid in small entity amounts if submitted with or subsequent to a written assertion of entitlement to small entity status. The paragraph would clarify that an exception exists under § 1.28(a) for refunds of the large entity portion of a fee within three months of payment thereof if the refund request is accompanied by a written assertion of entitlement to small entity status.

Paragraph (d)(1) of § 1.27 is proposed to be amended to reference § 1.28(b) as the means of changing small entity status. It would be clarified that where rights in an invention are assigned, or there is an obligation to assign, to a small entity subsequent to an assertion of entitlement to small entity status, a second assertion is not required. Paragraph (d)(2) would clarify that once small entity status is withdrawn a new written assertion would be required to again obtain small entity status.

Paragraph (e) of § 1.27 is proposed to be added to clarify the need to do a determination of entitlement to small entity status prior to asserting small entity status, and that the Office generally does not question assertions of entitlement to small entity status.

Paragraph (f)(1) of § 1.27 is proposed to be added to contain material transferred from current § 1.28. Paragraph (f)(2) is proposed to be added to revise the current reference to the party who can sign a notification of loss of entitlement to small entity status to require a party identified in § 1.33(b).

Paragraph (g) of § 1.27 is proposed to be added to contain material transferred from paragraphs (d)(1) and (d)(2) of current § 1.28 relating to fraud attempted or committed on the Office in regard to paying small entity fees.

Section 1.28: Section 1.28 is proposed to be amended to be entirely reformatted with some material transferred to § 1.27.

Section 1.28(a) is proposed to be amended to allow a three-month period (presently a two-month period) for refunds based on later establishment of small entity status. See further discussion in § 1.28(b)(1).

Section 1.28(b)(1) is proposed to be amended to refer to § 1.22(c). Section 1.22(c) sets forth that the filing date for an authorization to charge fees starts the period for refunds under § 1.28(a). The current time period for a refund request is two months from payment of the full fee and the date of payment for refund purposes can vary depending on the means the applicant used to pay the required fee. For example, if the applicant paid the required fee by check, the date of payment is the date on which the fee paper, including the check, was filed in the Office. If the applicant authorized a charge to a deposit account, however, the date of payment is the date the Office debited the deposit account. In view of the proposed change in practice under §§ 1.22(c) and 1.28(b)(1) to accord the same date of payment for checks and authorizations to charge deposit accounts, the refund period would be extended to three months in order to in-part offset any shortening of the refund time period that may result in starting the time period from the filing date of the fee paper instead of the debit date for an authorization to charge a deposit account. Additionally, in view of changes in practice under § 1.27 to ease the claiming of small entity status, the need for refunds should diminish, and the different payment date of an authorization to charge a deposit account for small entity refund purposes should not cause much inconvenience to applicants.

Section 1.28(b)(2) is proposed to be amended to state that the deficiency amount owed under § 1.28(c) is calculated by using the date on which the deficiency was paid in full.

Section 1.28(c) is proposed to be amended to require that deficiency payments must be submitted separately for each file (§ 1.28(c)(1)) and must include the itemization of the deficiency payment by identifying: type of fee along with the current fee amount (§ 1.28(c)(2)(ii)(A)), the small entity amount paid and when (§ 1.28 (c)(2)((ii)(B)), the deficiency owed for each individual fee paid in error (§ 1.28(c)(2)(ii)(C)), the total deficiency payment owed (§ 1.28(c)(2)(ii)(D)), and that any failure to comply with the separate payment and itemization requirements would allow the Office at its option to charge a processing fee or set a non-extendable one month period for compliance to avoid return of the paper (§ 1.28(c)(3)).

Paragraph by Paragraph Analysis

The title of § 1.28 is proposed to be revised to focus on refunds and on how errors in status are excused in view of transfer of material to § 1.27.

Paragraphs (a)–(c) of § 1.28 are proposed to be reformatted.

Paragraph (a)(1) of § 1.28 is proposed to be amended as paragraph (a).

Paragraph (a) of § 1.28 is proposed to be amended to clarify that the period for a refund runs from payment of the "full fee," and that it is the payment of the full fee that is considered the significant event relative to establishing status for a particular fee. Additionally, paragraph (a) would amend the time period for requesting a refund based upon later establishment of small entity status. The proposed time period would be three months measured from the filing date of the fee paper.

Paragraph (a)(2) of § 1.28 is proposed to be amended to have some subject matter transferred to § 1.27(b)(4). The next to last sentence, relating to filing a continuing or reissue application and referencing a small entity statement in the prior application or patent, would be deleted as unnecessary. The currently required reference to status in the prior application or patent would be replaced by the equally easily written assertion of § 1.27(b)(1). Written references to small entity status in a prior application, including submission of a copy of the small entity statement in a prior application, submitted in a continuing application subsequent to the effective date of any final rule, would be liberally construed under the proposed § 1.27(b)(1)(iii). Similarly, the last sentence of current paragraph (a)(2) would be deleted as the payment option for establishing small entity status in continuing or reissue applications has been expanded in § 1.27(b)(3) to include all applications.

Caution: Although the Office intends to liberally construe what is deemed to be an assertion of small entity status, the concept of entitlement must be clearly conveyed.

> *Example:* A prior application has been accorded small entity status. A continued prosecution application (CPA) under § 1.53(d) is filed with a general authorization to charge fees that does not state that the fees to be charged are small entity fees. Even though the CPA contains the same application number as its prior application (and the small entity statement), it would not be accorded small entity status and large entity filing fees would be immediately charged. This would be so because a new determination of entitlement to small entity status must be made upon filing of a new application, such as a CPA. Accordingly, in filing the CPA there must be some affirmative act to indicate that the determination has been done anew and small entity status is still appropriate. Where a copy of the small entity statement from the prior application, or a written assertion in the CPA application transmittal letter, or an authorization to charge small entity fees were present, the result would be reversed and small entity status would be accorded the CPA application on filing.

Paragraph (a)(3) of § 1.28 is proposed to be amended to have its subject matter transferred to § 1.27(d)(1).

Paragraph (b) of § 1.28 is proposed to be amended to have its subject matter transferred to § 1.27(f)(1) and (2). New paragraphs (b)(1) and (b)(2) are proposed to be added. Paragraph (b)(1) of § 1.28 would refer to § 1.22(c) to define the date a fee is paid for the purpose of starting the three-month period for refund. Current practice for authorizations to charge deposit accounts is to give benefit of the date that the deposit account is actually debited by the Office, which is a later time than when the paper authorizing charge of the fee to a deposit account is filed with the Office. Current practice would therefore be changed so that it is the date the paper is filed, not the date of debit of the fee, that would start the three-month refund period. Paragraph (b)(2) of § 1.28 would refer to § 1.22(c) to define the date when a deficiency payment is paid in full, which is the date that determines the amount of deficiency that is due.

> *Example:* A small entity issue fee has been paid in error in January and a paper under § 1.28(c) was submitted the following June with the deficiency payment. The deficiency payment of the issue fee was incorrectly determined so that the full amount owed (for the issue fee) was not submitted in June. If the mistake in the June payment is not discovered until the following November, the extra amount owed must be recalculated to take into account any October 1 increase in the issue fee.

Paragraph (c) of § 1.28 is proposed to be amended to recite that separate submissions, including separate payments and itemizations, are required for any deficiency payment. Paragraph (c)(1) would require that a deficiency paper/submission be limited to one application or patent file. Where, for example, the same set of facts has caused errors in payment in more than one application and/or patent file, a separate paper would need to be submitted in each file for which an error is to be excused. Paragraph (c)(2) would now require that for each fee that was erroneously paid in error the following itemization be provided: The particular fee (*e.g.*, basic filing fee, extension of time fee) (paragraph (c)(2)(ii)((A)), the small entity fee amount actually paid and when (for example, distinguishing between two one-month extension of time fees erroneously paid on two different dates) (paragraph (c)(2)(ii)(B)), the actual deficiency owed for each fee previously paid in error (paragraph (c)(2)(ii)(C)), and the total deficiency owed that is the sum of the individual deficiencies owed (paragraph (c)(2)(ii)(D)). Paragraph (c)(3) would address the failure to comply with the separate submission, including separate payment and itemization requirements of paragraph (c)(1) and (2) of this section. Paragraph (c)(3), upon failure to comply, would permit the Office at its option either to charge a processing fee (§ 1.17(i) would be suitably amended) to process the paper or require compliance within a one-month non-extendable time period to avoid return of the paper.

Paragraphs (d)(1) and (2) of § 1.28, are proposed to be amended to have the material relating to fraud attempted or committed on the Office as to paying of small entity fees, transferred to § 1.27(g). New paragraph (d) of § 1.28 is proposed to be added to clarify that any paper submitted under paragraph (c) of § 1.28 would also be treated as a notification of loss of small entity status under paragraph (f)(2) of § 1.27.

Section 1.33: Paragraph (a) of § 1.33 would be reformatted to create additional paragraphs (a)(1) and (a)(2) to separately identify the parties who can change a correspondence address depending upon the presence or absence of a § 1.63 oath/declaration. The revision is intended to make clear what may be a confusing practice to applicants as to which parties can set forth or change a correspondence address when an application does not yet have a § 1.63 oath or declaration by any of the inventors. See § 1.14(d)(4) for a similar change regarding status and access information. References to a § 1.63 oath/declaration are intended to mean an executed oath/declaration by any inventor, but not necessarily all the inventors.

Paragraph (a) of § 1.33 is proposed to be amended to provide that in a patent application the applicant must, either in an application data sheet (§ 1.76) or in a clearly identifiable manner elsewhere in any papers submitted with an application filing, specify a correspondence address to which the Office will send notices, letters and other communications in or about the application. It is now stated that where more than one correspondence address is specified, the Office would determine which one to establish as the correspondence address. This is intended to cover the situation where an unexecuted application is submitted with conflicting correspondence addresses in the application transmittal letter and in an unexecuted oath/declaration, or other similar situations.

Paragraph (a) of § 1.33 would request the submission of a daytime telephone number of the party to whom correspondence is to be addressed. While business is to be conducted on the written record, § 1.2, a daytime telephone number would be useful in initiating contact that could later be reduced to a writing. The phone number would be changeable by any party who could change the correspondence address.

Paragraph (a)(1) of § 1.33 would provide that any party filing the application and setting forth a correspondence address could later change the correspondence address provided that a § 1.63 oath/declaration by any of the inventors has not been submitted. The parties who may so change the correspondence address would include only the one inventor filing the application even if more than one inventor was identified on the application transmittal letter. If two of three inventors filed the application, the two inventors filing the application would be needed to change the correspondence address. Additionally, any registered practitioner named in the application transmittal letter, or a person who has the authority to act on behalf of the party that will be the assignee (if the application was filed by the party that will be the assignee), could change the correspondence address. A registered practitioner named in a letterhead would not be sufficient, but rather a clear identification of the individual as being a representative would be required. The intent is to permit a company (to whom the invention has been assigned, or to whom there is an obligation to assign the invention) who files an application, to designate the correspondence address, and to change the correspondence address, until such time as a (first) § 1.63 oath/declaration is filed. The mere filing of a § 1.63 oath/declaration, that does not include a correspondence address, including when the company is only a potential partial assignee would not affect any correspondence address previously established on filing of the application, or changed per paragraph (a)(1) of this section. The expression "party that will be the assignee" rather than assignee is used in that until a declaration is submitted, inventors have only been identified and any attempted assignment, or partial assignment, cannot operate for Office purposes until the declaration is supplied. Hence, the mere identification of a party as a party that will be an assignee or assignee would be sufficient for it to change the correspondence address without resort to § 3.73(b).

Paragraph (a)(2) of § 1.33 would retain the current requirements for changing a correspondence address when a § 1.63 oath/declaration by any of the inventors has been filed. Where a correspondence address was set forth or changed pursuant to paragraph (a)(1) (prior to the filing of a § 1.63 oath or declaration), that correspondence address remains in effect upon filing of a § 1.63 declaration and can then only be changed pursuant to paragraph (a)(2).

Paragraph (b) of § 1.33 would be simplified to make it easier to understand who are appropriate parties to file papers, particularly in view of the proposed change under § 3.71(b).

Paragraph (b)(3) of § 1.33 is proposed to be amended to add a reference to § 3.71.

Section 1.41: Section 1.41(a)(1) is proposed to be amended to indicate that a paper including the processing fee set forth in § 1.17(i) is required for supplying or changing the name(s) of the inventor(s) where an oath or declaration prescribed in § 1.63 is not filed during pendency of a nonprovisional application, rather than a petition including a petition fee, for consistency with the proposed amendment to § 1.17(i). Section 1.41(a)(2) is proposed to be amended to indicate that a paper including the processing fee set forth in § 1.17(q) is required for supplying or changing the name(s) of the inventor(s) where a cover sheet prescribed by § 1.53(c)(1) is not filed during the pendency of a provisional application, rather than a petition including a petition fee, for consistency with the proposed amendment to § 1.17(q). Section 1.41(a)(3) is proposed to be amended to delete the language concerning an alphanumeric identifier, and to provide that the name, residence, and citizenship of each person believed to be an actual inventor should be provided when the application papers pursuant to § 1.53(b) are filed without an oath or declaration or application papers pursuant to § 1.53(c) are filed without a cover sheet. Section 1.41(a)(4) is proposed to be added to set forth that the inventors who submitted an application under § 1.494 or § 1.495 are the inventors in the international application designating the United States.

Section 1.44: Section 1.44 is proposed to be removed and reserved to eliminate the requirement that proof of the power or authority of the legal representative be recorded in the Office or filed in an application under §§ 1.42 or 1.43.

Section 1.47: Section 1.47 is proposed to be amended to refer to "the fee set forth in § 1.17(h)" for consistency with the proposed amendment to § 1.17(h) and (i). See discussion of the proposed amendment to § 1.17. Section 1.47 is also proposed to be amended to add a new paragraph (c) providing that the Office will send notice of the filing of the application to all inventors who have not joined in the application at the address(es) provided in the petition under § 1.47, and will publish notice of the filing of the application in the *Official Gazette*. This provision is currently included in each of § 1.47(a) and § 1.47(b). Section 1.47(c) is also proposed to provide that the Office may dispense with such notice provisions in a continuation or divisional application where notice regarding the filing of the prior application has already been sent to the nonsigning inventor(s). The patent statute gives the Office great latitude as to the notice that must be given to an inventor who has not joined in an application for patent. *See* 35 U.S.C. 116, ¶2 ("after such notice to the omitted inventor as [the Commissioner] prescribes"), and 118 (upon such notice to [the inventor] as the Commissioner deems sufficient"). Providing notice to a non-joined inventor in a continuation or divisional application places a significant burden on the Office, especially when such continuation or divisional application is filed using a copy of the oath or declaration from a prior application under § 1.63(d). In addition, providing additional notice to the non-joined inventor in the continuation or divisional application provides little (if any) actual benefit to the non-joined inventor, as identical notice was previously given during the processing of the prior application. Thus, the Office considers it appropriate to dispense with notice under § 1.47 in situations (continuations or divisionals of an application accorded status under § 1.47) in which the non-joined inventor was previously given such notice in a prior application.

Section 1.48: Section 1.48 is proposed to be amended to have the title revised to reference the statutory basis for the rule, 35 U.S.C. 116.

Section 1.48 paragraphs (a) through (c) are proposed to be amended to: delete the recitation of "other than a reissue application" as such words are unnecessary in view of the indication in the title of the section that the section does not apply to reissue applications and the revision to paragraph (a) (discussed below), to change "When" to "If," and to add "nonprovisional" before "application" where it does not already appear.

Sections 1.48 paragraphs (a)(1) through (e)(1) would be revised to replace the reference to a "petition" with a reference to a "request." What is meant to be encompassed by the term "petition," as it is currently used in the section, may be better defined by the term "request." The presence of "petition" currently in the section is misleading to the extent that it may indicate to applicants that papers under this section have to be filed with the Office of Petitions when in fact amendments to correct the inventorship under § 1.48 are to be decided by the primary examiners in the Technology Centers and should be submitted there. *See* MPEP 1002.02(e). The requirements for a statement currently in § 1.48 paragraphs (a)(1), (c)(1), and (e)(1) would be placed in § 1.48 paragraphs (a)(2), (c)(2), and (e)(2) and corresponding changes made in subsequent paragraphs.

Section 1.48 paragraphs (b) and (d) are proposed to be revised to indicate that a request to correct the inventorship thereunder must be signed by a party as set forth in § 1.33(b) (which would enable a practitioner alone to sign all the needed papers). The inventors, whether being added, deleted or retained, are not required to participate in a correction under these paragraphs. Thus, the inventor(s) to be deleted pursuant to paragraph (b) in a nonprovisional application, or added pursuant to paragraph (d) in a provisional application, and those inventors that are retained in either situation, are not required to participate in the inventorship correction, such as by signing a statement of facts, or a new oath or declaration under § 1.63.

Section 1.48 paragraphs (a) through (e) are proposed to be revised to define the fee required as a "processing" fee, to delete the reference to a "petition," and to indicate that amendment of the application to correct the inventorship would require the filing of a request to correct the inventorship along with other items, as set forth in the respective paragraphs of this section. The latter change is not one of substance but a clarification that the amendment requirement of the statute, 35 U.S.C. 116, merely refers to the change in Office records (face of the application file wrapper corrected, notation on a previously submitted § 1.63 oath/declaration, change in Patent Application Location and Monitoring (PALM) data, and a corrected filing receipt issued) that would be made upon the grant of a § 1.48 request. Thus, amendment of the inventorship in an application is not made as an amendment under § 1.121. Where there is a need to make an actual § 1.121(a)(1) amendment, such as when a cover page of the specification recites the inventive entity, that should also be submitted. In the absence of such an amendment, the Office may, at its option, correct the inventor's names on the cover sheet or in the specification. Where an application needs correction of inventorship under § 1.48 and a paper is submitted with a title that does not set forth the paper as a request under § 1.48, but it is clear from the papers submitted that an inventorship correction is desired, a request for a correction of inventorship under § 1.48 will be inferred from the papers submitted and will be treated under § 1.48.

A request for a corrected filing receipt correcting a typing or office error in the names of the inventors will not ordinarily be treated under § 1.48. Any request to correct inventorship should be presented as a separate paper. For example, placing a request under § 1.48(b) to correct the inventorship in the remarks section of an amendment may cause the Office to overlook the request and not act on it.

Paragraph (f)(1) of § 1.48 is proposed to be clarified to recite that its provision for changing the inventorship only applies if an oath or declaration under § 1.63 has not been submitted by any of the inventors, and that submission of an oath or declaration under § 1.63 by any of the inventors is sufficient to correct an earlier identification of the inventorship.

Example 1: An unexecuted application is filed identifying A, B, and C as the inventors. A § 1.63 declaration is also submitted signed only by A and naming A, B, and C as the inventors. To complete the application (§ 1.53(f)) a § 1.63 oath or declaration by B and C is needed. In attempting to reply to a Notice to File Missing Parts of Application requiring the missing oath or declaration by B and C it is discovered that D is also an inventor. A declaration by A, B, C, and D if submitted without a petition under § 1.48(a) to correct the inventorship to A–D from A–C will not be accepted as a reply to the Notice to File Missing Parts of Application.

Thus, it should be clear that a first oath or declaration under § 1.63 completed by less than all the inventors initially identified, when the oath or declaration is submitted when the application is filed (or after), will under § 1.48(f)(1) lock in the inventorship, and the later filing of another declaration by a different but complete inventive entity will not be effective under § 1.48(f)(1) to correct the inventorship.

> *Example 2:* An application is filed identifying A, B, and C as the inventors in the application transmittal letter, and a § 1.63 declaration is concomitantly submitted only by A naming only A as the sole inventor. The inventorship of the application is A (because of the declaration of A). A later submitted § 1.63 declaration by A, B, and C would require a petition under § 1.48(a) to correct the inventorship to A, B, and C before the declaration by A, B, and C could be accepted.

Paragraph (f)(1) of § 1.48 is proposed to be amended to reference § 1.497(d) for submission of an executed oath or declaration naming an inventive entity different from the inventive entity set forth in the international stage when entering the national stage under 35 U.S.C. 371 and §§ 1.494 or 1.495.

Section 1.48(h) is proposed to be added to indicate that the provisions of this section do not apply to reissue applications, and referencing §§ 1.171 and 1.175 for correction of inventorship in reissue applications.

Section 1.48(i) is proposed to be added to reference §§ 1.324 and 1.634 for corrections of inventorship in patents and interference proceedings, respectively.

Section 1.48 paragraphs (a) through (i) are proposed to have titles added to make locating the appropriate paragraph easier.

Section 1.51: Section 1.51(b) is proposed to be amended to include a reference to § 1.53(d), as a proper continued prosecution application under § 1.53(d) in which the basic filing fee has been paid is a complete application under § 1.51(b).

Section 1.52: Section 1.52(a) and (b) are proposed to be amended to clarify the paper standard requirements for papers submitted as part of the record of a patent application. Section 1.52(a) sets forth the paper standard requirements for all papers which are to become a part of the permanent records of the Office, and § 1.52(b) sets forth the paper standard requirements for the application (specification, including the claims, drawings, and oath or declaration) and any amendments or corrections to the application. Papers making up the application or an amendment or correction to the application must meet the requirements of § 1.52 (a) and (b), but papers submitted for the record that do not make up the application (*e.g.*, a declaration under § 1.132) need not meet the requirements of § 1.52(b).

The Office is proposing in § 1.52(b)(6) an optional procedure for numbering the paragraphs of the specification, but not including the claims or the abstract. Although not required to do so, applicants would be strongly encouraged to present, at the time of filing, each paragraph of the specification as individually and consecutively numbered. The presentation of numbered paragraphs at the time of filing would facilitate the entry of amendments (in compliance with proposed § 1.121) during the prosecution of the application. If the paragraphs of the specification are not numbered at the time of filing, applicants would be urged, when the first response to an Office action is submitted, to supply a substitute specification including numbered paragraphs, consistent with the requirement of § 1.121 for amending the specification. Thereafter, amendments would be made through the use of numbered paragraph replacement.

The proposal to include paragraph numbering is to provide a consistent and uniform basis for the amendment practice being proposed in § 1.121 and as an aid to transitioning into total electronic filing. The proposed rule language establishes a procedure for numbering the paragraphs of the specification at the time of filing. This procedure would facilitate the entry of amendments by providing a uniform method for identifying paragraphs in the specification, thus overcoming any differences created by word processor formatting and pagination variations. Concurrently proposed changes to § 1.121 for amendment practice would additionally require the submission of clean copies of numbered replacement paragraphs, which would eliminate much of the red ink associated with hand entry of amendments and expedite the Optical

Character Recognition (OCR) scanning and reading employed in the patent printing process, ultimately resulting in patents containing fewer errors.

The Office will neither number the paragraphs or sections of the specification, nor accept any instructions from applicants to do the same.

The proposed procedure for paragraph numbering, in the interest of uniformity, encourages applicants to use four digit Arabic numerals enclosed within square brackets and including leading zeroes as the first element of the paragraph. The numbers and brackets should be highlighted in bold (*e.g.*, [0001], [0002]), and should appear as the first part of the paragraph immediately to the right of the left margin. Approximately four character spaces should follow the bracketed number before the beginning of the actual text of the paragraph. Paragraph (or section) headers, such as "Description of the Invention" or "Example 3," are not considered part of any paragraph and should not be numbered. Nontext elements, such as tables, mathematical formulae, etc., are considered part of the paragraph around or above the element, and should not be numbered separately. All portions of any nontext elements should be kept from extending to the left margin.

Response to Comments: Although paragraph numbering (as it appears in proposed § 1.52) was not an independent topic in the Advance Notice, the proposal did appear in conjunction with the replacement paragraph concept as part of Topic 13. While there was some opposition to paragraph numbering in the comments received relative to Topic 13 as being burdensome and inconsistent with the requirements of other countries, the Office proposes to move forward with this concept as the most effective plan currently under consideration for identifying paragraphs of the specification. The JPO and EPO have already begun to use paragraph numbering in their application and publication processing.

Some of the comments received in response to Topic 13 suggested identification of paragraphs by page and line number. Inasmuch as the Office proposal must be consistent with future electronic requirements, this suggestion of identification by page and line number could not be adopted in that fixed pages do not exist in documents created on a computer. Page and line numbering are affected by font size, line spacing and formatting and can vary between different hardware and software components. Once each paragraph has been individually identified and tagged with a number, however, all future processing of the application, whether by paper or electronic version, may be done uniformly and accurately by both the Office and the applicant.

Section 1.52(b)(7) is proposed to be added to provide that if papers submitted as part of the application do not comply with § 1.52 (b)(1) through (b)(5), the Office may require the applicant to provide substitute papers that comply with § 1.52(b)(1) through (b)(5), or the Office may convert the papers submitted by applicant into papers that do comply with § 1.52(b)(1) through (b)(5) and charge the applicant for the costs incurred by the Office in doing so (§ 1.21(j)).

Section 1.52(c) is proposed to be amended to provide that: (1) Alterations to the application papers must (rather than "should") be made before the oath or declaration is signed; (2) a substitute specification (§ 1.125) is required if the application papers do not comply with § 1.52(a) and (b) due to interlineations, erasures, cancellations or other alterations of the application papers; and (3) if an oath or declaration is a copy of the oath or declaration from a prior application, the application for which such copy is submitted may contain alterations that do not introduce matter that would have been new matter in the prior application.

Section 1.52(d) is proposed to be amended to provide separately for nonprovisional applications and provisional applications filed in a language other than English. Section 1.52(d)(1) is proposed to be added to provide that: (1) If a nonprovisional application is filed in a language other than English, an English language translation of the non-English-language application, a statement that the translation is accurate, and the processing fee set forth in § 1.17(i) are required; and (2) if these items are not filed with the application, applicant will be notified and given a period of time within which they must be filed in order to avoid abandonment. Section 1.52(d)(2) is proposed to be added to provide that: (1) If a provisional application is filed in a language other than English, an English language translation of the non-English-language provisional application will not be required in the provisional application; but (2) if a nonprovisional application claims the benefit of such provisional application, an English-language translation of the non-English-language provisional application and a statement that the translation is accurate must be supplied if the nonprovisional application is involved in an interference (§ 1.630), or when specifically required by the examiner.

Section 1.53: Section 1.53(c)(1) is proposed to be amended to clearly provide that the cover sheet required by § 1.51(c)(1) may be an application data sheet (§ 1.76).

Section 1.53(c)(2) is proposed to be amended for clarity and to refer to "the processing fee set forth in § 1.17(q)" for consistency with the proposed amendment to § 1.17(q).

Section 1.53(d)(4) is proposed to be amended to eliminate the reference to a petition under § 1.48 for consistency with the proposed amendment to § 1.48. Section 1.53(d) is also proposed to be amended to add a new § 1.53(d)(10) to provide a reference to § 1.103(b) for requesting a limited suspension of action in a continued prosecution application (CPA) under § 1.53(d).

Section 1.53(e)(2) is proposed to be amended to require that a petition under § 1.53(e) be accompanied by the fee set forth in § 1.17(h), regardless of whether the application is filed under § 1.53(b), § 1.53(c), or § 1.53(d). While provisional applications filed under § 1.53(c) are not subject to examination under 35 U.S.C. 131 (35 U.S.C. 111(b)(8)), petitions under § 1.53(e) in provisional applications under § 1.53(c) are as burdensome as petitions under § 1.53(e) in nonprovisional applications under § 1.53(b) or § 1.53(d). Therefore, it is appropriate to charge the petition fee set forth in § 1.17(h) for petitions under § 1.53(e) in applications filed under § 1.53(b), § 1.53(c), or § 1.53(d).

Section 1.53(f) and (g) are proposed to be amended for clarity and to include a reference to "or reissue" in the paragraph heading to clarify that the provisions of § 1.53(f) apply to all nonprovisional applications, which include continuation, divisional, and continuation-in-part applications, as well as reissue applications and continued prosecution applications. Section 1.53(f) is also proposed to be amended to provide that if applicant does not pay one of either the basic filing fee or the processing and retention fee set forth in § 1.21(l) during the pendency of the application (rather than within one year of the mailing of a Notice to File Missing Parts of Application), the Office may dispose of the application.

Section 1.55: Section 1.55(a) is proposed to be amended to refer to "the processing fee set forth in § 1.17(i)" for consistency with the proposed amendment to § 1.17(h) and (i). See discussion of the proposed amendment to § 1.17.

Section 1.55(a)(2)(i) through (iii) is proposed to clarify the current Office practice concerning when the claim for priority and the certified copy of the foreign application specified in 35 U.S.C. 119(b) must be filed. Specifically § 1.55(a)(2)(i) clarifies current Office practice that in an application filed under 35 U.S.C. 111(a) that the Office requires the claim for priority and the certified copy of the foreign application be filed before a patent is granted. Section 1.55(a)(2)(ii) clarifies current Office practice that in an application that entered the national stage of an international application after compliance with 35 U.S.C. 371, the time limits set in the PCT and the Regulations under the PCT control the time limit for making the claim for priority, while the certified copy of the foreign application must be filed before the patent is granted if the certified copy was not filed in accordance with the PCT and the Regulation under the PCT. Section 1.55(a)(2)(iii) clarifies current Office practice that the Office may require both the claim for priority and certified copy of the foreign application be filed at an earlier time than in §§ 1.55(a)(2)(i) or 1.55(a)(2)(ii) under certain circumstances.

Section 1.55(a)(2)(iv) is also proposed to provide that priority claims and documents may be submitted after payment of the issue fee but with no further review by the Office other than placement in the application file. Changes to the patent printing process will dramatically reduce the period between the date of issue fee payment and the date a patent is issued. See Filing of Continuing Applications, Amendments, or Petitions after Payment of Issue Fee, Notice, 1221 Off. Gaz. Pat. Office 14 (April 6, 1999); and Patents to Issue More Quickly After Issue Fee Payment, Notice, 1220 Off. Gaz. Pat. Office 42 (March 9, 1999). Thus, it is now difficult for the Office to match a petition containing a priority claim or certified priority document filed after payment of the issue fee with an application file, and determine whether the applicant has met the conditions of 35 U.S.C. 119(a)–(d) to make the priority claim, before the date the application will issue as a patent. Nevertheless, it is also undesirable to prohibit applicants from filing a priority claim or certified priority document between the date the issue fee is paid and the date a patent is issued. Therefore, the Office will permit applicants to file a priority claim or certified priority document (with the processing fee set forth in § 1.17(i)) between the date the issue fee is paid and the date a patent is issued. The Office will, however, merely place such submission in the application file but will not attempt to determine whether the applicant has met the conditions of 35 U.S.C. 119(a)–(d) to make the priority claim nor include the priority claim information in the text of the patent. In such a situation (as is currently the situation when a petition under § 1.55 is granted), the patent will not contain the priority claim information, and the patentee may request a certificate of correction under 35 U.S.C. 255 and § 1.323 at which point a determination of entitlement for such priority will be made.

Section 1.56: Section 1.56 is proposed to be amended to add a new § 1.56(e) to provide that in any continuation-in-part application, the duty under § 1.56 includes the duty to disclose to the Office all information known to the person to be material to patentability which became available between the filing date of the prior application and the national or PCT international filing date of the continuation-in-part application. Section 1.63(e) currently requires that the oath or declaration in a continuation-in-part application acknowledge that the duty under § 1.56 includes the duty to disclose to the Office all information known to the person to be material to patentability (as defined in § 1.56(b)) which became available between the filing date of the prior application and the national or PCT international filing date of the continuation-in-part application. Thus, the examiner must object to an oath or declaration in a continuation-in-part that does not contain this statement. By amending § 1.56 to expressly provide that the duty under § 1.56 includes this duty, an acknowledgment of the duty of disclosure under § 1.56 is an acknowledgment of this duty in a continuation-in-part application, and an express statement to that effect in the oath or declaration will no longer be required.

Section 1.59: Section 1.59 is proposed to be amended to refer "the fee set forth in § 1.17(h)" for consistency with the proposed amendment to § 1.17(h) and (i). See discussion of the proposed amendment to § 1.17.

Section 1.63: Section 1.63 is proposed to be amended for clarity and simplicity. Section 1.63(a) is proposed to be amended to set forth the oath or declaration requirements that are requirements of 35 U.S.C. 115 (and thus cannot be waived by the Office pursuant to § 1.183). Specifically, § 1.63(a) is proposed to be amended to provide that an oath or declaration filed under § 1.51(b)(2) as a part of a nonprovisional application must: (1) Be executed (i.e., signed) in accordance with either § 1.66 or § 1.68; (2) identify each inventor and country of citizenship of each inventor; and (3) state that the person making the oath or declaration believes the named inventor or inventors to be the original and first inventor or inventors of the subject matter which is claimed and for which a patent is sought.

Section 1.63(b) is proposed to be amended to provide that in addition to meeting the requirements of § 1.63(a), the oath or declaration must also: (1) Identify the application to which it is directed; (2) state that the person making the oath or declaration has reviewed and understands the contents of the application, including the claims, as amended by any amendment specifically referred to in the oath or declaration; and (3) state that the person making the oath or declaration acknowledges the duty to disclose to the Office all information known to the person to be material to patentability as defined in § 1.56. These requirements are currently located at § 1.63(a)(2), (b)(1), and (b)(3).

Section 1.63(c) is proposed to provide that an applicant may provide identifying information either in an application data sheet (§ 1.76) or in the oath or declaration. Permitting applicants to provide such identifying information in an application data sheet (rather than in the oath or declaration) should result in: (1) An increase in the use of application data sheets; and (2) a decrease in the need for supplemental oaths or declarations (providing omitted information) for applications in which an application data sheet was submitted.

Section 1.63(e) is proposed to be amended to eliminate the requirement that an oath or declaration in a continuation-in-part application state that the person making the oath or declaration also acknowledge that the duty under § 1.56 includes the duty to disclose to the Office all information known to the person to be material to patentability (as defined in § 1.56(b)) which became available between the filing date of the prior application and the national or PCT international filing date of the continuation-in-part application. See discussion of the proposed amendment to § 1.56(e).

Section 1.64: Section 1.64 is proposed to be amended to also refer to any supplemental oath or declaration (§ 1.67). In addition, § 1.64(b) is proposed to be amended to provide that if the person making the oath or declaration is the legal representative, the oath or declaration shall state that the person is the legal representative and shall also state the citizenship, residence and mailing address of the legal representative.

Section 1.67: Section 1.67(a) is proposed to be amended to also refer to § 1.162, and to provide that if the earlier-filed oath or declaration complied with § 1.63(a), the Office may permit the supplemental oath or declaration to be made by fewer than all of the inventors or by an applicant other than the inventor.

Section 1.67(c) is proposed to be deleted as unnecessary because it simply reiterates other provisions of the rules of practice. If the application was altered after the oath or declaration was signed (except as permitted by § 1.52(c)), § 1.52(c) requires a supplemental oath or declaration under § 1.67. If the oath or declaration was signed in blank (while incomplete), without review thereof by the person making the oath or declaration, or without review of the specification, including the claims, the oath or declaration does not meet the requirements of § 1.63. In this situation, § 1.67(a) requires a supplemental oath or declaration.

Section 1.72: Section 1.72(a) is proposed to be amended to state "[u]nless the title is supplied in an application data sheet (§ 1.76)" to clarify that the title is not requested to be a heading on the first page of the specification if supplied in an application data sheet. Section 1.72(b) is proposed to be amended to provide that "[t]he abstract in an application filed under 35 U.S.C. 111 may not exceed 150 words in length" to harmonize with PCT guidelines.

Section 1.76: A new § 1.76 is proposed to be added to provide for the inclusion of an application data sheet in an application. Section 1.76(a) is proposed to: (1) Explain that an application data sheet is a sheet or set of sheets containing bibliographic information concerning the associated patent application, which is arranged in a specified format; and (2) when an application data sheet is provided, the application data sheet becomes part of the application. While the use of an application data sheet is optional, the Office would prefer its use to help facilitate the machine reading of this important information. Entry of the information in this manner is more timely and accurate than the current practice of presenting the information on numerous other documents. Applicants benefit from the use of application data sheets by being provided with more accurate and timely filing receipts, by reducing the time required to collect bibliographic information and by having such information printed on the granted patents. The applicant also benefits by receiving an official notice of the receipt of papers from the Office at an earlier stage of the processing.

Section 1.76(b) is proposed to provide that bibliographic data as used in § 1.76(a) includes: (1) applicant information; (2) correspondence information; (3) specified application information; (4) representative information; (5) domestic priority information; and (6) foreign priority information. Section 1.76(b) as proposed also reminds applicants that the citizenship of each inventor must be provided in the oath or declaration under § 1.63 (as is required by 35 U.S.C. 115) even if this information is provided in the application data sheet.

Applicant information includes the name, residence, mailing address, and citizenship of each applicant (§ 1.41(b)). The name of each applicant must include the family name, and at least one given name without abbreviation together with any other given name or initial. If the applicant is not an inventor, this information also includes the applicant's authority (§§ 1.42, 1.43 and 1.47) to apply for the patent on behalf of the inventor.

Correspondence information includes the correspondence address, which may be indicated by reference to a customer number, to which correspondence is to be directed (*see* § 1.33(a)).

Application information includes the title of the invention, the total number of drawing sheets, whether the drawings are formal, any docket number assigned to the application, the type (*e.g.*, utility, plant, design, reissue utility, provisional) of application. Application information also indicates whether the application discloses any significant part of the subject matter of an application under a secrecy order pursuant to § 5.2 of this chapter (*see* § 5.2(c)).

Representative information includes the registration number of each practitioner, or the customer number, appointed with a power of attorney or authorization of agent in the application. Section 1.76(b)(4) is proposed to state that providing this information in the application data sheet does not constitute a power of attorney or authorization of agent in the application (*see* § 1.34(b)). This is because the Office does not expect the application data sheet to be executed (signed) by the party (applicant or assignee) who may appoint a power of attorney or authorization of agent in the application.

Domestic priority information includes the application number (series code and serial number), the filing date, the status (including patent number if available), and relationship of each application for which a benefit is claimed under 35 U.S.C. 119(e), 120, 121, or 365(c). Providing this information in the application data sheet constitutes the specific reference required by 35 U.S.C. 119(e) or 120. While the rules of practice (§ 1.78(a)(2) or § 1.78(a)(4)) require that this claim or specific reference be in the first line of the specification the patent statute requires that a claim to the benefit of (specific reference to) a provisional (35 U.S.C. 119(e)(1)) or nonprovisional (35 U.S.C. 120) be in the application. Since the application data sheet (if provided) is considered part of the application, the specific reference to an earlier filed provisional or nonprovisional application in the application data sheet meets the "specific reference" requirement of 35 U.S.C. 119(e)(1) or 120.

Foreign priority information includes the application number, country, and filing date of each foreign application for which priority is claimed, as well as any foreign application having a filing date before that of the application for which priority is claimed. Providing this information in the application data sheet constitutes the claim for priority as required by 35 U.S.C. 119(b) and § 1.55(a). The patent statute (35 U.S.C. 119(b)) does not require that a claim to the benefit of a prior foreign application take any particular form.

Section 1.76(c) as proposed indicates that inconsistencies between the information in the application data sheet (if provided) and the oath or declaration under § 1.63 will be resolved in favor of the application data sheet. This is because the application data sheet (and not the oath or declaration) is intended as the means by which applicants will provide information to the Office. Section 1.76(c) is also proposed to provide that a supplemental application data sheet may be submitted to correct or update information provided in a previous application data sheet.

Section 1.77: Section 1.77(a) is proposed to be separated into sections 1.77(a) and 1.77(b). New § 1.77(a) would list the order of the papers in a utility patent application, including the proposed application data sheet (*see* § 1.76). New § 1.77(b) would list the order of the sections in the specification of a utility patent application. Current § 1.77(b) is proposed to be redesignated 1.77(c).

Section 1.78: Section 1.78(a)(2) is proposed to be amended to provide that the specification must contain or be amended to contain a specific reference required by 35 U.S.C. 120 in the first sentence following the title, unless the reference is included in an application data sheet. Section 1.78(a)(4) is proposed to be amended to provide that the specification must contain or be amended to contain a specific reference required by 35 U.S.C. 119(e)(1) in the first sentence following the title, unless the reference is included in an application data sheet. See discussion of proposed § 1.76(b)(5).

Section 1.78(c) is proposed to be amended for consistency with § 1.110 and for clarity.

Section 1.84: Section 1.84 is proposed to be amended to delete some requirements that are more stringent than the requirements of the PCT, while retaining the provisions related to acceptance of color drawings/photographs which are, at this time, more lenient.

The Office is proposing to delete the petition requirements in § 1.84(a)(2) and § 1.84(b)(1) and the requirement for three copies of black and white photographs. This change would make § 1.84 consistent with current Office practice. See Interim Waiver of 37 CFR § 1.84(b)(1) for Petitions to Accept Black and White Photographs and Advance Notice of Change to M.P.E.P. § 608.02, Notice, 1213 Off. Gaz. Pat. Office 108 (August 4, 1998); and Interim Waiver of 37 CFR 1.84(b)(1) for Petitions to Accept Black and White Photographs Filed with only One Set of Photographs, Notice, 1211 Off. Gaz. Pat. Office 34 (June 9, 1998). In addition, paragraphs (d), (h), (i), (j), (k)(1) and (3), (m), (n), (p), (r), (s), and (x) of § 1.84 are proposed to be deleted for simplification. These paragraphs describe characteristics of patent drawings which are desirable because they assist in clearly communicating the disclosed invention, but which are not necessary for the reproduction of drawings. The requirements set forth in paragraphs (d), (h), (i), (j), (k)(1) and (3), (m), (n), (p), (r), (s), and (x) of § 1.84 will continue to be described in the MPEP and/or publications such as the Guide for the Preparation of Patent Drawings.

Section 1.84(g) is proposed to be changed to 1.84(f). In addition, the dimensions of sight on 21.6 cm by 27.9 cm (8½ by 11 inch) drawing sheets are proposed to be changed 17.0 cm by 24.4 cm (6¾ by 9⅝ inches) to standardize the sight with that for A4 paper.

In Topic 5 of the Advance Notice the Office proposed to harmonize patent drawing standards with those of the PCT. The Office received a number of comments. The majority of the comments welcomed a single standard for patent drawings in PCT and United States patent applications so long as applicants do not lose their ability to file color drawings/photographs or to use 8½ by 11 paper. Some expressed confusion about the exact requirements of the PCT and its regulations. Furthermore, many commented that drawing standards should be enforced in the same manner, and that drawings should not be objected to in the national stage if they were not objected to in the international stage. In this vein, several argued that only the patent examiners should be allowed to review the patent drawings. If the examiners could understand the invention from the drawings, no draftsperson should be permitted to make "petty objections" unrelated to how well the invention is disclosed in the drawings. On the other hand, several people commented that the standards for PCT applications are too low, since many PCT applications are published with illegible drawings or drawings that do not adequately communicate the invention. Several observed that the PCT rules do not permit color drawings or photographs and stated that the requirements of the two systems should be the same. Others observed that the PCT rules essentially require formal drawings on filing, which is contrary to U.S. practice, and argued that such a policy would be unnecessarily expensive to applicants.

Careful consideration of the comments and the business practice of drawing review has led the Office to conclude that, in general, drawings should only be objected to by the Office if they cannot be reproduced or there is an error in the drawings. The Office should accept drawings that would be acceptable under the PCT rules, but should not copy PCT rules solely for the sake of uniformity. A proper application of a low standard for drawing review will result in fewer drawings being objected to and fewer corrected or formal drawings being filed after allowance of a patent application. This should reduce delays during the printing cycle (during which time the Office waits for corrected or formal drawings to be filed). Applicants who submit informal drawings on filing will be unlikely to encounter a draftsperson's objection because few drawings will fail to meet the reduced standards. Any formal drawings filed after allowance which were not required by the Office, however, are unlikely to be included in the printed patent because the printing process will have begun before payment of the issue fee and the formal drawings are unlikely to catch up to the application file in time to be included in the printed patent.

Patents printed with high quality drawings look better and should be easier to understand. Applicants interested in having their patents printed with good quality drawings should be motivated by their own interests to submit good quality drawings. However, the Office should not spend resources to insist upon high-quality drawings when lesser quality drawings would suffice to communicate the invention and to meet the printer's requirements. Accordingly, if applicants submit drawings which are of inferior quality, but acceptable to the Office, applicants should not be surprised when a patent issues with those very same drawings.

Section 1.84 is also proposed to provide for a fee for processing and printing patents with color drawings or photographs in color rather than in black and white. The petition fee set forth in § 1.84(a)(2)(i) is proposed to be deleted and a fee commensurate with the Office costs of handling and printing color photographs will be charged instead.

Many comments were received welcoming printing of patents in color, and stating that applicants would be willing to pay any required fees for their patent to be printed in color.

When filing international applications under the PCT, applicants must remember to consult the PCT and its regulations regarding requirements of drawings, especially the provisions related to amendment or correction of drawings. While color drawings are permitted in U.S. patent applications, submission of color drawings in international applications is not permitted and may cause difficulties in international processing which cannot be overcome. Black and white drawings submitted after the international filing date to overcome objections to color drawings may be refused if they do not comply with the requirements of PCT Rule 91.1, which could result in significant loss to applicants.

Section 1.85: Section 1.85 is proposed to be amended to make the period for filing corrected or formal drawings in response to a Notice of Allowability a non-extendable period.

In Topic 7 of the Advance Notice the Office proposed to reduce the time for filing corrected or formal drawings after the mailing date of the "Notice of Allowability" from three months to one month. In response, many comments were received which explained that one month was too short of a period of time in which to make the necessary changes to the drawings. In addition, many stated that having two different time periods running against the applicant makes docketing of the required replies too complicated. Several comments received indicated that corrected or formal drawings should be required at the same time as the issue fee, with no opportunity for the drawings to be filed later. Others indicated that, while one month was too short of a period of time, two months would be adequate.

After consideration of the comments and the Office's business goal of decreasing cycle time for all inventions, the Office is proposing to amend § 1.85(c) to provide that corrected or formal drawings must be filed within three months of the date of mailing of the "Notice of Allowability" requiring such drawings, and that no extensions of time under § 1.136(a) or (b) will be permitted. Refusing to permit an extension of time when formal or corrected drawings cannot be filed within the three-month period and sufficient cause exists for an extension may appear to be harsh. A strong policy is considered necessary, however, to ensure that the drawings are filed within the set period. The Office has also considered that many applicants are in the habit of filing formal or corrected drawings with an extension of time and may, out of habit and ignorance of the rule change, continue to do so. These applicants will have to file a petition to revive under § 1.137(b) as the failure to timely file any formal drawings that were required will cause the application to go abandoned.

The Office is taking positive steps to make it easier for applicants to submit drawings which will be approved. See the changes proposed in § 1.84. Thus, the instances where formal drawings will be required when the case is allowable will be reduced as more drawings will be approved as submitted.

If the amendment to § 1.85 is adopted, the time period for filing any required supplemental oath or declaration in compliance with § 1.63 will be set to be the same non-extendable time period of three months from the date of mailing of the Notice of Allowability requiring the supplemental oath or declaration.

Section 1.91: Section 1.91(a)(3)(i) is proposed to be amended to refer to "[t]he fee set forth in § 1.17(h)" for consistency with the changes to § 1.17(h) and § 1.17(i). See discussion of changes to § 1.17(h) and § 1.17(i).

Section 1.96: The Office indicated in the Advance Notice that the submission of computer program listings on microfiche placed a burden on applicants and the Office, and that it was considering changes to § 1.96 to permit machine readable computer program listings to be submitted on electronic media in lieu of microfiche. See Changes to Implement the Patent Business Goals, 63 FR at 53510–12, 1215 Off. Gaz. Pat. Office at 99–100.

Section 1.96 is proposed to be amended to provide for voluminous program listings to be submitted on archival electronic media instead of microfiche. Section 1.96(b) is proposed to be amended to limit computer program listings that may be submitted as drawings or part of the specification to computer program listings that are contained on one sheet.

Under § 1.96 as proposed, any computer program listing may, and any computer program listing that would be contained on more than one sheet must, be submitted as a computer program listing appendix pursuant to § 1.96(c) (subject to the "transitional" practice discussed below).

Section 1.96(c) is specifically proposed to provide that a "computer program listing appendix" be submitted on a Compact Disk-Read Only Memory (CD–ROM) or Compact Disk-Recordable (CD–R). A CD–ROM is the only practical electronic medium of archival quality under the current standards of the National Archives and Records Administration (NARA). *See* 36 CFR 1228.188(c) and (d) and 1234.30. The Office considers CD–R to be an electronic medium having an archival quality equivalent to the archival quality of CD–ROM. The information so submitted will be considered a "computer program listing appendix" (rather than a microfiche appendix). Section 1.96(c) will continue to require a reference at the beginning of the specification as itemized in § 1.77(b)(4). As with a microfiche appendix, the contents of the "computer program listing appendix" on a CD–ROM or CD–R will not be printed with the published patent, but will be available at the Office on a medium to be specified by the Office. The contents of a "computer program listing appendix" on a CD–ROM or CD–R may not be amended pursuant to § 1.121, but must be submitted on a substitute CD–ROM or CD–R. Section 1.96(c) does not apply to international applications filed in the United States Receiving Office.

Section 1.96(c)(1) is proposed to provide that the availability of the computer program will be directly analogous to that of the microfiche. The Office will make the contents available for inspection, for example at electronic workstations in the Public Search Room. If needed, multiple CD–ROMs or CD–Rs may be used for the submissions pertaining to a single patent application, but each application with an electronic medium appendix must be supplied with its own copy of the medium or media. Section 1.96(c)(2) is proposed to provide submission requirements that refer to the relevant NARA standards in 36 CFR Part 1228 for submissions of Government electronic records to NARA. Section 1.96(c)(2) is also proposed to provide that a CD–ROM or CD–R "computer program listing appendix" must be labeled with the following information: (1) The name of each inventor (if known); (2) title of the invention; and (3) the docket number used by the person filing the application to identify the application (if applicable).

Even after adoption of this proposed change to § 1.96, the Office will continue to accept a computer program listing that complies with current § 1.96 (*i.e.*, a computer program listing contained on ten or fewer sheets as drawings or part of the specification, or a "computer program listing appendix" on microfiche) for some period of time (*e.g.*, two years) that will be specified in any final rule notice adopting this proposed change to § 1.96. Should these provisions be adopted, conforming changes may be made in the regulations to accommodate international applications in the national stage.

Comments: The comments (almost without exception) were supportive of this proposal. Comments specifically indicated that this proposal was "long overdue," and that the proposal should include provisional applications and other technologies including chemical and manufacturing processes requiring precise computer control. The comments provided advice including the concepts of safeguarding the information from alteration, of making the public access and examiner access easy, and of assuring the submissions are readable. The only negative comment was an expression of disbelief that the Office was equipped to handle electronic media submissions.

Response: The Office is proposing changes to § 1.96 to provide for voluminous program listings to be submitted on archival electronic media instead of microfiche. The effective date of the proposed change will be linked to the development and deployment of electronic systems at the Office to capture, store and retrieve information submitted on archival electronic media in a manner to assure the integrity and authenticity of the information, and provide its display as needed for the Office, the patentee (and applicants), and the public.

The proposed change to § 1.96 and § 1.821 *et seq.* (discussed below) contemplated for computer program listings and sequence listings would eliminate the need for submissions of hard to handle and reproduce microfiche computer program listings and voluminous paper sequence listings. To focus specifically on the Office's difficult paper handling problem, and to simplify this project so it can be deployed in a short time span, only the computer program listings and the nucleotide and/or amino acid sequences would be accepted in machine readable format.

Relationship to Office automation plans: These changes being proposed are understood to be the initial steps towards solutions to difficult Office paper-handling problems. The Office is planning for full electronic submission of applications and related documents by fiscal year 2003. The changes proposed in this notice are an initial step in that direction, permitting certain application and related material to be submitted on an acceptable archival medium.

Sections 1.97 and 1.98: The Office proposes to go forward, at the present time, with only one aspect of the plan for information disclosure statement (IDS) revision that was set forth in the Advance Notice: the proposal to require that an IDS include a legible copy of each cited pending U.S. application. The proposed IDS rules are also being revised for consistency and grammar, and to tie up a number of loose ends, as will be discussed below.

Other than the proposed requirement for a copy of each cited U.S. application, the IDS proposals as set forth in Topics 9 and 10 of the Advance Notice have been withdrawn. Accordingly, there is no proposal at this time for a statement of personal review nor for a unique description as were called for in the Advance Notice, and the amount of citations that may be submitted is not presently proposed to be limited. The Office issued a notice of hearing and request for public comments to obtain views of the public on issues associated with the identification and consideration of prior art during patentability determinations. See Notice of Public Hearing and Request for Comments on Issues Related to the Identification of Prior Art During the Examination of a Patent Application, Notice of Hearing and Request for Public Comments, 64 FR 28803 (May 27, 1999), 1223 Off. Gaz. Pat. Office 91 (June 15, 1999). Pursuant to that notice, the Office held public hearings on June 28th and July 14th of 1999 on the issues. These prior art issues are related to the changes presently being considered by the Office to impose requirements/limits on IDS submissions. Thus, it would be premature to go forward with a comprehensive new IDS alternative until the results of the hearings and comments submitted in response to the notice have been appropriately evaluated. It is contemplated that any new IDS alternatives will be advanced in any rulemaking notice which may result from the evaluation of the results of the public hearings and comments submitted in response to the notice.

The Office recently issued guidelines for reviewing requests for reexaminations and ongoing reexaminations for compliance with *In re Portola Packaging, Inc.*, 110 F.3d 786, 42 USPQ 2d 1295 (Fed. Cir. 1997). See Guidelines for Reexamination of Cases in View of In re Portola Packaging, Inc., 110 F.3d 786, 42 USPQ 2d 1295 (Fed. Cir. 1997), Notice, 64 FR 15346 (March 31, 1999), 1223 Off. Gaz. Pat. Office 124 (June 22, 1999). These guidelines are pertinent to the consideration given IDS citations, stating:

> Where the IDS citations are submitted but not described, the examiner is only responsible for cursorily reviewing the references. The initials of the examiner on the PTOL–1449 indicate only that degree of review unless the reference is either applied against the claims, or discussed by the examiner as pertinent art of interest, in a subsequent office action.

See Guidelines for Reexamination of Cases in View of In re Portola Packaging, Inc., 110 F.3d 786, 42 USPQ 2d 1295 (Fed. Cir. 1997), 64 FR at 15347, 1223 Off. Gaz. Pat. Office at 125 (response to comment 6).

The public should thus be aware that full consideration of all citations submitted in compliance with §§ 1.97 and 1.98 is *not* required on the part of the examiner. The examiner performs a *cursory* review of each IDS citation to the extent that he/she needs in order to determine whether he/she will evaluate the citation further. If the cursory review reveals the citation not to be useful, the examiner will simply stop looking at it. The examiner will be understood to have provided full consideration only where the examiner applies the IDS citation as a reference against the claims in the application being examined, or otherwise deems the citation useful to the examination and discusses that use. Further, the applying of the IDS citation as a reference, or the discussion of the use of the citation (where the citation is *not* applied as a reference), must be in writing:

> [T]he Office cannot presume that a prior art reference was previously relied upon to reject or discussed in a prior PTO proceeding if there is no basis in the written record to so conclude other than the examiner's initials or a check mark on a PTO 1449 form, or equivalent, submitted with an information disclosure statement. Thus, any discussion of prior art must appear on the record of a prior related PTO proceeding.

See Guidelines for Reexamination of Cases in View of In re Portola Packaging, Inc., 110 F.3d 786, 42 USPQ 2d 1295 (Fed. Cir. 1997), 64 FR at 15349, 1223 Off. Gaz. Pat. Office at 127 (endnote 7).

It is also noted that the Office intends to issue a notice dealing with printing of IDS citations on the face of the patent. Currently, all IDS citations which are listed on a PTO–1449 form, or an equivalent of the PTO–1449, and are initialed by the examiner, are printed on the face of the patent together with art cited by the examiner. In the notice, the public would be informed that IDS citations printed on the face of the patent will be distinguished from citations made by the examiner, using a separate printing field, markings, or some other means.

Specifics of the contemplated IDS revisions: The specifics of the contemplated revisions to § 1.97 and § 1.98 will now be discussed as to the one Advance Notice proposed change that is being retained, as to newly advanced changes, and as to Advance Notice proposed changes that are being dropped. The discussion is presented in the following twelve parts which separately address identifiable portions of the subject matter: (1) Deletion of unassociated text; (2) items cited in continued prosecution applications (CPAs); (3) filing the IDS before the mail date of final Office actions; (4) required fee and statement for IDS submission made after close of prosecution; (5) newly cited item in foreign office must be cited for the *first* time; (6) IDS that does not comply with either § 1.97 or § 1.98; (7) copies of cited U.S. applications required; (8) how to identify a cited U.S. application; (9) citation was previously made in parent application; (10) grammar and consistency; (11) aspects of Topic 9 in the Advance Notice not being pursued in this notice; and (12) comments generally directed at revision of the IDS rules.

Part (1) Deletion of Unassociated Text

The phrase "whichever event occurs last" appears at the end of paragraph (b)(3) of § 1.97, and thus it physically appears to apply only to paragraph (b)(3). In reality, "whichever event occurs last" should be associated with each of paragraphs (b)(1), (b)(2) and (b)(3). Accordingly, it is proposed to delete "whichever event occurs last" from paragraph (b)(3), and to insert "within any one of the following time periods" in paragraph (b). This would eliminate the unassociated text "whichever event occurs last" from paragraph (b)(3), while, at the same time, making it clear that the IDS will be entered if it is filed within any of the time periods of paragraphs (b)(1), (b)(2) or (b)(3). Additionally, paragraph (c) of § 1.97 is proposed to be revised, in conformance with paragraph (b), to delete "whichever occurs first."

Part (2) Items Cited in Continued Prosecution Applications (CPAs)

Section 1.97(b)(1) is proposed to be amended to insert "other than an application under § 1.53(d)" to eliminate the three-month window for filing an IDS in a CPA. Because of the streamlined processing for CPAs, it is expected that the examiner will issue an action on the merits before three months from the filing date. Under the current rule, should an examiner issue an action on the merits prior to three months from the filing date and an IDS is submitted after the Office action is mailed but within the three-month window, the examiner must redo the action to consider the IDS. A CPA is a continuing application, and, thus, applicant should have had ample opportunity to file an IDS. In addition, as pointed out below, it is being proposed to revise § 1.103 to provide for a request of a three-month suspension of action upon filing of a CPA; thus, in an unusual instance where a need to file an IDS newly arises, applicant can request the three-month suspension based upon that need. In view of the above, it is deemed appropriate to require that any IDS be filed before filing the CPA, or concurrently with the filing of the CPA.

Part (3) Filing the IDS Before the Mail Date of Final Office Actions

Paragraph (c) of § 1.97 would be revised to include, in addition to a final action under § 1.113 and a notice of allowance under § 1.311, other Office actions which close prosecution in the application. This would typically occur when an Office action under *Ex parte Quayle*, 1935 Dec. Comm'r Pat. 11 (1935), is issued. No reason is seen for including only two of the types of actions which close prosecution (that under Sec. 1.113, and that under Sec. 1.311), while not including other types.

Part (4) Required Fee and Statement for IDS Submission Made After Close of Prosecution:

Paragraph(d)(3) of § 1.97 would be revised to delete reference to the fee as a petition fee under § 1.17(i) and instead make reference to the fee as an IDS fee under § 1.17(p). There is no reason for the reduced fee of $130 that is currently recited by paragraph (d), as opposed to the larger $240 IDS fee set forth in paragraph (c). On the contrary, the paragraph (d) submission is made *later in the prosecution* than that of paragraph (c), and thus interrupts the process at least as much as the paragraph (c) submission. Therefore, the fee for the paragraph (d) submission should be at least as much the $240 IDS fee required for the paragraph (c) submission.

In addition, paragraph(d)(2) of § 1.97 has been deleted in its entirety, to remove all reference to the filing of a petition. A petition unduly complicates the matter, while there is really no issue to be decided other than the entry of the IDS, which issue is ordinarily decided by the patent examiner. As it is contemplated to be amended, paragraph (d) of § 1.97 would simply require (for an IDS submitted *after* the close of prosecution and before payment of the issue fee) the combination of the IDS fee and a statement as is specified in paragraph (e) of 164. 1.97.

Part (5) Newly Cited Item in Foreign Office Must Be Cited for the First Time

Section 1.97(e)(1) is proposed to be amended to specify that an item *first* cited in a communication from a foreign patent office in a counterpart foreign application not more than three months prior to the filing of the statement is entitled to special consideration for entry into the record. An item *first cited* by a foreign patent office (for example) a year before in a communication from that foreign patent office, which item is *once again cited* by another foreign patent office within three months prior to the filing of the statement in the Office, is not entitled to special consideration for entry, since applicant was aware of the item a year ago, yet did not submit that item.

Part (6) IDS That Does Not Comply With Either § 1.97 or § 1.98

Paragraph (i) of § 1.97 is proposed for revision to delete "filed before the grant of a patent." This phrase is surplusage since there can be no information disclosure statement after the grant of the patent. A submission of information items after the patent grant is a "prior art citation" which is made, and treated, under § 501.

Paragraph (i) of § 1.97 would also be revised to make it a little clearer as to what sections must be complied with, and to change the paragraph (i) plural recitation of information disclosure statements to a singular recitation, which would be in conformance with the rest of § 1.97.

Part (7) Copies of Cited U.S. Applications Required

The Office proposes to go forward, at the present time, with one aspect of the Advance Notice IDS proposal. Section 1.98(a)(2) would be revised to require that an IDS include a legible copy of each cited pending U.S. application. Thus, the current exception to the requirement for supplying citation copies set forth in § 1.98(a)(2)(ii) for pending U.S. applications would be eliminated.

The Office noted, in the Advance Notice, its concern that current § 1.98 does not require applicant to supply copies of U.S. *application* citations. It was pointed out that there is a real burden on the examiner to locate and copy one or more pending applications, thus delaying the examination of the application being examined (in which the U.S. application citation is made). Further, copying a cited application has the potential for interfering with the processing and examination of the cited application itself. Accordingly, § 1.98(a)(2) is proposed for revision to require, for each U.S. application citation listed, that applicant submit either a copy of the application specification, including the claims, and any drawing of the application, or as a minimum, the portion of the application which caused it to be listed, including any claims directed to the portion which caused it to be listed. This proposed revision would, additionally, be a benefit to the public since the copy of the application would be readily available upon issuance of the application as a patent.

Comments Received in Response to the Advance Notice: In response to the Advance Notice, a significant number of comments were in favor of adopting the requirement for copies of U.S. applications, and indicated that there should be no problem with requiring submission of copies. Comments noted that the submission of copies of cited applications will speed up the application process. It will decrease the time burden on examiners in obtaining and copying such applications. It will also avoid interruption of the examination of the application being cited, as otherwise, papers in the original file of the cited application must be removed and copied in order to be reviewed. Even further, it was noted that this revision of the rule should reduce risks of application papers in the cited cases being misplaced or lost.

A number of comments were concerned that submission of copies of multiple U.S. patent applications in an IDS will overwhelm the Office with an increased volume of paper. Some comments opposed the requirement for copies of U.S. patent applications on the grounds that it will place a difficult burden on counsel/applicants to provide the Office with a copy of each cited U.S. application. An example was given, where the client has an extensive patent portfolio distributed among several patent firms (*e.g.*, the result of licensing agreements or other conflicts of interest which require different counsel to be responsible for different cases in a portfolio). In such a scenario, counsel may not be able to receive/view copies of related applications due to constraints imposed by applicable ethical rules and thus may not be able to supply copies. Another example was given, where a practitioner may be aware that a pending application is relevant and may not have access to that pending application, since it is that of another party.

With respect to these grounds for opposition to the requirement, it should initially be noted that citation of another application in an IDS is relatively rare and, as such, should not significantly increase the volume of paper the Office must deal with. Also, in those few situations where U.S. applications are cited and counsel cannot provide copies of the applications, a petition could be submitted for waiver of the rules, and the petition would be decided on a case-by-case basis. In addition, if a practitioner is not permitted, due to ethical considerations, to review material that may be of significance in the prosecution of a particular application, it is not clear why the practitioner would be involved in the prosecution of that application. As to the comment relating to lack of access by practitioner, such lack of access may result from the fact that the application to be cited is that of a third party and is not available to the public, which includes the practitioner or the practitioner's client; the patent rules should not be a means whereby the Office will provide practitioner with a copy of a pending U.S. application merely because the practitioner or the client thereof has come across the application number.

It was suggested in the comments that review of the Office file is better than review of a supplied copy; *i.e.*, it is more useful for the examiner to review the Office file, which is more comprehensive, than to review the copies that applicant would send. As to this concern, the benefits of eliminating the Office's burden of obtaining and copying such applications, as well as avoiding interruption of examination of the cases being cited, are deemed to be greater than the possible benefit associated with the review of the Office file. If the submitted copy of a cited U.S. patent application is found by the examiner to be of sufficient relevance for further review of the application, at that point in time, the examiner can expend the extra effort to obtain and review the file. On the other hand, for the majority of the cited applications that are not worthy of looking into further, this extra expenditure of time and effort will be saved.

The comments further urged that if a cited U.S. application supplied with an IDS is later abandoned, a petition to expunge the copy of the cited application must be submitted to remove the application from the file, and the Office would then need to consider if the U.S. application is immaterial to patentability of the invention such that it can be expunged (*see* MPEP 724.05). This concern is noted; however, it should be the exception rather than the rule. The time expended in deciding the relatively few petitions to expunge that are filed should more than be counterbalanced by the reduction of the burden to obtain and copy applications and the avoidance of interruption of examination of the application being cited. In addition, even under the current system where application-citation copies are not required, a petition to expunge is still needed to expunge the listed application number, in cases where the content of that application citation is sufficiently identified in the record. Thus, the increase in petitions to expunge (generated by the proposal) should be very small indeed.

It was suggested that the examiner's time in obtaining U.S. application files could be saved by providing clerical support in the groups, which would function to assist the examiner with obtaining the cited application files. This, however, would be a large drain on Office resources, which are limited, and would still result in undesirable interruptions of examination of the application being cited.

It was suggested that, instead of requiring copies of all cited applications with the IDS, the Office should reserve the right to later request copies from applicant where specific application files are not easily available. As to this suggestion, it is first noted that it would not at all reduce the time that the cited application would be away from the examiner of the cited application, and thus does not deal with the problem of interruption of the examination of the application being cited. In addition, making a requirement from applicant for the application after the IDS is received (for difficult-to-obtain cases) slows the examination process since the examiner must wait for the copy, while if the copy were submitted with the IDS, the examiner could immediately begin the examination. Furthermore, a large expenditure of time would have been made in finding out that the application file is not easily available. Even after the application is obtained and reviewed, it is, at times, found that some portion is missing. At that time, the effort would already have been expended, and only then would the copy of the application first be required from applicant.

Part (8) How To Identify a Cited U.S. Application

Section 1.98(b) is proposed to be amended to require that each listed U.S. application to be identified by the inventors, application number and filing date.

Part (9) Citation Was Previously Made in Parent Application

Paragraph (d) of § 1.98 is proposed to be revised to make it clear that the mere submission of the citation in the parent application (by applicant) is not enough to take advantage of paragraph (d) when submitting the citation in the "child" application. A copy of the citation must have been submitted in the parent, and the submission of the citation made in the parent must have complied with § 1.97, except for an application filed under § 1.53(d).

A situation might arise where applicant would establish continuity with an existing application having listed U.S. applications for which copies were not supplied (under the current practice, *i.e.*, before the changes proposed in this notice would go into effect), and applicant would thereby take advantage of paragraph (d) of § 1.98 to have the cited applications reviewed in the newly filed "continuation" (i.e., filed after the changes proposed in this notice would go into effect) without submitting copies. To deal with this possibility, paragraph (d) of § 1.98 would be revised to require that where the cited U.S. application (the listed information) was not cited "by * * * the Office" (*i.e.*, not cited by the examiner in the parent), the information submission made in the prior application must have been in compliance with paragraphs (a) through (c) of § 1.98 as they are drafted in this notice. In other words, if the copy of the application papers (for the cited application) was not present in the parent, it must now be submitted in the continuation.

It might be argued that because a copy of the citation was submitted in the parent, paragraph (d) is satisfied even though the submission of the citation made in the parent did not comply with § 1.97. Paragraph (d) of § 1.98 as proposed for revision deals with this argument.

Part (10) Grammar and Consistency

All changes which are proposed in §§ 1.97 and 1.98 other than those explicitly identified above would be made for grammar and consistency within the sections. This includes, for example, deleting the last sentence of § 1.98(c) and inserting it as the last sentence of § 1.98(a)(3) where it more appropriately belongs.

Part (11) Aspects of Topic 9 in the Advance Notice Not Being Pursued Further

Statement of Personal Review: In the Advance Notice, it was proposed that the IDS submitter be required to state that he/she personally reviewed each submitted IDS citation to determine whether or not that citation is relevant to the claimed invention(s) and is appropriate to cite to the Office in the IDS. This statement of personal review would have to be made by a registered practitioner (where applicant is represented by a practitioner), or by at least one of the inventors (where applicant is not represented).

A large majority of the comments (in response to the Advance Notice) opposed requiring the statement of personal review as proposed in the Advance Notice. Opposition was based upon the following: (1) The required statement of personal review as proposed in the Advance Notice would greatly increase prosecution costs; (2) the impact of the cost burden imposed would be extremely hard on small entities and independent inventors, and may be contrary to the Office's Independent Inventor Initiative; (3) the proposed review by the practitioner (where applicant is represented) will result in a duplication of the prior efforts of inventors, in-house counsel (not representing the inventor before the Office), or foreign associates who initially provided the information (the practitioner must "second guess" the inventor, *etc.* as to whether the citation is relevant and how it is relevant); (4) the proposed practitioner review would provide new grounds for allegations of inequitable conduct (whether the subjective requirements of the personal review statement were complied with), and the possibility of malpractice as to the review conducted; (5) the statement of review is already inherent in any IDS (§ 10.18(b)(2), § 1.56), and an explicit statement is not needed;

(6) the proposed practitioner review would raise problems as to attorney-client relations, *e.g.*, conflict of interest, and potentially a breach of attorney-client privilege as to the review of the documents made; and (7) the statement of personal review would not be effective (it will not prevent marginally related and unrelated citations from being submitted), since one could make a cursory personal review of a citation, reach no decision, and simply submit the citation, with minimal comment.

There was some limited support for adoption of the proposal requiring a statement of personal review (at least in part); however, a substantial majority of the comments expressed opposition to the statement of personal review. The Office has taken note of the duplication of review effort, the potential increased costs, the subjectivity of the statement, the resulting potential for charges of inequitable conduct, and the conflict-of-interest problems that could be brought about by going forward with the proposed requirement for a statement of personal review. Accordingly, a decision has been made to not go forward with the requirement for a statement of personal review at this time.

Citations To Be Uniquely Described: The Advance Notice proposed that applicant be required to compare each of the citations to each of the independent claims, or specific dependent claim(s), in a meaningful way unique to each citation. The description of each citation would have to point out why applicant believes the citation to be unique in its teaching/showing relative to the claimed invention(s). Description would not be required for any ten citations, and for citations in a corresponding application by a foreign patent office, PCT international searching authority, or PCT international preliminary examining authority, provided the search report or office action in the English language is also submitted.

The comments in opposition to the unique description proposal were both numerous and varied as to the reasons for opposition. Reasons for opposition are summarized: (1) A potential for adverse future litigation implications, and for admissions which otherwise need not be made, would result from the proposal; (2) the proposal would impose an unreasonable cost and time burden upon the public; (3) the impact of the burden imposed would be extremely hard on small entities and independent inventors, and may be contrary to the Office's Independent Inventor Initiative; (4) the proposed description of the citations is unduly burdensome, and the many possible description permutations impose an impossible task (description would be needed to cover all claim meanings, art settings and potential art combinations, and would need to be updated each time the claims are amended); (5) reasonable minds will differ on which portions of a citation are significant, which citations are cumulative, and the relevant teachings of any particular citation; (6) the appropriate standard for determining if an item should be considered is whether the item is material, not whether it is cumulative (so, explanation of why the citation is not cumulative should not be imposed); (7) the description proposal discriminates against foreign applications and U.S. practitioners representing foreign applicants, since the U.S. practitioner, who is not the author of the case, is not completely familiar with the technology; (8) the proposed unique description requirement is not fair since examiners do not have this burden; (9) experience has shown that the submitted description may not be a useful tool to the examiner, and some examiners do/did not even read the descriptions; (10) the description proposal would provide a "role reversal" where applicant does the examiner's job of evaluating the citations but not as well, *i.e.*, the proposal appears to force applicant's representative to "play" examiner, review each of the citations, and essentially make a rejection for the examiner in an IDS; (11) there is no statute or case law that requires the applicant to comment on citations submitted to satisfy the duty to disclose (thus, applicant should not be charged with that responsibility); (12) it should take no longer for the examiner to evaluate IDS art than the time it takes him/her to review art when searching through shoes of patents; (13) no data/facts have been presented to show a need for the description of the citations; (14) the pre-set number of ten "free" citations (without description) proposed in the Advance Notice is an artificial and arbitrary number, and it would be difficult to decide which ten to choose (it encourages gamesmanship and planning in selecting which citations to describe); (15) the proposed selection of an arbitrary ten free citations opens up a "Pandora's Box" regarding inferences as to the particular ten citations selected; and (16) the number "ten" for the free citations is too small, and the number actually needed depends upon many factors surrounding the application such as complexity, technology, and number of claims.

Conclusion: The overwhelming majority of the comments expressed opposition to the unique description proposal of the Advance Notice. The Office has taken note of the large burden that would be imposed on applicants and attorneys by the description proposal of the Advance Notice, the potential for future adverse consequences stemming from doing the description or the choice not to describe, and the applicant's role reversal that would be imposed by the description proposal. Accordingly, a decision has been made to not go forward with the unique description proposal at this time.

Suggestions Regarding Topic 9: A substantial number of suggestions were submitted for modification of the Advance Notice Topic 9 proposal as to the required statement of personal review and the unique description requirement and its exceptions. It was also widely suggested that the Office charge fees for consideration and evaluation of an excessive number of submitted citations. These suggestions have not been accepted in view of the decision not to go forward with the Topic 9 proposal other than the requirement for copies of applications (as discussed above).

Part (12) Comments Generally Directed at Revision of the IDS Rules

Some comments on the Advance Notice IDS proposals were not directed to specific aspects of Topics 9 and 10, but commented on the IDS proposals on the whole. Those comments noted: (1) No reason nor incentive has been provided to the public to give up the current IDS system; (2) the proposed Advance Notice IDS changes do not serve the public nor applicant's interest, and would eliminate a significant number of application filings each year; (3) the current IDS submission rules work well and should not be changed (the Office should not over-react by adopting a drastic cure that would be more harmful than the disease); (4) it is not an excessive burden on the Office to review large numbers of submitted documents, but actually helps the process (this issue was previously visited during the promulgation of the current § 1.98, and the Office found that examiners' review of all submitted documents would not constitute an excessive burden); (5) the IDS proposals set forth in the Advance Notice will not be effective to discourage submissions to the point that the Office problem is solved since the duty of disclosure remains in effect, and on the other hand, the proposals will discourage pre-searches and other mechanisms for disclosure that strengthen patents; (6) the proposal imposes significant new limitations on the practitioner's ability to freely disclose information to the Office due to cost accountability to clients and potential adverse litigation consequences; (7) the Office desire to reduce application processing time via the IDS proposals would be expected to reduce the quality of examination, and that is an undesirable trade-off; (8) the IDS proposals conflict with world patent harmonization (the U.S. is the only patent-granting body in the world that requires citations of relevant art, and it runs counter to world patent harmonization that applicant's burden in this regard should now be increased by the proposals to further impose requirements on applicant not required by other patent granting bodies); (9) the IDS proposals are complicated; and (10) the Office's IDS problem is at least partly generated by MPEP 2004 which calls for citation of even questionable or marginal items.

Summary: The overall support for the IDS proposals as set forth in the Advance Notice was relatively limited, and, for the most part, where support was advanced, it was advanced as a qualified support. On the other hand, a large majority of the comments opposed the Advance Notice IDS proposals, often stating their objection to the proposals using strong language. Accordingly, the IDS proposals as set forth in Topics 9 and 10 of the Advance Notice have been withdrawn at this time (with the exception of the proposed requirement for a copy of each cited U.S. application, which did have some support and is being retained for reasons discussed both below and above).

The present IDS proposal addresses the major concerns of the comments in that it does not call for a statement of personal review, nor a unique description, as were called for in the Advance Notice. It also does not propose to limit the number of citations that may be submitted. As noted, the present IDS proposal does in fact retain one aspect of the Advance Notice IDS proposal—applicant would be required to provide a copy of the specification including the claims (and any drawing) of each U.S. application cited in the IDS, or the portion of the application which caused it to be listed, including any claims directed to that portion of the application. Any increase in applicant's burden due to this one retained aspect should be minor since: (1) The citation of U.S. applications represents a very small minority of documents cited, and (2) the original of the application is usually readily available to the applicant as a related application (and where not so, a petition can be filed requesting that a copy not be required in that isolated and rare case). The need for any such minor increase in burden is, however, heavily outweighed by the many benefits obtained. As pointed out above, the presence of the application copies with the IDS will (1) decrease the time burden on examiners in obtaining and copying the applications, (2) avoid interruption of examination of the cited cases, (3) reduce risks of application papers in the actual file of the cited applications being misplaced or lost, and (4) be advantageous to the public as such copies being in the application file would be readily available to the public upon issuance of the application as a patent.

The presently proposed IDS rules also include a number of revisions for consistency and grammar, and to tie up a number of loose ends as discussed above. These proposed revisions should not, however, represent any significant burden on the public.

Section 1.102: Section 1.102(d) is proposed to be amended to refer to "the fee set forth in § 1.17(h)" for consistency with the changes to § 1.17(h) and § 1.17(i). See discussion of changes to § 1.17(h) and § 1.17(i).

Section 1.103: Section 1.103 is proposed to be revised for clarity and to provide a procedure for obtaining a limited suspension of action in a continued prosecution application (CPA) under § 1.53(d). The heading of § 1.103 is proposed to be amended to add the phrase "by the Office" to clarify that this section does not apply to requests for suspension of action (or reply) by the applicant.

Section 1.103(a) is proposed to provide for suspension of action for cause. Specifically, § 1.103(a) is proposed to provide that on request of the applicant, the Office may grant a suspension of action under this paragraph for good and sufficient cause. Section 1.103(a) is also proposed to provide that: (1) The Office will not suspend action if reply by applicant to an Office action is outstanding; and (2) any petition for suspension of action under § 1.103(a) must specify a period of suspension not exceeding six months. Section 1.103(a) is proposed to specifically provide that any petition for suspension of action under § 1.103(a) must also include: (1) A showing of good and sufficient cause for suspension of action; and (2) the fee set forth in § 1.17(h), unless such cause is the fault of the Office. If an additional suspension period is desired applicant may submit another petition under § 1.103(a) requesting same.

Section 1.103(b) is proposed to provide for a limited suspension of action in a continued prosecution application (CPA) under § 1.53(d). Section 1.103(b) is specifically proposed to provide that on request of the applicant, the Office may grant a suspension of action under § 1.103(b) in a CPA for a period not exceeding three months. Section 1.103(b) is proposed to specifically provide that any request for suspension of action under § 1.103(b) must be filed with the request for a CPA and include the processing fee set forth in § 1.17(i).

Section 1.103(c) is proposed to provide that the Office will notify applicant if the Office suspends action on an application on its own initiative.

Section 1.103(d) is proposed to provide for suspension of action for public safety or defense. Section 1.103(b) is specifically proposed to provide that the Office may suspend action by order of the Commissioner if the following conditions are met: (1) The application is owned by the United States; (2) publication of the invention may be detrimental to the public safety or defense; and (3) the appropriate department or agency requests such suspension.

Section 1.103(e) is proposed to provide that the Office will suspend action for the entire pendency of an application if the Office has accepted a request to publish a statutory invention registration in the application, except for purposes relating to patent interference proceedings under Subpart E.

Section 1.105: Section 1.105 would be a new section containing paragraphs (a) through (c), relating to requirements by the Office that certain information be supplied.

Paragraph (a)(1) of § 1.105 would provide examiners or other Office employees explicit authority to require submission of such information as may be reasonably necessary for the Office to properly examine or treat a matter being addressed in an application under 35 U.S.C. 111 or 371, in a patent, or in a reexamination proceeding. Abandoned applications would also fall within the scope of the rule to provide for handling of petition matters. New § 1.105 is simply an explicit recitation of inherent authority that exists pursuant to 35 U.S.C. 131 and 132, and continues the practice of providing explicit authority to Office employees as was done with the Board of Patent Appeals and Interferences under § 1.196(d) and with trademark examiners under § 2.61.

The use of the authority under proposed paragraph (a)(1) of § 1.105 would be encouraged so that the Office can perform the best quality examination possible. The authority is not intended to be used by examiners without a reasonable basis, but to address legitimate concerns that may arise during the examination of an application or consideration of some matter. Any abuse in implementation of the authority, such as a requirement for information that is not in fact reasonably necessary to properly examine the application, would be addressed by way of petition under § 1.181. For example, the Office may, under appropriate circumstances, desire the authority to ask for:

1. The existence of any particularly relevant commercial data base that could be searched for a particular aspect of an invention, in certain technologies where pertinent prior art is highly likely to be found in a commercial data base.

2. Information that may not be required to be submitted by § 1.56, but that the examiner would deem useful on an application-by-application basis (which could be done prior to the application being taken up for examination, such as when the application is assigned to an examiner): (a) Submission of any published articles, authored by any of the inventors, that relate to a claimed invention, and (b) any non-patent literature or patents that were used to draft the application or in the invention process, such as where the invention is an improvement over the prior information.

3. A reply to a matter raised in a protest under § 1.291.

4. An explanation of technical material in a publication, such as one of the inventors' publications.

5. The identification of changes made in a reformatted continuing application filed under § 1.53(b).

6. A mark-up for a continuation-in-part application showing the new matter where there is an intervening reference.

7. Comments on a new Federal Circuit decision that appears on point.

The proposed § 1.105 is not intended to change current Office practice in regard to questions of fraud under § 1.56, and inquiries relating thereto would not be authorized. *See* MPEP 2010.

Paragraph (a)(2) of § 1.105 would provide a safety net by specifically recognizing that where the information required to be submitted is unknown and/or is not available, a complete response to the requirement for information would be a statement to that effect. There would be no requirement for a showing that in fact the information was unknown or not available such as by way of disclosing what was done to attempt to satisfy the requirement for information. Nonetheless, it should be understood that a good faith attempt must be made to obtain the information and a reasonable inquiry made once the information is requested even though the Office will not look behind the answer given. An Office employee should not continue to question the scope of a specific answer merely because it is not as complete as the Office employee desires.

Example: In a first action on the merits of an application with an effective filing date of May 1, 1999, the examiner notes the submission of a protest under § 1.291 relating to a public sale of the subject matter of the invention and requests a date of publication for a business circular authored by the assignee of the invention, which circular was submitted with the protest. It is expected that the attempt to respond to the requirement for information would involve contacting the assignee who would then make a good faith attempt to determine the publication date of the circular. The response to the requirement states that the publication date of the circular is "around May 1, 1998." As "around May 1, 1998" covers dates both prior and subsequent to May 1, 1998, a *prima facie* case under 35 U.S.C. 102(b) would not exist. The examiner cannot require that the response be more specific or hold the response to be incomplete based on such reply. The examiner can, however, in the next Office action seek confirmation that this is the most specific date that was obtained or can be obtained based on a reasonable inquiry being made if that is not already clear from the response to the initial requirement for information.

Paragraph (b) of § 1.105 would provide that the requirement for information may be included in an Office action, which would include a restriction requirement if appropriate, or can be sent as a separate letter independent of an Office action on the merits such as when the information required is critical to an issue or issues that need to be addressed in a subsequent Office action. It is expected that due to cycle time concerns the use of a requirement for information independent of an Office action on the merits would be limited.

Paragraph (c) of § 1.105 would provide that a response to a requirement for information or failure to respond thereto would be governed by §§ 1.135 and 1.136. Note the Example provided in the discussion of paragraph (a)(2) of § 1.105.

Section 1.111: The heading of § 1.111 is proposed to be amended to clarify that it applies to a reply by the applicant or patent owner to a non-final Office action. Section 1.111 is proposed to be amended to: (1) Provide a reference to § 1.104 concerning the first examination of an application; (2) change the reference to § 1.135 and § 1.136 (for time for reply to avoid abandonment) from paragraph (c) to paragraph (a); and (3) add the sentence "[a] second or subsequent supplemental reply will be entered unless disapproved by the Commissioner."

The Office indicated in the Advance Notice that it was considering charging a handling fee for all supplemental replies. The Office was specifically considering replacing the current practice of allowing unlimited supplemental replies to be filed without requiring any fee with a new practice in which a handling fee would be charged for each supplemental reply that is filed after the initial reply to an Office action has been filed.

While some comments supported this proposed change, a majority of comments opposed charging a handling fee for supplemental replies. The reasons given for opposition to the proposal included arguments that: (1) The proposal was simply a revenue-raising proposition; (2) the primary cause of supplemental replies crossing with an Office action is Office mail room delay and paper processing delays; (3) applicants may need to file a supplemental amendment due to later-discovered prior art. The comments also suggested that: (1) The PALM system be enhanced to flag supplemental replies to avoid issuing an Office action until any supplemental reply is matched with the application; and (2) examiners call applicants two weeks prior to acting on an application to determine whether a supplemental reply has been filed.

This notice does not propose changing the rules of practice to charge a handling fee for supplemental replies. Based upon the comments and its own evaluation, the Office has concluded that the proposed handling charge would not discourage the filing of supplemental replies, but would only result in such replies being filed with the handling fee.

The Office, however, is proposing a change to the rules of practice to provide that the entry of second or subsequent supplemental replies may be disapproved by the Commissioner. It is expected that disapproval of a second or subsequent supplemental amendment will be delegated to the appropriate Technology Center Group Director under MPEP 1002.02(c). As most supplemental replies cause only a minor inconvenience to the Office, the Office is not inclined to propose a change that would affect the ability to file a supplemental reply when such is warranted. There are, however, some applicants who routinely file preliminary or supplemental amendments that place a significant burden on the Office by: (1) Canceling the pending claims and adding many new claims; (2) adding numerous new claims; (3) being filed approximately two months from the date the original reply was filed (*i.e.*, when the examiner is likely to be preparing an Office action responsive to the original reply). These applicants also tend to be those having many applications simultaneously on file in the Office.

The provision that the entry of a second or subsequent supplemental reply may be disapproved by the Commissioner would give the Office the latitude to permit entry of those supplemental replies that do not unduly interfere with the preparation of an Office action, but would also give the Office the latitude to refuse entry of those supplemental replies that do unduly interfere with the preparation of an Office action. The factors that would be taken into consideration when deciding whether to disapprove entry of such a supplemental reply are: (1) The state of preparation of an Office action responsive to the initial reply; and (2) the nature of the change to the pending claims that would result from entry of the supplemental reply. That is, if the examiner has devoted a significant amount of time to preparing an Office action before such a supplemental amendment is matched with the application, it would be appropriate for the Office to disapprove entry of the supplemental amendment. If, however, such a supplemental amendment merely cancels claims (as opposed to canceling claims and adding claims, or simply adding claims), it would not be appropriate to disapprove entry of such a supplemental amendment even if the examiner has devoted a significant amount of time to preparing an Office action before such a supplemental amendment is matched with the application.

Obviously, if a supplemental reply is received in the Office (§ 1.6) after the mail date of the Office action responsive to the original reply and is not responsive to that Office action, the Office will continue the current practice of not mailing a new Office action responsive to that supplemental reply, but simply advising the applicant that the supplemental reply is non-responsive to such Office action and that a responsive reply (under § 1.111 or 1.113 as the situation may be) must be timely filed to avoid abandonment. Put simply, the mailing of an Office action responsive to the original reply will continue to cut off the applicant's right to have any later-filed supplemental reply considered by the Office.

The proposed change to § 1.111(a) in this notice: (1) Is not a revenue-raising proposition; and (2) will not affect the vast majority of supplemental replies. It will only apply to a supplemental reply if: (1) the applicant has already filed one (a first) supplemental reply; and (2) the supplemental reply is not matched with the application until after the examiner has devoted a significant amount of time to preparing an Office action.

The suggestion regarding enhancement to the PALM system is being taken under advisement. Such an enhancement, however, would not discourage the filing of the supplemental replies that place a burden on the Office, but would only inform the examiner that such a reply has not yet been matched with the application. In the absence of a procedure for disapproving the entry of such burdensome replies, the so-enhanced PALM system would simply advise the Office not to act on the affected application for extended periods of time, which would have an adverse effect on the Office's efforts to reduce cycle time.

The suggestion that examiners call applicants two weeks prior to acting on an application to determine whether a supplemental reply has been filed is not practicable. The Office issues hundreds of thousands of Office actions each year. Thus, implementing this suggestion would require the Office (examiners) to make hundreds of thousands of additional telephone calls to applicants each year.

Section 1.112: Section 1.112 is proposed to be amended to provide a reference to § 1.104 concerning the first examination of an application. Section 1.112 is proposed to be amended to add the phrase "or an appeal (§ 1.191) has been taken" to the last sentence. This addition is to clarify that once an appeal has been taken in an application, any amendment is subject to the provisions of § 1.116 (b) and (c), even if the appeal is in reply to a non-final Office action.

Section 1.115: A new Sec. 1.115 is proposed to be added to provide for preliminary amendments. The Office indicated in the Advance Notice that it was considering charging a handling fee for certain preliminary amendments. The Office was specifically considering replacing the current practice of allowing unlimited preliminary amendments to be filed without requiring any fee with a new practice in which a handling fee would be charged for each preliminary amendment filed later than a specified time period (one month) after the filing date of the application.

While some comments supported this proposed change, a majority of comments opposed charging a handling fee for certain preliminary amendments. The reasons given for opposition to the proposal included arguments that: (1) The proposal was simply a revenue-raising proposition; (2) the primary cause of preliminary amendments crossing with an Office action is Office mail room delay and paper processing delays; (3) applicants should not be forced to file preliminary amendments and other papers until after receiving a filing receipt and application number; and (4) applicants may need to file a preliminary amendment due to later-discovered prior art. The comments also suggested that: (1) The PALM system be enhanced to flag preliminary amendments to avoid issuing an Office action until the preliminary amendment is matched with the application; (2) examiners call applicants two weeks prior to acting on an application to determine whether a preliminary amendment has been filed; and (3) applicants filing a continued prosecution application under § 1.53(d) (CPA) be given a few weeks to file any necessary preliminary amendment.

The Office is not proposing a change to the rules of practice to charge a handling fee for certain preliminary amendments. Based upon the comments and its own evaluation, the Office has concluded the proposed handling charge would not discourage the filing of preliminary amendments, but would only result in such amendments being filed with the handling fee. The Office, however, is proposing a change to the rules of practice to provide that the entry of certain preliminary amendments may be disapproved by the Commissioner. See the discussion of § 1.111 for an explanation of the need for this change to the rules of practice.

Section 1.115(a) as proposed provides that a preliminary amendment is an amendment that is received in the Office (§ 1.6) on or before the mail date of the first Office action under § 1.104. That is, an amendment received in the Office (§ 1.6) after the mail date of the first Office action is not a preliminary amendment, even if it is non-responsive to the first Office action and seeks to amend the application prior to the first examination.

Section 1.115(b) is proposed to provide that a preliminary amendment will be entered unless disapproved by the Commissioner, and also provide that a preliminary amendment will not be disapproved if it is filed no later than: (1) Three months from the filing date of an application under § 1.53(b); (2) the filing date of a continued prosecution application under § 1.53(d); or (3) three months from the date the national stage is entered as set forth in § 1.491 in an international application. Thus, the entry of a preliminary amendment will not be disapproved under § 1.115(b) if it is filed within one of the periods specified in § 1.115(b)(1) through (b)(3). Nevertheless, if a "preliminary" amendment is filed after the mail date of the first Office action, it is not a preliminary amendment under § 1.115(a). If a ("preliminary") amendment is received in the Office (§ 1.6) after the mail date of the first Office action and is not responsive to the first Office action, the Office will continue the current practice of not mailing a new Office action responsive to that amendment, but simply advising the applicant that the amendment is non-responsive to first Office action and that a responsive reply must be timely filed to avoid abandonment. Put simply, the mailing of the first Office action will continue to cut off the applicant's right to have any later-filed preliminary amendment considered by the Office, even if that amendment is filed within the time periods specified in proposed § 1.115(b).

Section 1.115(c) is proposed to provide that the time periods specified in § 1.115(b) are not extendable.

It is expected that disapproval of a preliminary amendment filed outside the period specified in § 1.115(b) will be delegated to the appropriate Technology Center Group Director under MPEP 1002.02(c). The provision that the entry of a preliminary amendment filed outside the period specified in § 1.115(b) may be disapproved by the Commissioner would give the Office the latitude to permit entry of those preliminary amendments filed outside the period specified in § 1.115(b) that do not unduly interfere with the preparation of an Office action, but would also give the Office the latitude to refuse entry of those preliminary amendments filed outside the period specified in § 1.115(b) that do unduly interfere with the preparation of an Office action. As with the proposed change to § 1.111(a), the factors that would be taken into consideration when deciding whether to disapprove entry of such a preliminary amendment are: (1) The state of preparation of the first Office action; and (2) the nature of the change to the pending claims that would result from entry of the preliminary amendment.

The proposed change to § 1.115 in this notice: (1) Is not a revenue-raising proposition; and (2) will not affect the vast majority of preliminary amendments. It will only apply to a preliminary amendment if: (1) The preliminary amendment is filed outside the time periods specified in § 1.115(b)(1) through (b)(3); and (2) the preliminary amendment is not matched with the application until after the examiner has devoted a significant amount of time to preparing an Office action. The suggestions that the PALM system be enhanced and that examiners call applicants two weeks prior to acting on an application are addressed above in the discussion of § 1.111(a).

In an application filed under 35 U.S.C. 111(a) and § 1.53(b) or a PCT international application entering the national stage under § 1.491, the time periods specified in § 1.115(b) should give the applicant time between the mailing of a filing receipt and the mailing of a first Office action to file any necessary preliminary amendment. CPA practice under § 1.53(d), however, is designed to provide a first Office action sooner than if the application had been filed as a continuation under § 1.53(b) (or under former §§ 1.60 or 1.62). *See* Continued Prosecution Application (CPA) Practice, Notice, 1214 Off. Gaz. Pat. Office 32, 32 (September 8, 1998). An applicant filing a CPA under § 1.53(d) who needs time to prepare a preliminary amendment should file a request for suspension of action under § 1.103(b) with the CPA request. See discussion of § 1.103(b).

Section 1.121: Section 1.121 is proposed to be amended to change the manner of making amendments in non-reissue applications. The proposed practice to amend the specification by replacement of a section or paragraph (or claim) would eliminate the need for the Office to enter changes by handwriting in red ink. This change would result in a specification (including claims) in clean-copy form that can be Optical Character Recognition (OCR) scanned during the patent publishing process. The proposed practice also requires the applicant to provide a marked-up copy of the changed section or paragraphs (or claims), using the applicant's choice of marking system, which will aid the examiner in ascertaining the changes to the specification.

The proposed change to § 1.121 involves concurrent changes to § 1.52(b) (see discussion of § 1.52(b)(6)) to provide for numbering of the paragraphs of the specification, except for the claims. If the paragraphs of the specification are numbered as proposed in § 1.52, the applicant will be able to amend the specification by merely submitting a replacement paragraph (with the same number) with the desired changes made in the replacement paragraph.

As discussed above, the adoption of the proposed changes to § 1.121 will result in relatively clean (*e.g.*, without underlining, bracketing, or red ink) application specifications that can be OCR scanned as part of the printing process in the Office of Patent Publications, which will result in a higher quality of printed patents. Complete OCR scanning of the amended portions of the specification and claims is not possible today because insertions of words, phrases or sentences made by handwriting in red ink and deletions made by words which have been lined through with red ink are ignored by the scanner. Further, while text marked with underlining and bracketing can be scanned, extra processing is required to delete the brackets and the text within the brackets and to correct misreading of letters caused by the underlining. Thus, using clean replacement sections or paragraphs and claims will permit complete OCR scanning which is a faster and more accurate method of capturing the application for printing while eliminating an extensive amount of key-entry of subject matter. This should result in patents with fewer errors in need of correction by certificate of correction, which will be a clear benefit to the patentees and conserve Office resources.

In addition to submitting a replacement section or paragraph/claim to make an amendment, applicant would also be required to submit a marked-up copy of the section or paragraph/claim to show the differences between the original and the replacement. The marked-up copy may be created by any method applicant chooses, such as underlining and bracketing, redlining, or by any system designed to provide text comparison.

The proposed change to § 1.121 will make the amendment process simpler, reduce processing time and operating costs, and reduce the opportunity for error associated with amendment entry. In addition, it is consistent with standardizing processing of amendments in both paper and electronic format in anticipation of a total Electronic File Wrapper (EFW) environment, which is currently under development. Further, the changes being proposed are consistent with the Office's efforts to harmonize with PCT practice and any changes being contemplated for that system.

Section 1.121(a) is specifically proposed to be amended by replacing paragraphs (a)(1) through (a)(6) with new paragraphs (a)(1) through (a)(5), which treat the manner of making amendments in nonprovisional applications other than reissue applications. Section 1.121(b) relates to amendments in reissue applications and § 1.121(c) relates to amendments in reexamination proceedings.

Section 1.121(a)(1)(i) is proposed to provide procedures to delete, replace or add a paragraph to the specification of an application by requiring instructions for such accompanied by the replacement or added paragraph(s). By following the four-digit numbering system concurrently proposed in § 1.52(b)(6), applicants can easily refer to a specific paragraph by number and present an amendment thereto. Proposed § 1.121(a) requires that the replacement or added paragraph(s) not include any markings to indicate the changes that have been made. A copy of the replacement or added paragraph(s) marked-up to show the changes would be required to accompany the amendment as an aid to the examiner.

If a numbered paragraph is to be replaced by a single paragraph, the added replacement paragraph bearing the same number as the paragraph being replaced should be submitted. If more than one paragraph is to replace a single paragraph, the numbering of the added replacement paragraphs must begin first with the number of the paragraph being replaced, then subsequently by the number of the replaced paragraph together with a single decimal and sequential integers (*e.g.*, paragraph [0071] is replaced by [0071], [0071.1] and [0071.2]). Any paragraphs being added between existing paragraphs must take the number of the preceding paragraph followed by a decimal and sequential integers (*e.g.*, [0071.1] and [0071.2] are being inserted between paragraphs [0071] and [0072]). Unaffected paragraphs would retain their original numbers. Once an amendment is entered, subsequent amendments would be made *vis-a-vis* the numbering created by the previous amendment. Amendments to titles or headers, which are not considered paragraphs and thus not numbered, would be identified by reference to their location relative to a numbered paragraph (*e.g.*, "the title appearing after paragraph [0062]").

Section 1.121(a)(1)(ii) as proposed also permits applicants to amend the specification by replacement sections (*e.g.*, as provided in §§ 1.77(a), 1.154(a) or 1.163(c)). As with replacement paragraphs, the amended version of a replacement section would be required to be provided in clean form and not include any markings to show the changes which have been made. A marked-up version showing the changes must accompany the actual amendment as an aid to the examiner.

Section 1.121(a)(1)(ii) as proposed also permits applicants to amend the specification by submitting a substitute specification. Sections 1.52, 1.77, 1.154, 1.163 and 1.121(a) as proposed do not require applicants to number the paragraphs of the specification (§ 1.52(b)(6)) or provide section headings (§§ 1.77, 1.154, 1.163). Without numbered paragraphs of the specification or section headings, however, an applicant will be limited to amending the application by submitting a substitute specification. Thus, applicants submitting a substitute specification as a means of amending the application (including "transition applications" filed before but amended after this proposed change to § 1.121(a) is adopted) are urged to include numbered paragraphs in the substitute specification (in the manner proposed in § 1.52(b)(6)), so that further amendments may be made by replacement paragraphs in accordance with § 1.121(a)(1)(i). An accompanying marked-up copy showing amended portions of the specification would be required. The addition of paragraph numbers in a substitute specification, however, need not be considered as an amendment to the specification requiring a marked-up showing.

Further, in applications not having numbered paragraphs, even if no amendments to the specification are being made, applicants are urged to supply a substitute specification including numbered paragraphs (consistent with § 1.52 (b)(6)) as part of the response to the first Office action, so that any future amendments to the specification may be made by numbered paragraph replacement. As stated immediately above, a marked-up copy, showing paragraph numbers as the only change, is not required.

The Office will not, upon request of applicants, number the paragraphs or sections of the specification, or accept any instructions to do the same. The Office reserves the right, however, to number or renumber the paragraphs in the printed patent as part of the publication process.

Section 1.121(a)(1)(iv) as proposed requires that matter deleted by amendment pursuant to any of the earlier paragraphs of § 1.121 could only be reinstated by a subsequent amendment presenting the previously deleted subject matter. No unentering of previously entered amendments will be permitted.

Section 1.121(a)(2) as proposed requires that all amendments to the claims be presented as totally rewritten claims. Any rewriting of a claim will be construed as a direction to cancel the previous version of the claim. *See In re Byers*, 230 F.2d 451, 455, 109 USPQ 53, 55 (CCPA 1956) (amendment of a claim by inclusion of an additional limitation had exactly the same effect as if the claim as originally presented had been canceled and replaced by a new claim). The new (or rewritten) claim must be submitted in clean form with no markings showing the changes which have been made. A marked-up version of any amended claim must be submitted on pages separate from the amendment showing the changes which have been made by way of brackets (for deleted matter) and underlining (for added matter), or by any other suitable method of comparison, in order to clearly indicate the changes made by the amendment in a form that will assist the examiner in the examination process.

Section 1.121(a)(3) is proposed to be amended to clarify the requirements for amending figures of drawing in an application. A sketch showing changes in red must be filed for approval by the examiner before new drawings in compliance with § 1.84 can be filed.

Sections 1.121(a)(5) and (a)(6) will be redesignated without change as new § 1.121(a)(4) and (a)(5).

Section 1.121(b) is proposed to be amended to transfer the provisions for amending reissue applications to § 1.173 (see discussion of § 1.173). Section 1.121(b) is specifically proposed to simply include a reference to § 1.173 for amendment of reissue applications.

Most of the comments received were in support of the proposed change to amendment practice. Some criticisms and suggestions are addressed below.

Comment: A concern was raised by a number of commenters that replacement paragraphs would make the identification of changes more obscure than the present system of using bracketing and underlining, would place an extra burden on practitioners and their staffs, and would work against reducing paper submissions if applicants were required to submit marked-up copies of the desired changes.

Response: The proposed replacement paragraph requirement is necessary to facilitate the publication of patents more expeditiously and with fewer errors. The Office's goal is to eliminate the use of red ink and bracketing/underlining in the amendment of patent applications, since OCR techniques now employed in the preparation of patents for publication can best accommodate "clean copy" insertions of amended subject matter.

The submission of marked-up copies would, for a time, increase file size but would provide the examiner with an easy way to compare the most recent amendments with earlier versions in the application files. While it may be possible for examiners to compare the clean copy with the previous version in order to detect changes, in the interest of reduced cycle time, a review of a marked-up copy of an amendment has been determined to be most effective in the examination process. The proposed requirements would provide the needed comparative basis (for paper copies) during the transition phase into an EFW environment.

Comment: A number of comments were received which expressed concern about the harmonization of the Office's amendment requirements with those of PCT and/or other foreign countries.

Response: While PCT practice currently provides for the use of replacement pages, it appears that paragraph or section replacement is being considered worldwide as electronic filing requirements are being developed. Both the JPO and the EPO currently employ paragraph numbering in their application requirements and publication procedures. No other patent examining authority has yet developed procedures for transitioning into electronic filing and practice.

Comment: Several comments received questioned the ability of word processing software to handle paragraph numbering and renumbering without extensive clerical intervention.

Response: The objective of the proposed amendment practice and the concept of paragraph numbering is to easily identify a paragraph in the specification and to not disturb the numbering of the paragraphs preceding and following the amendments/insertions. It is being concurrently proposed that § 1.52 provide for paragraph numbering according to a four digit Arabic numeral arrangement enclosed in bold brackets to be placed at the beginning of each paragraph immediately to the right of the left margin, and followed by approximately four spaces, before beginning the paragraph text (*e.g.*, [0071]). If, according to the proposed changes to § 1.121, for example, paragraph [0071] is to be replaced, another paragraph of the same number should be inserted in its place. If several paragraphs are to replace a single deleted paragraph, [0071] should, for example, be replaced by [0071], [0071.1], and [0071.2]. The ability of word processing software to renumber the remaining paragraphs should not be necessary.

Comment: Several comments suggested identifying the replacement paragraphs by page number and line number, or through the use of replacement pages.

Response: The proposed changes to § 1.121 are intended, in part, to serve the Office and its customers during a transition into an EFW environment. Accordingly, paragraph replacement via paragraph numbering will most effectively achieve the desired results. Identification of paragraphs by page and line number does not consistently and uniformly refer to the same section of the specification due to formatting and pagination differences among various word processing programs.

Comment: Several comments received suggested that the Office more aggressively pursue total electronic filing.

Response: A total EFW environment is still several years away. The proposed changes must be workable during a transition into electronic filing, and, at the same time, serve all customers adequately, including those not yet able to adapt to word processing and advanced computer techniques.

Section 1.125: Section 1.125(b)(2) is proposed to be amended to require that all the changes to the specification (rather than simply all additions and deletions) be shown in a marked-up copy. Section 1.125(b)(2) is also proposed to be amended to provide that numbering the paragraphs of the specification of record is not considered a change that must be shown. Thus, the marked-up copy of the substitute specification need not show the numbering the paragraphs of the specification of record, and no marked-up copy of the substitute specification is required if the only change is numbering of the paragraph of the specification of record. Section 1.125(c) is proposed to be amended to encourage that the paragraphs of any substitute specification be numbered in a manner consistent with § 1.52(b)(6).

Section 1.131: The heading of § 1.131 is proposed to be amended to clarify that it applies to overcoming other activities in addition to cited patents or publication. Section 1.131(a) is proposed to be amended for simplicity.

Section 1.131(a) is specifically proposed to be amended to provide that when any claim of an application or a patent under reexamination is rejected, the inventor of the subject matter of the rejected claim, the owner of the patent under reexamination, or the party qualified under §§ 1.42, 1.43, or 1.47, may submit an appropriate oath or declaration to establish invention of the subject matter of the rejected claim prior to the effective date of the reference or activity on which the rejection is based. Section 1.131(a) as proposed would eliminate the provisions that specify which bases for rejection must be applicable for § 1.131 to apply. Instead, the approach would be that § 1.131 is applicable unless the rejection is based upon a U.S. patent to another or others which claims the same patentable invention as defined in § 1.601(n) or a statutory bar. This avoids the situation in which the basis for rejection is not a statutory bar (under 35 U.S.C. 102(a) based upon prior use by others in the United States) and should be capable of being antedated, but the rejection is not specified as a basis for rejection that must be applicable for § 1.131 to apply.

Section 1.131(a) is also proposed to be amended to provide that the effective date of a U.S. patent is the date that such U.S. patent is effective as a reference under 35 U.S.C. 102(e). MPEP 2136.03 provides a general discussion of the date a U.S. patent is effective as a reference under 35 U.S.C. 102(e). Finally, § 1.131(a) is proposed to be amended to provide that prior invention may not be established under § 1.131 if either: (1) The rejection is based upon a U.S. patent to another or others which claims the same patentable invention as defined in § 1.601(n); or (2) the rejection is based upon a statutory bar.

Section 1.132: Section 1.132 is proposed to be amended to eliminate the provisions that specify which bases for rejection must be applicable for § 1.132 to apply. Instead, the approach would be that § 1.132 is applicable unless the rejection is based upon a U.S. patent to another or others which claims the same patentable invention as defined in § 1.601(n). Section 1.132 is specifically proposed to be amended to state that: (1) when any claim of an application or a patent under reexamination is rejected or objected to, an oath or declaration may be submitted to traverse the rejection or objection; and (2) an oath or declaration may not be submitted under this section to traverse a rejection if the rejection is based upon a U.S. patent to another or others which claims the same patentable invention as defined in § 1.601(n).

Sections 1.131 and 1.132 are procedural in nature that they provide mechanisms for the submission of evidence to antedate or otherwise traverse a rejection; however, they do not address the substantive effect of the submission of such evidence on the objection or rejection at issue. *See, e.g., In re Zletz*, 893 F.2d 319, 322–33, 13 USPQ 2d 1320, 1322–23 (Fed. Cir. 1990)(§ 1.131 provides an *ex parte* mechanism whereby a patent applicant may antedate subject matter in a reference); *Newell Cos.* v. *Kenney Mfg.*, 864 F.2d 757, 768–69, 9 USPQ 2d 1417, 1426–27 (Fed. Cir. 1988)(the mere submission of evidence under § 1.132 does not mandate a conclusion of patentability). An applicant's compliance with §§ 1.131 or 1.132 means that the applicant is entitled to have the evidence considered in determining the patentability of the claim(s) at issue. It does not mean that the applicant is entitled as a matter of right to have the rejection or objection of the claim(s) withdrawn.

Section 1.133: Section 1.133(a) is proposed to be amended to provide that interviews must be conducted on "Office premises" (rather than "in the examiner's rooms"). The purpose of this proposed change is to account for interviews conducted in conference rooms or by video conference.

Section 1.136: Section 1.136(c) is proposed to be added to provide that if an applicant is notified in a "Notice of Allowability" that an application is otherwise in condition for allowance, the following time periods are not extendable if set in the "Notice of Allowability" or in an Office action having a mail date on or after the mail date of the "Notice of Allowability": (1) The period for submitting an oath or declaration in compliance with § 1.63; (2) the period for submitting formal drawings set under § 1.85(c); and (3) the period for making a deposit set under § 1.809(c). See discussion of the change to § 1.85(c).

Section 1.137: Section 1.137(c) is proposed to be amended to provide that any petition under § 1.137 in either a utility or plant application filed before June 8, 1995, must be accompanied by a terminal disclaimer and fee as set forth in § 1.321 dedicating to the public a terminal part of the term of any patent granted thereon equivalent to the lesser of: (1) The period of abandonment of the application; or (2) the period extending beyond twenty years from the date on which the application for the patent was filed in the United States or, if the application contains a specific reference to an earlier filed application(s) under 35 U.S.C. 120, 121, or 365(c), from the date on which the earliest such application was filed. This proposed change will further harmonize effective treatment under the patent term provisions of 35 U.S.C. 154(b) and (c) of utility and plant applications filed before June 8, 1995, with utility and plant applications filed on or after June 8, 1995. Section 1.137(c) is also proposed to provide that its terminal disclaimer requirement does not apply to applications for which revival is sought solely for purposes of copendency with a utility or plant application filed on or after June 8, 1995, or to lapsed patents.

Section 1.138: Section 1.138 is proposed to be amended to clarify the signature requirement for a letter (or written declaration) of express abandonment. Section 1.138(a) is proposed to provide that: (1) An application may be expressly abandoned by filing in the Patent and Trademark Office a written declaration of abandonment identifying the application; and (2) express abandonment of the application may not be recognized by the Office unless it is actually received by appropriate officials in time to act thereon before the date of issue. Section 1.138(b) is proposed to provide that a written declaration of abandonment must be signed by a party authorized under § 1.33(b)(1), (b)(3), or (b)(4) to sign a paper in the application, except that a registered attorney or agent not of record who acts in a representative capacity under the provisions of § 1.34(a) when filing a continuing application may expressly abandon the prior application as of the filing date granted to the continuing application.

Section 1.152: Section 1.152 is proposed to be revised to be consistent with the proposed changes to § 1.84 (deletion of the petition requirement for color photographs and color drawings). Section 1.152 was amended in 1997 to clarify Office practice that details disclosed in the drawings or photographs filed with a design application are considered to be an integral part of the disclosed and claimed design, unless disclaimed. See Changes to Patent Practice and Procedure, Final Rule Notice, 62 FR 53131, 53164 (October 10, 1997) 1203 Off. Gaz. Pat. Office 63, 91 (October 21, 1997). A recent decision by the Federal Circuit, however, has called this practice into question. *See In re Daniels*, 144 F.3d 1452, 46 USPQ 2d 1788 (Fed. Cir. 1988), *rev'g, Ex parte Daniels*, 40 USPQ 2d 1394 (BPAI 1996). Accordingly, the Office is proposing to amend § 1.152 to eliminate these provisions. See Removal of Surface Treatment From Design Drawings Permitted, Notice, 1217 Off. Gaz. Pat. Office 19 (December 1, 1998).

Section 1.154: Section 1.154(a) is proposed to be separated into §§ 1.154(a) and 1.154(b) and the material clarified. The order of the papers in a design patent application, including the proposed application data sheet (*see* § 1.76), is proposed to be listed in § 1.154(a). The order of the sections in the specification of a design patent application is proposed to be listed in § 1.154(b). New § 1.154(c) corresponds to § 1.77(c) and provides that the section heading should be in uppercase letters without underlining or bold type.

Section 1.155: Current § 1.155 is proposed to be eliminated as being unnecessarily duplicative of the provisions of §§ 1.311(a) and 1.316, which apply to the issuance of all patents, including designs. In its place, proposed § 1.155 is proposed to be redrafted to establish a procedure to create a "rocket docket" for design applications. The procedure will be available to all design applicants who first conduct a preliminary examination search and file a request for expedited treatment accompanied by a fee commensurate with the Office cost of the expedited treatment and handling (§ 1.17(t)). The Office will require a statement that a preexamination search was conducted which must also indicate the field of search and include an information disclosure statement in compliance with § 1.98. Formal drawings in compliance with § 1.84 are required. The applications will be individually examined with priority and the clerical processing will be conducted and/or monitored by specially designated personnel to achieve expeditious processing through initial application processing and the Design Examining Group. The Office will not examine an application that is not in condition for examination even if the applicant files a request for expedited examination under this section. The requirements announced in the Advance Notice relating to constructive election of the first presented invention have been dropped.

General Comments

Of the comments received in response to the proposal to creating a "Rocket Docket" for design applications, most of the comments generally favored the proposal, by roughly a two-to-one margin.

Comment: One commenter opined that the "ultra expedited" procedure is a much needed avenue for patentees concerned with the design and marketing of seasonal, high volume consumer goods and that the procedure would attract new customers and fulfill a critical need in many industries for patent protection to stop infringement and to deter would-be infringers. Moreover, the commenter opined that recent court interpretations of the marking provisions require patented products to be marked with the patent number no matter what monetary remedy the patentee pursues and that having all of the products marked with the patent number will maximize a patentee's protection by synchronizing protection with the retail market launch.

Response: The Office envisions that these provisions will fulfill a particular need by affording rapid design protection on an expedited basis so that designs may be readily patented and marked with a patent number before marketing. At the same time, a fee will be charged to recoup estimated expected costs incurred by the Office.

Comment: Two comments opposed the idea of giving one applicant priority over others based on a fee, or the opportunity to "buy a place in line," further reasoning that the granting of priority should be based on need.

Response: The applicant is not buying a place in line, but instead is merely compensating for the extra costs for expediting the examination of the design applications. Also, if priority were to be granted based upon need, a petition would be required to determine whether the standards for awarding priority had been met. By eliminating the determination of a petition (which is required to determine need or compliance in Petitions to Make Special), the significant time required to make the determination is eliminated.

Comment: Another comment stated that the fee was unjustified in view of the fact that the current "Petition to Make Special" is available at a reduced fee.

Response: Although the current system of making cases special by petition fulfills the needs of some applicants, an additional expedited process is necessary for a quicker, streamlined filing-to-issuance procedure that does not involve the lengthy process of deciding a petition based upon need or some other type of showing. Moreover, the Petition to Make Special procedure requires a petition to be decided once the application reaches the Design Group, whereas the expedited procedure is instituted once the fee is paid and the application is ready for examination. Further, the "Petition to Make Special" will continue to be made available. Although the § 1.155 expedited examination is more costly, the cost is warranted due to more comprehensive expedited procedures to reduce processing time.

Comment: One commenter also suggested that if the Office procedure for dealing with a petition to make special is too complex, then the answer should be to simplify the Petition to Make Special procedure.

Response: The Petition to Make Special procedures are adopted for treating variety of types of cases for which a determination must be made as to whether the subject matter qualifies under the procedure; *e.g.*, whether "the invention will materially enhance the quality of the environment." On the other hand, the expedited procedure of § 1.155 is an entirely different rule which is fee-based and which may be readily decided as part of a clerical function, thereby reducing processing time and costs since the application does not need to be reviewed by a high level official.

Comment: Two comments were directed to the amount of time the examiners spend on the searching of design applications. One commenter was alarmed by the belief that design applications were examined in groups of ten or twenty and questioned the fairness of not examining the application in the order of filing and of delaying examination until a group is filled. The same commenter reasoned that design applications are easy to search and therefore hiring additional design applications examiners should allow each design application to be examined in the order of filing. The same commenter postulated that applicants should not have to pay a surcharge and perform their own search in order to obtain the examination for which they have already paid. Another commenter stated that the examiners will require additional time for searching expedited cases.

Response: Only the search phase of the examination of design applications is conducted in groups. Generally, the remainder of the examination process is done individually, unless the subject matter is so close as to involve double patenting. However, the most time consuming part of the design patent application examination is the search for prior art. Unlike the utility patent examiner, the design examiner is not concerned about claim language, but is focusing on visual characteristics that can be readily evaluated and searched. To employ economies of scale, searching is best done in groups. Generally, the size of group depends on the clustering of filing dates and similarities in subject matter. Cases are not delayed since design examiners are required to work on the "oldest-date" case. Moreover, even though a group search may be conducted, the examination is done in order of filing and the cases are not delayed to fill a group. Typically, the examiner picks the oldest date case for examination and then tries to create a group of design applications with similar subject matter for efficiency in searching. As to the comment directed to increasing the number of examiners, to dramatically increase the number of examiners might result in less efficiency due to overlapping subject matter and is not necessarily an option available based on Office priorities and budget. As to the comment regarding the payment of a "surcharge," this is to cover the costs associated with expediting the search. It is recognized that more time is required to search cases individually than that required if the searching is done in groups. As to the requirement of a search performed by the applicant, this will not only enhance the quality of the search but also ensure that applicant is prudently filing for expedited status and making an informed choice. As to the impact of the processing time for expedited cases on those regularly filed, enough resources are being provided so that the handling of expedited cases will not influence the examination of other cases.

Comment: Two comments suggested that the concept be extended to both utility and design applications.

Response: This suggestion is not being adopted at this time, since due to limited resources, the idea is best limited to design applications where due to the relative ease of copying, there is often a need for rapid patent protection.

Comment: One comment supported the measure but asked for a *quid-pro-quo* short time goal of four months.

Response: The Design Group has indicated that they will set as an objective three months cycle-time for examination and one month cycle-time for printing and guidelines for the program shall be explained to the public in the MPEP.

Comment: One comment stated there was no need for an expedited procedure since design applications "are being examined as of late relatively quickly."

Response: Nonetheless, the proposal is responsive to public need for those applicants who are willing to pay an increased, cost-offsetting fee in view of the benefits arising from further decreases in patent prosecution time.

Comment: A few comments stated in opposition to the proposal that the best solution is to hire more examiners.

Response: Although additional manpower conceivably would reduce cycle time, the Office faces certain constraints on its ability to hire more examiners and it must utilize its resources as best it can in order to meet all of the Office's goals.

Comment: Several comments supportive in concept also had specific recommendations for streamlining the application process, including prepayment or preauthorization of the issue fee, and faxing and/or telephoning all communications.

Response: As to the prepayment or preauthorization of the issue fee, this suggestion is not being adopted for reasons similar to those presented in conjunction with the proposal to eliminate preauthorization of payment of the issue fee (§ 1.311). As to making all communications by facsimile or phone, this will be encouraged where practicable and when the applicant's representative supplies a facsimile number. Multiple references, however, may prove too cumbersome for transmission by facsimile.

Comment: One comment suggested that automatic refunds be given is short time goals were not met and that a "Public Advisory Committee" be established to monitor progress and to be a point of contact for suggestions from the public.

Response: The suggestion as to automatic refunds is not being adopted in view of the unpredictability of unforeseen circumstances which might justify the failure to achieve the goal as well as lack of statutory authority to give a refund because a processing goal is not met in time. As to the "Public Advisory Committee," the Office does not foresee the need for such a committee, and the most practical point of contact would be with the design group itself, which is always open to suggestions from the public.

Section 1.163: Section 1.163(b) is proposed to be eliminated to delete the requirement for two copies of the specification for consistency with the current Office practice. See Interim Waiver of 37 C.F.R. § 1.163(b) for Two Copies of a Specification of an Application for a Plant Patent, Notice, 1213 Off. Gaz. Pat. Office 109 (August 4, 1998). Section 1.163(c) us proposed to be separated into §§ 1.163(b) and 1.163(c). The order of the papers in a plant patent application, including the proposed application data sheet (*see* § 1.76) is proposed to be listed in § 1.163(b). The order of the sections in the specification of a plant patent application is proposed to be listed in § 1.163(c). New § 1.163(d) corresponds to § 1.77(c) and provides that the section headings should be in uppercase letters without underlining or bold type.

New sections 1.163(c)(4) and 1.163(c)(5) require the plant patent applicant to state the Latin name and the variety denomination for the plant claimed. The Latin name and the variety denomination of the claimed plant are usually included in the specification of the plant patent application. The Office, pursuant to the "International Convention for the Protection of New Varieties of Plants" (generally known by its French acronym as the UPOV convention), has been asked to compile a database of the plants patented and the database must include the Latin name and the variety denomination of each patented plant. Having this information in separate sections of the plant patent application will make the process of compiling this database more efficient.

Current §§ 1.163(c)(5) through 1.163(c)(10) are proposed to be redesignated §§ 1.163(c)(6) through 1.163 (c)(11), respectfully.

Section 1.163(c)(14) and 1.163(d) are proposed to be eliminated to delete the reference to a plant patent color coding sheet. The color codes and the color coding system are generally included in the specification. Repeating the color coding information in a color coding sheet increases the risk of error and inconsistencies.

Section 1.173: The proposed changes to § 1.173 regarding identifying all occurrences of claim broadening in a reissue application, which were published in the Advance Notice (Topic 16), have been dropped in view of comments received. A number of comments were directed to the undue burden which the rule change would place on applicants and the potential for future issues in litigation re § 1.56 violations.

It is now being proposed that § 1.173 be amended to consolidate the requirements for the filing of reissue applications currently in § 1.173, the requirements for amending reissue applications currently in § 1.121, and the requirements for filing drawings would be moved to § 1.173. The proposed language consolidates many procedural and formal requirements for reissue applications into a single section. Paragraphs for separate items within this section have been proposed, in order to set forth the requirements for the specification, claims and drawings in a format which is clearer and easier to understand.

The title § 1.173 is proposed to be changed to "Reissue specification, drawings, and amendments" to more aptly describe the inclusion of all filing and amendment requirements for the specification, including the claims, and the drawing of reissue applications in a single section.

Section 1.173(a), as proposed, sets forth the current requirements for the contents of a reissue application at filing, and the existing prohibition against new matter in a reissue application.

It is proposed in § 1.173(a)(1) to now require that the specification, including the claims, be furnished in the form of a copy of the printed patent with a single column of the patent appearing on each individual page of the specification of the reissue application. This format for submitting a reissue application is currently set out in MPEP 1411. Paragraph (a)(1) would also provide that amendments made to the specification at filing must be made according to paragraph (b) of this section.

Proposed paragraph (a)(2) of § 1.173 sets forth the requirements for the drawings at the time the reissue application is filed. If clean copies (*i.e.,* good quality photocopies free of any extraneous markings) of the drawings from the original patent are supplied by applicant at the time of filing the application and the copies meet the requirements of § 1.84, no further (formal) drawings would be required. The current provision of § 1.174 requiring temporary drawings would be eliminated in view of this proposed change to § 1.173. The Office will be able to print a reissue patent using clean copies of the patent drawings. How changes to the patent drawings may be made at the time of filing of the reissue application, or during the prosecution, would now be specifically set forth and must be made in accordance with the requirements of proposed paragraph (b)(3) of this section (which are essentially the requirements of current § 1.121(b)(3)(i) and (ii)). If applicant has failed to provide clean copies of the patent drawings, or if changes are made to the drawings during the reissue prosecution, drawings in compliance with § 1.84 would continue to be required at the time of allowance. It is also proposed to eliminate the practice of transferring drawings from the patent file since clean copies of patent drawings will be acceptable for use in the printing of the reissue patent.

Section 1.173(b), as proposed, now sets out that amendments in a reissue application made at the time of filing may be made either by physically incorporating the amendments within the body of the specification (including the claims) as filed, or by a preliminary amendment (separate paper).

Paragraphs (b)(1) and (b)(2) of § 1.173 incorporate the provisions of current § 1.121(b)(1) and (b)(2) as to the manner of amending the specification and claims, respectively.

Proposed § 1.173(b)(3) would incorporate the provisions currently set forth in § 1.121(b)(3) as to amending reissue drawings.

Paragraph (c) of § 1.173, as proposed, would now require, that whenever an amendment is made to the claims, either at the time of filing or during the prosecution, the amendment must be accompanied by a statement as to the status of all patent claims and all added claims, and an explanation as to the support in the disclosure for any concurrently made changes to the claims.

Paragraph (d), as proposed, would incorporate the provisions currently set forth in § 1.121(b)(1)(iii) and (b)(2)(i)(C) as to how changes in reissue applications are shown in the specification and claims, respectively.

Paragraphs (e), (f) and (g), as proposed, merely reiterate requirements for retaining original claim numbering, amending the disclosure when required, and making amendments relative to the original patent, as are set out currently in § 1.21(b)(2)(B), (b)(4), and (b)(6), respectively.

The current requirement of § 1.121(b)(5) prohibiting enlarging the scope of the claims more than two years after the patent grant has been eliminated from proposed § 1.173 as being redundant to existing statutory language in 35 U.S.C. 251.

Section 1.174: It is proposed that § 1.174 be eliminated (and reserved) in view of the inclusion of all filing and amendment requirements for reissue drawings into proposed § 1.173. Thus, in addition to the reissue filing requirements of current § 1.173, the reissue amendment requirements of current § 1.121(b) and the reissue drawing requirements of current § 1.174 would all be included in a single rule, proposed § 1.173. The proposed changes consolidating several current rules into a single section should make all reissue filing and amendment requirements quicker to locate and easier to understand.

Section 1.176: Section 1.176 is proposed to be amended to eliminate the prohibition against requiring division in a reissue application. The Federal Circuit has indicated that 35 U.S.C. 251 does not, under certain circumstances, prohibit an applicant in a reissue application from adding claims directed to an invention which is separate and distinct from the invention defined by the original patent claims. *See In re Amos,* 953 F.2d 613, 21 USPQ 2d 1271 (Fed. Cir. 1991). Section 1.176, however, presently prohibits the Office from making a restriction requirement in a reissue application. This prohibition in § 1.176, in combination with the Federal Circuit's decision in *Amos,* frequently places an unreasonable burden on the Office in requiring the examination of multiple inventions in a single reissue application.

Section 1.176 as proposed would allow the Office to make a restriction requirement in a reissue application between claims added in a reissue application and the original patent claims, where the added claims are directed to an invention which is separate and distinct from the invention(s) defined by the original patent claims. The criteria for making a restriction requirement in a reissue application between added claims and original claims would be the same as that applied in an original application. *See* MPEP 806 through 806.05(i). *See* the discussion of § 1.77 concerning the proposed treatment of multiple reissue applications and procedures following a restriction requirement in a reissue.

The Office would continue to not require restriction among original claims of the patent (*i.e.,* among claims that were in the patent prior to filing the reissue application). In order for restriction to be required between the original patent claims and added claims, the added claims must be directed toward inventions which are separate and distinct from the invention(s) defined by the original patent claims. Restriction between multiple inventions in the added claims would also be possible provided the added claims are drawn to several separate and distinct inventions.

The changes being considered are not intended to affect the type of errors that are or are not appropriate for correction under 35 U.S.C. 251 (*e.g.,* applicant's failure to timely file a divisional application is not considered to be the type of error that can be corrected by a reissue). *See In re Watkinson,* 900 F.2d 230, 14 USPQ 2d 1407 (Fed. Cir. 1990); *In re Mead,* 581 F.2d 251, 198 USPQ 412 (CCPA 1978); *and In re Orita,* 550 F.2d 1277, 193 USPQ 145 (CCPA 1977).

Section 1.11(b) currently exempts reissue continued prosecution applications (CPAs) under § 1.53(d) from the announcement of reissue filing in the *Official Gazette.* The proposed language of § 1.176(b) further clarifies that the examination of a CPA reissue its not subject to a two-month examination delay following its filing.

Section 1.77: It is proposed that § 1.177 be modified to eliminate current requirements that divisional reissues be limited to separate and distinct parts of the thing patented, and that they be issued simultaneously unless ordered by the Commissioner. It is proposed that the rule be expanded to include continuations of reissues as well as divisionals. As a result of comments received following publication in the Advance Notice (Topic 17), none of which were opposed to the proposed changes to § 1.177, the Office is moving forward with the changes proposed.

The Federal Circuit has indicated that 35 U.S.C. 251, ¶ 2, does not place stricter limitations on the filing of continuation or divisional reissue applications than is placed by 35 U.S.C. 120 and 121 on the filing of continuation or divisional non-reissue applications. *See In re Graff,* 111 F.3d 874, 876, 42 USPQ 2d 1471, 1473 (Fed. Cir. 1997). The Federal Circuit specifically stated:

> * * * [35 U.S.C. 251, ¶ 3,] provides that the general rules for patent applications apply also to reissue applications, and [35 U.S.C. 251, ¶ 2,] expressly recognizes that there may be more than one reissue patent for distinct and separate parts of the thing patented. [35 U.S.C. 251] does not prohibit divisional or continuation reissue applications, and does not place stricter limitations on such applications when they are presented by reissue, provided of course that the statutory requirements specific to reissue applications are met. *See* [35 U.S.C. 251, ¶ 3].
>
> * * * [35 U.S.C. 251, ¶ 2,] is plainly intended as enabling, not limiting. [35 U.S.C. 251, ¶ 2,] has the effect of assuring that a different burden is not placed on divisional or continuation reissue applications, compared with divisions and continuations of original applications, by codifying [*The Corn-Planter Patent,* 90 U.S. 181 (1874),] which recognized that more than one patent can result from a reissue proceeding. Thus, [35 U.S.C. 251, ¶ 2,] places no greater burden on [a] continuation reissue application than upon a continuation of an original application; [35 U.S.C. 251, ¶ 2,] neither overrides, enlarges, nor limits the statement in [35 U.S.C. 251, ¶ 3,] that the provisions of Title 35 apply to reissues.

Graff, 111 F.3d at 876–77, 42 USPQ 2d at 1473. Thus, the Federal Circuit has indicated that a continuation or divisional reissue application is not subject to any greater burden other than the burden imposed by 35 U.S.C. 120 and 121 on a continuation or divisional non-reissue application, except that a continuation or divisional reissue application must also comply with the statutory requirements specific to reissue applications (*e.g.,* the "error without any deceptive intention" requirement of 35 U.S.C. 251, ¶ 1).

Following *Graff,* the Office has adopted a policy of treating continuations/ divisionals of reissue applications in much the same manner as continuations/ divisionals of non-reissue applications. Accordingly, it is proposed that the current requirements of § 1.177 as to petitioning for non-simultaneous issuance of multiple reissues, suspending prosecution in an allowable reissue while the other is prosecuted, and limiting the content of each reissue to separate and distinct parts of the thing patented, all be eliminated. These requirements are considered unique to reissue continuations/divisionals, impose additional burdens on reissue applicants, and are not consistent with the Federal Circuit's discussion of 35 U.S.C. 251, ¶ 2, in *Graff.*

It is proposed that § 1.177(a) be changed to require that all multiple reissue applications from a single patent include as the first line of the respective specifications a cross reference to the other reissue application(s). The statement would provide the public with notice that more than one reissue application has been filed to correct an error (or errors) in a single patent. If one reissue has already issued without the appropriate cross reference, a certificate of correction would be issued to provide the cross reference in the issued reissue.

In § 1.177(b), it is proposed that all of the claims of the patent be presented in each application as amended, unamended or canceled, and that the same claim not be presented for examination in more than one application in its original unamended version. Any added claims would have to be numbered beginning with the next highest number following the last patent claim.

If the same or similar claims were presented in more than one of the multiple reissue applications, statutory double patenting (35 U.S.C. 101) or non-statutory (judicially created doctrine) double patenting considerations would be given by the examiner during examination, and appropriate rejections made. If needed to overcome the rejections, terminal disclaimers would be required in order to ensure common ownership of any non-distinct claims throughout each of the patents' lifetimes.

It is also being proposed concurrently that restriction between the original patent claims and any added claims to separate and distinct subject matter be permitted in reissue applications (see the proposed change to § 1.176). If one or more divisional applications are filed after such a restriction requirement, it is proposed in § 1.177(c) that the resulting multiple reissue applications would be issued alone or together, but each of the reissue applications would be required to include changes which correct an error in the original patent before it can be issued as a reissue patent. If one of the applications resulting from the restriction requirement was found to be allowable without any changes relative to the patent (*i.e.,* it includes only all the original patent claims), further action would be suspended until one other reissue application was allowable; then, the two would be recombined and issued as a single reissue patent. If the several reissue applications resulting from the restriction each included changes correcting some error in the original patent, the reissue applications could be issued separately, with an appropriate cross-reference to the other(s) in each of the respective specifications.

Section 1.178: Section 1.178 is proposed to be amended to no longer require an offer to surrender the original patent at the time of filling as part of the reissue application filing requirements. The inclusion of a sentence regarding the "offer" is frequently overlooked by reissue applicants at the time of filing and results in the Office sending out a Notice to File Missing Parts of Application (Missing Parts Notice). The time spent by the Office in preparing the Missing Parts Notice, the time needed by applicant to reply, and the further time needed by the Office to process applicant's "offer" reply, can all be saved by the proposed change. The requirement for actual surrender of the original patent (or a "statement" of its loss, as set out below) before the reissue application is allowed, however, is retained.

It is also proposed that § 1.178 be amended to change "affidavit or declaration" (attesting to the loss or inaccessibility of the original patent) to "statement." This proposed change would eliminate the verification requirements of the current rule, which are formalities covered by §§ 1.4 and 10.18. This change is in conformance with other similar changes to the patent rules which were effective on December 1, 1997, to ease the verification requirements of applicants. See Changes to Patent Practice and Procedure, 62 FR at 53175–78, 1203 Off. Gaz. Pat. Office at 100–03.

Section 1.193: Section 1.193(b)(1) is proposed to be amended to provide that appellant may file a reply brief to an examiner's answer "or a supplemental examiner's answer." The purpose of this proposed amendment is to clarify the current practice that the appellant may file a (or another) reply brief within two months of a supplemental examiner's answer (§ 1.193), but the appellant must file any request for an oral hearing within two months of the examiner's answer (§ 1.194).

Section 1.303: Section 1.303(a) is proposed to be amended to add the phrase "to an interference" between "any party" and "dissatisfied with the decision of the Board of Patent Appeals and Interferences" to correct an inadvertent omission.

Section 1.311: Section 1.311(b) is proposed to be amended to provide that an authorization to charge the issue fee (§ 1.18) to a deposit account may be filed in an individual application only after mailing of the notice of allowance (PTOL–85).

The suggestion of eliminating preauthorization of payment of the issue fee was discussed in Topic 19 of the Advance Notice and received a generally favorable response. Many patent attorneys stated that they considered preauthorization a dangerous practice that they would not use. Others thought that preauthorization was an important safety feature, and that the Office should fix the internal clerical problems which were motivating the change.

After considering all of the comments, the Office has decided to go forward with the proposal to eliminate the ability of applicants to preauthorize payment of the issue fee. Section 1.311(b), as currently written, causes problems for the Office that tend to increase Office processing time. The language used by applicants to authorize that fees be charged to a deposit account often varies from one application to another. As a result, conflicts arise between the Office and applicants as to the proper interpretation of authorizing language found in their applications. For example, some applicants are not aware that it is current Office policy to interpret broad language to "change any additional fees which may be required at any time during the prosecution of the application" as authorization to charge the issue fee on applications filed on or after October 1, 1982. *See* Deposit Account Authorization to Charge Issue Fee, Notice 1095 Off. Gaz. Pat. Office 44 (October 25, 1988), *reprinted at* 1206 Off. Gaz. Pat. Office 95 (January 6, 1998).

Even when the language preauthorizing payment of the issue fee is clear, the preauthorization can present problems for both the Office and practitioners. One problem is because it may not be clear to the Office whether a preauthorization is still valid after the practitioner withdraws or the practitioner's authority to act as a representative is revoked. If the Office charges the issue fee to the practitioner's deposit account, the practitioner may have difficulty getting reimbursement from the practitioner's former client. Another problem is that when the issue fee is actually charged at the time the notice of allowance is mailed, a notice to that effect is printed on the notice of allowance (PTOL–85) and applicant is given one month to submit/return the PTOL–85B with information to be printed on the patent. Applicants are sometimes confused, however, by the usual three-month time period provided for paying the issue fee and do not, therefore, return the PTOL–85B until the end of the normal there-month period. As the Office does not wait for the PTOL–85B to be returned to begin electronic capture of the data to be printed as a patent, any PTOL–85B received more than a month after the issue fee has been paid may not be matched with the application file in time for the information thereon to be included on the patent.

Clerical problems are not the main reason for proposing to eliminate the practice. The Office would like all of the information necessary for printing a patent to be in the application when the issue fee is paid. Thus, the Office is proposing to eliminate petitions under § 3.81(b), see below, and intends to no longer print any assignee data that is submitted after payment of the issue fee. As explained in the Advance Notice, it is not generally in applicant's best interest to pay the issue fee at the time the notice of allowance is mailed, since it is much easier to have a necessary amendment or an information disclosure statement considered if filed before the issue fee is paid rather than after the issue fee is paid. See current §§ 1.97 and 1.312(b). Also, once the issue fee has been paid, applicant's window of opportunity for filing a continuing application is reduced and the applicant no longer has the option of filing a continuation or divisional application as a continued prosecution application (CPA) under § 1.53(d). *See* Patents to Issue More Quickly After Issue Fee Payment, 1220 Off. Gaz. Pat. Office at 42, and Filing of Continuing Applications, Amendments, or Petitions after Payment of Issue Fee, 1221 Off. Gaz. Pat. Office at 14. Many applicants find the time period between the mailing date of the notice of allowance and the due date for paying the issue fee useful for re-evaluating the scope of protection afforded by the allowed claim(s) and for deciding whether to pay the issue fee and/or to file one or more continuing applications.

If prompt issuance of the patent is a high priority, after receipt of the notice of allowance applicant may promptly return the PTOL–85B (supplying any desired assignee and attorney information) and pay the issue fee. In this way. the Office will be able to process the payment of the issue fee and the information on the PTOL–85B as a part of a single processing step. Further, no time would be saved even if the issue fee was preauthorized for payment as the Office would still not have the assignee and attorney data which is taken from the PTOL–85B. Thus, it is not seen that the proposal to eliminate the preauthorization to pay the issue fee would have any adverse effects on our customers.

Section 1.312: Section 1.312(a) is proposed to be amended to change "case" to "application" for clarity. Section 1.312(b) is proposed to be amended to replace the required showing of good and sufficient reason of why the amendment is needed and was not earlier presented, to provide that any amendment pursuant to § 1.312 filed after the date the issue fee is paid must be accompanied by: (1) A petition under § 1.313(c)(1) to withdraw the application from issue; (2) an unequivocal statement that one or more claims are unpatentable; and (3) an explanation as to how the amendment is necessary to render such claim or claims patentable. The proposed change to § 1.312(b) is necessary because the change in the patent printing process (discussed above with respect to § 1.55 will dramatically reduce the period between the date of issue fee payment and the date a patent is issued. In view of the brief period between the date of issue fee payment and the date a patent is issued, the Office must limit amendments under § 1.312 to those necessary to avoid the issuance of a patent containing an unpatentable claim or claims. Other amendments must be filed prior to payment of the issue fee (preferably within one month of the mailing of a notice of allowance), or be sought in a continuing application (*see* § 1.313(c)(2)) or by certificate of correction under 35 U.S.C. 255 and § 1.323.

Section 1.313: Section 1.313(a) is proposed to be amended to provide that: (1) Applications may be withdrawn from issue for further action at the initiative of the Office or upon petition by the applicant; (2) to request that the Office withdraw an application from issue, the applicant must file a petition under this section including the fee set forth in § 1.17(h) and a showing of good and sufficient reasons why withdrawal of the application is necessary; and (3) if the Office withdraws the application from issue, the Office will issue a new notice of allowance if the Office again allows the application. The changes proposed to separate the language directed to actions by applicants and those actions by the Office are also proposed to increase the clarity of the section.

Section 1.313(b) is proposed to be amended to provide that once the issue fee has been paid, the Office will not withdraw the application from issue at its own initiative for any reason except: (1) a mistake on the part of the Office; (2) a violation of § 1.56 or illegality in the application; (3) unpatentability of one or more claims; or (4) for interference. Section 1.313(c) is proposed to provide that once the issue fee has been paid, the application will not be withdrawn from issue upon petition by the applicant for any reason except: (1) Unpatentability of one or more claims (*see* § 1.312(b)); or (2) for express abandonment (which express abandonment may be in favor of a continuing application). As discussed above, changes in the patent printing process will dramatically reduce the period between the date of issue fee payment and the date a patent is issued. The Office must streamline the provisions of current § 1.313(b) or the Office will not he able to render decisions on such petitions before the application is issued as a patent.

It is the Office's experience that petitions under current § 1.313(b) are rarely filed (and even more rarely granted) on the basis of: (1) A mistake on the part of the Office: (2) a violation of § 1.56 or illegality in the application; (3) unpatentability of one or more claims; or (4) for interference. Therefore, the Office is proposing to provide that the Office may withdraw applications from issue after payment of the issue fee at its own initiative for these bases, but limit petitions under current § 1.313(b) (§ 1.313(c) as proposed) to: (1) unpatentability of one or more claims; or (2) for express abandonment, (which express abandonment may be in favor of a continuing application). If a petition under § 1.313(c) filed on the basis of unpatentability of one or more claims (§ 1.313(c)(1)), that petition must (in addition to meeting the requirements of § 1.313(a)), be accompanied by an amendment (pursuant to § 1.312), an unequivocal statement that one or more claims are unpatentable, and an explanation as to how the amendment is necessary to render such claim or claims patentable. See discussion of § 1.312(b).

Obviously, if an applicant believes that an application should be withdrawn from issue (after payment of the issue fee) on the basis of a mistake on the part of the Office, a violation of § 1.56 or illegality in the application, or for interference, the applicant may contact the examiner and suggest that the examiner request the Group Director to withdraw the application from issue at the initiative of the Office. The applicant, however, cannot insist that the Office withdraw an application from issue (after payment of the issue fee) for these reasons.

Section 1.313(d) is proposed to provide that a petition under § 1.313 will not be effective to withdraw the application from issue unless it is actually received and granted by the appropriate officials before the date of issue. Section 1.313(d) is also proposed to advise applicants that withdrawal of an application from issue after payment of the issue fee may not be effective to avoid publication of application information. While the Office takes reasonable steps to stop the publication and dissemination of application information (*e.g.*, the patent document) once an application has been withdrawn from issue, withdrawal from issue after payment of the issue fee often occurs too late in the patent printing process to completely maintain the application in confidence. How much of the application information is actually disseminated depends upon how close to the issue date the application is withdrawn from issue. The change in the patent printing process (discussed above with respect to § 1.55) will make it less likely that the Office can completely stop the publication and dissemination of application information in an application withdrawn from issue under § 1.313 after payment of the issue fee.

Section 1.314: Section 1.314 is proposed to be amended to change the reference to the fee set forth in "§ 1.17(i)" to the fee set forth in "§ 1.17(h)." This change is for consistency with the changes to § 1.17(h) and § 1.17(i). See discussion of changes to § 1.17(h) and § 1.17(i).

Section 1.322: Section 1.322(a) is proposed to be amended to provide that: (1) The Office may issue a certificate of correction under the conditions specified in 35 U.S.C. 254 at the request of the patentee or the patentee's assignee or at its own initiative; and (2) the Office will not issue such a certificate at its own initiative without first notifying the patentee (including any assignee of record) at the correspondence address of record and affording the patentee an opportunity to be heard. Section 1.322 as proposed would continue to provide that if the request relates to a patent involved in an interference, the request must comply with the requirements of this section and be accompanied by a motion under § 1.635. The current language of § 1.322(a) permits a third party of request for a certificate for correction (a party "not owning an interest in the patent"), which has led third parties to conclude that they have standing to demand that the Office issue, or refuse to issue, a certificate of correction. Third parties do not have standing to demand that the Office issue, or refuse to issue, a certificate of correction. *See Hallmark Cards, Inc.* v. *Lehman,* 959 F. Supp. 539, 543–44, 42 USPQ 2d 1134, 1138 (D.D.C. 1997). Since the burden on the Office caused by such third-party requests now outweighs the benefit such information provides to the Office, the Office is proposing to amend § 1.322 such that a certificate of correction will be issued only at the request of the patentee or at the initiative of the Office.

Section 1.323: Section 1.323 is proposed to be amended to provide that the Office may issue a certificate of correction under the conditions specified in 35 U.S.C. 255 at the request of the patentee or the patentee's assignee, upon payment of the fee set forth in § 1.20(a). The language from 35 U.S.C. 255 currently in § 1.323 that provides the specific conditions under which a certificate of correction under § 1.323 will be issued is proposed to be eliminated for consistency with § 1.322 and because it is redundant to repeat the language of the statute in the rule. Section 1.323 as proposed would continue to provide that if the request relates to a patent involved in an interference, the request must comply with the requirements of this section and be accompanied by a motion under § 1.635.

Section 1.324: Section 1.324 would have the title revised to reference the statutory basis for the rule, 35 U.S.C. 256. It is particularly important to recognize that 35 U.S.C. 256, the statutory basis for corrections of inventorship in patents under § 1.324, is stricter than 35 U.S.C. 116, the statutory basis for corrections of inventorship in applications under § 1.48. 35 U.S.C. 256 requires "on application of all the parties and assignees," while 35 U.S.C. 116 does not have the same requirement. Thus, the flexibility under 35 U.S.C. 116, and § 1.48, wherein waiver requests under § 1.183 may be submitted (*e.g.,* MPEP 201.03, page 200–6, Statement of Lack of Deceptive Intention), is not possible under 35 U.S.C. 256, and § 1.324.

Section 1.324(b)(1) would be revised to eliminate the requirement for a statement from an inventor being deleted stating that the inventorship error occurred without deceptive intent. The revision would be made to conform Office practice to judicial practice as enunciated in *Stark* v. *Advanced Magnetics, Inc.,* 119 F.3d 1551, 43 USPQ 2d 1321 (Fed. Cir. 1997), which held that 35 U.S.C. 256 only requires an inquiry into the intent of a nonjoined inventor. The clause stating "such error arose without deceptive intent on his part" was interpreted by the court as being applicable only when there is an error where an inventor is not named, and not when there is an error where a person is named as an inventor. While the decision recognized that the Office's additional inquiry as to inventors named in error was appropriate under 35 U.S.C. 256 when read in conjunction with inequitable conduct standards, the Office no longer wishes to conduct an inquiry broader in scope than what would be conducted had the matter been raised in a court proceeding rather than under § 1.324.

Section 1.324(b)(2), which requires a statement from the current named inventors either agreeing to the requested change or stating that they have no disagreement to the requested change, would not be revised. Paragraph (b)(2) in combination with paragraph (b)(1) ensures compliance with the requirement of the statute for application by all the parties, which requirement is separate from the requirement that certain parties address the lack of deceptive intent in the inventorship error.

Section 1.324(c) would be a newly added paragraph for reference §§ 1.48, 1.497 and 1.634 for corrections of inventorship in national applications. international applications and interferences, respectively.

Section 1.366: Section 1.366(c) is proposed to be amended to continue to provide that a maintenance fee payment must include the patent number and the application number of the United States application for the patent on which the maintenance fee is being paid, but to further provide that if the payment includes identification of only the patent number (*i.e.,* does not identify the application number for the patent on which the maintenance fee is being paid), the Office may apply the payment to the patent identified by patent number in the payment or may return the payment. The Office requires the application number to detect situations in which a maintenance payment is submitted for the incorrect patent (*e.g.,* due to a transposition error in the patent number). Nevertheless, a significant number of maintenance fee payments contain only the patent number and not the application number for the patent on which the maintenance fee is being paid.

The proposed change to § 1.366(c) will permit the Office to streamline processing of maintenance fee payment that lack the application number for the patent on which the maintenance fee is being paid. The Office intends to treat payments that do not contain both a patent number and application number as follows: *First,* a reasonable attempt will be made to contact the person who submitted the payment (patentee or agent) by telephone to confirm the patent number and application number of the patent for which the maintenance fee is being paid. *Second,* if such an attempt is not successful but the payment includes at least a patent number, the payment will be processed as a maintenance fee paid for the patent number provided, and the person who submitted the payment will be sent a letter informing him or her of the patent number and application number of the patent to which the maintenance fee was posted and given a period of time within which to file a petition under § 1.377 (and $130) if the maintenance fee was not posted to the patent for which the payment was intended. If the payment does not include a patent number (*e.g.,* includes only an application number), the payment will be returned to the person who submitted the payment.

Section 1.446: Section 1.446 is proposed to be amended in such that its refund provisions are consistent with the refund provisions of § 1.26. See discussion of § 1.26.

Section 1.497: Section 1.497(b)(2) has been proposed to be amended in a manner consistent with § 1.64(b). Therefore, § 1.497(b)(2) is proposed to be amended to refer to any supplemental oath or declaration and to provide that if the person making the oath or declaration is the legal representative, the oath or declaration shall state that the person is the legal representative and shall state the citizenship, residence, and mailing address of the legal representative. In addition, § 1.497(b)(2) is proposed to be amended to clarify that facts submitted under §§ 1.42, 1.43, and 1.47 are not required to be in the § 1.497 oath or declaration. Section 1.497(d) is proposed to provide for the situation in which an oath or declaration filed pursuant to 35 U.S.C. 371(c)(4) and § 1.497 names an inventive entity different from the inventive entity set forth in the international stage. Section 1.497(d) is proposed to be added to provide that such an oath or declaration must be accompanied by: (1) A statement from each person being added as an inventor and from each person being deleted as an inventor that any error in inventorship in the international stage occurred without deceptive intention on his or her part; (2) the processing fee set forth in § 1.17(1); and (3) if an assignment has been executed by any of the original named inventors, the written consent of the assignee (*see* § 3.73(b)). Thus, naming a different inventive entity in an oath or declaration filed to enter the national stage under 35 U.S.C. 371 in an international application is not analogous to the filing of an oath or declaration to complete an application under 35 U.S.C. 111(a) (which operates itself to name the new inventive entity under §§ 1.41(a)(1) and 1.48(f)(1)). but is analogous to correction of inventorship under § 1.48(a).

Section 1.510: Paragraph (b)(4) of § 1.510 is proposed to be revised to correspond to paragraph (a) of § 1.173 as revised by the present notice, see the discussion as to the revision of § 1.173. It is considered advantageous for the reexamination and reissue provisions to correspond with each other to the maximum extent possible, in order to eliminate confusion.

Section 1.530: Paragraph (d) of § 1.530 is proposed to be revised, and paragraphs (e)–(i) are proposed to be added, to correspond to paragraph (b) *et seq.* of § 1.173 as revised by the present notice, see the discussion as to the revision of § 1.173. It is considered advantageous for the reexamination and reissue provisions to correspond with each other to the maximum extent possible, in order to eliminate confusion. Paragraphs (d)(3) and (d)(4) of § 1.530 are proposed to be redesignated as paragraphs (j) and (k) of § 1.530.

Section 1.530(1) is proposed to be added to make it clear that where the inventorship of a patent being reexamined is to be corrected, a petition for correction of inventorship which complies with § 1.324 must be submitted during the prosecution of the reexamination proceeding. If the petition under § 1.324 is granted, a certificate of correction indicating the change of inventorship will not be issued, because the reexamination certificate that will ultimately issue will contain the appropriate change-of-inventorship information (*i.e.,* the certificate of correction is in effect merged with the reexamination certificate). In the rare instances where the reexamination proceeding terminates but does not result in a reexamination certificate under § 1.570 (reexamination is vacated or the order for reexamination is denied), patentee may then request that the inventorship be corrected by a certificate of correction indicating the change of inventorship.

Section 1.550: Where an application has become abandoned for failure to timely respond, the application can be revived under 35 U.S.C. 133 upon an appropriate showing of unavoidable delay via petition for revival and a petition fee. Analogously, where a reexamination proceeding becomes terminated for failure to timely respond, the proceeding can be restored to pendency under 35 U.S.C. 133 upon an appropriate showing of unavoidable delay, again via a petition and fee. *See In re Katrapat, AG,* 6 USPQ 2d 1863, 1865–66 (Comm'r Pat. 1988).

In a situation where an appropriate showing of unavoidable delay cannot be made, an abandoned application can be revived upon an appropriate showing that the delay was unintentional via a petition and fee. The showing that the delay was unintentional is a lesser standard than that of unavoidable delay; however, the required petition fee for an unintentional delay petition is substantially larger than that of an unavoidable delay petition. This unintentional delay alternative has been found to be highly desirable to deal with situations where the higher standard for revival cannot be met; to eliminate paperwork, time, and effort in making the unavoidable delay showing; and to eliminate the need to request reconsideration if the initial petition for revival is dismissed or denied.

Despite the advantages of relief to petitioners via the unintentional delay alternative, there is no such alternative in reexamination proceedings. *See Katrapat,* 6 USPQ 2d at 1866–67. It would be desirable to provide an unintentional delay alternative by rulemaking. Unfortunately, the statute does not provide a basis for unintentional delay relief in reexamination proceedings that is analogous to that for an application. The statutory basis for revival of an application based upon the unintentional delay standard is 35 U.S.C. 41(a)(7). There is no such statutory basis for restoring a reexamination proceeding to pendency based upon the unintentional delay standard.

Section 1.550(c) is proposed to be revised to provide the reexamination patentee with unintentional delay relief for any reply filed within the full statutory time period for submission of the papers that were unintentionally delayed. This relief would be provided in the form of an extension of time under § 1.550(c), which would be granted when unintentional delay is established and the appropriate extension of time fee is paid.

This avenue of unintentional delay relief is expected to deal with the majority of reexamination proceedings terminated for untimely response. The reason for this is as follows. Late responses are most often generated because of one of three reasons: (1) The patentee does not realize that an extension must be requested prior to the response due date and thus, files the response after the due date together with an extension request; (2) the patentee flies the extension request shortly prior to the due date but fails to give reasons for the extension, and the time expires before a proper reexamination extension request can subsequently be provided and (3) the patentee is aware of the need for giving reasons and for filing or the request prior to the due date, however, the reminder docket system is not set up for the reexamination type of extension request and the request is not timely or properly made. In all three of these situations, the extension generally reaches the Office prior to the full six-month statutory period for submission of the response, especially given the fact that a one- or two-month shortened statutory period is set for response in reexamination. If there is time remaining in the statutory period, the Office can notify the patentee that an extension in accordance with § 1.550(c)(2) is needed to maintain pendency.

It is understood that the proposed revision will not provide relief to patentees in all cases with an unintentional termination of reexamination proceedings. However, in the absence of a statutory amendment to providing unintentional delay relief analogous to that of 35 U.S.C. 41(a)(7) for an application, the present rule change is believed to be the best avenue available to give patentees unintentional delay relief in reexamination proceedings.

Section 1.666: Section 1.666(b) is proposed to be amended to change the reference to the fee set forth in "§ 1.17(i)" to the fee set forth in "§ 1.17(h)." This change is for consistency with the changes to § 1.17(h) and § 1.17(i). See discussion of changes to § 1.17(h) and § 1.17(i).

Section 1.720: Section 1.720(b) is proposed to be amended to clarify that a patent extended under § 1.701 or § 1.790 would also be eligible for patent term extension. Section 1.720(g) is proposed to be amended to clarify that an application for patent term extension may be timely filed during the period of an interim extension under § 1.790.

Section 1.730: Section 1.730 is proposed to be amended to add new paragraphs (b), (c) and (d) which state who should sign the patent term extension application and what proof of authority may be required of the person signing the application. 35 U.S.C. 156 provides that an application for patent term extension must be filed by the patent owner of record or an agent of the patent owner. The Office interprets an agent of a patent owner to be either a licensee of the patent owner (for example, the party that sought permission from the Food and Drug Administration for permission to commercially use or sell a product, *i.e.,* the marketing applicant), or a registered attorney or agent. Proposed § 1.730(b) explains that, if the application is submitted by the patent owner, the correspondence must be signed by the patent owner or a registered practitioner. Proposed § 1.730(c) states that, if the application is submitted by an agent of the patent owner, the correspondence must be signed by a registered practitioner, and that the Office may require proof that the agent is authorized to act on behalf of the patent owner. Lastly, proposed § 1.730(d) states that the Office may require proof of authority of a registered practitioner who signs the application for patent term extension on behalf of the patent owner or the agent of the patent owner.

Section 1.740: Currently, for each product claim, method of use claim, and method of manufacturing claim which reads on the approved product, a showing is required demonstrating the manner in which each applicable claim reads on the approved product. Section 1.740(a)(9) is proposed to be amended to provide that the application for patent term extension only needs to explain how *one* product claim claims the approved product, if there is a claim the product. In addition, the application would only need to explain how one method of use claim claims the method of use of there approved product, if the is a claim to the method of use of the product. Lastly, the application would only need to explain how one claim claims the method of manufacturing the approved product, if there is a claim to the method of manufacturing the approved product. With this proposed change, applicants for patent term extension should be able to reduce the time required to prepare the application since at the most only three claims would have to be addressed rather than all the claims that read on the three categories. Each claim that claims the approved product, the method of use of the approved product, or the method of manufacturing the approved product would still be required to be listed. *See* 35 U.S.C. 156(d)(1)(B).

Section 1.740(a)(10) is proposed to be amended to separate the text into paragraphs (A), (B) and (C) to aid in comprehension of the text.

Section 1.740(a)(14) is proposed to amended to add "and" after the semicolon since the paragraph is now the next to last paragraph.

Section 1.740(a)(15)is proposed to be amended to change the semicolon to a period.

Section 1.740(a)(16) is proposed to be moved to § 1.740(b), the number of copies changed from two to three, and to eliminate the express "certification" requirement.

Section 1.740(a)(17) is proposed to be deleted as the requirement for an oath or declaration is being deleted in § 1.740(b).

Section 1.740(b) is proposed to be amended to delete the requirement for an oath or declaration since the averments set forth in § 1.740(b) are implicit in the submission of an application for patent term extension and the signature to the application.

Section 1.740(c) is proposed to be amended to increase the time period for response to a notice of informality for an application for patent term extension from one month to two months, where the notice of informality does not set time period.

Section 1.741: Section 1.741(a) is proposed to be amended to clarify the language to reference §§ 1.8 and 1.10 instead of referencing the rules and the titles of the rules. Section 1.741 (a)(5) is proposed to be amended to correct the format of the citation of the statute. Section 1.741(b) is proposed to be amended to provide that requests for review of a decision that the application for patent term extension is incomplete, or review of the filing date accorded to the application, must be filed as a petition under § 1.741 accompanied by the fee set forth in § 1.17(h), rather than a petition under § 1.181, and that the petition must be filed within two months of the date of the notice, and that the extension of time provisions of § 1.136 apply.

Section 1.780: Section 1.780, including the title, is proposed to be amended to use terminology consistent with current practice by inserting the term "order."

Section 1.809: Section 1.809(b) is proposed to be amended to change "respond" to "reply" (*see* § 1.111), and § 1.809(b)(1) is proposed to be amended to eliminate the language discussing payment of the issue fee. Section 1.809(c) is proposed to be amended to provide that if an application for patent is otherwise in condition for allowance except for a needed deposit and the Office has received a written assurance that an acceptable deposit will be made, applicant will be notified and given a period of time within which the deposit must be made in order to avoid abandonment. Section 1.809(c) is also proposed to be amended to provide that this time period is not extendable under § 1.136 (a) or (b) (*see* § 1.136(c)). Section 1.809(c) is also proposed to be amended to eliminate the language stating that failure to make a needed deposit will result in abandonment for failure to prosecute because abandonment for failure to prosecute occurs by operation of law when an applicant fails to timely comply with such a requirement (*see* 35 U.S.C. 133).

Section 1.821: The Office indicated in the Advance Notice that the submission of sequence listings on paper is a significant burden on the applicants and the Office, and that it was considering changes to § 1.821 *et seq.* to: (1) Permit a machine-readable submission of the nucleotide and/or amino acid sequence listings to be submitted in an appropriate archival medium; and (2) no longer require the voluminous paper submission of nucleotide and/or amino acid sequence listings. *See* Changes to Implement the Patent Business Goals, 63 FR at 53510–12, 1215 Off. Gaz. Pat. Office at 99–100.

Unlike a computer program listing appendix under § 1.96(c), a sequence listing under § 1.821 is part of the disclosure of the application. The Office, however, may accept electronically filed material in a patent application, regardless of whether it is considered "essential" or "nonessential." The patent statute requires that "[a]n application for patent shall be made * * * in writing to the Commissioner." 35 U.S.C. 111(a)(1) (emphasis added). With regard to the meaning of the "in writing" requirement of 35 U.S.C. 111(a)(1). "[i]n determining any Act of Congress, unless the context indicates otherwise * * *, "writing" includes printing and typewriting and reproduction of visual symbols by photographing, multigraphing, mimeographing, manifolding, or otherwise." 1 U.S.C. 1 (emphasis added); *see also* Fed. R. Evid. 1001(1) (writing defined as including magnetic impulse and electronic recording) and title XVII of the Omnibus Consolidated and Emergency Supplemental Appropriations Act, 1999, Pub. L. 105–277, 112 Stat. 2681 (1998) (the Government Paperwork Elimination Act). An electronic document (or an electronic transmission of a document) is a "reproduction of visual symbols." and the "in writing" requirement of 35 U.S.C. 111(a)(1) does not preclude the Office from accepting an electronically filed document. Likewise, there is nothing in the patent statute that precludes the Office from designating an "electronic" record of an application file as the Office's "official" copy of the application.

As discussed with regard to the proposed change to § 1.96, CD–ROM and CD–R are the only practical electronic media of archival quality. The CD–ROM or CD–R sequence listing would serve as the "original" of the sequence listing, yet still offer the conveniences of small size and ease in viewing. Thus, the Office is specifically considering revising § 1.821 *et seq.* to permit applicants to submit the official copy of the sequence listing either on paper or on CD–ROM or CD–R.

Section 1.821(c) is proposed to be amended to provide that a "Sequence Listing" must be submitted either: (1) on paper in compliance with § 1.823(a)(1) and (b); or (2) as a CD–ROM or CD–R in compliance with § 1.823(a)(2) and (b) that will be retained with the paper file. Section 1.821 is also proposed to be amended to provide that applicant may submit a second copy of the CD–ROM or CD–R "Sequence Listing" to satisfy the requirement for a "Sequence Listing" in a computer readable format pursuant to § 1.821(e), provided that the CD–ROM or CD–R "Sequence Listing" meets the requirements of § 1.824(c)(4). However, in order for a sequence listing to be a part of an international application, it must be filed in paper.

Section 1.821(e) and § 1.821(f) are proposed to be amended for consistency with the provisions in § 1.821(c) that permit the official copy of the "Sequence Listing" required by § 1.821(c) to be a paper or a CD–ROM or CD–R copy. Should these provisions be adopted, conforming changes may be made in the regulations to accommodate international applications in the national stage.

Section 1.823: The heading of § 1.823 is proposed to be amended for consistency with the provisions in § 1.821(c) that permit the official copy of the "Sequence Listing" required by § 1.821(c) to be a paper or a CD–ROM or CD–R copy. Section 1,823(a) is proposed to be amended to be divided into a paragraph (a)(i) that sets forth its current requirement as applying if the "Sequence Listing" submitted pursuant to § 1.821(c) is on paper, and a paragraph (a)(2) setting forth the requirements if the "Sequence Listing" submitted pursuant to § 1.821(c) is on a CD–ROM or CD–R. Section 1.823(a)(2) is proposed to provide that: (1) a "Sequence Listing" submitted on a CD–ROM or CD–R must be a text file in the American Standard Code for Information Interchange (ASCII) in accordance with the standards for that medium set forth in 36 CFR 1228.188(c)(2)(i) (no other format allowed); (2) the CD–ROM or CD–R "Sequence Listing" must be accompanied by documentation on paper that contains the machine format (*e.g.,* IBM–PC, Macintosh (etc.)), the operating system (*e.g.,* MS–DOS, Macintosh, Unix) and any other special information that is necessary to identify, maintain, and interpret the electronic "Sequence Listings"; and (3) a notation that "Sequence Listing" is submitted on a CD–ROM or CD–R must be placed conspicuously in the specification (*see* § 1.77(b)(11)). Section 1.823(a)(2) is also proposed to provide that the CD–ROM or CD–R "Sequence Listing" must be labeled with the following information: (1) The name of each inventor (if known); (2) title of the invention; (3) the sequence identifiers of the "Sequence Listings" on that CD–ROM or CD–R; and (4) the docket number used by the person filing the application to identify the application (if applicable). Finally, § 1.823(c)(4) is proposed to be amended to refer to CD–R (as well as the CD–ROM currently provided for). Should these provisions be adopted, conforming changes may be made in the regulations to accommodate international applications in the national stage.

Section 1.825: Section 1.825(a) is proposed to be amended to provide that any amendment to the CD–ROM or CD–R copy of the "Sequence Listing" submitted pursuant to § 1.821 must be made by submission of a new CD–ROM or CD–R containing a substitute "Sequence Listing," and that such amendments must be accompanied by a statement that indicates support for the amendment in the application-as-filed, and a statement that the new CD–ROM or CD–R includes no new matter. Section 1.825(b) is proposed to be amended to provide that any amendment to the CD–ROM or CD–R copy of the "Sequence Listing" pursuant to § 1.825(a) must be accompanied by a substitute copy of the computer readable form of the "Sequence Listing" required pursuant to § 1.821(e), including all previously submitted data with the amendment incorporated therein, and accompanied by a statement that the computer readable form copy is the same as the new CD–ROM or CD–R copy of the "Sequence Listing." Should these provisions be adopted, conforming changes may be made in the regulations to accommodate international applications in the national stage.

The comments are addressed above in the discussion of the proposed change to § 1.96. See discussion of § 1.96.

Part 3

Section 3.27: Section 3.27 is proposed to be amended to eliminate the reference to petitions under § 3.81(b) and the reference to a document required by Executive Order 9424 which does not affect title. See discussion of § 3.81(b).

Section 3.71: It is proposed that § 3.71 be revised as discussed immediately below. In conjunction with the proposed revision, the section would be broken into paragraphs (a) through (d), with each paragraph being given a heading, in order to more clearly delineate the topics of the paragraphs.

Proposed paragraph (a) of § 3.71 would clarify that the assignee must be of record in a U.S. national patent application in order to conduct prosecution in place of the inventive entity (the inventors of the application) or any previous assignee that was entitled to conduct prosecution.

Paragraph (b) of§ 3.71 has been proposed in order to clarify and define what is meant by the § 3.71(a) assignee which may conduct the prosecution of a U.S. national application for a patent.

A national patent application is owned by the inventor(s), an assignee or assignees of the inventor(s), or some combination of the two. All parties having a portion of the ownership must act together in order to be entitled to conduct the prosecution.

If there is an assignee of the entire right, title and interest in the patent application, § 3.71(b)(1) (as proposed) states that the single assignee may act alone to conduct the prosecution of an application.

If there is no assignee of the entire right, title and interest of the patent application, then two possibilities exist:

(1) The application has not been assigned; thus, ownership resides solely in the inventor(s) (*i.e.,* the applicant(s)). In this situation, § 3.71 does not apply (since there is no assignee), and the single inventor, or the combination of all the joint inventors, is needed to conduct the prosecution of an application.

(2) The application has been assigned; thus, there is at least one "partial assignee." As pointed out in § 3.71(b)(2), a partial assignee is any assignee of record who has less than the entire right, title and interest in the application. The application will be owned by the combination of all partial assignees and all inventors who have not assigned away their right, title and interest in the application. As proposed, § 3.71(b)(2) points out that where at least one inventor retains an ownership interest together with the partial assignee(s), the combination of all partial assignees and inventors retaining ownership interest is needed to conduct the prosecution of an application. Where no inventor retains an ownership interest, the combination of all partial assignees is needed to conduct the prosecution of an application.

To illustrate this, note as follows. Inventors A and B invent a process and file their application. Inventors A and B together may conduct prosecution. Inventor A then assigns his/her rights in the application to Corporation X. As soon as Corporation X (now a partial assignee) is made of record in the application as a partial assignee (by filing a statement pursuant to § 3.73(b) stating fifty percent ownership). Corporation X and Inventor B together may conduct prosecution. Corporation X and Inventor B then both assign their rights in the application to Corporation Y. As soon as Corporation Y (now an assignee of the entire right, title and interest) is made of record in the application as the assignee (by filing a statement pursuant to § 3.73(b) stating one-hundred percent ownership), Corporation Y may, by itself, conduct prosecution.

This definition of the assignee would apply wherever the assignee is permitted to take action in the prosecution of an application for patent.

Proposed paragraph (c) of § 3.71 defines the meaning of the term "of record" used in proposed paragraph (b) of § 3.71. An assignee is made of record in an application by filing a statement which is in compliance with § 3.73(b). Note that the assignee being made "of record" in an application is different than the recording of an assignment in the assignment records of the Office pursuant to § 3.11.

Proposed paragraphs (a) through (c) of § 3.71 have been drafted to allow for the situation where an assignee takes action in the prosecution of a reexamination proceeding (in addition to that where a patent application is involved). In a reexamination, the assignee has the entire right, title and interest in the patent upon which reexamination is based.

Proposed paragraph (d) of § 3.71, concerning trademarks, expands the list of actions an assignee may take or request. Specifically, an assignee may also rely on its federal trademark application or registration when filing papers against a third party. This subsection also corrects the inappropriate use of the term "prosecution" when referring to maintaining a registered trademark.

In various places in proposed § 3.71, "national" has been added before "application." Section 3.71 is directed to national applications as defined in § 1.9(a)(1) and not to international (PCT) applications. In an international (PCT) application the assignee is often the applicant for some, or all, of the designated states (except the U.S.) and may control prosecution as the applicant. Section 3.71 would apply to international applications after entry into the U.S. national stage under 35 U.S.C. 371.

Section 3.73: In Paragraph (a) of § 3.73, it is proposed to revise the second sentence to include a trademark registration, in addition to a trademark application which is currently recited. The sentence would read: "The original applicant is presumed to be the owner of a trademark application or registration, unless there is an assignment."

Under the proposal, paragraph (b) of § 3.73 would be revised for clarity and paragraph formatting. Additionally, paragraph (b) of § 3.73 is proposed to be revised to clarify that the statement establishing ownership must explicitly identify the assignee (by adding the language "a signed statement identifying the assignee * * *"). Paragraph (b) of § 3.73 is further proposed to be revised to make it clear that while the submission establishing ownership is separate from, and in addition to, the specific action taken by the assignee (*e.g.,* appointing a new attorney), the two may be presented together as part of the same paper. This would be done by adding that "The establishment of ownership by the assignee may be combined with the paper that requests or takes the action."

Currently, paragraph (b) of § 3.73 requires that the submission (statement) establishing ownership "must be signed by a party authorized to act on behalf of the assignee." Under the proposal, this language would be expanded upon by newly added paragraph (b)(2) of § 3.73 which would clarify what is acceptable to show that the party signing the submission is authorized to act on behalf of the assignee. (1) The submission could include a statement that the party signing the submission is authorized to act on behalf of the assignee. (2) Alternatively, the submission could be signed by a person having apparent authority to sign on behalf of the assignee, *e.g.,* an officer of the assignee.

In the first case, the statement that the party signing the submission is authorized to act on behalf of the assignee could be an actual statement included in the text of the submission that the signing person "is authorized to act on behalf of the assignee." Alternatively, it could be in the form of a resolution by the organization owning the property (*e.g.,* a corporate resolution, a partnership resolution) included with the submission.

In the second case, the title of the person signing must be given in the submission, and it must be one which empowers the person to act on behalf of the assignee, The president. vice-president, secretary, treasurer, and chairman of the board of directors are presumed to have authority to act on behalf of the organization. Modifications of these basic titles are acceptable, such as vice-president for sales, executive vice-president, assistant treasurer, vice-chairman of the board of directors. A title such as manager, director, administrator, or general counsel does not clearly set forth that the person is an officer of the organization, and as such, does not provide a presumption of authority to sign the statement on behalf of the assignee. A power of attorney from the inventors or the assignee to a practitioner to prosecute an application does not make that practitioner an official of an assignee and does not empower the practitioner to sign the statement on behalf of the assignee.

Proposed new paragraph (c)(1) of § 3.73 would require that the submission establishing ownership by the assignee must be submitted prior to, or at the same time, that the paper requesting or taking action is submitted. If the submission establishing ownership is not present, the action sought to be taken will not be given effect.

Proposed new paragraph (c)(2) of § 3.73 would point out that for patents, if an assignee of less than the entire right, title and interest (*i.e.,* a partial assignee) fails to indicate in the submission the extent (*e.g.,* by percentage) of its ownership interest, the Office may refuse to accept the submission.

Section 3.81: Section 3.81 is proposed to be amended to eliminate the provisions of § 3.8(b). As discussed above, changes in the patent printing process will dramatically reduce the period between the date of issue fee payment and the date a patent is issued. This change will eliminate the opportunity for providing an assignee name after the date the issue fee is paid.

Part 5

Section 5.1: Section 5.1 is proposed to be amended to locate its current text in § 5.1(a).

Section 5.1 is also proposed to be amended to add a § 5.1(b) to clarify that application as used in Part 5 includes provisional applications filed under 35 U.S.C. 111(b) (§ 1.9(a)(2)), nonprovisional applications filed under 35 U.S.C. 111(a) or entering the national stage from an international application after compliance with 35 U.S.C. 371 (§ 1.9(a)(3)), or international applications filed under the Patent Cooperation Treaty prior to entering the national stage of processing (§ 1.9(b)).

Section 5.1 is also proposed to be amended to add a § 5.1(c) to state current practice that: (1) Patent applications and documents relating thereto that are national security classified (*see* § 1.9(i)) and contain authorized national security markings (*e.g.,* "Confidential," "Secret" or "Top Secret") are accepted by the Office: and (2) national security classified documents filed in the Office must be either hand-carried to Licensing and Review or mailed to the Office in compliance with § 5.1(a).

Section 5.1 is also proposed to be amended to add a § 5.1(d) to provide that: (1) The applicant in a national security classified patent application must obtain a secrecy order pursuant to § 5.2(a); (2) if a national security classified patent application is filed without a notification pursuant to § 5.2(a), the Office will set a time period within which either the application must be declassified, or the application must be placed under a secrecy order pursuant to § 5.2(a), or the applicant must submit evidence of a good faith effort to obtain a secrecy order pursuant to § 5.2(a) from the relevant department or agency in order to prevent abandonment of the application; and (3) if evidence of a good faith effort to obtain a secrecy order pursuant to § 5.2(a) from the relevant department or agency is submitted by the applicant within the time period set by the Office, but the application has not been declassified or placed under a secrecy order pursuant to § 5.2(a), the Office will again set a time period within which either the application must be declassified, or the application must be placed under a secrecy order pursuant to § 5.2(a), or the applicant must submit evidence of a good faith effort to again obtain a secrecy order pursuant to § 5.2(a) from the relevant department or agency in order to prevent abandonment of the application. Section 5.1(d) as proposed sets forth the treatment of national security classified applications that is currently set forth in MPEP 130.

Section 5.1 is also proposed to be amended to add a § 5.1(e) to provide that a national security classified patent application will not be allowed pursuant to § 1.311 of this chapter until the application is declassified and any secrecy order pursuant to § 5.2(a) has been rescinded.

Section 5.1 is also proposed to be amended to add a § 5.1(f) to clarify that applications on inventions not made in the United States and on inventions in which a U.S. Government defense agency has a property interest will not be made available to defense agencies.

Section 5.2: Section 5.2(c) is proposed to be added to provide that: (1) An application disclosing any significant part of the subject matter of an application under a secrecy order pursuant to § 5.2(a) also falls within the scope of such secrecy order; (2) any such application that is pending before the Office must be promptly brought to the attention of Licensing and Review, unless such application is itself under a secrecy order pursuant to § 5.2(a); and (3) any subsequently filed application containing any significant part of the subject matter of an application under a secrecy order pursuant to § 5.2(a) must either be hand-carried to Licensing and Review or mailed to the Office in compliance with § 5.1(a).

Section 5.12: Section 5.12(b) is proposed to be amended to require that the fee set forth in § 1.17(h) is required for any petition under § 5.12 for a foreign filing license.

As a practical matter, all petitions under § 5.12 are treated on an expedited basis. Therefore, it is appropriate to require the fee set forth in § 1.17(h) for all petitions under § 5.12.

Part 10

Section 10.23: Section 10.23(c)(11) is proposed to be amended to add the phrase "[e]xcept as permitted by § 1.52(c)" for consistency with the proposed amendment to § 1.52(c).

Review Under the Paperwork Reduction Act of 1995 and Other Considerations

This Notice is in conformity with the requirements of the Regulatory Flexibility Act (5 U.S.C. 601 *et seq.*), Executive Order 12612 (October 26, 1987), and the Paperwork Reduction Act of 1995 (44 U.S.C. 3501 *et seq.*). It has been determined that this rulemaking is not significant for the purposes of Executive Order 12866 (September 30, 1993).

This notice involves information collection requirements which are subject to review by the Office of Management and Budget (OMB) under the Paperwork Reduction Act of 1995 (44 U.S.C. 3501 *et seq.*). The collections of information involved in this notice have been reviewed and previously approved by OMB under the following control numbers: 0651–0016, 0651–0020, 0651–0021, 0651–0022, 0651–0024, 0651–0027, 0651–0031, 0651–0032, 0032, 0651–0033, 0651–0034, 0651– and 0651–0037.

As required by the Paperwork Reduction Act of 1995 (44 U.S.C. 3507(d)), the Patent and Trademark Office has submitted an information collection package to OMB for its review and approval of the proposed information collections under OMB control numbers 0651–0031, 0651–0032, and 0651–0035. The Patent and Trademark Office is submitting information collection packages to OMB for its review and approval of these information collections because the following changes proposed in this notice do affect the information collection requirements associated with the information collections under OMB control numbers 0651–0031, 0651–0032, and 0651–0035: (1) The proposed change to §§ 1.27 and 1.28 will permit an applicant to establish small entity status in an application by a simple assertion of entitlement to small entity status (without a statement having a formalistic reference to § 1.9 or a standard form (PTO/SB/09/10/11/12)): (2) the proposed change to §§ 1.55, 1.63 and 1.78 would eliminate the need for an applicant using the application data sheet (§ 1.76) to provide priority claims in the oath or declaration or specification; (3) the proposed change to § 1.96 would require applicants to submit lengthy computer listings on a CD–ROM or CD–R (rather than microfiche); (4) the proposed change to §§ 1.821, 1.823, and 1.825 would permit applicants to submit sequence listings on a CD–ROM or CD–R (rather than paper); and (5) the proposed change to § 1.155 would allow an applicant to seek expedited examination of a design application by filing a request for expedited examination.

As discussed above, the notice also involves currently approved information collections under OMB control numbers: 0651–0016, 0651–0020, 0651–0021, 0651–0022, 0651–0024, 0651–0027, 0651–0033, 0651–0034, and 0651–0037. The Patent and Trademark Office is not resubmitting information collection packages to OMB for its review and approval of these information collections because the changes proposed in this notice do not affect the information collection requirements associated with the information collections under these OMB control numbers.

The title, description and respondent description of each of the information collections are shown below with an estimate of each of the annual reporting burdens. Included in each estimate is the time for reviewing instructions, gathering and maintaining the data needed, and completing and reviewing the collection of information. Any collections of information whose requirements will be revised as a result of the proposed rule changes discussed in this notice will be submitted to OMB for approval. The principal impact of the changes under consideration in this notice is to raise the efficiency and effectiveness of the Patent and Trademark Office's business processes to make the Patent and Trademark Office a more business-like agency and increase the level of the Patent and Trademark Office's service to the public.

OMB Number: 0651–0016.

Title: Rules for Patent Maintenance Fees.

Form Numbers: PTO/SB/45/47/65/66.

Type of Review: Approved through July of 1999.

Affected Public: Individuals or Households, Business or Other For-Profit, Not-for-Profit Institutions and Federal Government.

Estimated Number of Respondents: 273,800.

Estimated Time Per Response: 0.08 hour.

Estimated Total Annual Burden Hours: 22,640 hours.

Needs and Uses: Maintenance fees are required to maintain a patent, except design or plant patents, in force under 35 U.S.C. 41(b). Payment of maintenance fees are required at 3½, 7½ and 11½ years after the grant of the patent. A patent number and application number of the patent on which maintenance fees are paid are required in order to ensure proper crediting of such payments.

OMB Number: 0651–0020.

Title: Patent Term Extension.

Form Numbers: Note.

Type of Review: Approved through September of 2001.

Affected Publication: Individuals or households, businesses or other for-profit, not-for-profit institutions, farms, Federal Government, and state, local, or tribal governments.

Estimated Number of Respondents: 57.

Estimated Time Per Response: 22.8 hour.

Estimated Total Annual Burden Hours: 1,302 hours.

Needs and Uses: The information supplied to the PTO by an applicant seeking a patent term extension is used by the Patent and Trademark Office, the Department of Health and Human Services, and the Department of Agriculture to determine the eligibility of a patent for extension and to determine the period of any such extension. The applicant can apply for patent term and interim extensions petition the Patent and Trademark Office to review final eligibility decisions, and withdraw patent term extensions. If there are multiple patents, the applicant can designate which patents should be extended. An applicant can also declare their eligibility to apply for a patent term extension.

OMB Number: 0651–0021.

Title: Patent Cooperation Treaty.

Form Numbers: PCT/RO/101, ANNEX/134/144, PTO–1382, PCT/IPEA/401, PCT/IB/328.

Type of Review: Approved through May of 2000.

Affected Public: Individuals or Households, Business or Other For-Profit, Federal Agencies or Employees, Not-for-Profit Institutions, Small Businesses or Organizations.

Estimated Number of Respondent: 102,950.

Estimated Time Per Response: 0.9538 hour.

Estimated Total Annual Burden Hours: 98,195 hours.

Needs and Uses: The information collected is required by the Patent Cooperation Treaty (PCT). The general purpose of the PCT is to simplify the filing of patent applications on the same invention in different countries. It provides for a centralized filing procedure and a standardized application format.

OMB Number: 0651–0022.

Title: Deposit of Biological Materials for Patent Purposes.

Form Numbers: None.

Type of Review: Approved through December of 2000.

Affected Public: Individuals or Households, State or local Governments, Farms, Business or Other For-Profit, Federal Agencies or Employees, Not-for-Profit Institutions, Small Businesses or Organizations.

Estimated Number of Respondents: 3,300.

Estimated Time Per Response: 1.0 hour.

Estimated Total Annual Burden Hours: 3,300 hours.

Needs and Uses: Information on depositing or biological materials in depositories is required for (1) Office determination of compliance with the patent statute where the invention sought to be patented relies on biological material subject to deposit requirement, which includes notifying interested members of the public where to obtain samples of deposits, and (2) depositories desiring to be recognized as suitable by the Office.

OMB Number: 0651–0024.

Title: Requirements for Patent Applications Containing Nucleotide Sequence and/or Amino Acid Sequence Disclosures.

Form Numbers: None.

Type of Review: Approved through November or 1999.

Affected Public: Individuals or households, business or other for-profit institutions, not-for-profit institutions, and Federal Government.

Estimated Number of Respondents: 4,600.

Estimated Time Per Response: 80 minutes.

Estimated Total Annual Burden Hours: 6,133 hours.

Needs and Uses: This information is used by the Office during the examination process, the public and the patent bar. The Patent and Trademark Office also participates with the EPO and JPO in a Trilateral Sequence Exchange project, to facilitate the international exchange or published sequence data.

OMB Number: 0651–0027.

Title: Changes in Patent and Trademark Assignment Practices.

Form Numbers: PTO–1618 and PTO–1619, PTO/SB/15/41.

Type of Review: Approved through May of 2002.

Affected Public: Individuals or Households and Businesses or Other For-Profit.

Estimated Number of Respondents: 209,040.

Estimated Time Per Response: 0.5 hour.

Estimated Total Annual Burden Hours: 104,520 hours.

Needs and Uses: The Office records about 209,040 assignments or documents related to ownership of patent and trademark cases each year. The Office requires a cover sheet to expedite the processing of these documents and to ensure that they are properly recorded.

OMB Number: 0651–0031.

Title: Patent Processing (Updating).

Form Numbers: PTO/SB/08/21–27/31/42/43/61/62/63/64/67/68/91/92/96/97.

Type of Review: Approved through September of 2000.

Affected Public: Individuals or Households, Business or Other For-Profit Institutions, Not-for-Profit Institutions and Federal Government.

Estimated Number of Respondents: 2,040,630.

Estimated Time Per Response: 0.39 hours.

Estimated Total Annual Burden Hours: 788,421 hours.

Needs and Uses: During the processing for an application for a patent, the applicant/agent may be required or desire to submit additional information to the Office concerning the examination of a specific application. The specific information required or which may he submitted includes: Information Disclosure Statements; Terminal Disclaimers; Petitions to Revive; Express Abandonments; Appeal Notices; Petitions for Access; Powers to Inspect; Certificates of Mailing or Transmission; Statements under § 3.73(b); Amendments, Petitions and their Transmittal Letters; and Deposit Account Order Forms.

OMB Number: 0651–0032.

Title: Initial Patent Application.

Form Number: PTO/SB/01–07/13PCT/17–19/29/101–110.

Type of Review: Approved through September of 2000.

Affected Public: Individuals or Households, Business or Other For-Profit, Not-for-Profit Institutions and Federal Government.

Estimated Number of Respondents: 344,100.

Estimated Time Per Response: 8.7 hours.

Estimated Total Annual Burden Hours: 2,994,160 hours.

Needs and Uses: The purpose of this information collection is to permit the Office to determine whether an application meets the criteria set forth in the patent statute and regulations. The standard Fee Transmittal form, New Utility Patent Application Transmittal form, New Design Patent Application Transmittal form, New Plant Patent Application Transmittal form, Declaration, and Plant Patent Application Declaration will assist applicants in complying with the requirements of the patent statute and regulations, and will further assist the Office in processing and examination of the application.

OMB Number: 0651–0033.

Title: Post Allowance and Refiling.

Form Numbers: PTO/SB/13/14/44/50–57; PTOL–85b.

Type of Review: Approved through September of 2000.

Affected Public: Individuals or Households, Business or Other For-Profit, Not-for-Profit Institutions and Federal Government.

Estimated Number of Respondents: 135,250.

Estimated Time Per Response: 0.325 hour.

Estimated Total Annual Burden Hours: 43,893 hours.

Needs and Uses: This collection of information is required to administer the patent laws pursuant to title 35, U.S.C., concerning the issuance of patents and related actions including correcting errors in printed patents, refiling of patent applications, requesting reexamination of a patent, and requesting a reissue patent to correct an error in a patent. The affected public includes any individual or institution whose application for a patent has been allowed or who takes action as covered by the applicable rules.

OMB Number: 0651–0034.

Title: Secrecy/License to Export.

Form Numbers: None.

Type of Review: Approved through January of 2001.

Affected Public: Individuals or Households, Business or Other For-Profit, Not-for-Profit Institutions and Federal Government.

Estimated Number of Respondents: 2,187

Estimated Time Per Response: 0.67 hour.

Estimated Total Annual Burden Hours: 1,476 hours.

Needs and Uses: In the interest of national security, patent laws and regulations place certain limitations on the disclosure of information contained in patents and patent applications and on the filing of applications for patent in foreign countries.

OMB Number: 0651–0035.

Title: Address-Affecting Provisions.

Form Numbers: PTO/SB/81–84/121–125.

Type of Review: Approved through June of 1999.

Affected Public: Individuals or Households, Business or Other For-Profit, Not-for-Profit Institutions and Federal Government.

Estimated Number of Respondents: 263,520.

Estimated Time Per Response: 0.05 hour.

Estimated Total Annual Burden Hours: 13,386 hours.

Needs and Uses: Under existing law, a patent applicant or assignee may appoint, revoke or change a representative to act in a representative capacity. Also, an appointed representative may withdraw from acting in a representative capacity. This collection includes the information needed to ensure that Office correspondence reaches the appropriate individual.

OMB Number: 0651–0037.

Title: Provisional Applications.

Form Numbers: PTO/SB/16.

Type of Review: Approved through January of 2001.

Affected Public: Individuals or Households, Business or Other For-Profit, Not-for-Profit Institutions and Federal Government.

Estimated Number of Respondents: 25,000.
Estimated Time Per Response: 8.0 hour.
Estimated Total Annual Burden Hours: 200,000 hours.

Needs and Uses: The information included on the provisional application cover sheet is needed by the Office to identify the submission as a provisional application and not some other kind of submission, to promptly and properly process the provisional application, to prepare the provisional application filing receipt which is sent to the applicant, and to identify those provisional applications which must be reviewed by the Office for foreign filing licenses.

Notwithstanding any other provision of law, no person is required to respond to nor shall a person be subject to a penalty for failure to comply with a collection of information subject to the requirements of the Paperwork Reduction Act unless that collection of information displays a currently valid OMB control number.

As required by the Paperwork Reduction Act of 1995 (44 U.S.C. 3507(d)), the Patent and Trademark Office has submitted an information collection package to OMB for its review and approval of the proposed information collections under OMB control numbers 0651–0031, 0651–0032, and 0651–0035. As discussed above, the notice also involves currently approved information collections under OMB control numbers: 0651–0016, 0651–0020, 0651–0021, 0651–0022, 0651–0024, 0651–0027, 0651–0033, 0651–0034, and 0651–0037. The Patent and Trademark Office is not resubmitting information collection packages to OMB for its review and approval of these information collections because the changes proposed in this notice do not materially affect, or change the burden hours associated with, these information collections.

Interested persons are requested to send comments regarding these information collections, including suggestions for reducing this burden, to Robert J. Spar Director, Special Program Law Office, Patent and Trademark Office, Washington, D.C. 20231, or to the Office of Information and Regulatory Affairs of OMB, New Executive Office Building, 725 17th Street, NW, room 10235, Washington, DC 20503, Attention: Desk Officer for the Patent and Trademark Office.

The Chief Counsel for Regulation of Department of Commerce certified to the Chief Counsel for Advocacy, Small Business Administration, that the changes proposed in this rule, if adopted, would not have a significant impact on a substantial number of small entities (Regulatory Flexibility Act, 5 U.S.C. 605(b)). In furtherance of the Patent Business Goals, the Office is proposing changes to the rules of practice to eliminate unnecessary formal requirements, streamline the patent application process, and simplify and clarify procedures. In streamlining this process, the Office will be able to issue a patent in a shorter time by eliminating formal requirements that must be performed by the applicant, his or her representatives and the Office. All applicants will benefit from a reduced overall cost to them for receiving patent protection and from a faster receipt of their patents. In addition, small entities will benefit from the proposed changes to the requirements for establishing small entity status under § 1.27 for purposes of paying reduced patent fees under 35 U.S.C. 41(h). The currently used small entity statement forms are proposed to be eliminated. Small entity status would be established at any time by a simple assertion of entitlement 10 small entity status. A simpler procedure to establish small entity status would reduce processing time with the Office and would be a benefit to small entity applicants as it would eliminate the time-consuming and aggravating processing requirements that are mandated by the current rules.

The Patent and Trademark Office has determined that this notice has no Federalism implications affecting the relationship between the National Government and the States as outlined in Executive Order 12612.

List of Subjects

37 CFR Part 1

Administrative practice and procedure, Courts, Freedom of information, Inventions and patents, Reporting and recordkeeping requirements, Small businesses.

37 CFR Part 3

Administrative practice and procedure, Inventions and patents, Reporting and record keeping requirements.

37 CFR Part 5

Classified information, Foreign relations, Inventions and patents.

37 CFR Part 10

Administrative practice and procedure, Inventions and patents, Lawyers, Reporting and recordkeeping requirements.

For the reasons set forth in the preamble, 37 CFR parts 1, 3, 5, and 10 are proposed to be amended as follows:

PART 1—RULES OF PRACTICE IN PATENT CASES

1. The authority citation for 37 CFR part 1 is revised to read as follows:

Authority: 35 U.S.C. 6, unless otherwise noted.

2. Section 1.4 is proposed to be amended by revising paragraphs (b) and (c) to read as follows:

§ 1.4 Nature of correspondence and signature requirements.

* * * * *

(b) Since each file must be complete in itself, a separate copy of every paper to be filed in a patent or trademark application, patent file, trademark registration file, or other proceeding must be furnished for each file to which the paper pertains, even though the contents of the papers filed in two or more files may be identical. The filing of duplicate copies of correspondence in the file of an application, patent, trademark registration file, or other proceeding should be avoided, except in situations in which the Office requires the filing of duplicate copies. The Office may dispose of duplicate copies of correspondence in the file of an application, patent, trademark registration file, or other proceeding.

(c) Since different matters may be considered by different branches or sections of the Patent and Trademark Office, each distinct subject, inquiry or order must be contained in a separate paper to avoid confusion and delay in answering papers dealing with different subjects.

* * * * *

3. Section 1.6 is proposed to be amended by revising paragraph (d)(9) to read as follows:

§ 1.6 Receipt of correspondence.

* * * * *

(d) * * *

(9) Correspondence to be filed in an interference proceeding which consists of a preliminary statement under § 1.621; a transcript of a deposition under § 1.676 or of interrogatories, or cross-interrogatories; or an evidentiary record and exhibits under § 1.653.

* * * * *

4. Section 1.9 is proposed to be amended by removing and reserving paragraphs (c), (d) and (e), and revising paragraph (f) and adding a new paragraph (i) to read as follows:

§ 1.9 Definitions.

* * * * *

(f) *Small entities.* A small entity as used in this chapter means any party (person, small business concern, or nonprofit organization) under paragraphs (f)(1) through (f)(3) of this section.

(1) *Person:* A person, as used in § 1.27(b), means any inventor or other individual (*e.g.,* an individual to whom an inventor has transferred some rights in the invention), who *has not* assigned granted, conveyed, or licensed, and is under no obligation under contract or law to assign, grant, convey, or license, any rights in the invention. An inventor or other individual who *has* transferred some rights, or is under an obligation to transfer some rights in the invention to one or more parties, can also qualify for small entity status if all the parties who have had rights in the invention transferred to them also qualify for small entity status either as a person, small business concern, or nonprofit organization under this section.

(2) *Small business concern:* A small business concern, as used in § 1.27(b), means any business concern that:

(i) Has not assigned, granted, conveyed, or licensed, and is under no obligation under contract or law to assign, grant, convey, or license, any rights in the invention to any person, concern, or organization which would not qualify under this section for small entity status as a person, small business concern, or nonprofit organization.

(ii) Meets the size standards set forth in 13 CFR part 121 to be eligible for reduced patent fees. Questions related to size standards for a small business concern may be directed to: Small Business Administration, Size Standards Staff, 409 Third Street, SW, Washington, DC 20416.

(3) *Nonprofit organization.* A nonprofit organization, as used in § 1.27(b), means any nonprofit organization that:

(i) Has not assigned, granted, conveyed, or licensed, and is under no obligation under contract or law to assign, grant, convey, or license, any rights in the invention to any person who could not qualify for small entity status, or to any concern or organization which would not qualify as a small business concern, or a nonprofit organization under this section, and

(ii) Is either:

(A) A university or other institution of higher education located in any country;

(B) An organization of the type described in section 501(c)(3) of the Internal Revenue Code of 1986 (26 U.S.C. 501(c)(3)) and exempt from taxation under section 501(a) of the Internal Revenue Code (26 U.S.C. 501(a));

(C) Any nonprofit scientific or educational organization qualified under a nonprofit organization statute of a state of this country (35 U.S.C. 201(i)); or

(D) Any nonprofit organization located in a foreign country which would qualify as a nonprofit organization under paragraphs (f)(3)(ii)(B) or (f)(3)(ii)(C) of this section if it were located in this country.

(4) *License to a Federal Agency.* (i) For persons under paragraph (f)(1) of this section, a license to the Government resulting from a rights determination under Executive Order 10096 does not constitute a license so as to prohibit claiming small entity status.

(ii) For small business concerns and nonprofit organizations under paragraphs (f)(2) and (f)(3) of this section, a license to a Federal agency resulting from a funding agreement with that agency pursuant to 35 U.S.C. 202(c)(4) does not constitute a license.

* * * * *

(i) National security classified as used in this chapter means specifically authorized under criteria established by an Act of Congress or Executive order to be kept secret in the interest of national defense or foreign policy and, in fact, properly classified pursuant to such Act of Congress or Executive order.

5. Section 1.12 is proposed to be amended by revising paragraph (c)(1) to read as follows:

§ 1.12 Assignment records open to public inspection.

* * * * *

(c) * * *

(1) Be in the form of a petition including the fee set forth in § 1.17(h); or

* * * * *

6. Section 1.14 is proposed to be revised to read as follows:

§ 1.14 Patent applications preserved in confidence.

(a) *Confidentiality of patent application information.* Patent applications are generally preserved in confidence pursuant to 35 U.S.C. 122. Information concerning the filing, pendency, or subject matter of an application for patent, including status information, and access to the application, will only be given to the public as set forth in § 1.11 or in this section.

(1) *Status information* is:

(i) Whether the application is pending, abandoned, or patented; and

(ii) The application "numerical identifier" which may be:

(A) The eight digit application number (the two digit series code plus the six digit serial number); or

(B) The six digit serial number plus any of the filing date of the national application, the international filing date, or date or entry into the national stage.

(2) *Access* is defined as providing the application file for review and copying of any material.

(b) *When status information may be supplied.* Status information of an application may be supplied by the Office to the public if any of the following apply:

(1) Access to the application is available pursuant to paragraph (e) of this section;

(2) The application is referred to by its numerical identifier in a published patent document (*e.g.*, a U.S. patent or a published international application) or in a U.S. application open to public inspection (§ 1.11(b) or paragraph (e)(2)(i) of this section); or

(3) The application is a published international application in which the United States of America has been indicated as a designated state.

(c) *Copy of application-as-filed.* If a pending or abandoned application is incorporated by reference in a U.S. patent, a copy of that application-as-filed may be provided to any person upon written request including the fee set forth in § 1.19(b)(1).

(d) *Power to inspect a pending or abandoned application may be granted by a party named in the application file.* Access to an application may be provided to any person if the application file is available, and the application contains written authority (*e.g.*, a power to inspect) in that particular application granting access to such person that is signed by:

(1) An applicant;

(2) An attorney or agent of record;

(3) An authorized official of an assignee of record (made of record pursuant to § 3.71 of this chapter); or

(4) A registered attorney or agent named in papers accompanying the application papers filed under § 1.53 or the national stage documents filed under §§ 1.494 or 1.495, if an executed oath or declaration pursuant to § 1.63 or § 1.497 has not been filed.

(e) *Public access to a pending or abandoned application may be provided.* Access to an application may be provided to any person if a written request for access is submitted, the application file is available, and any of the following apply:

(1) The application is open to public inspection pursuant to § 1.11(b): or

(2) The application is abandoned, it is not within the file Jacket of a pending application under § 1.53(d), and it is referred to:

(i) In a U.S. patent; or

(ii) In another U.S. application which is open to public inspectIon either pursuant to § 1.11(b) or paragraph (e)(2)(i) or this section.

(f) *Applications that may be destroyed.* Applications that are abandoned or for which proceedings are otherwise terminated may be destroyed, and thus may not be available for access as permitted by paragraphs (d) or (e) of this section, after twenty years from their filing or deposit date. Exceptions may be made for applications to which particular attention has been called and which have been marked for preservation.

(g) *Applications reported to Department of Energy.* Applications for patents which appear to disclose, purport to disclose or do disclose inventions or discoveries relating to atomic energy are reported to the Department of Energy, which Department will be given access to the applications. Such reporting does not constitute a determination that the subject matter of each application so reported is in fact useful or is an invention or discovery, or that such application in fact discloses subject matter in categories specified by 42 U.S.C. 2181 (c) and (d).

(h) *Decisions by the Commissioner or the Board of Patent Appeals and Interferences.* Any decision by the Commissioner or the Board of Patent Appeals and Interferences which would not otherwise be open to public inspection may be published or made available for public inspection if:

(1) The Commissioner believes the decision involves an interpretation of patent laws or regulations that would be of precedential value; and

(2) The applicant, or a party involved in an interference for which a decision was rendered, is given notice and an opportunity to object in writing within two months on the ground that the decision discloses a trade secret or other confidential information. Any objection must identify the deletions in the text of the decision considered necessary to protect the information, or explain why the entire decision must be withheld from the public to protect such information. An applicant or party will be given time, not less than twenty days, to request reconsideration and seek court review before any portions of a decision are made public under this paragraph over his or her objection.

(i) *Publication pursuant to § 1.47.* Information as to the filing of an application will be published in the *Official Gazette* in accordance with § 1.47 (a) and (b).

(j) *International applications.* Copies of an application file for which the United States acted as the International Preliminary Examining Authority, or copies of a document in such an application file, will be furnished in accordance with Patent Cooperation Treaty (PCT) Rule 94.2 or 94.3, upon payment of the appropriate fee (§ 1.19(b)(2) or § 1.19(b)(3)).

(k) *Access or copies in other circumstances.* The Office, either *sua sponte* or on petition, may also provide access or copies of an application if necessary to carry out an Act of Congress or if warranted by other special circumstances. Any petition by a member of the public seeking access to, or copies of, any pending or abandoned application preserved in confidence pursuant to paragraph (a) of this section, or any related papers, must include:

(1) The fee set forth in § 1.17(h); and

(2) A showing that access to the application is necessary to carry out an Act of Coneess or that special circumstances exist which warrant petitioner being granted access to the application.

7. Section 1.17 is proposed to be amended by revising paragraphs (h), (i), (k), (l), (m), and (q) and adding paragraph (t) to read as follows:

§ 1.17 National application processing fees.

* * * * *

(h) For filing a petition to the Commissioner under a section listed below which refers to this paragraph $130.00
§ 1.12—for access to an assignment record.
§ 1.14—for access to an application.
§ 1.47—for filing by other than all the inventors or a person not the inventor.
§ 1.53(e)—to accord a filing date.
§ 1.59—for expungement and return of information.
§ 1.91—for entry of a model or exhibit.
§ 1.102—to make an application special.
§ 1.103(a)—to suspend action in application.
§ 1.182—for decision on a question not specifically provided for.
§ 1.183—to suspend the rules.
§ 1.295—for review of refusal to publish a statutory invention registration.
§ 1.313—to withdraw an application from issue.
§ 1.314—to defer issuance of a patent.
§ 1.377—for review of decision refusing to accept and record payment of a maintenance fee filed prior to expiration of a patent.
§ 1.378(e)—for reconsideration of decision on petition refusing to accept delayed payment of maintenance fee in an expired patent.
§ 1.550(c)(2)—for a petition for an extension of time to accept an unintentionally delayed response in a reexamination proceeding.
§ 1.644(e)—for petition in an interference.
§ 1.644(f)—for request for reconsideration of a decision on petition in an interference.
§ 1.666(b)—for access to an interference agreement.
§ 1.666(c)—for late filing of interference settlement agreement.
§ 1.741(b)—to accord a filing date to an application for extension of a patent term.
§ 5.12—for expedited handling of a foreign filing license.
§ 5.15—for changing the scope of a license.
§ 5.25—for retroactive license.

(i) Processing fee for taking action under a section listed below which refers to this paragraph 130.00
§ 1.28(c)(3)—for processing a non-itemized fee deficiency based on an error in small entity status.
§ 1.41—for supplying the name or names of the inventor or inventors after the filling date without an oath or declaration as prescribed by § 1.63, except in provisional applications.
§ 1.48—for correcting inventorship, except in provisional applications.
§ 1.52(d)—for processing a nonprovisional application filed with a specification in a language other than English.
§ 1.55—for entry of late priority papers.
§ 1.103(b)—for requesting limited suspension of action in continued prosecution application.
§ 1.497(d)—for filing an oath or declaration pursuant to 35 U.S.C. 371(c)(4) naming an inventive entity different from the inventive entity set forth in the international stage.

* * * * * *

(k) For accepting color drawings or color photographs (§ 1.84(a)) 200.00

(l) For filing a petition for the revival of an unavoidably abandoned application under 35 U.S.C. 111, 133, 364, or 371, or the unavoidably delayed payment of the issue fee under 35 U.S.C. 151 (§ 1.137(a)):
By a small entity (§ 1.9(f)) 55.00
By other than a small entity 110.00

(m) For filing a petition for the revival of an unintentionally abandoned application or the unintentionally delayed payment of the issue fee under 35 U.S.C. 41(a)(7) (§ 1.137(b)):
By a small entity (§ 1.9(f)) 605.00
By other than a small entity 1,210.00

* * * * * *

(q) Processing fee for taking action under a section listed below which refers to this paragraph	50.00
§ 1.41—to supply the name or names of the inventor or inventors after the filing date without a cover sheet as prescribed by § 1.51(c)(1) in a provisional application.	
§ 1.48—for correction of inventorship in a provisional application.	
§ 1.53(c)—to convert a nonprovisional application filed under § 1.53(b) to a provisional application under § 1.53(c)	

* * * * * *

(t) For filing a request for expedited examination under § 1.155(a)	900.00

8. Section 1.19 is proposed to be amended by revising its introductory text and paragraphs (a) and (b) and removing paragraph (h) to read as follows:

§ 1.19 Document supply fees.

The Patent and Trademark Office will supply copies of the following documents upon payment of the fees indicated. The copies will be in black and white unless the original document is in color, a color copy is requested and the fee for a color copy is paid.

(a) Uncertified copies of patents:	
(1) Printed copy of a patent, including a design patent, statutory invention registration, or defensive publication document:	
(i) Regular service	$3.00
(ii) Overnight delivery to PTO Box or overnight facsimile	6.00
(iii) Expedited service for copy ordered by expedited mail or facsimile delivery service and delivered to the customer within two workdays	25.00
(2) Printed copy of a plant patent in color	15.00
(3) Color copy of a patent (other than a plant patent) or statutory invention registration containing a color drawing	25.00
(b) Certified and uncertified copies of Office documents:	
(1) Certified or uncertified copy of patent application as filed:	
(i) Regular service	15.00
(ii) Expedited regular service	30.00
(2) Certified or uncertified copy of patent-related file wrapper and contents:	
(i) File wrapper and content of 400 or fewer pages	250.00
(ii) Additional fee for each additional 100 pages or portion thereof	25.00
(3) Certified or uncertified copy of Office records, per document except as otherwise provided in this section	25.00
(4) For assignment records, abstract of title and certification, per patent	25.00

* * * * * *

9. Section 1.22 is proposed to be amended by revising paragraph (b) and adding paragraph (c) to read as follows:

§ 1.22 Fee payable in advance.

* * * * *

(b) All fees paid to the Patent and Trademark Office must be itemized in each individual application, patent, trademark registration file, or other proceeding in such a manner that it is clear for which purpose the fees are paid. The Office may return fees that are not itemized as required by this paragraph. The provisions of § 1.5(a) do not apply to the resubmission of fees returned pursuant to this paragraph.

(c)(1) A fee paid by an authorization to charge such fee to a deposit account containing sufficient funds to cover the applicable fee amount (§ 1.25) is considered paid:

(i) On the date the paper for which the fee is payable is received in the Office (§ 1.6), if the paper including the deposit account charge authorization was filed prior to or concurrently with such paper;

(ii) On the date the paper including the deposit account charge authorization is received in the Office (§ 1.6), if the paper including the deposit account charge authorization is filed after the filing of the paper for which the fee is payable; and

(iii) On the date of the agreement, if the deposit account charge authorization is the result of an agreement between the applicant and an Office employee that is reduced to a writing.

(2) A fee paid other than by an authorization to charge such fee to a deposit account is considered paid on the date the applicable fee amount is received in the Office (§ 1.6).

(3) The applicable fee amount is determined by the fee in effect on the date such fee is paid in full.

10. Section 1.25 is proposed to be amended by revising paragraph (b) to read as follows:

§ 1.25 Deposit accounts.

* * * * *

(b) Filing, issue, appeal, international-type search report, international application processing, petition, and post-issuance fees may be charged against these accounts if sufficient funds are on deposit to cover such fees. A general authorization to charge all fees, or only certain fees, set forth in § 1.16 to § 1.18 to a deposit account containing sufficient funds may be filed in an individual application, either for the entire pendency of the application or with respect to a particular paper filed. An authorization to charge fees under § 1.16 in an application submitted under § 1.494, or § 1.495 will be treated as an authorization to charge fees under § 1.492. An authorization to charge fees set forth in § 1.18 to a deposit account is subject to the provisions of § 1.311(b). An authorization to charge to a deposit account the fee for a request for reexamination pursuant to § 1.510 and any other fees required in a reexamination proceeding in a patent may also be filed with the request for reexamination. An authorization to charge a fee to a deposit account will not be considered payment of the fee on the date the authorization to charge the fee is effective as to the particular fee to be charged unless sufficient funds are present in the account to cover the fee.

11. Section 1.26 is proposed to be amended by revising paragraph (a) and adding paragraph (b) to read as follows:

§ 1.26 Refunds.

(a) The Commissioner may refund a fee paid by mistake or in excess of that required. A change of purpose after the payment of a fee, as when a party desires to withdraw a patent or trademark filing for which the fee was paid, including an application, an appeal, or a request for an oral hearing, will not entitle a party to a refund of such fee. The Office will not refund amounts of twenty-five dollars or less unless a refund is specifically requested, and will not notify the payor of such amounts. If a party paying a fee or requesting a refund does not instruct the Office that refunds are to be credited to a deposit account, and does not provide the banking information necessary for making refunds by electronic funds transfer, the Commissioner may either require such banking information or use the banking information on the payment instrument to make a refund.

(b) Any request for refund must be filed within two years from the date the fee was paid, except as otherwise provided in this paragraph or in § 1.28(a). If the Office charges a deposit account by an amount other than an amount specifically indicated in an authorization (§ 1.25(b)), any request for refund based upon such charge must be filed within two years from the date of the deposit account statement indicating such charge, and include a copy of that deposit account statement. The time periods set forth in this paragraph are not extendable.

* * * * *

12. Section 1.27 is proposed to be revised to read as follows:

§ 1.27 Establishing status as small entity to permit payment of small entity fees; when a determination of entitlement to small entity status and notification of loss of entitlement to small entity status are required; fraud on the Office.

(a) *Establishment of small entity status permits payment of reduced fees.* A small entity, as defined in § 1.9(f), who has properly asserted entitlement to small entity status pursuant to paragraph (b) of this section will be accorded small entity status by the Office in the particular application or patent in which entitlement to small entity status was asserted. Establishment of small entity status allows the payment of certain reduced patent fees pursuant to 35 U.S.C. 41(h).

(b) *Assertion of small entity status.* Any party (person, small business concern or nonprofit organization) who has made a determination, pursuant to paragraph (e) of this section, of entitlement to be accorded small entity status pursuant to § 1.9(f) must, in order to establish small entity status for the purpose of paying small entity fees, make an assertion of entitlement to small entity status, pursuant to paragraph (b)(1) or (b)(3) of this section, in the application or patent in which such small entity fees are to be paid.

(1) *Assertion by writing.* Small entity status may be established by a written assertion of entitlement to small entity status. A written assertion must:

(i) Be clearly identifiable;

(ii) Be signed; and

(iii) Convey the concept of entitlement to small entity status, such as by stating that applicant is a small entity, or that small entity status is entitled to be asserted for the application or patent. While no specific words or wording are required to assert small entity status, the intent to assert small entity status must be clearly indicated in order to comply with the assertion requirement.

(2) *Parties who can sign the written assertion.* The written assertion can be signed by:

(i) One of the parties identified in § 1.33(b) (*e.g.*, an attorney or agent registered with the Office), § 3.73(b) of this chapter notwithstanding;

(ii) At least one of the inventors, § 1.33(b)(4) notwithstanding; or

(iii) An assignee of an undivided part interest, §§ 1.33(b)(3) and 3.73(b) of this chapter notwithstanding.

(3) *Assertion by payment of the small entity basic filing or national fee.* The payment, by any party, of the exact amount of one of the small entity basic filing fees set forth in § 1.16(a), (f), (g), (h), or (k), or one of the small entity national fees set forth in § 1.492(a)(1), (a)(2), (a)(3), (a)(4), or (a)(5), will be treated as a written assertion of entitlement to small entity status even if the type of basic filing or national fee is inadvertently selected in error.

(i) If the Office accords small entity status based on payment of a small entity fee that is not applicable to that application, any balance of the small entity fee that is applicable to that application will be due.

(ii) The payment of any small entity fee other than those set forth in paragraph (b)(3) (whether in the exact fee amount or not) of this section will not be treated as a written assertion of entitlement to small entity status and will not be sufficient to establish small entity status in an application or a patent.

(4) *Assertion required in related, continuing, and reissue applications.* Status as a small entity must be specifically established by an assertion in each related, continuing and reissue application in which status is appropriate and desired. Status as a small entity in one application or patent does not affect the status of any other application or patent, regardless of the relationship of the applications or patents. The refiling of an application under § 1.53 as a continuation, divisional, or continuation-in-part application (including a continued prosecution application under § 1.53(d)), or the filing of a reissue application, requires a new assertion as to continued entitlement to small entity status for the continuing or reissue application.

(c) *When small entity fees can be paid.* Any fee, other than the small entity basic filing fees and the small entity national fees of paragraph (b)(3) of this section, can be paid in the small entity amount only if it is submitted with, or subsequent to, the submission of a written assertion of entitlement to small entity status, except when refunds are permitted by § 1.28(a).

(d) *Only one assertion required.* (1) An assertion of small entity status need only be filed once in an application or patent. Small entity status, once established, remains in effect until changed pursuant to § 1.28(b) of this part. Where an assignment of rights or an obligation to assign rights to other parties who are small entities occurs subsequent to an assertion of small entity status, a second assertion is not required.

(2) Once small entity status is withdrawn pursuant to paragraph (f)(2) of this section, a new written assertion is required to again obtain small entity status.

(e) *Assertion requires a determination of entitlement to pay small entity fees.* Prior to submitting an assertion of entitlement to small entity status in an application, including a related, continuing, or reissue application, a determination of such entitlement should be made pursuant to the requirements of § 1.9(f). It should be determined that all parties holding rights in the invention qualify for small entity status. The Office will generally not question any assertion of small entity status that is made in accordance with the requirements of this section, but note paragraph (g) of this section.

(f)(1) *New determination of entitlement to small entity status is needed when issue and maintenance fees are due.* Once status as a small entity has been established in an application or patent, fees as a small entity may thereafter be paid in that application or patent without regard to a change in status until the issue fee is due or any maintenance fee is due.

(2) *Notification of loss of entitlement to small entity status is required when issue and maintenance fees are due.* Notification of a loss of entitlement to small entity status must be filed in the application or patent prior to paying, or at the time of paying, the earliest of the issue fee or any maintenance fee due after the date on which status as a small entity as defined in § 1.9(f) is no longer appropriate. The notification that small entity status is no longer appropriate must be signed by a party identified in § 1.33(b). Payment of a fee in other than the small entity amount is not sufficient notification that small entity status is no longer appropriate.

(g) *Fraud attempted or practiced on the Office.* (1) Any attempt to fraudulently establish status as a small entity, or to pay fees as a small entity, shall be considered as a fraud practiced or attempted on the Office.

(2) Improperly, and with intent to deceive, establishing status as a small entity, or paying fees as a small entity, shall be considered as a fraud practiced or attempted on the Office.

13. Section 1.28 is proposed to be revised to read as follows:

§ 1.28 Refunds when small entity status is later established; how errors in small entity status are excused.

(a) *Refunds based on later establishment of small entity status:* A refund pursuant to § 1.26 of this part, based on establishment of small entity status, of a portion of fees timely paid in full prior to establishing status as a small entity may only be obtained if an assertion under § 1.27(b) and a request for a refund of the excess amount are filed within three months of the date of the timely payment of the full fee. The three-month time period is not extendable under § 1.136. Status as a small entity is waived for any fee by the failure to establish the status prior to paying, at the time of paying, or within three months of the date of payment of, the full fee.

(b) *Date of payment.* (1) The three-month period for requesting a refund, pursuant to paragraph (a) of this section, starts on the date that a full fee has been paid as defined in § 1.22(c);

(2) The date when a deficiency payment is paid in full determines the amount of deficiency that is due, pursuant to paragraph (c) of this section, and is defined in § 1.22(c).

(c) *How errors in small entity status are excused.* If status as a small entity is established in good faith, and fees as a small entity are paid in good faith, in any application or patent, and it is later discovered that such status as a small entity was established in error, or that through error the Office was not notified of a loss of entitlement to small entity status as required by § 1.27(f)(2), the error will be excused upon: compliance with the separate submission and itemization requirements of paragraphs (c)(1) and (c)(2) of this section, and the deficiency payment requirement of paragraph (c)(2) of this section:

(1) *Separate submission required for each application or patent.* Any paper submitted under this paragraph must be limited to the deficiency payment (all fees paid in error), required by paragraph (c)(2) of this section, for one application or one patent. Where more than one application or patent is involved, separate submissions of deficiency payments (*e.g.*, checks) and itemizations are required for each application or patent. *See* § 1.4(b).

(2) *Payment of deficiency owed.* The deficiency owed, resulting from the previous erroneous payment of small entity fees, must be paid.

(i) *Calculation of the deficiency owed.* The deficiency owed for each previous fee erroneously paid as a small entity is the difference between the current fee amount (for other than a small entity) on the date the deficiency is paid in full and the amount of the previous erroneous (small entity) fee payment. The total deficiency payment owed is the sum of the individual deficiency owed amounts for each fee amount previously erroneously paid as a small entity;

(ii) *Itemization of the deficiency payment.* An itemization of the total deficiency payment is required. The itemization must include the following information:

(A) Each particular type of fee that was erroneously paid as a small entity, (*e.g.*, basic statutory filing fee, two-month extension of time fee) along with the current fee amount for a non-small entity;

(B) The small entity fee actually paid, and when. This will permit the Office to differentiate, for example, between two one-month extension of time fees erroneously paid as a small entity but on different dates;

(C) The deficiency owed amount (for each fee erroneously paid); and

(D) The total deficiency payment owed, which is the sum or total of the individual deficiency owed amounts set forth in paragraph (c)(2)(ii)(C) of this section.

(3) *Failure to comply with requirements.* If the requirements of paragraphs (c)(1) and (c)(2) of this section are not complied with, such failure will either: be treated as an authorization for the Office to process the deficiency payment and charge the processing fee set forth in § 1.17(i), or result in a requirement for compliance within a one-month non-extendable time period to avoid the return of the fee deficiency paper, at the option of the Office.

(d) *Payment of deficiency operates as notification of loss of status.* Any payment submitted under paragraph (c) of this section will be treated under § 1.27(f)(2) as a notification of a loss of entitlement to small entity status.

14. Section 1.33 is proposed to be amended by revising paragraphs (a) and (b) to read as follows:

§ 1.33 Correspondence respecting patent applications, reexamination proceedings, and other proceedings.

(a) *Correspondence address and daytime telephone number.* When filing an application, a correspondence address must be set forth in either an application data sheet (§ 1.76), or elsewhere in a clearly identifiable manner in any paper submitted with an application filing. If no correspondence address is specified, the Office may treat the mailing address of the first named inventor (if provided, see § 1.76(b)(1) and § 1.63(c)(2)) as the correspondence address. The Office will direct all notices, official letters, and other communications relating to the application to the correspondence address. The Office will not engage in double correspondence with an applicant and an attorney or agent, or with more than one attorney or agent except as deemed necessary by the Commissioner. If more than one correspondence address is specified, the Office will establish one as the correspondence address. For the party to whom correspondence is to be addressed, a daytime telephone number should be supplied in a clearly identifiable manner and may be changed by any party who may change the correspondence address. The correspondence address may be changed as follows:

(1) *Prior to filing of a § 1.63 oath or declaration by any of the inventors.* If a § 1.63 oath or declaration has not been filed by any of the inventors, the correspondence address may be changed by the party who filed the application. If the application was filed by a registered attorney or agent, any other registered practitioner named in the transmittal papers may also change the correspondence address. Thus, the inventor(s), any registered practitioner named in the transmittal papers accompanying the original application, or a party that will be the assignee who filed the application, may change the correspondence address in that application under this paragraph.

(2) *Where a § 1.63 oath or declaration has been filed by any of the inventors.* If a § 1.63 oath or declaration has been filed, or is filed concurrent with the filing of an application, by any of the inventors, the correspondence address may be changed by the parties set forth in paragraph (b) of this section, except for (b)(2).

(b) *Amendments and other papers:* Amendments and other papers filed in the application must be signed by:

(1) An attorney or agent of record appointed in compliance with § 1.34(b);

(2) A registered attorney or agent not of record who acts in a representative capacity under the provisions of § 1.34(a);

(3) An assignee as provided for under § 3.71(b) of this chapter; or

(4) All of the applicants (§ 1.41(b)) for patent, unless there is an assignee of the entire interest and such assignee has taken action in the application in accordance with § 3.71 of this chapter.

* * * * *

15. Section 1.41 is proposed to be amended by revising paragraph (a) to read as follows:

§ 1.41 Applicant for patent.

(a) A patent is applied for in the name or names of the actual inventor or inventors.

(1) The inventorship of a nonprovisional application is that inventorship set forth in the oath or declaration as prescribed by § 1.63, except as provided for in § 1.53(d)(4) and § 1.63(d). If an oath or declaration as prescribed by § 1.63 is not filed during the pendency of a nonprovisional application, the inventorship is that inventorship set forth in the application papers filed pursuant to § 1.53(b), unless applicant files a paper including the processing fee set forth in § 1.17(i) and supplying or changing the name or names of the inventor or inventors.

(2) The inventorship of a provisional application is that inventorship set forth in the cover sheet as prescribed by § 1.51(c)(1). If a cover sheet as prescribed by § 1.51(c)(1) is not filed during the pendency of a provisional application, the inventorship is that inventorship set forth in the application papers filed pursuant to § 1.53(c), unless applicant files a paper including the processing fee set forth in § 1.17(q) and supplying or changing the name or names of the inventor or inventors.

(3) In a nonprovisional application filed without an oath or declaration as prescribed by § 1.63 or a provisional application filed without a cover sheet as prescribed by § 1.51(c)(1), the name, residence, and citizenship of each person believed to be an actual inventor should be provided when the application papers pursuant to § 1.53(b) or (c) are filed.

(4) The inventors who submitted an application under §§ 1.494 or 1.495 are the inventors in the international application designating the United States.

* * * * *

§ 1.44 [Removed and reserved]

16. Section 1.44 is proposed to be removed and reserved.
17. Section 1.47 is proposed to be revised to read as follows:

§ 1.47 Filing when an inventor refuses to sign or cannot be reached.

(a) If a joint inventor refuses to join in an application for patent or cannot be found or reached after diligent effort, the application may be made by the other inventor on behalf of himself or herself and the nonsigning inventor. The oath or declaration in such an application must be accompanied by a petition including proof of the pertinent facts, the fee set forth in § 1.17(h), and the last known address of the nonsigning inventor. The nonsigning inventor may subsequently join in the application on filing an oath or declaration complying with § 1.63.

(b) Whenever all of the inventors refuse to execute an application for patent, or cannot be found or reached after diligent effort, a person to whom an inventor has assigned or agreed in writing to assign the invention, or who otherwise shows sufficient proprietary interest in the matter justifying such action, may make application for patent on behalf of and as agent for all the inventors. The oath or declaration in such an application must be accompanied by a petition including proof of the pertinent facts, a showing that such action is necessary to preserve the rights of the parties or to prevent irreparable damage, the fee set forth in § 1.17(h), and the last known address of all of the inventors. An inventor may subsequently join in the application on filing an oath or declaration complying with § 1.63.

(c) The Office will send notice of the filing of the application to all inventors who have not joined in the application at the address(es) provided in the petition under this section, and publish notice of the filing of the application in the *Official Gazette.* The Office may dispense with this notice provision in a continuation or divisional application, if notice regarding the filing of the prior application was given to the nonsigning inventor(s).

18. Section 1.48 is proposed to be revised to read as follows:

§ 1.48 Correction of inventorship in a patent application, other than are issue application, pursuant to 35 U.S.C. 116.

(a) *Nonprovisional application after oath/declaration filed.* If the inventive entity is set forth in error in an executed § 1.63 oath or declaration in a nonprovisional application, and such error arose without any deceptive intention on the part of the person named as an inventor in error or on the part of the person who through error was not named as an inventor, the inventorship of the nonprovisional application may be amended to name only the actual inventor or inventors. If the nonprovisional application is involved in an interference, the amendment must comply with the requirements of this section and must be accompanied by a motion under § 1.634. Amendment of the inventorship requires:

(1) A request to correct the inventorship that sets forth the desired inventorship change;

(2) A statement from each person being added as an inventor and from each person being deleted as an inventor that the error in inventorship occurred without deceptive intention on his or her part;

(3) An oath or declaration by the actual inventor or inventors as required by § 1.63 or as permitted by §§ 1.42, 1.43 or 1.47;

(4) The processing fee set forth in § 1.17(i); and

(5) If an assignment has been executed by any of the original named inventors, the written consent of the assignee (see § 3.73(b) of this chapter).

(b) *Nonprovisional application—fewer inventors due to amendment or cancellation of claims.* If the correct inventors are named in a nonprovisional application, and the prosecution of the nonprovisional application results in the amendment or cancellation of claims so that fewer than all of the currently named inventors are the actual inventors of the invention being claimed in the nonprovisional application, an amendment must be filed requesting deletion of the name or names of the person or persons who are not inventors of the invention being claimed. If the application is involved in an interference, the amendment must comply with the requirements of this section and must be accompanied by a motion under § 1.634. Amendment of the inventorship requires:

(1) A request, signed by a party set forth in § 1.33(b), to correct the inventorship that identifies the named inventor or inventors being deleted and acknowledges that the inventor's invention is no longer being claimed in the nonprovisional application; and

(2) The processing fee set forth in § 1.17(i).

(c) *Nonprovisional application—inventors added for claims to unclaimed subject matter.* If a nonprovisional application discloses unclaimed subject matter by an inventor or inventors not named in the application, the application may be amended to add claims to the subject matter and name the correct inventors for the application. If the application is involved in an interference, the amendment must comply with the requirements of this section and must be accompanied by a motion under § 1.634. Amendment of the inventorship requires:

(1) A request to correct the inventorship that sets forth the desired inventorship change;

(2) A statement from each person being added as an inventor that the addition is necessitated by amendment of the claims and that the inventorship error occurred without deceptive intention on his or her part;

(3) An oath or declaration by the actual inventors as required by § 1.63 or as permitted by §§ 1.42, 1.43 or 1.47;

(4) The processing fee set forth in § 1.17(i); and

(5) If an assignment has been executed by any of the original named inventors, the written consent of the assignee (see § 3.73(b) of this chapter).

(d) *Provisional application—adding omitted inventors.* If the name or names of an inventor or inventors were omitted in a provisional application through error without any deceptive intention on the part of the omitted inventor or inventors, the provisional application may be amended to add the name or names of the omitted inventor or inventors. Amendment of the inventorship requires:

(1) A request, signed by a party set forth in § 1.33(b), to correct the inventorship that identifies the inventor or inventors being added and states that the inventorship error occurred without deceptive intention on the part of the omitted inventor or inventors; and

(2) The processing fee set forth in § 1.17(q).

(e) *Provisional application—deleting the name or names of the inventor or inventors.* If a person or persons were named as an inventor or inventors in a provisional application through error without any deceptive intention on the part of such person or persons, an amendment may be filed in the provisional application deleting the name or names of the person or persons who were erroneously named. Amendment of the inventorship requires:

(1) A request to correct the inventorship that sets forth the desired inventorship change;

(2) A statement by the person or persons whose name or names are being deleted that the inventorship error occurred without deceptive intention on the part of such person or persons;

(3) The processing fee set forth in § 1.17(q); and

(4) If an assignment has been executed by any of the original named inventors, the written consent of the assignee (see § 3.73(b) of this chapter).

(f)(1) *Nonprovisional application—filing executed oath /declaration corrects inventorship.* If the correct inventor or inventors are not named on filing a nonprovisional application under § 1.53(b) without an executed oath or declaration under § 1.63 by any of the inventors, the first submission of an executed oath or declaration under § 1.63 by any of the inventors during the pendency of the application will act to correct the earlier identification of inventorship. See § 1.497(d) for submission of an executed oath or declaration to enter the national stage under 35 U.S.C. 371 and § 1.494 or § 1.495 naming an inventive entity different from the inventive entity set forth in the international stage.

(2) *Provisional application—filing cover sheet corrects inventorship.* If the correct inventor or inventors are not named on filing a provisional application without a cover sheet under § 1.51(c)(1), the later submission of a cover sheet under § 1.51(c)(1) during the pendency of the application will act to correct the earlier identification of inventorship.

(g) *Additional information may be required.* The Office may require such other information as may be deemed appropriate under the particular circumstances surrounding the correction of inventorship.

(h) *Reissue applications not covered.* The provisions of this section do not apply to reissue applications. See §§ 1.171 and 1.175 for correction of inventorship in a patent via a reissue application.

(i) *Correction of inventorship in patent or interference.* See § 1.324 for correction of inventorship in a patent, and § 1.634 for correction of inventorship in an interference.

19. Section 1.51 is proposed to be amended by revising paragraph (b) to read as follows:

§ 1.51 General requisites of an application.

* * * * *

(b) A complete application filed under § 1.53(b) or § 1.53(d) comprises:

(1) A specification as prescribed by 35 U.S.C. 112, including a claim or claims, see §§ 1.71 to 1.77;

(2) An oath or declaration, see §§ 1.63 and 1.68;

(3) Drawings, when necessary, see §§ 1.81 to 1.85; and

(4) The prescribed filing fee, see § 1.16.

* * * * *

20. Section 1.52 is proposed to be revised to read as follows:

§ 1.52 Language, paper, writing, margins.

(a) *Papers which are to become a part of the permanent Patent and Trademark Office records in the file of a patent application.* (1) All papers, other than drawings, which are to become a part of the permanent Patent and Trademark Office records in the file of a patent application must be on sheets of paper that are:

(i) Flexible, strong, smooth, non-shiny, durable, and white;

(ii) Either 21.0 cm by 29.7 cm (DIN size A4) or 21.6 cm by 27.9 cm (8½ by 11 inches), with each sheet including a top margin of at least 2.0 cm (¾ inch), a left side margin of at least 2.5 cm (1 inch), a right side margin of at least 2.0 cm (¾ inch), and a bottom margin of at least 2.0 cm (¾ inch);

(iii) Written on only one side in portrait orientation;

(iv) Plainly and legibly written either by a typewriter or machine printer in permanent dark ink or its equivalent; and

(v) Presented in a form having sufficient clarity and contrast between the paper and the writing thereon to permit the direct reproduction of readily legible copies in any number by use of photographic, electrostatic, photo-offset, and microfilming processes and electronic capture by use of digital imaging and optical character recognition.

(2) All papers which are to become a part of the permanent records of the Patent and Trademark Office should have no holes in the sheets as submitted.

(3) The provisions of this paragraph and paragraph (b) of this section do not apply to the pre-printed information on forms provided by the Office.

(4) See § 1.58 for chemical and mathematical formulae and tables, and § 1.84 for drawings.

(5) If papers are submitted as part of the permanent record, other than the drawings, that do not comply with paragraph (a)(1) of this section the Office may at its option:

(i) Convert the papers submitted by applicant into papers that do comply with paragraph (a)(1) of this section and charge the applicant the costs incurred by the Office in doing so (§ 1.21(j)); or

(ii) Require that the applicant provide substitute papers that comply with paragraph (a)(1) of this section within a set time period.

(b) *The application (specification, including the claims, drawings, and oath or declaration) and any amendments or corrections to the application.* (1) The application and any amendments or corrections to the application (including any translation submitted pursuant to paragraph (d) of this section), except as provided for in § 1.69 and paragraph (d) of this section, must:

(i) Comply with the requirements of paragraph (a) of this section; and

(ii) Be in the English language or be accompanied by a translation of any corrections or amendments into the English language together with a statement that the translation is accurate.

(2) The specification (including the abstract and claims), and any amendments to the specification, must have:

(i) Lines that are 1½ or double spaced;

(ii) Text written in a block (nonscript) type font or lettering style having capital letters which are at least 0.21 cm (0.08 inch) high; and

(iii) No more than a single column of text.

(3) The claim or claims must commence on a separate sheet (§ 1.75(h)).

(4) The abstract must commence on a separate sheet (§ 1.72(b)).

(5) The pages of the specification including claims and abstract must be numbered consecutively, starting with 1, the numbers being centrally located above or preferably, below, the text.

(6) Paragraphs in the specification, other than in the claims or abstract, should be individually and consecutively numbered using Arabic numerals, so as to unambiguously identify each paragraph. The number should consist of at least four numerals contained in square brackets, including leading zeros (*e.g.,* [0001]). The numbers and enclosing brackets should appear to the right of the left margin as the first item in each paragraph, before the first word of the paragraph, and should be highlighted in bold. A gap, equivalent to approximately four spaces, should follow the number. Nontext elements (*e.g.,* tables, mathematical or chemical formulas, chemical structures, and sequence data) are considered part of the numbered paragraph around or above the elements, and should not be independently numbered. Even if a nontext element extends to the left margin, it should not be numbered as a separate and independent paragraph. A list is also treated as part of the paragraph around or above the list, and should not be independently numbered. Paragraph or section headers (titles), whether abutting the left margin or centered on the page, are not considered paragraphs and should not be numbered.

(7) If papers are submitted as part of the application that do not comply with paragraphs (b)(1) through (b)(5) of this section, the Office may at its option:

(i) Convert the papers submitted by applicant into papers that do comply with paragraphs (b)(1) through (b)(5) of this section and charge the applicant the costs incurred by the Office in doing so (§ 1.21(j)); or

(ii) Require that the applicant provide substitute papers that comply with paragraphs (b)(1) through (b)(5) of this section within a set time period.

(c)(1) Any interlineation, erasure, cancellation or other alteration of the application papers filed must be made before the signing of any accompanying oath or declaration pursuant to § 1.63 referring to those application papers and should be dated and initialed or signed by the applicant on the same sheet of paper. Application papers containing alterations made after the signing of an oath or declaration referring to those application papers must be supported by a supplemental oath or declaration under § 1.67. In either situation, a substitute specification (§ 1.125) is required if the application papers do not comply with paragraphs (a) and (b) of this section.

(2) After the signing of the oath or declaration referring to the application papers, amendments may only be made in the manner provided by § 1.121.

(3) Notwithstanding the provisions of this paragraph, if an oath or declaration is a copy of the oath or declaration from a prior application, the application for which such copy is submitted may contain alterations that do not introduce matter that would have been new matter in the prior application.

(d) A nonprovisional or provisional application may be filed in a language other than English.

(1) *Nonprovisional application.* If a nonprovisional application is filed in a language other than English, an English language translation of the non-English language application, a statement that the translation is accurate, and the processing fee set forth in § 1.17(i) are required. If these items are not filed with the application, applicant will be notified and given a period of time within which they must be filed in order to avoid abandonment.

(2) *Provisional application:* If a provisional application is filed in a language other than English, an English language translation of the non-English language provisional application will not be required in the provisional application. If a nonprovisional application claims the benefit of such provisional application, however, an English language translation of the non-English language provisional application and a statement that the translation is accurate must be supplied if the nonprovisional application is involved in an interference (§ 1.630), or when specifically required by the examiner.

21. Section 1.53 is proposed to be amended by revising paragraphs (c)(1), (c)(2), (d)(4), (e)(2), (f) and (g) and adding paragraph (d)(10) to read as follows:

§ 1.53 Application number, filing date, and completion of application.

* * * * *

(c) * * *

(1) A provisional application must also include the cover sheet required by § 1.51(c)(1), which may be an application data sheet (§ 1.76), or a cover letter identifying the application as a provisional application. Otherwise, the application will be treated as an application filed under paragraph (b) of this section.

(2) An application for patent filed under paragraph (b) of this section may be converted to a provisional application and be accorded the original filing date of the application filed under paragraph (b) of this section. The grant of such a request for conversion will not entitle applicant to a refund of the fees which were properly paid in the application filed under paragraph (b) of this section. Such a request for conversion must be accompanied by the processing fee set forth in § 1.17(q) and be filed prior to the earliest of:

(i) Abandonment of the application filed under paragraph (b) of this section;

(ii) Payment of the issue fee on the application filed under paragraph (b) of this section;

(iii) Expiration of twelve months after the filing date of the application filed under paragraph (b) of this section; or

(iv) The filing of a request for a statutory invention registration under § 1.293 in the application filed under paragraph (b) of this section.

* * * * *

(d) * * *

(4) An application filed under this paragraph may be filed by fewer than all the inventors named in the prior application, provided that the request for an application under this paragraph when filed is accompanied by a statement requesting deletion of the name or names of the person or persons who are not inventors of the invention being claimed in the new application. No person may be named as an inventor in an

application filed under this paragraph who was not named as an inventor in the prior application on the date the application under this paragraph was filed, except by way of correction of inventorship under § 1.48.

* * * * *

(10) See § 1.103(b) for requesting a limited suspension of action in an application filed under this paragraph.

(e) * * *

(2) Any request for review of a notification pursuant to paragraph (e)(1) of this section, or a notification that the original application papers lack a portion of the specification or drawing(s), must be by way of a petition pursuant to this paragraph accompanied by the fee set forth in § 1.17(h). In the absence of a timely (§ 1.181(f)) petition pursuant to this paragraph, the filing date of an application in which the applicant was notified of a filing error pursuant to paragraph (e)(1) of this section will be the date the filing error is corrected.

* * * * *

(f) *Completion of application subsequent to filing—Nonprovisional (including continued prosecution and reissue) application.* (1) If an application which has been accorded a filing date pursuant to paragraph (b) or (d) of this section does not include the basic filing fee, or if an application which has been accorded a filing date pursuant to paragraph (b) of this section does not include an oath or declaration by the applicant pursuant to §§ 1.63, 1.162 or 1.175, and applicant has provided a correspondence address (§ 1.33(a)), applicant will be notified and given a period of time within which to pay the filing fee, file an oath or declaration in an application under paragraph (b) of this section, and pay the surcharge required by § 1.16(e) to avoid abandonment.

(2) If an application which has been accorded a filing date pursuant to paragraph (b) of this section does not include the basic filing fee or an oath or declaration by the applicant pursuant to §§ 1.63, 1.162 or 1.175, and applicant has not provided a correspondence address (§ 1.33(a)), applicant has two months from the filing date of the application within which to pay the basic filing fee, file an oath or declaration, and pay the surcharge required by § 1.16(e) to avoid abandonment.

(3) This paragraph applies to continuation or divisional applications under paragraphs (b) or (d) of this section and to continuation-in-part applications under paragraph (b) of this section.

(4) See § 1.63(d) concerning the submission of a copy of the oath or declaration from the prior application for a continuation or divisional application under paragraph (b) of this section.

(5) If applicant does not pay one of the basic filing fee or the processing and retention fee set forth in § 1.21(l) during the pendency of the application, the Office may dispose of the application.

(g) *Completion of application subsequent to filing—provisional application.* (1) If a provisional application which has been accorded a filing date pursuant to paragraph (c) of this section does not include the cover sheet required by § 1.51(c)(1) or the basic filing fee (§ 1.16(k)), and applicant has provided a correspondence address (§ 1.33(a)), applicant will be notified and given a period of time within which to pay the basic filing fee, file a cover sheet (§ 1.51(c)(1)), and pay the surcharge required by § 1.16(l) to avoid abandonment.

(2) If a provisional application which has been accorded a filing date pursuant to paragraph (c) of this section does not include the cover sheet required by § 1.51(c)(1) or the basic filing fee (§ 1.16(k)), and applicant has not provided a correspondence address (§ 1.33(a)), applicant has two months from the filing date of the application within which to pay the basic filing fee, file a cover sheet (§ 1.51(c)(1)), and pay the surcharge required by § 1.16(l) to avoid abandonment.

(3) If applicant does not pay the basic filing fee during the pendency of the application, the Office may dispose of the application.

* * * * *

22. Section 1.55 is proposed to be amended by revising paragraph (a) to read as follows:

§ 1.55 Claim for foreign priority.

(a) An applicant in a nonprovisional application may claim the benefit of the filing date of one or more prior foreign applications under the conditions specified in 35 U.S.C. 119(a) through (d), 172, and 365(b).

(1) The claim for priority must identify the foreign application for which priority is claimed, as well as any foreign application for the same subject having a filing date before that of the application for which priority is claimed, by specifying the application number, country (or intergovernmental organization), day, month, and year of its filing.

(2)(i) In an application filed under 35 U.S.C. 111(a), the claim for priority and the certified copy of the foreign application specified in 35 U.S.C. 119(b) must be filed before the patent is granted.

(ii) In an application that entered the national stage from an international application after compliance with 35 U.S.C. 371, the claim for priority must be made within the time limit set forth in the PCT and the Regulations under the PCT. If the certified copy of the foreign application has not been filed in accordance with the PCT and the Regulations under the PCT, it must be filed before the patent is granted.

(iii) When the application becomes involved in an interference (§ 1.630), when necessary to overcome the date of a reference relied upon by the examiner, or when deemed necessary by the examiner, the Office may require that the claim for priority and the certified copy of the foreign application be filed earlier than provided in paragraph (a)(2)(i) or (a)(2)(ii) of this section.

(iv) If the claim for priority or the certified copy of the foreign application is filed after the date the issue fee is paid, it must be accompanied by the processing fee set forth in § 1.17(i) but the patent will not include the priority claim unless corrected by a certificate of correction under 35 U.S.C. 255 and § 1.323 of this part.

(3) An English-language translation of a non-English-language foreign application is not required except when the application is involved in an interference (§ 1.630), when necessary to overcome the date of a reference relied upon by the examiner, or when specifically required by the examiner. If an English-language translation is required, it must be filed together with a statement that the translation of the certified copy is accurate.

* * * * *

23. Section 1.56 is proposed to be amended by adding a new paragraph (e) to read as follows:

§ 1.56 Duty to disclose information material to patent ability.

* * * * *

(e) In any continuation-in-part application, the duty under this section includes the duty to disclose to the Office all information known to the person to be material to patentability, as defined in paragraph (b) of this section, which became available between the filing date of the prior application and the national or PCT international filing date of the continuation-in-part application.

24. Section 1.59 is proposed to be amended by revising paragraph (b) to read as follows:

§ 1.59 Expungement of information or copy of papers in application file.

* * * * *

(b) An applicant may request that the Office expunge and return information, other than what is excluded by paragraph (a)(2) of this section, by filing a petition under this paragraph. Any petition to expunge and return information from an application must include the fee set forth in § 1.17(h) and establish to the satisfaction of the Commissioner that the return of the information is appropriate.

* * * * *

25. Section 1.63 is proposed to be amended by revising paragraphs (a), (b), (c) and (e) to read as follows:

§ 1.63 Oath or declaration.

(a) An oath or declaration filed under § 1.51(b)(2) as a part of a nonprovisional application must:

(1) Be executed (*i.e.,* signed) in accordance with either § 1.66 or § 1.68;

(2) Identify each inventor and country of citizenship of each inventor; and

(3) State that the person making the oath or declaration believes the named inventor or inventors to be the original and first inventor or inventors of the subject matter which is claimed and for which a patent is sought.

(b) In addition to meeting the requirements of paragraph (a), the oath or declaration must also:

(1) Identify the application to which it is directed;

(2) State that the person making the oath or declaration has reviewed and understands the contents of the application, including the claims, as amended by any amendment specifically referred to in the oath or declaration; and

(3) State that the person making the oath or declaration acknowledges the duty to disclose to the Office all information known to the person to be material to patentability as defined in § 1.56.

(c) Unless such information is supplied on an application data sheet in accordance with § 1.76, the oath or declaration must also identify:

(1) Each inventor, by full name, including the family name, and at least one given name without abbreviation together with any other given name or initial;

(2) The mailing address and residence (if different from the mailing address) of each inventor; and

(3) Any foreign application for patent (or inventor's certificate) for which a claim for priority is made pursuant to § 1.55, and any foreign application having a filing date before that of the application on which priority is claimed, by specifying the application number, country, day, month, and year of its filing.

* * * * *

(e) A newly executed oath or declaration must be filed in any continuation-in-part application, which application may name all, more, or fewer than all of the inventors named in the prior application.

26. Section 1.64 is proposed to be revised to read as follows:

§ 1.64 Person making oath or declaration.

(a) The oath or declaration (§ 1.63), including any supplemental oath or declaration (§ 1.67), must be made by all of the actual inventors except as provided for in §§ 1.42, 1.43, 1.47 or 1.67.

(b) If the person making the oath or declaration or any supplemental oath or declaration is not the inventor (§§ 1.42, 1.43, 1.47 or 1.67), the oath or declaration shall state the relationship of the person to the inventor, and, upon information and belief, the facts which the inventor is required to state. If the person signing the oath or declaration is the legal representative of a deceased inventor, the oath or declaration shall also state that the person is a legal representative and the citizenship, residence and mailing address of the legal representative.

27. Section 1.67 is proposed to be amended by revising paragraph (a) and removing paragraph (c) to read as follows:

§ 1.67 Supplemental oath or declaration.

(a) The Office may require a supplemental oath or declaration meeting the requirements of § 1.63 or § 1.162 to correct any deficiencies or inaccuracies present in the earlier filed oath or declaration. If the earlier filed oath or declaration complied with § 1.63(a), the Office may permit the supplemental oath or declaration to be made by fewer than all of the inventors or by an applicant other than the inventor.

* * * * *

28. Section 1.72 is proposed to be revised to read as follows:

§ 1.72 Title and abstract.

(a) Unless the title is supplied in an application data sheet (§ 1.76), the title of the invention, which should be as short and specific as possible, should appear as a heading on the first page of the specification.

(b) A brief abstract of the technical disclosure in the specification must commence on a separate sheet, preferably following the claims, under the heading "Abstract" or "Abstract of the Disclosure." The abstract in an application filed under 35 U.S.C. 111 may not exceed 150 words in length. The purpose of the abstract is to enable the Patent and Trademark Office and the public generally to determine quickly from a cursory inspection the nature and gist of the technical disclosure. The abstract will not be used for interpreting the scope of the claims.

29. A new § 1.76 is proposed to be added to read as follows:

§ 1.76 Application data sheet.

(a) An application data sheet is a sheet or sheets containing bibliographic data concerning a patent application arranged in a specified format. If an application data sheet is provided, the application data sheet is part of the application.

(b) Bibliographic data as used in paragraph (a) of this section includes:

(1) *Applicant information.* This information includes the name, residence, mailing address, and citizenship of each applicant (§ 1.41(b)). The name of each applicant must include the family name, and at least one given name without abbreviation together with any other given name or initial. If the applicant is not an inventor, this information also includes the applicant's authority (§§ 1.42, 1.43 and 1.47) to apply for the patent on behalf of the inventor. The citizenship of each inventor must be provided in the oath or declaration under § 1.63 even if it is provided in the application data sheet (35 U.S.C. 115).

(2) *Correspondence information.* This information includes the correspondence address, which may be indicated by reference to a customer number, to which correspondence is to be directed (*see* § 1.33(a)).

(3) *Application information.* This information includes the title of the invention, the total number of drawing sheets, whether the drawings are formal, any docket number assigned to the application, and the type (*e.g.*, utility, plant, design, reissue utility, provisional) of application, and whether the application discloses any significant part of the subject matter of an application under a secrecy order pursuant to § 5.2 of this chapter (see § 5.2(c)).

(4) *Representative information.* This information includes the registration number of each practitioner, or the customer number, having a power of attorney or authorization of agent in the application. Providing this information in the application data sheet does not constitute a power of attorney or authorization of agent in the application (*see* § 1.34(b)).

(5) *Domestic priority information.* This information includes the application number, the filing date, the status (including patent number if available), and re-

lationship of each application for which a benefit is claimed under 35 U.S.C. 119(e), 120, 121, or 365(c). Providing this information in the application data sheet constitutes the specific reference required by 35 U.S.C. 119(e) or 120 and § 1.78(a)(2) or § 1.78(a)(4) of this part.

(6) *Foreign priority information.* This information includes the application number, country, and filing date of each foreign application for which priority is claimed, as well as any foreign application having a filing date before that of the application for which priority is claimed. Providing this information in the application data sheet constitutes the claim for priority as required by 35 U.S.C. 119(b) and § 1.55(a) of this part.

(c) If an application contains an application data sheet, any inconsistency between the information provided in the application data sheet and the oath or declaration under § 1.63 will be resolved in favor of the information provided in the application data sheet. A supplemental application data sheet may be submitted to correct or update information provided in a previous application data sheet.

30. Section 1.77 is proposed to be revised to read as follows:

§ 1.77 Arrangement of application elements.

(a) The elements of the application, if applicable, should appear in the following order:

(1) Utility application transmittal form.
(2) Fee transmittal form.
(3) Application data sheet (see § 1.76).
(4) Specification.
(5) Drawings.
(6) Executed oath or declaration.

(b) The specification should include the following sections in order:

(1) Title of the invention, which may be accompanied by an introductory portion stating the name, citizenship and residence of the applicant.
(2) Cross-reference to related applications (unless included in the application data sheet).
(3) Statement regarding federally sponsored research or development.
(4) Reference to a "computer program listing appendix" (see § 1.96 (c)).
(5) Background of the invention.
(6) Brief summary of the invention.
(7) Brief description of the several views of the drawing.
(8) Detailed description of the invention.
(9) A claim or claims.
(10) Abstract of the disclosure.
(11) Sequence listing (see §§ 1.821 through 1.825).

(c) The text of the specification sections defined in paragraphs (b)(1) through (b)(3) and (b)(5) through (b)(11) of this section, if applicable, should be preceded by a section heading in uppercase and without underlining or bold type.

31. Section 1.78 is proposed to be amended by revising paragraphs (a)(2), (a)(4) and (c) to read as follows:

§ 1.78 Claiming benefit of earlier filing data and cross-references to other applications.

(a) * * *

(2) Except for a continued prosecution application filed under § 1.53(d), any nonprovisional application claiming the benefit of one or more prior filed copending nonprovisional applications or international applications designating the United States of America must contain a reference to each such prior application, identifying it by application number (consisting of the series code and serial number) or international application number and international filing date and indicating the relationship of the applications. Unless the reference required by this paragraph is included in an application data sheet (§ 1.76), the specification must contain or be amended to con-

tain such reference in the first sentence following the title. The request for a continued prosecution application under § 1.53(d) is the specific reference required by 35 U.S.C. 120 to the prior application. The identification of an application by application number under this section is the specific reference required by 35 U.S.C. 120 to every application assigned that application number. Cross-references to other related applications may be made when appropriate (see § 1.14).

* * * * *

(4) Any nonprovisional application claiming the benefit of one or more prior filed copending provisional applications must contain a reference to each such prior provisional application, identifying it as a provisional application, and including the provisional application number (consisting of series code and serial number). Unless the reference required by this paragraph is included in an application data sheet (§ 1.76), the specification must contain or be amended to contain such reference in the first sentence following the title.

* * * * *

(c) If an application or a patent under reexamination and at least one other application naming different inventors are owned by the same party and contain conflicting claims, and there is no statement of record indicating that the claimed inventions were commonly owned or subject to an obligation of assignment to the same person at the time the later invention was made, the Office may require the assignee to state whether the claimed inventions were commonly owned or subject to an obligation of assignment to the same person at the time the later invention was made, and, if not, indicate which named inventor is the prior inventor.

32. Section 1.84 is proposed to be revised to read as follows:

§ 1.84 Standards for drawings.

(a) *Drawings.* There are two acceptable categories for presenting drawings in utility patent applications:

(1) *Black ink.* Black and white drawings are normally required. India ink, or its equivalent that secures solid black lines, must be used for drawings, or

(2) *Color.* On rare occasions, color drawings may be necessary as the only practical medium by which to disclose the subject matter sought to be patented in a utility patent application or the subject matter of a statutory invention registration. The Patent and Trademark Office will accept color drawings in utility patent applications and statutory invention registrations only if color drawings are necessary for the understanding of the claimed invention and upon payment of the fee set forth in § 1.17(k) and submission of three sets of the color drawings. Color drawings are not permitted in international applications (see PCT Rule 11.13). If the subject matter of the application admits of illustration by a black and white drawing, the examiner may require a black and white drawing in place of the color drawing. The color drawings must be of sufficient quality so that all details in the drawings are reproducible in the printed patent. If color drawings are submitted, the specification must contain or be amended to contain the following language as the first paragraph of the brief description of the drawings:

> The file of this patent contains at least one drawing executed in color. Copies of this patent with color drawing(s) will be provided by the Patent and Trademark Office upon request and payment of the necessary fee.

(b)(1) *Photographs.* Photographs are not ordinarily permitted in utility patent applications. The Office will accept photographs in utility patent applications, however, if photographs are the only practicable medium for illustrating the claimed invention. If the subject matter of the application admits of illustration by a drawing, the examiner may require a drawing in place of the photograph. The photographs must be of sufficient quality so that all details in the photographs are reproducible in the printed patent.

(2) *Color photographs.* Color photographs will be accepted in utility patent applications if the conditions for accepting color drawings and photographs have been satisfied. See paragraphs (a)(2) and (b)(1) of this section.

(c) *Identification of drawings.* Identifying indicia, if provided, should include the title of the invention, inventor's name, and application number, or docket number (if any) if an application number has not been assigned to the application. If this information is provided, it must be placed on the front of each sheet and centered within the top margin.

(d) *Type of paper.* Drawings submitted to the Office must be made on paper which is flexible, strong, white, smooth, non-shiny, and durable. All sheets must be reasonably free from cracks, creases, and folds. Only one side of the sheet may be used for the drawing. Each sheet must be reasonably free from erasures and must be free from alterations, overwritings, and interlineations. Photographs must be developed on paper or be permanently mounted on Bristol board meeting the sheet-size requirements of paragraph (e) of this section and the margin requirements of paragraph (f) of this section. See paragraph (b) of this section for other requirements for photographs.

(e) *Size of paper.* All drawing sheets in an application must be the same size. One of the shorter sides of the sheet is regarded as its top. The size of the sheets on which drawings are made must be:

(1) 21.0 cm by 29.7 cm (DIN size A4); or

(2) 21.6 cm by 27.9 cm (8½ by 11 inches).

(f) *Margins.* The sheets must not contain frames around the sight (*i.e.,* the usable surface), but should have scan target points (*i.e.,* cross-hairs) printed on two catercorner margin corners. Each sheet must include a top margin of at least 2.5 cm (1 inch), a left side margin of at least 2.5 cm (1 inch), a right side margin of at least 1.5 cm (⅝ inch), and a bottom margin of at least 1.0 cm (⅜ inch), and must leave a sight no greater than 17.0 cm by 26.2 cm on 21.0 cm by 29.7 cm (DIN size A4) drawing sheets, and a sight no greater than 17.0 cm by 24.4 cm (6¾ by 9⅝ inches) on 21.6 cm by 27.9 cm (8½ by 11 inch) drawing sheets.

(g) *Scale.* The scale to which a drawing is made must be large enough to show the mechanism without crowding when the drawing is reduced in size to two-thirds in reproduction. Indications such as "actual size" or "scale ½" on the drawings are not permitted since these lose their meaning with reproduction in a different format.

(h) *Character of lines, numbers, and letters.* All drawings must be made by a process which will give them satisfactory reproduction characteristics. Every line, number, and letter must be durable, clean, black (except for color drawings), sufficiently dense and dark, and uniformly thick and well-defined. The weight of all lines and letters must be heavy enough to permit adequate reproduction. This requirement applies to all lines however fine, to shading, and to lines representing cut surfaces in sectional views. Lines and strokes of different thicknesses may be used in the same drawing where different thicknesses have a different meaning.

(i) *Legends.* Suitable descriptive legends may be used subject to approval by the Office, or may be required by the examiner where necessary for understanding of the drawing. They should contain as few words as possible.

(j) *Numbers, letters, and reference characters.* (1) Reference characters (numerals are preferred), sheet numbers, and view numbers must be plain and legible, and must not be used in association with brackets or inverted commas, or enclosed within outlines, *e.g.,* encircled. They must be oriented in the same direction as the view so as to avoid having to rotate the sheet.

(2) The English alphabet must be used for letters, except where another alphabet is customarily used, such as the Greek alphabet to indicate angles, wavelengths, and mathematical formulas.

(3) Numbers, letters, and reference characters must measure at least 0.32 cm (⅛ inch) in height.

(4) The same part of an invention appearing in more than one view of the drawing must always be designated by the same reference character, and the same reference character must never be used to designate different parts.

(5) Only reference characters mentioned in the description may appear in the drawings. Reference characters mentioned in the description must appear in the drawings.

(k) *Lead lines.* Lead lines are those lines between the reference characters and the details to which they refer. Such lines may be straight or curved and should be as short as possible. They must originate in the immediate proximity of the reference character and extend to the feature indicated. Lead lines must not cross each other. Lead lines are required for each reference character except for those which indicate the surface or cross section on which they are placed. Such a reference character must be underlined to make it clear that a lead line has not been left out by mistake. Lead lines must be executed in the same way as lines in the drawing. See paragraph (h) of this section.

(l) *Numbering of sheets of drawings.* The sheets of drawings should be numbered in consecutive Arabic numerals, starting with 1, within the sight as defined in paragraph (g) of this section. These numbers, if present, must be placed in the middle of the top of the sheet, but not in the margin. The numbers can be placed on the right-hand side if the drawing extends too close to the middle of the top edge of the usable surface. The drawing sheet numbering must be clear and larger than the numbers used as reference characters to avoid confusion. The number of each sheet may be shown by two Arabic numerals placed on either side of an oblique line, with the first being the sheet number and the second being the total number of sheets of drawings, with no other marking.

(m) *Numbering of views.* (1) The different views must be numbered in consecutive Arabic numerals, starting with 1, independent of the numbering of the sheets and, if possible, in the order in which they appear on the drawing sheet(s). Partial views intended to form one complete view, on one or several sheets, must be identified by the same number followed by a capital letter. View numbers must be preceded by the abbreviation "FIG." Where only a single view is used in an application to illustrate the claimed invention, it must not be numbered and the abbreviation "FIG." must not appear.

(2) Numbers and letters identifying the views must be simple and clear and must not be used in association with brackets, circles, or inverted commas. The view numbers must be larger than the numbers used for reference characters.

(n) *Security markings.* Authorized security markings may be placed on the drawings provided they are outside the sight, preferably centered in the top margin.

(o) *Corrections.* Any corrections on drawings submitted to the Office must be durable and permanent.

(p) See § 1.152 for design drawings, § 1.165 for plant drawings, and § 1.173 for reissue drawings.

33. Section 1.85 is proposed to be revised to read as follows:

§ 1.85 Corrections to drawings.

(a) If a drawing meets the requirements of § 1.84(d), (e) and (f) and is suitable for reproduction, but is not otherwise in compliance with § 1.84, the drawing may be admitted for examination.

(b) The Office will not release drawings for purposes of correction. If corrections are necessary, new corrected drawings must be submitted within the time set by the Office.

(c) If a corrected drawing is required or if a drawing does not comply with § 1.84 at the time an application is allowed, the Office may notify the applicant and set a three month period of time from the mail date of the notice of allowability within which the applicant must file a corrected or formal drawing in compliance with § 1.84 to avoid abandonment. This time period is not extendable under § 1.136(a) or (b).

34. Section 1.91 is proposed to be amended by revising paragraph (a)(3)(i) to read as follows:

§ 1.91 Models or exhibits not generally admitted as part of application or patent.

(a) * * *

(3) * * *

(i) The fee set forth in § 1.17(h); and

* * * * *

35. Section 1.96 is proposed to be amended by revising paragraphs (b) and (c) to read as follows:

§ 1.96 Submission of computer program listings.

* * * * *

(b) *Material which will be printed in the patent.* If the computer program listing is contained on one sheet, it may be submitted either as a drawing or as part of the specification.

(1) *Drawings.* If the listing is submitted as a drawing, it must be submitted in the manner and complying with the requirements for drawings as provided in § 1.84. At least one figure numeral is required on the sheet of drawing.

(2) *Specification.* (i) If the listing is submitted as part of the specification, it must be submitted in accordance with the provisions of § 1.52, at the end of the description but before the claims.

(ii) Any listing submitted as part of the specification must be a direct print-out (*i.e.,* not a copy) from the computer's printer with dark solid black letters not less than 0.21 cm high, on white, unshaded and unlined paper, and the sheet should be submitted in a protective cover. Any amendments must be made by way of submission of a substitute sheet.

(c) *As an appendix which will not be printed.* Any computer program listing may, and any computer program listing that would be contained on more than one sheet must, be submitted on a Compact Disk-Read Only Memory (CD–ROM) or Compact Disk-Recordable (CD–R), which must be referred to in the specification (see § 1.77(b)(4)). A CD–ROM or CD–R containing such a computer program listing is to be referred to as a "computer program listing appendix." The "computer program listing appendix" will not be part of the printed patent. Reference in the application to the "computer program listing appendix" must be made at the location indicated in § 1.77(b)(4). Any amendment to the "computer program listing appendix" must be by way of a new CD–ROM or CD–R containing a substitute computer program listing.

(1) *Availability of appendix.* Such "computer program listing appendix" will be available to the public for inspection, and copies thereof will be available for purchase with the file wrapper and contents, after a patent based on such application is granted or the application is otherwise made publicly available.

(2) *Submission requirements*—(i) A "computer program listing appendix" must be submitted on a CD–ROM or CD–R in accordance with the standards set forth in 36 CFR 1228.188(c) and (d).

(ii) The computer program listing must be written in American Standard Code for Information Interchange (ASCII) in the form of textual document files on a disk that complies with § 1.824(b). No other format shall be allowed. The CD–ROM or CD–R must be accompanied by documentation on paper in accordance with § 1.52(a) that contains the machine format (*e.g.,* IBM–PC, Macintosh)), the operating system (*e.g.,* MS–DOS, Macintosh, Unix) and any other special information that is necessary to identify, maintain, and interpret the "computer program listing appendix."

(iii) Multiple computer program listings for a single application may be placed on a single CD–ROM or CD–R. Multiple CD–ROMs or CD–Rs may be submitted for a single application if necessary. A separate CD–ROM or CD–R is required for each application containing a computer program listing that must be submitted on a "computer program listing appendix."

(iv) A CD–ROM or CD–R "computer program listing appendix" must be labeled with the following information:

(A) The name of each inventor (if known);

(B) Title of the invention;

(C) The docket number used by the person filing the application to identify the application (if applicable).

36. Section 1.97 is proposed to be amended by revising paragraphs (a) through (e) to read as follows:

§ 1.97 Filing of information disclosure statement.

(a) In order for an applicant for a patent or for a reissue of a patent to have an information disclosure statement in compliance with § 1.98 considered by the Office during the pendency of the application, it must satisfy one of paragraphs (b), (c), or (d) of this section.

(b) An information disclosure statement shall be considered by the Office if filed by the applicant within any one of the following time periods:

(1) Within three months of the filing date of a national application other than a continued prosecution application under § 1.53(d);

(2) Within three months of the date of entry of the national stage as set forth in § 1.491 in an international application; or

(3) Before the mailing date of a first Office action on the merits.

(c) An information disclosure statement shall be considered by the Office if filed after the period specified in paragraph (b) of this section, provided that the information disclosure statement is filed before the mailing date of any of a final action under § 1.113, a notice of allowance under § 1.311, or an action that otherwise closes prosecution in the application, and it is accompanied by one of:

(1) A statement as specified in paragraph (e) of this section; or

(2) The fee set forth in § 1.17(p).

(d) An information disclosure statement shall be considered by the Office if filed by the applicant after the period specified in paragraph (c) of this section, provided that the information disclosure statement is filed on or before payment of the issue fee and is accompanied by:

(1) A statement as specified in paragraph (e) of this section; and

(2) The fee set forth in § 1.17(p).

(e) A statement under this section must state either:

(1) That each item of information contained in the information disclosure statement was first cited in a communication from a foreign patent office in a counterpart foreign application not more than three months prior to the filing of the information disclosure statement; or

(2) That no item of information contained in the information disclosure statement was cited in a communication from a foreign patent office in a counterpart foreign application, and, to the knowledge of the person signing the certification after making reasonable inquiry, no item of information contained in the information disclosure statement was known to any individual designated in § 1.56(c) more than three months prior to the filing of the information disclosure statement.

* * * * *

37. Section 1.98 is proposed to be revised to read as follows:

§ 1.98 Content of information disclosure statement.

(a) Any information disclosure statement filed under § 1.97 shall include:

(1) A list of all patents, publications or other information submitted for consideration by the Office;

(2) A legible copy of:

(i) Each U.S. and foreign patent;

(ii) Each publication or that portion which caused it to be listed;

(iii) For each cited pending U.S. application, the application specification including the claims, and any drawing of the application, or that portion of the application which caused it to be listed including any claims directed to that portion; and

(iv) All other information or that portion which caused it to be listed; and

(3) A concise explanation of the relevance, as it is presently understood by the individual designated in § 1.56(c) most knowledgeable about the content of the information, of each patent, publication, or other information listed that is not in the English language. The concise explanation may be either separate from the specification or incorporated therein. If a written English-language translation of a non-English-language document, or portion thereof, is within the possession, custody, or control of, or is readily available to any individual designated in § 1.56(c), a copy of the translation shall accompany the information disclosure statement.

(b) Each U.S. patent listed in an information disclosure statement shall be identified by patentee, patent number and issue date. Each listed U.S. application shall be identified by the inventor, application number and filing date. Each listed foreign patent or published foreign patent application shall be identified by the country or patent office which issued the patent or published the application, an appropriate document number, and the publication date indicated on the patent or published application. Each listed publication shall be identified by author (if any), title, relevant pages of the publication, date, and place of publication.

(c) When the disclosures of two or more patents or publications listed in an information disclosure statement are substantively cumulative, a copy of one of the patents or publications may be submitted without copies of the other patents or publications provided that a statement is made that these other patents or publications are cumulative.

(d) A copy of any patent, publication, application, or other information listed in an information disclosure statement is not required to be provided if it was previously cited by or submitted to the Office in a prior application, provided that:

(1) The prior application is properly identified in the statement and relied on for an earlier filing date under 35 U.S.C. 120; and

(2) Where the listed information was not cited by the Office, the information submission made in the prior application complied with paragraphs (a) through (c) of this section, and except for an application filed under § 1.53(d) the submission made in the prior application complied with § 1.97.

38. Section 1.102 is proposed to be amended by revising paragraph (d) to read as follows:

§ 1.102 Advancement of examination.

* * * * *

(d) A petition to make an application special on grounds other than those referred to in paragraph (c) of this section must be accompanied by the fee set forth in § 1.17(h).

39. Section 1.103 is proposed to be revised to read as follows:

§ 1.103 Suspension of action by the Office.

(a) *Suspension for cause.* On request of the applicant, the Office may grant a suspension of action under this paragraph for good and sufficient cause. The Office will not suspend action if a reply by applicant to an Office action is outstanding. Any petition for suspension of action under this paragraph must specify a period of suspension not exceeding six months. Any petition for suspension of action under this paragraph must also include:

(1) A showing of good and sufficient cause for suspension of action; and

(2) The fee set forth in § 1.17(h), unless such cause is the fault of the Office.

(b) *Limited suspension of action in a continued prosecution application (CPA) under § 1.53(d).* On request of the applicant, the Office may grant a suspension of action under this paragraph in a continued prosecution application under § 1.53(d) for a period not exceeding three months. Any request for suspension of action under this paragraph must be filed with the request for an application under § 1.53(d), specify the period of suspension, and include the processing fee set forth in § 1.17(i).

(c) *Notice of suspension on initiative of the Office.* The Office will notify applicant if the Office suspends action by the Office on an application on its own initiative.

(d) *Suspension of action for public safety or defense.* The Office may suspend action by the Office by order of the Commissioner if the following conditions are met:

(1) The application is owned by the United States;

(2) Publication of the invention may be detrimental to the public safety or defense; and

(3) The appropriate department or agency requests such suspension.

(e) *Statutory invention registration.* The Office will suspend action for the entire pendency of an application if the Office has accepted a request to publish a statutory invention registration in the application, except for purposes relating to patent interference proceedings under subpart E of this part.

40. A new § 1.105 is proposed to be added to read as follows:

§ 1.105 Requirements for information.

(a)(1) In the course of examining or treating a matter in a pending or abandoned application filed under 35 U.S.C. 111 or 371 (including a reissue application), in a patent, or in a reexamination proceeding, the examiner or other Office employee may require the submission of such information as may be reasonably necessary to properly examine or treat the matter.

(2) Any reply that states that the information required to be submitted is unknown and/or is not available will be accepted as a complete reply.

(b) The requirement for information of paragraph (a)(1) of this section may be included in an Office action, or sent separately.

(c) A reply, or a failure to reply, to a requirement for information under this rule will be governed by §§ 1.135 and 1.136.

41. Section 1.111 is proposed to be amended by revising the heading and paragraphs (a) and (c) to read as follows:

§ 1.111 Reply by application or patent owner to a non-final Office action.

(a) If the Office action after the first examination (§ 1.104) is adverse in any respect, the applicant or patent owner, if he or she persists in his or her application for a patent or reexamination proceeding, must reply thereto and request reconsideration or further examination, with or without amendment. See § 1.135 and § 1.136 for time for reply to avoid abandonment. A second or subsequent supplemental reply will be entered unless disapproved by the Commissioner.

* * * * *

(c) In amending in reply to a rejection of claims in an application or patent under reexamination, the applicant or patent owner must clearly point out the patentable novelty which he or she thinks the claims present in view of the state of the art disclosed by the references cited or the objections made. The applicant or patent owner must also show how the amendments avoid such references or objections.

42. Section 1.112 is proposed to be revised to read as follows:

§ 1.112 Reconsideration before final action.

After reply by applicant or patent owner (§ 1.111) to a non-final action, the application or patent under reexamination will be reconsidered and again examined. The applicant or patent owner will be notified if claims are rejected, or objections or requirements made, in the same manner as after the first examination (§ 1.104). Applicant or patent owner may reply to such Office action in the same manner provided in § 1.111, with or without amendment, unless such Office action indicates that it is made final (§ 1.113) or an appeal (§ 1.191) has been taken.

43. A new § 1.115 is proposed to be added to read as follows:

§ 1.115 Preliminary amendments.

(a) A preliminary amendment is an amendment that is received in the Office (§ 1.6) on or before the mail date of the first Office action under § 1.104.

(b) A preliminary amendment will be entered unless disapproved by the Commissioner. A preliminary amendment will not be disapproved if it is filed no later than:

(1) Three months from the filing date of an application under § 1.53(b);

(2) The filing date of a continued prosecution application under § 1.53(d); or

(3) Three months from the date the national stage is entered as set forth in § 1.491 in an international application.

(c) The time periods specified in paragraph (b) of this section are not extendable.

44. Section 1.121 is proposed to be amended by revising paragraphs (a) and (b) to read as follows:

§ 1.121 Manner of making amendments.

(a) *Amendments in applications, other than reissue applications.* Amendments in applications, excluding reissue applications, are made by filing a paper, in compliance with § 1.52, directing that specified amendments be made.

(1) *Specification other than the claims*—(i) *Amendment by instruction to delete, replace or add a paragraph:* If the paragraphs of the specification are numbered as provided in § 1.52(b)(6), amendments to the specification, other than the claims, may be made by submitting an instruction, referencing the paragraph number, to delete one or more paragraphs of the specification, to replace a deleted paragraph with one or more replacement paragraphs, or to add one or more paragraphs, along with the replacement or added paragraph(s). The replacement or added paragraph(s) must not include any markings to indicate the changes that have been made. The amendment must be accompanied by a copy of any replacement paragraph(s), on one or more pages separate from the amendment, marked-up to show all the changes made by brackets (for deleted matter) or underlining (for added matter), or by any equivalent marking system. If a deleted paragraph is replaced by a single paragraph, the replacement paragraph must retain the same number as the deleted paragraph. If a deleted paragraph is replaced by more than one paragraph, the numbering of the replacement paragraphs must begin with the number of the deleted paragraph with following paragraphs beginning with the number of the deleted paragraph followed by a single decimal and sequential integers (*e.g.,* paragraph 0071 is replaced by 0071, 0071.1, and 0071.2). Any paragraph(s) added between existing paragraphs must have the same number as the paragraph immediately above the added one, followed by a period and a new sequential number series (*e.g.,* 0071.1, 0071.2). When numbered paragraphs are added or deleted by amendment, the numbering of any unaffected paragraphs must remain unchanged. Subsequent amendments which may involve further replacement paragraphs are added in the same manner using existing paragraph numbers along with increasing numbers following a decimal. For clarity, a total renumbering of all previously added paragraphs or the submission of a substitute specification with totally renumbered paragraphs may be required.

(ii) *Amendment by replacement section.* If the sections of the specification contain section headings as provided in § 1.77(b), § 1.154(b), or § 1.163(c), amendments to the specification, other than the claims, may be made by referring to the section heading along with an instruction to delete that section of the specification and to replace such deleted section with a replacement section. The replacement section must be in clean form and must not include any markings to indicate the changes that have been made. The amendment must be accompanied by a copy of the replacement section, on one or more pages separate from the amendment, marked-up to show all changes made by brackets (for deleted matter) or underlining (for added matter), or by any equivalent marking system.

(iii) *Amendment by substitute specification.* The specification, other than the claims, may also be amended by submission of a substitute specification in compliance with § 1.125. If the paragraphs of the specification are not numbered as provided in § 1.52(b)(6), and the sections of the specification do not contain section headings as provided in § 1.77(b), § 1.154(b), or § 1.163(c), the specification, other than the claims, may be amended only by submission of a substitute specification in compliance with § 1.125. The paragraphs of the substitute specification, other than the claims, should be individually numbered in Arabic numerals so that any further amendment to the specification may be made by replacement paragraph(s) in accordance with paragraph (a)(1)(i) of this section. The amendment must be accompanied by a copy of the substitute specification marked-up to show all changes made by brackets (for deleted matter), or underlining (for added matter), or by any equivalent marking system.

(iv) Matter deleted by amendment pursuant to paragraph (a)(1) of this section can be reinstated only by a subsequent amendment presenting the previously deleted matter.

(2) *Claims.* Amendments to a claim must be made by rewriting such claim with all changes (*e.g.,* additions, deletions, modifications) included therein, or by directions to cancel or delete such claim. The rewriting of a claim (with the same or a new number) will be construed as directing the deletion of the previous version of that claim. A rewritten or newly added claim must be in clean form without markings as to the changes from the previous version of the claim or a canceled claim. If a claim is amended by rewriting such claim with the same number, the amendment must be accompanied by a copy of the rewritten claim, on one or more pages separate from the amendment, marked-up to show all the changes made by brackets (for deleted matter) or underlining (for added matter) or by any equivalent marking system, relative to the previous version of that claim. A claim canceled by amendment (deleted in its entirety) can be reinstated only by a subsequent amendment presenting the claim as a new claim with a new claim number.

(3) *Drawings.* Application drawings are amended in the following manner: Any change to the patent drawings must be submitted as a sketch on a separate paper showing the proposed changes in red for approval by the examiner. Upon approval by the examiner, new drawings in compliance with § 1.84 including the changes must be filed.

(4) *Disclosure consistency.* The disclosure must be amended, when required by the Office, to correct inaccuracies of description and definition, and to secure substantial correspondence between the claims, the remainder of the specification, and the drawings.

(5) *No new matter.* No amendment may introduce new matter into the disclosure of an application.

(b) *Amendments in reissue applications.* Any amendment to the description and claims of a reissue application must be made in accordance with § 1.173.

* * * * *

45. Section 1.125 is proposed to be amended by revising paragraphs (b)(2) and (c) to read as follows:

§ 1.125 Substitute specification.

* * * * *

(b) * * *

(2) A marked-up copy of the substitute specification showing all the changes to (including the matter being added to and the matter being deleted from) the specification of record. Numbering the paragraphs of the specification of record is not considered a change that must be shown pursuant to this paragraph.

(c) A substitute specification submitted under this section must be submitted in clean form without markings as to amended material. The paragraphs of any substitute specification, other than the claims, should be individually numbered in Arabic numerals so that any amendment to the specification may be made by replacement paragraph in accordance with § 1.121(a)(1)(i).

* * * * *

46. Section 1.131 is proposed to be amended by revising its heading and paragraph (a) to read as follows:

§ 1.131 Affidavit or declaration of prior invention.

(a) When any claim of an application or a patent under reexamination is rejected, the inventor of the subject matter of the rejected claim, the owner of the patent under reexamination, or the party qualified under §§ 1.42, 1.43, or 1.47, may submit an appropriate oath or declaration to establish invention of the subject matter of the rejected claim prior to the effective date of the reference or activity on which the rejection is based. The effective date of a U.S. patent is the date that such U.S. patent is effective as a reference under 35 U.S.C. 102(e). Prior invention may not be established under this section in any country other than the United States, a NAFTA country, or a WTO member country. Prior invention may not be established under this section before December 8, 1993, in a NAFTA country other than the United States, or before January 1, 1996, in a WTO member country other than a NAFTA country. Prior invention may not be established under this section if either:

(1) The rejection is based upon a U.S. patent to another or others which claims the same patentable invention as defined in § 1.601(n); or

(2) The rejection is based upon a statutory bar.

* * * * *

47. Section 1.132 is proposed to be revised to read as follows:

§ 1.132 Affidavits or declarations traversing rejections or objections.

When any claim of an application or a patent under reexamination is rejected or objected to, the inventor of the subject matter of the rejected claim, an oath or declaration may be submitted to traverse the rejection or objection. An oath or declaration may not be submitted under this section to traverse a rejection if the rejection is based upon a U.S. patent to another or others which claims the same patentable invention as defined in § 1.601(n).

48. Section 1.133 is proposed to be amended by revising paragraph (a) to read as follows:

§ 1.133 Interviews.

(a) Interviews with examiners concerning applications and other matters pending before the Office must be conducted on Office premises and within office hours, as the respective examiners may designate. Interviews will not be permitted at any other time or place without the authority of the Commissioner. Interviews for the discussion of the patentability of pending applications will not occur before the first Office action. The examiner may require that an interview be scheduled in advance.

* * * * *

49. Section 1.136 is proposed to be amended by adding paragraph (c) to read as follows:

§ 1.136 Extensions of time.

* * * * *

(c) If an applicant is notified in a "Notice of Allowability" that an application is otherwise in condition for allowance, the following time periods are not extendable if set in the "Notice of Allowability" or in an Office action having a mail date on or after the mail date of the "Notice of Allowability":

(1) The period for submitting an oath or declaration in compliance with § 1.63;
(2) The period for submitting formal drawings set under § 1.85(c); and
(3) The period for making a deposit set under § 1.809(c).

50. Section 1.137 is proposed to be amended by revising paragraph (c) to read as follows:

§ 1.137 Revival of abandoned application or lapsed patent.

* * * * *

(c)(1) Any petition to revive pursuant to this section in a design application must be accompanied by a terminal disclaimer and fee as set forth in § 1.321 dedicating to the public a terminal part of the term of any patent granted thereon equivalent to the period of abandonment of the application. Any petition to revive pursuant to this section in either a utility or plant application filed before June 8, 1995, must be accompanied by a terminal disclaimer and fee as set forth in § 1.321 dedicating to the public a terminal part of the term of any patent granted thereon equivalent to the lesser of:

(i) The period of abandonment of the application; or

(ii) The period extending beyond twenty years from the date on which the application for the patent was filed in the United States or, if the application contains a specific reference to an earlier filed application(s) under 35 U.S.C. 120, 121, or 365(c), from the date on which the earliest such application was filed.

(2) Any terminal disclaimer pursuant to paragraph (c)(1) of this section must also apply to any patent granted on a continuing utility or plant application filed after June 8, 1995, or a continuing design application, that contains a specific reference under 35 U.S.C. 120, 121, or 365(c) to the application for which revival is sought.

(3) The provisions of paragraph (c)(1) of this section do not apply to applications for which revival is sought solely for purposes of copendency with a utility or plant application filed on or after June 8, 1995, or to lapsed patents.

* * * * *

51. Section 1.138 is proposed to be revised to read as follows:

§ 1.138 Express abandonment.

(a) An application may be expressly abandoned by filing in the Patent and Trademark Office a written declaration of abandonment identifying the application. Express abandonment of the application may not be recognized by the Office unless it is actually received by appropriate officials in time to act thereon before the date of issue.

(b) A written declaration of abandonment must be signed by a party authorized under § 1.33(b)(1), (b)(3) or (b)(4) to sign a paper in the application, except as otherwise provided in this paragraph. A registered attorney or agent not of record who acts in a representative capacity under the provisions of § 1.34(a) when filing a continuing application may expressly abandon the prior application as of the filing date granted to the continuing application.

52. Section 1.152 is proposed to be revised to read as follows:

§ 1.152 Design drawings.

The design must be represented by a drawing that complies with the requirements of § 1.84, and must contain a sufficient number of views to constitute a complete disclosure of the appearance of the design. Appropriate and adequate surface shading should be used to show the character or contour of the surfaces represented. Solid black surface shading is not permitted except when used to represent the color black as well as color contrast. Broken lines may be used to show visible environmental structure, but may not be used to show hidden planes and surfaces which cannot be seen through opaque materials. Alternate positions of a design component, illustrated by full and broken lines in the same view are not permitted in a design drawing. Photographs and ink drawings are not permitted to be combined as formal drawings in one application. Photographs submitted in lieu of ink drawings in design patent applications must not disclose environmental structure but must be limited to the design for the article claimed.

53. Section 1.154 is proposed to be revised to read as follows:

§ 1.154 Arrangement of application elements.

(a) The elements of the design application, if applicable, should appear in the following order:

(1) Design application transmittal form.
(2) Fee transmittal form.
(3) Application data sheet (see § 1.76).
(4) Specification.
(5) Drawings or photographs.
(6) Executed oath or declaration (see § 1.153(b)).

(b) The specification should include the following sections in order:

(1) Preamble, stating name of the applicant, title of the design, and a brief description of the nature and intended use of the article in which the design is embodied.

(2) Cross-reference to related applications (unless included in the application data sheet).

(3) Statement regarding federally sponsored research or development.
(4) Description of the figure or figures of the drawing.
(5) Feature description.
(6) A single claim.

(c) The text of the specification sections defined in paragraph (b) of this section, if applicable, should be preceded by a section heading in uppercase and without underlining or bold type.

54. Section 1.155 is proposed to be revised to read as follows:

§ 1.155 Expedited examination of design patents.

(a) The applicant may request that the Office expedite the examination of a design application. To qualify for expedited examination:

(1) The application must include drawings in compliance with § 1.84;
(2) The applicant must have conducted a preexamination search; and
(3) The applicant must file a request for expedited examination including:

(i) The fee set forth in § 1.17(t); and

(ii) A statement that a preexamination search was conducted. The statement must also indicate the field of search and include an information disclosure statement in compliance with § 1.98.

(b) The Office will not examine an application that is not in condition for examination (*e.g.*, missing basic filing fee) even if the applicant files a request for expedited examination under this section.

55. Section 1.163 is proposed to be revised to read as follows:

§ 1.163 Specification and arrangement of application elements.

(a) The specification must contain as full and complete a disclosure as possible of the plant and the characteristics thereof that distinguish the same over related known varieties, and its antecedents, and must particularly point out where and in what manner the variety of plant has been asexually reproduced. For a newly found plant, the specification must particularly point out the location and character of the area where the plant was discovered.

(b) The elements of the plant application, if applicable, should appear in the following order:

(1) Plant application transmittal form.
(2) Fee transmittal form.
(3) Application data sheet (see § 1.76).

(4) Specification.
(5) Drawings (in duplicate).
(6) Executed oath or declaration (§ 1.162).

(c) The specification should include the following sections in order:

(1) Title of the invention, which may include an introductory portion stating the name, citizenship, and residence of the applicant.

(2) Cross-reference to related applications (unless included in the application data sheet).

(3) Statement regarding federally sponsored research or development.
(4) Latin name of the genus and species of the plant claimed.
(5) Variety denomination.
(6) Background of the invention.
(7) Brief summary of the invention.
(8) Brief description of the drawing.
(9) Detailed botanical description.
(10) A single claim.
(11) Abstract of the disclosure.

(d) The text of the specification or sections defined in paragraph (c) of this section, if applicable, should be preceded by a section heading in upper case, without underlining or bold type.

56. Section 1.173 is proposed to be revised to read as follows:

§ 1.173 Reissue specification, drawings, and amendments.

(a) *Contents of a reissue application.* An application for reissue must contain the entire specification, including the claims, and the drawings of the patent. No new matter shall be introduced into the application.

(1) *Specification, including claims.* The entire specification, including the claims, of the patent for which reissue is requested must be furnished in the form of a copy of the printed patent, but with only a single column of the printed patent securely mounted, or otherwise reproduced in permanent form, on a single page. If an amendment of the reissue application is to be included, it must be made pursuant to paragraph (b) of this section.

(2) *Drawings.* Applicant must submit a clean copy of each drawing sheet of the printed patent at the time the reissue application is filed. If such copy complies with § 1.84, no further drawings will be required. Where a drawing of the reissue application is to include any changes relative to the patent being reissued, the changes to the drawing must be made in accordance with paragraph (b)(3) of this section. The Office will not transfer the drawings from the patent file to the reissue application.

(b) *Making amendments in a reissue application.* An amendment in a reissue application is made either upon filing, by incorporating the changes physically within the specification, including the claims, using markings pursuant to paragraph (d) of this section, or by filing an amendment paper as a preliminary amendment or during prosecution directing that specified changes be made to the application specification, including the claims, or to the drawings.

(1) *Specification other than the claims.* Changes to the specification, other than to the claims, must be made by submission of the entire text of an added or rewritten paragraph, including markings pursuant to paragraph (d) of this section, except that an entire paragraph may be deleted by a statement deleting the paragraph without presentation of the text of the paragraph. The precise point in the specification must be identified where any added or rewritten paragraph is located.

(2) *Claims.* An amendment paper must include the entire text of each claim being changed by such amendment paper and of each claim being added by such amendment paper. For any claim changed by the amendment paper, a parenthetical expression "amended," "twice amended," *etc.*, should follow the claim number. Each changed patent claim and each added claim must include markings pursuant to paragraph (d) of this

section, except that a patent claim or added claim should be canceled by a statement canceling the claim without presentation of the text of the claim.

(3) *Drawings.* Any change to the patent drawings must be submitted as a sketch on a separate paper showing the proposed changes in red for approval by the examiner. Upon approval by the examiner, new drawings in compliance with § 1.84 including the approved changes must be filed. Amended figures must be identified as "Amended," and any added figure must be identified as "New." In the event that a figure is canceled, the figure must be surrounded by brackets and identified as "Canceled."

(c) *Status of claims and support for claim changes.* Whenever there is an amendment to the claims pursuant to paragraph (b) of this section, there must also be supplied, on pages separate from the pages containing the changes, the status (*i.e.*, pending or canceled), as of the date of the amendment, of all patent claims and of all added claims, and an explanation of the support in the disclosure of the patent for the changes to the claims made by the amendment paper.

(d) *Changes shown by markings.* Any changes relative to the patent being reissued which are made to the specification, including the claims, upon filing, or by an amendment paper in the reissue application, must include the following markings:

(1) The matter to be omitted by reissue must be enclosed in brackets; and

(2) The matter to be added by reissue must be underlined.

(e) *Numbering of patent claims preserved.* Patent claims may not be renumbered. The numbering of any claims added in the reissue application must follow the number of the highest numbered patent claim.

(f) *Amendment of disclosure may be required.* The disclosure must be amended, when required by the Office, to correct inaccuracies of description and definition, and to secure substantial correspondence between the claims, the remainder of the specification, and the drawings.

(g) *Amendments made relative to patent.* All amendments must be made relative to the patent specification, including the claims, and drawings, which are in effect as of the date of filing of the reissue application.

§ 1.174 [Removed and Reserved]

57. Section 1.174 is proposed to be removed and reserved.

58. Section 1.176 is proposed to be revised to read as follows:

§ 1.176 Examination of reissue.

(a) A reissue application will be examined in the same manner as a non-reissue nonprovisional application, and will be subject to all the requirements of the rules related to non-reissue applications. Restriction between subject matter of the original patent claims and previously unclaimed subject matter may be required.

(b) The examiner will act on applications for reissue in advance of other nonprovisional applications. An application for reissue, other than a continued prosecution application under § 1.53(d), will not be acted on sooner than two months after the announcement of the filing of the reissue application in the *Official Gazette.*

59. Section 1.177 is proposed to be revised to read as follows:

§ 1.177 Issuance of multiple reissue patents.

(a) The Office may reissue a patent as multiple reissue patents. If applicant files more than one application for the reissue of a single patent, each such application must contain or be amended to contain in the first sentence of the specification a notice stating that more than one reissue application has been filed and identifying each of the reissue applications by relationship, application number and filing date. The Office may correct any reissue patent resulting from an application to which this paragraph applies and not containing the required notice by certificate of correction under § 1.322.

(b) If applicant files more than one application for the reissue of a single patent, each claim of the patent being reissued must be presented in each of the reissue applications as an amended, unamended, or canceled (shown in brackets) claim, with each such claim bearing the same number as in the patent being reissued. The same claim of the patent being reissued may not be presented in its original unamended form for examination in more than one of such multiple reissue applications. The numbering of any added claims in any of the multiple reissue applications must follow the number of the highest numbered original patent claim.

(c) If any one of the several reissue applications by itself fails to correct an error in the original patent as required by 35 U.S.C. 251, but is otherwise in condition for allowance, the Office may suspend action in the allowable application until all issues are resolved as to at least one of the remaining reissue applications. The Office may also merge two or more of the multiple reissue applications into a single reissue application. No reissue application containing only unamended patent claims and not correcting an error in the original patent will be passed to issue by itself.

60. Section 1.178 is proposed to be revised to read as follows:

§ 1.178 Original patent.

The application for a reissue should be accompanied by an offer to surrender the original patent. The application should also be accompanied by the original patent, or if the original is lost or inaccessible, by a statement to that effect. The application may be accepted for examination in the absence of the original patent or the statement, but one or the other must be supplied before the application is allowed. If a reissue is refused, the original patent will be returned to applicant upon request.

61. Section 1.193 is proposed to be amended by revising paragraph (b)(1) to read as follows:

§ 1.193 Examiner's answer and reply brief.

* * * * *

(b)(1) Appellant may file a reply brief to an examiner's answer or a supplemental examiner's answer within two months from the date of such examiner's answer or supplemental examiner's answer. See § 1.136(b) for extensions of time for filing a reply brief in a patent application and § 1.550(c) for extensions of time for filing a reply brief in a reexamination proceeding. The primary examiner must either acknowledge receipt and entry of the reply brief or withdraw the final rejection and reopen prosecution to respond to the reply brief. A supplemental examiner's answer is not permitted, unless the application has been remanded by the Board of Patent Appeals and Interferences for such purpose.

* * * * *

62. Section 1.303 is proposed to be amended by revising paragraph (a) to read as follows:

§ 1.303 Civil action under 35 U.S.C. 145, 146, 306.

(a) Any applicant or any owner of a patent involved in a reexamination proceeding dissatisfied with the decision of the Board of Patent Appeals and Interferences, and any party to an interference dissatisfied with the decision of the Board of Patent Appeals and Interferences may, instead of appealing to the U.S. Court of Appeals for the Federal Circuit (§ 1.301), have remedy by civil action under 35 U.S.C. 145 or 146, as appropriate. Such civil action must be commenced within the time specified in § 1.304.

* * * * *

63. Section 1.311 is proposed to be amended by revising paragraph (b) to read as follows:

§ 1.311 Notice of allowance.

* * * * *

(b) An authorization to charge the issue fee (§ 1.18) to a deposit account may be filed in an individual application only after mailing of the notice of allowance.

64. Section 1.312 is proposed to be revised to read as follows:

§ 1.312 Amendments after allowance.

(a) No amendment may be made as a matter of right in an application after the mailing of the notice of allowance. Any amendment pursuant to this paragraph filed before the payment of the issue fee may be entered on the recommendation of the primary examiner, approved by the Commissioner, without withdrawing the application from issue.

(b) Any amendment pursuant to paragraph (a) of this section filed after the date the issue fee is paid must be accompanied by a petition under § 1.313(c)(1) to withdraw the application from issue, an unequivocal statement that one or more claims are unpatentable, and an explanation as to how the amendment is necessary to render such claim or claims patentable.

65. Section 1.313 is proposed to be revised to read as follows:

§ 1.313 Withdrawal from issue.

(a) Applications may be withdrawn from issue for further action at the initiative of the Office or upon petition by the applicant. To request that the Office withdraw an application from issue, the applicant must file a petition under this section including the fee set forth in § 1.17(h) and a showing of good and sufficient reasons why withdrawal of the application is necessary. If the Office withdraws the application from issue, the Office will issue a new notice of allowance if the Office again allows the application.

(b) Once the issue fee has been paid, the Office will not withdraw the application from issue at its own initiative for any reason except:

(1) A mistake on the part of the Office;

(2) A violation of § 1.56 or illegality in the application;

(3) Unpatentability of one or more claims; or

(4) For interference.

(c) Once the issue fee has been paid, the application will not be withdrawn from issue upon petition by the applicant for any reason except:

(1) Unpatentability of one of more claims, which petition must be accompanied by a statement of such unpatentability and an amendment in compliance with § 1.312(b); or

(2) Express abandonment of the application. Such express abandonment may be in favor of a continuing application.

(d) A petition under this section will not be effective to withdraw the application from issue unless it is actually received and granted by the appropriate officials before the date of issue. Withdrawal of an application from issue after payment of the issue fee may not be effective to avoid publication of application information.

66. Section 1.314 is proposed to be revised to read as follows:

§ 1.314 Issuance of patent.

If applicant timely pays the issue fee, the Office will issue the patent in regular course unless the application is withdrawn from issue (§ 1.313), or the Office defers issuance of the patent. To request that the Office defer issuance of a patent, applicant must file petition under this section including the fee set forth in § 1.17(h) and a showing of good and sufficient reasons why it is necessary to defer issuance of the patent.

67. Section 1.322 is proposed to be amended by revising paragraph (a) to read as follows:

§ 1.322 Certificate of correction of Office mistake.

(a) The Office may issue a certificate of correction under the conditions specified in 35 U.S.C. 254 at the request of the patentee or the patentee's assignee or on its own initiative. If the request relates to a patent involved in an interference, the request must comply with the requirements of this section and be accompanied by a motion under § 1.635. The Office will not issue such a certificate on its own initiative without first notifying the patentee (including any assignee of record) at the correspondence address of record as specified in § 1.33(a) and affording the patentee an opportunity to be heard.

* * * * *

68. Section 1.323 is proposed to be revised to read as follows:

§ 1.323 Certificate of correction of applicant's mistake.

The Office may issue a certificate of correction under the conditions specified in 35 U.S.C. 255 at the request of the patentee or the patentee's assignee, upon payment of the fee set forth in § 1.20(a). If the request relates to a patent involved in an interference, the request must comply with the requirements of this section and be accompanied by a motion under § 1.635.

69. Section 1.324 is proposed to be amended by revising its heading and paragraph (b)(1) and adding paragraph (c) to read as follows:

§ 1.324 Correction of inventorship in patent, pursuant to 35 U.S.C. 256.

* * * * *

(b) * * *

(1) Where one or more persons are being added, a statement from each person who is being added as an inventor that the inventorship error occurred without any deceptive intention on his or her part;

* * * * *

(c) For correction of inventorship in an application see §§ 1.48 and 1.497, and in an interference see § 1.634.

70. Section 1.366 is proposed to be amended by revising paragraph (c) to read as follows:

§ 1.366 Submission of maintenance fees.

* * * * *

(c) In submitting maintenance fees and any necessary surcharges, identification of the patents for which maintenance fees are being paid must include the patent number, and the application number of the United States application for the patent on which the maintenance fee is being paid. If the payment includes identification of only the patent number (*i.e.,* does not identify the application number of the United States application for the patent on which the maintenance fee is being paid), the Office may apply the payment to the patent identified by patent number in the payment or may return the payment.

* * * * *

71. Section 1.446 is proposed to be amended by revising paragraphs (a) and (b) to read as follows:

§ 1.446 Refund of international application filing and processing fees.

(a) Money paid for international application fees, where paid by actual mistake or in excess, such as a payment not required by law or Treaty and it Regulations, may be refunded. A mere change of purpose after the payment of a fee will not entitle a party to a refund of such fee. The Office will not refund amounts of twenty-five dollars or less unless a refund is specifically requested, and will not notify the payor of such amounts. If the payor or party requesting a refund does not provide the banking information necessary for making refunds by electronic funds transfer, the Office may use the banking information provided on the payment instrument to make any refund by electronic funds transfer.

(b) Any request for refund under paragraph (a) must be filed within two years from the date the fee was paid. If the Office charges a deposit account by an amount other than an amount specifically indicated in an authorization under § 1.25(b), any request for refund based upon such charge must be filed within two years from the date of the deposit account statement indicating such charge, and include a copy of that deposit account statement. The time periods set forth in this paragraph are not extendable.

* * * * *

72. Section 1.497 is proposed to be amended by revising paragraph (b)(2) and adding paragraph (d) to read as follows:

§ 1.497 Oath or declaration under 35 U.S.C. 371(c)(4).

* * * * *

(b) * * *

(2) If the person making the oath or declaration or any supplemental oath or declaration is not the inventor (§§ 1.42, 1.43, or 1.47), the oath or declaration shall state the relationship of the person to the inventor, and, upon information and belief, the facts which the inventor would have been required to state. If the person signing the oath or declaration is the legal representative of a deceased inventor, the oath or declaration shall also state that the person is a legal representative and the citizenship, residence and mailing address of the legal representative.

* * * * *

(d) If the oath or declaration filed pursuant to 35 U.S.C. 371(c)(4) and this section names an inventive entity different from the inventive entity set forth in the international stage, the oath or declaration must be accompanied by:

(1) A statement from each person being added as an inventor and from each person being deleted as an inventor that any error in inventorship in the international stage occurred without deceptive intention on his or her part;

(2) The processing fee set forth in § 1.17(i); and

(3) If an assignment has been executed by any of the original named inventors, the written consent of the assignee (see § 3.73(b)).

73. Section 1.510 is proposed to be amended by revising paragraph (b)(4) to read as follows:

§ 1.510 Request for reexamination.

* * * * *

(b) * * *

(4) The entire specification, including the claims, of the patent for which reexamination is requested, in the form of a copy of the printed patent, but with only a single column of the printed patent securely mounted, or otherwise reproduced in permanent form, on a single sheet. A clean copy of each drawing sheet of the printed patent must also be furnished. Additionally, a copy of any disclaimer, certificate of correction, or reexamination certificate issued in the patent must be included.

* * * * *

74. Section 1.530 is proposed to be amended by revising its heading and paragraph (d), and adding paragraphs (e) through (l) to read as follows:

§ 1.530 Statement; amendment by patent owner; inventorship change.

* * * * *

(d) *Making amendments in a reexamination proceeding.* A proposed amendment in a reexamination proceeding is made by filing a paper directing that proposed specified changes be made to the patent specification, including the claims, or to the drawings. An amendment paper directing that proposed specified changes be made in a reexamination proceeding may be submitted as an accompaniment to a request filed by the patent owner in accordance with § 1.510(e), as part of a patent owner statement in accordance with paragraph (b) of this section, or, where permitted, during the conduct of the reexamination proceeding pursuant to § 1.550(a).

(1) *Specification other than the claims.* Changes to the specification, other than to the claims, must be made by submission of the entire text of an added or rewritten paragraph including markings pursuant to paragraph (f) of this section, except that an entire paragraph may be deleted by a statement deleting the paragraph, without presentation of the text of the paragraph. The precise point in the specification must be identified where any added or rewritten paragraph is located.

(2) *Claims.* An amendment paper must include the entire text of each patent claim which is being proposed to be changed by such amendment paper and of each new claim being proposed to be added by such amendment paper. For any claim changed by the amendment paper, a parenthetical expression "amended," "twice amended," *etc.*, should follow the claim number. Each patent claim proposed to be changed and each proposed added claim must include markings pursuant to paragraph (f) of this section, except that a patent claim or proposed added claim should be canceled by a statement canceling the claim, without presentation of the text of the claim.

(3) *Drawings.* Any change to the patent drawings must be submitted as a sketch on a separate paper showing the proposed changes in red for approval by the examiner. Upon approval of the changes by the examiner, only new sheets of drawings including the changes and in compliance with § 1.84 must be filed. Amended figures must be identified as "Amended," and any added figure must be identified as "New." In the event a figure is canceled, the figure must be surrounded by brackets and identified as "Canceled."

(e) *Status of claims and support for claim changes.* Whenever there is an amendment to the claims pursuant to paragraph (d) of this section, there must also be supplied, on pages separate from the pages containing the changes, the status (*i.e.*, pending or canceled), as of the date of the amendment, of all patent claims and of all added claims, and an explanation of the support in the disclosure of the patent for the changes to the claims made by the amendment paper.

(f) *Changes shown by markings.* Any changes relative to the patent being reexamined which are made to the specification, including the claims, must include the following markings:

(1) The matter to be omitted by the reexamination proceeding must be enclosed in brackets; and

(2) The matter to be added by the reexamination proceeding must be underlined.

(g) *Numbering of patent claims preserved.* Patent claims may not be renumbered. The numbering of any claims added in the reexamination proceeding must follow the number of the highest numbered patent claim.

(h) *Amendment of disclosure maybe required.* The disclosure must be amended, when required by the Office, to correct inaccuracies of description and definition, and to secure substantial correspondence between the claims, the remainder of the specification, and the drawings.

(i) *Amendments made relative to patent.* All amendments must be made relative to the patent specification, including the claims, and drawings, which are in effect as of the date of filing the request for reexamination.

(j) *No enlargement of claim scope.* No amendment may enlarge the scope of the claims of the patent or introduce new matter. No amendment may be proposed for entry in an expired patent. Moreover, no amendment, other than the cancellation of claims, will be incorporated into the patent by a certificate issued after the expiration of the patent.

(k) *Amendments not effective until certificate.* Although the Office actions will treat proposed amendments as though they have been entered, the proposed amendments will not be effective until the reexamination certificate is issued.

(l) *Correction of inventorship in reexamination proceedings.* (1) When it appears that the correct inventor or inventors were not named in a patent being reexamined through error without deceptive intention on the part of the actual inventor or inventors, the Commissioner may, on petition of all the parties and the assignees and satisfactory proof of the facts and payment of the fee set forth in § 1.20(b), or on order of a court before which such matter is called in question, include in the reexamination certificate to be issued under § 1.570 an amendment naming only the actual inventor or inventors. The petition must be submitted as part of the reexamination proceeding, and must satisfy the requirements of § 1.324.

(2) Notwithstanding paragraph (l)(1) of this section, if a petition to correct inventorship satisfying the requirements of § 1.324 is filed in a reexamination proceeding, and the reexamination proceeding is terminated other than in a reexamination certificate under § 1.570, a certificate of correction indicating the change of inventorship stated in the petition will be issued upon request by the patentee.

75. Section 1.550 is proposed to be amended by revising paragraphs (a) through (c) to read as follows:

§ 1.550 Conduct of reexamination proceedings.

(a) All reexamination proceedings, including any appeals to the Board of Patent Appeals and Interferences, will be conducted with special dispatch within the Office. After issuance of the reexamination order and expiration of the time for submitting any responses thereto, the examination will be conducted in accordance with §§ 1.104, 1.105, 1.110–1.113, 1.115, and 1.116 and will result in the issuance of a reexamination certificate under § 1.570.

(b) The patent owner will be given at least thirty days to respond to any Office action. Such response may include further statements in response to any rejections and/or proposed amendments or new claims to place the patent in a condition where all claims, if amended as proposed, would be patentable.

(c)(1) On or before the day on which an action by the patent owner is due in a reexamination proceeding, the time for taking action by a patent owner will be extended only for sufficient cause, and for a reasonable time specified. Any request for such extension must be filed on or before the day on which action by the patent owner is due, but in no case will the mere filing of a request effect any extension. See § 1.304(a) for extensions of time for filing a notice of appeal to the U.S. Court of Appeals for the Federal Circuit or for commencing a civil action.

(2) After the day on which an action by the patent owner is due in a reexamination proceeding, the time for taking action by a patent owner will be extended only upon the granting of a petition for extension of time to accept late papers on the grounds that submission of the papers was unintentionally delayed. A petition must be;

(i) Accompanied by papers effecting the action by the patent owner required to continue prosecution of the reexamination proceeding;

(ii) Accompanied by the petition fee as set forth in § 1.17(h);

(iii) Accompanied by a statement that the delay was unintentional. The Commissioner may require additional information where there is a question whether the delay was unintentional; and

(iv) Filed as a complete petition within the full statutory time period for submission of the papers that were unintentionally delayed.

* * * * *

76. Section 1.666 is proposed to be amended by revising paragraph (b) to read as follows:

§ 1.666 Filing of interference settlement agreements.

* * * * *

(b) If any party filing the agreement or understanding under paragraph (a) of this section so requests, the copy will be kept separate from the file of the interference, and made available only to Government agencies on written request, or to any person upon petition accompanied by the fee set forth in § 1.17(h) and on a showing of good cause.

* * * * *

77. Section 1.720 is proposed to be amended by revising paragraphs (b) and (g) to read as follows:

§ 1.720 Conditions for extension of patent term.

* * * * *

(b) The term of the patent has never been previously extended, except for extensions issued pursuant to § 1.701, § 1.760, or § 1.790;

* * * * *

(g) The term of the patent, including any interim extension issued pursuant to § 1.790, has not expired before the submission of an application in compliance with § 1.741; and

* * * * *

78. Section 1.730 is proposed to be revised to read as follows:

§ 1.730 Applicant for extension of patent term; signature requirements.

(a) Any application for extension of a patent term must be submitted by the owner of record of the patent or its agent and must comply with the requirements of § 1.740.

(b) If the application is submitted by the patent owner, the application must be signed either by:

(1) The patent owner in compliance with § 3.73(b) of this chapter; or

(2) A registered practitioner on behalf of the patent owner.

(c) If the application is submitted on behalf of the patent owner by an agent of the patent owner (*e.g.*, a licensee of the patent owner), the application must be signed by a registered practitioner on behalf of the agent. The Office may require proof that the agent is authorized to act on behalf of the patent owner.

(d) If the application is signed by a registered practitioner, the Office may require proof that the practitioner is authorized to act on behalf of the patent owner or agent of the patent owner.

79. Section 1.740 is proposed to be amended by revising its heading, the introductory text of paragraph (a), and paragraphs (a)(9), (a)(10), (a)(14), (a)(15), (b) and (c) to read as follows:

§ 1.740 Formal requirements for application for extension of patent term; correction of informalities.

(a) An application for extension of patent term must be made in writing to the Commissioner. A formal application for the extension of patent term must include:

* * * * *

(9) A statement that the patent claims the approved product or a method of using or manufacturing the approved product, and a showing which lists each applicable patent claim and demonstrates the manner in which at least one such patent claim reads on:

(i) The approved product, if the listed claims include any claim to the approved product;

(ii) The method of using the approved product, if the listed claims include any claim to the method of using the approved product; and

(iii) The method of manufacturing the approved product, if the listed claims include any claim to the method of manufacturing the approved product;

(10) A statement beginning on a new page, of the relevant dates and information pursuant to 35 U.S.C. 156(g) in order to enable the Secretary of Health and Human Services or the Secretary of Agriculture, as appropriate, to determine the applicable regulatory review period as follows:

(i) For a patent claiming a human drug, antibiotic, or human biological product;

(A) The effective date of the investigational new drug (IND) application and the IND number;

(B) The date on which a new drug application (NDA) or a Product License Application (PLA) was initially submitted and the NDA or PLA number; and

(C) The date on which the NDA was approved or the Product License issued;

(ii) For a patent claiming a new animal drug;

(A) The date a major health or environmental effects test on the drug was initiated, and any available substantiation of that date, or the date of an exemption under subsection (j) of section 512 of the Federal Food, Drug, and Cosmetic Act became effective for such animal drug;

(B) The date on which a new animal drug application (NADA) was initially submitted and the NADA number; and

(C) The date on which the NADA was approved;

(iii) For a patent claiming a veterinary biological product;

(A) The date thc authority to prepare an experimental biological product under the Virus-Serum-Toxin Act became effective;

(B) The date an application for a license was submitted under the Virus-Serum-Toxin Act; and

(C) The date the license issued;

(iv) For a patent claiming a food or color additive:

(A) The date a major health or environmental effects test on the additive was initiated and any available substantiation of that date;

(B) The date on which a petition for product approval under the Federal Food, Drug and Cosmetic Act was initially submitted and the petition number; and

(C) The date on which the FDA published a **Federal Register** notice listing the additive for use;

(v) For a patent claiming a medical device:

(A) The effective date of the investigational device exemption (IDE) and the IDE number, if applicable, or the date on which the applicant began the first clinical investigation involving the device if no IDE was submitted and any available substantiation of that date;

(B) The date on which the application for product approval or notice of completion of a product development protocol under section 515 of the Federal Food, Drug and Cosmetic Act was initially submitted and the number of the application; and

(C) The date on which the application was approved or the protocol declared to be completed;

* * * * *

(14) The prescribed fee for receiving and acting upon the application for extension (see § 1.20(j)); and

(15) The name, address, and telephone number of the person to whom inquiries and correspondence relating to the application for patent term extension are to be directed.

(b) The application under this section must be accompanied by two additional copies of such application.

(c) If an application for extension of patent term is informal under this section, the Office will so notify the applicant. The applicant has two months from the mail date of the notice, or such time as is set in the notice, within which to correct the informality. Unless the notice indicates otherwise, this time period may be extended under the provisions of § 1.136.

80. Section 1.741 is proposed to be amended by revising its heading, the introductory text of paragraph (a) and paragraphs (a)(5) and (b) to read as follows:

§ 1.741 Complete application given a filing date; petition procedure.

(a) The filing date of an application for extension of a patent term is the date on which a complete application is received in the Office or filed pursuant to the procedures set forth in § 1.8 or § 1.10. A complete application must include:

* * * * *

(5) Sufficient information to enable the Commissioner to determine under subsections (a) and (b) of 35 U.S.C. 156 the eligibility of a patent for extension and the rights that will be derived from the extension and information to enable the Commissioner and the Secretary of Health and Human Services or the Secretary of Agriculture to determine the length of the regulatory review period; and

* * * * *

(b) If an application for extension of patent term is incomplete under this section, the Office will so notify the applicant. If applicant requests review of a notice that an application is incomplete, or review of the filing date accorded an application under this section, applicant must file a petition pursuant to this paragraph accompanied by the fee set forth in § 1.17(h) within two months of the mail date of the notice that the application is incomplete, or the notice according the filing date complained of. Unless the notice indicates otherwise, this time period may be extended under the provisions of § 1.136.

81. Section 1.780 is proposed to be revised to read as follows:

§ 1.780 Certificate or order of extension of patent term.

If a determination is made pursuant to § 1.750 that a patent is eligible for extension and that the term of the patent is to be extended, a certificate of extension, under seal, or an order granting interim extension under 35 U.S.C. 156(d)(5), will be issued to the applicant for the extension of the patent term. Such certificate or order will be recorded in the official file of the patent and will be considered as part of the original patent. Notification of the issuance of the certificate or order of extension will be published in the *Official Gazette* of the Patent and Trademark Office. Notification of the issuance of the order granting an interim extension under 35 U.S.C. 156(d)(5), including the identity of the product currently under regulatory review, will be published in the *Official Gazette* of the Patent and Trademark Office and in the **Federal Register.** No certificate of, or order granting, an extension will be issued if the term of the patent cannot be extended, even though the patent is otherwise determined to be eligible for extension. In such situations, the final determination made pursuant to § 1.750 will indicate that no certificate or order will issue.

82. Section 1.809 is proposed to be amended by revising paragraphs (b) introductory text, (b)(1) and (c) to read as follows:

§ 1.809 Examination procedures.

* * * * *

(b) The applicant for patent or patent owner shall reply to a rejection under paragraph (a) of this section by—

(1) In the case of an applicant for patent, making an acceptable original or replacement or supplemental deposit or assuring the Office in writing that an

acceptable deposit will be made, or, in the case of a patent owner, requesting a certificate of correction of the patent which meets the terms of paragraphs (b) and (c) of § 1.805, or

* * * * *

(c) If an application for patent is otherwise in condition for allowance except for a needed deposit and the Office has received a written assurance that an acceptable deposit will be made, applicant will be notified and given a period of time within which the deposit must be made in order to avoid abandonment. This time period is not extendable under § 1.136(a) or (b) (see § 1.136(c)).

* * * * *

83. Section 1.821 is proposed to be amended by revising paragraphs (c), (e) and (f) to read as follows:

§ 1.821 Nucleotide and/or amino acid sequence disclosures in patent applications.

* * * * *

(c) Patent applications which contain disclosures of nucleotide and/or amino acid sequences must contain such nucleotide and/or amino acid sequences disclosure and associated information as a separate part of the disclosure using the symbols and format in accordance with the requirements of §§ 1.822 and 1.823. This disclosure is hereinafter referred to as the "Sequence Listing." Each sequence disclosed must appear separately in the "Sequence Listing." Each sequence set forth in the "Sequence Listing" shall be assigned a separate sequence identifier. The sequence identifiers shall begin with 1 and increase sequentially by integers. If no sequence is present for a sequence identifier, the code "000" shall be used in place of the sequence. The response for the numeric identifier <160> (see § 1.823(b)) shall include the total number of SEQ ID NOs, whether followed by a sequence or by the code "000." The "Sequence Listing" must be submitted either on:

(1) Paper in compliance with § 1.823; or

(2) A Compact Disk-Read Only Memory (CD–ROM) or Compact Disk-Recordable (CD–R) in compliance with § 1.823. Applicant may submit a second copy of such a CD–ROM or CD–R "Sequence Listing" to satisfy the requirement for a "Sequence Listing" in a computer readable format pursuant to paragraph (e) of this section, provided that the CD–ROM or CD–R "Sequence Listing" meets the requirements of § 1.824(b) and (c)(4).

* * * * *

(e) In addition to the submission of the "Sequence Listing" referred to in paragraph (c) of this section, a copy of this "Sequence Listing" must also be submitted in computer readable form in accordance with the requirements of § 1.824. The computer readable form submitted pursuant to this paragraph must be a copy of the "Sequence Listing" submitted pursuant to paragraph (c) of this section and will not necessarily be retained as a part of the patent application file. If the computer readable form of a new application is to be identical with the computer readable form of another application of the applicant on file in the Patent and Trademark Office, reference may be made to the other application and computer readable form in lieu of filing a duplicate computer readable form in the new application if the computer readable form in the other application was compliant with all of the requirements of this subpart. The new application shall be accompanied by a letter making such reference to the other application and computer readable form, both of which shall be completely identified. In the new application, applicant must also request the use of the compliant computer readable form (CRF) "Sequence Listing" that is already on file for the other application and must state that the paper or CD–ROM or CD–R copy of the "Sequence Listing" in the new application is identical to the computer readable (CRF) copy filed for the other application.

(f) In addition to the paper or CD–ROM or CD–R copy required by paragraph (c) of this section and the computer readable form required by paragraph (e) of this section, a statement that the content of the paper, CD–ROM, or CD–R submission under paragraph (c) of this section and the computer readable (CRF) copy under paragraph (e) of this section are the same must be submitted with the computer readable form (*e.g.*, a statement that "the information recorded in computer readable form is identical to the paper (or CD–ROM or CD–R) copy of the sequence listing submitted under § 1.821(c)" submitted under § 1.821(c)).

* * * * *

84. Section 1.823 is proposed to be amended by revising its heading and paragraph (a) to read as follows:

§ 1.823 Requirements for nucleotide and/or amino acid sequences as part of the application.

(a)(1) If the "Sequence Listing" required by § 1.821(c) is submitted on paper: The "Sequence Listing" setting forth the nucleotide and/or amino acid sequence and associated information in accordance with paragraph (b) of this section, must begin on a new page and must be titled "Sequence Listing." The "Sequence Listing" preferably should be numbered independently of the numbering of the remainder of the application. Each page of the "Sequence Listing" should contain no more than 66 lines and each line should contain no more than 72 characters. A fixed-width font should be used exclusively throughout the "Sequence Listing."

(2) If the "Sequence Listing" required by § 1.821(c) is submitted on a CD–ROM or CD–R: The "Sequence Listing" must be submitted as a text file in the American Standard Code for Information Interchange (ASCII) in accordance with the standards for that medium set forth in 36 CFR 1228.188(c) and (d). No other format shall be allowed. The CD–ROM or CD–R "Sequence Listing" must also be accompanied by documentation on paper that is adequate to identify, maintain, and interpret the electronic "Sequence Listing." A notation that a "Sequence Listing" is submitted on a CD–ROM or CD–R must be placed conspicuously in the specification (see § 1.77(b)(11)). The CD–ROM or CD–R "Sequence Listing" also must be labeled with the following information:

(i) The name of each inventor (if known);

(ii) The title of the invention;

(iii) The sequence identifiers of the "Sequence Listings" on the CD–ROM or CD–R; and

(iv) The docket number used by the person filing the application to identify the application (if applicable).

* * * * *

84a. Section 1.824 is proposed to be amended by revising paragraph (c)(4) to read as follows:

§ 1.824 Form and format for nucleotide and/or amino acid sequence submissions in computer readable form.

* * * * *

(c) * * *

(4) CD–ROM or CD–R: Format ISO 9660 or High Sierra Format.

* * * * *

85. Section 1.825 is proposed to be amended by revising paragraphs (a) and (b) to read as follows:

§ 1.825 Amendments to or replacement of sequence listing and computer readable copy thereof.

(a) Any amendment to the paper copy of the "Sequence Listing" submitted pursuant to § 1.821 must be made by submission of substitute sheets. Any amendment to the CD–ROM or CD–R copy of the "Sequence Listing" submitted pursuant to § 1.821 must be made by submission of a new CD–ROM or CD–R containing a substitute "Sequence Listing." Amendments must be accompanied by a statement that indicates support for the amendment in the application-as-filed, and a statement that the substitute sheets or new CD–ROM or CD–R includes no new matter.

(b) Any amendment to the paper, CD–ROM, or CD–R copy of the "Sequence Listing" pursuant to paragraph (a) of this section must be accompanied by a substitute copy of the computer readable form of the "Sequence Listing" required pursuant to § 1.821(e), including all previously submitted data with the amendment incorporated therein, and accompanied by a statement that the computer readable form copy is the same as the substitute paper or new CD–ROM or CD–R copy of the "Sequence Listing."

* * * * *

PART 3—ASSIGNMENT, RECORDING AND RIGHTS OF ASSIGNEE

86. The authority citation for 37 CFR part 3 continues to read as follows:

Authority: 15 U.S.C. 1123; 35 U.S.C. 6.

87. Section 3.27 is proposed to be revised to read as follows:

§ 3.27 Mailing address for submitting documents to be recorded.

Documents and cover sheets to be recorded should be addressed to the Commissioner of Patents and Trademarks, Box Assignment, Washington, D.C. 20231, unless they are filed together with new applications.

88. Section 3.71 is proposed to be revised to read as follows:

§ 3.71 Prosecution by assignee.

(a) *Patents—Conducting of prosecution.* One or more assignees as defined in paragraph (b) of this section may, after becoming of record pursuant to paragraph (c) of this section, conduct prosecution of a national patent application or a reexamination proceeding to the exclusion of either the inventive entity, or the assignee(s) previously entitled to conduct prosecution.

(b) *Patents—Assignee(s) who can prosecute.* The assignee(s) who may conduct either the prosecution of a national application for patent or a reexamination proceeding are:

(1) *A single assignee.* An assignee of the entire right, title and interest in the application or patent being reexamined who is of record, or

(2) *Partial assignee(s) together or with inventor(s).* All partial assignees, or all partial assignees and inventors who have not assigned their right, title and interest in the application or patent being reexamined, who together own the entire right, title and interest in the application or patent being reexamined. A partial assignee is any assignee of record having less than the entire right, title and interest in the application or patent being reexamined.

(c) *Patents—Becoming of record.* An assignee becomes of record either in a national patent application or a reexamination proceeding by filing a statement in compliance with § 3.73(b).

(d) *Trademarks.* The assignee of a trademark application or registration may prosecute a trademark application; submit documents to maintain a trademark registration; or file papers against a third party in reliance on the assignee's trademark application or registration, to the exclusion of the original applicant or previous assignee. The assignee must establish ownership in compliance with § 3.73(b).

89. Section 3.73 is proposed to be revised to read as follows:

§ 3.73 Establishing right of assignee to take action.

(a) The inventor is presumed to be the owner of a patent application, and any patent that may issue therefrom, unless there is an assignment. The original applicant is presumed to be the owner of a trademark application or registration, unless there is an assignment.

(b)(1) In order to request or take action in a patent or trademark matter, the assignee must establish its ownership of the patent or trademark property to the satisfaction of the Commissioner. The establishment of ownership by the assignee may be combined with the paper that requests or takes the action. Ownership is established by submitting to the Office a signed statement identifying the assignee, accompanied by either:

(i) Documentary evidence of a chain of title from the original owner to the assignee (*e.g.,* copy of an executed assignment). The documents submitted to establish ownership may be required to be recorded pursuant to § 3.11 in the assignment records of the Office as a condition to permitting the assignee to take action in a matter pending before the Office; or

(ii) A statement specifying where documentary evidence of a chain of title is recorded in the assignment records of the Office (*e.g.,* reel and frame number).

(2) The submission establishing ownership must show that the party signing the submission is a party authorized to act on behalf of the assignee by:

(i) Including a statement that the party signing the submission is authorized to act on behalf of the assignee; or

(ii) Being signed by a person having apparent authority to sign on behalf of the assignee, *e.g.,* an officer of the assignee.

(c) For patent matters only:

(1) Establishment of ownership by the assignee must be submitted prior to, or at the same time as, the paper requesting or taking action is submitted.

(2) If the submission under this section is by an assignee of less than the entire right, title and interest, such assignee must indicate the extent (by percentage) of its ownership interest or the Office may refuse to accept the submission.

90. Section 3.81 is proposed to be revised to read as follows:

§ 3.81 Issue of patent to assignee.

For a patent application, if an assignment of the entire right, title, and interest is recorded before the issue fee is paid, the patent may issue in the name of the assignee. If the assignee holds an undivided part interest, the patent may issue jointly to the inventor and the assignee. If the patent is to issue solely or jointly to that assignee, the name of the assignee must be provided at the time the issue fee is paid.

PART 5—SECRECY OF CERTAIN INVENTIONS AND LICENSES TO EXPORT AND FILE APPLICATIONS IN FOREIGN COUNTRIES

91. The authority citation for 37 CFR part 5 would continue to read as follows:

Authority: 35 U.S.C. 6, 41, 181–188, as amended by the Patent Law Foreign Filing Amendments Act of 1988, Pub. L. 100–418, 102 Stat. 1567; the Arms Export Control Act, as amended, 22 U.S.C. 2751 *et seq.*; the Atomic Energy Act of 1954, as amended, 42 U.S.C. 2011 *et seq.*; and the Nuclear Non-Proliferation Act of 1978, 22 U.S.C. 3201 *et seq.*; and the delegations in the regulations under these Acts to the Commissioner (15 CFR 370.10(j). 22 CFR 125.04, and 10 CFR 810.7).

92. Section 5.1 is proposed to be revised to read as follows:

§ 5.1 Applications and correspondence involving national security.

(a) All correspondence in connection with this part, including petitions, should be addressed to "Assistant Commissioner for Patents (Attention Licensing and Review), Washington, D.C. 20231."

(b) Application as used in this part includes provisional applications filed under 35 U.S.C. 111(b) (§ 1.9(a)(2) of this chapter), nonprovisional applications filed under 35 U.S.C. 111(a) or entering the national stage from an international application after compliance with 35 U.S.C. 371 (§ 1.9(a)(3)), or international applications filed under the Patent Cooperation Treaty prior to entering the national stage of processing (§ 1.9(b)).

(c) Patent applications and documents relating thereto that are national security classified (see § 1.9(i) of this chapter) and contain authorized national security markings (*e.g.*, "Confidential," "Secret" or "Top Secret") are accepted by the Office. National security classified documents filed in the Office must be either hand-carried to Licensing and Review or mailed to the Office in compliance with paragraph (a) of this section.

(d) The applicant in a national security classified patent application must obtain a secrecy order pursuant to § 5.2(a). If a national security classified patent application is filed without a notification pursuant to § 5.2(a), the Office will set a time period within which either the application must be declassified, or the application must be placed under a secrecy order pursuant to § 5.2(a), or the applicant must submit evidence of a good faith effort to obtain a secrecy order pursuant to § 5.2(a) from the relevant department or agency in order to prevent abandonment of the application. If evidence of a good faith effort to obtain a secrecy order pursuant to § 5.2(a) from the relevant department or agency is submitted by the applicant within the time period set by the Office, but the application has not been declassified or placed under a secrecy order pursuant to § 5.2(a), the Office will again set a time period within which either the application must be declassified, or the application must be placed under a secrecy order pursuant to § 5.2(a), or the applicant must submit evidence of a good faith effort to again obtain a secrecy order pursuant to § 5.2(a) from the relevant department or agency in order to prevent abandonment of the application.

(e) A national security classified patent application will not be allowed pursuant to § 1.311 of this chapter until the application is declassified and any secrecy order pursuant to § 5.2(a) has been rescinded.

(f) Applications on inventions made outside the United States and on inventions in which a U.S. Government defense agency has a property interest will not be made available to defense agencies.

93. Section 5.2 is proposed to be amended by adding a new paragraph (c) to read as follows:

§ 5.2 Secrecy order.

* * * * *

(c) An application disclosing any significant part of the subject matter of an application under a secrecy order pursuant to paragraph (a) of this section also falls within the scope of such secrecy order. Any such application that is pending before the Office must be promptly brought to the attention of Licensing and Review, unless such application is itself under a secrecy order pursuant to paragraph (a) of this section. Any subsequently filed application containing any significant part of the subject matter of an application under a secrecy order pursuant to paragraph (a) of this section must either be hand-carried to Licensing and Review or mailed to the Office in compliance with § 5.1(a).

94. Section 5.12 is amended by revising paragraph (b) to read as follows:

§ 5.12 Petition for license.

* * * * *

(b) A petition for license must include the fee set forth in § 1.17(h), the petitioner's address, and full instructions for delivery of the requested license when it is to be delivered to other than the petitioner. The petition should be presented in letter form.

PART 10—REPRESENTATION OF OTHERS BEFORE THE PATENT AND TRADEMARK OFFICE

95. The authority citation for 37 CFR part 10 would continue to read as follows:

Authority: 5 U.S.C. 500, 15 U.S.C. 1123; 35 U.S.C. 6, 31, 32, 41.

96. Section 10.23 is proposed to be amended by revising paragraph (c)(11) to read as follows:

§ 10.23 Misconduct.

* * * * *

(c) * * *

(11) Except as permitted by § 1.52(c) of this chapter, knowingly filing or causing to be filed an application containing any material alteration made in the application papers after the signing of the accompanying oath or declaration without identifying the alteration at the time of filing the application papers.

* * * * *

Dated: September 17, 1999.

Q. Todd Dickinson,
Acting Assistant Secretary of Commerce and Acting Commissioner of Patents and Trademarks.
[FR Doc. 99–24922 Filed 10–1–99; 8:45 am]

Appendix D-10

Changes to Implement Patent Term Adjustment Under Twenty-Year Patent Term; Notice of Proposed Rulemaking

65 FR 17215
Department of Commerce
Patent and Trademark Office
37 CFR Part 1
RIN 0651—AB06

Agency: United States Patent and Trademark Office, Commerce

Action: Notice of Proposed Rulemaking

* * *

PART 1—RULES OF PRACTICE IN PATENT CASES

1. The authority citation for 37 CFR Part 1 is revised to read as follows:

Authority: 35 U.S.C. 2(b)(2), unless otherwise noted.

2. Section 1.18 is amended by revising the section heading, adding and reserving paragraph (d), and adding paragraphs (e) and (f) to read as follows:

§1.18 Patent post allowance (including issue) fees.

* * * * *

(d) [Reserved]

(e) For filing an application for patent term adjustment under §1.705—$200.00

(f) For filing a request for reinstatement of all or part of the term reduced pursuant to §1.704(b) in an application for patent term adjustment under §1.705—$450.00

Subpart F—Adjustment and Extension of Patent Term

3. The heading of subpart F is revised to read as set forth above.

4. An undesignated center heading is added to Subpart F §1.701 to read as follows:

ADJUSTMENT OF PATENT TERM DUE TO EXAMINATION DELAY

5. Section 1.701 is amended by revising the section heading and adding paragraph (e) to read as follows:

§1.701 Extension of patent term due to examination delay under the Uruguay Round Agreements Act (original applications, other than designs, file donor after June 8, 1995, and before May 29, 2000).

* * * * *

(e) The provisions of this section apply only to original patents, except for design patents, issued on applications filed on or after June 8, 1995.

6. Sections 1.702 through 1.705 are added to read as follows:

§1.702 Grounds for adjustment of patent term due to examination delay under the Patent Term Guarantee Act of 1999 (original applications, other than designs, file donor after May 29, 2000).

(a) *Failure to take certain actions within specified time frames.* Subject to the provisions of 35 U.S.C. 154(b) and this subpart, the term of an original patent shall be adjusted if the issuance of the patent was delayed due to the failure of the Office to:

(1) Mail at least one of a notification under 35 U.S.C. 132 or a notice of allowance under 35 U.S.C. 151 not later than fourteen months after the date on which the application was filed under 35 U.S.C. 111(a) or fulfilled the requirements of 35 U.S.C. 371;

(2) Respond to a reply under 35 U.S.C. 132 or to an appeal taken under 35 U.S.C. 134 not later than four months after the date on which the reply was filed or the appeal was taken;

(3) Act on an application not later than four months after the date of a decision by the Board of Patent Appeals and Interferences under 35 U.S.C. 134 or 135 or a decision by a Federal court under 35 U.S.C. 141, 145, or 146 where allowable claims remain in the application; or

(4) Issue a patent not later than four months after the date on which the issue fee was paid under 35 U.S.C. 151 and all outstanding requirements were satisfied.

(b) *Failure to issue a patent within three years of the actual filing date of the application.* Subject to the provisions of 35 U.S.C. 154(b) and this subpart, the term of an original patent shall be adjusted if the issuance of the patent was delayed due to the failure of the Office to issue a patent within three years after the actual filing date of the application, not including:

(1) Any time consumed by continued examination of the application under 35 U.S.C. 132(b);

(2) Any time consumed by an interference proceeding under 35 U.S.C. 135(a);

(3) Any time consumed by the imposition of a secrecy order under 35 U.S.C. 181;

(4) Any time consumed by review by the Board of Patent Appeals and Interferences or a Federal court; or

(5) Any delay in the processing of the application by the Office that was requested by the applicant.

(c) *Delays caused by interference proceedings.* Subject to the provisions of 35 U.S.C. 154(b) and this subpart, the term of an original patent shall be adjusted if the issuance of the patent was delayed due to interference proceedings under 35 U.S.C. 135(a).

(d) *Delays caused by secrecy order.* Subject to the provisions of 35 U.S.C. 154(b) and this subpart, the term of an original patent shall be adjusted if the issuance of the patent was delayed due to the application being placed under a secrecy order under 35 U.S.C. 181.

(e) *Delays caused by successful appellate review.* Subject to the provisions of 35 U.S.C. 154(b) and this subpart, the term of an original patent shall be adjusted if the issuance of the patent was delayed due to review by the Board of Patent Appeals and Interferences under 35 U.S.C. 134 or by a Federal court under 35 U.S.C. 141 or 145, if the patent was issued pursuant to a decision reversing an adverse determination of patentability.

(f) The provisions of this section and §§1.703 through 1.705 apply only to original applications, except applications for a design patent, filed on or after May 29, 2000, and patents issued on such applications.

§1.703 Period of adjustment of patent term due to examination delay.

(a) The period of adjustment under §1.702(a) is the sum of the following periods, to the extent that the periods are not overlapping:

(1) The number of days, if any, in the period beginning on the date fourteen months after the date on which the application was filed under 35 U.S.C. 111(a) or fulfilled the requirements of 35 U.S.C. 371 and ending on the date of mailing of either an action under 35 U.S.C. 132, or a notice of allowance under 35 U.S.C. 151, whichever occurs first;

(2) The number of days, if any, in the period beginning on the date four months after the date a reply under §1.111 was filed and ending on the date of mailing of an action under 35 U.S.C. 132, or a notice of allowance under 35 U.S.C. 151, whichever occurs first;

(3) The number of days, if any, in the period beginning on the date four months after the date a reply in compliance with §1.113 was filed and ending on the date of mailing of an action under 35 U.S.C. 132, or a notice of allowance under 35 U.S.C. 151, whichever occurs first;

(4) The number of days, if any, in the period beginning on the date four months after the date a notice of appeal to the Board of Patent Appeals and Interferences under 35 U.S.C. 134 and §1.191 was filed and ending on the date of mailing of an examiner's answer under §1.193, an action under 35 U.S.C. 132, or a notice of allowance under 35 U.S.C. 151, whichever occurs first;

(5) The number of days, if any, in the period beginning on the date four months after the date of a final decision by the Board of Patent Appeals and Interferences or by a Federal court in an appeal under 35 U.S.C. 141 or a civil action under 35 U.S.C. 145 or 146 in an application containing allowable claims and ending on the date of mailing of either an action under 35 U.S.C. 132 or a notice of allowance under 35 U.S.C. 151, whichever occurs first; and

(6) The number of days, if any, in the period beginning on the date four months after the date the issue fee was paid and all outstanding requirements were satisfied and ending on the date a patent was issued.

(b) The period of adjustment under §1.702(b) is the number of days, if any, in the period beginning on the date three years after the actual filing date of the application and ending on the date a patent was issued, but not including the sum of the following periods:

(1) The number of days, if any, in the period beginning on the date on which a request for continued examination of the application under 35 U.S.C. 132(b) was filed and ending on the date the patent was issued;

(2)(i) The number of days, if any, in the period beginning on the date an interference was declared or redeclared to involve the application in the interference and ending on the date that the interference was terminated with respect to the application; and

(ii) The number of days, if any, in the period beginning on the date prosecution in the application was suspended by the Office due to interference proceedings under 35 U.S.C. 135(a) not involving the application and ending on the date of the termination of the suspension;

(3)(i) The number of days, if any, the application was maintained in a sealed condition under 35 U.S.C. 181;

(ii) The number of days, if any, in the period beginning on the date of mailing of an examiner's answer under §1.193 in the application under secrecy order and ending on the date the secrecy order was removed;

(iii) The number of days, if any, in the period beginning on the date applicant was notified that an interference would be declared but for the secrecy order and ending on the date the secrecy order was removed; and

(iv) The number of days, if any, in the period beginning on the date of notification under §5.3(c) of this chapter and ending on the date of mailing of the notice of allowance under §1.311; and,

(4) The number of days, if any, in the period beginning on the date on which a notice of appeal to the Board of Patent Appeals and Interferences was filed under 35 U.S.C. 134 and §1.191 and ending on the date of a final decision by the Board of Patent Appeals and Interferences or by a Federal court in an appeal under 35 U.S.C. 141 or a civil action under 35 U.S.C. 145.

(c) The period of adjustment under §1.702(c) is the sum of the following periods, to the extent that the periods are not overlapping:

(1) The number of days, if any, in the period beginning on the date an interference was declared or redeclared to involve the application in the interference and ending on the date that the interference was terminated with respect to the application; and

(2) The number of days, if any, in the period beginning on the date prosecution in the application was suspended by the Office due to interference proceedings under 35 U.S.C. 135(a) not involving the application and ending on the date of the termination of the suspension.

(d) The period of adjustment under §1.702(d) is the sum of the following periods, to the extent that the periods are not overlapping:

(1) The number of days, if any, the application was maintained in a sealed condition under 35 U.S.C. 181;

(2) The number of days, if any, in the period beginning on the date of mailing of an examiner's answer under §1.193 in the application under secrecy order and ending on the date the secrecy order was removed;

(3) The number of days, if any, in the period beginning on the date applicant was notified that an interference would be declared but for the secrecy order and ending on the date the secrecy order was removed; and

(4) The number of days, if any, in the period beginning on the date of notification under §5.3(c) of this chapter and ending on the date of mailing of the notice of allowance under §1.311.

(e) The period of adjustment under §1.702(e) is the sum of the number of days, if any, in the period beginning on the date on which a notice of appeal to the Board of Patent Appeals and Interferences was filed under 35 U.S.C. 134 and §1.191 and ending on the date of a final decision in favor of the applicant by the Board of Patent Appeals and Interferences or by a Federal court in an appeal under 35 U.S.C. 141 or a civil action under 35 U.S.C. 145.

(f) The adjustment will run from the expiration date of the patent as set forth in 35 U.S.C. 154(a)(2). To the extent that periods of adjustment attributable to the grounds specified in §1.702 overlap, the period of adjustment granted under this section shall not exceed the actual number of days the issuance of the patent was delayed. The term of a patent entitled to adjustment under §1.702 and this section shall be adjusted for the sum of the periods calculated under paragraphs (a) through (e) of this section, to the extent that such periods are not overlapping, less the sum of the periods calculated under §1.704. The date indicated on any certificate of mailing or transmission under §1.8 shall not be taken into account in this calculation.

(g) No patent the term of which has been disclaimed beyond a specified date shall be adjusted under §1.702 and this section beyond the expiration date specified in the disclaimer.

§1.704 Reduction of period of adjustment of patent term.

(a) The period of adjustment of the term of a patent under §1.703(a) through (e) shall be reduced by a period equal to the period of time during which the applicant failed to engage in reasonable efforts to conclude prosecution (processing or examination) of the application.

(b) With respect to the ground for adjustment set forth in §1.702(a) through (e), and in particular the ground of adjustment set forth in §1.702(b), an applicant shall be deemed to have failed to engage in reasonable efforts to conclude processing or examination of the application for the cumulative total of any periods of time in excess of three months that are taken to reply to any notice or action by the Office making any rejection, objection, argument, or other request, measuring such three-month period from the date the notice or action was mailed or given to the applicant, in which case the period of adjustment set forth in §1.703 shall be reduced by the number of days, if any, beginning on the date three months after the date of mailing of the Office communication notifying the applicant of the rejection, objection, argument, or other request and ending on the date the reply was filed.

(c) Circumstances that constitute a failure of the applicant to engage in reasonable efforts to conclude processing or examination of the application also include the following circumstances, which will result in the following reduction of the period of adjustment set forth in §1.703 to the extent that the periods are not overlapping:

(1) Suspension of action under §1.103 at the applicant's request, in which case the period of adjustment set forth in §1.703 shall be reduced by the number of days, if any, beginning on the date a request for suspension of action under §1.103 was filed and ending on the date of the termination of the suspension;

(2) Deferral of issuance of a patent under §1.314, in which case the period of adjustment set forth in §1.703 shall be reduced by the number of days, if any, beginning on the date a request for deferral of issuance of a patent under §1.314 was filed and ending on the date the patent was issued;

(3) Abandonment of the application or late payment of the issue fee, in which case the period of adjustment set forth in §1.703 shall be reduced by the number of days, if any, beginning on the date of abandonment or the date after the day the issue fee was due and ending on the date of mailing of the decision reviving the application or accepting late payment of the issue fee;

(4) Failure to file a petition to withdraw the holding of abandonment or to revive an application within two months from the mailing date of a notice of abandonment, in which case the period of adjustment set forth in §1.703 shall be reduced by the number of days, if any, beginning on the date two months from the mailing date of a notice of abandonment and ending on the date a petition to withdraw the holding of abandonment or to revive the application was filed;

(5) Conversion of a provisional application under 35 U.S.C. 111(b) to a nonprovisional application under 35 U.S.C. 111(a) pursuant to 35 U.S.C. 111(b)(5), in which case the period of adjustment set forth in §1.703 shall be reduced by the number of days, if any, beginning on the date the application was filed under 35 U.S.C. 111(b) and ending on the date a request in compliance with §1.53(c)(3) to convert the provisional application into a nonprovisional application was filed;

(6) Failure to file the basic filing fee (§1.16(a) or (g)), any English language translation required by §1.52(d), or an oath or declaration (§1.63) executed by all of the inventors in an application under 35 U.S.C. 111(a), in which case the period of adjustment set forth in §1.703 shall be reduced by the number of days, if any, beginning on the date the application was filed and ending on the later of the date the applicant supplied the basic filing fee (§1.16), supplied any English language translation required by §1.52(d), and either supplied an oath or declaration (§1.63) executed in compliance with §1.64 or, if the oath or declaration was not executed by all of the inventors, the earliest of date the application was accorded status under §1.47 or four months after a grantable petition under §1.47 was filed;

(7) Failure to fulfill the requirements of 35 U.S.C. 371(c) and §1.494 or §1.495 in an international application, in which case the period of adjustment set forth in §1.703 shall be reduced by the number of days, if any, beginning on the date the application was filed under 35 U.S.C. 363 and the later of the date the application fulfilled the requirements of 35 U.S.C. 371(c) and §1.494 or §1.495 or,

if the oath or declaration (§1.497) is not executed by all of the inventors, the earliest of date the application was accorded status under §1.47 or four months after a grantable petition under §1.47 was filed;

(8) Failure to request the national stage of processing in an international application if the application fulfills the requirements of 35 U.S.C. 371(c) and §1.494 or §1.495 before the expiration of the applicable time period set forth in §1.494(b) or §1.495(b), in which case the period of adjustment set forth in §1.703 shall be reduced by the number of days, if any, beginning on the date the application was filed under 35 U.S.C. 363 and ending on the earlier of date of expiration of the applicable time period in §1.494(b) or §1.495(b) or the date on which an express request for national stage of processing is filed;

(9) Failure to file an application with a specification on papers in compliance with §1.52 and having a title and abstract in compliance with §1.72, drawings in compliance with §1.84 (if applicable), and a sequence listing in compliance with §§1.821 through 1.825 (if applicable), in which case the period of adjustment set forth in §1.703 shall be reduced by the number of days, if any, beginning on the filing date of the application and ending on the date the application contains a specification on papers in compliance with §1.52 and having an abstract (§1.72(b)), drawings in compliance with §1.84 (if applicable), and a sequence listing in compliance with §§1.821 through 1.825 (if applicable);

(10) Submission of a preliminary amendment or other preliminary paper less than one month before the mailing of an Office action under 35 U.S.C. 132 or notice of allowance under 35 U.S.C. 151 that requires the mailing of a supplemental Office action or notice of allowance, in which case the period of adjustment set forth in §1.703 shall be reduced by the number of days, if any, beginning on the mailing date of the original Office action or notice of allowance and ending on the mailing date of the supplemental Office action or notice of allowance;

(11) Submission of a reply having an omission under §1.135(c), in which case the period of adjustment set forth in §1.703 shall be reduced by the number of days, if any, beginning on the date the reply having an omission was filed and ending on the date that the omission was filed;

(12) Submission of a supplemental reply or other paper after a reply has been filed, in which case the period of adjustment set forth in §1.703 shall be reduced by the number of days, if any, beginning on the date the initial reply was filed and ending on the date that the supplemental reply or other such paper was filed;

(13) Failure to file an appeal brief (and brief fee) in compliance with §1.192 with a notice of appeal to the Board of Patent Appeals and Interferences under 35 U.S.C. 134 and §1.191, in which case the period of adjustment set forth in §1.703 shall be reduced by the number of days, if any, beginning on the date a notice of appeal to the Board of Patent Appeals and Interferences under 35 U.S.C. 134 and §1.191 was filed and ending on the day an appeal brief in compliance with §1.192 was filed, or, if no appeal brief under §1.192 is filed, ending on the day an amendment in compliance with §1.113 was filed;

(14) Submission of an amendment or other paper after a decision by the Board of Patent Appeals and Interferences, other than a decision designated as containing a new ground of rejection under §1.196(b) or statement under §1.196(c), or a decision by a Federal court less than one month before the mailing of an Office action under 35 U.S.C. 132 or notice of allowance under 35 U.S.C. 151 that requires the mailing of a supplemental Office action or supplemental notice of allowance, in which case the period of adjustment set forth in §1.703 shall be reduced by the number of days, if any, beginning on the mailing date of the original Office action or notice of allowance and ending on the mailing date of the supplemental Office action or notice of allowance;

(15) Submission of an amendment under §1.312 or other paper after a notice of allowance has been given or mailed, in which case the period of adjustment set forth in §1.703 shall be reduced by the lesser of:

(i) The number of days, if any, beginning on the date the amendment under §1.312 or other paper was filed and ending on the mailing date of the

Office action or notice in response to the amendment under §1.312 or such other paper; or

(ii) Four months; and

(16) Further prosecution via a continuing application, in which case the period of adjustment set forth in §1.703 shall not include any period that is prior to the actual filing date of the application that resulted in the patent.

§1.705 Patent term adjustment determination.

(a) The notice of allowance will include notification of any patent term adjustment under 35 U.S.C. 154(b).

(b) Any request for reconsideration of the patent term adjustment indicated in the notice of allowance, except as provided in paragraph (d) of this section, and any request for reinstatement of all or part of the term reduced pursuant to §1.704(b) must be by way of an application for patent term adjustment. An application for patent term adjustment under this section must be filed no later than payment of the issue fee but may not be filed earlier than the date of mailing of the notice of allowance. An application for patent term adjustment under this section must be accompanied by:

(1) The fee set forth in §1.18(e); and

(2) A statement of the facts involved, specifying:

(i) The correct patent term adjustment and the basis or bases under §1.702 for the adjustment;

(ii) The relevant dates as specified in §1.703(a) through (e) for which an adjustment is sought and the adjustment as specified in §1.703(f) to which the patent is entitled;

(iii) Whether the patent is subject to a terminal disclaimer and any expiration date specified in the terminal disclaimer; and

(iv) (A) Any circumstances during the prosecution of the application resulting in the patent that constitute a failure to engage in reasonable efforts to conclude processing or examination of such application as set forth in §1.704; or

(B) That there were no circumstances constituting a failure to engage in reasonable efforts to conclude processing or examination of such application as set forth in §1.704.

(c) Any application for patent term adjustment under this section that requests reinstatement of all or part of the term reduced pursuant to §1.704(b) for failing to reply to a rejection, objection, argument, or other request within three months of the date of mailing of the Office communication notifying the applicant of the rejection, objection, argument, or other request must also be accompanied by:

(1) The fee set forth in §1.18(f); and

(2) A showing to the satisfaction of the Director that, in spite of all due care, the applicant was unable to reply to the rejection, objection, argument, or other request within three months of the date of mailing of the Office communication notifying the applicant of the rejection, objection, argument, or other request. The Office shall not grant any request for reinstatement for more than three additional months for each reply beyond three months of the date of mailing of the Office communication notifying the applicant of the rejection, objection, argument, or other request.

(d) If the patent is issued on a date other than the projected date of issue and this change necessitates a revision of the patent term adjustment indicated in the notice of allowance, the patent will indicate the revised patent term adjustment. If the patent indicates a revised patent term adjustment due to the patent being issued on a date other than the projected date of issue, any request for reconsideration of the patent term adjustment indicated in the patent must be filed within thirty days of the date the patent issued and must comply with the requirements of paragraphs (b)(1) and (b)(2) of this section.

(e) The periods set forth in this section are not extendable.

(f) No submission or petition on behalf of a third party concerning patent term adjustment under 35 U.S.C. 154(b) will be considered by the Office. Any such submission or petition will be returned to the third party, or otherwise disposed of, at the convenience of the Office.

7. A undesignated center heading is added to Subpart F before §1.710 to read as follows:

EXTENSION OF PATENT TERM DUE TO REGULATORY REVIEW

Dated: March 24, 2000.

Q. Todd Dickinson,
Assistant Secretary of Commerce and Commissioner of Patents and Trademarks.
[FR Doc. 00-7938 Filed 3-30-00; 8:45 am]

Appendix D-11

Changes to Implement Eighteen-Month Publication of Patent Applications; Proposed Rule

65 FR 17946
Department of Commerce
Patent and Trademark Office
37 CFR Parts 1 and 5
RIN 0651—AB05

Agency: United States Patent and Trademark Office, Commerce

Action: Notice of Proposed Rulemaking

* * *

PART 1—RULES OF PRACTICE IN PATENT CASES

1. The authority citation for 37 CFR Part 1 is revised to read as follows:

Authority: 35 U.S.C. 2(b)(2), unless otherwise noted.

2. Section 1.9 is amended by revising paragraph (c) to read as follows:

§1.9 Definitions.

* * * * *

(c) A published application as used in this chapter means an application for patent which has been published under 35 U.S.C. 122(b).

* * * * *

3. Section 1.11 is amended by revising paragraph (a) to read as follows:

§1.11 Files open to the public.

(a) The specification, drawings, and all papers relating to the file of an abandoned published application, except if a redacted copy of the application was used for the patent application publication, a patent, or a statutory invention registration are open to inspection by the public, and copies may be obtained upon the payment of the fee set forth in §1.19(b)(2). See §2.27 for trademark files.

* * * * *

4. Section 1.12 is amended by revising paragraphs (a)(1) and (b) to read as follows:

§1.12 Assignment records open to public inspection.

(a)(1) Separate assignment records are maintained in the Patent and Trademark Office for patents and trademarks. The assignment records, relating to original or reissue patents, including digests and indexes, for assignments recorded on or after May 1, 1957, published patent applications, and assignment records relating to pending or abandoned trademark applications and to trademark registrations, for assignments recorded on or after January 1, 1955, are open to public inspection at the Patent and Trademark Office, and copies of those assignment records may be obtained upon request and payment of the fee set forth in §1.19 and §2.6 of this chapter.

* * * * *

(b) Assignment records, digests, and indexes relating to any pending or abandoned patent application which has not been published under 35 U.S.C. 122(b) are not available to the public. Copies of any such assignment records and information with respect thereto shall be obtainable only upon written authority of the applicant or applicant's assignee or attorney or agent or upon a showing that the person seeking such information is a bona fide prospective or actual purchaser, mortgagee, or licensee of such application, unless it shall be necessary to the proper conduct of business before the Office or as provided by these rules.

* * * * *

5. Section 1.13 is revised to read as follows:

§1.13 Copies and certified copies.

(a) Non-certified copies of patents, patent application publications, and trademark registrations and of any records, books, papers, or drawings within the jurisdiction of the United States Patent and Trademark Office and open to the public, will be furnished by the United States Patent and Trademark Office to any person, and copies of other records or papers will be furnished to persons entitled thereto, upon payment of the fee therefor.

(b) Certified copies of patents, patent application publications, and trademark registrations and of any records, books, papers, or drawings within the jurisdiction of the United States Patent and Trademark Office and open to the public or persons entitled thereto will be authenticated by the seal of the United States Patent and Trademark Office and certified by the Director, or in his or her name attested by an officer of the United States Patent and Trademark Office authorized by the Director, upon payment of the fee for the certified copy.

6. Section 1.14 is amended by revising paragraphs (a), (b), (c) and (e), and adding paragraphs (h), (i) and (j) to read as follows:

§1.14 Patent applications preserved in confidence.

(a) *Confidentiality of patent application information.* Patent applications that have not been published under 35 U.S.C. 122(b) are generally preserved in confidence pursuant to 35 U.S.C. 122(a). Information concerning the filing, pendency, or subject matter of an application for patent, including status information, and access to the application, will only be given to the public as set forth in §1.11 or in this section.

(1) *Status information* is:

(i) Whether the application is pending, abandoned, or patented;

(ii) Whether the application has been published under 35 U.S.C. 122(b); and

(iii) The application "numerical identifier" which may be:

(A) The eight digit application number (the two digit series code plus the six digit serial number); or

(B) The six digit serial number plus any one of the filing date of the national application, the international filing date, or date of entry into the national stage.

(2) *Access* is defined as providing the application file for review and copying of any material.

(b) *When status information may be supplied.* Status information of an application may be supplied by the Office to the public if any of the following apply:

(1) Access to the application is available pursuant to paragraph (e) of this section;

(2) The application is referred to by its numerical identifier in a published patent document (*e.g.*, a U.S. patent, a U.S. patent application publication, or an international application publication), or in a U.S. application open to public inspection (§1.11(b), or paragraph (e)(2)(i) or (e)(2)(ii) of this section); or

(3) The application is a published international application in which the United States of America has been indicated as a designated state.

(4) The application claims the benefit of the filing date of an application for which status information may be provided pursuant to paragraphs (b)(1) through (b)(3) of this section.

(c) *When copies may be supplied.* A copy of an application-as-filed or a file wrapper and contents may, subject to paragraph (j) of this section (addresses international applications), be supplied by the Office to the public if any of the following apply:

(1) *Application-as-filed.* If a U.S. patent application publication or patent incorporates by reference, or includes a specific reference under 35 U.S.C. 119(e) or 120 to, a pending or abandoned application, a copy of that application-as-filed may be provided to any person upon written request, including the fee set forth in §1.19(b)(1).

(2) *File wrapper and contents.* A copy of the specification, drawings, and all papers relating to the file of an abandoned or pending published application may be provided to any person upon written request, including the fee set forth in §1.19(b)(2). If a redacted copy of the application was used for the patent application publication, the copy of the specification, drawings, and papers may be limited to a redacted copy.

* * * * *

(e) *Public access to a pending or abandoned application may be provided.* Access to an application may, subject to paragraph (j) of this section, be provided to any person if a written request for access is submitted, the application file is available, and any of the following apply:

(1) The application is open to public inspection pursuant to §1.11(b); or

(2) The application is abandoned, it is not within the file jacket of a pending application under §1.53(d), and it is referred to:

(i) In a U.S. patent application publication or patent; or

(ii) In another U.S. application which is open to public inspection either pursuant to §1.11(b) or paragraph (e)(2)(i) of this section.

* * * * *

(h) [Reserved]

(i) *International applications.* (1) Copies of international application files for international applications filed on or after November 29, 2000, and which designate the U.S. and which have been published in accordance with PCT Article 21(2), or copies of a document in such application files, will be furnished in accordance with Patent Cooperation Treaty (PCT) Articles 30 and 38 and PCT Rules 94.2 and 94.3, upon written request including a showing that the publication of the application has occurred and that the U.S. was designated, and upon payment of the appropriate fee (§1.19(b)(2) or §1.19(b)(3)), if:

(i) With respect to the Home Copy, the international application was filed with the U.S. Receiving Office;

(ii) With respect to the Search Copy, the U.S. acted as the International Searching Authority; or

(iii) With respect to the Examination Copy, the United States acted as the International Preliminary Examining Authority, an International Preliminary Examination Report has issued, and the United States was elected.

(2) A copy of an English language translation of an international application, which has been filed in the Patent and Trademark Office pursuant to 35 U.S.C. 154(2)(d)(4) will be furnished upon written request including a showing that the publication of the application in accordance with PCT Article 21(2) has occurred and that the U.S. was designated, and upon payment of the appropriate fee (§1.19(b)(2) or §1.19(b)(3)).

(3) Access to international application files for international applications filed on or after November 29, 2000, and which designate the U.S. and which have been published in accordance with PCT Article 21(2), or copies of a document in such application files, will be furnished in accordance with Patent Cooperation Treaty (PCT) Articles 30 and 38 and PCT Rules 94.2 and 94.3, upon written request including a showing that the publication of the application has occurred and that the U.S. was designated.

(4) In accordance with PCT Article 30, copies of an international application-as-filed under paragraph (c)(1) of this section will not be provided prior to the international publication of the application pursuant to PCT Article 21(2).

(5) Access to international application files under paragraphs (e) and (i)(3) of this section will not be permitted with respect to the Examination Copy in accordance with PCT Article 38.

(j) *Access or copies in other circumstances*. The Office, either *sua sponte* or on petition, may also provide access or copies of all or part of an application if necessary to carry out an Act of Congress or if warranted by other special circumstances. Any petition by a member of the public seeking access to, or copies of, all or part of any pending or abandoned application preserved in confidence pursuant to paragraph (a) of this section, or any related papers, must include:

(1) The fee set forth in §1.17(h); and

(2) A showing that access to the application is necessary to carry out an Act of Congress or that special circumstances exist which warrant petitioner being granted access to all or part of the application.

7. Section 1.17 is amended by revising its heading and paragraphs (h), (i), (l), (m) and (p) and adding paragraph (u) to read as follows:

§1.17 Patent application and reexamination processing fees.

* * * * *

(h) For filing a petition under one of the following sections which refers to this paragraph: 130.00

§1.12—for access to an assignment record.
§1.14—for access to an application.
§1.47—for filing by other than all the inventors or a person not the inventor.
§1.53(e)—to accord a filing date.
§1.59—for expungement and return of information.
§1.84—for accepting color drawings or photographs.
§1.91—for entry of a model or exhibit.
§1.102—to make an application special.
§1.103(a)—to suspend action in application.
§1.138(c)—to expressly abandon an application to avoid publication.
§1.182—for decision on a question not specifically provided for.
§1.183—to suspend the rules.
§1.295—for review of refusal to publish a statutory invention registration.
§1.313—to withdraw an application from issue.
§1.314—to defer issuance of a patent.
§1.377—for review of decision refusing to accept and record payment of a maintenance fee filed prior to expiration of a patent.
§1.378(e)—for reconsideration of decision on petition refusing to accept delayed payment of maintenance fee in an expired patent.
§1.644(e)—for petition in an interference.

§1.644(f)—for request for reconsideration of a decision on petition in an interference.

§1.666(b)—for access to an interference settlement agreement.

§1.666(c)—for late filing of interference settlement agreement.

§1.741(b)—to accord a filing date to an application for extension of a patent term.

§5.12—for expedited handling of a foreign filing license.

§5.15—for changing the scope of a license.

§5.25—for retroactive license.

(i) Processing fee for taking action under one of the following sections which refers to this paragraph: 130.00

§1.28(c)(3)—for processing a non-itemized fee deficiency based on an error in small entity status.

§1.41—for supplying the name or names of the inventor or inventors after the filing date without an oath or declaration as prescribed by §1.63, except in provisional applications.

§1.48—for correcting inventorship, except in provisional applications.

§1.52(d)—for processing a nonprovisional application filed with a specification in a language other than English.

§1.55—for entry of late priority papers.

§1.99(e)—for processing a belated submission under §1.99.

§1.103(b)—for requesting limited suspension of action in continued prosecution application.

§1.217—for processing a redacted copy of a paper submitted in the file of an application in which a redacted copy was submitted for the patent application publication.

§1.221—for requesting voluntary publication or republication of an application.

§1.497(d)—for filing an oath or declaration pursuant to 35 U.S.C. 371(c)(4) naming an inventive entity different from the inventive entity set forth in the international stage.

* * * * *

(l) For filing a petition for the revival of an unavoidably abandoned application under 35 U.S.C. 111, 133, 364, or 371, for delayed payment of the issue fee under 35 U.S.C. 151, or for the revival of an unavoidably terminated reexamination proceeding under 35 U.S.C. 133 (§1.137(a)):

By a small entity (§1.9(f)): 55.00
By other than a small entity: 110.00

(m) For filing a petition for revival of an unintentionally abandoned application, for the unintentionally delayed payment of the fee for issuing a patent, or for the revival of an unintentionally terminated reexamination proceeding under 35 U.S.C. 41(a)(7) (§1.137(b)):

By a small entity (§1.9(f)): 605.00
By other than a small entity: 1,210.00

* * * * *

(p) For an information disclosure statement under §1.97(c) or (d) or a submission under §1.99: 240.00

* * * * *

(u) For the acceptance of an unintentionally delayed claim for priority under 35 U.S.C. 119, 120, 121, or 365 (§§1.55 and 1.78); 1,210.00

8. Section 1.18 is amended by revising its heading and adding paragraph (d) to read as follows:

§1.18 Patent post-allowance (including issue) fees.

* * * * *

(d) Publication fee: 300.00

§1.24 [Removed and Reserved]

9. Section 1.24 is removed and reserved.
10. Section 1.52 is amended by revising paragraph (d) to read as follows:

§1.52 Language, paper, writing, margins.

* * * * *

(d) A nonprovisional or provisional application may be filed in a language other than English.

(1) *Nonprovisional application.* If a nonprovisional application is filed in a language other than English, an English language translation of the non-English language application, a statement that the translation is accurate, and the processing fee set forth in §1.17(i) are required. If these items are not filed with the application, applicant will be notified and given a period of time within which they must be filed in order to avoid abandonment.

(2) *Provisional application.* If a provisional application is filed in a language other than English, an English language translation of the non-English language provisional application will not be required in the provisional application. See §1.78(a) for the requirements for claiming the benefit of such provisional application in a nonprovisional application.

11. Section 1.55 is amended by revising paragraph (a) and adding paragraph (c) to read as follows:

§1.55 Claim for foreign priority.

(a) An applicant in a nonprovisional application may claim the benefit of the filing date of one or more prior foreign applications under the conditions specified in 35 U.S.C. 119(a) through (d), 172, and 365(a) and (b).

(1)(i) In an original application filed under 35 U.S.C. 111(a), the claim for priority must be presented during the pendency of the application, and within the later of four months from the actual filing date of the application or sixteen months from the filing date of the prior foreign application. This time period is not extendable. The claim must identify the foreign application for which priority is claimed, as well as any foreign application for the same subject matter and having a filing date before that of the application for which priority is claimed, by specifying the application number, country (or intellectual property authority), day, month, and year of its filing. The time period in this paragraph does not apply to an application for a design patent.

(ii) In an application that entered the national stage from an international application after compliance with 35 U.S.C. 371, the claim for priority must be made during the pendency of the application and within the time limit set forth in the PCT and the Regulations under the PCT.

(2) The claim for priority and the certified copy of the foreign application specified in 35 U.S.C. 119(b) or PCT Rule 17 must, in any event, be filed before the patent is granted. If the claim for priority or the certified copy of the foreign application is filed after the date the issue fee is paid, it must be accompanied by the processing fee set forth in §1.17(i), but the patent will not include the priority claim unless corrected by a certificate of correction under 35 U.S.C. 255 and §1.323 of this part.

(3) When the application becomes involved in an interference (§1.630), when necessary to overcome the date of a reference relied upon by the examiner, or when deemed necessary by the examiner, the Office may require that the claim for priority and the certified copy of the foreign application be filed earlier than provided in paragraphs (a)(1) or (a)(2) of this section.

(4) An English-language translation of a non-English-language foreign application is not required except when the application is involved in an inter-

ference (§1.630), when necessary to overcome the date of a reference relied upon by the examiner, or when specifically required by the examiner. If an English-language translation is required, it must be filed together with a statement that the translation of the certified copy is accurate.

* * * * *

(c) Unless such claim is accepted in accordance with the provisions of this paragraph, any claim for priority under 35 U.S.C. 119(a)–(d), or 365(a) or (b) not presented within the time period provided by paragraph (a) of this section is considered to have been waived. If a claim for priority under 35 U.S.C. 119(a)–(d) or 365(a) or (b) is presented after the time period provided by paragraph (a) of this section, the claim may be accepted if the claim identifying the prior foreign application by specifying its application number, country, and the day, month and year of its filing was unintentionally delayed. A petition to accept a delayed claim for priority under 35 U.S.C. 119(a)–(d) or 365(a) or (b) must be accompanied by:

(1) The surcharge set forth in §1.17(u); and

(2) A statement that the entire delay between the date the claim was due under paragraph (a)(1) of this section and the date the claim was filed was unintentional. The Director may require additional information where there is a question whether the delay was unintentional.

12. Section 1.72 is amended by revising paragraph (a) to read as follows:

§1.72 Title and abstract.

(a) The title of the invention may include only characters capable of being created by a keyboard and may not exceed 500 characters in length. The title should be as short and specific as possible. Unless the title is supplied in an application data sheet (§1.76), the title of the invention should appear as a heading on the first page of the specification.

* * * * *

13. Section 1.78 is amended by revising paragraphs (a)(2), (a)(3), and (a)(4), and adding new paragraphs (a)(5) and (a)(6) to read as follows:

§1.78 Claiming benefit of earlier filing date and cross references to other applications.

(a)(1) * * *

(2) Except for a continued prosecution application filed under §1.53(d), any nonprovisional application claiming the benefit of one or more prior filed copending nonprovisional applications or international applications designating the United States of America must contain a reference to each such prior application, identifying it by application number (consisting of the series code and serial number) or international application number and international filing date and indicating the relationship of the applications. This reference must be submitted during the pendency of the application, and within the later of four months from the actual filing date of the application or sixteen months from the filing date of the prior application. This time period is not extendable. Unless the reference required by this paragraph is included in an application data sheet (§1.76), the specification must contain or be amended to contain such reference in the first sentence following the title. If the application claims the benefit of an international application, the first sentence of the specification must include an indication of whether the international application was published under PCT Article 21(2) in English (regardless of whether benefit for such application is claimed in the application data sheet). The request for a continued prosecution application under §1.53(d) is the specific reference required by 35 U.S.C. 120 to the prior application. The identification of an application by application number under this section is the specific reference required by 35 U.S.C. 120 to every application as-

signed that application number. Cross references to other related applications may be made when appropriate (see §1.14). Except as provided in paragraph (a)(3) of this section, the failure to timely submit the reference required by 35 U.S.C. 120 and this paragraph is considered a waiver of any benefit under 35 U.S.C. 120, 121, or 365(c) to such prior application. The time period set forth in this paragraph does not apply to an application for a design patent.

(3) If the reference required by 35 U.S.C. 120 and paragraph (a)(2) of this section is presented in a nonprovisional application after the time period provided by paragraph (a)(2) of this section, the claim under 35 U.S.C. 120, 121, or 365(c) for the benefit of a prior filed copending nonprovisional application or international application designating the United States of America may be accepted if the reference identifying the prior application by application number or international application number and international filing date was unintentionally delayed. A petition to accept an unintentionally delayed claim under 35 U.S.C. 120, 121, or 365(c) for the benefit of a prior filed application must be accompanied by:

(i) The surcharge set forth in §1.17(u); and

(ii) A statement that the entire delay between the date the claim was due under paragraph (a)(2) of this section and the date the claim was filed was unintentional. The Director may require additional information where there is a question whether the delay was unintentional.

(4) A nonprovisional application other than for a design patent may claim an invention disclosed in one or more prior filed provisional applications. In order for a nonprovisional application to claim the benefit of one or more prior filed provisional applications, each prior provisional application must name as an inventor at least one inventor named in the later filed nonprovisional application and disclose the named inventor's invention claimed in at least one claim of the later filed nonprovisional application in the manner provided by the first paragraph of 35 U.S.C. 112. In addition, each prior provisional application must be entitled to a filing date as set forth in §1.53(c), and the basic filing fee set forth in §1.16(k) must be paid within the time period set forth in §1.53(g).

(5) Any nonprovisional application claiming the benefit of one or more prior filed copending provisional applications must contain a reference to each such prior provisional application, identifying it as a provisional application, and including the provisional application number (consisting of series code and serial number), and, if the provisional application is filed in a language other than English, an English language translation of the non-English language provisional application and a statement that the translation is accurate. This reference and English language translation of a non-English language provisional application must be submitted during the pendency of the nonprovisional application, and within the later of four months from the actual filing date of the nonprovisional application or sixteen months from the filing date of the prior provisional application. This time period is not extendable. Unless the reference required by this paragraph is included in an application data sheet (§1.76), the specification must contain or be amended to contain such reference in the first sentence following the title. Except as provided in paragraph (a)(6) of this section, the failure to timely submit the reference and English language translation of a non-English language provisional application required by 35 U.S.C. 119(e) and this paragraph is considered a waiver of any benefit under 35 U.S.C. 119(e) to such prior provisional application.

(6) If the reference or English language translation of a non-English language provisional application required by 35 U.S.C. 119(e) and paragraph (a)(5) of this section is presented in a nonprovisional application after the time period provided by paragraph (a)(5) of this section, the claim under 35 U.S.C. 119(e) for the benefit of a prior filed provisional application may be accepted during the pendency of the nonprovisional application if the claim identifying the prior application by pro-

visional application number and any English language translation of a non-English language provisional application were unintentionally delayed. A petition to accept an unintentionally delayed claim under 35 U.S.C. 119(e) for the benefit of a prior filed provisional application must be accompanied by:

(i) The surcharge set forth in §1.17(u); and

(ii) A statement that the entire delay between the date the claim was due under paragraph (a)(5) of this section and the date the claim was filed was unintentional. The Director may require additional information where there is a question whether the delay was unintentional.

* * * * *

14. Section 1.84 is amended by revising paragraphs (a)(2), (e), and (j) to read as follows:

§1.84 Standards for drawings.

(a) * * *

(2) *Color*. On rare occasions, color drawings may be necessary as the only practical medium by which to disclose the subject matter sought to be patented in a utility or design patent application or the subject matter of a statutory invention registration. The color drawings must be of sufficient quality such that all details in the drawings are reproducible in black and white in the printed patent. Color drawings are not permitted in international applications (see PCT Rule 11.13), or in an application, or copy thereof, submitted under the Office electronic filing system. The Office will accept color drawings in utility or design patent applications and statutory invention registrations only after granting a petition filed under this paragraph explaining why the color drawings are necessary. Any such petition must include the following:

(i) The fee set forth in §1.17(h);

(ii) Three (3) sets of color drawings;

(iii) A black and white photocopy that accurately depicts, to the extent possible, the subject matter shown in the color drawing; and

(iv) An amendment to the specification to insert (unless the specification contains or has been previously amended to contain) the following language as the first paragraph of the brief description of the drawings:

The patent or application file contains at least one drawing executed in color. Copies of this patent or patent application publication with color drawing(s) will be provided by the Patent and Trademark Office upon request and payment of the necessary fee.

* * * * *

(e) *Type of paper*. Drawings submitted to the Office must be made on paper which is flexible, strong, white, smooth, non-shiny, and durable. All sheets must be reasonably free from cracks, creases, and folds. Only one side of the sheet may be used for the drawing. Each sheet must be reasonably free from erasures and must be free from alterations, overwritings, and interlineations. Photographs must be developed on paper meeting the sheet-size requirements of paragraph (f) of this section and the margin requirements of paragraph (g) of this section. See paragraph (b) of this section for other requirements for photographs.

* * * * *

(j) *Front page view*. One of the views should be suitable for inclusion on the front page of the patent application publication and patent as the illustration of the invention. Applicant may suggest a single view (by figure number) for inclusion on the front page of the patent application publication and patent.

* * * * *

15. Section 1.85 is amended by revising paragraph (a) to read as follows:

§1.85 Corrections to drawings.

(a) A utility or plant application will not be placed on the files for examination until objections to the drawings have been corrected. Except as provided in §1.215(c), any patent application publication will not include drawings filed after the application has been placed on the files for examination. Unless applicant is otherwise notified in an Office action, objections to the drawings in a utility or plant application will not be held in abeyance, and a request to hold objections to the drawings in abeyance will not be considered a *bona fide* attempt to advance the application to final action (§1.135(c)). If a drawing in a design application meets the requirements of §1.84(e), (f), and (g) and is suitable for reproduction, but is not otherwise in compliance with §1.84, the drawing may be admitted for examination.

* * * * *

16. Section 1.98 is amended by revising paragraphs (a)(2) and (b) to read as follows:

§1.98 Content of information disclosure statement.

(a) * * *

(2) A legible copy of:

(i) Each U.S. patent application publication and U.S. and foreign patent;

(ii) Each publication or that portion which caused it to be listed;

(iii) For each cited pending U.S. application, the application specification including the claims, and any drawing of the application, or that portion of the application which caused it to be listed including any claims directed to that portion; and

(iv) All other information or that portion which caused it to be listed; and

* * * * *

(b) Each U.S. patent listed in an information disclosure statement shall be identified by patentee, patent number, and issue date. Each U.S. patent application publication listed in an information disclosure statement shall be identified by applicant, patent application publication number, and publication date. Each listed U.S. application shall be identified by the inventor, application number, and filing date. Each listed foreign patent or published foreign patent application shall be identified by the country or patent office which issued the patent or published the application, an appropriate document number, and the publication date indicated on the patent or published application. Each listed publication shall be identified by author (if any), title, relevant pages of the publication, date, and place of publication.

* * * * *

17. A new §1.99 is added to read as follows:

§1.99 Third party submission in published application.

(a) A submission by a member of the public of patents or publications relevant to a pending published application will be entered in the application file if the submission complies with the requirements of this section and the application is still pending when the submission and application file are brought before the examiner.

(b) A submission under this section must identify the application to which it is directed by application number and include:

(1) The fee set forth in §1.17(p);

(2) A listing of the patents or publications submitted for consideration by the Office;

(3) A copy of each listed patent or publication in written form or at least the pertinent portions thereof; and

(4) An English language translation of all the necessary and pertinent parts of any non-English language patent or publication in written form relied upon.

(c) The submission under this section must be served upon the applicant in accordance with §1.248.

(d) A submission under this section may not include any explanation of the patents, publications, or any other information, and is limited to twenty total patents or publications.

(e) A submission under this section must be filed within two months of the date of publication of the application (§1.215(a)) or prior to the mailing of a notice of allowance (§1.311), whichever is earlier. Any submission under this section not filed within this period is permitted only when the patents or publications could not have been submitted to the Office earlier, and must also be accompanied by the processing fee set forth in §1.17(i). A submission by a member of the public to a pending published application that does not comply with the requirements of this section will be returned or discarded.

(f) A member of the public may include a self-addressed postcard with a submission to receive an acknowledgment by the Office that the submission has been received. A member of the public filing a submission under this section will not receive any communications from the Office relating to the submission other than the return of a self-addressed postcard. In the absence of a request by the Office, an applicant has no duty to, and need not, reply to a submission under this section. The limited involvement of the member of the public filing a submission pursuant to this section ends with the filing of the submission, and no further submission on behalf of the member of the public will be considered, except for additional prior art, or unless such submission raises new issues which could not have been earlier presented.

18. Section 1.104 is amended by revising paragraph (d)(1) to read as follows:

§1.104 Nature of examination.

* * * * *

(d) *Citation of references*. (1) If domestic patents are cited by the examiner, their numbers and dates, and the names of the patentees will be stated. If domestic patent application publications are cited by the examiner, their publication number, publication date, and the names of the applicants will be stated. If foreign published applications or patents are cited, their nationality or country, numbers and dates, and the names of the patentees will be stated, and such other data will be furnished as may be necessary to enable the applicant, or in the case of a reexamination proceeding, the patent owner, to identify the published applications or patents cited. In citing foreign published applications or patents, in case only a part of the document is involved, the particular pages and sheets containing the parts relied upon will be identified. If printed publications are cited, the author (if any), title, date, pages or plates, and place of publication, or place where a copy can be found, will be given.

* * * * *

19. Section 1.130 is amended by revising its heading and paragraph (a) to read as follows:

§1.130 Affidavit or declaration to disqualify commonly owned patent or published application as prior art.

(a) When any claim of an application or a patent under reexamination is rejected under 35 U.S.C. 103 on a U.S. patent or U.S. patent application publication which is not prior art under 35 U.S.C. 102(b), and the inventions defined by the claims in the application or patent under reexamination and by the claims in the patent or published application are not identical but are not patentably distinct, and the inventions are owned by the same party, the applicant or owner of the patent under reexamination may disqualify the patent or patent application publication as prior art. The patent or patent application publication can be disqualified as prior art by submission of:

(1) A terminal disclaimer in accordance with §1.321(c); and

(2) An oath or declaration stating that the application or patent under reexamination and patent or published application are currently owned by the same party, and that the inventor named in the application or patent under reexamination is the prior inventor under 35 U.S.C. 104.

* * * * *

20. Section 1.131 is amended by revising its heading and paragraph (a) to read as follows:

§1.131 Affidavit or declaration of prior invention.

(a) When any claim of an application or a patent under reexamination is rejected, the inventor of the subject matter of the rejected claim, the owner of the patent under reexamination, or the party qualified under §§1.42, 1.43, or 1.47, may submit an appropriate oath or declaration to establish invention of the subject matter of the rejected claim prior to the effective date of the reference or activity on which the rejection is based. The effective date of a U.S. patent, U.S. patent application publication, or international application publication under PCT Article 21(2) is the date that it is effective as a reference under 35 U.S.C. 102(e). Prior invention may not be established under this section in any country other than the United States, a NAFTA country, or a WTO member country. Prior invention may not be established under this section before December 8, 1993, in a NAFTA country other than the United States, or before January 1, 1996, in a WTO member country other than a NAFTA country. Prior invention may not be established under this section if either:

(1) The rejection is based upon a U.S. patent or U.S. patent application publication of a pending or patented application to another or others which claims the same patentable invention as defined in §1.601(n); or

(2) The rejection is based upon a statutory bar.

* * * * *

21. Section 1.132 is revised to read as follows:

§1.132 Affidavits or declarations traversing rejections or objections.

When any claim of an application or a patent under reexamination is rejected or objected to, an oath or declaration may be submitted to traverse the rejection or objection. An oath or declaration may not be submitted under this section to traverse a rejection if the rejection is based upon a U.S. patent or a U.S. patent application publication of a pending or patented application to another or others which claims the same patentable invention as defined in §1.601(n).

22. Section 1.137 is revised to read as follows:

§1.137 Revival of abandoned application, terminated reexamination proceeding, or lapsed patent.

(a) *Unavoidable.* Where the delay in reply by applicant or patent owner was unavoidable, a petition may be filed to revive an abandoned application, a terminated reexamination proceeding, or a lapsed patent pursuant to this paragraph. A grantable petition pursuant to this paragraph must be accompanied by:

(1) The reply required to the outstanding Office action or notice, unless previously filed;

(2) The petition fee as set forth in §1.17(l);

(3) A showing to the satisfaction of the Director that the entire delay in filing the required reply from the due date for the reply until the filing of a grantable petition pursuant to this paragraph was unavoidable; and

(4) Any terminal disclaimer (and fee as set forth in §1.20(d)) required pursuant to paragraph (d) of this section.

(b) *Unintentional.* Where the delay in reply by applicant or patent owner was unintentional, a petition may be filed to revive an abandoned application, a terminated reexamination proceeding, or a lapsed patent pursuant to this paragraph. A grantable petition pursuant to this paragraph must be accompanied by:

(1) The reply required to the outstanding Office action or notice, unless previously filed;

(2) The petition fee as set forth in §1.17(m);

(3) A statement that the entire delay in filing the required reply from the due date for the reply until the filing of a grantable petition pursuant to this paragraph was unintentional. The Director may require additional information where there is a question whether the delay was unintentional; and

(4) Any terminal disclaimer (and fee as set forth in §1.20(d)) required pursuant to paragraph (d) of this section.

(c) *Reply*. In a nonprovisional application abandoned for failure to prosecute, the required reply may be met by the filing of a continuing application. In a nonprovisional utility or plant application filed after June 8, 1995, and abandoned for failure to prosecute, the required reply may also be met by the filing of a request for continued examination in compliance with §1.114. In an application or patent, abandoned or lapsed for failure to pay the issue fee or any portion thereof, the required reply must include payment of the issue fee or any outstanding balance thereof. In an application, abandoned for failure to pay the publication fee, the required reply must include payment of the publication fee.

(d) *Terminal disclaimer*. (1) Any petition to revive pursuant to this section in a design application must be accompanied by a terminal disclaimer and fee as set forth in §1.321 dedicating to the public a terminal part of the term of any patent granted thereon equivalent to the period of abandonment of the application. Any petition to revive pursuant to this section in either a utility or plant application filed before June 8, 1995, must be accompanied by a terminal disclaimer and fee as set forth in §1.321 dedicating to the public a terminal part of the term of any patent granted thereon equivalent to the lesser of:

(i) The period of abandonment of the application; or

(ii) The period extending beyond twenty years from the date on which the application for the patent was filed in the United States or, if the application contains a specific reference to an earlier filed application(s) under 35 U.S.C. 120, 121, or 365(c), from the date on which the earliest such application was filed.

(2) Any terminal disclaimer pursuant to paragraph (d)(1) of this section must also apply to any patent granted on a continuing utility or plant application filed after June 8, 1995, or a continuing design application, that contains a specific reference under 35 U.S.C. 120, 121, or 365(c) to the application for which revival is sought.

(3) The provisions of paragraph (d)(1) of this section do not apply to applications for which revival is sought solely for purposes of copendency with a utility or plant application filed on or after June 8, 1995, to lapsed patents, or to reexamination proceedings.

(e) *Request for reconsideration*. Any request for reconsideration or review of a decision refusing to revive an abandoned application or lapsed patent upon petition filed pursuant to this section, to be considered timely, must be filed within two months of the decision refusing to revive or within such time as set in the decision. Unless a decision indicates otherwise, this time period may be extended under the provisions of §1.136 for an abandoned application or lapsed patent; under the provisions of §1.550(c) for a terminated *ex parte* reexamination proceeding filed under §1.510; and under the provisions of §1.956 for a terminated *inter partes* reexamination proceeding filed under §1.913.

(f) *Abandonment for failure to notify the Office of a foreign filing*. A nonprovisional application abandoned pursuant to 35 U.S.C. 122(b)(2)(B)(iii) for failure to timely notify the Office of the filing of an application in a foreign country or under a multinational treaty that requires publication of applications eighteen months after filing, may be revived only pursuant to paragraph (b) of this section. The reply requirement of paragraph (c) of this section is met by the notification of such filing in a foreign country or under a multinational treaty, but the filing of a petition under this section will not operate to stay any period for reply that may be running against the application.

(g) *Provisional applications.* A provisional application, abandoned for failure to timely respond to an Office requirement, may be revived pursuant to this section. Subject to the provisions of 35 U.S.C. 119(e)(3) and §1.7(b), a provisional application will not be regarded as pending after twelve months from its filing date under any circumstances.

23. Section 1.138 is revised to read as follows:

§1.138 Express abandonment.

(a) An application may be expressly abandoned by filing in the Patent and Trademark Office a written declaration of abandonment identifying the application. Express abandonment of the application may not be recognized by the Office unless it is actually received by appropriate officials in time to act thereon before the date of issue or publication.

(b) A written declaration of abandonment must be signed by a party authorized under §1.33(b)(1), (b)(3) or (b)(4) to sign a paper in the application, except as otherwise provided in this paragraph. A registered attorney or agent not of record who acts in a representative capacity under the provisions of §1.34(a) when filing a continuing application may expressly abandon the prior application as of the filing date granted to the continuing application.

(c) An applicant seeking to abandon an application to avoid publication of the application (see §1.211(a)(1)) must submit a declaration of express abandonment by way of a petition under this section including the fee set forth in §1.17(h) in sufficient time to permit the appropriate officials to recognize the abandonment and remove the application from the publication process. Applicant should expect that the petition will not be granted and the application will be published in regular course unless such declaration of express abandonment and petition are received by the appropriate officials more than four weeks prior to the projected date of publication.

24. Section 1.165 is amended by revising paragraph (b) to read as follows:

§1.165 Plant drawings.

* * * * *

(b) The drawings may be in color. The drawing must be in color if color is a distinguishing characteristic of the new variety. Two copies of color drawings or photographs and a black and white photocopy that accurately depicts, to the extent possible, the subject matter shown in the color drawing or photograph must be submitted.

25. A new, undesignated center heading and new sections 1.211, 1.213, 1.215, 1.217, 1.219, and 1.221 are added to Subpart B to read as follows:

Publication of Applications

§1.211 Publication of applications.

(a) Each U.S. national application for patent filed in the Office under 35 U.S.C. 111(a) and each international application in compliance with 35 U.S.C. 371 will be published promptly after the expiration of a period of eighteen months from the earliest filing date for which a benefit is sought under title 35, United States Code, unless:

(1) The application is recognized by the Office as no longer pending;

(2) The application is national security classified (see §5.2(c)), subject to a secrecy order under 35 U.S.C. 181, or under national security review;

(3) The application has issued as a patent in sufficient time to be removed from the publication process; or

(4) The application was filed with a nonpublication request in compliance with §1.213(a).

(b) Provisional applications under 35 U.S.C. 111(b) shall not be published, and design applications under 35 U.S.C. chapter 16 and reissue applications under 35 U.S.C. chapter 25 shall not be published under this section.

(c) An application filed under 35 U.S.C. 111(a) will not be published until it includes the basic filing fee (§1.16(a) or 1.16(g)), any English translation required by §1.52(d), and an executed oath or declaration under §1.63. The Office may delay publishing any application until it includes a specification on papers in compliance with §1.52 and having an abstract (§1.72(b)), drawings in compliance with §1.84, and a sequence listing in compliance with §§1.821 through 1.825 (if applicable), and until any petition under §1.47 is granted.

(d) The Office may refuse to publish an application, or to include a portion of an application in the patent application publication (§1.215), if publication of the application or portion thereof would violate Federal or state law, or if the application or portion thereof contains offensive or disparaging material.

(e) The publication fee set forth in §1.18(d) must be paid in each application published under this section before the patent will be granted. If an application is subject to publication under this section, the sum specified in the notice of allowance under §1.311 will also include the publication fee which must be paid within three months from the date of mailing of the notice of allowance to avoid abandonment of the application. This three-month period is not extendable. If the application is not published under this section, the publication fee (if paid) will be refunded.

§1.213 Nonpublication request.

(a) If the invention disclosed in an application has not been and will not be the subject of an application filed in another country, or under a multilateral international agreement, that requires publication of applications eighteen months after filing, the application will not be published under 35 U.S.C. 122(b) and §1.211 provided:

(1) A request (nonpublication request) is submitted with the application upon filing;

(2) The request states in a conspicuous manner that the application is not to be published under 35 U.S.C. 122(b);

(3) The request contains a certification that the invention disclosed in the application has not been and will not be the subject of an application filed in another country, or under a multilateral agreement, that requires publication at eighteen months after filing; and

(4) The request is signed in compliance with §1.33(b).

(b) The applicant may rescind a nonpublication request at any time. A request to rescind a nonpublication request under paragraph (a) of this section must:

(1) Identify the application to which it is directed;

(2) State in a conspicuous manner that the request that the application is not to be published under 35 U.S.C. 122(b) is rescinded; and

(3) Be signed in compliance with §1.33(b).

(c) If an applicant who has submitted a nonpublication request under paragraph (a) of this section subsequently files an application directed to the invention disclosed in the application in which the nonpublication request was submitted in another country, or under a multilateral international agreement, that requires publication of applications eighteen months after filing, the applicant must notify the Office of such filing within forty-five days after the date of the filing of such foreign or international application. The failure to timely notify the Office of the filing of such foreign or international application shall result in abandonment of the application in which the nonpublication request was submitted (35 U.S.C. 122(b)(2)(B)(iii)).

§1.215 Patent application publication.

(a) The publication of an application under 35 U.S.C. 122(b) shall include a patent application publication. The date of publication shall be indicated on the patent application publication. The patent application publication will be based upon the application papers deposited on the filing date of the application, except for preliminary amendments, as well as the executed oath or declaration submitted to complete the application, and any application papers or drawings submitted in reply to a preexamination notice requiring a title and abstract in compliance with §1.72, application papers in compliance with §1.52, drawings in compliance with §1.84, or a sequence listing in compliance with §§1.821 through 1.825, except as otherwise provided in this section.

(b) If applicant wants the patent application publication to include assignee information, the applicant must include a separate paper indicating that such information is being provided for inclusion on the patent application publication. Assignee information might not be included on the patent application publication if such paper is not included with the application on filing. Assignee information as used in this paragraph means the name and address of the assignee of the entire right, title, and interest in an application. Providing this information does not substitute for compliance with any requirement of part 3 of this chapter to have an assignment recorded by the Office.

(c) At applicant's option, the patent application publication will be based upon the copy of the application (specification, drawings, and oath or declaration) as amended during examination, provided that applicant supplies such a copy in compliance with the Office electronic filing system requirements within one month of the actual filing date of the application or fourteen months of the earliest filing date for which a benefit is sought under title 35, United States Code, whichever is later.

(d) If the copy of the application submitted pursuant to paragraph (c) of this section does not comply with the Office electronic filing system requirements, the Office will publish the application as provided in paragraph (a) of this section. If, however, the Office has not started the publication process, the Office may use an untimely filed copy of the application supplied by the applicant under paragraph (c) of this section in creating the patent application publication.

§1.217 Publication of a redacted copy of an application.

(a) If an applicant has filed applications in one or more foreign countries, directly or through a multilateral international agreement, and such foreign-filed applications or the description of the invention in such foreign-filed applications is less extensive than the application or description of the invention in the application filed in the Office, the applicant may submit a redacted copy of the application filed in the Office for publication, eliminating any part or description of the invention that is not also contained in any of the corresponding applications filed in a foreign country. The Office will publish the application as provided in §1.215(a) unless the applicant files a redacted copy of the application in compliance with this section within sixteen months after the earliest filing date for which a benefit is sought under title 35, United States Code.

(b) The redacted copy of the application must be submitted in compliance with the Office electronic filing system requirements. The title of the invention in the redacted copy of the application must correspond to the title of the application at the time the redacted copy of the application is submitted to the Office. If the redacted copy of the application does not comply with the Office electronic filing system requirements, the Office will publish the application as provided in §1.215(a).

(c) The applicant must also concurrently submit in paper (§1.52(a)) to be filed in the application:

(1) A certified copy of each foreign-filed application that corresponds to the application for which a redacted copy is submitted;

(2) A translation of each such foreign-filed application that is in a language other than English, and a statement that the translation is accurate;

(3) A marked-up copy of the application showing the redactions in brackets; and

(4) A certification that the redacted copy of the application eliminates only the part or description of the invention that is not contained in any application

filed in a foreign country, directly or through a multilateral international agreement, that corresponds to the application filed in the Office.

(d) The Office will provide a copy of the complete file wrapper and contents of an application for which a redacted copy was submitted under this section to any person upon written request pursuant to §1.14(c)(2), unless applicant complies with the requirements of paragraphs (d)(1), (d)(2), and (d)(3) of this section.

(1) Applicant must accompany the submission required by paragraph (c) of this section with the following:

(i) A copy of any Office correspondence previously received by applicant including any desired redactions, and a second copy of all Office correspondence previously received by applicant showing the redacted material in brackets; and

(ii) A copy of each submission previously filed by the applicant including any desired redactions, and a second copy of each submission previously filed by the applicant showing the redacted material in brackets.

(2) In addition to providing the submission required by paragraphs (c) and (d)(1) of this section, applicant must:

(i) Within one month of the date of mailing of any correspondence from the Office, file a copy of such Office correspondence including any desired redactions, and a second copy of such Office correspondence showing the redacted material in brackets; and

(ii) With each submission by the applicant, include a copy of such submission including any desired redactions, and a second copy of such submission showing the redacted material in brackets.

(3) Each submission under paragraph (d)(1) or (d)(2) of this paragraph must also be accompanied by the processing fee set forth in §1.17(i) and a certification that the redactions included therein are limited to the elimination of material that is relevant only to the part or description of the invention that were not contained in the redacted copy of the application submitted for publication.

(e) The provisions of §1.8 do not apply to the time periods set forth in this section.

§1.219 Early publication.

(a) Applications that will be published under §1.211 may be published earlier than as set forth in §1.211(a) at the request of the applicant. Any request for early publication must be accompanied by the publication fee set forth in §1.18(d). If the applicant does not submit a copy of the application in compliance with the Office electronic filing system requirements, the Office will publish the application as provided in §1.215(a). No consideration will be given to requests for publication on a certain date, and such requests will be treated as a request for publication as soon as possible.

§1.221 Voluntary publication or republication of patent application publication.

(a) Any request for publication of an application filed before, but pending on, November 29, 2000, and any request for republication of an application previously published under §1.211, must include a copy of the application in compliance with the Office electronic filing system requirements and be accompanied by the publication fee set forth in §1.18(d) and the processing fee set forth in §1.17(i). If the request does not comply with the requirements of this paragraph or the copy of the application does not comply with the Office electronic filing system requirements, the Office will not publish the application and will refund the publication fee.

(b) The Office will grant a request for a corrected or revised patent application publication other than as provided in paragraph (a) of this section only when the Office makes a material mistake which is apparent from Office records. Any request for a corrected or revised patent application publication other than as provided in paragraph (a) of this section must be filed within two months from the date of the patent application publication. This period is not extendable.

26. Section 1.291 is amended by revising paragraph (a)(1) to read as follows:

§1.291 Protests by the public against pending applications.

(a) * * *

(1) The protest is submitted prior to the date the application was published or the mailing of a notice of allowance under §1.311, whichever occurs first; and

* * * * *

27. Section 1.292 is amended by revising paragraph (b)(3) to read as follows:

§1.292 Public use proceedings.

* * * * *

(b) * * *

(3) The petition is submitted prior to the date the application was published or the mailing of a notice of allowance under §1.311, whichever occurs first.

* * * * *

28. Section 1.311 is revised to read as follows:

§1.311 Notice of allowance.

(a) If, on examination, it shall appear that the applicant is entitled to a patent under the law, a notice of allowance will be sent to the applicant at the correspondence address indicated in §1.33. The notice of allowance shall specify a sum constituting the issue fee which must be paid within three months from the date of mailing of the notice of allowance to avoid abandonment of the application. The sum specified in the notice of allowance may also include the publication fee, in which case the issue fee and publication fee (§1.211(f)) must both be paid within three months from the date of mailing of the notice of allowance to avoid abandonment of the application. This three-month period is not extendable.

(b) An authorization to charge the issue or other post-allowance fees set forth in §1.18 to a deposit account may be filed in an individual application only after mailing of the notice of allowance.

29. A new §1.417 is added to read as follows:

§1.417 Submission of translation of international application.

The submission of the international publication or an English language translation of an international application pursuant to 35 U.S.C. 154(d)(4) must clearly identify the international application to which it pertains (§1.5(a)) and, unless it is being submitted pursuant to §1.494 or §1.495, be clearly identified as a submission pursuant to 35 U.S.C. 154(d)(4). Otherwise, the submission will be treated as a filing under 35 U.S.C. 111(a). Such submissions should be marked "Box PCT."

30. Section 1.494 is amended by revising paragraph (f) to read as follows:

§1.494 Entering the national stage in the United States of America as a Designated Office.

* * * * *

(f) The documents and fees submitted under paragraphs (b) and (c) of this section must, except for a copy of the international publication or translation of the international application that is identified as provided in §1.417, be clearly identified as a submission to enter the national stage under 35 U.S.C. 371. Otherwise, the submission will be considered as being made under 35 U.S.C. 111(a).

* * * * *

31. Section 1.495 is amended by revising paragraph (g) to read as follows:

§1.495 Entering the national stage in the United States of America as an Elected Office.

* * * * *

(g) The documents and fees submitted under paragraphs (b) and (c) of this section must, except for a copy of the international publication or translation of the international application that is identified as provided in §1.417, be clearly identified as a submission to enter the national stage under 35 U.S.C. 371. Otherwise, the submission will be considered as being made under 35 U.S.C. 111(a).

* * * * *

PART 5—SECRECY OF CERTAIN INVENTIONS AND LICENSES TO EXPORT AND FILE APPLICATIONS IN FOREIGN COUNTRIES

32. The authority citation for 37 CFR Part 5 is revised to read as follows:

Authority: 35 U.S.C. 2(b)(2), 41, 181–188, as amended by the Patent Law Foreign Filing Amendments Act of 1988, Pub. L. 100-418, 102 Stat. 1567; the Arms Export Control Act, as amended, 22 U.S.C. 2751 *et seq.*; the Atomic Energy Act of 1954, as amended, 42 U.S.C. 2011 *et seq.*; and the Nuclear Non Proliferation Act of 1978, 22 U.S.C. 3201 *et seq.*; and the delegations in the regulations under these Acts to the Director (15 CFR 370.10(j), 22 CFR 125.04, and 10 CFR 810.7).

33. Section 5.1 as proposed to be revised at 64 FR 53844 is amended by revising paragraph (e) to read as follows:

§5.1 Applications and correspondence involving national security.

* * * * *

(e) An application will not be published under §1.211 of this chapter or allowed under §1.311 of this chapter if publication or disclosure of the application would be detrimental to national security. An application under national security review will not be published at least until six months from its filing date or three months from the date the application was referred to a defense agency, whichever is later. A national security classified patent application will not be published under §1.211 of this chapter or allowed under §1.311 of this chapter until the application is declassified and any secrecy order under §5.2(a) has been rescinded.

* * * * *

Dated: March 24, 2000.

Q. Todd Dickinson,
Assistant Secretary of Commerce and Commissioner of Patents and Trademarks.
[FR Doc. 00-7939 Filed 4-4-00; 8:45 am]

Appendix D-12

American Inventors Protection Act of 1999—Information Exchange

[The following Q&A was taken from the U.S. Patent and Trademark Office website on December 20, 2000. The Q&A is periodically updated and may be found at <http://www.uspto.gov/web/offices/dcom/olia/aipa/infoexch.htm>.]

American Inventors Protection Act of 1999

What's New on the AIPA Web Site

Information Exchange

A. *Request for Continued Examination (RCE)*

A1. What is a request for continued examination (RCE)?

Section 4403 of the "American Inventors Protection Act of 1999" amends 35 U.S.C. §132 to provide, at the request of the applicant, for continued examination of an application for a fee (request for continued examination or RCE practice), without requiring the applicant to file a continuing application under 37 CFR 1.53(b) or a continued prosecution application (CPA) under 37 CFR 1.53(d).

To implement RCE practice, the Office has added 37 CFR 1.114 to provide a procedure under which an applicant may obtain continued examination of an application by filing a submission and paying a specified fee, even if the application is under a final rejection, appeal, or a notice of allowance.

For the Final Rule, see *Request for Continued Examination Practice and Changes to Provisional Application Practice*; Final Rule, 65 FR 50092 (Aug. 16, 2000), 1238 Off. Gaz. Pat. Office 13 (Sept. 5, 2000).

For the Interim Rule, see *Changes to Application Examination and Provisional Application Practice*, Interim Rule, 65 FR 14865 (Mar. 20, 2000), 1233 Off. Gaz. Pat. Office 47 (Apr. 11, 2000).

A2. To what applications do the RCE provisions of 37 CFR 1.114 apply?

The provisions of 37 CFR 1.114 apply to utility or plant applications filed under 35 U.S.C. §111(a) on or after June 8, 1995, or international applications filed under 35 U.S.C. §363 on or after June 8, 1995. The request for continued examination provisions of 37 CFR 1.114 do not apply to: (1) a provisional application; (2) an application for a utility or plant patent filed under 35 U.S.C. §111(a) before June 8, 1995; (3) an international application filed under 35 U.S.C. §363 before June 8, 1995; (4) an application for a design patent; or (5) a patent under reexamination. *See* 37 CFR 1.114(e).

A3. When may applicant file a request for continued examination (RCE) under 37 CFR 1.114?

An applicant may obtain continued examination of an application by filing a submission and the fee set forth in 37 CFR 1.17(e) (currently, $710.00 for a large entity and $355.00 for a small entity) prior to the earliest of: (1) the date a patent is granted (but after payment of the issue fee only if a petition under 37 CFR 1.313 is granted); (2) abandonment of the application; or (3) the date applicant seeks court review of a decision by the Board of Patent Appeals and Interferences (unless the court action is terminated). *See* 37 CFR 1.114(a). An applicant cannot request continued examination of an application until after the prosecution in the application is closed. *See* 37 CFR 1.114(a).

Note: 37 CFR 1.114 in the Final Rule requires that prosecution in an application be closed (i.e., the application is under appeal, or the last Office action is a final action, a notice of allowance, or an action that otherwise closes prosecution in the application such as an Office action under *Ex parte Quayle*, 1935 Comm'r Dec. 11 (1935)) before an applicant can request continued examination of the application. Thus, a RCE would not be acceptable if the last Office action was a non-final rejection.

A4. What is/is not a submission under 37 CFR 1.114?

A submission as used in 37 CFR 1.114 includes, but is not limited to, an information disclosure statement, an amendment to the written description, claims, or drawings, new arguments, or new evidence in support of patentability. *See* 37 CFR 1.114(c). The definition for a "submission" in 37 CFR 1.114 is the same as the definition in 37 CFR 1.129(a). If reply to an Office action under 35 U.S.C. §132 is outstanding, the submission must meet the reply requirements of 37 CFR 1.111. *See* 37 CFR 1.114(c). Thus, an applicant may file a submission under 37 CFR 1.114 containing only an information disclosure statement (37 CFR 1.97 and 1.98) in an application subject to a notice of allowance under 35 U.S.C. §151. An appeal brief or a reply brief (or related papers) will not be considered a submission under 37 CFR 1.114. *See* 37 CFR 1.114(d). The submission, however, may consist of the arguments in a previously filed appeal brief or reply brief, or may simply consist of a statement that incorporates by reference the arguments in a previously filed appeal brief or reply brief. In addition, a previously filed amendment after final may satisfy this submission requirement.

A5. What is the status of unentered after final amendments upon the filing of a RCE (and fee)?

Upon the filing of a RCE (and fee), the finality of the last Office action is *withdrawn*. Any previously filed unentered amendments, amendments filed with the RCE, and any amendments filed prior to the mailing of the next Office action (after the RCE) are to be entered. Any conflicting amendments should be clarified for entry by the applicant upon filing the RCE (and fee). Absent specific instructions for entry, all amendments filed as of the date the RCE is filed are entered in the order in which they were filed.

A6. What submission is required if applicant has submitted arguments after final which were (1) entered by the examiner (2) not found persuasive by the examiner in the prior prosecution and (3) an advisory action to that effect was mailed?

Prior to submitting the request for continued examination (and fee), the final rejection continues as modified by the advisory action. The request for continued examination (and fee) may be accompanied by new arguments or amendments. The request for continued examination, however, need not be accompanied by new arguments or amendments. The fact that the previously submitted arguments were not found persuasive does not preclude them as a submission under 37 CFR 1.114, provided that such arguments are responsive within the meaning of 37 CFR 1.111 to the Office action. Consideration of whether any submission is responsive within the meaning of 37 CFR 1.111 to the last outstanding Office action is done without factoring in the "final" status of such outstanding Office action. Thus, a reply which might not be acceptable as a reply under 37 CFR 1.113 when the application is under a final rejection may very well be acceptable as a reply under 37 CFR 1.111.

A7. How should a conditional RCE be treated?

If a submission is accompanied by a "conditional" RCE and payment of the RCE fee (37 CFR 1.17(e) (*i.e.*, an authorization to charge the 37 CFR 1.17(e) fee to a deposit account in the event that the submission would not otherwise be entered), the Office will treat the "conditional" RCE and payment as if a RCE and payment of the fee set forth in 37 CFR 1.17(e) had been filed.

A8. How should new matter in an amendment entered pursuant to 37 CFR 1.114 be treated?

35 U.S.C. §132(a) provides that "[n]o amendment shall introduce new matter into the disclosure of the invention." Any amendment entered pursuant to 37 CFR 1.114 that is determined to contain new matter should be treated in the same manner that a reply under 37 CFR 1.111 determined to contain new matter is currently treated. *See* MPEP 706.03(o). In those instances in which an applicant seeks to add new matter to the disclosure of an application, the procedure in 37 CFR 1.114 is not available, and the applicant must file a continuation-in-part application under 37 CFR 1.53(b) containing such new matter. In addition, as 35 U.S.C. §132(b) and 37 CFR 1.114 provide continued examination of an application (and not examination of a continuing application), the applicant cannot file a RCE to obtain continued examination on the basis of claims that are independent and distinct from the claims previously claimed and examined as a matter of right (i.e., applicant cannot switch inventions) (*see* 37 CFR 1.145).

A9. Can the next Office action after the filing of a request for continued examination under 37 CFR 1.114 be made final?

The action immediately subsequent to the filing of a RCE with a submission and fee under 37 CFR 1.114 may be made final only if the conditions set forth in MPEP 706.07(b) for making a first action final in a continuing application are met.

A10. What if a request for continued examination under 37 CFR 1.114 is filed in an application under final rejection?

If an applicant timely files a RCE with the fee set forth in 37 CFR 1.17(e) and a submission, the Office will withdraw the finality of any Office action to which a reply is outstanding and the submission will be entered and considered. *See* 37 CFR 1.114(d). If the application is under final rejection, a submission meeting the reply requirements of 37 CFR 1.111 must be timely received to continue prosecution of an application. In other words, the mere request for, and payment of the fee for, continued examination will not operate to toll the running of any time period set in the previous Office action for reply to avoid abandonment of the application.

A11. What if a RCE is filed with a submission and the required fee after final rejection but the submission does not meet the reply requirements of 37 CFR 1.111?

If reply to an Office action is outstanding and the submission is not fully responsive to the prior Office action, then it must be a *bona fide* attempt to provide a complete reply to the prior Office action in order for the RCE to toll the period for reply. If the submission is a *bona fide* attempt to provide a complete reply, applicant should be informed that the submission is not fully responsive to the prior Office action, along with the reasons why, and given a new shortened statutory period of one month or thirty days (whichever is longer) to complete the reply. *See* 37 CFR 1.135(c). If the submission is not a *bona fide* attempt to provide a complete reply, the RCE will not toll the period for reply and the application will be abandoned after the expiration of the statutory period for reply.

A12. What if a request for continued examination under 37 CFR 1.114 is filed in an allowed application?

The phrase "withdraw the finality of any Office action" in 37 CFR 1.114(d) includes the withdrawal of the finality of a final rejection, as well as the closing of prosecution by an Office action under *Ex parte Quayle*, 1935 Comm'r Dec. 11 (1935), or notice of allowance under 35 U.S.C. §151 (or notice of allowability). Therefore, if an applicant files a RCE with the fee set forth in 37 CFR 1.17(e) and a submission in an application which has been allowed, prosecution will be reopened. If the issue fee has been paid, however, payment of the fee for a RCE and a submission without a petition under 37 CFR 1.313 to withdraw the application from issue will not avoid issuance of the application as a patent.

A13. If a request for continued examination under 37 CFR 1.114 is filed in an allowed application after the issue fee has been paid and a petition under 37 CFR 1.313 is also filed and granted, does the applicant have to pay the issue fee again if the application is thereafter allowed?

No. If the issue fee has been paid and prosecution is reopened, the applicant may not obtain a refund of the issue fee. If, however, the application is subsequently allowed, applicant may request that the previously submitted issue fee be applied toward payment of the issue fee required by the new notice of allowance.

A14. What if a request for continued examination under 37 CFR 1.114 is filed in an application after the filing of Notice of Appeal to the Board of Patent Appeals and Interferences but prior to a decision on the appeal?

If an applicant files a request for continued examination under 37 CFR 1.114 after the filing of a Notice of Appeal to the Board of Patent Appeals and Interferences, but prior to a decision on the appeal, it will be treated as a request to withdraw the appeal and to reopen prosecution of the application before the examiner. *See* 37 CFR 1.114(d). Thus, the filing of a request for continued examination under §1.114 in an application containing an appeal awaiting a decision on the appeal will be treated as a withdrawal of the appeal by the applicant, regardless of whether the request for continued examination under 37 CFR 1.114 includes the appropriate fee (37 CFR 1.17(e)) or a submission (37 CFR 1.114(c)).

If a RCE is filed in an application after appeal to the Board of Patent Appeals and Interferences but the request does not include the fee required by 37 CFR 1.17(e) or the submission required by 37 CFR 1.114, or both, the examiner should withdraw the appeal pursuant to 37 CFR 1.114. The proceedings as to the rejected claims are considered terminated. Therefore, if no claim is allowed, the application is abandoned. *See* MPEP 1215.01. If there is at least one allowed claim, the application should be passed to issue on the allowed claim(s). If there is at least one allowed claim but formal matters are outstanding, applicant should be given a shortened statutory period of one month or thirty days (whichever is longer) in which to correct the formal matters.

A15. What if a request for continued examination under 37 CFR 1.114 is filed in an application after a decision by the Board of Patent Appeals and Interferences but before further appeal or civil action?

The filing of a request for continued examination (accompanied by the fee and a submission) after a decision by the Board of Patent Appeals and Interferences, but before the filing of a Notice of Appeal to the Court of Appeals for the Federal Circuit (Federal Circuit) or the commencement of a civil action, will also result in the finality of the rejection or action being withdrawn and the submission being considered. In addition to the *res judicata* effect of a Board of Patent Appeals and Interferences decision in an application (*see* MPEP 706.03(w)), a Board of Patent Appeals and Interferences decision in an application is the "law of the case," and is thus controlling in that application and any subsequent, related application. *See* MPEP 1214.01 (where a new ground of rejection is entered by the Board of Patent Appeals and Interferences pursuant to 37 CFR 1.196(b), argument without either amendment of the claims so rejected or the submission of a showing of facts can only result in a final rejection of the claims, since the examiner is without authority to allow the claims unless amended or unless the rejection is overcome by a showing of facts not before the Board of Patent Appeals and Interferences). As such, a submission containing arguments without either amendment of the rejected claims or the submission of a showing of facts will not be effective to remove such rejection.

A16. What if a request for continued examination under 37 CFR 1.114 is filed in an application after the filing of a Notice of Appeal to the Federal Circuit or the commencement of a civil action?

The procedure set forth in 37 CFR 1.114 is not available in an application after the filing of a Notice of Appeal to the Federal Circuit or the commencement of a civil action, unless the appeal or civil action is terminated and the application is still pending. If a RCE is filed in an application that has undergone court review, the application should be brought to the attention of the SPE or SPRE to determine whether the RCE is proper.

A17. Can a CPA still be filed after May 29, 2000?

37 CFR 1.53(d)(1)(i) has been amended to provide that continued prosecution application (CPA) practice under 37 CFR 1.53(d) does not apply to applications (other than design) if the prior application has a filing date on or after May 29, 2000. Thus, an application (except for a design application) must have an actual filing date before May 29, 2000 for the applicant to be able to file a CPA of that application. While the Office uses the filing date (and application number) of the prior application of a CPA for identification purposes, the filing date of a CPA under 37 CFR 1.53(d) is the date the request for a CPA is filed. *See* 37 CFR 1.53(d)(2). Thus, if a CPA of an application (other than for a design patent) is filed on or after May 29, 2000, 37 CFR 1.53(d)(1)(i) does not permit the filing of a further CPA, regardless of the filing date of the prior application as to the first CPA (*i.e.*, the filing date used for identification purposes for the CPA).

A18. What if applicant files a request for a CPA of a utility or plant application that was filed on or after May 29, 2000?

In the event that an applicant files a request for a CPA of a utility or plant application that was filed on or after May 29, 2000 (to which CPA practice no longer applies), the Office will automatically treat the improper CPA as a request for continued examination of the prior application (identified in the request for CPA) under new 37 CFR 1.114. If an applicant files a request for a CPA of an application to which CPA practice no longer applies and does not want the request for a CPA to be treated as a request for continued examination under 37 CFR 1.114 (*e.g.*, the CPA is a divisional CPA), the applicant may file a petition under 37 CFR 1.53(e) requesting that the improper CPA be converted to an application under 37 CFR 1.53(b). The requirements for such a petition under 37 CFR 1.53(e) are identical to those set forth in MPEP 201.06(b) for converting an improper file wrapper continuing (FWC) application under former 37 CFR 1.62 to an application under 37 CFR 1.53(b). The Office will not grant such a petition, however, unless it is before the appropriate deciding official before an Office action has been mailed in response to the request for continued examination under 37 CFR 1.114 (as the improper CPA is being treated). If an Office action has been mailed in response to the request for continued examination under 37 CFR 1.114, the applicant should then simply file an application under 37 CFR 1.53(b) within the period for reply to such Office action.

A19. How does the RCE procedure under 37 CFR 1.114 differ from the transitional procedure set forth in 37 CFR 1.129(a) and CPA procedure set forth in 37 CFR 1.53(d)?

The request for continued examination (RCE) procedure in 37 CFR 1.114 should not be confused with the transitional procedure for the further limited examination of patent applications set forth in 37 CFR 1.129(a) or the continued prosecution application (CPA) procedure set forth in 37 CFR 1.53(d). This chart provides a comparison of the three different procedures.

http://www.uspto.gov/web/offices/dcom/olia/aipa/RCECPA.pdf

A20. Are there new form paragraphs for use in treating a RCE?

The Office has developed new form paragraphs for use by examiners when acting on an application in which a RCE has been filed. The Office is in the process of adding these paragraphs to both ActionWriter and the Office Action Creation System (OACS). *These form paragraphs are reproduced below: (click hyperlink)*

A21. If a RCE is filed after the mailing of a Notice of Allowance but before payment of the issue fee, is a petition under 37 CFR 1.313 to withdraw the application from issue required?

No. If a RCE (with the fee and a submission) is filed in an allowed application prior to payment of the issue fee, a petition to withdraw the application from issue is not required. If the issue fee has been paid, however, filing of a RCE (with the fee and a submission) without a petition to withdraw the application from issue will not avoid issuance of the application as a patent. *See* 37 CFR 1.114(a).

A22. In an allowed application and before payment of the issue fee, is a petition under §1.313 to withdraw the application from issue required for consideration of a request for continued examination under §1.114?

No, a petition to withdraw an application from issue is not required if a request for continued examination under §1.114 is filed prior to payment of the issue fee.

A23. If I filed a provisional application on June 8, 1995, and haven't done anything since then (so there is no pending application), does the new law now enable me to file the same application as a regular application, claim priority from the provisional, and obtain the benefit of provisional's filing date?

On its face, Section 4801(c) of the American Inventors Protection Act of 1999 seems to create the ultimate submarine patent, and I wonder how the PTO intends to prevent this result. If you filed a provisional application on June 8, 1995, §4801 of the AIPA extended its period of pendency from June 8, 1996 (a Saturday) until June 10, 1996 and eliminated the copendency requirement for a nonprovisional application to claim the benefit of that provisional application. Section 4801 of the AIPA, however, did not eliminate the requirement in 35 U.S.C. 119(e)(1) that a nonprovisional application be filed within twelve months of the filing date of the provisional application for the nonprovisional application to claim the benefit of the filing date of the provisional application. Under 35 U.S.C. 21(b), if this twelve-month period expires on a non-business day (June 8, 1996), it is extended to expire on the next business day (June 10, 1996). Thus, you cannot claim the benefit of the filing date of the provisional application filed on June 8, 1995 in a nonprovisional application filed after June 10, 1996.

A24. Does amended 35 USC 119(e) enable a nonprovisional application to claim priority based on a corresponding provisional application when the nonprovisional is filed more than 12 months after the filing of the provisional? Please explain.

No, 35 U.S.C. 119(e)(1) still requires that a nonprovisional application be filed within twelve months of the filing date of the provisional application for the nonprovisional application to claim the benefit of the filing date of the provisional application.

A25. The legislation amended 119(e)(2) to remove the requirement of copendency for a provisional application. However, 119(e)(1) was not amended so it has retained the copendency requirement for filing a nonprovisional application claiming priority from a provisional. 37 CFR 1.78 has been amended to remove the copendency requirement entirely. This seems inconsistent with 119(e)(1). Please clarify this issue.

35 U.S.C. 119(e)(1) requires that a nonprovisional application be filed within twelve months of the filing date of the provisional application for the nonprovisional application to claim the benefit of the filing date of the provisional application. It does not require copendency for the nonprovisional application to claim the benefit of that provisional application. It is not necessary for the rules of practice to reiterate statutory requirements (it is sufficient that the statute contains the requirements) and that a rule does not reiterate all the pertinent statutory requirements does not make the rule inconsistent with the statute.

A26. An applicant filed a RCE within 3 months from the mailing of a non-final Office action (i.e., the prosecution in the application is not closed). With the RCE, the applicant submitted an amendment responsive to the Office action in compliance with 37 CFR 1.111 and the proper fee. (a) Is the RCE proper? (b) If the RCE is improper, will the amendment be entered and considered by the examiner to avoid abandonment of the application?

(a) The answer would depend on the filing date of the RCE.

If the RCE was filed *before August 16, 2000*, then the *RCE would be proper* because under the RCE Interim Rule, a RCE may be filed before the prosecution in an application is closed. See *Changes to Application Examination and Provisional Application Practice*, Interim Rule, 65 FR 14865 (Mar. 20, 2000), 1233 Off. Gaz. Pat. Office 47 (Apr. 11, 2000).

If the RCE, however, was filed *on or after August 16, 2000*, then the *RCE would be improper* because under the RCE Final Rule, a RCE may not be filed before the prosecution in an application is closed. *See* 37 CFR 1.114(a) and *Request for Continued Examination Practice and Changes to Provisional Application Practice; Final Rule*, 65 FR 50092 (Aug. 16, 2000), 1238 Off. Gaz. Pat. Office 13 (Sept. 5, 2000).

For the purpose of filing a RCE, the prosecution in an application is closed when the application is under appeal, or the last Office action is a final action, a notice of allowance or a *Qualye* action.

(b) Even though the RCE is improper (because it was filed on or after August 16, 2000 and before the prosecution is closed), the amendment submitted with the RCE would still be entered and considered by the examiner since it was timely filed and responsive to the non-final Office action in compliance with 37 CFR 1.111.

B. *Patent Term Adjustment*

B1. In view of the Patent Term Guarantee, does the United States Patent and Trademark Office plan to print an explicit indication of the expiration date on the face of a patent so that the expiration date can be ascertained without having to add the patent term extension to the original patent term?

The United States Patent and Trademark Office does not print the expiration date on issued patents because the actual date a patent will expire is dependent upon a number of future events. The actual date any particular patent will expire is, for example, dependent upon whether: (1) all maintenance fees are timely paid; (2) the patent is disclaimed, either by a statutory disclaimer of all claims or a terminal disclaimer; (3) all of the claims of the patent are canceled during a reexamination proceeding; or (4) an extension under 35 U.S.C. 156 is granted. Since less than forty percent of patentees pay all three maintenance fees, an expiration date based upon a calculation of date that is twenty years from the earliest filing date under 35 U.S.C. 111(a), 120, 121, 363, or 365(c) plus any calculated extension under 35 U.S.C. 154(b) would be incorrect and misleading over sixty percent of the time. However, the front page of the patent will indicate the number of days of term adjustment to which the patent is entitled.

B2. May an applicant obtain patent term adjustment even if prosecution is less than 3 years?

Yes, assuming the application is eligible, patent term adjustment is available under either 35 USC 154(b)(1)(A) (administrative delays) or (C) (interferences, secrecy orders and successful appeals) regardless of how long the application was pending in the Office. See proposed 37 CFR 1.702(a), (c), (d), and (e).

Example: An application is filed 6/1/00. A notice of allowance is mailed 9/1/01. The issue fee is paid and all formal requirements are satisfied on 12/1/01. The patent is not issued until 5/1/02. As the patent was not issued in four months following the payment of the issue fee, the period of delay from 4/2/02 to 5/1/02 would give rise to patent term adjustment pursuant 35 USC 154(b)(1)(A)(iv) and proposed 37 CFR 1.702(a)(4) and 1.703(a)(6).

B3. Is an application for patent term adjustment under 37 CFR 1.705(c) required to include the fee set forth in 1.18(f) and the fee set forth in 1.18(e) or only the fee set forth in 1.18(f)?

Both fees. Even an application for term adjustment that is only requesting reinstatement of part of a period of adjustment by showing, in spite of all due care, that the applicant was unable to respond to any rejection, objection, argument or any other request made by the Office within a three-month period starting the date of mailing of the Office action or requirement, is required to pay the fee for an application for term adjustment set forth in 1.18(e) as well as the fee for a due care showing set forth in 1.18(f). In other words, an application under 37 CFR 1.705(c) is also required to comply with 37 CFR 1.705(b).

B4. When must an application be filed in order for the National Stage of an International Application to be eligible for Patent Term Adjustment (PTA)?

The international application must have an international filing date of May 29, 2000 or later. The date on which the international application either complies with 35 USC 371(c) or enters the National Stage is not relevant for determining eligibility for PTA. *See* section 4405(a) of the AIPA, 35 USC §363, and 37 CFR §1.702(f).

B5. If an International Application is filed before May 29, 2000 and is pending on or after May 29, 2000, may a continuing application filed under 35 USC 111(a) be filed on or after May 29, 2000, to seek the benefit of Patent Term Adjustment (PTA)?

Yes, the filing date of the continuing application controls, thus, if the continuing application is filed on or after May 29, 2000, the continuing application is eligible for PTA. *See* section 4405(a) of the AIPA, 35 USC §§111(a) and 120, and 37 CFR §1.702(f).

B6. 37 CFR 1.704(c)(10) provides that submission of an amendment under 37 CFR 1.312 or other paper after a notice of allowance has been mailed is a circumstance that constitutes a failure of the applicant to engage in reasonable efforts to conclude processing or examination of an application. Are formal drawings an "other paper" within the meaning of 37 CFR 1.704(c)(10), such that the submission of formal drawings after a notice of allowance is mailed will result in reduction of any patent term adjustment? What if the drawings are required by the notice of allowance?

Yes (regardless of whether formal drawings are required by the notice of allowance). 37 CFR 1.85 no longer permits applicants to request that a requirement for correction of drawings be held in abeyance until a notice of allowance is mailed. *See* Changes to Implement Eighteen-Month Publication of Patent Applications, Final rule, 65 Fed. Reg. 57023, 57032, 57055 (Sept. 20, 2000). Applicants must file any formal drawings prior to the mailing of a notice of allowance to avoid a reduction of any patent term adjustment.

C. *Eighteen-Month Publication*

C1. Is there any information on the United States Patent and Trademark Office Web site regarding automation plans related to Pre-Grant Publication of Applications?

Yes, please see the Pre-Grant Publication Global Concept of Operations document, posted on the AIPA web page, under the heading "Presentations."

C2. Will Divisionals, Continuations-in-Part, and/or Continuations based on original applications filed before the critical date be subject to the mandatory publication?

Yes. Any nonprovisional application (other than for a design patent) filed on or after November 29, 2000 is subject to the eighteen-month publication provisions of the AIPA. This includes continuation, divisional, and continuation-in-part applications of applications filed prior to November 29, 2000. It does not matter whether the continuing application was filed under 37 CFR 1.53(b), or as a continued prosecution application (CPA) under 37 CFR 1.53(d). Since a request for continued examination under 35 U.S.C. 132(b) and 37 CFR 1.114 is not a continuing application, filing a request for continued examination of an application filed prior to November 29, 2000 will not make that application subject to the eighteen-month publication provisions of the AIPA.

C3. Where can I find the form of the declaration under Subtitle E of the American Inventors Protection Act of 1999 that no foreign filing is planned for the invention described in a new application?

The form is not yet available, but it is under development. As soon as it is ready it will be made available on the PTO Web site.

C4. Does the American Inventors Protection Act of 1999 address the issue of royalty payments by companies who knowingly violate an invention claimed in a published patent application for infringement that occurs before the patent grant date?

The American Inventors Protection Act of 1999 (AIPA) does indeed address this issue. In the AIPA, Subtitle E - Domestic Publication of Patent Applications Published Abroad, Section 4504 on Provisional Rights addresses this very issue. By the terms of the AIPA, an eventual patentee will be able to obtain a reasonable royalty from any person, having actual notice, who "infringes" the claimed invention during the period beginning on the date of publication of the application and ending on the date the patent is issued. The right to recover a reasonable royalty is based upon actual notice and is only available if the invention as claimed in the patent is substantially identical to the invention as claimed in the published patent application.

C5. Does the Office intend to provide guidance as to the meaning of the term "substantially identical" as used in AIPA §4504 to define when reasonable royalties will be available (35 U.S.C. 154(d)(2))?

No, because the PTO is not charged with administering provisional rights.

C6. Can an examiner reject a claim in an application being examined under 35 USC 135(b)(2) as being statutorily barred by the publication of another application?

Yes. Applicants have one year from the publication date of a published application to present the same or substantially the same claim as a claim in a published application. When the claim is, however, presented later than one year after the publication date, a rejection under 35 USC 135(b)(2) is proper. Thus, a rejection under §135(b)(2) should be made when:

(1) The effective filing date of the claim in an application being examined is later than the publication date of the published application;

(2) The application being examined is claiming the same invention as claimed in the application publication, i.e., the claim in the application being examined is the same as, or for the same or substantially the same subject matter as, the published claim in the application publication; and

(3) The presentation of the claim in the application being examined is later than one year after the publication date of the published application.

Note:

(1) A rejection under 35 USC 102(a) and 102(e) should also be made, since the effective filing date of the claim in the application being examined is later than the publication date of the published application.

(2) The published application could be a U.S. patent application or an international application designating the United States.

C7. Patents filed after 11/29/00 will be published by the USPTO 18 months after the filing unless the applicant requests an earlier publication or the applicant requests that the application not be published. The patent rights allow for a reasonable royalty from the date of publication to the date of issuance.

(1) Can I request that my application be published even though I filed before 11/29/00?

(2) If so, can I request immediate publication or must I wait until 11/29/00?

Initially, the right to reasonable royalties is subject to a number of conditions: *e.g.*, (1) actual notice of the published application must be given; and (2) the patent claims must be substantially identical to the claims in the published application. In answer to your questions: (1) Yes, provided that the application is pending on November 29, 2000 and your request complies with applicable USPTO regulations (proposed 37 CFR 1.211); and (2) You must wait until November 29, 2000 to make such a request (the statutory provisions and implementing regulations will not take effect until November 29, 2000).

C8. Is there a mechanism by which the USPTO intends to assess whether or not any foreign filings have been made contrary to the certification provided by the applicant under 35 USC 22(b)(2)(B)(i), and whether or not the notice requirements of section 122(b)(2)(iii) have subsequently been met?

The Office does not have any current plans to routinely monitor compliance with either the certification or notice requirements of 35 USC 122(b)(2). Applicants are advised that the Office's failure to note that an application has gone abandoned as a matter of law for failing to provide the proper notice has no effect on the abandoned status of the application (will not operate to prevent the abandonment of the application), regardless of any indication of allowability from the Office.

Also, is there a mechanism by which the USPTO intends to provide notice to applicants that their patent applications have been "regarded as abandoned" for having failed to provide notice of any foreign filings within 45 days thereof, as required by section 122(b)(2)(iii)?

The Office does not have any current plans to routinely provide notice to applicant that their patent applications have been "regarded as abandoned." Should the examiner become aware of the foreign filing, e.g., during the prior art search, the examiner does have the authority to formally hold the application abandoned.

C9. Will references in a submission under 37 CFR §1.99 be placed in the application file and forwarded to the examiner if the submissions includes explanation or references that are highlighted?

Section 1.99 provides that a submission by a member of the public of patents or publications relevant to a pending published application will be entered in the application file if the submission complies with the requirements of §1.99 and the application is still pending when the submission and application file are brought before the examiner. Section 1.99(d) provides that a submission under §1.99 may not include any explanation of the references, or any other information. The Office will dispose of any explanation or information if included in a submission under §1.99. To ensure that there is no protest, the Office will review submissions under §1.99 to determine whether they are limited to patents and publications before the submission is placed in the file of the application and forwarded to the examiner. The submission under §1.99 will not be placed in the file of the application, if the explanation of the references and any other information included in the submission are integrated in the references and cannot be extracted easily, or if the references are highlighted.

C10. If I file a PCT application designating the U.S. and then before International Bureau publishes the PCT application I abandon the application, may I submit a non-publication request under 37 CFR 1.213 with a filing of a U.S. application under 35 USC 111, that discloses the same subject matter as disclosed in the PCT application?

No, the mere filing of the PCT application precludes the proper use of a non-publication request, since the invention disclosed in the US application was the subject of an application that was filed under an international agreement requiring publication at 18 months (the PCT). 35 USC 122(b)(2)(B)(i) states that "If an applicant makes a request upon filing, certifying that the invention disclosed in the application has not and will not be the subject of an application filed in another country, or under a multilateral international agreement, that requires publication of applications 18 months after filing, . . ."

The trigger in the statute is not the publication, but rather the trigger is the act of filing in a foreign country that requires publication, or under international agreement that requires publication. Thus 37 CFR 1.213(a)(3) is consistent with the statutory requirement. The statute simply does not allow for abandonment of the foreign application, or application under a multilateral international agreement, prior to foreign publication at 18 months in order to provide for an appropriate request for non-publication in the US application.

D. *102(e)*

D1. If an International Application (IA) was published by the International Bureau (IB) in language other than English (i.e., German) and designates the United States, is there any action that can be done (i.e., filing a translation or getting it republished in English) to make the published IA eligible to be prior art under amended 35 U.S.C. 102(e)(1)?

Assuming the new §102(e)(1), as amended by AIPA, is applicable to the IA, 35 U.S.C. 102(e)(1) clearly states that an IA only receives a 102(e)(1) date if the IA is published under PCT Article 21(2)(a) in English and designates the United States. Therefore, the IA must be published by the International Bureau pursuant to PCT Article 21(2)(a) (normal 18 month publication) in English and must designate the United States in order to be prior art under 35 U.S.C. 102(e)(1). Any filing of a translation or later publication in English will not be effective in obtaining a 102(e)(1) date for the IA published by the IB in a language other than English.

E. *103(c)*

E1. Does a Continued Prosecution Application qualify for the new provisions of 35 U.S.C. 103(c) as specified in Section 4807 of the American Inventors Protection Act?

Yes, see Guidelines Concerning the Implementation of Changes to 35 U.S.C. 102(g) and 103(c) and the Interpretation of the Term "Original Application" in the American Inventors Protection Act of 1999, Notice, 1233 Off. Gaz. Pat. Office 2 (April 11, 2000).

E2. Q & A: Under the amended 35 U.S.C. 103(c), what type of evidence will provide proof that the inventions were commonly owned by, or subject to an obligation of assignment to, the same person, at the time the invention was made?

To disqualify a reference under 35 U.S.C. 103(c), applicant needs to supply evidence that the invention described in the application for patent and the invention described in the "prior art" reference applied against the application were commonly owed by, or subject to an obligation of assignment to, the same person, *at the time the invention in the application for patent was made*.

The time requirement "at the time the invention was made" is required by statute. *See* 35 U.S.C. 103(c). The assignment records kept by the USPTO do not supply the necessary evidence for the time requirement nor are such records required to have such timing information. Therefore, the following evidence is sufficient to provide proof of common ownership by, or subject to an obligation of assignment to, the same person at the time the invention was made:

For recorded assignments, applicant provides:

1. a statement of the location of the assignments recorded in the USPTO in accordance with 37 CFR 3.11 which convey the entire rights in the application and the reference to the same person(s) or organization(s),
2. **and** a statement from applicant(s) or their registered practitioner that the application for patent and the "prior art" reference applied against the application were commonly owed by, or subject to an obligation of assignment to, the same person, *at the time the invention in the application for patent was made;* **or**

For unrecorded assignments, applicant provides:

1. copies of unrecorded assignments which convey the entire rights in the application and the reference to the same person(s) or organization(s), **and**
2. a statement from applicant(s) or their registered practitioner that the application for patent and the "prior art" reference applied against the application were commonly owed by, or subject to an obligation of assignment to, the same person, *at the time the invention in the application for patent was made;* **or**

Applicant provides an affidavit or declaration by the common owner stating:

1. there was common ownership by, or an obligation of assignment to, the same person for the application and the "prior art" reference *at the time the invention was made*, **and**
2. why the affiant believes there was common ownership; **or**
3. applicant provides other evidence that established common ownership by, or an obligation of assignment to, the same person for the application and the "prior art" reference *at the time the invention was made*, e.g., a court decision determining the owner.

In circumstances where the common owner is a corporation or other organization, an affidavit or declaration averring ownership may be signed by an official of the corporation or organization empowered to act on behalf of the corporation or organization.

Last Update: October, 2000

Appendix D-13

American Inventors Protection Act of 1999—Comparison of CPA Practice, URAA Transitional Practice Under 37 CFR 1.129(a), and New Request for Continued Examination (RCE) Practice

[The following table was taken from the U.S. Patent and Trademark Office website. The table is updated from time to time and may be found at <http://www.uspto.gov/web/offices/dcom/olia/aipa/comparison_of_cpa_practice.htm>.]

	Continued prosecution application (CPA) under 37 CFR 1.53(d)	**URAA transitional practice under 37 CFR 1.129(a)**	**Request for continued examination (RCE) under 37 CFR 1.114**
1	CPA practice is not applicable to provisional applications or during reexamination Note: CPA practice has been made inapplicable to any utility or original plant applications filed on or after May 29, 2000 (including reissue)	37 CFR 1.129(a) practice is applicable only to original utility or original plant applications filed before or on June 8, 1995, and which have been pending for at least two years as of June 8, 1995 (date-wise virtual mutual exclusivity with RCE practice)	RCE practice is not applicable to provisional applications, design applications, applications filed before June 8, 1995, or during reexamination
2	A CPA may be filed before the prosecution in an application is closed	A submission under 37 CFR 1.129(a) must be filed after final rejection and before an appeal brief is filed	After August 16, 2000, a RCE must be filed after the prosecution in an application is closed
3	Statutory authority: 35 U.S.C. §§111(a), 120, and 121	Statutory authority: Section 532(a)(2)(A) of Pub. L. 103-465 (uncodified)	Statutory authority: 35 U.S.C. §132(b)
4	The Office treats a CPA as continued examination of the same application, but it is technically/legally a new application	Further examination under 37 CFR 1.129(a) is in fact continued examination of the same application	A RCE is in fact continued examination of the same application
5	The applicant may defer paying the filing fee for a CPA under 37 CFR 1.53(g)	The applicant may not defer paying the fee for a submission under 37 CFR 1.129(a)	The applicant may not defer paying the fee for a RCE
6	The fee for a CPA must be the statutory filing fee: basic filing fee plus any applicable excess claims fees (even if previously paid in the prior application)	The Office sets the fee (fee need not include excess claims fee for claims previously paid for): the fee is set at an amount equal to the basic filing fee of a utility application (small entity reduction is available)	The Office sets the fee for a RCE (RCE fee need not include excess claims fee for claims previously paid for): the RCE fee is set at an amount equal to the basic filing fee of a utility application (small entity reduction is available)

	Continued prosecution application (CPA) under 37 CFR 1.53(d)	**URAA transitional practice under 37 CFR 1.129(a)**	**Request for continued examination (RCE) under 37 CFR 1.114**
7	A patent issuing on a CPA filed on or after May 29, 2000, is entitled to the patent term adjustment provisions of the AIPA, regardless of the filing date of any prior application of the CPA. A patent issuing on a CPA is **not** entitled to any patent term adjustment accumulated during prosecution of any prior application of the CPA	An application that is eligible for the transitional practice of 37 CFR 1.129(a) is **not** entitled to the patent term adjustment provisions of the AIPA	Filing a RCE on or after May 29, 2000, will **not** cause an application to be entitled to the patent term adjustment provisions of the AIPA. If an application is entitled to the patent term adjustment provisions of the AIPA (*i.e.*, was itself filed on or after May 29, 2000), filing a RCE cuts-off the applicant's ability to accumulate any additional patent term adjustment against the three-year pendency provision, but does not otherwise affect patent term adjustment
8	No limit on the number of times an applicant may file a CPA to obtain continued examination	An applicant may have only two (2) submissions entered as a matter of right under 37 CFR 1.129(a)	No limit on the number of times an applicant may file a RCE to obtain continued examination
9	A CPA is not entitled to the benefit of a Certificate of Mailing under 37 CFR 1.8	A submission under 37 CFR 1.129(a) is entitled to the benefit of a Certificate of Mailing under 37 CFR 1.8	A RCE is entitled to the benefit of a Certificate of Mailing under 37 CFR 1.8
10	Applicants may file a continuation or divisional CPA, but not a CIP CPA	Applicants may not switch inventions (divisional equivalent) as a matter of right or add new matter (CIP equivalent)	Applicants may not switch inventions (divisional equivalent) as a matter of right or add new matter (CIP equivalent)
11	A CPA abandons the (previously) pending application: appeals to the BPAI or courts in the prior application become moot automatically	A submission under 37 CFR 1.129(a) does not abandon the (previously and currently) pending application: no appeal issues because Office requires such submission to be filed before an appeal (to BPAI) brief is filed	A RCE does not abandon the (previously and currently) pending application: appeals to the BPAI are dismissed by operation of 37 CFR 1.114 but any pending court action must be dismissed to restore jurisdiction over the application to the Office

	Continued prosecution application (CPA) under 37 CFR 1.53(d)	URAA transitional practice under 37 CFR 1.129(a)	Request for continued examination (RCE) under 37 CFR 1.114
12	Inventorship carries over unless the applicant provides a statement deleting inventors	Inventorship carries/ continues: any change must be via 37 CFR 1.48	Inventorship carries/ continues: any change must be via 37 CFR 1.48
13	Small entity status does not carry (but can be claimed by reference to status in prior application or payment of small entity filing fee)	Small entity status carries/continues	Small entity status carries/continues
14	A CPA accompanied by an amendment (preliminary) cancelling all claims makes the CPA improper (not entitled to a filing date)	Submission under 37 CFR 1.129(a) accompanied by an amendment cancelling all claims is simply a non-responsive amendment	RCE accompanied by an amendment cancelling all claims is simply a non-responsive amendment
15	Submission need not include a reply that is a *bona fide* attempt to advance the application	Submission must include a reply that is a *bona fide* attempt to advance the application (37 CFR 1.111)	Submission must include a reply that is a *bona fide* attempt to advance the application (37 CFR 1.111) if a reply to an Office action is outstanding
16	A CPA filed on or after November 29, 2000, will be subject to the eighteen-month publication provisions of the AIPA, and the changes to 35 U.S.C. §102(e)	Submission on or after November 29, 2000, does not subject application to the eighteen-month publication provisions of the AIPA or the changes to 35 U.S.C. §102(e); voluntary publication may be requested	Submission on or after November 29, 2000, does not subject application to the eighteen-month publication provisions of the AIPA or the changes to 35 U.S.C. §102(e); voluntary publication may be requested
17	A CPA based on the national stage of an international application is an application filed under 35 U.S.C. §111(a) and thus it is subject to restriction practice in accordance with 37 CFR 1.141–1.146	If a submission is filed in a national stage application under 35 U.S.C. §371, the application is still subject to unity of invention practice in accordance with 37 CFR 1.475 and 1.499	If a submission is filed in a national stage application under 35 U.S.C. §371, the application is still subject to unity of invention practice in accordance with 37 CFR 1.475 and 1.499

Appendix D-14

Patent Business Goals—Final Rule—Explanatory Materials

[The following explanatory materials concerning the Patent Business Goals final rule have been published on the U.S. Patent and Trademark Office web site.]

Question : Answers

A. Small Entity Status (37 CFR 1.27)

A1. If an application is filed prior to September 8, 2000 with the small entity basic filing fee and an assertion that the applicant is a small entity, but no small entity statement in compliance with former 37 CFR 1.27: (1) what must the applicant do to establish small entity status; (2) is a surcharge under 37 CFR 1.16(e) (or (l)) required; and (3) does it matter whether the Office has issued a Notice to File Missing Parts of Application as of September 8, 2000?

(1) Nothing is necessary to establish small entity status. The change to 37 CFR 1.27 applies to the application as of September 8, 2000, that is, the applicant is considered to have established small entity status in the application on September 8, 2000.

(2) The (small entity) surcharge under 37 CFR 1.16 is required. The appropriate basic filing fee was not present on filing (since the application was filed before September 8, 2000, and small entity status was not established until September 8, 2000), and 37 CFR 1.53(f) (or (g)) requires payment of the surcharge under 37 CFR 1.16(e) (or (l)) if the appropriate basic filing fee is not present on filing.

(3) No. Regardless of whether the Office has issued a Notice to File Missing Parts of Application as of September 8, 2000, the appropriate basic filing fee was not present on filing and 37 CFR 1.53(f) (or (g)) requires payment of the surcharge under 37 CFR 1.16(e) (or (l)) if the appropriate basic filing fee is not present on filing.

B. Standards for Drawings (37 CFR 1.84)

B1. Why are all applications with drawings reviewed in the Office of Initial Patent Examination? Can applications which are not going to be published as part of the pre-grant publication process be reviewed later?

All applications with drawings need to be reviewed in OIPE to determine whether the drawings are capable of reproduction (can be copied and/or scanned in black and white) and are in the English language. Further compliance with 37 CFR 1.84 will not be required by OIPE. Reproducible drawings are required even if an application is not going to be published, so that the Office will be able to provide a certified copy of the application for foreign priority and other purposes. Furthermore, since applicants may rescind a non-publication request, all applications need to be reviewed according to the same standards regardless of whether they are to be published. In addition, an English translation of the application is required pursuant to 37 CFR 1.52(d)(1). Aside from the non-English text and for the need to have a black and white copy of color drawings/photographs in plant applications (see 37 CFR 1.165(b)), this drawing review during scanning is the same review that has been performed for several years. The Office does not anticipate requiring very many more drawing corrections in OIPE as a result of pre-grant publication.

As a result of this minimal screening, the Office will not be requiring applicant to submit "formal drawings" during preexamination under 37 CFR 1.215(a), the Office will merely require drawings that can be copied and are in the English language. Drawings that are filed in reply to a preexamination notice requiring drawings that can be copied in black and white or are in the English language will be rescanned and included in the patent application publication. If applicant desires to have better drawings included in the pre-grant publication, the drawings will have to be submitted in paper on filing or in electronic form through the Electronic Filing System (EFS) within one month of the filing date of the application, or fourteen months from any priority date claimed 35 U.S.C. §§119, 120, 121 or 365(c). See 37 CFR 1.215(c).

Applicants should also note that the Office may require "formal drawings" at allowance merely because applicant originally indicated the drawings as informal. In addition, the patent examiner may find errors in the drawings and require correction of the drawings. If the application was filed after May 29, 2000, any formal or corrected drawings filed after allowance will result in a reduction to any patent term adjustment. See 37 CFR 1.704(c)(10).

C. Title and Abstract (37 CFR 1.72)

C1. Must the title of the invention appear as a heading on the first page of the specification?

No. The title of the invention is not required (nor has it been under the previous version of §1.72) to be part of the specification. To the extent that practitioners feel an important identification purpose is served by supplying a title on the specification, it should appear as a heading on the first page of the specification. Alternatively, the title may now be supplied in an application data sheet (§1.76).

C2. How long may the abstract be?

The abstract may not exceed 150 words in length. This is a departure from the former 37 CFR 1.72, which allowed an abstract to be up to 250 words in length. The reduction in the number of words allowed in the abstract is necessary to harmonize USPTO practice with PCT guidelines.

C3. What will happen if an application is filed with an abstract that has more than 150 words?

When an application is originally filed with an abstract having more than 150 words, the Office of Initial Patent Examination (OIPE) will send applicant a notice to correct the abstract (with a period for reply of two months). The application file will be held in OIPE and not released to the assigned Technology Center for examination until an acceptable abstract is filed. The mere presence of an abstract which fails to comply with amended §1.72 will not prevent an application from being accorded a filing date. It will, however, delay the initiation of the examination. Failure to comply to the notice within 3 months, in an application subject to Patent Term Adjustment, may cause a reduction of any patent term adjustment.

D. Certificate of Correction of Office Mistake (37 CFR 1.322)

D1. Under what conditions may the Commissioner issue a certificate of correction to correct a mistake in a patent incurred through the fault of the Office?

The Commissioner may pursuant to 35 U.S.C. 254 issue a certificate of correction to correct a mistake in a patent incurred through the fault of the Office, which mistake is clearly disclosed in the records of the Office, (1) At the request of the patentee or the patentee's assignee, (2) Acting sua sponte for mistakes that the Office discovers, and (3) Acting on information about a mistake supplied by a third party.

D2. Do third parties have standing to demand that the Office issue or refuse to issue a certificate of correction?

No. Third parties do not having standing to demand that the Office issue or refuse to issue a certificate of correction. See Hallmark Card, Inc. v. Lehman, 959 F. Supp. 539, 543–44, 42 USPQ2d 1134, 1138 (D.D.C. 1997). The Office is, however, cognizant of the need for the public to have correct information about published patents and may therefore accept information about mistakes in patents from third parties and may issue certificates of correction based upon that information (whether or not it is accompanied by a specific request for issuance of a certificate of correction).

D3. Where third parties submit information or a request for a certification of correction, will the Office correspond with the third parties about their submission or request?

No. The Office does not intend to correspond with third parties about the information they submitted either to inform the third parties of whether it intends to issue a certificate of correction or to issue a denial of any request for issuance of a certificate of correction that may accompany the information. The Office will confirm to the party submitting such information that such information has in fact been received by the Office if a stamped, self-addressed post card has been submitted. See MPEP 503. The status of the patent file, including issuance of any certificate of correction, may be monitored via the web using the Patent Application Information Retrieval (PAIR) system.

D4. Is there a fee for submission of information by a third party?

No. A fee has not been imposed for submission of information by a third party.

D5. Will papers containing a submission of information or request for a certificate of correction submitted by a third party be made record of and kept in the patent file?

No. Papers containing a submission of information or request for a certificate of correction submitted by a third party will not be made of record in the file that they relate to or be retained by the Office.

D6. Will all mistakes incurred by the Office and identified by the patentee, the patentee's assignee, the Office, or a third party be corrected?

No. The Office intends to retain its discretion and may not issue a certificate of correction even if a mistake is identified, particularly if the identified mistake is not a significant one that would justify the cost and time to issue a certificate of correction.

D7. Where the Office discovers a mistake or receives a submission of information or request for a certificate of correction from a third party, will the patentee be notified prior to the issuance of any certificate of correction?

Yes. The Office will not issue a certification of correction under 37 CFR 1.322 without first notifying the patentee (including any assignee of record) at the correspondence address of record as specified in §1.33(a) and affording the patentee or an assignee an opportunity to be heard.

E. Amendment by Paragraph Replacement (37 CFR 1.121)

E1. If an applicant elects to utilize optional paragraph numbering as per §1.52(b)(6), would amendments to the specification (under §1.121) which add new paragraphs require a renumbering of all the paragraphs?

No. If the method for numbering paragraphs suggested by the Office is used, a single new paragraph replacing a single original paragraph would retain the same number as the paragraph being replaced. If more than one paragraph replaces a single original paragraph, the additional paragraphs would be numbered with sequential integers following a single decimal, e.g., [0071], [0071.1] and [0071.2] would replace original paragraph [0071]. Original unamended paragraphs before and after the affected paragraph would retain their original numbering.

E2. Are there software products currently on the market which will automatically number paragraphs?

Yes. At the very least, recent releases of Word (Office 97 or later) and WordPerfect (9.0) have features for automatically numbering paragraphs.

E3. What is the effective date for implementing the requirements for amendments by replacement paragraph/claims?

Mandatory compliance with the revised rule is not required until March 1, 2001. It is suggested, however, that applicants adopt the revised procedures on or after November 7, 2000, in order to adjust to the changes in amendment practice. The time period prior to November 7 will be used by the Office to train technical support personnel on the changes of the new rule.

On or after March 1, 2001, all amendments must comply with revised §1.121.

E4. How do I amend claims which were previously amended prior to the change to 37 CFR 1.121?

After the effective date of the rule change, the latest amended version of a claim must be presented in clean form, including all changes made by the current, as well as any earlier, amendment. A marked-up version showing changes made by only the current amendment must accompany the clean version.

Applicants will also be able to submit a clean set of all pending claims, consolidating all previous versions of pending claims from a series of separate amendments into a single clean version in a single amendment paper. This submission of a clean version of all of the pending claims will be construed as directing the cancellation of all previous versions of any pending claims. No marked-up version will be required to accompany the clean version where no changes other than the consolidation are being made.

E5. What if I fail to amend my specification/claims according to the revised rule after March 1, 2001?

The amendment may be considered not fully responsive and treated by the examiner under 37 CFR 1.135(c). The examiner, however, will not give applicant additional time for correcting amendments submitted after final rejection. See MPEP Sec. 714.03.

F. Reissue

F1. If amendment by paragraph replacement is now required by the Office for amendments submitted during prosecution, how should I amend the specification in a reissue application at the time of filing?

Amendment of a reissue specification at the time of filing can be accomplished either by (1) paragraph replacement in a preliminary amendment, or (2) "cut and paste" of a two column copy of the original patent, whereby minor changes are inserted at a cut portion of a column and the remainder of the column rejoined. Unlike amendment practice for non-reissue applications, no clean copy of a replacement paragraph should be submitted; rather, underlining and bracketing (to show additions and deletions, respectively) must be employed in the paragraph to be inserted. No accompanying marked-up version of the amended paragraph should be submitted.

F2. Can I merely make a request for transfer of drawings (from the patent file to the reissue application) to satisfy the drawing requirements for a reissue application?

The Office will no longer grant or act on a request for transfer of drawings. If good quality copies of the patent drawings are submitted at the time of filing, and the drawing copies satisfy the requirements of §1.84, the copies will be accepted in lieu of formal drawings, and the reissue patent will be printed using the copies of the drawings.

F3. If a reissue application is filed which broadens the claims of the invention of the original patent as well as adds claims to a different invention, will the broadened claims of the original invention still be considered to be constructively elected under revised §1.176?

Yes. Even though the original patent claims have been broadened, they are still considered as being drawn to the same invention as was claimed in the original patent. Short of a disclaimer of the original claims being filed in the reissue application, claims to the invention claimed in the original patent (even if broadened) will always be considered the elected invention in a first reissue application which additionally contains claims to another invention. If the constructively elected broadened claims correct a legitimate error in the original patent, the first reissue application may be able to issue prior to the completed examination of any later filed divisional applications. If no error is corrected by the constructively elected claims, and the claims are found to be allowable, prosecution of the first reissue application may have to be suspended pending the completion of the examination of any later filed divisional application, at which time the claims will be recombined into a single application for issuance.

F4. If multiple reissue applications are filed, into which application should the original patent claims be placed, and how should the claims be numbered in each of the applications?

The original patent claims should be submitted in each of the multiple reissue applications as either (1) unamended, (2) amended (including underlined and/or bracketed material), or (3) deleted (bracketed) claims. They should retain their original numbering in each of the multiple reissues. Claims added to any of the reissues should be numbered beginning with the next highest number following the last original claim. Unamended original claims may only appear in one of the reissue applications for examination.

Last Modified: Monday, October 17, 2000

A Brief Summary of Some Significant Rule Changes

***Unless otherwise specificed in the rule, the effective date for the PBG-FINAL RULE is November 7, 2000.**

Amendment Practice (37 CFR 1.121)
- Specification/Claims
  - Amendment by paragraph replacement or rewritten claim in clean form
  - Marked-up version showing changes must be supplied

See § 1.121 Slides on PBG-FINAL RULE Webpage for suggested amendment FORMAT (Optional now; mandatory March 1, 2001)

Small Entity Status (37 CFR 1.27) - FORMS NO LONGER REQUIRED (Eff. Sept. 8, 2000):
- Mere written assertion (e.g., use check box on Application Transmittal Forms) is acceptable

Abstract and Title Length (37 CFR 1.72)
- Abstract now limited to 150 words (PBG)
- Title now limited to 500 characters (AIPA)

Application Data Sheet (ADS) (37 CFR 1.76) NEW
- Use of ADS encouraged for more accurate capture of bibliographic data. Data in ADS not needed in declaration.

After Allowance Practice (37 CFR 1.85(c) and 1.136)
- No extensions of time permitted to file corrected or formal drawings

Elimination of Issue Fee Preauthorizations (37 CFR 1.311)
- Preauthorizations prior to Notice of Allowance no longer permitted

Rocket Docket Established for Designs (37 CFR 1.155)
- Extra submissions plus $900 fee is required

Proof of Authority of Legal Representative (37 CFR 1.44) THIS RULE HAS BEEN DELETED. (Eff. Sept. 8, 2000):
- Oath/Dec. (§1.63) should identify legal rep for deceased/incapacitated inventor

Parts of Applications on CD-R or CD-ROM (37 CFR 1.52 (e), 1.58, 1.96 & 1.821)
- Large tables, computer program listings, and bio-sequences now allowed on CD

Patent Business Goals Final Rule

65 *Fed. Reg.* 54604 (September 8, 2000)

1238 *Off. Gaz. Pat. Office* 77 (September 19, 2000)

USPTO's PBG-FINAL RULE webpage has helpful related information at one location:
http://www.uspto.gov/web/offices/dcom/olia/pbg/index.html)

This site includes: a Listing of Affected Rules, Training & Implementation Materials including Training Slides, Q & A's, Summaries, Effective Date Chart, Forms Changed by Recent Rules, etc.

Contact:
Bob Spar (703) 308-5107 or
Hiram Bernstein (703) 305-8713
for any PBG Change.

Joe Narcavage (703) 305-1795
for 37 CFR 1.121
Amendment Practice Changes

Eugenia Jones (703) 306-5586
for 37 CFR 1.27 Small Entity
Changes

37 CFR 1.2

MPEP BOOKMARK

Changes to the Patent Rules

October 24, 2000 **Volume 1, Issue 1**

This is the first in a series of Patent News Bulletins to assist you in keeping up to date with significant rule changes which affect your area. Keep this copy to use as a bookmark for your present MPEP, or view this bulletin again on the USPTO Website http://www.uspto.gov/web/offices/dcom/olia/pbg/index.html.

Simplified Small Entity Status Practice. Now only an assertion is required. 37 CFR 1.27

The rule package "Changes to the Patent Business Goals - Final Rule," published in the Federal Register on September 8, 2000, 65 Fed. Reg. 54603 (Sept. 8, 2000), and the Official Gazette on September 19, 2000, 1238 Off. Gaz. Pat. Office 77 (September 19, 2000). The PBG rule package makes a number of revisions to Title 37.

The entire final rule may be accessed through the USPTO homepage. Click on the button "PBG - Final Rule."

Areas primarily affected by this rule change include:
(1) Office of Initial Patent Examination
(2) PCT Operations
(3) Tech Centers
(4) Office of Patent Publication

Any questions related to this change in practice should be directed to Eugenia Jones, Legal Advisor, (306-5586), or Hiram Bernstein, Senior Legal Advisor, (305-8713), OPLA.

Effective September 8, 2000, small entity status can be established at any time by a simple written assertion of entitlement to small entity status. Specific forms are no longer required but may continue to be used. The Office will liberally construe any written reference to small entity status to be a request for small entity status. Certain Office forms (e.g., application transmittal forms) have been modified to include a box which can be checked to establish small entity status: http://www.uspto.gov/web/forms/index.html. The new standard for obtaining small entity status also applies to applications or papers filed before September 8, 2000, where status has not yet been accorded. A surcharge is required if an application was filed prior to September 8, 2000, which did not comply with the former 37 CFR 1.27, but in which small entity status was established as of September 8, 2000, under amended 37 CFR 1.27, unless the large entity basic filing fee or a general authorization to charge fees to a deposit account was present on filing.

Small entity status is easy to establish, forms are no longer required.

Payment of any exact small entity basic filing (§§ 1.16(a), (f), (g), (h), or (k)) or basic national fee (§§ 1.492(a)(1)-(a)(5)) is also considered an assertion of small entity status. This is so even if the wrong exact basic filing fee or national fee is selected for the type of application being filed. Payment of any other fee in its exact small entity amount will **not** result in small entity status without a specific written assertion of entitlement to small entity status. In other words, if small entity status was not established when the basic filing or basic national fee was paid, a later claim to small entity status requires an actual written assertion and not merely payment of a small entity fee.

The parties who can assert small entity status have been expanded to include a registered practitioner (who need not actually be of record), one of the inventors (instead of all of the inventors), or a partial assignee (instead of all the assignees). An assertion of small entity status by an assignee, however, must be filed by a party identified in 37 CFR 1.33(b) (e.g., a registered attorney or agent).

Even though payment of an exact small entity basic filing fee or basic national fee is sufficient to assert small entity status, the Office encourages applicants to file a written assertion of small entity status as well as pay the exact amount of the small entity basic filing or basic national fee. A written assertion will provide small entity status should applicant fail to pay the exact small entity basic filing or basic national fee.

Applicants still need to make a thorough investigation of all facts and circumstances before making an assertion of entitlement to small entity status.

MPEP 509.02 & 509.03

37 CFR 1.12

MPEP BOOKMARK

Changes to the Patent Rules

October 24, 2000 **Volume 1, Issue 3**

This is the third in a series of Patent News Bulletins to assist you in keeping up to date with significant rule changes which affect your area. Keep this copy to use as a bookmark for your present MPEP, or view this bulletin again on the USPTO Website .

Simplified Amendment Practice.
Replacement paragraphs/sections/claims to be used. 37 CFR 1.121

The rule package "Changes to the Patent Business Goals - Final Rule," published in the Federal Register on September 8, 2000, 65 Fed. Reg. 54603 (Sept. 8, 2000), and the Official Gazette on September 19, 2000, 1238 Off. Gaz. Pat. Office 77 (September 19, 2000). The PBG rule package makes a number of revisions to Title 37.

The entire final rule may be found at the USPTO Website at ***http://www.uspto.gov/web/offices/dcom/olia/pbg/index.html.***

Areas and individuals primarily affected by this rule change include: (1)Patent Examiners and Tech Support Staff in the Technology Centers (2) Office of Patent Publication

Any questions related to this change in practice should be directed to Joe Narcavage, Special Projects Exr., (703-305-1795) OPLA.

Mandatory compliance with the revised rule is not required until March 1, 2001. It is suggested that applicants adopt the revised procedures on or after November 7, 2000, in order to adjust to the changes in amendment practice.

Under the new amendment practice, amendments to the specification must be made by the submission of clean new or replacement paragraph(s), section(s), specification, or claim(s). This practice will provide a specification (including claims) in clean, or substantially clean, form that can be effectively captured and converted by optical character recognition (OCR) scanning during the patent printing process.

Amendment by paragraph/claim replacement in clean form.

The new practice requires applicant to provide, in addition to the clean version of a replacement paragraph/section/claim, a marked-up version using applicant's choice of a conventional marking system to indicate the changes, which will aid the examiner in identifying the changes that have been made. The marked-up version must be based on the previous version and indicate (by markings) how the previous version has been modified to produce the clean version submitted in the current amendment. The term "previous version" means the version of record in the application as originally filed or from a previously entered amendment.

The following format is suggested in an amendment paper: (1) a clean version of each replacement paragraph/section/claim with clear instructions for entry; (2) starting on a separate page, any remarks/arguments (37 CFR 1.111); and (3) starting on a separate page, a marked-up version entitled "**Version with markings to show changes made**."

Applicants will also be able to submit a clean set of all pending claims, consolidating all previous versions of pending claims from a series of separate amendments into a single clean version in a single amendment paper. This submission of a clean version of all of the pending claims will be construed as directing the cancellation of all previous versions of any pending claims. No marked-up version will be required to accompany the clean version where no changes other than the consolidation are being made.

The amended rule encourages issuance of applications with an examiner's amendment without practitioners/applicants having to file a formal amendment. Additions or deletions of subject matter in the specification, including the claims, may continue to be made in an examiner's amendment at the time of allowance by instructions to make any change at a precise location in the specification or the claims. An examiner's amendment may incorporate a printed copy of a fax or e-mail amendment submitted by applicant. Only that part of the e-mail or fax directed to a clean version, or a portion of, a paragraph/claim to be added should be printed and attached to the examiner's amendment, with a paper copy of the entire e-mail or fax being entered in the file. The electronic version of the e-mail is not required to be saved once the printed e-mail (and any attachments) becomes part of the application file record.

MPEP 714+ & 1302.04

37 CFR 1.32

MPEP BOOKMARK

Changes to the Patent Rules

October 24, 2000 Volume 1, Issue 4

This is the fourth in a series of Patent News Bulletins to assist you in keeping up to date with significant rule changes which affect your area. Keep this copy to use as a bookmark for your present MPEP, or view this bulletin again on the USPTO Website http://www.uspto.gov/web/offices/dcom/olia/pbg/index.html.

Certificate of Correction Practice.

Sua Sponte and Third Party Corrections. 37 CFR 1.322

The rule package "Changes to the Patent Business Goals - Final Rule," published in the Federal Register on September 8, 2000, 65 Fed. Reg. 54603 (Sept. 8, 2000), and the Official Gazette on September 19, 2000, 1238 Off. Gaz. Pat. Office 77 (Sept. 19, 2000). The PBG rule package makes a number of revisions to Title 37.

The entire final rule may be accessed through the USPTO homepage. Click on the button "PBG - Final Rule."

Areas and individuals primarily affected by this rule change include:
(1) Tech Centers - Supervisory Patent Examiners (SPEs) and Special Program Examiners (SPREs)
(2) Office of Patent Publication

Any questions related to this change in practice should be directed to Joe Narcavage, Special Projects Exr., (305-1795), OPLA.

The Office may issue a certificate of correction to correct a mistake in a patent, incurred through the fault of the Office, which mistake is clearly disclosed in the records of the Office. Effective November 7, 2000, the certificate of correction may be issued (1) at the request of patentee or the patentee's assignee, (2) sua sponte by the Office for mistakes that the Office discovers, or (3) based on information supplied by a third party.

Third parties may submit information or requests for certificates of correction.

Regarding information supplied by a third party, 37 CFR 1.322(a)(2)(i) provides that there is no obligation on the Office to act on or respond to submissions of information or requests to issue a certificate of correction by a third party. Additionally, 37 CFR 1.322(a)(2)(ii) provides that a paper submitted by a third party under this section will not be made of record in the file that it relates to nor be retained by the Office. The Office, however, will review such paper to determine whether the Office wishes to proceed with a certificate of correction based on the information supplied in such a paper.

The wording of former 37 CFR 1.322(a) led third parties to conclude that they had standing to demand that the Office issue, or refuse to issue, a certificate of correction. Third parties, however, do not have standing to demand that the Office issue, or refuse to issue, a certificate of correction and 37 CFR 1.322(a)(2), therefore, has been amended accordingly. See Hallmark Cards, Inc. v. Lehman, 959 F. Supp. 539, 543-44, 42 USPQ2d 1134, 1138 (D.D.C. 1997).

When such information is received by the Office, the Office will not correspond with third parties about the information they submitted, but will merely confirm to the party submitting such information that such information has in fact been received by the Office if a stamped, self-addressed post card has been submitted. See MPEP 503.

MPEP 1480 & 1485

PBG - FINAL RULE:

Affected Rules

RULES AMENDED

The final rulemaking includes changes to the following sections of 37 CFR:

1.4, 1.6, 1.9, 1.12, 1.14, 1.17, 1.19, 1.22, 1.25, 1.26, 1.27, 1.28, 1.33, 1.34, 1.36, 1.41, 1.47, 1.48, 1.51, 1.52, 1.53, 1.55, 1.56, 1.58, 1.59, 1.63, 1.64, 1.67, 1.72, 1.77, 1.78, 1.84, 1.85, 1.91, 1.96, 1.97, 1.98, 1.102, 1.104, 1.111, 1.112, 1.115, 1.121, 1.125, 1.131, 1.132, 1.133, 1.136, 1.137, 1.138, 1.152, 1.154, 1.155, 1.163, 1.173, 1.176, 1.177, 1.178, 1.181, 1.193, 1.303, 1.311, 1.314, 1.322, 1.323, 1.324, 1.366, 1.446, 1.497, 1.510, 1.530, 1.550, 1.565, 1.666, 1.720, 1.730, 1.740, 1.741, 1.780, 1.821, 1.823, 1.824, 1.825, 3.27, 3.71, 3.73, 3.81, 5.1, 5.2, 5.12, and 10.23.

RULES DELETED AND ADDED

Sections of 37 CFR that are deleted: §§ 1.44 and 1.174,
Sections of 37 CFR that are added: §§ 1.76, 1.105, and 1.115.

Back to Top

Back to PBG Final Rule Page

USPTO HOME PAGE

Last Modified: Friday, October 13, 2000

PBG - Final Rule
Effective Dates of Individual Rule Changes

Rule	Title	Permitted Date	Mandatory /Effective Date
1.4	Nature of correspondence and signature requirements.		November 7, 2000
1.6	Receipt of correspondence.		November 7, 2000
1.9	Definitions.		November 7, 2000
1.12	Assignment records open to public inspection.		November 7, 2000
1.14	Patent applications preserved in confidence.		November 7, 2000
1.17	Patent application processing fees.		November 7, 2000
1.19	Document supply fees.		November 7, 2000
1.22	Fees payable in advance.		November 7, 2000
1.25	Deposit accounts.		November 7, 2000
1.26	Refunds.		November 7, 2000
1.27	Statement of status as small entity.		September 8, 2000
1.28	Effect on fees of failure to establish status, or change status, as a small entity.		November 7, 2000
1.33	Correspondence respecting patent applications, reexamination proceedings, and other proceedings.		November 7, 2000
1.34	Recognition for representation.		November 7, 2000
1.36	Revocation of power of attorney or authorization; withdrawal of attorney or agent.		November 7, 2000
1.41	Applicant for patent.		November 7, 2000
1.44	Proof of authority.		September 8, 2000
1.47	Filing when an inventor refuses to sign or cannot be reached.		November 7, 2000
1.48	Correction of inventorship in a patent application, other than a reissue application.		November 7, 2000
1.51	General requisites of an application.		November 7, 2000
1.52	Language, paper, writing, margins.		November 7, 2000
1.53	Application number, filing date, and completion of application.		November 7, 2000
1.55	Claim for foreign priority.		November 7, 2000
1.56	Duty to disclose information material to patentability.		November 7, 2000
1.58	Chemical and mathematical formulae and tables.		November 7, 2000
1.59	Expungement of information or copy of papers in application file.		November 7, 2000
1.63	Oath or declaration.		November 7, 2000
1.64	Person making oath or declaration.		November 7, 2000
1.67	Supplemental oath or declaration.		November 7, 2000
1.72	Title and abstract.		November 7, 2000
1.76	Application Data Sheet		November 7, 2000
1.77	Arrangement of application elements.		November 7, 2000
1.78	Claiming benefit of earlier filing date and cross-references to other applications.		September 8, 2000
1.84	Standards for drawings.		November 7, 2000

1.85	Corrections to drawings.		November 7, 2000
1.91	Models or exhibits not generally admitted as part of application or patent.		November 7, 2000
1.96	Submission of computer program listings.	November 8, 2000	March 1, 2001
1.97	Filing of information disclosure statement.		November 7, 2000
1.98	Content of information disclosure statement.		November 7, 2000
1.102	Advancement of examination.		November 7, 2000
1.104	Nature of examination.		November 7, 2000
1.105	Requirements for Information		November 7, 2000
1.111	Reply by applicant or patent owner.		November 8, 2000
1.112	Reconsideration before final action.		November 7, 2000
1.115	Preliminary amendments		November 8, 2000
1.121	Manner of making amendments	November 7, 2000	March 1, 2001
1.125	Substitute specification.		November 7, 2000
1.131	Affidavit or declaration of prior invention to overcome cited patent or publication.		September 8, 2000
1.132	Affidavits or declarations traversing grounds of rejection.		September 8, 2000
1.133	Interviews.		November 7, 2000
1.136	Extensions of time.		November 7, 2000
1.137	Revival of abandoned application or lapsed patent.		September 8, 2000
1.138	Express abandonment.		November 7, 2000
1.152	Design drawings.		September 8, 2000
1.154	Arrangement of application elements.		November 7, 2000
1.155	Issue of design patents.		September 8, 2000
1.173	Specification.		November 8, 2000
1.174	Drawings.		November 7, 2000
1.176	Examination of reissue.		November 7, 2000
1.177	Reissue in divisions.		November 7, 2000
1.178	Original patent.		November 7, 2000
1.181	Petition to the Commissioner.		November 7, 2000
1.193	Examiner's answer and reply brief.		November 7, 2000
1.303	Civil action under 35 U.S.C. 145, 146, 306.		November 7, 2000
1.311	Notice of Allowance.		November 7, 2000
1.314	Issuance of patent.		September 8, 2000
1.322	Certificate of correction of Office mistake.		November 8, 2000
1.323	Certificate of correction of applicant's mistake.		November 7, 2000
1.324	Correction of inventorship in patent.		September 8, 2000
1.366	Submission of maintenance fees.		September 8, 2000
1.446	Refund of international application filing and processing fees.		November 7, 2000
1.497	Oath or declaration under 35 U.S.C. 371(c)(4).		November 7, 2000
1.510	Request for reexamination.		November 8, 2000
1.530	Statement; amendment by patent owner.		November 7, 2000
1.550	Conduct of reexamination proceedings.		November 7, 2000
1.565	Concurrent office proceedings.		November 7, 2000
1.666	Filing of interference settlement agreements.		November 7, 2000
1.720	Conditions for extension of patent term.		November 7, 2000
1.730	Applicant for extension of patent term.		November 7, 2000
1.740	Application for extension of patent term.		September 8, 2000
1.741	Filing date of application.		November 7, 2000

1.760	Interim extension of patent term under 35 U.S.C. 156(e)(2).		September 8, 2000
1.780	Certificate of extension of patent term.		November 7, 2000
1.821	Nucleotide and/or amino acid sequence disclosures in patent applications.		November 7, 2000
1.823	Requirements for nucleotide and/or amino acid sequences as part of the application papers.		November 7, 2000
1.824	Form and format for nucleotide and/or amino acid sequence submissions in computer readable form.		November 7, 2000
1.825	Amendments to or replacement of sequence listing and computer readable copy thereof.		November 7, 2000
3.27	Mailing address for submitting documents to be recorded.		November 7, 2000
3.71	Prosecution by assignee.		November 7, 2000
3.73	Establishing right of assignee to take action.		November 7, 2000
3.81	Issue of patent to assignee.		November 7, 2000
5.1	Correspondence.		November 7, 2000
5.2	Secrecy order.		November 7, 2000
5.12	Petition for license.		November 7, 2000
10.23	Misconduct.		November 7, 2000

Appendix D-15

The American Inventors Protection Act—Comments

[The following comments on the American Inventors Protection Act have been published on the U.S. Patent and Trademark Office web site.]

American Inventors Protection Act of 1999

American Inventors Protection Act of 1999 is Law

By Talis Dzenitis

The "American Inventors Protection Act of 1999" was signed into law (P.L. 106-113) on November 29, 1999, as part of the conference report (H. Rept. 106-479) on H.R. 3194, Consolidated Appropriations Act, Fiscal Year 2000. The text of the American Inventors Protection Act of 1999 is contained in Title IV of S. 1948, the "Intellectual Property and Communications Omnibus Reform Act of 1999." S. 1948 was enacted by reference in Division B of the conference report on H.R. 3194.

The new law presents the PTO with a number of challenges as well as opportunities. PTO staff is laboring over the preparation of the rules package to implement the substantive law changes including 18-month publication and patent extension provisions. The initial costs of setting up these new systems are likely to be substantial and may require a request to Congress for supplemental funding. The new law's recasting of PTO as a performance-based organization gives PTO substantial autonomy in managing its budget, personnel, procurement and other administrative functions, and will permit it to run in a more business-like manner.

Some key provisions of the American Inventors Protection Act of 1999, as signed into law, are as follows:

Subtitle A—The "Inventors' Rights Act of 1999"

This subtitle, effective 60 days after enactment, helps protect inventors against deceptive practices of certain invention promotion companies. The title requires invention promoters to disclose in writing the number of positive and negative evaluations of inventions they have given over a five-year period and their customers' success in receiving net financial profit and license agreements as a direct result of the invention promotion services.

Customers injured by failure to disclose the required information or by any material false or fraudulent representation by the invention promoter can bring a civil action to recover statutory damages up to $5,000 or actual damages. Damages of up to three times the amount awarded are available for intentional or willful violations.

The subtitle directs the Comptroller General, in consultation with the Director, to conduct a study and submit a report to Congress, within six months after enactment, on the potential risks to the U.S. biotechnology industry relating to biological deposits in support of biotechnology patents.

The Director is prohibited from entering into an agreement to provide copies of specifications and drawings of U.S. patents and applications to non-NAFTA or non-WTO member countries without the express authorization of the Secretary of Commerce. The Commissioner (see subtitle G) of Patents is required to make all complaints received by the PTO involving invention promoters publicly available, along with any responses by the invention promoters.

Subtitle B—The "Patent and Trademark Fee Fairness Act of 1999"

This subtitle reduces certain patent fees, effective 30 days after enactment. The Section 41(a)(1)(A) original filing fee, the Sec. 41(a)(4)(A) reissue fee and the Sec. 41(a)(10) international application fees are each reduced from $760 to $690. The initial maintenance fee is reduced from $940 to $830.

Effective upon enactment, the Director (see subtitle G) is authorized in fiscal year 2000 to adjust trademark fees without regard to fluctuations in the CPI. The subtitle also includes language to emphasize that trademark fees can only be used for trademark-related activities.

The subtitle also requires the Director to conduct and submit to the House and Senate Judiciary Committees, within one year of enactment, a study of alternative fee structures that could be adopted by PTO to encourage maximum participation by the inventor community.

Subtitle C—The "First Inventor Defense Act of 1999"

Subtitle C provides a defense against charges of patent infringement for a party who had, in good faith, actually reduced the subject matter to practice at least one year before the effective filing date of the patent, and commercially used the subject matter before the effective filing date. The defense is limited to methods of "doing or conducting business."

Establishment of the defense does not invalidate the subject patent.

The subtitle is effective upon enactment but does not apply to any pending infringement action or to any subject matter for which an adjudication of infringement, including a consent judgment, has been made before the date of enactment.

Subtitle D—The "Patent Term Guarantee Act of 1999"

This subtitle extends the term of patents, in accordance with regulations prescribed by the Director, to compensate for certain PTO processing delays and for delays in the prosecution of applications pending more than three years. Extensions are available for delays in issuance of a patent due to interference proceedings, secrecy orders, and appellate review. Diligent applicants are guaranteed a minimum 17-year patent term.

Extension authority under this title applies only to applications filed on or after the date six months after enactment.

This subtitle also requires the Director to prescribe regulations to provide for the continued examination of an application, at the request of the applicant. The Director is authorized to establish appropriate fees for continued examination, with a 50% reduction for small entities. The continued examination provisions take effect six months after enactment and apply to all applications filed on or after June 8, 1995.

Subtitle E—The "Domestic Publication of Foreign Filed Patent Applications Act of 1999"

This subtitle provides for publication of patent applications 18 months after filing unless the applicant requests otherwise upon filing and certifies that the invention has not and will not be the subject of an application filed in a foreign country. Provisional rights are available to patentees to obtain reasonable royalties if others make, use, sell, or import the invention during the period between publication and grant.

If the foreign-filed application is less extensive than that filed with the PTO, the applicant may submit and request publication of a redacted version by the PTO.

This title also provides a prior art effect for published patent applications; requires the GAO to conduct a three-year study of applicants who file only in the United States; and requires the Director to recover the cost of early publication by charging a separate publication fee after notice of allowance is given.

The subtitle's provisions take effect one year after the date of enactment and apply to patent applications filed on or after that date.

Subtitle F—The "Optional Inter Partes Reexamination Procedure Act of 1999"

This subtitle establishes a reexamination alternative that expands the participation of third-party requesters by permitting those parties to submit a written response each time the patent owner files a response to the PTO. Those third-party requesters who choose to use the optional procedure, however, will not be able to appeal adverse decisions beyond the Board of Patent Appeals and Interferences. Also, they will not be able to challenge, in any later civil action, any fact determined during the process of the optional reexamination procedure.

The Director must submit to Congress within five years a report evaluating whether the optional reexamination proceedings are inequitable to any of the parties in interest and, if so, recommendations for appropriate changes.

Subtitle F takes effect on the date of enactment and its provisions apply to any patent that issues from an application filed on or after that date.

Subtitle G—The "Patent and Trademark Office Efficiency Act"

Subtitle G establishes the PTO as an agency within the Department of Commerce, subject to the policy direction of the Secretary of Commerce. The PTO retains responsibility for decisions regarding the management and administration of its operations and exercises independent control of its budget allocations and expenditures, personnel decisions and processes, procurements and other administrative and management functions. The subtitle takes effect four months after the date of enactment. The subtitle requires that the patent and trademark operations shall be treated as separate operating units within the Office.

The new PTO is headed by an Under Secretary of Commerce for Intellectual Property and Director of the USPTO, appointed by the President with the advice and consent of the Senate. A Deputy Under Secretary of Commerce for Intellectual Property and Deputy Director of the USPTO is appointed by the Secretary of Commerce upon nomination by the Director.

The Secretary of Commerce appoints a Commissioner for Patents and a Commissioner for Trademarks to serve as chief operating officers for the respective units for a term of five years. The Commissioners will enter into annual performance agreements with the Secretary and will be eligible for up to 50% bonuses based on their performance under those agreements.

The PTO is not subject to any administratively or statutorily imposed limitation on positions or personnel.

Officers and employees of the PTO continue to be subject to the provisions of Title 5 of the United States Code relating to Federal employees.

The Secretary of Commerce appoints, within three months of enactment, nine members each to a Patent Public Advisory Committee and a Trademark Public Advisory Committee. The Committees will review and advise the Director on matters involving policies, goals, performance, budget and user fees, and will prepare annual reports on their efforts within 60 days after the end of each fiscal year. The Federal Advisory Committee Act is not applicable to the Committees.

Subtitle H—Miscellaneous Patent Provisions

This subtitle makes a number of technical and clarifying changes to patent law and provides authority for the electronic filing, maintenance and publication of documents.

The Director may not cease to maintain paper or microform collections of patents and trademarks for public use without providing notice and opportunity for public comment and without first submitting a report detailing such plan to the House and Senate Judiciary Committees. That report must include a description of the mechanisms in place to ensure the integrity of such collections and the data contained therein as well as to ensure prompt public access to the most current available information and a certification that the implementation of such plan will not negatively impact the public.

Last Update: May 25, 2000

Appendix D-16

Patent Business Goals—Overview

[The following comments on the Patent Business Goals final rule have been published on the U.S. Patent and Trademark Office web site.]

Revised (November 15, 2000) Rule by Rule Overview of the PBG - Final Rule

Contents

Part I: Introduction

The focus in Part II is on the changes in practice resulting from the final rule - *Changes to Implement the Patent Business Goals*. Significant clarifications are also identified. Conforming amendments in the rules are generally not listed. Cross references to related rules have been provided.

The final rule has been published as follows:
Federal Register 65 *Fed. Reg.* 54603 (September 8, 2000)
Official Gazette 1238 *Off. Gaz. Pat. Office* 77 (September 19, 2000)

The Office intends to publish a notice of correction to note inadvertent errors in the published rules, update changes in implementation, and address other technical issues.

The Office of Patent Legal Administration (OPLA) of the Office of the Deputy Commissioner for Patent Examination Policy has a webpage on the final rule entitled PBG - Final Rule webpage (http://www.uspto.gov/web/offices/dcom/olia/pbg/index.html)

For further information, contact either:

Robert J. Spar, Director ((703) 308-5107), Hiram H. Bernstein ((703) 305-8713), or Robert Bahr ((703) 305-0471), Senior Legal Advisors, Office of Patent Legal Administration.

Part II: Brief Summary of Changes by Rule (Section) Order

§1.4(b)	*Nature of correspondence and signature requirements:* Provides that the Office may dispose of duplicate copies of correspondence (not required to be filed in duplicate), and that a separate copy must be supplied of each paper for every file it is to be considered in.
§1.14	*Patent Applications preserved in confidence:* Completely re-written so as to define "status" and "access," and to make it easier to understand when status information about, and access to, an application are available, and to whom.
§1.14(d)(4)	Clarifies that a registered attorney or agent named in papers accompanying an application may give a power to inspect the application if an executed oath or declaration under §1.63 has not been filed.
§1.14(e)	Access is no longer given to an abandoned application simply because it claims benefit of the filing date of another application that is open to public inspection (former §1.14(a)(3)(iv)(C) dropped).
§1.19(b)(2)	*Document supply fees:* Fee for a copy of a patent-related file wrapper (previously $150 total) is $200 for the first 400 or fewer pages, plus $40 for each additional 100 or fewer pages. An additional fee of $25 is charged for certification.
§1.19(b)(3)	New fee of $55 for the first copy of patent-related file-wrapper contents that were submitted on compact disc, and $15 for each additional copy. See §§1.52(e), 1.96 and 1.821 et seq.
§1.19(g)	Eliminated the practice of comparing and certifying documents not produced by the Office.
§1.19(h)	Removed the $25 fee for obtaining a corrected filing receipt as the Office now performs that service without charge.
§1.22	*Fee payable in advance:* The preamble (of the rulemaking) states that the Office will no longer treat authorizations to charge a deposit account, for purposes of refund payments under §§1.26 and 1.28, as a payment as of the date that the deposit account is actually debited. Instead, such payment will be treated the same as a payment by check. Thus, the date the payment is received in the Office is considered to be the date that the payment is made (and not any §1.8 date, however, if §1.10 is used, the certificate of express mail date will govern for refund purposes and not the actual date the payment arrives at the Office).
§1.22(b)	Where a single payment is made that represents more than one fee, an itemization of fees being paid is now required. Where an itemization is not supplied, the payment may be returned.
§1.26(a)	*Refunds:* Refunds by electronic transfer are made easier as the Office may issue a credit to a bank account (from information on a check), a credit card account, or an Office deposit account, without the need to first obtain a specific authorization to do so.
§1.26(b)	The period for requesting a refund has been changed from within a "reasonable time" (a subjective standard) to within "two years" from the date of payment (note the change in practice re §1.22), or the date of a deposit account statement where the Office charges an amount other than what was indicated in the authorization.
§1.27	*Definition of small entities and establishing status as a small entity to permit payment of small entity fees; when a determination of en-*

titlement to small entity status and notification of loss of entitlement to small entity status are required; fraud on the Office: A simplified procedure for asserting a claim for small entity status will be effective on the date of publication of the amended rule in the Federal Register.

§1.27(a) Contains definitions of small entities transferred from former §1.9(f), which have also been revised.

§1.27(a)(4)(i) Removes bar to small entity status for a person granting a license to the U.S. government from a rights determination under Executive Order 10096.

§1.27(c)(1) Small entity status can be established by a simple written assertion of entitlement to small entity status without use of a specialized form. The Office will liberally construe any written reference to small entity status to be a request for small entity status.

§1.27(c)(2) The parties who can assert small entity status are expanded to include a registered practitioner (who need not actually be of record), one of the inventors (instead of all the inventors), or a partial assignee (instead of all the assignees). Note: An assignee assertion (of small entity status) must be filed by a §1.33(b) party, §1.27(c)(2)(iii).

§1.27(c)(3) Payment of any exact small entity basic filing (§§1.16(a), (f), (g), (h), or (k)) or basic national fee (§§1.492(a)(1)–(a)(5)) is sufficient to assert and obtain small entity status (even if incorrectly identified for the type of application being filed), which expands the practice from continuing and reissue applications under former §1.28(a)(2). Payment of any other small entity fee in its exact amount, e.g., the issue fee, will not result in small entity status absent a specific written assertion of entitlement to small entity status, §1.27(d).

§1.28(a) *Refunds when small entity status is later established; how errors in small entity status are excused:* The period for requesting a refund based on small entity status is increased to 3 months from 2 months (from the date of payment of the large entity fee).

§1.28(c)(1) Any paper correcting an error in claiming small entity status where one or more small entity fees were erroneously paid must be limited to the payment error(s) in one application, or in one patent file.

§1.28(c)(2)(i) Where the fee paid in error was subject to a fee decrease, the deficiency owed is equal to the amount previously paid (rather than being based on the new lower large entity fee less the small entity amount paid in error).

§1.28(c)(2)(ii) Submissions of deficiency payments for errors in claiming small entity status must be itemized.

§1.28(c)(3) Failure to comply with the separate submission and itemization requirements of §§1.28(c)(1) and (2) can be treated as an authorization for the Office to process the deficiency payment and charge a processing fee. Alternatively, at the option of the Office, a requirement can be mailed by the Office for compliance with the rule within a one month non-extendable time period to avoid return of the fee deficiency paper.

§1.33(a) *Correspondence respecting patent applications, reexamination proceedings, and other proceedings:* The correspondence address must be specified in a clearly identifiable manner or in a newly proposed Application Data Sheet (§1.76), or correspondence will be forwarded to the first named inventor. A request is added for a daytime telephone number.

§1.33(a)(1) Prior to filing a §1.63 oath/declaration, the correspondence address may be changed by the party filing the application, including: (1) those inventors who filed the application (versus all the listed inventors), (2) a party that will be a (full or partial) assignee (as the inventors are only identified and not named until the oath/declaration is filed), (3) the attorney or agent, or (4) any other practitioner who did not file the application but was named in the application transmittal papers as a representative (but not simply identified in the letterhead as a member of the firm).

§1.41(a)(4) *Applicant for patent:* Clarification that §1.48(f) (§1.63 declaration names the inventors) does not apply to applications entering the national stage. To change the inventorship from what is set forth in the international application, a §1.48(a) petition is required as is set forth in §1.497(d).

§1.44 Reserved. The accompanying proof requirement for the power or authority of the legal representative for a dead inventor (§1.42), or an insane or legally incapacitated inventor (§1.43), is deleted. Identification of the party as the legal representative in the executed oath/dec is sufficient.

§1.47(c) *Filing when an inventor refuses to sign or cannot be reached:* When processing a continuation or divisional application, the Office will not send another §1.47 notice to the non-signing inventor as a §1.47 notice was sent to the non-signing inventor when the prior application was accorded status under 37 CFR 1.47. Similarly, the Office will not publish another notice in the Official Gazette for a continuation or divisional application.

§1.48(f)(1) *Correction of inventorship in a patent application, other than a reissue application, pursuant to 35 U.S.C. 116:* Clarification to indicate that once an executed declaration is submitted by any of the inventors, the inventorship is set and §1.48(f) no longer applies.

§1.52(b)(6) *Language, paper, writing, margins, compact disc specification:* Provides for the option of numbering paragraphs in the specification, not including the claims, abstract, or non-text elements, to support the change to §1.121 relating to amendment by replacement paragraphs.

§1.52(e) Provides for the electronic submission of a computer program listing (§1.96), a nucleotide and/or amino acid sequence listing (§1.821(c)), or a large table (§1.58). A statement under §1.77(b)(4) is needed to incorporate by reference to parts of the specification submitted on compact disc.

§1.53(e)(2) *Application number, filing date, and completion of application:* The petition fee relating to a notification of failure to meet filing date requirements for a provisional application under §1.53(c) is raised to the same level as the petition fee relating to applications under §§1.53(b) and (d) ($50 to $130).

§1.53(f)(5) An application retention fee may be submitted in place of the filing fee where an application is not desired to be examined but is to be used for its priority date under 35 U.S.C. 120 for the filing of a continuing application. The one year period for submitting a retention fee to retain the (prior) application is replaced with a requirement that the retention fee be submitted during the pendency of the prior application (in timely response to a Notice to File Missing Parts of Application as may be extended under §1.136).

§1.55(a) *Claim for foreign priority:* No longer permits a petition for entry of a claim for foreign priority *after the issue fee is paid.* While a priority claim may still be filed (along with the processing fee), it would not be reviewed for compliance with the conditions of 35 U.S.C. 119(a)–(d) and the patent will not contain a priority claim. The patentee, however, could then file a request for a certificate of correction under §1.323 to have the priority claim reviewed for compliance with 35 U.S.C. 119 (a)–(d).

§1.56(e) *Duty to disclose information material to patentability:* Adds an explicit duty to disclose all information known to be material to patentability as defined under §1.56(b) which became available between the filing date of the prior application and the national or PCT international filing date of a continuation-in-part application. This change does away with the need for a separate CIP §1.63 oath or declaration that contains the provision that now would be explicitly added to §1.56(b). The §1.63 oath/dec form will be modified but will continue to recite the material added to §1.56(e) as comments indicated such citation is helpful.

§1.58(b) *Chemical and mathematical formula and tables:* Requires that tables submitted in electronic form (see §1.96(c) and §1.821(c)) must maintain row and column formatting and proper page presentation of formulas.

§1.63(a)(1) *Oath or declaration:* Clarifies that there is no (minimum) age requirement for an inventor to sign the oath or declaration, rather competency to understand what is being signed is needed.

§1.63(c) Permits certain information (mailing address and residence, and foreign application information) to be on an Application Data Sheet (new Rule 1.76) rather than in the §1.63 oath/dec. Missing or incorrect information need not, therefore, be submitted or corrected by way of a supplemental oath/dec.

Note: The term "mailing address" has been replaced by the term "post office address" for clarity because many applicants have expressed confusion about the term "post office address." The two terms have the same meaning and there is no change in the requirement that an applicant state where mail is normally received. §1.63(c)(1).

§1.64(b) *Person making oath or declaration:* If the person signing the oath or declaration is the legal representative of a deceased or incapacitated inventor, the legal representative must provide the citizenship, residence and mailing address of the legal representative (in addition to that of the deceased or incapacitated inventor).

§1.67(a) *Supplemental oath or declaration:* Supplemental oaths/declarations may be completed by fewer than all the inventors (or an applicant other than an inventor) to correct deficiencies or inaccuracies that applied to less than all the inventors. Submission (as opposed to execution) of such a completed oath/dec remains, however, controlled by §§1.33(a) and (b), e.g., a supplemental declaration completed by one of several inventors must be submitted by a practitioner or with a cover sheet signed by all the inventors if a power of attorney has not been given.

§1.72(b) *Title and abstract:* The word length of the abstract, for consistency with PCT, is required not to exceed 150 words, replacing the MPEP 608.01(b) range of 50–250 words.

§1.76 *Application data sheet:* A new rule that optionally provides for an "Application Data Sheet" (ADS) containing bibliographic data (§1.76(b)) in a specified format in both provisional and nonprovisional applications. An ADS or a supplemental ADS (§1.76(c)), can be used by practitioners to supply certain bibliographic information or to correct information that, prior to the rule change, had to be supplied by a §1.63 oath or declaration, or corrected by a supplemental oath/dec.

§1.76(b)(3) The ADS optionally provides for the submission of certain examination related information, e.g., class/subclass for assigning the application to be examined, and the art unit or Technology Center where the application should be examined in, and other information, such as a suggested drawing figure for publication purposes. The Office particularly desires classification information for provisional applications (although not to be examined, they provide a useful indicator for future filings of nonprovisional applications).

§1.76(d) Provides how the Office will treat inconsistencies between an ADS and an oath/dec in terms of which governs, and that the Office will initially capture information from the ADS and not the §1.63 oath/dec notwithstanding which governs.

§1.78(a)(2) *Claiming benefit of earlier filing date and cross-reference to other applications:* Permits the specific priority reference required by 35 U.S.C. §120 to be in the Application Data Sheet (ADS) of §1.76 rather than in the first sentence of the specification following the title. (This will be used in creating the patent front page.)

§1.84 *Standards for drawings:* Drawing standards are mostly retained in the rule to provide guidance as to producing a high quality drawing. The Office, however, will focus on what is needed to scan the drawings for publishing patent applications, and patents, and for communicating the invention to the examiner. As a result less notices of drawing informalities are expected to be issued. (The proposals for printing patents in color and eliminating the petition for color drawings or color photographs were not implemented.)

§1.84(b) Eliminates requirement for three copies of a photograph. Replaces petition requirement to accept a photograph with a list of examples when a photograph is acceptable, but examiner may require drawing in place of photograph where a drawing would better illustrate the invention.

§1.85(c) *Correction to drawings:* Extensions of time are no longer permitted to extend the three month period for filing corrected or formal drawings from the Notice of Allowability. See §1.136(c). The change applies only to a Notice of Allowability mailed on or after sixty days from publication of the rule in the Federal Register.

§1.96(c) *Submission of computer program listings:* Requires computer program listings over 300 lines to be submitted on CD-ROM or CD-R as the official copy and eliminates microfiche submissions. See also §§1.52(e), 1.77(b)(4), and 1.821. Listings under 300 lines may be submitted on paper or compact disc. Submissions may be made under the former rule until March 1, 2001.

§1.97(b)(1) *Filing information disclosure statement:* The 3 month window for filing an IDS submission in a CPA (§1.53(d)) is eliminated - since CPAs are treated as amended applications by examiners and subject to short turnover times. Note: Section 1.103 has been revised, by the PG Pubs rulemaking, so as to permit applicants to request a three month suspension of action by the Office if such a period is desired, e.g., in order to submit an IDS, a preliminary amendment, or an affidavit under §1.132.

§1.97(c) The limitation "or an action that otherwise closes prosecution" is added to provide for types of actions other than final actions and notices of allowance that close prosecution, e.g., *Ex parte Quayle*, 1935 Dec. Comm'r Pat. 11 (1935). The fee has been reduced from $240 to $180 (§1.17(p)), and it is made the same as the fee for IDS's submitted after allowance under §1.97(d).

§1.97(d)(2) The fee has been increased from $130 to $180 (§1.17(p)), and it is made the same as the fee for IDS's submitted after a first Office action but before the close of prosecution under §1.97(c).

§1.97(e)(1) Added requirement that the item of information be cited for the "first" time in a communication in a counterpart application from a foreign patent office not more than three months prior to its submission in the U.S. application. (This avoids the abuse which occurs when a document was first cited in a search report, then submitted to the Office within three months after it was again cited in an examination report from the same foreign office, or it is submitted within three months after is it cited for a second time from a different foreign patent office - but the second citation (improperly) occurs more than three months prior to submission to the USPTO).

§1.98(a)(2) *Content of information disclosure statement:* Section 1.98(a)(2)(iii) requires submission of copies of U.S. patent applications that are being cited in IDS statements.

§1.98(d)(2) If a U.S. application was cited in an IDS prior to the effective date of the change to §1.98(a)(2) (now requiring a copy of the cited application) but a copy of the cited application was not supplied, as was permissible under the former rule, a copy of the cited application must be supplied if cited in any continuing application where the citation is made after the effective date of the changes to §§1.98(a) and (d).

§1.105 *Requirement for information:* A new rule that provides explicit authority for an examiner or other Office employee to require the submission of such information as may be reasonably necessary to properly examine an application or treat a matter therein. The requirement for information may be included in an Office action that includes other matters or sent separately. Any reply that states that the information required to be submitted is unknown and/or is not readily available will be accepted as a complete reply. Specific non-exclusive examples are provided in the rule: existence of a particularly relevant commercial data base, whether a prior art search was made, and if so, what was searched, non-patent literature by any of the inventors that relates to the claimed invention, information used in the inventive process or to draft the application, where the claimed invention is an improvement, identification of what is being improved, and identification of any use of the claimed invention known to any of the inventors at the time the application was filed notwithstanding the date of the use.

§1.111 *Reply by applicant or patent owner to a non-final Office action:* The Commissioner has the right to disapprove entry of a second, or subsequent, supplemental reply (a third reply) where the second, or subsequent, supplemental reply unduly interferes with an Office action being prepared in response to the previous reply or replies. Factors that will be considered for disapproval are: the state of preparation of an Office action responsive to the previous reply or replies as of the date of receipt by the Office of the second, or subsequent, supplemental reply, and the nature of any changes to the specification or claims that would result from entry of the second, or subsequent, supplemental reply. Implementation will apply to second, or subsequent, supplemental replies filed on or after sixty days from the date of publication of the rule in the Federal Register. See also §1.115.

§1.115 *Preliminary amendments:* A new rule. The Commissioner has the right to disapprove entry for preliminary amendments, not filed within three months of the filing date for non-CPAs, or not filed when the CPA is filed, that unduly interfere with the preparation of an Office action. See the factors set forth in §1.111 for disapproval related to second, or subsequent, supplemental replies. The three month window for filing the preliminary amendment is not extendable. Implementation will apply to applications filed on or after 60 days from the date of publication of the rule in the Federal Register.

§1.121 *Manner of making amendments in applications:* Amendments must be made by submission of a "clean" replacement paragraph/section/claim. The paragraph being amended can be identified in any unambiguous manner, such as by using page and line numbering or paragraph numbers. (The Office will not accept a direction to add paragraph numbers to currently pending applications.) An entire paragraph/claim can be deleted by an instruction.

Addition/deletion of specific words or sentences would no longer be permitted. A marked up version of the replacement paragraph/section/claim showing all changes made must also be submitted. §1.121(c)(1)(ii). See also §1.52(b)(6). A clean set of all pending claims can be submitted. §1.121(c)(3).

The presentation of a clean version of a claim that is not accompanied by a marked up version will constitute an assertion that the clean version of the claim has not been modified relative to the immediate prior version. §1.121(c)(3).

An exception is made for examiner's amendments. Re-writing of a paragraph or claim, and a marked up version are not required, while deletion of specific words or sentences are permitted. Examiner's amendments may rely on material from faxes or e-mails as attachments, §1.121(g).

Amendments may be made under the former rule until March 1, 2001.

§1.131(a) *Affidavit or declaration of prior invention:* Expands use of rule, e.g., to include overcoming a rejection based on a prior knowledge or use under 35 U.S.C. 102(a).

§1.132 *Affidavits or declarations traversing rejections or objections:* Expands use of rule, e.g., to include overcoming a rejection based on a prior knowledge or use under 35 U.S.C. 102(a).

§1.137(c) *Revival of abandoned application or lapsed patent:* For revivals of utility and plant applications filed before June 8, 1995, the period needed to be disclaimed is no longer the entire period of abandonment but only the period extending beyond 20 years from the earliest filing date if it is a lesser period than the period of abandonment.

Additionally, the terminal disclaimer provisions no longer apply in pre June 8, 1995 applications (except designs) where revival is sought solely for purposes of copendency with a utility or plant application filed on or after June 8, 1995, since the 20 year term of the later application begins from the 35 U.S.C. §120 benefit date of the earlier application.

§1.152 *Design drawings:* Eliminates provisions, formerly found in §1.152(b), relating to the integral nature of indicia disclosed in drawings or photographs filed with a design application to conform to *In re Daniels*, 46 USPQ2d 1788 (Fed. Cir. 1998).

§1.155 *Expedited examination of design applications:* The section is redrafted to establish a procedure to create an expedited processing and examination procedure for design applications. A preexamination search, a statement that the search was made with an indication of the field of search, an IDS based on the search, formal drawings in compliance with §1.84, and a $900 fee are required.

§1.163 *Specification and arrangement of application elements in a plant application:* The Latin name of the genus and species of a plant, and the variety denomination are required to be supplied in a plant application to aid in search and examination. §§1.163(c)(4) and (5).

§1.163(c)(14) Removes the requirement for a plant color coding sheet.

§1.173(a)(1) *Reissue specification, drawings, and amendments:* Requires a reissue specification and claims to be furnished as a copy of the printed patent in double column format on single sided sheets only (same as §1.510). Also requires submission of a copy of any disclaimer (§1.321), certificate of correction (§§1.322–1.324), or any reexamination certificate (§1.570).

§1.173(a)(2) Transfer of the drawings from the patent file to the reissue application is no longer permitted. New drawings, such as copies from the printed patent, are required.

§1.173(c) Status of all patent claims and all added claims is required whenever an amendment is made (either at the time of filing or during prosecution). An explanation of support in the disclosure of the patent must be submitted when changes to the claims are made at filing (in addition to the current requirement of when an amendment is made during prosecution).

§1.176(b) *Examination of reissue:* The prohibition against requiring division in reissues is eliminated, and a restriction will now be permitted between: (a) claims to previously unclaimed subject matter added in a reissue application, and (b) the original patent claims. There shall be a constructive election of the subject matter of the original patent claims unless all the patent claims are disclaimed on filing. The prohibition on the Office issuing an Official action within two months from the announcement date in the *Official Gazette* was removed.

§1.177 *Issuance of multiple reissue patents:* Eliminates the requirements: a) that divisional reissues be limited to separate and distinct parts of the thing patented, b) that divisional reissues issue simultaneously unless otherwise ordered by the Commissioner, c) for a petition to avoid simultaneous issuance, and d) of referral to the Commissioner upon filing of the divisional reissue.

The rule is expanded to include continuations of reissues as well as divisionals, and requires that all multiple applications for reissue of a single patent include a cross reference to the other reissue application(s). Where one reissue issues without the appropriate cross reference, the Office will issue a certificate of correction under §1.322 to provide the cross reference. (These are changes consequential to *In re Graff*, 42 USPQ2d 1471 (Fed. Cir. 1997) and *In re Amos*, 953 F.2d 613, 21 USPQ2d 1271 (Fed. Cir. 1991)).

§1.178(a) *Original patent; continuing duty of applicant:* Where the original patent is lost or inaccessible and an offer to surrender it in a reissue application cannot therefore be made, a statement rather than an affidavit or declaration is now required to inform the Office of the loss or lack of access.

An offer to surrender the original patent (that has not been lost or is not inaccessible) is no longer required to accompany the filing of a reissue application (although the original patent must be surrendered before the reissue can be allowed).

§1.178(b) The Office's attention must be called to any prior or concurrent proceedings in which the patent (for which reissue is requested) is or was involved, such as interferences, reissues, reexaminations, or litigation and the results of such proceedings.

§1.181(f) *Petitions to the Commissioner:* Clarifies the rule to apply its two month period from the mailing date of the Office action or notice from which relief is requested to any petition under part 1, such as §§1.182 and 1.183, unless otherwise provided. The rule is also clarified that the two month period is not extendable. The clarifications are in response to *Helfgott v. Dickinson*, 209 F.3d 1328, 1333 n.3, 54 USPQ2d 1425, 1428 n.3 (Fed. Cir. 2000).

§1.311(b) *Notice of allowance:* Authorizations to charge the issue fee may be filed only after the mailing of the notice of allowance. Where an incorrect issue fee, or a completed fee transmittal form (PTOL-85(B)) without payment is submitted (so that it is clear that there is an intent to pay the issue fee), however, either will operate as a valid request to charge the correct issue fee to any deposit account identified in a previously filed authorization to charge fees.

§1.322 *Certificate of correction of Office mistake:* Clarifies certificate of correction (C of C) practice re third parties. While third parties may request that the Office consider issuing a C of C (after notification to the patent owner), they have no standing to require that the Office do so. Papers from third parties requesting C of Cs will be disposed of rather than made of record after the Office reviews these requests.

§1.324(b)(1) *Correction of inventorship in patent, pursuant to 35 U.S.C. 256:* Eliminates the requirement for a statement from the inventor being deleted from a patent that the inventorship error occurred without deceptive intent, to conform to *Stark v. Advanced Magnetics, Inc.*, 119 F.3d 1551, 43 USPQ2d 1321 (Fed. Cir. 1997).

§1.366(c) *Submission of maintenance fees:* Provides that both the patent number and the application number be supplied. Where one is missing, the Office intends to first attempt to telephone the party who submitted the payment. If contact is unsuccessful: (1) Where the maintenance fee payment only identifies the patent number (and not also the application number), the Office may apply the payment to the identified patent or return the payment; and (2) Where only the application number is identified, the payment will be returned.

§1.497(d) *Oath or declaration under 35 U.S.C. 371(c)(4):* Clarifies that §1.48(f) national practice does not apply to correction of inventorship by submission of a declaration in a national stage application, as correction must be by the way indicated in the rule (which is analogous to §1.48(a)). See also §1.41(a).

§1.510 *Request for reexamination:* A copy of a patent for which reexamination is requested must be submitted in double column format on single sided sheets only (see also §1.173(a)(1)).

§1.740(a)(9) *Formal requirements for application for extension of patent term; correction of informalities:* Replaces requirement for explaining how each applicable claim reads on the categories of approved product, or method of using, or method of manufacturing, with the requirement that the explanation is needed for only one claim in each category.

§1.740(b) The requirement for an oath/declaration is deleted, and a total of three copies of the application is required to reflect that two copies are sent to the FDA.

§1.741(b) Review of a notice that an application for extension of patent term is incomplete, or review of the filing date accorded an application therefor, now requires a petition and petition fee, and the period for filing the petition is extendable under §1.136 unless the notice indicates otherwise.

§1.821+ *Nucleotide and/or amino acid sequence disclosures in patent applications:* For nucleotide and/or amino acid sequences, no change is made to computer readable form (CRF) practice under §1.821(e), but the paper version under §1.821(c) can continue to be on paper or may now be on a compact disc, CD-ROM, or CD-R. Tables (§1.58) over 50 pages (§1.52(e)(1)(iii)) may also be submitted on a compact disk, §1.823(a)(2). See also §§1.52(e), and 1.96.

§3.71 *Prosecution by assignee:* Revises definitions of a single assignee and partial assignees to be linked to being of record in the patent application/proceeding and to set forth how each may become of record and thereby intervene to control prosecution in a patent application/proceeding.

§3.73 *Establishing right of assignee to take action:* Clarifies that the documentary evidence required must include proof of who is the assignee. Clarifies that the §3.73(b) submission is required in addition to (although it may be combined with) the specific action taken (e.g., appointing an attorney) by the assignee. Requires that a partial assignee in a patent application/proceeding indicate in the submission the extent of its ownership interest, to help account for the entire ownership interest.

§3.81(b) *Issue of patent to assignee:* Eliminates the need for a petition in order to submit assignments after payment of the issue fee. Processing by the Office to have the assignee reflected in the published patent, however, is subject to time restraints inherent in the issue process.

The assignment need no longer be recorded among the Office's assignment records before the Office will issue a patent to the assignee as the Office will now accept a §3.73(b) statement (submitted with the assignment information or one already present in the file if it is still valid).

§5.12 *Petition for license:* Requires a petition fee (§1.17(h)) for all petitions for a foreign filing license (rather than just expedited petitions) since all such petitions are treated on an expedited basis.

Part III: List of All Rules Changed

The final rulemaking includes changes to the following sections of 37 CFR:

1.4, 1.6, 1.9, 1.12, 1.14, 1.17, 1.19, 1.22, 1.25, 1.26, 1.27, 1.28, 1.33, 1.34, 1.36, 1.41, 1.47, 1.48, 1.51, 1.52, 1.53, 1.55, 1.56, 1.58, 1.59, 1.63, 1.64, 1.67, 1.72, 1.77, 1.78, 1.84, 1.85, 1.91, 1.96, 1.97, 1.98, 1.102, 1.104, 1.111, 1.112, 1.115, 1.121, 1.125, 1.131, 1.132, 1.133, 1.136, 1.137, 1.138, 1.152, 1.154, 1.155, 1.163, 1.173, 1.176, 1.177, 1.178, 1.181, 1.193, 1.303, 1.311, 1.314, 1.322, 1.323, 1.324, 1.366, 1.446, 1.497, 1.510, 1.530, 1.550, 1.565, 1.666, 1.720, 1.730, 1.740, 1.741, 1.780, 1.821, 1.823, 1.824, 1.825, 3.27, 3.71, 3.73, 3.81, 5.1, 5.2, 5.12, and 10.23.

Part IV: Rules Deleted and Added

Sections of 37 CFR that are deleted: §§1.44 and 1.174,
Sections of 37 CFR that are added: §§1.76, 1.105, and 1.115.

Part V: Coordination with AIPA rulemaking packages

The USPTO is currently in the process of implementing the American Inventors Protection Act (AIPA) of 1999, which includes the following four patents rulemakings:

1) **Request for Continued Examination (RCE)**, "Changes to Application Examination and Provisional Application Practice," 65 Fed. Reg. 14865 (March 20, 2000), 1233 Off. Gaz. Pat. Office 47 (April 11, 2000) **(Interim Rule)**; and 65 Fed. Reg. 50091 (August 16, 2000) **(Final Rule)**, which sets forth changes from the Interim Rule. **Thus, both the Interim Rule, as modified by the Final Rule, must be considered.**
2) **Patent Term Adjustment (PTA),** "Changes to Implement Patent Term Adjustment Under Twenty-Year Patent Term," 65 Fed. Reg. 17215 (March 31, 2000), 1233 Off. Gaz. Pat. Office 109 (April 25, 2000) **(Proposed Rule)**, and 65 Fed. Reg. 56365 (Sept. 18, 2000) **(Final Rule)**.
3) **Eighteen-Month or Pre-Grant Publication (PG Pub),** "Changes to Implement Eighteen-Month Publication of Patent Applications," 65 Fed. Reg. 17945 (April 5, 2000), 1233 Off. Gaz. Pat. Office 121 (April 25, 2000) **(Proposed Rule)**, and 65 Fed. Reg. 56365 (Sept. 18, 2000) **(Final Rule)**.
4) ***Inter Partes* Reexamination,** "Rules to Implement Optional *Inter Partes* Reexamination Proceedings," 65 Fed. Reg. 18153 (April 6, 2000), 1234 Off. Gaz. Pat. Office 93 (May 23, 2000) **(Proposed Rule)**.

To coordinate this final PBG rule and the four rulemakings to implement the AIPA, it was necessary to shift some of the proposed changes in the PBG proposed rulemaking to two of the AIPA rulemaking packages.

First: The following three changes are set forth in the **RCE** rulemaking:

(1) The change to 37 CFR 1.103 that provides for a request for up to a three month suspension of a first Office action in a CPA application under §1.53(d) (§1.103(b)) and in an RCE under (new) §1.114 (§1.103(c));

(2) The change to 37 CFR 1.312 that prohibits the filing of amendments after payment of the issue fee (except as permitted in 37 CFR 1.313); and
(3) The change to 37 CFR 1.313 that limits the reasons an applicant can request withdrawal of an application from issue to: 1) unpatentability (in which case the petition must include a statement that the claim(s) is unpatentable; 2) to file an RCE; and 3) for express abandonment (which may be in favor of a continuing application). The reasons the USPTO can withdraw an application from issue on its own initiative, as set forth in 37 CFR 1.313, are not changed.

Second: The change to §1.52(d), that modifies the requirement for supplying a translation of a non-English language provisional application, is included in the **PG Pub** final rulemaking. If a provisional application is filed in a foreign language, an English language translation will no longer have to be filed in the provisional application. Instead, the translation of the non-English language provisional application can be filed in the nonprovisional application at the time the claim for priority to the provisional application is made in the nonprovisional application.

Part VI: Proposed Changes to Rules Which Were Not Implemented

The PBG final rule did **not** go forward with proposals related to: §1.14 (eliminating the availability of some types of status information), §1.22 (defining date of payment of fees), and §1.809 (eliminating the extensions of time for making deposits after an indication that the application is otherwise in condition for allowance). Modifications were made in many other proposals, e.g., §1.84 only some of the drawing requirements which were proposed to be eliminated were eliminated, and §1.121 eliminating requirement for specification amendment by replacement specification if paragraph numbering were not used.

Appendix D-17

Patent Business Goals—News Bulletin

37 CFR 1.324

MPEP BOOKMARK

Changes to the Patent Rules

October 24, 2000 Volume 1, Issue 2

This is the second in a series of Patent News Bulletins to assist you in keeping up to date with significant rule changes which affect your area. Keep this copy to use as a bookmark for your present MPEP, or view this bulletin again on the USPTO Website http://www.uspto.gov/web/offices/dcom/olia/pbg/index.html.

Correction of Inventorship in a Patent. 37 CFR 1.324

The rule package "Changes to the Patent Business Goals - Final Rule," published in the Federal Register on September 8, 2000, 65 Fed. Reg. 54603 (Sept. 8, 2000), and the Official Gazette on September 19, 2000, 1238 Off. Gaz. Pat. Office 77 (September 19, 2000). The PBG rule package makes a number of revisions to Title 37.

The entire final rule may be accessed through the USPTO homepage. Click on the button "PBG - Final Rule."

Areas and individuals primarily affected by this rule change include: Tech Center - Supervisory Patent Examiners (SPEs) and Special Program Examiners (SPREs)

Any questions related to this change in practice should be directed to Eugenia Jones, Legal Advisor, (306-5586), OPLA.

Effective September 8, 2000, 37 CFR 1.324 (b)(1) is amended to eliminate the requirement for a statement from an inventor being deleted stating that an inventorship error occurred without deceptive intent. The change is made to conform Office practice to Stark v. Advanced Magnetics, Inc., 119 F.3d 1551, 43 USPQ2d 1321 (Fed. Cir. 1997), which held that 35 U.S.C. 256 only requires inquiry into the intent of a nonjoined inventor. It should be noted, however, that 37 CFR 1.324(b)(2) still requires a statement from the current named inventors either agreeing to the requested change or stating that they have no disagreement in regard to the requested change. Thus, an inventor being deleted from a patent must submit a statement under 37 CFR 1.324(b)(2). 37 CFR 1.324(b)(2) in combination with 37 CFR1.324(b)(1) ensures compliance with the requirement of 35 U.S.C. 256 for application for correction of inventorship in a patent by all parties. This requirement is separate from the requirement that certain parties address the lack of deceptive intent in the inventorship error.

An inventor being deleted from a patent does not have to state that the inventorship error occurred without deceptive intent.

Supervisory Patent Examiners are advised to use the latest version of 37 CFR 1.324 when deciding petitions to correct inventorship under 37 CFR 1.324. Form Paragraph 10.16 has been modified to reflect the change and will be available in the Office Action Correspondence Subsystem (OACS) in the near future. The body of the text of Form Paragraph 10.16, as modified, is as follows:

"A petition to correct inventorship as provided by 37 CFR 1.324 requires (1) a statement from each person who is being added as an inventor that the inventorship error occurred without any deceptive intention on their part, (2) a statement from the current named inventors who have not submitted a statement as per "(1)" either agreeing to the change of inventorship or stating that they have no disagreement in regard to the requested change, (3) a statement from all assignees of the parties submitting a statement under "(1)" and "(2)" agreeing to the change of inventorship in the patent; (such statement must comply with the requirements of 37 FR 3.73(b)); and (4) the fee set forth in 37 FR 1.20(b). This petition lacks item(s)__."

MPEP 1481

Appendix D-18

Business Methods Patent Initiative: An Action Plan

INDUSTRY OUTREACH

1. **Customer Partnership:** Establish formal Customer Partnership with the software, Internet and electronic commerce industry similar to that in place with the biotechnology industry. The Partnership will meet quarterly to discuss mutual concerns, share USPTO plans and operational efforts in this technology area, and discuss solutions to common problems.

2. **Roundtable Forum:** The USPTO will convene a Roundtable Forum with Stakeholders in Summer 2000 to discuss issues and possible solutions surrounding business method patents.

3. **Industry Feedback:** A greater effort will be made to obtain industry feedback on prior art resources used by the USPTO, solicit input on other databases and information collections and sources, and expand prior art collections.

QUALITY

1. **Enhance Technical Training:**

    - Enhance technical currency for examiners and continue current training efforts/partnerships with industry associations and various individual corporate sponsors.

    - Business practice specialists will be pursued to serve as a resource for examiners on alleged common or well known industry practices, terminology scope and meaning, and industry standards in four basic areas: banking/finance, general e-commerce, insurance, and Internet infrastructure.

    - The USPTO will publish the areas of training needs for comment and offers to provide such training.

2. **Revise Examination Guidelines:** The Examination Guidelines for Computer-Related Inventions and the relevant training examples will be revised in light of the *State Street Bank* and *AT&T v. Excel* decisions.

3. **Expand Current Search Activities:**

   - **Mandatory Search:** A mandatory search for all applications in Class 705 to include a classified U.S. patent document search, and a text search of U.S. patent documents, foreign patent documents, and non-patent literature (NPL), with NPL searches to include required search areas mapped/correlated to U.S. classification system for Class 705, which will provide a more fully developed prior art record;

   - **Second Review:** A new second-level review of all allowed applications in Class 705 will be required, with an eye toward ensuring compliance with search requirements, reasons for allowance, and a determination whether the scope of the claims should be reconsidered; and

   - **Expand Sampling Size:** The sampling size for quality review by the Office of Patent Quality Review will be substantially expanded, and a new in-process review of Office actions will be introduced with an emphasis on the field of search of the prior art and patentability determinations under 102/103.

Source: PTO website at >http://www.uspto.gov/web/offices/com/sol/actionplan.html>. Visited 5/30/00.

Appendix D-19

A USPTO White Paper: Automated Financial or Management Data Processing Methods (Business Methods)

TABLE OF CONTENTS

EXECUTIVE SUMMARY

Recently there has been a marked increase in public attention to the operations of the United Sates Patent and Trademark Office (USPTO), and specifically, the workgroup responsible for examining patent applications in automated business data processing technologies, Class 705. On March 29, 2000, the USPTO announced a plan to improve the quality of the examination process in technologies related to electronic commerce and business methods. This white paper discusses the patent history of business data processing, the transition this technology is beginning, and the initiatives the USPTO is engaged in to keep pace with this transition and to improve quality in the examination of this technology.

Origin and Evolution – Business data processing has followed an unbroken evolutionary path from mechanical technology up to today's software controlled microprocessors. Automated business data processing itself dates back over a hundred years. The business method claim format has been used in various forms throughout that period. The increase in its use today is an inevitable end result of our progress over the last century.

Class 705 (Modern Business Data Processing) – This class contains numerous small groupings and four major groupings directed to specific and general business data processing machines and methods. These machines and methods still heavily reflect the electrical and computer engineering that underlay them. Class 705 saw about 1% of the total patent applications filed at the USPTO in FY 1999. Its 2658 applications did not even place it among the top five Communications and Information Processing technologies.

Resources In Transition – In 1998, the State Street decision triggered an awareness of the "business method claim" as a viable form of patent protection. We are at the beginning of a change in the approach to how inventors choose to describe their inventions. This change is in turn driving a shift in the required examiner knowledge base for the examination of Class 705 inventions. As it has for over a century, the USPTO is responding appropriately and is adapting its knowledge base as the needs of business patent examination evolve.

Improving Quality – It is universally agreed that high quality examination by USPTO Patent Examiners must be ensured. Quality initiatives are continuously updated. This white paper highlights initiatives in place prior to March 2000, as well as, quality initiatives announced in March by Q. Todd Dickinson, Under Secretary of Commerce for Intellectual Property and Director of the United States Patent and Trademark Office.

Customer Partnerships – These are important to improving quality as the USPTO gauges the future needs of Class 705. Customers will know first the future evolution of business data processing technology. Customers' application filings will control the transition of patent application format towards the "business method form" and any future shift that will be required in the knowledge base of Class 705 examiners. They are also in a unique position to assist in providing training needed as part of adapting the knowledge base.

I. INTRODUCTION

On September 23, 1975, Ivan E. Sutherland of the Rand Corporation received the 1975 Award for Outstanding Accomplishment of the Systems, Man, and Cybernetics Society. In his acceptance address entitled "Computerized Commerce"[1], Mr. Sutherland states "What we should be building is a system of computerized commerce: a "smart" communications network which can remember, process, forward, remind and schedule as well as merely communicating". Mr. Sutherland continues "Computers will become the repositories of manufacturing know-how. Parts lists, purchasing specifications, lists of qualified vendors, design information, fabrication directions, and production history will all be stored in computers. Individuals will be free to take on new tasks more easily than ever before, because the instructions required for those tasks will be available through a variety of on-line computer terminals".

In the mid-1990s, Mr. Sutherland's proposed "smart" communication network, now called "Electronic Commerce" or "e-commerce" began finding its niche in the business world. In recent years, the growth of the business technologies, especially the electronic commerce business industry has been phenomenal. This growth has resulted in an increase of business technology patent application filings. Concomitant with this increase in filings there has been a marked increase in public attention to the operations of Workgroup 2760 of the United States Patent and Trademark Office (USPTO) currently responsible for examining patent applications in business related data processing methods and technologies, Class 705.

One prominent portion of business method patents is the area of "Automated Financial/Management Business Data Processing Method Patents." Such automated business methods are found in U.S. Patent Class 705.

[1] "Computerized Commerce"; Ivan E. Sutherland; September 1975. Acceptance address for the 1975 Award for Outstanding Accomplishment of the Systems, Man, Cybernetics Society, San Francisco, California, September 23, 1975.

II. ORIGINS OF FINANCIAL/MANAGEMENT BUSINESS PATENTS - PRODUCT, APPARATUS AND METHOD

The creation of a patent system was one of the acts performed by the First Congress of the United States. The first patent statute was passed on April 5, 1790, by the Congress of the twelve United States and signed into law on April 10 by President Washington. Rhode Island ratified the Constitution and joined the Union 49 days later on May 29, 1790. The "Commissioners for the Promotion of the Useful Arts" granted the first United States patent on July 31, 1790. The Commission consisted of Secretary of State Thomas Jefferson, Secretary of War Henry Knox, and Attorney General Edmund Randolph. This first patent was to a chemical method for making potash and pearl ash.[2]

Financial apparatus and method patents date back to this period. These early financial patents were largely paper-related products and methods. The first financial patent was granted on March 19, 1799, to Jacob Perkins of Massachusetts for an invention for "Detecting Counterfeit Notes." All details of Mr. Perkins invention, which we presume was a device or process in the printing art, were lost in the great Patent Office fire of 1836. We only know of its existence from other sources. Mr. Perkins was perhaps our young nation's most prolific early inventor with nearly 1% of all patents from our first quarter century. Upon his death in 1849, his obituary filled three pages of the Commissioner of Patents annual report to Congress.[3] The first financial patent for which any detailed written description survives was to a printing method entitled "A Mode of Preventing Counterfeiting" granted to John Kneass on April 28, 1815. The first fifty years of the U.S. Patent Office saw the granting of forty-one financial patents in the arts of bank notes (2 patents), bills of credit (1), bills of exchange (1), check blanks (4); detecting and preventing counterfeiting (10), coin counting (1), interest calculation tables (5), and lotteries (17).[4] Financial patents in the paper-based technologies have been granted continuously for over two-hundred years. See Appendix A for sample Patents.

---

[2] Kenneth W. Dobyns, The Patent Office Pony: A History of the Early Patent Office, Sergeant Kirkland's Museum and Historical Society (1994).

[3] "One of the most important of his inventions was in the engraving of bank bills. [Fifty] years ago counterfeiting was carried on with an audacity and a success which would seem incredible at the present time. The ease with which the clumsy engravings of the bank bills of the day were imitated, was a temptation to every knave who could scratch copper; and counterfeits flooded the country, to the serious detriment of trade. Perkins invented the stereotype check-plate, which no art of counterfeiting could match; and a security was thus given to bank paper which it had never known.";

The Patent Office, Report of the Commissioner of Patents for the Year 1849, Part I. Arts and Manufactures (1850).

[4] Edmund Burke Commissioner of Patents, List of Patents for Inventions and Designs, Issued by the United States from 1790 to 1847 (1847).

Automated financial/management business data processing method patents cannot trace their origins back to the founding of our nation. However, contrary to popular view, they did not suddenly spring into being in the late 1990's. On January 8, 1889, the era of automated financial/management business data processing method patents was born. United States patents 395,781; 395,782; and 395,783 were granted to inventor-entrepreneur Herman Hollerith on that date.[5] See Appendix B for Mr. Hollerith's Patents. Mr. Hollerith's method and apparatus patents automated the tabulating and compiling of statistical information for businesses and enterprises. They were acclaimed nationally and viewed as revolutionizing business data processing. The protection of his patents allowed his fledgling Tabulating Machine Company to succeed and thrive. In 1924, Thomas J. Watson, Sr. changed the company name to International Business Machine Corporation. Hollerith manual punch cards (IBM punch cards) and his methods for processing business data were still being used up until the birth of the personal computer era.[6]

The financial/management business data processing method patents of today are more numerous and more sophisticated than those of 1889. However, this is not a function of the business method ingenuity of our forebears. Rather, this is directly a function of high cost, low speed, and limited availability of automated data processing machines in the 1890's versus the low cost, high speed, and wide spread use of today's computers. Put another way, we invented some automated business data processing methods over the last one hundred years, but we spent the bulk of that time perfecting the automated business data processing machines upon which we will run the methods. It is only recently that data processing systems have become sufficiently developed to begin to allow us to fully tap our ingenuity in the business method arts.

The development of today's business data processing systems follows an unbroken evolutionary path back to simple manually operated mechanical registering devices that predate electrically controlled Hollerith type machines. See Appendix C - 1870 to 1905. Purely mechanical business data processing reached its zenith in the early 20th century. For about $100 ($2000 today), a 1909 merchant could purchase a cash register system that even now is one of the most sophisticated mechanical devices ever constructed. See

[5] http://www.invent.org/book/book-text/57.html and http://www.computer-museum.org/collections/hollerith.html

[6] Business Method Patents, i.e. automated financial/management business data processing method patents, were patented long before the USPTO's "Examination Guidelines for Computer-Related Inventions," 1184 Off. Gaz. Pat. Office 87 (March 26, 1996) and the decision in *State Street Bank & Trust v. Signature Financial Group, Inc.*, 149 F.3d 1368, 47 USPQ2d 1596 (Fed. Cir. 1998), cert. Denied, __U.S.__, 119 S. Ct. 851 (1999). *State Street* merely modified the test used to determine "statutory subject matter." It is important to understand that many business data processing methods were deemed statutory subject matter under the old "Business Method Exemption" test. For example, the claims in *State Street* were deemed by the USPTO to meet the statutory subject matter requirement under the old test.

Appendix D - 1906 to 1920. Unfortunately, business data processing was simplistic in even the most powerful of these totally mechanical registering systems. None were able to match the data processing power of the electrical-mechanical systems such as the Hollerith tabulator. However, manufacturing cost was a key issue and it was not until the 1930s that electrical-mechanical superseded purely mechanical in day-to-day business data processing systems. See Appendix E - 1921 to 1940.

The full arrival of electricity as a component in business data processing system was a watershed event. Electrical-mechanical devices provided far more business data processing power than their mechanical predecessors did. By the 1930s it was cost effective to build far more complex data processing systems. A pattern was set that has repeated itself in successive evolutionary steps since the 1930s. Electrical-mechanical switches were replaced by individual transistors. Individual transistors were replaced in turn by small-scale integrated circuits which were replaced by large-scale integrated circuits. Each new generation resulted in increased business data processing power and new inventions. However, one key thing was not significantly improved by each of these generations. Even with the arrival of larger-scale integrated circuits, each data processing system had to be individually designed at the transistor level and hard-wired to perform the correct business data processing functions. The time from innovation through design and manufacturing to market was too long and needed to be improved. The replacement of specific function large-scale integrated circuits by software controlled microprocessors allowed this to occur and was the latest evolutionary step to bring us to the business data processing systems of today. See Appendix F - 1941-1995.

III. CLASS 705 – MODERN BUSINESS DATA PROCESSING

A. TYPE OF TECHNOLOGY

Class 705 encompasses machines and their corresponding methods for performing data processing or calculation operations, where the machine or method is utilized in the 1) practice, administration, or management of an enterprise, or 2) processing of financial data, or 3) determination of the charge for goods or services. This is the formal definition of the subject matter classified in Class 705. See Appendix G for a sample of patents issued on May 30, 2000.

In layman's terms, Class 705 is a collection of 20+ financial and management data processing areas. These including data processing in specific enterprises such as Insurance, Stock/Bond Trading, Health Care Management, Reservation Systems, Postage Meter Systems (Computerized) as well as more general enterprise functions such as Electronic Shopping, Auction Systems, and Business Cryptography. The four largest groupings in Class 705 are those directed to the general business operations of:

1) Determining Who Your Customers Are, and The Products/Services They Need/Want

    Operations Research - Market Analysis

2) Informing Customers You Exist, Showing Them Your Products & Services, and Getting Them to Purchase

    Advertising Management
    Catalog Systems
    Incentive Programs
    Redemption of Coupons

3) Exchanging Money and Credit Before, During, and After the Business Transaction

    Credit and Loan Processing
    Point of Sale Systems
    Billing
    Funds Transfer
    Banking
    Clearinghouses
    Tax Processing
    Investment Planning

4) Tracking Resources, Money, And Products

    Human Resource Management
    Scheduling
    Accounting
    Inventory Monitoring

B. ENGINEERING IN SUPPORT OF BUSINESS

The systems and methods of Class 705 are directed to diverse business functions. However, a strong understanding of certain non-business fields is required to fully understand many inventions in this class. Patent applications being examined in Class 705 still strongly reflect the basic engineering that underlay each invention. Electrical and computer engineering (e.g., databases, communication systems) will continue to be a dominant feature of business data processing for generations to come. A strong electrical and computer engineering foundation is as important as a strong foundation in any of the diverse business functions.

These and other shared non-business fields allow unique patent examining flexibility across certain communications and information processing technologies. This is particularly true in technologies where large amounts of data must be stored and communicated from one location to another prior to performance of some final end function such as product sales. Patent examiners, from what appears on the surface to be diverse technologies, can readily assist each other with respect to shared non-business fields.

C. PATENT ASSIGNEES 1977-1999

Class 705 was created in 1997 from the business and cost/price sections of computer classes 395 and 364. These two sections having originally evolved from class 235 - Registers, beginning in the late 1960's. The evolution of the technologies in Class 705 can be seen by reviewing the assignees of Business Methods in the three periods 1977-1989, 1990-1994, and 1995-1999.

Ranking	1977-1989 (13 year span)		1990-1994 (5 year span)		1995-1999 (5 year span)	
1	Pitney-Bowes	134	Pitney-Bowes	47	Pitney-Bowes	77
2	Sharp Corporation	39	IBM	32	*Fujitsu LTD	64
3	Omron Electronics	31	Hitachi	23	IBM	58
4	IBM	26	Sharp	11	NCR	30
5	Casio	21	Omron	9	Hitachi	27
6	Tokyo Electric	21	*Alcatel Business System	9	*Citibank	22
7	Hitachi	10	NCR	6	*EDS	21
8	NCR	7	*AT&T	6	*Microsoft	20
9	Toshiba	6	*Unisys	6	* Neopost	16
10	Merrill Lynch Attalla Technovations	5 5	Casio * Frama A.G.	5 5	*Matsushita Electric Industrial	16

* indicates a new assignee from previous period

In the period prior to 1990, the Business Methods patents were heavily focused on computerized postage metering and cash register systems. By the end of 1994 heavier emphasis was placed on financial transaction systems which moved postage metering to the second place category. By the end of 1999, electronic shopping and financial transaction systems were the two dominant categories moving postage metering systems down to third. A review of the newly filed applications shows that postage metering will be moved to the fourth spot by the emerging technology of advertising management systems.

D. PATENT APPLICATION FILINGS

Class 705 has seen strong filing growth in FY 1998 and FY 1999. However, it represented only about 1% of the total patent applications filed at the USPTO in FY 1999. The *2658* applications filed in Class 705 did not even place it among the top five Communication and Information Processing technologies.

The digital and multiplex communication technologies of Classes 370 and 375 which form the backbone of all modern communication systems saw *7131* patent applications in FY 1999. Class 345 - Display data processing (e.g., graphical user interfaces, web browsers) saw *3898* applications; Class 455 - Telecommunications (e.g., radio, cellular telephones) saw *3480* applications; Class 709 – Networked computer data processing saw 3190 applications; Class 707 – Databases and Word Processors saw *3068* applications; and Classes 360 and 369 - Dynamic Information Storage (e.g., disk drives) saw *2905* applications.

Collectively the communications and information technologies saw 57,000 applications in FY 1999. Class 705 received less than 5 % of that total.

IV. RESOURCES IN TRANSITION

A component of addressing the needs of an emerging technology is expansion of available resources commensurate in scope to the expansion of the technology. This is particularly true in the people resource intensive profession of patent examining. Additional resources can only help the Office to continue to meet its statutory mandates. The key resource is the patent examiner who is supported by the other resources of the USPTO.

A. PATENT EXAMINERS

1. Primary And Non-Primary Patent Examiners

Patent examining is a profession learned through 5 to 7 years of on the job training reinforced by classroom training. It is analogous to the master-apprentice system. Primary Examiners and their managers are the Office's master patent professionals. These master professionals are delegated signatory authority from the Under Secretary of Commerce for Intellectual Property and Director of the United States Patent and Trademark Office to grant patents for the United States. Non-Primary patent examiners are the Office's apprentices in the process of learning their profession. All work by a non-Primary Examiner must be reviewed and signed by a person with signatory authority. Class 705 began Fiscal 1998 with three Primary Examiners and nine non-Primary Examiners.

Patent examiners are the key resource of Class 705. Critical to the managed growth of this technology is an adequate supply of this key resource.

2. Internal Transfers

The first step in expanding the examining resources available to Class 705 was to find individuals with appropriate backgrounds among the current examining corps. Since late 1997, a number of Examiners volunteered to transfer to Class 705. This group included several electrical engineers each with a Masters of Business Administration, an examiner with banking management experience, and a Ph.D. in Information Science with 30 years work experience developing business information systems.

B. HIRING

2000 Hiring - Preparation for Transition

Workgroup 2760 will hire sufficient Class 705 examiners in FY 2000 to cover attrition and modest expansion. However, expansion of the number of Class 705 examiners will not be the primary focus for this year.

Class 705 is in the first stage of a transition period. In 1998, the State Street decision triggered an awareness of the "business method claim" as a viable form of patent protection. As noted in Section II above, such patents express the practical application (useful, concrete and tangible result) of technology that is the essence of an innovation. This segment of Class 705 is transitioning away from technology towards the end result the inventor is attempting to achieve with that technology. Inventors are changing the approach to how they choose to describe their inventions. This change is in turn driving a shift in the knowledge base of the Class 705 examiners.

However, it must be noted that most patent applications being examined in Class 705 still strongly reflect the implementing or enabling engineering (see Section III B) used to carryout the practical application being claimed. Databases, communication systems, circuits, and wires (i.e. electrical and computer engineering) will continue to be a dominant feature of business data processing for generations to come. A business data processing method is implemented on a data processing machine which is still reflected in the patent application. The USPTO will also continue to grant patent protection for the business data processing machine itself. See Appendix G for a sample of patents issued on May 30, 2000.

In FY 2000, the focus for Class 705 is to ensure that high quality is maintained by its examiners as this transition moves forward. Numerous quality efforts are being implemented as discussed below. Such quality efforts are resource intensive. The collective result of these efforts will be proportional to the USPTO's ability to marshal the needed resources.

C. RESULTS TO DATE

1. Profile - An Appropriate Balance

Today thirty-eight examiners work in Class 705. This is an increase from twelve in late 1997. The total number, knowledge, and experience pool has been increased. Seventeen of the 38 examiners have advanced or multiple degrees. Of these 4 have an MBA or other business degrees, 4 have a JD degree, 4 have Ph.D. degrees, and 7 have Masters Degrees.

Every examiner in Class 705 has data processing and computer education or experience. The majority of examination in Class 705 is still centered on the data processing and computer technologies used to perform business functions. See Appendix G.

For over 100 years the USPTO has maintained quality by adapting its knowledge base continuously as business technologies have evolved. It has adjusted the mix of training and experience of its examiners. The USPTO will continue to maintain an appropriate mix of electrical engineering, computer science, and business knowledge balanced to the contents of the business data processing inventions it is asked to examine.

2. Business Industry Experience - Shifting the Knowledge Base

The patent applications of Class 705 have begun a transition to become more business function focused. Although still present in these patent applications, implementing technologies such as databases, communication systems, and circuits are becoming less prominent. However, as was previously discussed, this transition has only begun. As this transition continues the USPTO is appropriately responding by increasing examiner training and hiring, particularly by increasing the number of examiners with 3 years of business industry work experience.

Fourteen (14) patent examiners working in Class 705 have business industry work experience that pertains directly to the examination of patent applications in Class 705. Of these, ten have three or more years of work experience in various fields including Banking, Securities, Business Development, Marketing Analysis, Real Estate Analysis, Business Consulting, Management, Sales, Insurance, Business Information Systems, and Financial Analysis. This is 26% of the current Class 705 examiners. The combined business industry work experience of these 14 examiners is over 120 years.

Resources must be made available to continue to attract and retain greater numbers of these skilled experts. Without sufficient resources to continue both training and hiring, it is possible that as business data processing inventions continue to evolve the USPTO knowledge base will not keep pace with that change.

D. SCIENTIFIC & TECHNICAL INFORMATION CENTER – ELECTRONIC INFORMATION CENTER (STIC – EIC)

Patent examining in Class 705 is filled with challenges. This class contains diverse business topics (e.g. insurance and inventory systems). Prior art references can be found in many diverse sources (e.g. an Internet web site, a sales brochure, or a 120-year-old textbook). There is poor tabulation of all the available references for a particular topic (e.g. not all the insurance prior art is found in one location).

The STIC – EIC provides search and library support to help examiners meet these challenges. The professional searchers of the EIC routinely perform non-patent literature (NPL) searches requested by Class 705 examiners. The number of EIC professional searchers has expanded from two in 1995 to twelve in FY 2000. Although the EIC provides searching for all 703 examiners in Technology Center 2700, requests from the Class 705 examiners represented their largest technology specific group of search requests during FY 1998 and FY 1999. In the first half of FY 2000, this trend continued.

Among the library support functions currently being performed by the EIC are the locating of additional electronic business literature sources; the continued expansion of a conventional library of business books; and the retrieval of hard copies of pertinent NPL documents requested by examiners.

STIC is currently working on an initiative to collate examining resources into a web-based tool for Class 705 examiners. This tool will connect with databases, web sites, electronic and print literature resources on Class 705 topics.

V. IMPROVING QUALITY

A. INTRODUCTION

It is universally agreed that high quality examination by USPTO Patent Examiners must be ensured. Quality initiatives are continuously updated. The detailed discussion below highlights initiatives in place prior to March 2000, as well as, quality initiatives announced in March by Q. Todd Dickinson, Under Secretary of Commerce for Intellectual Property and Director of the United States Patent and Trademark Office. Each new quality initiative follows the pre-March 2000 initiative discussion it relates to most closely.

The mission of the USPTO is to help our customers get patents. However, not all applications are patentable. The patent examiner is tasked with helping the inventor including pointing out patentable inventions disclosed but not claimed in the originally presented claims. The examiner is also tasked with analyzing the scope of the claims and determining if sufficient evidence exists to meet the burden of proof to deny the granting of a patent on some or all of the presented claims. The patent statute is quite specific: "A person shall be entitled to a patent unless" this burden of proof is met. In Class 705, the examiners are able to grant patents on presented claim(s) about 57% of the time.

B. HYBRID EXAMINER-TRAINER

To assist first-line supervisors with training and review of work, Workgroup 2760 is using Examiner-Trainers in the Class 705 arts to promote consistent examination. An Examiner-Trainer is a Primary Examiner that spends 50% of the time examining patent applications, and 50% of the time training others in legal, procedural, and technological aspects of patent examining. On each application they examine, the new examiners work extremely closely with the Examiner-Trainers learning patent examining practice and procedure. In this way, the workgroup was able to properly train and integrate all their new hires in Fiscal Years 1999 and 2000.

C. TRAINING

1. Procedural

All examiners receive legal, procedural and technical training throughout their career at the USPTO.

When first hired, patent examiners undergo two weeks of intensive training in patent examining procedure. Here, the new employees learn the various statutes (35 USC) and rules (37 CFR) that govern the patent system. Using generic examples and lectures, they also learn how to properly examine an application and provide feedback (in the form of an Action) to the applicant. Upon successful completion of this course, the new examiners are released to the art units/workgroups for further training.

Upon their arrival in Workgroup 2760, the new Class 705 examiners learn of the policies and procedures of Workgroup 2760 and Technology Center 2700. Their orientation covers the workgroup training manual (to be discussed later in this paper), administrative procedures of the workgroup and of the technology center, and a discussion of training opportunities available.

Within the first month, new examiners are also trained on the various electronic and computerized systems used within the USPTO for searching, preparing actions, and tracking workflow. Either the workgroup or the technology center provides most of this training.

After approximately 2 months on the job, the new Class 705 examiners attend two more weeks of intensive training (called Introduction to Practice and Procedure - IPP) where they learn more aspects of searching and writing actions. Managers from the Technology Center teach the IPP course. These examiners receive training in the computer arts as they examine their own application.

Following the two week long IPP course, the new examiners begin attending weekly courses on advanced practice and procedure. Topics include affidavit practice, Patent Cooperation Treaty (PCT) procedures, and 35 U.S.C. 101 training.

2. Workgroup 2760 Training Manual

Typically, a new examiner works side by side with an experienced examiner (called a Primary Examiner) learning how to analyze an application, search the invention, and provide feedback to the applicant in the form of a written Action. In Workgroup 2760, to provide more guidance for the examiner, the managers working in cooperation with the Primary Examiners developed a training manual for the workgroup. The initial chapters of the manual focus on three critical steps: analyzing the disclosure and claims, searching for the invention, and preparing a written report (office action) to be sent to the inventor.

The intent of the training manual is to bring the new examiner up to speed with the basics of examining within 6 months. The manual also ensures that all examiners, new and experienced, are consistent in the manner they examine patent applications. The manual contains over 100 pages directed to analyzing the specification, searching, writing the action, handling amendments, responding to amendments, and samples of each. The manual is distributed to each new examiner within days of their entry into the workgroup. The Examiner Trainers provide an orientation for the new examiners and among other activities, acquaint the new examiner to the training manual. Over the two years since it's introduction to the examiners, the 2760 training manual has been used to assist in the apprentice training of new business patent examiners.

3. Search Strategy Training

A proper search is the mainstay of the U.S. Patent system. It usually takes years of training to fully develop the skills required to ascertain a proper search strategy after analyzing an application. The examiner must be trained in the art of analyzing the scope of the claims and searching. With this in mind, the managers and Primary Examiners of Workgroup 2760 have formulated standardized base search strategies for the varying aspects of the business technology. Thus, once an examiner knows the technology and concepts cited in the application, the examiner can utilize the standardized search strategy to determine not only where to search in the U.S. Patent system, but also which data files to search in Dialog and/or STN. While each application is unique and requires individual attention, these strategies assist a patent examiner, new or experienced, in searching the appropriate areas and finding references relevant to the application at hand.

To further assist the Class 705 examiners, a search strategy advisory panel comprised of managers and experienced examiners has been established to assist all Class 705 examiners in developing a search strategy for the application under examination. This panel may also be used to provide legal and procedural assistance.

4. Commercial and NPL Databases

During the first month of an examiner's career, and as new systems are introduced, the USPTO through the Patent Academy teach examiners how to search the U.S. patent databases (known as EAST and WEST). Commercial databases, searched by Class 705 examiners, provide "non-patent literature" (NPL) documents such as professional journals, magazines, and conference proceedings. Some commercial databases also offer abstracts of foreign documents.

Workgroup 2760, with the support of the Technology Center and the USPTO Academy, provides both basic and advanced training to the Class 705 examiners in DIALOG and STN/CAS. These courses utilize specific examples compiled by the workgroup managers and the Examiner Trainers so the trainees are searching "real world" situations during their training.

If examiners do not wish to search the commercial databases themselves, they can request a commercial database search by the Electronic Information Center (EIC) – a branch of the USPTO's Scientific and Technological Center (STIC) supported by Technology Center 2700. The EIC staff includes 12 professional searchers who perform the searches for these examiners. One searcher also collects new and interesting business information (including web sites) and provides them to the Class 705 examiners in a daily e-mail newsletter.

Non-patent literature (NPL) encompasses a wide variety of diverse published materials, such as textbooks, newspaper articles, magazine articles, sales brochures, professional journals, and conference proceedings. A patent examiner can find patented art in the U.S. Patent database for many business technologies. However, for rapidly emerging technologies, and/or simple accounting procedures, the U.S. Patent database is of less value. The Class 705 examiner will rely on NPL to provide the relevant art in these situations.

Begun in 1994, the EIC of Technology Center 2700 has worked hard to more readily provide NPL to the examiner. To assist the patent examiner in finding relevant NPL, the USPTO provides access to scientific and business related articles in over 900 databases through two commercial NPL database providers –

1. DIALOG
2. STN/CAS

All Class 705 examiners receive training in one or more of these two commercial database providers. The training is taught in two parts. The first part is an orientation into how the database operates, and how to establish a simple search query. The second part of the course is hands on with specific examples related to the business arts.

5. March 2000 Initiatives on Searching

Examiners perform a mandatory search for all applications in Class 705 to include a classified U.S. patent document search, and a text search of U.S. patent documents, foreign patent documents, and non-patent literature (NPL). The NPL searches include required search areas mapped/correlated to the U.S. classification system for Class 705.

For example, if an examiner is searching an insurance patent application classified in class 705/4, the examiner would have to search the 22 mandatory general business databases as well as the 3 mandatory databases specific to insurance. See figures NPL-1 to NPL-4 for a listing of class 705 core databases.

In addition to these mandatory databases, the examiner would search all appropriate databases from among the 900 available databases (e.g. Software Patent Institute [SPI], IEEE/IEE Electronic Library [IEL Online], etc.).

CLASS 705 CORE DATABASES

Non-Patent Literature Core Databases

All Class 705 applications will be searched in the following databases:

ABI/INFORM® [Bell & Howell Information and Learning]
Business & Industry™ [Responsive Database Services, Inc.]
Business Week [The McGraw-Hill Companies Publications Online]
Business Wire [Business Wire]
Computer Database™ [The Gale Group]
Conference Papers Index [Cambridge Scientific Abstracts]
Dissertation Abstracts Online [Bell & Howell Information and Learning]
Globalbase™ [The Gale Group]
Inside Conferences [The British Library]
INSPEC [INSPEC, Inc.]
Internet & Personal Computing Abstracts® [Information Today, Inc.]
The McGraw-Hill Companies Publications Online [The McGraw-Hill Companies, Inc.]
Microcomputer Software Guide Online® [R. R. Bowker Company]
New Product Announcements /Plus® (*NPA/Plus)* [The Gale Group]
Newsletter Database™ [The Gale Group]
Newspapers

- *Financial Times Abstracts*
- *New York Times Abstracts*
- *San Jose Mercury News*
- *Wall Street Journal Abstracts*

PR Newswire [PR Newswire Association, Inc.]
PROMT® [The Gale Group]
Softbase: Reviews, Companies, and Products [Information Sources, Inc.]
Trade & Industry Database™ [The Gale Group] *Wilson Applied Science and Technology Abstracts* [The H.W. Wilson Company]
World Reporter [The Dialog Corporation, Dow Jones & Company, and Financial Times Information]

Figure NPL-1

Subject Specific Databases

Many databases contain significant non-patent literature resources relevant to specific Class 705 subclasses. Therefore, additional core databases are listed for the subclasses indicated in this section. Examiners are required to search these databases during the examination of cases classified under these subclasses. In this list, the subclass numbers have been listed to the left of the subclass description.

2 **Health Care Management**

In addition to Core databases, search:

American Medical Association Journals [The American Medical Association]
BIOSIS Previews® [BIOSIS®]
EMBASE® [Elsevier Science, B.V.]
Health & Wellness Database^{SM} [The Gale Group]
Health News Daily [F-D-C Reports, Inc.]
HealthSTAR® [U.S. National Library of Medicine (NLM)]
MEDLINE® [U.S. National Library of Medicine (NLM)]
New England Journal of Medicine [Massachusetts Medical Society]
SciSearch® [Institute for Scientific Information® (ISI®)]

If drugs/pharmaceuticals are involved. . . . .

Drug News & Perspectives [Prous Science Publishers]
International Pharmaceutical Abstracts [American Society of Health-System Pharmacists]
Pharmaceutical and Healthcare Industry News Database [PJB Publications Ltd.]
Pharmaceutical News Index (PNI®) [Bell & Howell Information and Learning]

4 **Insurance**

In addition to Core databases, search:

American Banker Financial Publications [American Banker-Bond Buyer]
Insurance Periodicals Index [NILS Publishing Company]
The Journal of Commerce [The Journal of Commerce, Inc.]

7 **Operations Research**

In addition to Core databases, search:

Inventory Monitoring Databases

Figure NPL-2

13 **Transportation Facility Access**

In addition to Core databases, search:

Aerospace/Defense Markets & Technology® [The Gale Group]
Aerospace Database [AEROPLUS ACCESS]
The Journal of Commerce [The Journal of Commerce, Inc.]
NTIS - National Technical Information Service [National Technical Information Service, U.S. Department of Commerce]
Transportation Research Information Services [Transportation Research Board]

14 **Advertising/Coupon Redemption/Incentives**

In addition to Core databases, search:

Business Dateline® [Bell & Howell Information and Learning]
Marketing & Advertising Reference Service® [The Gale Group]

Newspapers

The Atlanta Journal/The Atlanta Constitution
The Arizona Republic/The Phoenix Gazette (Phoenix)
The Sun (Baltimore)
The Boston Globe
Chicago Tribune
The Christian Science Monitor
Detroit Free Press
The Denver Post
Houston Chronicle
Independent (London)
The Irish Times
Los Angeles Times
The Miami Herald
Newsday and New York Newsday
The Oregonian (Portland)
The Plain Dealer (Cleveland)
The Philadelphia Inquirer
Rocky Mountain News (Denver)
San Francisco Chronicle
St. Louis Post-Dispatch
St. Petersburg Times
Times/Sunday Times (London)
USA Today
Washington Post Online

Figure NPL-3

26 Electronic Shopping

In addition to Core databases, search:
Advertising/Coupon Redemption/Incentives Databases
Magazine Database™ [The Gale Group]

28 Inventory Monitoring

In addition to Core databases, search:
Ei Compendex® [Engineering Information, Inc.]
ISMEC: Mechanical Engineering Abstracts [Cambridge Scientific Abstracts]
JICST-EPlus - Japanese Science & Technology [Japan Information Center for Science and Technology (JICST)]
NTIS: National Technical Information Service [National Technical Information Service, U.S. Department of Commerce]
SciSearch® [Institute for Scientific Information (ISI®)]
Social SciSearch® [Institute for Scientific Information (ISI®)]

35 Banking/Finance/Investments

In addition to Core databases, search:
American Banker Financial Publications [American Banker-Bond Buyer]
Banking Information Source [Bell & Howell Information and Learning]
Bond Buyer Full Text [American Banker-Bond Buyer]
DIALOG Finance and Banking Newsletters [The Dialog Corporation]
EconLit [American Economic Association]

36 Portfolio Selection

In addition to Core databases, search:
Banking/Finance/Investment Databases

37 Trading, Matching or Bidding

In addition to Core databases, search:
Banking/Finance/Investment Databases

38 Credit Processing or Loan Processing

In addition to Core databases, search:
Banking/Finance/Investment Databases

39 Including Funds Transfer or Credit Transaction

In addition to Core databases, search:
Banking/Finance/Investment Databases
Knight-Ridder/Tribune Business News™ [Knight-Ridder/Tribune Business News]

Figure NPL-4

6. Technical

The patent examiner's training does not end with procedural training. The workgroup also provides technical training to both the new and the experienced Class 705 examiner. In keeping with the latest trends in "electronic business practice", the Class 705 examiners have received training over the last two years in – Computer networking, Computer organization and architecture, Electronic Payments, Electronic Catalogs, and Computer Security

Courses in the planning stage for the year 2000 include –

1. Advanced Computer Networking
2. Financial Transaction (including ATM)
3. Smart Cards
4. General Accounting Procedures

The intent of the technical training course is to provide the examiners with current information in the various fields of endeavor, and the history of that field. In this way, every Class 705 patent examiner has the same baseline of knowledge regardless of previous training or course work.

7. Field Trips, Conferences, and Seminars

Field trips to industry are important to the examining process as such trips give the examiner first hand knowledge of the inventive process and augment technological knowledge and expertise. Such trips also enable the examiner to sit down with the inventors to see the patent process through the eyes of the customer. Field trips also enable the examiner to understand the efforts put into the inventive process and the application process by the applicant. Workgroup 2760 is planning a business field trip during the summer of 2000 to Wall Street.

Conferences and seminars are important to the examining process as they provide tutorials and information on new technology and processes. In November of 2000, Workgroup 2760 is planning to send a contingent of Class 705 examiners to New York City to the Financial Tech Conference, which covers technologies used in insurance, banking and Wall Street.

8. March 2000 Initiatives on Training

Workgroup 2760 will maintain technical currency for examiners and continue current training efforts/partnerships with industry associations and various individual corporate sponsors.

Business practice specialists will be pursued from industry to serve as a resource for examiners on common or well known industry practices, terminology, scope and meaning, and industry standards in four basic areas: banking/finance, general e-commerce, insurance, and Internet infrastructure.

The USPTO will publish the areas of training needs for public comment and outside offers to provide such training.

D. MARCH 2000 INITIATIVES FOR ADDITIONAL REVIEW

A new second-level review of all allowed applications in Class 705 is required to ensure compliance with the mandatory search requirements, clarity and completeness of reasons for allowance, and to determine whether the scope of the claims should be reconsidered.

The sampling size for quality review by the Office of Patent Quality Review is being substantially expanded for Class 705.

The Examination Guidelines for Computer-Related Inventions and the relevant training examples are being revised in light of the *State Street Bank* and *AT&T v. Excel* decisions.

E. MEASURE OF QUALITY EFFORTS

The value of the quality initiatives is dependent upon associated measurement systems. Workgroup 2760 has two measuring components in place to measure their quality and the effectiveness of any initiatives implemented.

In-Process Review

Since 1998, Workgroup 2760, as well as TC 2700, have been performing in-process reviews of applications after a first office action to assist them in determining areas for quality improvement within the business area. These reviews check numerous items in the office actions but have a particular emphasis on the field of search of the prior art and patentability determinations under 35 U.S.C. 102 and 103. The data from each of these in-process reviews is compiled and provided to the workgroup managers. Results from these reviews are used to determine areas for improvement in application prosecution. Over the past two years, several areas have been identified and addressed with appropriate training by the Tech Center Quality Assurance Specialist (QAS).

VI. CUSTOMER PARTNERSHIP

In 1999, Technology Center 2700 and Workgroup 2760 began customer outreach initiatives and the formation of customer partnerships directed to Class 705.

On October 26, 1999, a *Customer Focus Session on Quality of USPTO Prior Art Searches in the Business Method Area* was held to identify strengths and weaknesses in the quality of searches being completed at the USPTO. This session included officials of the USPTO and a number of patent practitioners from the East Coast. Valuable information was received from customers that will be utilized in crafting initiatives to improve performance.

Technology Center 2700 has begun the process of forming customer partnerships to jointly address the issues of examination in Class 705. These customer partnerships will be a key mechanism in continuing to properly address the patent examination impacts of business data processing. Customer partnerships will allow the USPTO to properly gauge numerous items. Customers of the USPTO will know first the future evolution of business data processing. Their application filings will control the transition of patent application format towards the "business method form" and any future shift that will be required in the knowledge base of Class 705 examiners. They are also in a unique position to assist in providing training needed as part of shifting thc knowledge base.

VII. CONCLUSION

The growth of the business technology industry has been reflected in the increase in the quantity and complexity of patent applications filed in Class 705. This paper has discussed many initiatives that have been implemented to improve quality and begin customer partnerships for Class 705. More will be required in the future to meet the needs of this emerging technology and the needs of our customers. The USPTO management is committed to the successful examination of these applications to ensure continued growth and innovation in this important area.

APPENDIX A

Patent Number	Issue Date	Inventor	Title
X2301	April 28, 1815	Kneas	Bank Note Printing *Note this is a restored Patent taken from court records
871	August 3, 1838	Watson	Bank Note
63889	April 16, 1857	Hawes	Hotel-Register
138,891	May 13, 1873	Hunter	Revenue Stamps
575,731	January 26, 1897	Powers et al.	Insurable Property Chart
853,852	May 14, 1907	Adams	Insurance System
1,406,561	February 14, 1922	Howard	Business Form
3,556,563	July 9, 1969	Scheinberg et al.	Booklet and Cards For Use In A Limited Credit System

APPENDIX B

Patent Number	Issue Date	Inventor	Title
395,781	January 8, 1889	Hollerith	Art of Compiling Statistics
395,782	January 8, 1889	Hollerith	Art of Compiling Statistics
395,783	January 8, 1889	Hollerith	Art of Compiling Statistics

APPENDIX C

Patent Number	Issue Date	Inventor	Title
209,827	November 12, 1878	Moss et	Ticket Printing and Recording-Machine
774,322	November 8, 1904	Hepfer	Profit Sharing Sales Counter

APPENDIX D

Patent Number	Issue Date	Inventor	Title
915,090	March 16, 1909	Fuller	Cash Register
920,110	May 4, 1909	Cleal et al.	Cash Register

APPENDIX E

Patent Number	Issue Date	Inventor	Title
1,710,691	April 30, 1929	Carroll	Combined Sorter and Tabulator
2,052,444	August 25, 1936	Breitling	Bookkeeping Machine
2,126,615	August 9, 1938	Campbell	Accounting Machine

APPENDIX F

Patent Number	Issue Date	Inventor	Title
2,594,865	April 29, 1952	Bumstead	System for Making Reservations
2,916,212	December 8, 1959	Yoshiharu Mita	Electro-Analog Model Equipment of National Economic System
3,017,103	January 16, 1962	Goldberg et al.	Service Charge Calculation System
3,018,050	January 23, 1962	Barrell	Economic Data Computer
3,638,003	January 25, 1972	Meixner	Credit-Accumulating Arrangement
4,365,314	December 21, 1982	Badagnani et al.	Electronic Accounting Machine With Split Display
5,058,009	October 15, 1991	Yoshino et al.	Financial Calculator for Calculating, Graphically Displaying and Confirming Results of Loan Amortization Calculation

APPENDIX G

Patent Number	Issue Date	Inventor	Title
6,070,147	May 30, 2000	Harms et al.	Customer Identification and Marketing Analysis Systems
6,070,148	May 30, 2000	Mori et al.	Electronic Commerce System and Method for Providing Commercial Information in Electronic Commerce System
6,070,149	May 30, 2000	Tavor et al.	Virtual Sales Personnel

Appendix D-20

Rules to Implement Optional *Inter Partes* Reexamination Proceedings: Proposed Rule

65 FR 18154
Department of Commerce
Patent and Trademark Office
37 CFR Part 1
RIN 0651—AB04

Agency: United States Patent and Trademark Office, Commerce

Action: Notice of Proposed Rulemaking

* * *

PART 1—RULES OF PRACTICE IN PATENT CASES

1. The authority citation for 37 CFR Part 1 would continue to read as follows:

Authority: 35 U.S.C. 6, unless otherwise noted.

2. Section 1.4(a)(2) is proposed to be revised to read as follows:

§1.4 Nature of correspondence and signature requirements.

(a) * * *

(2) *Correspondence in and relating to a particular application or other proceeding in the Office.* See particularly the rules relating to the filing, processing, or other proceedings of national applications in Subpart B, §§1.31 to 1.378; of international applications in Subpart C, §§1.401 to 1.499; of *ex parte* reexaminations of patents in Subpart D, §§1.501 to 1.570; of interferences in Subpart E, §§1.601 to 1.690; of extension of patent term in Subpart F, §§1.710 to 1.785; of *inter partes* reexaminations of patents in Subpart H, §§1.902 to 1.997; and of trademark applications §§2.11 to 2.189.

* * * * *

3. Section 1.6(d)(5) is proposed to be revised to read as follows:

§1.6 Receipt of Correspondence.

* * * * *

(d) * * *

(5) A request for reexamination under §1.510 or §1.913.

4. Sections 1.17(l) and (m) are proposed to be revised to read as follows:

§1.17 Patent application and reexamination processing fees.

* * * * *

(l) For filing a petition for the revival of an unavoidably abandoned application under 35 U.S.C. 111, 133, 364, or 371, for the delayed payment of the issue fee under 35 U.S.C. 151, or for the revival of an unavoidably terminated reexamination proceeding under 35 U.S.C. 133 (§1.137(a)):

By a small entity (§1.9(f))	$55.00
By other than a small entity	110.00

(m) For filing a petition for revival of an unintentionally abandoned application, for the unintentionally delayed payment of the fee for issuing a patent, or for the revival of an unintentionally terminated reexamination proceeding under 35 U.S.C. 41(a)(7) (§1.137)(b)):

By a small entity (§1.9(f))	$605.00
By other than a small entity	1,210.00

* * * * *

5. Section 1.20(c) is proposed to be revised to read as follows:

§1.20 Post-issuance and reexamination fees.

* * * * *

(c) In reexamination proceedings

(1) For filing a request for *ex parte* reexamination (§1.510(a))	$2,520.00
(2) For filing a request for *inter partes* reexamination (§1.915(a))	8,800.00

* * * * *

6. Section 1.25(b) is proposed to be revised to read as follows:

§1.25 Deposit accounts.

* * * * *

(b) Filing, issue, appeal, international-type search report, international application processing, petition, and post-issuance fees may be charged against these accounts if sufficient funds are on deposit to cover such fees. A general authorization to charge all fees, or only certain fees, set forth in §§1.16 to 1.18 to a deposit account containing sufficient funds may be filed in an individual application, either for the entire pendency of the application or with respect to a particular paper filed. An authorization to charge to a deposit account the fee for a request for reexamination pursuant to §1.510 or §1.913 and any other fees required in a reexamination proceeding of a patent may also be filed. An authorization to charge a fee to a deposit account will not be considered payment of the fee on the date the authorization to charge the fee is effective as to the particular fee to be charged unless sufficient funds are present in the account to cover the fee.

7. Section 1.26(c) is proposed to be revised to read as follows:

§1.26 Refunds.

* * * * *

(c) If the Director decides not to institute a reexamination proceeding, for *ex parte* reexaminations filed under §1.510 a refund of $1,690.00 will be made to the reexamination requester. For *inter partes* reexaminations filed under §1.913, a refund of $7,970 will be made to the reexamination requester. Reexamination requester should indicate the form in which any refund should be made (*e.g.*, by check, electronic funds transfer, credit to a deposit account, *etc.*). Generally, reexamination refunds will be issued in the form that the original payment was provided.

8. Section 1.112 is proposed to be revised to read as follows:

§1.112 Reconsideration before final action.

After reply by applicant or patent owner (§1.111) to a non-final action, the application or the patent under reexamination will be reconsidered and again examined. The applicant, or in the case of a reexamination proceeding the patent owner and any third-party requester, will be notified if claims are rejected, objections or requirements made, or decisions favorable to patentability are made, in the same manner as after the first examination. Applicant or patent owner may reply to such Office action in the same manner provided in §1.111, with or without amendment, unless such Office action indicates that it is made final (§§1.113), or in an *inter partes* reexamination, that it is an action closing prosecution (§1.949) or a right of appeal notice (§1.953).

9. Section 1.113(a) is proposed to be revised to read as follows:

§1.113 Final rejection or action.

(a) On the second or any subsequent examination or consideration by the examiner the rejection or other action may be made final, whereupon applicant's, or for *ex parte* reexaminations filed under §1.510 patent owner's, reply is limited to appeal in the case of rejection of any claim (§1.191), or to amendment as specified in §1.116. Petition may be taken to the Director in the case of objections or requirements not involved in the rejection of any claim (§1.181). Reply to a final rejection or action must include cancellation of, or appeal from the rejection of, each rejected claim. If any claim stands allowed, the reply to a final rejection or action must comply with any requirements or objections as to form. For final actions in an *inter partes* reexamination filed under §1.913, see §1.953.

* * * * *

10. Sections 1.116(a) and (c) are proposed to be revised to read as follows:

§1.116 Amendments after final action, action closing prosecution, right of appeal notice, or appeal.

(a) After a final rejection or other final action (§1.113) in an application or in an *ex parte* reexamination filed under §1.510, or an action closing prosecution (§1.949) in an *inter partes* reexamination filed under §1.913, amendments may be made canceling claims or complying with any requirement of form expressly set forth in a previous Office action. Amendments presenting rejected claims in better form for consideration on appeal may be admitted. The admission of, or refusal to admit, any amendment after a final rejection, a final action, an action closing prosecution or any related proceedings, will not operate to relieve the application or patent under reexamination from its condition as subject to appeal or to save the application from abandonment under §1.135, or the reexamination from termination. No amendment can be made in an *inter partes* reexamination proceeding after the right of appeal notice under §1.953 except as provided for in paragraph (c) of this section.

* * * * *

(c) No amendment can be made as a matter of right in appealed cases. After decision on appeal, amendments can only be made as provided in §§1.198 and 1.981, or to carry into effect a recommendation under §§1.196 or 1.977.

11. Section 1.121(c) is proposed to be revised to read as follows:

§1.121 Manner of making amendments.

* * * * *

(c) *Amendments in reexamination proceedings*. Any proposed amendment to the description and claims in patents involved in reexamination proceedings in both *ex parte* reexaminations filed under §1.510 and *inter partes* reexaminations filed under §1.913 must be made in accordance with §1.530(d).

12. Section 1.136(a)(2) and (b) are proposed to be revised to read as follows:

§1.136 Extensions of time.

(a) * * *

(2) The date on which the petition and the fee have been filed is the date for purposes of determining the period of extension and the corresponding amount of the fee. The expiration of the time period is determined by the amount of the fee paid. A reply must be filed prior to the expiration of the period of extension to avoid abandonment of the application (§1.135), but in no situation may an applicant reply later than the maximum time period set by statute, or be granted an extension of time under paragraph (b) of this section when the provisions of this paragraph are available. See §1.136(b) for extensions of time relating to proceedings pursuant to §§1.193(b), 1.194, 1.196 or 1.197; §1.304 for extensions of time to appeal to the U.S. Court of Appeals for the Federal Circuit or to commence a civil action; §1.550(c) for extensions of time in *ex parte* reexamination proceedings, §1.956 for extensions of time in *inter partes* reexamination proceedings; and §1.645 for extensions of time in interference proceedings.

* * * * *

(b) When a reply cannot be filed within the time period set for such reply and the provisions of paragraph (a) of this section are not available, the period for reply will be extended only for sufficient cause and for a reasonable time specified. Any request for an extension of time under this paragraph must be filed on or before the day on which such reply is due, but the mere filing of such a request will not effect any extension under this paragraph. In no situation can any extension carry the date on which reply is due beyond the maximum time period set by statute. See §1.304 for extensions of time to appeal to the U.S. Court of Appeals for the Federal Circuit or to commence a civil action; §1.645 for extensions of time in interference proceedings; §1.550(c) for extensions of time in *ex parte* reexamination proceedings; and §1.956 for extensions of time in *inter partes* reexamination proceedings.

13. Section 1.137 is proposed to be amended by revising its heading, the introductory text of paragraph (a), the introductory text of paragraph (b), and paragraph (d) to read as follows:

§1.137 Revival of abandoned application, lapsed patent, or terminated reexamination proceeding.

(a) *Unavoidable*. Where the delay in reply was unavoidable, a petition may be filed to revive an abandoned application, a reexamination proceeding terminated under §§1.550(d) and 1.957(b) and (c), or a lapsed patent pursuant to this paragraph. A grantable petition pursuant to this paragraph must be accompanied by:

* * * * *

(b) *Unintentional*. Where the delay in reply was unintentional, a petition may be filed to revive an abandoned application, a reexamination proceeding terminated under §§1.550(d) and 1.957(b) and (c), or a lapsed patent pursuant to this paragraph. A grantable petition pursuant to this paragraph must be accompanied by:

* * * * *

(d) Any request for reconsideration or review of a decision refusing to revive an abandoned application, a terminated reexamination proceeding, or lapsed patent upon petition filed pursuant to this section, to be considered timely, must be filed within two months of the decision refusing to revive or within such time as set in the decision. Unless a decision indicates otherwise, this time period may be extended under the provisions of §1.136 for an abandoned application or lapsed patent; under the provisions of §1.550(c) for a terminated *ex parte* reexamination proceeding filed under §1.510; and under the provisions of §1.956 for a terminated *inter partes* reexamination proceeding filed under §1.913.

* * * * *

14. Sections 1.181(a) and (c) are proposed to be revised to read as follows:

§1.181 Petition to the Director.

(a) Petition may be taken to the Director:

(1) From any action or requirement of any examiner in the *ex parte* prosecution of an application, or in the *ex parte* or *inter partes* prosecution of a reexamination proceeding which is not subject to appeal to the Board of Patent Appeals and Interferences or to the court;

(2) In cases in which a statute or the rules specify that the matter is to be determined directly by or review by the Director; and

(3) To invoke the supervisory authority of the Director in appropriate circumstances.

(4) For petitions in interferences, see §1.644.

* * * * *

(c) When a petition is taken from an action or requirement of an examiner in the *ex parte* prosecution of an application, or in the *ex parte* or *inter partes* prosecution of a reexamination proceeding, it may be required that there have been a proper request for reconsideration (§1.111) and a repeated action by the examiner. The examiner may be directed by the Director to furnish a written statement, within a specified time, setting forth the reasons for his or her decision upon the matters averred in the petition, supplying a copy thereof to the petitioner.

* * * * *

15. Section 1.191(a) is proposed to be revised to read as follows:

§1.191 Appeal to Board of Patent Appeals and Interferences.

(a) Every applicant for a patent or for reissue of a patent, and every owner of a patent under *ex parte* reexamination filed under §1.510 for a patent that issued from an original application filed in the United States before November 29, 1999, any of whose claims has been twice or finally (§1.113) rejected, may appeal from the decision of the examiner to the Board of Patent Appeals and Interferences by filing a notice of appeal and the fee set forth in §1.17(b) within the time period provided under §§1.134 and 1.136 for reply. Notwithstanding the above, for an *ex parte* reexamination proceeding filed under §1.510 for a patent that issued from an original application filed in the United States on or after November 29, 1999, no appeal may be filed until the claims have been finally rejected (§1.113). Appeals to the Board of Patent Appeals and Interferences in *inter partes* reexamination proceedings filed under §1.913 are controlled by §§1.959 through 1.981. Sections 1.191 through 1.198 are not applicable to appeals in *inter partes* reexamination proceedings filed under §1.913.

16. Section 1.301 is proposed to be revised to read as follows:

§1.301 Appeal to U.S. Court of Appeals for the Federal Circuit.

Any applicant or any owner of a patent involved in any *ex parte* reexamination proceeding filed under §1.510, dissatisfied with the decision of the Board of Patent Appeals and Interferences, and any party to an interference dissatisfied with the decision of the Board of Patent Appeals and Interferences, may appeal to the U.S. Court of Appeals for the Federal Circuit. The appellant must take the following steps in such an appeal: In the U.S. Patent and Trademark Office, file a written notice of appeal directed to the Director (see §§1.302 and 1.304); and in the Court, file a copy of the notice of appeal and pay the fee for appeal as provided by the rules of the Court. For *inter partes* reexamination proceedings filed under §1.913, §1.983 is controlling.

17. Section 1.303 is proposed to be amended by revising paragraphs (a) and (b) and by adding a new paragraph (d) to read as follows:

§1.303 Civil action under 35 U.S.C. 145, 146, 306.

(a) Any applicant or any owner of a patent involved in an *ex parte* reexamination proceeding filed under §1.510 for a patent that issues from an original application filed in the United States before November 29, 1999, dissatisfied with the decision of the Board of Patent Appeals and Interferences, and any party to an interference dissatisfied with the decision of the Board of Patent Appeals and Interferences may, instead of appealing to the U.S. Court of Appeals for the Federal Circuit (§1.301), have remedy by civil action under 35 U.S.C. 145 or 146, as appropriate. Such civil action must be commenced within the time specified in §1.304.

(b) If an applicant in an *ex parte* case or an owner of a patent involved in an *ex parte* reexamination proceeding filed under §1.510 for a patent that issues from an original application filed in the United States before November 29, 1999, has taken an appeal to the U.S. Court of Appeals for the Federal Circuit, he or she thereby waives his or her right to proceed under 35 U.S.C. 145.

* * * * *

(d) For an *ex parte* reexamination proceeding filed under §1.510 for a patent that issues from an original application filed in the United States on or after November 29, 1999, and for an *inter partes* reexamination proceeding filed under §1.913, no remedy by civil action under 35 U.S.C. 145 is available.

18. Sections 1.304(a)(1) and (a)(2) are proposed to be revised to read as follows:

§1.304 Time for appeal or civil action.

(a)(1) The time for filing the notice of appeal to the U.S. Court of Appeals for the Federal Circuit (§1.302) or for commencing a civil action (§1.303) is two months from the date of the decision of the Board of Patent Appeals and Interferences. If a request for rehearing or reconsideration of the decision is filed within the time period provided under §1.197(b), §1.658(b), or §1.979(a), the time for filing an appeal or commencing a civil action shall expire two months after action on the request. In interferences the time for filing a cross-appeal or cross-action expires:

(i) 14 days after service of the notice of appeal or the summons and complaint; or

(ii) Two months after the date of decision of the Board of Patent Appeals and Interferences, whichever is later.

(2) The time periods set forth in this section are not subject to the provisions of §§1.136, 1.550(c), 1.956, or §1.645(a) or (b).

* * * * *

19. The heading for Subpart D is proposed to be revised to read as follows:

Subpart D—*Ex Parte* Reexamination of Patents

* * * * *

20. Section 1.501 is proposed to be amended by revising its heading and paragraph (a) to read as follows:

§1.501 Citation of prior art in patent and *ex parte* reexamination files.

(a) At any time during the period of enforceability of a patent, any person may cite to the Office in writing prior art consisting of patents or printed publications which that person states to be pertinent and applicable to the patent and believes to have a bearing on the patentability of any claim of the patent. If the citation is made by the patent owner, the explanation of pertinency and applicability may include an explanation of how the claims differ from the prior art. Such citations shall be entered in the patent file except as set forth in this section. Citations by the patent owner under §1.555 and by an *ex parte* reexamination requester under either §1.510 or §1.535 will be entered in the reexamination file during a reexamination proceeding. The entry in the patent file of citations submitted after the date of an order to reexamine pursuant to §1.525 by persons other than the patent owner, or an *ex parte* reexamination requester under either §1.510 or §1.535, will be delayed until the reexamination proceeding has been terminated. See §1.902 for processing of prior art citations in patent files and the reexamination file during an *inter partes* reexamination proceeding filed under §1.913.

* * * * *

21. The undesignated center heading following §1.501 is proposed to be revised to read as follows:

Request for *Ex Parte* Reexamination

22. Section 1.510 is proposed to be amended by revising its heading and the text of paragraphs (a) and (b)(4) to read as follows:

§1.510 Request for *ex parte* reexamination.

(a) Any person may, at any time during the period of enforceability of a patent, file a request for an *ex parte* reexamination by the Office of any claim of the patent on the basis of prior art patents or printed publications cited under §1.501. The request must be accompanied by the fee for requesting reexamination set in §1.20(c)(1).

(b) Any request for *ex parte* reexamination must include the following parts:

* * * * *

(4) A copy of the entire patent including the front face, drawings, and specification/ claims (in double column format) for which reexamination is requested, and a copy of any disclaimer, certificate of correction, or reexamination certificate issued in the patent. All copies must have each page plainly written on only one side of a sheet of paper.

* * * * *

23. Section 1.515 is proposed to be revised to read as follows:

§1.515 Determination of the request for *ex parte* reexamination.

(a) Within three months following the filing date of a request for an *ex parte* reexamination, an examiner will consider the request and determine whether or not a substantial new question of patentability affecting any claim of the patent is raised by the request and the prior art cited therein, with or without consideration of other patents or printed publications. The examiner's determination will be based on the claims in effect at the time of the determination and will become a part of the official file of the patent and will be mailed to the patent owner at the address as provided for in §1.33(c) and to the person requesting reexamination.

(b) Where no substantial new question of patentability has been found, a refund of a portion of the fee for requesting *ex parte* reexamination will be made to the requester in accordance with §1.26(c).

(c) The requester may seek review by a petition to the Director under §1.181 within one month of the mailing date of the examiner's determination refusing *ex parte* reexamination. Any such petition must comply with §1.181(b). If no petition is timely filed or if the decision on petition affirms that no substantial new question of patentability has been raised, the determination shall be final and nonappealable.

24. Section 1.520 is proposed to be revised to read as follows:

§1.520 *Ex parte* reexamination at the initiative of the Director.

The Director, at any time during the period of enforceability of a patent, may determine whether or not a substantial new question of patentability is raised by patents or printed publications which have been discovered by the Director or which have been brought to the Director's attention even though no request for reexamination has been filed in accordance with §1.510 or §1.913. The Director may initiate *ex parte* reexamination without a request for reexamination pursuant to §1.510 or §1.913. Normally requests from outside the Office that the Director undertake reexamination on his own initiative will not be considered. Any determination to initiate *ex parte* reexamination under this section will become a part of the official file of the patent and will be mailed to the patent owner at the address as provided for in §1.33(c).

25. The undesignated center heading following §1.520 is proposed to be revised to read as follows:

Ex Parte Reexamination

26. Section 1.525 is proposed to be revised to read as follows:

§1.525 Order for *ex parte* reexamination.

(a) If a substantial new question of patentability is found pursuant to §1.515 or §1.520, the determination will include an order for *ex parte* reexamination of the patent for resolution of the question. If the order for *ex parte* reexamination resulted from a petition pursuant to §1.515(c), the *ex parte* reexamination will ordinarily be conducted by an examiner other than the examiner responsible for the initial determination under §1.515(a).

(b) The notice published in the *Official Gazette* under §1.11(c) will be considered to be constructive notice and *ex parte* reexamination will proceed.

27. Section 1.530 is proposed to be amended by revising its heading and paragraphs (a), (b), (c) and (d), introductory text, to read as follows:

§1.530 Statement by patent owner in *ex parte* reexamination; amendment by patent owner in *ex parte* reexamination or *inter partes* reexamination.

(a) Except as provided in §1.510(e), no statement or other response by the patent owner in an *ex parte* reexamination proceeding shall be filed prior to the determinations made in accordance with §1.515 or §1.520. If a premature statement or other response is filed by the patent owner it will not be acknowledged or considered in making the determination.

(b) The order for *ex parte* reexamination will set a period of not less than two months from the date of the order within which the patent owner may file a statement on the new question of patentability including any proposed amendments the patent owner wishes to make.

(c) Any statement filed by the patent owner shall clearly point out why the subject matter as claimed is not anticipated or rendered obvious by the prior art patents or printed publications, either alone or in any reasonable combinations. Where the reexamination request was filed by a third-party requester, any statement filed by the patent owner must be served upon the *ex parte* reexamination requester in accordance with §1.248.

(d) *Amendments in reexamination proceedings*. Amendments in both *ex parte* and *inter partes* reexamination proceedings are made by filing a paper, in compliance with paragraph (d)(5) of this section, directing that specified amendments be made.

* * * * *

28. Section 1.535 is proposed to be revised to read as follows:

§1.535 Reply by third-party requester in *ex parte* reexamination.

A reply to the patent owner's statement under §1.530 may be filed by the *ex parte* reexamination requester within two months from the date of service of the patent owner's statement. Any reply by the *ex parte* requester must be served upon the patent owner in accordance with §1.248. If the patent owner does not file a statement under §1.530, no reply or other submission from the *ex parte* reexamination requester will be considered.

29. Section 1.540 is proposed to be revised to read as follows:

§1.540 Consideration of responses in *ex parte* reexamination.

The failure to timely file or serve the documents set forth in §1.530 or in §1.535 may result in their being refused consideration. No submissions other than the statement pursuant to §1.530 and the reply by the *ex parte* reexamination requester pursuant to §1.535 will be considered prior to examination.

30. Section 1.550 is proposed to be revised to read as follows:

§1.550 Conduct of *ex parte* reexamination proceedings.

(a) All *ex parte* reexamination proceedings, including any appeals to the Board of Patent Appeals and Interferences, will be conducted with special dispatch within the Office. After issuance of the *ex parte* reexamination order and expiration of the time for submitting any responses thereto, the examination will be conducted in accordance with §§1.104 through 1.116, and will result in the issuance of an *ex parte* reexamination certificate under §1.570.

(b) The patent owner in an *ex parte* reexamination proceeding will be given at least thirty days to respond to any Office action. Such response may include further statements in response to any rejections or proposed amendments or new claims to place the patent in a condition where all claims, if amended as proposed, would be patentable.

(c) The time for taking any action by a patent owner in an *ex parte* reexamination proceeding will be extended only for sufficient cause and for a reasonable time specified. Any request for such extension must be filed on or before the day on which action by the patent owner is due, but in no case will the mere filing of a request affect any extension. See §1.304(a) for extensions of time for filing a notice of appeal to the U.S. Court of Appeals for the Federal Circuit or for commencing a civil action.

(d) If the patent owner fails to file a timely and appropriate response to any Office action or any written statement of an interview required under §1.560(b), the *ex parte* reexamination proceeding will be terminated and the Director will proceed to issue a certificate under §1.570 in accordance with the last action of the Office.

(e) If a response by the patent owner is not timely filed in the Office.

(1) The delay in filing such response may be excused if it is shown to the satisfaction of the Director that the delay was unavoidable; a petition to accept an unavoidably delayed response must be filed in compliance with §1.137(a); or

(2) The response may nevertheless be accepted if the delay was unintentional; a petition to accept an unintentionally delayed response must be filed in compliance with §1.137(b).

(f) The reexamination requester will be sent copies of Office actions issued during the *ex parte* reexamination proceeding. After filing of a request for *ex parte* reexamination by a third-party requester, any document filed by either the patent owner or the third-party requester must be served on the other party in the reexamination proceeding in the manner provided by §1.248. The document must reflect service or the document may be refused consideration by the Office.

(g) The active participation of the *ex parte* reexamination requester ends with the reply pursuant to §1.535, and no further submissions on behalf of the reexamination requester will be acknowledged or considered. Further, no submissions on behalf of any third parties will be acknowledged or considered unless such submissions are:

(1) In accordance with §§1.510 or 1.535; or

(2) Entered in the patent file prior to the date of the order for *ex parte* reexamination pursuant to §1.525.

(h) Submissions by third parties, filed after the date of the order for *ex parte* reexamination pursuant to §1.525, must meet the requirements of and will be treated in accordance with §1.501(a).

31. Section 1.552 is proposed to be revised to read as follows:

§1.552 Scope of reexamination in *ex parte* reexamination proceedings.

(a) Claims in an *ex parte* reexamination proceeding will be examined on the basis of patents or printed publications and, with respect to subject matter added or deleted in the reexamination proceeding, on the basis of the requirements of 35 U.S.C. 112.

(b) Claims in an *ex parte* reexamination proceeding will not be permitted to enlarge the scope of the claims of the patent.

(c) Issues other than those indicated in paragraphs (a) and (b) of this section will not be resolved in a reexamination proceeding. If such issues are raised by the patent owner or third-party requester during a reexamination proceeding, the existence of such issues will be noted by the examiner in the next Office action, in which case the patent owner may desire to consider the advisability of filing a reissue application to have such issues considered and resolved.

32. Section 1.555 is proposed to be amended by revising its heading to read as follows:

§1.555 Information material to patentability in *ex parte* reexamination and *inter partes* reexamination proceedings.

* * * * *

33. Section 1.560 is proposed to be revised to read as follows:

§1.560 Interviews in *ex parte* reexamination proceedings.

(a) Interviews in *ex parte* reexamination proceedings pending before the Office between examiners and the owners of such patents or their attorneys or agents of record must be conducted in the Office at such times, within Office hours, as the respective examiners may designate. Interviews will not be permitted at any other time or place without the authority of the Director. Interviews for the discussion of the patentability of claims in patents involved in *ex parte* reexamination proceedings will not be conducted prior to the first official action thereon. Interviews should be arranged for in advance. Requests that reexamination requesters participate in interviews with examiners will not be granted.

(b) In every instance of an interview with an examiner in an *ex parte* reexamination proceeding, a complete written statement of the reasons presented at the interview as warranting favorable action must be filed by the patent owner. An interview does not remove the necessity for response to Office actions as specified in §1.111. Patent owner's response to an outstanding Office action after the interview does not remove the necessity for filing the written statement. The written statement must be filed as a separate part of a response to an Office action outstanding at the time of the interview, or as a separate paper within one month from the date of the interview, whichever is later.

34. Section 1.565 is proposed to be revised to read as follows:

§1.565 Concurrent Office proceedings which include an *ex parte* reexamination proceeding.

(a) In an *ex parte* reexamination proceeding before the Office, the patent owner shall call the attention of the Office to any prior or concurrent proceedings in which the patent is or was involved such as an interference, reissue, *ex parte* reexamination, *inter partes* reexamination, or litigation and the results of such proceedings. See §1.985 for notification of prior or concurrent proceedings in an *inter partes* reexamination proceeding.

(b) If a patent in the process of *ex parte* reexamination is or becomes involved in litigation, the Director shall determine whether or not to suspend the reexamination. See §1.987 for *inter partes* reexamination proceedings.

(c) If *ex parte* reexamination is ordered while a prior *ex parte* reexamination proceeding is pending and prosecution has not been terminated, the *ex parte* reexamination proceedings will be consolidated and result in the issuance of a single certificate under §1.570. For merger of *inter partes* reexamination proceedings, see §1.989(a). For merger of *ex parte* reexamination and *inter partes* reexamination proceedings, see §1.989(b).

(d) If a reissue application and an *ex parte* reexamination proceeding on which an order pursuant to §1.525 has been mailed are pending concurrently on a patent, a decision will normally be made to merge the two proceedings or to suspend one of the two proceedings. Where merger of a reissue application and an *ex parte* reexamination proceeding is ordered, the merged examination will be conducted in accordance with §§1.171 through 1.179 and the patent owner will be required to place and maintain the same claims in the reissue application and the *ex parte* reexamination proceeding during the pendency of the merged proceeding. The examiner's actions and responses by the patent owner in a merged proceeding will apply to both the reissue application and the *ex parte* reexamination proceeding and be physically entered into both files. Any *ex parte* reexamination proceeding merged with a reissue application shall be terminated by the grant of the reissued patent. For merger of a reissue application and an *inter partes* reexamination, see §1.991.

(e) If a patent in the process of *ex parte* reexamination is or becomes involved in an interference, the Director may suspend the reexamination or the interference. The Director will not consider a request to suspend an interference unless a motion (§1.635) to suspend the interference has been presented to, and denied by, an administrative patent judge and the request is filed within ten (10) days of a decision by an administrative patent judge denying the motion for suspension or such other time as the administrative patent judge may set. For concurrent *inter partes* reexamination and interference of a patent, see §1.993.

35. The undesignated center heading following §1.565 is proposed to be revised to read as follows:

Ex Parte Reexamination Certificate

36. Section 1.570 is proposed to be revised to read as follows:

§1.570 Issuance of *ex parte* reexamination certificate after *ex parte* reexamination proceedings.

(a) Upon the conclusion of *ex parte* reexamination proceedings, the Director will issue an *ex parte* reexamination certificate in accordance with 35 U.S.C. 307 setting forth the results of the *ex parte* reexamination proceeding and the content of the patent following the *ex parte* reexamination proceeding.

(b) An *ex parte* reexamination certificate will be issued in each patent in which an *ex parte* reexamination proceeding has been ordered under §1.525 and has not been merged with any *inter partes* reexamination proceeding pursuant to §1.989(a). Any statutory disclaimer filed by the patent owner will be made part of the *ex parte* reexamination certificate.

(c) The *ex parte* reexamination certificate will be mailed on the day of its date to the patent owner at the address as provided for in §1.33(c). A copy of the *ex parte* reexamination certificate will also be mailed to the requester of the *ex parte* reexamination proceeding.

(d) If an *ex parte* reexamination certificate has been issued which cancels all of the claims of the patent, no further Office proceedings will be conducted with regard to that patent or any reissue applications or any reexamination requests relating thereto.

(e) If the *ex parte* reexamination proceeding is terminated by the grant of a reissued patent as provided in §1.565(d), the reissued patent will constitute the *ex parte* reexamination certificate required by this section and 35 U.S.C. 307.

(f) A notice of the issuance of each *ex parte* reexamination certificate under this section will be published in the *Official Gazette* on its date of issuance.

37. Subpart H is proposed to be added to read as follows:

Subpart H—*Inter Partes* Reexamination of Patents

Prior Art Citations

Sec.

1.902 Processing of prior art citations during an *inter partes* reexamination proceeding.

Requirements for *Inter Partes* Reexamination Proceedings

1.903 Service of papers on parties in *inter partes* reexamination.
1.904 Notice of *inter partes* reexamination in *Official Gazette*.
1.905 Submission of papers by public in *inter partes* reexamination.
1.906 Scope of reexamination in *inter partes* reexamination proceeding.
1.907 *Inter partes* reexamination prohibited.
1.913 Persons eligible to file request for *inter partes* reexamination.
1.915 Content of request for *inter partes* reexamination.
1.919 Filing date of request for *inter partes* reexamination.
1.923 Examiner's determination on the request for *inter partes* reexamination.
1.925 Partial refund if request for *inter partes* reexamination is not ordered.
1.927 Petition to review refusal to order *inter partes* reexamination.

Inter Partes Reexamination of Patents

1.931 Order for *inter partes* reexamination.

Information Disclosure in *Inter Partes* Reexamination

1.933 Patent owner duty of disclosure in *inter partes* reexamination proceedings.

Office Actions and Responses (Before the Examiner) in *Inter Partes* Reexamination

1.935 Initial Office action usually accompanies order for *inter partes* reexamination.
1.937 Conduct of *inter partes* reexamination.
1.939 Unauthorized papers in *inter partes* reexamination.
1.941 Amendments by patent owner in *inter partes* reexamination.
1.943 Requirements of responses, written comments, and briefs in *inter partes* reexamination.
1.945 Response to Office action by patent owner in *inter partes* reexamination.
1.947 Comments by third-party requester to patent owner's response in *inter partes* reexamination.
1.948 Limitations on submission of prior art by third-party requester following the order for *inter partes* reexamination.
1.949 Examiner's Office action closing prosecution in *inter partes* reexamination.
1.951 Options after Office action closing prosecution in *inter partes* reexamination.
1.953 Examiner's Right of Appeal Notice in *inter partes* reexamination.

Interviews Prohibited in *Inter Partes* Reexamination

1.955 Interviews prohibited in *inter partes* reexamination proceedings.

Extensions of Time, Termination of Proceedings, and Petitions to Revive in *Inter Partes* Reexamination

Appeal to the Board of Patent Appeals and Interferences in *Inter Partes* Reexamination

Patent Owner Appeal to the United States Court of Appeals for the Federal Circuit in *Inter Partes* Reexamination

Concurrent Proceedings Involving Same Patent in *Inter Partes* Reexamination

Reexamination Certificate in *Inter partes* Reexamination

Prior Art Citations

§1.902 Processing of prior art citations during an *inter partes* reexamination proceeding.

Citations by the patent owner in accordance with §1.933 and by an *inter partes* reexamination third-party requester under §§1.915 or 1.948 will be entered in the *inter partes* reexamination file. The entry in the patent file of other citations submitted after the date of an order for reexamination pursuant to §1.931 by persons other than the patent owner, or the third-party requester under either §1.915 or §1.948, will be delayed until the *inter partes* reexamination proceeding has been terminated.

Requirements for *Inter Partes* Reexamination Proceedings

§1.903 Service of papers on parties in *inter partes* reexamination.

The patent owner and the third-party requester will be sent copies of Office actions issued during the *inter partes* reexamination proceeding. After filing of a request for *inter partes* reexamination by a third-party requester, any document filed by either the patent owner or the third-party requester must be served on every other party in the reexamination proceeding in the manner provided in §1.248. Any document must reflect service or the document may be refused consideration by the Office. The failure of the patent owner or the third-party requester to serve documents may result in their being refused consideration.

§1.904 Notice of *inter partes* reexamination in *Official Gazette*.

A notice of the filing of an *inter partes* reexamination request will be published in the *Official Gazette*. The notice published in the *Official Gazette* under §1.11(c) will be considered to be constructive notice of the *inter partes* reexamination proceeding and *inter partes* reexamination will proceed.

§1.905 Submission of papers by public in *inter partes* reexamination.

Unless specifically provided for, no submissions on behalf of any third parties other than third-party requesters as defined in 35 U.S.C. 100(e) will be considered unless such submissions are in accordance with §1.915 or entered in the patent file prior to the date of the order for reexamination pursuant to §1.931. Submissions by third parties, other than third-party requesters, filed after the date of the order for reexamination pursuant to §1.931, must meet the requirements of §1.501 and will be treated in accordance with §1.902. Submissions which do not meet the requirements of §1.501 will be returned.

§1.906 Scope of reexamination in *inter partes* reexamination proceeding.

(a) Claims in an *inter partes* reexamination proceeding will be examined on the basis of patents or printed publications and, with respect to subject matter added or deleted in the reexamination proceeding, on the basis of the requirements of 35 U.S.C. 112.

(b) Claims in an *inter partes* reexamination proceeding will not be permitted to enlarge the scope of the claims of the patent.

(c) Issues other than those indicated in paragraphs (a) and (b) of this section will not be resolved in an *inter partes* reexamination proceeding. If such issues are raised by the patent owner or the third-party requester during a reexamination proceeding, the existence of such issues will be noted by the examiner in the next Office action, in which case the patent owner may desire to consider the advisability of filing a reissue application to have such issues considered and resolved.

§1.907 *Inter partes* reexamination prohibited.

(a) Once an order to reexamine has been issued under §1.931, neither the third-party requester, nor its privies, may file a subsequent request for *inter partes* reexamination of the patent until an *inter partes* reexamination certificate is issued under §1.997, unless authorized by the Director.

(b) Once a final decision has been entered against a party in a civil action arising in whole or in part under 28 U.S.C. 1338 that the party has not sustained its burden of proving invalidity of any patent claim in suit, then neither that party nor its privies may thereafter request *inter partes* reexamination of any such patent claim on the basis of issues which that party, or its privies, raised or could have raised in such civil action, and an *inter partes* reexamination requested by that party, or its privies, on the basis of such issues may not thereafter be maintained by the Office.

(c) If a final decision in an *inter partes* reexamination proceeding instituted by a third-party requester is favorable to patentability of any original, proposed amended, or new claims of the patent, then neither that party nor its privies may thereafter request *inter partes* reexamination of any such patent claims on the basis of issues which that party, or its privies, raised or could have raised in such *inter partes* reexamination proceeding.

§1.913 Persons eligible to file request for *inter partes* reexamination.

Except as provided for in §1.907, any person other than the patent owner or its privies may, at any time during the period of enforceability of a patent which issued from an original application filed in the United States on or after November 29, 1999, file a request for *inter partes* reexamination by the Office of any claim of the patent on the basis of prior art patents or printed publications cited under §1.501.

§1.915 Content of request for *inter partes* reexamination.

(a) The request must be accompanied by the fee for requesting *inter partes* reexamination set in §1.20(c)(2).

(b) A request for *inter partes* reexamination must include the following parts:

(1) An identification of the patent by patent number and every claim for which reexamination is requested.

(2) A citation of the patents and printed publications which are presented to provide a substantial new question of patentability.

(3) A statement pointing out each substantial new question of patentability based on the cited patents and printed publications, and a detailed explanation of the pertinency and manner of applying the patents and printed publications to every claim for which reexamination is requested.

(4) A copy of every patent or printed publication relied upon or referred to in paragraphs (b)(1)–(3) of this section, accompanied by an English language translation of all the necessary and pertinent parts of any non-English language document.

(5) A copy of the entire patent including the front face, drawings, and specification/claims (in double column format) for which reexamination is requested, and a copy of any disclaimer, certificate of correction, or reexamination certificate issued in the patent. All copies must have each page plainly written on only one side of a sheet of paper.

(6) A certification by the third-party requester that a copy of the request has been served in its entirety on the patent owner at the address as provided for in §1.33(c). The name and address of the party served must be indicated. If service was not possible, a duplicate copy of the request must be supplied to the Office.

(7) A certification by the third-party requester that the estoppel provisions of §1.907 do not prohibit the *inter partes* reexamination.

(8) A statement identifying the real party in interest to the extent necessary for a subsequent person filing an *inter partes* reexamination request to determine whether that person is a privy.

(c) If an *inter partes* request is filed by an attorney or agent identifying another party on whose behalf the request is being filed, the attorney or agent must have a power of attorney from that party or be acting in a representative capacity pursuant to §1.34(a).

(d) If the *inter partes* request does not meet all the requirements of §1.915(b), the person identified as requesting *inter partes* reexamination may be so notified and given an opportunity to complete the formal requirements of the request within a specified time. Failure to comply with the notice may result in the *inter partes* reexamination proceeding being vacated.

§1.919 Filing date of request for *inter partes* reexamination.

(a) The filing date of a request for *inter partes* reexamination is the date on which the request satisfies the fee requirement of §1.915(a).

(b) If the request is not granted a filing date, the request will be placed in the patent file as a citation of prior art if it complies with the requirements of §1.501.

§1.923 Examiner's determination on the request for *inter partes* reexamination.

Within three months following the filing date of a request for *inter partes* reexamination under §1.919, the examiner will consider the request and determine whether or not a substantial new question of patentability affecting any claim of the patent is raised by the request and the prior art citation. The examiner's determination will be based on the claims in effect at the time of the determination and will become a part of the official file of the patent and will be mailed to the patent owner at the address as provided for in §1.33(c) and to the third-party requester. If the examiner determines that no substantial new question of patentability is present, the examiner shall refuse the request and shall not order *inter partes* reexamination.

§1.925 Partial refund if request for *inter partes* reexamination is not ordered.

Where *inter partes* reexamination is not ordered, a refund of a portion of the fee for requesting *inter partes* reexamination will be made to the requester in accordance with §1.26(c).

§1.927 Petition to review refusal to order *inter partes* reexamination.

The third-party requester may seek review by a petition to the Director under §1.181 within one month of the mailing date of the examiner's determination refusing to order *inter partes* reexamination. Any such petition must comply with §1.181(b). If no petition is timely filed, or if the decision on petition affirms that no substantial new question of patentability has been raised, the determination shall be final and non-appealable.

Inter Partes Reexamination of Patents

§1.931 Order for *inter partes* reexamination.

(a) If a substantial new question of patentability is found, the determination will include an order for *inter partes* reexamination of the patent for resolution of the question.

(b) If the order for *inter partes* reexamination resulted from a petition pursuant to §1.927, the *inter partes* reexamination will ordinarily be conducted by an examiner other than the examiner responsible for the initial determination under §1.923.

Information Disclosure in *Inter Partes* Reexamination

§1.933 Patent owner duty of disclosure in *inter partes* reexamination proceedings.

(a) Each individual associated with the patent owner in an *inter partes* reexamination proceeding has a duty of candor and good faith in dealing with the Office, which includes a duty to disclose to the Office all information known to that individual to be material to patentability in a reexamination proceeding as set forth in §1.555(a) and (b). The duty to disclose all information known to be material to patentability in an *inter partes* reexamination proceeding is deemed to be satisfied by filing a paper in compliance with the requirements set forth in §1.555(a) and (b).

(b) The responsibility for compliance with this section rests upon the individuals designated in paragraph (a) of this section, and no evaluation will be made by the Office in the reexamination proceeding as to compliance with this section. If questions of compliance with this section are discovered during a reexamination proceeding, they will be noted as unresolved questions in accordance with §1.906(c).

Office Actions and Responses (Before the Examiner) in *Inter Partes* Reexamination

§1.935 Initial Office action usually accompanies order for *inter partes* reexamination.

The order for *inter partes* reexamination will usually be accompanied by the initial Office action on the merits of the reexamination.

§1.937 Conduct of *inter partes* reexamination.

(a) All *inter partes* reexamination proceedings, including any appeals to the Board of Patent Appeals and Interferences, will be conducted with special dispatch within the Office, unless the Director makes a determination that there is good cause for suspending the reexamination proceeding.

(b) The *inter partes* reexamination proceeding will be conducted in accordance with §§1.104 through 1.116, the sections governing the application examination process, and will result in the issuance of an *inter partes* reexamination certificate under §1.997, except as otherwise provided.

(c) All communications between the Office and the parties to the *inter partes* reexamination which are directed to the merits of the proceeding must be in writing and filed with the Office for entry into the record of the proceeding.

§1.939 Unauthorized papers in *inter partes* reexamination.

(a) If an unauthorized paper is filed by any party at any time during the *inter partes* reexamination proceeding it will not be considered and may be returned.

(b) Unless otherwise authorized, no paper shall be filed prior to the initial Office action on the merits of the *inter partes* reexamination.

§1.941 Amendments by patent owner in *inter partes* reexamination.

Amendments by patent owner in *inter partes* reexamination proceedings are made by filing a paper in compliance with §§1.530(d) and 1.943.

§1.943 Requirements of responses, written comments, and briefs in *inter partes* reexamination.

(a) The form of responses, written comments, briefs, appendices, and other papers must be in accordance with the requirements of §1.530(d)(5).

(b) Responses by the patent owner and written comments by the third-party requester shall not exceed 50 pages in length, excluding amendments, appendices of claims, and reference materials such as prior art references.

(c) Appellant briefs by the patent owner and the third-party requester shall not exceed 30 pages or 14,000 words in length, excluding appendices of claims and reference materials such as prior art references. All other briefs by any party shall not exceed 15 pages in length or 7,000 words. If the page limit for any brief is exceeded, a certificate is required stating the number of words contained in the brief.

§1.945 Response to Office action by patent owner in *inter partes* reexamination.

The patent owner will be given at least 30 days to file a response to any Office action on the merits of the *inter partes* reexamination.

§1.947 Comments by third-party requester to patent owner's response in *inter partes* reexamination.

Each time the patent owner files a response to an Office action on the merits, a third-party requester may once file written comments within a period of 30 days from the date of service of the patent owner's response. These comments shall be limited to issues raised by the Office action or the patent owner's response. The time for submitting comments by the third-party requester may not be extended.

§1.948 Limitations on submission of prior art by third-party requester following the order for *inter partes* reexamination.

After the *inter partes* reexamination order, the third-party requester may only cite additional prior art as defined under §1.501 if it is filed as part of a comments submission under §§1.947, 1.951(a) and 1.951(d), and is limited to prior art:

(a) Which is necessary to rebut a finding of fact by the examiner;

(b) Which is necessary to rebut a response of the patent owner; or,

(c) Which became known or available to the third-party requester after the filing of the request for *inter partes* reexamination proceeding where a discussion of the pertinency of each reference to the patentability of at least one claim is included. Prior art submitted under this paragraph (c) must be accompanied by a statement as to when the prior art first became known or available to the third-party requester.

§1.949 Examiner's Office action closing prosecution in *inter partes* reexamination.

Upon consideration of the issues a second or subsequent time, or upon allowance of all claims, the examiner shall issue an Office action treating all claims present in the *inter partes* reexamination, which may be an action closing prosecution. The Office action shall set forth all rejections and determinations not to make a proposed rejection, and the grounds therefor. An Office action will not usually close prosecution if it includes a new ground of rejection which was not previously addressed by the patent owner, unless the new ground was necessitated by an amendment.

§1.951 Options after Office action closing prosecution in *inter partes* reexamination.

(a) After an action closing prosecution in an *inter partes* reexamination, a third-party requester may once file comments limited to the issues raised in the Office action closing prosecution. Such comments must be filed within the time set for response in the Office action closing prosecution.

(b) When a third-party requester does file comments, the patent owner may once file comments responsive to the third-party requester's comments within 30 days from the date of service of the third-party requester's comments on the patent owner.

(c) After an Office action closing prosecution in an *inter partes* reexamination, the patent owner may once file comments limited to the issues raised in the Office action closing prosecution. The comments can include a proposed amendment to the claims, which amendment will be subject to the criteria of §1.116 as to whether or not it shall be admitted. The comments must be filed within the time set for response in the Office action closing prosecution.

(d) When the patent owner does file comments, a third-party requester may once file comments responsive to the patent owner's comments within 30 days from the date of service of patent owner's comments on the third-party requester.

§1.953 Examiner's Right of Appeal Notice in *inter partes* reexamination.

(a) Upon considering the comments of the patent owner and the third-party requester subsequent to the Office action closing prosecution in an *inter partes* reexamination, or upon expiration of the time for submitting such comments, the examiner shall issue a Right of Appeal Notice, unless the examiner reopens prosecution and issues another Office action on the merits.

(b) *Expedited Right of Appeal Notice:* At any time after the patent owner's response to the initial Office action on the merits in an *inter partes* reexamination, the patent owner and all third-party requesters may stipulate that the issues are appropriate for a final action, which would include a final rejection and/or a final determination favorable to patentability, and may request the issuance of a Right of Appeal Notice. The request must have the concurrence of the patent owner and all third-party requesters present in the proceeding and must identify all the appealable issues, and the positions of the patent owner and all third-party requesters on those issues. If the examiner determines that no other issues are present or should be raised, a Right of Appeal Notice limited to the identified issues shall be issued. Any appeal by the parties shall be conducted in accordance with §§1.959–1.983.

(c) The Right of Appeal Notice shall be a final action, which includes a final rejection setting forth each ground of rejection and/or final decision favorable to patentability including each determination not to make a proposed rejection, an identification of the status of each claim, and the reasons for decisions favorable to patentability and/or the grounds of rejection for each claim. No amendment can be made in response to the Right of Appeal Notice. The Right of Appeal Notice shall set a one-month time period for either party to appeal. If no notice of appeal is filed, the *inter partes* reexamination proceeding will be terminated, and the Director will proceed to issue a certificate under §1.997 in accordance with the Right of Appeal Notice.

Interviews Prohibited in *Inter Partes* Reexamination

§1.955 Interviews prohibited in *inter partes* reexamination proceedings.

There will not be any interviews in an *inter partes* reexamination proceeding which discuss the merits of the proceeding.

Extensions of Time, Termination of Proceedings, and Petitions to Revive in *Inter Partes* Reexamination

§1.956 Patent owner extensions of time in *inter partes* reexamination.

The time for taking any action by a patent owner in an *inter partes* reexamination proceeding will be extended only for sufficient cause and for a reasonable time specified. Any request for such extension must be filed on or before the day on which action by the patent owner is due, but in no case will the mere filing of a request effect any extension. See §1.304(a) for extensions of time for filing a notice of appeal to the U.S. Court of Appeals for the Federal Circuit.

§1.957 Failure to file a timely, appropriate or complete response or comment in *inter partes* reexamination.

(a) If the third-party requester files an untimely or inappropriate comment, notice of appeal or brief in an *inter partes* reexamination, the paper will be refused consideration.

(b) If no claims are found patentable, and the patent owner fails to file a timely and appropriate response in an *inter partes* reexamination proceeding, the reexamination proceeding will be terminated and the Director will proceed to issue a certificate under §1.997 in accordance with the last action of the Office.

(c) If claims are found patentable, and the patent owner fails to file a timely and appropriate response to any Office action in an *inter partes* reexamination proceeding, further prosecution will be limited to the claims found patentable at the time of the failure to respond, and to any claims added thereafter which do not expand the scope of the claims which were found patentable at that time.

(d) When action by the patent owner is a *bona fide* attempt to respond and to advance the prosecution, and is substantially a complete response to the Office action, but consideration of some matter or compliance with some requirement has been inadvertently omitted, an opportunity to explain and supply the omission may be given.

§1.958 Petition to revive terminated *inter partes* reexamination or claims terminated for lack of patent owner response.

(a) If a response by the patent owner is not timely filed in the Office, the delay in filing such response may be excused if it is shown to the satisfaction of the Director that the delay was unavoidable. A petition to accept an unavoidably delayed response must be filed in compliance with §1.137(a).

(b) Any response by the patent owner not timely filed in the Office may nevertheless be accepted if the delay was unintentional. A petition to accept an unintentionally delayed response must be filed in compliance with §1.137(b).

Appeal to the Board of Patent Appeals and Interferences in *Inter Partes* Reexamination

§1.959 Notice of appeal and cross appeal to Board of Patent Appeals and Interferences in *inter partes* reexamination.

(a)(1) Upon the issuance of a Right of Appeal Notice under §1.953, the patent owner involved in an *inter partes* reexamination proceeding may appeal to the Board of Patent Appeals and Interferences with respect to the final rejection of any claim of the patent by filing a notice of appeal within the time provided in the Right of Appeal Notice and paying the fee set forth in §1.17(b).

(2) Upon the issuance of a Right of Appeal Notice under §1.953, a third-party requester involved in an *inter partes* reexamination proceeding may appeal to the Board of Patent Appeals and Interferences with respect to any final decision favorable to the patentability, including any final determination not to make a proposed rejection, of any original or proposed amended or new claim of the patent by filing a notice of appeal within the time provided in the Right of Appeal Notice and paying the fee set forth in §1.17(b).

(b)(1) Within fourteen days of service of a third-party requester's notice of appeal under paragraph (a)(2) of this section, and upon payment of the fee set forth in §1.17(b), a patent owner who has not filed a notice of appeal may file a notice of cross appeal with respect to the final rejection of any claim of the patent.

(2) Within fourteen days of service of a patent owner's notice of appeal under paragraph (a)(1) of this section, and upon payment of the fee set forth in §1.17(b), a third-party requester who has not filed a notice of appeal may file a notice of cross appeal with respect to any final decision favorable to the patentability, including any final determination not to make a proposed rejection, of any original or proposed amended or new claim of the patent.

(c) The notice of appeal or cross appeal in an *inter partes* reexamination proceeding must identify the claim(s) with respect to which an appeal is being taken, and must be signed by the patent owner or third-party requester, or their duly authorized attorney or agent.

(d) An appeal or cross appeal when taken must be taken from all the rejections of the claims under rejection in a Right of Appeal Notice which the patent owner proposes to contest, or from all the determinations favorable to patentability, including any final determination not to make a proposed rejection, in a Right of Appeal Notice which a third-party requester proposes to contest. Questions relating to matters not affecting the merits of the invention may be required to be settled before an appeal is decided.

(e) The times for filing a notice of appeal or cross-appeal may not be extended.

§1.961 Jurisdiction over appeal in *inter partes* reexamination.

Jurisdiction over the *inter partes* reexamination proceeding passes to the Board of Patent Appeals and Interferences upon transmittal of the file, including all briefs and examiner's answers, to the Board of Patent Appeals and Interferences. Prior to the entry of a decision on the appeal, the Director may sua sponte order the *inter partes* reexamination proceeding remanded to the examiner, for action consistent with the Director's order.

§1.962 Appellant and respondent in *inter partes* reexamination defined.

For the purposes of *inter partes* reexamination, appellant is any party, whether the patent owner or a third-party requester, filing a notice of appeal or cross appeal. If more than one party appeals or cross appeals, each appealing or cross appealing party is an appellant with respect to the claims to which his or her appeal or cross appeal is directed. A respondent is any third-party requester responding under §1.967 to the appellant brief of the patent owner, or the patent owner responding under §1.967 to the appellant brief of any third-party requester. No third-party requester may be a respondent to the appellant brief of any other third-party requester.

§1.963 Time for filing briefs in *inter partes* reexamination.

(a) An appellant brief in an *inter partes* reexamination must be filed no later than two months from the latest of the filing date of the last-filed notice of appeal or cross appeal or if any party to the *inter partes* reexamination is entitled to file an appeal or cross appeal but fails to timely do so, the expiration of time for filing (by the last party entitled to do so) such notice of appeal or cross appeal. The time for filing an appellant brief may not be extended.

(b) Once an appellant brief has been properly filed, any respondent brief must be filed within one month from the date of service of the appellant brief. The time for filing a respondent brief may not be extended.

(c) The examiner will consider both the appellant and respondent briefs and may prepare an examiner's answer under §1.969.

(d) Any appellant may file a rebuttal brief under §1.971 within one month of the date of the examiner's answer. The time for filing a rebuttal brief may not be extended.

(e) No further submission will be considered and any such submission will be treated in accordance with §1.939.

§1.965 Appellant brief in *inter partes* reexamination.

(a) Appellant(s) may once, within time limits for filing set forth in §1.963, file a brief in triplicate and serve the brief on all other parties to the *inter partes* reexamination proceeding in accordance with §1.903. The brief must be signed by the appellant, or the appellant's duly authorized attorney or agent, and must be accompanied by the requisite fee set forth in §1.17(c). The brief must set forth the authorities and arguments on which appellant will rely to maintain the appeal. Any arguments or authorities not included in the brief will be refused consideration by the Board of Patent Appeals and Interferences, unless good cause is shown.

(b) On failure of a party to file an appellant brief, accompanied by the requisite fee, within the time allowed, that party's appeal shall stand dismissed.

(c) The appellant brief shall contain the following items under appropriate headings and in the order indicated below, unless the brief is filed by a party who is not represented by a registered practitioner. The brief may include an appendix containing only those portions of the record on which reliance has been made.

(1) *Real Party in Interest.* A statement identifying the real party in interest.

(2) *Related Appeals and Interferences.* A statement identifying by number and filing date all other appeals or interferences known to the appellant, the appellant's legal representative, or assignee which will directly affect or be directly affected by or have a bearing on the decision of the Board of Patent Appeals and Interferences in the pending appeal.

(3) *Status of Claims.* A statement of the status of all the claims, pending or canceled. If the appellant is the patent owner, the appellant must also identify the rejected claims whose rejection is being appealed. If the appellant is a third-party requester, the appellant must identify the claims that the examiner has made a determination favorable to patentability, which determination is being appealed.

(4) *Status of Amendments.* A statement of the status of any amendment filed subsequent to the close of prosecution.

(5) *Summary of Invention.* A concise explanation of the invention or subject matter defined in the claims involved in the appeal, which shall refer to the specification by column and line number, and to the drawing(s), if any, by reference characters.

(6) *Issues.* A concise statement of the issues presented for review. No new ground of rejection can be proposed by a third-party requester appellant.

(7) *Grouping of Claims.* If the appellant is the patent owner, for each ground of rejection in the right of appeal notice which appellant contests and which applies to a group of two or more claims, the Board of Patent Appeals and Interferences shall select a single claim from the group and shall decide the appeal as to

the ground of rejection on the basis of that claim alone unless a statement is included that the claims of the group do not stand or fall together and, in the argument under paragraph (c)(8) of this section, appellant explains why the claims of this group are believed to be separately patentable. Merely pointing out differences in what the claims cover is not an argument as to why the claims are separately patentable.

(8) *Argument*. The contentions of appellant with respect to each of the issues presented for review in paragraph (c)(6) of this section, and the bases therefor, with citations of the authorities, statutes, and parts of the record relied on. Each issue should be treated under a separate, numbered heading.

(i) For each rejection under 35 U.S.C. 112, first paragraph, or for each determination favorable to patentability including a determination not to make a proposed rejection under 35 U.S.C. 112, first paragraph, which appellant contests, the argument shall specify the errors in the rejection or the determination and how the first paragraph of 35 U.S.C. 112 is complied with, if the appellant is the patent owner, or is not complied with, if the appellant is a third-party requester, including, as appropriate, how the specification and drawing(s), if any,

(A) Describe, if the appellant is the patent owner, or fail to describe, if the appellant is a third-party requester, the subject matter defined by each of the appealed claims, and

(B) Enable, if the appellant is the patent owner, or fail to enable, if the appellant is a third-party requester, any person skilled in the art to make and use the subject matter defined by each of the appealed claims, and

(ii) For each rejection under 35 U.S.C. 112, second paragraph, or for each determination favorable to patentability including a determination not to make a proposed rejection under 35 U.S.C. 112, second paragraph, which appellant contests, the argument shall specify the errors in the rejection, if the appellant is the patent owner, or the determination, if the appellant is a third-party requester, and how the claims do, if the appellant is the patent owner, or do not, if the appellant is a third-party requester, particularly point out and distinctly claim the subject matter which the inventors regard as the invention.

(iii) For each rejection under 35 U.S.C. 102 or for each determination favorable to patentability including a determination not to make a proposed rejection under 35 U.S.C. 102 which appellant contests, the argument shall specify the errors in the rejection, if the appellant is the patent owner, or determination, if the appellant is a third-party requester, and why the appealed claims are, if the appellant is the patent owner, or are not, if the appellant is a third-party requester, patentable under 35 U.S.C. 102, including any specific limitations in the appealed claims which are or are not described in the prior art.

(iv) For each rejection under 35 U.S.C. 103 or for each determination favorable to patentability including a determination not to make a proposed rejection under 35 U.S.C. 103 which appellant contests, the argument shall specify the errors in the rejection, if the appellant is the patent owner, or determination, if the appellant is a third-party requester, and, if appropriate, the specific limitations in the appealed claims which are or are not described in the prior art, and shall explain how such limitations render the claimed subject matter obvious, if the appellant is a third-party requester, or unobvious, if the appellant is the patent owner, over the prior art. If the rejection or determination is based upon a combination of references, the argument shall explain why the references, taken as a whole, do or do not suggest the claimed subject matter, and shall include, as may be appropriate, an explanation of why features disclosed in one reference may or may not properly be combined with features disclosed in another reference. A general argument that all the limitations are or are not described in a single reference does not satisfy the requirements of this paragraph.

(v) For any rejection other than those referred to in paragraphs (c)(8)(i) to (iv) of this section or for each determination favorable to patentability including any determination not to make a proposed rejection other than those referred to in paragraphs (c)(8)(i) to (iv) of this section which appellant contests, the argument shall specify the errors in the rejection, if the appellant is the patent owner, or determination, if the appellant is a third-party requester, and the specific limitations in the appealed claims, if appropriate, or other reasons, which cause the rejection or determination to be in error.

(9) *Appendix.* An appendix containing a copy of the claims appealed by the appellant.

(10) *Certificate of Service.* A certification that a copy of the brief has been served in its entirety on all other parties to the reexamination proceeding. The names and addresses of the parties served must be indicated.

(d) If a brief is filed which does not comply with all the requirements of paragraph (c) of this section, appellant will be notified of the reasons for non-compliance and provided with a non-extendable period of one month within which to file an amended brief. If the appellant does not file an amended brief during the one-month period, or files an amended brief which does not overcome all the reasons for non-compliance stated in the notification, that appellant's appeal will stand dismissed.

§1.967 Respondent brief in *inter partes* reexamination.

(a) Respondent(s) in an *inter partes* reexamination appeal may once, within time limit for filing set forth in §1.963, file a respondent brief in triplicate and serve the brief on all parties in accordance with §1.903. The brief must be signed by the party, or the party's duly authorized attorney or agent, and must be accompanied by the requisite fee set forth in §1.17(c). The brief must set forth the authorities and arguments on which respondent will rely. Any arguments or authorities not included in the brief will be refused consideration by the Board of Patent Appeals and Interferences, unless good cause is shown. The respondent brief shall be limited to issues raised in the appellant brief to which the respondent brief is directed. A third-party respondent brief may not address any brief of any other third-party.

(b) The respondent brief shall contain the following items under appropriate headings and in the order here indicated, and may include an appendix containing only those portions of the record on which reliance has been made.

(1) *Real Party in Interest.* A statement identifying the real party in interest.

(2) *Related Appeals and Interferences.* A statement identifying by number and filing date all other appeals or interferences known to the respondent, the respondent's legal representative, or assignee (if any) which will directly affect or be directly affected by or have a bearing on the decision of the Board of Patent Appeals and Interferences in the pending appeal.

(3) *Status of Claims.* A statement accepting or disputing appellant's statement of the status of claims. If appellant's statement of the status of claims is disputed, the errors in appellant's statement must be specified with particularity.

(4) *Status of Amendments.* A statement accepting or disputing appellant's statement of the status of amendments. If appellant's statement of the status of amendments is disputed, the errors in appellant's statement must be specified with particularity.

(5) *Summary of Invention.* A statement accepting or disputing appellant's summary of the invention or subject matter defined in the claims involved in the appeal. If appellant's summary of the invention or subject matter defined in the claims involved in the appeal is disputed, the errors in appellant's summary must be specified with particularity.

(6) *Issues.* A statement accepting or disputing appellant's statement of the issues presented for review. If appellant's statement of the issues presented for review is disputed, the errors in appellant's statement must be specified with particularity. A counter statement of the issues for review may be made. No new ground of rejection can be proposed by a third-party requester respondent.

(7) *Argument.* A statement accepting or disputing the contentions of the appellant with each of the issues. If a contention of the appellant is disputed, the

errors in appellant's argument must be specified with particularity, stating the basis therefor, with citations of the authorities, statutes and parts of the record relied on. Each issue should be treated under a separate heading. An argument may be made with each of the issues stated in the counter statement of the issues, with each counter-stated issue being treated under a separate heading. The provisions of §§1.965(c)(8)(iii) and (iv) shall apply to any argument raised under 35 U.S.C. 102 or 103.

(8) *Certificate of Service*. A certification that a copy of the respondent brief has been served in its entirety on all other parties to the reexamination proceeding. The names and addresses of the parties served must be indicated.

(c) If a respondent brief is filed which does not comply with all the requirements of paragraph (b) of this section, respondent will be notified of the reasons for non-compliance and provided with a non-extendable period of one month within which to file an amended brief. If the respondent does not file an amended brief during the one-month period, or files an amended brief which does not overcome all the reasons for non-compliance stated in the notification, the respondent brief will not be considered.

§1.969 Examiner's answer in *inter partes* reexamination.

(a) The primary examiner in an *inter partes* reexamination appeal may, within such time as directed by the Director, furnish a written statement in answer to the patent owner's and/or third-party requester's appellant brief or respondent brief including, as may be necessary, such explanation of the invention claimed and of the references, the grounds of rejection, and the reasons for patentability including grounds for not adopting a proposed rejection. A copy of the answer shall be supplied to all parties to the reexamination proceeding. If the primary examiner finds that the appeal is not regular in form or does not relate to an appealable action, he or she shall so state.

(b) An examiner's answer may not include a new ground of rejection.

(c) Where a third-party requester is a party to the appeal, an examiner's answer may not include a new determination not to make a proposed rejection of a claim.

§1.971 Rebuttal brief in *inter partes* reexamination.

Within one month of the examiner's answer in an *inter partes* reexamination appeal, any appellant may once file a rebuttal brief in triplicate. The rebuttal brief of the patent owner may be directed to the examiner's answer and/or any respondent brief. The rebuttal brief of any third-party requester may be directed to the examiner's answer and/or the respondent brief of the patent owner. The rebuttal brief of a third-party requester may not be directed to the respondent brief of any other third-party requester. No new ground of rejection can be proposed by a third-party requester appellant. The time for filing a rebuttal brief may not be extended. The rebuttal brief must include a certification that a copy of the rebuttal brief has been served in its entirety on all other parties to the reexamination proceeding. The names and addresses of the parties served must be indicated.

§1.973 Oral hearing in *inter partes* reexamination.

(a) An oral hearing in an *inter partes* reexamination appeal should be requested only in those circumstances in which an appellant or a respondent considers such a hearing necessary or desirable for a proper presentation of the appeal. An appeal decided without an oral hearing will receive the same consideration by the Board of Patent Appeals and Interferences as an appeal decided after oral hearing.

(b) If an appellant or a respondent desires an oral hearing, he or she must file a written request for such hearing accompanied by the fee set forth in §1.17(d) within two months after the date of the examiner's answer. The time for requesting an oral hearing may not be extended.

(c) An oral argument may be presented at oral hearing by, or on behalf of, the primary examiner if considered desirable by either the primary examiner or the Board of Patent Appeals and Interferences.

(d) If an appellant or a respondent has requested an oral hearing and has submitted the fee set forth in §1.17(d), a hearing date will be set, and notice given to all parties to the reexamination proceeding, and to the primary examiner. The notice shall set a period within which all requests for oral hearing shall be submitted by any other party to the appeal desiring to participate in the oral hearing, which period will not be extended. A hearing will be held as stated in the notice, and oral argument will be limited to thirty minutes for each appellant and respondent who has requested an oral hearing, and twenty minutes for the primary examiner unless otherwise ordered before the hearing begins. No appellant or respondent will be permitted to participate in an oral hearing unless he or she has requested an oral hearing and submitted the fee set forth in §1.17(d).

(e) If no request and fee for oral hearing have been timely filed by an appellant or a respondent, the appeal will be assigned for consideration and decision on the written record.

§1.975 Affidavits or declarations after appeal in *inter partes* reexamination.

Affidavits, declarations, or exhibits submitted after the *inter partes* reexamination has been appealed will not be admitted without a showing of good and sufficient reasons why they were not earlier presented.

§1.977 Decision by the Board of Patent Appeals and Interferences; remand to examiner in *inter partes* reexamination.

(a) The Board of Patent Appeals and Interferences, in its decision, may affirm or reverse each decision of the examiner on all issues raised on each appealed claim, or remand the reexamination proceeding to the examiner for further consideration. The reversal of the examiner's determination not to make a rejection proposed by the third-party requester constitutes a decision adverse to the patentability of the claims which are subject to that proposed rejection which will be set forth in the decision of the Board of Patent Appeals and Interferences as a new ground of rejection under paragraph (b) of this section. The affirmance of the rejection of a claim on any of the grounds specified constitutes a general affirmance of the decision of the examiner on that claim, except as to any ground specifically reversed.

(b) Should the Board of Patent Appeals and Interferences have knowledge of any grounds not raised in the appeal for rejecting any pending claim, it may include in the decision a statement to that effect with its reasons for so holding, which statement shall constitute a new ground of rejection of the claim. A decision which includes a new ground of rejection shall not be considered final for purposes of judicial review. When the Board of Patent Appeals and Interferences makes a new ground of rejection, the patent owner, within one month from the date of the decision, must exercise one of the following two options with respect to the new ground of rejection to avoid termination of the appeal proceeding as to the rejected claim:

(1) The patent owner may submit an appropriate amendment of the claim so rejected or a showing of facts relating to the claim, or both. The reexamination proceeding will be remanded to the examiner for consideration. The statement of the Board of Patent Appeals and Interferences shall be binding upon the examiner unless an amendment or showing of facts not previously of record be made which, in the opinion of the examiner, overcomes the new ground of rejection.

(2) The patent owner may file a request for rehearing of the decision of the Board of Patent Appeals and Interferences under §1.979(a).

(c) The Board of Patent Appeals and Interferences, in its decision, may include an explicit statement that a claim may be allowed in amended form. The decision shall not be considered a final decision for purposes of judicial review if the patent owner, within one month of the date of the decision, submits an appropriate amendment of the claim in conformity with such statement, in which event the reexamination proceeding will be remanded to the examiner. The statement shall be binding on the examiner in the absence of new references or new grounds of rejection.

(d) Where the patent owner has responded under paragraph (b)(1) or (c) of this section, any third-party requester, within one month of the date of service of the patent owner response, may once file comments on the response. Such written comments must be limited to the issues raised by the decision of the Board of Patent Appeals and Interferences and the patent owner's response. Any third-party requester that had not previously filed an appeal or cross appeal and is seeking under this subsection to file comments or a reply to the comments is subject to the appeal and brief fees under §§1.17(b) and (c), respectively, which must accompany the comments or reply.

(e) Following any response by the patent owner under paragraph (b)(1) or (c) of this section and any written comments from a third-party requester under paragraph (d) of this section, the reexamination proceeding will be remanded to the examiner. The examiner will consider any response under paragraph (b)(1) or (c) of this section and any written comments by a third-party requester under paragraph (d) of this section and issue a determination that the rejection should be maintained or has been overcome.

(f) Within one month of the examiner's determination pursuant to paragraph (e) of this section, the patent owner or any third-party requester may once submit comments in response to the examiner's determination. Within one month of the date of service of comments in response to the examiner's determination, any party may file a reply to the comments. Any third-party requester that had not previously filed an appeal or cross appeal and is seeking under this subsection to file comments or a reply to the comments is subject to the appeal and brief fees under §§1.17(b) and (c), respectively, which must accompany the comments or reply.

(g) After submission of any comments and any reply pursuant to paragraph (f) of this section, or after time has expired therefor, the reexamination proceeding will be returned to the Board of Patent Appeals and Interferences which shall reconsider the matter and issue a new decision. The new decision is deemed to incorporate the earlier decision, except for those portions specifically withdrawn.

(h) The time periods set forth in paragraphs (b) and (c) of this section are subject to the extension of time provisions of §1.956. The time periods set forth in subsections (d) and (f) may not be extended.

§1.979 Action following decision by the Board of Patent Appeals and Interferences or dismissal of appeal in *inter partes* reexamination.

(a) Parties to the appeal may file a request for rehearing of the decision within one month of the date of:

(1) The original decision of the Board of Patent Appeals and Interferences under §1.977(a),

(2) The original §1.977(b) decision under the provisions of §1.977(b)(2),

(3) The expiration of the time for the patent owner to take action under §1.977(b)(2) or (c), or

(4) The new decision of the Board of Patent Appeals and Interferences under §1.977(g).

(b) Within one month of the date of service of any request for rehearing under paragraph (a) of this section, or any further request for rehearing under paragraph (c) of this section, any party to the appeal may once file comments in opposition to the request for rehearing or the further request for rehearing. The comments in opposition must be limited to the issues raised in the request for rehearing or the further request for rehearing.

(c) If a party to an appeal files a request for rehearing under paragraph (a) of this section, or a further request for rehearing under this section, the Board of Patent Appeals and Interferences will issue a decision on rehearing which decision is deemed to incorporate the earlier decision, except for those portions specifically withdrawn. If the decision on rehearing becomes, in effect, a new decision, and the Board of Patent Appeals and Interferences so states, then any party to the appeal may, within one month of the new decision, once file a further request for rehearing of the new decision under this subsection.

(d) Any request for rehearing shall state with particularity the points believed to have been misapprehended or overlooked in rendering the decision and also state all other grounds upon which rehearing is sought.

(e) The patent owner may not appeal to the U.S. Court of Appeals for the Federal Circuit under §1.983 until all parties' rights to request rehearing have been exhausted, at which time the decision of the Board of Patent Appeals and Interferences is final and appealable by the patent owner.

(f) An appeal by a third-party requester is considered terminated by the dismissal of the third-party requester's appeal, the failure of the third-party requester to timely request rehearing under §§1.979(a) or (c), or a final decision under §1.979(e). The date of such termination is the date on which the appeal is dismissed, the date on which the time for rehearing expires, or the decision of the Board of Patent Appeals and Interferences is final. An appeal by the patent owner is considered terminated by the dismissal of the patent owner's appeal, the failure of the patent owner to timely request rehearing under §§1.979(a) or (c), or the failure of the patent owner to timely file an appeal to the U.S. Court of Appeals for the Federal Circuit under §1.983. The date of such termination is the date on which the appeal is dismissed, the date on which the time for rehearing expires, or the date on which the time for the patent owner's appeal to the U.S. Court of Appeals for the Federal Circuit expires. If an appeal to the U.S. Court of Appeals for the Federal Circuit has been filed, the patent owner's appeal is considered terminated when the mandate is received by the Office. Upon termination of an appeal, if no other appeal is present, the reexamination proceeding will be terminated and the Director will issue a certificate under §1.997.

(g) The times for requesting rehearing under paragraph (a) of this section, for requesting further rehearing under paragraph (c) of this section, and for submitting comments under paragraph (b) of this section may not be extended.

§1.981 Reopening after decision by the Board of Patent Appeals and Interferences in *inter partes* reexamination.

Cases which have been decided by the Board of Patent Appeals and Interferences will not be reopened or reconsidered by the primary examiner except under the provisions of §1.977 without the written authority of the Director, and then only for the consideration of matters not already adjudicated, sufficient cause being shown.

Patent Owner Appeal to the United States Court of Appeals for the Federal Circuit in *Inter Partes* Reexamination

§1.983 Patent owner appeal to the United States Court of Appeals for the Federal Circuit in *inter partes* reexamination.

The patent owner in a reexamination proceeding who is dissatisfied with the decision of the Board of Patent Appeals and Interferences may, subject to §1.979(e), appeal to the U.S. Court of Appeals for the Federal Circuit. The appellant must take the following steps in such an appeal:

(1) In the U.S. Patent and Trademark Office file a timely written notice of appeal directed to the Director in accordance with §§1.302 and 1.304; and

(2) In the Court, file a copy of the notice of appeal and pay the fee, as provided for in the rules of the Court.

Concurrent Proceedings Involving Same Patent in *Inter Partes* Reexamination

§1.985 Notification of prior or concurrent proceedings in *inter partes* reexamination.

(a) In any *inter partes* reexamination proceeding, the patent owner shall call the attention of the Office to any prior or concurrent proceedings in which the patent is or was involved, including but not limited to interference, reissue, reexamination, or litigation and the results of such proceedings.

(b) Notwithstanding any provision of the rules, any person at any time may file a paper in an *inter partes* reexamination proceeding notifying the Office of a prior or concurrent proceedings in which the same patent is or was involved, including but not limited to interference, reissue, reexamination, or litigation and the results of such proceedings. Such paper must be limited to merely providing notice of the other proceeding without discussion of issues of the current *inter partes* reexamination proceeding. Any paper not so limited will be returned to the sender.

§1.987 Suspension of *inter partes* reexamination proceeding due to litigation.

If a patent in the process of *inter partes* reexamination is or becomes involved in litigation, the Director shall determine whether or not to suspend the *inter partes* reexamination proceeding.

§1.989 Merger of concurrent reexamination proceedings.

(a) If any reexamination is ordered while a prior *inter partes* reexamination proceeding is pending for the same patent, a decision may be made to merge the two proceedings or to suspend one of the two proceedings. Where merger is ordered, the merged examination will normally result in the issuance of a single reexamination certificate under §1.997.

(b) An *inter partes* reexamination proceeding filed under §1.913 which is merged with an *ex parte* reexamination proceeding filed under §1.510 will result in the merged proceeding being governed by §§1.902–1.997, except that the rights of any third-party requester of the *ex parte* reexamination shall be governed by §§1.510–1.560.

§1.991 Merger of concurrent reissue application and *inter partes* reexamination proceeding.

If a reissue application and an *inter partes* reexamination proceeding on which an order pursuant to §1.931 has been mailed are pending concurrently on a patent, a decision may be made to merge the two proceedings or to suspend one of the two proceedings. Where merger of a reissue application and an *inter partes* reexamination proceeding is ordered, the merged proceeding will be conducted in accordance with §§1.171 through 1.179 and the patent owner will be required to place and maintain the same claims in the reissue application and the *inter partes* reexamination proceeding during the pendency of the merged proceeding. In a merged proceeding the third-party requester may participate to the extent provided under §§1.902–1.997, except such participation shall be limited to issues within the scope of *inter partes* reexamination. The examiner's actions and any responses by the patent owner or third-party requester in a merged proceeding will apply to both the reissue application and the *inter partes* reexamination proceeding and be physically entered into both files. Any *inter partes* reexamination proceeding merged with a reissue application shall be terminated by the grant of the reissued patent.

§1.993 Suspension of concurrent interference and *inter partes* reexamination proceeding.

If a patent in the process of *inter partes* reexamination is or becomes involved in an interference, the Director may suspend the *inter partes* reexamination or the interference. The Director will not consider a request to suspend an interference unless a motion under §1.635 to suspend the interference has been presented to, and denied by, an administrative patent judge and the request is filed within ten (10) days of a decision by an administrative patent judge denying the motion for suspension or such other time as the administrative patent judge may set.

§1.995 Third-party requester's participation rights preserved in merged proceeding.

When a third-party requester is involved in one or more proceedings including an *inter partes* reexamination proceeding, the merger of such proceedings will be accomplished so as to preserve the third-party requester's right to participate to the extent specifically provided for in these regulations. In merged proceedings involving different requesters, any paper filed by one party in the merged proceeding shall be served on all other parties of the merged proceeding.

Reexamination Certificate in *Inter Partes* Reexamination

§1.997 Issuance of *inter partes* reexamination certificate.

(a) Upon the conclusion of an *inter partes* reexamination proceeding, the Director will issue a certificate in accordance with 35 U.S.C. 316 setting forth the results of the *inter partes* reexamination proceeding and the content of the patent following the *inter partes* reexamination proceeding.

(b) A certificate will be issued in each patent in which an *inter partes* reexamination proceeding has been ordered under §1.931. Any statutory disclaimer filed by the patent owner will be made part of the certificate.

(c) The certificate will be sent to the patent owner at the address as provided for in §1.33(c). A copy of the certificate will also be sent to the third-party requester of the *inter partes* reexamination proceeding.

(d) If a certificate has been issued which cancels all of the claims of the patent, no further Office proceedings will be conducted with regard to that patent or any reissue applications or any reexamination requests relating thereto.

(e) If the *inter partes* reexamination proceeding is terminated by the grant of a reissued patent as provided in §1.991, the reissued patent will constitute the reexamination certificate required by this section and 35 U.S.C. 316.

(f) A notice of the issuance of each certificate under this section will be published in the *Official Gazette*.

Dated: March 30, 2000.

Q. Todd Dickinson,
Under Secretary of Commerce for Intellectual Property and Director of the United States, Patent and Trademark Office.
[FR Doc. 00-8284 Filed 4-5-00; 8:45 am]

Table of Cases

*References are to chapter and footnote number (e.g., **2:** 27 refers to footnote 27 in supplement chapter 2). MV indicates an update in this supplement to a footnote in the main volume (e.g., **MV2:** 189 refers to footnote 189 in main volume chapter 2). For the updates to the main volume, only new cases are included in the table. Alphabetization is letter-by-letter (e.g., "Marketing" precedes "Mark I Mktg. Corp.").*

D

Duve, In re, Civ. No. App. 97-1095 (Fed. Cir. Feb. 26, 1999) (unpublished) ***2:*** 5

E

Eagle Iron Works v. McLanahan Corp., 429 F.2d 1375, 166 USPQ 225 (3d Cir. 1970) ***12:*** 301, 331
Eastman Kodak Co. v. Goodyear Tire & Rubber Co., 114 F.3d 1547, 42 USPQ 2d 1737 (Fed. Cir. 1997), *overruled by* Cybor Corp. v. FAS Techs., Inc., 138 F.3d 1448, 46 USPQ 2d 1169 (Fed. Cir. 1998) ***2:*** 50
Ecolochem, Inc. v. Southern Cal. Edison Co., 227 F.3d 1361, 56 USPQ 2d 1065 (Fed. Cir. 2000), *cert. denied,* 121 S. Ct. 1607 (2001) ***6:*** 7
Edwards, In re, 440 F.2d 1380, 169 USPQ 480 (C.C.P.A. 1971) ***7:*** 39
Egbert v. Lippmann, 104 U.S. 333 (1881) ***6:*** 44; ***7:*** 203
Eibel Process Co. v. Minnesota & Ontario Paper Co., 261 U.S. 45 (1923) ***MV6:*** 328
E.I. du Pont de Nemours & Co. v. Phillips Petroleum Co., 849 F.2d 1430, 7 USPQ 2d 1129 (Fed. Cir. 1988) ***1:*** 53; ***2:*** 39, 45
Eisenberg v. Alimed, Inc., Civ. App. No. 98-317 (Fed. Cir. Aug. 8, 2000) (unpublished) ***2:*** 66
Ekchian v. Home Depot, Inc., 104 F.3d 1299, 41 USPQ 2d 1364 (Fed. Cir. 1997) ***9:*** 9
Electro Med. Sys., S.A. v. Cooper Life Sciences, Inc., 34 F.3d 1048, 32 USPQ 2d 1017 (Fed. Cir. 1994) ***2:*** 52, 103; ***9:*** 48
Elekta Instrument S.A. v. O.U.R. Scientific Int'l, Inc., 214 F.3d 1302, 54 USPQ 2d 1910 (Fed. Cir. 2000) ***2:*** 54
Eli Lilly & Co. v. Barr Labs.
  222 F.3d 973, 55 USPQ 2d 1609 (Fed. Cir. 2000) ***MV8:*** 443
  251 F.3d 955, 58 USPQ 2d 1865 (Fed. Cir. 2001) ***8:*** 98, 99, 102; ***10:*** 83–85
Elizabeth, City of v. American Nicholson Pavement Co., 97 U.S. (7 Otto.) 126 (1878) ***6:*** 24
Elkay Mfg. Co. v. Ebco Mfg. Co., 192 F.3d 973, 52 USPQ 2d 1109 (Fed. Cir. 1999), *cert. denied,* 529 U.S. 1066 (2000) ***2:*** 113, 160, 161, 163, 164; ***9:*** 39–42; ***10:*** 22, 23
Eltgroth, In re, 419 F.2d 918, 164 USPQ 221 (C.C.P.A. 1970) ***8:*** 54
Emert, In re, 124 F.3d 1458, 44 USPQ 2d 1149 (Fed. Cir. 1997) ***7:*** 61; ***10:*** 65
EMI Group N. Am., Inc. v. Intel Corp., 157 F.3d 887, 48 USPQ 2d 1181 (Fed. Cir. 1998), *cert. denied,* 526 U.S. 1112 (1999) ***2:*** 82, 169; ***10:*** 90
Engel Indus., Inc. v. Lockformer Co., 946 F.2d 1528, 20 USPQ 2d 1300 (Fed. Cir. 1991) ***8:*** 96, 98
Envirco Corp. v. Clestra Cleanroom, Inc., 209 F.3d 1360, 54 USPQ 2d 1449 (Fed. Cir. 2000) ***7:*** 102–07
Environmental Designs, Ltd. v. Union Oil Co. of Cal., 713 F.2d 693, 218 USPQ 865 (Fed. Cir. 1983) ***7:*** 57
Envirotech Corp. v. Al George, Inc., 730 F.2d 753, 221 USPQ 473 (Fed. Cir. 1984) ***2:*** 45; ***8:*** 52
Enzo APA & Son, Inc. v. Geapag A.G., 134 F.3d 1090, 45 USPQ 2d 1368 (Fed. Cir. 1998) ***3:*** 27, 30
Enzo Biochem, Inc. v. Calgene, Inc., 188 F.3d 1362, 52 USPQ 2d 1129 (Fed. Cir. 1999) ***8:*** 3, 4, 28–31, 45–49
Essilor Int'l v. Nidek Co., Civ. App. No. 98-1558 (Fed. Cir. Oct. 29, 1999) (unpublished) ***9:*** 80–82, 111; ***MV9:*** 545
Estee Lauder, Inc. v. L'Oreal, S.A., 129 F.3d 588, 44 USPQ 2d 1610 (Fed. Cir. 1997) ***4:*** 5
Ethicon
  v. Quigg, 849 F.2d 1422, 7 USPQ 2d 1152 (Fed. Cir. 1988) ***1:*** 2
  v. United States Surgical Corp., 149 F.3d 1309, 47 USPQ 2d 1272 (Fed. Cir. 1998) ***2:*** 77, 81
Etter, In re, 756 F.2d 852, 225 USPQ 1 (Fed. Cir.), *cert. denied,* 464 U.S. 828 (1985) ***12:*** 173, 174
Evans Med. Ltd. v. American Cyanamid Co., 52 USPQ 2d 1455 (Fed. Cir. 1999) (unpublished) ***7:*** 138, 139; ***8:*** 64–67
Ex parte. *See name of party*

F

Feist Publications, Inc. v. Rural Tel. Serv. Co., 499 U.S. 340, 18 USPQ 2d 1275 (1991) ***1:*** 26
Ferrari S.P.A. Esercizio Fabriche Automobile Corse v. Roberts, 944 F.2d 1235, 20 USPQ 2d 1001 (6th Cir. 1991) ***1:*** 46
Festo Corp. v. Shoketsu Kinzoku Kogyo Kabushiki Co., 234 F.3d 558, 56 USPQ 2d 1865 (Fed. Cir. 2000), *cert. granted,* 121 S. Ct. 2519 (2001) ***2:*** 117–36, 138, 139, 172
Filmtec Corp. v. Allied-Signal Inc., 939 F.2d 1568, 19 USPQ 2d 1508 (Fed. Cir. 1991) ***3:*** 20–23
Finnigan Corp. v. United States International Trade Comm'n, 180 F.3d 1354, 51 USPQ 2d 1001 (Fed. Cir. 1999) ***6:*** 76
Fiskars Inc. v. Hunt Mfg. Co., 221 F.3d 1318, 55 USPQ 2d 1569 (Fed. Cir. 2000), *cert. denied,* 121 S. Ct. 1603 (2001) ***2:*** 147
Florida Prepaid Postsecondary Educ. Expense Bd. v. College Sav. Bank, 527 U.S. 627, 51 USPQ 2d 1081 (1999) ***1:*** 17, 19; ***3:*** 1
Fonar Corp. v. Johnson & Johnson, 821 F.2d 627, 3 USPQ 2d 1109 (Fed. Cir. 1987) ***2:*** 189; ***9:*** 23
Fontijn v. Okamoto, 518 F.2d 610, 186 USPQ 97 (C.C.P.A. 1975) ***12:*** 332
Fortel Corp. v. Phone-Mate, Inc., 825 F.2d 1577, 3 USPQ 2d 1991 (Fed. Cir. 1987) ***12:*** 242
Fotland, In re, 779 F.2d 31, 228 USPQ 2d 193 (Fed. Cir. 1985) ***12:*** 80
Fouche, In re, 439 F.2d 1237, 169 USPQ 429 (C.C.P.A. 1971) ***8:*** 52
Fracalossi, In re, 681 F.2d 792, 215 USPQ 569 (C.C.P.A. 1982) ***6:*** 57; ***7:*** 8
Freeman, In re, 30 F.3d 1459, 31 USPQ 2d 1444 (Fed. Cir. 1994) ***12:*** 211
Fretheim v. Department of the Air Force, 49 USPQ 2d 1316 (U.S. Dep't Comm. 1998) ***3:*** 40, 41

M

Q

R

S

T

U

V

Index

Alphabetization is word-by-word (e.g., "Ex parte prosecution" precedes "Examination of applications").

E

U

W

About the Author

Irah Donner concentrates on the counseling, acquisition, and enforcement of all forms of intellectual property rights, with emphasis on business method, Internet, and computer software applications. Mr. Donner frequently conducts technology audits, advising technology-based companies, such as wireless, fiber optic, Internet, and financial-related companies, on strategies for protecting their intellectual property, including preparing and prosecuting patent applications directed to the above technologies, as well as others. He also provides counseling in e-commerce and doing business over the Internet.

Before pursuing a career in law, Mr. Donner worked as a control engineer, designing software implemented feedback controllers for paralyzed muscle at the Cleveland Veterans Administration Hospital. He also designed software applications for large-scale computer systems at Bell Communications Research (BELLCORE) in the facility analysis and control field.

Mr. Donner is a member of the DC Technology Council and the Information Technology & Telecommunications Committee of the Northern Virginia Technology Council. He has served on the editorial board of *IEEE COMPUTER* magazine and published a monthly column for the Computer Law Department. He is currently an associate editor for the American Bar Association (ABA) *Computer Litigation* legal journal, and is a former circuit reporter for the ABA *IP Litigation* legal journal.

Mr. Donner is author of the books *Patent Prosecution: Practice and Procedure Before the U.S. Patent Office* (BNA 1996 and 1999 editions, and 1997, 1998, 2000, and 2001 Supplements), *Patent Prosecution Case Digest* (BNA 1996, 1997, 1998, 1999, 2000, and 2001 editions), *Patent Prosecution Forms* (BNA 1998), and *Guidelines and Tips for Prosecuting Computer Inventions and Designs* (DB Publishing 1998). He has published many articles on subjects including the patenting of computer software- and hardware-related applications. Mr. Donner is also the inventor of eight U.S. patents, and has another four patent applications pending in the U.S. Patent Office. Mr. Donner is admitted to practice in the District of Columbia, New York, New Jersey, the Federal Circuit Court of Appeals, and the U.S. Patent and Trademark Office.

Mr. Donner received a J.D. degree, *magna cum laude*, from Case Western Reserve University School of Law, where he also served on the editorial board of the *CWRU Law Review*. He received an M.S. degree in systems engineering and a B.S. degree with high honors from Case School of Engineering.

Mr. Donner lives in Silver Spring, Maryland, with his wife Batsheva and four children: Zachary, Avital, Jason, and Elana.